Lecture Notes in Computer Science 7573

Commenced Publication in 1973
Founding and Former Series Editors:
Gerhard Goos, Juris Hartmanis, and Jan van Leeuwen

Andrew Fitzgibbon Svetlana Lazebnik
Pietro Perona Yoichi Sato
Cordelia Schmid (Eds.)

Computer Vision – ECCV 2012

12th European Conference on Computer Vision
Florence, Italy, October 7-13, 2012
Proceedings, Part II

Springer

Volume Editors

Andrew Fitzgibbon
Microsoft Research Ltd., Cambridge, CB3 0FB, UK
E-mail: awf@microsoft.com

Svetlana Lazebnik
University of North Carolina, Dept. of Computer Science
Chapel Hill, NC 27599, USA
E-mail: lazebnik@cs.unc.edu

Pietro Perona
California Institute of Technology
Pasadena, CA 91125, USA
E-mail: perona@caltech.edu

Yoichi Sato
The University of Tokyo, Institute of Industrial Science
Tokyo 153-8505, Japan
E-mail: ysato@iis.u-tokyo.ac.jp

Cordelia Schmid
INRIA, 38330 Montbonnot, France
E-mail: cordelia.schmid@inria.fr

ISSN 0302-9743
e-ISSN 1611-3349
ISBN 978-3-642-33708-6
e-ISBN 978-3-642-33709-3
DOI 10.1007/978-3-642-33709-3
Springer Heidelberg Dordrecht London New York

Library of Congress Control Number: 2012947663

CR Subject Classification (1998): I.4.6, I.4.8, I.4.1-5, I.4.9, I.5.2-4, I.2.10, I.3.5, F.2.2

LNCS Sublibrary: SL 6 – Image Processing, Computer Vision, Pattern Recognition, and Graphics

Typesetting: Camera-ready by author, data conversion by Scientific Publishing Services, Chennai, India

Printed on acid-free paper

Springer is part of Springer Science+Business Media (www.springer.com)

Foreword

The European Conference on Computer Vision is one of the top conferences for researchers in this field and is held biennially in alternation with the International Conference on Computer Vision. It was first held in 1990 in Antibes (France) with subsequent conferences in Santa Margherita Ligure (Italy) in 1992, Stockholm (Sweden) in 1994, Cambridge (UK) in 1996, Freiburg (Germany) in 1998, Dublin (Ireland) in 2000, Copenhagen (Denmark) in 2002, Prague (Czech Republic) in 2004, Graz (Austria) in 2006, Marseille (France) in 2008, and Heraklion (Greece) in 2010. To our great delight, the 12th conference was held in Florence, Italy.

ECCV has an established tradition of very high scientific quality and an overall duration of one week. ECCV 2012 began with a keynote lecture from the honorary chair, Tomaso Poggio. The main conference followed over four days with 40 orals, 368 posters, 22 demos, and 12 industrial exhibits. There were also 9 tutorials and 21 workshops held before and after the main event. For this event we introduced some novelties. These included innovations in the review policy, the publication of a conference booklet with all paper abstracts and the full video recording of oral presentations.

This conference is the result of a great deal of hard work by many people, who have been working enthusiastically since our first meetings in 2008. We are particularly grateful to the Program Chairs, who handled the review of about 1500 submissions and co-ordinated the efforts of over 50 area chairs and about 1000 reviewers (see details of the process in their preface to the proceedings). We are also indebted to all the other chairs who, with the support of our research teams (names listed below), diligently helped us manage all aspects of the main conference, tutorials, workshops, exhibits, demos, proceedings, and web presence. Finally we thank our generous sponsors and Consulta Umbria for handling the registration of delegates and all financial aspects associated with the conference.

We hope you enjoyed ECCV 2012. Benvenuti a Firenze!

October 2012

Roberto Cipolla
Carlo Colombo
Alberto Del Bimbo

Preface

Welcome to the proceedings of the 2012 European Conference on Computer Vision in Florence, Italy! We received 1437 complete submissions, the largest number of submissions in the history of ECCV. Forty papers were selected for oral presentation and 368 papers for poster presentation, resulting in acceptance rates of 2.8% for oral, 25.6% for poster, and 28.4% in total.

The following is a brief description of the review process. After the submission deadline, each paper was assigned to one of 54 area chairs (28 from Europe, 21 from the USA and Canada, and 4 from Asia) with the help of the Toronto Paper Matching System (TMS). TMS, developed by Laurent Charlin and Richard Zemel, is beginning to be used by an increasing number of conferences, including NIPS, ICML, and CVPR. To ensure the best possible assignment of papers to area chairs, the program chairs manually selected several area chair candidates for each paper based on the suggestions generated by TMS. After automatic load balancing and conflict resolution, each AC was finally assigned approximately 30 papers closely matching their expertise.

Area chairs then made reviewer suggestions (an average of seven per paper), which were load-balanced and conflict-resolved, giving 3 reviewers for each paper and a maximum of 11 papers per reviewer. The ACs were assisted in this process by TMS, which was also used for automatically selecting potential reviewers, matching each submitted paper based on the reviewers' representative publications. These suggestions came from a pool of potential reviewers composed from names of people who have reviewed for recent vision conferences, self-nominations (any member of the community could fill out a form on the ECCV website asking to be a reviewer), and nominations by ACs. From an initial pool of 863 reviewers, 638 ended up reviewing at least one paper. This was the first time that TMS had been used this extensively in the review process for a vision conference (CVPR 2012 used a restricted version of the system for assigning papers to area chairs), and in the end, we were very pleased with its performance. An important improvement over previous conferences was that initial reviewer suggestions were generated entirely in parallel by the ACs, without the "race" for good reviewers that the previous methods have implicitly encouraged. Area chairs were then given the opportunity to correct infelicities in the load balancing before the final list was generated. We extend our heartfelt thanks to the area chairs, who participated vigorously in this process, to maximize the quality of the review assignments.

For the decision process, we introduced one major innovation. We replaced the physical area chair meeting and the conventional AC buddy system with virtual meetings of AC triplets (this system was first tried out for BMVC 2011 and found to work very well). After the conclusion of the review, rebuttal, and discussion periods, the AC triplets met on the phone or on Skype (and, in just one case, in person), jointly discussed all their papers, and made acceptance/rejection decisions. Thus, the reviews and consolidation reports for each paper were carefully examined by three ACs, ensuring a fair and thorough assessment. A program chair assisted in each AC triplet meeting to maintain the consistency in the decision process and to provide any necessary support. Furthermore, each triplet recommended a small number of top-ranked papers (typically one to three) for oral presentation, and the program chairs took these candidates and made the final oral vs. poster decisions.

Double-blind reviewing policies were strictly maintained throughout the entire process – neither the area chairs nor the reviewers knew the identity of the authors, and the authors did not know the identity of the reviewers and ACs. Based on feedback from authors, reviewers, and area chairs, we believe we successfully maintained the integrity of the paper selection process, and we are very excited about the quality of the resulting program.

We wish to thank everyone involved for their time and dedication to making the ECCV 2012 program possible. The success of ECCV 2012 entirely relied on the time and effort invested by the authors into producing high-quality research, on the care taken by the reviewers in writing thorough and professional reviews, and on the commitment by the area chairs to reconciling the reviews and writing detailed and precise consolidation reports. We also wish to thank the general chairs, Roberto Cipolla, Carlo Colombo, and Alberto Del Bimbo, and the other organizing committee members for their top-notch handling of the event.

Finally, we would like to commemorate Mark Everingham, whose untimely death has shocked and saddened the entire vision community. Mark was an area chair for ECCV and also an organizer for one of the workshops; his hard work and dedication were absolutely essential in enabling us to put together a high-quality conference program. We salute his record of exemplary service and intellectual contributions to the discipline of computer vision. Mark, you will be missed!

October 2012

Andrew Fitzgibbon
Svetlana Lazebnik
Pietro Perona
Yoichi Sato
Cordelia Schmid

Organization

General Chairs

Roberto Cipolla	University of Cambridge, UK
Carlo Colombo	University of Florence, Italy
Alberto Del Bimbo	University of Florence, Italy

Program Coordinator

Pietro Perona	California Institute of Technology, USA

Program Chairs

Andrew Fitzgibbon	Microsoft Research, Cambridge, UK
Svetlana Lazebnik	University of Illinois at Urbana-Champaign, USA
Yoichi Sato	The University of Tokyo, Japan
Cordelia Schmid	INRIA, Grenoble, France

Honorary Chair

Tomaso Poggio	Massachusetts Institute of Technology, USA

Tutorial Chairs

Emanuele Trucco	University of Dundee, UK
Alessandro Verri	University of Genoa, Italy

Workshop Chairs

Andrea Fusiello	University of Udine, Italy
Vittorio Murino	Istituto Italiano di Tecnologia, Genoa, Italy

Demonstration Chair

Rita Cucchiara	University of Modena and Reggio Emilia, Italy

Industrial Liaison Chair

Björn Stenger	Toshiba Research Europe, Cambridge, UK

Web Chair

Marco Bertini	University of Florence, Italy

Publicity Chairs

Terrance E. Boult	University of Colorado at Colorado Springs, USA
Tat Jen Cham	Nanyang Technological University, Singapore
Marcello Pelillo	University Ca' Foscari of Venice, Italy

Publication Chair

Massimo Tistarelli	University of Sassari, Italy

Video Processing Chairs

Sebastiano Battiato	University of Catania, Italy
Giovanni M. Farinella	University of Catania, Italy

Travel Grants Chair

Luigi Di Stefano	University of Bologna, Italy

Travel Visa Chair

Stefano Berretti	University of Florence, Italy

Local Committee Chair

Andrew Bagdanov	MICC, Florence, Italy

Local Committee

Lamberto Ballan
Laura Benassi
Marco Fanfani
Andrea Ferracani
Claudio Guida
Lea Landucci
Giuseppe Lisanti
Iacopo Masi
Fabio Pazzaglia
Federico Pernici
Lorenzo Seidenari
Giuseppe Serra

Area Chairs

Simon Baker	Microsoft Research, USA
Horst Bischof	Graz University of Technology, Austria
Michael Black	Max Planck Institute, Germany
Richard Bowden	University of Surrey, UK
Michael S. Brown	National University of Singapore, Singapore
Joachim Buhmann	ETH Zurich, Switzerland
Alyosha Efros	Carnegie Mellon University, USA
Mark Everingham	University of Leeds, UK
Pedro Felzenszwalb	Brown University, USA

Rob Fergus	New York University, USA
Vittorio Ferrari	ETH Zurich, Switzerland
David Fleet	University of Toronto, Canada
David Forsyth	University of Illinois at Urbana-Champaign, USA
Kristen Grauman	University of Texas at Austin, USA
Martial Hebert	Carnegie Mellon University, USA
Aaron Hertzmann	University of Toronto, Canada
Derek Hoiem	University of Illinois at Urbana-Champaign, USA
Katsushi Ikeuchi	The University of Tokyo, Japan
Michal Irani	The Weizmann Institute of Science, Israel
David Jacobs	University of Maryland, USA
Sing Bing Kang	Microsoft Research, USA
David Kriegman	University of California, San Diego, USA
Kyros Kutulakos	University of Toronto, Canada
Christof Lampert	Institute of Science and Technology, Austria
Ivan Laptev	INRIA, France
Victor Lempitsky	Yandex, Russia
Steve Lin	Microsoft Research, China
Jitendra Malik	University of California, Berkeley, USA
Jiří Matas	Czech Technical University, Czech Republic
Yasuyuki Matsushita	Microsoft Research, China
Tomas Pajdla	Czech Technical University, Czech Republic
Patrick Pérez	Thomson-Technicolor, France
Marc Pollefeys	ETH Zurich, Switzerland
Jean Ponce	Ecole Normale Supérieure, France
Long Quan	Hong Kong Univ. of Science and Technology, China
Deva Ramanan	University of California, Irvine, USA
Stefan Roth	TU Darmstadt, Germany
Carsten Rother	Microsoft Research, UK
Yoav Schechner	Technion, Israel
Bernt Schiele	Max Planck Institute, Germany
Christoph Schnörr	University of Heidelberg, Germany
Stan Sclaroff	University of Boston, USA
Josef Sivic	Ecole Normale Supérieure, France
Peter Sturm	INRIA, France
Carlo Tomasi	Duke University, USA
Antonio Torralba	Massachusetts Institute of Technology, USA
Tinne Tuytelaars	University of Leuven, Belgium
Jakob Verbeek	INRIA, France
Yair Weiss	The Hebrew University of Jerusalem, Israel
Christopher Williams	University of Edinburgh, UK
Ramin Zabih	Cornell University, USA
Lihi Zelnik	Technion, Israel
Andrew Zisserman	University of Oxford, UK
Larry Zitnick	Microsoft Research, USA

Reviewers

Vitaly Ablavsky
Lourdes Agapito
Sameer Agarwal
Amit Agrawal
Karteek Alahari
Karim Ali
Saad Ali
S. Ali Eslami
Daniel Aliaga
Neil Alldrin
Marina Alterman
Jose M. Alvarez
Brian Amberg
Cosmin Ancuti
Juan Andrade
Mykhaylo Andriluka
Anton Andriyenko
Elli Angelopoulou
Roland Angst
Relja Arandjelovic
Helder Araujo
Pablo Arbelaez
Antonis Argyros
Kalle Åström
Vassilis Athitsos
Josep Aulinas
Shai Avidan
Tamar Avraham
Yannis Avrithis
Yusuf Aytar
Luca Ballan
Lamberto Ballan
Atsuhiko Banno
Yinzge Bao
Adrian Barbu
Nick Barnes
João Pedro Barreto
Adrien Bartoli
Arslan Basharat
Dhruv Batra
Sebastiano Battiato
Jean-Charles Bazin
Fethallah Benmansour
Alexander Berg
Tamara Berg
Hakan Bilen
Matthew Blaschko
Michael Bleyer
Liefeng Bo
Daniele Borghesani
Terrance Boult
Lubomir Bourdev
Y-Lan Boureau
Kevin Bowyer
Edmond Boyer
Steven Branson
Mathieu Brédif
William Brendel
Michael Bronstein
Gabriel Brostow
Matthew Brown
Thomas Brox
Marcus Brubaker
Darius Burschka
Tiberio Caetano
Barbara Caputo
Stefan Carlsson
Gustavo Carneiro
Joao Carreira
Yaron Caspi
Carlos Castillo
Jan Cech
Turgay Celik
Ayan Chakrabarti
Tat Jen Cham
Antoni Chan
Manmohan Chandraker
Ming-Ching Chang
Lin Chen
Xilin Chen
Daozheng Chen
Wen-Huang Cheng
Yuan Cheng
Tat-Jun Chin
Han-Pang Chiu
Minsu Cho
Tae Choe
Ondrej Chum
Albert C.S. Chung
John Collomosse
Tim Cootes
Florent Couzine-Devy
David Crandall
Keenan Crane
Antonio Criminisi
Shengyang Dai
Dima Damen
Larry Davis
Andrew Davison
Fernando De la Torre
Joost de Weijer
Teofilo deCampos
Vincent Delaitre
Amael Delaunoy
Andrew Delong
David Demirdjian
Jia Deng
Joachim Denzler
Konstantinos Derpanis
Chaitanya Desai
Thomas Deselaers
Frederic Devernay
Thang Dinh
Santosh Kumar Divvala
Piotr Dollar
Justin Domke
Gianfranco Doretto
Matthijs Douze
Tom Drummond
Lixin Duan
Olivier Duchenne
Zoran Duric
Pinar Duygulu
Charles Dyer
Sandra Ebert
Michael Elad
James Elder
Ehsan Elhamifar
Ian Endres

Olof Enqvist
Sergio Escalera
Jialue Fan
Bin Fan
Gabriele Fanelli
Yi Fang
Ali Farhadi
Ryan Farrell
Raanan Fattal
Paolo Favaro
Rogerio Feris
Sanja Fidler
Robert Fisher
Pierre Fite-Georgel
Boris Flach
François Fleuret
Wolfgang Förstner
Andrea Fossati
Charless Fowlkes
Jan-Michael Frahm
Jean-Sebastien Franco
Friedrich Fraundorfer
William Freeman
Oren Freifeld
Mario Fritz
Yasutaka Furukawa
Andrea Fusiello
Adrien Gaidon
Juergen Gall
Andrew Gallagher
Simone Gasparini
Peter Gehler
Yakup Genc
Leifman George
Guido Gerig
Christopher Geyer
Abhijeet Ghosh
Andrew Gilbert
Ross Girshick
Martin Godec
Roland Goecke
Michael Goesele
Siome Goldenstein
Bastian Goldluecke
Shaogang Gong
German Gonzalez
Raghuraman Gopalan
Albert Gordo
Lena Gorelick
Paulo Gotardo
Stephen Gould
Helmut Grabner
Etienne Grossmann
Matthias Grundmann
Jinwei Gu
Steve Gu
Li Guan
Peng Guan
Matthieu Guillaumin
Jean-Yves Guillemaut
Ruiqi Guo
Guodong Guo
Abhinav Gupta
Mohit Gupta
Tony Han
Bohyung Han
Mei Han
Edwin Hancock
Jari Hannuksela
Kenji Hara
Tatsuya Harada
Daniel Harari
Zaid Harchaoui
Stefan Harmeling
Søren Hauberg
Michal Havlena
James Hays
Xuming He
Kaiming He
Varsha Hedau
Nicolas Heess
Yong Heo
Adrian Hilton
Stefan Hinterstoisser
Minh Hoai
Jesse Hoey
Anthony Hoogs
Joachim Hornegger
Alexander Hornung
Edward Hsiao
Wenze Hu
Changbo Hu
Gang Hua
Xinyu Huang
Rui Huang
Wonjun Hwang
Ichiro Ide
Juan Iglesias
Ivo Ihrke
Nazli Ikizler-Cinbis
Slobodan Ilic
Ignazio Infantino
Michael Isard
Hervé Jégou
C.V. Jawahar
Rodolphe Jenatton
Hueihan Jhuang
Qiang Ji
Jiaya Jia
Hongjun Jia
Yong-Dian Jian
Hao Jiang
Zhuolin Jiang
Shuqiang Jiang
Sam Johnson
Anne Jorstad
Neel Joshi
Armand Joulin
Frederic Jurie
Ioannis Kakadiaris
Zdenek Kalal
Joni-K. Kamarainen
Kenichi Kanatani
Atul Kanaujia
Ashish Kapoor
Jörg Kappes
Leonid Karlinsky
Kevin Karsch
koray kavukcuoglu
Rei Kawakami
Hiroshi Kawasaki
Verena Kaynig
Qifa Ke
Ira Kemelmacher-Shlizerman

Aditya Khosla
Tae-Kyun Kim
Jaechul Kim
Seon Joo Kim
Kris Kitani
Jyri Kivinen
Hedvig Kjellstrom
Jan Knopp
Kevin Koeser
Pushmeet Kohli
Nikos Komodakis
Kurt Konolige
Filip Korc
Andreas Koschan
Adriana Kovashka
Josip Krapac
Dilip Krishnan
Zuzana Kukelova
Neeraj Kumar
M. Pawan Kumar
Junghyun Kwon
Dongjin Kwon
Junseok Kwon
Florent Lafarge
Shang-Hong Lai
Jean-Francois Lalonde
Michael Langer
Douglas Lanman
Diane Larlus
Longin Jan Latecki
Erik Learned-Miller
Seungkyu Lee
Kyong Joon Lee
Honglak Lee
Yong Jae Lee
Bastian Leibe
Ido Leichter
Frank Lenzen
Matt Leotta
Vincent Lepetit
Anat Levin
Maxime Lhuillier
Rui Li
Stan Li
Hongsheng Li
Ruonan Li
Hongdong Li
Feng Li
Yunpeng Li
Fuxin Li
Li-Jia Li
Zicheng Liao
Shengcai Liao
Jongwoo Lim
Joseph Lim
Yen-Yu Lin
Dahua Lin
Daniel Lin
Haibin Ling
James Little
Ce Liu
Xiaobai Liu
Ming-Yu Liu
Xiaoming Liu
Tyng-Luh Liu
Yunlong Liu
Wei Liu
Jingen Liu
Marcus Liwicki
Liliana Lo Presti
Roberto Lopez-Sastre
Jiwen Lu
Zheng Lu
Le Lu
Simon Lucey
Julien Mairal
Michael Maire
Subhransu Maji
Yasushi Makihara
Dimitrios Makris
Tomasz Malisiewicz
Jiri Matas
Iain Matthews
Stefano Mattoccia
Thomas Mauthner
Steven Maybank
Walterio Mayol-Cuevas
Scott McCloskey
Stephen McKenna
Gerard Medioni
Jason Meltzer
Talya Meltzer
Heydi Mendez-Vazquez
Thomas Mensink
Fabrice Michel
Branislav Micusik
Krystian Mikolajczyk
Niloy Mitra
Anurag Mittal
Philippos Mordohai
Francesc Moreno-Noguer
Greg Mori
Bryan Morse
Yadong Mu
Yasuhiro Mukaigawa
Lopamudra Mukherjee
Andreas Müller
Jane Mulligan
Daniel Munoz
A. Murillo
Carlo Mutto
Hajime Nagahara
Vinay Namboodiri
Srinivasa Narasimhan
Fabian Nater
Shawn Newsam
Kai Ni
Feiping Nie
Juan Carlos Niebles
Claudia Nieuwenhuis
Ko Nishino
Sebastian Nowozin
Jean-Marc Odobez
Peter O'Donovan
Sangmin Oh
Takeshi Oishi
Takahiro Okabe
Takayuki Okatani
Aude Oliva
Carl Olsson
Bjorn Ommer
Eng-Jon Ong
Anton Osokin
Matthew O'Toole
Mustafa Özuysal

Maja Pantic
Caroline Pantofaru
George Papandreou
Toufiq Parag
Vasu Parameswaran
Devi Parikh
Sylvain Paris
Minwoo Park
Dennis Park
Ioannis Patras
Ioannis Pavlidis
Nadia Payet
Kim Pedersen
Ofir Pele
Shmuel Peleg
Yigang Peng
Amitha Perera
Florent Perronnin
Adrian Peter
Maria Petrou
Patrick Peursum
Tomas Pfister
James Philbin
Justus Piater
Hamed Pirsiavash
Robert Pless
Thomas Pock
Gerard Pons-Moll
Ronald Poppe
Fatih Porikli
Mukta Prasad
Andrea Prati
Jerry Prince
Nicolas Pugeault
Novi Quadrianto
Vincent Rabaud
Rahul Raguram
Srikumar Ramalingam
Narayanan Ramanathan
Marc'Aurelio Ranzato
Konstantinos Rapantzikos
Nikhil Rasiwasia
Mohammad Rastegari
James Rehg
Erik Reinhard
Xiaofeng Ren
Christoph Rhemann
Antonio Robles-Kelly
Emanuele Rodolà
Mikel Rodriguez
Antonio Rodriguez-Sanchez
Marcus Rohrbach
Javier Romero
Charles Rosenberg
Bodo Rosenhahn
Samuel Rota Bulò
Peter Roth
Amit Roy-Chowdhury
Dmitry Rudoy
Olga Russakovsky
Bryan Russell
Chris Russell
Radu Rusu
Michael Ryoo
Mohammad Sadeghi
Kate Saenko
Amir Saffari
Albert Salah
Mathieu Salzmann
Dimitris Samaras
Aswin Sankaranarayanan
Benjamin Sapp
Radim Sara
Scott Satkin
Imari Sato
Eric Saund
Daniel Scharstein
Walter Scheirer
Kevin Schelten
Raimondo Schettini
Konrad Schindler
Joseph Schlecht
Frank Schmidt
Uwe Schmidt
Florian Schroff
Rodolphe Sepulchre
Uri Shalit
Shiguang Shan
Ling Shao
Abhishek Sharma
Eli Shechtman
Yaser Sheikh
Alexander Shekhovtsov
Ilan Shimshoni
Takaaki Shiratori
Jamie Shotton
Nitesh Shroff
Zhangzhang Si
Leonid Sigal
Nathan Silberman
Karen Simonyan
Vivek Singh
Vikas Singh
Maneesh Singh
Sudipta Sinha
Greg Slabaugh
Arnold Smeulders
Cristian Sminchisescu
William A. P. Smith
Kevin Smith
Noah Snavely
Cees Snoek
Michal Sofka
Qi Song
Xuan Song
Anuj Srivastava
Michael Stark
Bjorn Stenger
Yu Su
Yusuke Sugano
Ju Sun
Min Sun
Deqing Sun
Jian Sun
David Suter
Yohay Swirski
Rick Szeliski
Yuichi Taguchi
Yu-Wing Tai
Jun Takamatsu
Hugues Talbot
Robby Tan

Xiaoou Tang
Marshall Tappen
Jonathan Taylor
Christian Theobalt
Tai-Peng Tian
Joseph Tighe
Radu Timofte
Sinisa Todorovic
Federico Tombari
Akihiko Torii
Duan Tran
Tali Treibitz
Bill Triggs
Nhon Trinh
Ivor Tsang
Yanghai Tsin
Aggeliki Tsoli
Zhuowen Tu
Pavan Turaga
Ambrish Tyagi
Martin Urschler
Raquel Urtasun
Jan van Gemert
Daniel Vaquero
Andrea Vedaldi
Ashok Veeraraghavan
Olga Veksler
Alexander Vezhnevets
Sara Vicente
Sudheendra Vijayanarasimhan
Pascal Vincent
Carl Vondrick
Chaohui Wang
Yang Wang
Jue Wang
Hanzi Wang
Song Wang
Gang Wang
Hongcheng Wang
Jingdong Wang
Lu Wang
Yueming Wang
Ruiping Wang
Kai Wang
Alexander Weiss
Andreas Wendel
Manuel Werlberger
Tomas Werner
Gordon Wetzstein
Yonatan Wexler
Oliver Whyte
Richard Wildes
Oliver Williams
Thomas Windheuser
David Wipf
Kwan-Yee K. Wong
John Wright
Shandong Wu
Yi Wu
Changchang Wu
Jianxin Wu
Ying Wu
Jonas Wulff
Jing Xiao
Jianxiong Xiao
Wei Xu
Li Xu
Yong Xu
Yi Xu
Yasushi Yagi
Takayoshi Yamashita
Ming Yang
Ming-Hsuan Yang
Qingxiong Yang
Jinfeng Yang
Weilong Yang
Ruigang Yang
Jianchao Yang
Yi Yang
Bangpeng Yao
Angela Yao
Mohammad Yaqub
Lijun Yin
Kuk-Jin Yoon
Tianli Yu
Qian Yu
Lu Yuan
Xiaotong Yuan
Christopher Zach
Stefanos Zafeiriou
Andrei Zaharescu
Matthew Zeiler
Yun Zeng
Guofeng Zhang
Li Zhang
Lei Zhang
Xinhua Zhang
Shaoting Zhang
Jianguo Zhang
Ying Zheng
S. Kevin Zhou
Changyin Zhou
Shaojie Zhuo
Todd Zickler
Darko Zikic
Henning Zimmer
Daniel Zoran
Silvia Zuffi

Sponsoring Companies and Institutions

Gold Sponsors

Google

NATIONAL ROBOTICS ENGINEERING CENTER (NREC)

Silver Sponsors

Adobe

Microsoft Research

MITSUBISHI ELECTRIC

MOBILEYE

NVIDIA

POINT GREY

technicolor

TOSHIBA Leading Innovation

TOYOTA

Bronze Sponsors

DATALOGIC INDUSTRIAL AUTOMATION

IBM Research

ST life.augmented

Institutional Sponsors

Università degli Studi di Firenze

UNIVERSITY OF CAMBRIDGE

ENTE CASSA DI RISPARMIO DI FIRENZE

Table of Contents

Poster Session 2

Object-Centric Spatial Pooling for Image Classification 1
Olga Russakovsky, Yuanqing Lin, Kai Yu, and Li Fei-Fei

Statistics of Patch Offsets for Image Completion 16
Kaiming He and Jian Sun

Spectral Demons – Image Registration via Global Spectral Correspondence 30
Herve Lombaert, Leo Grady, Xavier Pennec, Nicholas Ayache, and Farida Cheriet

MatchMiner: Efficient Spanning Structure Mining in Large Image Collections 45
Yin Lou, Noah Snavely, and Johannes Gehrke

V1-Inspired Features Induce a Weighted Margin in SVMs 59
Hilton Bristow and Simon Lucey

Unsupervised Discovery of Mid-Level Discriminative Patches 73
Saurabh Singh, Abhinav Gupta, and Alexei A. Efros

Self-similar Sketch 87
Andrea Vedaldi and Andrew Zisserman

Depth Matters: Influence of Depth Cues on Visual Saliency 101
Congyan Lang, Tam V. Nguyen, Harish Katti, Karthik Yadati, Mohan Kankanhalli, and Shuicheng Yan

Quaternion-Based Spectral Saliency Detection for Eye Fixation Prediction 116
Boris Schauerte and Rainer Stiefelhagen

Human Activities as Stochastic Kronecker Graphs.................... 130
Sinisa Todorovic

Facial Action Transfer with Personalized Bilinear Regression 144
Dong Huang and Fernando De La Torre

Point of Gaze Estimation through Corneal Surface Reflection in an Active Illumination Environment 159
Atsushi Nakazawa and Christian Nitschke

Order-Preserving Sparse Coding for Sequence Classification 173
Bingbing Ni, Pierre Moulin, and Shuicheng Yan

Min-Space Integral Histogram 188
Séverine Dubuisson and Christophe Gonzales

On Learning Higher-Order Consistency Potentials for Multi-class Pixel Labeling 202
Kyoungup Park and Stephen Gould

Sparse Coding and Dictionary Learning for Symmetric Positive Definite Matrices: A Kernel Approach 216
Mehrtash T. Harandi, Conrad Sanderson, Richard Hartley, and Brian C. Lovell

Learning Class-to-Image Distance via Large Margin and L1-Norm Regularization 230
Zhengxiang Wang, Shenghua Gao, and Liang-Tien Chia

Taxonomic Multi-class Prediction and Person Layout Using Efficient Structured Ranking 245
Arpit Mittal, Matthew B. Blaschko, Andrew Zisserman, and Philip H.S. Torr

Robust Point Matching Revisited: A Concave Optimization Approach 259
Wei Lian and Lei Zhang

Learning Discriminative Spatial Relations for Detector Dictionaries: An Application to Pedestrian Detection 273
Enver Sangineto, Marco Cristani, Alessio Del Bue, and Vittorio Murino

Learning Deformations with Parallel Transport 287
Donglai Wei, Dahua Lin, and John Fisher III

Multi-channel Shape-Flow Kernel Descriptors for Robust Video Event Detection and Retrieval 301
Pradeep Natarajan, Shuang Wu, Shiv Vitaladevuni, Xiaodan Zhuang, Unsang Park, Rohit Prasad, and Premkumar Natarajan

Tracking Using Motion Patterns for Very Crowded Scenes 315
Xuemei Zhao, Dian Gong, and Gérard Medioni

Long-Range Spatio-Temporal Modeling of Video with Application to Fire Detection 329
Avinash Ravichandran and Stefano Soatto

GMCP-Tracker: Global Multi-object Tracking Using Generalized Minimum Clique Graphs 343
Amir Roshan Zamir, Afshin Dehghan, and Mubarak Shah

Heliometric Stereo: Shape from Sun Position 357
Austin Abrams, Christopher Hawley, and Robert Pless

Shape from Single Scattering for Translucent Objects 371
Chika Inoshita, Yasuhiro Mukaigawa, Yasuyuki Matsushita, and Yasushi Yagi

Scale Invariant Optical Flow 385
Li Xu, Zhenlong Dai, and Jiaya Jia

Structured Image Segmentation Using Kernelized Features 400
Aurélien Lucchi, Yunpeng Li, Kevin Smith, and Pascal Fua

Salient Object Detection: A Benchmark 414
Ali Borji, Dicky N. Sihite, and Laurent Itti

Automatic Segmentation of Unknown Objects, with Application to Baggage Security 430
Leo Grady, Vivek Singh, Timo Kohlberger, Christopher Alvino, and Claus Bahlmann

Multi-scale Clustering of Frame-to-Frame Correspondences for Motion Segmentation 445
Ralf Dragon, Bodo Rosenhahn, and Jörn Ostermann

Oral Session 2: Learning and large-Scale Recognition

Fourier Kernel Learning 459
Eduard Gabriel Băzăvan, Fuxin Li, and Cristian Sminchisescu

Efficient Optimization for Low-Rank Integrated Bilinear Classifiers 474
Takumi Kobayashi and Nobuyuki Otsu

Metric Learning for Large Scale Image Classification: Generalizing to New Classes at Near-Zero Cost 488
Thomas Mensink, Jakob Verbeek, Florent Perronnin, and Gabriela Csurka

Leafsnap: A Computer Vision System for Automatic Plant Species Identification 502
Neeraj Kumar, Peter N. Belhumeur, Arijit Biswas, David W. Jacobs, W. John Kress, Ida C. Lopez, and João V.B. Soares

Large Scale Visual Geo-Localization of Images in Mountainous Terrain 517
Georges Baatz, Olivier Saurer, Kevin Köser, and Marc Pollefeys

Poster Session 3

Manifold Statistics for Essential Matrices 531
Gijs Dubbelman, Leo Dorst, and Henk Pijls

Covariance Propagation and Next Best View Planning for 3D Reconstruction 545
Sebastian Haner and Anders Heyden

Dilated Divergence Based Scale-Space Representation for Curve Analysis 557
Max W.K. Law, KengYeow Tay, Andrew Leung, Gregory J. Garvin, and Shuo Li

A Parameterless Line Segment and Elliptical Arc Detector with Enhanced Ellipse Fitting 572
Viorica Pătrăucean, Pierre Gurdjos, and Rafael Grompone von Gioi

Detecting and Reconstructing 3D Mirror Symmetric Objects 586
Sudipta N. Sinha, Krishnan Ramnath, and Richard Szeliski

3D Reconstruction of Dynamic Scenes with Multiple Handheld Cameras 601
Hanqing Jiang, Haomin Liu, Ping Tan, Guofeng Zhang, and Hujun Bao

Joint Face Alignment: Rescue Bad Alignments with Good Ones by Regularized Re-fitting 616
Xiaowei Zhao, Xiujuan Chai, and Shiguang Shan

Dynamic Facial Expression Recognition Using Longitudinal Facial Expression Atlases 631
Yimo Guo, Guoying Zhao, and Matti Pietikäinen

Crosstalk Cascades for Frame-Rate Pedestrian Detection 645
Piotr Dollár, Ron Appel, and Wolf Kienzle

Query Specific Fusion for Image Retrieval ... 660
Shaoting Zhang, Ming Yang, Timothee Cour, Kai Yu, and Dimitris N. Metaxas

Size Matters: Exhaustive Geometric Verification for Image Retrieval Accepted for ECCV 2012 ... 674
Henrik Stewénius, Steinar H. Gunderson, and Julien Pilet

Scene Aligned Pooling for Complex Video Recognition ... 688
Liangliang Cao, Yadong Mu, Apostol Natsev, Shih-Fu Chang, Gang Hua, and John R. Smith

Discovering Latent Domains for Multisource Domain Adaptation ... 702
Judy Hoffman, Brian Kulis, Trevor Darrell, and Kate Saenko

Visual Recognition Using Local Quantized Patterns ... 716
Sibt ul Hussain and Bill Triggs

Randomized Spatial Partition for Scene Recognition ... 730
Yuning Jiang, Junsong Yuan, and Gang Yu

Nested Sparse Quantization for Efficient Feature Coding ... 744
Xavier Boix, Gemma Roig, Christian Leistner, and Luc Van Gool

Comparative Evaluation of Binary Features ... 759
Jared Heinly, Enrique Dunn, and Jan-Michael Frahm

Negative Evidences and Co-occurences in Image Retrieval: The Benefit of PCA and Whitening ... 774
Hervé Jégou and Ondřej Chum

WαSH: Weighted α-Shapes for Local Feature Detection ... 788
Christos Varytimidis, Konstantinos Rapantzikos, and Yannis Avrithis

Sparselet Models for Efficient Multiclass Object Detection ... 802
Hyun Oh Song, Stefan Zickler, Tim Althoff, Ross Girshick, Mario Fritz, Christopher Geyer, Pedro Felzenszwalb, and Trevor Darrell

Nested Pictorial Structures ... 816
Steve Gu, Ying Zheng, and Carlo Tomasi

Performance Capture of Interacting Characters with Handheld Kinects ... 828
Genzhi Ye, Yebin Liu, Nils Hasler, Xiangyang Ji, Qionghai Dai, and Christian Theobalt

Dynamic Eye Movement Datasets and Learnt Saliency Models for Visual Action Recognition ... 842
Stefan Mathe and Cristian Sminchisescu

Coherent Filtering: Detecting Coherent Motions from Crowd Clutters 857
Bolei Zhou, Xiaoou Tang, and Xiaogang Wang

Robust 3D Action Recognition with Random Occupancy Patterns 872
Jiang Wang, Zicheng Liu, Jan Chorowski, Zhuoyuan Chen, and Ying Wu

Author Index 887

Object-Centric Spatial Pooling for Image Classification

Olga Russakovsky[1], Yuanqing Lin[2], Kai Yu[3], and Li Fei-Fei[1]

[1] Stanford University
{olga,feifeili}@cs.stanford.edu
[2] NEC Laboratories America
ylin@nec-labs.com
[3] Baidu Inc.
yukai@baidu.com

Abstract. Spatial pyramid matching (SPM) based pooling has been the dominant choice for state-of-art image classification systems. In contrast, we propose a novel *object-centric spatial pooling* (OCP) approach, following the intuition that knowing the location of the object of interest can be useful for image classification. OCP consists of two steps: (1) inferring the location of the objects, and (2) using the location information to pool foreground and background features separately to form the image-level representation. Step (1) is particularly challenging in a typical classification setting where precise object location annotations are not available during training. To address this challenge, we propose a framework that learns object detectors using only image-level class labels, or so-called weak labels. We validate our approach on the challenging PASCAL07 dataset. Our learned detectors are comparable in accuracy with state-of-the-art weakly supervised detection methods. More importantly, the resulting OCP approach significantly outperforms SPM-based pooling in image classification.

1 Introduction

Image object recognition has been a major research direction in computer vision. Its goal is two-fold: deciding *what* objects are in an image (classification) and *where* these objects are in the image (localization). Intuitively, if we know which objects are present, determining their location should be easier; alternatively, if we know where to look, recognizing the objects should be easier. Therefore, it is natural to think of these two tasks jointly [1–9].

However, in practice, classification and localization are often treated separately. Object localization is generally deemed as a harder problem than image classification even when precise object location annotations are available during training. In the purely image classification setting, it may be seen as a detour to attempt to localize objects. As a result, current state-of-the-art image classification systems don't go through the trouble of inferring object location information [10–14]. Most classification systems are based on spatial pyramid matching

A. Fitzgibbon et al. (Eds.): ECCV 2012, Part II, LNCS 7573, pp. 1–15, 2012.

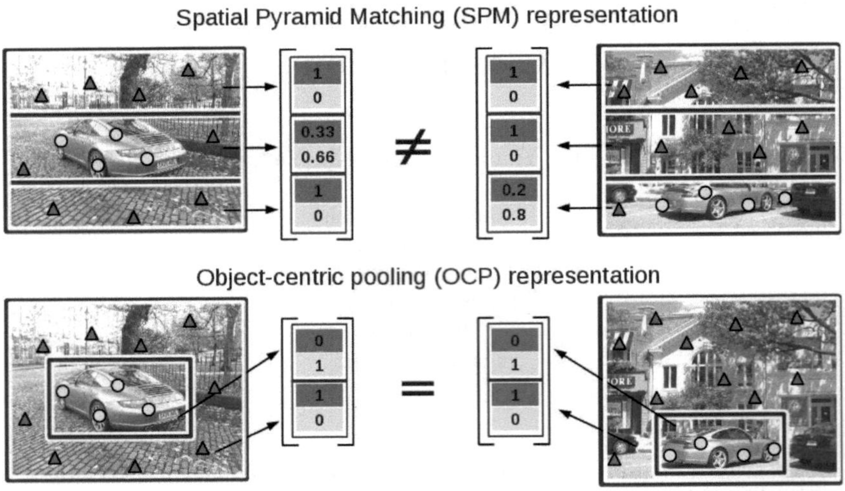

Fig. 1. We present *object-centric spatial pooling* (OCP), a method which first localizes the object of interest and then pools foreground object features separately from background features. In contrast, Spatial Pyramid Matching (SPM) based pooling [15] (top), the most common spatial pooling method for object classification, results in inconsistent image features when the object of interest (here, a car) appears in different locations within images, making is more difficult to learn an appearance model of the object. For the purpose of easy illustration, circles (yellow) denote object-related local features, triangles (green) denote background-related local features, and the numbers indicate the fraction of the respective local features in each pooling region.

(SPM) [15] which pools low-level image features over pre-defined coarse spatial bins, with little effort to localize the objects [10–12].

This paper proposes a novel *object-centric spatial pooling* (OCP) approach for image classification. In contrast to SPM pooling, OCP first infers the location of the object of interest and then pools low level features separately in the foreground and background to form the image-level representation. As shown in Figure 1, if the location of the object of interest (a car in this case) is available, OCP tends to produce more consistent feature vectors than SPM pooling. Therefore, object location information can be very useful for further pushing the state-of-the-art performance of image classification.

Of course, the challenge for OCP is deriving accurate enough location information for improving classification performance. If the derived location information is not sufficiently accurate, it can end up hurting classification accuracy. There is interesting previous work on learning object detectors using only image-level class labels (or weak labels) [16, 17]. Although these methods yield impressive localization results, they are formulated as detection tasks and have not been shown to be helpful for improving image classification performance. Methods such as [1–7] attempt to localize objects to improve image classification accuracy but only demonstrate results on simple datasets such as subsets of

Caltech101 classes. In contrast, we evaluate our proposed OCP method on the highly cluttered PASCAL07 data [14], where we are able to localize objects with accuracy comparable to state-of-the-art weakly supervised object localization methods [16, 17] as well as to significantly improve image classification performance. To the best of our knowledge, this paper is the first to use weakly supervised object detection to improve image classification on PASCAL07, which is considered a challenging object detection dataset even when bounding box annotations are provided for training.

2 Related Work

Classification. Many state-of-the-art image classification systems follow the popular image feature extraction procedure [10–12] shown in Figure 2. First, for each image, low-level descriptors like DHOG [18] or LBP [19] are sampled on a dense grid. They are then coded into higher dimensions through vector quantization, local coordinate coding (LCC) [10] or sparse coding [12]. Finally the coded vectors are pooled together, typically using SPM [15] pooling, to form the image-level representation. Much research in image classification has been focused on the former two steps, namely on different types of low-level descriptors [18–20] and coding methods [10, 12, 21–23]. In this paper we focus on the spatial pooling step, replacing the popular SPM with our object-centric pooling.

Methods such as [1–7] use localization information learned in a weakly supervised way to help boost classification accuracy by focusing on pooling low-level object features without background features. However, most of them only validate their approach on less cluttered and mostly centered datasets such as subsets of Caltech101 categories, Oxford Flowers 17 dataset, etc. For example, recently Feng et al. [7] presented a geometric pooling approach which resizes each image to the same size and learns a class-specific weighting factor for each grid position in an image. On the Caltech101 dataset, where most images are roughly aligned and centered, this method greatly improves over the previous state-of-the-art [10]. However, it has difficulty handling cluttered images like the ones of PASCAL07 [14]. Further, Nguyen et al. [1] and Bilen et al. [2] explicitly mention that some degree of context information (like road for cars) needs to be included into the detected object bounding box in order to be useful for image classification. This leads to very rough object localization even on simple datasets. In

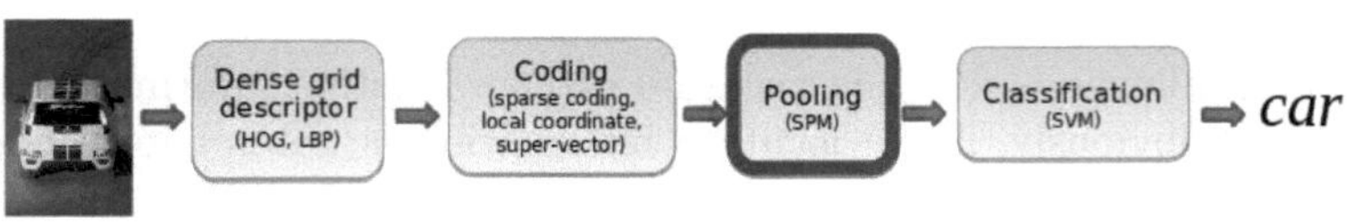

Fig. 2. A popular image classification pipeline of state-of-the-art methods [10–12]. In this paper we focus on the pooling step and propose an object-centric spatial pooling approach which achieves superior classification accuracy compared to the SPM pooling.

contrast, our work deals with high intra-class variability in object location and our proposed generic object-centric spatial pooling approach yields both classification improvements as well as competitive object localization results on the challenging PASCAL07 data.

If object location information is available during training, methods such as [24, 25] have been used to detect the object of interest, and [8, 9] showed how to use the output of object detectors to boost classification performance. There are two main differences compared our approach. First, we focus on the purely classification setting where no annotations beyond image-level class labels are available during training. Second, we learn a joint model for both localization and classification instead of combining the scores of the two tasks as post-processing.

Weakly Supervised Localization. There is a large body of work on weakly supervised object localization [16, 17, 26–28]. Most of these methods use HOG-type low-level features [18] which are faster for detection but have been shown to be inferior than bag-of-words models for classification [10, 25]. The current state of the art is the work of Pandey and Lazebnik [17] which uses deformable parts-based models [24] trained discriminatively in a weakly supervised fashion for object localization. In contrast, our goal here is image classification (not object localization) although we do utilize localization as an intermediate step.

3 Object-Centric Spatial Pooling (OCP) for Image Classification

Let's first use an empirical experiment to quantitatively see how object location information can dramatically improve image classification performance. On the PASCAL07 classification dataset [14], we trained two classifiers for each object class: one classifier using features extracted from the full image, and the other classifier using features extracted only from the provided tight bounding boxes around the objects. We followed [10] in extracting image features and training linear classifiers. Both classifiers were trained on the training set and tested on the validation set. The former classifier (trained on full images) yielded 52.0% mean average precision (mAP), whereas the latter classifier (trained and tested on tight bounding boxes) achieved an astonishing 69.7% mAP. In comparison the current state-of-the-art classification result with a single type of low-level descriptor (which used a more involved coding method as well as significant post-processing) [11] is just 59.2% mAP. Therefore, it is evident that learning to properly localize the object in the image holds great promise for improving classification accuracy.

Now, the challenge is deriving accurate enough location information to help classification. Obviously, if the location information is not reliable enough, it can easily end up hurting classification performance instead. Reliable localization becomes very challenging on generic dataset like PASCAL07 [14] where objects vary greatly in appearance and viewpoint, are often occluded, and appear in highly cluttered and unstructured scenes. In fact, most work on weakly supervised localization uses simpler datasets [1, 2, 26–28]. Recently, Deselaers et al. [16] were the first to tackle PASCAL07. To simplify the problem, however, they trained object class models separately for different viewpoints of objects. We are interested in learning generic object detectors without any additional annotations and evaluating classification performance on the original 20 object classes. To the best of our knowledge we are the first to do so.

To this end, we introduce a novel framework of *object-centric spatial pooling* (OCP) for image classification. OCP consists of two steps: (1) inferring the location of the objects of interested; and (2) pooling low-level features from the foreground and the background separately to form the image-level representation. In order to infer the object locations, we propose an iterative procedure for learning object detectors from only image class labels (or weak labels). Very different from existing methods for learning weakly supervised object detectors [16, 17], our approach directly optimizes the classification objective function and uses object detection as an intermediate step. This is described in Section 3.1. More importantly, OCP enables feature sharing between classification and detection: the resulting feature representation of OCP can be seen as both a bounding box representation (for detection) and an image representation (for classification). This is described in detail in Section 3.2. As we show in Section 4, such feature sharing plays an essential role in improving classification performance.

3.1 Classification Formulation

We assume we are dealing with the binary image classification problem since multi-class classification is often solved in practice by training one-versus-all binary classifiers. Given N data pairs, $\{\mathbf{I}_i, y_i\}_{i=1}^N$, where I_i is the ith image and $y_i \in \{+1, -1\}$ is a binary label of the image, the SVM formulation for binary image classification with OCP becomes

$$\min_{\mathbf{w},b} \frac{1}{2}||\mathbf{w}||^2 + C\sum_{i}^{N} \xi_i \tag{1}$$

$$\text{s.t.} \quad y_i \max_{B \in \mathcal{BB}(i)} \left[\mathbf{w}^T \mathcal{P}_B(I_i) + b\right] \geq 1 - \xi_i \tag{2}$$

$$\xi_i \geq 0 \quad \forall i \tag{3}$$

where $\mathbf{w}$ is SVM weight vector, b is bias term, $\mathcal{P}_B(I_i)$ is the image feature representation of image I_i using OCP with given bounding box B, and $\mathcal{BB}(i)$ is the collection of all bounding box windows within image I_i. $\mathcal{BB}(i)$ can be obtained by either densely sampling sliding windows or by using salient regions [25]. We do not require any ground truth localization information in this optimization.

Interestingly, the above formulation can also be viewed as multi-instance learning (MIL) for object detection [1]. However, as in [1], the traditional MIL formation often only uses the foreground for constructing the bounding box features and discards the background information. This has its drawbacks in both detection and classification. As a result, the method of [1] was not able to accurately localize objects even on simpler datasets such as Caltech101; it tended to choose regions which were larger than the object of interest to encompass contextual information for classification. We fix these drawbacks by using a foreground-background representation, as described below. As a result, we are able to localize objects on the significantly more challenging PASCAL07 [14] with accuracy comparable to state-of-the-art weakly supervised object localization methods [16, 17].

3.2 Foreground-Background Feature Representation

In the classification formulation in Eq. 3, the foreground-background feature representation of OCP provides a natural mechanism for feature sharing between classification and detection. In fact, even for standalone detection and classification, the foreground-background feature representation is advantageous compared to traditional foreground-only feature representation.

Foreground-Background for Classification. The foreground-background feature representation provides stronger classification performance than its foreground-only counterpart. This is not surprising since the background provides strong scene context for classification [4, 29]. For example, for the class *boat*, the surrounding water in the image may provide a strong clue that this image contains a boat; similarly, seeing road at the bottom of an image can strongly indicate that this image is likely about *cars*. Going back to the classifiers trained on the tight bounding boxes as described at the beginning of Section 3, if we replace the foreground-only feature representation with the foreground-background representation, we further improve the classification mAP from 69.7% to 71.1%. This highlights the fact that the foreground-background feature representation carries important information for classification which may be missing in the foreground-only representation. This is illustrated in Figure 3.

Foreground-Background for Detection. Object detectors trained with the foreground-background features also tend to yield more accurate bounding boxes during detection. Since the foreground and background models are learned jointly, they will prevent the object appearance features from leaking into the background, and context features from leaking into the foreground. This is illustrated in Figure 4. To validate the effectiveness of the foreground-background feature representation for detection, we also experimented on PASCAL07, training fully supervised object detectors using the foreground-only and the foreground-background feature representation respectively. It was no surprise that the

Fig. 3. Example images which were misclassified using just the foreground representation but correctly classified when using the foreground-background representation

Fig. 4. Bounding boxes bb_1 and bb_2 have a similar foreground-only feature representation, but they are very different under the foreground-background representation. Here, the numbers denote the count of object-related descriptors. For bb_1, parts of object that leaked into the background will be greatly discounted by the background model.

foreground-background feature representation yielded significantly better detection performance. Here we skip the details of the experiments for simplicity since supervised detection is not the major focus of this paper. In Figure 6 in the experimental results section, however, we show the differences in detections made with the foreground-only and the foreground-background model in our OCP framework.

With the foreground-background representation of OCP, optimizing the formulation in Eq. 3 can be seen as a simultaneous detection and classification procedure. This is because the foreground-background representation can be seen as both a bounding box representation (for detection) and an image-level representation (for classification).

3.3 Optimization

Now that we have defined our objective and our foreground-background feature representation, we discuss how to optimize this formulation. The optimization in Eq. 1 is non-convex because of the maximization operation in the constraints, thus we need to be careful during optimization to avoid local minima. In particular, since we are not given any localization information during training, our optimization algorithm consists of an outer loop that bootstraps the background region from the foreground and an inner loop that trains the apperance model.

Outer Loop: Bootstrapping Background Regions. In a purely classification setting, no foreground and background annotations are provided initially. We initialize the background region by cropping out a 16-pixel border of each image. Then the outer loops bootstraps the background by gradually shrinking the smallest bounding box considered in the bounding box search ($\mathcal{BB}(i)$ in Eq. 1). Thus we begin localizing using large windows and iteratively allow smaller and smaller windows as we learn more and more accurate models. As the background region is allowed to grow, the algorithm learns more and more accurate background models. If the algorithm goes too aggressively, it will end up in bad local minima. For example, if the localization is so inaccurate that many features from the object of interest appear in the background region, the model would learn that objects features actually belong to the background. This would lead to bad classification models which are hard to correct in later iterations. However, as long as such bad local minima are avoided, the specific rate of shrinking the foreground region does not affect performance in our experiments.

Inner Loop: Learning the Appearance Model for Detection. Given the current constraint on the background size, we need to learn the best object appearance model. This is done in two steps: (1) detection, where given the current appearance model we find the best possible object location from positive images (images that are known to contain the object of interest); and (2) classification, where given the proposed bounding boxes from positive images as positive examples and a large sample of bounding boxes from negative images as negative examples, we construct the bounding box representation using OCP and then train a binary SVM classifier for discriminating the positive bounding boxes from the negative bounding boxes. In contrast to more common treatments which would need another loop to bootstrap the difficult negative bounding boxes and iteratively improve the SVM model, here we get rid of this loop by solving an SVM optimization directly with all (often millions) negative bounding boxes.

We make use of the candidate image regions proposed in an unsupervised fashion by [25] to avoid both sampling too many negative windows for classification and running sliding windows search for detection. Since the candidate bounding boxes aim to achieve high recall rate ($> 96\%$), we ended up with 1000$\sim$3000 candidate bounding boxes per image. For PASCAL07, we have 5011 images in the training and validation sets. Therefore, for each inner loop, we need to solve for 20 binary SVMs with about 10 million data examples. Furthermore, our feature representation for OCP is very high-dimensional: we used a codebook of 8192 for LLC coding [10], pool the low-level features on the foreground region using 1×1 and 3×3 SPM pooling regions [15], and separately pool all low-level features features in the background, thus resulting in a feature vector of dimension $8192 \times 11 = 90112$. Indeed, if we save all the feature vectors from the 5011 images, this would require more than 700G of space. Most off-the-shelf SVM solvers would not be able to handle such a large-scale problem. So, we developed a stochastic gradient descent algorithm with averaging using a similar idea to [30]. We were able to run an inner loop in 7$\sim$8 hours and to finish the training (inner look and outer loop) in about 3 days on a single machine.

4 Experiments

We validate our approach on the challenging PASCAL07 dataset [14], containing 5011 images for training and validation, and 4952 images for testing. This dataset consists of 20 object categories, with object instances ocurring in a variety of scales, locations and viewpoints.

Image Representation. For low-level features, we extract DHOG [18] features with patch sizes 16×16, 25×25, 31×31 and 46×46. We then run Linear Locality-Constrained (LLC) coding [10] using a codebook of size 8192 and 5 nearest neighbors. For the baseline representation, we pool the DHOG features using 1×1 and 3×3 SPM pooling regions [15] over the full image. Thus each image is represented using a feature vector of dimension $8192 \times 10 = 81920$. For our object-centric pooling, we use the same SPM representation but on the foreground region and also pool over all low-level features in the background separately, thus giving us a feature dimension of $8192 \times 11 = 90112$.

4.1 Joint Classification and Localization

The main insight behind our approach is that object classification and detection can be mutually beneficial. In particular, as the classification accuracy improves we expect detection accuracy to improve as well, and vice versa. We begin by verifying that this is indeed the case. Figure 5 shows the steady improvement in mean average precision on both classification and detection over the iterations (outer loop) of our algorithms. As a baseline (iteration 0), we use a classifier trained on full images with the SPM spatial pooling representation, which is equivalent to assuming an empty background region in foreground-background representation. Interestingly, even after just one iteration, our classification mAP is already 54.8%, which is 0.5% greater than the 54.3% SPM classification result.[1] In the end our OCP method achieves 57.2% classification mAP, significantly outperforming the SPM representation. In fact, it significantly outperforms even a much richer 4-level SPM representation of size 8192×30 which achieves only 54.8% classification mAP. On the detection side, our approach was able to improve the baseline of 6.10% detection mAP to the final 15.0%.

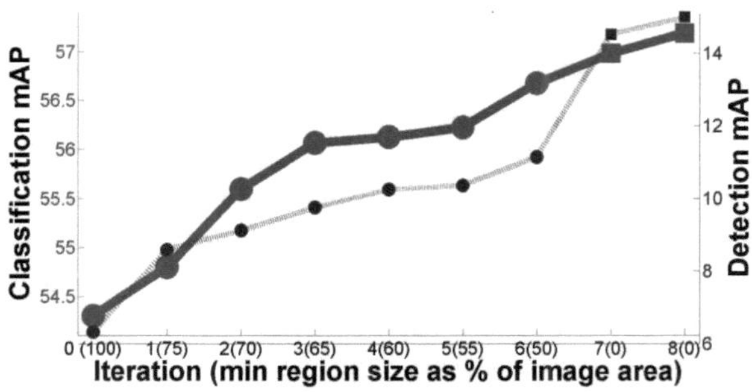

Fig. 5. Classification and detection mAP on the PASCAL07 test set over the iterations of our joint detection and classification approach. The red solid line is classification mAP, and the blue dotted line is detection mAP. We see a steady joint improvement of classification and detection accuracy.

[1] We make use of only one type of low-level image descriptor in contrast to [9, 31], and don't do any additional post-processing of the features in contrast to [10, 11]. The work of [10] gives 59.3% classification mAP on this dataset when using LLC coding, but this relied on significant post-processing of the resulting image features. To simplify the comparison, we do not involve the post-processing.

It is important to note that jointly optimizing detection and classification using OCP as in Eq. 3 plays an essential role in achieving the joint improvements for classification and detection. As we show below, when detection and classification are optimized separately, higher detection accuracy may not always means higher classification accuracy.

4.2 Image Classification

OCP significantly boost of classification accuracy on most of the 20 object classes, as shown in Table 1. In particular, OCP achieves significant improvement on the following categories: dog (7.3% improvement), bottle (7.1%), bicycle (6.8%), sheep (6.2%), diningtable (5.9%), bus (4.6%), motorbike (4.3%) and even 1.3% on the notoriously difficult potted plant category. Noticeably, many of these categories are relatively small objects (like bottles) embedded in cluttered environments. OCP greatly improves classification accuracy on these categories by making an effort to localize the objects.

Table 1. Classification AP of object-centric spatial pooling compared to the standard SPM spatial pooling on the PASCAL07 test set

Method	aero	bicycle	bird	boat	bottle	bus	car	cat	chair	cow	dining
SPM	72.5	56.3	**49.5**	63.5	22.4	60.1	76.4	57.5	**51.9**	42.2	48.9
OCP	**74.2**	**63.1**	45.1	**65.9**	**29.5**	**64.7**	**79.2**	**61.4**	51.0	**45.0**	**54.8**

Method	dog	horse	motbike	person	plant	sheep	sofa	train	tv	Mean
SPM	38.1	75.1	62.8	82.9	20.5	38.1	46.0	**71.7**	50.5	54.3
OCP	**45.4**	**76.3**	**67.1**	**84.4**	**21.8**	**44.3**	**48.8**	70.7	**51.7**	**57.2**

There are three categories that proved difficult for OCP to improve: chairs (−0.9%), trains (−1.0%) and birds (−4.4%). For the bird and chair categories, the objects are often occluded (e.g., birds are often occluded by trees, and chairs are often occluded by people sitting on them), which make them very challenging for detection even when bounding box annotations are available (see [14, 24]). For the slight drop in the train category, since trains are already relatively well-centered in images, SPM pooling alone yields very satisfactory classification accuracy (71.7%) and is difficult to further improve.

We also investigate using the foreground-only (instead of the foreground-background) feature representation when optimizing Eq. 3.[2] This foreground-only representation leads to an improvement from the baseline SPM model – the mAP increases from 54.3% to 55.7%. This is a 1.4% improvement as compared to the 2.9% improvement as in the case of our foreground-background

[2] This experiment is a more assertive version of the technique described in Nguyen et al. [1]: the optimization framework is similar to [1] but with significantly stronger low-level descriptors (HOG descriptors [18] with LLC coding [10] compared to vector-quantized SIFT [20]) and with much more negative training data.

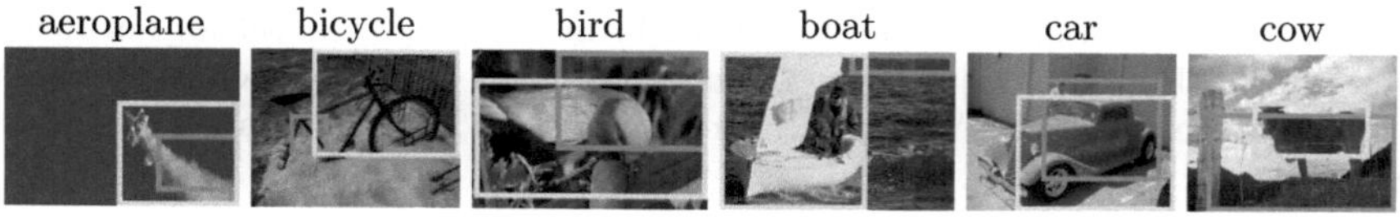

Fig. 6. Images where object-centric pooling with the foreground-background model (yellow) localizes objects more accurately than the foreground-only model (green)

representation. Figure 6 illustrates some location results, showing that foreground-background representation often yields better localization.

4.3 Weakly Supervised Object Localization

Even though our primary goal is image classification, the proposed object-centric spatial pooling also accurately localizes the objects of interest. PASCAL07 is a very challenging dataset for weakly supervised localization (where bounding box information is not available during training). Only a few recent works have tackled this data (Deselaers et al. [16] and Pandey and Lazebnik [17]). They focused on localizing only a handful of the object classes and use the available viewpoint annotations during training to assist learning. In contrast, we work on the full dataset without using these additional annotations to mimic the purely classification setting.

Weakly supervised localization can be evaluated directly on the training set (in our case the PASCAL07 trainval set) since only image-level class labels are available during training. Following [16, 17] we compute localization accuracy as the percentage of training image in which an instance was correctly localized by the highest-scoring detection according to the PASCAL criterion (window intersection over the union $\geq 50\%$). On the 14 classes of PASCAL07-*all*[3] introduced by [16], our localization accuracy is 27.4%, which is comparable to 26% of [16] using additional viewpoint annotations and 30.0% of [17].

As we're most interested in inferring object location on unseen images, we evaluate the detection accuracy on the test set as well. Table 2 compares our detection average precision on six PASCAL07-6x2 classes [16] evaluated on all test images with the current state-of-the-art in weakly supervised localization. We obtain 22.8%, outperforming the previous best 20.8% of [17] which used additional viewpoint annotations. On all 20 classes, we obtained 15.0% detection mAP compared to 29.1% mAP of the state-of-the-art deformable part-based model that used bounding box labels for detector training [24].

Figure 7 shows some examples of our detection results on PASCAL07 test set. Localization is often quite reasonable, which is amazing considering the difficulty of the dataset and the lack of any bounding box annotations during training. Even on images with multiple object instances our method is sometimes able to separate out the different instances.

[3] PASCAL07-*all* includes all classes of PASCAL07 except bird, car, cat, cow, dog and sheep [16].

Table 2. Comparison of detection AP on the PASCAL07-6x2 test set for our method versus [16, 17]. Both [16, 17] split up the objects by left and right viewpoint to make the models easier to learn. We do not make use of these additional labels and learn a single model for each object.

Method	aeroplane		bicycle		boat		bus		horse		motorbike		Average
	left	right	left	right	left	right	left	right	left	right	left	right	
Deselaers [16]	9.1	23.6	33.4	49.4	0.0	0.0	0.0	16.4	9.6	9.1	20.9	16.1	16.0
Pandey [17]	7.5	21.1	38.5	44.8	0.3	0.5	0	0.3	45.9	17.3	43.8	27.2	20.8
OCP	**30.8**		25.0		**3.6**		**26.0**		21.3		29.9		**22.8**

Fig. 7. Foreground regions detected by the object-centric pooling framework on PASCAL07 test images. The models are learned without any ground truth localization information. Yellow boxes correspond to correct detections and red boxes are failed detections. On images where multiple instances of a object class are presented, we show the top few detections after running non-maximal suppression.

Interestingly, when we used the location information derived from the deformable part-based model mentioned above [24] learned with the help of bounding box annotations, images features constructed using our image representation with the foreground-background pooling yielded a classification mAP of 56.9%. This is inferior to the aforementioned 57.2% classification mAP obtained using

OCP, where our proposed approach in Eq. 3 did not use any bounding box annotations and only achieved 15.0% detection mAP. This strongly highlights the importance of the formulation in Eq. 3, which uses classification as the major optimization objective and jointly optimizes detection and classification when solving the optimization.

5 Conclusion

We presented an object-centric spatial pooling (OCP) approach for improving classification performance. The challenge of OCP is training reliable object detectors with no available bounding box annotations as in a typical classification setting. We propose a framework that directly optimizes classification objective with detection being treated as an intermediate step. The key to this framework is the foreground-background feature representation by OCP that naturally enables feature sharing between detection and classification. Our results on the challenging PASCAL07 dataset show that not only is the proposed OCP approach able to improve the classification accuracy compared to using SPM pooling, but it also yields very reasonable object detection results. We believe this is an important step toward better image understanding – not only deciding *what* objects are in an image but also figuring out *where* these objects are.

Our future work includes incorporating bounding box annotations during training (from all or just a subset of images) to further improve the classification performance. We are also very interested in exploiting even more powerful visual features than the simple LLC feature as used in this paper. As demonstrates by the motivation experiment described in the beginning of Section 3, there is much room for improving classification performance by utilizing location information. This paper is just an initial step toward that direction.

Acknowledgements. This work was done while Olga Russakovsky was a summer intern and Kai Yu was a research staff member at NEC Labs. Li Fei-Fei was supported partially by a MURI grant from ONR. Many thanks to Jia Deng at Stanford and to Anelia Angelova, Timothee Cour, Chang Huang and Shenghuo Zhu at NEC Labs for helpful discussions.

References

1. Nguyen, M.H., Torresani, L., de la Torre, F., Rother, C.: Weakly supervised discriminative localization and classification: a joint learning process. In: ICCV (2009)
2. Bilen, H., Namboodiri, V.P., Gool, L.V.: Object and action classification with latent variables. In: BMVC (2010)
3. Chai, Y., Lempitsky, V., Zisserman, A.: BiCoS: A bi-level co-segmentation method for image classification. In: CVPR (2011)
4. Murphy, K., Torralba, A., Eaton, D., Freeman, W.: Object detection and localization using local and global features. Lecture Notes in Compute Science (2006)

5. Crandall, D.J., Huttenlocher, D.P.: Weakly Supervised Learning of Part-Based Spatial Models for Visual Object Recognition. In: Leonardis, A., Bischof, H., Pinz, A. (eds.) ECCV 2006. LNCS, vol. 3951, pp. 16–29. Springer, Heidelberg (2006)
6. Zhang, Y., Chen, T.: Weakly supervised object recognition and localization with invariant high order features. In: BMVC (2010)
7. Feng, J., Ni, B., Tian, Q., Yan, S.: Geometric ℓ_p-norm feature pooling for image classification. In: CVPR (2011)
8. Hedi, H., Frederic, J., Cordelia, S.: Combining efficient object localization and image classification. In: ICCV (2009)
9. Song, Z., Chen, Q., Huang, Z., Hua, Y., Yan, S.: Contextualizing object detection and classification. In: CVPR (2011)
10. Wang, J., Yang, J., Yu, K., Lv, F., Huang, T., Gong, Y.: Locality-constrained Linear Coding for image classification. In: CVPR (2010)
11. Zhou, X., Yu, K., Zhang, T., Huang, T.S.: Image Classification Using Super-Vector Coding of Local Image Descriptors. In: Daniilidis, K., Maragos, P., Paragios, N. (eds.) ECCV 2010, Part V. LNCS, vol. 6315, pp. 141–154. Springer, Heidelberg (2010)
12. Yang, J., Yu, K., Gong, Y., Huang, T.: Linear spatial pyramid matching using sparse coding for image classification. In: CVPR (2009)
13. Berg, A., Deng, J., Satheesh, S., Su, H., Fei-Fei, L.: Large scale visual recognition challenge (2010-2011), `http://www.image-net.org/challenges/LSVRC/2011/`
14. Everingham, M., Van Gool, L., Williams, C.K.I., Winn, J., Zisserman, A.: The Pascal Visual Object Classes (VOC) challenge. IJCV 88, 303–338 (2010)
15. Lazebnik, S., Schmid, C., Ponce, J.: Beyond bags of features: Spatial Pyramid Matching for recognizing natural scene categories. In: CVPR (2006)
16. Deselaers, T., Alexe, B., Ferrari, V.: Localizing Objects While Learning Their Appearance. In: Daniilidis, K., Maragos, P., Paragios, N. (eds.) ECCV 2010, Part IV. LNCS, vol. 6314, pp. 452–466. Springer, Heidelberg (2010)
17. Pandey, M., Lazebnik, S.: Scene recognition and weakly supervised object localization with deformable part-based models. In: ICCV (2011)
18. Dalal, N., Triggs, B.: Histograms of Oriented Gradients for Human Detection. In: CVPR (2005)
19. Ahonen, T., Hadid, A., Pietikinen, M.: Face description with local binary patterns: Application to face recognition. PAMI 28 (2006)
20. Lowe, D.G.: Distinctive image features from scale-invariant keypoints. IJCV 60, 91–110 (2004)
21. Huang, Y., Huang, K., Tan, T.: Salient coding for image classification. In: CVPR (2011)
22. Gao, S., Chia, L.T., Tsang, I.W.: Multi-layer group sparse coding – for concurrent image classification and annotation. In: CVPR (2011)
23. Perronnin, F., Sánchez, J., Mensink, T.: Improving the Fisher Kernel for Large-Scale Image Classification. In: Daniilidis, K., Maragos, P., Paragios, N. (eds.) ECCV 2010, Part IV. LNCS, vol. 6314, pp. 143–156. Springer, Heidelberg (2010)
24. Felzenszwalb, P., Girshick, R., McAllester, D., Ramanan, D.: Object detection with discriminatively trained part based models. PAMI 32 (2010)
25. ovan de Sande, K.E.A., Uijlings, J.R.R., Gevers, T., Smeulders, A.W.M.: Segmentation as selective search for object recognition. In: ICCV (2011)
26. Russell, B.C., Freeman, W.T., Effros, A.A., Sivic, J., Zisserman, A.: Using multiple segmentations to discover objects and their extent in image collections. In: CVPR (2006)

27. Kim, G., Torralba, A.: Unsupervised detection of regions of interest using iterative link analysis. In: NIPS (2009)
28. Chum, O., Zisserman, A.: An exemplar model for learning object classes. In: CVPR (2007)
29. Oliva, A., Torralba, A.: The role of context in object recognition. Trends in Cognitive Sciences 11 (2007)
30. Lin, Y., Lv, F., Cao, L., Zhu, S., Yang, M., Cour, T., Yu, K., Huang, T.: Large-scale image classification: Fast feature extraction and SVM training. In: CVPR (2011)
31. Guillaumin, M., Verbeek, J., Schmid, C.: Multimodal semi-supervised learning for image classification. In: CVPR (2010)

Statistics of Patch Offsets for Image Completion

Kaiming He and Jian Sun

Microsoft Research Asia

Abstract. Image completion involves filling missing parts in images. In this paper we address this problem through the statistics of patch offsets. We observe that if we match similar patches in the image and obtain their offsets (relative positions), the statistics of these offsets are sparsely distributed. We further observe that a few dominant offsets provide reliable information for completing the image. With these offsets we fill the missing region by combining a stack of shifted images via optimization. A variety of experiments show that our method yields generally better results and is faster than existing state-of-the-art methods.

1 Introduction

Image completion involves the issue of filling missing parts in images. This is a non-trivial task in computer vision/graphics: on one hand, the completed images must be visually plausible; on the other hand, the algorithm must be efficient, because in practice image completion is often applied with user interactions and needs quick feedbacks. For today's consumer-level multi-mega-pixel cameras, high-quality and fast image completion is still a challenging problem.

One category of image completion methods are diffusion-based [1–5]. These methods are mainly designed for filling narrow or small holes (known as "inpainting") but work less well for large missing regions because they are less suitable for synthesizing semantic textures or structures.

Another category of methods that are more effective for large holes are exemplar-based. We further categorize them into two groups: *matching-based* and *MRF-based*. Matching-based methods [6–10] explicitly match patches in the region to be filled with those in the known region and copy the content. This makes it possible to synthesize textures [6] and more complex content [7–10]. The methods in [6–8] progress in greedy fashions, whereas [9] adopts a global cost function called *coherence measure*, where each patch in the filled region is optimally similar to a known patch. This measure helps to yield more coherent results and is later generalized for image retargeting/reshuffling [11]. But because the underlying cost has multiple disconnected local optima, this method is very sensitive to initialization and to the optimization strategy.

Matching-based methods are computationally expensive. A fast PatchMatch method [12] largely relieves this problem and is combined with [9]. The *Content Aware Fill* in Adobe Photoshop, implementing [9, 12] as reported in [13], is arguably the current state-of-the-art image completion software in terms of quality and speed.

A. Fitzgibbon et al. (Eds.): ECCV 2012, Part II, LNCS 7573, pp. 16–29, 2012.

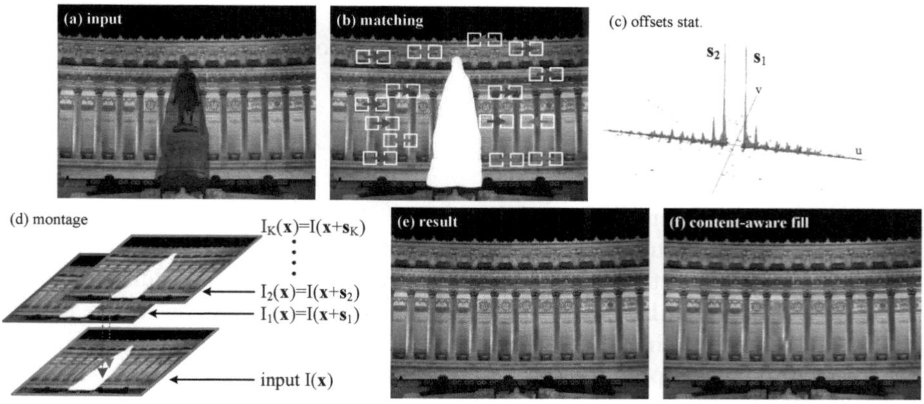

Fig. 1. Algorithm outline. (a) Input image with a mask overlayed. (b) Matching similar patches in the known region. (c) The statistics of the offsets of the similar patches. The offsets corresponding to the highest peaks are picked out. (d) Combining a set of shifted images with the given offsets. (e) Our result. (f) Result of Content-Aware Fill.

Exemplar-based methods can also be realized by optimizing discrete Markov Random Fields (MRFs), as in Priority-BP [14] and Shift-map [15]. Rather than match patches, these methods rearrange the patch/pixel locations to complete the image. The labels to be optimized in the MRFs are absolute locations [14] or relative offsets [15]. The MRFs are optimized via belief propagation (BP) [14] or graph-cuts [15]. Though avoiding matching patches, these methods are computationally expensive: the time complexity is linear in the number of labels and also in the number of unknown pixels, so is quadratic in the image pixel number. Even with the help of a hierarchical solver [15] or label pruning [14], they may still take tens of seconds to process small images (*e.g.*, 400×300).

We notice that exemplar-based methods, either matching-based or MRF-based, must implicitly or explicitly assign each unknown pixel/patch an *offset* - the relative location from where it copies the content. But existing methods do not predict reliable offsets beforehand, and generally allow any possible offsets. We will show this is not beneficial. In terms of quality, unrestricted labels may lead to unexpected bias for MRF optimization (*cf.* Sec. 3.3), or make the coherence measure [9] difficult to be optimized (*cf.* Sec. 3.4). In terms of speed, a huge label set demands very long running time for MRF-based methods.

In this paper we propose a novel method for high-quality and fast image completion. We observe that if we match similar patches in the image, the statistics of patch offsets are sparsely distributed (as in Fig. 1(c)): a majority of patches have similar offsets, forming several prominent peaks in the statistics. Such dominant offsets describe how the patterns are most possibly repeated, and thus provide clues for completing the missing region. We observe that these offsets are predictive for completing linear structures, textures, and repeated objects. With a few (*e.g.*, 60) pre-selected dominant offsets, we combine a stack of shifted images in the missing region via optimization. A variety of experiments show our method performs generally better and is faster than many state-of-the-art methods, including the Content-Aware Fill in Photoshop.

2 Algorithm

In this section we describe the pipeline of our algorithm. We provide reasoning in the next section. Our method has three steps: (i) matching similar patches; (ii) computing offsets statistics; (iii) filling the hole by combining shifted images.

(i) Matching Similar Patches. We first match similar patches *in the known region* and obtain their offsets (Fig. 1(b)). Formally, for each patch P in the known region, we compute its offset $\mathbf{s}$ to its most similar patch:

$$\mathbf{s}(\mathbf{x}) = \arg\min_{\mathbf{s}} \|P(\mathbf{x}+\mathbf{s}) - P(\mathbf{x})\|^2 \quad s.t. \quad |\mathbf{s}| > \tau. \tag{1}$$

Here, $\mathbf{s} = (u, v)$ is the 2-d coordinates of the offset, $\mathbf{x} = (x, y)$ is the position of a patch, and $P(\mathbf{x})$ is a patch centered at $\mathbf{x}$. The similarity is measured by sum of squared differences between two patches. The threshold τ is to preclude nearby patches. This constraint is to avoid trivial statistics as we will soon discuss.

(ii) Computing Offset Statistics. Given all the offsets $\mathbf{s}(\mathbf{x})$, we compute their statistics by a 2-d histogram $h(u, v)$:

$$h(u, v) = \sum_{\mathbf{x}} \delta\left(\mathbf{s}(\mathbf{x}) = (u, v)\right), \tag{2}$$

where $\delta(\cdot)$ is 1 when the argument is true and 0 otherwise. We pick out the K highest peaks of this histogram (details in Sec. 4). They correspond to K dominant offsets. We empirically use $K = 60$ throughout this paper.

Fig. 1(c) shows an example of this histogram. There are two major peaks in the horizontal direction. The offsets given by these peaks indicates how the patterns are repeated in the image. In Sec. 3 we will discuss various cases and explain why these dominant offsets are useful for image completion.

(iii) Combining Shifted Images via Optimization. Given the K offsets, we treat image completion as a *photomontage* [16] problem (Fig. 1(d)): the missing region is filled by combining a stack of shifted images. Formally, we optimize the following MRF energy function:

$$E(L) = \sum_{\mathbf{x}\in\Omega} E_d(L(\mathbf{x})) + \sum_{(\mathbf{x},\mathbf{x}') \,\mid\, \mathbf{x}\in\Omega, \mathbf{x}'\in\Omega} E_s(L(\mathbf{x}), L(\mathbf{x}')). \tag{3}$$

Here Ω is the unknown region (with boundary conditions), and $(\mathbf{x}, \mathbf{x}')$ are 4-connected neighbors. L is the *labeling* where the labels represent the pre-selected offsets $\{\mathbf{s}_i\}_{i=1}^{K}$ or $\mathbf{s}_0 = (0, 0)$[1]. Intuitively, "$L(\mathbf{x}) = i$" means that we copy the pixel at $\mathbf{x} + \mathbf{s}_i$ to the location $\mathbf{x}$.

[1] Here $\mathbf{s}_0$ happens if and only if on boundary pixels.

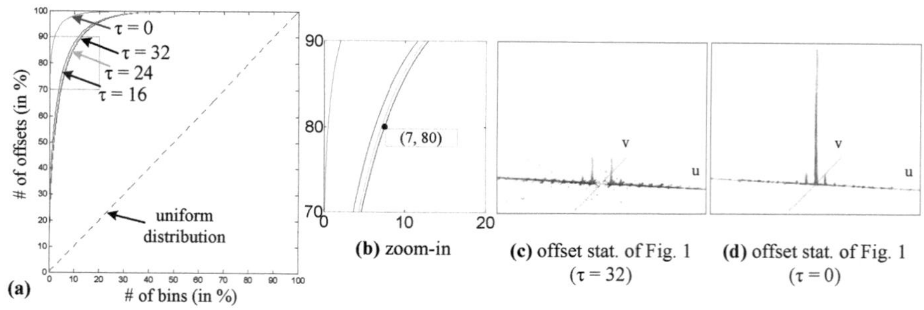

Fig. 2. (a): cumulative distributions of offsets, averaged over 5,000 images. (b): zoon-in of (a). (c)(d): offset statistics of Fig. 1 using τ=32 or τ=0 (shown in the same scale).

The data term E_d is 0 if the label is valid (*i.e.*, $\mathbf{x} + \mathbf{s}$ is a known pixel); otherwise it is $+\infty$. The smoothness term E_s penalizes the incoherent seams. Denoting $a = L(\mathbf{x})$ and $b = L(\mathbf{x}')$, we define E_s as:

$$E_s(a, b) = \|I(\mathbf{x} + \mathbf{s}_a) - I(\mathbf{x} + \mathbf{s}_b)\|^2 + \|I(\mathbf{x}' + \mathbf{s}_a) - I(\mathbf{x}' + \mathbf{s}_b)\|^2. \quad (4)$$

Here $I(\mathbf{x})$ is the RGB color of $\mathbf{x}$. Note $I(\cdot + \mathbf{s})$ is a shifted image given fixed $\mathbf{s}$. If $\mathbf{s}_a \neq \mathbf{s}_b$, there is a seam between $\mathbf{x}$ and $\mathbf{x}'$. Thus (4) penalizes such a seam that the two shifted images $I(\cdot + \mathbf{s}_a)$ and $I(\cdot + \mathbf{s}_b)$ are not similar near this seam. This smoothness term is essentially similar to the those defined in GraphCuts texture [17], Photomontage [16], or Shift-map [15]. We optimize the energy (3) using multi-label graph-cuts [18]. Fig. 1(e) shows a result.

3 Analysis

Given the algorithm described above, we have the following observations.

3.1 Sparsity of Offsets Statistics

One of our key observations is that the offsets statistics are sparse (Fig. 1(c)). We verify this in the *MSRA Salient Object Database* [19] which contains 5,000 images with manually labeled salient objects. We omit these objects and compute the offsets statistics in the background. Note the background still contains various structures or less salient objects. We use 8×8 patches and test τ=16, 24, or 32 in Eq.(1). For each image, we sort the histogram bins in the descending order of their magnitude (*i.e.*, the number of offsets in a bin), and we cumulate the bins. The cumulative distribution, averaged over 5,000 images, is shown in Fig. 2(a). We can see the offsets are sparsely distributed: *e.g.*, when τ=32, about 80% of the offsets are in 7% of all possible bins. We also observe the cumulative distribution changes only a little with different τ values (16, 24, or 32) (Fig. 2(a)(b)). This means the sparsity is insensitive to τ in a wide spectrum.

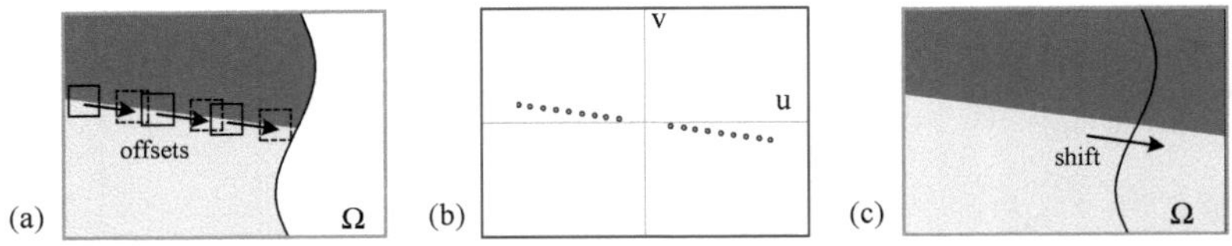

Fig. 3. Illustration of completing linear structures. (a): matching similar patches. (b): ideal dominant offsets. (c) filling the hole by shifting the image using these offsets. Note this figure is for illustration only. The real examples are in Fig. 4.

Fig. 4. Linear structures. Top: input. Middle: dominant offsets. Bottom: our results. (a) Long/thin objects. (b) Linear color edges. (c)(d) Linear textural edges.

It is worth mentioning that the non-nearby constraint ($|\mathbf{s}| > \tau$) in (1) is important. A recent work on natural image statistics [20] shows that the best match of a patch is most probably located near itself. We verify this by setting $\tau = 0$ (thus a patch can match any other patch rather than itself). We can see that the offsets statistics have a single dominant peak around $(0, 0)$ (Fig. 2(d)). Although the offsets distribution is even sparser (see Fig. 2(a)), the zero offset is insignificant for inferring the structures in the hole.

3.2 Offsets Statistics for Image Completion

We further observe that the dominant offsets (with the non-nearby constraint) are informative for filling the hole under at least three situations: (i) linear structures, (ii) regular/random textures, and (iii) repeated objects.

Linear structures include the cases of long and thin objects (Fig. 4(a)), color edges (Fig. 4(b)), and textural edges (Fig. 4(c)(d)). In these examples, we use a

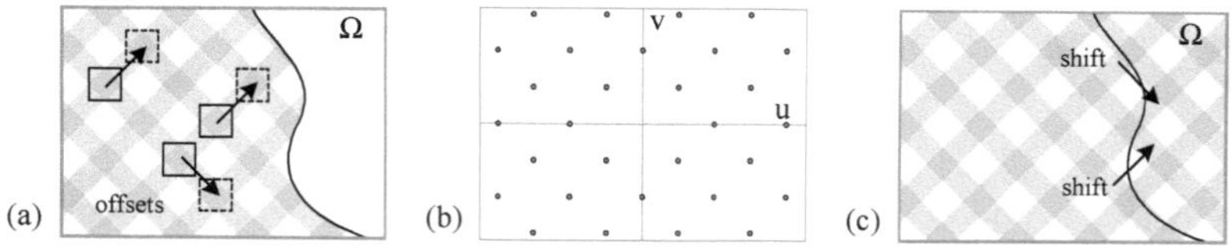

Fig. 5. Illustration of completing textures. The notations are as in Fig. 3.

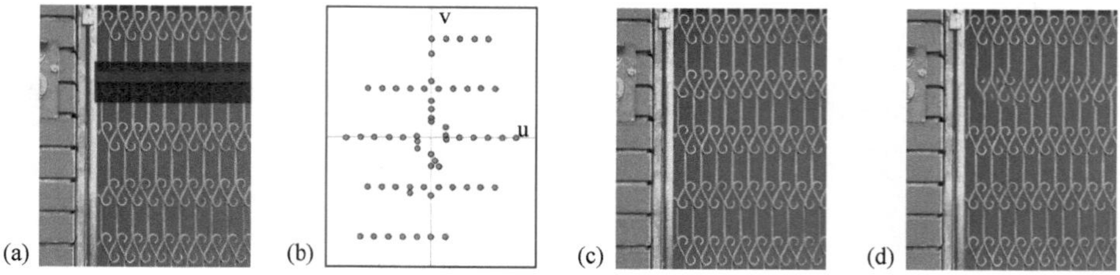

Fig. 6. Regular textures. (a): input. (b): dominant offsets. They describe how the textures are repeated. (c): our result. (d): result of Content-Aware Fill.

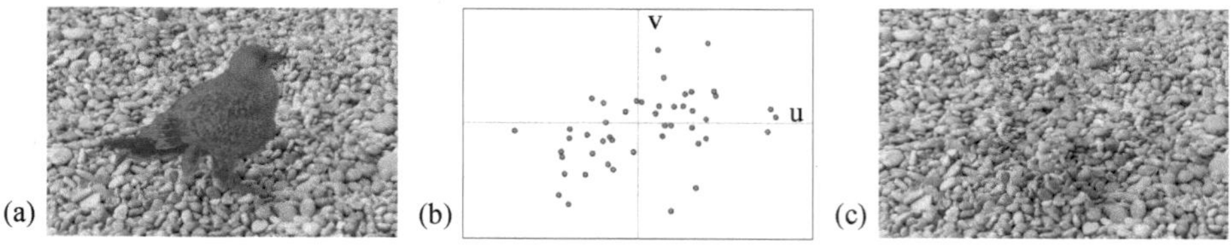

Fig. 7. Random textures. (a): input. (b): dominant offsets. (c): our result.

dot to denote a dominant offset in the histogram. As illustrated in Fig. 3(a), a patch on a linear structure can find its match that is also on this structure. The offsets statistics will exhibit a series of peaks along the direction of the structure (Fig. 3(b)), as observed in the real examples in Fig. 4. We can complete this linear structure by shifting the image along this direction (Fig. 3(c)). Note that our method is tolerant to the structures that are not salient (*e.g.*, Fig. 4(c)) or that are not strictly straight (*e.g.*, Fig. 4(d)); it is sufficient if the structures have a "trend" along one or a few directions.

Textures can yield prominent patterns in the offset statistics. Ideally, a *regular* texture should generate a regular pattern of dominant offsets describing how the textures are repeated (Fig. 5). This is observed in real images (Fig. 6). We can complete the texture by shifting the image using these offsets. On the other hand, an *irregular* texture generates random patterns (Fig. 7). In this case our method behaves just like the Graphcut texture algorithm [17].

Repeated objects can also generate prominent peaks in the offset statistics. This is helpful in synthesizing semantic content. As shown in Fig. 8, the partially missing circles yield peaks in the offsets that correspond to the relative positions of the circles. We can complete each circle by shifting another circle with these

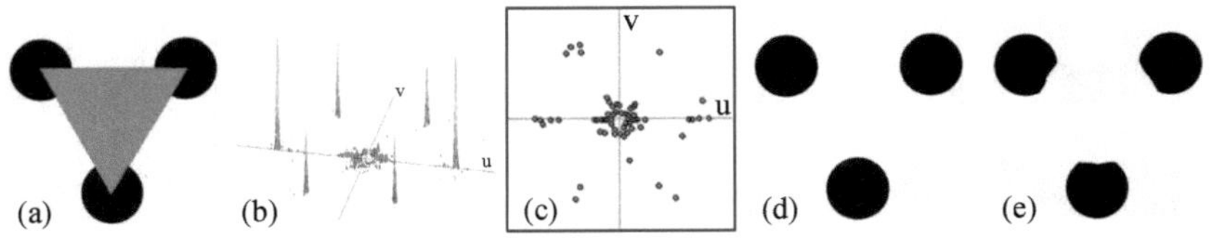

Fig. 8. Repeated circles. (a): input with a missing region in red. (b): offset histogram. (c): dominant offsets found by our algorithm. (d): our result (this is a real result, not a synthetic illustration). (e): result of Content-Aware Fill.

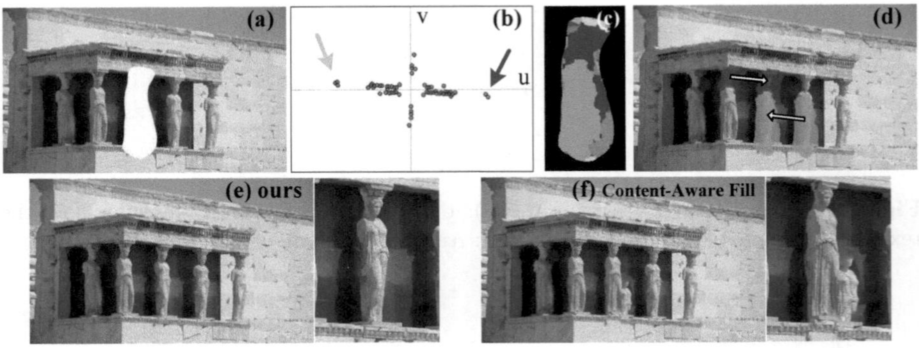

Fig. 9. Repeated objects. (a): input with a sculpture missing. (b): dominant offsets. The arrows indicate the offsets of the relative positions of the sculptures. (c): the label map obtained by graph-cuts: each color represents an offset. (d): the hole is mainly filled by copying the other sculptures, using the offsets indicated in (b). (e) our result and zoom-in. (f) result of Content-Aware Fill and zoom-in.

offsets. In Fig. 9 we show a real example in which our algorithm faithfully recovers a fully missing sculpture. We find that matching-based methods (like [9]) might produce unsatisfactory results (see Fig. 8(e) and Fig. 9(f)), mainly because they are unaware of how the objects are repeated.

Our method has the advantage that it need not consider the above cases separately. It can handle all of them or a mixture of them in the same framework.

3.3 Offsets Sparsity and Optimized Energy

Our method has an energy function (3) similar to the Shift-map method [15]. The main difference is that Shift-map allows all possible offsets. Thus our solution space is a very small subset of the one of Shift-map. Theoretically, Shift-map can achieve a smaller energy than our method (this is observed in experiments). However, we find that the results of Shift-map may have unexpected bias, and their visual quality is very often unsatisfactory even if their energy is much lower than ours. In Fig. 10 we optimize the energy (3) respectively using our sparse offsets (Fig. 10(b)) and using all possible offsets (Fig. 10(c)). The later is the

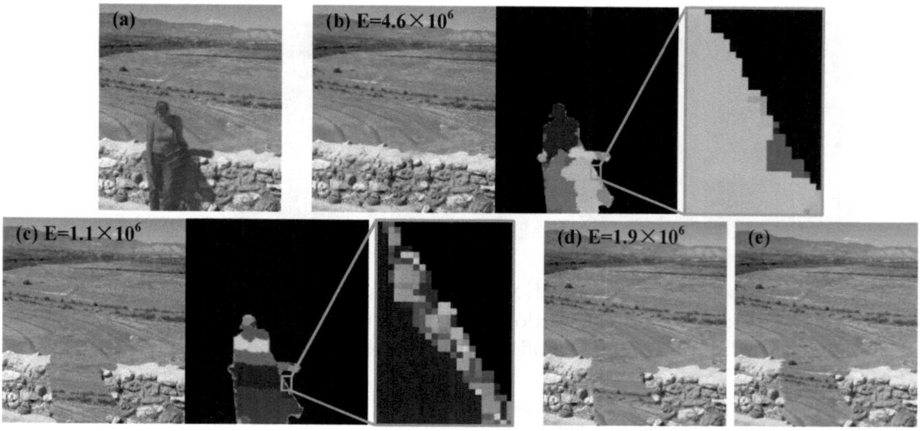

Fig. 10. Offsets sparsity and optimized energy. (a): input. (b): our result and the label map. Energy: E=4.6×10^6, running time: t=0.5s. (c): the result using all possible offsets. E=1.1×10^6, t=4300s. (In this case the number of labels is K=3.8×10^5, and the number of unknown pixels is N=2.2×10^4.) (d): the result of a hierarchical solver [15]. E=1.9×10^6, t=83s. (e): the result from the authors' demo [21] (with gradient smoothness terms).

way of Shift-map [15] (except that [15] has an extra gradient smoothness term). As expected, our energy (4.6×10^6) is much larger than the energy of Shift-map (1.1×10^6). But our result is visually superior.

We investigate this unexpected phenomenon through the graph-cuts label maps (Fig. 10(b)(c)). We find that with a huge number of offsets, the Shift-map method decreases the energy by "inserting" a great many insignificant labels into the seam (see the zoom-in of Fig. 10(c)). These labels correspond to a few isolated pixels that occasionally "connect" the content on both sides of the seam. But when the offset candidates are in a great number, these "occasional" pixels are not rare. We further observe that this problem is inherent and cannot be safely avoided by a hierarchical solver [15] (Fig. 10(d)) or by combining the gradient smoothness term (Fig. 10(e), obtained from the authors' demo [21]). On the contrary, our method is less influenced by this problem (Fig. 10(b)). Actually, exemplar-based methods tend to fill the missing region by copying large segments (like patches or regions). This means that only a few offsets should take effect, which is ensured by our method. The above experiments and analysis indicate that *limiting the solution space is important for improving the quality in image completion.*

Although a small number of offsets can improve quality (and also speed), it is non-trivial to select a few reliable candidate offsets (*e.g.*, 60) out of all possible ones (usually $10^4 - 10^6$). We compare some naive offset selection methods in Fig. 11. We generate the same number (K=60) of offsets, either on a regular grid (Fig. 11(b)), randomly (Fig. 11(c)), or by our method (Fig. 11(d)). We observe that the alternative methods cannot produce satisfactory results, because the

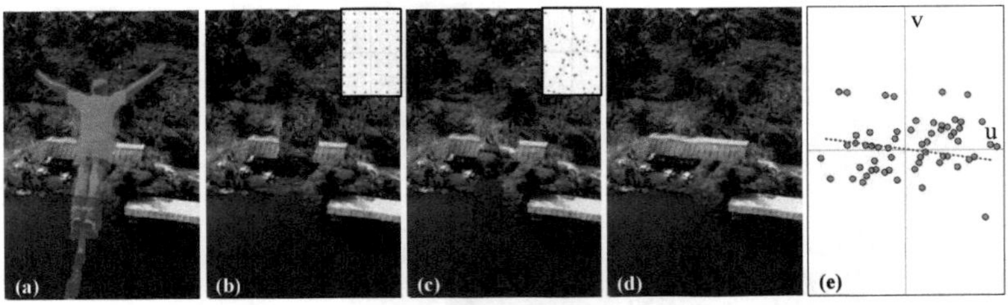

Fig. 11. Comparisons of offsets selection methods. (a): input. (b): the result of regularly spaced offsets. (c): the result of randomly distributed offsets. (d): our result. (e): our offsets. The dash line indicates the offsets used to complete the structure of the roof.

Fig. 12. (a) input. (b) our results. (c) the results of [9], obtained via Content-Aware Fill. The coherence measure is given in each image (computed before Poisson blending).

predefined offsets do not capture sufficient information to predict the missing structures.

3.4 Coherence Measure

Interestingly, we also observe that our method often leads to a better coherence measure [9] even though it does not explicitly optimize this measure. The coherence measure in [9] is defined as:

$$d_{\text{coherence}} = \frac{1}{N} \sum_{P \in \Omega} \min_{Q \in \overline{\Omega}} \|P - Q\|^2, \tag{5}$$

where P is a patch in the synthesized region Ω, and Q is a patch in the known region $\overline{\Omega}$. This measure penalizes any patch P in the synthesized region if its best match Q in the known region is not similar to it.

The method in [9] explicitly optimizes the coherence measure by the EM (Expectation-Maximization) algorithm. Because the solution space when defined at the single finest scale is very large and very irregular, the optimization in [9] adopts a multi-scale fashion to avoid bad local minima. We empirically observe that in this manner a few offset values take major effect in the final solution, and they are determined in coarser scales and hardly changed in finer scales. Thus the multi-scale fashion in [9] also plays a role of *limiting the solution space*[2].

On the contrary, our method directly selects the offsets beforehand. In Fig. 12 we show two examples of our method and [9]. We find that our coherence measure is smaller. This indicates that our statistics-based offset selection works better in these cases to reduce the coherence measure. This partially explains why our method has better quality than [9], as in Fig. 12 and many other examples.

4 Implementation Details

Matching Similar Patches. To efficiently compute $\mathbf{s}$ in (1), we apply a recent nearest-neighbor field algorithm [23] where we additionally reject any patch that disobeys the constraint in the search procedure. This step takes <0.1s for an 800×600 region. We use 8×8 patches and perform matching in a rectangle that is 3 times larger (in length) than the bounding box of the hole. The threshold τ in Eq.(1) is 1/15 of the max of the rectangle's width and height.

Finding Dominant Offsets. The histogram in (2) is further smoothed by a Gaussian filter (σ=$\sqrt{2}$). A "peak" in the smoothed histogram is a bin whose magnitude is locally maximal in a d×d window (d=8).

Combining Shifted Images. The time complexity of graph-cuts [18] is $O(NK)$, where N is the number of unknown pixels and K is the number of labels. The time of our graph-cuts step is 0.2-0.5 seconds for a 800×600 image with 10-20% pixels missing. As a comparison, it takes over one hour to solve such an image in full resolution if all possible offsets are allowed (K=10^4-10^6, like Fig. 10(c)), or tens of seconds using a hierarchical solver [15] with the coarsest level as small as 100×100 pixels (like Fig. 10(d)). Thus our method is 1-2 orders of magnitude faster than Shift-map [15].

Our method is scalable for multi-mega-pixel images because K is fixed. But in practice we find it unnecessary to optimize in full resolution. We downsample the image (by a scale l) to 800×600 and apply the entire algorithm. Then we upsample the resulting label map to full resolution by nearest-neighbor interpolation and multiply the offsets by l. To correct small misalignments we optimize (3) in full resolution, but allow each pixel to take 5 offsets: the upsampled offset and 4 relative offsets[3]. We only solve for the pixels that are in $\frac{l}{2}$-pixel around the seams. This upsampling takes <0.1s for typical 2Mp images using the code in [24]. We have also tested our algorithm in full resolution without downsampling, and found the visual qualities are similar.

A Poisson fusion [25] is applied to further hide small seams. We adopt a recent $O(N)$ time Poisson solver [26]. In our implementation it takes 50ms/Mp.

[2] Contemporary with our work, a recent paper [22] also observes that the method of [9] updates mainly around the boundaries of coherent regions at finer scales. This means that the majority of the used offsets have been limited in the coarser scales.

[3] If the upsampled shift is $\mathbf{s} = (u, v)$, then the other 4 shifts are $(u \pm \frac{l}{2}, v)$ and $(u, v \pm \frac{l}{2})$.

Fig. 13. Comparisons with Content-Aware Fill. Left: input. Middle: our results. Right: results of Content-Aware Fill. The artifacts are highlighted by the arrows. Image size (from top to down): 0.6Mp, 2Mp, 4Mp, 10Mp. The running time is in Fig. 14.

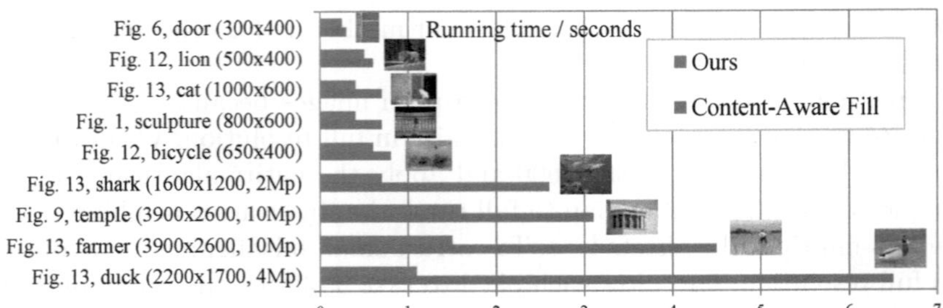

Fig. 14. Running timing comparisons with Content-Aware Fill. The bars are sorted in the ascending order of Content-Aware Fill's time. The two-scale solution does not take effect in the first five examples.

5 Experimental Results

In all the experiments in this paper, we strictly fix all the parameters. This shows the robustness of our algorithm in various cases. Note some other methods

Fig. 15. Comparisons with state-of-the-art methods. (a) Input (640×430). (b) Ours (0.18s). (c) Content-Aware Fill (0.3s). (d) Priority-BP [28] (117s). (e) Shift-map [15] (13s). (f) Criminisi *et al.*'s [7] (6.9s).

require manually tuned parameters for each individual image. Our algorithm is also very robust to various patch sizes (see the supplementary material).

Comparison with Content-Aware Fill. We believe *Content-Aware Fill* in Photoshop [13] is a well-tuned, optimized, and perhaps enhanced version of [9, 12]. Thus we compare with [9, 12] by this implementation[4]. The comparisons are in Fig. 13 and also in Fig. 1, 6, 8, 9, 12 (more in supplementary materials).

In Fig. 14 we compare the speed with Content-Aware Fill on a PC with an Intel Core i7 3.0GHz CPU and 8G RAM. Both methods are using quad cores[5]. For small images where the two-scale solution does not take effect (the first five examples in Fig. 14), our method is slightly faster than Content-Aware Fill. For mega-pixel images our method is 2-5 times faster.

Comparisons with other State-of-the-Art Methods. In Fig. 15 we further compare with Priority-BP [28], Shift-map [15], and Criminisi *et al.*'s method [7]. Our method faithfully recovers the texture edges here, and is much faster than the other three methods (see the caption in Fig. 15). More comparisons are in Fig. 16, Fig. 17, and in the supplementary materials.

Limitations. Our method may fail when the desired offsets do not form dominant statistics. Fig. 18(a-c) show our failure case. We can partially solve this problem by manually introducing offsets. *E.g.*, we can paint an extra stroke on the image (Fig. 18(d)), and treat this image as a new source for patch statistics. This stroke contributes to the statistics and overcomes the problem (Fig. 18(e)). Some other failure examples are in the supplementary materials.

[4] We have also tested [9, 12] using the code in [27], but we find it is non-trivial to tune universally acceptable parameters.

[5] Our method benefits *less* than Content-Aware Fill in multi-core, mainly because the EM algorithm and PatchMatch are fully parallelized but the graph-cut is not. In our method, the parallelism is mainly for matching patches and Poisson blending.

Fig. 16. Comparison with Priority-BP [14]. For this 256×163 image Priority-BP takes 40s in a well parallelized quad-core implementation, while our method takes 0.09s. Also note Priority-BP cannot recover the pattern in the lamp.

Fig. 17. Comparison with Shift-map [15]. In the zoom-in we show how Shift-map behaves near inconsistent seams. This result is obtained from the authors' demo [21]. We have tried various parameter settings but observed similar artifacts.

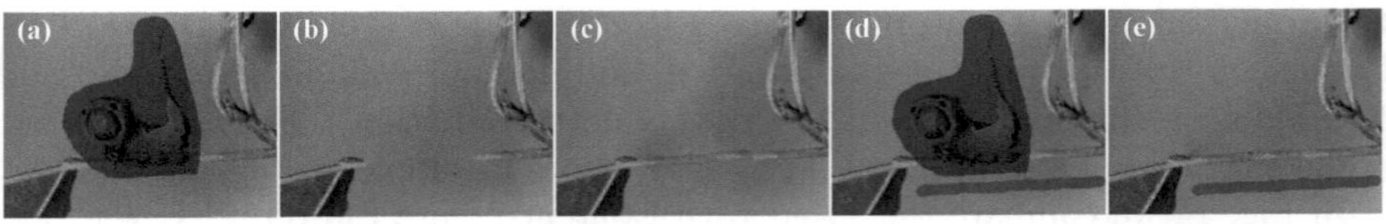

Fig. 18. Failure case. (a) Input. (b) Our result. (c) Result of Content-Aware Fill. (d) An extra stroke is casually painted on the image. (e) Our result of (d).

6 Conclusion

Image statistics have been proven essential in computer vision. Gradient-domain statistics have been applied in denoising [29], deconvolution [30], and inpainting [3], whereas recent patch-domain statistics have been shown very successful in denoising [29] and super-resolution [31]. Our method, which is based on the internal statistics of patch offsets, can be further studied in such context.

References

1. Bertalmio, M., Sapiro, G., Caselles, V., Ballester, C.: Image inpainting. In: SIGGRAPH, pp. 417–424 (2000)
2. Ballester, C., Bertalmio, M., Caselles, V., Sapiro, G., Verdera, J.: Filling-in by joint interpolation of vector fields and gray levels. In: TIP, pp. 1200–1211 (2001)
3. Levin, A., Zomet, A., Weiss, Y.: Learning how to inpaint from global image statistics. In: ICCV, pp. 305–312 (2003)

4. Bertalmio, M., Vese, L., Sapiro, G., Osher, S.: Simultaneous structure and texture image inpainting. In: CVPR (2003)
5. Roth, S., Black, M.J.: Fields of experts: a framework for learning image priors. In: CVPR, pp. 860–867 (2005)
6. Efros, A.A., Leung, T.K.: Texture synthesis by non-parametric sampling. In: ICCV, pp. 1033–1038 (1999)
7. Criminisi, A., Perez, P., Toyama, K.: Object removal by exemplar-based inpainting. In: CVPR (2003)
8. Drori, I., Cohen-Or, D., Yeshurun, H.: Fragment-based image completion. In: SIGGRAPH, pp. 303–312 (2003)
9. Wexler, Y., Shechtman, E., Irani, M.: Space-time video completion. In: CVPR (2004)
10. Sun, J., Yuan, L., Jia, J., Shum, H.-Y.: Image completion with structure propagation. In: SIGGRAPH, pp. 861–868 (2005)
11. Simakov, D., Caspi, Y., Shechtman, E., Irani, M.: Summarizing visual data using bidirectional similarity. In: CVPR, pp. 1–8 (2008)
12. Barnes, C., Shechtman, E., Finkelstein, A., Goldman, D.B.: PatchMatch: A randomized correspondence algorithm for structural image editing. In: SIGGRAPH, pp. 1–8 (2009)
13. Adobe, http://www.adobe.com/technology/graphics/content_aware_fill.html
14. Komodakis, N., Tziritas, G.: Image completion using efficient belief propagation via priority scheduling and dynamic pruning. In: TIP, pp. 2649–2661 (2007)
15. Pritch, Y., Kav-Venaki, E., Peleg, S.: Shift-map image editing. In: ICCV (2009)
16. Agarwala, A., Dontcheva, M., Agrawala, M., Drucker, S., Colburn, A., Curless, B., Salesin, D., Cohen, M.: Interactive digital photomontage. In: SIGGRAPH (2004)
17. Kwatra, V., Schödl, A., Essa, I., Turk, G., Bobick, A.: Graphcut textures: image and video synthesis using graph cuts. In: ACM SIGGRAPH 2003 Papers (2003)
18. Boykov, Y., Veksler, O., Zabih, R.: Fast approximate energy minimization via graph cuts. In: TPAMI, pp. 1222–1239 (2001)
19. Liu, T., Sun, J., Zheng, N.-N., Tang, X., Shum, H.-Y.: Learning to detect a salient object. In: CVPR (2007)
20. Zontak, M., Irani, M.: Internal statistics of a single natural image. In: CVPR (2011)
21. Shift-map On-line Demo, http://www.vision.huji.ac.il/shiftmap/
22. Darabi, S., Shechtman, E., Barnes, C., Goldman, D.B., Sen, P.: Image Melding: Combining Inconsistent Images using Patch-based Synthesis. In: SIGGRAPH (2012)
23. He, K., Sun, J.: Computing nearest-neighbor fields via propagation-assisted kd-trees. In: CVPR (2012)
24. Multi-label Graph Cuts, http://vision.csd.uwo.ca/code/
25. Pérez, P., Gangnet, M., Blake, A.: Poisson image editing. In: SIGGRAPH (2003)
26. Farbman, Z., Fattal, R., Lischinski, D.: Convolution pyramids. In: SIGGRAPH Asia, 175:1–175:8 (2011)
27. Mansfield, A., Prasad, M., Rother, C., Sharp, T., Kohli, P., Van Gool, L.: Transforming image completion. In: BMVC (2011)
28. Komodakis, N., Tziritas, G.: Image completion using global optimization. In: CVPR, pp. 442–452 (2006)
29. Katkovnik, V., Foi, A., Egiazarian, K., Astola, J.: From local kernel to nonlocal multiple-model image denoising. In: IJCV, pp. 1–32 (2010)
30. Fergus, R., Singh, B., Hertzmann, A., Roweis, S.T., Freeman, W.T.: Removing camera shake from a single photograph. In: SIGGRAPH, pp. 787–794 (2006)
31. Glasner, D., Bagon, S., Irani, M.: Super-resolution from a single image. In: ICCV (2009)

Spectral Demons – Image Registration via Global Spectral Correspondence

Herve Lombaert[1,2], Leo Grady[3], Xavier Pennec[2], Nicholas Ayache[2], and Farida Cheriet[1]

[1] Ecole Polytechnique de Montreal, Canada
[2] INRIA Sophia Antipolis, France
[3] Siemens Corporate Research, Princeton, NJ

Abstract. Image registration is a building block for many applications in computer vision and medical imaging. However the current methods are limited when large and highly non-local deformations are present. In this paper, we introduce a new direct feature matching technique for non-parametric image registration where efficient nearest-neighbor searches find global correspondences between intensity, spatial and geometric information. We exploit graph spectral representations that are invariant to isometry under complex deformations. Our direct feature matching technique is used within the established Demons framework for diffeomorphic image registration. Our method, called *Spectral Demons*, can capture very large, complex and highly non-local deformations between images. We evaluate the improvements of our method on 2D and 3D images and demonstrate substantial improvement over the conventional Demons algorithm for large deformations.

1 Introduction

The comparison of images or the need to find correspondences between them is key to many computer vision applications and crucial to establishing accurate diagnostics in medical imaging. Current methods register images with Euler-Lagrangian approaches that typically model elastic and viscous (non-rigid) deformations (recent state-of-the-art is surveyed in [1]). Parametric models ([2,3]) take advantage of restraining the optimization to a few parameters, while non-parametric models use the entire space of displacement fields. Recently, optimization is performed in the diffeomorphism group [4,5,6,7,8,9] (differentiability and reversibility of the transformation) that prevents an invalid folding of space and guarantees a smooth one-to-one mapping between points. The update schemes underlying these methods rely, however, on forces derived from the image gradients and are therefore fundamentally limited by their *local scope* (e.g., gradients are null in textureless areas and optimization is undermined by local minima). The typical response is to use a multilevel scheme to capture larger deformations in a higher resolution but fundamentally does not solve the local scope of their gradient-based update schemes.

In order to capture complex large deformations, we introduce a new approach for image registration based on a *direct feature matching* technique with a *global scope* that uses simple nearest-neighbor searches in a multi-dimensional space comprising information on *image texture* (e.g., pixel intensities), *space* (e.g., Euclidean

A. Fitzgibbon et al. (Eds.): ECCV 2012, Part II, LNCS 7573, pp. 30–44, 2012.

coordinates of pixels) and on *global image geometry*. For the latter, graph spectral representations [10], which are invariant to isometry (preserving geodesic distances), can capture large and complex deformations. Spectral methods [10,11,12,13,14] are popular for general graph partitioning and are applied in computer vision for mesh matching [15,16,17,18] and shape retrieval [19]. Pioneered in the late 80s, [12,13,14], spectral correspondence methods match points in shapes by comparing eigenvectors of a proximity matrix derived from the mesh structure. Recent work (surveyed in [20,21]) uses different types of proximity matrices, graph structures and spectrum deformations [15,16,18]. However, spectral representations of images (strongly linked with Normalized Cuts [22,23]) have never been used for image registration.

Our new direct feature matching technique provides a geometric component with a *global scope* that can be used for image registration, i.e., the nearest-neighbor search finds correspondences with the best compromise in image similarity, spatial regularity and geometric similarity. Unfortunately, diffeomorphism is not guaranteed since a simple nearest-neighbor search could leave unassigned correspondences. Therefore, our approach for image registration is to perform our direct feature matching technique within a diffeomorphic framework such as the efficient symmetric *Log-Demons* algorithm [24,25]. The new method, called **Spectral Demons**, enables a symmetric and diffeomorphic registration of images undergoing *large* and *complex* deformations. We describe in the next section our new direct feature matching and briefly review the *Log-Demons* algorithm. The results evaluate the capability and robustness of the *Spectral Demons* to register images with highly non-local deformations.

2 Method

Our registration approach aims at exploiting the *global scope* and the speed of nearest-neighbor search methods in order to capture very large deformations between two images. We begin our methodology with our simple and direct feature matching technique followed by how spectral representations are built for images. We finish by explaining how our new direct feature matching technique can be used within a diffeomorphic framework for image registration with very large deformations.

2.1 Direct Feature Matching

Image registration warps a moving image M toward a fixed image F through a transformation ϕ that maps points from F to M (i.e., features $\mathbf{F}(\cdot)$, such as point coordinates $\mathbf{x}(\cdot) = (x, y)$ or image intensity $I(\cdot)$, match those in the transformed features $\mathbf{M}(\phi(\cdot))$, or simply $\mathbf{F} \mapsto \mathbf{M} \circ \phi$). A *direct* approach for feature matching would find the point correspondence with a nearest-neighbor search in the feature space (e.g., with a Voronoi tessellation or a k-d tree) such that $\phi(i) = \text{argmin}_{j \in M} \|\mathbf{F}(i) - \mathbf{M}(j)\|^2$ (e.g., if point $j \in M$ has the closest intensity from the one of point $i \in F$, then $\phi(i) = j$). Obviously, matching 1D features such as image intensity would result in a highly unsmooth mapping lacking any spatial regularity (points with the closest intensities might be far apart in the images). Spatial regularity can be introduced by incorporating Euclidean coordinates in the feature space where points now have the extended coordinates $\mathbf{F} = (\alpha_i I_F, \alpha_s \mathbf{x}_F)$ and $\mathbf{M} = (\alpha_i I_M, \alpha_s \mathbf{x}_M)$ (with weights α_i and α_s). A nearest-neighbor search in such extended space effectively provides similarity in pixel intensity and closeness in space between corresponding pixels and minimizes the similarity criterion:

$$\mathrm{Sim}(F, M, \phi) = (I_F - I_{M\circ\phi})^2 + \frac{\alpha_s^2}{\alpha_i^2}\, \|\mathbf{x}_F - \mathbf{x}_{M\circ\phi}\|^2 \tag{1}$$

However, such method lacks information on the image geometry (how to naturally match objects in different poses?) and does not produce a diffeomorphic mapping (a one-to-one mapping is not guaranteed). Each issue is addressed below.

2.2 Spectral Correspondence

The spectral representation of shapes [10,11,12,13,14,15,16,18] has the strong property of being invariant to *isometry*, i.e., corresponding points between shapes in different poses would share the same *spectral coordinates* (or signature) even if they are far away in space (e.g., a point on a nose tip has a geometric description that is unique even if moved in space). By adding these spectral coordinates in our feature space, we enforce an intrinsic *geometric consistency* in our matching technique.

Spectral Graph Theory. From the pixels of I_Ω (the portion of an image I bounded by a contour Ω), the connected undirected graph $\mathscr{G} = (\mathscr{V}, \mathscr{E})$ is constructed with the vertices $\mathscr{V}$ representing pixels and the edges $\mathscr{E}$ defined by the neighborhood structure of these vertices. Such graph can be represented with its adjacency matrix W in terms of affinity weights [11] where high weights are given to edges within a region of uniform intensity and low weights are given to edges crossing region boundaries, e.g., $W_{i,j} = \exp\left(-(I(i) - I(j))^2/2\sigma^2\right)/\|\mathbf{x}(i) - \mathbf{x}(j)\|^2$ if $(i,j) \in \mathscr{E}$ and 0 otherwise (parameter σ depends on the image noise and is set, without being limited, to $\sigma = \mathrm{mean}\{|I(i) - I(j)|\}_{(i,j)\in\mathscr{E}}$). The (diagonal) degree matrix D provides the total weighting of all edges connected to each vertex ($D_{ii} = \sum_j W_{i,j}$) and the Laplacian matrix is defined by $L = D - W$. Here, we consider the general Laplacian operator on a graph $\mathcal{L} = G^{-1}(D - W)$ [11], i.e., a $|\mathscr{V}| \times |\mathscr{V}|$ sparse matrix where G is the (diagonal) node weighting matrix, e.g., $G = D$.

Spectral Coordinates. The graph spectrum [10] computed from the decomposition of the Laplacian $\mathcal{L} = \mathbf{X}^T \Lambda \mathbf{X}$ comprises the eigenvalues (in increasing order) $\Lambda = \mathrm{diag}(\lambda_0, \lambda_1, \ldots, \lambda_{|\mathcal{V}|})$ and their associated eigenvectors $\mathbf{X} = \left(\mathscr{X}^{(0)}, \mathscr{X}^{(1)}, \ldots, \mathscr{X}^{(|\mathcal{V}|)}\right)$ ($\mathbf{X}$ is a $|\mathscr{V}| \times |\mathscr{V}|$ sparse matrix where each column $\mathscr{X}^{(\cdot)}$ is an eigenvector). The first eigenvector $\mathscr{X}^{(0)}$ is the stationary distribution (related to the expected return time of a random walker). The following eigenvectors associated with the non-zero eigenvalues are the fundamental modes of vibrations of the shape (with free ends) depicted by I_Ω (in a Riemannian sense). We thus prefer the term eigenmode since they are effectively functions over I_Ω (visualized as images, see Fig. 1). The eigenmodes of lower modal frequencies are harmonics depicting coarse geometric properties of I_Ω while those associated with higher eigenvalues depict finer geometric details in I_Ω. Moreover, the oscillations at a modal frequency λ occur around nodal sets (where the eigenmode values equal 0) that reside on prominent demarcations of the shape geometry. For instance, graph-based segmentation methods (e.g., [22,23]) rely on the nodal set of $\mathscr{X}^{(1)}$, called the Fiedler vector [10], to find a binary partition of an image. The number

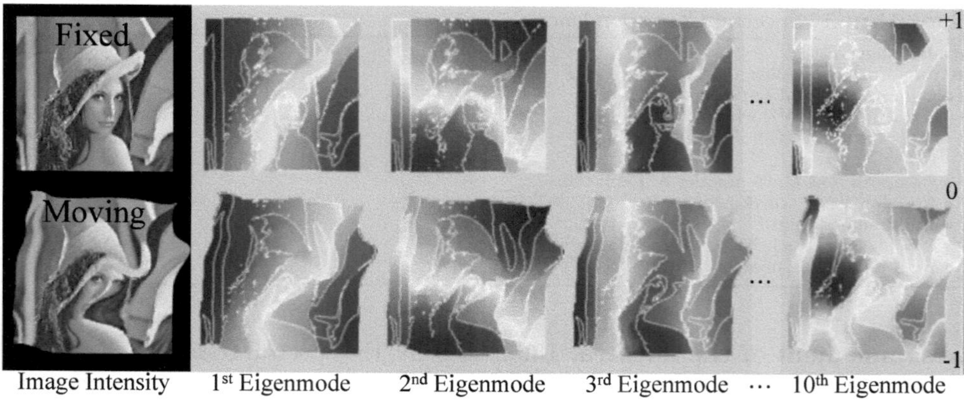

Fig. 1. The eigenmodes of the graph Laplacian are used as geometric descriptors. They remain stable under complex deformations (i.e., invariant to isometry). The lower eigenmodes describe coarse geometric properties, while higher eigenmodes describe finer details in the images (the image contours are overlaid on the eigenmodes).

of half waves in these oscillations (or the number of extrema in the eigenmodal values) is also given by the algebraic multiplicity of their eigenvalue, n_λ.

In our approach (summarized in Alg. (1)), we consider the first k eigenmodes of lower modal frequencies $\mathscr{X}^{(1..k)}$ (i.e., the strongest intrinsic geometric descriptors). Their components represent the k-dimensional *spectral coordinates* $\mathscr{X}$ in a spectral domain[1] where each point i has the coordinates $\mathscr{X}(i) = \left(\mathscr{X}^{(1)}(i), \mathscr{X}^{(2)}(i), \ldots, \mathscr{X}^{(k)}(i)\right)$ (a truncated line of matrix $\mathbf{X}$). The spectral representation $\mathscr{X}$ has the strong property of being invariant to isometry, i.e., if F and M are images of the same object in different poses, equivalent points would share similar coordinates $\mathscr{X}_F$ and $\mathscr{X}_M$. We use this property to improve our direct feature matching by extending Eq. (2) with these spectral coordinates (weighted with α_g). A nearest-neighbor search between $\mathbf{F} = (\alpha_i I_F, \alpha_s \mathbf{x}_F, \alpha_g \mathscr{X}_F)$ and $\mathbf{M} = (\alpha_i I_M, \alpha_s \mathbf{x}_M, \alpha_g \mathscr{X}_M)$ provides similarity in intensity, space and in intrinsic geometric characteristics, effectively minimizing:

$$\text{Sim}(F, M, \phi) = (I_F - I_{M\circ\phi})^2 + \frac{\alpha_s^2}{\alpha_i^2} \left\|\mathbf{x}_F - \mathbf{x}_{M\circ\phi}\right\|^2 + \frac{\alpha_g^2}{\alpha_i^2} \left\|\mathscr{X}_F - \mathscr{X}_{M\circ\phi}\right\|^2, \quad (2)$$

where $\mathscr{X}_{M\circ\phi}$ are the spectral coordinates of the corresponding points in the transformed image $M \circ \phi$.

The choice of the number of spectral components $k = n_{\lambda_1}$ is motivated by the Colin de Verdière's number [26] which is in this case the multiplicity of the Fiedler vector n_{λ_1} and is also related [26] to the maximal dimension of a space in which the graph $\mathcal{G}$ can be mapped (i.e., the eigenspace of the Fiedler eigenvalue reveals the principal symmetries in I_Ω and, $n_{\lambda_1} \leq 2$ in 2D, $n_{\lambda_1} \leq 3$ in 3D). More complex symmetries in the cyclic or dihedral group could be considered with a higher k, but is not required in our method.

[1] In our notation $\mathbf{x}$ is the Euclidean coordinates (e.g., x, y, z in 3D) and superscripted $\mathscr{X}^{(u)}$ is the uth component of the spectral coordinates $\mathscr{X}$

Algorithm 1. Spectral Correspondence

Input: Images F, M.
Output: Correspondence c mapping F to M

- Compute general Laplacians $\mathcal{L}_F$, $\mathcal{L}_M$.
  $\mathcal{L} = D^{-1}(D - W)$, where
  $W_{ij} = \exp\left(-(I(i) - I(j))^2/2\sigma^2\right)/\|\mathbf{x}(i) - \mathbf{x}(j)\|^2$
  $D_{ii} = \sum_j W_{ij}$,
- Compute first k eigenmodes of Laplacians
- Reorder $\mathscr{X}_M$ with respect to $\mathscr{X}_F$ (Eq. (3))
- Build embeddings:
  $\mathbf{F} = (I_F, \mathbf{x}_F, \mathscr{X}_F)$; $\mathbf{M} = (I_M, \mathbf{x}_M, \mathscr{X}_M)$
- Find c mapping nearest points $\mathbf{F} \mapsto \mathbf{M}$

Rearrangement of the Spectra. Unfortunately, the spectral coordinates $\mathscr{X}_F$ and $\mathscr{X}_M$ of points in F and M may not be directly comparable as a result of two phenomena. *Firstly*, there is a sign and scaling ambiguity between corresponding eigenmodes (if $\mathscr{X}^{(\cdot)}$ is an eigenmode of $\mathcal{L}$, so is $-\alpha\mathscr{X}^{(\cdot)}$) which requires a sign check and a scaling correction between $\mathscr{X}_F$ and $\mathscr{X}_M$. *Secondly*, the order of the eigenmodes is undefined within an eigenspace (if two eigenmodes $\mathscr{X}^{(u)}, \mathscr{X}^{(v)}$ share the same eigenvalue, their order (u, v) may differ between two images). The order is additionally perturbed with imperfections in isometry (near-symmetry creates close but not equal eigenvalues and may change order between images). We rearrange the spectral coordinates using two new simple heuristics.

The *first* issue is addressed by scaling the values of each eigenmodes in order to fit the range $[-1; +1]$. The nodal set (where $\mathscr{X}^{(\cdot)} = 0$) is thought to remain on a prominent geometric feature (an axis of symmetry in a Riemannian sense) and should not be changed. We scale thus the positive values (where $\mathscr{X}^{(\cdot)} > 0$) with $\mathscr{X}^{(\cdot)+} \leftarrow \mathscr{X}^{(\cdot)+}/\max\{\mathscr{X}^{(\cdot)+}\}$ and the negative values (where $\mathscr{X}^{(\cdot)} < 0$) with $\mathscr{X}^{(\cdot)-} \leftarrow \mathscr{X}^{(\cdot)-}/\min\{\mathscr{X}^{(\cdot)-}\}$. The *second* issue is addressed by finding the optimal permutation π such that $\mathscr{X}_F^{(\cdot)}$ and $\mathscr{X}_M^{\pi\circ(\cdot)}$ correspond with each other. The Hungarian algorithm (also used in [16,18]) minimizes the following 2D dissimilarity matrix:

$$C(u,v) = \sqrt{\frac{1}{|I_\Omega|}\sum_{i\in I_\Omega}\left(\mathscr{X}_F^{(u)}(i) - \mathscr{X}_M^{(v)}(i)\right)^2} + \sqrt{\sum_{i,j}\left(h_F^{\mathscr{X}_F^{(u)}}(i,j) - h_M^{\mathscr{X}_M^{(v)}}(i,j)\right)^2} \quad (3)$$

The first term is the difference in eigenmodal values between the images and, the second term measures the dissimilarities between the joint histograms $h(i, j)$ (a 2D matrix where the element (i, j) is the joint probability of having at the same time a pixel with intensity i and eigenmodal value $\mathscr{X}^{(\cdot)} = j$). The sign ambiguity can be removed by using, instead, the dissimilarity matrix $Q(u, v) = \min\{C(u, v), C(u, -v)\}$. To keep the notation simple, in the next sections, we assume that the spectral coordinates have been appropriately signed, scaled and reordered.

The ordered spectral coordinates provides our geometric component in our new direct feature matching. We now briefly review how diffeomorphism can be achieved for image registration.

2.3 Diffeomorphic Registration

The minimization of Eq. (2) does not guarantee a one-to-one mapping between points (only closest points are assigned and undefined correspondences are possible). Such

Algorithm 2. Exponential $\phi = \exp(v)$

Input: Velocity field v.
Output: Diffeomorphic map $\phi = \exp(v)$.
- Choose N such that $2^{-N}v$ is close to 0 e.g., such that $\max ||2^{-N}v|| \leq 0.5$ pixels
- Scale velocity field $\phi \leftarrow 2^{-N}v$.

for N times **do**
- Square $\phi \leftarrow \phi \circ \phi$.

end for

Algorithm 3. The Log-Demons Framework

Input: Images F, M and initial velocity field v
Output: Transformation $\phi = \exp(v)$ from F to M
repeat
- Find updates $u_{F\to M}$ mapping F to $M \circ \exp(v)$
- Find updates $u_{M\to F}$ mapping M to $F \circ \exp(-v)$
- Average updates: $u \leftarrow \frac{1}{2}(u_{F\to M} - u_{M\to F})$.
- Smooth updates: $u \leftarrow K_{\text{fluid}} \star u$
- Update velocity field: $v \leftarrow \log(\exp(v) \circ \exp(u))$ (approximated with $v \leftarrow v + u$)
- Smooth velocity field: $v \leftarrow K_{\text{diff}} \star v$.

until convergence

property however exists in classical methods for diffeomorphic registration such as the *Log-Demons* algorithm [24]. Arising from the theory of Lie groups, a diffeomorphic transformation ϕ (on a Lie group structure) is related to the exponential map of a velocity field v (a Lie algebra), i.e., $\phi = \exp(v)$. In the case of stationary velocity fields, a practical and fast approximation is possible with the scaling-and-squaring method [24] (Alg. (2)). As an aside, the inverse of the transformation is simply $\phi^{-1} = \exp(-v)$.

The *Log-Demons* framework alternates, similarly to the Maxwell's demon, between the optimization of a similarity term, e.g., $\text{Sim}(F, M \circ \exp(v)) = (I_F - I_{M\circ\exp(v)})^2$, and a regularization term, e.g., $\text{Reg}(v) = \|\nabla v\|^2$, through the introduction of a hidden variable (the correspondences c) which allows a small error between alternations, e.g., $\text{dist}(c, \phi) = \|c - v\|$. Moreover, invariance to the order of the input images is possible with the symmetric extension of the algorithm [25,9]. The energy of the symmetric *Log-Demons* can be written:

$$E(F, M, \exp(c), \exp(v)) = \tfrac{1}{2}\alpha_i^2 \left(\text{Sim}\left(F, M \circ \exp(c)\right) + \text{Sim}\left(F \circ \exp(-c), M\right)\right) + \alpha_x^2 \text{dist}(c, v)^2 + \alpha_T^2 \text{Reg}(v), \tag{4}$$

where the Euler-Lagrangian updates are computed directly on the stationary velocity field v and consist of the average of the forward and backward updates $u_{F\to M}, u_{M\to F}$ mapping F to $M \circ \exp(c)$ and, M to $F \circ \exp(-c)$ such as (see [24] for more details):

$$u_{F\to M} = -\frac{I_F - I_{M\circ\phi}}{\|\nabla I_{M\circ\phi}\|^2 + \alpha_x^2 |I_F - I_{M\circ\phi}|^2} \nabla I_{M\circ\phi}. \tag{5}$$

In the first step, the transformation ϕ is fixed and the updates are computed (optionally smoothed with a kernel K_{fluid}, e.g., Gaussian with σ_{fluid}). In the second step, the velocity field is updated $v \leftarrow v + u$ (optionally smoothed with the a kernel $K_{\text{diffusion}}$, e.g., Gaussian with $\sigma_{\text{diffusion}}$, see [27]). The general symmetric diffeomorphic Demons framework is summarized in Alg. (3).

2.4 Spectral Demons

At this stage, we have described two methods. The first (the direct feature matching technique, Eq. (2)) can capture large deformations between images but does not guarantee diffeomorphism and symmetry. The second (the Demons algorithm, Eq. (4)) offers these properties but suffers from the local scope of the update forces dervied

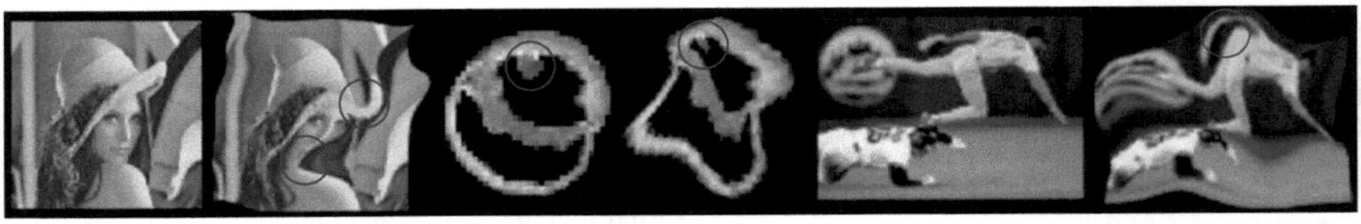

Fig. 2. Pairs of images used in the synthetic experiments (Lena, heart, baseball player). Each left image is a fixed image, each right side is a moving image generated with a random deformation of at most 25 pixels (difficulties in red). These transformations provide our ground truth.

from the image gradient (Eq. (5)). Both methods can benefit from the incorporation, with very little modifications, of our spectral correspondence approach in the *Log-Demons* framework.

The so-called *Spectral Demons* algorithm takes advantage of the efficient diffeomorphic framework offered by Alg. (3) and finds the correspondences between images F and M using our *global* spectral approach in place of using *local* gradient based updates. To be more precise, the first two steps of Alg. (3) (originally computing updates with Eq. (5)) now perform spectral correspondence between images F and $M \circ \exp(v)$ using Alg. (1) (and respectively between M and $F \circ \exp(-v)$). This modification enables large jumps in each iteration where points are moving toward their isometric equivalent even if they are far away in space. This virtually enables the capture of very large deformations (with invariance to isometry) between images as well as a faster convergence of the algorithm. The underlying energy being minimized has the form of Eq. (4) where its similarity term is expressed with Eq. (2).

Multilevel Scheme. A multilevel scheme is also possible with the *Spectral Demons* where large deformations are assumed to be related with coarse geometric information. Spectral updates can thus be safely used in a lower resolution level, while finer details and local deformations remain computed in the higher levels of resolutions using the classical update forces based on the image gradient. This multilevel scheme keeps the computation of the eigenmodes tractable. On the same note, the computation of the eigenmodes can be used with the efficient Lanczos method (used by Matlab) which has a running time of $O(n\sqrt{n}) + O(n^2)$ [22], where n is the number of pixels in I_Ω, while spectral matching can be performed with a k-d tree which is built in $O(n \log^2 n)$ and queried in $O(\log n)$.

3 Results

We evaluate here the performance of the *Log-Demons* (our benchmark) and *Spectral Demons* (our method) by registering images with large and highly non-local deformations. In our controlled experiments, the full power of the *Spectral Demons* can be appreciated with drastic deformations of the images. Accurate measurements, with known ground truth, are used to evaluate the improvements in registration accuracy with respect to the *Log-Demons*. We additionally provide a real application where two human brains are registered.

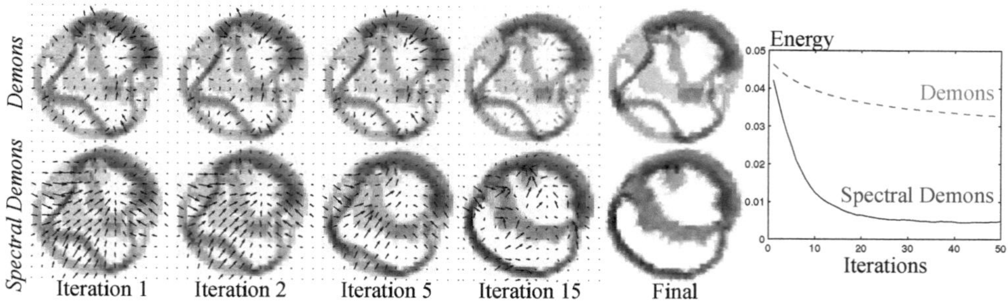

Fig. 3. Comparison of the iterations in the *Log-Demons* and the *Spectral Demons* (our method) within the same resolution level. The update forces (indicated with the arrows and scaled for visualization) have a local scope with the *Log-Demons* and a global scope with the *Spectral Demons*. This global scope allows a faster convergence while the *Log-Demons* remains in a local minimum.

3.1 Controlled Experiments

In the first controlled experiment, we evaluate the fundamental difference between the update schemes of the *Log-Demons* and *Spectral Demons*. To do so, we analyze the convergence rate of both algorithms and, since we are not interested here in their final performance, we compare them within the same level of resolution. The algorithms use the same parameter set ($\sigma_{\text{fluid,diffuse}} = 1, \alpha_x = 1, k = 2, \alpha_g = 0.05, \alpha_s = 0.15, \alpha_i = 0.8$). We register the images on Fig. 2 (Lena has size 128^2, the heart is 75^2 and the baseball player is 110×75). Each moving image is generated with random diffeomorphic deformations ϕ_{truth} with displacements of at most 25 pixels, i.e., we take the exponential map of a random velocity field generated with 15 random displacements (control points randomly located) diffused across the image (Gaussian smoothing $\sigma = 10$ pixels). Notably, Lena's hat, her neck and, the player's arm are the highest registration challenges, while the cardiac image (a 2D slice of an MRI) shows a papillary muscle (red circle on Fig. 2) severely deformed and almost fully collapsed (the muscle forms, however, a dent in the image and provides a signature that *Spectral Demons* can understand). The iterations of the *Log-Demons* and *Spectral Demons* are compared in Fig. 3. It shows that within the same level of resolution, the update forces computed with spectral correspondence are coherent spatially and geometrically, i.e., points move toward their geometric equivalent, however the update forces derived from the image gradient lack any global information on the shape geometry and put the *Log-Demons* into an erroneous local minimum.

The use of a multilevel scheme allows the *Log-Demons* to capture larger deformations (Fig. 4) but does not change the inherent local scope of its update forces. For instance, *Log-Demons* even with 4 levels of resolution ultimately fails in recovering the extreme deformations on the anterior side of the heart, while *Spectral Demons* without a multilevel scheme can successfully register the whole myocardium with a 71% improvement in performance (mean square differences (or MSE) of intensities with ground truth from 19.9×10^{-3} to 5.7×10^{-3}). The performance is further improved when 4 levels are used (down to 2.4×10^{-3} MSE, or a 88% improvement in the heart registration). Similar results are observable with the other images. Lena's hat, her neck and, the player's arm are successfully registered using the *Spectral Demons*

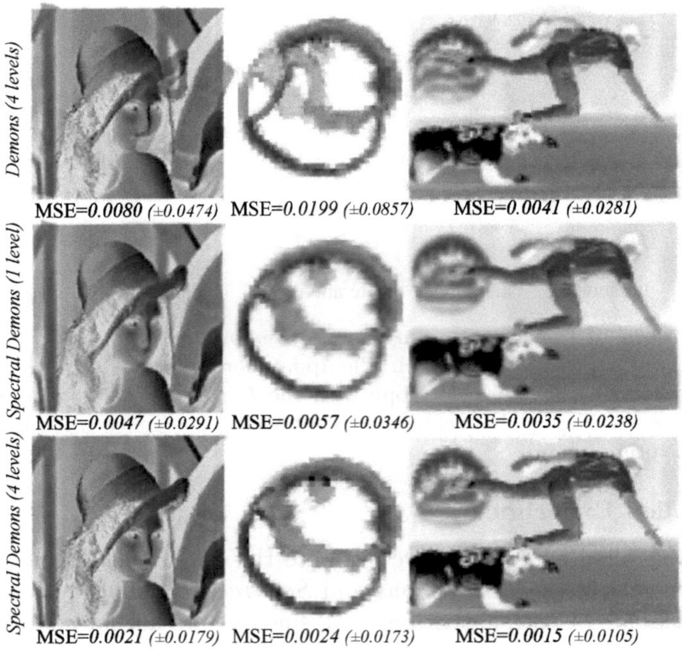

Fig. 4. Final registrations for (*top row*) Multilevel *Log-Demons* with 4 levels, (*middle row*) *Spectral Demons* with 1 level, (*bottom row*) Multilevel *Spectral Demons* with 4 levels. The fixed image is in blue and misalignments of the registered image are in red. The mean square differences of intensities are reported along their standard deviations. *Log-Demons* is limited in areas of high deformations, while *Spectral Demons* can capture these large deformations.

with respectively 73% improvement over *Log-Demons* in Lena's image and 63% in the baseball image.

Additionally, the quality of the computed registration maps ϕ is evaluated in terms of difference of displacements (in pixels) with the ground truth $\|\phi - \phi_{\mathrm{truth}}\|$. The *Log-Demons* results in registration maps (Fig. 5) with larger errors in high deformation areas (e.g., Lena's hat or neck), whereas the *Spectral Demons* results in a smoother registration map with significantly less errors (62% less) in these same areas.

The cost of the global scope offered by *Spectral Demons* is increased computation time. For instance, on Lena's image, 50 iterations requires 55.82 seconds with *Log-Demons* and 178.32 seconds with *Spectral Demons*; on the heart image, 21.01 seconds with *Log-Demons* and 41.03 seconds with *Spectral Demons*; and on the baseball player's image, 42.06 seconds with *Log-Demons* and 102.17 seconds with *Spectral Demons*. We used unoptimized Matlab code on a Core 2 Duo, 2.53GHz.

Robustness to Deformation. The *Spectral Demons*' robustness to deformation is evaluated on Lena's image by exaggerating the previous synthetic transformation from $\phi_0 = \exp(0v)$ (zero displacements) to $\phi_2 = \exp(2v)$ (creating a maximal displacement of 40 pixels, see samples on Fig. 6). The performance is evaluated with the transformation differences (in pixels) from the ground truth. Both *Log-Demons* and *Spectral Demons* perform with sub-pixel accuracy on deformations below 20

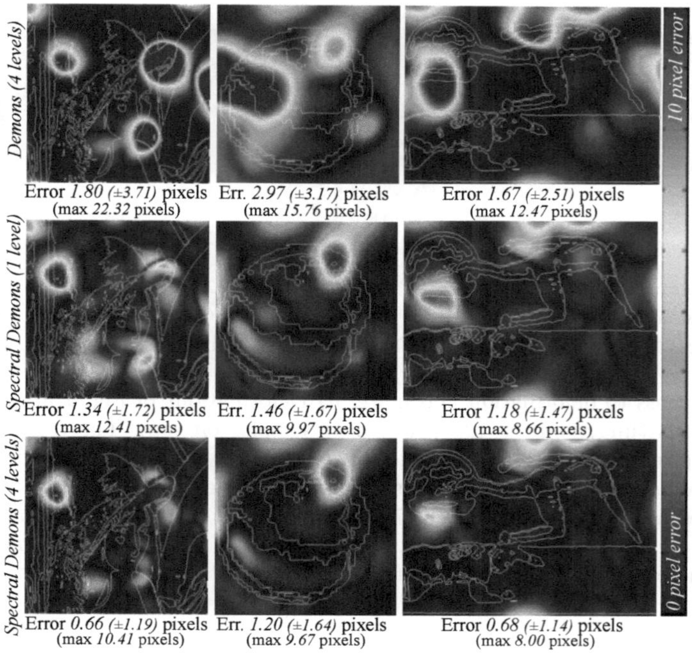

Fig. 5. Differences (in pixels) between computed transformations and ground truth for (*top row*) Multilevel *Log-Demons*, (*middle row*) *Spectral Demons* and, (*bottom row*) Multilevel *Spectral Demons*. The fixed images are overlaid on the error maps. The Multilevel *Spectral Demons* decreases the error by 60% from the Multilevel *Log-Demons*.

pixels, however they differ with larger deformations where our method shows a greater robustness, e.g., with a deformation of 40 pixels (more than 30% of the image size) the average transformation error is 5.9 pixels with *Log-Demons* and 1.6 pixels with *Spectral Demons* (a 73% decrease).

Robustness to Noise. The analysis on the robustness to noise reveals the current limitations of both algorithms. An increasing Gaussian noise is added to Lena's image, from $\sigma = 0$ to 0.25 (samples on Fig. 6). *Spectral Demons* performs better with noise $\sigma < 0.075$, however the comparison with control images (the unregistered noisy images) reveals that *Log-Demons* stops transforming the images when noise is increased (due to trapping in a local minimum). For instance, Fig. 6 shows that when using *Log-Demons* with noise $\sigma = 0.13$, the registered image is similar to its initial state, while *Spectral Demons*, even though with a larger average error (6.8 pixels versus 3.7 pixels), continues to recover large deformations (see the hat area on Fig. 6). With noise $\sigma > 0.2$, the corrupted images become problematic for *Spectral Demons* (graph edge weights are almost null and may need a different heuristic weighting), whereas *Log-Demons* is almost immediately trapped in a local minimum.

3.2 Registration of Medical Images

The performance of the *Spectral Demons* is evaluated in a medical application with the registration of brain MR images from the Internet Brain Segmentation Repository

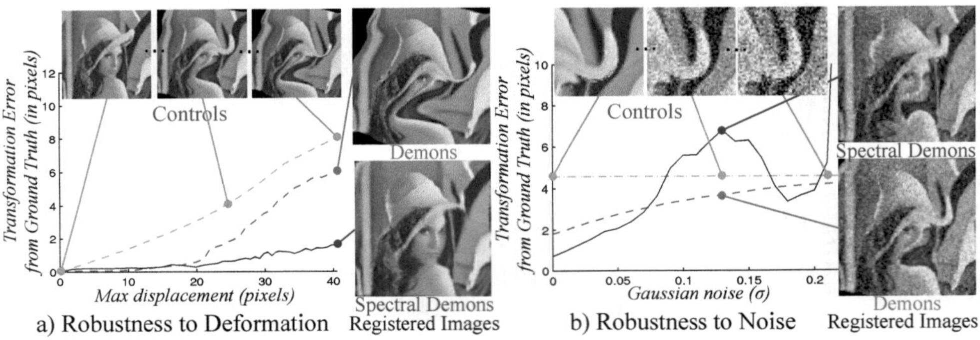

Fig. 6. Robustness to deformation and noise. *a)* Deformations of Fig. 2 are amplified to a max of 40 pixels (image size is 128^2, deformed samples on top). The transformation differences with ground truth (y-axis in pixels) are smaller with *Spectral Demons* (*blue*) than with *Log-Demons* (*red*). *b)* Gaussian noise is used (samples around the hat area). *Spectral Demons* looses advantage after $\sigma > 0.075$, however even with a lower error, *Log-Demons* stops moving when increasing noise (error is similar with untransformed images (controls, in *green*)), whereas *Spectral Demons* continues to recover large deformations.

(IBSR, `http://www.cma.mgh.harvard.edu/ibsr`, our images are 64^3 volumes). The brain presents a wide variety of shapes and internal structures across individuals. While the cerebral cortex is particularly convoluted and is the focus of many specific surface matching techniques ([28,29,17,18]), the registration of internal components in the brain, such as the white or gray matter, requires a volumetric approach. We chose two individuals that have lateral ventricles with different sizes (Fig. 7, the moving image shows a longer ventricle). We evaluate the registration accuracy with the overlap of the provided manual segmentations of the white and gray matter (measured with the Dice metric defined as the ratio $2(A \cap B)/(|A| + |B|)$ with 1 being an optimal overlap) as well as with the mean squared differences of pixel intensities between the fixed and registered images. The original (unregistered) setting has a Dice metric of 0.65 in the white matter and 0.69 in the gray matter. Both algorithms (using 4 levels) increase the overlap of the white and gray matter to respectively above 0.71 and 0.75, with a slight advantage to the *Spectral Demons*, however the comparison of the mean squared differences of intensities reveals a 4% improvement in accuracy and precision when using *Spectral Demons* (from 29.0×10^{-3} error in the original setting, decreasing to 20.8×10^{-3} with *Log-Demons* and to 19.9×10^{-3} with *Spectral Demons*). This experiment showed that *Spectral Demons* offers an improved performance in a real application when registering medical images.

The computation and the current implementation shows again that there is room for improvements with our method. With downsampled images of size 32^3, 50 iterations requires 108.49 seconds with *Log-Demons* and 201.43 seconds with *Spectral Demons*. Notably, memory becomes problematic with our unoptimized Matlab code as volumes beyond 32^3 require the decomposition of Laplacian matrices larger than $32^3 \times 32^3$ (although extremely sparse, our current code is not optimized for such large matrices).

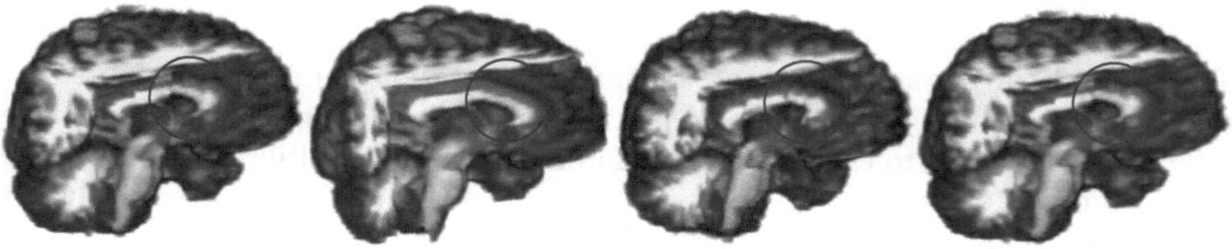

	Fixed	Moving (Original)	Registered Moving (Demons)	Registered Moving (Spectral Demons)
Difference (MSE) with Fixed		$29.0\ (\pm 51.3)\ x10^{-3}$	$20.8\ (\pm 37.7)\ x10^{-3}$ ↘	$19.9\ (\pm 36.2)\ x10^{-3}$ ↘
Dice metric white matter		0.6515	0.7126 ↗	0.7166 ↗
Dice metric gray matter		0.6931	0.7572 ↗	0.7784 ↗

Fig. 7. Registration in 3D between two brains from healthy subjects using *Log-Demons* and *Spectral Demons* (both with 4 levels). While observations show apparently similar results (ventricles are circled), the mean square differences of intensities (MSE) between the fixed and registered images reveal an increase of 4% in accuracy and precision when using *Spectral Demons*. The Dice metrics of the white and gray matter (measuring segmentation overlaps) also increase with *Spectral Demons*.

3.3 Note on Image Segmentation

The Laplacian eigenmodes have been demonstrated to have important properties in the field of spectral graph theory [10,22,30,11] by providing a probabilistic foundation [23,31] for graph-based segmentation methods. In particular, the normalized cut problem [22] finds a segmentation x by minimizing $\frac{x^T L x}{x^T D x}$ (revealed by the Fiedler vector of the normalized Laplacian $D^{-\frac{1}{2}} L D^{-\frac{1}{2}}$ [23]). *Spectral Demons* considers the more general Laplacian operator $\mathcal{L}$ and effectively exploits for registration the same global image description used by normalized cuts for segmentation, i.e., eigenmodes of the (general) Laplacian operator are used for image registration. Since the Fiedler vector is an inherent part of our algorithm, binary segmentations of images come at no extra cost by taking either the positive or negative values of the Fiedler vector, $\mathscr{X}^{(1)+}$ or $\mathscr{X}^{(1)-}$. For example, the implicit segmentation of Lena's image, shown on the *right* (with overlaid image contours), was obtained with the nodal sets of the first and second eigenmodes (positive values of the Fiedler vector gave warmer colors, negative values gave cooler colors, see also 1st and 2nd eigenmodes on Fig. 1)). Nodal sets of higher frequency eigenmodes may additionally reveal important geometric features for meaningful segmentation, however, an exhaustive experimental study on the segmentation aspect of our registration method goes beyond the scope of this paper.

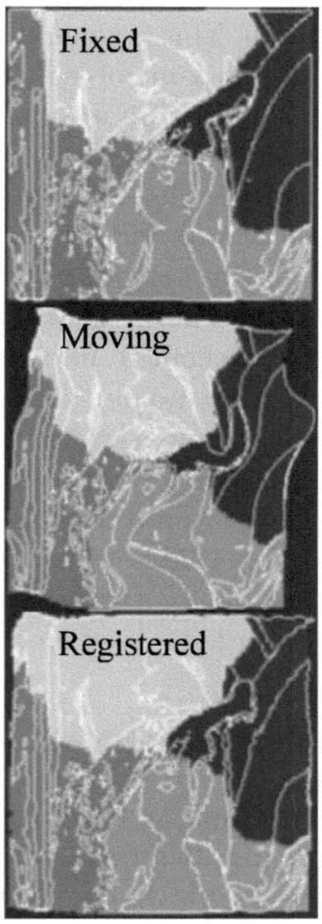

Implicit Segmentation from nodal sets

4 Conclusion

The methods in the state-of-the-art of image registration are currently limited by the local scope of their underlying update schemes (based on image gradients). The typical response tries to capture larger deformations with a multilevel scheme where large jumps are possible with images of lower resolutions. Although sufficient for most applications, a multilevel scheme does not change the inherent local scope of update forces derived from the image gradient and finds its limitation with very large deformations. We proposed a fundamentally new update scheme based on a direct feature matching technique that uses image, spatial and geometric information. The *global scope* of our new update scheme is captured through spectral representations of images that are invariant to isometry. Our approach consists of finding point correspondences with a nearest-neighbor search in a multi-dimensional space that embeds pixel intensity, Euclidean coordinates and spectral coordinates. Such direct feature matching technique can be used within classical frameworks for image registration. Among them, the *Log-Demons* algorithm [9] provides symmetry and diffeomorphism of the registration. Our new registration method, called *Spectral Demons*, successfully captures large, complex and highly non-local deformations. We evaluated its performance with displacements of more than 30% of the image size and observed an improvement of 73% over the *Log-Demons*. Here, we assumed that registered images have a similar topology (same global shape) with no occlusions, holes, or missing parts. This is generally true in most applications as we are often interested in comparing the same object or similar ones (e.g., the same organ in medical imaging). Future work will aim at improving our main limitation, the computational cost of the spectral decomposition, for instance by pre-computing the eigenmodes before registration and warping them during registration in order to avoid costly spectral decompositions in each iteration. We will also investigate the use of the Nyström approximation [32] (by sampling the Laplacian matrix). Additionally, the strong links with image segmentation [23,31] will be studied more carefully. Image registration may also further benefit from employing global optimization framework. Nevertheless, we believe that our fundamentally new approach, relying on the *global* image structure to drive correspondences via spectral representations, is a significant contribution in the state-of-the-art of image registration, i.e., our registration respects the *global* Riemannian structure of the image (isomorphism, brought by *spectral coordinates*) on top of the differentiable structure (diffeomorphism, from state-of-the-art methods). The *Spectral Demons* algorithm can improve applications that employ objects or study organs undergoing very large, complex and highly non-local deformations.

References

1. Crum, W.R., Hartkens, T., Hill, D.L.: Non-rigid image registration: theory and practice. Br. J. of Radiology 77, 140–153 (2004)
2. Rueckert, D., Sonoda, L.I., Hayes, C., Hill, D.L., Leach, M.O., Hawkes, D.J.: Non-rigid registration using free-form deformations: application to breast MR images. IEEE TMI 18, 712–721 (1999)
3. Chui, H., Rangarajan, A.: A new algorithm for non-rigid point matching. In: CVPR, pp. 44–51 (2000)

4. Miller, M.I., Trouvé, A., Younes, L.: On the metrics and Euler-Lagrange equations of computational anatomy. An. Review of Biomed. Eng. 4, 375–405 (2002)
5. Beg, M.F., Miller, M.I., Trouvé, A., Younes, L.: Computing large deformation metric mappings via geodesic flows of diffeomorphisms. IJCV 61, 139–157 (2005)
6. Bossa, M., Hernandez, M., Olmos, S.: Contributions to 3D Diffeomorphic Atlas Estimation: Application to Brain Images. In: Ayache, N., Ourselin, S., Maeder, A. (eds.) MICCAI 2007, Part I. LNCS, vol. 4791, pp. 667–674. Springer, Heidelberg (2007)
7. Allassonnière, S., Amit, Y., Trouvé, A.: Towards a coherent statistical framework for dense deformable template estimation. Royal Stat. Soc. 69, 3–29 (2007)
8. Durrleman, S., Fillard, P., Pennec, X., Trouvé, A., Ayache, N.: Registration, atlas estimation and variability analysis of white matter fiber bundles modeled as currents. NeuroImage 55, 1073–1090 (2011)
9. Vercauteren, T., Pennec, X., Perchant, A., Ayache, N.: Diffeomorphic demons: efficient non-parametric image registration. NeuroImage 45, 61–72 (2009)
10. Chung, F.R.K.: Spectral Graph Theory. AMS (1997)
11. Grady, L.J., Polimeni, J.R.: Discrete Calculus: Applied Analysis on Graphs for Computational Science. Springer (2010)
12. Umeyama, S.: An eigendecomposition approach to weighted graph matching problems. IEEE TPAMI 10, 695–703 (1988)
13. Scott, G.L., Longuet-Higgins, H.C.: An algorithm for associating the features of two images. Royal Soc. Bio. Sciences 244, 21–26 (1991)
14. Shapiro, L.S., Brady, J.M.: Feature-based correspondence: an eigenvector approach. Image and Vision Computing 10, 283–288 (1992)
15. Jain, V., Zhang, H.: Robust 3D shape correspondence in the spectral domain. In: Int. Conf. on Shape Modeling and App. (2006)
16. Mateus, D., Horaud, R., Knossow, D., Cuzzolin, F., Boyer, E.: Articulated shape matching using Laplacian eigenfunctions and unsupervised point registration. In: CVPR, pp. 1–8 (2008)
17. Reuter, M.: Hierarchical shape segmentation and registration via topological features of Laplace-Beltrami eigenfunctions. IJCV 89, 287–308 (2009)
18. Lombaert, H., Grady, L., Polimeni, J.R., Cheriet, F.: Spectral correspondence for brain matching. In: IPMI, pp. 660–670 (2011)
19. Egozi, A., Keller, Y., Guterman, H.: Improving shape retrieval by spectral matching and meta similarity. IEEE Trans. Image Processing 19, 1319–1327 (2010)
20. Zhang, H., Van Kaick, O., Dyer, R.: Spectral mesh processing. Eurographics 29 (2010)
21. van Kaick, O., Zhang, H., Hamarneh, G., Cohen-Or, D.: A survey on shape correspondence. Eurographics 30, 1681–1707 (2011)
22. Shi, J., Malik, J.: Normalized cuts and image segmentation. IEEE TPAMI 22, 888–905 (2000)
23. Meila, M., Shi, J.: Learning segmentation by random walks. In: NIPS (2000)
24. Vercauteren, T., Pennec, X., Perchant, A., Ayache, N.: Non-parametric Diffeomorphic Image Registration with the Demons Algorithm. In: Ayache, N., Ourselin, S., Maeder, A. (eds.) MICCAI 2007, Part II. LNCS, vol. 4792, pp. 319–326. Springer, Heidelberg (2007)
25. Vercauteren, T., Pennec, X., Perchant, A., Ayache, N.: Symmetric Log-Domain Diffeomorphic Registration: A Demons-Based Approach. In: Metaxas, D., Axel, L., Fichtinger, G., Székely, G. (eds.) MICCAI 2008, Part I. LNCS, vol. 5241, pp. 754–761. Springer, Heidelberg (2008)
26. Tlusty, T.: A relation between the multiplicity of the second eigenvalue of a graph Laplacian, Courant's nodal line theorem and the substantial dimension of tight polyhedral surfaces. Electronic Journal of Linear Algebra 16, 315–324 (2010)

27. Cachier, P., Bardinet, E., Dormont, D., Pennec, X., Ayache, N.: Iconic feature based nonrigid registration: the PASHA algorithm. CVIU 89, 272–298 (2003)
28. Fischl, B., Sereno, M., Tootell, R., Dale, A.: High-resolution intersubject averaging and a coordinate system for the cortical surface. H. Brain Map. 8, 272–284 (1999)
29. Yeo, B.T., Sabuncu, M.R., Vercauteren, T., Ayache, N., Fischl, B., Golland, P.: Spherical demons: Fast diffeomorphic Landmark-Free surface registration. IEEE TMI 29 (2010)
30. Luxburg, U.: A tutorial on spectral clustering. Stat. and Comp. 17, 395–416 (2007)
31. Robles-Kelly, A.: Segmentation via Graph-Spectral Methods and Riemannian Geometry. In: Gagalowicz, A., Philips, W. (eds.) CAIP 2005. LNCS, vol. 3691, pp. 661–668. Springer, Heidelberg (2005)
32. Drineas, P., Mahoney, M.W.: On the Nyström method for approximating a Gram matrix for improved Kernel-Based learning. J. Mach. Learn. Res. 6, 2153–2175 (2005)

MatchMiner: Efficient Spanning Structure Mining in Large Image Collections

Yin Lou, Noah Snavely, and Johannes Gehrke

Department of Computer Science, Cornell University
{yinlou,snavely,johannes}@cs.cornell.edu

Abstract. Many new computer vision applications are utilizing large-scale datasets of places derived from the many billions of photos on the Web. Such applications often require knowledge of the visual connectivity structure of these image collections—describing which images overlap or are otherwise related—and an important step in understanding this structure is to identify *connected components* of this underlying image graph. As the structure of this graph is often initially unknown, this problem can be posed as one of exploring the connectivity between images as quickly as possible, by intelligently selecting a subset of image pairs for feature matching and geometric verification, without having to test all $O(n^2)$ possible pairs. We propose a novel, scalable algorithm called MatchMiner that efficiently explores visual relations between images, incorporating ideas from relevance feedback to improve decision making over time, as well as a simple yet effective *rank distance* measure for detecting outlier images. Using these ideas, our algorithm automatically prioritizes image pairs that can potentially connect or contribute to large connected components, using an information-theoretic algorithm to decide which image pairs to test next. Our experimental results show that MatchMiner can efficiently find connected components in large image collections, significantly outperforming state-of-the-art image matching methods.

1 Introduction

The last decade has witnessed explosive growth in the availability of image data. Thousands of photos are added every minute to online repositories, such as Flickr and Facebook, with views covering large parts of the Earth. A number of new geometric computer vision applications have been built on top of such large-scale photo collections of places [4,5]. A key requirement of these systems is to identify the connectivity of an image collection in the form of an *image graph* where each image is a node, and where an edge connects each pair of images that visually overlap. For unstructured image collections, the structure of this graph is initially unknown—i.e., we do not know which pairs of images match, and accordingly what edges exist—and thus needs to be discovered, usually using the tools of feature matching and RANSAC-based geometric verification [7] to test the existence of edges (i.e., overlapping images). However, this matching and verification process is relatively expensive, so it is desirable to obtain an image graph that is as complete as possible while rigorously matching and verifying a minimal number of edges.

In addition, given an image collection, it is often unnecessary to discover a complete description of the underlying image graph, as a much sparser graph contains sufficient

A. Fitzgibbon et al. (Eds.): ECCV 2012, Part II, LNCS 7573, pp. 45–58, 2012.

Fig. 1. A visual path from Il Vittoriano to the inside of the Colosseum in our Forum dataset. Each consecutive image pair exhibits spatial overlap. In an image graph, links between densely-connected subgraphs are important for applications such as 3D reconstruction and visualization as they contribute to a more complete scene and a more accurate 3D model.

information for many applications. For example, if the graph underlying a set of n images is complete (i.e., each image overlaps every other image), then a star graph (one with $n-1$ edges, each connecting one node to a central node) might be a sufficient description of the graph for certain applications, as compared to exhaustively matching all n choose 2 pairs of images. In the context of structure from motion (SfM), a sparse graph is sometimes even more desirable than a complete description; for instance, Agarwal et al. take an image graph and apply a sparsification technique to derive a simpler "skeletal" graph for efficiently reconstruction [1,8]. On the other hand, breaking the graph into two separate connected components (CCs) is undesirable, as it can lead to separate, disconnected models for SfM methods. As a motivating example, Figure 1 shows a "visual path" through a set of images of Rome (out of a collection of nearly 75K images) connecting two landmarks, the Il Vittoriano Monument and the Colosseum. While both of these landmarks are densely photographed, photos linking the two are much more difficult to find, hence finding such connections is critical to connecting these two monuments in a 3D model. This motivates our goal of discovering the large CCs of an image collection as completely, and as efficiently, as possible.

We do this through a method that proposes edges to verify through feature matching and spatial verification. If each edge verification step on an image pair successfully finds that the pair indeed matches, then problem would be much easier—we would need to test at most $n-1$ edges to find a spanning forest for the image collection. In practice, however, it is difficult to know in advance which pairs to test, as many pairs of images do not match. Many state-of-the-art image matching systems [4,8,9] use techniques based on image retrieval techniques (such as bag-of-words and inverted files [10]) to determine likely matches, but these metrics are not always good predictors of whether two images match. While several techniques have been proposed to improve retrieval performance [11,12] based on the idea of refining the query and retrieve images repeatedly, many of them introduce overhead at the retrieval stage since the similarities have to be recomputed, which substantially increases the total running time.

Another source of difficulty comes from the fact that large-scale image datasets often contain many "singleton" images, i.e., images that match no or very few other images, such as a closeup of a pigeon, and verifications on such images are wasted. Even worse, some near-singleton images contain confusing features that result in them being similar to other images under bag-of-words methods. Detecting such "bad" singleton images is expensive because in the worst case we have to verify a query image against all other images in the dataset to conclude whether the query image is indeed a singleton. Currently, most large-scale matching systems do not explicitly model such outlier images, and hence waste computation time trying to match them.

Contributions. To address these problems, we develop an efficient and effective algorithm called **MatchMiner** that applies to large-scale collections of images of scenes to discover large CCs. MatchMiner works by intelligently maintaining a shortlist of image pairs to match, and re-ranking this shortlist over time based on feedback from successful and unsuccessful prior matches. We show that a novel algorithm based on relevance feedback can be employed in MatchMiner to effectively re-rank image pairs while introducing little overhead in the image retrieval process. This algorithm significantly improves the success rate of finding true matching pairs. To prevent singleton images from appearing in the shortlists of other images, we also propose a simple yet effective measure called *rank distance* to prune out false positives and to increase the probability of success. Finally, we use an information-theoretic model of the problem to choose edges that minimize a objective based on expected entropy given estimated prior probabilities of matches based on visual similarities.

We demonstrate the effectiveness of MatchMiner on several image collections with ground truth obtained by exhaustive matching, as well as larger collections with tens or hundreds of thousands of images. Our experiments show that MatchMiner can effectively identify large CCs in an image graph with a relatively small number of matching operations, and that for large problems it can produce significantly better results than current techniques, such as Image Webs [9], given the same budget of matches performed.

2 Related Work

Several techniques have been proposed to match large-scale image collections. Probably the most related method is Image Webs [9], whose matching system has two phases. The first phase proposes image pairs based on visual similarity using a standard bag-of-visual-words model. Potential image pairs that straddle different connected components (CCs) are given priority for verification. This phase results in a (hopefully large) set of CCs. In the second phase, spectral graph theory is employed to increase the connectivity within each CC. Our work differs in that we are mainly interested in finding as complete a set of CCs as possible, as this is critical to many applications including 3D reconstruction. To the best of our knowledge, our work is the first to incorporate practical relevance feedback methods in the domain of large-scale image matching.

Chum and Matas formulated the problem as one of clustering and presented a method based on min-wise hashing to quickly generate cluster seeds (image pairs) whose similarity is above a user-defined threshold [13]. These seeds are then spatially verified to filter out false positives. To increase recall, they then grow these seeds using query expansion [12]. One problem with their approach is that the quality of their final graph structure highly depends on those initial seeds, and their method can easily miss important connections between components of the image set.

Structure within CCs is also important in many problems. Techniques such as skeletal graphs [1] and dominating sets [3] attempt to sparsify the graph while retaining important structures. However, these techniques often require a (near) complete set of edges within CCs given in advance, while our formulation of the problem aims at discovering those CCs and therefore can be viewed as an initial step in such systems. Other work takes a probabilistic approach to identifying important structures in a graph [2].

Large-scale matching is a key component in many city-scale 3D reconstruction systems [4,8]. For instance, Frahm *et al.* build a reconstruction on a single PC using GPUs [4], leveraging GIST features and compact binary codes in a clustering algorithm for very fast image matching. Iconic images in these clusters are then chosen and connected between clusters. However, they sacrifice graph quality for efficiency, and thus they may lose important connections between landmarks, breaking a scene up into several separate connected components; our goal is to find not just "easy" clusters, but to connect even weakly connected subsets of images, such as those shown in Figure 1.

Our technique is also related to recent image retrieval techniques based on bag-of-visual-words models [11,12]. As in our work, some of these methods modify the image query to either reduce the effect of confusing visual words or enhance the power of relevant words. *Recursive average query expansion* [12] constructs a new query by averaging verified results of the original query, i.e., a new query vector is formed using positive feedback. *Incremental spatial re-ranking* [11] automatically detects tf-idf failure (too few features landing in the same visual words are geometrically consistent), incrementally builds a statistical model of the query object, and learns relevant spatial context to boost retrieval performance. Despite their effectiveness, most of these methods introduce significant overhead in the retrieval stage of large-scale image matching since the similarities between the query and database images must be recomputed using the updated query. This is especially problematic in our setting, where *all* images are potential queries. We address this with a query modification technique that is extremely efficient and can take into account negative information.

3 MatchMiner Algorithm

As mentioned in the introduction, we formulate the process of finding structure in a large image collection as that of finding all of the large connected components (CCs) of the underlying image graph. While this is not the only possible way to formulate the matching problem, it fits with our goal of connecting up the images as best as possible, so that later processing stages (e.g., of an SfM pipeline) can obtain as complete models as possible. To that end, imagine that by some process we can obtain the "ground truth" image graph (e.g., by exhaustively matching all pairs of images),[1] and hence the ground truth CCs. Our task is then to quickly discover these ground truth components (without prior knowledge), by testing as few image pairs as possible. While we may only be able to find an approximation of the ground truth CCs in a reasonable time, e.g., due to weak edges that are difficult to discover, we want the approximate set of CCs we find to be as complete as possible. More formally,

[1] Note that this $O(n^2)$ process is intractable for very large image collections, which is why we require approximate methods.

Definition 1 (Spanning Structure Mining). *Given an image set $\mathcal{I} = \{I_1, ..., I_n\}$ and a geometric verification predicate $GV(I_i, I_j)$, the ground truth image graph G_g is formed by creating a node for each image and by creating an edge between images I_i and I_j if $GV(I_i, I_j)$ holds for $i \neq j$. We want to efficiently find all large connected components of G_g, which we refer to as the* spanning structure *of G_g.*

We define GV as a standard feature matching and geometric verification procedure, involving SIFT matching [6] with approximate nearest neighbor search and a ratio test for classifying true and false feature matches. These feature matches are then verified using a RANSAC-based estimation of the fundamental or essential matrix, depending on the availability of camera calibration information [7].

Our approach works by proposing sets of image pairs to match, based on visual similarities and rank information accumulated as the algorithm proceeds. Initially, we use a standard bag-of-visual-words approach to model visual similarity. We train a vocabulary tree offline on 50,000 images of a single city to yield 1 million visual words. For each image in the input collection $\mathcal{I}$, its SIFT descriptors are assigned to the approximately closest visual word. The image is then represented as a histogram of visual words (a vector of length 1M), weighted using standard *tf-idf* weighting [10]. In this paper, we use the same vocabulary tree for all experiments, and we use the dot product on normalized vectors as our image similarity metric.

3.1 Algorithm Overview

Our image matching method, called **MatchMiner**, consists of two steps. In Step 1, each image is issued as a query image, and highly ranked images are given priority for verification. This step employs Rocchio's relevance feedback [14] to improve the quality of retrieval results. In Step 2, we re-rank image pairs for testing with a preference for merging large CCs. We propose a *rank distance* to eliminate spurious image pairs, and use visual similarity to estimate the probability that a match will succeed. Note that in both steps, we skip verifying image pairs that are already in the same CC, as well as image pairs that have already been tested. We follow the standard practice [8,9] of setting a verification budget, i.e., the maximum number of image pairs that may be tested; we use a budget of $K \times |\mathcal{I}|$ (i.e., on average each image is matched to at most K other images), and we terminate after the budget is exhausted, returning whatever CCs are found. We now describe these two steps in detail.

3.2 Step 1: Finding Initial Connected Components

Initially each image forms its own connected component, and each image is issued as a query to retrieve visually similar images. Over time, to maintain a high probability of success in linking CCs, we update each query using a modified version of Rocchio's relevance feedback [14]. In Rocchio's relevance feedback, a query vector Q_t is modified based on a shortlist of retrieved images. In our case, geometric verification (GV) is performed on the top k most similar images to a query, which partitions the k images into a positive set $\mathcal{P}$ and a negative set $\mathcal{N}$. These sets are used as feedback to create a new virtual query vector Q_{t+1} (before normalization), based on the following formula,

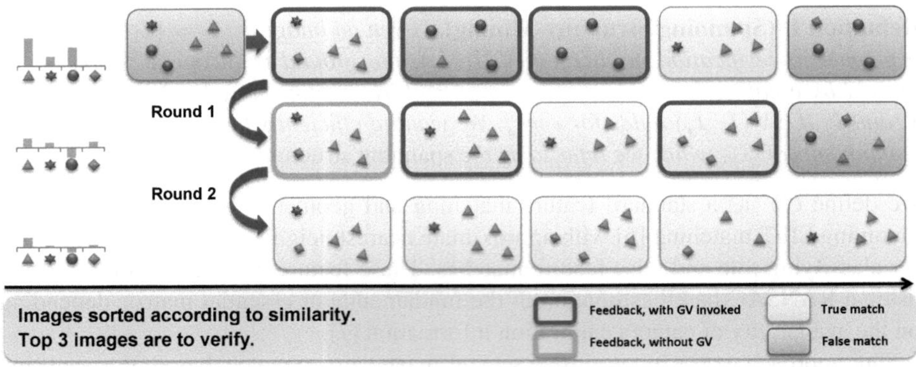

Fig. 2. Illustration of Step 1. The visual word distribution of the initial and modified query vectors are shown on the left. Row 1 uses the original query vector, and rows 2 and 3 use queries with feedback incorporated. The algorithm skips images already in the same CC of the query image, such as the third image in row 2.

$$Q_{t+1} = Q_t + \frac{\alpha^{t+1}}{|\mathcal{P}|} \sum_{I \in \mathcal{P}} I - \frac{\beta^{t+1}}{|\mathcal{N}|} \sum_{I \in \mathcal{N}} I \tag{1}$$

where α and β are dampening factors to prevent topic drift, and I denotes original bag-of-words vector for an image. The new query vector is then normalized and used to retrieve a new set of relevant images. In our experience, setting $\alpha = \beta = 0.8$ gave good retrieval results. Unlike in most settings for Rocchio's relevance feedback, we allow negative weights on features, as this produced better results in our experiments.

Figure 2 illustrates an example of Step 1. The query image (purple) is first used to retrieve a shortlist of images (Row 1). We verify the top 3 images in the shortlist (in dark blue boxes) to get feedback. Here, the feedback indicates that purple circles are "noisy" and therefore down-weighted in the next query. The new query vector is normalized, and images are retrieved again (Row 2). We do not match images that are already in the same CC; for example, we skip the third image in row 2. The query is again refined according to feedback to retrieve more true matches in the shortlist. Note that as we keep refining the query, the shortlist generally becomes cleaner, and in addition the algorithm is able to find important features that are not in original query (the blue diamond in this example). It is easy to see that in Step 1, the algorithm invokes GV at most $Tk \times |\mathcal{I}|$ times, where T is the number of rounds of relevance feedback.

There are several reasons why we use Rocchio's relevance feedback to modify the query. First, we find that it significantly improves accuracy even after one or two rounds of relevance feedback, as new query vectors are created with a bias towards features in $\mathcal{P}$, and against features in $\mathcal{N}$. Second, Rocchio's relevance feedback is very efficient. Note that the new query vector is a linear combination of the old query vector and image vectors in the shortlist; moreover, the dot product is linear in the first argument: $\langle ax + by, z\rangle = a\langle x, z\rangle + b\langle y, z\rangle$, which means that we do not need to recompute the similarity between the new query and image vectors from scratch. Instead, we simply reuse precomputed dot products between images to compute the similarity between the new query and other image vectors, a very fast operation. Although geometric verification is the bottleneck of the whole system, we still desire an efficient re-ranking scheme since it is a heavily used subroutine.

In summary, Step 1 performs T rounds of relevance feedback, where each round considers the top k images in each image's shortlist. T and k are chosen so that the overall budget $K \times |\mathcal{I}|$ is not exhausted. Step 1 returns an initial set of CCs and the number of geometric verifications that have already been spent.

3.3 Step 2: Merging Connected Components

After Step 1, we have discovered a set of initial connected components, and have used up some portion of the verification budget. As others have observed, we find that the probability of geometric consistency of neighbors for a given image decreases quickly with the rank of the neighbor in the shortlist, and so verification on image pairs proposed solely based on visual similarity can frequently fail after a point; the verification budget would not be used fruitfully if we continue to match such pairs. Therefore in Step 2, we use a weighting function $w(\cdot)$ to re-rank the shortlists of each image, aiming to increase the probability of success. Each image retrieves its top neighbor with highest weight, and geometric verification is performed on such pairs until the verification budget is exhausted. Again, we avoid matching images already in the same CC.

As our objective is to create large CCs, we prefer a weighting function that proposes image pairs that can potentially merge two CCs into an even larger CC. We formalize this intuition using the concept of entropy.

Minimizing Entropy. Let $\mathcal{C}$ denote a set of connected components, where each component $c \in \mathcal{C}$ is a subset of images. The *entropy* of $\mathcal{C}$, denoted $H(\mathcal{C})$, is defined as:

$$H(\mathcal{C}) = -\sum_{c \in \mathcal{C}} p(c) \cdot \log p(c), \tag{2}$$

where $p(c)$ is the probability that an image arbitrarily selected from the dataset belongs to connected component c, i.e., $p(c) = \frac{|c|}{|\mathcal{I}|}$.

When initially every image forms its own CC, the entropy of this set of components is at its maximum, $\log |\mathcal{I}|$. If we are able to connect all images into one CC, then the entropy is 0. As we merge CCs, the entropy strictly decreases monotonically until and unless we find exactly all CCs in G_g (i.e., we find the ground truth CCs). Thus our task can be re-formulated as minimizing $H(\mathcal{C})$ given the verification budget.

Intuitively, if we merge two small CCs, the entropy $H(\mathcal{C})$ will not decrease by much. However, when two CCs are merged into a large one, $H(\mathcal{C})$ will quickly decrease. We now show this more formally. Consider two images that straddle two CCs and are geometrically consistent; we can thus merge these CCs, c_x and c_y. Let $x = |c_x|$ and $y = |c_y|$. The entropy $H(\mathcal{C})$ upon merging c_x and c_y will decrease as $\Delta H(\mathcal{C}) = \frac{x}{n} \log \frac{n}{x} + \frac{y}{n} \log \frac{n}{y} - \frac{x+y}{n} \log \frac{n}{x+y}$. Let $z = x + y$. It can be easily shown that $\frac{\partial \Delta H(\mathcal{C})}{\partial z} \propto \frac{1}{n} \log \frac{z}{z-y}$. Thus, as z goes to infinity, $\frac{\partial \Delta H(\mathcal{C})}{\partial z}$ converges to 0, which means we reach a local maxima of $\Delta H(\mathcal{C})$. This shows that if we fix a component c_y, we should merge it with the largest CC possible so as to obtain the largest decrease in $H(\mathcal{C})$.

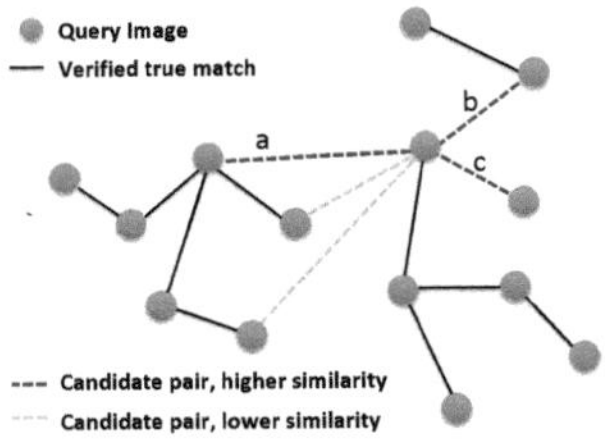

(a) Illustration of entropy-descent strategy of choosing edges to verify. The algorithm will pick edge a to verify, as it is strong and spans large CCs.

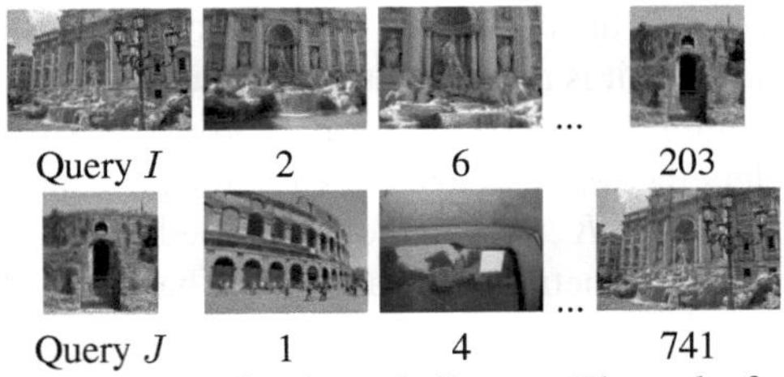

(b) Motivation for the rank distance. The rank after two rounds of relevance feedback is shown below the image. Image J is proposed by similarity to image I, but pruned by the rank distance.

Fig. 3. Illustration of Step 2. (a) Image pairs will be chosen to maximize the reduction in expected entropy, except for (b) pairs with large rank distance that are pruned.

We can use this idea to define a weighting function $w(\cdot)$ as the *expected reduction in entropy*, $E_I(J)$, for matching an image J to a query image I—the decrease in entropy weighted by the probability of a successful merge:

$$w_I(J) = E_I(J) = p_I(J) \cdot \Delta H(\mathcal{C}) \tag{3}$$

where $p_I(J)$ is an estimated probability of success of the merge. We define this probability later in this section. Note that after Step 1, we need to choose pairs (I, J) very carefully, as the probability of success for an arbitrary merge is low.

Figure 3(a) illustrates how a query image (the green node) chooses its next image to verify. Black lines are already verified true matches and red dashed lines are candidate pairs to verify; darker red indicates higher similarity. Although there are three strong candidates, our method chooses edge a since its expected decrease in entropy is highest.

Eliminating Singleton Images. Large-scale, unstructured image datasets often contain a significant number of singleton images ("distractor" or "noise" images) that match no other image, such as a closeup of a random cobblestone or of water. Worse, we have observed that these often contain confusing visual words that cause those images to be relatively highly ranked in the shortlists of other images. We propose a simple yet effective method to eliminate these images.

Consider two images I and J, and assume I is a "good" image, while J is an outlier image. In Step 1, when we use J as a query, all of the verifications will fail. However, each round of relevance feedback adds negative feedback pushing J away from these initially similar (according to the bag-of-words model), yet non-matching images. After T rounds, the refined query will be far away from those non-matching images. Let $Rank_I(J)$ denote the rank for image I using image J as a query in Step 1. Although $Rank_I(J)$ might be small because of noisy features present in J, $Rank_J(I)$ will often be large since this is not a "true" match. Figure 3(b) illustrates this effect with a real example from one of our datasets. Based on this observation, we propose as a distance function the *rank distance* $R(I, J)$ for a pair of images I and J, defined as the harmonic mean of $Rank_J(I)$ and $Rank_I(J)$:

$$R(I,J) = 2Rank_I(J)Rank_J(I)/(Rank_I(J) + Rank_J(I)) \tag{4}$$

If either of $Rank_J(I)$ or $Rank_I(J)$ is large, $R(I,J)$ is large, indicating that the pair (I,J) may not be promising. Our experiments show that we can use this ranking to prune many (near) singleton images effectively and increase the probability of performing successful matches.

Probability of Successful Match. We now define the probability of geometric consistency $p_I(J)$ using similarity and rank information. Let $\mathrm{SimNeighbor}_{N_s}(I)$ denote the set of the top N_s most visually similar neighbors to a query image I. We model the likelihood of geometric consistency as a normal distribution $\mathcal{N}(0,\sigma_s)$. Similarly, let $\mathrm{RankNeighbor}_{N_r}(I_i)$ denote a set of closest N_r neighbors to the query image I_i, based on rank distance $R(I,J)$. We wish to highly score images that are both visually similar to the query image, and highly ranked in each other's rank list; accordingly, we define the estimated probability of geometric consistency as follows:

$$p_I(J) \propto \begin{cases} \frac{1}{\sqrt{2\pi}\sigma_s} e^{-\frac{(s-1)^2}{2\sigma_s{}^2}}, & J \in \mathrm{SimNeighbor}_{N_s}(I) \cap \mathrm{RankNeighbor}_{N_r}(I) \\ 0, & \text{otherwise} \end{cases} \tag{5}$$

where s is the original similarity of image I and J.

We use the original queries (rather than modified queries) because we observe that true matches can sometimes be pushed down by relevance feedback in the ranking. However, since the original similarity function is very noisy, we need to filter out false matches and have found the rank distance an effective way to do so.

4 Experiments

To evaluate the effectiveness of MatchMiner, we performed experiments on several medium- and large-scale datasets. We downloaded five datasets from Flickr[2]: **Acropolis, Pantheon, St. Paul's, Forum**, and **Washington DC**, using keyword search. Images in the Acropolis, Forum, and Washington DC datasets come with geotags, while the other images do not. We sample two small datasets according to their geotags, forming smaller datasets Forum 1 and Forum 2. The ground truth image graphs for Forum 1, Forum 2, Acropolis, Pantheon, and St. Paul's are computed by exhaustive geometric verification on all image pairs, as these are small enough so that exhaustive matching is tractable. Table 1 summarizes these datasets.

4.1 Effectiveness of Relevance Feedback

Step 1 of MatchMiner uses relevance feedback; to understand how much relevance feedback improves the accuracy, we first compare relevance feedback with dot product and recursive average query expansion [12], using Average Precision (AP) @k. Each image in a dataset is issued as a query and all retrieved images are ranked solely based on their

[2] `http://www.flickr.com`

Table 1. Datasets. Each row lists: *Name*, the name of the dataset; *# Images*, the number of images in the dataset; CC_1, the size of the largest connected component in the ground truth image graph (if known); $|V_g|$, the number of images that are not singletons (i.e., in their own CC) in the ground truth image graph; μ_I, the average number of features per image; and σ_I, the standard deviation of number of features per image.

Name	# Images	CC_1	$\|V_g\|$	μ_I	σ_I
Forum 1	1069	320	692	7741	6379
Forum 2	2911	1213	1937	6528	4957
Acropolis	2961	2105	2451	3969	2242
Pantheon	1123	855	947	10784	13309
St. Pauls	3000	2045	2372	11388	10191
Forum	74391	-	-	7748	5752
DC	375531	-	-	5379	5161

similarity to the query. Precision@k of a query Q is computed as $|\{I \mid GV(Q,I)\}|/k$, and AP@k is obtained by averaging Precision@k for all queries. In these experiments, each round of relevance feedback and recursive average query expansion examines the top five images in the shortlist. We compare with average query expansion because it is a state-of-the-art retrieval method with little overhead in the retrieval process. Figure 4 shows the AP@k on five datasets. Relevance feedback achieves significantly better AP@k than dot product and recursive average query expansion for the top images in the ranked lists. As we are mainly focused on low Ks, i.e., a relatively small verification budget, we conclude that relevance feedback is quite suitable for Step 1. Note that two rounds of relevance feedback produce excellent retrieval performance while consuming a relatively small amount of the verification budget (at most 10 verifications per query), and therefore we use two rounds for all further experiments.

4.2 Effectiveness of Rank Distance

Step 2 in MatchMiner is a combination of favoring merging large CCs and avoiding matching singleton images. We first evaluate the effectiveness of rank distance in pruning singleton images. Recall that in Step 2, for each image I in the dataset, we verify its next k images after relevance feedback. In this experiment, we propose those k images according to $p_I(J)$ and plot the average number of false edges in those k images that are pruned by using rank distance, where $N_s = N_r = 200$. Figure 5 shows the results on five datasets. By using rank distance, we can prune almost half of the images among k images without invoking actual verification. This means at least half of the top k images in N_s of Step 2 are false matches to the query, but they will be pruned by looking at N_r, which can give a large savings and increase the probability that we encounter an important edge between two CCs. On all of our datasets, the rate of pruning true edges stays consistently below 0.1%, i.e., the rank distance rarely makes mistakes.

4.3 Evaluation Metric

In order to evaluate our results, we need some measure of how similar two sets of connected components are. For this we use *normalized mutual information* [15], a popular

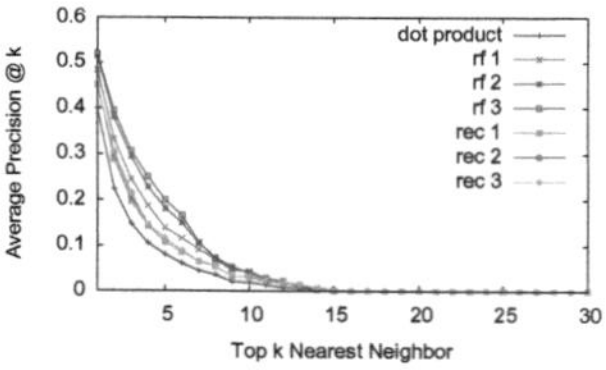

(a) Forum 1

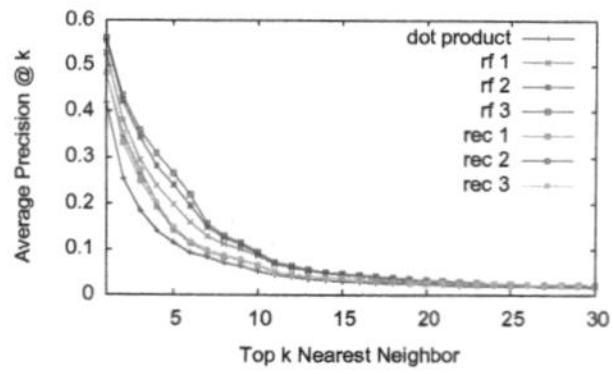

(b) Forum 2

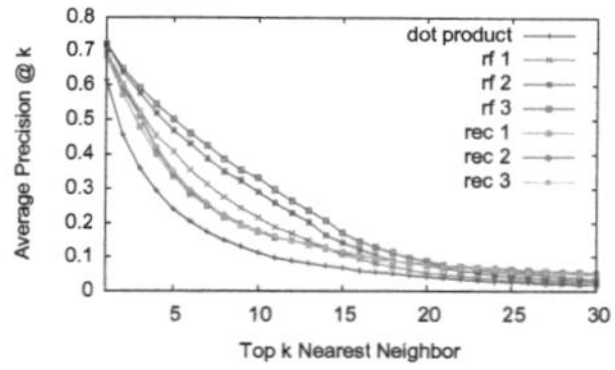

(c) Acropolis

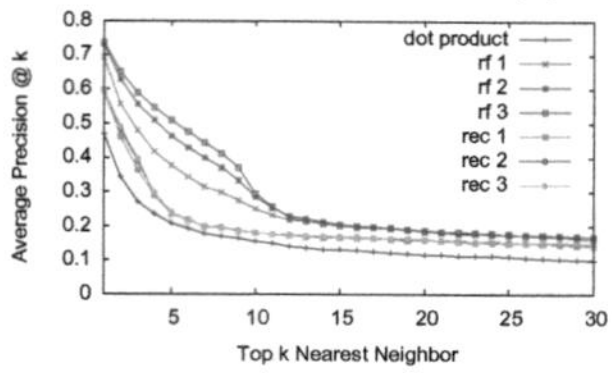

(e) Pantheon

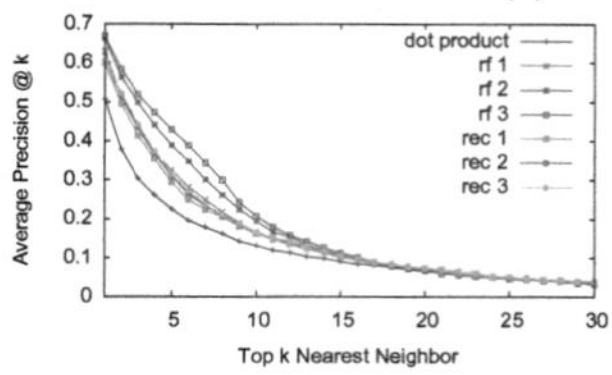

(f) St. Pauls

Fig. 4. Average precision @ k for dot product, one round of relevance feedback (rf 1), two rounds of relevance feedback (rf 2), three rounds of relevance feedback (rf 3), one round of recursive average query expansion (rec 1), two rounds of recursive average query expansion (rec 2) and three rounds of recursive average query expansion (rec 3).

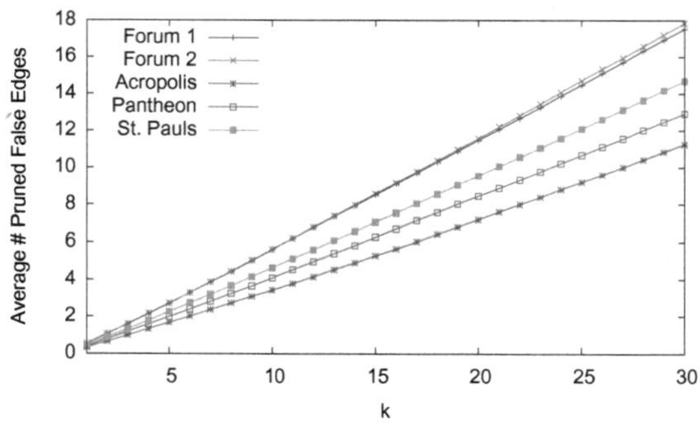

Fig. 5. Avg. number of false edges pruned by rank distance in the k images considered in Step 2

similarity measurement for clustering algorithms; we adopt this to measure similarity of two connected component sets.

Let $\mathcal{C}^*$ denote the set of CCs in the ground truth graph G_g and $\mathcal{C}$ the spanning structure to compare to the ground truth. We define the mutual information of the two sets as follows:

$$MI(\mathcal{C};\mathcal{C}^*) = H(\mathcal{C}) - H(\mathcal{C}|\mathcal{C}^*) = \sum_{c\in\mathcal{C},c^*\in\mathcal{C}^*} p(c,c^*)\cdot\log\frac{p(c,c^*)}{p(c)\cdot p(c^*)} \tag{6}$$

where $p(c)$ and $p(c^*)$ are the same probabilities defined in Equation 2, and $p(c,c^*)$ is the joint probability that the arbitrarily selected image belongs to both c and c^*, i.e., $p(c,c^*) = \frac{|c\cap c^*|}{|\mathcal{I}|}$. In our experiments, we use the normalized mutual information $\overline{MI}$:

$$\overline{MI}(\mathcal{C};\mathcal{C}^*) = MI(\mathcal{C};\mathcal{C}^*)/\max(H(\mathcal{C}),H(\mathcal{C}^*)) \tag{7}$$

Table 2. Mining results on five datasets.

(a) $K = 20$.

Dataset	Algo.	CC_1	$\lvert V_c\rvert$	$\overline{MI}$
Forum 1	Image Webs	105	563	0.80
	MatchMiner	266	598	0.90
Forum 2	Image Webs	728	1670	0.80
	MatchMiner	908	1744	0.85
Acropolis	Image Webs	1894	2239	0.79
	MatchMiner	1948	2305	0.83
Pantheon	Image Webs	639	847	0.59
	MatchMiner	765	869	0.74
St. Pauls	Image Webs	1816	2145	0.80
	MatchMiner	1883	2187	0.84

(b) $K = 30$.

Dataset	Algo.	CC_1	$\lvert V_c\rvert$	$\overline{MI}$
Forum 1	Image Webs	180	606	0.85
	MatchMiner	271	622	0.91
Forum 2	Image Webs	788	1745	0.83
	MatchMiner	937	1761	0.87
Acropolis	Image Webs	1951	2307	0.84
	MatchMiner	1978	2324	0.86
Pantheon	Image Webs	659	855	0.62
	MatchMiner	788	900	0.80
St. Pauls	Image Webs	1845	2179	0.82
	MatchMiner	1934	2248	0.89

It is easy to verify that $\overline{MI}(\mathcal{C};\mathcal{C}^*)$ ranges from 0 to 1. $\overline{MI}(\mathcal{C};\mathcal{C}^*) = 1$ if we find the exact same CCs as the ground truth, and $\overline{MI}(\mathcal{C};\mathcal{C}^*) = 0$ if two sets are independent. In general, a higher score indicates a more complete set of connected components. It is easy to verify that minimizing $H(\mathcal{C})$ (as described in Section 3.3) is equivalent to maximizing $\overline{MI}$ and therefore Step 2 of MatchMiner explicitly maximizes $\overline{MI}$.

4.4 Mining Performance Comparison

To evaluate our results compared to ground truth, we perform several sets of experiments on different Ks (defining different verification budgets). We compare our approach to Image Webs [9]; we only compare our results with the output of their Phase 1 because their Phase 2 aims at increasing connectivity within connected components, which cannot improve $\overline{MI}$ and the spanning structure of the graph.

Tables 2(a) and 2(b) show results for $K = 20$ and 30, respectively. Each table shows the size of the largest connected component (CC_1), the number of non-singleton images in the resulting spanning structure ($|V_c|$), and the normalized mutual information ($\overline{MI}$) achieved compared to the ground truth. All of the five datasets have a single large connected component that captures the majority of the scene, so CC_1 is another important measure of success. We allow two rounds of relevance feedback in Step 1 ($T = 2$), and we set $N_s = N_d = 200$.

The results suggest MatchMiner significantly outperforms Image Webs at our task. Note that when $K = 20$, MatchMiner already outperforms Image Webs when $K = 30$ on most datasets, which demonstrates the effectiveness of our approach.

4.5 Mining Results on Large-scale Datasets

We implemented a distributed version of MatchMiner on a shared cluster with 53 nodes. Each node in the cluster has 2 quad-core Xeon processors running at 2.66 GHz with 16 GB memory. Experiments are performed on two large datasets, Forum and Washington DC, and results are summarized in Table 3. Since the ground truth graphs for these

Table 3. Results for large datasets. $K = 20$ for all experiments. CC_1 and CC_2 denote the size of the largest and second largest connected component, respectively. $|V_c|$ is the number of non-singleton images. *Components* shows the distribution of large connected components. $H(\mathcal{C})$ is the entropy of the mining result. *Time* is the total running time of the system (not including extracting SIFT features and learning bag-of-visual-words vectors).

Dataset	Algorithm	CC_1	CC_2	$\|V_c\|$	Components			$H(\mathcal{C})$	Time
					$=2$	$=3$	≥ 4		
Forum	Image Webs	6944	6649	40689	2919	860	1011	11.92	1hr40min
	MatchMiner	13871	3088	40604	2753	812	944	11.62	1hr39min
Washington DC	Image Webs	11249	3772	146035	19526	5083	6386	16.76	6hr13min
	MatchMiner	16922	2804	140273	17276	4554	5865	16.64	6hr21min

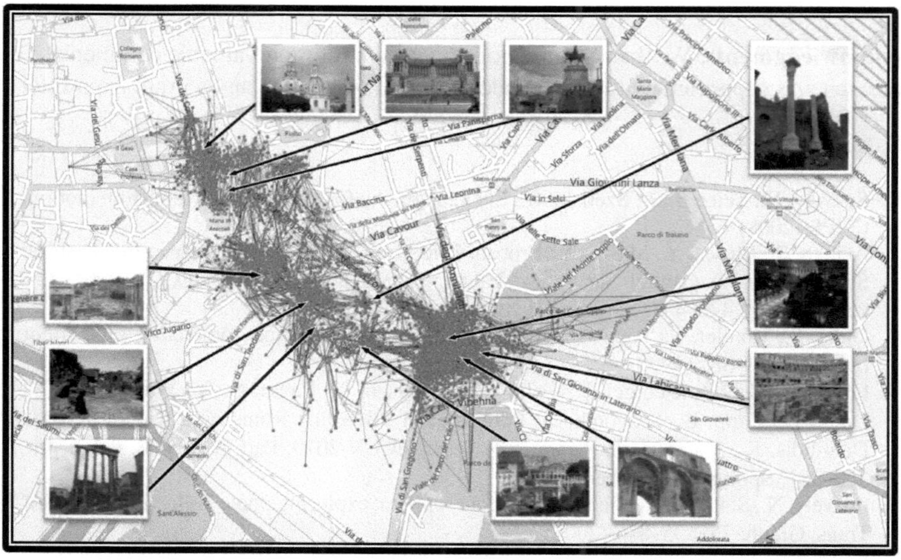

Fig. 6. Visualization of largest connected component of the image graph for Forum

two datasets are intractable to compute, we use $H(\mathcal{C})$ instead of $\overline{MI}$ to measure the quality of a set of CCs, where lower $H(\mathcal{C})$ indicates a higher $\overline{MI}$. Again, MatchMiner achieves significantly better results than Image Webs. These experiments demonstrate that MatchMiner is effective at finding large-scale spanning structure, and when parallelized can find such structure very efficiently.

The distributions of the number of CCs of different sizes are also shown in Table 3. Image Webs tends to find more small CCs (e.g., size 2 and 3). However, those small CCs are not useful in most applications based on image graphs and we are mainly interested in large CCs. Comparing the numbers of large CCs, we can see MatchMiner merges more CCs and therefore the number of large CCs is much smaller than that of Image Webs. This shows that our information-theoretic framework can prevent the system being trapped by small uninformative CCs, and that the verification budget is used to match potential image pairs that can merge large CCs, guided by the decrease of entropy.

Figure 6 shows the largest CC of the Forum dataset produced by MatchMiner, rendered on a map based on geotags and with sample images shown; discovered edges are shown as line segments. MatchMiner successfully captures links spanning several landmarks, including Il Vittoriano, the Roman Forum, and the Colosseum. The algorithm also finds links between daytime and nighttime components of the Colosseum.

5 Conclusion

In this paper, we formulate the problem of discovering the structure of an image graph as a mining task called spanning structure mining, and we describe our novel MatchMiner algorithm that solves this problem very efficiently as compared to the state of the art. In future work, we would like to further improve our algorithms, especially focusing on finding noise images and eliminating them even earlier in the process.

Acknowledgments. We thank anonymous reviewers for their valuable comments. This research was supported by the NSF under grants IIS-0964027 and a grant from Intel.

References

1. Snavely, N., Seitz, S.M., Szeliski, R.: Skeletal graphs for efficient structure from motion. In: CVPR (2008)
2. Avidan, S., Moses, Y., Moses, Y.: Probabilistic Multi-view Correspondence in a Distributed Setting with No Central Server. In: Pajdla, T., Matas, J(G.) (eds.) ECCV 2004. LNCS, vol. 3024, pp. 428–441. Springer, Heidelberg (2004)
3. Guha, S., Khuller, S.: Approximation algorithms for connected dominating sets. Algorithmica 20, 374–387 (1998)
4. Frahm, J.-M., Fite-Georgel, P., Gallup, D., Johnson, T., Raguram, R., Wu, C., Jen, Y.-H., Dunn, E., Clipp, B., Lazebnik, S., Pollefeys, M.: Building Rome on a Cloudless Day. In: Daniilidis, K., Maragos, P., Paragios, N. (eds.) ECCV 2010, Part IV. LNCS, vol. 6314, pp. 368–381. Springer, Heidelberg (2010)
5. Snavely, N., Seitz, S.M., Szeliski, R.: Photo tourism: exploring photo collections in 3d. ACM Trans. Graph. 25, 835–846 (2006)
6. Lowe, D.G.: Distinctive image features from scale-invariant keypoints. IJCV 60 (2004)
7. Hartley, R., Zisserman, A.: Multiple View Geometry in Computer Vision, 2nd edn. Cambridge University Press (2003)
8. Agarwal, S., Snavely, N., Simon, T., Seitz, S.M., Szeliski, R.: Building rome in a day. In: ICCV (2009)
9. Heath, K., Gelfand, N., Ovsjanikov, M., Aanjaneya, M., Guibas, L.J.: Image webs: Computing and exploiting connectivity in image collections. In: CVPR (2010)
10. Nistér, D., Stewénius, H.: Scalable recognition with a vocabulary tree. In: CVPR (2006)
11. Chum, O., Mikulík, A., Perdoch, M., Matas, J.: Total recall ii: Query expansion revisited. In: CVPR (2011)
12. Chum, O., Philbin, J., Sivic, J., Isard, M., Zisserman, A.: Total recall: Automatic query expansion with a generative feature model for object retrieval. In: ICCV (2007)
13. Chum, O., Matas, J.: Large-scale discovery of spatially related images. IEEE Trans. Pattern Anal. Mach. Intell. 32, 371–377 (2010)
14. Rocchio, J.J.: Relevance feedback in information retrieval. In: The SMART Retrieval System: Experiments in Automatic Document Processing, pp. 313–323. Prentice-Hall Inc. (1971)
15. Xu, W., Liu, X., Gong, Y.: Document clustering based on non-negative matrix factorization. In: SIGIR (2003)

V1-Inspired Features Induce a Weighted Margin in SVMs

Hilton Bristow[1,2] and Simon Lucey[2]

[1] Queensland University of Technology, Australia
[2] Commonwealth Scientific and Industrial Research Organisation, Australia
{hilton.bristow,simon.lucey}@csiro.au

Abstract. Image representations derived from simplified models of the primary visual cortex (V1), such as HOG and SIFT, elicit good performance in a myriad of visual classification tasks including object recognition/detection, pedestrian detection and facial expression classification. A central question in the vision, learning and neuroscience communities regards *why* these architectures perform so well. In this paper, we offer a unique perspective to this question by subsuming the role of V1-inspired features directly within a linear support vector machine (SVM). We demonstrate that a specific class of such features in conjunction with a linear SVM can be reinterpreted as inducing a weighted margin on the Kronecker basis expansion of an image. This new viewpoint on the role of V1-inspired features allows us to answer fundamental questions on the uniqueness and redundancies of these features, and offer substantial improvements in terms of computational and storage efficiency.

1 Introduction

One of the fundamental unanswered questions in computer vision regards how to best represent object appearance in the face of geometric and photometric distortions. The computational neuroscience community faces a parallel challenge, trying to understand how the human visual system attains a high degree of invariance whilst maintaining high selectivity. Our understanding of invariant representations stems largely from the works on the mammalian primary visual cortex (V1) [7]. Here, local object appearance and shape can be well categorised by the distribution of local edge directions, without precise knowledge of their spatial location. This is the premise behind HOG [4] and SIFT [12], among other features inspired by V1.

Jarrett *et al.* [8] showed that many V1-inspired features follow a similar pipeline of filtering an image through a large filter bank, followed by a non-linear rectification step, and finally a blurring/histogramming step.[1] Canonical features such as HOG and SIFT employ filter banks with strong selectivity to spatial frequency, orientation and scale (*e.g.* oriented edge filters, Gabor filters,

[1] We ignore photometric normalisation for brevity, but owing to its importance in the efficacy of the descriptor [8], we show how to reintroduce it later.

A. Fitzgibbon et al. (Eds.): ECCV 2012, Part II, LNCS 7573, pp. 59–72, 2012.

etc.). More recently however, weakly selective architectures such as random filters in convolutional networks have shown good performance in object classification tasks [15]. This brings into question the purpose of filters and the intrinsic properties of invariant representations in visual recognition.

From a practical perspective, most V1-inspired features use an over-complete representation based on filtered versions of images, incurring a storage cost linear in the number of filters. Whilst this seems reasonable at a glance, consider a simple example of storing 200000 50×50 images in double precision. In the case of raw pixels this amounts to only 3.72 GB of storage, a manageable figure on current desktop hardware. Filtering these images with 40 Gabor filters (5 scales and 8 orientations), commonly used in facial expression recognition [9], storage blows out to an untenable 149 GB. Strategies have been proposed to curb storage complexity, however they are largely based on heuristic subsampling or data dependent matrix factorisations that do not generalise well to new problems or datasets.

The role of V1-inspired features has been studied largely in isolation to the learning architecture used for classification. One criticism of ignoring the learning strategy when studying features is that structure unimportant to the classifier may be preserved, resulting in (i) additional computational burden, and (ii) ambiguity in representation. A fundamental motivation of our work is to consider these entities as intimately coupled. Analysing them as a whole yields insights that would not otherwise be apparent.

Contributions. We make three specific contributions in this paper:

- We show that a particular class of V1-inspired features can be rewritten as a linear function of the Kronecker expansion of an image (§2). This linear transform can be viewed as a data-independent matrix which induces a weighted margin in max-margin learning (§4).
- We postulate that a lower dimensional matrix should be able to approximate the same prior but at a substantially lower computational cost (§3), and empirically show that this is indeed the case (§5). This reduces both the storage complexity of the data and the time taken to train the resulting SVM, in theory enabling training on significantly larger datasets with little loss in classification performance.
- We demonstrate that reinterpreting the role of V1-inspired features as a weighted margin reveals some valuable insights into: (i) the uniqueness of the filters commonly used in these architectures, and (ii) the capacity of a linear SVM using V1-inspired features tending towards a quadratic kernel SVM (§4).

Empirical results are detailed in §5 across a number of visual classification tasks. Matlab code is available at `hiltonbristow.com/software`.

Prior Art. Ashraf *et al.* [1] originally explored the link between feature extraction and a weighted margin for visual classification tasks. By restricting their scope to linear features, they view filtering as a weighted margin on the data in the Fourier domain. We instead explore an inherently nonlinear embedding, more akin to current models of early biological vision. Due to the high dimensionality of the resulting problem (not encountered by Ashraf *et al.* by virtue of the convolution theorem), we seek to explicitly represent the feature maps in a lower dimensional space.

Vedaldi and Zisserman [17] and Bo *et al.* [3] both propose methods for explicitly representing kernels so lower dimensional approximations can be found, independent of data. The appeal of both approaches is the speedup in training and evaluation time that can be enjoyed by learning a linear rather than kernel SVM. Vedaldi considers the case of approximately representing the implicit feature associated with additive kernels (*i.e.* kernels useful for matching histograms) whilst Bo considers the case of incorporating preprocessed oriented edge energies, along with spatial position and colour directly into the kernel function. Our method, by contrast, relates the raw image pixel intensities directly with the feature pipeline. By having this direct relationship we can gain fundamental insights into the importance of particular architectures and redundancies in V1-inspired features to actual classification performance within a linear SVM.

2 Problem Formulation

Feature representations such as HOG and SIFT, and other more exotic architectures such as convolutional networks, crudely approximate the function of V1 complex cells. They commonly involve (1) edge orientation detection, (2) nonlinear rectification to increase edge bandwidth and discard edge step direction, (3) contrast normalisation to remove photometric variation, and (4) downsampling/pooling to histogram the resulting edge directions. We show now that a specific form of this pipeline can be expressed through a mixture of Kronecker products and convolution operations.

V1 Form. Given a vectorised input image of intensities $\mathbf{x} \in \Re^D$, coarse edge orientation detection can be cast as a 2D convolution operation with a bank of oriented filters, $\{\mathbf{g}_f\}_{f=1}^F$. A simple pointwise quadratic function, cast here as the Hadamard product ($\odot$) between two filtered versions of an image fulfils both the rectification and nonlinearity steps. Spatial pooling is achieved through 2D convolution ($*$) of the rectified response with a boxcar filter $\mathbf{b}$. The feature map $\Phi(\mathbf{x})$ can thus be expressed as,

$$\Phi(\mathbf{x}) = [\Phi_1(\mathbf{x}), \Phi_2(\mathbf{x}), \ldots, \Phi_F(\mathbf{x})]^T \tag{1}$$

where,

$$\Phi_f(\mathbf{x}) = \mathbf{b} * [(\mathbf{g}_f * \mathbf{x}) \odot (\mathbf{g}_f * \mathbf{x})] \ . \tag{2}$$

This particular architecture has taken the name "convolutional square pooling" and has shown good performance across a range of tasks [2]. Many variations on this feature pipeline have been advocated in literature previously, such as the use of max rather than average pooling, a sigmoid nonlinear function after rectification, and the estimation of orientation energies using an arctangent function on the horizontal and vertical edge energies. Motivations for the specific form used in this paper are that it: (i) is similar in philosophy to these other variants, (ii) still offers excellent performance when applied to a variety of classification tasks, and (iii) has greater flexibility in manipulation, thus leading to our re-interpretation as a weighted margin within a linear SVM.

Kronecker Form. Manipulation of the form in Equation 2 is limiting due to the Hadamard product ($\odot$). By defining a relation between the Hadamard and Kronecker product ($\otimes$) however, we can exploit some properties of the latter.

Theorem 21 *The Hadamard product between any two equal size vectors* $\mathbf{x}_i \in \Re^D$ *and* $\mathbf{x}_j \in \Re^D$ *can be written as,*

$$\mathbf{x}_i \odot \mathbf{x}_j = \mathbf{M}(\mathbf{x}_i \otimes \mathbf{x}_j) \tag{3}$$

such that $\mathbf{M} \in \Re^{D \times D^2}$. We can explictly define $\mathbf{M}$ as,

$$\mathbf{M} = \begin{bmatrix} \mathbf{e}_1^T \otimes \mathbf{e}_1^T \\ \vdots \\ \mathbf{e}_D^T \otimes \mathbf{e}_D^T \end{bmatrix} \tag{4}$$

given that $\mathbf{e}_i \in \Re^D$ is a vector of zeros with 1 at the i-th element.

Replacing 2D convolution operations (*e.g.* $\mathbf{g} * \mathbf{x}$) with convolution matrices (*e.g.* $\mathbf{Gx}$) and applying Theorem 21 to Equation 2, the response to a single filter can be written as,

$$\begin{aligned} \Phi_f(\mathbf{x}) &= \mathbf{BM}[(\mathbf{G}_f\mathbf{x}) \otimes (\mathbf{G}_f\mathbf{x})] \\ &= \mathbf{BM}(\mathbf{G}_f \otimes \mathbf{G}_f)(\mathbf{x} \otimes \mathbf{x}) \ . \end{aligned} \tag{5}$$

The full response to a bank of filters can be written as,

$$\Phi(\mathbf{x}) = \mathbf{L}(\mathbf{x} \otimes \mathbf{x}) \tag{6}$$

where,

$$\mathbf{L} = \begin{bmatrix} \mathbf{BM}(\mathbf{G}_1 \otimes \mathbf{G}_1) \\ \vdots \\ \mathbf{BM}(\mathbf{G}_F \otimes \mathbf{G}_F) \end{bmatrix} \ . \tag{7}$$

For two V1-inspired feature maps $\Phi(\mathbf{x}_i)$ and $\Phi(\mathbf{x}_j)$, the kernel is defined as the inner product of the maps,

$$\mathcal{K}(\mathbf{x}_i, \mathbf{x}_j) = \langle \Phi(\mathbf{x}_i), \Phi(\mathbf{x}_j) \rangle \ . \tag{8}$$

Since the feature maps have a closed form expression, the kernel can be written explicitly as,

$$\begin{aligned} \Phi(\mathbf{x}_i)^T \Phi(\mathbf{x}_j) &= (\mathbf{x}_i \otimes \mathbf{x}_i)^T \mathbf{L}^T \mathbf{L} (\mathbf{x}_j \otimes \mathbf{x}_j) \qquad (9) \\ &= (\mathbf{x}_i \otimes \mathbf{x}_i)^T \mathbf{S} (\mathbf{x}_j \otimes \mathbf{x}_j) \qquad (10) \end{aligned}$$

where $\mathbf{L} \in \Re^{DF \times D^2}$ implies that the rank of $\mathbf{S}$ is at most DF. Thus after some manipulation, the form of V1-inspired features can be rearranged with the filter and data terms isolated. This suggests that the feature map is only dependent on the *joint* response from the filters and blur kernels, and that the weighting matrix $\mathbf{S}$ can be completely precomputed in the absence of data.

3 Computational Efficiency

Whilst $\mathbf{S}$ is rank deficient, its high dimensionality (*i.e.* $D^2 \times D^2$) makes it infeasible to work with directly. In practice, we wish to find a matrix of rank $K \ll DF$ that makes a good approximation to $\mathbf{S}$ whilst never explicitly computing $\mathbf{S}$ or its eigenvectors.

Indirectly Computing the Eigenvectors. From the thin singular value decomposition (SVD) of $\mathbf{L}$,

$$\mathbf{L} = \mathbf{U}\boldsymbol{\Sigma}\mathbf{V}^T \tag{11}$$

the right singular vectors $\mathbf{V} \in \Re^{DF \times D^2}$ correspond to the eigenvectors of $\mathbf{L}^T\mathbf{L} = \mathbf{S} \in \Re^{D^2 \times D^2}$, and the left singular vectors $\mathbf{U} \in \Re^{DF \times DF}$ to the eigenvectors of $\mathbf{L}\mathbf{L}^T$ which we denote $\mathbf{S}^* \in \Re^{DF \times DF}$. The eigenvectors $\mathbf{V}$ of $\mathbf{S}$ can be found efficiently by first computing the eigenvectors $\mathbf{U}$ of $\mathbf{S}^*$, then from Equation 11,

$$\mathbf{V}^T = (\boldsymbol{\Sigma}^T\mathbf{U}^T\mathbf{U}\boldsymbol{\Sigma})^{-1}(\mathbf{U}\boldsymbol{\Sigma})^T\mathbf{L} \tag{12}$$

$$= \boldsymbol{\Sigma}^{-1}\mathbf{U}^T\mathbf{L}\,. \tag{13}$$

Letting $\hat{\mathbf{U}}, \hat{\boldsymbol{\Sigma}}, \hat{\mathbf{V}}$ be components of the SVD of $\mathbf{L}$ with the K largest magnitude singular values preserved, and $\hat{\Phi}(.)$ the corresponding low dimensional feature map, then

$$\mathbf{S} \approx \hat{\mathbf{V}}\hat{\boldsymbol{\Sigma}}^2\hat{\mathbf{V}}^T\,. \tag{14}$$

The distribution of singular values in $\mathbf{S}^*$ suggests how well a rank reduction will preserve the information in $\mathbf{S}$. Figure 1 shows the eigenspectra of typical $\mathbf{S}$ matrices constructed from a number of filter representations. The spectra hint at the significant redundancies that can be exploited to reduce storage and computational costs associated with computing the low rank feature map. The $\sim \frac{1}{f}$ slope of the spectra correlates well with statistics observed in natural images.

Applying the Eigenvectors. An explicit representation of $\mathbf{S}$ is unnecessary since the goal is to find an efficient closed-form expression for the feature maps. Thus,

$$\Phi(\mathbf{x}_i)^T\Phi(\mathbf{x}_j) \approx (\mathbf{x}_i \otimes \mathbf{x}_i)^T\hat{\mathbf{V}}\hat{\boldsymbol{\Sigma}}^2\hat{\mathbf{V}}^T(\mathbf{x}_j \otimes \mathbf{x}_j) \tag{15}$$

and since the kernel is separable, a single feature map in isolation becomes,

$$\hat{\Phi}(\mathbf{x}_i) = \hat{\boldsymbol{\Sigma}}\hat{\mathbf{V}}^T(\mathbf{x}_i \otimes \mathbf{x}_i)\,. \tag{16}$$

Substituting Equation 13 into Equation 16 gives,

$$\hat{\Phi}(\mathbf{x}_i) = \hat{\mathbf{U}}^T\mathbf{L}(\mathbf{x}_i \otimes \mathbf{x}_i)\,. \tag{17}$$

Whilst $\mathbf{L}$ is sparse for compact support filters, storage in memory quickly becomes prohibitive with increasing image size. For our earlier example of a 50×50 pixel input and 40 filters with 20×20 pixel support, storing the full $\mathbf{L}$ matrix will

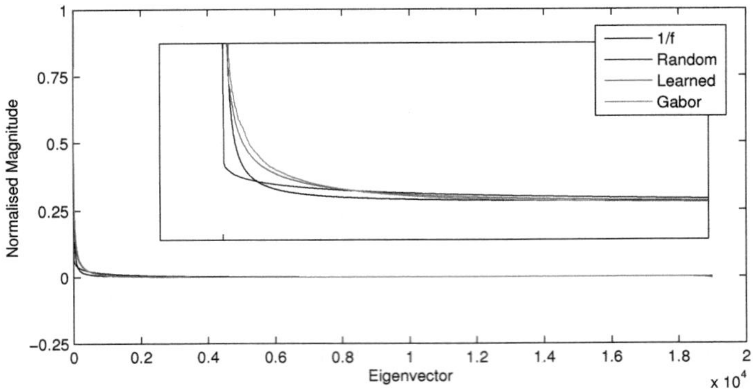

Fig. 1. The eigenspectrum of **S** for a number of filter representations. The $\sim \frac{1}{f}$ distribution suggests a low rank approximation could be found, which preserves most of the variance in **S**. The magnified region shows in greater detail the energy distribution of the largest eigenvalues. The learned filters (using the method of [10]) have the most compact energy spectrum, followed by the Gabor filters, with the random filters having the broadest spectrum.

require on the order of 657 GB. We know however, that the joint portion $\mathbf{L}(\mathbf{x} \otimes \mathbf{x})$ can be efficiently computed using the original method of convolutions via,

$$\mathbf{L}(\mathbf{x} \otimes \mathbf{x}) = \begin{bmatrix} \mathbf{b} * [(\mathbf{g}_1 * \mathbf{x}) \odot (\mathbf{g}_1 * \mathbf{x})] \\ \vdots \\ \mathbf{b} * [(\mathbf{g}_F * \mathbf{x}) \odot (\mathbf{g}_F * \mathbf{x})] \end{bmatrix} . \tag{18}$$

By taking this approach, only $\hat{\mathbf{\Sigma}}$ and $\hat{\mathbf{U}}$ ever need be explicitly computed. For the example above, storing $\hat{\mathbf{U}}$ of rank $K = D$ will consume only 1.86 GB of memory.

Computing the feature map of Equation 1 incurs a cost of $O(DF \log D)$ operations and storage $O(DF)$. Computing the proposed feature map of Equation 17 incurs an added $O(KDF)$ operations but storage is only $O(K)$ where $K \ll DF$. Our feature map therefore realises a tradeoff between computational complexity and storage complexity, and results in a representation that is manageable for large amounts of high dimensional data, and as shown following, tractable in time when learning an SVM.

4 V1-Inspired Features and SVMs

Support vector machines have seen extensive use in visual classification tasks, and have proved particularly successful in tasks involving V1-inspired features [4]. Linear SVMs have a number of inherent advantages over kernel SVMs: (i) faster learning times, (ii) the ability to learn from larger datasets, (iii) low computation cost during evaluation as the summation over support weights and vectors can be pre-computed, and most importantly, (iv) for some applications identical if not superior performance to nonlinear kernels (*e.g.*, RBF, polynomial, tanh) [5].

Given a set of training features and labels $\{\Phi(\mathbf{x}), y_i\}_{i=1}^{l}$, $\Phi(\mathbf{x}) \in \Re^{DF}$, $y_i \in \{+1, -1\}$ a linear SVM attempts to find the solution to the following optimisation problem,

$$\min_{\mathbf{w},\xi_i \geq 0} \frac{1}{2}\mathbf{w}^T\mathbf{w} + C\sum_{i=1}^{l}\xi_i \qquad (19)$$
$$\text{subject to } y_i\mathbf{w}^T\Phi(\mathbf{x}_i) \geqslant 1 - \xi_i, \quad i = 1 \ldots l$$

where C is a penalty parameter and ξ_i are the slack variables introduced to offset the effects of outliers in the final solution.[2]

It is well understood in SVM literature that the $\mathbf{w}^T\mathbf{w}$ term in Equation 19 is inversely proportional to the margin of the solution. Maximising this margin is central to the generalisation properties of SVMs. The type of margin being maximised in this feature space is based on an unweighted (i.e. Euclidean) distance. Inspired by [1], however, we can demonstrate that an equivalent form of Equation 19 can be obtained by solving,

$$\min_{\mathbf{v},\xi_i \geq 0} \frac{1}{2}\mathbf{v}^T\mathbf{S}^{-1}\mathbf{v} + C\sum_{i=1}^{l}\xi_i \qquad (20)$$
$$\text{subject to } y_i\mathbf{v}^T(\mathbf{x}_i \otimes \mathbf{x}_i) \geqslant 1 - \xi_i, \quad i = 1 \ldots l$$

where the role of features has been completely subsumed into the weighted margin term $\mathbf{v}^T\mathbf{S}^{-1}\mathbf{v}$. The solutions to Equation 19 ($\mathbf{w} \in \Re^{DF}$) and 20 ($\mathbf{v} \in \Re^{D^2}$) are related by $\mathbf{w} = \mathbf{L}\mathbf{v}$ where $\mathbf{L} \in \Re^{DF \times D^2}$ is previously defined in Equation 10. A key realisation here is that the role of the features is completely described as a margin manipulation – the weighting term is only applied to the margin term and not the data term.

Capacity of the Classifier. This result links well with previous work of Shivaswamy and Jebara [16] concerning what "type" of margin should be maximised during the estimation of a max margin classifier such as an SVM. In this work Shivaswamy and Jebara discussed the importance of selecting the "correct" kind of margin when learning an SVM and how maximising a margin based on Euclidean distance might not always be the best choice in terms of classifier generalisation. In fact when one sets $\mathbf{S} = \mathbf{I}$ then the solution to the objective in Equation 20 reverts to a classical kernel SVM since,

$$(\mathbf{x}_i \otimes \mathbf{x}_i)^T\mathbf{I}(\mathbf{x}_j \otimes \mathbf{x}_j) = (\mathbf{x}_i^T\mathbf{x}_j)^2 \qquad (21)$$

where the kernel employed is a homogeneous second-order polynomial. Understanding how V1-inspired features improve the capacity of a linear SVM will

[2] The bias b is accounted for in $\mathbf{w} \leftarrow [\mathbf{w}^T, b]$ by $\Phi(\mathbf{x}) \leftarrow [\Phi(\mathbf{x})^T, 1]^T$ but is omitted here for clarity.

become important in our experiments section (§5). It is more reasonable to compare the classification performance of V1-inspired features to a quadratic kernel than to (a linear kernel on) raw pixels, since the latter has substantially less capacity.

Complexity in SVM Training and Prediction. When training an SVM classifier, we modify Equation 19 to instead use our low dimensional feature map $\hat{\Phi}(\mathbf{x})$, which yields an optimisation over a lower (K) dimensional $\hat{\mathbf{w}}$,

$$\min_{\hat{\mathbf{w}},\xi_i\geq 0} \frac{1}{2}\hat{\mathbf{w}}^T\hat{\mathbf{w}} + C\sum_{i=1}^{l}\xi_i \tag{22}$$
$$\text{subject to } y_i\hat{\mathbf{w}}^T\hat{\Phi}(\mathbf{x}_i) \geqslant 1 - \xi_i, \quad i = 1\ldots l\,.$$

Further to the space-time tradeoffs of §3, our method also realises a preprocessing-learning tradeoff, which has benefits when training large datasets and enumerating over different training schemes. We do not, however, have to make that same tradeoff during prediction. By taking advantage of the form of $\hat{\Phi}(\mathbf{x})$ from Equation 13, we can promote $\hat{\mathbf{w}}$ from a K dimensional space to a DF dimensional space through $\mathbf{w} = \mathbf{U}\hat{\mathbf{w}}$, such that for a vectorised test image $\mathbf{x}_i$,

$$\mathbf{w}^T\Phi(\mathbf{x}_i) \equiv \hat{\mathbf{w}}^T\hat{\Phi}(\mathbf{x}_i) \tag{23}$$

where $\Phi(\mathbf{x})$ is the original feature map of Equation 1.

Uniqueness of Filters. The structured form of the $\mathbf{S}$ matrix gives us an insight into the role of filters in the margin manipulation, specifically the uniqueness of the filter responses and their joint contribution to the invariant representation. The matrix $\mathbf{S} = \mathbf{L}\mathbf{L}^T$ can be represented as a concatenation of $F \times F$ sub-matrices,

$$\begin{aligned}\mathbf{L}_i\mathbf{L}_j^T &= \mathbf{BM}(\mathbf{G}_i \otimes \mathbf{G}_i)(\mathbf{G}_j \otimes \mathbf{G}_j)^T\mathbf{M}^T\mathbf{B}^T \\ &= \mathbf{BM}(\mathbf{G}_i\mathbf{G}_j^T) \otimes (\mathbf{G}_i\mathbf{G}_j^T)\mathbf{M}^T\mathbf{B}^T\,.\end{aligned} \tag{24}$$

From this form one can see that the role of the individual filters in this form is not unique since $\mathbf{G}_i\mathbf{A}\mathbf{A}^{-1}\mathbf{G}_j^T = \mathbf{G}_i\mathbf{G}_j^T$ where $\mathbf{A}$ is any arbitrary full rank transform matrix. Further, it is possible to show that the interaction of these filters $\mathbf{G}_i\mathbf{G}_j^T$ is unique up to a sign ambiguity.[3] Finally, it is possible to see where spatial invariance stems from in the weighting matrix $\mathbf{S}$ since for $i = j$ local phase is lost, and when $i \neq j$ only relative phase is preserved.

5 Experiments

Here we evaluate our methodology on MNIST, Caltech 101 and Cohn Kanade+ datasets to illustrate the applicability of our method to a range of computer

[3] Since $\mathbf{x}\otimes\mathbf{x} = \text{vec}(\mathbf{x}\mathbf{x}^T)$ where we know through the SVD that one can recover $\mathbf{x}$ up to a sign. Here we assume $\mathbf{x} = \text{vec}(\mathbf{G}_i\mathbf{G}_j^T)$ from Equation 24.

vision domains. Since we have already motivated the scalability of our method to large datasets through our initial thought experiment, we instead focus on showing our rank reduced features remain competitive on established benchmarks. We mimic the experimental setup of other authors who have used similar V1-inspired features.

For each of the experiments we consider 5 cases: (i) rank DF $\mathbf{S}$ matrix, (ii) rank D $\mathbf{S}$ matrix, (iii) random filters rather than frequency and orientation selective filters, (iv) $\mathbf{S} \rightarrow \mathbf{I}$ corresponding to a quadratic kernel on the pixels, and (v) pixels. Where we say rank($\mathbf{S}$) $= D$, we take D to be the dimensionality of the vectorised input image. In the case of frequency and orientation selective filters, we use a bank of log Gabor filters. In the case of random filters, we use the same number of filters as the Gabor case, and ensure that each filter has zero mean and unit norm. For each convolution, we only keep the central area that is the same size as the input image.

Reintroducing Photometric Normalisation. Jarrett *et al.* [8] show that rectification and photometric normalisation are the single most important factors in improving the performance of a recognition system. We too note this to be the case, especially in images exhibiting large photometric variation, as observed in natural images (*e.g.* Caltech 101).

Given a pointwise processing stage $\Psi(.)$ that maps $\Re^{DF} \rightarrow \Re^{DF}$ Equation 17 can be extended to

$$\Phi(\mathbf{x}) = \mathbf{U}^T \Psi\big(\mathbf{L}(\mathbf{x} \otimes \mathbf{x})\big) . \tag{25}$$

This allows us to include mid-processing such as photometric normalisation without loss of generality.

MNIST. MNIST is a handwritten character recognition dataset containing 60000 training examples and 10000 test examples of the characters $0-9$. Each character is roughly centred in a 28×28 window and quantised to 8-bit grayscale. Although MNIST is an ageing dataset, LeCun's convolutional network architecture – which for a single layer closely follows our parametric form – has shown particularly impressive performance at the task [8].

We use 48 Gabor filters at 12 orientations and 4 frequencies each of size 28×28, and a boxcar filter of size 3×3. We remove the photometric normalisation step from our model, but preprocess each image by power normalisation. Due to the large number of training data and the resulting descriptor dimensionality of 37632, we opt to train the resulting linear SVM in the prime. Average classification performance is shown in Figure 2(a).

Caltech101. Caltech 101 is a "natural" object recognition dataset containing 101 object classes, each with $40-800$ instances. The objects are roughly centred and in similar poses, though vary in appearance. Pinto has pointed to a number of flaws in the dataset and argues that it lacks true real-world variability, and supports his claims by achieving good performance with a simple biologically motivated feature representation [14]. We mimic his setup and achieve similar performance whilst illustrating some advantages of our method.

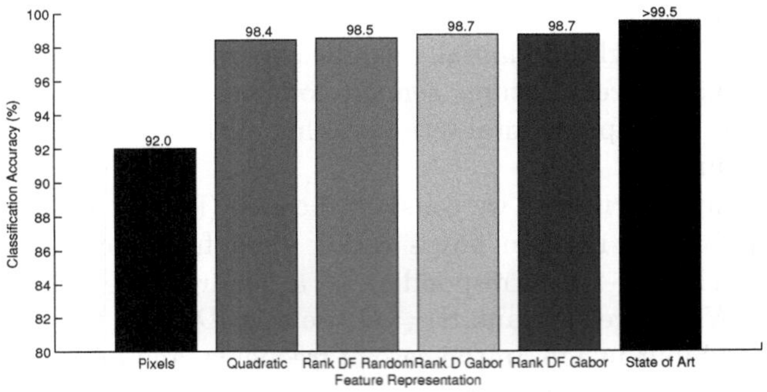

(a) MNIST

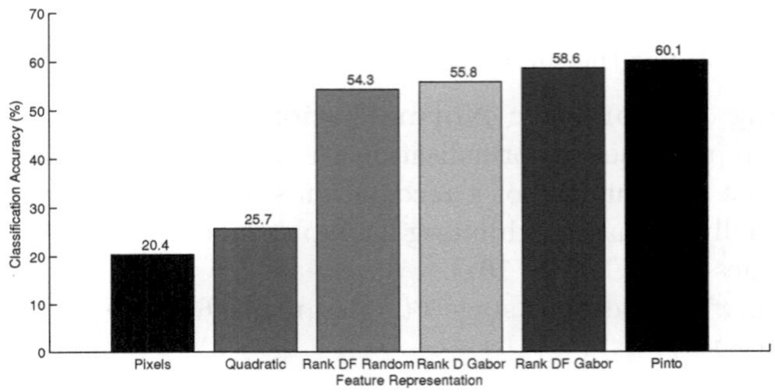

(b) Caltech 101

Fig. 2. Average classification performance across all classes of the (a) MNIST, and (b) Caltech 101 dataset for different feature descriptor representations. (Pixels) raw pixels, (Quadratic) quadratic kernel on raw pixels, (Rank DF Random) the full **S** matrix constructed from random filters, (Rank D Gabor) a low rank approximation to the full **S** matrix constructed from Gabor filters, (Rank DF Gabor) the full **S** matrix constructed from Gabor filters, (State of Art) State of the Art benchmark for MNIST taken from a survey of 60 algorithms, (Pinto) the reference method of Pinto [14].

We use 92 Gabor filters at 16 orientations and 6 scales each of size 43×43, and a boxcar filter of size 17×17. We preprocess the images by resizing and cropping each to fit a 150×150 pixel box. We modify our model to include a downsampling matrix which subsamples each filter response by a factor of 5 (to a 30×30 image). Average classification performance is shown in Figure 2(b).

PCA on Responses. To deal with the "curse of dimensionality", many papers have been devoted to finding low dimensional approximations to descriptors using PCA, LDA or nonlinear dimensionality reduction methods [11,18,6]. These methods have two inherent problems: the reduction is data dependent and needs to be recomputed for each new set of data, and the reduction must occur in the original dimensionality and may not be feasible in time or space.

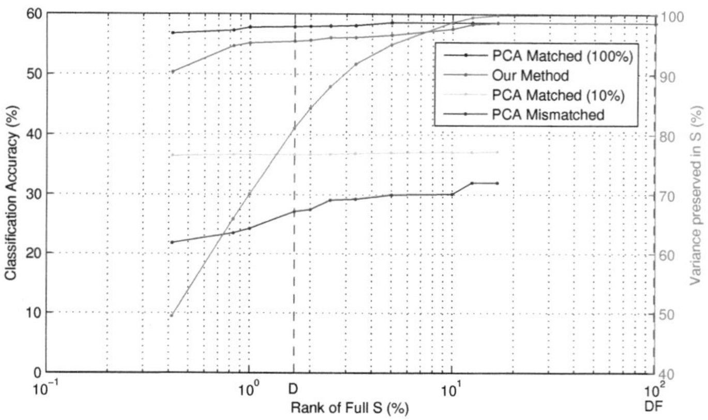

Fig. 3. A comparison of dimensionality reduction techniques on the Caltech 101 dataset. Performance is measured as average classification accuracy across classes as a function of descriptor dimensionality. (PCA Matched 100%) PCA loadings calculated from the entire training set. (Our Method) Dimensionality reduction using a low rank approximation to **S**. (PCA Matched 10%) PCA loadings calculated from 10% of the training set, with equal class representation. (PCA Mismatched) PCA loadings calculated from Cohn Kanade+ dataset. The green curve shows the variance of **S** preserved as a function of the rank. A descriptor of rank D not only models 80% of the variance in the original DF representation, but achieves similar classification performance. PCA consistently performs $\sim 4\%$ better, but only in well-matched conditions.

Equation 17 suggests that the matrix **U** acts to transform the feature onto a low rank orthonormal basis which preserves the highest modes of variance - in essence PCA. The advantages of this approach are twofold: the reduction can be precomputed in the absence of data and the reduction is based on the filter components that are likely to be discriminative rather than the observed modes of deformation specific to each training set. Figure 3 shows the classification performance of our method as a function of feature length, using the Caltech 101 setup with Gabor filters. A number of PCA schemas are shown for comparison. PCA Matched (10%) and PCA Mismatched show how PCA fails to generalise when the data used to calculate the loadings either does not span the full extent of geometric variability in the training and testing sets, or is from a different domain entirely. Our method suffers neither of these drawbacks, yet approaches the performance of PCA with loadings calculated from the full training set (PCA Matched (100%)).

Cohn Kanade+. Cohn Kanade+ is an expression recognition dataset consisting of 68-point landmark, broad expression and FACS labels across 123 subjects and 593 sequences. Each sequence varies in length and captures the neutral expression in the first frame and the peak formation of facial expression in the last. We follow the experimental setup of Lucey *et al.* [13], however we consider only the broad expressions and discard the AU labels.

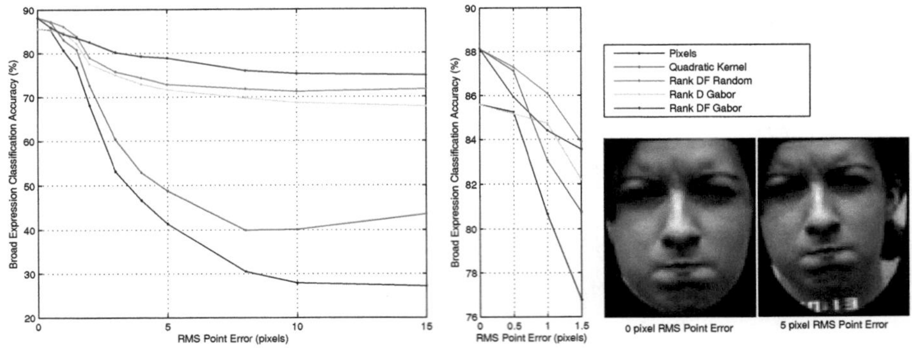

Fig. 4. Classification performance on Cohn Kanade+ broad expressions as a function of increasing registration error. Feature representations have better robustness to registration error. The central magnified panel shows that with perfect registration, the rank DF representations converge to a quadratic kernel and the rank D representations converge to (a linear kernel on) raw pixels. A quadratic kernel represents the inherent capacity of our V1-like feature parameterisation in a linear SVM learning scheme.

We register each face to a canonical geometric template then measure classification accuracy across all expressions with increasing registration error. Results are shown in Figure 4.

6 Discussion

The application of V1-inspired features can be reinterpreted as a weighted margin on the on the Kronecker basis expansion of an image. This insight becomes clearer in Equation 20 when viewed in the context of training a linear SVM. The prior on the margin is a global spatial weighting on the responses to oriented edge filters, which appear to encode some phase invariance along with relationships between frequency and orientation bands. The Cohn Kanade+ dataset was used to explore the weighted margin insight under known ground-truth geometric distortions. The results of Figure 4 reveal a pervasive insight. Image features give better robustness to registration error than raw pixel representations. With perfect registration however, the performance of rank DF representations converge to a quadratic kernel on the raw pixels, whilst the performance of the rank D representations converge to (a linear kernel on) raw pixels.

This suggests that in the absence of geometric noise, the filter prior over the data has no influence. The process of *gaining invariance* importantly does not improve performance outright; but rather only in the face of geometric mismatch. With perfect registration the class separation is sufficiently large that a prior on the margin has no effect on the discriminability of the decision hyperplane. It is only with increasing registration error and increasing nonlinearity of the true decision boundary that the prior helps guide the separating hyperplane to a good solution.

Casting the prior in a lower dimensional space whilst retaining good performance shows the function of features is more about generalisation than increasing classifier capacity. This prior encodes information important in gaining invariance to geometric variability with substantially lower capacity than a quadratic kernel. Nonetheless, the results of experiments on MNIST (Figure 2(a)) and Caltech 101 (Figure 2(b)) show that for a 60-fold decrease in dimensionality, the rank D approximation to $\mathbf{S}$ suffers only a $0 - 3\%$ decrease in performance.

Insights aside, the crux of the rank reduction lies in its relationship to and advantage over regular PCA. Because PCA is data dependent, it relies on an explicit representation of the entire training set, and a strong affinity between the observed geometric variability in the training and testing sets. As the amount and availability of crowd-sourced data increases, so too does the need for data-independent dimensionality reduction schemes. The $\mathbf{S}$ matrix is data agnostic and a rank reduction on this matrix is equivalent to an optimisation over the most important frequency components and their spatial support. Further, we show in Figure 3 that this approach is comparable with PCA. In essence, our choice of filters conveys our intuition about what spatial and frequency content is semantically important in images. A rank reduction on $\mathbf{S}$ acts to preserve the most important parts of this prior.

In light of this, we end by making two comments: (i) the choice of filters is still important as they constitute an assumed prior over the image statistics, however (ii) rather than expressing the prior indirectly through filters (which are not unique), we should consider treating the application of V1-inspired features as a machine learning task with a prior on natural image statistics and directly optimise for a weighted margin (which *is* unique) using conventional and well-established machine learning techniques.

7 Conclusions and Future Work

This paper has presented a new form for V1-inspired features, with filter terms decoupled from data terms. By integrating the learning strategy into the feature design, we reveal that the filter matrix prior acts to weight the margin in an SVM with an implicit quadratic kernel capacity. We speculated from the redundant eigenspectrum of this matrix that a low dimensional approximation to this matrix should be able to approximate the same margin manipulation but at greatly reduced computational cost, and showed this to be the case across a range of visual classification tasks. This approach enables a data independent dimensionality reduction scheme, appropriate for large-scale learning.

This work has freed the V1-inspired feature from its canonical parametrisation into a form more readily accepted by existing machine learning techniques. This unleashes a wealth of new questions about the optimality of V1-inspired features, the structure of $\mathbf{S}$ and the "best" weighting matrix.

Acknowledgements. Dr Simon Lucey is the recipient of an Australian Research Council Future Fellowship (project number FT0991969).

References

1. Ashraf, A.B., Lucey, S., Chen, T.: Reinterpreting the application of Gabor filters as a manipulation of the margin in linear support vector machines. Pattern Analysis and Machine Learning 32(7), 1335–1341 (2010)
2. Bergstra, J., Desjardins, G., Lamblin, P., Bengio, Y.: Quadratic polynomials learn better image features. Technical report, Universite de Montreal (2009)
3. Bo, L., Ren, X., Fox, D.: Kernel Descriptors for Visual Recognition. In: Advances in Neural Information Processing Systems, pp. 1–9 (2010)
4. Dalal, N., Triggs, B.: Histograms of oriented gradients for human detection. In: Computer Vision and Pattern Recognition, pp. 886–893 (2005)
5. Fan, R., Chang, K., Hsieh, C., Wang, X., Lin, C.: LIBLINEAR: A library for large linear classification. The Journal of Machine Learning Research 9, 1871–1874 (2008)
6. Fodor, I.: A survey of dimension reduction techniques. Technical report, Lawrence Livermore National Laboratory (2002)
7. Hubel, D., Wiesel, T.: Receptive fields, binocular interaction and functional architecture in the cat's visual cortex. The Journal of Physiology 160(1), 106 (1962)
8. Jarrett, K., Kavukcuoglu, K., Ranzato, M.A., LeCun, Y.: What is the best multistage architecture for object recognition? In: International Conference on Computer Vision, pp. 2146–2153 (September 2009)
9. Lades, M., Vorbruggen, J., Buhmann, J., Lange, J., von der Malsburg, C., Wurtz, R., Konen, W.: Distortion invariant object recognition in the dynamic link architecture. IEEE Transactions on Computers 42(3), 300–311 (1993)
10. Lee, H., Battle, A., Raina, R., Ng, A.: Efficient sparse coding algorithms. In: Advances in Neural Information Processing Systems, vol. 19, p. 801 (2007)
11. Liu, C., Wechsler, H.: Gabor feature based classification using the enhanced fisher linear discriminant model for face recognition. IEEE Transactions on Image Processing 11(4), 467–476 (2002)
12. Lowe, D.: Object recognition from local scale-invariant features. In: International Conference on Computer Vision, vol. 2, pp. 1150–1157 (1999)
13. Lucey, P., Lucey, S., Cohn, J.: Registration invariant representations for expression detection. In: International Conference on Digital Image Computing: Techniques and Applications, vol. (i), pp. 255–261 (2010)
14. Pinto, N., Cox, D.D., DiCarlo, J.J.: Why is real-world visual object recognition hard? PLoS computational biology 4(1), e27 (2008)
15. Saxe, A., Koh, P., Chen, Z., Bhand, M., Suresh, B., Ng, A.: On random weights and unsupervised feature learning. In: Advances in Neural Information Processing Systems, pp. 1–9 (2010)
16. Shivaswamy, P., Jebara, T.: Relative margin machines. In: Advances in Neural Information Processing Systems, vol. 21, pp. 1–8 (2008)
17. Vedaldi, A., Zisserman, A.: Efficient additive kernels via explicit feature maps. Computer Vision and Pattern Recognition, vol. (iii), pp. 3539–3546 (2010)
18. Yang, M., Zhang, L.: Gabor Feature Based Sparse Representation for Face Recognition with Gabor Occlusion Dictionary. In: Daniilidis, K., Maragos, P., Paragios, N. (eds.) ECCV 2010, Part VI. LNCS, vol. 6316, pp. 448–461. Springer, Heidelberg (2010)

Unsupervised Discovery of Mid-Level Discriminative Patches

Saurabh Singh, Abhinav Gupta, and Alexei A. Efros

Carnegie Mellon University, Pittsburgh, PA 15213, USA
http://graphics.cs.cmu.edu/projects/discriminativePatches/

Abstract. The goal of this paper is to discover a set of *discriminative patches* which can serve as a fully unsupervised mid-level visual representation. The desired patches need to satisfy two requirements: 1) to be representative, they need to occur frequently enough in the visual world; 2) to be discriminative, they need to be different enough from the rest of the visual world. The patches could correspond to parts, objects, "visual phrases", etc. but are not restricted to be any one of them. We pose this as an unsupervised discriminative clustering problem on a huge dataset of image patches. We use an iterative procedure which alternates between clustering and training discriminative classifiers, while applying careful cross-validation at each step to prevent overfitting. The paper experimentally demonstrates the effectiveness of discriminative patches as an unsupervised mid-level visual representation, suggesting that it could be used in place of visual words for many tasks. Furthermore, discriminative patches can also be used in a supervised regime, such as scene classification, where they demonstrate state-of-the-art performance on the MIT Indoor-67 dataset.

1 Introduction

Consider the image in Figure 1. Shown in green are the two most confident visual words [1] detected in this image and the corresponding visual word clusters. Shown in red are the two most confident detections using our proposed mid-level discriminative patches, computed on the same large, unlabeled image dataset as the visual words *without any supervision*. For most people, the representation at the top seems instantly more intuitive and reasonable. In this paper, we will show that it is also simple to compute, and offers very good discriminability, broad coverage, better purity, and improved performance compared to visual word features. Finally, we will also show how our approach can be used in a supervised setting, where it demonstrates state-of-the-art performance on scene classification, beating bag-of-words, spatial pyramids [2], ObjectBank [3], and scene deformable-parts models [4] on the MIT Indoor-67 dataset [5].

What are the right primitives for representing visual information? This is a question as old as the computer vision discipline itself, and is unlikely to be settled anytime soon. Over the years, researchers have proposed a plethora of different visual features spanning a wide spectrum, from very local to full-image,

A. Fitzgibbon et al. (Eds.): ECCV 2012, Part II, LNCS 7573, pp. 73–86, 2012.

Fig. 1. The top two detected Visual Words (bottom) vs. Mid-level Discriminative Patches (top), trained without any supervision and on the same large unlabeled dataset

and from low-level (bottom-up) to semantic (top-down). In terms of spatial resolution, one extreme is using the pixel itself as a primitive. However there is generally not enough information at a pixel level to make a useful feature – it will fire all the time. At the other extreme, one can use the whole image as a primitive which, while showing great promise in some applications [6,7], requires extraordinarily large amounts of training data, since one needs to represent all possible spatial configurations of objects in the world explicitly. As a result, most researchers have converged on using features at an intermediate scale: that of an image patch.

But even if we fix the resolution of the primitive, there is still a wide range of choices to be made regarding *what* this primitive aims to represent. From the low-level, bottom-up point of view, an image patch simply represents the appearance at that point, either directly (with raw pixels [8]), or transformed into a different representation (filterbank response vector [9], blurred [10,11] or spatially-binned [12,13] feature, etc). At a slightly higher level, combining such patches together, typically by clustering and histogramming, allows one to represent texture information (e.g., textons [9], dense bag-of-words [2], etc). A bit higher still are approaches that encode image patches only at sparse interest-points in a scale- and rotation-invariant way, such as in SIFT matching [12]. Overall, the bottom-up approaches work very well for most problems involving exact instance matching, but their record for generalization, i.e. finding *similar* instances, is more mixed. One explanation is that at the low-level it is very hard to know which parts of the representation are the important ones, and which could be safely ignored.

As a result, recently some researchers have started looking at high-level features, which are already impregnated with semantic information needed to generalize well. For example, a number of papers have used full-blown object detectors, e.g. [14], as features to describe and reason about images (e.g. [15,3,16]). Others have employed discriminative part detectors such as poselets [17], attribute detectors [18], "visual phrases" [19], or "stuff" detectors [20] as features.

However, there are significant practical barriers to the wide-spread adaptation of such top-down semantic techniques. First, they all require non-trivial amounts of hand-labeled training data per each semantic entity (object, part, attribute, etc). Second, many semantic entities are just not discriminative enough visually to act as good features. For example, "wall" is a well-defined semantic category (with plenty of training data available [21]), but it makes a lousy detector [21] simply because walls are usually plain and thus not easily discriminable.

In this paper, we consider *mid-level* visual primitives, which are more adaptable to the appearance distributions in the real world than the low-level features, but do not require the semantic grounding of the high-level entities. We propose a representation called *mid-level discriminative patches*. These patches could correspond to parts, objects, "visual phrases", etc. but are not restricted to be any one of them. What defines them is their *representative and discriminative property*: that is, that they can be detected in a large number of images with high recall and precision. But unlike other discriminative methods which are weakly supervised, either with image labels (e.g.,[22]) or bounding-box labels (e.g., [14]), our discriminative patches can be discovered in a *fully unsupervised* manner – given only a large pile of unlabeled images[1]. The key insight of this paper is to pose this as an unsupervised discriminative clustering problem on a huge unlabeled dataset of image patches. We use an iterative procedure which alternates between clustering and training discriminative classifiers (linear SVMs), while applying careful cross-validation at each step to prevent overfitting. Some of the resulting discriminative patches are shown in Figure 2.

Prior Work: Our goals are very much in common with prior work on finding good mid-level feature representations, most notably the original "visual words" approach [1]. Given sparse key-point detections over a large dataset, the idea is to cluster them in SIFT space in an effort to yield meaningful common units of visual meaning, akin to words in text. However, in practice it turns out that while some visual words do capture high-level object parts, most others "end up encoding simple oriented bars and corners and might more appropriately be called 'visual phonemes' or even 'visual letters'." [24]. The way [24] addressed these shortcomings was by using image segments as a mid-level unit for finding commonality. Since then, there has been a large body of work in the general area of unsupervised object discovery [25,26,27,28,29,30,31]. While we share some of the same conceptual goals, our work is quite different in that: 1) we do not explicitly aim to discover whole semantic units like objects or parts, 2) unlike [25,27,30], we do not assume a single object per image, 3) whereas in object discovery there is no separate training and test set, we explicitly aim to discover patches that are detectable in novel images. Because only visual words [1] have all the above properties, that will be our main point of comparison.

Our paper is very much inspired by poselets [17], both in its goal of finding representative yet discriminative regions, and its use of HOG descriptors and

[1] N.B.: The term "unsupervised" has changed its meaning over the years. E.g., while the award-winning 2003 paper of Fergus et al. [23] had "unsupervised" in its title, it would now be considered a weakly supervised method.

Fig. 2. Examples of discovered discriminative patches that were highly ranked

linear SVMs. However, poselets is a heavily-supervised method, employing labels at the image, bounding box, and part levels, whereas our approach aims to solve a much harder problem without any supervision at all, so direct comparisons between the two would not be meaningful. Our work is also informed by [32], who show that discriminative machinery, such as a linear SVM, could be successfully used in a fully unsupervised manner.

2 Discovering Discriminative Patches

Given an arbitrary set of unlabeled images (the "discovery dataset" $\mathcal{D}$), our goal is to discover a relatively small number of *discriminative patches* at arbitrary resolution which can capture the "essence" of that data. The challenge is that the space of potential patches (represented in this paper by HOG features [13]) is extremely large since even a single image can generate tens of thousands of patches at multiple scales.

2.1 Approach Motivation

Of our two key requirements for good discriminative patches – to occur frequently, and to be sufficiently different from the rest of the visual world – the first one is actually common to most other object discovery approaches. The standard solution is to employ some form of unsupervised clustering, such as k-means, either on the entire dataset or on a randomly sampled subset. However, running k-means on our mid-level patches does not produce very good clusters, as shown on Figure 3 (Initial KMeans). The reason is that unsupervised clustering like k-means has no choice but to use a low-level distance metric (e.g. Euclidean, $L1$, cross-correlation) which does not work well for medium-sized patches, often combining instances which are in no way visually similar. Of course, if we somehow knew that a set of patches *were* visually similar, we could easily train a discriminative classifier, such as a linear SVM, to produce an appropriate similarity metric for these patches. It would seem we have a classic chicken-and-egg problem: the clustering of the patches depends on a good similarity, but learning a similarity depends on obtaining good clusters.

But notice that we can pose this problem as a type of iterative discriminative clustering. In a typical instantiation, e.g. [33], an initial clustering of data is followed by learning a discriminative classifier for each cluster. Based on the discriminatively-learned similarity, new cluster memberships can be computed by reassigning data points to each cluster, *etc.*. In principle, this procedure will satisfy both of our requirements: the clustering step will latch onto frequently occurring patches, while the classification step will make sure that the patches in the clusters are different enough from the rest, and thus discriminative. However, this approach will not work on our problem "as is" since it is infeasible to use a discovery dataset large enough to be representative of the entire visual world – it will require too many clusters.

To address this, we turn the classification step of discriminative clustering into a *detection* step, making each patch cluster into a detector, trained (using a linear SVM) to find other patches like those it already owns. This means that each cluster is now trained to be discriminative not just against the other clusters in the discovery dataset $\mathcal{D}$, but against the rest of the *visual world*, which we propose to model by a "natural world dataset" $\mathcal{N}$. The only requirement of $\mathcal{N}$ is that it be very large (thousands of images, containing tens of millions of patches), and drawn from a reasonably random image distribution (we follow [32] in simply using random photos from the Internet). Note that $\mathcal{N}$ is not a "negative set", as it can (and most likely will) contain visual patterns also found in $\mathcal{D}$ (we also experimented with $\mathcal{D} \subset \mathcal{N}$).

It is interesting to note the similarity between this version of discriminative clustering and the root filter latent updates of [14]. There too, a cluster of patches (representing an object category) is being iteratively refined by making it more discriminative against millions of other image patches. However, whereas [14] imposes overlap constraints preventing the cluster from moving too far from the supervised initialization, in our unsupervised formulation the clusters are completely unconstrained.

Fig. 3. Few examples to show how our iterative approach, starting with initial k-means clustering, converges to consistent clusters (Iter 4). While standard discriminative clustering approach (second row) also converges in some cases (1st column), in vast majority of cases it memorizes and overfits. Note that our approach allows clusters to move around in x,y and scale space to find better members (Oval in 3rd column).

Alas, our proposed discriminative clustering procedure is still not quite enough. Consider Figure 3 which shows three example clusters: the top row is simple initialization using k-means, while the second row shows the results of the discriminative clustering described above. The left-most cluster shows good improvement compared to initialization, but the other two clusters see little change. The culprit seems to be the SVM – it is so good at "memorizing" the training data, that it is often unwilling to budge from the initial cluster configuration. To combat this, we propose an extremely simple but surprisingly effective solution – cross-validation training. Instead of training and classifying the same data, we divide our input dataset into two equal, non-overlapping subsets. We perform a step of discriminative clustering on the training subset, but then apply our learned discriminative patches on the validation subset to form clusters there. In this way, we are able to achieve better generalization since the errors in the training set are largely uncorrelated with errors in the validation set, and hence the SVM is not able to overfit to them. We then exchange the roles of training and validation, and repeat the whole process until convergence. Figure 3 shows the iterations of our algorithm for the three initial patch clusters (showing top 5 patches in each cluster). Note how the consistency of the clusters improves significantly after each iteration. Note also that the clusters can "move around" in x, y and scale space to latch onto the more discriminative parts of the visual space (see the circled train in the right-most column).

2.2 Approach Details

Initialization: The input to our discovery algorithm is a "discovery dataset" $\mathcal{D}$ of unlabeled images as well as a much larger "natural world dataset" $\mathcal{N}$ (in this

Algorithm 1. Discover Top n Discriminative Patches

Require: Discovery set $\mathcal{D}$, Natural World set $\mathcal{N}$

$\mathcal{D} \Rightarrow \{D_1, D_2\}$; $\mathcal{N} \Rightarrow \{N_1, N_2\}$ ▷ Divide $\mathcal{D}, \mathcal{N}$ into equal sized disjoint sets
$S \Leftarrow rand\_sample(D_1)$ ▷ Sample random patches from D_1
$K \Leftarrow kmeans(S)$ ▷ Cluster patches using KMeans
while not $converged()$ **do**
  for all i such that $size(K[i]) \geq 3$ **do** ▷ Prune out small ones
    $C_{new}[i] \Leftarrow svm\_train(K[i], N_1)$ ▷ Train classifier for each cluster
    $K_{new}[i] \Leftarrow detect\_top(C[i], D_2, m)$ ▷ Find top m new members in other set
  end for
  $K \Leftarrow K_{new}$; $C \Leftarrow C_{new}$
  $swap(D_1, D_2)$; $swap(N_1, N_2)$ ▷ Swap the two sets
end while
$A[i] \Leftarrow purity(K[i]) + \lambda \times discriminativeness(K[i]) \; \forall \, i$ ▷ Compute scores
return $select\_top(C, A, n)$ ▷ Sort according to scores and select top n patches

paper we used 6,000 images randomly sampled from Flickr.com). First, we divide both $\mathcal{D}$ and $\mathcal{N}$ into two equal, non-overlapping subsets (D_1, N_1 and D_2, N_2) for cross-validation. For all images in $\mathcal{D}_1$, we compute HOG descriptors [13] at multiple resolutions (at 7 different scales). To initialize our algorithm, we randomly sample S patches from $\mathcal{D}_1$ (about 150 per image), disallowing highly overlapping patches or patches with no gradient energy (e.g. sky patches) and then run standard k-means clustering in HOG space. Since we do not trust k-means to generalize well, we set k quite high ($k = S/4$) producing tens of thousands of clusters, most with very few members. We remove clusters with less than 3 patches (eliminating 66% of the clusters), ending up with about 6 patches per image still active.

Iterative Algorithm: Given an initial set of clusters K, we train a linear SVM classifier [13] for each cluster, using patches within the cluster as positive examples and *all* patches of N_1 as negative examples (iterative hard mining is used to handle the complexity). If $D_1 \subset N_1$, we exclude near-duplicates from N_1 by normalized cross-correlation > 0.4. The trained discriminative classifiers are then run on the held-out validation set D_2, and new clusters are formed from the top m firings of each detector (we consider all SVM scores above -1 to be firings). We limit the new clusters to only $m = 5$ members to keep cluster purity high – using more produces much less homogeneous clusters. On the other hand, if a cluster/detector fires less than 2 times on the validation set, this suggests that it might not be very discriminative and is killed. The validation set now becomes the training set and the procedure is repeated until convergence (i.e. the top m patches in a cluster do not change). In practice, the algorithm converges in 4-5 iterations. The full approach is summarized in Algorithm 1.

Parameters: The size of our HOG descriptor is 8x8 cells (with a stride of 8 pixels/cell), so the minimum possible patch is 80x80 pixels, while the maximum could be as large as full image. We use a linear SVM (C=0.1), with 12 iterations of hard negative mining. For more details, consult the source code on the website.

Fig. 4. Visualizing images (left) in terms of their most discriminative patches (right). The patch detectors were fired on a novel image and the high-scoring patch detections were averaged together, weighted by their scores.

2.3 Ranking Discriminative Patches

Our algorithm produces a dictionary of a few thousand discriminative patches of varying quality. Our next task is to rank them, to find a small number of the most discriminative ones. Our criteria for ranking consists of two terms:
Purity: Ideally, a good cluster should have all its member patches come from the same visual concept. However, measuring purity in an unsupervised setting is impossible. Therefore, we approximate the purity of each cluster in terms of the classifier confidence of the cluster members (assuming that cross-validation removed overfitting). Thus, the purity score for a cluster is computed by summing up the SVM detection scores of top r cluster members (where $r > m$ to evaluate the generalization of the cluster beyond the m training patches).
Discriminativeness: In an unsupervised setting, the only thing we can say is that a highly discriminative patch should fire *rarely* in the natural world. Therefore, we define discriminativeness of a patch as the ratio of the number of firings on $\mathcal{D}$ to the number of firings on $\mathcal{D} \cup \mathcal{N}$ (of course, we do not want patches that never fire at all, but these would have already been removed in cross-validation training).

All clusters are ranked using a linear combination of the above two scores. Figure 2 shows a set of top-ranked discriminative patch clusters discovered with our approach. Note how sometimes the patches correspond to object parts, such as "horse legs" and "horse muzzle", sometimes to whole objects, such as "plates", and sometimes they are just discriminative portions of an object, similar to poselets (e.g., see the corner of trains). Also note that they exhibit surprisingly good visual consistency for a fully unsupervised approach. The ability of discriminative patches to fire on visually similar image regions is further demonstrated in Figure 4, where the patch detectors are applied to a novel image and high-scoring detections are displayed with the average patch from that cluster. In a way, the figure shows what our representation captures about the image.

3 Discovering "Doublets"

While our discriminative patch discovery approach is able to produce a number of visually good, highly-ranked discriminative patches, some other potentially promising ones do not make it to the top due to low purity. This happens when

Fig. 5. Cluster clean-up using "doublets". A visually non-homogeneous cluster (b) that has learned more than one concept, when coupled into a doublet with a high quality cluster (a), gets cleaned up (c).

Fig. 6. Examples of discovered discriminative "doublets" that were highly ranked

a cluster converges to two or more "concepts" because the underlying classifier is able to generalize to both concepts simultaneously (e.g., Figure 5b). However, often the two concepts have different firing patterns with respect to some other mid-level patch in the dictionary, e.g., motorcycle wheel in Figure 5a. Therefore, we propose to employ second-order spatial co-occurrence relationships among our discriminative patches as a way of "cleaning them up" (Figure 5c). Moreover, discovering these second-order relationships can provide us with "doublets" [34] (which could be further generalized to grouplets [22,35]) that can themselves be highly discriminative and useful as mid-level features in their own right.

To discover doublets, we start with a list of highly discriminative patches that will serve as high-quality "roots". For each root patch, we search over all the other discovered discriminative patches (even poor-quality ones), and record their relative spatial configuration in each image where they both fire. The pairs that exhibit a highly spatially-correlated firing pattern become potential doublets. We rank the doublets by applying them on the (unlabeled) validation set. The doublets are ranked high if in images where both patches fire, their relative spatial configuration is consistent with what was observed in the training set. In Figure 6 we show some examples of highly discriminative doublets. Notice that not only is the quality of discriminative patches good, but also the spatial relationships within the doublet are intuitive.

4 Quantitative Evaluation

As with other unsupervised discovery approaches, evaluation is difficult. We have shown a number of qualitative results (Figures 2, 6), and there are many more on the website. For the first set of quantitative evaluations (as well as for all the qualitative results except Figure 8), we have chosen a subset of of PASCAL VOC 2007 [36] (1,500 images) as our discovery dataset. We picked PASCAL

VOC because it is a well-known and difficult dataset, with rich visual diversity and scene clutter. Moreover, it provides annotations for a number of object classes which could be used to evaluate our unsupervised discovery. However, since our discovered patches are not meant to correspond to semantic objects, this evaluation metric should be taken with quite a few grains of salt.

One way to evaluate the quality of our discriminative patch clusters is by using the standard unsupervised discovery measures of "purity" and "coverage" (e.g., [31]). *Purity* is defined by what percentage of cluster members correspond to the same visual entity. In our case, we will use PASCAL semantic category annotations as a surrogate for visual similarity. For each of the top 1000 discovered patches, we first assign it to one of the semantic categories using majority membership. We then measure purity as percentage of patches assigned to the same PASCAL semantic label. *Coverage* is defined as the number of images in the dataset "covered" (fired on) by a given cluster.

Figure 7 reports the purity and coverage of our approach and a number of baselines. For each one, the graphs show the cumulative purity/coverage as number of clusters being considered is increased (the clusters are sorted in the decreasing order of purity). We compare our approach with Visual Words [1] and Russell et. al [24] baseline, plus a number of intermediate results of our method: 1) HOG K-Means (visual word analog for HOG features), 2) Initial Clustering (SVMs trained on the K-Means clusters without discriminative re-clustering), and 3) No Cross-Validation (iterative, discriminatively-trained clusters but without cross-validation). In each case, the numbers indicate area-under-the-curve (AUC) for each method. Overall, our approach demonstrates substantial gain in purity without sacrificing much coverage as compared to the established approaches. Moreover, each step of our algorithm improves purity. Note in particular the substantial improvement afforded by the cross-validation training procedure compared to standard training.

As we mentioned, however, the experiment above under-reports the purity of our clusters, since semantic equivalence is not the same as visual similarity. Therefore, we performed an informal perceptual experiment with human subjects, measuring the *visual purity* of our clusters. We selected the top 30 clusters from the dataset. For each cluster, we asked human labelers to mark which of the cluster's top ten firings on the validation set are visually consistent with the cluster. Based on this measure, average visual purity for these clusters was 73%.

4.1 Supervised Image Classification

Unsupervised clustering approaches, such as visual words, have long been used as features for supervised tasks, such as classification. In particular, bag of visual words and spatial pyramids [2] are some of the most popular current methods for image classification. Since our mid-level patches could be considered the true visual words (as opposed to "visual letters"), it makes sense to see how they would perform on a supervised classification task. We evaluate them in two different settings: 1) unsupervised discovery, supervised classification, and 2) supervised discovery, supervised classification.

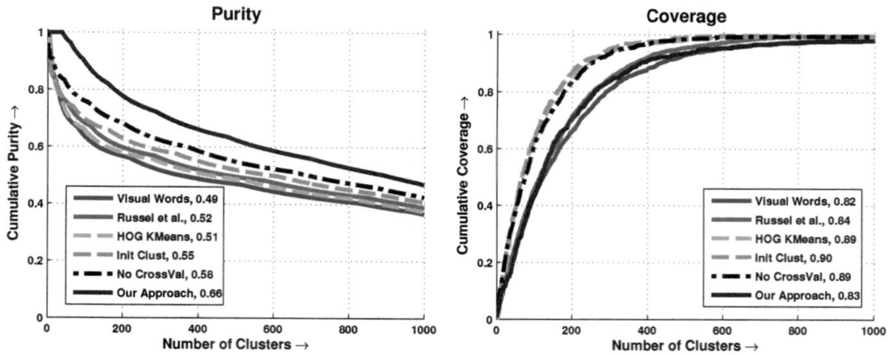

Fig. 7. Quantitative comparison of discriminative patches compared to the baseline approaches. Quality of clustering is evaluated in terms of the area under the curve for cumulative purity and coverage.

Table 1. Quantitative Evaluation: Average Classification on MIT Indoor-67 dataset. *Current state-of-the-art. †Best performance from various vocabulary sizes.

GIST	29.7
Spatial Pyramid HOG (*SPHOG*)†	29.8
Spatial Pyramid SIFT (*SP*)†	34.4
ROI-GIST [5]	26.5
Scene DPM [4]	30.4
MM-Scene [37]	28.0
Object Bank [3]	37.6
Ours	**38.1**

Ours+GIST	44.0
Ours+SP	46.4
Ours+GIST + SP	47.5
Ours+DPM	42.4
Ours+GIST+DPM	46.9
Ours+SP+DPM	46.4
GIST+SP+DPM [4]	43.1*
Ours+GIST+SP+DPM	**49.4**

Unsupervised Discriminative Patches

Using the discriminative patches discovered from the same PASCAL VOC discovery dataset as before, we would like to see if they could make better visual words for a supervised image classification task. Our baseline is the standard spatial pyramid of visual words (using 1000 visual words) using their public code [2]. For our approach, we construct spatial pyramid using top 1000 discriminative patches. Classification was performed using a simple linear SVM and performance was evaluated using Average Precision. Standard visual words scored 0.54 AP, while using our discriminative patches, the score was 0.65 AP. We further expanded our feature representation by adding the top 250-ranking doublets as extra visual words, resulting in a slight improvement to 0.66 AP.

Supervised Discriminative Patches

We further want to evaluate the performance of our approach when it is allowed to utilize more supervision for a fair comparison with several existing supervised approaches. Instead of discovering the discriminative patches from a common pool of all the images, we can also discover them on a per-category basis. In this experiment, we perform supervised scene classification using the challenging MIT Indoor-67 dataset [5], containing 67 scene categories. Using the provided scene

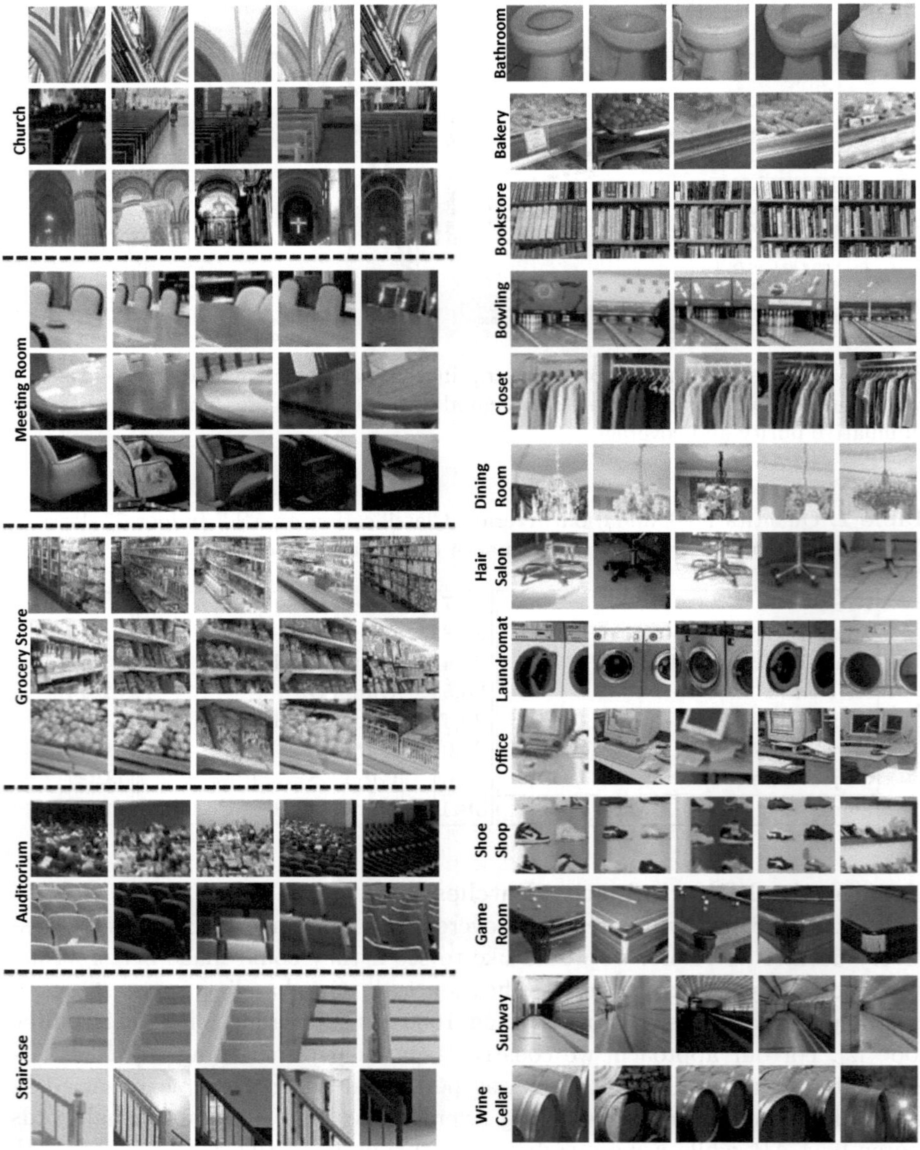

Fig. 8. Top discriminative patches for a sampling of scenes in the MIT Indoor-67 Scene dataset [5]. Note how these capture various visual aspects of a typical scene.

labels, we discover discriminative patches for each scene independently, while treating all other images in the dataset as the "natural world".

Figure 8 shows top few most discriminative patches discovered this way for a number of categories from the dataset. It is interesting to see that the discriminative patches capture aspects of scenes that seem very intuitive to us. In particular the discriminative patches for the *Church* category capture the arches and the benches; the ones for the *Meeting Room* capture the center table and the seats. These discriminative patches are therefore capturing the essence of the scene in terms of these highly consistent and repeating patterns and hence providing a simple yet highly effective mid-level representation. Inspired by these results, we have also applied a similar approach to discovering "What makes Paris look like Paris" [38] using geographic labels as the weak supervisory signal.

To perform classification, top 210 discovered patches of each scene are aggregated into a spatial pyramid using maxpooling over the discriminative patch scores as in [3]. We again use a linear SVM in a one-vs-all classification. The results are reported in Table 1. Comparison with HOG visual words (SPHOG) shows the huge performance gain resulting from our algorithm when operating in the same feature space. Further, our simple method by itself outperforms all others that have been tested on this dataset [5,4,37,3]. Moreover, combining our method with the currently best-performing combination approach of [4] yields **49.4**% performance which, to our knowledge, is the best on this dataset.

Acknowledgments. The authors would like to thank Martial Hebert, Tomasz Malisiewicz, Abhinav Shrivastava and Carl Doersch for many helpful discussions. This work was supported by ONR Grant N000141010766.

References

1. Sivic, J., Zisserman, A.: Video Google: A text retrieval approach to object matching in videos. In: ICCV (2003)
2. Lazebnik, S., Schmid, C., Ponce, J.: Beyond bags of features: Spatial pyramid matching for recognizing natural scene categories. In: CVPR (2006)
3. Li, L.-J., Su, H., Xing, E.P., Fei-fei, L.: Object bank: A high-level image representation for scene classification and semantic feature sparsification. In: NIPS (2010)
4. Pandey, M., Lazebnik, S.: Scene recognition and weakly supervised object localization with deformable part-based models. In: ICCV (2011)
5. Quattoni, A., Torralba, A.: Recognizing indoor scenes. In: CVPR (2009)
6. Torralba, A., Fergus, R., Freeman, W.T.: 80 million tiny images: a large database for non-parametric object and scene recognition. PAMI (2008)
7. Hays, J., Efros, A.A.: im2gps: estimating geographic information from a single image. In: CVPR (2008)
8. Ullman, S., Vidal-Naquet, M., Sali, E.: Visual features of intermediate complexity and their use in classification. Nature America (2002)
9. Leung, T., Malik, J.: Representing and recognizing the visual appearance of materials using three-dimensional textons (2001)
10. Brown, M., Szeliski, R., Winder, S.: Multi-image matching using multi-scale oriented patches. In: CVPR (2005)
11. Berg, A.C., Malik, J.: Geometric blur for template matching. In: CVPR (2001)
12. Lowe, D.: Distinctive image features from scale-invariant keypoints. IJCV (2004)
13. Dalal, N., Triggs, B.: Histograms of oriented gradients for human detection. In: CVPR (2005)
14. Felzenszwalb, P., McAllester, D., Ramanan, D.: A discriminatively trained, multiscale, deformable part model. In: CVPR (2008)

15. Torresani, L., Szummer, M., Fitzgibbon, A.: Efficient Object Category Recognition Using Classemes. In: Daniilidis, K., Maragos, P., Paragios, N. (eds.) ECCV 2010, Part I. LNCS, vol. 6311, pp. 776–789. Springer, Heidelberg (2010)
16. Payet, N., Todorovic, S.: Scene shape from texture of objects. In: CVPR (2011)
17. Bourdev, L., Malik, J.: Poselets: Body part detectors trained using 3d human pose annotations. In: ICCV (2009)
18. Farhadi, A., Endres, I., Hoiem, D.: Attribute-centric recognition for cross-category generalization. In: CVPR (2010)
19. Sadeghi, M.A., Farhadi, A.: Recognition using visual phrases. In: CVPR (2011)
20. Shotton, J., Winn, J.M., Rother, C., Criminisi, A.: *TextonBoost*: Joint Appearance, Shape and Context Modeling for Multi-class Object Recognition and Segmentation. In: Leonardis, A., Bischof, H., Pinz, A. (eds.) ECCV 2006. LNCS, vol. 3951, pp. 1–15. Springer, Heidelberg (2006)
21. Choi, M.J., Lim, J.J., Torralba, A., Willsky, A.S.: Exploiting hierarchical context on a large database of object categories. In: CVPR (2010)
22. Yao, B., Fei-Fei, L.: Grouplet: A structured image representation for recognizing human and object interactions. In: CVPR (2010)
23. Fergus, R., Perona, P., Zisserman, A.: Object class recognition by unsupervised scale-invariant learning. In: CVPR (2003)
24. Russell, B.C., Freeman, W.T., Efros, A.A., Sivic, J., Zisserman, A.: Using multiple segmentations to discover objects and their extent in image collections. In: CVPR (2006)
25. Todorovic, S., Ahuja, N.: Unsupervised category modeling, recognition, and segmentation in images. PAMI (2008)
26. Kim, G., Faloutsos, C., Hebert, M.: Unsupervised Modeling of Object Categories Using Link Analysis Techniques. In: CVPR (2008)
27. Lee, Y.J., Grauman, K.: Foreground focus: Unsupervised learning from partially matching images. IJCV (2009)
28. Lee, Y.J., Grauman, K.: Object-graphs for context-aware category discovery. In: CVPR (2010)
29. Lee, Y.J., Grauman, K.: Learning the easy things first: Self-paced visual category discovery. In: CVPR (2011)
30. Kim, G., Torralba, A.: Unsupervised Detection of Regions of Interest using Iterative Link Analysis. In: NIPS (2009)
31. Kang, H., Hebert, M., Kanade, T.: Discovering object instances from scenes of daily living. In: ICCV (2011)
32. Shrivastava, A., Malisiewicz, T., Gupta, A., Efros, A.A.: Data-driven visual similarity for cross-domain image matching. ACM ToG (SIGGRAPH Asia) (2011)
33. Ye, J., Zhao, Z., Wu, M.: Discriminative k-means for clustering. In: NIPS (2007)
34. Sivic, J., Russell, B.C., Efros, A.A., Zisserman, A., Freeman, W.T.: Discovering object categories in image collections. In: ICCV (2005)
35. Karlinsky, L., Dinerstein, M., Ullman, S.: Unsupervised feature optimization (ufo): Simultaneous selection of multiple features with their detection parameters. In: CVPR (2009)
36. Everingham, M., Gool, L.V., Williams, C.K.I., Winn, J., Zisserman, A.: The PASCAL Visual Object Classes Challenge (2007)
37. Zhu, J., Li, L.-J., Li, F.-F., Xing, E.P.: Large margin learning of upstream scene understanding models. In: NIPS (2010)
38. Doersch, C., Singh, S., Gupta, A., Sivic, J., Efros, A.A.: What makes paris look like paris? ACM Transactions on Graphics (SIGGRAPH) 31 (2012)

Self-similar Sketch

Andrea Vedaldi and Andrew Zisserman

Department of Engineering Science, University of Oxford
{vedaldi,az}@robots.ox.ac.uk

Abstract. We introduce the self-similar sketch, a new method for the extraction of intermediate image features that combines three principles: detection of self-similarity structures, nonaccidental alignment, and instance-specific modelling. The method searches for self-similar image structures that form nonaccidental patterns, for example collinear arrangements. We demonstrate a simple implementation of this idea where self-similar structures are found by looking for SIFT descriptors that map to the same visual words in image-specific vocabularies. This results in a visual word map which is searched for elongated connected components. Finally, segments are fitted to these connected components, extracting linear image structures beyond the ones that can be captured by conventional edge detectors, as the latter implicitly assume a specific appearance for the edges (steps). The resulting collection of segments constitutes a "sketch" of the image. This is applied to the task of estimating vanishing points, horizon, and zenith in standard benchmark data, obtaining state-of-the-art results. We also propose a new vanishing point estimation algorithm based on recently introduced techniques for the continuous-discrete optimisation of energies arising from model selection priors.

Keywords: self-similarity, feature detector, vanishing point estimation, UFL.

1 Introduction

Almost all computer vision methods start by computing features of the image. This is done in addressing geometric tasks such as three dimensional reconstruction from multiple views, as well as semantic tasks such as the recognition of natural object categories. Useful features extract stable image structures which are relevant to the task at hand, factoring the useful information from nuisances of the imaging process. A typical example are the many co-variant image region detectors [1–3] and the corresponding invariant descriptors [4] used in wide-baseline matching to identify fragments of 3D dimensional scenes regardless of viewpoint.

Due to the lack of a theory that can indicate what an optimal feature design should be, one usually looks for reasonable properties such as viewpoint invariance [5], robustness, and speed. Standard feature *detectors* such as Harris' corners [6], Canny's edges [7], the Laplacian and Hessian detectors [8], and their

A. Fitzgibbon et al. (Eds.): ECCV 2012, Part II, LNCS 7573, pp. 87–100, 2012.

Fig. 1. Self-similar sketches. The figure shows a few example images, the quantised local descriptors, and the fitted line segments constituting the sketch. The calculation is straightforward and relatively efficient.

affine co-variant extensions [1, 2], look for simple structures such as corners, blobs, and steps. In these cases, the appearance of the detected structures is defined analytically by looking at the extrema of one or more operators of the image scale space. Alternatively, it can be *learned* from example data [9, 10] to go past the restrictions of the analytical approach.

In this work we propose a novel design for feature detectors which does *not* require defining (either analytically or through example data) the *appearance* of the detected structures at all. Our approach, which we call *self-similar sketch*, combines in a novel way three known principles: (i) self-similarity [11], (ii) nonaccidental alignment [12–14], and (iii) instance-specific modelling [15]. The idea of self-similarity, as proposed by [11], is to abstract from the image appearance by searching for occurrences of visually similar structures within an image. Spatial arrangements of self-similar structures are then recorded and used as feature *descriptors*. By contrast, the self-similar sketch looks for nonaccidental arrangements (in the following examples straight line segments) of self-similar structures and use these as a basis for feature *detectors*. Moreover, the method used to detect the self-similar structures, *i.e.*, computing an image-specific visual vocabulary [16] (Sect. 2), can be seen as estimating an appearance model of each detected structure on an instance-by-instance basis.

Fig. 2. Construction of the self-simlar sketch. From left to right: input image, label $l(u, v)$ associated to each pixel (different colours correspond to different labels), regions selected as elongated overlaid by the corresponding line segment, and the final sketch.

The paper explores a particularly simple example of the self-similar sketch construction that can be summarised in a few words: (i) local descriptors are extracted densely from the image, (ii) these are discretised based on an image-specific vocabulary, and (iii) the aligned occurrences of identical visual words are extracted as line segments. The result can be thought of as a sketch of the image abstracting away from the details of the local appearance while capturing shape by coarse straight strokes (Fig. 1, 2, Sect. 2).

Compared to traditional feature designs, perhaps the most striking difference is that the self-similar sketch does not attempt to characterise the *appearance* of the detected structure (*e.g.*, as blobs or steps). Instead, the feature appearance is completely instance-dependent, and the features are defined solely based on a nonaccidental alignment principle. The details of the construction are reported in Sect. 2.

As an example application, Sect. 4 demonstrates using the self-similar sketch for the extraction of vanishing points and the estimation of the horizon location on standard benchmark data. For vanishing point estimation, a method inspired by [17, 18] (Sect. 3) is used to simultaneously group of line segments into vanishing points, determine the number and locations of such points, and reject potential line outliers. By carefully modelling the uncertainty of line detector output (Sect 3.3), this method is competitive with state-of-the-art algorithms even when standard edge detectors are used (Sect. 4). When the algorithm is used in combination with the self-similar sketch, however, the performance is improved significantly and results may exceed the state-of-the-art by a margin.

2 Self-similar Sketch

This section describes in detail the extraction of the self-similar sketch outlined in Sect. 1. Fig. 2 illustrates the main steps.

Given an input image $I(u, v)$, $(u, v) \in \Omega$, where Ω is a discrete set of pixel locations, the construction starts by extracting a dense set of local appearance descriptors $\{\Psi(u,v),(u,v)\in\Omega\}$ from the image. While many different choices of $\Psi(u,v)$ are possible, in this paper we consider SIFT features [4] as these can be extracted very efficiently at a dense set of locations if their orientation and scale are fixed. Very low-contrast SIFT descriptors are mapped to the null vector to avoid wasting resources by coding unstable image structures in the next step.

The descriptors $\{\Psi(u,v):(u,v)\in\Omega\}$ are then quantised in a small image-specific vocabulary $\{\mathbf{c}_1,\dots,\mathbf{c}_k\}$ of $k\approx 100$ visual words by using k-means clustering. While the number of descriptors is potentially large, the small size of the vocabulary means that even a simple implementation of the k-means algorithm is usually sufficient to complete the computation quickly (it is also possible to subsample the set of descriptors used to estimate the k-means centres).

After quantisation, line segments are efficiently extracted by using a method analogous to [19]. First, each image pixel (u,v) is assigned the label $l(u,v)$ corresponding to the visual word $\mathbf{c}_{l(u,v)}$ closest to the local descriptor $\Psi(u,v)$. Then the connected components of the label map $l(u,v)$ are extracted, in our example using the standard 4-neighbours topology. The area $A(R)$ and major $\mu_1(R)$ and minor $\mu_2(R)$ axis of inertia of each connected component $R\subset\Omega$ are computed (this can be done efficiently in a single pass over the image by using appropriate accumulators), and the regions R that have sufficiently large area $A(R)\geq A_0$ and aspect ratio $\mu_1(R)/\mu_2(R)>r$ are deemed as *elongated* and marked as detected.

Once these elongated regions are extracted, a line segment is fitted to each of them. The segment passes through the centroid of the region R, is aligned to the major axis of inertia of the region, and extends to touch a bounding box tightly containing the region itself. In the following, each segment will be represented by the two extrema $(\mathbf{x}_1,\mathbf{x}_2)$. The collection of all the segments extracted in this manner constitutes the self-similar sketch. Example results are reported in Fig. 2 and Sect. 4.

3 Vanishing Points from the Self-similar Sketch

This section discusses an example application of the self-similar sketch, namely the automatic extraction of vanishing points and related geometric entities such as the horizon. Recall that a *vanishing point* is an image point where the projection of parallel three dimensional lines converge. The estimation of the image vanishing points [20–26] is a standard step in several geometry-based applications. For example, in a so-called Manhattan world one has ideally three groups of three dimensional parallel lines, corresponding to the vertical direction (the side of buildings) and two orthogonal ones, parallel to the ground (the bases of buildings), forming an orthonormal system. Thus, by identifying these characteristic directions, it is possible to estimate the camera orientation. In a slightly more complex scenario, there are a number of directions that are parallel to the ground but not necessarily orthogonal, corresponding to vertical structures whose base may not be aligned. In this case, vanishing points can still be useful to estimate other important geometric parameters, such as the location of the horizon. In particular, the estimation of the horizon has been shown to be a useful cue for higher level tasks, including object categorisation and scene interpretation [27].

3.1 Geometry

This section reviews briefly the geometry of vanishing points and the relative equations. Given a point $(u, v) \in \Omega$ in the image reference frame, its coordinates $\mathbf{x} \in \mathbb{R}^3$ in the camera reference frame are given by

$$\mathbf{x} = \begin{bmatrix} \rho(u - c_u) \\ \rho(v - c_v) \\ 1 \end{bmatrix}$$

where ρ is a pixel size in units of focal length and (u_c, v_c) are the coordinates of the camera principal point (in pixels). When the pixel size and the principal points are unknown, a sensible choice [21] is to assume that the principal point lies at the centre of the image and that $\rho = 2/W$, where W is the image width in pixels (this corresponds to assuming a field of view is of 90 degrees).

A line segment is defined by two extrema $(\mathbf{x}_1, \mathbf{x}_2)$ in the image plane. The corresponding line can be obtained by intersecting the image plane with the plane π passing through $\mathbf{x}_1, \mathbf{x}_2$ and the camera centre $\mathbf{0}$. Therefore, the line can be represented as the unit vector $\ell \in \mathbb{S}^2$ normal to the plane π, where $\mathbb{S}^2$ denotes the Gaussian (unit) sphere. This vector is given by

$$\ell = \frac{\hat{\mathbf{x}}_1\mathbf{x}_2}{\|\hat{\mathbf{x}}_1\mathbf{x}_2\|} \tag{1}$$

where $\hat{\cdot}$ denotes the hat operator (*i.e.*, $\hat{\mathbf{x}}_1\mathbf{x}_2 = \mathbf{x}_1 \times \mathbf{x}_2$).

Let $\ell_1, \ldots, \ell_n$ be lines whose image converges to the same vanishing point. Then the vectors $\ell_1, \ldots, \ell_n$ belong to a plane π' passing through the camera centre. If $\mathbf{v} \in \mathbb{S}^2$ is the vector normal to π', then all the vectors ℓ_i are orthogonal to it, *i.e.*, $\langle \ell_i, \mathbf{v} \rangle = 0$. Moreover, the image of the vector $\mathbf{v}$ is the vanishing point.

Given n lines $\ell_1, \ldots, \ell_n$, the goal is to associate them to m vanishing points $\mathbf{v}_i, \ldots \mathbf{v}_m$ in such a way that the equations

$$\langle \mathbf{v}_{q_i}, \ell \rangle = 0, \quad i = 1, \ldots, n \tag{2}$$

are satisfied. Here $q_i \in \{1, \ldots, m\}$ are n label assignments mapping the n lines to up to m vanishing points. In general, not only the associations q_i and vanishing points $\mathbf{v}_i$ are unknown, but also the number m of the latter must be determined. Moreover, measurements are affected by noise and can be contaminated by outliers. The next section introduces an effective statistical model that can handle all this automatically.

3.2 Statistics and Objective Function

This section introduces a statistical model for associating lines to vanishing points, estimating the number and location of these, and handling potential outliers in the measurements. The association is represented by n label assignments

$q_i \in \{1, \dots, m, m+1\}$, where the additional label $m+1$ indicates that a line is an outlier (by convention we set the corresponding vanishing point vector $\mathbf{v}_{m+1} = 0$ to zero). The goal is to find a small number of vanishing points that can explain all the lines that are inliers. This can be obtained by trading off the number of vanishing point used to "explain" the lines and the likelihood of the fit, as expressed by the minimisation of the energy function

$$E(q_1, \dots, q_n; \mathbf{v}_1, \dots, \mathbf{v}_m) = -\sum_{i=1}^{n} \log p(\ell_i | \mathbf{v}_{q_i}, \sigma_i) + \gamma \sum_{j=1}^{m+1} [\exists i : q_i = j]. \quad (3)$$

The first term is the negative log-likelihood of the vanishing points given the measured lines and the second term is the number of vanishing points that are associated to at least one line. Choosing a large parameter γ discourages selecting too many vanishing points, avoiding overfitting the data. This formulation is a special case of, for example, [17].

The probability density $p(\ell | \mathbf{v}, \sigma)$ is the likelihood of the vanishing point $\mathbf{v}$ given the measured line ℓ and accounts for the measurement error, including the outlier case $\mathbf{v} = 0$. According to (2), in the ideal case all the line vectors ℓ_i are orthogonal to $\mathbf{v}_{q_i}$. A simple model [21] is therefore to assume that $\langle \ell_i, \mathbf{v} \rangle$ has a null mean Gaussian distribution, *i.e.*,

$$-\log p(\ell | \mathbf{v}, \sigma) = \begin{cases} \frac{1}{2} \langle \ell, \mathbf{v} \rangle^2 / \sigma^2 + \frac{1}{2} \log 2\pi\sigma, & \mathbf{v} \neq 0, \\ \frac{1}{2} \log 2\pi\sigma_0, & \mathbf{v} = 0 \quad \text{(outlier)}. \end{cases} \quad (4)$$

Here the standard deviation σ should be proportional to the uncertainty induced by measurement errors. The parameter σ_0 is a nominal standard deviation corresponding to the outlier case, expressed in this way to make tuning more intuitive. The next section introduces a simple yet effective method for tuning σ based on the uncertainty of each line segment.

3.3 Measurement Model

This section suggests how to choose the standard deviations σ_i in (3) in order to reflect the accuracy of the line segment detection. When the line segments are obtained as discussed in Sect. 2, they are affected by an error $\tilde{\mathbf{x}}_i = \mathbf{x}_i + \mathbf{e}_i$, where $\mathbf{e}_i = (e_{1i}, e_{2i}, 0)^\top$ is a small displacement in the image plane. The modulus of the error can be bounded by a parameter $\delta \geq \|\mathbf{e}_i\|$ equal to half the width of the elongated region R used to extract that segment, which for simplicity is assumed to be proportional to its minor axis of inertia $\mu_2(R)$ (Sect. 2). Let $\tilde{\ell} = \hat{\tilde{\mathbf{x}}}_1 \mathbf{x}_2 / \|\hat{\tilde{\mathbf{x}}}_1 \mathbf{x}_2\|$ be the line perturbed by the error at the extrema of the segment. The uncertainty on the projection of the line ℓ on the vanishing point vector $\mathbf{v}$ is then bounded by the Cauchy-Schwartz inequality:

$$|\langle \mathbf{v}, \tilde{\ell} \rangle - \langle \mathbf{v}, \ell \rangle| \leq \|\mathbf{v}\| \|\tilde{\ell} - \ell\| = \|\tilde{\ell} - \ell\|.$$

The difference between the perturbed and exact line is given by

$$\tilde{\ell} - \ell = \frac{\hat{\tilde{\mathbf{x}}}_1 \tilde{\mathbf{x}}_2}{\|\hat{\tilde{\mathbf{x}}}_1 \tilde{\mathbf{x}}_2\|} - \frac{\hat{\mathbf{x}}_1 \mathbf{x}_2}{\|\hat{\mathbf{x}}_1 \mathbf{x}_2\|} \approx \frac{\hat{\tilde{\mathbf{x}}}_1 \tilde{\mathbf{x}}_2 - \hat{\mathbf{x}}_1 \mathbf{x}_2}{\|\hat{\mathbf{x}}_1 \mathbf{x}_2\|} = \frac{\hat{\mathbf{x}}_1 \mathbf{e}_2 - \hat{\mathbf{x}}_2 \mathbf{e}_1 + \hat{\mathbf{e}}_2 \mathbf{e}_1}{\|\hat{\mathbf{x}}_1 \mathbf{x}_2\|}.$$

Since $\hat{\mathbf{x}}_1\mathbf{e}_2 = (-e_{22}, e_{12}, x_{11}e_{22} - x_{21}e_{12})^\top$, then, in the worst case, one obtains that $e_{12} = \delta x_{21}/\sqrt{x_{11}^2 + x_{21}^2}$ and $e_{21} = -\delta x_{11}/\sqrt{x_{11}^2 + x_{21}^2}$, so that $\|\hat{\mathbf{x}}_1\mathbf{e}_2\|^2 < \delta^2(1 + x_{11}^2 + x_{21}^2)$. Since $\|\hat{\mathbf{e}}_2\mathbf{e}_1\|^2 \leq \delta^4$, one obtains

$$|\langle \mathbf{v}, \tilde{\ell}\rangle - \langle \mathbf{v}, \ell\rangle| \leq \|\tilde{\ell} - \ell\| \leq \delta \frac{\sqrt{\|\mathbf{x}_1\|^2 + \|\mathbf{x}_2\|^2 + \delta^2}}{\|\mathbf{x}_1 \times \mathbf{x}_2\|}. \tag{5}$$

It is then natural to set the standard deviation σ in the likelihood (4) proportional to the right-hand side of (5).

3.4 Optimisation

The optimisation of the energy function (3) is quite challenging as one has to simultaneously allocate vanishing points to lines as well as determine how many should be used. This is the same problem addressed, for example, by the PEARL algorithm of [17, 18], and in fact a special case which reduces to the *uncapacitated facility location* (UFL [18]) algorithm as there are no pairwise terms in the energy. While not explored here, pairwise terms could be used in the estimation of vanishing points in order to encourage image lines that are nearly parallel and spatially close to converge to the same vanishing point. The algorithm combines four steps, initialisation, α-expansion, re-estimation, and re-sampling, as detailed next.

Initialisation. The algorithm starts by considering a large set of candidate vanishing points $\mathbf{v}_1, \ldots, \mathbf{v}_m$. These can be sampled from data in various ways. In our implementation, one vanishing point is generated from each line ℓ_i by setting $\mathbf{v}_i \propto (0, 0, 1) \times \ell_i$. This choice corresponds to initialising a vanishing point at infinity in the direction of each line ℓ_i.

α-Expansion. Given a label $\alpha \in \{1, \ldots, m, m+1\}$ to expand, one searches which label assignments q_i should switch to α in order to maximally decrease the energy (3). There are two cases to be considered:

- If the label α is already active (*i.e.*, $\exists i : q_i = \alpha$) switching any assignment q_i to α does not pay the cost γ of activating a new label. Given this observation, there are two cases for which switching improves the likelihood. The first one is that the likelihood of α for the line ℓ_i is better:

$$-\log p(\ell_i|\mathbf{v}_\alpha, \sigma_i) < -\log p(\ell_i|\mathbf{v}_{q_i}, \sigma_i). \tag{6}$$

  The second one is that switching *all the current assignments* $I = \{i : q_j = \beta\}$ to some label $\beta \neq \alpha$ back to α lowers the energy accounting for the additional reward γ obtained by making the label β inactive:

$$-\sum_{i\in I} \log p(\ell_i|\mathbf{v}_\alpha, \sigma_j) < -\sum_{i\in I} \log p(\ell_i|\mathbf{v}_{q_i}, \sigma_i) + \gamma, \tag{7}$$

- If on the contrarily α is inactive in the current labelling (*i.e.*, $\forall i : q_i \neq \alpha$), then conditions similar to (6) and (7) still apply, but one needs to check whether the overall improvement is larger than the cost γ of activating the new label α before switching.

Once a new assignment q^α is obtained from q by using these rules, the move is accepted if it lowers the energy:

$$E(q_1^\alpha, \dots, q_n^\alpha; \mathbf{v}_1, \dots, \mathbf{v}_m) < E(q_1, \dots, q_n; \mathbf{v}_1, \dots, \mathbf{v}_m).$$

Re-Estimation. After labels have been reassigned by an α-expansion step, one can further improve the energy by updating the vanishing points to optimally match the lines currently assigned to them. Given the likelihood (4), this amounts to calculating

$$\mathbf{v}_j^* = \operatorname*{argmin}_{\mathbf{v} \in \mathbb{S}^2} \sum_{i:q_i=j} \frac{\langle \ell_i, \mathbf{v} \rangle^2}{\sigma_i^2} \tag{8}$$

Then the vanishing point $\mathbf{v}_j^*$ is obtained [21] as the unit eigenvector of $M^\top M$, where the columns of the matrix M are the vectors ℓ_i/σ_i, $i : q_i = j$.

Re-Sampling. After a few iterations of α-expansion and re-estimation, the algorithm may converge to a locally optimal solution. This can be further improved by proposing new candidate vanishing points. In practice, the next time an inactive label α is expanded, rather than using the current value of $\mathbf{v}^\alpha$, this can be replaced by the vanishing point obtained by intersecting two lines ℓ_i, ℓ_j selected at random, or by intersecting the lines $\{\ell_i : q_i = j \vee q_i = k\}$ obtained by merging two active labels j and k (in this case $\mathbf{v}^\alpha$ is computed using (8)).

4 Experiments

This section evaluates empirically the self-similar sketch applied to the task of estimating vanishing points. The comparison includes: (i) the algorithm of Sect. 3 with the self-similar sketch (Sect. 2), (ii) the algorithm of Sect. 3 with lines obtained as in Sect. 2 but based on the image gradient (which reduces to [19] and is used by Video Compass [21]), (iii) the current state-of-the-art geometric parsing algorithm of [24, 28] based on Canny's edges, (iv) Tardif's method [23], and (v) Video Compass [21].

Video Compass [21] is a carefully tuned expectation-maximisation (EM) algorithm that, similarly to the method of Sect. 3.4, fits lines to vanishing points on the Gauss sphere, hence using an algebraic error. *Tardif's method* [23] uses J-Linkage to non-iteratively associate line segments to vanishing points and refines the solution by using EM iterations, measuring errors directly on the image plane. *Geometric parsing* [24] proposes and integrated energy formulation that simultaneously groups edges into lines, lines into vanishing points, and use the latter to estimate the horizon an zenith.

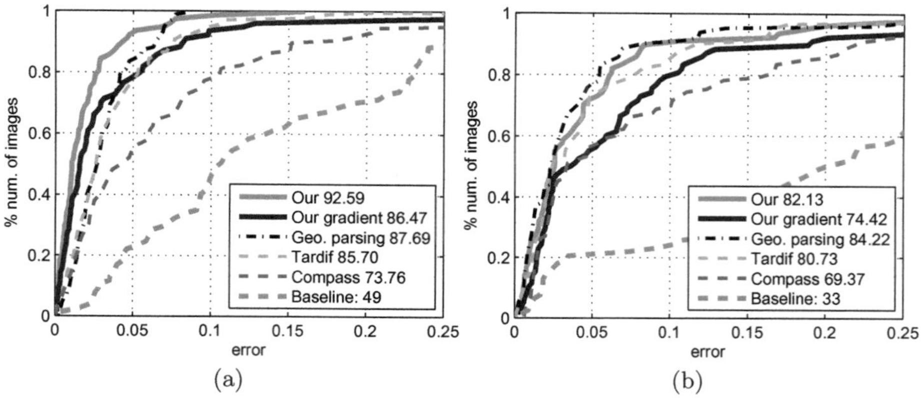

Fig. 3. Quantitative evaluation of the horizon estimation. (a) York Urban and (b) Eurasian Cities datasets. The figure compares our estimation algorithm combined with the self-similar sketch, the same with gradient-based features, three competing methods, and the baseline obtained by setting the horizon to be an horizontal line in the image centre. See the text for details.

Datasets. The methods are evaluated on the same datasets and with the same protocol of [24], and in fact we report their results for all but the proposed methods. The methods are evaluated on two datasets: (i) York Urban [22] consisting of 102 images mostly following the Manhattan world assumption (three main orthogonal vanishing points) taken indoor and outdoor around the same location and (ii) the significantly harder Eurasian dataset of [24], including scenes from different parts of the world (hence with different appearance statistics), more varied viewpoints, and poorer fit to the Manhattan assumption. Both datasets come with a few accurately hand annotated systems of vanishing lines for each image that are used to estimate the ground truth parameters during evaluation. Images are split into validation and testing as explained in [24].

Task and Performance Metric. [24] proposes as performance metric the quality of the recovered horizon line, as the latter can be obtained directly from un-calibrated images (camera calibration is not available for Eurasian Cities). Following the protocol in [24], the horizon is estimated into two steps: first the zenith (vertical direction) is used to estimate the orientation of the horizon (as the zenith is orthogonal to it) and then the other vanishing points are used to estimate the horizon offset. In principle, in estimating the horizon offset only the vanishing points corresponding to three dimensional lines parallel to the ground should be used. While the sophisticated model in [24] explicitly identifies such vanishing points, here we use the simple heuristic of letting all the vanishing points vote for the horizon based on their mass (number of line segments converging to them). Performance is reported in term of the percentage of test images that achieve an error smaller or equal than a given threshold, obtaining corresponding performance curves as the threshold is varied (Fig. 3). We also

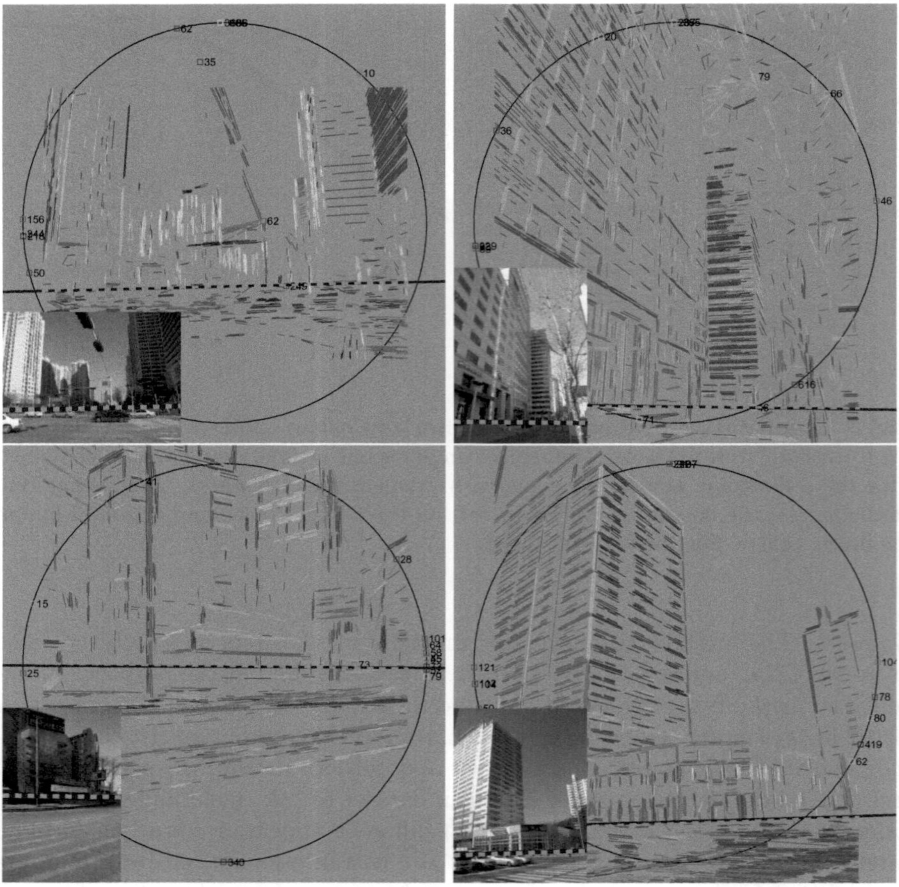

Fig. 4. Vanishing points and horizon estimation. Example images, vanishing points, and horizon (in solid blue the estimated one and in dashed green the ground truth one) on the Eurasian Cities dataset. The coloured line segments correspond to the self-similar sketch elements that converge to one of the vanishing points. Each vanishing point is marked by a square along with the number of segments converging to it. For the vanishing points outside the circle only the direction (with respect to the image centre) is shown.

report a numerical value as the percentage of area under the curve in the subset $[0, 0.25] \times [0, 1]$ (*i.e.*, focusing on the low-error region of the plots).

4.1 Implementation Details

For the fast extraction of dense SIFT features and k-means clustering we use the public implementation of these two algorithms in VLFeat [29] with default values. No image smoothing is applied before extraction of the SIFT features and the size of a spatial bin is set to two pixels. The number of visual words for each

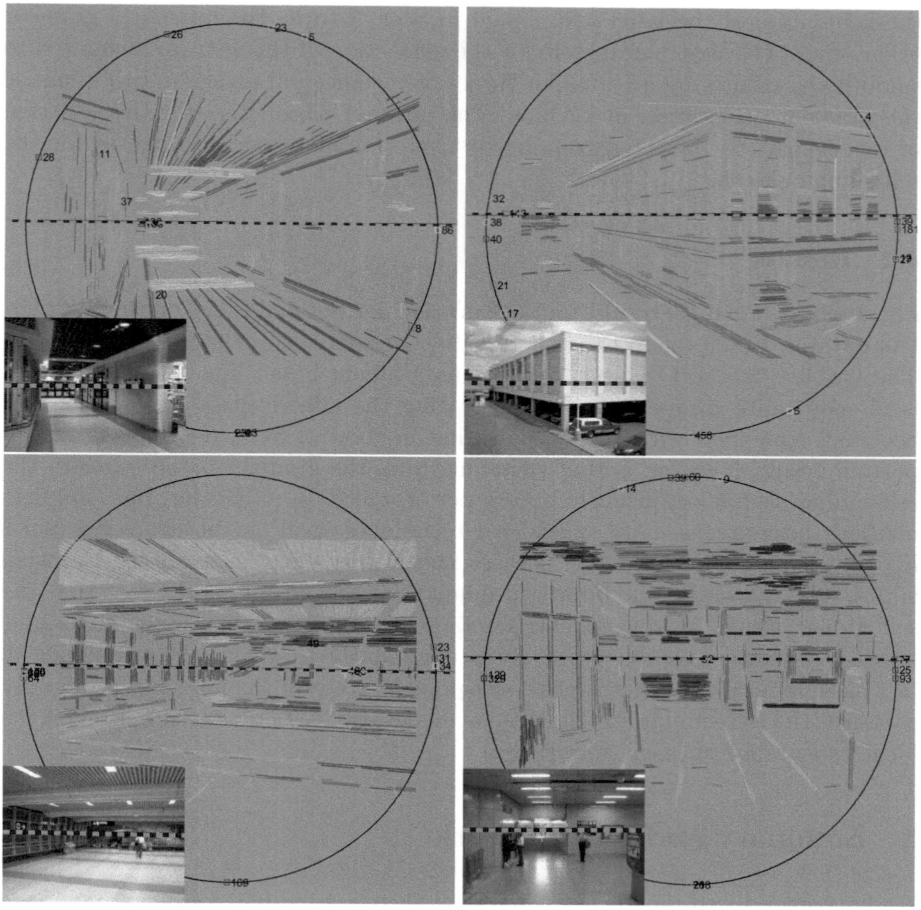

Fig. 5. Vanishing points and horizon estimation. The same of Fig. 4 but for the York Urban dataset.

image-dependent vocabulary was set to 100, although different values (*e.g.*, 50 or 150) did not change results substantially. The minimum area of an elongated connected component was set to 17 and 20 pixels respectively on the Eurasian Cities and the York Urban dataset and the minimum ratio between minor and major moment of inertia of the regions was set to 7 and 9 respectively. Increasing such values may select a more reliable but smaller set of linear structures in the images and can affect performance somewhat due to the limitations of the model of Sect. 3.2 and the fact that the optimisation method of Sect. 3.4 might still be confused by too many outliers and get stuck into a bad local optimum. The computation of the sketch requires only a few seconds on a standard laptop computer with an un-optimised MATLAB implementation.

The self-similar sketch is compared to the method of [19] for the extraction of line segments from an image. [19] can be implemented simply by changing the generation of the label map $l(u, v)$ in Sect. 2 to be the quantised gradient orientation. The best parameters for the extraction of this feature amounted to smooth the images by a Gaussian kernel of variance 0.5 pixels and to quantise the gradient orientation in 12 bins. The optimal parameters for the selection of the elongated connected components were found to be the same as for the self-similar sketch.

4.2 Results

Fig. 4 reports example results on the Eurasian dataset and Fig. 5 on the York Urban dataset. Fig. 3 reports the quantitative comparison of the various methods. The baseline method of Sect. 3 with the gradient-based line segments of [19] is already quite competitive, demonstrating the effectiveness of the model of Sect. 3.2 combined with the optimisation method of Sect. 3.4. The most important result, however, is that switching from the gradient-based edges to the self-similar sketch significantly boosts performance. In particular, our complete method outperforms more specialised techniques such as the geometric parsing of [24] on the York Urban dataset and is very close to it on the Eurasian Cities. The reason for the improved quality of these results is the fact that the self-similar sketch is able to extract many additional linear image structures beyond standard edge detectors. By looking at the gradient, these methods in fact assume implicitly that edges correspond to steps of the intensity profile. By contrast, the self-similar sketch does not make any particular assumption on the local appearance of linear structures.

5 Summary and Future Work

We have introduced the idea of self-similar sketch, a method for detecting image features without committing to their appearance beforehand. The self-similar sketch looks for self-similar structures in an image that happen to be arranged in a non-accidental manner. A simple implementation of this idea was obtained by clustering SIFT features with an image-dependent vocabulary and looking for collinear occurrences of identical visual words. The resulting linear structures are more reliable than standard gradient-based edge extraction methods when applied to the task of estimating vanishing points, zenith, and horizon in natural images. As part of this evaluation, recent methods for the optimisation of discrete-continuous energies arising from automatic model selection problems have been found to perform very well.

This paper has examined only a simple example of self-similar sketch. Future directions include exploring different ways of computing self similarity and the use of other type of nonaccidental cues. Particularly interesting cases include the extraction of curved structures and of groups of collinear, parallel ones. Most importantly, we plan to explore the use of the sketch in semantic image analysis tasks such as object detection and image categorisation. A simple way to do so is to compute descriptors on top of the detected sketch features. By enabling abstracting from instance-specific details, this would be similar to the original self-similar sketch descriptors [11], while incorporating the notion of alignment/non-accidentally. The qualitative examples of Fig. 1 suggest that this may be a promising direction.

Acknowledgments. This work was supported by VisRec no. 228180 and the Oxford Violette and Samuel Glasstone Research Fellowships in Science.

References

1. Baumberg, A.: Reliable feature matching across widely separated views. In: CVPR, pp. 1774–1781. IEEE Press, New York (2000)
2. Mikolajczyk, K., Schmid, C.: An Affine Invariant Interest Point Detector. In: Heyden, A., Sparr, G., Nielsen, M., Johansen, P. (eds.) ECCV 2002, Part I. LNCS, vol. 2350, pp. 128–142. Springer, Heidelberg (2002)
3. Matas, J., Chum, O., Urban, M., Pajdla, T.: Robust wide baseline stereo from maximally stable extremal regions. In: Rosin, P.L., Marshall, A.D. (eds.) BMVC, British Machine Vision Association (2002)
4. Lowe, D.G.: Object recognition from local scale-invariant features. In: ICCV, pp. 1150–1157 (1999)
5. Vedaldi, A., Soatto, S.: Features for recognition: Viewpoint invariance for non-planar scenes. In: ICCV, pp. 1474–1481. IEEE Press, New York (2005)
6. Harris, C., Stephens, M.: A combined corner and edge detector. In: Proc. of The Fourth Alvey Vision Conference, pp. 147–151 (1988)
7. Canny, J.: A computational approach to edge detection. IEEE Trans. on Patt. Analysis and Machine Intell. 8 (1986)
8. Lindeberg, T.: Principles for automatic scale selection. Technical Report ISRN KTH/NA/P 98/14 SE, Royal Institute of Technology (1998)
9. Arbelaez, P., Maire, M., Fowlkes, C., Malik, J.: Contour detection and hierarchical image segmentation. IEEE Trans. on Patt. Analysis and Machine Intell. 33, 898–916 (2011)
10. Rosten, E., Drummond, T.: Machine Learning for High-Speed Corner Detection. In: Leonardis, A., Bischof, H., Pinz, A. (eds.) ECCV 2006. LNCS, vol. 3951, pp. 430–443. Springer, Heidelberg (2006)
11. Shechtman, E., Irani, M.: Matching local self-similarities across images and videos. In: CVPR. IEEE Press, New York (2007)
12. Biederman, I.: Recognition-by-components: A theory of human image understanding. Psychological Review 94 (1987)
13. Agin, G.J., Binford, T.O.: Computer description of curved objects. IEEE Trans. Comp.s 25, 439–449 (1976)
14. Gibson, B.M., Gosselin, O.F., Gosselin, F., Schyns, P.G., Wasserman, E.A.: Nonaccidental properties underlie shape recognition in mammalian and nonmammalian vision. Current Biology 17 (2007)
15. Jojic, N., Caspi, Y.: Capturing image structure with probabilistic index maps. In: CVPR (1), pp. 212–219 (2004)
16. Deselaers, T., Ferrari, V.: Global and efficient self-similarity for object classification and detection. In: CVPR, pp. 1633–1640. IEEE Press, New York (2010)

17. Isack, H.N., Boykov, Y.: Energy-based geometric multi-model fitting. Int. Journal of Comp. Vision 97, 123–147 (2012)
18. Delong, A., Osokin, A., Isack, H.N., Boykov, Y.: Fast approximate energy minimization with label costs. Int. Journal of Comp. Vision 96, 1–27 (2012)
19. Kahn, P., Kitchen, L.J., Riseman, E.M.: A fast line finder for vision-guided robot navigation. IEEE Trans. Patt. Anal. Mach. Intell. 12, 1098–1102 (1990)
20. Schaffalitzky, F., Zisserman, A.: Planar grouping for automatic detection of vanishing lines and points. Image Vision Comput. 18, 647–658 (2000)
21. Kŏsecká, J., Zhang, W.: Video Compass. In: Heyden, A., Sparr, G., Nielsen, M., Johansen, P. (eds.) ECCV 2002, Part IV. LNCS, vol. 2353, pp. 476–490. Springer, Heidelberg (2002)
22. Denis, P., Elder, J.H., Estrada, F.J.: Efficient Edge-Based Methods for Estimating Manhattan Frames in Urban Imagery. In: Forsyth, D., Torr, P., Zisserman, A. (eds.) ECCV 2008, Part II. LNCS, vol. 5303, pp. 197–210. Springer, Heidelberg (2008)
23. Tardif, J.P.: Non-iterative approach for fast and accurate vanishing point detection. In: ICCV, pp. 1250–1257. IEEE Press, New York (2009)
24. Barinova, O., Lempitsky, V.S., Tretiak, E., Kohli, P.: Geometric Image Parsing in Man-Made Environments. In: Daniilidis, K., Maragos, P., Paragios, N. (eds.) ECCV 2010, Part II. LNCS, vol. 6312, pp. 57–70. Springer, Heidelberg (2010)
25. Flint, A., Mei, C., Reid, I.D., Murray, D.W.: Growing semantically meaningful models for visual slam. In: CVPR, pp. 467–474. IEEE Press, New York (2010)
26. Flint, A., Murray, D.W., Reid, I.: Manhattan scene understanding using monocular, stereo, and 3d features. In: Metaxas, D.N., Quan, L., Sanfeliu, A., Gool, L.J.V. (eds.) ICCV, pp. 2228–2235. IEEE Press, New York (2011)
27. Hoiem, D., Efros, A.A., Hebert, M.: Closing the loop in scene interpretation. In: CVPR. IEEE Press, New York (2008)
28. Tretiak, E., Barinova, O., Kohli, P., Lempitsky, V.S.: Geometric image parsing in man-made environments. Int. Journal of Comp. Vision 97, 305–321 (2012)
29. Vedaldi, A., Fulkerson, B.: VLFeat: an open and portable library of computer vision algorithms. In: Bimbo, A.D., Chang, S.F., Smeulders, A.W.M. (eds.) ACM Multimedia, pp. 1469–1472. ACM (2010)

Depth Matters: Influence of Depth Cues on Visual Saliency

Congyan Lang[1,3,⋆], Tam V. Nguyen[1,⋆], Harish Katti[2,⋆], Karthik Yadati[2], Mohan Kankanhalli[2], and Shuicheng Yan[1]

[1] Department of ECE, National University of Singapore, Singapore
{tamnguyen,eleyans}@nus.edu.sg
[2] School of Computing, National University of Singapore, Singapore
{harishk,nyadati,mohan}@comp.nus.edu.sg
[3] Department of Computer Science, Beijing Jiaotong University, China
cylang@bjtu.edu.cn

Abstract. Most previous studies on visual saliency have only focused on static or dynamic 2D scenes. Since the human visual system has evolved predominantly in natural three dimensional environments, it is important to study whether and how depth information influences visual saliency. In this work, we first collect a large human eye fixation database compiled from a pool of 600 2D-vs-3D image pairs viewed by 80 subjects, where the depth information is directly provided by the Kinect camera and the eye tracking data are captured in both 2D and 3D free-viewing experiments. We then analyze the major discrepancies between 2D and 3D human fixation data of the same scenes, which are further abstracted and modeled as novel depth priors. Finally, we evaluate the performances of state-of-the-art saliency detection models over 3D images, and propose solutions to enhance their performances by integrating the depth priors.

1 Introduction

Human visual exploration and selection of specific regions for detailed processing is permitted by the visual attention mechanism [1]. The eyes remain nearly stationary during fixation events as humans look at details in selected locations, which makes eye movements a valuable proxy to understand human attention. Visual saliency refers to the preferential fixation on conspicuous or meaningful regions in a scene [2] that have also been shown to correspond with important objects and their relationships [5]. Visual saliency is thus crucial in determining human visual experience and also relevant to many applications, such as automatic image collection browsing and image cropping.

Visual saliency has been extensively studied in signal processing, computer vision, machine learning, psychology and vision research literatures (e.g., [6,7,1,8,9]). However, most saliency models disregard the fact that human visual system operates in real 3D environments, while these models only investigate the cues from 2D images and the eye fixation data are captured in a 2D scene. However, stereoscopic contents provide additional depth cues that are used by

⋆ Indicates equal contribution.

A. Fitzgibbon et al. (Eds.): ECCV 2012, Part II, LNCS 7573, pp. 101–115, 2012.

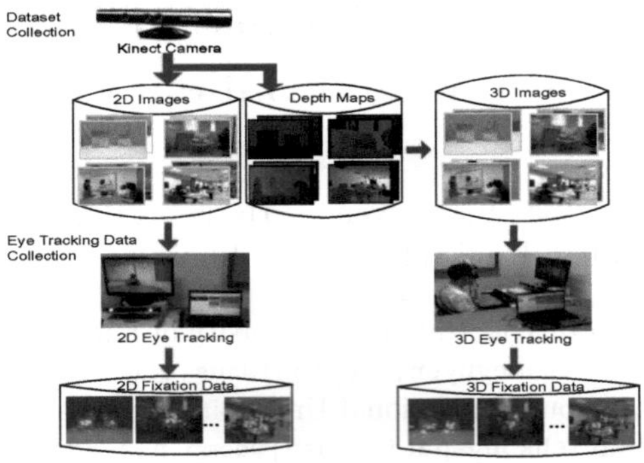

Fig. 1. Flowchart on 2D-vs-3D fixation dataset NUS-3DSaliency construction. We collect eye-tracking data on both 2D and 3D viewing settings and each 2D or 3D image was viewed by at least 14 observers. Eye fixations are recorded for each observer. The final fixation maps are generated by averaging locations across all the observers' fixations.

humans in the understanding of their surrounding and play an important role in visual attention [10]. Are the observer's fixations different when viewing 3D images compared to 2D images? How do the current state-of-the-art saliency models perform with additional depth cues? Not only are these questions interesting and important, answering them can also significantly benefit areas in computer vision research, such as autonomous mobile systems, 3D content surveillance and retrieval, advertising design, and adaptive image display on small devices.

In this paper, we conduct a comparative and systematic study of visual saliency in 2D and 3D scenes. Whereas existing eye tracking datasets captured for 2D images contain hundreds of images, the largest available eye tracking dataset for 3D scenes contains only a limited size of 28 stereo images [11]. A comprehensive eye tracking dataset for 3D scenes is yet to be developed. Motivated by these limitations, we collect a larger eye fixation dataset for 2D-vs-3D scenes. A 3D camera with active infra-red illumination (Microsoft "Kinect" [3]) offers the capability to easily extract scene depth information in order to extend 2D stimulus to 3D versions. Using an eye tracker, we collect eye fixation data to create human fixation maps which represent where viewers actually look in 2D and 3D versions of each scene. This large eye fixation dataset will be released for public usage. Our work further aims at quantitatively assessing the contribution of depth cues in visual attention in 3D scenes and proposing depth priors to improve the performances of state-of-the-art saliency detection models. In summary, the contributions of our work mainly include:

1. The eye-fixation dataset NUS-3DSaliency is collected from a pool of 600 images and 80 participants in both 2D and 3D scenes.
2. We analyze and quantify the difference between 2D and 3D eye fixation data. Based on the observations, the novel depth priors are proposed and integrated into saliency detection models.
3. We comprehensively evaluate the performances of state-of-the-art saliency detection models augmented with proposed depth priors on 2D and 3D eye fixation data.

2 Related Work

In order to understand what human attend to and qualitatively evaluate computational models, eye tracking data are used to create the human fixation maps, which will offer an excellent repository of ground truth for saliency model research. Most eye tracking datasets [7,12,13,5] are constructed for 2D scenes and most saliency models only investigate the cues from 2D images or videos. In contrast, relatively few studies have investigated visual attention modeling on 3D contents. Recently, several researchers have pioneered visual attention research on stereoscopic 3D contents. Jansen et al. [11] examined the influence of disparity on human behavior in visual inspection of 2D and 3D still images. They collected eye tracking data from 14 participants across 28 stereo images in a free-viewing task on 2D and 3D versions. A recent study [14] collected 21 video clips and the corresponding eye gaze data in both versions. However, compared with 2D eye tracking datasets, a comprehensive eye tracking dataset for 3D scenes is still absent. We believe that the studies on a rich and comprehensive 3D eye tracking dataset can offer interesting and important insights into how eye fixations are driven in real 3D environment. Motivated by this requirement, we collect a large 3D image database in this work, and then capture eye tracking data from an average of 14 participants per image across both 2D and 3D versions of 600 images.

Depth cues provide additional important information about contents in the visual field and can be regarded as relevant features for saliency detection [15] and action recognition [29]. Stereoscopic contents bring important additional binocular cues for enhancing human depth perception. Although there have been several efforts [16,17,18,19] to include the depth channel into computational attention models, a major problem in extracting depth from stereo input is the computation time needed to process disparities. In this paper, we study the discrepancies in human fixation data when viewing 2D and 3D scenes. The influence of depth on visual saliency is then studied and serves as the basis for learning depth priors to model 3D saliency.

3 Dataset Collection and Analysis

3.1 Dataset Collection

Our dataset aims to provide a comprehensive and diverse coverage of visual scenes for eye tracking analysis. We choose indoor and outdoor scenes that have natural co-occurrence of common objects. Furthermore, we systematically generate variants of scenes by varying parameters like depth ranges of different objects, number and size of objects and degree of interaction or activity depicted in the scene. We use the Kinect camera, which consists of an infra-red projector-camera pair as the depth camera that measures per pixel disparity, to capture a 640×480 pixel color image and its corresponding depth image at the same time. To the best of our knowledge, this is the largest 3D eye tracking dataset available to date for visual attention research, in terms of the total number of images and size of subject pool.

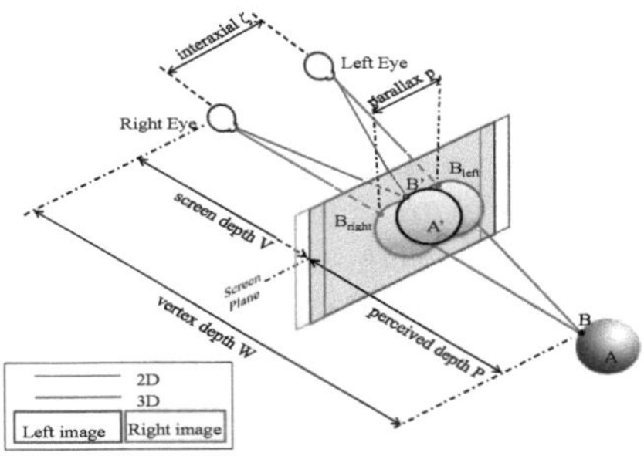

Fig. 2. The relationship between 2D and 3D fixations. The fixation location captured from participant viewing at B is the same for both 2D and 3D experiment setups. Screen depth W is the distance from the participant to the screen, while perceive depth P is calculated based on the depth value.

Stereoscopic Image Pair Generation for 3D Display. Following the collection of the color and depth image pair, the next step is to create 3D stimulus which involves generating left and right images. Prior to generating left-right image pair, some pre-processing on the captured images are required. We first perform calibration on both depth and color cameras to find the transformation between their images in a similar way as [4]. Next, we over-segment the color image into superpixels [20]. Each pixel, whose original depth value equal to 0, is assigned the average depth of the nearest neighbors in 8 directions in the same superpixel. Finally, we apply a default Laplacian filter with a 3 × 3 kernel for pixels whose depth values equal to 0 until all missing depth pixels are filled.

The stereoscopic image pair is produced by extracting parallax values from the smoothed depth map D and applying them to the left image I^l and right image I^r. For each pixel of the input color image I, the value of the parallax is obtained from its depth value. Figure 2 shows the relationship between 2D and 3D fixation. In both 2D and 3D viewing, for example, the fixation location for viewing B is recorded as the same position by the eye tracker. Considering the input image as a virtual central view, the left and right views are then obtained by shifting the input image pixels by a value ρ , $\rho = parallax/2$. In particular, the left image I^l and right image I^r can be obtained as $I^l(x_p^l) = I^r(x_p^r) = I(x_p)$, where x_p denotes the coordinate of the pixel in the color image I, the coordinate of the pixel in each view is calculated as $x_p^l = x_p + \rho, x_p^r = x_p - \rho$. Following Figure 2, the *parallax* is calculated as follows:

$$parallax = \zeta \times (1 - \frac{V}{W}), \tag{1}$$

where ζ is the interaxial gap between two eyes, averaged as $60mm$, V is the screen depth or the distance from eyes to the screen and fixed as $80cm$ in our experiment setup, W is the vertex depth, equal to the summation of screen depth V and perceived depth P. For each pixel x in the image I, the perceived depth $P(x)$ can be calculated as $P(x) = D(x) \times \tau$, where τ ($\tau = 39.2$) is the ratio between the maximum depth distance captured by Kinect (10,000mm) and the

Fig. 3. Exemplar data in our eye fixation dataset NUS-3DSaliency. From left to right columns: color image and raw depth map captured by Kinect camera, smoothed depth map, 2D fixation map, and 3D fixation map.

maximum value in the depth image D (255). Since our dataset aims to provide the comprehensive and diverse coverage of visual scenes for eye tracking analysis, we reject images that are similar or have significantly overlapping content with other images in the dataset. Furthermore, images with significant artifacts after the smoothing process were rejected as an effort to minimize problematic images.

Participants. The participants (students and staff members of a university) ranged from 20 to 33 years old (μ=24.3, σ=3.1), among them 26 females and 54 males with normal or corrected-to-normal vision. All participants are naive to the purpose of the study and sign consent forms for public distribution of recorded eye-fixation data.

Data Collection Procedure. We use a block based design and free viewing paradigm. The subject views two blocks of 100 images that are unique and randomly chosen from the pool of 600 images, one of the blocks is entirely 2D and the other one entirely 3D. 3D images were viewed by using active shutter glasses on a 3D LCD display and 2D images were shown on the same screen in 2D display mode and the active shutter glasses switched off. In order to record subject eye gaze data, we used an infra-red illumination based remote eye-tracker from SensoMotoric Instruments Gmbh. The eye-tracker gives less than 1° error on successful calibration. The eye tracker was calibrated for each participant using a 9-point calibration and validation method. Then images were presented in random order for 6 seconds followed by a gray mask for 3 seconds.

Human Fixation Maps. Human fixation maps are constructed from the fixations of viewers for 2D and 3D images to globally represent the spatial distribution of human fixations. Similar to [21], in order to produce a continuous fixation map of an image, we convolve a Gaussian filter across all corresponding viewers's fixation locations. Six examples of 2D and 3D fixation maps are shown

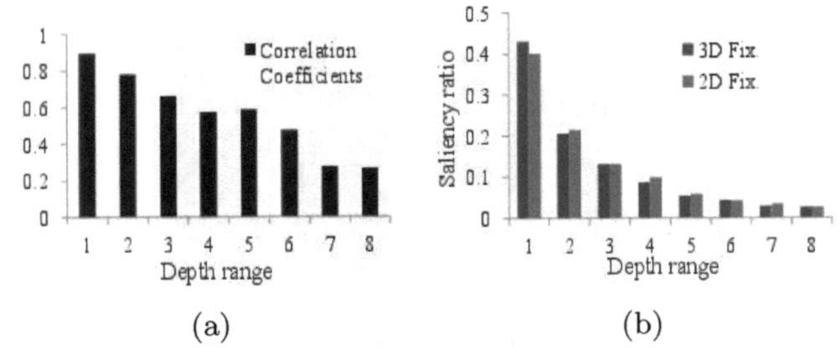

Fig. 4. (a) The correlation coefficients between 2D and 3D fixations in different depth ranges. We observe lower correlation coefficients for farther depth ranges.(b) Saliency ratio in different depth ranges for 2D and 3D scenes respectively. The participants show to fix at closer depth ranges more often than farther depth ranges.

in Figure 3, the brighter pixels on the fixation maps denote the higher salience values.

3.2 Observations and Statistics

Using the recorded eye tracker data, we mainly investigate whether spatial distributions of fixations are different when human subjects view 3D images compared to 2D version. The interrelated observations are summarized as follows.

Observation 1: *Depth cues modulate visual saliency to a greater extent at farther depth ranges. Furthermore, humans fixate preferentially at closer depth ranges.*

In order to study the difference between 2D and 3D versions with respect to different depth range, fixation data for each 2D image I and its corresponding 3D image I', are divided into n ($n = 8$) depth ranges. Then for each depth range $r_b, b \in \{1, \cdots, n\}$, we compute the similarity between the 2D and 3D fixation distributions. We use the correlation coefficients (CC)[22] as similarity measure between two fixation maps. Figure 4(a) shows lower correlation coefficients for farther depth ranges.

Furthermore, in order to create a quantitative statistic of the relationship between the fixation distributions and depth ranges, we define saliency ratio as the description of fixation distribution. For the image I, we first compute saliency ratio $\gamma(r_b)$ as a function of the depth range, $\gamma(r_b) = \sum_x S(x)\delta(D(x) \in r_b)/\sum_x S(x)$, where $\delta(D(x) \in r_b)$ is set to 1 if x is in the depth range r_b. Figure 4(b) shows the saliency ratio vs. the depth range for 2D and 3D fixation data respectively. Looking at the data from the entire fixation dataset, the saliency ratio systematically decreases with the increase in depth range. A linear-best-fit of 2D(3D) saliency ratio with depth planes yields negative slopes $-0.045(-0.047)$ and indicates a statistically decreasing trend with increasing depth planes. From our analysis of fixation distribution and 2D-vs-3D correlation statistics over the entire dataset, we observe, (a) the larger discrepancy between 2D and 3D fixation data at further depth planes and, (b) the greater attenuation of visual attention at farther depth planes.

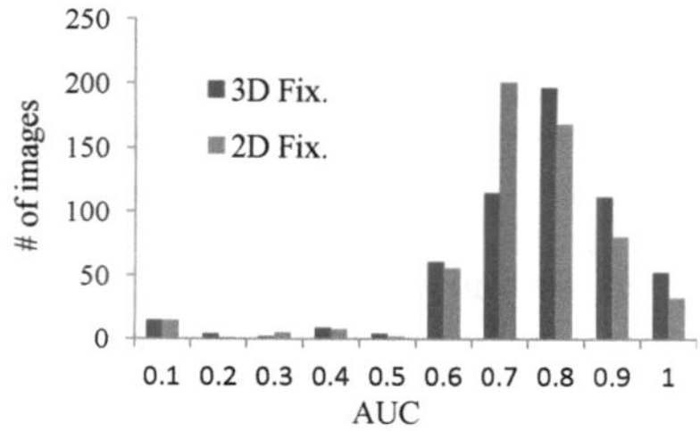

Fig. 5. We examine the ability of 2D/3D fixation map to predict the labeled interesting objects and histogram of the AUC values for 2D and 3D fixation dataset are comparatively shown is blue and red colors, respectively.

Observation 2: *A few interesting objects account for majority of the fixations and this behavior is consistent across both 2D and 3D.*

Such interesting objects such as human faces, body parts, text, cars and other conspicuous objects are discussed in [12]. Other studies such as [23] have shown that the eye fixations are correlated to the locations of such objects. In order to analyze this relationship, we follow the method in [12] by manually labeling objects of interest. To form more object-like contours, annotation of such regions is done by over-segmentation using superpixels [20] for each color image in our dataset. Despite occupying only 7.6% of the image area on average, the area corresponding to interesting objects account for 54.2% and 51.2% of the fixation points for 3D and 2D respectively. To quantitatively measure how well a 2D/3D fixation map predicts interesting objects on a given 2D/3D image, we compute the AUC value [8], the area under receiver operating characteristic (ROC) curve for each image. We use the labeled objects of interest as ground truth along with the fixation map as the predicted map of the image, this method effectively marginalizes out the influence of depth planes and helps to understand the role

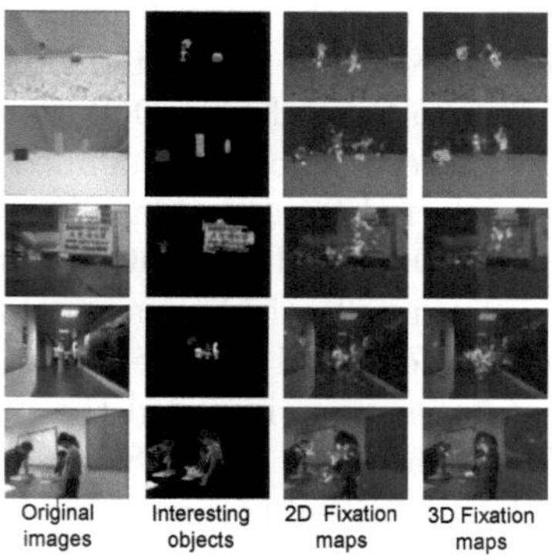

Fig. 6. Exemplar interesting objects manually labeled and fixation maps for 2D and 3D images. It indicates that the participants frequently fixed on such areas.

Fig. 7. Examples with low and high depth-of-field values

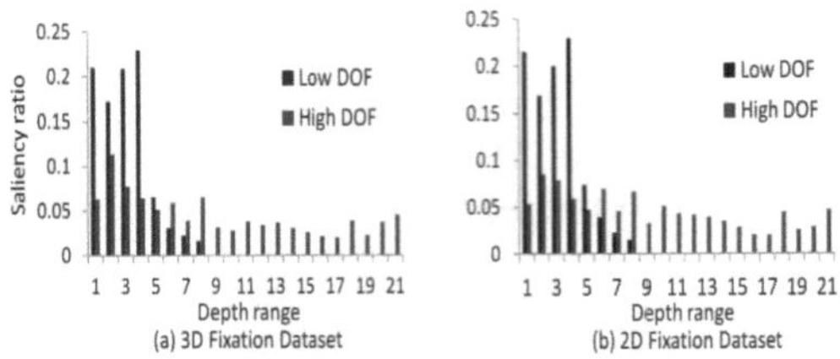

Fig. 8. Saliency ratio as a function of depth range. The saliency ratio distribution for 200 lowest depth-of-field images and for 200 highest depth-of-field images calculated on (a) 3D and (b) 2D fixation dataset respectively. The plot indicates that depth-of-field has influence on the allocation of attention in both 2D and 3D images.

of objects in isolation. Figure 5 shows the distribution of the AUC value for 600 labeled images. The average AUC for the entire 3D fixation dataset is 0.7399 and 0.7046 for 2D fixation dataset. Figure 6 gives examples of interesting objects along with corresponding fixation maps. These results suggest that the 2D and 3D fixation points show good correspondence with a few interesting objects.

Observation 3: *The relationship between depth and saliency is non-linear and characteristic for low and high depth-of-field scenes.*

Importantly, we observe that strong correlation exists between the depth-of-field (DOF) of the image and the fixation distribution. The DOF value ℓ of the image I is inferred from the distance between farthest and nearest depth values. In this experiment, we assign depth values into n ($n = 21$) depth ranges. The ℓ is defined as $\ell = |\overline{h^s} - \overline{h^t}|$, where $\overline{h^s}$ and $\overline{h^t}$ denotes the mean of the depth value for the pixels in the nearest and farthest depth ranges. Figure 7 shows some examples corresponding to the different DOF values. To demonstrate the influence of DOF, we analyze the saliency ratio defined in Observation 2 on two subsets of 200 images each selected from our dataset, one low-DOF subset and one high-DOF subset.The low DOF and high DOF partitions have a significant overlap of object types and this effectively marginalizes out the influence of objects. Similar to the statistic described in Observation 2, we create the statistic of the relationship between saliency ratio γ and the depth range for these two image subsets respectively. As shown in Figure 8, the saliency ratio distribution on different depth ranges have noticeable discrepancies between low DOF and high DOF images, as well as the distribution is non-linear. We find that 2D(3D) low DOF and corresponding 2D(3D) high DOF saliency ratio distributions in Figure 8 are dissimilar at $p = 0.05$ using a non parametric Kolmogorov-Smirnov test, on the other hand, saliency ratio distribution for 2D low(high) DOF shows

Table 1. The CC (correlation coefficient) comparison of fixation distribution on the 2D and 3D fixation data

DOF	0-0.25	0.25-0.5	0.5-0.75	0.75-1	*Avg.*
CC	0.8066	0.5495	0.2721	0.3057	0.4835

similarity to 3D low(high) DOF at $p = 0.05$. Motivated by this observation, we use the Gaussian Mixture Models (GMM) to model the distribution and the further implementation will be described in the next section.

Observation 4: *The additional depth information led to an increased difference of fixation distribution between 2D and 3D version, especially, when there are multiple salient stimuli located in different depth planes.*

In order to study the difference between 2D and 3D versions, we divide the image dataset into four groups according the DOF values and compute the correlation coefficients between two fixation maps for the four groups respectively. Table 1 shows lower correlation coefficients for high DOF image groups. Figure 9 shows the fixation maps from the lower and higher depth-of-field images in 2D and 3D versions respectively.

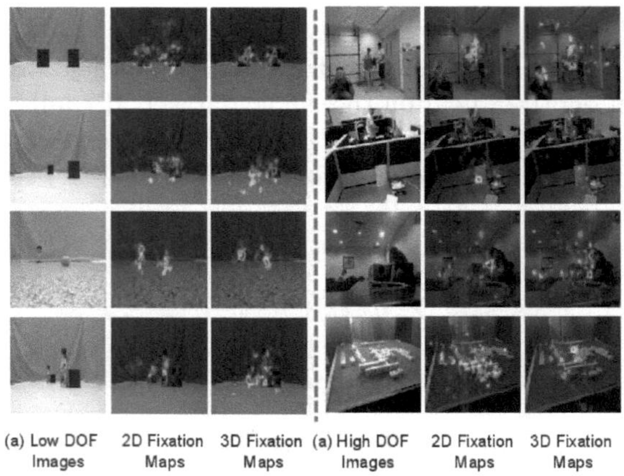

Fig. 9. Fixation maps and fixation distributions for 2D and 3D images. The results indicate a clear difference between 2D and 3D fixation maps with the increased Depth-of-field of the images.

4 Saliency Detection with Depth Priors

Based upon the above observations, we seek the global-context depth priors in order to improve the performance of the state-of-the-art saliency detection models. In this section, we propose to model the relationship between depth and saliency by approximating the joint density with a Mixture of Gaussians.

4.1 Learning Depth Priors

Formally, let D and S represent the depth image and fixation map of the image I, respectively. And d and s denote N-dimensional vector formed by orderly concatenating the patches from a regular partition of the image D and S respectively, N is the number of patches in the image. For the vector s, larger (smaller) magnitude implies that the patch is more salient (less salient). ℓ is the depth-of-field value introduced in the Section 3.2. The joint density between saliency response and depth distribution is written as

$$p(s, d|\ell) = \sum_{k=1}^{K} p(k)p(s|\ell, k)p(d|\ell, k), \tag{2}$$

where k indicates the kth component of the GMM. From the joint distribution we calculate the conditional density required for the depth modulated saliency:

$$\begin{aligned} p(s|d, \ell) &= \frac{p(s, d|\ell)}{\sum_{k=1}^{K} p(k)p(d|\ell, k)} \\ &\propto \sum_{c=1}^{C} q_c(\ell) \sum_{k=1}^{K} \pi_k \mathcal{N}(s; \mu_k^c, \Lambda_k^c)\mathcal{N}(d; \nu_k^c, \Upsilon_k^c), \end{aligned} \tag{3}$$

where $q_c(\cdot)$ is a quantization function for the depth-of-field. We compute a C-bins histogram of depth-of-field on the whole dataset. If ℓ falls into the cth bin, $q_c(\ell) = 1$, otherwise, $q_c(\ell) = 0$. Finally, the conditional expected saliency of the test image I_t, with the depth vector d_t and depth-of-field ℓ_t, is the weighted sum of K linear regressors:

$$\begin{aligned} s_t &= \sum_{c=1}^{C} q_c(\ell_t) \frac{\sum_{k=1}^{K} \mu_k^c * w_k^c}{\sum_{k=1}^{K} w_k^c}, \\ w_k^c &= \pi_k \mathcal{N}(d_t; \nu_k^c, \Upsilon_k^c). \end{aligned} \tag{4}$$

The model parameters are obtained from the training dataset and the EM algorithm is applied for fitting Gaussian mixtures. For the image I_t, its corresponding depth saliency map can be defined as the predicted saliency s_t. Note that s_t has a non-linear dependency with respect to the image depth distribution d_t.

4.2 Saliency Detection Augmented with Depth Priors

In order to investigate whether the depth priors are helpful for determining saliency, we extend seven existing methods to include the learned depth priors: Itti model (IT) [1], graph based visual saliency (GBVS) [8], frequency-tuned model (FT) [24], self-information (AIM) [7], incremental coding length (ICL) [25], local steering kernel (LSK) [26] and low-rank representation based model (LRR) [27]. The bottom-up saliency value predicted by the original models is denoted as $\psi(x)$. The final saliency can be achieved[1] by simply using summation $\oplus$ or point-wise multiplication $\otimes$ as the fusion of two components. The final saliency is described by the equation:

$$S(x) = \psi(x)(\oplus/\otimes)p(s(x)|d(x), \ell). \tag{5}$$

5 Experiments and Results

In this section, we evaluate the saliency detection performance of the state-of-the-art models on our 2D and 3D fixation of NUS-3DSaliency dataset. Furthermore, we quantitatively assess the effectiveness of the depth priors improving the performances of saliency prediction algorithms.

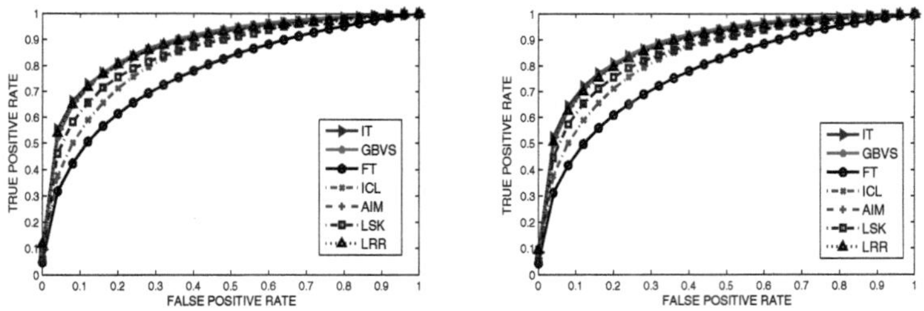

(a) 2D fixation dataset (b) 3D fixation dataset

Fig. 10. ROC curves of different models. The results are from seven bottom-up saliency detection models by integrating depth priors to predict 2D and 3D fixation individually.

All saliency models use default parameter settings given by the corresponding authors. In order to learn depth priors, each image is resized to 200×200 pixels and regularly partitioned into 15×15 patches for training Gaussian models. The entire dataset is divided into four groups ($C = 4$) according to the depth-of-field value of each image. Depth saliency prediction is satisfactory with $K = 5$ as the number of the Gaussian components. For each image group, we randomly separate into 5 subsets, 4 subsets as the training set to learn the parameters of GMM and the remaining subset for testing. All the selected models are evaluated based on the following widely-used ROC and AUC. We also compute the correlation coefficients (CC) [22] between the fixation map and the predicted saliency map for evaluation.

5.1 Comparison of State-of-the-art Models

In this study, we examine the capability of seven bottom-up visual attention models to predict both the 2D and 3D fixation data in a free-viewing task.

[1] Due to the space limitation, we do not further report how to more elegantly integrate depth priors into the models themselves, and only do simple late fusion in this work. We will explore the methods along this direction in our further work.

Table 2. The AUC and CC (correlation coefficient) comparison of different saliency models without the depth priors on the 2D and 3D eye fixation dataset

Criteria	AUC		CC	
Method	2D Fix.	3D Fix.	2D Fix.	3D Fix.
IT	0.7270	0.7299	0.2706	0.2594
GBVS	0.7486	0.7506	0.2986	0.2844
FT	0.5707	0.5726	0.1402	0.1388
ICL	0.7676	0.7673	0.3095	0.2759
AIM	0.7293	0.7308	0.2868	0.2531
LSK	0.7142	0.7158	0.2658	0.2425
LRR	**0.8045**	**0.7971**	**0.3155**	**0.2975**
2D Fix.	—	0.7982	—	0.3797
3D Fix.	0.8156	—	0.3797	—

Table 3. The AUC and CC (correlation coefficient) comparison of different saliency models with the depth priors on the 2D and 3D eye fixation dataset

Criteria	Method	2D Fix.	2D Fix.	3D Fix.	3D Fix.
		⊕	⊗	⊕	⊗
AUC	IT	0.8521	0.8536	0.8490	0.8539
	GBVS	0.8541	**0.8562**	0.8509	**0.8546**
	FT	0.7995	0.7458	0.7971	0.7449
	AIM	0.8502	0.8517	0.8495	0.8503
	ICL	0.8406	0.8088	0.8455	0.8077
	LSK	0.8496	0.8233	0.8453	0.8237
	LRR	0.8511	0.8495	0.8556	0.8463
CC	IT	0.4000	0.4202	0.3752	0.3977
	GBVS	0.4128	**0.4346**	0.3903	**0.4128**
	FT	0.3355	0.2804	0.3148	0.2680
	AIM	0.3651	0.4180	0.3419	0.3913
	ICL	0.4126	0.3704	0.3850	0.3248
	LSK	0.4064	0.3764	0.3793	0.3511
	LRR	0.4065	0.4085	0.3847	0.3953

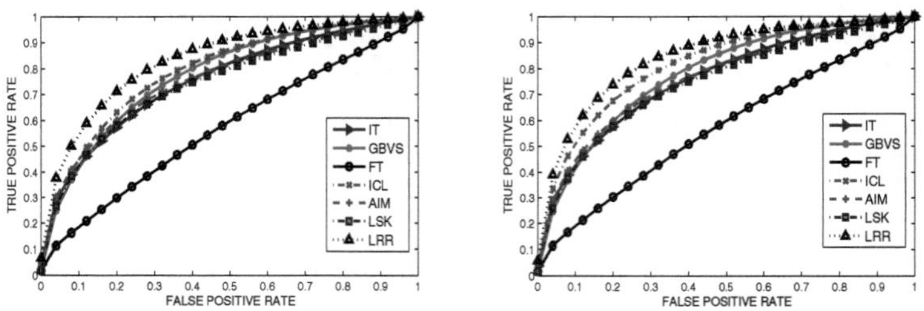

(a) 2D fixation data (b) 3D fixation data

Fig. 11. ROC curves of different models. The results are from seven bottom-up saliency detection models to predict on the 2D and 3D fixation data individually.

Figure 11 and Table 2 show the comparison results. First of all, most of models performed well for predicting human fixation when viewing 2D scenes. LRR exhibits stronger consistence with human eye fixations than the other models. We also evaluate the performance on 2D(3D) fixation maps to predict the 3D(2D) fixation maps. Interestingly, the AUC for the 2D fixation maps to predict 3D version is equal to 0.7982. On the contrary, the AUC of 0.8156 is obtained using 3D fixation maps to predict 2D fixation maps.

In contrast to 2D scenes, 3D scenes contain the additional information regarding the depth cue. This additional information could change the saliency of regions that are present in both 2D and 3D images. Here we show that the overall saliency is comparable in 2D and 3D scenes in terms of AUC. Thus, the bottom-up saliency models should also predict a fraction of the allocation of attention in 3D scenes. However, all models conducted on 2D scenes perform significantly better than 3D versions in terms of correlation coefficients. It further suggests that in a 3D attention model, depth could be considered as the important cue for saliency detection.

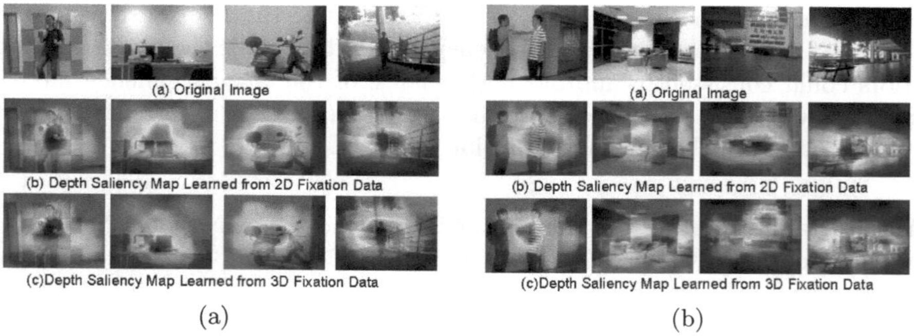

Fig. 12. Representative examples in depth saliency prediction on 2D and 3D scenes respectively. (a) The predicted depth saliency maps are similar between 2D and 3D versions due to the scenes with one conspicuous area/object clearly standing out from the others. (b) The results show an obvious difference of the predicted depth saliency maps between 2D and 3D versions when multiply attractive objects or no conspicuous stimuli in the scenes.

5.2 Depth Priors for Augmented Saliency Prediction

In this subsection, we assess the influence of the depth priors on saliency detection. To evaluate quantitatively the effectiveness of the proposed depth priors, the results of saliency models integrating depth priors are shown in Table 3. The ROC curves are illustrated in Figure 10. These results show that the models with predicted depth priors perform consistently better than those without such depth priors. Overall we observe a 6% to 7% increase in predictive power using depth based cues. Another important aspect brought out in Table 2 a multiplicative modulating effect explains the influence of depth on saliency better than a linear weighted summation model, the latter has been used popularly in literature to combine results saliency maps derived from individual features [28].

Furthermore, Figure 12 gives some predicted saliency maps using depth priors alone (denoted as depth saliency map). On the one hand, the predicted depth saliency maps are similar in their spatial distribution between 2D and 3D versions when there is one conspicuous area or object clearly standing out from the others. On the other hand, when the scenes include multiple objects or no conspicuous objects, there is a noticeable difference between the predicted depth saliency maps of 2D and 3D cases.

6 Conclusions and Future Work

In this paper, we introduce the eye fixation dataset NUS-3DSaliency compiled from 600 images for both 2D and 3D scenes viewed by 80 participants. Using the state-of-the-art models for saliency detection, we have shown new performance bounds for this task. We expect that the newly built 3D eye fixation dataset would help the community advance the study of visual attention in a real 3D environment. Furthermore, based on the analysis of the relationship between depth and saliency, extending the saliency models to include the proposed depth priors could consistently improve performance of the current saliency models. In future work, we are interested in how to integrate depth priors into various models instead of the current late fusion methods.

Acknowledgements. This work is partially supported by National Nature Science Foundation of China (90820013, 61033013, 61100142), Beijing Jiaotong University Science Foundation No. 2011JBM219; MOE project MOE2010-T2-1-087, Singapore; and the A*STAR PSF Grant No. 102-101-0029 on "Characterizing and Exploiting Human Visual Attention for Automated Image Understanding and Description".

References

1. Itti, L., Koch, C., Niebur, E.: A model of saliency-based visual attention for rapid scene analysis. TPAMI (1998)
2. Toet, A.: Computational versus psychophysical bottom-up image saliency: A comparative evaluation study. TPAMI (2011)
3. Kinect: `http://www.xbox.com/kinect`
4. `http://nicolas.burrus.name/index.php/Research/Kinect/Calibration`
5. Ramanathan, S., Katti, H., Sebe, N., Kankanhalli, M., Chua, T.-S.: An Eye Fixation Database for Saliency Detection in Images. In: Daniilidis, K., Maragos, P., Paragios, N. (eds.) ECCV 2010, Part IV. LNCS, vol. 6314, pp. 30–43. Springer, Heidelberg (2010)
6. Avraham, T., Lindenbaum, M.: Esaliency (extended saliency): Meaningful attention using stochastic image modeling. TPAMI (2010)
7. Bruce, N., Tsotsos, J.: Saliency based on information maximization. In: NIPS (2006)
8. Harel, J., Koch, C., Perona, P.: Graph-based visual saliency. In: NIPS (2006)
9. Tsotsos, J., Culhane, S., Wai, W., Lai, Y., Davis, N.: Modelling visual attention via selective tuning. Artificial Intelligence (1995)
10. Wolfe, J., Horowitz, T.: What attributes guide the deployment of visual attention and how do they do it? Neuroscience (2004)
11. Jansen, L., Onat, S., Konig, P.: Influence of disparity on fixation and saccades in free viewing of natural scenes. JOV (2009)
12. Judd, T., Ehinger, K., Durand, F., Torralba, A.: Learning to predict where humans look. In: ICCV (2009)
13. Cerf, M., Frady, E., Koch, C.: Faces and text attract gaze independent of the task: Experimental data and computer model. JOV (2010)
14. Quan, H., Schiaatti, L.: Examination of 3d visual attention in stereoscopic video content. SPIE-IST Electronic Imaging (2011)
15. Nakayama, K., Silverman, G.: Serial and parallel processing of visual feature conjunctions. Nature (1986)
16. Jang, Y.-M., Ban, S.-W., Lee, M.: Stereo Saliency Map Considering Affective Factors in a Dynamic Environment. In: Ishikawa, M., Doya, K., Miyamoto, H., Yamakawa, T. (eds.) ICONIP 2007, Part II. LNCS, vol. 4985, pp. 1055–1064. Springer, Heidelberg (2008)

17. Aziz, M., Mertsching, B.: Pre-attentive detection of depth saliency using stereo vision. In: AIPR (2010)
18. Frintrop, S., Rome, E., Núchter, A., Surmann, H.: A bimodal laser-based attention system. CVIU (2005)
19. Ouerhani, N., Hugli, H.: Computing visual attention from scene depth. In: ICPR (2000)
20. Achanta, R., Shaji, A., Smith, K., Lucchi, A., Fua, P., Susstrunk, S.: SLIC Superpixels. EPFL Technical Report (2010)
21. Velichkovsky, B., Pomplun, M., Rieser, J., Ritter, H.: Eye-movement-based research paradigms. In: Visual Attention and Cognition (2009)
22. Ouerhani, N., Wartburg, R., Hugli, H.: Empirical validation of the saliency-based model of visual attention. Electronic Letters on CVIA (2004)
23. Meur, O., Chevet, J.: Relevance of a feed-forward model of visual attention for goal-oriented and free-viewing tasks. TIP (2010)
24. Achanta, R., Hemami, S., Estrada, F., Susstrunk, S.: Frequency-tuned salient region detection. In: CVPR (2009)
25. Hou, X., Zhang, L.: Dynamic visual attention: searching for coding length increments. In: NIPS (2008)
26. Seo, H., Milanfar, P.: Static and space-time visual saliency detection by self-resemblance. JOV (2009)
27. Lang, C., Liu, G., Yu, J., Yan, S.: Saliency detection by multi-task sparsity pursuit. TIP (2011)
28. Itti, L., Koch, C.: Feature combination strategies for saliency-based visual attention systems. J. Electronic Imaging (2001)
29. Ni, B., Wang, G., Moulin, P.: HuDaAct: A color-depth video database for human daily activity recognition. In: ICCV Workshop (2011)

Quaternion-Based Spectral Saliency Detection for Eye Fixation Prediction

Boris Schauerte and Rainer Stiefelhagen

Karlsruhe Institute of Technology
Institute for Anthropomatics, Vincenz-Prießnitz-Str. 3
76131 Karlsruhe, Germany

Abstract In recent years, several authors have reported that spectral saliency detection methods provide state-of-the-art performance in predicting human gaze in images (see, e.g., [1–3]). We systematically integrate and evaluate quaternion DCT- and FFT-based spectral saliency detection [3,4], weighted quaternion color space components [5], and the use of multiple resolutions [1]. Furthermore, we propose the use of the eigenaxes and eigenangles for spectral saliency models that are based on the quaternion Fourier transform. We demonstrate the outstanding performance on the Bruce-Tsotsos (Toronto), Judd (MIT), and Kootstra-Schomacker eye-tracking data sets.

1 Introduction

There are many aspects that influence the human visual attention, but probably one of the most well-studied is that visual stimuli and objects that visually stand out of the surrounding environment automatically attract the human attention and, consequently, gaze. In the last two decades, many computational models of bottom-up visual attention have been proposed that model and try to help understand this inherent attractiveness, i.e. the visual saliency, of arbitrary stimuli and objects in a scene (see, e.g., [6]). Moreover, predicting where humans look is not only an interesting question in cognitive psychology, neurophysics, and neurobiology, but it has proven to be an important information for many application areas, e.g.: for efficient scene exploration and analysis in robotics (see, e.g., [7,8]), information visualization using image retargeting (see, e.g., [9,10]), or predicting the attractiveness of advertisement (see [11]).

In recent years, starting with the work by Hou *et al.* in 2007 [12], spectral saliency models attracted a lot of interest (see, e.g., [1,3–5,7,12–15]). These approaches manipulate the image's frequency spectrum to highlight sparse salient regions (see also [16,17]) and provide state-of-the-art performance, e.g., on psychological patterns (see [12]), for salient region detection (see [12]), and spatio-temporal eye fixation prediction (see [2,5]). But, what makes these approaches particularly attractive is the unusual combination of state-of-the-art performance and computational efficiency that is inherited from the fast Fourier transform. An interesting development in this area is the use of quaternions as a holistic representation to process color images as a whole [3,4]. The quaternion algebra

A. Fitzgibbon et al. (Eds.): ECCV 2012, Part II, LNCS 7573, pp. 116–129, 2012.

makes it possible to process color images as a whole without the need to process the image channels separately and, in consequence, tear apart the color information[1]. Given the definition of (real-valued) spectral saliency models, it does not seem possible to calculate them on color images without separation of the image channels if it were not for the quaternion algebra and its hypercomplex discrete Fourier transform (DFT) and discrete cosine transform (DCT) definitions.

In this paper, we combine and extend the previous work on spectral saliency detection. Most importantly, we integrate and investigate the influence of quaternion component weights as proposed by Bian *et al.* [5], adapt the multiscale model by Peters *et al.* [1] and evaluate its effect on the quaternion-based approaches, and propose and evaluate the use of the quaternion eigenaxis and eigenangle for saliency algorithms that rely on the quaternion Fourier transform (see, e.g., [4, 12, 13]). Furthermore, we evaluate the choice of the color spaces that have been applied in previous work (see, e.g., [2]) and also address the influence of the quaternion DFT and quaternion DCT transformation axis. We evaluate all algorithms on the Bruce-Tsotsos (Toronto), Judd (MIT), and Kootstra-Schomacker data sets (see [18–20]) and analyze how well these models can predict where humans look at in natural scenes. To this end, we use the well-known area under curve (AUC) of the receiver operator characteristic (ROC) as a measure of the predictive power (see, e.g., [2]).

In summary, we are able to improve the state-of-the-art on the Toronto, and Kootstra-Schomacker data set in terms of the area under the ROC curve. On the Judd data set, our approach is outperformed by Judd's algorithm and we achieve only the second best performance. This can be explained by the fact that Judd's algorithm explicitly models the influence of higher level concepts, which are very prominent in Judd's data set. However, the evaluated spectral saliency algorithms achieve the performance at a fraction of the computational requirements of Judd's algorithm. The proposed use of the eigenaxis and eigenangle substantially improves the performance of the quaternion Fourier approach (PQFT; see [4]) and makes it the second best choice after the quaternion DCT signature saliency (QDCT; see [3]). The use of multiple scales significantly improves the results and the use of appropriately weighted color spaces is essential to achieve outstanding performance using quaternion-based spectral saliency detection.

2 Related Work

Visual saliency is a concept that has been derived from human perception and describes how likely it is that a stimulus attracts the attention (see, e.g., [6]). Many factors influence the human attention and we have to distinguish between bottom-up, data-driven as well as top-down, knowledge-driven aspects. In this paper, we consider the traditional concept of visual saliency that is primarily linked to the bottom-up attention that automatically attracts the human gaze.

[1] A simple, illustrated example and discussion of the disadvantage of processing an image's color channels separately can be found in [5, Sec. 3.1].

One of the most influential works is the feature integration theory by Treisman and Gelade [21], which is probably the first model that used several feature dimensions to calculate a *saliency map* of the image that tries to estimate how salient each image region is. Since then many different saliency models have been proposed to calculate such maps; for example, the well-known model by Itti and Koch [22], attention by information maximization (AIM) [18], saliency using natural statistics (SUN) [23], graph-based visual saliency (GBVS) [24], context-aware saliency (CAS) [9,10], and Judd's model that is based on machine learning [19]. However, since reviewing the existing approaches is beyond the scope of this paper, we refer the interested reader to the survey by Frintrop *et al.* [6]. In the following, we summarize the most closely related work.

The first spectral approach for visual saliency detection was presented in 2007 by Hou *et al.* [12]. Since then, several spectral saliency models have been proposed (see, e.g., [1,4,5,12–15]). Hou *et al.* proposed the use of the Fourier transform to calculate the visual saliency of an image. To this end, – processing each color channel separately – the image is Fourier transformed and the magnitude components are attenuated (spectral residual). Then, the inverse Fourier transform is calculated using the manipulated magnitude components in combination with the original phase angles. The saliency map is obtained by calculating the absolute value of each pixel of this inverse transformed image and subsequent Gaussian smoothing. This way Hou *et al.* achieved state-of-the-art performance for salient region (proto-object) detection and psychological test patterns. However, although Hou *et al.* were the first to propose this method for saliency detection, it has been known for at least three decades that suppressing the magnitude components in the frequency domain highlights signal components such as lines, edges, or narrow events (see [16,17]).

In 2008 [1], Peters *et al.* analyzed the role of Fourier phase information in predicting visual saliency. They extended the model of Hou *et al.* by linearly combining the saliency of the image at several scales. Then, they analyzed how well this model predicts eye fixations and found that "salience maps from this model significantly predicted the free-viewing gaze patterns of four observers for 337 images of natural outdoor scenes, fractals, and aerial imagery" [1].

Also in 2008 [4], Guo *et al.* proposed the use of quaternions as a holistic color image representation for spectral saliency calculation. This was possible because quaternions provide a powerful algebra that allows to realize a hypercomplex Fourier transform (see [25]), which was first demonstrated to be applicable for color image processing by Sangwine [26,27]. Thus, Guo *et al.* were able to Fourier transform the image as a whole and did not have to process each color channel separately[1]. Furthermore, this made it possible to use the scalar part of the quaternion image as 4th channel to integrate a motion component. However, in contrast to Hou *et al.*, Guo *et al.* did not use the spectral residual. Most interestingly, Guo *et al.* were able to determine salient people in videos and outperformed the models of Itti *et al.* [22] and Walther *et al.* [28]. In 2010 [13], a multiresolution attention selection mechanism was introduced, but the definition of the main saliency model remained unchanged. However, most interestingly, further

Fig. 1. Visualization (see [30] on how to interpret it) of the quaternion Fourier spectrum of an example image for two transformation axes (1&2). Left-to-right, top-to-bottom: original, eigenangles (1), eigenaxes (1), magnitude (1), eigenangles (2), and eigenaxes (2). This illustration is best viewed in color.

experiments demonstrated that the approach outperformed several established approaches in predicting eye gaze on still images.

In 2009 [5], Bian *et al.* adapted the work by Guo *et al.* by weighting the quaternion components[2]. Furthermore, they provide a biological justification for spectral visual saliency models and proposed the use of the YUV color space, in contrast to the use of the previously applied intensity and color opponents (ICOPP) [4,13], and RGB [12]. This made it possible to outperform the models of Bruce *et al.* [18], Gao *et al.* [29], Walther and Koch [28], and Itti and Koch [22] when predicting human eye fixations on video sequences.

In 2012 [2], Hou *et al.* proposed and theoretically analyzed the use of the discrete cosine transform (DCT) for spectral saliency detection. They showed that this approach outperforms (in terms of the AUC) all other evaluated state-of-the-art approaches – e.g., Itti and Koch [22], AIM [18], GBVS [24], and SUN [23] – in predicting human eye fixations on the Toronto data set [18]. Furthermore, Hou *et al.* pointed out the importance of choosing an appropriate color space.

Also in 2012 [3], Schauerte *et al.* used the definition of a quaternion DCT and quaternion signatures to calculate the visual saliency and was able to outperform the real-valued approach by Hou *et al.* [2]. This way they improved the state-of-the-art in predicting where humans look in the presence and absence of faces.

3 Saliency Model

3.1 Basic Quaternion Definitions

Quaternion Algebra: Quaternions form a 4D algebra $\mathbf{H}$ over the real numbers and are – in principle – an extension of the 2D complex numbers [31]. A quaternion q is defined as $q = a + bi + cj + dk \in \mathbf{H}$ with $a, b, c, d \in \mathbf{R}$, where i, j, and k provide the basis to define the (Hamilton) product of two quaternions q_1 and q_2 ($q_1, q_2 \in \mathbf{H}$):

$$q_1 q_2 = (a_1 + b_1 i + c_1 j + d_1 k)(a_2 + b_2 i + c_2 j + d_2 k)\,, \tag{1}$$

[2] Please note that the mentioned SW approach [5] is in principle equivalent to the PFT approach by Guo *et al.* [4].

where $i^2 = j^2 = k^2 = ijk = -1$. Since, for example, by definition $ij = k$ while $ji = -k$ the Hamilton product is not commutative. Accordingly, we have to distinguish between left-sided and right-sided multiplications (marked by L and R, respectively, in the following). A quaternion q is called real, if $x = a + 0i + 0j + 0k$, and pure imaginary, if $q = 0 + bi + cj + dk$. We can define the operators $S(q) = a$ and $V(q) = bi + cj + dk$ that extract the scalar part and the imaginary part of a quaternion $q = a + bi + cj + dk$, respectively. As for complex numbers, we can define conjugate quaternions $\bar{q} = a - bi - cj - dk$ as well as the norm $|q| = \sqrt{q \cdot \bar{q}}$. Furthermore, we can define the quaternion scalar product $* : \mathbf{H} \times \mathbf{H} \rightarrow \mathbf{R}$

$$s = q_1 * q_2 = a_1 a_2 + b_1 b_2 + c_1 c_2 + d_1 d_2 \,. \tag{2}$$

Eigenaxis and Eigenangle: Euler's formula for the polar representation using the complex exponential generalizes to (hypercomplex) quaternion form

$$e^{\mu \Phi} = \cos \Phi + \mu \sin \Phi \,, \tag{3}$$

where μ is a unit pure quaternion (see [27] and [13]). Consequently, any quaternion q may be represented in a polar representation such as:

$$q = |q| e^{\gamma \Phi} \tag{4}$$

with the norm $|q|$, its *eigenaxis* γ

$$\gamma = f_\gamma(q) = \frac{V(q)}{|V(q)|} \,, \tag{5}$$

and the corresponding *eigenangle* Φ

$$\Phi = f_\Phi(q) = \arctan\left(\frac{|V(q)| \operatorname{sgn}(V(q) * \gamma)}{S(q)}\right) \tag{6}$$

with respect to the eigenaxis γ, which is a unit pure quaternion, and where $\operatorname{sgn}(\cdot)$ is the signum function (see [27]). The eigenaxis γ specifies the quaternion direction in the 3-dimensional space of the imaginary, vector part and can be seen as being a generalization of the imaginary unit of complex numbers. Analogously, the eigenangle Φ corresponds to the argument of a complex number.

3.2 Quaternion Images

Every image $\mathbf{I} \in \mathbb{R}^{M \times N \times C}$ – with at most 4 color components, i.e. $C \leq 4$ – can be represented using a $M \times N$ quaternion matrix

$$\begin{aligned} \mathbf{I}_Q &= \mathbf{I}_4 + \mathbf{I}_1 i + \mathbf{I}_2 j + \mathbf{I}_3 k & (7) \\ &= \mathbf{I}_4 + \mathbf{I}_1 i + (\mathbf{I}_2 + \mathbf{I}_3 i) j \quad \text{(symplectic form)}, & (8) \end{aligned}$$

where $\mathbf{I}_c$ denotes the $M \times N$ matrix of the cth image channel. It is common to represent the (potential) 4th image channel as the scalar part (see, e.g., [27]), because when using this definition it is possible to work with pure quaternions for the most common color spaces such as, e.g., RGB, YUV and Lab.

Weighted Quaternion Color Components: Naturally, as done by Bian *et al.* [5] and also related to the recent trend to learn feature dimension weights (see, e.g., [32] and [19]), we can model the relative importance of the color space components for the visual saliency by introducing a quaternion component weight vector $\mathbf{w} = [w_1\ w_2\ w_3\ w_4]^{\mathrm{T}}$ and adapting Eq. 7 appropriately:

$$\mathbf{I}_{\mathrm{Q}} = w_4\mathbf{I}_4 + w_1\mathbf{I}_1 i + w_2\mathbf{I}_2 j + w_3\mathbf{I}_3 k\,. \tag{9}$$

In case of equal influence of each color component, i.e. uniform weights, Eq. 7 is a scaled version of Eq. 9, which is practically equivalent for our application.

3.3 Quaternion Transforms and Transformation Axis

Quaternion Discrete Fourier Transform: We can transform a $M \times N$ quaternion matrix $\mathbf{f}$ using the definition of the quaternion Fourier transform $\mathscr{F}_{\mathrm{Q}}^{\mathrm{L}}$ [30]:

$$\mathscr{F}_{\mathrm{Q}}^{\mathrm{L}}[\mathbf{f}](u,v) = \mathbf{F}_{\mathrm{Q}}^{\mathrm{L}}(u,v) \tag{10}$$

$$\mathbf{F}_{\mathrm{Q}}^{\mathrm{L}}(u,v) = \frac{1}{\sqrt{MN}} \sum_{m=0}^{M-1} \sum_{n=0}^{N-1} e^{-\eta 2\pi((mv/M)+(nu/N))}\mathbf{f}(m,n)\,,$$

see Fig. 1 for an example. The corresponding inverse quaternion discrete Fourier transform $\mathscr{F}_{\mathrm{Q}}^{-\mathrm{L}}$ is defined as:

$$\mathscr{F}_{\mathrm{Q}}^{-\mathrm{L}}[\mathbf{F}](m,n) = \mathbf{f}_{\mathrm{Q}}^{\mathrm{L}}(m,n) \tag{11}$$

$$\mathbf{f}_{\mathrm{Q}}^{\mathrm{L}}(m,n) = \frac{1}{\sqrt{MN}} \sum_{u=0}^{M-1} \sum_{v=0}^{N-1} e^{\eta 2\pi((mv/M)+(nu/N))}\mathbf{F}(u,v)\,.$$

Here, η is a unit pure quaternion that serves as an axis and determines a direction in the color space. Although the choice of η is arbitrary, it is not without consequence (see [30, Sec. V]) and can influence the results. For example, in RGB a good axis candidate would be the "gray line" and thus $\eta = (i+j+k)/\sqrt{3}$. In fact, as discussed by Ell and Sangwine [30], this would decompose the image into luminance and chrominance components.

Quaternion Discrete Cosine Transform: Similarly, it is possible to define a quaternion discrete cosine transform:

$$\mathscr{D}_{\mathrm{Q}}^{\mathrm{L}}[\mathbf{f}](u,v) = \frac{2}{\sqrt{MM}} \sum_{m=0}^{M-1} \sum_{n=0}^{N-1} \eta f(m,n) \beta_{u,m}^{M} \beta_{v,n}^{N} \tag{12}$$

$$\mathscr{D}_{\mathrm{Q}}^{-\mathrm{L}}[\mathbf{F}](m,n) = \frac{2}{\sqrt{MM}} \sum_{u=0}^{M-1} \sum_{v=0}^{N-1} \eta F(u,v) \beta_{u,v}^{M} \beta_{m,n}^{N} \tag{13}$$

with $\beta_{u,m}^{M} = \cos\left[\frac{\pi}{M}(m+\frac{1}{2})u\right]$ (see, e.g., [3]). However, as can be seen when comparing Eq. 10 and 12, the definition of $\mathscr{D}_{\mathrm{Q}}^{\mathrm{L}}$ is substantially different from

Fig. 2. Example images (top) from the data sets (see Sec. 4.1) that illustrate the difference of the PQFT (middle) and proposed EigenPQFT (bottom) saliency maps

$\mathscr{F}_{\mathrm{Q}}^{\mathrm{L}}$, because the factors $\beta_{u,m}^{M}$ are real-valued instead of the hypercomplex terms of $\mathscr{F}_{\mathrm{Q}}^{\mathrm{L}}$, as discussed by Schauerte *et al.* [3]. However, both definitions share the concept of a unit pure quaternion η that serves as a transformation axis.

3.4 Eigenaxis and -angle Spectral Saliency

Similar to the real-numbered definition of the spectral residual by Hou *et al.* [12], let $\mathbf{A}_{\mathrm{Q}}$ denote the amplitude, $\mathbf{E}_{\gamma}$ the eigenaxes, and the eigenangles $\mathbf{E}_{\Theta}$ (see Sec. 3.1) of the quaternion image $\mathbf{I}_{\mathrm{Q}}$:

$$\mathbf{E}_{\gamma}(x,y) = f_{\gamma}(\mathbf{I}_{\mathrm{Q}}(x,y)) \tag{14}$$

$$\mathbf{E}_{\Theta}(x,y) = f_{\Theta}(\mathbf{I}_{\mathrm{Q}}(x,y)) \tag{15}$$

$$\mathbf{A}_{\mathrm{Q}}(x,y) = |\mathbf{I}_{\mathrm{Q}}(x,y)| \,. \tag{16}$$

Then, we calculate the log amplitude and a low-pass filtered log amplitude using a Gaussian filter $h_{\sigma_{\mathrm{A}}}$ with the standard deviation σ_{A} to obtain the spectral residual R_Q:

$$\mathbf{L}_{\mathrm{Q}}(x,y) = \log \mathbf{A}_{\mathrm{Q}}(x,y) \tag{17}$$

$$\mathbf{R}_{\mathrm{Q}}(x,y) = \mathbf{L}_{\mathrm{Q}}(x,y) - \left[\mathbf{h}_{\sigma_{\mathrm{A}}} * \mathbf{L}_{\mathrm{Q}}\right](x,y) \,. \tag{18}$$

Finally, we can calculate the *Eigen Spectral Residual* (*EigenSR*) saliency map S_{ESR} using the spectral residual R_Q, the eigenaxis E_{γ}, and the eigenangle E_{Θ}:

$$S_{\mathrm{ESR}} = \mathscr{S}_{\mathrm{ESR}}(\mathbf{I}_{\mathrm{Q}}) = \mathbf{h}_{\sigma_{\mathrm{S}}} * \left|\mathscr{F}_{\mathrm{Q}}^{-\mathrm{L}}\left[e^{\mathbf{R}_Q + \mathbf{E}_{\gamma} \circ \mathbf{E}_{\Theta}}\right]\right| , \tag{19}$$

where $\circ$ denotes the Hadamard product and $\mathbf{h}_{\sigma_{\mathrm{S}}}$ is a Gauss filter with standard deviation σ_{S}. If σ_{A} approaches zero, then the spectral residual $\mathbf{R}_Q$ will become $\mathbf{0}$, i.e. $\lim_{\sigma_{\mathrm{A}} \to 0^+} \mathbf{R}_{\mathrm{Q}}(x,y) = 0$, in which case we refer to the model as the *Eigen Spectral Whitening* model (*EigenSW* or *EigenPQFT*).

If the input image is a single-channel image, then the quaternion definitions and equations are reduced to their real-valued counterparts, in which case Eq. 19

is identical to the single-channel real-numbered definition by Hou *et al.* [12]. Our EigenSR and EigenPQFT definition that is presented in Eq. 19 differs from Guo's PQFT [4] definition in two aspects: First, it – in principle – preserves Hou's spectral residual definition [12]. Second, it relies on the combination of the eigenaxes and eigenangles instead of the combination of a single unit pure quaternion and the corresponding phase spectrum (see [13, Eq. 16] and [4, Eq. 20]), see Fig. 2 for an illustration.

3.5 Multiple Scales

The above saliency definitions only consider a fixed, single scale (see, e.g., [2–5, 13]). But, the scale is an important parameter when calculating the visual saliency and an integral part of many saliency models (see, e.g., [6]). For spectral approaches the scale is (implicitly) defined by the resolution of the image I_{Q} (see, e.g., [33]). Consequently, as proposed by Peters and Itti [1], it is possible to calculate a multiscale saliency map $\mathbf{S}^M$ by combining the spectral saliency of the image at different image scales. Let $\mathbf{I}_{\mathrm{Q}}^m$ denote the quaternion image at scale $m \in M$, then

$$S^M = \mathscr{S}^M(\mathbf{I}_{\mathrm{Q}}) = h_{\sigma_{\mathrm{M}}} * \sum_{m \in M} \phi_R(\mathscr{S}(\mathbf{I}_{\mathrm{Q}}^m)), \qquad (20)$$

where ϕ_R rescales the matrix to the target saliency map resolution R and $h_{\sigma_{\mathrm{M}}}$ is an additional, optional Gauss filter.

4 Evaluation and Discussion

4.1 The Data Set, Algorithms, and Measures

Data Sets: To evaluate the considered saliency algorithms, we use the following eye-tracking data sets: The Toronto data set by Bruce and Tsotsos (see [18]), which consists of 120 images (681 × 511 pixels) and the corresponding eye-tracking data of 20 subjects that were free-viewing each image for 4 seconds. The data set by Kootstra and Schomacker [20], which consists of 100 images (1024 × 768 pixels) and eye-tracking data of 31 subjects that free-viewed the images. The images are subdivided into 5 categories and were selected from the McGill calibrated color image database [34]. Furthermore, we use the data set by Judd et al. (see [19]), which is also known as MIT data set and is the largest publicly available data set. It consists of 1003 images (varying resolution and aspect ratio) and eye-tracking data of 15 viewers.

Algorithms: We evaluate the following spectral saliency methods[3]: spectral residual (SR) [12], pure Fourier transform aka. spectral whitening (PFT) [4,13], PFT at multiple scales (ΔPFT) [1], pure quaternion Fourier transform (PQFT)

[3] Please note that our reference implementations are publicly available and free (BSD License) to allow for fair benchmarking and evaluation by other authors in the future.

[4,13], DCT signature (DCT) [2], and quaternion DCT signature (QDCT) [3]. We mark algorithms that use multiple scales with a preceding Δ (imagine a stylized image pyramid). To serve as a reference, we use the following algorithms[4] as baselines: the Itti and Koch model [22], graph-based visual saliency (GBVS) [24], context-aware saliency (CAS) [9, 10], attention using information maximization [18], and Judd's model [19].

We evaluate how well the proposed algorithms perform for all color spaces that have been applied in the closely related literature, i.e.: red-green-blue (RGB) (see, e.g., [2, 12]), CIELAB (Lab) (see [2]), intensity and red-green/blue-yellow color opponents (ICP) (see [4, 13]), and YUV which consists of the luma Y and the two chrominance components U and V (see [5]).

ΔPQFT, EigenPQFT, ΔEigenPQFT, EigenSR, ΔEigenSR, and ΔQDCT are methods that are first introduced and evaluated in this paper. Except for the PQFT in combination with YUV that was proposed by Bian *et al.* [5], the influence of the quaternion component weight has not been evaluated for any quaternion-based algorithm.

Evaluation Measure: We follow the evaluation procedure described by Hou *et al.* [2] and use the center-bias corrected area under the receiver operating characteristic curve as performance measure. As has been shown in prior art (see, e.g., [33]), the human gaze is often biased toward the center of an image. To remove this bias (see [2] and [35]), we define a positive and a negative sample set of eye fixation points for each image. The positive sample set contains the fixation points of all subjects on that image. The negative sample set contains the union of all eye fixation points across all images from the same data set, but excluding the samples of the positive sample set. Each saliency map can be thresholded and the resulting binarized (saliency) map can be considered to be a binary classifier that tries to separate positive and negative samples. Thus, for each threshold, the true positive rate is the proportion of the positive samples that fall in the positive region of the binarized (saliency) map. Analogously, the false positive rate can be calculated by using the negative sample set. Sweeping over all thresholds leads to the receiver operating characteristic (ROC) curves. The area under the ROC curves is a widely used compact measure for the ability of the saliency map to predict human eye fixations. Chance would lead to an AUC of 0.5, values < 0.5 indicate a negative correlation, and values > 0.5 indicate a positive correlation (perfect prediction is 1.0).

4.2 Experimental Results and Discussion

We kept the image resolution fixed at 64×48 pixels in the evaluation, because in preparatory pilot experiments this resolution has constantly shown to provide very good results on all data sets and is the resolution most widely used in the

[4] When available, we used the publicly available reference implementation from the authors. For the Itti and Koch model we used the implementation by Harel [24], which achieved a better performance than the iLab Neuromorphic Vision Toolkit (iNVT).

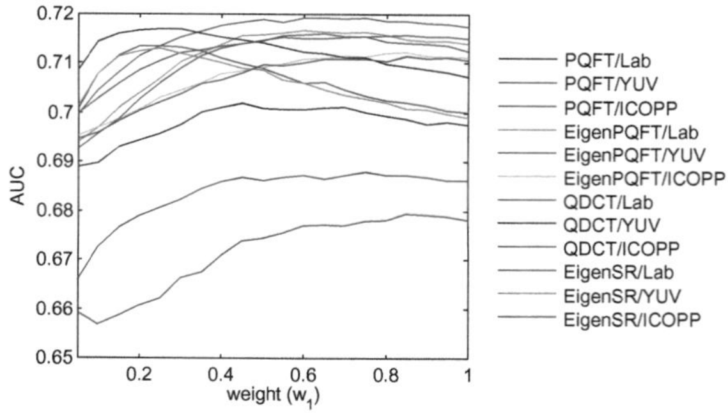

Fig. 3. Example of the influence of quaternion color component weights on the AUC performance for QDCT, EigenPQFT, EigenSR, and PQFT on the Toronto data set. Using the default quaternion transformation axis $\eta = (i + j + k)/\sqrt{3}$.

literature (see, e.g., [2,3]). For multiscale approaches 64×48 pixels is consequently the base resolution. For the Gaussian filtering of the saliency maps, we use the fast recursive filter implementation by Geusebroek *et al.* [36].

The achievable performance depends substantially on the data set, see Tab. 1. We can rank the data sets by the maximum area under the ROC curve that spectral algorithms achieved and obtain the following descending order: Toronto, Judd, and Kootstra. This order can most likely be explained with the different characteristics of the images in each data set. Two image categories are dominant within the Toronto data set: street scenes and objects. Furthermore, the images have relatively similar characteristics. The Judd data set contains many images from two categories: images that depict landscapes and images that show people. The second category is problematic for low-level approaches that do not consider higher-level influences on visual attention such as, e.g., the presence of people and faces in images. This also is the most important aspect why Judd's model excels on this data set. The Kootstra data set is the data set with the highest data variability. It contains five image categories, close-up as well as landscape images, and images with and without a strong photographer bias.

RGB is the color space with the worst performance. While Lab provides the best performance on the Toronto data set, it is outperformed by YUV and ICOPP on the Kootstra and Judd data set. Since YUV is the best color model on the Kootstra and Judd data set and is close to the performance of Lab on the Toronto data set, we advise the use of the YUV color space.

Within each color space and across all data sets the performance ranking of the algorithms is relatively stable, see Tab. 1. We can observe that with naive parameters the performance of the quaternion-based approaches may be lower than the performance of their real-valued counterparts. The extent of this effect depends on the color space as well as on the algorithm. For example, for QDCT this effect does not exist on the RGB and ICOPP color spaces and for Lab only on the Kootstra data set. However, over all data sets this effect is most apparent for the YUV color space. But, the YUV color space is also the color space that profits

Table 1. Area under the receiver-operator characteristic curve (ROC AUC) of the evaluated algorithms (0.5 is chance level, > 0.5 indicates positive correlation, and an AUC of 1.0 represents perfect prediction). In the default configuration, the algorithms use a uniform color component weight (except for the approach by Bian *et al.*, which is denoted as PQFT/Bian), and the uniform transform axis $\eta = (i+j+k)/\sqrt{3}$. In the optimized configuration, we use appropriate quaternion component weights and non-standard axes. The overall optimal quaternion component weight vectors are roughly $[0.5\ 1\ 1\ 0]^T$, $[0.2\ 1\ 1\ 0]^T$, and $[0.8\ 1\ 1\ 0]^T$ for Lab, YUV, and ICOPP, respectively. The best overall performance can be achieved with a smoothing filter standard deviation (σ_s and σ_M for single-scale and multiscale, respectively) of roughly 0.039 (image widths). The optimal axis depends on the algorithm as well as on the color space. But, interestingly, for RGB the most reliable axis is in fact the "gray line", see Sec. 3.3. In general, the influence of the quaternion FFT and DCT transformation axis is secondary to the influence of the quaternion component weights. But, a badly chosen quaternion transformation axis can substantially degrade the performance.

	Area under the Receiver Operating Characteristic curve (mean)											
	Toronto				Kootstra				Judd			
Method	Lab	YUV	ICP	RGB	Lab	YUV	ICP	RGB	Lab	YUV	ICP	RGB
	Weighted Color Space and Non-Standard Axis											
ΔQDCT	.7201	.7188	.7174	.7091	.6104	.6125	.6110	.6007	.6589	.6751	.6712	.6622
QDCT	.7195	.7170	.7158	.7066	.6085	.6119	.6106	.5994	.6528	.6656	.6623	.6552
ΔEigenPQFT	.7183	.7160	.7144	.7035	.6053	.6082	.6064	.5963	.6527	.6658	.6617	.6559
EigenPQFT	.7180	.7137	.7122	.7006	.6058	.6073	.6063	.5934	.6483	.6611	.6568	.6493
ΔEigenSR	.7175	.7153	.7133	.7014	.6050	.6077	.6056	.5941	.6508	.6649	.6603	.6534
EigenSR	.7162	.7129	.7112	.6990	.6038	.6068	.6044	.5912	.6467	.6601	.6554	.6470
ΔPQFT	.7085	.6969	.6927	.6930	.5943	.5994	.5922	.5868	.6467	.6503	.6429	.6468
PQFT	.7042	.6881	.6826	.6891	.5930	.5970	.5913	.5861	.6404	.6416	.6379	.6398
PQFT/Bian	.7035	.6880	.6817	.6884	.5928	.5961	.5911	.5861	.6404	.6411	.6375	.6396
	Uniform Color Space Weights and Standard Axis											
ΔQDCT	.7191	.7107	.7070	.7088	.6050	.6036	.6078	.6002	.6539	.6648	.6618	.6620
QDCT	.7180	.7079	.7039	.7056	.6036	.6005	.6079	.5987	.6517	.6572	.6552	.6551
ΔEigenPQFT	.7148	.7030	.7024	.7026	.6005	.5963	.6045	.5959	.6490	.6530	.6548	.6556
EigenPQFT	.7141	.7006	.6982	.7006	.5984	.5939	.6023	.5934	.6461	.6496	.6518	.6491
ΔEigenSR	.7142	.7135	.7006	.7013	.6003	.5951	.6028	.5937	.6477	.6504	.6534	.6531
EigenSR	.7132	.6998	.6969	.6988	.5975	.5930	.6007	.5909	.6448	.6486	.6502	.6466
ΔPQFT	.7022	.6925	.6868	.6927	.5803	.5826	.5877	.5850	.6431	.6441	.6380	.6465
PQFT	.6974	.6858	.6796	.6884	.5788	.5808	.5860	.5846	.6368	.6368	.6271	.6396
	Non-Quaternion Spectral Baseline Algorithms											
DCT	.7137	.7131	.7014	.6941	.6052	.6089	.6049	.5907	.6465	.6604	.6556	.6461
ΔPFT	.7177	.7170	.7079	.7014	.6072	.6107	.6084	.5945	.6502	.6601	.6583	.6523
PFT	.7140	.7120	.7025	.6958	.6057	.6079	.6058	.5908	.6445	.6590	.6572	.6446
SR	.7156	.7144	.7051	.6983	.6059	.6090	.6061	.5916	.6462	.6599	.6573	.6461
	Baseline Algorithms (algorithm-specific feature spaces)											
CAS	.6921				.6034				.6622			
AIM	.6986				.5749				.6662			
Judd	.6847				.5793				.7696			
GBVS	.6703				.5791				.6539			
Itti	.6492				.5672				.6433			

most from non-uniform quaternion component weights with an optimal weight vector around $[0.2\ 1\ 1\ 0]^T$, which indicates that the unweighted influence of the luminance component is too high. When weighted appropriately, as mentioned before, we achieve the overall best results using the YUV color space.

The influence of quaternion component weights is substantial, see Tab. 1, and depends on the color space. As discussed it is most important for the YUV color space. However, it is also substantial for Lab and ICOPP. Most importantly, the best weights are relatively constant over all data sets. Accordingly, we advise the use of the following weight vectors $[0.5\ 1\ 1\ 0]^T$, $[0.2\ 1\ 1\ 0]^T$, and $[0.8\ 1\ 1\ 0]^T$ for Lab, YUV, and ICOPP, respectively. In general, the influence of the quaternion transformation axis is secondary to the influence of the quaternion component weights. However, a badly chosen axis can significantly degrade the performance.

The influence of multiple scales varies depending on the data set. For the Toronto data set the influence is small, which can be explained by the fact that the resolution of 64×48 pixels is nearly optimal for this data set (see [2]). On the Kootstra data set the influence is also relatively small, which may be due to the heterogeneous image data. The highest influence of multiple scales can be seen on the Judd data set (e.g., compare ΔQDCT with QDCT).

We achieve the best single-scale as well as multiscale performance with the quaternion DCT approach. With respect to their overall performance we can rank the algorithms as follows: QDCT, EigenPQFT, EigenSR, and PQFT. With the exception of Judd's model on the Judd data set (discussed earlier), quaternion-based spectral approaches and especially QDCT are able to outperform the baseline methods on all three data sets. Furthermore, the proposed EigenPQFT is a substantial improvement over Guo's PQFT and is the 2nd best quaternion-based approach. It is also able to achieve a better performance than the low-level baseline algorithms on all three data sets. In consequence, using quaternion-based saliency detection, quaternion component weights and multiple scales, we are able to improve the state-of-the-art in predicting human gaze points.

The spectral approaches inherit the $O(N \log_2 N)$ arithmetic complexity of the discrete fast Fourier transform and in practice also benefit from highly optimized fast Fourier implementations. Thus, without going into any detail, the (quaternion) FFT- and DCT-based models that we evaluated can be implemented to operate in less than one millisecond (single-scale) on an off the shelf PC (Intel Core i5 @ 3GHz). This is an important aspect for practical applications and a fraction of the computational requirements of most other approaches such as, e.g., Judd (more than 30,000× slower on Judd's data set), CAS (more than 40,000× slower), and AIM (more than 100,000× slower).

5 Conclusion

We analyzed quaternion-based spectral saliency approaches which use the quaternion Fourier or cosine spectrum to calculate the visual saliency. Using the Toronto, Kootstra and Judd eye-tracking data sets, we are able to show the suitability of these approaches to predict human gaze in images and demonstrated the influence of multiple scales, color space weights, and quaternion transformation axes. We integrated these aspects and presented a consistent and comprehensive evaluation of spectral saliency models for predicting human eye fixations. We were able to achieve the best results for low-level approaches (i.e., without explicitly modeling the influence of higher level aspects such as, e.g., faces) on all three data sets in terms of the area under the receiver-operator characteristic curve.

In our opinion, the most important future work for spectral saliency detection would be to define an appropriate color/feature space. As can be seen in the results the color space has an important influence, but color space weighting can only be seen as an intermediate step toward a more appropriate feature space.

Acknowledgements. This work was realized as part of the Quaero Programme, funded by OSEO, French State agency for innovation.

References

1. Peters, R., Itti, L.: The role of fourier phase information in predicting saliency. Journal of Vision 8, 879 (2008)
2. Hou, X., Harel, J., Koch, C.: Image signature: Highlighting sparse salient regions. IEEE Trans. Pattern Anal. Mach. Intell. 34, 194–201 (2012)
3. Schauerte, B., Stiefelhagen, R.: Predicting human gaze using quaternion dct image signature saliency and face detection. In: Proc. Workshop on the Applications of Computer Vision (2012)
4. Guo, C.L., Ma, Q., Zhang, L.M.: Spatio-temporal saliency detection using phase spectrum of quaternion fourier transform. In: Proc. Int. Conf. Comp. Vis. Pat. Rec. (2008)
5. Bian, P., Zhang, L.: Biological plausibility of spectral domain approach for spatiotemporal visual saliency. In: Advances in Neural Information Processing Systems (2009)
6. Frintrop, S., Rome, E., Christensen, H.I.: Computational visual attention systems and their cognitive foundation: A survey. ACM Trans. Applied Perception 7(1), 6:1–6:39 (2010)
7. Meger, D., Forssén, P.E., Lai, K., et al.: Curious george: An attentive semantic robot. Robotics and Autonomous Systems 56(6), 503–511 (2008)
8. Schauerte, B., Kühn, B., Kroschel, K., Stiefelhagen, R.: Multimodal saliency-based attention for object-based scene analysis. In: Proc. Int. Conf. Intell. Robots Syst. (2011)
9. Goferman, S., Zelnik-Manor, L., Tal, A.: Context-aware saliency detection. In: Proc. Int. Conf. Comp. Vis. Pat. Rec. (2010)
10. Goferman, S., Zelnik-Manor, L., Tal, A.: Context-aware saliency detection. IEEE Trans. Pattern Anal. Mach. Intell. (2012)
11. Ma, Z., Qing, L., Miao, J., Chen, X.: Advertisement evaluation using visual saliency based on foveated image. In: Proc. Int. Conf. Multimedia and Expo. (2009)
12. Hou, X., Zhang, L.: Saliency detection: A spectral residual approach. In: Proc. Int. Conf. Comp. Vis. Pat. Rec. (2007)
13. Guo, C., Zhang, L.: A novel multiresolution spatiotemporal saliency detection model and its applications in image and video compression. IEEE Trans. Image Process. 19, 185–198 (2010)

14. Achanta, R., Süsstrunk, S.: Saliency detection using maximum symmetric surround. In: Proc. Int. Conf. Image Process. (2010)
15. Li, J., Levine, M.D., An, X., He, H.: Saliency detection based on frequency and spatial domain analysis. In: Proc. British Mach. Vis. Conf. (2011)
16. Oppenheim, A., Lim, J.: The importance of phase in signals. Proc. IEEE 69, 529–541 (1981)
17. Huang, T., Burnett, J., Deczky, A.: The importance of phase in image processing filters. IEEE Trans. Acoust., Speech, Signal Process. 23, 529–542 (1975)
18. Bruce, N., Tsotsos, J.: Saliency, attention, and visual search: An information theoretic approach. Journal of Vision 9, 1–24 (2009)
19. Judd, T., Ehinger, K., Durand, F., Torralba, A.: Learning to predict where humans look. In: Proc. Int. Conf. Comp. Vis. (2009)
20. Kootstra, G., Nederveen, A., de Boer, B.: Paying attention to symmetry. In: Proc. British Mach. Vis. Conf. (2008)
21. Treisman, A.M., Gelade, G.: A feature-integration theory of attention. Cog. Psy. 12, 97–136 (1980)
22. Itti, L., Koch, C., Niebur, E.: A model of saliency-based visual attention for rapid scene analysis. IEEE Trans. Pattern Anal. Mach. Intell. 20, 1254–1259 (1998)
23. Zhang, L., Tong, M.H., Marks, T.K., Shan, H., Cottrell, G.W.: Sun: A bayesian framework for saliency using natural statistics. Journal of Vision 8 (2008)
24. Harel, J., Koch, C., Perona, P.: Graph-based visual saliency. In: Advances in Neural Information Processing Systems (2007)
25. Ell, T.: Quaternion-fourier transforms for analysis of two-dimensional linear time-invariant partial differential systems. In: Int. Conf. Decision and Control (1993)
26. Sangwine, S.J.: Fourier transforms of colour images using quaternion or hypercomplex, numbers. Electronics Letters 32, 1979–1980 (1996)
27. Sangwine, S.J., Ell, T.A.: Colour image filters based on hypercomplex convolution. In: IEEE Proc. Vision, Image and Signal Processing, vol. 147, pp. 89–93 (2000)
28. Walther, D., Koch, C.: Modeling attention to salient proto-objects. Neural Networks 19, 1395–1407 (2006)
29. Gao, D., Mahadevan, V., Vasconcelos, N.: On the plausibility of the discriminant center-surround hypothesis for visual saliency. Journal of Vision 8, 1–18 (2008)
30. Ell, T., Sangwine, S.: Hypercomplex fourier transforms of color images. IEEE Trans. Image Process. 16, 22–35 (2007)
31. Hamilton, W.R.: Elements of Quaternions. University of Dublin Press (1866)
32. Zhao, Q., Koch, C.: Learning a saliency map using fixated locations in natural scenes. Journal of Vision 11, 1–15 (2011)
33. Judd, T., Durand, F., Torralba, A.: Fixations on low-resolution images. Journal of Vision 11 (2011)
34. Olmos, A., Kingdom, F.A.A.: A biologically inspired algorithm for the recovery of shading and reflectance images. Perception 33, 1463–1473 (2004)
35. Tatler, B., Baddeley, R., Gilchrist, I.: Visual correlates of fixation selection: Effects of scale and time. Vision Research 45, 643–659 (2005)
36. Geusebroek, J.M., Smeulders, A., van de Weijer, J.: Fast anisotropic gauss filtering. IEEE Trans. Image Process. 12, 938–943 (2003)

Human Activities as Stochastic Kronecker Graphs

Sinisa Todorovic

Oregon State University, Corvallis, Oregon
sinisa@eecs.oregonstate.edu

Abstract. A human activity can be viewed as a space-time repetition of activity primitives. Both instances of the primitives, and their repetition are stochastic. They can be modeled by a generative model-graph, where nodes correspond to the primitives, and the graph's adjacency matrix encodes their affinities for probabilistic grouping into observable video features. When a video of the activity is represented by a graph capturing the space-time layout of video features, such a video graph can be viewed as probabilistically sampled from the activity's model-graph. This sampling is formulated as a successive Kronecker multiplication of the model's affinity matrix. The resulting Kronecker-power matrix is taken as a noisy permutation of the adjacency matrix of the video graph. The paper presents our: 1) model-graph; 2) memory- and time-efficient, weakly supervised learning of activity primitives and their affinities; and 3) inference aimed at finding the best expected correspondences between the primitives and observed video features. Our results demonstrate good scalability on UCF50, and superior performance to that of the state of the art on individual, structured, and collective activities of UCF YouTube, Olympic, and Collective datasets.

1 Introduction

This paper is about detecting and localizing human activities in real-world videos. Both individual activities of people (e.g., triple-jump), and collective activities of groups of people (e.g., waiting in line) are considered in a unified framework. We define an activity as a hierarchical, space-time repetition of activity primitives. The primitives have probabilistic affinities to recursively combine into observable spatiotemporal patterns of the activity. The main advantage of such a definition over existing, alternative formulations is that the essence of the activity can be compactly captured only via a (small) set of primitives, their affinities, and an operator for their recursive grouping. This, in turn, allows for memory- and time-efficient, scalable learning and inference algorithms.

Our motivation comes from an observation that an activity may consist of a number of subactivities, where each subactivity is an activity on its own right. This recursion ends with activity primitives. For example, in a collective activity of jogging, the individual activity of running is stochastically repeated by multiple actors within the group, where each running activity represents a repetition of characteristic protrusions of the legs, and swinging of the arms.

Given a video of an activity, we capture the spatiotemporal repetition of activity primitives by a graph. Nodes in the video graph correspond to video features (e.g., KLT tracks of Harris corners [1]). Their neighbor relationships in space and time are captured

A. Fitzgibbon et al. (Eds.): ECCV 2012, Part II, LNCS 7573, pp. 130–143, 2012.

by the graph's adjacency matrix, also referred to as video matrix. We posit that video graphs representing instances of an activity class are probabilistically sampled from a generative model-graph of the activity. Nodes of this model-graph represent the activity primitives. Their probabilistic affinities for recursive grouping into video features are captured by the affinity matrix, also referred to as initiator matrix. As an operator for generating video graphs from the model-graph, we use the Kronecker product. Specifically, the grouping of the activity primitives is formulated as a successive Kronecker-multiplication of the initiator matrix. Consequently, the resulting video matrices can be viewed as stochastic realizations of a Kronecker-power of the initiator matrix.

We learn the model-graph of the activity under weak supervision. From the above, the goal of our learning is to discover the set of activity primitives, and estimate their affinities from a set of training video graphs. The goal of our inference is to identify a subset of primitives, and how they have recursively grouped so as to generate the observed video features. In this paper, we exploit the structure of the Kronecker power of a matrix to specify memory- and time-efficient inference and learning algorithms that take linear time in the number of video features.

Our results demonstrate good scalability on the benchmark UCF50 dataset, as well as superior performance to that of the state of the art on individual, structured, and collective activities in UCF YouTube, Olympic, and Collective datasets.

Related Work – We are not aware of any work in computer vision that uses Kronecker graphs to represent images or videos. The most related to ours is the work on modeling video segmentation graphs for activity recognition by an archetype graph, whose inference and learning are formulated as a weighted least squares estimation [2]. Their model, however, is not compact, requiring the numbers of model nodes and edges to exceed those found in the segmentation graphs of training videos. By contrast, our generative model-graph stores only the affinity matrix of a relatively small number of activity primitives. Other related work has focused on 2D shape recognition by modeling image graphs with mixture of trees [3], generative Delaunay graph [4], and tree-union [5]. Kronecker graphs have been successfully used for modeling social networks [6]. This line of work, however, focuses on modeling *local* structural properties of a *single* large social network (e.g., shrinking node diameter, densification power law, etc.). They do not need to make a distinction between two distinct sets of nodes representing foreground and background. Our model-graph, instead, is aimed at capturing both local and global space-time relations captured by a set of video graphs. Also, we need to take into account that only a subset of nodes in each video graph represent foreground. A compact generative model, called video epitomes, has been used for video super-resolution and video interpolation [7]. Similar to our activity primitives, the epitomes compactly capture the essence of a large number of space-time cubes from training videos. Related is also the action-bank representation of activities [8]. However, this approach requires a manual specification of the bank of elementary actions, and their detectors, instead of automatically discovering activity primitives.

While recent work typically focuses on a particular type of activities [9] — in particular, on single-actor punctual and repetitive activities [10–12], or exclusively on activities with distinct temporal structure [2,13–15], or exclusively on collective activities [16,17]

— we present a unified framework that is capable of addressing all these activity types in challenging, realistic (YouTube) videos.

Overview – Our approach consists of three computational modules: feature extraction, inference, and learning. *Feature extraction:* Given a video, motion features are extracted in the form of trajectory snippets, which can be either KLT tracks of Harris corners [1], or Lagrangian particle trajectories [18]. These features have been demonstrated by prior work as robust against many challenges of real-world videos, including large variations in camera motions, object pose and scale, and illumination. The neighboring tracks are then linked in the video graph. *Inference:* Our inference identifies the activity whose model-graph most likely generated foreground features of the video. Specifically, inference estimates correspondences between nodes of the activity model and nodes of the video graph in two steps. Given a model-graph, we first apply the Kronecker product to its initiator matrix a number of times. This results in a Kronecker-power matrix, whose random permutations of rows and columns are taken as the adjacency matrix of the video graph. Second, we find the expected correspondences between the Kronecker-power matrix, and the video's adjacency matrix via summing out the random permutations. This immediately estimates the subset of activity primitives, and the way they have recursively combined so as to generate the observed video features. *Learning:* Given a set of graphs representing training videos of an activity class, we learn a model-graph that most likely generated the training graphs. The three-fold goal of learning is to estimate: i) initiator matrix, ii) number of times the Kronecker product needs to be successively applied to the initiator matrix to generate the training graphs, and (iii) optimal correspondences (i.e., permutations) between the Kronecker-power of the initiator matrix, and the adjacency matrices of the training video graphs.

In the sequel, Sec. 2 reviews main properties of the Kronecker product, Sec. 3 formalizes our activity model, Sec. 4 presents our inference and its complexity, Sec. 5 specifies our learning algorithm, Sec. 6 describes our feature extraction, and Sec. 7 presents our experimental evaluation.

2 A Brief Review of the Kronecker Product

This section closely follows the review presented in [6], for completeness. Our activity model is characterized by the initiator square matrix Θ of size $N \times N$, whose elements θ_{ij} take values in $[0, 1]$. Θ is used to recursively construct a sequence of $N^k \times N^k$ matrices $\{\Theta^{[k]} : k = 2, ..., K\}$, where $\Theta^{[K]}$ is taken as a random permutation of the adjacency matrix of the video graph. The sequence $\{\Theta^{[k]}\}$ is produced by a successive application of the Kronecker product to Θ, as specified in the following two definitions.[1]

Def. 1: The Kronecker product of an $n \times m$ matrix $A = [a_{ij}]$ and $n' \times m'$ matrix B is the $(n \cdot n') \times (m \cdot m')$ matrix $C = A \otimes B = \begin{bmatrix} a_{11}B \; ... \; a_{1m}B \\ ... \\ a_{n1}B \; ... \; a_{nm}B \end{bmatrix}$.

Def. 2: The kth Kronecker power of matrix Θ is matrix $\Theta^{[k]} = \Theta^{[k-1]} \otimes \Theta$.

[1] For simplicity, we use a single Θ. This can be trivially extended by using a number of distinct initiator matrices of different sizes, which can be Kronecker-multiplied to obtain $\Theta^{[k]}$.

Since $\Theta \in [0,1]^{N\times N}$, the Kronecker power matrix $\Theta^{[k]} \in [0,1]^{N^k\times N^k}$ can be viewed as encoding a probability distribution of Bernoulli edges in an ensemble of graphs $\{\mathcal{G}\}$ with N^k nodes, as explained in Sec. 3. Suppose that $\{\mathcal{G}\}$ represent video graphs of activity instances. Then, every $\mathcal{G}$ can be probabilistically sampled from $\Theta^{[k]}$ by including edges between nodes u and v in $\mathcal{G}$ with corresponding probabilities $\theta^{[k]}_{uv}$.

The structure of the Kronecker product allows for an efficient computation of each element $\theta^{[k]}_{uv}$ in $O(k)$ time, as follows. Let us look at a relationship between rows of Θ and rows of $\Theta^{[k]}$. Define u, v as the indices of rows of $\Theta^{[k]}$, $u = 1, ..., N^k$ and $v = 1, ..., N^k$. Then, from Def. 1 and Def. 2, every row u of $\Theta^{[k]}$ can be described with a sequence $(u_1, \ldots, u_l, \ldots, u_k)$ of rows l of Θ, where $u_l \in \{1, ..., N\}$, $l = 1, ..., k$. Similarly, another row v of $\Theta^{[k]}$ corresponds to the sequence $(v_1, \ldots, v_l, \ldots, v_k)$ of rows of Θ, where $v_l \in \{1, ..., N\}$, $l = 1, ..., k$. It follows that the probability that edge (u, v) is present in $\mathcal{G}$ is computed as $\theta^{[k]}_{uv} = \prod_{l=1}^{k} \theta_{u_l v_l}$, which can be equivalently expressed as the following $O(k)$ time computation:

$$\theta^{[k]}_{uv} = \prod_{l=0}^{k-1} \theta_{\mathrm{mod}_N(\frac{u-1}{N^l})+1, \mathrm{mod}_N(\frac{v-1}{N^l})+1}, \quad u = 1, ..., N^k,\ v = 1, ..., N^k. \quad (1)$$

From the above, observable features of a video graph, represented as nodes of $\mathcal{G}$, can be interpreted as ordered sequences of activity primitives. Since nodes u of $\mathcal{G}$ can be described by sequences of rows of Θ, $(u_1, ..., u_k)$, we can view the rows of Θ as encoding the activity primitives. From such an interpretation, elements θ_{ij} of Θ can be viewed as probabilistic affinities between primitives i and j. This is because the probability of an edge in $\mathcal{G}$, $\theta^{[k]}_{uv}$, is computed as a product of k elements θ_{ij}, as in (1). Thus, the greater the affinities θ_{ij}, the larger the linking probability $\theta^{[k]}_{uv}$. In addition, our use of the successive Kronecker products of Θ for generating $\mathcal{G}$ can be interpreted as an effective encoding of both homophily and heterophily of the primitives. For homophily, pairs of nodes (u, v) in $\mathcal{G}$ described by similar sequences of the primitives, $(u_1, ..., u_k)$ and $(v_1, ..., v_k)$, are more likely to link in $\mathcal{G}$ when Θ has high value elements on the main diagonal. For heterophily, pairs of nodes in $\mathcal{G}$ with different sequences of the primitives are more likely to link in $\mathcal{G}$ when Θ has high value elements off the main diagonal.

3 The Model

This section extends the Kronecker graph model presented in [6] by explicitly accounting for a video's foreground and background. We assume that the space-time domain of a video, $\mathcal{D}$, is partitioned into foreground and background, $\mathcal{D} = \mathcal{D}_{\text{fg}} \cup \mathcal{D}_{\text{bg}}$, and $\mathcal{D}_{\text{fg}} \cap \mathcal{D}_{\text{bg}} = \emptyset$. $\mathcal{D}_{\text{fg}}$ is represented by a graph, $\mathcal{G} = (V, E)$, where V is a set of nodes corresponding to foreground video features and $|V| = N^k$, and E is a set of edges capturing neighbor relationships of foreground features and $|E| \ll N^{2k}$. We say that $\mathcal{G}$ explains the foreground, $\mathcal{D}_{\text{fg}} = \mathcal{D}(\mathcal{G})$, where every node $v \in V$ explains the corresponding foreground video part, $\mathcal{D}_{\text{fg}} = \cup_{v\in V}\mathcal{D}_v$. Let $p(\mathcal{D}_{\text{fg}}|\mathcal{G})$ denote the foreground likelihood. Also, let $q(\mathcal{D}_{\text{bg}})$ denote a generic pdf of background, made implicit in our derivation. Then, the likelihood of the video data can be defined as

$$p(\mathcal{D}|\mathcal{G}) = p(\mathcal{D}_{\text{fg}}|\mathcal{G})q(\mathcal{D}_{\text{bg}})\frac{q(\mathcal{D}_{\text{fg}})}{q(\mathcal{D}_{\text{fg}})} = q(\mathcal{D})\frac{p(\mathcal{D}_{\text{fg}}|\mathcal{G})}{q(\mathcal{D}_{\text{fg}})} = q(\mathcal{D})\prod_{v\in V}\frac{p(\mathcal{D}_v|\mathcal{G})}{q(\mathcal{D}_v)}. \quad (2)$$

In (2), each ratio $\frac{p(\mathcal{D}_v|\mathcal{G})}{q(\mathcal{D}_v)} = \psi(\boldsymbol{x}_v)$ can be viewed as a confidence of a foreground-background classifier (i.e., detector) applied to a descriptor vector $\boldsymbol{x}_v$ of video features extracted from domain $\mathcal{D}_v$.

Following the formalism of [6], given the $N \times N$ initiator matrix Θ, our generative model-graph assigns the likelihood $p(\mathcal{G}|\Theta)$ to the video graph $\mathcal{G}$. To define $p(\mathcal{G}|\Theta)$, we use the following generative process. We first Kronecker-multiply Θ to create an $N^k \times N^k$ Kronecker power matrix $\Theta^{[k]}$, as described in Sec. 2. Elements of $\Theta^{[k]}$ are viewed as probabilities of the presence of corresponding edges in $\mathcal{G}$. Since the assignment of node IDs in $\mathcal{G}$ is arbitrary, it is necessary to explicitly account for the permutation π that maps rows and columns of the adjacency matrix of $\mathcal{G}$ to the rows and columns of $\Theta^{[k]}$. Specifically, edges $(u,v) \in E$ are modeled as independent Bernoulli random variables, parameterized by the corresponding elements $\theta^{[k]}_{\pi_u\pi_v}$ of $\Theta^{[k]}$, where π_u denotes uth element of random permutation π. Thus, the likelihood of $\mathcal{G}$ is

$$p(\mathcal{G}|k,\Theta,\pi) = \prod_{(u,v)\in E} \theta^{[k]}_{\pi_u\pi_v} \prod_{(u,v)\notin E} (1-\theta^{[k]}_{\pi_u\pi_v}). \tag{3}$$

From (2) and (3), we define the joint pdf of $\mathcal{D}$ and $\mathcal{G}$ as

$$p(\mathcal{D},\mathcal{G}|k,\Theta) = q(\mathcal{D}) \prod_{v\in V} \psi(\boldsymbol{x}_v) \sum_\pi \prod_{(u,v)\in E} \theta^{[k]}_{\pi_u\pi_v} \prod_{(u,v)\notin E} (1-\theta^{[k]}_{\pi_u\pi_v}) p(\pi). \tag{4}$$

We assume that a priori all model-data correspondences are equally likely, i.e., the prior distribution $p(\pi)$ is uniform.

From (4), the model of each activity class $a \in \mathcal{A}$ is defined by (ψ_a, Θ_a, k_a).

4 Inference

Suppose we are given a video showing an activity class, $a^* \in \mathcal{A}$, whose model-graph has initiator matrix, Θ_{a^*}, of size $N_{a^*} \times N_{a^*}$. The $N^k_{a^*}$ foreground features of the video form a spatiotemporal configuration $\mathcal{G}_{a^*}$. Edges of $\mathcal{G}_{a^*}$ are sampled from the Kronecker power matrix $\Theta^{[k]}_{a^*}$ under a random permutation. Our inference evaluates the joint log-pdf of $\mathcal{D}$ and $\mathcal{G}_a$, given by (4), for all activity models $\{(\psi_a, \Theta_a, k_a) : \forall a \in \mathcal{A}\}$, and selects the activity a^* which gives the highest joint log likelihood:

$$a^* = \arg\max_{a\in\mathcal{A}} \Big[\sum_{v\in V_a} \log \psi_a(\boldsymbol{x}_v) + \log \sum_\pi p(\mathcal{G}_a|k_a,\Theta_a,\pi)p(\pi) \Big]. \tag{5}$$

From (5), inference consists of two computational stages, summarized in Alg. 1 and Alg. 2. The first stage identifies $\mathcal{G}_a$ using the first term in (5), while the second stage evaluates the likelihood of edges present in $\mathcal{G}_a$ using the second term in (5).

In the first stage of inference, for a particular activity a, we apply its foreground-background detector, ψ_a, to all features extracted from the video, as explained in Sec. 6. Then, the N^k_a most confident foreground features are taken to form the set of nodes V_a of $\mathcal{G}_a$. Inference accounts for their confidences via the term $\sum_{v\in V_a} \log \psi_a(\boldsymbol{x}_v)$ in (5). A subset of node pairs $(u,v) \in V_a \times V_a$ representing neighboring video features are then linked to form the set of edges E_a of $\mathcal{G}_a$.

In the second stage of inference, we estimate the likelihood $\sum_\pi p(\mathcal{G}_a|k,\Theta_a,\pi)p(\pi)$. To this end, we use the standard Markov Chain Monte Carlo (MCMC) simulation, as explained next.

4.1 Probabilistic Sampling of Permutations

In this section, we drop the subscript a in notation, implying that inference is conducted for a particular activity model. As in [6], we use the standard Metropolis-Hastings (MH) algorithm to sample permutations $\{\pi^{(\tau)} : \tau = 1, ..., T\}$. These sample permutations are then used to compute the second term in (5) as

$$\sum_{\pi} p(\mathcal{G}|k, \Theta, \pi)p(\pi) \approx \tfrac{1}{T} \sum_{\tau=1}^{T} p(\mathcal{G}|k, \Theta, \pi^{(\tau)}). \tag{6}$$

In each iteration τ, MH samples $\pi^{(\tau)}$ from the posterior distribution

$$p(\pi|\mathcal{G}, k, \Theta) = \frac{p(\mathcal{G}, k, \Theta, \pi)}{\sum_{\pi'} p(\mathcal{G}, k, \Theta, \pi')} = \frac{p(\mathcal{G}|k, \Theta, \pi)p(k, \Theta)p(\pi)}{\sum_{\pi'} p(\mathcal{G}, k, \Theta, \pi')}. \tag{7}$$

This generates a Markov chain in which state $\pi^{(\tau+1)}$ depends only on the previous state $\pi^{(t)}$. The MH jumps between the states are reversible, and governed by a proposal distribution, which we assume is uniform. The proposal to jump from $\pi^{(\tau)}$ to $\pi^{(\tau+1)}$ is accepted if the acceptance rate, $\alpha \sim U[0, 1]$, satisfies

$$\begin{aligned} \alpha &< \min\left\{1, \tfrac{p(\pi^{(\tau+1)}|\mathcal{G},k,\Theta)}{p(\pi^{(\tau)}|\mathcal{G},k,\Theta)}\right\} = \min\left\{1, \tfrac{p(\mathcal{G}|k,\Theta,\pi^{(\tau+1)})}{p(\mathcal{G}|k,\Theta,\pi^{(\tau)})}\right\} \\ &= \min\left\{1, \frac{\prod_{(u,v)\in E} \theta^{[k]}_{\pi_u^{(\tau+1)}\pi_v^{(\tau+1)}} \prod_{(u,v)\notin E} \left(1-\theta^{[k]}_{\pi_u^{(\tau+1)}\pi_v^{(\tau+1)}}\right)}{\prod_{(u,v)\in E} \theta^{[k]}_{\pi_u^{(\tau)}\pi_v^{(\tau)}} \prod_{(u,v)\notin E} \left(1-\theta^{[k]}_{\pi_u^{(\tau)}\pi_v^{(\tau)}}\right)}\right\}, \end{aligned} \tag{8}$$

where the priors $p(k, \Theta)$, $p(\pi)$, and $\sum_{\pi'} p(G, k, \Theta, \pi')$ cancel out.

We expect that there will be a relatively small number of permutations yielding high values of $p(\mathcal{G}|k, \Theta, \pi)$. To avoid sampling zero-likelihood permutations, as in [6], we design a Markov chain which would stay longer in a high-likelihood region of the permutation space. The Markov chain ensures that the MH jumps remain reversible. To this end, we select an edge in $\mathcal{G}$ uniformly at random, and swap the IDs of its two nodes. Note that this is biased toward swapping IDs of nodes with high degrees, since they have more edges in $\mathcal{G}$. This is suitable, since such nodes represent foreground video features co-occurring with many other foreground features, resulting in a more accurate sampling of permutations over foreground features, as desired. The balance condition of reversible MH jumps holds as graph edges are sampled uniformly at random. We call this procedure Swap2Nodes($\mathcal{G}$).

4.2 Reducing Complexity of Inference

Following the derivation of [6], evaluation of (8) and (6) can be made both computationally and memory efficient.

First, for memory efficiency, we do not store the adjacency matrix $\Theta_a^{[k]}$ for each activity a. Instead, we store only the initiator matrices Θ_a, $\forall a \in \mathcal{A}$, which have significantly smaller sizes $N_a \times N_a$. Consequently, every time the Bernoulli probability $\theta_{uv}^{[k]}$ is needed in (8) and (6), we use (1), which takes $O(k)$ time.

Second, note that in (8) permutations $\pi^{(\tau)}$ and $\pi^{(\tau+1)}$ differ only at two positions. This means that most terms in (8) cancel out, except for edges where $(\pi_u^{(\tau)}, \pi_v^{(\tau)}) \neq (\pi_u^{(\tau+1)}, \pi_v^{(\tau+1)})$. This makes complexity of sampling T permutations $O(Tk)$.

Third, to compute (6), there is no need to evaluate every $p(\mathcal{G}|k, \Theta, \pi^{(\tau)})$ anew, for $\tau = 1, ..., T$. Instead, from (3), it suffices to compute the initial likelihood $p(\mathcal{G}|k, \Theta, \pi^{(1)})$, and then to update the subsequent likelihoods, by traversing two rows and columns of matrix $\Theta^{[k]}$, for edges where $(\pi_u^{(\tau)}, \pi_v^{(\tau)}) \neq (\pi_u^{(\tau+1)}, \pi_v^{(\tau+1)})$.

What remains to be explained is the complexity of evaluating $p(\mathcal{G}|k, \Theta, \pi^{(1)})$. A naive evaluation of (3), which considers all N^{2k} node pairs in $\mathcal{G}$, takes $O(kN^{2k})$. Instead, as in [6], we first calculate the likelihood $p(\overline{\mathcal{G}}|k, \Theta, \pi)$ for an empty graph $\overline{\mathcal{G}}$ with the same number of nodes as $\mathcal{G}$ but zero edges, and then correct for the edges that appear in $\mathcal{G}$. From (3), and using the Taylor approximation $\log(1-x) \approx -x - \frac{1}{2}x^2$, it is straightforward to derive that $\log p(\overline{\mathcal{G}}|k, \Theta, \pi) = \sum_{u=1}^{N^k} \sum_{v=1}^{N^k} \log(1 - \theta_{\pi_u \pi_v}^{[k]}) \approx -(\sum_{i,j=1}^{N} \theta_{ij})^k - \frac{1}{2}(\sum_{i,j=1}^{N} \theta_{ij}^2)^k$. The Taylor approximation of $\log p(\overline{\mathcal{G}}|k, \Theta, \pi)$ reduces complexity from $O(kN^{2k})$ to $O(kN^2)$. Then, we account for edges in $\mathcal{G}$ as

$$\log p(\mathcal{G}|k, \Theta, \pi) \approx -(\sum_{i,j=1}^{N} \theta_{ij})^k - \frac{1}{2}(\sum_{i,j=1}^{N} \theta_{ij}^2)^k + \sum_{(u,v)\in E} \left(\log \theta_{\pi_u \pi_v}^{[k]} - \log(1 - \theta_{\pi_u \pi_v}^{[k]})\right). \tag{9}$$

From (9), computing $p(\mathcal{G}|k, \Theta, \pi)$ takes $O(k|E|)$. In comparison with the naive approach (3), the approximation in (9) is efficient, since $\mathcal{G}$ is typically sparse, $|E| \ll N^{2k}$.

In summary, inference has complexity $O(k(T + |E|))$. As the number of edges in $\mathcal{G}$ is of the same order as the number of nodes, inference is linear in the number of extracted video features. Inference is summarized in Alg. 1 and Alg. 2.

Algorithm 1. Inference

Input: Models $\{(\psi_a, \Theta_a, k_a) : a \in \mathcal{A}\}$;
Descriptors of video features $\{\boldsymbol{x}_v\}$
Output: Activity a^*; Foreground $\mathcal{G}_{a^*}$

for $a \in \mathcal{A}$ **do**
  Detect foreground features $\{\psi_a(\boldsymbol{x}_v)\}$;
  Form $\mathcal{G}_a$ from N_a^k most confident foreground features;
  Sample permutations $\{\pi^{(\tau)}\}$ as in Alg. 2;
  Compute $\frac{p(\mathcal{D}, \mathcal{G}_a | k_a, \Theta_a)}{q(\mathcal{D})}$ in (4) using (6);
end
Find a^* using (5);

Algorithm 2. MCMC

Input: Initiator matrix Θ; video graph $\mathcal{G}$;
number of iterations T
Output: Permutations $\{\pi^{(\tau)}:\tau=1, \ldots, T\}$

Initialize random node IDs $\pi^{(1)}$;
Compute $p(\mathcal{G}|\Theta, \pi^{(1)})$ using (9) and (1);
for $\tau = 1 : T - 1$ **do**
  repeat
    Sample $\pi^{(\tau+1)}$ by Swap2Nodes($\mathcal{G}$);
    Sample $\alpha \sim U[0, 1]$;
    Update the ratio in (8);
  until $\alpha <$ *The ratio in (8)* ;
end

5 Learning

Suppose we are given a set of graphs $\mathbb{G} = \{\mathcal{G}_t = (V_t, E_t) : t = 1, 2, ...\}$, representing foreground features of training videos of an activity class. We assume that $\forall t$, $|V_t| =$

N^k, for a positive integer k. For now, we will assume that N and k are known, and then later relax this assumption. The goal of learning is to estimate an $N \times N$ initiator matrix Θ. We learn Θ by maximizing the log-likelihood of the training graphs, $\Theta^* = \arg\max_\Theta L_\Theta$, where $L_\Theta = \sum_{t=1}^{T} \log\left[\sum_\pi p(\mathcal{G}_t|k,\Theta,\pi)p(\pi)\right]$. Thus, we extend the learning of Θ^* from a single network, presented in [6], to learning from a set of graphs. We compute the gradient of L_Θ as

$$\frac{\partial L_\Theta}{\partial \Theta} = \sum_t \frac{\sum_\pi \frac{\partial p(\mathcal{G}_t|k,\Theta,\pi)}{\partial \Theta} p(\pi)}{\sum_\pi p(\mathcal{G}_t|k,\Theta,\pi)p(\pi)} = \sum_t \sum_\pi \frac{\partial \log p(\mathcal{G}_t|k,\Theta,\pi)}{\partial \Theta} p(\pi|k,\mathcal{G}_t,\Theta). \tag{10}$$

Note that (10) has a convenient form that allows for the MCMC sampling of permutations, $\pi^{(\tau)}$, τ=1,...,T, as in Alg. 2, and estimating $\frac{\partial L_\Theta}{\partial \Theta} \approx \sum_t \frac{1}{T} \sum_{\tau=1}^{T} \frac{\partial \log p(\mathcal{G}_t|k,\Theta,\pi^{(\tau)})}{\partial \Theta}$.

To compute $\partial \log p(\mathcal{G}_t|k,\Theta,\pi^{(\tau)})/\partial\Theta$, we use the Taylor approximation given by (9). From (9), this gradient entails computing $\frac{\partial \log \theta_{uv}^{[k]}}{\partial \theta_{ij}}$ for all pairs of activity primitives i and j, where $i, j \in \{1, ..., N\}$, and for all ordered sequences $u = (u_1, \ldots, u_l, \ldots, u_k)$ and $v = (v_1, \ldots, v_l, \ldots, v_k)$, where $u_l, v_l \in \{1, ..., N\}$ (see Sec. 2). Let f_{ij}^{uv} denote a frequency that the pair of activity primitives i and j appear in the pair of ordered sequences u and v, where $\exists l$, $u_l = i$ and $v_l = j$. Then, we derive that $\frac{\partial \log \theta_{uv}^{[k]}}{\partial \theta_{ij}} = \frac{f_{ij}^{uv}}{\theta_{ij}}(\frac{1}{1-\theta_{uv}^{[k]}})$. This closed-form solution of $\partial \log p(\mathcal{G}_t|k,\Theta,\pi^{(\tau)})/\partial\Theta$ allows efficient computation of the gradient for a given permutation $\pi^{(\tau)}$.

As explained in Sec. 4.2, we efficiently compute $\partial \log p(\mathcal{G}_t|k,\Theta,\pi^{(\tau)})/\partial\Theta$ over a number of probabilistically sampled permutations by exploiting the fact that two consecutive permutations $\pi^{(\tau)}$ and $\pi^{(\tau+1)}$ differ only at two positions. Thus, given the gradient $\partial \log p(\mathcal{G}_t|k,\Theta,\pi^{(\tau)})/\partial\Theta$, we account for the swap of the two rows and columns of $\Theta^{[k]}$, and thus only update the gradients of these individual parameters in $\partial \log p(\mathcal{G}_t|k,\Theta,\pi^{(\tau+1)})/\partial\Theta$. Since the space of permutations on N^k nodes is $(N^k)!$, we will be able to explore only a small fraction of that space, and thus may converge to a local maximum. As we empirically show in Sec. 7, we are not sensitive to this: multiple restarts result in equivalent estimates of Θ^* (permuted).

Next, we consider how to determine k and N, and thus the right size of matrix Θ. As in [6], we use the standard Bayes Information Criterion (BIC). This is justified because, our likelihood $p(\mathcal{G}|k,\Theta,\pi)$ is an exponential 1 family distribution, for which BIC holds. Since the categorical number of our model parameters is N^{2k}, BIC$(N,k) = -L_{\Theta_N^*} + \frac{1}{2}N^2 \log N^{2k}$. As most model-selection methods, we exhaustively examine the values $N = 4:10$, and $k = 2:6$, and find the minimum BIC(N^*, k^*) with the best tradeoff between model complexity and quality of the fit.

6 Feature Extraction

This section presents our feature extraction. Since our focus here is on modeling a spatiotemporal graph of video features – not on particular features – we use two recent, easy-to-implement approaches that were thoroughly evaluated in the literature [1, 18].

Our first approach uses KLT tracks of Harris corners [1]. The KLT tracks are described using the standard, log-polar, 24-bin, Shape Context (SC) descriptor. We break each track into a number of consecutive, straight-line fragments connecting high-curvature points of the track. The number of line fragments is automatically estimated, so that an average error of the piece-wise linear approximation of a track is sufficiently low ($\epsilon \leq 2$ pixels). For example, for a KLT track of length 50 frames, the approximation typically yields 10–20 straight line fragments (or just 1, when the KLT track is a straight line). The orientation and magnitude of the motion vector along each fragment is then encoded into one of 24 bins of the SC.

Our second approach uses Lagrangian particle (LP) trajectories of the foreground motions in the video [18]. The LP tracks are obtained by advecting dense optical flow over time. They capture the ensemble motions of a scene, including both camera-induced and object-induced components. The LP tacks that correspond to moving objects are separated from those arising from the camera motion using a low rank optimization, presented in [18]. The resulting LP tacks of moving objects are described using a descriptor of the chaotic invariants [18], aimed at encoding underlying dynamics of each track. These descriptors are then clustered with K-means, and the clusters' centroids are taken as the representative LP trajectories.

We associate with the extracted track-based features descriptor vectors $\mathcal{X} = \{\boldsymbol{x}_z : z = 1, 2, ...\}$. The tracks are classified as belonging to the foreground or background (see Sec. 3) with a linear SVM, $\psi_a(\boldsymbol{x}_z)$, with the complexity parameter $C = 1$. The SVM is learned on tracks that fall within annotated bounding boxes in training videos for each activity class $a \in \mathcal{A}$. Note that our feature extraction is simpler than that of recent methods, e.g., [11] ([16]), which run part-based person or object detectors (or sophisticated multi-target trackers), and then use detector responses (or multi target tracks) as input for activity recognition.

The margin-based confidence of the linear SVM is used to select a total of $N_a^{k_a}$ most confident foreground features, and link them into a video graph, $\mathcal{G}_a = (V_a, E_a)$ for activity class $a \in \mathcal{A}$. An edge $(u, v) \in E_a$ links the corresponding foreground tracks if they are neighbors in the space-time volume of the video. We say that the tracks are neighbors in two cases: if they overlap in time (i.e., co-occur in some of their subintervals), or follow each other by δ frames. We empirically set $\delta = 5$ to handle accidental breaks of tracks due to noise. This produces a sparse graph $\mathcal{G}_a$ where the number of edges $|E_a|$ is of the order of $|V_a| = N_a^{k_a}$.

7 Results

Evaluation is conducted on collective activities and individual activities.

The collective activities dataset[2] consists of videos showing six activity classes: Crossing, Waiting, Queuing, Talking, Dancing, and Jogging. This dataset tests our performance on the behaviors of groups of people under realistic conditions, including background clutter, and mutual occlusions of actors. For training and testing, we use the standard split of $2/3$ and $1/3$ of the videos from each class, respectively. Labels of

[2] http://www.eecs.umich.edu/vision/activity-dataset.html

every 10th frame are provided in terms of bounding boxes around people performing the activity, their pose, and activity class.

UCF-YT, UCF50: UCF-YT[3] and UCF50[3] show punctual or repetitive activities occurring in challenging YouTube videos with large variations in camera motion, object appearance and pose, object scale, viewpoint, cluttered background, and illumination. UCF-YT consists of 1600 videos, of approximately 150 frames each, showing 11 activity classes (mostly various sports). There are about 100 clips per action. We use the recommended split of UCF-YT into 2/3 training set and 1/3 test set [11], as well as Leave-One-Out (LOO) validation. UCF50 consists of 6685 videos of 50 activity classes, mostly including sports activities. Each activity is represented by more than 100 videos. For training and testing on UCF50, we use 2/3 and 1/3 of the videos from each class, respectively.

Olympic dataset [14] consists of 50 YouTube videos for each of 16 activity classes. Each activity represents a temporal sequence of primitive activities (e.g., running, jumping, landing, and standing-up). As in [14], we use 80% of videos from the dataset for training, and the rest for testing. Challenges of this dataset arise from very similar, and thus hard-to-discriminate temporal structures of the activity classes.

Metrics: We evaluate video classification accuracy on all datasets, and recall and precision of localizing foreground video parts on the Collective dataset. Localization error is estimated only on accurately classified instances. A true positive is declared if the intersection of a bounding box that we place around detected foreground features, and the ground-truth bounding box is larger than 50% of their union.

Variants: To evaluate sensitivity to certain design choices, we define Var0 as our default approach, and then make changes in one computational step at a time, resulting in variants Var1 and Var2. Var0 uses Lagrangian particle (LP) tracks as features (Sec. 6), and a linear SVM to classify the tracks as foreground or background, where the SVM is learned on the annotated foreground tracks of training videos. For UCF-YT and UCF50, we train the SVM on "positive" tracks that fall in a bounding box centered at the image center, since the datasets do not provide ground-truth bounding boxes of activities. Typically, we extract on the order of 10^3 foreground features. From our experiments, this preprocessing step is sufficiently reliable to yield a high recall of true foreground tracks. On all Collective videos, the SVM gives on average 82.4% recall and 32.7% precision of foreground LP tracks. This preprocessing result is improved by our inference in Alg. 1. Fig. 1 illustrates the results of foreground (magenta) vs. background (cyan) classification of LP tracks in an example frame from a Kayaking video of UCF50 (only a subset of LP tracks is shown for visibility). The white bounding box in Fig. 1 encloses all tracks estimated as foreground. As can be seen, this preprocessing step is capable of addressing very challenging YouTube videos with large camera motions, and dynamic backgrounds. In learning and inference, Var0 samples $T = 10^4$ permutations. Fig. 2 shows how Alg. 1 maximizes the log-likelihood in (9), for 10 restarts, on an example Kayaking video from UCF50. As can be seen, multiple restarts of sampling permutations result in the same, accurate inference. We empirically observe the same trend across all datasets used. Even in cases when restarts yield different log-likelihoods, the highest log-likelihood value typically gives accurate classification. Since our learning

[3] http://vision.eecs.ucf.edu/datasetsActivities.html

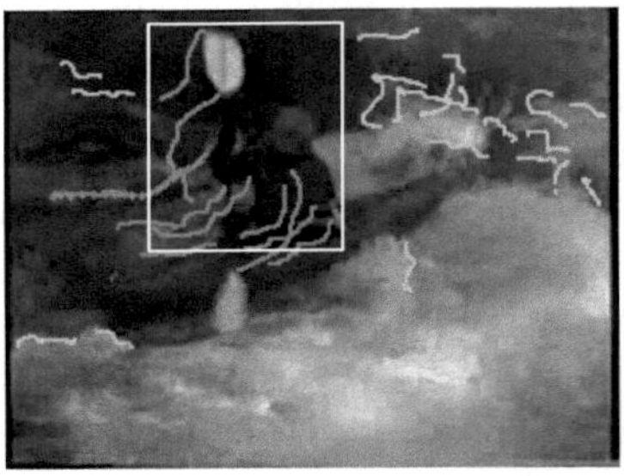

Fig. 1. UCF50 Kayaking: SVM detection of foreground (magenta) and background (cyan) LP tracks; only a subset of LP tracks is shown for clarity

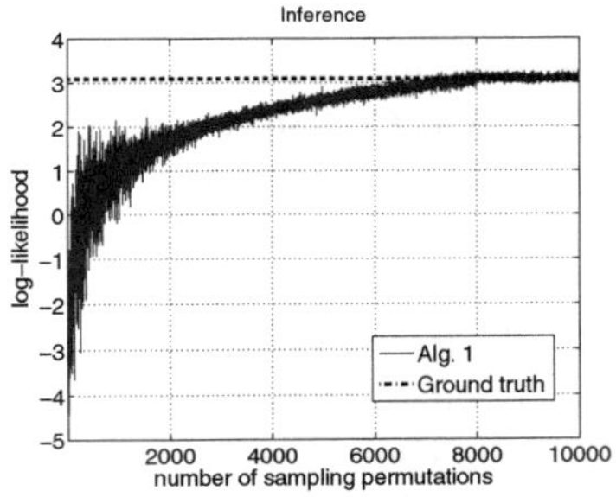

Fig. 2. 10 restarts of Alg. 1 for the video shown in Fig. 1

uses the same Alg. 2, we also empirically observe that multiple restarts of learning in most cases yield the same model parameters Θ. Var1 uses KLT tracks as features. Var2 does not classify tracks into foreground and background, but constructs the video graph from all features.

Quantitative Results: On UCF50, Var0 achieves $81.03 \pm 4.7\%$ average per-class accuracy, demonstrating our scalability, i.e., that we can successfully handle a large number of activity classes, under extreme YouTube conditions. We outperform the $76.2 \pm 11.7\%$ average per-class accuracy of the action-bank approach [8]. This improvement is significant, considering that [8] uses a manually specified bank of elementary actions, whose detector responses are more sophisticated features than our LP tracks.

In Tab. 3, we compare our performance on UCF-YT with the state of the art [10, 12], using the standard LOO validation, as well as with [11] using their setup of 2/3–1/3 dataset split for training and testing. Tab. 3 also shows the performance of Global bag-of-words—a baseline that uses an SVM classifier on the global histogram of STIP codewords [19]. As can be seen in Tab. 3, Var0 outperforms Var1, suggesting that the LP tracks and associated descriptors are better low-level video representation than KLT tracks for our approach. Also, classifying features into foreground and background yields more than 4% gain in accuracy relative to Var2 where this classification is not done. Var0 outperforms the state of the art by more than 5% in LOO setting, and 8% in the dataset-split setting. Also, all our variants are superior to existing methods, which suggests that the main power of our approach does not come from particular features used, or their preprocessing, but from the Kronecker graph modeling of activities.

Tab. 5 shows our superior performance to [2, 14, 19] on Olympic videos. Both Tab. 3 and Tab. 5 demonstrate that we are effective at classifying individual activities with complex temporal structures in unscripted real-world video.

Tab. 4 presents Var0's confusion table on Collective. Our mean per-class accuracy is $90.57 \pm 3.6\%$, which improves the recent $82.0 \pm 6.4\%$ accuracy of [16]. This improvement is significant, considering that [16] uses part-based people detections as input to their MRF-based approach, which are more sophisticated features than our LP tracks.

Fig. 6 illustrates our localization results on two example videos from the Collective dataset. Fig. 7 shows that Var0 achieves the average precision of 69.5% and recall of

Fig. 3. Average per-class accuracy in [%] on UCF-YT for LOO validation, and 2/3–1/3 dataset split

Method	Accuracy LOO	Accuracy Splits
Var0	$\mathbf{92.1 \pm 1.4}$	$\mathbf{86.8 \pm 2.2}$
Var1	88.4 ± 1.8	83.9 ± 2.6
Var2	89.0 ± 1.9	82.6 ± 1.9
[11]	83.7	78.6
[12]	N/A	76.5
[10]	87.3	N/A
global BOW	81.9	63.1

Fig. 4. Confusion table of Var0's accuracy in [%] on Collective activities

	Cross	Wait	Queue	Talk	Dance	Jog
Cross	86.87	3.15	0	0	0	9.98
Wait	2.08	89.09	8.02	0	0.82	0
Queue	0	13.10	86.90	0	0	0
Talk	0.59	3.03	3.33	93.04	0	0
Dance	6.73	2.29	0.67	0	90.31	0
Jog	2.76	0	0	0	0	97.24

Fig. 5. Classification accuracy in [%] on Olympic data

Sport	Var0	[2]	[14]	[19]
high-jump	79.1	75.8	68.9	52.4
long-jump	81.4	78.6	74.8	66.8
triple-jump	72.3	69.7	52.3	36.1
pole-vault	86.2	85.5	82.0	47.8
g-vault	92.2	89.4	86.1	88.6
shot-put	74.3	65.9	62.1	56.2
snatch	83.3	72.1	69.2	41.8
clean-jerk	91.3	86.2	84.1	83.2
javelin	86.7	77.8	74.6	61.1
hammer	81.2	79.4	77.5	65.1
discus	72.3	62.2	58.5	37.4
diving-pl.	90.2	89.9	87.2	91.5
diving-sp.	89.1	82.2	77.2	80.7
basketball	88.3	79.7	77.9	75.8
bowling	85.9	78.7	72.7	66.7
tennis	73.2	63.8	49.1	39.6
Average	**82.9**	77.3	71.1	62.0

76.2% at the point of equal error rate on Collective dataset. This ROC plot is generated by manually varying the number of most confident foreground features, N^k, selected to form the video graph $\mathcal{G}$ in inference. The use of the learned N and k values gives average precision of 72.8% and recall of 70.3%. This suggests that Alg. 1 conservatively selects low-level features toward improving precision of activity localization.

Running Time: The computation time of our MATLAB implementation of inference is less than 15s on an Intel Core i7-2600, 8GB RAM PC on UCF-YT videos, for $T = 10^4$, $N = 7$, $k = 4$. Our learning additionally optimizes over $N = 4 : 10$, and thus has the computation time of about 20min for 100 training videos from UCF-YT.

8 Conclusion

Capturing spatiotemporal layouts of video features has been argued as instrumental for accurate activity recognition. While graph based representations are capable of effectively encoding feature layouts, they are typically not suitable for applications with stringent requirements in terms of time complexity and scalability. This is typically due to their prohibitively expensive inference and learning. In this paper, we have addressed this fundamental problem by exploiting the recursive structure of human activities.

We have formulated an activity as a spatiotemporal layout of ordered sequences of activity primitives. The primitives are stochastically grouped into ordered sequences to generate observable video features. Such a formulation is fundamentally efficient in both memory and time, because videos of activity instances can be compactly represented by a relatively small set of activity primitives, their probabilistic affinities for

Fig. 6. Examples of Crossing and Waiting from the Collective activities dataset. A subset of foreground (magenta) and background (cyan) KLT tracks is shown for clarity. The bounding box encloses the estimated foreground.

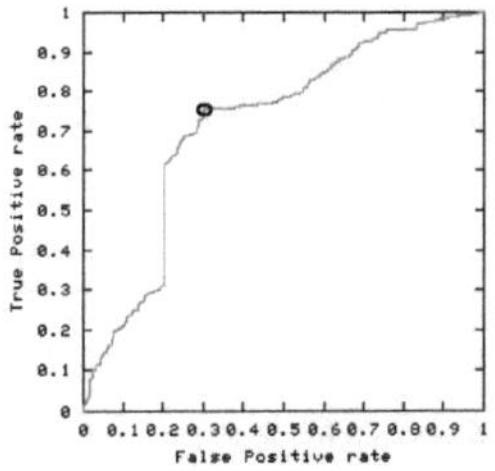

Fig. 7. Average ROC on Collective dataset with marked equal error rate

grouping into video features, and the grouping operator. We have used the Kronecker product as the grouping operator. Building upon recent work on modeling social networks [6], we have exploited the structure of the Kronecker product to specify the inference and learning algorithms with linear-time complexity in the number of video features.

Our formulation has enabled detection and localization of different types of activities — including individual, structured, and collective activities — within a unified framework. This advances prior work which typically addresses only a single activity type. Our results demonstrate good scalability and superior performance to that of the state of the art on benchmark datasets, including UCF50, UCF YouTube, Olympic, and Collective activities datasets. Evaluation of our design choices suggests that the main power of our approach does not come from particular features used, or their preprocessing, but from the compositional modeling of activities, operationalized by the Kronecker product.

Acknowledgement. The support of the National Science Foundation under grant NSF IIS 1018490 is gratefully acknowledged.

References

1. Messing, R., Pal, C., Kautz, H.A.: Activity recognition using the velocity histories of tracked keypoints. In: ICCV (2009)
2. Brendel, W., Todorovic, S.: Learning spatiotemporal graphs of human activities. In: ICCV (2011)
3. Torsello, A., Hancock, E.R.: Learning shape-classes using a mixture of tree-unions. IEEE TPAMI 28, 954–967 (2006)
4. Torsello, A.: An importance sampling approach to learning structural representations of shape. In: CVPR (2008)
5. Todorovic, S., Ahuja, N.: Unsupervised category modeling, recognition, and segmentation in images. IEEE TPAMI 30, 1–17 (2008)
6. Leskovec, J., Chakrabarti, D., Kleinberg, J.M., Faloutsos, C., Ghahramani, Z.: Kronecker graphs: An approach to modeling networks. Journal of Machine Learning Research 11, 985–1042 (2010)
7. Cheung, V., Frey, B.J., Jojic, N.: Video epitomes. IJCV 76, 141–152 (2008)

8. Sadanand, S., Corso, J.J.: Action bank: A high-level representation of activity in video. In: CVPR (2012)
9. Aggarwal, J.K., Ryoo, M.S.: Human activity analysis: A review. ACM Comput. Surv. 43, 16:1–16:43 (2011)
10. Kovashka, A., Grauman, K.: Learning a hierarchy of discriminative space-time neighborhood features for human action recognition. In: CVPR (2010)
11. Lan, T., Wang, Y., Mori, G.: Discriminative figure-centric models for joint action localization and recognition. In: ICCV (2011)
12. Bhattacharya, S., Sukthankar, R., Jin, R., Shah, M.: A probabilistic representation for efficient large scale visual recognition tasks. In: CVPR (2011)
13. Gupta, A., Srinivasan, P., Shi, J.B., Davis, L.S.: Understanding videos, constructing plots learning a visually grounded storyline model from annotated videos. In: CVPR (2009)
14. Niebles, J.C., Chen, C.-W., Fei-Fei, L.: Modeling Temporal Structure of Decomposable Motion Segments for Activity Classification. In: Daniilidis, K., Maragos, P., Paragios, N. (eds.) ECCV 2010, Part II. LNCS, vol. 6312, pp. 392–405. Springer, Heidelberg (2010)
15. Pei, M., Jia, Y., Zhu, S.-C.: Parsing video events with goal inference and intent prediction. In: ICCV (2011)
16. Choi, W., Shahid, K., Savarese, S.: Learning context for collective activity recognition. In: CVPR (2011)
17. Lan, T., Wang, Y., Yang, W., Robinovitch, S., Mori, G.: Discriminative latent models for recognizing contextual group activities. IEEE TPAMI (2011)
18. Wu, S., Oreifej, O., Shah, M.: Action recognition in videos acquired by a moving camera using motion decomposition of Lagrangian particle trajectories. In: ICCV (2011)
19. Laptev, I., Marszalek, M., Schmid, C., Rozenfeld, B.: Learning realistic human actions from movies. In: CVPR (2008)

Facial Action Transfer with Personalized Bilinear Regression

Dong Huang and Fernando De La Torre

Robotics Institute, Carnegie Mellon University

Abstract. Facial Action Transfer (FAT) has recently attracted much attention in computer vision due to its diverse applications in the movie industry, computer games, and privacy protection. The goal of FAT is to "clone" the facial actions from the videos of one person (source) to another person (target). In this paper, we will assume that we have a video of the source person but only one frontal image of the target person. Most successful methods for FAT require a training set with annotated correspondence between expressions of different subjects, sometimes including many images of the target subject. However, labeling expressions is time consuming and error prone (i.e., it is difficult to capture the same intensity of the expression across people). Moreover, in many applications it is not realistic to have many labeled images of the target. This paper proposes a method to learn a personalized facial model, that can produce photo-realistic person-specific facial actions (e.g., synthesize wrinkles for smiling), from **only** a neutral image of the target person. More importantly, our learning method does not need an explicit correspondence of expressions across subjects. Experiments on the Cohn-Kanade and the RU-FACS databases show the effectiveness of our approach to generate video-realistic images of the target person driven by spontaneous facial actions of the source. Moreover, we illustrate applications of FAT to face de-identification.

Keywords: Facial action transfer, Bilinear regression.

1 Introduction

Facial Action Transfer (FAT) from a source person to a target person (from which we only have one image) has attracted much attention in computer vision and computer graphics due to its increasing number of applications. Beyond the film making industry, such technology is also applicable to preserve privacy of subjects in video (i.e., face de-identification) [1,2], online image and video collections [3], and virtual avatars [4]. A major challenge of FAT is to transfer subtle facial actions from the source to the target to create video-realistic outputs. Throughout the paper we will refer to this problem as FAT instead of facial expression transfer to emphasize that our method is able to deal with subtle and spontaneous facial movement, rather than only imitating some predefined expressions (e.g., happy, sad, disgust) [5,6].

There are four major challenges on FAT: (1) Typically, the facial structure (shape) and texture (appearance) of the source and target subjects are quite different, as well as the dynamics of the facial actions. There are person-specific facial features in the source images (e.g., glasses, freckles, wrinkles, eyelashes) that the target person might not have. Directly copying the shape and appearance changes from the source to the target (e.g., [7]) can result in artifacts in the rendered target person. (2) Although

A. Fitzgibbon et al. (Eds.): ECCV 2012, Part II, LNCS 7573, pp. 144–158, 2012.

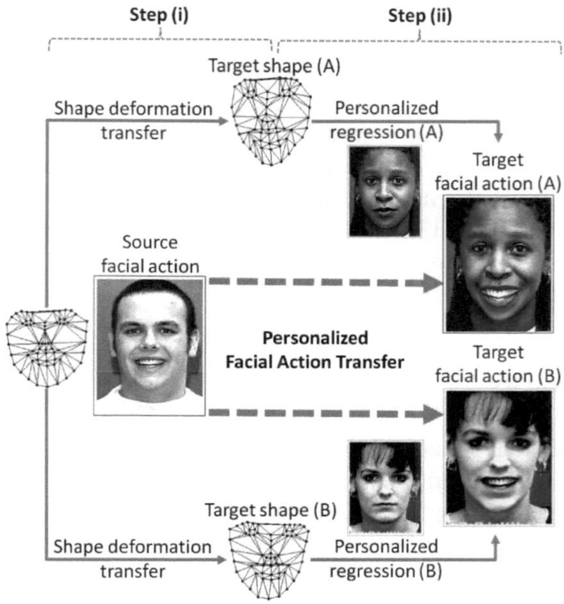

Fig. 1. Overview of our personalized FAT method. The facial action of the source person (a smile) is transferred to both subjects (A) and (B) in two steps: (i) Shape deformation transfer, where the shape change of the source w.r.t. his neutral face is transferred to the targets; (ii) Generate the appearance changes using personalized bilinear regression. Observe how the wrinkles of the smile are adapted (i.e. personalized) to subject (A) and (B).

shape deformation transfer has been successfully applied to computer graphics problems [8,9,10,11], transferring the appearance/texture remains an unsolved problem due to the high dimensionality of the image data and potential nonlinearity of the facial actions. (3) An ideal algorithm should be able to factorize identity, expression and pose changes. However, this factorization is very difficult in practice, because the facial motions are combinations of the movement of facial muscles, head motion and person-specific features. Moreover, existing methods that decouple identity from expression (e.g., tensor and regression based methods [12,13,14,5,6]) require correspondences across predefined expressions (e.g., happy, sad, disgust) for different subjects. Labeling the correspondence of facial expressions across subjects is time-consuming and error prone. Even if all subjects are instructed to pose with the same expression, they cannot perform the facial action with exactly the same style and intensity. (4) In real world scenarios (e.g., interviews, movies), facial behaviors are spontaneous and usually combined with pose changes. The complexity of these facial actions are beyond the representation ability of predefined expressions (e.g., happy, sad, disgust) that could be posed and labeled in controlled environments.

To solve these problems, this paper proposes a two-step approach for FAT (see Fig. 1). In the first step, our method transfers the shape of the source person to the target subject (A) and (B) using the triangle-based deformation transfer method [10]. In the second step, our method generates the appearance of the target person using a personalized mapping from shape changes to appearance changes. Our main hypothesis is that the physical structure of the face (e.g., bones, muscles and skin) defines a consistent and measurable pattern that relates the movements (shape changes) of facial components to the appearance changes [15] for a particular person. Based on this intuition, our method learns a bilinear regression between the shape and appearance changes from training images. A major contribution of this work is to personalize the shape-to-appearance regression with **only** one sample of the target subject. More importantly, unlike previous methods [12,13,14,4,5,6], **our learning method does not require the correspondence of expressions across training subjects**. Fig. 1 illustrates the main idea of our method.

2 Previous Works

Existing approaches to FAT can be broadly grouped into two categories: direct transfer methods and learning-based transfer methods.

Direct transfer methods copy the shape and/or appearance changes of the source person to the target face image. [8,9] represents the face by a densely partitioned triangle mesh, usually containing 10^4 triangles. The shape changes under a given expression are transferred to the target face as a set of local affine transformations while preserving the connectivity of the target triangles. These methods do not transfer appearance changes. Liu et al. [7] proposed a geometric warping algorithm in conjunction with the Expression Ratio Image (ratio between the appearance of the neutral image and the image of a given expression) to copy subtle appearance details such as wrinkles and cast shadows to the target. This method tends to produce artifacts on the target face image since the appearance details to be transferred are not adapted to the target subject.

Learning-based FAT methods learn a transformation from a training set of face images that have been labeled across expressions. The correspondence is determined manually or semi-automatically [5,6,4,16]. Existing learning-based FAT can be broadly classified into two major approaches: the regression-based and tensor-based methods.

Regression-based methods include two modalities: (1) Regression between expressions [5,6] that learns a mapping from a reference expression (e.g., neutral) to the expressions to be transferred (e.g., smile). Given a reference face of a target person, the smile face of the target person can be predicted with the regression specifically learned for the smile expression. A major limitation of this method is its inability to represent untrained expressions. (2) Regression between subjects [4,16]. This method learns a mapping between multiple pairs of corresponding expressions performed by both the source and target subjects, and then uses the learned regression to transfer new expressions. In the case, that there are no corresponding images between expressions of different people, [4] generates the correspondent images by learning a regression from the neutral face to the pre-defined expression, similar to [5,6], and apply this mapping to the neutral of the target subject. In addition, [4] learns a generic regressor from the shape to the appearance. In our work, we extend this approach by personalizing the regressor using only one training sample, achieving a highly photo-realistic result. [16] learns two Active Appearance Models (AAMs), one for the source and one for the target. It performs FAT by learning a mapping between AMMs' coefficients. This method also requires solving for the correspondence between the expressions of the target and source, which is not possible in many realistic applications.

Tensor-based approaches [12,13,14] perform Higher-Order Singular Value Decomposition (HOSVD) to factorize the facial appearance into identity, expression, pose and illumination. Given the factorization, expression transfer [17,18,19] is done by first computing the identity coefficients of the new testing person, and then reassembling the identity factor with expression factors learned by the HOSVD. A major drawback of tensor-based approaches is the need of carefully labeled correspondences across expression, pose and illumination. [20,21] generalize the tensor-based approaches to build non-linear manifolds of human body actions and facial expressions. Similar to the standard tensor-based approaches, these methods require to solve for the correspondence of states on the manifold (content) across different subjects (style).

The existing learning-based FAT methods rely on the the availability and labeling accuracy of the similar expression in faces of different subjects. However, labeling expression is time consuming and error prone (i.e., it is hard to capture and solve correspondence for expressions under different intensities). In addition, in many applications it is not possible to have labeled training samples for the target. This paper proposes a more practical approach to FAT that does not require expression correspondence across subjects. Moreover, we are able to generate photo-realistic rendering using a personalized bilinear regression that only requires one frontal image of the target.

3 Personalized FAT

This section describes how to transfer the shape and appearance changes to achieve a personalized FAT method.

3.1 Transferring Shape Changes

Let $\mathbf{x}_i^{neu} \in \Re^{v \times 1}$ (see notation [1]) be a vector containing the two-dimensional coordinates of 66 landmarks ($v = 2 \times 66 = 132$) for the ith subject under the neutral expression ($i = 1, \cdots, p$) (see Fig. 1). By performing Delaunay triangulation using these landmarks, the face region is partitioned into 106 triangles. $\mathbf{X}_i^e = \{\mathbf{x}_i^{e_1}, \cdots, \mathbf{x}_i^{e_{n_i}}\} \in \Re^{v \times n_i}$ is a matrix that contains the landmark coordinates of the n_i face images for the ith subject performing different facial actions (i.e., subscript "e").

The first step to transfer shape changes is to compute the shape deformation from the neutral to the facial expression of the source subject. We used an affine transformation between triangles [10] (See Fig. 2). In the second step, we will transfer the triangle-wise shape transformation to the target subject.

The mapping between the neutral and a given facial expression of the source person (first step) is done as follows. Let the vectors $\{\mathbf{v}_{s_j}^{(1)}, \mathbf{v}_{s_j}^{(2)}, \mathbf{v}_{s_j}^{(3)}\} \in \Re^{2 \times 3}$ contain the

[1] Bold capital letters denote matrices $\mathbf{X}$, bold lower-case letters a column vector $\mathbf{x}$. $\mathbf{x}_j$ represents the jth column of the matrix $\mathbf{X}$. All non-bold letters represent scalar variables. $diag$ is an operator that transforms a vector to a diagonal matrix or takes the diagonal of the matrix into a vector. $vec(\cdot)$ vectorizes a matrix into a vector. $\mathbf{I}_k \in \Re^{k \times k}$ denotes the identity matrix. $\mathbf{1}_n \in \Re^n$ is a vector of all 1s. $vec(\mathbf{A})$ rearrange the elements of $\mathbf{A}$ in a vector. $\|\mathbf{x}\|_2$ denotes the L2-norm of the vector $\mathbf{x}$. $\|\mathbf{A}\|_F^2$ designates the Frobenious norm of matrix $\mathbf{A}$.

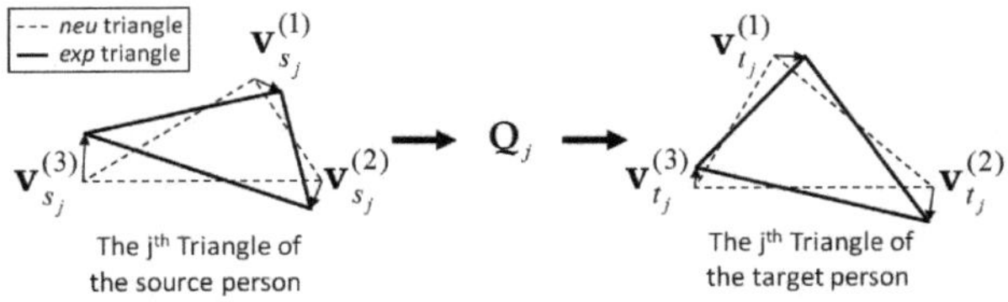

Fig. 2. Transfer shape changes for the jth triangle of the source person (with vertex $\{\mathbf{v}_{s_j}^{(1)}, \mathbf{v}_{s_j}^{(2)}, \mathbf{v}_{s_j}^{(3)}\}$) to the corresponding triangle of the target person (with vertex $\{\mathbf{v}_{t_j}^{(1)}, \mathbf{v}_{t_j}^{(2)}, \mathbf{v}_{t_j}^{(3)}\}$). The dash and thick edged triangles represent the neutral expression and other expression, respectively. $\mathbf{Q}_j$ is the affine transformation matrix to be transferred.

two dimensional coordinates of the three vertices for the jth triangle of the source person ($j = 1, \cdots, 106$). The matrix $\mathbf{V}_{s_j} = [\mathbf{v}_{s_j}^{(2)} - \mathbf{v}_{s_j}^{(1)}, \mathbf{v}_{s_j}^{(3)} - \mathbf{v}_{s_j}^{(1)}] \in \Re^{2\times 2}$ is the translation-free representation of this triangle. We compute the affine transformation $\mathbf{Q}_j \in \Re^{2\times 2}$ for the triangle from neutral to an expression by minimizing: $\min_{\mathbf{Q}_j} \left\|\mathbf{V}_{s_j}^{exp} - \mathbf{Q}_j\mathbf{V}_{s_j}^{neu}\right\|_F^2$, where $\mathbf{V}_{s_j}^{exp}$ and $\mathbf{V}_{s_j}^{neu}$ represent the jth triangle containing the landmarks of source facial expression to be transferred and the source neutral face, respectively.

After computing all triangle-wise shape changes between the neutral and a different expression of the source person, the next step is to transfer the shape changes to the target person. Let $\widetilde{\mathbf{X}}_t^e \in \Re^{2\times 66}$ be a rearranged version of the target shape vector $\mathbf{x}_t^e = vec(\widetilde{\mathbf{X}}_t^e) \in \Re^{132\times 1}$. Applying $\mathbf{Q}_j$'s individually to the target neutral shape might result in disconnected vertexes. To solve this problem, we jointly transfer the transformations by minimizing:

$$\min_{\mathbf{x}_t^e} \sum_{j=1}^{106} w_j \left\|\mathbf{V}_{t_j}^{exp} - \mathbf{Q}_j\mathbf{V}_{t_j}^{neu}\right\|_F^2, \tag{1}$$

where $\mathbf{V}_{t_j}^{exp} = \widetilde{\mathbf{X}}_t^e\mathbf{S}_j \in \Re^{2\times 2}$, $\mathbf{S}_j \in \Re^{66\times 2}$ is a matrix of elements $\{-1, 0, 1\}$ that transforms $\widetilde{\mathbf{X}}_t^e$ to a translation-free representation $\mathbf{V}_{t_j}^{exp}$ for the jth triangle, and w_j is the weighting coefficient proportional to the number of pixels within the jth triangle. Eq. (1) is a least-square problem and has a closed-form solution as:

$$\mathbf{x}_t^e = vec\left[\sum_{j=1}^{106} w_j\mathbf{Q}_j\mathbf{V}_{t_j}^{neu}\mathbf{S}_j^T\left(\sum_{l=1}^{106} w_l\mathbf{S}_l\mathbf{S}_l^T\right)^{-1}\right]. \tag{2}$$

3.2 Estimating Appearance Changes from Shape Changes

Once we have transferred the shape changes, our next step is to transfer appearance changes. We normalized the pixel intensity (appearance) of a face image by warping the pixels within each triangle to their corresponding pixels on a common template. $\mathbf{y}_i^{neu} \in \Re^{d\times 1}$ is the normalized appearance vector (d pixels) for the ith subject. $\mathbf{Y}_i^e = \{\mathbf{y}_i^{e_1}, \cdots, \mathbf{y}_i^{e_{n_i}}\} \in \Re^{d\times n_i}$ contains the appearance vectors for the n_i face images. Directly transferring appearance changes is extremely difficult due to the high dimensionality of the image data and potentially nonlinearity of the facial actions. This process typically produces unwanted artifacts (see Fig 5 "Copy"). A key observation is that there is a strong correlation between the shape changes and the appearance changes performed by the same person. Fig. 3 shows the projection onto the first three principal components of the shape and appearance for 4 sequences of the same person. The shape and appearance are projected independently, and then an affine transformation is computed to align shape to appearance. As we can observe (also numerically validated in Sec.4.1.), there is a strong correlation between shape and appearance, that allows us to predict the appearance from the shape. See caption of Fig. 3 for more details.

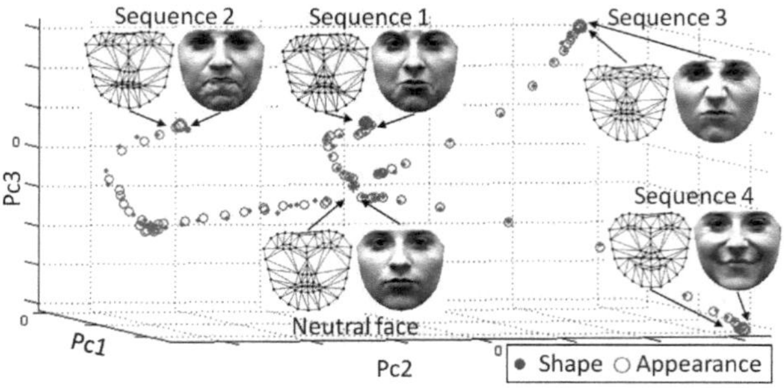

Fig. 3. Low dimensional embedding that shows the correlation between shape ("•") and appearance changes ("○") for four image sequences (82 face images in total) of subject "S014" in the Cohn-Kanade (CK) database [22]. The circles ("○") are the projections of appearance changes of each face image with respect to the neutral face ($\mathbf{y}^e - \mathbf{y}^{neu}$) along the first three principal components (denoted by axis Pc1-Pc3). The dots ("•") represent shape changes ($\mathbf{x}^e - \mathbf{x}^{neu}$) projected in the three principal components after linear regression (alignment) to ($\mathbf{y}^e - \mathbf{y}^{neu}$).

After transferring the shape changes to the target, and assuming that we have training samples of the target person, we could build a person-specific model by explicitly learning a mapping $\mathbf{T}$ between shape ($\mathbf{x}$) and appearance ($\mathbf{y}$) that minimizes:

$$\min_{\mathbf{T}} \sum_{e \in \Omega_i} \|(\mathbf{y}_i^e - \mathbf{y}_i^{neu}) - \mathbf{T}(\mathbf{x}_i^e - \mathbf{x}_i^{neu})\|_2^2, \tag{3}$$

where Ω_i is the index set of available instances of the ith subject performing different facial actions, $\mathbf{T} \in \Re^{d \times v}$ is the regression matrix that maps the displacement of facial landmarks to the change of pixel intensity. Solving Eq. (3) leads to a person-specific regression matrix $\mathbf{T}$. The column space of $\mathbf{T}$ correlates with the appearance changes and its row space with the shape changes of the ith subject.

In realistic scenarios, we will not have training samples of the target subject. An alternative is to learn a generic regression using images from the training subjects but ignoring images from the target subjects. However, as we will show in the experimental part, the learned generic regression can only predict the averaged appearance changes for all training subjects but it fails to model specific facial features from the target image. In addition, training instances would need to be well-sampled in order to generalize to all facial actions to be transferred. In the following section, we propose to personalize the mapping $\mathbf{T}$ given only a neutral face image of the target.

3.3 Personalizing the Regression

For the ith person ($i = 1, \cdots, p$), the person-specific mapping $\mathbf{T}_i \in \Re^{d \times v}$ minimizes

$$E(\mathbf{T}_i) = \|\mathbf{Y}_{\Delta i} - \mathbf{T}_i \mathbf{X}_{\Delta i}\|_F^2 = \left\|\mathbf{Y}_{\Delta i} - \mathbf{B}_i \mathbf{A}_i^T \mathbf{X}_{\Delta i}\right\|_F^2, \quad (4)$$

where $\mathbf{Y}_{\Delta i} = \mathbf{Y}_i - \mathbf{y}_i^{neu} \mathbf{1}_{n_i}^T \in \Re^{d \times n_i}$ and $\mathbf{X}_{\Delta i} = \mathbf{X}_i - \mathbf{x}_i^{neu} \mathbf{1}_{n_i}^T \in \Re^{v \times n_i}$ contain the appearance and shape changes w.r.t. the neutral face, for all images belonging to the ith person. To avoid the curse of dimensionality and reduce the amount of parameters to estimate, the row and column subspaces of $\mathbf{T}_i$ are explicitly modeled by the outer product of two matrices $\mathbf{T}_i = \mathbf{B}_i \mathbf{A}_i^T$ [5], so that the column space of $\mathbf{B}_i \in \Re^{d \times k}$ and $\mathbf{A}_i \in \Re^{v \times k}$ are respectively correlated with the shape and appearance subspace of this person ($k = rank(\mathbf{T}_i)$). A necessary condition for the existence of a minimum of E (in Eq. (4)) w.r.t. $\mathbf{B}_i$ and $\mathbf{A}_i$ has to satisfy $\frac{\partial E}{\partial \mathbf{B}_i} = \mathbf{0}$ and $\frac{\partial E}{\partial \mathbf{A}_i} = \mathbf{0}$, which leads to

$$\mathbf{B}_i = \mathbf{Y}_{\Delta i} \mathbf{X}_{\Delta i}^T \mathbf{A}_i (\mathbf{A}_i^T \mathbf{X}_{\Delta i} \mathbf{X}_{\Delta i}^T \mathbf{A}_i)^{-1}, \quad (5)$$

$$\mathbf{A}_i = (\mathbf{X}_{\Delta i} \mathbf{X}_{\Delta i}^T)^{-1} \mathbf{X}_{\Delta i} \mathbf{Y}_{\Delta i}^T \mathbf{B}_i (\mathbf{B}_i^T \mathbf{B}_i)^{-1}. \quad (6)$$

Eq. (5) and (6) imply that the columns of $\mathbf{B}_i$ and $\mathbf{A}_i$ are in the subspaces spanned by the appearance changes $\mathbf{Y}_{\Delta i}$ and the shape changes $\mathbf{X}_{\Delta i}$ respectively. If we solve Eq. (4) over all facial actions performed by the ith subject, the column spaces of $\mathbf{B}_i$ and $\mathbf{A}_i$ are optimized to capture the specific shape and appearance changes for this subject, respectively. However, as mentioned before the person-specific model is not available in many applications, and the generic model is not accurate enough. Our goal in this section is to personalize $\mathbf{B}_i$ and $\mathbf{A}_i$ using only one neutral face.

A key aspect to build a personalized model from one sample, is to realize that from a neutral image, we can predict many different facial expressions [5,6,4,16]. Observe that the neutral image has enough information to generate an approximation of the texture of a particular face under several expressions. That is, $\mathbf{Y}_{\Delta i} \approx [\mathbf{R}_1 \mathbf{y}_i^{neu} \ \cdots \ \mathbf{R}_n \mathbf{y}_i^{neu}]$, where $\mathbf{R}_i$ is a regressor for a particular expression ($i = 1, \cdots, n$). However, learning this expression-specific regressions requires carefully posed expressions and labeling expression across all subjects [5,6,4,16].

In this paper, we overcome this limitation by explicitly learning the mapping from the appearance and shape of a neutral face to the person-specific matrices $\mathbf{B}_i$ and $\mathbf{A}_i$ for all training subjects ($i = 1, \cdots, p$). Following recent work on subspace regression [23], we learn a mapping between a neutral face and a subspace of shape and appearance. That is, the person-specific subspace is parameterized as: $\mathbf{B}_i \approx [\mathbf{W}_1 \mathbf{y}_i^{neu} \cdots \mathbf{W}_k \mathbf{y}_i^{neu}]$, where $\mathbf{W}_k \in \Re^{d \times d}$. In practice the number of parameters for each $\mathbf{W}_k$ is large and some rank constraints have to be imposed to avoid overfitting. Alternatively, to solve this problem we kernealize the previous expression as: $vec(\mathbf{B}_i) \approx \mathbf{B} \varphi_y(\mathbf{y}_i^{neu})$, where $\mathbf{B} \in \Re^{dk \times w_y}$ is a transformation matrix, and $\varphi_y(\cdot) \in \Re^{w_y}$ is a kernel mapping of the neutral appearance from the d spaces to a w_y (possible infinite) dimensional space. Observe that, the columns of matrix $\mathbf{B}$ span the dk dimensional space of person-specific matrices $\mathbf{B}_i$'s that model possible appearance changes for all subjects ($i = 1, \cdots, p$). Similarly, $vec(\mathbf{A}_i) \approx \mathbf{A} \varphi_x(\mathbf{x}_i^{neu})$ where $\mathbf{A} \in \Re^{vk \times w_x}$ spans the vk dimensional spaces of person-specific matrices $\mathbf{A}_i$'s that model possible shape changes for all subjects ($i = 1, \cdots, p$), and $\varphi_x(\cdot) \in \Re^{w_x}$ is kernel mapping of the neutral shape.

As in traditional kernel methods, we will assume that the rows of the matrix $\mathbf{B}$ can be expanded as the combination of $\varphi_y(\mathbf{Y}^{neu})$, i.e., $\mathbf{B} = \mathbf{R}_B\varphi_y(\mathbf{Y}^{neu})^T$, where $\mathbf{R}_B \in \Re^{dk \times p}$ is a coefficient matrix and $\mathbf{Y}^{neu}$ contains all neutral appearances for $i = 1, .., p$. Similarly, the row vectors of $\mathbf{A}$ can be spanned by $\varphi_x(\mathbf{X}^{neu})$, i.e., $\mathbf{A} = \mathbf{R}_A\varphi_x(\mathbf{X}^{neu})^T$, where $\mathbf{X}^{neu}$ contains all neutral shapes. Using the kernel trick, we can re-write $\mathbf{B}_i$ and $\mathbf{A}_i$ in a more compact form as:

$$\mathbf{B}_i \approx \mathbf{T}_B(\mathbf{k}_{\mathbf{y}_i^{neu}} \otimes \mathbf{I}_k), \quad \mathbf{A}_i \approx \mathbf{T}_A(\mathbf{k}_{\mathbf{x}_i^{neu}} \otimes \mathbf{I}_k), \tag{7}$$

where $\mathbf{T}_B \in \Re^{d \times kp}$ contains re-organized elements of $\mathbf{R}_B$, $\mathbf{T}_A \in \Re^{v \times kp}$ contains re-organized elements of $\mathbf{R}_A$. $\mathbf{k}_{\mathbf{y}_i^{neu}} = \varphi(\mathbf{Y}^{neu})^T\varphi(\mathbf{y}_i^{neu}) \in \Re^p$ is the kernel vector measuring the similarity between the ith person with other subjects for the neutral appearance. Similarly, $\mathbf{k}_{\mathbf{x}_i^{neu}} = \varphi(\mathbf{X}^{neu})^T\varphi(\mathbf{x}_i^{neu}) \in \Re^p$ is the kernel vector measuring the similarity between the ith person with other subjects for neutral shapes.

Now we can rewrite the error in Eq. (4) by combining it with Eq. (7) as:

$$\min_{\mathbf{T}_B,\mathbf{T}_A} E(\mathbf{T}_B, \mathbf{T}_A) = \sum_{i=1}^{p} \left\|\mathbf{Y}_{\Delta i} - \mathbf{T}_B\mathbf{M}_i\mathbf{T}_A^T\mathbf{X}_{\Delta i}\right\|_F^2, \tag{8}$$

where $\mathbf{M}_i = (\mathbf{k}_{\mathbf{y}_i^{neu}} \otimes \mathbf{I}_k)(\mathbf{k}_{\mathbf{x}_i^{neu}} \otimes \mathbf{I}_k)^T \in \Re^{kp \times kp}$. To estimate $\mathbf{T}_B$ and $\mathbf{T}_A$, we use an alternated least square (ALS) method to monotonically reduce the error of E. ALS alternates between optimizing for $\mathbf{T}_A$ while $\mathbf{T}_B$ is fixed, and vice versa. This is guaranteed to converge to a critical point of E. The update equations for ALS are:

$$\mathbf{T}_B = \left(\sum_{i=1}^{p} \mathbf{Y}_{\Delta i}\mathbf{X}_{\Delta i}^T\mathbf{T}_A\mathbf{M}_i^T\right)\left(\sum_{i=1}^{p} \mathbf{M}_i\mathbf{T}_A^T\mathbf{X}_{\Delta i}\mathbf{X}_{\Delta i}^T\mathbf{T}_A\mathbf{M}_i^T\right)^{-1}, \tag{9}$$

$$vec(\mathbf{T}_A) = \left(\sum_{i=1}^{p} \mathbf{H}_i \otimes \mathbf{G}_i\right)^{-1} vec\left(\sum_{i=1}^{p} \mathbf{X}_{\Delta i}\mathbf{Y}_{\Delta i}^T\mathbf{T}_B\mathbf{M}_i\right), \tag{10}$$

where $\mathbf{H}_i = \mathbf{M}_i^T\mathbf{T}_B^T\mathbf{T}_B\mathbf{M}_i$ and $\mathbf{G}_i = \mathbf{X}_{\Delta i}\mathbf{X}_{\Delta i}^T$. Given an initial guess of $\mathbf{T}_B$ and $\mathbf{T}_A$, Eq. (9) and (10) are alternated until convergence.

For a new target person t, we represent the neutral face by the shape $\mathbf{x}_t^{neu}$ and appearance $\mathbf{y}_t^{neu}$, and compute the personalized regression matrices as $\mathbf{B}_t = \mathbf{T}_B(\mathbf{k}_{\mathbf{y}_t^{neu}} \otimes \mathbf{I}_k)$ and $\mathbf{A}_t = \mathbf{T}_A(\mathbf{k}_{\mathbf{x}_t^{neu}} \otimes \mathbf{I}_k)$. Given the target shape change transferred from the source (Section 3.1), the target appearance change $\mathbf{y}_{\Delta t}^e$ is predicted using the personalized bilinear regression as $\mathbf{y}_{\Delta t}^e = \mathbf{B}_t\mathbf{A}_t^T(\mathbf{x}_t^e - \mathbf{x}_t^{neu})$. Finally, the appearance vector of the target person under expression "e" is computed as $\mathbf{y}_t^e = \mathbf{y}_t^{neu} + \mathbf{y}_{\Delta t}^e$.

4 Experiments

This section provides quantitative and qualitative evaluation of our method on two challenging databases: **(1) Cohn-Kanade (CK) database** [22]: This database contains posed facial action sequences for 100 adults. There are small changes in pose and illumination in the sequences. Each person has several sequences performing different

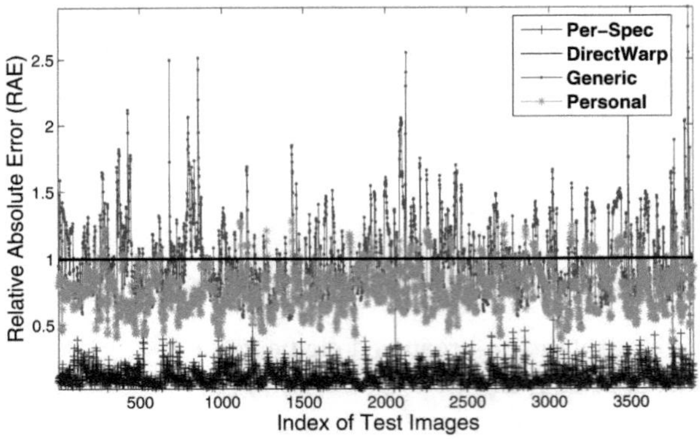

Fig. 4. Comparison of appearance reconstruction error over a random testing set from the CK database. RAE is computed for 4 methods: "Per-Spec", "Direct warp", "Generic" and our method "Personal". Note "Personal" uses only one neutral image per target subject.

expressions for about 20 frames, beginning at neutral and ending in the peak of the expression. We used 442 sequences posed by 98 persons for which the 66 landmarks per frame were available. The total number of images used in our experiments is 8036. **(2) RU-FACS database** [24]: This database consists of videos of 34 young adults recorded during an interview of approximately 2 minutes, duration in which they lied or told the truth in response to an interviewer's questions. Head pose was mostly frontal with small to moderate out-of-plane head motion. Image data from five subjects could not be analyzed due to image artifacts. Thus, image data from 29 subjects was used.

4.1 Reconstruction Ability of the Shape-to-Appearance Mapping

In the first experiment, we evaluated how well several shape-to-appearance mapping methods (Section 3.2 and 3.3) can reconstruct the facial appearance of subjects in the CK database. We compared the performance of four approaches: (1) "Generic" mapping, computed for all subjects similar to [4] as explained in Section 3.2; (2) Person-specific mapping ("Per-Spec"), where we learn a different regressor $\mathbf{T}_i$ for each subject (Eq. (4)); (3) Our personalized bilinear mapping ("Personal") estimated given only a neutral face of each person (Eq. (8)); (4) "Direct warp", which is the baseline method where we directly warped the pixels of neutral appearances $\mathbf{y}^{neu}$ to a common template. We computed the Relative Absolute Error (RAE) between the estimated and the ground truth appearances on the common template as: $RAE = \frac{|\mathbf{y}^{exp} - \tilde{\mathbf{y}}^{exp}|}{|\mathbf{y}^{exp} - \mathbf{y}^{neu}|}$, where $\tilde{\mathbf{y}}^{exp}$ is the

Table 1. Comparison of averaged RAE of appearances for four methods on CK database over 20 repetitions. Note "Per-Spec" reproduces the appearances of training images for each target subject while "Personal" predicts the appearances using only one neutral face per subject.

	Per-Spec	Direct warp	Generic	Personal (Our method)
RAE	$0.11 \pm 0.07\%$	$1 \pm 0\%$	$0.93 \pm 0.29\%$	$0.74 \pm 0.15\%$

estimated appearance and $\mathbf{y}^{exp}$ is the ground truth appearances. Observe that the baseline method ("Direct warp") produces the same appearance as the neutral face on the common template (i.e. $\widetilde{\mathbf{y}}^{exp} = \mathbf{y}^{neu}$) and its RAE is 1 for all images.

For each subject, we consider the neutral face as the average of the first frame over all the sequences (between 2 and 6) for each subject. We randomly selected half of the subjects (49) for training and cross-validation, and the other 49 subjects are used for testing. We used Gaussian kernels in Eq. (7) to respectively measure the similarity among neutral shapes and appearances. The bandwidth parameters for the neutral shape and appearance Gaussian kernel were chosen by cross-validation. We repeated the experiments 20 times. The average and standard deviation are summarized in Table 1. Fig. 4 shows an instance of the RAE on a randomly selected test set.

As shown in Fig. 4 and Table 1, the "Generic" mapping produces the largest error because it computes the averaged appearance changes which, in many cases, are not the appearances the target (test) subject can produce. As expected from Fig. 3, the "Per-Spec" method achieves the least error because it learns the person-specific regression using the data of this particular subject. This further validates the strong correlation between shape-appearance used in Sec.3.2. Note this is the ideal scenario, where we have images of the subject to train and test. Unfortunately, the "Per-Spec" mapping is typically not available in practice because of the lack of training samples for the target person (only one frontal image is available). Finally, our method ("Personal") produces lower RAE than the generic mapping using only a neutral face of each person.

4.2 Facial Action Transfer

This section presents qualitative (visual) evaluation for FAT on the CK database. Note that this is a different experiment from the one in the previous section. Now our goal is to transfer the expression to a different subject, and not to reconstruct the appearance from the shape of the same subject.

We used 49 subjects to learn the regressors as explained in the previous section. The other 49 subjects are used as target subjects. The source for these 49 targets are randomly selected from the other 49 training subjects. We transfer the facial actions of the source (Fig. 5 the "Source" column) to the target subjects. Fig. 5 shows the results for four methods: (1) Copying directly the shape and appearance changes from the source to the target similar to [7], the "Copy" column; (2) Person-specific mapping learned from available instances of each target person (for evaluation only, instances usually are not available in practice), the "Per-Spec" column; (3) The generic mapping computed for all training subjects [4], the "Generic" column; and (4) our personalized regression, estimated from a neutral face of the target, the last column: "Personal". Here we do not compare with "Direct warp" as in the previous subsection because it produces no appearance changes. The pixels within the mouth (e.g., teeth) in Fig. 5-7 are directly warped from the images of the source subject.

As shown in Fig. 5, the direct coping method ("Copy") does not adapt the expression changes of the source subjects to the specific facial features of the targets. It produced strong artifacts around eye brows, cheeks and jaws on the target faces. The person-specific method (the "Per-Spec" column) performed very well in reconstructing the appearance in the last experiment; however, it behaved poorly in the experiment of

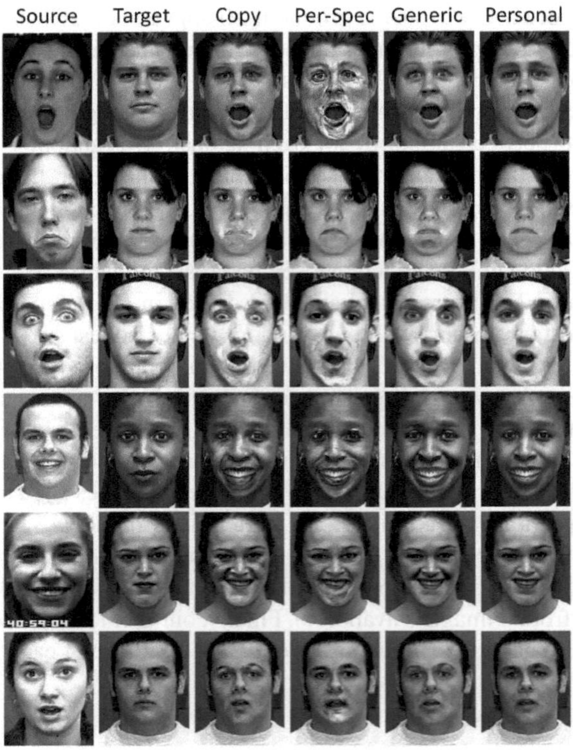

Fig. 5. Facial action transfer from the source persons (the "Source" column) to the target persons (the neutral faces in the "Target" column) using the direct copying ("Copy"), personal specific mapping ("Per-Spec"), the generic mapping ("Generic") and our method ("Personal")

transferring the expression. In this case, we learn the regression from shape to appearance using the video of the target person, but there is no guarantee that the expression performed by the source will be represented in the available data of the target person. This is the reason why the person-specific method performs poorly. In fact, it is usually difficult to get well-sampled instances of the target subject. The generic mapping ("Generic") generates averaged appearance changes, which in many cases does not fit the specific facial features of the target subjects. Our method ("Personal") estimates the personalized regression from only a neutral face of the target person, and it produces video-realistic personalized facial actions. Although the ground truth for the transferred expressions are not available, the result of our personal mapping is the one that is visually more video-realistic [2].

4.3 Face De-Identification

Advances in camera and computing equipment hardware in recent years have made it increasingly easy to capture and store extensive amounts of video data. This, among

[2] See more results at http://www.andrew.cmu.edu/user/dghuang/fat.htm

other things, creates many opportunities for the sharing of video sequences. In order to protect the privacy of subjects visible in the scene, automated methods to de-identify the images, particularly the face region, are necessary [1]. So far the majority of privacy protection schemes currently used in practice rely on ad-hoc methods such as pixelation or blurring of the face. This section explores the use of our method for face de-identification in real interviews when there is subtle, spontaneous facial expressions combined with pose changes using the RU-FACS database.

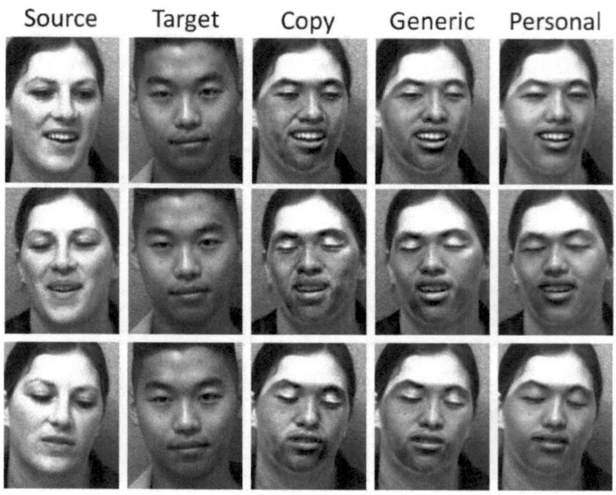

Fig. 6. Application of FAT to de-identification: replacing the identity of the source persons (the "Source" column) with that of the target person (the "Target" column) performing the same facial actions. Three methods compared: Direct copying ("Copy"), the generic mapping ("Generic") and our method ("Personal"). The "Copy" and "Generic" columns produce artifacts on the cheek, eyelids and around the mouth. To clearly illustrate the de-identified/replaced face region on the source images, we do not adapt the target skin to the source skin.

As shown in Fig. 6-7, we transferred the facial actions of the source person (the "Source" column) to the target person (the "Target" column), and then warped the transferred target facial image patch back to the image of the source person. In this way, we replaced the identity of the source person with the target person performing the same facial actions. Three methods compared are: Direct copying ("Copy"), the generic mapping ("Generic") and our method ("Personal"). For each pair of source and target persons in Fig. 6-7, we show three instances of de-identification including various head poses and subtle facial actions. In all the instances, both "Copy" and "Generic" generate exceptional bright or dark texture in cheeks, eyelids, jaw and eyebrows. This is because the shape and appearance changes imposed in those regions are not suitable for the target facial features. Using the personalized regression estimated from one target neutral face, our method ("Personal") produces the realistic personalized facial actions compatible with the target facial features such as eyes, nose, lips and the skin. We ex-

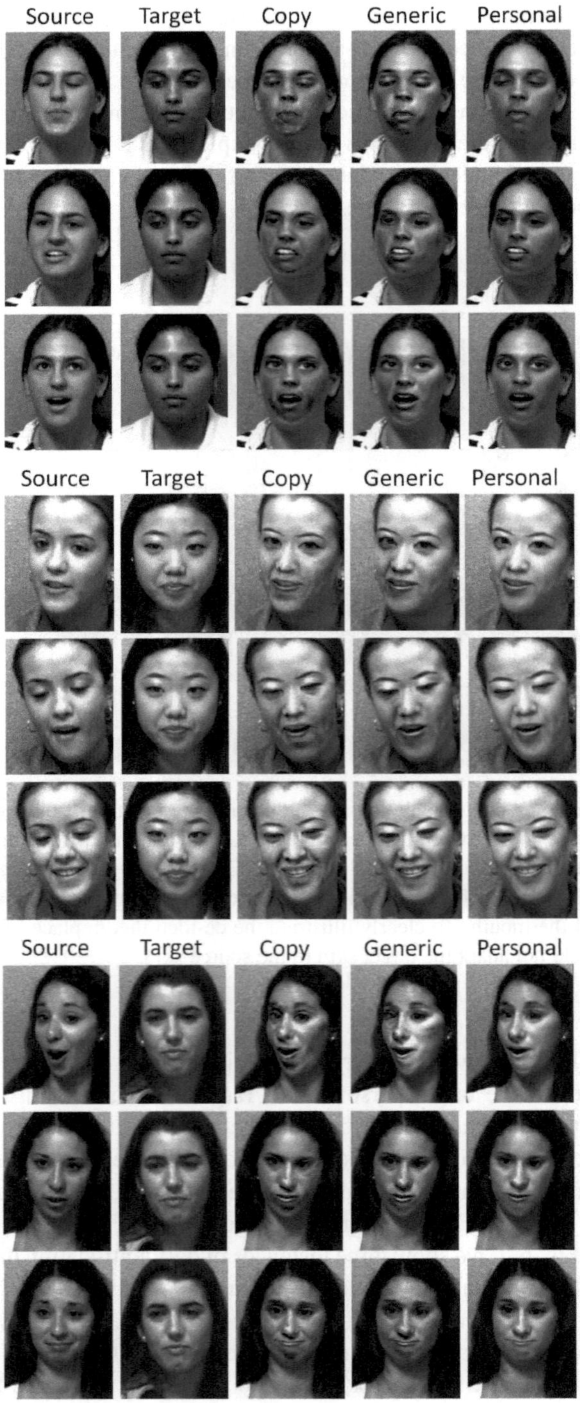

Fig. 7. Application of FAT to face de-identification (continued with Fig. 6). The "Copy" and "Generic" columns produce artifacts on the cheek, eyebrows and the jaw.

plicitly use a person of different color skin as target to illustrate the de-identification process.

5 Conclusion

This paper presents a personalized supervised bilinear regression method for FAT. We have illustrated how our algorithm can outperform state-of-the-art methods for generating video-realistic face images of a target subject from a source video. Moreover, we illustrated how our method can also be used for face de-identification in the challenging RU-FACS database. The main reason for the superior performance of our method is that is able to personalize the relation between the shape and appearance changes using only one target neutral face. This brings two main advantages: (1) Our learning method does not rely on expression correspondences which are difficult to obtain; (2) To transfer the facial actions to a new person, our method only requires the neutral face of the person, which is a realistic assumption in many scenarios. Further improvements of our method can be achieved by using local models for different face regions and better regression methods to model the relations between the bilinear regression matrices and the neutral face. Finally, although we have illustrated the benefits of our approach on the problem of FAT, our method is more general and can be applied to other appearence/texture synthesis problems.

References

1. Gross, R., Sweeney, L., De la Torre, F., Baker, S.: Model-based face de-identification. In: CVPR Workshop on Privacy Research in Vision (2006)
2. Frome, A., Cheung, G., Abdulkader, A., Zennaro, M.: B. Wu, A.B., Adam, H., Neven, H., Vincent, L.: Largescale privacy protection in google street view. In: ICCV (2009)
3. Senior, A. (ed.): Protecting Privacy in Video Surveillance. Springer (2009)
4. Saragih, J., Lucey, S., Cohn, J.: Real-time avatar animation from a single image. In: AFGR (2011)
5. Huang, D., De la Torre, F.: Bilinear Kernel Reduced Rank Regression for Facial Expression Synthesis. In: Daniilidis, K., Maragos, P., Paragios, N. (eds.) ECCV 2010, Part II. LNCS, vol. 6312, pp. 364–377. Springer, Heidelberg (2010)
6. Zhang, Q., Liu, Z., Guo, B., Shum, H.: Geometry-driven photorealistic facial expression synthesis. In: ACM SIGGRAPH/Eurographics Symposium on Computer Animation, pp. 177–186 (2003)
7. Liu, Z., Shan, Y., Zhang, Z.: Expressive expression mapping with ratio images. In: Ann. Conf. on Computer Graphics and Interactive Techniques (2001)
8. Noh, J., Neumann, U.: Expression cloning. SIGGRAPH, 277–288 (2001)
9. Chai, J., Xiao, J., Hodgins, J.: Vision-based control of 3d facial animation. In: Eurographics (2003)
10. Sumner, R., Popovic, J.: Deformation transfer for triangle meshes. SIGGRAPH 23, 399–405 (2004)
11. Anguelov, D., Srinivasan, P., Koller, D., Thrun, S., Rodgers, J., Davis, J.: Scape: shape completion and animation of people. SIGGRAPH 24, 408–416 (2005)
12. Vasilescu, M.A.O., Terzopoulos, D.: Multilinear Analysis of Image Ensembles: TensorFaces. In: Heyden, A., Sparr, G., Nielsen, M., Johansen, P. (eds.) ECCV 2002, Part I. LNCS, vol. 2350, pp. 447–460. Springer, Heidelberg (2002)

13. Tenenbaum, J., Freeman, W.: Separating style and content with bilinear models. Neural Computation 12, 1247–1283 (2000)
14. Wang, H., Ahuja, N.: Facial expression decomposition. In: ICCV (2003)
15. Chung, K.: Gross Anatomy (Board Review). Lippincott Williams & Wilkins, Hagerstown (2005)
16. De La Hunty, M., Asthana, A., Goecke, R.: Linear facial expression transfer with active appearance models. In: ICPR (2010)
17. Abboud, B., Davoine, F.: Appearance factorization for facial expression analysis. In: BMVC (2004)
18. Vlasic, D., Brand, M., Pfister, H., Popovic, J.: Face transfer with multiliner models. ACM Trans. Graphics 24, 426–433 (2005)
19. Macedo, I., Brazil, E., Velho, L.: Expression transfer between photographs through multilinear aam's. In: SIBGRAPI, pp. 239–246 (2006)
20. Elgammal, A., Lee, C.: Separating style and content on a nonlinear manifold. In: CVPR, pp. 478–485 (2004)
21. Wang, Y., Huang, X., Lee, C., Zhang, S., Li, Z., Samaras, D., Metaxas, D., Elgammal, A., Huang, P.: High resolution acquisition, learning and transfer of dynamic 3D facial expressions. Computer Graphic Forum 23, 677–686 (2004)
22. Kanade, T., Cohn, J.F., Tian, Y.: Comprehensive database for facial expression analysis. In: AFGR (2000)
23. Kim, M., Zhang, Z., De la Torre, F., Zhang, W.: Subspace regression: Predicting a subspace from one sample. In: Asian Conference on Computer Vision, ACCV (2010)
24. Bartlett, M., Littlewort, G., Frank, M., Lainscsek, C., Fasel, I., Movellan, J.: Automatic recognition of facial actions in spontaneous expressions. Journal of Multimedia 1, 22–35 (2006)

Point of Gaze Estimation through Corneal Surface Reflection in an Active Illumination Environment

Atsushi Nakazawa[1,2,*] and Christian Nitschke[1,*]

[1] Cybermedia Center, Osaka University
1-32 Machikaneyama, Toyonaka, Osaka 560-0032, Japan
{nakazawa,christian.nitschke}@cmc.osaka-u.ac.jp

[2] PRESTO, Japan Science and Technology Agency (JST)
4-1-8 Honmachi, Kawaguchi, Saitama 332-0012, Japan

Abstract. Eye gaze tracking (EGT) is a common problem with many applications in various fields. While recent methods have achieved improvements in accuracy and usability, current techniques still share several limitations. A major issue is the need for external calibration between the gaze camera system and the scene, which commonly restricts to static planar surfaces and leads to parallax errors. To overcome these issues, the paper proposes a novel scheme that uses the corneal imaging technique to directly analyze reflections from a scene illuminated with structured light. This comprises two major contributions: First, an analytic solution is developed for the forward projection problem to obtain the gaze reflection point (GRP), where light from the point of gaze (PoG) in the scene reflects at the corneal surface into an eye image. We also develop a method to compensate for the individual offset between the optical axis and true visual axis. Second, introducing active coded illumination enables robust and accurate matching at the GRP to obtain the PoG in a scene image, which is the first use of this technique in EGT and corneal reflection analysis. For this purpose, we designed a special high-power IR LED-array projector. Experimental evaluation with a prototype system shows that the proposed scheme achieves considerable accuracy and successfully supports depth-varying environments.

1 Introduction

Eye movements contribute a key part to the interpreting and understanding of a person's wishes, needs, tasks, cognitive processes, affective states, and interpersonal relations. As this information is relevant to a large number of applications in a variety of fields, eye gaze tracking (EGT) is a common problem with a long history [1]. These days, most popular and usable approaches are vision-based techniques [2]. This sort of systems employ an eye camera to capture a

* Both authors contributed equally to this work.

A. Fitzgibbon et al. (Eds.): ECCV 2012, Part II, LNCS 7573, pp. 159–172, 2012.

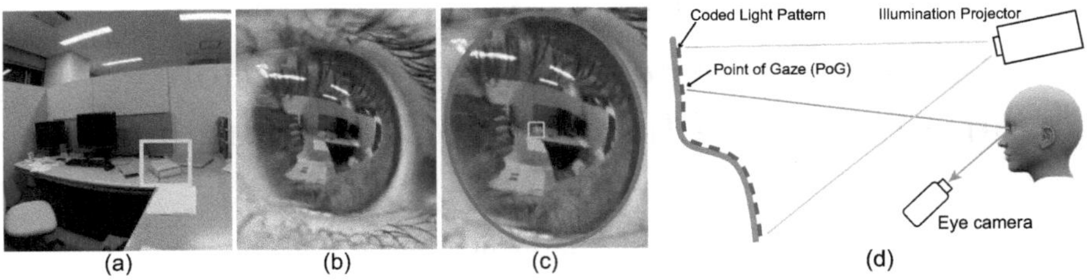

Fig. 1. Corneal reflection and point of gaze (PoG). (a) An environment image showing a book a person is looking at (yellow square). (b) A corresponding corneal reflection image. Note, that this picture is taken in a finely controlled setup, where the camera is placed relatively near to the eye. (c) Estimated iris contour (magenta ellipse) and gaze reflection point (GRP), where light from the PoG is reflected (yellow square). Here, we can see that the GRP coincides with the book. The proposed method analytically obtains the GRP based on a geometric eye model and a reflection model of the corneal surface. (d) A schematic illustration of the PoG estimation approach in an active illumination environment, where the scene is illuminated using coded structured light projection. This allows robust and accurate matching of the GRP in a corneal image to locate the corresponding PoG in a scene image, even from low quality eye images.

close-up view of a person's eye and estimate its pose w.r.t. the camera, then output the point of gaze (PoG) as a location in a planar scene or an image of the environment. For example, the pupil-center/corneal-reflection (PCCR) technique [3] obtains the pose of the eye using the center or contour of the pupil and corneal surface reflections (glints) from point light sources (usually IR LEDs). This technique is the foundation for many current EGT systems; however, it has two major drawbacks: First, mapping the pose of the eye to the PoG requires *system calibration* to obtain the geometric relationship between eye camera and scene. In remote systems, where the relationship is static, calibration determines the pose of the eye camera w.r.t. the scene. In mobile head-mounted systems, where the relationship is dynamic, calibration determines the pose of the eye camera w.r.t. an environment camera that points in the direction of the person's face. In either case, calibrations require a lot of setup effort. Second, due to the fundamental concepts in calculating the PoG, systems potentially suffer from a *parallax issue*. In remote systems the PoG is calculated as the intersection of the gaze ray and a scene model. Since such a model is usually difficult to obtain, systems restrict to simple target scenes like computer screens and walls, or provide functionalities of parallax compensation by manual specification of the scene depth. Moreover, this requires re-calibration when the configuration is changed. In mobile head-mounted systems the PoG is calculated by mapping the gaze ray to an image of the scene assuming a virtual 'calibration plane'. In either case, parallax errors occur under depth-varying scene conditions.

In this paper, we show a novel PoG estimation approach for remote and head-mounted systems that overcomes the issues using a *direct mapping* strategy (Fig. 1). Since the cornea of the human eye reflects the light from the surrounding environment, an image of the eye contains a reflected image of the scene. Using this observation, we calculate the pose of the eye and the corneal surface location, where light from the PoG reflects into the eye image. Directly matching at the reflected PoG, then, obtains the location of the PoG in an environment image. This approach solves the discussed issues and allows for dynamic depth-varying environments as it does not require any mapping functions.

Therefore, this work introduces two novel points: First, we find the so-called gaze-reflection point (GRP), where light from the PoG reflects at the corneal surface into the eye camera. This relates to the forward projection problem, for which Agrawal et al. recently derived a first analytic solution [4]. Unfortunately, their method is not applicable for this more general case, where the PoG is defined up to an unknown distance along the gaze ray. We, therefore, introduce a novel analytic method for obtaining the GRP based on a geometric eye model and a reflection model of the corneal surface. We further provide a one-point calibration technique that is required once per user, and largely increases accuracy by compensating for the individual offset between optical and visual axis in human vision. Second, we introduce the idea of using active coded illumination for robust and accurate correspondence matching between a corneal image and a direct view of the scene (Fig. 1(d)). Because corneal reflections suffer from low image quality, low intensity, superimposed iris texture, and unknown geometric distortion, this kind of matching is difficult to achieve with passively captured images. To compensate for this, we describe an active strategy using a novel LED-array projector to assign scene locations with temporal-coded patterns that can be identified from within both, corneal and scene images.

The remainder of the paper is organized as follows: Section 2 surveys related work. Section 3 describes a geometric eye model and a reflection model for the corneal surface to develop a method for obtaining the GRP. Section 4 describes the concept of direct matching and introduces the coded illumination projector. Sections 5 to 7 show experimental results, followed by discussion and conclusion.

2 Related Work

In the following, we discuss the relation of this work to the fields of corneal reflection analysis, eye gaze tracking and active coded illumination.

Corneal Reflection Analysis: The environmental light distribution around a person can be obtained from corneal images. Backes et al. [5] estimate the point spread function of the corneal reflection system and apply it to recover clear environment images using non-blind deconvolution. Nishino and Nayar [6] formalize the imaging characteristics of the eye-camera geometry as a non-central catadioptric system [7] that requires per-frame calibration through eye pose estimation. They describe a number of applications including environment map extraction, gaze target (PoG) estimation and face relighting. However, the gaze target estimation technique has several drawbacks compared to our approach: (1) It requires a more complex eye model with known eyeball size, and the back projection of the whole corneal image. (2) It does not model the individual offset between optical and visual axis, which is not accurate. (3) It obtains the PoG only in the (low quality) corneal image. (4) It uses passively captured corneal reflections that do not allow for robust matching.

Eye Gaze Tracking (EGT): Traditional PCCR approaches rely on a trained mapping from eye-image derived data (e.g., appearance, 2D or 3D geometric features) to the PoG on a target surface [2]. This approach is simple but involves a number of drawbacks. In particular, it assumes a static geometric relation between eye, camera, and a planar scene, which requires tedious calibration, and leads to decreased accuracy from unavoidable drift of the eye camera w.r.t. the head and a parallax variation with scene depth. More recent approaches achieve head-pose invariance by explicitly modeling the 3D geometry of the setup. The eye is tracked through a remote stationary high-resolution camera or a dynamic camera system [8,9]. In these systems, the PoG is obtained as the intersection of gaze ray and target surface. These approaches achieve reduced intrusiveness, but are more complex as they require domain knowledge. Also, they still involve a combination of drawbacks such as complicated extrinsic calibration of cameras and light sources, and accuracy degradation when the geometric relation changes. Several interesting techniques use machine learning to automatically obtain a gaze mapping to a computer screen by exploiting mouse click positions [10] or visual saliency maps of display content [11]. While not requiring a dedicated calibration or attached devices, this assumes particular application scenarios, relies on the properties of human perception, and obtains only low accuracy.

Coded structured light is widely used to identify environment locations, for scene reconstruction [12] and object tagging [13]. Non-intrusiveness for human observers is accomplished by exploiting the imperceptibility of complement patterns at high framerates or invisible IR light. Because commodity projectors are optimized for the visible spectrum, IR projection commonly requires special devices. Lee et al. [14] describe a high-resolution, scalable, and general-purpose solution that replaces the lamp of a DLP projector by an array of IR and visible-light LEDs; however, its luminance is insufficient for our application. Special LED arrays have been previously applied in EGT to allow automatic and robust extraction of corneal reflections [15]. While referred to as *structured light*, this relates only to the geometric alignment of the LED array.

3 Calculation of the Gaze Reflection Point

The GRP is obtained as follows: First, the three-dimensional pose of the eye w.r.t. the eye camera is found through a geometric model-based iris contour fitting. Then, the GRP is calculated using the eye pose and a reflection model at the corneal surface. In addition, a corrected GRP is obtained by compensating for the individual offset between optical and visual axis. We will now describe each step in detail.

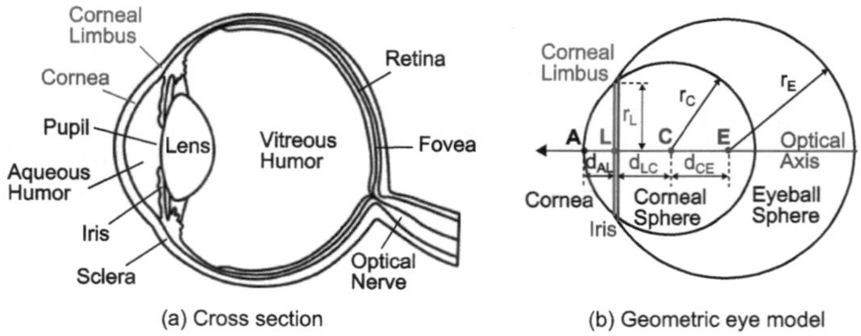

Fig. 2. (a) Cross section of the human eye and (b) geometric eye model with spherical curvature for eyeball and cornea

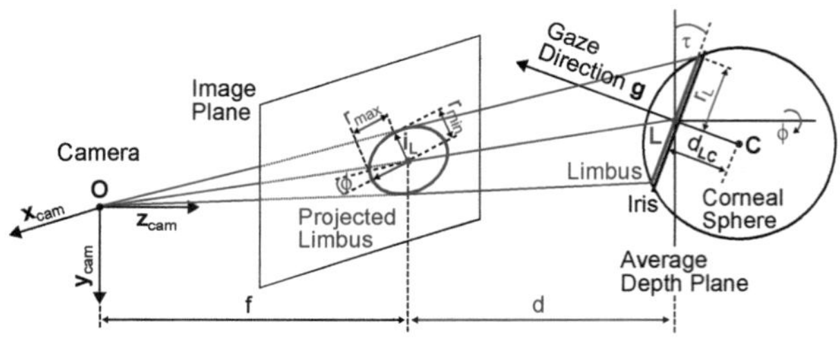

Fig. 3. 3D eye pose estimation from the projected limbus (iris contour)

3.1 Geometric Eye Model

Fig. 2(a) shows a cross-section of the eye. The human eyeball is not a plain sphere; it can be subdivided into two main segments: the anterior and the posterior. Both segments can be approximated by two overlapping spheres of different size (Fig. 2(b)). We use this geometric model to estimate the 3D pose of the eye and the location of the GRP in the image. Although there have been several discussions as to whether the eyeball shape is more complex than the model, and whether or not its anatomic parameters vary among humans, several previous studies have shown that this simplified model is sufficiently accurate [16]. The cornea is modeled as a spherical cap that is cut off from the corneal sphere by the limbus plane. The average radius of the limbus r_L is approximately 5.6 mm [17].

3.2 Eye Pose Estimation

We assume weak perspective projection since the depth of a tilted limbus is much smaller than the distance between eye and camera. Thus, the almost circular limbus projects to an ellipse that is described by five parameters: the center $\mathbf{i}_L$, the major and minor radii $r_{\max}$ and $r_{\min}$, and the rotation angle ϕ (Fig. 3). As the iris is delimited by the limbus, we estimate these values by fitting an ellipse to the projected iris contour.

Eye pose estimation is initialized from the pupil contour obtained through the dark-pupil method that exploits the relatively high light absorption of the

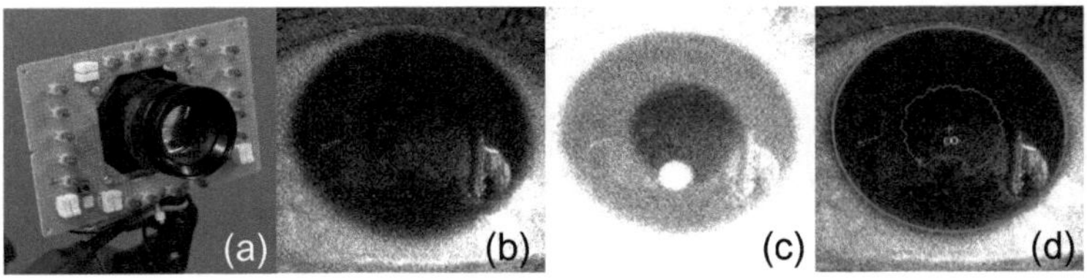

Fig. 4. Iris contour detection using the dark-pupil method. (a) The eye camera with a concentric ring of IR LEDs. (b) First frame (under normal lighting). (c) Second frame (under IR illumination). The bright spot denotes the reflection of the IR illumination. (d) Detected pupil contour (red) from the dark-pupil method. The magenta ellipse and '+' denote the estimated limbus contour and center position. The cyan circle indicates the center of the corneal sphere that coincides with the reflection of the IR illumination. Green and yellow circles indicate the GRP and the corrected GRP (GRP*).

pupil compared to other eye regions. The method uses two corneal images, taken under normal lighting and under illumination from a concentric ring of IR-LEDs around the camera lens (Fig. 4(a)–(c)). We subtract and threshold these frames to segment the pupil region, and apply a RANSAC-based ellipse-fitting to estimate its contour $B(x, y, c_x, c_y, a, b, \phi)$, where (c_x, c_y) is the center, a and b are the two radii, and ϕ is the rotation angle. We initialize the iris contour parameters using c_x, c_y, ϕ, and calculate the radii a_0, b_0 as in

$$eval_0(c_x, c_y, a, b, \phi) = \sum_{x,y} E_x(x, y) \cdot \mathrm{sgn}(c_x - x) \cdot B(x, y, c_x, c_y, a, b, \phi), \quad (1)$$

$$[a_0, b_0] = \arg\max_{a,b} eval_0(c_x, c_y, a, b, \phi), \quad (2)$$

where $E_x(x, y)$ are the x-differentials of the eye image and $a_0 > a$, $b_0 > b$. We only use x-differentials to avoid the effects of eyelid occlusion edges.

The gaze direction $\mathbf{g}$ is approximated by the optical axis of the eye, and theoretically obtained as in

$$\mathbf{g} = \left[\sin\tau \sin\phi \; -\sin\tau \cos\phi \; -\cos\tau\right]^{\mathrm{T}}. \quad (3)$$

The angle ϕ is known as the rotation of the limbus ellipse in the image plane. The angle $\tau = \pm\arccos(r_{\min}/r_{\max})$ corresponds to the tilt of the limbus plane w.r.t. the image plane. The center of the corneal sphere $\mathbf{C}$ is located at distance $d_{\mathbf{LC}}(= 5.6$ mm) from the limbus center[1] $\mathbf{L}$ along $-\mathbf{g}$. The center $\mathbf{C}$ and the radius r_C, approximately 7.7 mm [17], describe the corneal sphere that enables to model the light-reflection properties of the corneal surface.

Finally, we apply an iterative optimization to obtain accurate eye pose parameters. Since the cornea is a spherical surface, its projected center must coincide

[1] The position of the limbus center can be calculated from the center of the detected ellipse and the distance to the camera $d = f \cdot r_L/r_{\max}$ as in $\mathbf{L} = d\mathbf{K}^{-1}\mathbf{i}_{\mathbf{L}}$, where $\mathbf{K}$ is the camera matrix and f the focal length in pixels. However, this is not required for the calculation of the GRP.

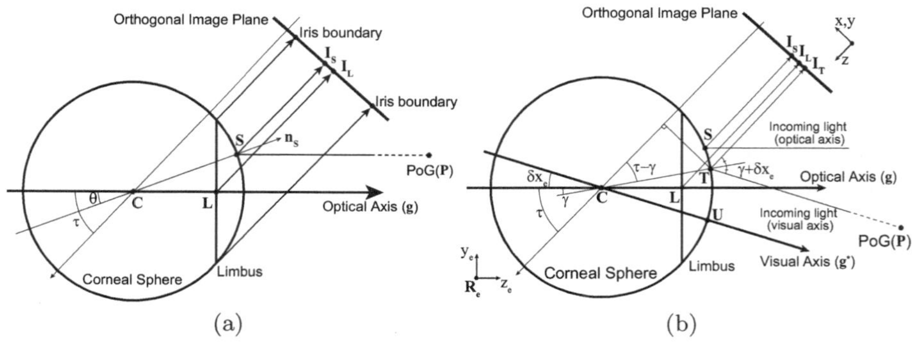

Fig. 5. (a) Corneal reflection and gaze-reflection point (GRP). The light-ray parallel to the gaze direction reflects at the GRP into the image of an eye-observation camera. (b) The optical axis and visual axis of the human eye. The light ray from the optical axis is reflected at the GRP **S**, and the calibration point is reflected at the calibration reflection point (CRP) **T**. The angular difference between these two axes (δx, δy) is obtained to compensate the individual offset. This illustration shows the cross section at the short axis of the projected limbus.

with the the centroid of the IR-LED ring reflection that represents the corneal image of the camera itself (Fig. 4(a),(c)). We formulate this constraint as an additional error term in equation (1) as in

$$eval_1(c_x, c_y, a, b, \phi) = \sum_{x,y} E_x(x, y) \cdot \operatorname{sgn}(c_x - x) \cdot B(x, y, c_x, c_y, a, b, \phi) + \alpha \cdot \|\mathbf{p}_{\mathrm{LED}} - \mathbf{p}_{\mathrm{CC}}\|, \quad (4)$$

and estimate the optimal iris contour parameters through iterative minimization. Here, $\mathbf{p}_{\mathrm{LED}}$ is the surface reflection point of the IR-LED, $\mathbf{p}_{\mathrm{CC}}$ is the projected corneal center, and α is a positive constant that is determined experimentally. The combined image- and geometric-model-based evaluation enables increased accuracy and robustness compared to existing iris-contour based eye pose estimation methods.

3.3 GRP Estimation from the Optical Axis of the Eye

According to the law of reflection, possible solutions for the GRP are not arbitrarily distributed on the surface of the corneal sphere, but on a circular subspace, arising from the intersection with the plane of reflection, that contains incident ray, reflected ray, and surface normal $\mathbf{n}_\mathbf{S}$, and, thus, camera center **O**, corneal sphere center **C**, PoG **P**, and GRP **S**. Assuming weak perspective projection, the plane of reflection intersects the semi-minor axis of the projected limbus (ellipse) and is orthogonal to the image plane. Fig. 5(a) illustrates the light reflection in the plane. We can formulate the reflection of the light ray parallel to the optical axis of the eye at the GRP as follows:

$$\mathbf{C}\cdot\mathbf{n_S} = \mathbf{g}\cdot\mathbf{n_S}, \quad \mathbf{C} = \begin{bmatrix}0 \; 1\end{bmatrix}^{\mathrm{T}}, \quad \mathbf{g} = \begin{bmatrix}\cos\tau \; \sin\tau\end{bmatrix}^{\mathrm{T}}, \quad \mathbf{n_S} = \begin{bmatrix}\cos\theta \; \sin\theta\end{bmatrix}^{\mathrm{T}}. \tag{5}$$

We then solve for the corneal angle θ that defines the GRP, using the known eye gaze angle τ as in

$$\begin{aligned}\theta &= \arctan((1 - \sin\tau)/\cos\tau) \\ &= \tau/2.\end{aligned} \tag{6}$$

The distance between the limbus center and the GRP in the local orthogonal image plane is defined as in

$$|\mathbf{I_S} - \mathbf{I_L}| = r_C \sin\theta - d_{\mathbf{LC}} \sin\tau. \tag{7}$$

Assuming the average depth plane for weak perspective projection to be located at the center of the limbus $\mathbf{L}$, then, the location of the GRP $\mathbf{i_{S'}}$ is given as in

$$\mathbf{i_S} = \mathbf{i_L} + s \cdot \mathbf{v}_{sm} \, |\mathbf{I_S} - \mathbf{I_L}|, \quad s = r_{\max}/r_L, \tag{8}$$

where s is the scale factor of the weak perspective projection, $\mathbf{i_L}$ is the center of the limbus ellipse, and $\mathbf{v}_{sm}$ is its semi-minor axis.

3.4 Calibration and Application of Individual Parameters

Many studies report that the optical axis of a human eye differs by an individual offset from the visual axis, which is the true gaze direction [2]. This difference can be described by static offset angles in a facial coordinate system, where z_{face} is the facial frontal direction, x_{face} is the direction from left to right eye, and y_{face} is orthogonal to x_{face} and z_{face}. The offset angles around x_{face} (tilt) and y_{face} (pan) are commonly within $1.5 \sim 3$ and $4 \sim 5$ deg. However, a one-time personal calibration is needed to obtain accurate values for a particular user. We introduce a one-point calibration technique to obtain these parameters through the analysis of a corneal reflection image.

In the calibration process, a user gazes a calibration point, such as a highly illuminated scene location or marker. We calculate the GRP and manually find the reflection of the calibration point (calibration reflection point (CRP)) in the corneal reflection image. We then introduce a coordinate system $\mathbf{R}_{\mathrm{e}} = [\mathbf{x}_{\mathrm{e}} \, \mathbf{y}_{\mathrm{e}} \, \mathbf{z}_{\mathrm{e}}]$ at the limbus center, where $\mathbf{x}_{\mathrm{e}}$ and $\mathbf{y}_{\mathrm{e}}$ correspond to the three-dimensional vectors of the long and short axes of the projected limbus, respectively. Fig. 5(b) illustrates the cross section at the short axis ($\mathbf{y}_{\mathrm{e}}\mathbf{z}_{\mathrm{e}}$-plane). In this plane, the angle γ between the optical axis and the CRP is described as in

$$|\mathbf{I_L} - \mathbf{I_T}| = \frac{|\mathbf{v}_{sm} \cdot (\mathbf{i_T} - \mathbf{i_L})|}{s}, \tag{9}$$

$$\gamma = \tau - \arcsin(d_{\mathbf{LC}} \cdot \cos\tau + \frac{|\mathbf{I_L} - \mathbf{I_T}|}{r_C}), \tag{10}$$

where $\mathbf{I_T}$ and $\mathbf{i_T}$ are the location of the CRP and its projection in the corneal image, respectively. Considering a surface reflection at the CRP, then the offset angle δx_e between the optical and the visual axis in this plane is defined as in

$$2 \cdot (\gamma + \delta x_\mathrm{e}) = \tau + \delta x_\mathrm{e}, \tag{11}$$

$$\delta x_\mathrm{e} = \tau - 2 \cdot \gamma. \tag{12}$$

Similarly, the angle δy_e in the $\mathbf{x}_\mathrm{e}\mathbf{z}_\mathrm{e}$-plane is defined as in

$$\delta y_e = 2 \cdot \arcsin(\frac{\mathbf{v}_{lm} \cdot (\mathbf{i_T} - \mathbf{i_L})}{s \cdot r_C}), \tag{13}$$

where $\mathbf{v}_{lm}$ is the major axis of the limbus ellipse.

Assuming the camera to be located in front of the face, the offset angles can be transformed into the camera coordinate system as in

$$\delta x = \arctan(\frac{\mathbf{e}_\mathrm{y}^\mathrm{T}\mathbf{R}_\mathrm{e}\mathbf{u}}{\mathbf{e}_\mathrm{z}^\mathrm{T}\mathbf{R}_\mathrm{e}\mathbf{u}}), \tag{14}$$

$$\delta y = \arctan(\frac{\mathbf{e}_\mathrm{x}^\mathrm{T}\mathbf{R}_\mathrm{e}\mathbf{u}}{\mathbf{e}_\mathrm{z}^\mathrm{T}\mathbf{R}_\mathrm{e}\mathbf{u}}), \tag{15}$$

$$\mathbf{u} = \left[\sin \delta y_\mathrm{e} \; \sin \delta x_\mathrm{e} \sqrt{1 - \sin^2 \delta x_\mathrm{e} - \sin^2 \delta y_\mathrm{e}}\right]^\mathrm{T}, \tag{16}$$

$$\mathbf{e}_\mathrm{x} = [1\;0\;0]^\mathrm{T},\; \mathbf{e}_\mathrm{y} = [0\;1\;0]^\mathrm{T}, \mathbf{e}_\mathrm{z} = [0\;0\;1]^\mathrm{T}.$$

Once the transformed offset angles are obtained, the corrected GRP (GRP*) can be estimated using the corrected eye coordinate system $\mathbf{R}_\mathrm{e}^*$ that is rotated by $(\delta x, \delta y)$ from the original eye coordinate system $\mathbf{R}_\mathrm{e}$. Using $\mathbf{R}_\mathrm{e}^*$, we obtain the corrected angle τ^* and the semi-minor axis of the projected limbus $\mathbf{v}_{sm}^*$ as in

$$\tau^* = \arccos(\mathbf{e}_\mathrm{z}^\mathrm{T}\mathbf{R}_\mathrm{e}^*\mathbf{e}_\mathrm{z}), \tag{17}$$

$$\mathbf{v}_{sm}^* = (\begin{bmatrix} \mathbf{e}_\mathrm{x}^\mathrm{T} \\ \mathbf{e}_\mathrm{y}^\mathrm{T} \end{bmatrix} \mathbf{R}_e^*\mathbf{e}_\mathrm{y}) / \left\| \begin{bmatrix} \mathbf{e}_\mathrm{x}^\mathrm{T} \\ \mathbf{e}_\mathrm{y}^\mathrm{T} \end{bmatrix} \mathbf{R}_e^*\mathbf{e}_\mathrm{y} \right\|, \tag{18}$$

$$\mathbf{R}_\mathrm{e}^* = \mathbf{R}_x(\delta x)\mathbf{R}_y(\delta y)\mathbf{R}_\mathrm{e}, \tag{19}$$

where $\mathbf{R}_x$ and $\mathbf{R}_y$ are the rotation matrices around the x and y axes, respectively. Applying τ^*, $\mathbf{v}_{sm}^*$, and equations (7) and (8), we obtain the position of the GRP* that reflects the light from the true visual axis of the particular eye.

4 Direct Matching Using Coded Illumination

4.1 LED Array Projector

Coded illumination is the key component for matching the GRP in a corneal reflection image to find the PoG in the scene. For this purpose, we designed a novel programmable LED-array projector (LED-AP) that produces high-power and high-frequency coded light beams to achieve real-time PoG estimation (Fig. 6).

It comprises an array of LED-lens units, LED power modules and a controller (Fig. 7). We evaluate two types of LEDs: high-power visible-light and IR LEDs to produce imperceptible IR illumination. Each LED can be toggled on/off within 0.05 ms according to control signals from an Arduino micro-controller. As each LED's illumination is modulated with a unique temporal coding sequence, the system can identify projected light-spots by decoding the series of eye (Fig. 8(c)–(e)) and environment images. The direction of an LED can be manually adjusted so that the illumination covers the whole scene or particular objects of interest. The number of LEDs defines the spatial resolution of the coverage area, which is usually lower than that of data projectors. To compensate for this, we employ the following linear interpolation technique for PoG estimation: First, we recover the codes from the sequences of corneal reflection and environment images, and obtain the center of the moments of the LED light-spots. In the corneal reflection image, we calculate the relative position of the GRP w.r.t. four neighboring light-spots, and use this to locate the PoG in the environment image.

4.2 Coding Strategy

For temporal modulation of the LED-AP illumination, we implemented both, a binary code and a Hamming(7,4) code [18]. While the binary code is simple and short-length, the Hamming(7,4) code allows to correct a single-bit errors but encodes 4 data bits into 7 bits by adding 3 parity bits. Each implementation requires one frame for pupil detection using the dark-pupil method before starting a temporal code block. Fig. 9 shows the signal ordering.

5 Experiments

We evaluate the proposed method and compare it to a mapping-based PCCR technique that is commonly used in existing EGT systems.

PCCR is implemented using two kinds of IR illumination: a previously described on-axis IR-LED ring around the camera lens to realize the dark-pupil method and a single off-axis IR-LED that is static w.r.t. the eye camera. In the calibration step, four eye images are captured, where a subject gazes the corners of a rectangle on a calibration plane. Detecting pupil centers and glints from the off-axis IR-LED allows to calculate an affine matrix that maps the pupil center/glint vector to the corresponding calibration point in the scene coordinate system. At the gaze estimation step, this mapping function is used to obtain the PoG from the pupil center and glint in a corneal image.

Experimental Setup: We performed experiments with five subjects in an indoor environment under normal lighting conditions. Fig. 7 (d) shows the experimental setup. We use Point Grey Dragonfly Express cameras (640×480 pixels, B/W, 30 Hz) and MATLAB 2011b with the Image Processing Toolbox on a PC (Linux, Intel Core i7-960 3.06 GHz, 8 GB RAM). The eye camera has a horizontal angle of view of approximately 9 deg, where the projected limbus radius is approximately 100 pixels. To evaluate the effects of depth variation in

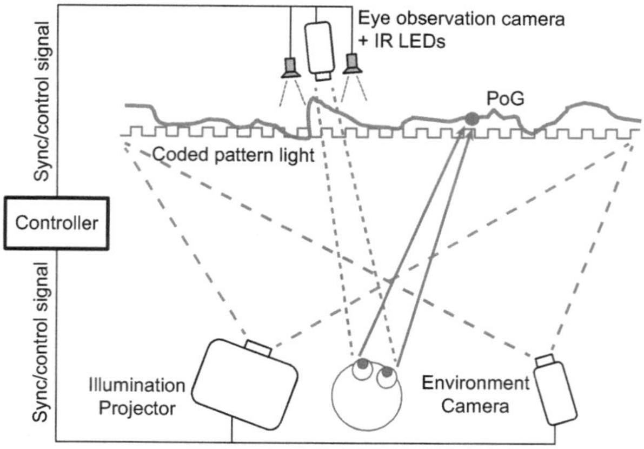

Fig. 6. System configuration. The system consists of an eye-observation camera with IR LEDs, an environment camera and an LED-array projector.

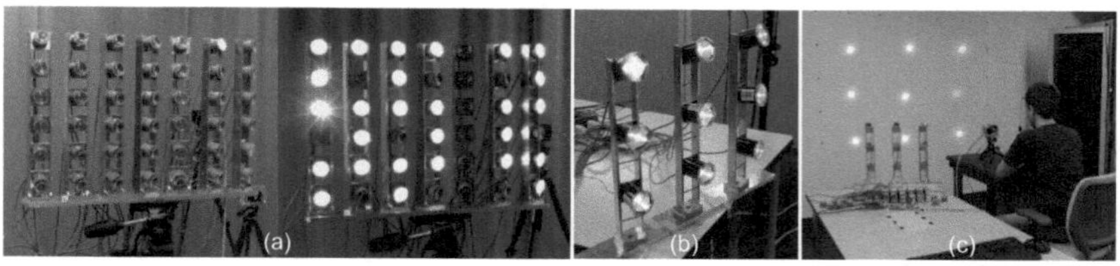

Fig. 7. LED array projector (LED-AP). (a) LED array (42-LED configuration). Each unit consists of a high-luminance LED (visible light or IR-light) with a Fresnel lens. (b) LED array (9-LED configuration). (c) Experimental setup and projected illumination patterns.

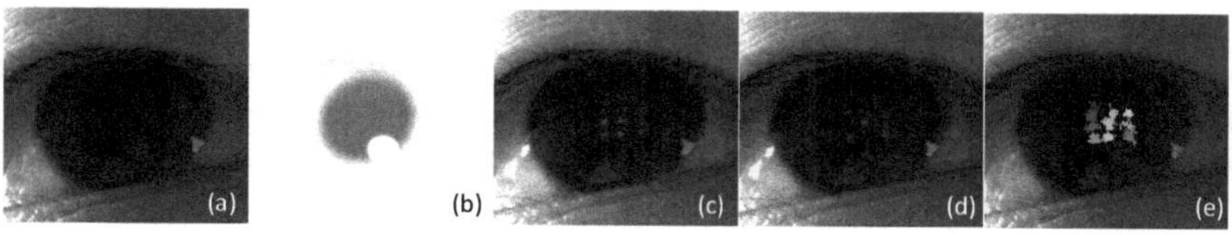

Fig. 8. Corneal images obtained with the LED-AP implementation. (a) Frame #1 (under normal lighting). (b) Frame #2 (under IR illumination). (c) Frame #3, (d) frame #13, and (e) decoded result from a sequence of temporal-coded patterns with the reflections of 9 light spots.

Frame #	1	2	3	4	5	....
IR LED RING	OFF	ON	OFF	OFF	OFF	....
LED-AP	OFF	OFF	ALL ON	CODE#1	CODE#2	....

Fig. 9. Signal ordering for the concentric ring of IR-LEDs attached around the lens of the eye camera, and the LED-AP. At frames #1 and #2, the IR-LED ring is turned on and off for pupil detection. At frame #3, the LED-AP is completely turned on to obtain the reference illumination for subsequent signal code frames.

Table 1. Mean PoG estimation error [deg]

	Condition 1 (depth = 1900 mm)		Condition 2 (depth = 3000 mm)	
	Proposed method	PCCR	Proposed method	PCCR
User 1	0.960	0.973	0.909	3.084
User 2	0.913	1.032	0.642	4.350
User 3	0.916	0.963	0.756	3.560
User 4	0.947	0.890	0.759	3.951
User 5	0.761	1.121	0.914	4.240
Mean	**0.899**	0.996	**0.796**	3.837

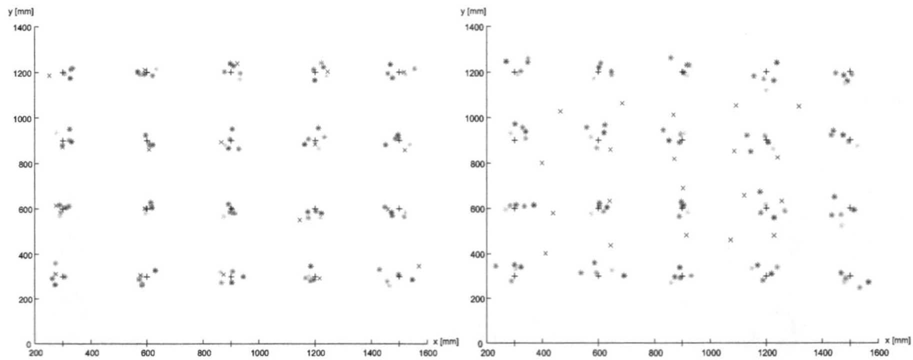

(a) Condition 1 (depth = 1900 mm) (b) Condition 2 (depth = 3000 mm)

Fig. 10. Result of PoG estimation under condition 1 and 2. '+' indicate ground-truth markers, and '*' indicate PoG estimation results from the proposed method. 5 users are represented by different colors. Red 'x' indicate results of implicit EGT for user 1. The light-spots of the 9 LEDs are located at the plane coordinates (1490, 1200), (895, 1200), (300, 1200), (1430, 750), (835, 750), (300, 750), (1450, 300), (820, 300) and (320, 300) [mm]. The eye positions are located at (900, 600, 1900) and (900, 600, 3000) [mm] at condition 1 and 2, respectively.

the scene, subjects are seated at both, 1900 (condition 1) and 3000 mm (condition 2), in front of a wall, where 20 ground-truth markers are attached. The subjects are asked to gaze the markers, where we calculate the angular errors between ground-truth and estimated PoGs. Individual parameters are calibrated at condition 1 and also applied at condition 2. The eye camera is placed slightly below a subject's face at a distance of 600 mm in front of the eyes. The environment camera is placed behind the subject so as to capture the entire scene. We used 9-LED illumination for these experiments, where the coordinates of the light-spots are described in Fig. 10.

Results: Table 1 shows the angular errors, obtained with the subject's right eyes are located at $(x, y, z) = (900, 600, 1900)$ and $(900, 600, 3000)$ [mm]. Fig. 10 shows the PoG estimation results at conditions 1 and 2. The proposed method results in an error of less than 1 deg at both conditions. However, the PCCR method suffers from a reduced performance at condition 2. Please refer to a supplementary video[2] for results in more complex environments.

6 Discussion

The proposed method performs with considerable accuracy, although it does not require body-attached devices and allows free head movement. A novel one-point personal calibration technique successfully increased the accuracy under all experimental conditions. Moreover, we confirmed that the method supports PoG estimation under a varying scene depth.

The performance of the implemented single-glint PCCR technique is found to decrease when the depth of the scene changes from the one at which calibration was performed, which relates to an increasing parallax error for the calibrated mapping function. On the contrary, the proposed approach relies on an uncalibrated direct matching between corneal reflection and environment image, which performs accurately and stably under varying depth conditions.

We implemented and evaluated two temporal-coding patterns for LED-AP illumination. Even though, the Hamming(7,4) code requires more frames than the binary code, there was only little difference in the decoding results for corneal reflection images under the current experimental setup.

Eyelid occlusion is a common problem in any EGT system. In the proposed approach, this does not affect the PoG mapping as the GRP is located near the center of the pupil. However, it increases the error in iris-contour based eye pose estimation, where more robust and accurate strategies need to be investigated.

PoG estimation using the LED-AP assumes local planarity between the light spots in the scene. Increasing the intensity and number of LEDs can, therefore, potentially increase the accuracy under complex geometry and decoding errors, e.g., from object occlusion and noise.

7 Conclusion

The paper introduced a novel point of gaze estimation scheme that overcomes two major limitations of existing methods, namely, (1) the requirement for calibration of a static relationship between eye, eye camera and scene, and (2) a parallax error that occurs when the depth of the scene varies. The proposed approach comprises two major contributions: First, an analytic solution is developed to calculate the gaze reflection point (GRP), where light from the point of gaze (PoG) reflects into an eye image. This includes compensation for the individual offset between optical and visual axis. Second, active coded illumination enables robust and accurate matching at the GRP to obtain the PoG in a scene image, which is also the first use of this technique in EGT and corneal reflection analysis. Experimental evaluation with a specially-designed high-power IR LED-array projector shows that the proposed scheme achieves considerable accuracy and successfully supports depth-varying environments.

[2] http://www.ime.cmc.osaka-u.ac.jp/~nakazawa/wiki/index.php?EGT

Acknowledgement. This work was supported by the JST Precursory Research for Embryonic Science and Technology (PRESTO) program, Japan.

References

1. Young, L., Sheena, D.: Survey of eye movement recording methods. Behav. Res. Meth. Instrum. 7, 397–429 (1975)
2. Hansen, D.W., Ji, Q.: In the eye of the beholder: A survey of models for eyes and gaze. IEEE Trans. Pattern Anal. Mach. Intell. 32, 478–500 (2010)
3. Guestrin, E.D., Eizenman, M.: General theory of remote gaze estimation using the pupil center and corneal reflections. IEEE Trans. Biomed. Eng. 53, 1124–1133 (2006)
4. Agrawal, A., Taguchi, Y., Ramalingam, S.: Beyond Alhazen's problem: Analytical projection model for non-central catadioptric cameras with quadric mirrors. In: Proc. CVPR, pp. 2993–3000 (2011)
5. Backes, M., Chen, T., Dürmuth, M., Lensch, H.P.A., Welk, M.: Tempest in a teapot: Compromising reflections revisited. In: Proc. IEEE SP, pp. 315–327 (2009)
6. Nishino, K., Nayar, S.K.: Corneal imaging system: Environment from eyes. Int. J. Comput. Vision 70, 23–40 (2006)
7. Sturm, P., Ramalingam, S., Tardif, J.P., Gasparini, S., Barreto, J.: Camera models and fundamental concepts used in geometric computer vision. Found. Trends. Comput. Graph. Vis. 6, 1–183 (2011)
8. Kim, S.M., Sked, M., Ji, Q.: Non-intrusive eye gaze tracking under natural head movements. In: Proc. IEEE IEMBS, pp. 2271–2274 (2004)
9. Reale, M., Hung, T., Yin, L.: Viewing direction estimation based on 3D eyeball construction for HRI. In: Proc. CVPRW, pp. 24–31 (2010)
10. Sugano, Y., Matsushita, Y., Sato, Y., Koike, H.: An Incremental Learning Method for Unconstrained Gaze Estimation. In: Forsyth, D., Torr, P., Zisserman, A. (eds.) ECCV 2008, Part III. LNCS, vol. 5304, pp. 656–667. Springer, Heidelberg (2008)
11. Sugano, Y., Matsushita, Y., Sato, Y.: Appearance-based gaze estimation using visual saliency. IEEE Trans. Pattern Anal. Mach. Intell., 1 (2012)
12. Salvi, J., Fernandez, S., Pribanic, T., Llado, X.: A state of the art in structured light patterns for surface profilometry. Pattern Recogn. 43, 2666–2680 (2010)
13. Zhang, L., Subramaniam, N., Lin, R., Raskar, R., Nayar, S.: Capturing images with sparse informational pixels using projected 3D tags. In: Proc. IEEE VR, pp. 11–18 (2008)
14. Lee, J.C., Hudson, S., Dietz, P.: Hybrid infrared and visible light projection for location tracking. In: Proc. ACM UIST, pp. 57–60 (2007)
15. Li, F., Kolakowski, S., Pelz, J.: Using structured illumination to enhance video-based eye tracking. In: Proc. IEEE ICIP, pp. 373–376 (2007)
16. Nitschke, C., Nakazawa, A., Takemura, H.: Display-camera calibration using eye reflections and geometry constraints. Comput. Vis. Image Underst. 115, 835–853 (2011)
17. Snell, R.S., Lemp, M.A.: Clinical Anatomy of the Eye, 2nd edn. Blackwell Publishing, Malden (1997)
18. Moon, T.K.: Error Correction Coding: Mathematical Methods and Algorithms. Wiley-Interscience (2005)

Order-Preserving Sparse Coding for Sequence Classification

Bingbing Ni[1], Pierre Moulin[2], and Shuicheng Yan[3]

[1] Advanced Digital Sciences Center, Singapore
[2] University of Illinois at Urbana-Champaign, US
[3] National University of Singapore, Singapore
bingbing.ni@adsc.com.sg, moulin@ifp.uiuc.edu, eleyans@nus.edu.sg

Abstract. In this paper, we investigate order-preserving sparse coding for classifying multi-dimensional sequence data. Such a problem is often tackled by first decomposing the input sequence into individual *frames* and extracting features, then performing sparse coding or other processing for each frame based feature vector independently, and finally aggregating individual responses to classify the input sequence. However, this heuristic approach ignores the underlying temporal order of the input sequence frames, which in turn results in suboptimal discriminative capability. In this work, we introduce a temporal-order-preserving regularizer which aims to preserve the temporal order of the reconstruction coefficients. An efficient Nesterov-type smooth approximation method is developed for optimization of the new regularization criterion, with guaranteed error bounds. Extensive experiments for time series classification on a synthetic dataset, several machine learning benchmarks, and a challenging real-world RGB-D human activity dataset, show that the proposed coding scheme is discriminative and robust, and it outperforms previous art for sequence classification.

1 Introduction

Sparse coding has been successfully used in various computer vision applications [1] [2] [3]. Sparse coding compactly represents objects as a linear combination of a small number of elements of a dictionary, however there often exist *group* structures in basis data (dictionary). To handle such structures, two alternative methods, Elastic Net [4] and group Lasso [5] have been proposed. They favor the selection of few groups of the correlated dictionary samples to represent the testing data. Often we may estimate models from multiple related data sources. For example, in object recognition, we may extract K types of image representations from K different types of features associated with the same visual input. By minimizing the sum of ℓ_2 norms of the blocks of coefficients associated with each covariate group across different feature representations, similar sparsity patterns in all modalities are encouraged [6]. In [7], the objective of joint sparsity is achieved by imposing an $\ell_{2,1}$ mixed-norm penalty on the reconstruction coefficients.

A. Fitzgibbon et al. (Eds.): ECCV 2012, Part II, LNCS 7573, pp. 173–187, 2012.

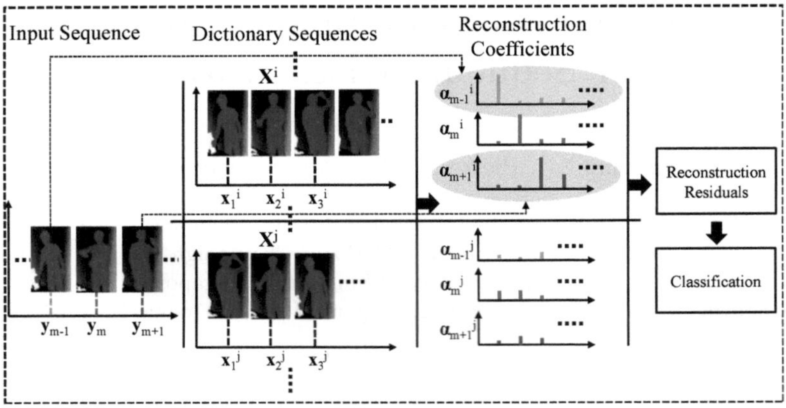

Fig. 1. Motivation of the proposed work, applied to human motion sequence classification. The input sequence receives a strong response from dictionary sequence i as their temporal ordering structures are similar. In contrast, the response from dictionary sequence j is low as its temporal structure is different, although individual frames of the input sequence are similar to those of the sequence j. Similarly to [7], the reconstruction residual is used for classification. See the color pdf for better view.

In this work, we are interested in a different problem setting: the input is a sequence of feature vectors instead of a single feature vector, and there exist dependencies among the input feature vectors. An example is a multidimensional time series such as audio data, which admit a natural temporal ordering structure across instantaneous feature vectors at successive time stamps. A heuristic solution is to apply sparse coding to the feature vector for each input frame (*i.e.*, time stamp) individually, and then compute and aggregate reconstruction coefficients for individual frames over the entire audio sequence for classification [8]. The temporal structure of the sequence conveys discriminative information. Treating each frame independently would discard this important information. However, this problem has been largely ignored in current sparse coding literature.

We address this problem by developing an order-preserving sparse coding scheme for discriminatively representing multidimensional time series, as illustrated in Figure 1. Our main contribution is to introduce a temporal order preserving regularization scheme. The regularizer penalizes misfit of the temporal order of the reconstruction coefficients for individual frames with respect to the temporal order of the input sequence. To the best of our knowledge, this is the first attempt to address this temporal consistency issue for sparse coding. The resulting optimization problem is convex but nonsmooth. We therefore develop an efficient Nesterov-type smooth approximation method [9] for optimization. Extensive experiments on time series classification over a synthetic dataset, several machine learning benchmarks, and a challenging real world RGB-D human activity dataset, demonstrate that the proposed scheme is discriminative and robust, and outperforms previous art for time series classification.

2 Related Work

Time series classification is an active research topic. Hidden Markov models (HMMs) [10] is the most popular way for sequence classification. A segmental hidden Markov model (HMM) was recently used to characterize waveform shape for recognition [11]. The limitations of HMM methods are the Markovian assumption and the complexity in training. Dynamic Time Warping (DTW) [12] is also widely used for time series classification. Rodrigues et al. [13] proposed a DTW decision tree method for time series classification. Hayashi et al. [14] used DTW distances to embed time series into a lower dimensional space by Laplacian eigenmap. Xi et al. [15] proposed numerosity reduction to accelerate nearest-neighbor DTW. However, similar to HMM based methods, the computational burden of DTW-based methods is generally high. Another tool for sequence classification is Recurrent Neural Networks (RNN) [16], which is a modification of a general Neural Network architecture that considers temporal structure. However, training the model using back propagation is also complex.

In this work, we present our classification scheme and experimentally compare it with the above methods as well as with multi-resolution symbolic representation [17]. RNN is not used for comparison here because it is generally slow in training and it is less discriminative than other methods. As our method inherits the discriminative capability of conventional sparse coding scheme and further boosts this capability by explicitly encoding temporal ordering structures, it significantly outperforms previous work in classification accuracy. It requires no training and is efficient in testing. Note that *n-gram* model [18] is also used for sequence modeling for speech recognition; however, it lacks explicit representation of long range dependency, and it is very sensitive to temporal scaling. In contrast, our proposed regularization scheme does not have these limitations. The *n-gram* model is therefore not used in our comparisons. Although some works [19] [20] [21] also concern sparse coding for temporal varying signals (events, images), their regularization frameworks only use traditional temporal smoothness constraints. None of these works directly considers temporal ordering.

3 Order-Preserving Sparse Coding

3.1 Notation

We first introduce the notation used in this work. The input is a multi-dimensional time series $Y = [\mathbf{y}_1, \mathbf{y}_2, \cdots, \mathbf{y}_t]$, where each $\mathbf{y}_i$ is a D-dimensional feature vector, and t denotes the length of the time series. We are given a basis dictionary denoted as $\mathcal{X} = \{(X_1, y_1), (X_2, y_2), \cdots, (X_S, y_S)\}$, where S is the number of dictionary sequences. Each sequence X_j is a time series represented as $X_j = [\mathbf{x}_1^j, \mathbf{x}_2^j, \cdots, \mathbf{x}_{t_j}^j]$, where t_j is the length of the j-th sequence and y_j is the corresponding class label. Each $\mathbf{x}_i^j$ is a D-dimensional feature vector normalized to unit ℓ_2 norm. Note that t_j may vary from sequence to sequence. The label y_j has K possible values in the set $\{1, 2, \cdots, K\}$. If we stack all the sequences in the dictionary one by one with the temporal order within sequence retained, we can represent the dictionary by a $D \times N$ matrix $X = [X_1, X_2, \cdots, X_S]$, where $N = \sum_{j=1}^{S} t_j$ is the total number of feature vectors. Let the N-dimensional vector $\boldsymbol{\alpha}_i$ denote the reconstruction coefficients for the input vector $\mathbf{y}_i$, which is expressed as a linear combination of all dictionary entries. Let $\boldsymbol{\alpha} = (\boldsymbol{\alpha}_1; \boldsymbol{\alpha}_2; \cdots; \boldsymbol{\alpha}_t)$, and $\boldsymbol{\alpha}_i^j$ be the t_j-dimensional reconstruction coefficients for input vector i from the dictionary sequence j. Using this convention, we further denote by $\boldsymbol{\alpha}^j = (\boldsymbol{\alpha}_1^j; \boldsymbol{\alpha}_2^j; \cdots; \boldsymbol{\alpha}_t^j)$ the reconstruction coefficients from the dictionary sequence j.

3.2 Temporal-Order-Preserving Regularizer

Sparse coding provides a discriminative way for encoding signals. A straightforward way to represent an input sequence within the sparse coding framework is to first decompose the input sequence into frame-based representations (feature vectors at each time stamp), then perform sparse coding for each frame based feature vector independently, and finally aggregate individual responses (reconstruction coefficients) for classification. However, this heuristic approach is suboptimal because the time series has very strong temporal correlation across individual frames. We refer to this correlation is as a temporal ordering structure. For example, in speech recognition, reordering of a given sequence of phonemes may lead to a totally different sentence and meaning. Ignoring temporal ordering information results in loss of discriminative capability in sparse coding.

Our proposed regularization scheme explicitly addresses this problem in sparsely encoding time series data. As a prerequisite, we require that the reconstruction coefficients for all individual feature vectors of the input sequence should be nonzero on only a few dictionary sequences. As the input sequence normally matches only a few dictionary sequences, spreading the reconstruction coefficients throughout all dictionary sequences degrades the representation discriminative capability. To address this problem, we adopt an $\ell_{2,1}$ norm group-sparsity regularizer as in multitask joint sparse coding [7]. Long sequence can be decomposed into shorter ones for more sparsity. Thus the first term of our regularization criterion is

$$G(\boldsymbol{\alpha}) = \sum_{j=1}^{S} \|\boldsymbol{\alpha}^j\|_2. \tag{1}$$

The second term of our regularization criterion is the temporal order preserving regularizer. The goal is to prevent the reconstruction coefficients of the input feature vector i (at the time stamp i of the input sequence) from the j-th dictionary sequence from being temporally *behind* those of the input vector $i+1$ (at the time stamp $i+1$ of the input sequence). In other words, the nonzero reconstruction coefficients for individual feature vectors obey the same temporal order as the corresponding feature vectors in the input sequence. To encourage this, we consider the expression

$$(\mathbf{w}_j^T(\boldsymbol{\alpha}_i^j - \boldsymbol{\alpha}_{i+1}^j))_+ = \max\{\mathbf{w}_j^T(\boldsymbol{\alpha}_i^j - \boldsymbol{\alpha}_{i+1}^j), 0\}, \tag{2}$$

where $\mathbf{w}_j$ is a vector that has the same length as the corresponding dictionary sequence j and it is element-wise increasing. More specifically, $\mathbf{w}_j$ satisfies the condition: $\mathbf{w}_j(a) < \mathbf{w}_j(b), \forall a < b$, where $\mathbf{w}_j(a)$ denotes the a-th element of vector $\mathbf{w}_j$. With this property, $\mathbf{w}_j^T \boldsymbol{\alpha}_i^j$ approximates the temporal position of the responses for the i-th input vector $\mathbf{y}_i$ from dictionary sequence j. When the sum of all entries in $\boldsymbol{\alpha}_i^j$ is one, the sum $\mathbf{w}_j^T \boldsymbol{\alpha}_i^j$ can be considered as the approximated temporal position. When the sum of the entries in $\boldsymbol{\alpha}_i^j$ is not equal to one, the sum $\mathbf{w}_j^T \boldsymbol{\alpha}_i^j$ can be considered as the importance weighted version of the approximated temporal position. Therefore $\mathbf{w}_j^T \boldsymbol{\alpha}_i^j > \mathbf{w}_j^T \boldsymbol{\alpha}_{i+1}^j$ means that the approximated temporal position of the response for the $(i+1)$-th input vector on dictionary sequence j precedes that of the i-th input vector, which is the case to penalize. We call $\mathbf{w}_j$ as temporal-structure-prior-multiplier, and in this work we choose a simple form of $\mathbf{w}_j$, *i.e.*, element-wise linear, to reflect the time ordering information as:

$$\mathbf{w}_j = \left(\frac{1}{t_j}, \frac{2}{t_j}, \cdots, \frac{t_j - 1}{t_j}, 1\right)^T. \tag{3}$$

The **temporal-order-preserving regularization** term is obtained by summing (2) over all consecutive frames of the input sequence and over all dictionary sequences, namely,

$$P(\boldsymbol{\alpha}) = \sum_{i=1}^{t-1} \sum_{j=1}^{S} \max(\mathbf{w}_j^T \boldsymbol{\alpha}_i^j - \mathbf{w}_j^T \boldsymbol{\alpha}_{i+1}^j, 0). \tag{4}$$

An illustration of the effect of the regularizer (4) is given in Figure 2. Observe that *unordered* reconstruction coefficients receive large penalty, and when re-

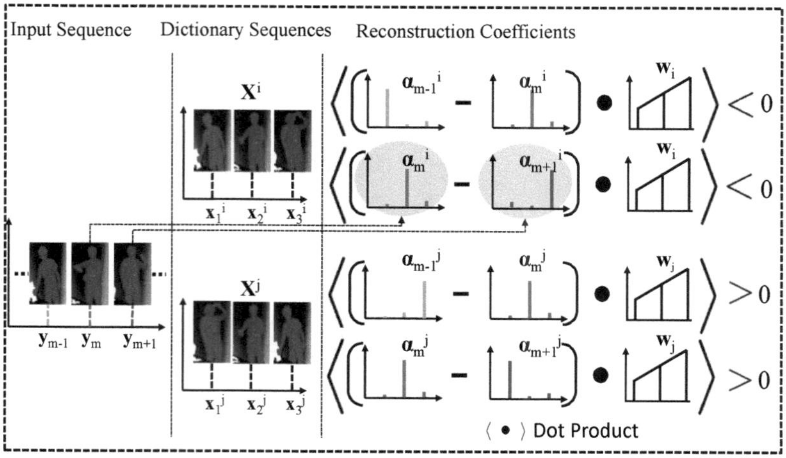

Fig. 2. Effect of applying the regularizer (4). Note that the reconstruction coefficients that follow the temporal order of the input sequence are not penalized by the expression (upper two rows). Those that do not are penalized (bottom two rows). See the color pdf for better view.

construction coefficients are *ordered*, this term vanishes. Note that the inverse is not true, *i.e.*, zero penalty does not necessary indicate temporally-ordered reconstruction.

3.3 Objective Function

Here we formally state our regularization criterion. The reconstruction error term is

$$f(\boldsymbol{\alpha}) = \frac{1}{2}\sum_{i=1}^{t} \|\mathbf{y}_i - X\boldsymbol{\alpha}_i\|_2^2, \tag{5}$$

which is a convex, smooth, differentiable function with Lipschitz constant $L_f = \|X^T X\|_F$, where $\|.\|_F$ denotes the Frobenius norm.

Recall that the group-sparsity regularizer given in (1) is

$$G(\boldsymbol{\alpha}) = \sum_{j=1}^{S} \|\boldsymbol{\alpha}^j\|_2.$$

This is an $\ell_{2,1}$ mixed-norm, which is convex and nonsmooth. However, $\|\boldsymbol{\alpha}^j\|_2$ can be written as

$$\|\boldsymbol{\alpha}^j\|_2 = \max_{\|\mathbf{v}_j\|_2 \le 1} \langle \boldsymbol{\alpha}^j, \mathbf{v}_j \rangle. \tag{6}$$

We use the Nesterov smooth approximation method of [9] and approximate (6) by the smooth function:

$$q_{\mu,j}(\boldsymbol{\alpha}^j) = \max_{\|\mathbf{v}_j\|_2 \le 1} \{\langle \boldsymbol{\alpha}^j, \mathbf{v}_j \rangle - \frac{1}{2}\mu\|\mathbf{v}_j\|_2^2\}, \tag{7}$$

where μ is a parameter that controls the approximation accuracy. The unique minimizer of (7), denoted as $\mathbf{v}_j(\boldsymbol{\alpha}^j)$, can be derived as

$$\mathbf{v}_j(\boldsymbol{\alpha}^j) = \begin{cases} \frac{\boldsymbol{\alpha}^j}{\mu}, & 0 \le \|\boldsymbol{\alpha}^j\|_2 \le \mu\ ; \\ \frac{\boldsymbol{\alpha}^j}{\|\boldsymbol{\alpha}^j\|_2}, & \|\boldsymbol{\alpha}^j\|_2 > \mu. \end{cases} \tag{8}$$

The approximation of (1) is therefore obtained as

$$G_\mu(\boldsymbol{\alpha}) = \sum_{j=1}^{S} q_{\mu,j}(\boldsymbol{\alpha}^j). \tag{9}$$

Recall that the temporal-order-preserving regularization function is given by $P(\boldsymbol{\alpha})$ in (4). By simple manipulation, we can rewrite $P(\boldsymbol{\alpha})$ more compactly as:

$$P(\boldsymbol{\alpha}) = \sum_{i=1}^{S\times(t-1)} \|(W_i\boldsymbol{\alpha})_+\|_1, \tag{10}$$

Here each W_i, $i = 1, 2, \cdots, (t-1) \times S$, is an N-dimensional row vector given by $W_{(h-1)\times S+j} = (0, \cdots, 0, \mathbf{w}_j^T, 0, \cdots, 0, -\mathbf{w}_j^T, 0, \cdots, 0)$, for $h = 1, 2, \cdots, t-1$, $j = 1, 2, \cdots, S$. The positions of $\mathbf{w}_j^T$ and $-\mathbf{w}_j^T$ correspond to those of $\boldsymbol{\alpha}_h^j$ and $\boldsymbol{\alpha}_{h+1}^j$ in $\boldsymbol{\alpha}$, respectively. As mentioned above, the regularizer (10) encourages order preserving for the reconstruction coefficients for individual feature vectors of the input sequence. Again, $(.)_+$ denotes $\max(., 0)$. The function $\|(W_i\boldsymbol{\alpha})_+\|_1$ is convex and nonsmooth. Moreover,

$$\|(W_i\boldsymbol{\alpha})_+\|_1 = \max_{0 \le v_i \le 1} \langle W_i\boldsymbol{\alpha}, v_i \rangle. \tag{11}$$

By using the Nesterov smooth approximation method of [9], (11) can be approximated by the following smooth function

$$p_{\mu,i}(\boldsymbol{\alpha}) = \max_{0 \le v_i \le 1} \{\langle W_i\boldsymbol{\alpha}, v_i \rangle - \frac{1}{2}\mu\|v_i\|_2^2\}, \tag{12}$$

where μ is the parameter that controls the approximation accuracy. For fixed $\boldsymbol{\alpha}$, the unique minimizer of (12) can be derived as:

$$v_i(\boldsymbol{\alpha}) = \min\{1, \max(0, \frac{W_i\boldsymbol{\alpha}}{\mu})\}. \tag{13}$$

We then construct a smooth approximation of $P(\boldsymbol{\alpha})$ as:

$$P_\mu(\boldsymbol{\alpha}) = \sum_{i=1}^{S\times(t-1)} p_{\mu,i}(\boldsymbol{\alpha}). \tag{14}$$

The *nonsmoothed* objective function is defined as

$$F(\boldsymbol{\alpha}) = \frac{1}{2}\sum_{i=1}^{t} \|\mathbf{y}_i - X\boldsymbol{\alpha}_i\|_2^2 + \lambda_1 \sum_{j=1}^{S} \|\boldsymbol{\alpha}^j\|_2 + \lambda_2 \sum_{i=1}^{S\times(t-1)} \|(W_i\boldsymbol{\alpha})_+\|_1. \tag{15}$$

This is a convex but nonsmooth function. According to (9) and (14), $F(\boldsymbol{\alpha})$ can be approximated by the convex and smooth function as:

$$F_\mu(\boldsymbol{\alpha}) = f(\boldsymbol{\alpha}) + \lambda_1 G_\mu(\boldsymbol{\alpha}) + \lambda_2 P_\mu(\boldsymbol{\alpha}). \tag{16}$$

We adopt (16) as our regularization criterion. The gradient of $F_\mu(\boldsymbol{\alpha})$ is $\nabla F_\mu(\boldsymbol{\alpha}) = \nabla f(\boldsymbol{\alpha}) + \lambda_1 \nabla G_\mu(\boldsymbol{\alpha}) + \lambda_2 \nabla P_\mu(\boldsymbol{\alpha})$, and the corresponding Lipschitz constant is $L_{F_\mu} = L_f + \lambda_1 L_{G_\mu} + \lambda_2 L_{P_\mu}$.

To minimize the objective function $F_\mu(\boldsymbol{\alpha})$, we use the efficient accelerated proximal gradient (APG) method [22], which has the rate of convergence $O(1/n^2)$, where n is the iteration number. In terms of the desired residue ϵ, *i.e.*, $|F_\mu - \min F_\mu| \le \epsilon$, by choosing $\mu \approx \epsilon$ we have that the rate of convergence is $O(1/\epsilon)$. Algorithm 1 gives the detailed description of the optimization procedure. The regularization parameters λ_1 and λ_2 are chosen by cross-validation on a small validation subset. In particular, we enumerate the value of λ_1 and λ_2 within the set $\{0.1, 1.0, 10, 100, 1000\}$ and select the optimal one by cross-validation.

Inputs : $X \in \mathbb{R}^{D\times N}$, $\{W_i \in \mathbb{R}^{1\times N}, i = 1, 2, \cdots, S(t-1)\}$, λ_1, λ_2, μ, $\{\mathbf{y}_i, i = 1, \cdots, t\}$.
Output: $\boldsymbol{\alpha} = (\boldsymbol{\alpha}_1; \boldsymbol{\alpha}_2; \cdots; \boldsymbol{\alpha}_t) \in \mathbb{R}^{tN}$.
Initialization: Calculate $L_{F_\mu} = L_f + \lambda_1 L_{G_\mu} + \lambda_2 L_{P_\mu}$. Initialize $\boldsymbol{\alpha}_0, \boldsymbol{\beta}_0 \in \mathbb{R}^{tN}$ to be zero vectors, and let $\gamma_0 = 0$, $k = 0$.
repeat
  $\boldsymbol{u}_k = (1-\gamma_k)\boldsymbol{\alpha}_k + \gamma_k \boldsymbol{\beta}_k$,
  Calculate the gradient $\nabla F_\mu(\boldsymbol{u}_k)$.
  $\boldsymbol{\beta}_{k+1} = \boldsymbol{\beta}_k - \frac{1}{\gamma_k L_{F_\mu}} \nabla F_\mu(\boldsymbol{u}_k)$,
  $\boldsymbol{\alpha}_{k+1} = (1-\gamma_k)\boldsymbol{\alpha}_k + \gamma_k \boldsymbol{\beta}_{k+1}$,
  $\gamma_{k+1} = \frac{2}{k+1}$, $k \leftarrow k+1$.
until *Converged* ;

Algorithm 1. Minimization algorithm for (16)

3.4 Analysis

In this subsection, we analyze the approximations (9) and (14).

Proposition 1. *$G_\mu(\boldsymbol{\alpha})$ is a μ-accurate approximation to $G(\boldsymbol{\alpha})$, that is*

$$G_\mu(\boldsymbol{\alpha}) \leq G(\boldsymbol{\alpha}) \leq G_\mu(\boldsymbol{\alpha}) + \frac{1}{2}\mu S. \tag{17}$$

Proof. By (7) we have

$$0 \leq q_{\mu,j}(\boldsymbol{\alpha}^j) \leq \max_{0\leq \|\mathbf{v}_j\|_2 \leq 1} \langle \boldsymbol{\alpha}^j, \mathbf{v}_j \rangle = \|\boldsymbol{\alpha}^j\|_2. \tag{18}$$

Summing (18) over j, we obtain the upper bound

$$G_\mu(\boldsymbol{\alpha}) = \sum_{j=1}^{S} q_{\mu,j}(\boldsymbol{\alpha}^j) \leq \sum_{j=1}^{S} \|\boldsymbol{\alpha}^j\|_2 = G(\boldsymbol{\alpha}). \tag{19}$$

Since $0 \leq \|\mathbf{v}_j\|_2 \leq 1$, we also obtain the lower bound

$$q_{\mu,j}(\boldsymbol{\alpha}) \geq \max_{0\leq \|\mathbf{v}_j\|_2 \leq 1} \langle \boldsymbol{\alpha}^j, \mathbf{v}_j \rangle - \frac{1}{2}\mu = \|\boldsymbol{\alpha}^j\|_2 - \frac{1}{2}\mu. \tag{20}$$

Summing (20) over j we obtain

$$G_\mu(\boldsymbol{\alpha}) \geq G(\boldsymbol{\alpha}) - \frac{1}{2}\mu S. \tag{21}$$

Combining (19) and (21) yields (17).

Theorem 1. *The function $G_\mu(\boldsymbol{\alpha})$ is convex and continuously differentiable. Moreover, its gradient $\nabla G_\mu(\boldsymbol{\alpha}) = \sum_{j=1}^{S} \mathbf{v}_j(\boldsymbol{\alpha}^j)$ is Lipschitz continuous with constant $L_{G_\mu} = \frac{tN}{\mu}$.*

Proof. It follows directly from [9] that for $1 \le j \le S$, $\nabla q_{\mu,j}(\boldsymbol{\alpha}^j) = \mathbf{v}_j(\boldsymbol{\alpha}^j)$. The function $q_{\mu,j}(\boldsymbol{\alpha}^j)$ is Lipschitz continuous with constant $L_{G_{\mu,j}} = \frac{t \times t_j}{\mu}$. We thus have $L_{G_\mu} = \sum_{j=1}^{S} \frac{t \times t_j}{\mu} = \frac{tN}{\mu}$.

Proposition 2. *$P_\mu(\boldsymbol{\alpha})$ is a μ-accurate approximation to $P(\boldsymbol{\alpha})$, that is*

$$P_\mu(\boldsymbol{\alpha}) \le P(\boldsymbol{\alpha}) \le P_\mu(\boldsymbol{\alpha}) + \frac{1}{2}\mu S(t-1). \tag{22}$$

Proof. By definition we have

$$0 \le p_{\mu,i}(\boldsymbol{\alpha}) \le \max_{0 \le v_i \le 1} \langle W_i\boldsymbol{\alpha}, v_i\rangle = \|(W_i\boldsymbol{\alpha})_+\|_1. \tag{23}$$

Summing (23) over i, we obtain

$$P_\mu(\boldsymbol{\alpha}) = \sum_{i=1}^{S(t-1)} p_{\mu,i}(\boldsymbol{\alpha}) \le \sum_{i=1}^{S(t-1)} \|(W_i\boldsymbol{\alpha})_+\|_1 = P(\boldsymbol{\alpha}). \tag{24}$$

Since $0 \le v_i \le 1$, we have

$$p_{\mu,i}(\boldsymbol{\alpha}) \ge \max_{0 \le v_i \le 1} \langle W_i\boldsymbol{\alpha}, v_i\rangle - \frac{1}{2}\mu = \|(W_i\boldsymbol{\alpha})_+\|_1 - \frac{1}{2}\mu. \tag{25}$$

Summing both sides of (25) over i, we obtain

$$P_\mu(\boldsymbol{\alpha}) \ge P(\boldsymbol{\alpha}) - \frac{1}{2}\mu S(t-1). \tag{26}$$

Combining (24) and (26) yields (22).

Theorem 2. *The function $P_\mu(\boldsymbol{\alpha})$ is convex and continuously differentiable. Moreover, its gradient $\nabla P_\mu(\boldsymbol{\alpha}) = \sum_{i=1}^{S(t-1)} W_i^T v_i(\boldsymbol{\alpha})$ is Lipschitz continuous with constant $L_{P_\mu} = \frac{1}{\mu}\sum_{i=1}^{S(t-1)} \|W_i\|_2^2$.*

Proof. It follows directly from [9] that for $1 \le i \le S(t-1)$, $\nabla p_{\mu,i}(\boldsymbol{\alpha}) = W_i^T v_i(\boldsymbol{\alpha})$, and it is Lipschitz continuous with constant $L_{P_{\mu,i}} = \frac{1}{\mu}\|W_i\|_2^2$. We thus obtain $L_{P_\mu} = \frac{1}{\mu}\sum_{i=1}^{S(t-1)} \|W_i\|_2^2$.

3.5 Time Series Classification Rule

We denote by $X^{(j)} = [X_{j_1}, X_{j_2}, \cdots]$ the set of dictionary sequences from the j-th class. Here X_{j_i} denotes the i-th sequence in $X^{(j)}$ that belongs to the j-th class. Let $\boldsymbol{\alpha}^{(j)}$ denote the corresponding reconstruction coefficients for $X^{(j)}$. One can approximate the input sequence Y by using only the optimal coefficients associated with the j-th class as $X^{(j)}\boldsymbol{\alpha}^{(j)}$. According to the classification rule defined in [7], the predicted class label is the one with the lowest total reconstruction error:

$$j_{opt} = \arg\min_j \|Y - X^{(j)}\boldsymbol{\alpha}^{(j)}\|_F^2. \tag{27}$$

4 Experiments

To evaluate the effectiveness of our proposed method, we conduct experiments on multidimensional time series classification on a synthetic dataset, three machine learning benchmarks, and a real-world RGB-D human activity dataset. We also compare the proposed method with other state-of-the-art time series classification algorithms.

4.1 Synthetic Dataset

We first generate eight two-dimensional dictionary sequences $(X_1, X_2, \cdots, X_8)$. They are generated from eight polynomial functions: $f^1(i) = \frac{\pi}{4}$; $f^2(i) = \frac{\pi}{5}$; $f^3(i) = \frac{\pi}{10}$; $f^4(i) = \frac{\pi}{10}i$; $f^5(i) = \frac{\pi}{10}(4-i)$; $f^6(i) = \frac{\pi}{10}(i-2)^2$;$f^7(i) = \frac{2\pi}{5} - \frac{\pi}{10}(i-2)^2$; and $f^8(i) = \frac{\pi}{5}|\sin(\frac{\pi}{2}i)| + \frac{\pi}{10}$. From these functions, we generate eight length-5 two-dimensional time series as

$$X_j = \begin{bmatrix} \sin(f^j(0)) \ \sin(f^j(1)) \cdots \ \sin(f^j(4)) \\ \cos(f^j(0)) \ \cos(f^j(1)) \cdots \ \cos(f^j(4)) \end{bmatrix}, \quad j = 1, 2, \cdots, 8. \tag{28}$$

For all sequences, we add independent Gaussian noise samples with zero mean and variance 0.2 to both dimensions at each time stamp. We select the fourth sequence from the dictionary as the test time series input, *i.e.*, $Y = X_4$. Each dictionary sequence is labeled as different class. For comparison, we use a) sparse coding (SC) which computes reconstruction coefficients for each frame of the input sequence individually; b) multitask group sparse coding (Group-SC) [7]; and c) the proposed order-preserving sparse coding method (MTO-SC). Reconstruction coefficients are shown in Figure 3. We can observe that 1) reconstruction coefficients from sparse coding are similar among different dictionary sequences and therefore the representation is less discriminative. This is because sparse

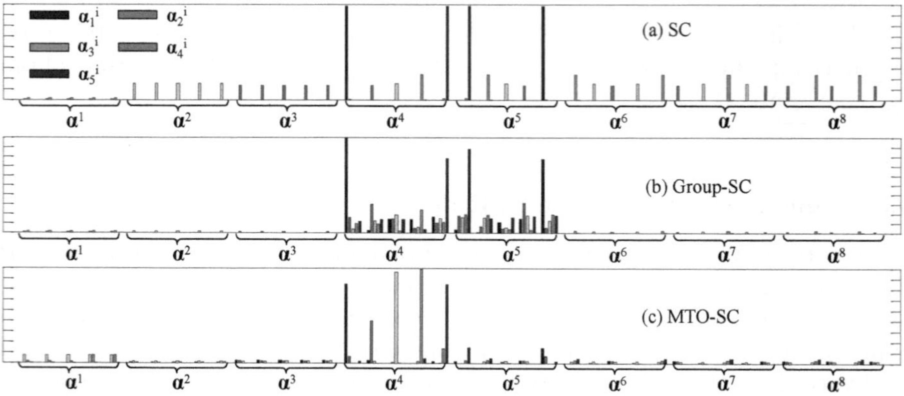

Fig. 3. Reconstruction coefficients of the input time series on the synthetic dataset using three algorithms: (a) sparse coding; (b) group sparse coding, and (c) Order-preserving sparse coding. See the color pdf for better view.

coding does not utilize any structure information of either the dictionary or the input sequence; 2) reconstruction coefficients from multitask group sparse coding [7] are nonzero on few sequences; however, without enforcing the temporal order constraint, dictionary sequences with similar individual features but different ordering structures receive similar reconstruction coefficients, which results in ambiguities; and 3) as our method explicitly encourages temporal order preservation, the reconstruction coefficients well follow the temporal ordering of the input sequence.

4.2 Machine Learning Benchmarks

We apply the proposed algorithm on three benchmark time series datasets:

- **UCI Australian Sign Language signs (High Quality) Dataset** [23]: it consists of 2565 samples of Auslan signs captured from 9 native signers using high-quality position trackers. It contains 95 different signs, with 27 samples per sign. The average length of each sign is about 60 frames. Each frame is represented as a 15 dimensional feature vector consisting of hand position (X, Y, Z), roll, yaw, pitch, bend measurements of different fingers. For the ease of experiment, we randomly selected 4 subsets of the whole dataset with each subset containing 20 categories, denoted by AusLan1, AusLan2, AusLan3 and AusLan4, respectively.
- **UCI Spoken Arabic Digits Dataset** [24]: it contains times series of mel-frequency cepstrum coefficients (MFCCs) corresponding to spoken Arabic digits. It includes data from 44 male and 44 female native Arabic speakers, capturing 8800 (10 digits $\times 10$ repetitions $\times 88$ speakers) time series of 13 Frequency Cepstral Coefficients (MFCCs). The average length of each sample is about 40 frames.
- **CMU Motion Capture Dataset (CMU MoCap)** [25]: we use the same subset as in [26] which includes 5 actions, *i.e.*, jumping, golf swing, running, climbing and walking. The dataset contains 225 sequences with average length of 300 frames. Each frame is represented by rotation angles of 11 joints and end points including head, shoulders, elbows, hands, knees and feet.

For all above datasets, we randomly split them into training and testing sets of equal size. The random split is performed 10 times and all the reported testing results are averaged over the 10 random choices of the training and testing partition. For each frame, we normalize the feature vector to be of unit ℓ_2 norm. We compare our method (MTO-SC) with the following state-of-the-art time series classification methods: 1) Segmental Hidden Markov Model [11] (S-HMM); 2) DTW-based decision tree method [13] (DTW-DT); 3) DTW-based distance embedding [14] (DTW-DE); 4) numerosity reduction based DTW [15] (NR-DTW); 5) multi-resolution symbolic representation [17] (MSR); 6) sparse coding which is performed for every individual input frame (SC) followed by majority voting; and 7) multitask group sparse coding [7] (Group-SC). For all competing algorithms, their corresponding parameters (*e.g.*, λ_1 and λ_2 in MTO-SC, number of

Table 1. Classification accuracy [mean(std. dev.)] for different algorithms on different datasets

Dataset	AusLan1	AusLan2	AusLan3	AusLan4	ArabSpokenDigit	CMU MoCap
S-HMM	75.46(1.39)	80.07(2.04)	82.30(1.77)	80.02(1.74)	54.30(1.37)	79.53(1.93)
DTW-DT	79.70(2.01)	82.73(1.98)	84.98(1.49)	83.76(1.91)	58.73(1.76)	82.97(1.64)
DTW-DE	79.93(1.49)	84.96(2.34)	85.41(1.84)	84.11(2.40)	59.60(2.40)	83.21(1.84)
NR-DTW	79.63(1.95)	85.43(1.91)	85.03(2.30)	83.09(2.21)	57.32(1.98)	83.60(1.28)
MSR	80.33(2.20)	89.77(1.35)	87.96(1.90)	85.98(1.90)	64.90(2.45)	85.36(1.92)
SC	83.09(1.89)	90.46(1.09)	90.00(1.66)	86.78(1.72)	45.98(2.10)	84.00(1.57)
Group-SC	84.19(1.76)	89.97(1.12)	91.50(1.89)	87.18(1.92)	46.04(1.99)	84.56(1.73)
MTO-SC	**91.40**(1.53)	**96.73**(1.80)	**95.53**(1.79)	**92.45**(1.81)	**75.80**(2.25)	**92.65**(1.09)

hidden states for HMM and number of neighborhood samples for DTW, etc.) are set by cross-validation on a validation subset.

We implemented these algorithms using Matlab 2010 on a 2.63 GHz machine with 8GB of memory. The average testing time per sample on AusLan1 dataset for S-HMM, NR-DTW (the fastest DTW-based method among the three), MSR, SC, Group-SC and MTO-SC are 3.5, 11.5, 2.8, 2.0, 2.2 and 2.4 seconds, respectively. We see that MTO-SC is among the most efficient methods in testing. For training, S-HMM, DTW-DT, DTW-DE, NR-DTW and MSR take about 4, 13, 3, 2.5 and 1.5 minutes, respectively, and the rest do not require training.

In Table 1, we report the mean classification accuracies averaged over 10 random splits with standard deviations. Observe that MTO-SC achieves the highest classification accuracy, owing to its capability in encoding temporal ordering structure for time series classification. To evaluate algorithmic robustness, we also add Gaussian noise to the AusLan1 dataset with zero mean and standard deviation in $\{0.1, 0.2, 0.3\}$ in three different experiments. The classification results are shown in Figure 4. Observe that our MTO-SC method is significantly more robust than its competitors.

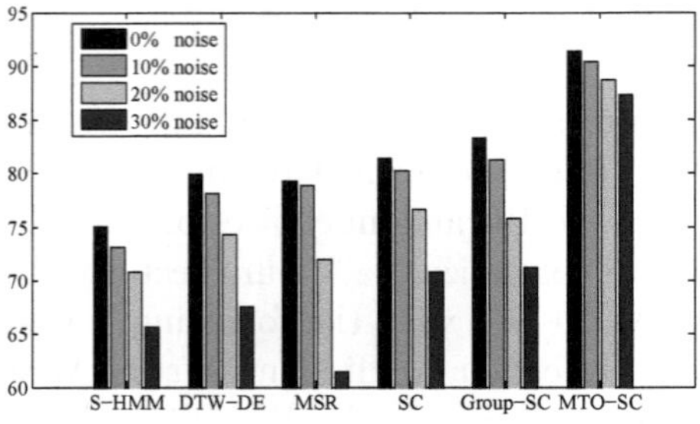

Fig. 4. Classification accuracies for different algorithms on the AusLan1 dataset under different noise conditions

4.3 Human Activity Recognition

In this experiment, we use the RGB-D human activity dataset [27]. The video dataset is captured using the Kinect sensor, which produces 640 × 480 color-depth image sequences with human 3D motion sequences, namely, each activity sample can be represented as a sequence of 3D joint positions (or angles), similar to those in the CMU MoCap dataset. The dataset consists of five scenarios: office, kitchen, bedroom, bathroom, and living room. Three to four common activities were identified for each location, giving a total of twelve unique activities collected from 4 subjects (with an additional *neutral activity* category). We use similar feature representation as in [27], where each frame is represented as a combination of body pose, hand position, motion information and object contextual information. We use the leave-one-subject-out scheme, hence subjects in the testing samples do not occur in the training samples. We compare the multiclass classification accuracies for various algorithms including the proposed MTO-SC method, the time series classification methods compared in the previous experiment and SVM, One-level MEMM and hierarchical maximum entropy Markov model, which are also evaluated in [27]. The classification accuracies are summarized in Table 2 and the class confusion matrix for our method is illustrated in Figure 5. We observe that our method outperforms the other methods.

Table 2. Classification accuracy (%) on RGB-D human activity dataset

Method	S-HMM	DTW-DT	DTW-DE	NR-DTW	MSR	SVM	MEMM	HMEMM	SC	Group-SC	MTO-SC
Accuracy	55.78	58.71	57.66	57.02	60.34	50.67	61.98	63.75	59.60	58.73	**65.32**

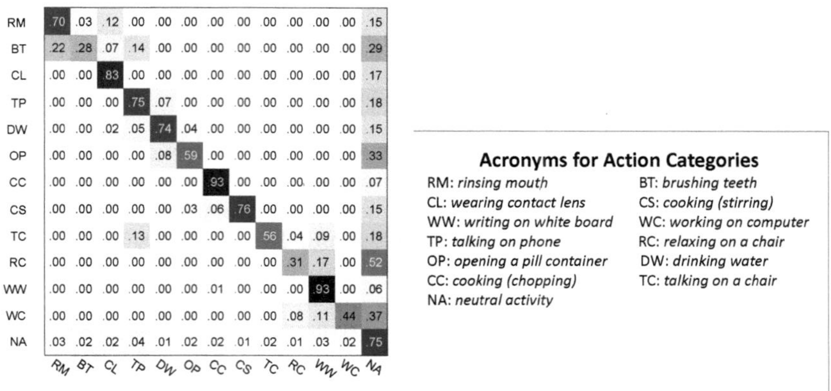

Fig. 5. Class confusion matrix for the proposed MTO-SC method on RGB-D human activity dataset

5 Conclusions and Future Work

We have proposed an order-preserving sparse coding scheme for time series classification. Extensive experiments demonstrate that this scheme is highly discriminative and robust. We will further consider learning a weighted reconstruction for different frames of the input sequence with the proposed order-preserving regularization scheme.

Acknowledgments. This study is supported by the research grant for the Human Sixth Sense Programme at the Advanced Digital Sciences Center from Singapore's Agency for Science, Technology and Research (A*STAR).

References

1. Wright, J., Yang, A., Ganesh, A., Sastry, S., Ma, Y.: Robust face recognition via sparse representation. IEEE Transactions on Pattern Analysis and Machine Intelligence 31, 210–227 (2009)
2. Elad, M., Aharon, M.: Image denoising via sparse and redundant representations over learned dictionaries. IEEE Transactions on Image Processing 15, 3736–3745 (2006)
3. Rao, S., Tron, R., Vidal, R., Ma, Y.: Motion segmentation via robust subspace separation in the presence of outlying, incomplete, or corrupted trajectories. In: CVPR (2008)
4. Zou, H., Hastie, T.: Regularization and variable selection via the elastic net. Journal of the Royal Statistical Society B 67, 301–320 (2005)
5. Yuan, M., Lin, Y.: Model selection and estimation in regression with grouped variables. Journal of the Royal Statistical Society B 68, 49–67 (2006)
6. Zhang, J.: A probabilistic framework for multi-task learning. Technical report, CMU-LTI-06-006 (2006)
7. Yuan, X., Yan, S.: Visual classification with multi-task joint sparse representation. In: CVPR (2010)
8. Raina, R., Battle, A., Lee, H., Packer, B., Ng, A.Y.: Self-taught learning: Transfer learning from unlabeled data. In: ICML (2007)
9. Nesterov, Y.: Smooth minimization of non-smooth functions. Mathematical Programming, 127–152 (2005)
10. Rabiner, L.R., Juang, B.H.: An introduction to hidden markov models. IEEE Magazine on Accoustics, Speech and Signal Processing 3, 4–16 (1986)
11. Kim, S., Smyth, P.: Segmental hidden markov models with random effects for waveform modeling. Journal of Machine Learning Research 7, 945–969 (2006)
12. Myers, C.S., Rabiner, L.R.: A comparative study of several dynamic time-warping algorithms for connected word recognition. The Bell System Technical Journal (60)
13. Rodríguez, J.J., Alonso, C.J.: Interval and dynamic time warping-based decision trees. In: ACM Symposium on Applied Computing, pp. 548–552 (2004)
14. Hayashi, A., Mizuhara, Y., Suematsu, N.: Embedding time series data for classification. Machine Learning and Data Mining in Pattern Recognition, 356–365 (2005)
15. Xi, X., Keogh, E., Shelton, C., Wei, L., Ratanamahatana, C.A.: Fast time series classification using numerosity reduction. In: ICML, pp. 1033–1040 (2006)

16. Nanopoulos, A., Alcock, R., Manolopoulos, Y.: Feature-based classification of time series data. Information Processing and Technology, 49–61 (2001)
17. Megalooikonomou, V., Wang, Q., Li, G., Faloutsos, C.: A multiresolution symbolic representation of time series. In: ICDE, pp. 668–679 (2005)
18. Manning, C.D., Schütze, H.: Foundations of statistical natural language processing. MIT press (1999)
19. Cadieu, C., Olshausen, B.: Learning transformational invariants from natural movies. In: NIPS, pp. 209–216 (2008)
20. Kim, T., Shakhnarovich, G., Urtasun, R.: Sparse coding for learning interpretable spatio-temporal primitives. In: NIPS, pp. 1117–1125 (2010)
21. Zhao, B., Fei-Fei, L., Xing, E.P.: Online detection of unusual events in videos via dynamic sparse coding. In: CVPR (2011)
22. Tseng, P.: On accelerated proximal gradient methods for convex-concave optimization. Submitted to SIAM Journal on Optimization (2008)
23. Kadous, M.W.: Temporal classification: Extending the classification paradigm to multivariate time series. PhD Thesis, School of Computer Science and Engineering, University of New South Wales (2002)
24. Hammami, N., Bedda, M.: Improved tree model for arabic speech recognition. In: Internationl Conference on Computer Science and Information Technology, pp. 521–526 (2010)
25. `http://mocap.cs.cmu.edu/`
26. Shen, Y., Ashraf, N., Foroosh, H.: Action recognition based on homography constraints. In: ICPR (2008)
27. Sung, J., Ponce, C., Selman, B., Saxena, A.: Human activity detection from rgbd images. CoRR abs/1107.0169 (2011)

Min-Space Integral Histogram

Séverine Dubuisson and Christophe Gonzales

Laboratoire d'Informatique de Paris 6,
Université Pierre et Marie Curie
{severine.dubuisson,christophe.gonzales}@lip6.fr

Abstract. In this paper, we present a new approach for quickly computing the histograms of a set of unrotating rectangular regions. Although it is related to the well-known Integral Histogram (IH), our approach significantly outperforms it, both in terms of memory requirements and of response times. By preprocessing the region of interest (ROI) computing and storing a temporary histogram for each of its pixels, IH is effective only when a large amount of histograms located in a small ROI need be computed by the user. Unlike IH, our approach, called *Min-Space Integral Histogram*, only computes and stores those temporary histograms that are strictly necessary (less than 4 times the number of regions). Comparative tests highlight its efficiency, which can be up to 75 times faster than IH. In particular, we show that our approach is much less sensitive than IH to histogram quantization and to the size of the ROI.

Keywords: Integral histogram, multiple histogram computation.

1 Introduction

The complex nature of images implies that a large amount of data needs to be stored in histograms (colors, edges, *etc.*), hence making their computations time consuming. In many applications, large sets of histograms need be computed frequently, hence making it a computational bottleneck. This explains why fast histogram computation has received some attention in the literature [1,2,3,4].

An image yields a distribution over a color space by mapping each of its pixels into its color. The histogram H of an $N \times M$ image $\mathcal{I}$ is defined by $H(k) = \sum_{x=1}^{N}\sum_{y=1}^{M}\{\mathcal{I}(x,y) = k\}$, where $\mathcal{I}(x,y)$ is a pixel, $k = 0,\dots,K-1$ is its value (in this paper, this is a color value, but gray intensities, gradient orientations, etc., could also be considered). Binning the probability distribution induced by H is a way to summarize it, and the applied quantization (bin size) controls the rate of summarization. In such a case, histogram H is divided into B bins $b = 0,\dots,B-1$, and is defined by:

$$H(b) = \sum_{x=1}^{N}\sum_{y=1}^{M}\left\{\mathcal{I}(x,y) \in \left[b\frac{K}{B}, (b+1)\frac{K}{B}\right[\right\}.$$

The classical approach to compute an histogram of a $w \times h$ region R consists of browsing all its pixels, hence yielding a time complexity of $O(wh)$.

A. Fitzgibbon et al. (Eds.): ECCV 2012, Part II, LNCS 7573, pp. 188–201, 2012.

In this paper, we propose a novel approach to speed-up multiple histogram computation by reducing computational redundancies. We will show that this new method outperforms the well-known Integral Histogram (IH) both in terms of memory requirements and of response times.

Our approach requires that the ROI in which the histograms need be computed is known in advance, that it is still applicable to some major problems of interest in computer vision, especially in visual object tracking methods that generate multiple tracking hypotheses for each frame, where an hypothesis corresponds to an unrotated rectangular patch in the frame. This includes, for instance, grid-based localization methods as well as particle filters [5], and also some recent approaches that use sets of fragments to model objects [6,7,8,9]. Actually, our motivation for developing Min Space Histograms (MSIH) was particle filtering-based tracking.

The paper is organized as follows. Section 2 first presents a short overview of the main approaches that have been proposed in the literature to speed-up histogram computation. In particular, it recalls IH's approach. Section 3 then describes our new approach: we first present the overview of the method and, then, we detail it, including its time and space complexity. Section 4 gives some comparative results for the computation of a set of histograms, both in terms of response times and memory requirements. Three approaches are compared; the classical one, IH and our method. Finally, concluding remarks are given in Section 5.

2 Fast Histograms Computations

The classical approach would certainly be sufficient for practical applications did the latter need computing only very few histograms. Unfortunately, in practice, applications often have to repeatedly compute large sets of histograms and, in those cases, a more efficient approach is compulsory to get admissible response times. To achieve this, it can be observed that the rectangular regions where histograms are computed often overlap, thus inducing some redundancies. Exploiting the latter is the key idea underlying fast histograms computation.

One of the first works in this direction was proposed in [1], in the context of image filtering (median filter). Considering the histogram H_R of a region R, that of another region Q is computed by removing from H_R the histogram of the pixels that belong to R but not to Q and adding that of the pixels that belong to Q but not to R. This approach can be very efficient when the two regions considered have a large intersection. Similar in spirit, the method proposed in [2] breaks up region R into the union of its columns in the image, and all the column histograms are kept up to date in constant time using a two-step approach. In [3], the authors propose the distributive histogram based on a distributive property of disjoint regions combined with a per-column histogram maintenance and a row-based update of these column histograms. This approach can be easily extended to cope with non-rectangular regions and multi-scale processing.

When massive amounts of histograms need be computed, IH [4] proves to be particularly effective and, actually, it is now used in many practical applications, especially in recent tracking algorithms [6]. Consider a set of regions $\{R_1, \ldots, R_n\}$ where histograms need be computed. We will call them "goal histograms" (GH). Each region R_i is identified by a quadruple $\langle x_i, y_i, w_i, h_i \rangle$ where (x_i, y_i) are the coordinates of the bottom right corner of the region in the image and w_i and h_i refer to the width and height of the region respectively. Instead of computing directly the goal histograms, IH preprocesses the image to compute efficiently a set of "temporary histograms" (TH) that prove to be sufficient to compute all the GHs. More formally, let R be the smallest rectangular area containing all the R_i, $i = 1, \ldots, n$, i.e., R is the image's region of interest (ROI). IH's preprocess consists of computing for each pixel p of the ROI the histogram $TH(p)$ of the upper left region of p. To perform this efficiently, it exploits the following formula, for any pair of coordinates (x, y) of the ROI:

$$TH(x,y) = \mathcal{I}(x,y) + TH(x-1,y) + TH(x,y-1) - TH(x-1,y-1). \quad (1)$$

THs are computed from the upper left corner of the ROI to the bottom right one and, thus, each TH is inferred from the previously computed THs using only three arithmetic operations. This guarantees the efficiency of the method. Once this preprocess is completed, for each region R_i, $i = 1, \ldots, n$, the goal histogram H_{R_i} of region R_i is simply computed as:

$$H_{R_i} = TH(x_i, y_i) - TH(x_i - w_i, y_i) - TH(x_i, y_i - h_i) + TH(x_i - w_i, y_i - h_i). \quad (2)$$

Again, the three operations involved in Eq. (2) make IH particularly effective. However, IH has two major drawbacks. First, if the ROI is large, IH consumes a large amount of memory to store one TH per ROI's pixel. Actually, if the ROI is an $N \times M$ region and if B is the total number of bins per histogram[1], then, the memory used by the THs is of size $N \times M \times B$. Second, when the number of GHs is relatively small, the classical approach that directly computes all the GHs significantly outperforms IH as the latter needs to compute many THs. In the next section, we will propose a new approach addressing both problems.

Note that all the methods presented above try to speed-up histogram computations by reducing the redundancies between the computations of the GHs in the current image (see [3] for a comparative study). But other types of redundancies can also be exploited, as in [10] where, relying on the spatial differences arising between consecutive frames, the Temporal Histogram proves to be quite effective. In the latter, to compute an histogram in a given frame, the corresponding histogram in the preceding frame is simply updated taking into account only the differences between the preceding frame and the current one. In our paper, we focus on the first type of redundancy: that between the regions of the current image and we provide in the next section a novel algorithm that significantly outperforms both IH and the classical algorithm in most cases.

[1] When the image contains several channels, B refers to the product of the number of bins per channel, e.g., $B = 512$ for 3 channels of 8 bins each.

3 Min-Space Integral Histogram

The Min-Space Integral Histogram (MSIH) is quite similar in spirit to IH. Actually, it computes some THs that correspond to histograms of the upper left region of some pixels. However, unlike IH, it does not store one histogram per pixel in the ROI but rather one per TH that is involved in Eq. (2). In other words, MSIH only requires the THs of the pixels corresponding to the corners of regions R_i[2]. In addition to these points, it also uses one additional temporary histogram during its whole preprocess. Hence it never computes more than $(4n+1)$ THs, thus significantly reducing the memory consumption compared to IH. In addition, this reduction also induces a significant speed-up.

3.1 Overview of the Method

The basic idea of MSIH is summarized in Fig. 1. Consider we wish to compute the histograms of the seven regions of Fig. 1.a and assume that the ROI is a 100×100-pixel area. Then IH has to store 10000 THs although only those corresponding to the points in blue and red on Fig. 1.b, i.e., 28 THs, are actually used in Eq. (2) to compute the histograms of the seven areas. MSIH focuses on these 28 THs. To do so, it first determines the grid where these points are located (the gray lines in Fig. 1.b). Note that this grid contains only 12 rows and 14 columns, hence an overall of 168 cells instead of 10000 for the ROI. Then, MSIH parses this grid from left to right and from top to bottom and computes incrementally the THs in an Integral Histogram-like manner. The basic idea is the following: let $TH(i,j)$ denote the TH at the ith row and jth column of the grid, then:

$$TH(i,j) = \sum_{(x,y)\in G_{ij}} \mathcal{I}(x,y) + TH(i-1,j) + TH(i,j-1) - TH(i-1,j-1), \quad (3)$$

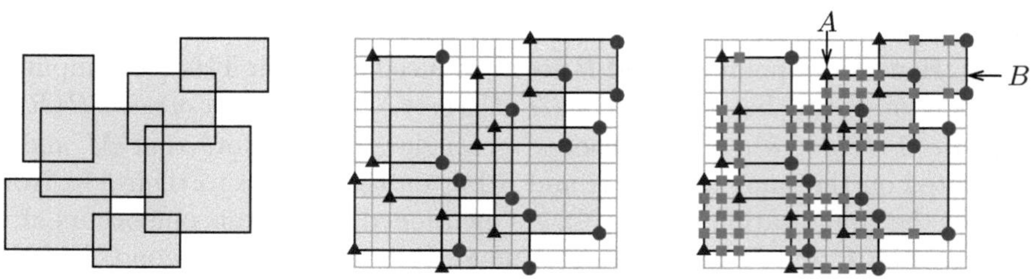

a) 7 regions b) MSIH's grid c) THs and GHs

Fig. 1. The key idea of MSIH

[2] To be precise, like IH, for each region $R_i = \langle x_i, y_i, w_i, h_i \rangle$, MSIH uses the THs corresponding to the points of coordinates (x_i, y_i), $(x_i - w_i, y_i)$, $(x_i, y_i - h_i)$ and $(x_i - w_i, y_i - h_i)$ in the image, which do not correspond exactly to the corners of R_i.

where G_{ij} is the rectangular area of the image defined by the extremal points $(G_X(i-1)+1, G_Y(j-1)+1)$ and $(G_X(i), G_Y(j))$, with $G_X(i)$ and $G_Y(j)$ representing the X and Y-coordinates in the image of the pixel corresponding to the ith row and jth column of the grid respectively. This simple scheme already outperforms IH both in terms of memory consumption (only 168 THs are stored instead of 10000) and in terms of response time (since it involves much fewer arithmetic operations on histograms). But this basic idea can be refined because, computing $TH(i,j)$ for every row and column of the grid is not necessary. Actually, as we will see, computing only those THs that are represented as green squares, blue triangles and red circles on Fig. 1.c is sufficient to compute the histograms of seven regions R_i of interest. This results in a significant improvement as there are only 91 squares, triangles and circles compared to 168 cells on the grid (12 rows by 14 columns). Note that the green points just correspond to points where histogram computations are needed, they do not involve any memory requirement: as mentioned before, at most $(4n+1)$ THs will be kept in memory (here only 29 THs are stored). Finally, we will see that even Eq. (3) itself can be improved so that it involves only 2 arithmetic operations over histograms instead of three, hence further speeding up the method.

3.2 Determination of the Temporary Histograms

Eq. (3) is the stepping stone of our TH computation: to the values of the pixels of a rectangular region G_{ij} are added or subtracted 3 previously computed THs: those of the regions above and to the left of G_{ij} and the TH of their intersection. So, the green squares shall be determined in order to enforce that whenever a region G_{ij} is involved in Eq. (3), these three THs do exist. To understand how this can simply be achieved, consider Fig. 2.a. The blue triangles and red circles correspond to the left and right corners of the regions respectively. Consider the computation of S's TH. If THs are computed from left to right and from top to bottom, then those of N, K and R have already been computed. Thus, to avoid parsing pixels of the image more than once, we shall combine the previously computed THs and add to this combination the pixels of the polygon $NMRSKJ$. Unfortunately, this one is not a rectangle, hence ruling out an application of Eq. (3). However, if points M and P are introduced and their THs are computed, then that of S can be computed as $TH(S) = \sum_{(x,y)\in G_S} \mathcal{I}(x,y) + TH(R) + TH(P) - TH(M)$, where G_S denotes rectangle $SPMR$. Note that M and P are located on the same rows as R and S but on the column to their left. Now, consider the computation of $TH(N)$. As mentioned above, this one occurs after the THs of C, F and M have been computed. But, as above, polygon $CFMN$ is not a rectangle. So, to exploit Eq. (3), we shall add a new green square J. Then, $TH(N) = \sum_{(x,y)\in G_N} \mathcal{I}(x,y) + TH(M) + TH(J) - TH(F)$, where G_N denotes rectangle $NJFM$. For the same reason, the computation of $TH(M)$ requires creating new point E. More generally, this suggests that whenever a TH needs be computed at point (i,j), that at point $(i-1,j)$ shall be computed as well. If the latter is not a corner of a region R_i of interest, then it shall be a green square. However, this rule applies only to the points of the grid that belong to some region R_i: those that are outside all the regions need not be computed. For instance, on Fig. 2.a, although the TH of K is needed, that of D is clearly unnecessary. This rule is general and is precisely that applied on Fig. 1.c to determine the 63 green squares. This leads to Algorithm 1 whose correctness is proved in Proposition 1.

Proposition 1. *The grid resulting from Algorithm 1 is such that the THs of all its nonempty points, i.e., those in red, blue or green, can be computed parsing the pixels of the ROI at most once and using Eq. (3) where only the THs of points belonging to regions $R_1, \ldots, R_n$ are taken into account.*

Proof. We shall first prove by induction that, in lines 5–9, nb_current_regions counts precisely the number of regions R_k whose right and left corners are located in columns $i+1, \ldots, w$ and $1, \ldots, i$ respectively. Of course, at the beginning of the algorithm, this property holds since V_T and V_B are initialized with zeros. Assume that the property holds on the $(i+1)$th rightmost columns of the grid and let us show that it also holds on the ith one. Vectors V_T and V_B are updated on lines 14 and 19: whenever the right side of a new region R_k is encountered (lines 10–14), $V_T[t_k]$ and $V_B[b_k+1]$ are incremented, where t_k and b_k are the grid Y-coordinates of the top and bottom corners of R_k respectively. Thus, within loop 6–9, the increment of $V_T[t_k]$ and $V_B[b_k+1]$ will induce on line 7 that nb_current_regions will be incremented by 1 as well only on rows $t_k, \ldots, b_k$, i.e.,on the rows where region R_k is located. Similarly, when the left side of region R_k is encountered, i.e., on loop 16–19, line 19 will do the inverse process, i.e., it will decrease by 1 nb_current_regions on all the rows $t_k, \ldots, b_k$. Hence, overall, nb_current_regions precisely counts the number of regions whose right sides have already been examined but not their left sides yet.

Thus, green squares are constructed on line 9 whenever i) there exist regions whose right sides have been encountered in the columns already processed, i.e., on the right, but whose left sides have not been encountered yet; and ii) in the right column, there exists either a green, blue or red point. Condition ii) indicates the we shall systematically construct green squares on columns on the left of nonempty points and condition i) removes only those green points that would be created on areas of the grid where no region R_k is located (like point D in Fig. 2.a). Consequently, if a nonempty point, say S has another point R above it (see Fig. 2.a), then, on their left column, line 9 will create two points

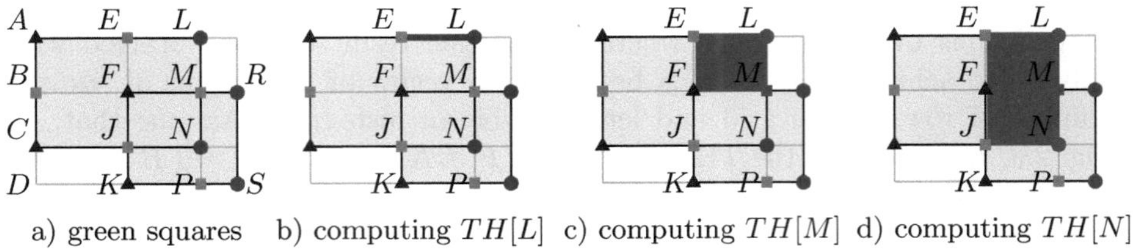

Fig. 2. Computing green squares and the THs of a given column

```
Input: a set of regions {R_1, ..., R_n}, a w × h grid G
initialize G: all cells are set to "empty" points (neither green nor blue nor red)
// create 2 vectors V_T, V_B counting, for each row, the number of
// top and bottom R_i's corners processed yet on that row
V_T, V_B ← vectors of size h + 1 filled with 0's
// fill the grid from right to left
for i = w downto 1 do
    // if there is a column on the right, create green the squares:
    if i ≠ w then
        nb_current_regions ← 0
        for j = 1 to h do
            nb_current_regions ← nb_current_regions + V_T[j] − V_B[j]
            if nb_current_regions > 0 and G[i + 1, j] ≠ empty point then
                G[i, j] ← green square
    // fill G with the regions whose corners are on its ith column
    R ← {regions R_k whose right sides are located on the ith column of G}
    foreach R_k = ⟨x_k, y_k, w_k, h_k⟩ ∈ R do
        convert image coordinates (y_k, y_k − h_k) into grid coordinates (b_k, t_k)
        G[i, b_k] ← red circle;   G[i, t_k] ← red circle
        V_T[t_k] ← V_T[t_k] + 1;   V_B[b_k + 1] ← V_B[b_k + 1] + 1
    L ← {regions R_k whose left sides are located on the ith column of G}
    foreach R_k = ⟨x_k, y_k, w_k, h_k⟩ ∈ L do
        convert image coordinates (y_k, y_k − h_k) into grid coordinates (b_k, t_k)
        G[i, b_k] ← blue triangle;   G[i, t_k] ← blue triangle
        V_T[t_k] ← V_T[t_k] − 1;   V_B[b_k + 1] ← V_B[b_k + 1] − 1
```

Algorithm 1. Determination of the points where THs are computed

P and M unless those are outside any region R_k (like point D). Thus, Eq. (3) can be applied and the proposition holds. □

We shall now see how the THs can be computed efficiently on the grid, minimizing the number of arithmetic operations over histograms.

3.3 Efficient Computation of the Temporary Histograms

As suggested by Eq. (3), we shall construct the THs on the grid from left to right and from top to bottom. But applying directly Eq. (3), as would be done to construct the THs of IH, is not efficient because this would involve 3 operations over histograms whereas the same result can be obtained with only 2. To achieve this, let H_{col} be a column vector of histograms of size the number of rows of the grid and let H_{tmp} be an histogram. Assume that, on Fig. 2.a, H_{col} contains the THs of points E, F, J, K, i.e., $H_{col}[1] = TH[E]$ (resp. $H_{col}[2] = TH[F], H_{col}[3] = TH[J], H_{col}[4] = TH[K]$) is the histogram of the union of the subparts of the regions R_k that lie above and to the left of E (resp. F, J, K). Let us now compute the THs of L, M, N, P. First, each time we process a new column in the grid, H_{tmp} is cleared so that it contains no pixel. Now, add to H_{tmp} the pixels of line $]E, L]$ as shown in red on Fig. 2.b. Then, to be a valid TH for L, we should add to H_{tmp} the histogram of the area on the left of E, which corresponds precisely to $H_{col}[1]$. Thus, adding H_{tmp} to $H_{col}[1]$, the latter contains $TH[L]$. Next, add to H_{tmp} the pixels of rectangle $MFEL$ (excluding lines $[E, L]$ and $[E, F]$). Then H_{tmp} contains the histogram of rectangle $MFEL$ excluding only line $[E, F]$ as shown in Fig. 2.c. So, as $H_{col}[2] = TH[F]$ contains the histogram of the area above and to the left of F, after adding H_{tmp} to $H_{col}[2]$, the latter contains $TH[M]$. Similarly, after adding to H_{tmp} the pixels of rectangles $NJFM$ (excluding lines $[F, M]$ and $[F, J]$), H_{tmp} contains the histogram of rectangle $NJEL$ excluding line $[E, J]$ (see Fig. 2.d). Hence, adding H_{tmp} to $H_{col}[3] = TH[J]$, we get $TH[N]$. By processing as shown above, we thus reduce the number of arithmetic operations over histograms. This leads to Algorithm 2 whose correctness is shown in Proposition 2.

Input: an image $\mathcal{I}$, a $w \times h$ grid G
Output: the set TH of temporary histograms of the blue and red points of G

$H_{col} \leftarrow$ a vector of size h of empty histograms
$H_{tmp} \leftarrow$ an empty histogram; $TH \leftarrow \emptyset$
for $i = 1$ **to** w **do**
  clear H_{tmp}
  for $j = 1$ **to** h **do**
    if $G[i, j]$ *is a red circle, a blue triangle or a green square* **then**
      let R be the rectangle from the last rows and columns where THs were computed in the grid (e.g., $NJFM$ for $H_{col}[3]$ in Fig. 2)
      add to H_{tmp} the pixels of rectangle R
      add H_{tmp} to $H_{col}[j]$
      if $G[i, j]$ *is a blue triangle or a red circle* **then**
        save $H_{col}[j]$ into $TH[i, j]$
        if *there exists no nonempty point on* $G[k, j]$ *for* $k > i$ **then**
          delete $H_{col}[j]$ from memory
return *the set TH of histograms*

Algorithm 2. Computation of the Temporary Histograms

Proposition 2. *Applying Eq. (2) with the THs resulting from Algorithm 2 yields correct histograms* H_{R_i}.

Proof. First, note that adding any histogram Δ_1 to both $TH(x_i, y_i)$ and $TH(x_i - w_i, y_i)$ and adding any histogram Δ_2 to $TH(x_i, y_i - h_i)$ and $TH(x_i - w_i, y_i - h_i)$, then, in Eq. (2), H_{R_i} is unaffected. So, in this proof, a temporary histogram $TH[i, j]$ is said to be valid if it represents the histogram of the area above and to the left of point $G[i, j]$ minus some histogram Δ and, for all points $G[k, j]$ such that the whole segment $[G[i, j], G[k, j]]$ belongs to $\bigcup_{k=1}^{n} R_k$, $TH[k, j]$ represents the histogram of the area above and to the left of point $G[k, j]$ minus Δ. For instance, in Fig. 1.c, all the THs on segment $[A, B]$ should subtract the same Δ.

This is sufficient to ensure that the same Δ will be removed from both $TH(x_i, y_i)$ and $TH(x_i - w_i, y_i)$ (resp. $TH(x_i, y_i - h_i)$ and $TH(x_i - w_i, y_i - h_i)$) in Eq. (2).

The rest of the proof is by induction. For the leftmost column of the grid, after executing lines 4–13, H_{col} clearly contains the THs of every nonempty grid point of the column since, at each iteration, $H_{col}[j] = H_{tmp}$ and, by line 7, the latter incrementally contains all the pixels from the top of the grid to the jth row. Assume now that, until the $(i-1)$th column, H_{col} contains valid THs. At the beginning of the processing of the ith column, H_{tmp} is cleared and, each time j is incremented, H_{tmp} is updated by adding precisely the image pixels that it lacked to be the histogram of all the points between columns $i-1$ and i of the grid from the top up to the jth row. Therefore, adding H_{tmp} to $H_{col}[j]$ as done in line 9, the latter actually contains a valid histogram of the area above and to the left of $G[i, j]$. Hence the property also holds on column i.

Therefore, at each step H_{col} contains valid THs. As lines 10–11 save those corresponding to blue and red points, i.e., to the corners of regions $R_1, \ldots, R_n$, set TH returned by Algorithm 2 contains valid THs. Applying Eq. (2) on them thus produces the same result as IH. □

Proposition 3. *Algorithm 2 never keeps in memory more than* $(4n + 1)$ *THs. For a* $w \times h$ *grid, a* $N \times M$ *ROI and* B *bins, the time complexity of MSIH is* $O(n \log n + whB + NM)$ *whereas that of IH is in* $O(NMB)$.

Proof. Concerning the number of THs used by Algo. 2, remark that whenever a row has no more nonempty point, line 13 removes the TH stored in $H_{col}[j]$. Thus, there are never more THs in vector H_{col} than the number of columns where there exist nonempty points. By construction of the grid, each green square and blue triangle have at least one red point on their right. Hence, the number of THs in H_{col} is never higher than the number of red points, i.e., the number of right corners, still to be examined by the algorithm. As there are at most $4n$ corners in $R_1, \ldots, R_n$, the algorithm never uses more than $(4n+1)$ THs (including H_{tmp}).

For the time complexity, determining the rows and columns of the grid can be done in $O(4n \log 2n)$ by sorting the set of X and Y-coordinates of the corners of regions R_i. For Algo. 1, the initialization of the grid is made in $O(w \times h)$ as well as the execution of lines 4–9. Parsing once the set of R_i's, we can determine in $O(n)$ all the sets $\mathcal{R}$ and $\mathcal{L}$ that will be used on lines 10 and 15. As the union of all those sets correspond to the set of corners of the R_k's, the overall complexity of lines 10–19 is in $O(4n)$. Except the parsing of the image on line 7, there are w histograms clearings (line 4), hence a complexity of $O(wB)$. In addition, line 9 is executed at most wh times, hence a complexity of whB, and line 11 is executed at most $4n$ times. Finally, as the image pixels are parsed only once, if the ROI has size $N \times M$, then all the executions of line 7–8 involve a complexity of $N \times M$. Overall, the construction of all the THs is in $O(n \log n + whB + NM)$. □

4 Experimental Results

In this section, we compare three approaches in terms of computation times and memory requirements: the classical histogram approach (CH) consisting of computing the goal histograms by scanning all the pixels of their regions, the Integral Histogram (IH) which computes one TH per pixel of the ROI (see Section 2), and our approach, the Min-Space Integral Histogram (MSIH), which was described in Section 3. For this purpose, n centers of regions R_i are randomly generated using a normal distribution centered on some location (x, y) with a covariance matrix $\begin{pmatrix} \sigma_x & 0 \\ 0 & \sigma_y \end{pmatrix}$. The size $w_i \times h_i$ of the regions can also vary, but this does not play an important role in our tests. Histograms are computed on HSV images, and their number of bins B is equal to $(B_H \times B_S \times B_V)$. To make them easier to read, all the curves presenting the results of the experiments are Y-logscaled, and correspond to averages over 20 runs. The response times of IH and MSIH include the computation of the THs and the goal histograms (GH).

4.1 Computations Times

Number of Computed Histograms. Fig. 3.(a) reports the computation times of the $(6 \times 6 \times 4)$-bin histograms of regions R_i of size 10×10, 50×50 and 100×100 respectively, in function of the number n of regions (n are 1000 times the numbers indicated on the X-axis). As may be expected, CH linearly depends on n. For small regions, e.g., on the left graph, and for small amounts of GHs (e.g., $n < 50$), CH clearly outperforms IH because the computation of its THs is too time expensive. In all benchmarks, MSIH proved to be the fastest method, especially when regions R_i are large. MSIH outperforms IH even when numerous GHs need be computed, which corresponds to situations where IH is known to be very effective. In all our tests, MSIH is 1.5 (small regions, $n = 20000$) to 40 (large regions, $n = 50$) times faster than IH.

Quantization of Histograms. One of the major drawbacks of IH is its sensitivity to the quantization of histograms: the computation of the THs (one per pixel) requires a lot of operations (and memory) when B increases. Fig. 3.(b) shows comparative results for the computation of the histograms of $n = 1000$ regions R_i of sizes 10×10, 50×50 and 100×100 respectively, in function of the number of bins per channel. To simplify, we suppose here that all channels are identically quantized. CH requires the highest computation times, and our MSIH the lowest ones. For IH and MSIH, computation times increase with B, but MSIH is less affected than IH. In all our tests, MSIH is 1.5 (small regions, $B = 2 \times 2 \times 2$) to 20 (medium regions, $B = 8 \times 8 \times 8$) times faster than IH.

Percentage of Region Overlap. The percentage of region overlap reflects the spatial dispersion of regions: the more spatially dispersed the regions, the smallest the overlap. In our tests, σ_x and σ_y control this percentage. This one is defined by $\%_{\text{overlap}} = 100 \times \frac{N_\cap}{N_T}$, where $N_\cap$ and N_T are the number of pixels belonging to at least two regions and belonging to at least one region respectively. Fig. 4 displays the times to compute $n \in \{100, 500, 1000\}$ $(6 \times 6 \times 4)$-bin

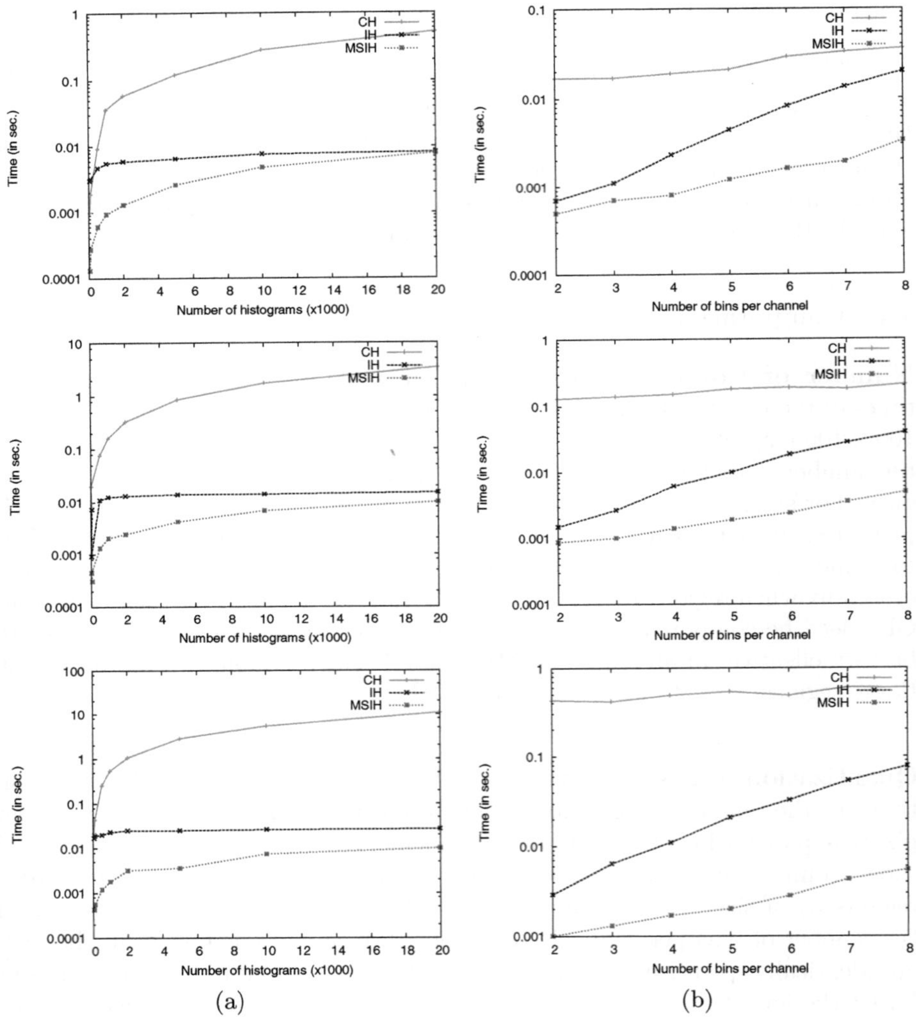

Fig. 3. Computation times (logscale) for CH, IH and MSIH depending on: (a) the number n (multiples of 1000) of regions R_i of sizes $\{10 \times 10, 50 \times 50, 100 \times 100\}$ from top to bottom; GHs are $(6 \times 6 \times 4)$-bin histograms; (b) the number of bins per channels (3 channels); $n = 1000$ regions of sizes $\{10 \times 10, 50 \times 50, 100 \times 100\}$ from top to bottom

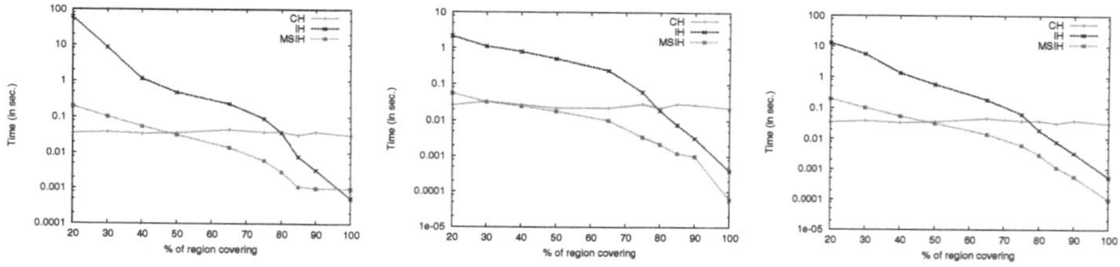

Fig. 4. Computation times (logscale) for CH, IH and MSIH depending on the percentage of region overlap, with $(6 \times 6 \times 4)$-bin histograms and regions of size 30×30, and $n = \{100, 500, 1000\}$ from left to right

histograms of 30×30 regions. CH is independent of the percentage of overlapping because all pixels are scanned to populate its histograms. For both IH and MSIH, computation times decrease when $\%_{\text{overlap}}$ increases because the size of the ROI in which they work decrease as well. For instance, in our tests with $n = 1000$ GHs, when 20% of the regions are overlapping, the average size of the ROI is 2800×2800 whereas it is only 30×30 for a 100% overlapping: this explains the discrepancy between the corresponding response times. Note however that MSIH is from 6 ($n = 100$, 100% overlapping) to 73 ($n = 100$, 20% overlapping) times faster than IH. This highlights the fact that IH is much more sensitive to the size of the ROI than our method: CH even outperforms IH when there is less than 90% of overlapping whereas it outperforms MSIH only when there is less than 20% of overlapping, which seldom happens in practice. Note that the profiles of the curves remain unchanged when the size of regions varies (even from very small regions to large ones).

4.2 Memory Requirements

The memory consumption of IH and MSIH depends linearly on the numbers of THs they store, which are denoted as $\#\text{histo}_{\text{IH}}$ and $\#\text{histo}_{\text{MSIH}}$ (blue and red points) respectively. Actually, each histogram is simply a B-length vector. Thus, the memory gain of running MSIH instead of IH, i.e., the percentage of IH's THs that MSIH does not need to store, is given by $100 \times \left(1 - \frac{\#\text{histo}_{\text{MSIH}}}{\#\text{histo}_{\text{IH}}}\right)$. Table 1 highlights how this gain is related to the number n and to the size of the regions R_i. Observe that MSIH always computes fewer THs than IH. This is especially true when large regions are considered and n is small (MSIH's gain can rise up to 99%). This is due to the fact that, when regions become large, the size of the ROI increases, which increases accordingly the number of histograms stored by IH. Table 2 highlights the impact of the percentage of region overlap, for different values of n. A first remark concerns the fact that, for fixed values of n, $\#\text{histo}_{\text{MSIH}}$ is not very dependent on $\%_{\text{overlap}}$. On the contrary, $\#\text{histo}_{\text{IH}}$ drastically increases when this percentage decreases because the size of the ROI increases. In average, MSIH stores 1500 times fewer histograms than IH for

Table 1. Comparison of memory requirements for IH and MSIH to compute $(6\times 6\times 4)$-bin histograms of regions (overlapping percentage: 95%), depending on n and $w_i \times h_i$

	$n =$	100	500	1000	5000	20000
small region 10×10	size of ROI	76×79	89×89	93×95	105×105	112×111
	$\#\text{histo}_{\text{IH}}$	6004	7921	8835	11025	12432
	$\#\text{histo}_{\text{MSIH}}$	376	1510	2400	4548	6137
	Gain	94%	81%	73%	59%	51%
medium region 50×50	size of ROI	117×117	128×128	134×135	144×144	150×151
	$\#\text{histo}_{\text{IH}}$	13689	16384	18090	20736	22650
	$\#\text{histo}_{\text{MSIH}}$	390	1720	3018	7593	11742
	Gain	98%	90%	84%	64%	49%
large region 100×100	size of ROI	166×167	179×178	183×184	194×194	238×237
	$\#\text{histo}_{\text{IH}}$	27722	31862	33672	37636	56406
	$\#\text{histo}_{\text{MSIH}}$	387	1723	3017	7641	19568
	Gain	99%	95%	92%	80%	66%

Table 2. Comparison of memory requirements for IH and MSIH to compute $(6\times 6\times 4)$-bin histograms of regions of size 30×30 depending on the overlapping percentage and the number n of regions R_i

	$\% =$	30	50	70	90
$n = 100$	size of ROI	740×722	465×433	206×197	77×75
	$\#\text{histo}_{\text{IH}}$	534280	201345	40582	5775
	$\#\text{histo}_{\text{MSIH}}$	400	399	397	374
	Gain	99.9%	99.9%	99.1%	94%
$n = 500$	size of ROI	1899×1964	1287×1211	629×654	106×109
	$\#\text{histo}_{\text{IH}}$	3729636	1558557	411366	11554
	$\#\text{histo}_{\text{MSIH}}$	1999	1996	1986	1701
	Gain	99.9%	99.9%	99.6%	86%
$n = 1000$	size of ROI	2571×2711	1704×1627	713×714	171×180
	$\#\text{histo}_{\text{IH}}$	6969981	2772408	509082	30780
	$\#\text{histo}_{\text{MSIH}}$	3996	3989	3940	3385
	Gain	99.9%	99.9%	99.3%	90%

$\%_{\text{overlap}} = 30\%$ and for any value of n. But when $\%_{\text{overlap}} = 90\%$, MSIH stores only 10 times fewer histograms.

5 Conclusion

We have introduced a new approach for fast multiple histogram computation that significantly reduces response times as well as memory consumptions, compared to both the classical approach and the well-known Integral Histogram. The idea relies on the fact that the number of temporary histograms that are computed by Integral Histograms can be reduced (up to 1500 times less). This induces a significant decrease of the computation times (up to 75 times less) as well as of memory requirement. Our current works concern the generalization of our algorithm to the computation of histograms of rotated regions.

References

1. Tang, G., Yang, G., Huang, T.: A fast two-dimensional median filtering algorithm. IEEE Transactions on Acoustics, Speech and Signal Processing 27, 13–18 (1979)
2. Perreault, S., Hebert, P.: Median filtering in constant time. IEEE Transactions on Image Processing 16, 2389–2394 (2007)
3. Sizintsev, M., Derpanis, K., Hogue, A.: Histogram-based search: A comparative study. In: Proc. of CVPR, pp. 1–8 (2008)
4. Porikli, F.: Integral histogram: A fast way to extract histograms in Cartesian spaces. In: Proc. of CVPR, pp. 829–836 (2005)
5. Gordon, N., Salmond, D., Smith, A.: Novel approach to nonlinear/non-Gaussian Bayesian state estimation. IEE Proceedings of Radar and Signal Processing 140, 107–113 (1993)
6. Adam, A., Rivlin, E., Shimshoni, I.: Robust fragments-based tracking using the integral histogram. In: Proc. of CVPR, pp. 798–805 (2006)
7. Babenko, B., Yang, M.H., Belongie, S.: Visual tracking with online multiple instance learning. In: Proc. of CVPR, pp. 983–990 (2009)
8. Mei, X., Ling, H.: Robust visual tracking using l1 minimization. In: Proc. of ICCV (2009)
9. Erdem, E., Dubuisson, S., Bloch, I.: Fragment based tracking with adaptive cue integration. Computer Vision and Image Understanding 116, 827–841 (2012)
10. Dubuisson, S.: Tree-structured image difference for fast histogram and distance between histograms computation. Pattern Recognition Letters 32, 411–422 (2011)

On Learning Higher-Order Consistency Potentials for Multi-class Pixel Labeling

Kyoungup Park[1,2] and Stephen Gould[1]

[1] College of Engineering and Computer Science, Australian National University
[2] NICTA, Australia
{kyoungup.park,stephen.gould}@anu.edu.au

Abstract. Pairwise Markov random fields are an effective framework for solving many pixel labeling problems in computer vision. However, their performance is limited by their inability to capture higher-order correlations. Recently proposed higher-order models are showing superior performance to their pairwise counterparts. In this paper, we derive two variants of the higher-order lower linear envelop model and show how to perform tractable move-making inference in these models. We propose a novel use of this model for encoding consistency constraints over large sets of pixels. Importantly these pixel sets do not need to be contiguous. However, the consistency model has a large number of parameters to be tuned for good performance. We exploit the structured SVM paradigm to learn optimal parameters and show some practical techniques to overcome huge computation requirements. We evaluate our model on the problems of image denoising and semantic segmentation.

1 Introduction

Many challenging problems in computer vision, such as semantic segmentation [1,2], geometric interpretation [3] and image denoising [4], can be formulated in terms of pixel labeling. Here the goal is to assign a label to each pixel in an image from some predefined label set. Conditional random fields (CRFs) are a powerful framework for solving these problems. Usually, the CRFs encode labeling preferences via unary terms conditioned on local pixel features and a pairwise smoothness prior over adjacent pixels. However, this encoding scheme fails to model the complex structure of objects in images.

Shotton et al. [2] attempted to enforce consistency globally by learning an image-specific appearance model for each object class and encoded as hidden variables in the CRF. This approach has the benefit of encoding consistency between disconnected regions. However, the approach is necessarily iterative since appearance models need to be estimated from an initial prediction of the pixel labeling, and errors in these predictions can negatively affect the quality of the results. Moreover, the introduction of hidden variables into the model complicates parameter learning.

Many authors have demonstrated the improvement over pairwise CRFs by incorporating higher-order constraints, which encode complex relationships over

A. Fitzgibbon et al. (Eds.): ECCV 2012, Part II, LNCS 7573, pp. 202–215, 2012.

the image. One important class of higher-order constraint enforces consistency over contiguous regions in the image. The consistency model, for example, starts from P^n Potts model [5], which favors the same label to be assigned to all pixels within the region. However, the P^n Potts model can be quite brittle especially on poorly estimated regions. For instance, if all pixels in a clique do not take the same label, the same penalty is incurred regardless of the number of inconsistent pixels. To overcome this problem, Kohli et al. [6] proposed the Robust P^n Potts model and reported impressive segmentation results due to better modeling of superpixel regions. Their model defines a penalty proportional to the number of inconsistent labels up to some maximum penalty. This model has been generalized to an arbitrary number of linear functions that define lower and upper envelops [7]. However, model performance is still sensitive to the superpixel definition of regions. One possible remedy is provided by Ladicky et al. [8], who combined multiple contiguous regions hierarchically and included a generalization of the Robust P^n model.

With the significant improvements promised by higher-order terms, the issue of learning the model parameters efficiently and effectively has become an important research question. As the number of parameters increases by the introduction of the higher-order potential, cross-validation–typically used for pairwise models–is not effective. Szummer et al. [9] show the max-margin framework is efficient solution for learning parameters in pairwise CRF models, especially using graph cuts. Gould [10] proposed an alternative energy minimization construction for the case of binary consistency potentials and resolved the learning issue with a modified max-margin framework. On top of the standard max-margin framework, they included additional linear constraints by adding a second-order curvature constraint to ensure that the higher-order potentials remain concave functions. Komodakis [11] showed an alternative interpretation of the max-margin learning using the dual-decomposition method.

In this paper, we explore variants of the higher-order potential that encodes a preference for consistency over large (and possibly disjoint) regions. Building on the work of Gould [10], we generalize the binary case to the multi-class case. Our model defines a concave penalty function over the number of pixels within a predefined region (or clique) that is annotated with a given label. Importantly, we do not restrict the pixel sets to contiguous local regions. In our experiments, we show that the non-local regions are beneficial in encoding global labeling constraints. We derive α-expansion and $\alpha\beta$-swap moves that can be generalized to multi-class lower linear envelop functions. Our paper also provides efficient and effective learning methods for the large number of parameters. We show how the max-margin learning method is affected by our approximate inference to find the optimal parameters, and propose a number of heuristics to reduce the heavy computation required by the max-margin method.

Our contributions in this paper include: First, we derive two different extensions (i.e., min or *sum*) of the binary lower linear envelop function to the multi-class case with approximate move-making inference. The derivation generalizes the higher-order consistency terms with the lower linear envelop function.

Second, we explore the max-margin learning for our extended higher-order terms and reduce the training time significantly with approximate solutions for large-scale training examples. Third, we apply our model to the task of multi-class pixel labeling with non-local consistency constraints. Our approach is evaluated on the 21-class MSRC image segmentation data set.

2 Background

We begin by providing a brief background to submodular energy functions and move-making inference for multi-class conditional random fields (CRFs).[1]

Submodular Energy Functions. Consider a binary pairwise conditional Markov random field (CRF) over variables $\boldsymbol{y} = (y_1, \ldots, y_n) \in \{0,1\}^n$ and observed features $\boldsymbol{x}$. Let $\mathcal{V} = \{1, \ldots, n\}$ denote the set of *nodes* and $\mathcal{E} \subset \mathcal{V} \times \mathcal{V}$ denotes the set of *edges*. Then we can write the energy function for the CRF as

$$E(\boldsymbol{y}; \boldsymbol{x}, \boldsymbol{\theta}) = \sum_{i \in \mathcal{V}} \psi_i^U(y_i; \boldsymbol{x}) + \sum_{(i,j) \in \mathcal{E}} \psi_{ij}^P(y_i, y_j; \boldsymbol{x}) \tag{1}$$

where $\boldsymbol{\theta}$ are the model parameters. The terms $\psi_i^U(y_i; \boldsymbol{x})$ are known as *unary potentials* and capture the labeling preference for a single variable in the random field. The terms $\psi_{ij}^P(y_i, y_j; \boldsymbol{x})$ are known as *pairwise potentials* and define a preference over two variables. The pairwise terms are typically defined over a sparse subset $\mathcal{E}$ of all possible variables pairs (i.e. adjacent pixels in the image). If two nodes $(i, j) \in \mathcal{E}$, then the node i and the node j are said to be *neighbors*. In pixel labeling problems, it is usual to use the pairwise term to smooth via a contrast sensitive term of the form

$$\psi_{ij}(y_i, y_j; \boldsymbol{x}) = \lambda [\![y_i \neq y_j]\!] \exp\left\{ -\frac{1}{2\beta} \|x_i - x_j\|^2 \right\} \tag{2}$$

where $[\![\cdot]\!]$ is the indicator function which takes 1 when the argument is true and 0 otherwise, x_i is the color vector for pixel i, and λ and β are global and image specific constants that determine the strength of the smoothness prior.

An equivalent representation for the pairwise binary CRF is as a quadratic pseudo-Boolean function (QPBF) [12]. Here we write the energy function $E : \{0,1\}^n \to \mathbf{R}$ in *posiform* as

$$\begin{aligned} E(\boldsymbol{y}; \boldsymbol{x}, \boldsymbol{\theta}) = {} & \theta_{const}(\boldsymbol{x}) + \sum_{i \in \mathcal{V}} \theta_{i;0}(\boldsymbol{x}) \overline{y}_i + \theta_{i;1}(\boldsymbol{x}) y_i \\ & + \sum_{(i,j) \in \mathcal{E}} \theta_{ij;00}(\boldsymbol{x}) \overline{y}_i \overline{y}_j + \theta_{ij;01}(\boldsymbol{x}) \overline{y}_i y_j + \theta_{ij;10}(\boldsymbol{x}) y_i \overline{y}_j + \theta_{ij;11}(\boldsymbol{x}) y_i y_j \end{aligned} \tag{3}$$

[1] We will use the terms MRF and CRF interchangeably from now on.

where $\overline{y}_i = 1 - y_i$ and all coefficients $\theta_{a;b}(\boldsymbol{x})$ are non-negative with the possible exception of the constant term θ_{const}.[2] The coefficients can be constant or some functions of the observed features $\boldsymbol{x}$. With respect to the pixel labeling problem, we have $\theta_{ij;00} = \theta_{ij;11} = 0$ and $\theta_{ij;01} = \theta_{ij;10} = \lambda \exp\left\{-\frac{1}{2\beta}\|x_i - x_j\|^2\right\}$.

A pseudo-Boolean function is called submodular if and only if $f(\boldsymbol{u}) + f(\boldsymbol{v}) \geq f(\boldsymbol{u} \vee \boldsymbol{v}) + f(\boldsymbol{u} \wedge \boldsymbol{v})$ for all binary vectors $\boldsymbol{u}, \boldsymbol{v} \in \{0,1\}^n$. An equivalent condition for the binary pairwise CRFs (i.e., quadratic pseudo-Boolean function) can be written in posiform notation with $\theta_{ij;00} = \theta_{ij;11} = 0$ for all variable pairs $(i,j) \in \mathcal{E}$. Note that the contrast sensitive smoothness prior (Eq. (2)) is submodular. In the computer vision literature submodularity is sometimes referred to as regularity [13].

The goal of inference is to find the assignment $\hat{\boldsymbol{y}}$ with minimum energy. Message-passing algorithms can be suitable for the objective, but it is well known that for submodular pairwise energy functions this can be done efficiently by finding the minimum-cut in a suitably constructed graph [14,15,16]. Unfortunately, in general for multi-label CRFs (or indeed, non-submodular binary CRFs), inference is intractable and we need to resort to approximate routines.

Move-Making Inference. Generally, most energy minimization problems are NP-hard [13]. However, there are good approximate solutions available. For example, some move-making algorithms reduce the energy minimization to sequence of smaller problems which are submodular. Here, each move restricts the label space of variables to at most two values from the label set. The algorithm starts from an initial labeling. Then, it searches move spaces to minimize the energy relative to the previous assignment. If no improvement is found after searching over the restricted label space, the solution is considered to converge to a local minimum. The algorithm can be formalized as follows: Consider the current assignment $\boldsymbol{y}^{prev} \in \mathcal{L}^n$, where $\mathcal{L}$ is the set of possible labels to each variable. If the energy $E(\boldsymbol{y}_t)$ from $\boldsymbol{y}_t \in \{\boldsymbol{y}^{prev}\} \cup \mathcal{Y}^t$ is less than $E(\boldsymbol{y}^{prev})$, the assignment $\boldsymbol{y}_t$ is updated as $\boldsymbol{y}^{next}$ at the iteration t, where $\mathcal{Y}^t$ is a possible movement at the iteration t. Otherwise, $\boldsymbol{y}^{prev}$ is kept as $\boldsymbol{y}^{next}$.

An early example of move-making algorithms is Iterated Conditional Modes (ICM) [17]. For a variable, it finds the optimal solution conditioned on all other variables. However, the update of a single variable makes its convergence slow and can easily get stuck in poor local optima. The more advanced examples of move-making algorithms are α-expansion and $\alpha\beta$-swap [15]. In α-expansion, a label from $\mathcal{L}$ is chosen iteratively. Each variable can switch to the chosen label α or keep the current label, which expands the current label α to other regions as long as the energy is reduced. It continues to iterate through the label set until the energy reduces no more. Similarly, during $\alpha\beta$-swap, two labels from $\mathcal{L}$ are iteratively selected. Then it makes moves by swapping only between variables with either of the two labels and retains all other variable assignments. In summary, the three algorithms are characterized as follows:

[2] Note that this representation is not unique.

- **ICM**: for a given variable $i \in \mathcal{V}$, we choose the $y_i^{next} \in \mathcal{L}$ that minimizes the energy with $y_i^{next} = y_j^{prev}$ for all $j \neq i$.
- **α-expansion**: for all i, we choose the $y_i^{next} \in \{y_i^{prev}, \alpha\}$ that jointly minimize the energy.
- **$\alpha\beta$-swap**: for all i such that $y_i^{prev} \in \{\alpha, \beta\}$, we choose the $y_i^{next} \in \{\alpha, \beta\}$ that jointly minimize the energy and $y_j^{next} = y_j^{prev}$ for all other variables.

For α-expansion and $\alpha\beta$-swap, an efficient graph-cut based algorithm has been proposed to minimize the energy functions composed of pairwise potential functions [16,13].

3 Higher-Order Consistency Potentials

The usual form of the energy function for a CRF model is composed of the sum of unary and pairwise potentials. The unary potential ψ_i is represented as the negative log of the likelihood of a label assigned to a node i while the pairwise potential ψ_{ij} encodes the interaction between the neighborhood nodes. The Potts model is an example of the pairwise potential to impose image smoothness. In spite of its improvement in removing noise, the pairwise terms can over smooth resulting in poor object boundaries. Due to the limitations of the pairwise potential model, the development of more sophisticated models with higher-order terms have been developed (see Eq. (4)). These higher degree potentials ψ_c^H are capable of capturing more powerful statistics over images.

$$E(\boldsymbol{y}; \boldsymbol{x}, \boldsymbol{\theta}) = \sum_{i \in \mathcal{V}} \psi_i^U(y_i) + \sum_{(i,j) \in \mathcal{E}} \psi_{ij}^P(y_i, y_j) + \sum_{c \in \mathcal{C}} \psi_c^H(\boldsymbol{y}_c) \tag{4}$$

In this section, we describe two variants of lower linear envelop functions introduced by [7]. These can encode arbitrary concave functions over the number of variables taking a given assignment. Gould [10] showed that the potentials can be represented by pairwise submodular energy functions for the case of binary MRFs. We extend the binary lower linear envelope functions to multi-class inference problem using α-expansion and $\alpha\beta$-swap move algorithms.

Generalized Multi-class Representation. Here we extend and generalize the binary lower linear envelope potential functions described in Gould [10] to a multi-class problem. Consider an arbitrary set of multi-class variables $\boldsymbol{y}_c = \{y_i \mid i \in c\}$ where $c \subseteq \{1, \ldots, n\}$. We define our multi-class consistency potential as

$$\psi_c^H(\boldsymbol{y}_c) = \bigoplus_{l \in \mathcal{L}} \min_{k=1,\ldots,K_l} \{a_k^l \sum_{i \in c} \omega_i [\![y_i = l]\!] + b_k^l\} \tag{5}$$

where (a_k^l, b_k^l) are parameter pairs of each k-th linear envelop function for label l. We assume that the parameters are sorted by a_k^l in decreasing order for each label, which means that $a_k^l > a_{k+1}^l$ and $b_k^l < b_{k+1}^l$ for each label l. Thus, a set of K_l linear functions composes piecewise linear envelop functions to assign a penalty for each label l being inconsistent over the subset $\boldsymbol{y}_c$. The aggregation $\bigoplus$ can represent {min or $\sum$} to measure various penalties over the cliques. We consider three cases for the same objective:

1. $\psi_c^H(\boldsymbol{y}_c) = \min_l \min_k \{b_k^l + a_k^l \sum_{i \in c} [\![y_i = l]\!]\}$
2. $\psi_c^H(\boldsymbol{y}_c) = \sum_l \min_k \{b_k^l + a_k^l \sum_{i \in c} [\![y_i = l]\!]\}$
3. $\psi_c^H(\boldsymbol{y}_c) = \min_{k'} \{b_{k'} + a_{k'} \sum_{i \in c} [\![y_i = l_{k'}]\!]\}$

Case 1 finds the least potential function among all label set with K_l functions and is identical to Case 3 just with different parameterizations over all sorted functions. Case 2 is the extended form of the binary case [10], which minimizes the sum of the penalties over each lower linear envelop function. Note that the per-variable weight ω_i is set as one for convenience.

α-Expansion Move. From the generalized higher-order potential function, we derive the α-expansion move for approximate minimization of the linear envelop potential functions. Let $\boldsymbol{y}^{prev} \in \mathcal{L}^n$ be the current best assignment of labels and $S_l = \{i \mid y_i^{prev} = l\}$ be the subset whose variables are assigned to label l. For α-expansion, we constrain the moves to $y_i^{next} \in \{y_i^{prev}, \alpha\}$. To encode the expansion moves, the binary transfer vector $\boldsymbol{t}$ is defined as

$$y_i^{next} = \begin{cases} y_i^{prev} \ (\neq \alpha) & \text{if } t_i = 0 \\ \alpha & \text{if } t_i = 1 \ . \end{cases} \tag{6}$$

Then, we can rewrite the restricted potential function with the new variables;

$$\begin{aligned} \psi_c^\alpha(\boldsymbol{t}) &= \bigoplus_{l \in \mathcal{L}} \min_k \left\{ a_k^l \sum_{i \in S_l} \{t_i [\![l = \alpha]\!] + \bar{t}_i [\![l \neq \alpha]\!]\} + b_k^l \right\} \\ &= \left(\bigoplus_{l \neq \alpha} \min_k \{a_k^l \sum_{i \in S_l} \bar{t}_i + b_k^l\} \right) \oplus \left(\min_k \{a_k^\alpha (\sum_{i \notin S_\alpha} t_i + N_\alpha) + b_k^\alpha\} \right) \end{aligned} \tag{7}$$

where $N_l = |S_l|$. Replacing $\bar{t}_i = 1 - t_i$ and substituting each coefficient and subset with

$$\tilde{a}_k^l = \begin{cases} -a_k^l & \text{for } l \neq \alpha \\ a_k^\alpha & \text{for } l = \alpha \end{cases}, \ \tilde{b}_k^l = b_k^l + a_k^l N_l, \ \text{and } \tilde{S}_l = \begin{cases} S_l & \text{for } l \neq \alpha \\ \overline{S}_\alpha & \text{for } l = \alpha \end{cases}, \tag{8}$$

we have the general form of a lower linear envelop function over binary variables

$$\psi_c^\alpha(\boldsymbol{t}) = \bigoplus_{l \in \mathcal{L}} \min_k \{\tilde{a}_k^l \sum_{i \in \tilde{S}_l} t_i + \tilde{b}_k^l\} \ . \tag{9}$$

$\alpha\beta$-Swap Move. Similarly defining the transfer vector $\boldsymbol{t}$ as

$$y_i^{next} = \begin{cases} \alpha & \text{if } t_i = 0 \\ \beta & \text{if } t_i = 1 \end{cases} \quad \forall i \in S_\alpha \cup S_\beta \ , \tag{10}$$

we arrive at

$$\psi_c^{\alpha\beta}(\boldsymbol{t}) = \left(\bigoplus_{l=\alpha,\beta} \min_k \{\tilde{a}_k^l \sum_{i \in S_\alpha \cup S_\beta} t_i + \tilde{b}_k^l\} \right) \bigoplus_{l \neq \alpha,\beta} C_l \tag{11}$$

where $C_l = \min_k\{a_k^l N_l + b_k^l\}$ is a constant to account for all variables excluded from the move. Again, this is a lower linear envelop function over binary variables.

Applying Auxiliary Variables. In addition to the transfer vector $\boldsymbol{t}$ above, we need to transform the higher-order potential functions to the form of quadratic pseudo-Boolean function for energy minimization to be tractable. For simplicity, we assume that each class has K linear functions and there are $|\mathcal{L}|$ different classes. However, our method extends to the general case of $K_l \neq K_{l'}$. In [10], an alternative way to minimize over the piecewise linear functions is introduced using binary auxiliary variables. The minimization over K linear functions can be encoded by introducing $K - 1$ binary auxiliary variables. Extended to the multi-class case, the required binary variables z_k^l are $|\mathcal{L}|(K-1)$ for the set of all labels. Here we take an example of replacing the aggregation with '$\sum$'.[3] Then, we can derive the QPBF representation for α-expansion as

$$\hat{\psi}_c^\alpha(\boldsymbol{t}, \boldsymbol{z}) = \min_{\boldsymbol{z}} \tilde{E}_c^\alpha(\boldsymbol{t}, \boldsymbol{z}^\alpha) + \sum_{l \neq \alpha} \tilde{E}_c^l(\boldsymbol{t}, \boldsymbol{z}^l) \tag{12}$$

where
$$\begin{aligned} \tilde{E}_c^\alpha(\boldsymbol{t}) = a_K^\alpha \sum_{i \notin S_\alpha} t_i + a_K^\alpha N_\alpha + b_1^\alpha + \sum_{k=1}^{K-1} \overline{z}_k^\alpha (a_k^\alpha - a_{k+1}^\alpha) \sum_{i \notin S_\alpha} t_i \\ + \sum_{k=1}^{K-1} \overline{z}_k^\alpha (a_k^\alpha - a_{k+1}^\alpha) N_\alpha + \sum_{k=1}^{K-1} z_k^\alpha (b_{k+1}^\alpha - b_k^\alpha) \end{aligned} \tag{13}$$

and

$$\tilde{E}_c^l(\boldsymbol{t}) = b_1^l + a_K^l \sum_{i \in S_l} \bar{t}_i + \sum_{k=1}^{K-1} z_k^l (a_k^l - a_{k+1}^l) \sum_{i \in S_l} \bar{t}_i + \sum_{k=1}^{K-1} \overline{z}_k^l (b_{k+1}^l - b_k^l)\,. \tag{14}$$

Note that contrasting the description in [10], the explicit constraints to enforce $z_k^l \geq z_{k+1}^l$ is not required any more because the constraints are implicitly sufficient to get the minimum energy. Now, we have the restricted submodular potential functions, which can be minimized in time polynomial in the number of variables using the graph cuts algorithm. Figure 1 illustrate the st-graph constructions for both the move-making algorithms.

[3] Unlike the $\alpha\beta$-swap move, the α-expansion should be derived for '$\sum$' because of the submodularity condition.

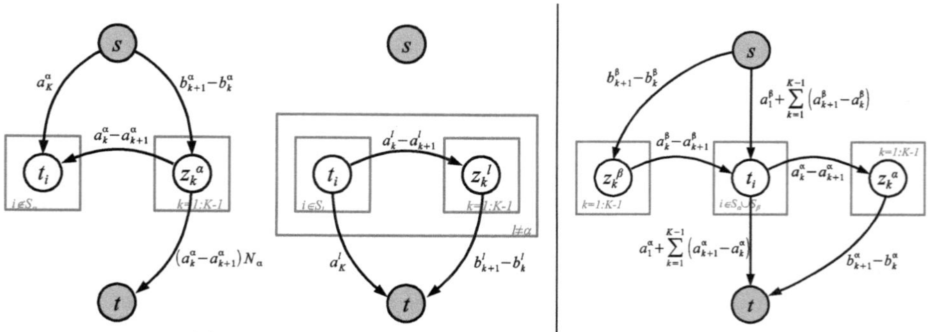

(a) α-expansion (b) $\alpha\beta$-swap

Fig. 1. st-graphs for α-expansion and $\alpha\beta$-swap moves. The rectangles indicate replication of nodes.

4 Learning Parameters with Structured SVM

In this section, we describe how to learn the parameters including our lower linear envelop potentials. Our multi-class model needs to learn $2 + (K+1)|\mathcal{L}|$ parameters for unary, pairwise and higher-order terms. The cross-validation approach usually employed for pairwise learning is not a feasible method for this large number of parameters. To learn parameters efficiently, we adopt a variant of the max-margin framework by [18,19].

Let an energy function $E(\boldsymbol{y};\boldsymbol{\theta}) = \boldsymbol{\theta}^\top \phi(\boldsymbol{y})$ be parameterized as linear combination of features $\phi(\boldsymbol{y}) \in \mathbb{R}^m$ and weights $\boldsymbol{\theta} \in \mathbb{R}^m$ where m is the number of the parameters. The framework learns weights for the energy function given a training set $\mathcal{Y} = \{\boldsymbol{y}_t\}_{t=1}^T$ and the objective function with constraints is

$$\underset{\boldsymbol{\theta},\,\boldsymbol{\xi}\succeq 0}{\text{minimize}} \quad \frac{1}{2}\|\boldsymbol{\theta}\|^2 + \frac{C}{T}\sum_{t=1}^{T}\xi_t \tag{15}$$

$$\text{subject to } E(\boldsymbol{y};\boldsymbol{\theta}) - E(\boldsymbol{y}_t;\boldsymbol{\theta}) \geq \Delta(\boldsymbol{y},\boldsymbol{y}_t) - \xi_t \qquad \boldsymbol{y} \in \mathcal{Y}_t,\ \forall t$$

$$\mathbf{G}\boldsymbol{\theta} \geq \mathbf{0} \tag{16}$$

where $\mathcal{Y}_t \subseteq \mathcal{L}^n$ is the set of all possible assignments for t-th training example and C is a regularization constant. The loss Δ compensates the large margin for each high loss example. To solve the above quadratic program, the constrains should be satisfied by all the possible assignments $\boldsymbol{y}$. Due to the large number of the possible assignments, this optimization problem can be solved by cutting-plane method by finding the most violated ones first; other potential constraints are then guaranteed to have larger margin than the subset of constraints. The Hamming loss Δ is suitable to be decomposed to the unary potential and we can get the most violated constraints by graph-cuts algorithm ($\boldsymbol{y}^* = \text{argmin}_{\boldsymbol{y}} E(\boldsymbol{y};\boldsymbol{\theta}) - \Delta(\boldsymbol{y},\boldsymbol{y}_t)$).

In order to learn the parameters by the max-margin framework, our higher-order term requires re-parameterization. Let $\psi_c^H(\boldsymbol{y};\boldsymbol{\theta}) = \boldsymbol{\theta}^\top \phi(\boldsymbol{y})$. The feature vector $\phi(\boldsymbol{y}) = \{\phi^l \mid l \in \mathcal{L}, \phi^l \in \mathbb{R}^{K+1}\}$ represents the consistency of the clique by the number of pixels for each label l (i.e. $\phi_k^l(\boldsymbol{y}) = \sum_c \sum_{i \in c} [\![y_i = l]\!]$). And the coefficients are converted to the parameters to learn such as $a_k^l = \theta_k^l - \theta_{k-1}^l$ and $b_k^l = \theta_k^l - k a_k^l$ for $k = 1, \ldots, K+1$. The additional constraint (16) enforces the parameters $\boldsymbol{\theta}$ of our higher-order potentials to be the concave function (refer to [10] for further details).[4]

Max-margin learning is a powerful framework but computationally expensive on large data sets. Specifically, it demands comprehensive search for violated constraints from all training examples at every iteration. Intuitively, we can borrow some idea from stochastic gradient descent to speed convergence. Instead of testing the whole training set, taking a subset of the examples at each iteration results in decrease of the computational complexity. For example, if an example had no violated constraints found before, the example will be discarded for inference of most violated constraint. After skipping all examples, we seek violated constraints for all examples again. This method still guarantees to converge to optimal parameters because it finally satisfies all constraints for the training examples. Another heuristic speed-up is to reduce the number of iterations in move-making inference. During training, we know the ground-truth labels of the training examples, therefore we expect that the minimum energy assignment tends to belong to the ground-truth labels. By reducing the label set to only ground-truth labels in the move-making algorithm, the loss-augmented inference time as a main part of the training time, can be saved at the risk of missing the most violated constraints. Choosing the optimal move space is a topic of active research area (see [20]).

5 Experiments

Denoising with Synthetic Data. This synthetic experiment is a toy example that verifies the overall performance of the algorithm on a denoising task. The input data is an artificially generated checkerboard image. Here we generate 8×8 checkerboards and each square contains 16×16 variables assigned with one of five labels consistently. The unary potential is $\psi_i^U(y_i) = \theta^{unary} x_i(y_i)$ and generated with noise as $x_i(y_i) = \mathcal{U}[1,2] - 0.3\mathcal{U}[0,1][\![y_i = y_i^*]\!]$ where y_i^* is a ground truth label for the pixel i and $\mathcal{U}[0,1]$ is the uniform distribution. The pairwise potential is $\psi_{ij}^P(y_i, y_j) = \theta^{pair}[\![y_i \neq y_j]\!]$ and defined between every pair of adjacent variables. Each checkerboard coincides with a consistency clique for the input of the higher-order term. We set the number of the linear envelop functions per label to $K = 5$.

Figure 2 compares the denoised images inferred with all the parameters learned by the max-margin learning. As expected, the pairwise model does not recover the noisy image perfectly (Fig. 2b and 2f). However, we can see the images 2c and 2d, where parameters have been learned by α-expansion, are coincident with the ground truth. When $\alpha\beta$-swap is used, the performance is slightly worse (see 2g and 2h). With the higher-order terms involved, the value of the pairwise

[4] To ensure the energy function remains submodular, θ^{pair} must be non-negative.

parameter became negligible,[5] which indicates that the higher-order term is more dominant than the pairwise term because the higher-order consistency term is the generalized form of the pairwise term in the experiment. Another interesting point is that move-making algorithms are approximate solutions to the global minimum energy [15] and the approximate inference for generating constraints in learning can lead the max-margin framework to perform poorly [21], which explains that the learning with $\alpha\beta$-swap move left some noise in the image.

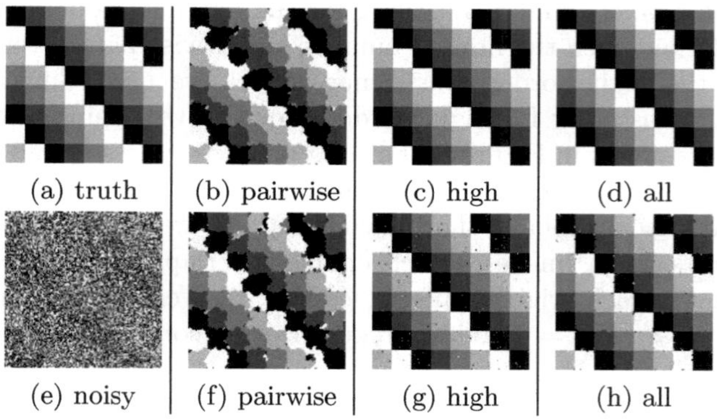

Fig. 2. Results from our synthetic data. 2a is the ground truth with 5 different labels and 2e is the noisy image. 2b - 2d are results by α-expansion. 2f - 2h are results by $\alpha\beta$-swap move.

Multi-class Segmentation. We evaluate the performance of our model conducting semantic segmentation on the MSRC data set (23 classes)[6]. While there exist very powerful models for achieving state-of-the-art results on this data set (e.g., Ladicky et al. [8] use sophisticated features and a hierarchical CRF model), our interest is in evaluating the learning algorithm for higher-order consistency potentials. We, therefore, choose a simpler baseline model consisting of a pairwise smoothness prior and unary potentials learned from local color and texture features. As is standard with this data set, we removed the two scarcest classes ('horse' and 'mountain') by filling with the 'void' label. Based on the previously published works on this data set, we divided the image set into 315 training and 276 test images. This separation repeated with five random shuffles.

The baseline (unary, pairwise) models follow the standard pixelwise MRF models.[7] The unary potentials are encoded by boosted decision trees via multiclass logistic regression classifier. The features are derived from 17 filters over images. The pairwise potentials are contrast-dependent smoothness terms for 8 neighbors defined as $\psi^P_{ij}(y_i, y_j) = [\![y_i \neq y_j]\!] \exp\left\{-\frac{1}{2\beta}\|x_i - x_j\|^2\right\}$ where β is the average squared distance between adjacent color vectors and x_i and x_j are RGB

[5] The ratio is about 42 times ($\theta^{unary} = 7.33 \times 10^{-4}$ and $\theta^{pair} = 1.76 \times 10^{-5}$).
[6] `http://www.cs.cmu.edu/~tmalisie/projects/bmvc07/`
[7] `http://drwn.anu.edu.au`

Fig. 3. Separate pixel sets for non-local regions and contiguous regions. The five pixel sets by GMM are illustrated followed by mean-shift clustering.

color vectors for pixel i and j. Learning for the baseline model was conducted by cross-validation given the limited number of pairwise parameters.

Regarding the higher-order consistency model, we used Gaussian Mixture Model (GMM) clustering for higher-order cliques: five groups of clusters over pixel colors.[8] As shown in Figure 3, the superpixels vary in size and shape unlike the checkerboards. Different to contiguous clustering, the GMM clustering defines non-local regions globally sharing common features (i.e. colors or textures) over similar objects in images, which enables overlapped or disjointed object parts to belong to each original object (see Fig. 3). We set the number of linear functions per class as $K = 3$ and the regularization constant as $C = 1$.

Table 1. Averaged results with standard deviation for five experiments on 21-class MSRC data set ((B)='Baseline', (V)='Validation', (R)='Reduced Set')

Model	Evaluation Accuracy		Time (d:h:m)
	Overall	Class	
Unary(B)	58.44±1.04	42.40±1.08	26m
Unary+Pair(B)	73.23±2.39	58.69±4.21	2h53m
Unary+Pair	71.65±1.20	59.18±1.42	1h19m
Unary+Pair(R)	71.19±1.25	58.64±1.50	9m
Unary+Pair(V)	76.09±1.21	64.66±1.55	1h5m
Unary+Pair(RV)	74.11±1.39	62.38±1.75	43m
Unary+High	73.22±1.22	61.23±1.27	8h8m
Unary+High(V)	73.06±1.17	60.86±0.75	7h51m
Full	**79.47**±1.38	69.55±0.94	2d15h21m
Full(R)	75.51±1.59	66.48±1.92	11h46m
Full(V)	**79.68**±1.42	69.48±1.17	2d6h28m
Full(RV)	76.02±1.74	67.48±1.95	1d9h46m

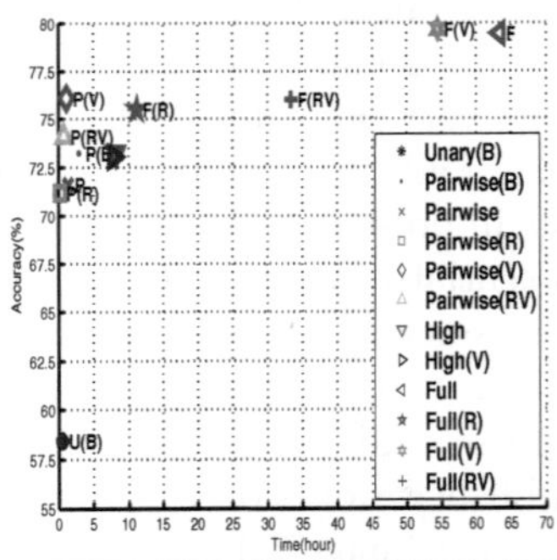

Table 1 shows overall results from various models.[9] The full models performed best in accuracy (79.7%). Unlike the previous experiment with the synthetic data, the experiments with consistency terms alone do not always outperform the result from the pairwise experiment. We recall that simple clustering over

[8] Other clustering methods such as mean-shift clustering or mixture of clustered regions can be considered.

[9] The experiment was performed on a workstation with an Intel Xeon E5520 CPU (2.27GHz) and 32GB RAM (10 cores were used).

pixel colors decomposed objects apart into some classes (i.e. the human has different colors of limbs and clothing) and sometimes, a clique combines more than one object classes together. In case of the pairwise parameter learning, the validation process was effective on gaining the optimal parameters while the learning without validation missed the best parameters. For max-margin learning, validation may be required due to: a) loss in constraints may not represent sufficiently large margin for minimum energy, b) the move-making inference is approximate solution, and c) some amount of 'void' labeling can not be estimated properly in learning. Naturally, the training and the inference times increase as the number of parameters and variables increase. Our heuristic methods such as skipping non-violated examples and cutting down label set in inference reduced the training time significantly. However, cutting down the label set sometimes results in degraded accuracy as shown in Table 1.

(a) image (b) truth (c) unary (d) pairwise (e) high (f) all

Fig. 4. Improved examples with the higher-order consistency terms. The black region represents 'void'. Best viewed in color.

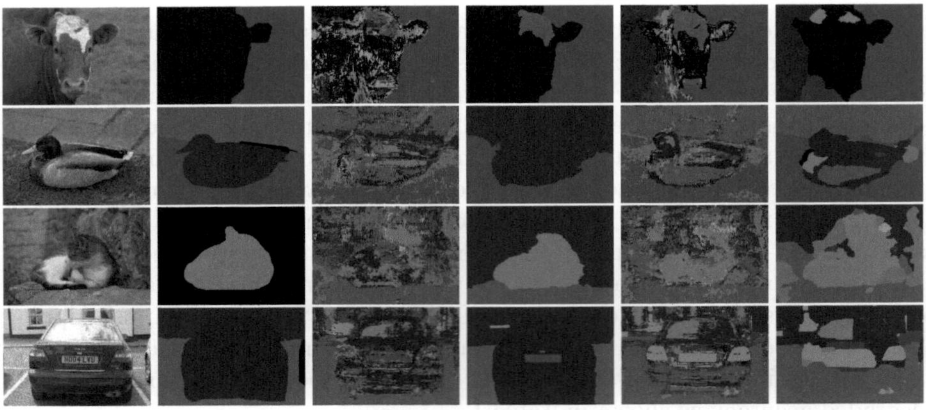

(a) image (b) truth (c) unary (d) pairwise (e) high (f) all

Fig. 5. Degraded examples including the higher-order consistency terms

Figure 4 and Figure 5 show some examples of where the inclusion of the consistency potential improved and degraded the results respectively. We can see that the higher-order terms provide clear contours and accurate object segmentation comparing to the pairwise term model. Note that our model with the definition of non-local regions, for example, segmented the fence correctly with holes in it, which differentiates from the use of contiguous local regions (see Fig. 3). However, the higher-order terms can also degrade performance. Due to the coarse color-based clustering, some objects have been labeled with a few different labels instead of a single one. We suspect including multiple overlapping or hierarchical clustering, this difficulty would be alleviated and performance improved.

6 Conclusion

In this paper we addressed the problem of parameter learning for multi-class lower linear envelop energy functions. We first showed how to perform approximate inference via move-making and thus how to employ max-margin parameter learning. Our results demonstrated that the higher-order terms were very successful in MRF inference tasks such as image denoising and semantic segmentation. However, the higher-order terms impose heavy computation cost on inference and learning due to the large number of parameters and variables. In our max-margin learning procedure, we proposed adaptive methods based on subset optimization for reducing the training time.

It remains an open question how to best define the regions for the higher-order terms. We utilized simple color based non-local regions for the higher-order cliques and saw the improved results. But, we believe that there is still room for improvement, for example, through more sophisticated clique discovery and learning higher-order terms conditioned on refined image features.

Acknowledgments. This research is supported by the Australian Research Council. Kyoungup Park is funded by National ICT Australia (NICTA).

References

1. He, X., Zemel, R., Carreira-Perpinán, M.: Multiscale conditional random fields for image labeling. In: CVPR (2004)
2. Shotton, J., Winn, J.M., Rother, C., Criminisi, A.: *TextonBoost*: Joint Appearance, Shape and Context Modeling for Multi-class Object Recognition and Segmentation. In: Leonardis, A., Bischof, H., Pinz, A. (eds.) ECCV 2006. LNCS, vol. 3951, pp. 1–15. Springer, Heidelberg (2006)
3. Hoiem, D., Efros, A., Hebert, M.: Recovering surface layout from an image. International Journal of Computer Vision 75, 151–172 (2007)
4. Roth, S., Black, M.: Fields of experts. International Journal of Computer Vision 82, 205–229 (2009)
5. Kohli, P., Kumar, M., Torr, P.: P3 & beyond: Solving energies with higher order cliques. In: CVPR (2007)
6. Kohli, P., Ladický, L., Torr, P.: Robust higher order potentials for enforcing label consistency. International Journal of Computer Vision 82, 302–324 (2009)
7. Kohli, P., Kumar, M.: Energy minimization for linear envelope MRFs. In: CVPR (2010)
8. Ladicky, L., Russell, C., Kohli, P., Torr, P.: Associative hierarchical CRFs for object class image segmentation. In: ICCV (2009)
9. Szummer, M., Kohli, P., Hoiem, D.: Learning CRFs Using Graph Cuts. In: Forsyth, D., Torr, P., Zisserman, A. (eds.) ECCV 2008, Part II. LNCS, vol. 5303, pp. 582–595. Springer, Heidelberg (2008)
10. Gould, S.: Max-margin learning for lower linear envelope potentials in binary markov random fields. In: ICML (2011)
11. Komodakis, N.: Efficient training for pairwise or higher order CRFs via dual decomposition. In: CVPR (2011)
12. Boros, E., Hammer, P.: Pseudo-boolean optimization. Discrete Applied Mathematics 123, 155–225 (2002)
13. Kolmogorov, V., Zabin, R.: What energy functions can be minimized via graph cuts? PAMI (2004)
14. Szeliski, R., Zabih, R., Scharstein, D., Veksler, O., Kolmogorov, V., Agarwala, A., Tappen, M., Rother, C.: A comparative study of energy minimization methods for markov random fields with smoothness-based priors. PAMI (2008)
15. Boykov, Y., Veksler, O., Zabih, R.: Fast approximate energy minimization via graph cuts. PAMI (2001)
16. Boykov, Y., Kolmogorov, V.: An experimental comparison of min-cut/max-flow algorithms for energy minimization in vision. PAMI (2004)
17. Besag, J.: On the statistical analysis of dirty pictures. Journal of the Royal Statistical Society. Series B (Methodological), 259–302 (1986)
18. Tsochantaridis, I., Hofmann, T., Joachims, T., Altun, Y.: Support vector machine learning for interdependent and structured output spaces. In: ICML (2004)
19. Taskar, B., Chatalbashev, V., Koller, D., Guestrin, C.: Learning structured prediction models: A large margin approach. In: ICML (2005)
20. Batra, D., Kohli, P.: Making the right moves: Guiding alpha-expansion using local primal-dual gaps. In: CVPR (2011)
21. Finley, T., Joachims, T.: Training structural SVMs when exact inference is intractable. In: ICML (2008)

Sparse Coding and Dictionary Learning for Symmetric Positive Definite Matrices: A Kernel Approach

Mehrtash T. Harandi[1], Conrad Sanderson[1], Richard Hartley[2], and Brian C. Lovell[1]

[1] NICTA, PO Box 6020, St Lucia, QLD 4067, Australia
University of Queensland,
School of ITEE, QLD 4072, Australia
[2] NICTA, Locked Bag 8001, Canberra, ACT 2601, Australia
Australian National University, Canberra, ACT 0200, Australia

Abstract. Recent advances suggest that a wide range of computer vision problems can be addressed more appropriately by considering non-Euclidean geometry. This paper tackles the problem of sparse coding and dictionary learning in the space of symmetric positive definite matrices, which form a Riemannian manifold. With the aid of the recently introduced Stein kernel (related to a symmetric version of Bregman matrix divergence), we propose to perform sparse coding by embedding Riemannian manifolds into reproducing kernel Hilbert spaces. This leads to a convex and kernel version of the Lasso problem, which can be solved efficiently. We furthermore propose an algorithm for learning a Riemannian dictionary (used for sparse coding), closely tied to the Stein kernel. Experiments on several classification tasks (face recognition, texture classification, person re-identification) show that the proposed sparse coding approach achieves notable improvements in discrimination accuracy, in comparison to state-of-the-art methods such as tensor sparse coding, Riemannian locality preserving projection, and symmetry-driven accumulation of local features.

1 Introduction

Sparse representation (SR), the linear decomposition of a signal using a few atoms of a dictionary, has led to notable results for various image processing and computer vision tasks [1,2]. While significant steps have been taken towards expanding the theory of SR, such representations in non-Euclidean spaces have received comparatively little attention. This paper tackles the problem of sparse coding within the space of symmetric positive definite (SPD) matrices.

SPD matrices are fundamental building blocks in computer vision and machine learning. A notable example is the covariance descriptor [3], which offer a compact way of describing regions/cuboids in images/videos and fusion of multiple features. Covariance descriptors have been exploited in several applications, such as diffusion tensor imaging [4], action recognition [5,6,7], pedestrian detection [3], face recognition [8,9], texture classification [9,10], and tracking [11].

SPD matrices form a cone of zero curvature and can be analysed using the geometry of Euclidean space. However, several studies have shown that a Riemannian structure of negative curvature is more suitable for analysing SPD matrices [4,12]. More specifically, Pennec et al. [4] introduced the Affine Invariant Riemannian Metric (AIRM) and

A. Fitzgibbon et al. (Eds.): ECCV 2012, Part II, LNCS 7573, pp. 216–229, 2012.

showed that the induced Riemannian structure is invariant to inversion and similarity transforms. The AIRM is perhaps the most widely used similarity measure for SPD matrices. Nevertheless, efficiently and accurately handling the Riemannian structure is non-trivial as basic computations on Riemannian manifolds (such as similarities and distances) involve non-linear operators. This not only hinders the development of optimisation algorithms but also incurs a significant numerical burden.

To address the above drawbacks, in this paper we propose to perform the sparse coding of SPD matrices by embedding Riemannian manifolds into reproducing kernel Hilbert spaces (RKHS) [13]. This is in contrast to directly embedding into Euclidean spaces [7,6,14].

Related Work. Sra et al. [14] used the cone of SPD matrices and the Frobenius norm as a measure of similarity between SPD matrices. While this results in a regularised non-negative least-squares approach, it does not consider the Riemannian geometry induced by AIRM.

Guo et al. [6] and Yuan et al. [7] separately proposed to solve sparse representation by a log-Euclidean approach, where a Riemannian problem is converted to an Euclidean one by embedding manifolds into tangent spaces. While log-Euclidean approaches benefit from simplicity, the true geometry of the manifold is not taken into account. More specifically, on a tangent space only distances to the pole of space are true geodesic distances. As such, the pairwise distances between arbitrary points on the tangent space do not represent the structure of the manifold.

Sivalingam et al. [9] used Burg divergence [15] as a metric and reformulated the Riemannian[1] SR problem as a determinant maximisation problem. This has the advantage of avoiding the explicit manifold embedding, as well as resulting in a convex MAXDET problem [16] that can be solved by interior point methods. However, there are two downsides: the solution is computationally very expensive, and the relations between Burg divergence and the geometry of Riemannian manifolds were not well established.

Contributions. With the aid of the recently introduced Stein kernel [17], which is related to AIRM via a tight bound, we propose a Riemannian sparse solver by embedding Riemannian manifolds into RKHS. We show that the embedding leads to a convex and kernelised version of the Lasso problem [1], which can be solved efficiently. We furthermore propose a sparsity-maximising algorithm for dictionary learning within the space of SPD matrices, closely tied to the Stein kernel. Lastly, we show that the proposed sparse coding approach obtains superior performance on several visual classification tasks (face recognition, texture classification, person re-identification), in comparison to several state-of-the-art methods: tensor sparse coding [9], log-Euclidean sparse representation [6,7], Gabor feature based sparse representation [18], and Riemannian locality preserving projection [10].

We continue the paper as follows. Section 2 begins with an overview of Bregman divergence and the Stein kernel. Section 3 describes the proposed kernel solution of Riemannian sparse coding, followed by Section 4, which covers the problem of dictionary learning on Riemannian manifolds. In Section 5 we compare the performance of

[1] We loosely use 'Riemannian' to refer to the Riemannian manifold formed by SPD matrices.

the proposed method with previous approaches on several visual classification tasks. The main findings and possible future directions are summarised in Section 6.

2 Background

In this section we first overview the properties of Bregman matrix divergences, including a special case known as the symmetric Stein divergence. This leads to the Stein kernel, which can be used to embed Riemannian manifolds into RKHS.

2.1 Bregman Matrix Divergences

The *Bregman* matrix divergence for two symmetric matrices $\boldsymbol{X}$ and $\boldsymbol{Y}$ is defined as [15]:

$$D_\zeta(\boldsymbol{X},\boldsymbol{Y}) \triangleq \zeta(\boldsymbol{X}) - \zeta(\boldsymbol{Y}) - \langle \nabla_\zeta(\boldsymbol{Y}), \boldsymbol{X}-\boldsymbol{Y}\rangle \tag{1}$$

where $\langle \boldsymbol{A},\boldsymbol{B}\rangle = \mathrm{Tr}\left(\boldsymbol{A}^T\boldsymbol{B}\right)$ and ζ is a real valued, strictly convex function on symmetric matrices. Bregman divergences are non-negative, definite, and in general asymmetric. Among the several ways to symmetrise them, the *Jensen-Shannon* symmetrisation is often used [15]:

$$D_\zeta^{JS}(\boldsymbol{X},\boldsymbol{Y}) \triangleq \frac{1}{2}D_\zeta\left(\boldsymbol{X},\frac{\boldsymbol{X}+\boldsymbol{Y}}{2}\right) + \frac{1}{2}D_\zeta\left(\boldsymbol{Y},\frac{\boldsymbol{X}+\boldsymbol{Y}}{2}\right) \tag{2}$$

If $\zeta = -\log\left(\det\left(\boldsymbol{X}\right)\right)$, then the symmetric Stein divergence is obtained from (2):

$$S(\boldsymbol{X},\boldsymbol{Y}) \triangleq \log\left(\det\left(\frac{\boldsymbol{X}+\boldsymbol{Y}}{2}\right)\right) - \frac{1}{2}\log\left(\det\left(\boldsymbol{X}\boldsymbol{Y}\right)\right), \text{ for } \boldsymbol{X},\boldsymbol{Y} \succ 0 \tag{3}$$

The space induced by AIRM on symmetric positive definite matrices of dimension d is a Riemannian manifold Sym_+^d of negative curvature. For two points $\boldsymbol{X},\boldsymbol{Y} \in Sym_+^d$, the AIRM is defined as $d_g^2 = \|\log_{\boldsymbol{X}}(\boldsymbol{Y})\|_{\boldsymbol{X}}^2 = \mathrm{Tr}\left\{\log^2\left(\boldsymbol{X}^{-\frac{1}{2}}\boldsymbol{Y}\boldsymbol{X}^{-\frac{1}{2}}\right)\right\}$, where $\log_{\boldsymbol{X}}(\boldsymbol{Y}) = \boldsymbol{X}^{\frac{1}{2}}\log\left(\boldsymbol{X}^{-\frac{1}{2}}\boldsymbol{Y}\boldsymbol{X}^{-\frac{1}{2}}\right)\boldsymbol{X}^{\frac{1}{2}}$. The symmetric Stein divergence and Riemannian metric over Sym_+^d manifolds are related in several aspects. Two important properties are summarised below.

Property 1. Let $\boldsymbol{X},\boldsymbol{Y} \in Sym_+^d$, and $\delta_T(\boldsymbol{X},\boldsymbol{Y}) = \max_{1\le i\le d}\{|\log \Lambda\left(\boldsymbol{X}\boldsymbol{Y}^{-1}\right)|\}$ be the Thompson metric [19] with $\Lambda\left(\boldsymbol{X}\boldsymbol{Y}^{-1}\right)$ representing the vector of eigenvalues of $\boldsymbol{X}\boldsymbol{Y}^{-1}$. The following sandwiching inequality between the symmetric Stein divergence and Riemannian metric exists [17]:

$$S(\boldsymbol{X},\boldsymbol{Y}) \le \frac{1}{8}d_g^2(\boldsymbol{X},\boldsymbol{Y}) \le \frac{1}{4}\delta_T(\boldsymbol{X},\boldsymbol{Y})\left(S(\boldsymbol{X},\boldsymbol{Y}) + d\log d\right) \tag{4}$$

Property 2. The curve $\gamma(p) \triangleq \boldsymbol{X}^{\frac{1}{2}}\left(\boldsymbol{X}^{-\frac{1}{2}}\boldsymbol{Y}\boldsymbol{X}^{-\frac{1}{2}}\right)^p\boldsymbol{X}^{\frac{1}{2}}$ parameterises the unique geodesic between the SPD matrices $\boldsymbol{X}$ and $\boldsymbol{Y}$. On this curve the Riemannian geodesic distance satisfies $d_g(\boldsymbol{X},\gamma(p)) = p\,d_g(\boldsymbol{X},\boldsymbol{Y}); p \in [0,1]$ [12]. The symmetric Stein divergence satisfies a similar but slightly weaker result, $S(\boldsymbol{X},\gamma(p)) \le pS(\boldsymbol{X},\boldsymbol{Y})$.

The first property establishes a bound between the geodesic distance and Stein divergence, providing motivation for addressing Riemannian problems via the divergence. The second property reinforces the motivation by explaining that the behaviour of Stein divergences along geodesic curves is similar to true Riemannian geometry.

2.2 Stein Kernel

Definition 1. *Let $\Omega = \{\boldsymbol{X}_1, \boldsymbol{X}_2, \cdots, \boldsymbol{X}_N\}$ be a non-empty set on Riemannian manifold Sym_+^d. A function $\varphi : \Omega \times \Omega \to \mathbb{R}_+$ is a Riemannian kernel if φ is symmetric for all $\boldsymbol{X}, \boldsymbol{Y} \in \Omega$, ie., $\varphi(\boldsymbol{X}, \boldsymbol{Y}) = \varphi(\boldsymbol{Y}, \boldsymbol{X})$, and the following inequality is satisfied for all $a_i \in \mathbb{R}$:*

$$\sum_{i,j} a_i a_j \varphi(\boldsymbol{X}_i, \boldsymbol{X}_j) \geq 0$$

Under a mild condition (explained afterwards), the following function forms a Riemannian kernel [17]:

$$k(\boldsymbol{X}, \boldsymbol{Y}) = e^{-\sigma S(\boldsymbol{X}, \boldsymbol{Y})} = 2^{d\sigma} \frac{\sqrt{\det(\boldsymbol{X})^\sigma \det(\boldsymbol{Y})^\sigma}}{\det(\boldsymbol{X} + \boldsymbol{Y})^\sigma} \tag{5}$$

We shall refer to this kernel as the *Stein kernel* from here on. The following theorem states the condition under which Stein kernel is positive definite.

Theorem 1. *Let $\Omega = \{\boldsymbol{X}_1, \boldsymbol{X}_2, \cdots, \boldsymbol{X}_N\}; \boldsymbol{X}_i \in Sym_+^d$ be a set of Riemannian points. The $N \times N$ matrix $K_\sigma = [k_\sigma(i,j)]; 1 \leq i, j \leq N$, with $k_\sigma(i,j) = k(\boldsymbol{X}_i, \boldsymbol{X}_j)$, defined in* (5)*, is positive definite iff:*

$$\sigma \in \left\{\frac{1}{2}, \frac{2}{2}, \cdots, \frac{d-1}{2}\right\} \cup \left\{\tau \in \mathbb{R} : \tau > \frac{1}{2}(d-1)\right\} \tag{6}$$

Interested readers can follow the proof in [17]. For values of σ outside of the above set, it is possible to convert a pseudo kernel into a true kernel, as discussed for example in [20]. The determinant of an $d \times d$ SPD matrix can be efficiently computed by Cholesky decomposition in $O\left(d^3\right)$. As such, the complexity of computing Stein kernel is $O\left(3d^3 + 3\sigma\right)$.

3 Kernel Sparse Coding

Sparse coding on Riemannian manifolds in general means that a given query point on a manifold can be expressed as a sparse "combination" of dictionary elements. Our idea here is to embed the manifold into RKHS and replace the idea of "combination" on manifolds with the general concept of linear combination in Hilbert spaces. More specifically, given a Riemannian dictionary $\mathbb{D} = \{\boldsymbol{D}_1, \boldsymbol{D}_2, \cdots, \boldsymbol{D}_N\}; \boldsymbol{D}_i \in Sym_+^d$, and an embedding function $\phi : Sym_+^d \to \mathbb{H}$, for a Riemannian point $\boldsymbol{X}$ we seek for a sparse vector $\boldsymbol{v} \in \mathbb{R}^N$ such that $\phi(\boldsymbol{X})$ admits the sparse representation $\boldsymbol{v}$ over $\{\phi(\boldsymbol{D}_1), \phi(\boldsymbol{D}_2), \cdots, \phi(\boldsymbol{D}_N)\}$. In other words, we are interested in solving the following kernelised version of the Lasso problem [1]:

$$\min_{\boldsymbol{v} \in \mathbb{R}^N} \left(\left\| \phi(\boldsymbol{X}) - \sum_{i=1}^N v_i \phi(\boldsymbol{D}_i) \right\|^2 + \lambda \left\| \boldsymbol{v} \right\|_1 \right) \tag{7}$$

The first term in (7) can be expanded as:

$$\begin{aligned} &\left\| \phi(\boldsymbol{X}) - \sum_{i=1}^N v_i \phi(\boldsymbol{D}_i) \right\|^2 \\ &= k(\boldsymbol{X}, \boldsymbol{X}) - 2\sum_{i=1}^N v_i k(\boldsymbol{X}, \boldsymbol{D}_i) + \sum_{i=1}^N \sum_{j=1}^N v_i v_j k(\boldsymbol{D}_j, \boldsymbol{D}_i) \\ &= k(\boldsymbol{X}, \boldsymbol{X}) - 2\boldsymbol{v}^T \boldsymbol{\mathcal{K}}(\boldsymbol{X}, \mathbb{D}) + \boldsymbol{v}^T \mathbb{K}(\mathbb{D}, \mathbb{D}) \boldsymbol{v} \end{aligned} \tag{8}$$

where $\mathcal{K} = [a_i]_{N\times 1};\ a_i = k(\boldsymbol{X}, \boldsymbol{D}_i)$ and $\mathbb{K} = [a_{ij}]_{N\times N};\ a_{ij} = k(\boldsymbol{D}_i, \boldsymbol{D}_j)$. This reveals that the optimisation problem in (7) is convex and similar to its counterpart in Euclidean space, except for the definition of $\mathcal{K}$ and $\mathbb{K}$. Consequently, greedy or relaxation solutions can be adapted to obtain the sparse codes [1]. To solve problem (7) we used CVX [21], a package for specifying and solving convex programs[2].

3.1 Classification Using Sparse Codes

There are two main approaches for classification based on the obtained sparse codes (vectors) for a given query sample: **(i)** directly, and **(ii)** indirectly, with the aid of an Euclidean-based classifier. We elucidate the two approaches below.

(i) If the atoms in sparse dictionary $\mathbb{D}$ have associated class labels (ie. each atom in the dictionary is a training sample), the sparse codes can be directly used for classification. This approach is applicable only to closed-set identification tasks. Let $\boldsymbol{v}_i = [v_{i,1}\delta(l(1)-i),\ v_{i,2}\delta(l(2)-i),\ \cdots,\ v_{i,N}\delta(l(N)-i)]^T$ be the class-specific sparse codes, where $l(j)$ is the class label of atom $\boldsymbol{D}_j$ and $\delta(x)$ is the discrete Dirac function [22]. An efficient way of using class-specific sparse codes is through computing residual errors [2]. In this case, the residual error of query sample $\boldsymbol{X}$ for class i is defined as:

$$\varepsilon_i(\boldsymbol{X}) = \left\|\phi(\boldsymbol{X}) - \sum\nolimits_{j=1}^{N} v_j\phi(\boldsymbol{D}_j)\delta(l(j)-i)\right\|^2 \tag{9}$$

which can be computed via the use of a Riemannian kernel in a similar manner to (8). The class with the minimum residual error is deemed to represent the query. Alternatively, the similarity between query sample $\boldsymbol{X}$ to class i can be defined as $S_i(\boldsymbol{X})$=$h_i(\boldsymbol{v})$. The function $h_i(\boldsymbol{v})$ can be linear like $\sum_{j=1}^{j=N} v_j\delta(l(j)-i)$ or even non-linear like $\max\left(v_j\delta(l(j)-i)\right)$.

(ii) If the atoms in the sparse dictionary $\mathbb{D}$ are not labelled (eg. $\mathbb{D}$ is a generic dictionary not tied to any particular class [23]), the generated sparse codes (vectors) for both training and query data can be fed to Euclidean-based classifiers, such as support vector machines [22]. The sparse code is hence interpreted as a feature vector, which in essence means that a classification problem on a Riemannian manifold is converted to an Euclidean classification problem. This approach is applicable to both closed-set and open-set classification tasks.

4 Learning Riemannian Dictionaries

If the indirect classification of sparse codes is required (as elucidated in the preceding section) a Riemannian dictionary is first required. Given a set of Riemannian points $\Omega = \{\boldsymbol{X}_1, \boldsymbol{X}_2, \cdots, \boldsymbol{X}_m\}; \boldsymbol{X}_i \in Sym_+^d$, learning a dictionary $\mathbb{D} = \{\boldsymbol{D}_1, \boldsymbol{D}_2, \cdots, \boldsymbol{D}_N\}; \boldsymbol{D}_i \in Sym_+^d$ can be formulated as jointly minimising the energy function

$$J = \left\{\sum\nolimits_{j=1}^{m}\left(\left\|\phi(\boldsymbol{X}_j) - \sum\nolimits_{i=1}^{N} v_{j,i}\phi(\boldsymbol{D}_i)\right\|^2 + \lambda\left\|\boldsymbol{v}_j\right\|_1\right)\right\} \tag{10}$$

over the dictionary and the sparse codes $\mathbb{V} = \{\boldsymbol{v}_1, \boldsymbol{v}_2, \cdots, \boldsymbol{v}_m\}; \boldsymbol{v}_i \in \mathbb{R}^N$, ie., $\min_{\mathbb{D},\mathbb{V}}(J)$.

[2] The SPAMS package can also be used: `http://spams-devel.gforge.inria.fr/`

Among the various solutions to the problem of dictionary learning in Euclidean spaces, iterative methods like K-SVD have received much attention [1]. Borrowing the idea from Euclidean spaces, we propose to minimise the energy in (10) iteratively. After initialising the dictionary $\mathbb{D}$, for example by Riemannian clustering using the Karcher mean [4], we iterate between a sparse coding step and a dictionary update step. In the sparse coding step, $\mathbb{D}$ is fixed and $\mathbb{V}$ is computed. In the dictionary update step, $\mathbb{V}$ is fixed while $\mathbb{D}$ is updated, with each dictionary atom updated independently.

The derivative of (10) with respect to $\boldsymbol{D}_r$, while $\mathbb{V}$ and other atoms are fixed, is:

$$\frac{\partial J}{\partial \boldsymbol{D}_r} = \sum\nolimits_{j=1}^{m} \left(-2v_{j,r} \frac{\partial k(\boldsymbol{X}_j, \boldsymbol{D}_r)}{\partial \boldsymbol{D}_r} + \sum\nolimits_{i=1}^{N} v_{j,i} v_{j,r} \frac{\partial k(\boldsymbol{D}_i, \boldsymbol{D}_r)}{\partial \boldsymbol{D}_r} \right) \tag{11}$$

As $\nabla_{\boldsymbol{X}} S(\boldsymbol{X}, \boldsymbol{Y}) = (\boldsymbol{X} + \boldsymbol{Y})^{-1} - \frac{1}{2}\boldsymbol{X}^{-1}$, (11) can be further simplified to:

$$\begin{aligned} \frac{\partial J}{\partial \boldsymbol{D}_r} = {} & 2\beta \sum\nolimits_{j=1}^{m} v_{j,r} k(\boldsymbol{X}_j, \boldsymbol{D}_r) \left((\boldsymbol{X}_j + \boldsymbol{D}_r)^{-1} - \frac{1}{2}\boldsymbol{D}_r^{-1} \right) \\ & - \beta \sum\nolimits_{j=1}^{m} \sum\nolimits_{i=1}^{N} v_{j,i} v_{j,r} k(\boldsymbol{D}_i, \boldsymbol{D}_r) \left((\boldsymbol{D}_i + \boldsymbol{D}_r)^{-1} - \frac{1}{2}\boldsymbol{D}_r^{-1} \right) \end{aligned} \tag{12}$$

Since (12) contains linear and non-linear terms of $\boldsymbol{D}_r$ (eg. inverse and kernel terms), a closed-form solution for computing its root, ie., $\boldsymbol{D}_r$, cannot be sought. As such, we propose an alternative solution by exploiting previous values of $k(\cdot, \boldsymbol{D}_r)$ and $(\boldsymbol{D}_i - \boldsymbol{D}_r)^{-1}$ in the updating step. More specifically, rearranging (12) and estimating $k(\cdot, \boldsymbol{D}_r)$ as well as $(\boldsymbol{D}_i - \boldsymbol{D}_r)^{-1}$ by their previous values, atom $\boldsymbol{D}_r$ at iteration $t + 1$ is updated using:

$$\boldsymbol{D}_r^{(t+1)} = \frac{2}{\sum_{j=1}^{m} v_{j,r} \left(\boldsymbol{v}_j^T \boldsymbol{k}(\mathbb{D}, \boldsymbol{D}_r) - 2k(\boldsymbol{X}_j, \boldsymbol{D}_r) \right)} \left(F^{(t)}(r) + G^{(t)}(r) \right)^{-1} \tag{13}$$

where

$$F^{(t)}(r) = \sum\nolimits_{j=1}^{m} 2v_{j,r} k^{(t)}(\boldsymbol{X}_j, \boldsymbol{D}_r) \left(\boldsymbol{X}_j + \boldsymbol{D}_r^{(t)} \right)^{-1} \tag{14}$$

$$G^{(t)}(r) = \sum\nolimits_{j=1}^{m} \sum\nolimits_{i=1}^{N} v_{j,r} v_{j,i} k^{(t)}(\boldsymbol{D}_i, \boldsymbol{D}_r) \left(\boldsymbol{D}_i^{(t)} + \boldsymbol{D}_r^{(t)} \right)^{-1} \tag{15}$$

To avoid the degenerative case (due to numerical inconsistency), atoms are normalised by their second norms at the end of each iteration. Algorithm 1 assembles all the above details into pseudo-code for dictionary learning.

5 Experiments

Two sets of experiments[3] are presented in this section. In the first set, we evaluate the performance of the proposed Riemannian SR (RSR) method (as described in Section 3) without dictionary learning. Each atom in the dictionary is a training sample. This is to contrast RSR to previous state-of-the-art methods on several popular closed-set classification tasks. We use the residual error approach for classification, as described in Eqn. (9).

In the second set, the performance of the RSR method is evaluated in conjunction with dictionaries learned via three methods: random, Riemannian k-means, and the proposed dictionary learning technique (as described in Section 4).

[3] Matlab/Octave source code is available at `http://itee.uq.edu.au/~uqmhara1`

Algorithm 1. Dictionary learning over Sym_+^d using the Stein kernel

Input:

- training set $\mathbb{X}=\{\boldsymbol{X}_i\}_{i=1}^m$ from the underlying Riemannian manifold, where each $\boldsymbol{X}_i \in Sym_+^d$ is a SPD matrix
- Stein kernel function $k(\boldsymbol{X}, \boldsymbol{Y})$, as defined in Eqn. (5)
- $nIter$, the number of iterations

Output:

- Riemannian dictionary $\mathbb{D} = \{\boldsymbol{D}_i\}_{i=1}^N$

Initialise the dictionary $\mathbb{D}^{(1)} = \left\{\boldsymbol{D}_i^{(1)}\right\}_{i=1}^N$ by selecting N samples from $\mathbb{X}$ randomly, or by clustering $\mathbb{X}$ on the manifold [24]

for $t = 1 \to nIter$ **do**
  Compute $k^{(t)}(\boldsymbol{X}_i, \boldsymbol{D}_j^{(t)}),\ 1 \leq i \leq m,\ 1 \leq j \leq N$
  Compute $k^{(t)}(\boldsymbol{D}_i^{(t)}, \boldsymbol{D}_j^{(t)}),\ 1 \leq i, j \leq N$
  Solve $\min\limits_{\boldsymbol{v}_j \in \mathbb{R}^N} -2\boldsymbol{v}_j^T \boldsymbol{\mathcal{K}}(\boldsymbol{X}_j, \mathbb{D}^{(t)}) + \boldsymbol{v}^T \mathbb{K}(\mathbb{D}^{(t)}, \mathbb{D}^{(t)})\boldsymbol{v} + \lambda \|\boldsymbol{v}_j\|_1, \ \forall j, \boldsymbol{X}_j \in \mathbb{X}$
  for $r = 1 \to N$ **do**
    Compute $G^{(t)}(r) = \sum_{j=1}^m \sum_{i=1}^N v_{j,r} v_{j,i} k^{(t)}(\boldsymbol{D}_i^{(t)}, \boldsymbol{D}_r^{(t)}) \left(\boldsymbol{D}_i^{(t)} + \boldsymbol{D}_r^{(t)}\right)^{-1}$
    Compute $F^{(t)}(r) = \sum_{j=1}^m 2v_{j,r} k^{(t)}(\boldsymbol{X}_j, \boldsymbol{D}_r^{(t)}) \left(\boldsymbol{X}_j + \boldsymbol{D}_r^{(t)}\right)^{-1}$
    $\boldsymbol{D}_r^{\texttt{temp}} \leftarrow \frac{2}{\sum_{j=1}^m v_{j,r}\left(\boldsymbol{v}_j^T \boldsymbol{k}(\mathbb{D}^{(t)}, \boldsymbol{D}_r^{(t)}) - 2k(\boldsymbol{X}_j, \boldsymbol{D}_r^{(t)})\right)} \left(F^{(t)}(r) + G^{(t)}(r)\right)^{-1}$
    $\boldsymbol{D}_r^{(t+1)} \leftarrow \frac{\boldsymbol{D}_r^{\texttt{temp}}}{\left\|\boldsymbol{D}_r^{\texttt{temp}}\right\|_2}$
  end for
end for

5.1 Riemannian Sparse Representation

Synthetic Data. We first consider a multi-class classification problem over Sym_+^3 using synthetic data. We compared the proposed RSR against Tensor Sparse Coding (TSC) [9] and log-Euclidean Sparse Representation (logE-SR) [6,7]. The data used in the experiments constitutes 512 random samples from 4 classes. Half of the samples were used for training and the rest were used as test data.

To create a Riemannian manifold, samples were generated over a particular tangent space and then mapped back to the manifold using the exponential map [12]. The positions of tangent spaces were chosen randomly and samples in each class obeyed a normal distribution. By fixing the mean of each class and increasing the class variance we created two classification problems: 'easy' and 'hard'. To draw useful statistics, the data creation process was repeated 100 times.

Table 1 shows the average recognition accuracy and the total running time (in seconds). All algorithms were implemented in Matlab and executed on a 3 GHz Intel CPU. In terms of recognition accuracy, RSR obtains superior performance when compared with previous state-of-the-art approaches. We note that by increasing the class variance, samples from the four classes are intertwined, leading to a decrease in recognition accuracy. The performance of logE-SR is higher than TSC, which might be due the to fact

Table 1. Average recognition accuracy (in %) and wall-clock time for the synthetic classification tasks using log-Euclidean sparse representation [6,7], tensor sparse coding [9] and the proposed RSR approach. Run time is represented by combining the times for the easy and hard tasks.

		logE-SR [6,7]	TSC [9]	RSR (proposed)
recognition accuracy	easy	68.08 ± 2.5	60.04 ± 6.8	$\mathbf{83.05 \pm 3.0}$
	hard	53.67 ± 3.2	50.35 ± 4.9	$\mathbf{66.72 \pm 2.7}$
run-time	easy+hard	6 sec	11107 sec	41 sec

that the generated data can be modelled by Gaussian distribution over tangent space, hence favouring the tangent-based solution.

Focusing on run time, Table 1 suggests that logE-SR has the lowest complexity while TSC has the highest. The proposed RSR method is substantially faster than TSC, while delivering the highest recognition accuracy.

Face Recognition. We used the 'b' subset of the FERET dataset [25], which includes 1400 images from 198 subjects. The images were closely cropped around the face and downsampled to 64×64. Examples are shown in Figure 1.

We performed four tests with various pose angles. Training data was composed of images marked 'ba', 'bj' and 'bk' (ie., frontal faces with expression and illumination variations). Images with 'bd', 'be', 'bf' and 'bg' labels (ie., non-frontal faces) were used as test data. For Riemannian-based methods, a 43×43 covariance descriptor described a face image, using the following features:

$$F_{x,y} = [\, I(x,y),\ x,\ y,\ |G_{0,0}(x,y)|,\ \cdots,\ |G_{0,7}(x,y)|,\ |G_{1,0}(x,y)|,\ \cdots,\ |G_{4,7}(x,y)|\,]$$

where $I(x,y)$ is the intensity value at position x, y and $G_{u,v}(x,y)$ is the response of a 2D Gabor wavelet [26] centered at x, y with orientation u and scale v:

$$G_{u,v}(x,y) = \frac{k_v^2}{4\pi^2} \sum\nolimits_{t,s} e^{-\frac{k_v^2}{8\pi^2}\left((x-s)^2+(y-t)^2\right)} \left(e^{ik_v((x-t)cos(\theta_u)+(y-s)sin(\theta_u))} - e^{-2\pi^2}\right)$$

with $k_v = \frac{1}{\sqrt{2^{v-1}}}$ and $\theta_u = \frac{\pi u}{8}$.

Table 2 shows a comparison of RSR against logE-SR [6,7], TSC [9], and two purely Euclidean sparse representations, PCA-SRC [2] and Gabor SR (GSR) [18]. In all cases the proposed RSR method obtains the highest accuracy. Furthermore, the proposed approach significantly outperforms state-of-the-art Euclidean solutions, especially for test images with label 'bg'.

Texture Classification. We performed a classification task using the Brodatz texture dataset [27]. Examples are shown in Fig. 2. We followed the test protocol devised in [9] and generated nine test scenarios with various number of classes. This includes

Table 2. Recognition accuracy (in %) for the face recognition task using PCA-SRC [2], Gabor SR (GSR) [18], log-Euclidean sparse representation (logE-SR) [6,7], Tensor Sparse Coding (TSC) [9], and the proposed RSR approach

	PCA-SR [2]	GSR [18]	logE-SR [6,7]	TSC [9]	RSR (proposed)
bg	26.0	79.0	46.5	44.5	**86.0**
bf	61.0	97.0	91.0	73.5	**97.5**
be	55.5	93.5	81.0	73.0	**96.5**
bd	27.5	77.0	34.5	36.0	**79.5**
average	42.50	86.63	63.25	56.75	**89.88**

5-texture ('5c', '5m', '5v', '5v2', '5v3'), 10-texture ('10', '10v') and 16-texture ('16c', '16v') mosaics. To create a Riemannian manifold, each image was first downsampled to 256×256 and then split into 64 regions of size 32×32. The feature vector for any pixel $I(x,y)$ is $F(x,y) = \left[I(x,y), \left|\frac{\partial I}{\partial x}\right|, \left|\frac{\partial I}{\partial y}\right|, \left|\frac{\partial^2 I}{\partial x^2}\right|, \left|\frac{\partial^2 I}{\partial y^2}\right| \right]$. Each region is described by a 5×5 covariance descriptor of these features. For each test scenario, five covariance matrices per class were randomly selected as training data and the rest was used for testing. The random selection of training/testing data was repeated 20 times.

Fig. 3 compares the proposed RSR method against logE-SR [6,7] and TSC [9]. The proposed RSR approach obtains the highest recognition accuracy on all test scenarios except for the '5c' test, where it has slightly worse performance than TSC.

Person Re-identification. We used the modified ETHZ dataset [31]. The original ETHZ dataset was captured using a moving camera [28], providing a range of variations in the appearance of people. The dataset is structured into 3 sequences. Sequence 1 contains 83 pedestrians (4,857 images), Sequence 2 contains 35 pedestrians (1,936 images), and Sequence 3 contains 28 pedestrians (1,762 images). See Fig. 4 for examples.

We downsampled all images to 64×32 pixels. For each subject we randomly selected 10 images for training and used the rest for testing. Random selection of training and testing data was repeated 20 times to obtain reliable statistics. To describe each image, the covariance descriptor was computed using the following features:

$$F_{x,y} = \left[\, x,\ y,\ R_{x,y},\ G_{x,y},\ B_{x,y},\ R'_{x,y},\ G'_{x,y},\ B'_{x,y},\ R''_{x,y},\ G''_{x,y},\ B''_{x,y} \,\right]$$

where (x,y) is the position of a pixel, while $R_{x,y}$, $G_{x,y}$ and $B_{x,y}$ represent the corresponding colour information. The gradient and Laplacian for colour C are represented by $C'_{x,y} = [|\partial C/\partial x|, |\partial C/\partial y|]$ and $C''_{x,y} = [|\partial^2 C/\partial x^2|, |\partial^2 C/\partial y^2|]$, respectively.

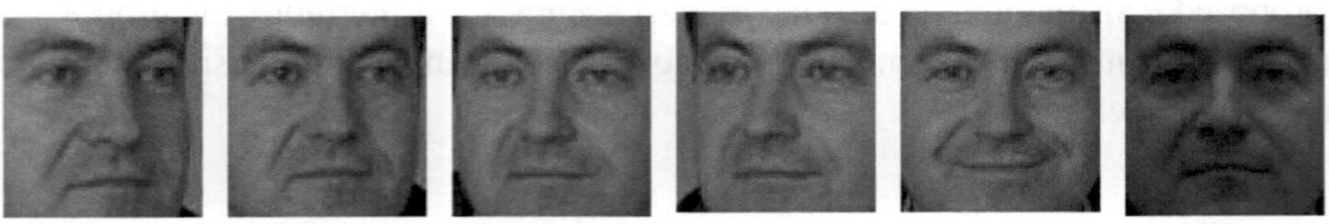

bd be bf bg bj bk

Fig. 1. Examples of closely-cropped faces from the FERET 'b' subset

Fig. 2. Examples from the Brodatz texture dataset [27]

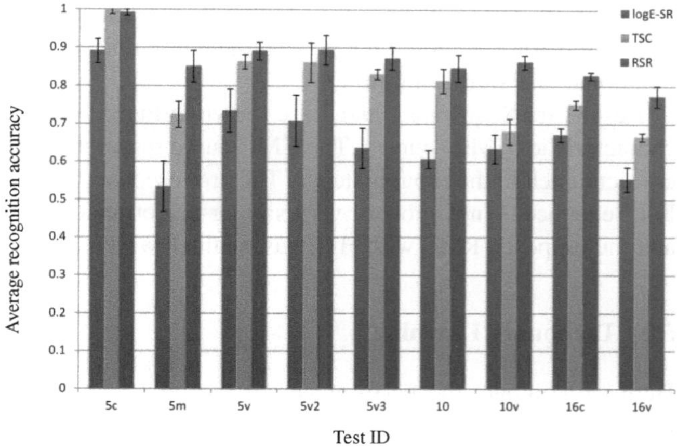

Fig. 3. Performance on the Bordatz texture dataset [27] using log-Euclidean sparse representation (logE-SR) [6,7], Tensor Sparse Coding (TSC) [9] and the proposed RSR approach. The black bars indicate standard deviations.

Fig. 4. Examples of pedestrians in the ETHZ dataset [28]

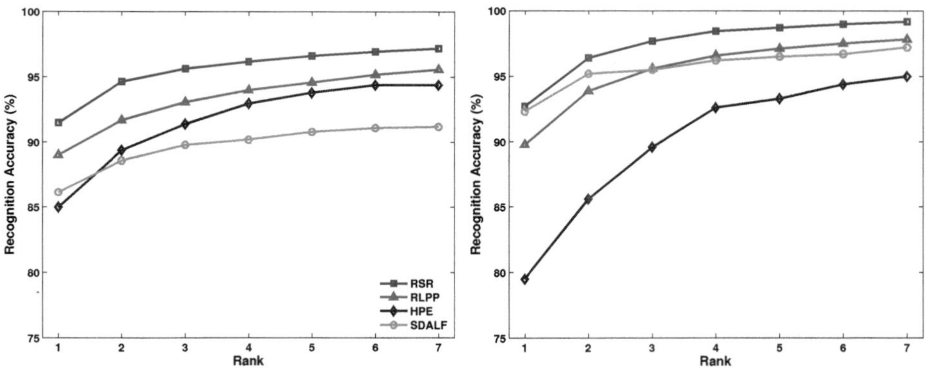

Fig. 5. Performance on Sequences 1 and 2 of the ETHZ dataset (left and right panels, respectively), in terms of Cumulative Matching Characteristic curves. The proposed RSR method is compared with Histogram Plus Epitome (HPE) [29], Symmetry-Driven Accumulation of Local Features (SDALF) [30] and Riemannian Locality Preserving Projection (RLPP) [10].

We compared the proposed RSR method with several techniques previously used for pedestrian detection: Histogram Plus Epitome (HPE) [29], Symmetry-Driven Accumulation of Local Features (SDALF) [30], and Riemannian Locality Preserving Projection

(RLPP) [10]. The performance of logE-SR was below HPE method and is not shown. The results for TSC could not be generated in a timely manner, due to the heavy computational load of the algorithm.

Results for Sequence 1 and 2 are shown in Fig. 5, in terms of cumulative matching characteristic (CMC) curves. The CMC curve represents the expectation of finding the correct match in the top n matches. The proposed method obtains the highest accuracy. For Sequence 3 (not shown), very similar performance is obtained by SDALF, RLPP and the proposed RSR, with HPE having the lowest performance.

5.2 Dictionary Learning

Here we compare the performance of the proposed Riemannian dictionary learning technique (as described in Section 4), with the performances of dictionaries obtained by random sampling and Riemannian k-means. We first use synthetic data to show that the proposed method obtains a lower representation error in RKHS, followed by classification experiments on texture data.

Synthetic Data. We synthesised 512 Riemannian samples from a set of 32 source points in Sym_{+}^{5}. The source points can be considered as a form of ground-truth. The synthesised samples were then used for dictionary creation by Riemannian k-means [24] and the proposed algorithm.

To generate each source point, an SPD matrix was created by computing the covariance of 100 random samples of a 5 dimensional normal distribution. The mean and variance of the distribution are different for each source point. To synthesise each of the 512 Riemannian samples, we uniformly selected $T = 4$ source points and combined them with random positive weights, where the weights obeyed a normal distribution with zero mean and unit variance.

The performance is measured in terms of representation error in RKHS, ie. Eqn. (10). Fig. 6 shows the representation error as the algorithms iterate, with the proposed algorithm obtaining a lower error than Riemannian k-means.

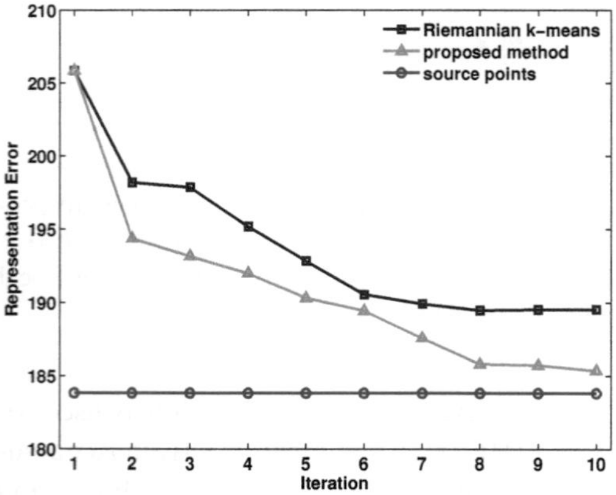

Fig. 6. Representation error of learned dictionaries in RKHS, Eqn. (10), for synthetic data. The proposed method (Section 4) is compared with Riemannian k-means [24]. The source points can be interpreted as a form of ground-truth.

Table 3. Recognition accuracy (in %) for the texture classification task with dictionary learning. In all cases the proposed RSR approach was used, coupled with a dictionary generated via three separate methods: random dictionary generation, Riemannian k-means [24], and the proposed learning algorithm (Section 4).

random	k-means	learning
46.09 ± 1.5	53.20 ± 1.1	60.65 ± 0.9

Texture Classification. Here we consider a multi-class classification problem, using 111 texture images of the Brodatz texture dataset [27]. From each image we randomly extracted 50 blocks of size 32×32. To train the dictionary, 20 blocks from each image were randomly selected, resulting in a dictionary learning problem with 2200 samples. From the remaining blocks, 20 per image were used as probe data and 10 as gallery samples. The process of random block creation and dictionary generation was repeated twenty times. The average recognition accuracies over probe data are reported here. In the same manner as in Section 5.1, we used the feature vector $F(x,y)=\left[I(x,y), \left|\frac{\partial I}{\partial x}\right|, \left|\frac{\partial I}{\partial y}\right|, \left|\frac{\partial^2 I}{\partial x^2}\right|, \left|\frac{\partial^2 I}{\partial y^2}\right|\right]$ to create the covariance, where the first dimension is the grayscale intensity, and the remaining dimensions capture first and second order gradients.

We used the proposed RSR approach to obtain the sparse codes, coupled with a dictionary generated via three separate methods: random dictionary generation, Riemannian k-means algorithm [24], and the proposed learning algorithm (Section 4). The sparse codes were then classified using a nearest-neighbour classifier.

For the randomly generated dictionary case, the classification rates are averaged over 10 runs, with each run using a different random dictionary. For all methods, dictionaries of size $k=\{8, 16, 24, \cdots, 128\}$ were trained. The best results for each approach (ie., the results for the dictionary size that obtained the highest recognition accuracy) are reported in Table 3. For the random dictionary, $k = 64$; for the k-means dictionary, $k = 96$; for the proposed dictionary learning algorithm, $k = 24$. The results show that the proposed algorithm leads to a considerable gain in accuracy.

6 Main Findings and Future Directions

With the aim of addressing sparse representation on Riemannian manifolds, proposed to seek the solution through embedding the manifolds into RKHS, with the aid of the recently introduced Stein kernel. This led to a relaxed and extended version of the Lasso problem [1] on Riemannian manifolds.

Experiments on several classification tasks (face recognition, texture classification, person re-identification) show that the proposed approach achieves notable improvements in discrimination accuracy, in comparison to state-of-the-art methods such as tensor sparse coding, Riemannian locality preserving projection, and symmetry-driven accumulation of local features. We conjuncture that this stems from better exploitation of Riemannian geometry, as the Stein kernel is related to geodesic distances via a tight bound. The proposed sparse coding method is also considerably faster than the state-of-the-art MAXDET reformulation used by Tensor Sparse Coding [9].

We have furthermore proposed an algorithm for learning a Riemannian dictionary, closely tied to the Stein kernel. In comparison to Riemannian k-means [24], the proposed algorithm obtains a lower representation error in RKHS and leads to improved classification accuracies.

Future directions include using the Stein kernel for solving large margin classification problems on Riemannian manifolds. This translates to designing a machinery that maximises a margin on SPD matrices based on Stein divergence, which can be considered as an extension of support vector machines [13] to tensor spaces.

Acknowledgements. NICTA is funded by the Australian Government as represented by the Department of Broadband, Communications and the Digital Economy, as well as by the Australian Research Council through the ICT Centre of Excellence program.

References

1. Elad, M.: Sparse and Redundant Representations: From Theory to Applications in Signal and Image Processing. Springer (2010)
2. Wright, J., Yang, A.Y., Ganesh, A., Sastry, S.S., Ma, Y.: Robust face recognition via sparse representation. IEEE Trans. Pattern Analysis and Machine Intelligence (PAMI) 31(2), 210–227 (2009)
3. Tuzel, O., Porikli, F., Meer, P.: Pedestrian detection via classification on Riemannian manifolds. IEEE Trans. Pattern Analysis and Machine Intelligence 30(10), 1713–1727 (2008)
4. Pennec, X.: Intrinsic statistics on Riemannian manifolds: Basic tools for geometric measurements. Journal of Mathematical Imaging and Vision 25(1), 127–154 (2006)
5. Lui, Y.M.: Advances in matrix manifolds for computer vision. Image and Vision Computing 30(6–7), 380–388 (2012)
6. Guo, K., Ishwar, P., Konrad, J.: Action recognition using sparse representation on covariance manifolds of optical flow. In: IEEE Conf. Advanced Video and Signal Based Surveillance, pp. 188–195 (2010)
7. Yuan, C., Hu, W., Li, X., Maybank, S., Luo, G.: Human Action Recognition under Log-Euclidean Riemannian Metric. In: Zha, H., Taniguchi, R.-i., Maybank, S. (eds.) ACCV 2009, Part I. LNCS, vol. 5994, pp. 343–353. Springer, Heidelberg (2010)
8. Pang, Y., Yuan, Y., Li, X.: Gabor-based region covariance matrices for face recognition. IEEE Transactions on Circuits and Systems for Video Technology 18(7), 989–993 (2008)
9. Sivalingam, R., Boley, D., Morellas, V., Papanikolopoulos, N.: Tensor Sparse Coding for Region Covariances. In: Daniilidis, K., Maragos, P., Paragios, N. (eds.) ECCV 2010, Part IV. LNCS, vol. 6314, pp. 722–735. Springer, Heidelberg (2010)
10. Harandi, M.T., Sanderson, C., Wiliem, A., Lovell, B.C.: Kernel analysis over Riemannian manifolds for visual recognition of actions, pedestrians and textures. In: IEEE Workshop on the Applications of Computer Vision (WACV), pp. 433–439 (2012)
11. Hu, W., Li, X., Luo, W., Zhang, X., Maybank, S., Zhang, Z.: Single and multiple object tracking using log-Euclidean Riemannian subspace and block-division appearance model. IEEE Trans. Pattern Analysis and Machine Intelligence (in press) doi:10.1109/TPAMI.2012.42
12. Bhatia, R.: Positive Definite Matrices. Princeton University Press (2007)
13. Shawe-Taylor, J., Cristianini, N.: Kernel Methods for Pattern Analysis. Cambridge University Press (2004)
14. Sra, S., Cherian, A.: Generalized Dictionary Learning for Symmetric Positive Definite Matrices with Application to Nearest Neighbor Retrieval. In: Gunopulos, D., Hofmann, T., Malerba, D., Vazirgiannis, M. (eds.) ECML PKDD 2011, Part III. LNCS, vol. 6913, pp. 318–332. Springer, Heidelberg (2011)

15. Kulis, B., Sustik, M.A., Dhillon, I.S.: Low-rank kernel learning with Bregman matrix divergences. Journal of Machine Learning Reseach 10, 341–376 (2009)
16. Boyd, S., Vandenberghe, L.: Convex Optimization. Cambridge University Press, New York (2004)
17. Sra, S.: Positive definite matrices and the symmetric Stein divergence. Preprint: (arXiv:1110.1773) (2012)
18. Yang, M., Zhang, L.: Gabor Feature Based Sparse Representation for Face Recognition with Gabor Occlusion Dictionary. In: Daniilidis, K., Maragos, P., Paragios, N. (eds.) ECCV 2010, Part VI. LNCS, vol. 6316, pp. 448–461. Springer, Heidelberg (2010)
19. Thompson, A.C.: On certain contraction mappings in a partially ordered vector space. Proceedings of the American Mathematical Society 14, 438–443 (1963)
20. Chen, Y., Garcia, E.K., Gupta, M.R., Rahimi, A., Cazzanti, L.: Similarity-based classification: Concepts and algorithms. Journal of Machine Learning Research 10, 747–776 (2009)
21. Grant, M., Boyd, S.: CVX: Matlab software for disciplined convex programming, version 1.21 (April 2011), `http://cvxr.com/cvx/`
22. Bishop, C.M.: Pattern Recognition and Machine Learning. Springer (2006)
23. Wong, Y., Harandi, M.T., Sanderson, C., Lovell, B.C.: On robust biometric identity verification via sparse encoding of faces: holistic vs local approaches. In: IEEE International Joint Conference on Neural Networks, pp. 1762–1769 (2012)
24. Goh, A., Vidal, R.: Clustering and dimensionality reduction on Riemannian manifolds. In: IEEE Conf. Computer Vision and Pattern Recognition, pp. 1–7 (2008)
25. Phillips, P., Moon, H., Rizvi, S., Rauss, P.: The FERET evaluation methodology for face-recognition algorithms. IEEE Trans. Pattern Analysis and Machine Intelligence 22(10), 1090–1104 (2000)
26. Lee, T.S.: Image representation using 2d Gabor wavelets. IEEE Trans. Pattern Analysis and Machine Intelligence 18, 959–971 (1996)
27. Randen, T., Husøy, J.H.: Filtering for texture classification: A comparative study. IEEE Trans. Pattern Analysis and Machine Intelligence 21(4), 291–310 (1999)
28. Ess, A., Leibe, B., Van Gool, L.: Depth and appearance for mobile scene analysis. In: Int. Conf. Computer Vision (ICCV), pp. 1–8 (2007)
29. Bazzani, L., Cristani, M., Perina, A., Farenzena, M., Murino, V.: Multiple-shot person re-identification by HPE signature. In: Int. Conf. Pattern Recognition, pp. 1413–1416 (2010)
30. Farenzena, M., Bazzani, L., Perina, A., Murino, V., Cristani, M.: Person re-identification by symmetry-driven accumulation of local features. In: IEEE Conf. Computer Vision and Pattern Recognition, pp. 2360–2367 (2010)
31. Schwartz, W.R., Davis, L.S.: Learning discriminative appearance-based models using partial least squares. In: Brazilian Symposium on Computer Graphics and Image Processing, pp. 322–329 (2009)

Learning Class-to-Image Distance via Large Margin and L1-Norm Regularization

Zhengxiang Wang[1,2], Shenghua Gao[1,3], and Liang-Tien Chia[1]

[1] Nanyang Technological University, Singapore
[2] Fujitsu Research & Development Center Co., Ltd, Beijing, China
[3] Advanced Digital Sciences Center, Singapore
{wang0460,gaos0004,asltchia}@ntu.edu.sg

Abstract. Image-to-Class (I2C) distance has demonstrated its effectiveness for object recognition in several single-label datasets. However, for the multi-label problem, where an image may contain several regions belonging to different classes, this distance may not work well since it cannot discriminate local features from different regions in the test image and all local features have to be counted in the I2C distance calculation. In this paper, we propose to use Class-to-Image (C2I) distance and show that this distance performs better than I2C distance for multi-label image classification. However, since the number of local features in a class is huge compared to that in an image, the calculation of C2I distance is much more expensive than I2C distance. Moreover, the label information of training images can be used to help select relevant local features for each class and further improve the recognition performance. Therefore, to make C2I distance faster and perform better, we propose an optimization algorithm using L1-norm regularization and large margin constraint to learn the C2I distance, which will not only reduce the number of local features in the class feature set, but also improve the performance of C2I distance due to the use of label information. Experiments on MSRC, Pascal VOC and MirFlickr datasets show that our method can significantly speed up the C2I distance calculation, while achieves better recognition performance than the original C2I distance and other related methods for multi-labeled datasets.

1 Introduction

Recently Image-to-Class (I2C) distance [1] is proposed to overcome the information loss during feature quantization process in traditional bag-of-words (BOW) model and has demonstrated its effectiveness for object recognition in several single-label datasets. In the I2C distance, a feature set for each class is constructed by gathering all local features in the training images belonging to this class, while the test image is also represented by a set of densely sampled local features. The I2C distance from a test image to a certain class is defined as the sum of Euclidean distance between every local feature in the test image and its Nearest Neighbor (NN) in the class. In [1], they have shown I2C distance performs better than bag-of-words model in several single-label datasets, though

A. Fitzgibbon et al. (Eds.): ECCV 2012, Part II, LNCS 7573, pp. 230–244, 2012.

the whole feature set must be kept during the test phase and therefore increases the memory usage.

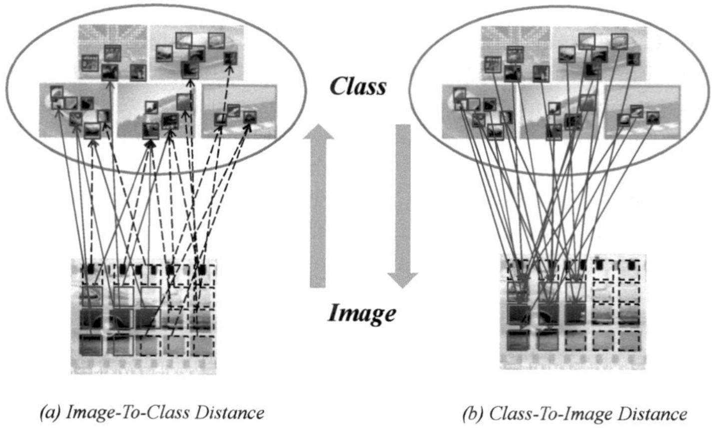

Fig. 1. The illustration of I2C distance (a) and C2I distance (b). Red and black rectangles represent the local features located at the region of "car" and "street" respectively. The NN search directions are represented by arrows from one side to the other side. Red and black arrows represent the NN match between same region and different regions respectively. Though region "street" may not be useful in the "car" class, the NN match from region "street" to "car" in I2C distance (a) cannot be avoided, while in C2I distance (b) it can be avoided.

However, the I2C distance may not perform well in a multi-label problem. In this problem, a test image may contain several regions belonging to different classes. Therefore the resulting feature set for this test image contains local features belonging to multiple different classes and all local features have to be counted in the I2C distance calculation, since it is unknown which local feature belongs to which class before the I2C distance calculation. Consider an example test image in Figure 1 (a), which mainly contains two regions: "car" and "street". When measuring the distance to each class, local features in every region of the test image are counted in the final I2C distance. In this example, local features located at "street" region are also counted in the I2C distance to class "car", while distances between these features and their NNs in the class "car" (marked as black arrows) are useless and will make the I2C distance to class "car" inaccurate. Such problem also exists when measuring the distance between this image and class "street". Since it is even more difficult to first detect the region of "car" and "street" in this test image before the I2C distance calculation, the I2C distance may not be suitable for the multi-label problem.

In this paper, we propose to use Class-to-Image (C2I) distance to measure the distance between image and class for the multi-label problem. We could assume all local features in each class are relevant to this class, either by manually removing irrelevant local features or using some feature selection technologies. Therefore we define the C2I distance as an inverse version of the I2C distance: the Euclidean distance between each local feature in the class feature set and its NN in the feature set of the test image is summed up to form its C2I distance. Such an inversion can solve the problem that I2C distance encounters in the multi-label problem. We explain that by taking the same test image as example. Figure 1 (b) shows the formation of C2I distance from class "car" to the test image. The feature set of class "car" is constructed during the training phase and we should assume most of its elements are located at the regions of "car". If a test image contains a car as in this example, the local features in class "car" will have better opportunities to find their NNs located at the regions of car in this test image and thus a smaller C2I distance than other images without a car. Irrelevant local features in the region of other objects such as "street" in this test image is less likely to be matched as NN features from class "car" and therefore less likely to influence the measurement accuracy of C2I distance compared to I2C distance.

There are two problems in C2I distance. First, the success of C2I distance in the previous example relies on the assumption that most of the local features in the feature set of class "car" are located at the regions of "car". Since the training images also contain multiple regions, we do not know which local features belong to class "car" and which do not. Manually labeling every region to its class label can solve this problem but this is very expensive and most datasets only provide a list of class labels for each training image without pixel-wise or bounding box label information. Second, the number of local features in a class is usually much more than that in an image, resulting in a time-consuming C2I distance calculation when compared to I2C distance.

To solve these problems, in this work, we propose an optimization algorithm using large margin constraint and L1-norm regularization to learn the C2I distance. The feature set of each class is first constructed by gathering all local features in the training images belonging to this class, same as that in I2C distance. Then we associate a weight to every local feature to distinguish the different importance of each local feature, and formulate an optimization problem to learn these weights. We try to use the label information to select relevant local features based on their weights and reduce the size of feature set by L1-norm regularization. Therefore, the objective function of our optimization problem is comprised of two parts: the error term and the regularization term. In the error term, label information is utilized by constraining in each triplet that the C2I distance to the relevant image should be smaller than that to irrelevant image with a large margin. In the regularization term, we use L1-norm on the weight vector to generate a sparse solution as in [2,3]. To solve this optimization problem, we also propose an efficient gradient descent based solver, which can update the weights and converge to the global optimum quickly. After the learning procedure, most of the weights get zero values due to the L1-norm regularization and those local features with zero weight can be removed from the feature set, while the remaining local features with non-zero weight are preserved to make up the feature set. This reduction not only speeds up the C2I distance calculation, but also decreases the memory usage. Using this optimization algorithm, we are able to get better recognition performance with the learned C2I distance even though the size of the resulting feature set is much smaller.

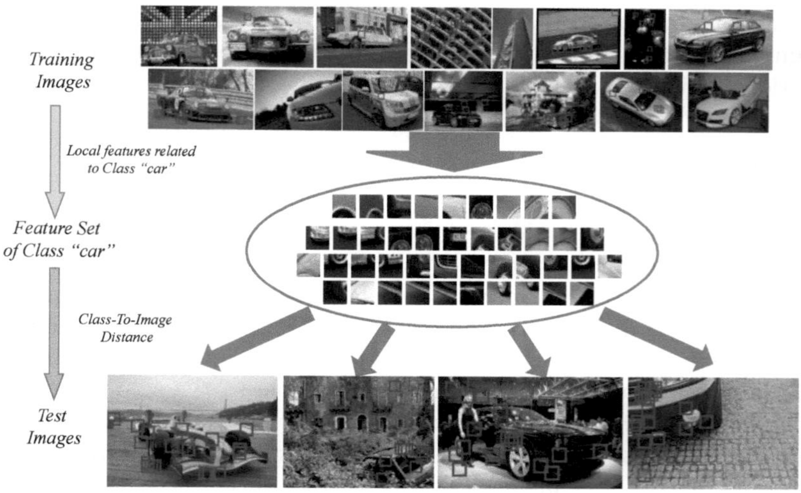

Fig. 2. The example of C2I distance from training feature set of class "car" to some test images containing a car object

We show in Figure 2 the example of our learned C2I distance from the training feature set of the class "car" for consistent description, to some test images containing the car. Local features are initially densely sampled from training images having a label of class "car". After the learning algorithm of our optimization framework, only those local features with non-zero weight (Marked with red rectangles in the Figure 2) are preserved to make up the final feature set. The local features of test image are also densely sampled to form the image feature set. To evaluate the C2I distance from the class "car" to each test image, every local feature in class "car" needs to find its NN in the feature set of each test image (Those local features matched as NN features in the test images are also marked with red rectangles in Figure 2, and we can see that most of them are correctly located at the region of car). The sum of Euclidean distance from every local feature in class "car" to its NN feature in a test image multiplied by the learned weight is defined as the C2I distance to this image. We summarize the main contributions of this paper as follows:

- We propose to use C2I distance for the multi-label problem and show that this distance performs better than I2C distance when test images contain multiple class labels.
- We propose an optimization algorithm using large margin constraint and L1-norm regularization to learn the C2I distance. With this optimization algorithm, we are able to get better recognition performance, while the size of feature set is significantly reduced.
- To solve this optimization problem, we propose an efficient gradient descent based solver, which can update the weight and converge to global optimum quickly.

We organize the rest of this paper as follows. Section 2 briefly reviews previous research related to our work. We describe the objective function and learning algorithm in Section 3, and evaluate its performance compared with other methods in Section 4. Finally, we conclude this paper in Section 5.

2 Related Work

Recent research tries to avoid the information loss in feature quantization process, some methods measure the distance from set to set directly and some use other strategies [4]. The former one can be roughly divided into three types: The first one is I2I distance as proposed by Frome *et al.* [5,6], which shows good performance in image classification and retrieval. However, its recognition performance in image classification is not comparable to the second type of I2C distance proposed in [1], which achieves state-of-the-art performance in several single-label datasets. The effectiveness of I2C distance attracts many later research work on it. For example, Wang *et al.* [7,8] learn a per-class Mahalanobis distance metric and weighted I2C distance for improving the recognition performance, Behmo *et al.* [9] learn an optimal NBNN by hinge-loss minimization to further enhance its generalization ability, Tuytelaars *et al.* [10] propose a kernelized version of I2C distance as complimentary to standard bag-of-words based kernels, McCann and Lowe [11] modify the formulation of I2C distance and propose a local NBNN method, which can not only speed up the distance calculation, but also improve the recognition performance.

However, I2C distance is not suitable for the multi-label problem since it cannot distinguish local features from different regions in a test image. This problem can be solved by the third type of C2I distance as shown in previous section. Wang *et al.* [12,13] first use this distance for multi-instance learning problems. However, they do not discuss the advantage of C2I distance over I2C distance for the multi-label problem. The reduction of local features for C2I distance calculation is also ignored, which is an important issue to make C2I distance practical since the number of local features in a class is much more than that in an image. Our work addresses this problem and uses L1-norm regularization to learn a sparse solution, so that the irrelevant local features receive a zero weight and can be removed directly from the feature set, which can not only accelerate the distance calculation, but also reduce the memory usage during the test phase. Our work is similar to the weight learning method in [8]. Both methods use large margin constraint while [8] use L2-norm regularization but we use L1-norm. This is also the difference between C2I and I2C distances. In I2C distance, it is not necessary to use L1-norm regularization since no local feature in each class requires to be removed before the NN search. Other similar methods of using large margin or weighting model for the multi-label problem includes [14,15].

3 Learning Class-to-Image Distance

We briefly describe the notations used in this paper before describing the objective function of our optimization problem. For a class C_i, all the local features extracted from the training images belonging to this class are gathered together to make up the initial feature set of this class, and are denoted as $F_{C_i} = \{f_{C_i1}, f_{C_i2}, \ldots, f_{C_im_i}\}$, where m_i represents the total number of local features in C_i and each local feature is denoted as $f_{C_ik} \in R^d, \forall k \in \{1, \ldots, m_i\}$. Similarly, the feature set of an image X_j is denoted as $F_{X_j} = \{f_{X_j1}, f_{X_j2}, \ldots, f_{X_jm_j}\}$, where m_j represents the total number of local features in image X_j. To calculate the C2I distance from class C_i to image X_j, every local feature f_{C_ik} in F_{C_i} needs to find its NN feature in F_{X_j}, which we denote as $f_{C_ik}^{X_j}$. The sum of Euclidean distance between every local feature f_{C_ik} in F_{C_i} and its NN feature $f_{C_ik}^{X_j}$ is defined as the C2I distance from class C_i to image X_j and is denoted as $Dist(C_i, X_j)$:

$$Dist(C_i, X_j) = \sum_{k=1}^{m_i} \| f_{C_ik} - f_{C_ik}^{X_j} \|^2 \tag{1}$$

where

$$f_{C_ik}^{X_j} = \mathop{\arg\min}_{t=\{1,\ldots,m_j\}} \| f_{C_ik} - f_{X_j,t} \|^2 \tag{2}$$

We associate a weight W_{C_ik} to every local feature f_{C_ik} in class C_i to distinguish the different importance of each local feature and learn a weighted C2I distance. All the weights can be put into a long vector W and a distance vector $D(C_i, X_j)$ is constructed as well with the same dimension to W, so the weighted C2I distance is formulated as:

$$W^T \cdot D(C_i, X_j) = \sum_{k=1}^{m_i} W_{C_ik} \cdot \| f_{C_ik} - f_{C_ik}^{X_j} \|^2 \tag{3}$$

The objective function of our optimization problem is composed of two terms: the regularization term and the error term. In the error term, we form the triplet constraints by selecting one class with one relevant image and one irrelevant image for each triplet and constrain that the C2I distance from class C_i to the relevant image X_p should be smaller than the distance to the irrelevant image X_n with a large margin:

$$W^T \cdot D(C_i, X_n) - W^T \cdot D(C_i, X_p) \geq 1 - \xi_{ipn} \tag{4}$$

where ξ_{ipn} is a slack variable in order to allow soft-margin. With these triplet constraints, the learned weights are able to discriminate the different importance of local features in the class. Higher important local features are likely to get higher value weight and less important local features will get smaller weight, while irrelevant local features will get zero value weight and are removed from the feature set.

In the regularization term, if we impose L2-norm regularization on the weight vector W like standard SVM framework, the sparseness of the weight vector cannot be guaranteed. Since the number of local features in a class is usually very large, the sparsity of the learned weight is very important to make C2I distance practical. Therefore, in this paper we use L1-norm regularization in the objective function and try to learn a more sparse weight vector. The objective function of our optimization framework with L1-norm regularization is formulated as follows:

$$\min_{W} O(W) = ||W||_1 + C \sum_{i,p,n} \xi_{ipn} \tag{5}$$

$$\begin{aligned} s.t. \forall\ i,p,n:\ & W^T \cdot (D(C_i, X_n) - D(C_i, X_p)) \geq 1 - \xi_{ipn} \\ & \xi_{ipn} \geq 0 \\ \forall\ k:\ & W(k) \geq 0 \end{aligned}$$

where C is used to control the trade-off between regularization term and error term. With this objective function, less important and irrelevant local features will be more likely to receive a zero weight and be removed from the feature set, making the size of final feature set smaller and therefore accelerating the C2I distance calculation. To solve this new optimization problem, we propose a gradient descend based method, which is able to effectively and efficiently update the weight vector.

Since we guarantee the non-negativeness of weight vector, the L1-norm $||W||_1$ can be reformulated as $W^T \cdot e$ where e is a constant vector with all entries to be 1 and same dimension to W, and this optimization problem is convex w.r.t. W. Therefore, the gradient descend based method can be used to iteratively update the weight vector and is guaranteed to converge to the global optimum. In each iteration, the weight vector is updated by taking a small step along the negative gradient direction to reduce the objective function and then negative components are truncated to zero to ensure the non-negativeness. To calculate the gradient of the objective function over the weight vector W, we first rewrite this objective function by replacing the slack variable ξ_{ipn} using the triplet constraints. To simplify, we denote $D(C_i, X_n) - D(C_i, X_p)$ by X_{ipn}. Since

$$\xi_{ipn} = 0 \quad if \qquad W^T \cdot X_{ipn} \geq 1 \tag{6}$$

and

$$\begin{aligned} \xi_{ipn} > 0 \ \ if & \qquad W^T \cdot X_{ipn} < 1 \\ and & \qquad W^T \cdot X_{ipn} + \xi_{ipn} = 1 \end{aligned} \tag{7}$$

at each iteration t, we can first scan over all triplets to find a set of unsatisfied triplets where $\xi_{ipn} > 0$. We denote N^t as the set of triplet indices such that $(i,p,n) \in N^t$ if $\xi_{ipn} > 0$. Then the objective function at t^{th} iteration can be rewritten as:

$$O(W) = W^T \cdot e + C \sum_{(i,p,n) \in N^t} (1 - W^T \cdot X_{ipn}) \tag{8}$$

The gradient $G(W^t)$ at t^{th} iteration can be calculated by taking the derivative of the above objective function w.r.t. W:

$$G(W^t) = e - C \cdot (e^T \cdot \sum_{(i,p,n) \in N^t} X_{ipn}) \tag{9}$$

Therefore, the weight vector W^t at t^{th} iteration is calculated as:

$$W^t = W^{t-1} - \alpha \cdot G(W^t) \tag{10}$$

where α is the step size, which is tuned during the iterations using the method in [16]. To satisfy the non-negativeness, all negative components of the weight vector are truncated to zero after each updating. Since the whole optimization problem is convex w.r.t. W, it is guaranteed to converge to the global optimum after iterative updating.

The main computation bottleneck in this solving method is the calculation of N^t in each iteration t, since every triplet constraint needs to be checked by calculating ${W^t}^T \cdot X_{ipn}$ (If ${W^t}^T \cdot X_{ipn} < 1$, then $\xi_{ipn} > 0$ and $(i, p, n) \in N^t$). This calculation is time-consuming as the dimension of W and X_{ipn} depends on the initial feature set size and is usually very huge, and the number of triplets is also large. To accelerate this calculation, we can keep an active set for triplets that have been violating the constraints and scanning only the triplets in the active set during each iteration. The full scanning over all triplets is only made at the beginning of the algorithm and every 10-20 iterations. Meanwhile, since the weight vector is usually very sparse after a few iterations, the calculation of ${W^t}^T \cdot X_{ipn}$ can be accelerated as only the non-negative components are involved in the calculation. The whole work flow of updating the weight vector for each class is summarized in Algorithm 1.

Algorithm 1. The Algorithm for Solving Our Optimization Problem

Input: step size α, parameter C and pre-calculated data X_{ipn}
$W^0 := e$ {Initialize the weight vector with all entries equal to 1}
Set $t := 0$
repeat
  Compute N^t by checking each error term ξ_{ipn}
  Update $G(W^t)$:
    $G(W^t) := e - C \cdot (e^T \cdot \sum_{(i,p,n) \in N^t} X_{ipn})$
  Update W^t:
    $W^t := W^{t-1} - \alpha \cdot G(W^t)$
  Truncate negative components of W^t to 0
  Calculate new objective function
  $t := t + 1$
until Objective function converged
Output: Weight Vector W

4 Experiment

In this section, We evaluate the performance of our method and compare it with other related methods on three multi-label image datasets: MSRC [1], Pascal VOC 2011 [17] and MirFlickr [18].

4.1 Dataset Setup

We briefly describe the setup for each of the three datasets as follows:

MSRC dataset contains 591 images and 21 class labels, and the average number of class labels per image is 2.46. We use 10-fold cross validation on this dataset. Specifically, the dataset is divided into 10 parts and each time 9 parts are used for training and the rest one is used for test, and the average result over 10 runs is reported.

VOC2011 dataset is a much larger dataset, which contains a total of 28,952 images annotated into 20 classes. However, the majority of images in this dataset are single-labeled, on average about 1.44 labels per image. To better evaluate our method for the multi-label problem, we select a subset where most of images have more than one label. Specifically, We randomly select images with multiple labels such that each class contains at least 50 training and 50 test images, which leads to 1777 images used in our experiment and the average number of class labels per image is increased to 2.12. This random selection is conducted 5 times and the average result is reported.

MirFlickr dataset consists of 25000 images downloaded from Flickr.com. There are 1386 tags which occur in at least 20 images. We use the most common 30 content based tags as suggested by [18] in our experiment and select at least 100 image for each class, resulting in average 2.47 class labels per image. The selected image collections are equally divided into the training and test sets and we run 5 random partitions to report the average result.

In each dataset, we use SIFT feature [19] as our descriptor densely sampled at every 10 pixels to make up the feature set for training and test images. We evaluate our method of Learning the C2I distance with weight learned using L1-norm regularization, which is denoted as **"LC2I-L1"**, and compare it to:

- **"LC2I-L1-FS"**, which only uses the local features with non-zero weight to calculate the C2I distance but does not multiply with the learned weight, to show the performance of our Feature Selection strategy;
- **"C2I"**, the original C2I distance summed up by Euclidean distance from all local features without feature selection and weighting;
- **"C2I-DVW-FS"**, C2I distance with the Feature Selection method of selecting Discriminative Visual Words used in [20];
- **"LC2I-L2"**, the Learned C2I distance with weight learned using L2-norm regularization, which is solved using the method in [5].

[1] `http://research.microsoft.com/en-us/projects/objectclassrecognition/`

We also compare with other related methods:

- **"I2C"**, the original NBNN method in [1];
- **"LI2C"**, the Learning of weighted I2C distance [8];
- **"Local NBNN"**, an improved I2C distance [11];
- **"NBNN Kernel"** [10], I2C distance as input of One-vs-All SVM with histogram intersection kernel
- **"BoW"**, Bag-of-Words model [21] for image representation with One-vs-All SVM of histogram intersection kernel.

We use mean average precision (MAP) to evaluate and compare different methods in our experiment as in [17]. All the NN searches involved in C2I and I2C distance calculations are approximated by kd-tree implemented by VLFeat [22], with 5 kd-trees in each feature set and a maximum of 100 comparisons for each NN search, which does not show much difference on the final MAP compared to that of accurate NN search.

4.2 Experiment Result

Table 1 shows the result of different methods on the three datasets, and we can see that the proposed method, "LC2I-L1" significantly outperforms all other methods. In particular, the improvement over the original C2I distance can be divided into two parts: feature selection by removing local features with zero value weight and the discrimination of different importance for the preserved local features by their associated non-zero weight.

The improvement over the first one of feature selection can be seen by comparing the performance of "LC2I-L1-FS" to "C2I". "LC2I-L1-FS" only uses the weight to select relevant local features without weighting in C2I distance calculation, and its improvement over the original C2I distance shows that this feature selection is able to remove the irrelevant local features that deteriorate the performance of C2I distance. These irrelevant local features have to be put into the initial feature set of each relevant class because the training images may also

Table 1. Performance comparison using MAP

Method	MSRC	VOC2011	MirFlickr
LC2I-L1	**0.6379 ± 0.0020**	**0.3522 ± 0.0036**	**0.2561 ± 0.0029**
LC2I-L1-FS	0.5679 ± 0.0037	0.3238 ± 0.0035	0.2306 ± 0.0061
C2I	0.3438 ± 0.0007	0.2180 ± 0.0016	0.1591 ± 0.0014
C2I-DVW-FS [20]	0.3387 ± 0.0041	0.2035 ± 0.0007	0.1534 ± 0.0012
LC2I-L2 [5]	0.5864 ± 0.0010	0.3016 ± 0.0001	0.2078 ± 0.0009
I2C (NBNN) [1]	0.3549 ± 0.0016	0.1508 ± 0.0011	0.1548 ± 0.0023
LI2C [8]	0.5231 ± 0.0017	0.1690 ± 0.0003	0.1619 ± 0.0016
Local NBNN [11]	0.6019 ± 0.0052	0.2669 ± 0.0018	0.1979 ± 0.0021
NBNN Kernel [10]	0.6054 ± 0.0033	0.2693 ± 0.0041	0.1782 ± 0.0009
BoW [21]	0.6110 ± 0.0024	0.3096 ± 0.0014	0.2299 ± 0.0033

belong to multiple classes but the information that which region in the image belongs to which class is not provided since this pixel-wise or bounding box human labeling is expensive. Due to the inclusion of these irrelevant local features, the original C2I distance does not show better performance compared to I2C distance on MSRC and MirFlickr datasets as shown in Table 1. However, with the feature selection to remove these irrelevant local features, the performance of C2I distance can be largely improved, as comparing "LC2I-L1-FS" to "C2I".

The improvement over the second part of non-zero weighting can be recognized by comparing the performance of "LC2I-L1" to "LC2I-L1-FS". This improvement shows the learned weight not only provides a feature selection strategy to reduce the size of feature set and remove irrelevant local features, but also discriminates the different importance of the preserved local features in the final feature set by their associated non-zero weight to further improve the C2I distance, which validates the effectiveness of our learning algorithm.

Compared to I2C distance related methods, our learned C2I distance is able to achieve better recognition performance under the multi-label problem. Though I2C distance of non-learning methods like NBNN and Local NBNN may benefit from a larger feature set sampled from denser grids, their performances are still worse than our method. To verify this, we have tried sampling at every 4 pixels and find Local NBNN is only slightly improved to 0.2846 in VOC2011 dataset. It should be noted the improvement over I2C distance methods is based on the multi-label problem. When more images are single-labeled, e.g. in the full VOC dataset, such large improvement is not expected. Due to the computation limitation of our working machine for the heavy NN search in distance calculation, we only try class "aeroplane", "bicycle", "car", "chair" and "person" for the full VOC 2007 dataset, and find the performance of our method is worse than I2C distance (0.502 vs 0.649 [23]), while in our multi-label subset version of these classes, our method significantly outperform NBNN (0.467 vs 0.247).

We also compare the performance of learning weight using L1-norm regularization to L2-norm. By comparing "LC2I-L1" to "LC2I-L2" in Table 1, we can see that even using L1-norm to learn a sparser solution, the recognition performance is still better than using L2-norm, which again shows the effectiveness of our learning algorithm. Meanwhile, the sparsity of the resulting feature set learned by L1-norm is much lower than L2-norm. This is shown in Table 2, where the sparsity is represented by the percentage of the number of preserved local features compared to the original feature set. With L1-norm regularization, only 3.35% local features are preserved in MSRC dataset and in VOC2011 and MirFlickr datasets, this is reduced to only 0.26% and 0.31% respectively. This is a much larger reduction on both computational cost of C2I distance calculation and memory usage, since their complexities are linear to the size of class feature set. To verify this reduction, we show in Table 3 the average running time of distance calculation for a test image over all classes and Table 2 shows the memory usage for loading the training feature sets of all classes. All of the experiments are running on a single core of **Intel x86 Xeon CPU E7320@2.13GHz** and **16GB** memory.

Table 2. sparsity comparison (Percentage of the number of local features compared to the original feature set)

Method	MSRC	VOC2011	MirFlickr
LC2I-L1	**3.35% ± 0.14**	**0.26% ± 0.01**	**0.31% ± 0.02**
LC2I-L2 [5]	12.50% ± 0.10	5.86% ± 0.16	1.58% ± 0.32
C2I-DVW-FS [20]	18.45% ± 0.15	16.20% ± 0.09	16.85% ± 0.12
C2I,I2C [1]	100%	100%	100%

Table 3. running time comparison (second)

Method	MSRC	VOC2011	MirFlickr
LC2I-L1	**0.61 ± 0.03**	**0.63 ± 0.05**	**0.61 ± 0.04**
LC2I-L2 [5]	3.02 ± 0.22	5.64 ± 0.53	1.86 ± 0.15
C2I-DVW-FS [20]	9.12 ± 0.41	21.08 ± 1.53	22.20 ± 1.01
C2I	51.95 ± 1.07	132.88 ± 5.03	129.72 ± 3.05
I2C [1]	5.08 ± 0.13	7.44 ± 0.61	14.29 ± 0.33
Local NBNN [11]	1.18 ± 0.09	3.04 ± 0.22	3.57 ± 0.15

Table 4. memory usage comparison (MB)

Method	MSRC	VOC2011	MirFlickr
LC2I-L1	**5.91 ± 0.04**	**6.12 ± 0.05**	**5.38 ± 0.08**
LC2I-L2 [5]	31.19 ± 0.51	65.38 ± 2.44	20.34 ± 0.40
C2I-DVW-FS [20]	101.88 ± 1.49	240.25 ± 3.72	254.08 ± 4.13
C2I,I2C [1]	547.88 ± 3.26	1508.94 ± 10.28	1512.23 ± 15.11

Compared to I2C distance, the original C2I distance needs much more expensive computational cost since the number of local features in a class is much more than that in an image, while both methods need the same amount of memory usage to store the whole feature sets of classes for distance calculation. However, with our learning method using L1-norm regularization, only a very small number of local features are preserved in the final feature set for each class. Therefore, the computational cost of our C2I distance can be even lower than I2C distance, and the memory usage is greatly reduced. Even compared to Local NBNN, which is the most efficient method in I2C distance computation so far, our method still needs less running time for distance calculation.

The method of "C2I-DVW-FS" clusters the feature set of each class to 1000 visual words and selects the top 64 most discriminative visual words. Local features belonging to these visual words are selected to make up the final feature set for each class and used in C2I distance. However, the result in Table 1 and Table 2 shows that its recognition performance is even worse than the original C2I distance, probably because label information is not utilized in the clustering and selection procedure. Therefore this method cannot distinguish relevant local features used in C2I distance. Meanwhile, its sparsity is not as good as our learning method. In summary, our learned C2I distance not only achieves better recognition performance, but also greatly reduces the computational cost and memory usage.

4.3 The Influence of Parameter C

We also analyze the impact of the trade-off parameter C in the objective function 5. Table 5 shows the MAP and sparsity under different C values ranging from 10^{-3} to 10^{1} on MSRC dataset. With the increase of C, the size of the feature set is always increased, meaning more local features are preserved and more computational cost and memory usage are required. This can be recognized as the increase of C makes the objective function pay less emphasis on the sparsity of the weight vector and therefore resulting in more local features preserved. However, when C is increasing, the recognition performance is first increased but then decreased, as a large value of C might put too much emphasis on the error term to cause over-fitting. The best MAP is achieved when C is equal to 10^{-2} on MSRC dataset. If we further increase C after this peak point, both the recognition performance and efficiency are getting worse.

Table 5. MAP and sparsity of our method over different C value on MSRC dataset

C	MAP	Sparsity
10^{-3}	0.6027 ± 0.0031	$1.73\% \pm 0.03$
10^{-2}	0.6379 ± 0.0020	$3.35\% \pm 0.14$
10^{-1}	0.6054 ± 0.0007	$8.71\% \pm 0.23$
10^{0}	0.5727 ± 0.0020	$14.97\% \pm 0.51$
10^{1}	0.5669 ± 0.0007	$20.55\% \pm 0.95$

5 Conclusion

In this paper, we have discussed the drawback of I2C distance in classifying multi-label images and proposed to use C2I distance for dealing with multi-label image classification. To select relevant local features for each class and speed up the C2I distance calculation, we associated a weight for each local feature densely sampled from images, and proposed an optimization algorithm using large margin constraint and L1-norm regularization to learn these weights. We also proposed a gradient descend based solver to efficiently and effectively update these weights in the learning procedure. Experiments on three multi-label datasets have shown that our learning algorithm can not only improve the performance of C2I distance and outperform other related methods, but also significantly reduce the number of local features in the class feature set and greatly improve the efficiency.

However, it should be noted such performance and efficiency improvements in the test phase is a trade-off of the additional training phase for learning the C2I distance. The original C2I distance calculation in the training phase is computation expensive since this is done before the learning procedure. Therefore, when there are a large number of local features in the original feature set, an initial local feature selection before the learning procedure may be required to alleviate the computational cost of distance calculation in the training phase, which would be a possible future direction.

Acknowledgement. This study is done when Zhengxiang Wang and Shenghua Gao were studying in Nanyang Technological University and is supported by Fujitsu Research & Development Center Co., Ltd and the research grant for the Human Sixth Sense Programme at the Advanced Digital Sciences Center from Singapore's Agency for Science, Technology and Research (A*STAR).

References

1. Boiman, O., Shechtman, E., Irani, M.: In defense of nearest-neighbor based image classification. In: CVPR (2008)
2. Bradley, P.S., Mangasarian, O.L.: Feature selection via concave minimization and support vector machines. In: ICML (1998)
3. Yuan, G.X., Chang, K.W., Hsieh, C.J., Lin, C.J.: A comparison of optimization methods and software for large-scale L1-regularized linear classification. JMLR 11(52) (2010)
4. Perronnin, F., Liu, Y., Sanchez, J., Poirier, H.: Large-scale image retrieval with compressed fisher vectors. In: CVPR (2010)
5. Frome, A., Singer, Y., Sha, F., Malik, J.: Learning globally-consistent local distance functions for shape-based image retrieval and classification. In: ICCV (October 2007)
6. Frome, A., Singer, Y., Malik, J.: Image retrieval and classification using local distance functions. In: NIPS, vol. 19 (2006)
7. Wang, Z., Hu, Y., Chia, L.-T.: Image-to-Class Distance Metric Learning for Image Classification. In: Daniilidis, K., Maragos, P., Paragios, N. (eds.) ECCV 2010, Part I. LNCS, vol. 6311, pp. 706–719. Springer, Heidelberg (2010)
8. Wang, Z., Hu, Y., Chia, L.T.: Improved learning of i2c distance and accelerating the neighborhood search for image classification. Pattern Recognition 44(10-11), 2384–2394 (2011)
9. Behmo, R., Marcombes, P., Dalalyan, A., Prinet, V.: Towards Optimal Naive Bayes Nearest Neighbor. In: Daniilidis, K., Maragos, P., Paragios, N. (eds.) ECCV 2010, Part IV. LNCS, vol. 6314, pp. 171–184. Springer, Heidelberg (2010)
10. Tuytelaars, T., Fritz, M., Saenko, K., Darrell, T.: The nbnn kernel. In: ICCV, pp. 1824–1831 (2011)
11. McCann, S., Lowe, D.G.: Local naive bayes nearest neighbor for image classification. In: CVPR (2012)
12. Wang, H., Nie, F., Huang, H.: Learning instance specific distance for multi-instance classification. In: AAAI (2011)
13. Wang, H., Huang, H., Kamangar, F., Nie, F., Ding, C.: Maximum margin multi-instance learning. In: NIPS, vol. 24 (2011)
14. Verbeek, J., Guillaumin, M., Mensink, T., Schmid, C.: Image annotation with tagprop on the mirflickr set. In: MIR (2010)
15. Lampert, C.H.: Maximum margin multi-label structured prediction. In: NIPS, vol. 24 (2011)
16. Weinberger, K.Q., Saul, L.K.: Distance metric learning for large margin nearest neighbor classification. JMLR 10, 207–244 (2009)
17. Everingham, M., Van Gool, L., Williams, C.K.I., Winn, J., Zisserman, A.: The PASCAL Visual Object Classes Challenge 2011 (VOC 2011) (2011) (Results)
18. Huiskes, M.J., Thomee, B., Lew, M.S.: New trends and ideas in visual concept detection: The mir flickr retrieval evaluation initiative. In: MIR, pp. 527–536 (2010)

19. Lowe, D.G.: Distinctive image features from scale-invariant keypoints. IJCV 60(2) (2004)
20. Chum, O., Zisserman, A.: An exemplar model for learning object classes. In: CVPR (2007)
21. Sivic, J., Zisserman, A.: Video Google: a text retrieval approach to object matching in videos. In: ICCV (2003)
22. Vedaldi, A., Fulkerson, B.: VLFeat: An open and portable library of computer vision algorithms (2008), `http://www.vlfeat.org/`
23. Timofte, R., Gool, L.V.: Iterative nearest neighbors for classification and dimensionality reduction. In: CVPR (2012)

Taxonomic Multi-class Prediction and Person Layout Using Efficient Structured Ranking

Arpit Mittal[1], Matthew B. Blaschko[2], Andrew Zisserman[1], and Philip H. S. Torr[3]

[1] Department of Engineering Science, University of Oxford, UK
[2] Center for Visual Computing, École Centrale Paris, France**
[3] Department of Computing, Oxford Brookes University, UK

Abstract. In computer vision efficient multi-class classification is becoming a key problem as the field develops and the number of object classes to be identified increases. Often objects might have some sort of structure such as a taxonomy in which the mis-classification score for object classes close by, using tree distance within the taxonomy, should be less than for those far apart. This is an example of multi-class classification in which the loss function has a special structure. Another example in vision is for the ubiquitous pictorial structure or parts based model. In this case we would like the mis-classification score to be proportional to the number of parts misclassified.

It transpires both of these are examples of structured output ranking problems. However, so far no efficient large scale algorithm for this problem has been demonstrated. In this work we propose an algorithm for structured output ranking that can be trained in a time linear in the number of samples under a mild assumption common to many computer vision problems: that the loss function can be discretized into a small number of values.

We show the feasibility of structured ranking on these two core computer vision problems and demonstrate a consistent and substantial improvement over competing techniques. Aside from this, we also achieve state-of-the art results for the PASCAL VOC human layout problem.

1 Introduction

Multi-class classification has become of increasing interest as the computational power of computers increases. Standard approaches to multi-class image labeling typically penalize incorrect predictions equally: a motorbike mis-classified as a bicycle receives the same penalty as a motorbike mis-classified as a cow. If taxonomic knowledge is included, a system can be designed to penalize misclassifications proportional to their taxonomic losses (e.g. the distance along a taxonomic tree, so that for instance misclassifying a car as a van might be

** M. B. Blaschko is also associated with Équipe Galen, INRIA Saclay, Île-de-France, France and Université Paris-Est, LIGM (UMR CNRS), Center for Visual Computing, École des Ponts ParisTech, France.

A. Fitzgibbon et al. (Eds.): ECCV 2012, Part II, LNCS 7573, pp. 245–258, 2012.

Fig. 1. Sample high ranked results of person layout detection task for the VOC 2010 test dataset. The blue rectangle represents the provided bounding box of the person, green rectangles are the detected hands and red rectangle is the detected head respectively. Our method yields the best results despite high variation in pose and occlusion.

better than misclassifying it as a banana). We refer to the problem of multi-class classification with a structured loss defined by a taxonomy as *taxonomic multi-class prediction*. A taxonomy defines a limited number of losses, which are logarithmic in the number of classes [1].

Person layout is another example of a multi-class problem. The person layout problem of the PASCAL VOC challenge [2] involves predicting the bounding box for several parts of a person (head, hands and feet). It is a very challenging task with evaluation over real-world images comprising a variety of different view-points and highly varied human layout configurations. The success of the layout prediction is judged by the correct prediction for the presence/absence of the parts and also by their correct localization. The natural loss underlying this problem can be computed from the number of incorrectly predicted parts.

The output space of both these problems is structured and can be solved by the structured output support vector machine (SOSVM) [3,4], which generalizes the support vector machine to the case of complex or interdependent output spaces. SOSVM has been successfully applied to core computer vision tasks such as stereo vision [5], object detection [6], and segmentation [7]. Furthermore, both multi-class taxonomic prediction and person layout exhibit an inherent order among the different instances. For any class in the tree multi-class taxonomic prediction the class taxonomy defines the ordering of predicted classes according to the distance in the tree. In the person layout problem, instances having more correctly predicted parts are ranked higher than those with less correctly predicted parts. As such, it is clear that these problems could benefit from the use of structured output *ranking*, which has been shown to improve over the SOSVM when predictions involve ranking results [8,9,10].

Although structured output ranking often performs better than the SOSVM for problems with certain structured losses, it has previously not been feasible to train the ranking objective with all pairs of training samples when the number of samples is large [11]. The number of constraints in an SVM or SOSVM is linear in the number of training samples, whilst structured output ranking is quadratic. As standard computer vision datasets contain thousands of samples, complexity quadratic in the number of samples is typically infeasible. In all the efficient formulations of structured output ranking proposed so far, the constraints are defined either between ground-truth and one (most) incorrect prediction per training image [8] or between predictions above and below a certain threshold value [9,10]. If these formulations are generalised for all pairs of predictions (our case), it would result in an $\mathcal{O}(n^2)$ algorithm. In this paper we show that training of the structured output ranking objective can be performed with linear complexity if the structured output loss has a small number of discrete values. We demonstrate the applicability of this linear time algorithm to the two quite disparate tasks: taxonomic multi-class prediction (Section 4) and person layout (Section 5).

We show that learning with structured output ranking consistently surpasses the predictive performance of SVM, SOSVM, ordinal regression and other related methods.

2 Structured Output Ranking – Review

For a given training set, $(x_1, y_1), ..., (x_n, y_n)$, where x_i is the input and y_i is the output, structured output prediction [3] learns a compatibility function $f(x_i, y_i) = \langle w, \phi(x_i, y_i)\rangle$ that assigns a scalar value indicating the fitness of the structured prediction y_i to x_i. To do so, a combined feature representation $(\phi(x_i, y_i))$ is used and the training problem involves the learning of a classifying hyperplane (w) for this joint feature map. For computer vision problems, $x_i \in \mathcal{R}^d$ is the ith image represented as a d-dimensional feature vector, and $y_i \in \mathcal{Y}$ is a sample in a structured output space. The domain of $\mathcal{Y}$ is application specific. For multi-class prediction, $\mathcal{Y} \equiv \{1, ..., c\}$, where c is the number of class labels. For human layout, $\mathcal{Y} \equiv \mathcal{R}^{4r}$, where r is the number of body parts each represented by four co-ordinates of its bounding box.

Ordinal Regression. In ordinal regression [12] (which is not a structured output), the output y_i is a scalar value indicating the ordering (rank) of x_i. Thus, for this problem $y_i \in \{1, ..., R\}$, so that the values $1, ..., R$ are related on an ordinal scale. R is the number of rank values. The goal is to learn a ranking function $h(x) = w^T x$, such that higher ranked pairs are assigned higher score, i.e., $h(x_i) > h(x_j) \iff y_i > y_j$. This results in the following optimization problem:

$$\min_{w,\xi} \frac{1}{2}\|w\|^2 + C\sum_{i,j} \xi_{ij} \qquad s.t., \xi_{ij} \geq 0, \tag{1}$$

$$w^T x_i - w^T x_j \geq 1 - \xi_{ij}$$

where (i, j) are the ordered indices of training samples, such that $y_i > y_j$. This formulation finds a solution that minimizes the number of training examples that are swapped w.r.t. their desired order.

Structured Output Ranking. In structured output *ranking*, the goal is to learn a compatibility function $f(x_i, y_i) = w^T\phi(x_i, y_i)$, such that input-output pairs with lower loss (e.g. fewer mispredicted parts in the case of human layout) are assigned higher compatibility score. To do so, a loss value $\Delta(y_i)$ is defined for every input-output pair (x_i, y_i) which represents the loss associated with the prediction y_i in the image x_i. In this case (x_i, y_i) now correspond to a training set including incorrect predictions y_i for the x_i as well as correct predictions. We will write Δ_i in place of $\Delta(y_i)$ in the sequel. The compatibility function f is learned such that it holds, $f(x_i, y_i) > f(x_j, y_j) \iff \Delta_i < \Delta_j$. Structured output ranking generalises ordinal regression to structured space and does so by modifying the hinge loss paid for misordered pairs. The objective function is modified as follows such that it pays a loss proportional to the difference in losses for misordering:

$$\min_{w,\xi} \frac{1}{2}\|w\|^2 + C \sum_{(i,j)\in\mathcal{P}} \xi_{ij} \qquad s.t., \xi_{ij} \geq 0, \tag{2}$$

$$w^T\phi(x_i, y_i) - w^T\phi(x_j, y_j) \geq 1 - \frac{\xi_{ij}}{\Delta_j - \Delta_i}$$

where $\mathcal{P}$ denotes the set of ordered training sample pairs such that the structured output loss, of the sample Δ_i, of sample i is less than the loss, Δ_j, of sample j.

This form (2) of the objective function is referred as slack rescaling. Another common form, margin rescaling, uses the difference in the losses to change the margin directly rather than scaling the slack variable. Due to space restrictions, in the paper we will only consider the case of slack rescaling.

3 Linear Time Constraint Generation

The above formulation has $m \in \mathcal{O}(n^2)$ number of constraints and slack variables, where n is the number of training samples. Although the objective function can contain a number of constraints quadratic in the number of structured output predictions, many vision applications have loss functions that have a fixed number of discrete values, L. For instance, the VOC detection overlap score [2] is a continuous value lying between 0 and 1. However, if it is rounded to tenths of a decimal then we get 11 discrete values. A limited number of discrete loss values also arise in taxonomic multi-class prediction (Section 4) and part based models with thresholded loss (Section 5). Having a small number of loss values enables us to adapt the cutting plane strategy of Joachims [13], achieving a linear time complexity to optimize over a quadratic number of constraints. It is to be noted that in [13], algorithms are given for SVM classification and ordinal regression, which are very different from the problem we are addressing.

We propose an equivalent 1-slack formulation [13] of structured output ranking that uses a single slack variable $\xi = \sum_{(i,j)\in\mathcal{P}} \xi_{ij}$ resulting in the following cutting plane optimization problem:

$$\min_{w,\xi} \frac{1}{2}\|w\|^2 + C\xi, \qquad s.t., \xi \geq 0, \tag{3}$$

$$\frac{1}{m}\sum_{(i,j)\in\mathcal{P}} c_{ij}(w^T\phi(x_i, y_i) - w^T\phi(x_j, y_j)) \geq \frac{1}{m}\sum_{(i,j)\in\mathcal{P}} c_{ij} - \frac{\xi}{\Delta_j - \Delta_i}$$

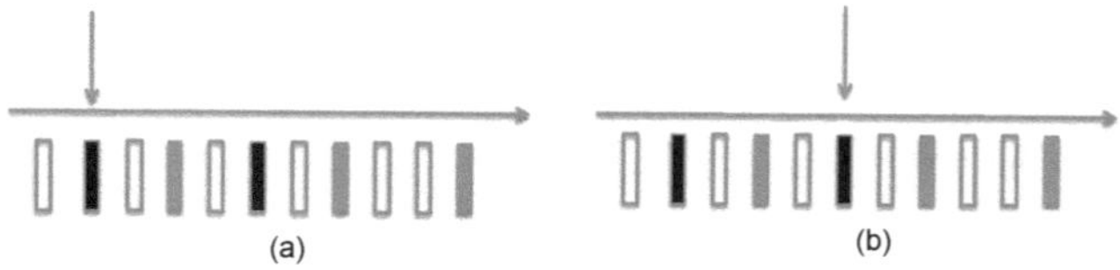

Fig. 2. Linear time constraint generation method. For a particular w the data-points with training pairs (x_i, y_i) are ordered in decreasing compatibility scores $w^T\phi(x_i, y_i)$ (shown by the horizontal arrow sign). The vertical arrow represents the current position of the scan through the data. Gray bars are all the data-points with training pairs having the given loss value l. Black bars are the data-points with training pairs which have loss $l' > l$. For simplicity of the explanation, the margin is considered to be zero. In this case, a constraint is violated when a black bar is placed earlier than a gray bar in the sorted list. In (a), the first black bar will violate constraints with the three subsequent gray bars and in (b), the second black bar will violate constraints with the two remaining gray bars. If an account is maintained of all the subsequent gray bars in the list, then all the violated constraints (i, j) having $\Delta_i = l$ can be obtained in a single scan through the data.

Here $c_{ij} \in \{0,1\}$ is the indicator variable stating whether the constraint between samples i and j has been included in the summation. The indicator c_{ij} is 1 if the corresponding constraint in (2) is violated and zero otherwise, i.e., $c_{ij} = |(\Delta_i < \Delta_j) \wedge ((w^T\phi(x_i, y_i)) - (w^T\phi(x_j, y_j)) < 1)|$. Thus, a constraint is violated when the training samples are scored such that the difference in the scores of lower loss sample and higher loss sample is less than the margin. While the above formulation (3) has 2^n constraints one for each possible value of c_{ij}, it has only one slack variable ξ shared across all constraints. Each constraint in this formulation correspond to the sum of a sub-set of constraints from formulation (2) selected by c_{ij}.

Cutting plane optimization of Equation (3) consists of alternating between optimizing the objective with a fixed set of constraints, and finding violated constraints of the current function estimate. The core of the learning algorithm is to determine, for a given w, the most violated constraints.

For a given loss value l, all the violated constraints for pairs (i, j) such that $\Delta_i = l$ can be obtained in linear time using a strategy analogous to the one proposed in [13] for ordinal regression. To do so, first the training samples are sorted in terms of decreasing compatibility scores $(w^T\phi(x_i, y_i))$. If a sample j with $\Delta_j > l$ is scored such that difference between the scores of samples i and j is less than one (i.e., the margin is violated), it will also violate all the subsequent samples, i' with $\Delta_{i'} = l$ in the sorted list (i.e., having $w^T\phi(x_{i'}, y_{i'}) < 1 + w^T\phi(x_j, y_j)$). Thus by book-keeping all the samples having loss value l, all the violated constraints for pairs (i, j) having $\Delta_i = l$ can be found in one pass through the training data. Figure 2 illustrates the method. If the number of possible loss values is small, then this gives a linear time solution for generating all the violated constraints (by going through each of the loss values in this manner). The complete learning method is summarized in Algorithm 1. Source code of a reference implementation is available from our website at: `http://www.robots.ox.ac.uk/~vgg/software/struct_rank/`.

Algorithm 1. 1-slack optimization for structured output ranking with slack rescaling

1: Input: $S = ((\phi(x_1, y_1), \Delta_1), ..., (\phi(x_n, y_n), \Delta_n)), C, \epsilon$
2: $L = (\Delta_1, \Delta_2, ..., \Delta_n)$
3: sort L in decreasing order
4: $W \leftarrow \emptyset$
5: **repeat**
6: $\quad (w, \xi) \leftarrow argmin_{w,\xi \geq 0} \frac{1}{2} w^T w + C\xi$
$\quad s.t. \forall (c^+, c^-) \in W : \frac{1}{m} w^T \sum_{i=1}^{n} (c_i^+ - c_i^-)\phi(x_i, y_i) \geq \frac{1}{2m} \sum_{i=1}^{n} (c_i^+ + c_i^-) - \xi$
7: $\quad$ sort S by decreasing $w^T \phi(x_i, y_i)$
8: $\quad c^+ \leftarrow 0; c^- \leftarrow 0$
9: $\quad$ **for** $l = l_2, ..., l_{|L|}$ **do**
10: $\qquad n_l \leftarrow$ number of examples with $\Delta_i = l$
11: $\qquad i \leftarrow 1; j \leftarrow 1; a \leftarrow 0; b \leftarrow 0; d \leftarrow 0$
12: $\qquad$ **while** $i \leq n$ **do**
13: $\qquad\quad$ **if** $\Delta_i == l$ **then**
14: $\qquad\qquad$ **while** $(j \leq n) \wedge (w^T \phi(x_i, y_i) - w^T \phi(x_j, y_j)) < 1$ **do**
15: $\qquad\qquad\quad$ **if** $\Delta_j > l$ **then**
16: $\qquad\qquad\qquad b++; d \leftarrow d + \Delta_j; c_j^- \leftarrow c_j^- + (n_l - a)(\Delta_j - \Delta_i)$
17: $\qquad\qquad\quad$ **end if**
18: $\qquad\qquad\quad j++$
19: $\qquad\qquad$ **end while**
20: $\qquad\qquad a++; c_i^+ \leftarrow c_i^+ + d - b\Delta_i$
21: $\qquad\quad$ **end if**
22: $\qquad\quad i++$
23: $\qquad$ **end while**
24: $\quad$ **end for**
25: $\quad W \leftarrow W \cup \{(c^+, c^-)\}$
26: **until** $\frac{1}{2m} \sum_{i=1}^{n} (c_i^+ + c_i^-) - \frac{1}{m} \sum_{i=1}^{n} (c_i^+ - c_i^-)(w^T \phi(x_i, y_i)) \leq \xi + \epsilon$
27: **return** (w, ξ)

In the algorithm, we have used variables c_i^+ and c_i^- which are the weighted counts of violations in which the ith sample occurs with positive sign (i.e. $c_{ij} = 1$) and negative sign (i.e. $c_{ji} = 1$) respectively. In slack rescaling, these weights are related to c_{ij} by $\frac{1}{m} \sum_{(i,j) \in \mathcal{P}} (\Delta_j - \Delta_i) c_{ij} = \frac{1}{2m} \sum_{i=1}^{n} (c_i^+ + c_i^-)$. In each iteration, the algorithm computes the optimum over the current working set W (line 6). In lines 9–24, it finds all the violated constraints and adds them to the current working set W (line 25). Unlike ordinal regression, the variables c_i^+ and c_i^- are scaled by the loss values, which results in the scaling of hinge loss of the objective function with the difference in loss values of samples. As long as the number of loss values, $|L|$, is independent of the number of samples, computation of the outer loop (lines 9–24) is therefore also linear in the number of samples. The linear time algorithm for ordinal regression proposed in [13] is a special case of our method. Plugging $\phi(x_i, y_i) = x_i$ and replacing $\Delta_j - \Delta_i$ with 1, our method reduces to ordinal regression.

4 Taxonomic Multi-class Prediction

Class hierarchies (otherwise known as taxonomies) are especially important in computer vision when scaling classification and detection to large numbers of categories [14]. In this work, class hierarchies are learned in a ranking setting. This is done by using the taxonomic loss as the Δ value in the structured output ranking objective. We define the taxonomic loss as the minimum path length between the two classes in the taxonomic graph, resulting in a number of loss values logarithmic in the number of classes to be predicted [15]. A class nearer to the reference class in the taxonomic graph is ranked higher. For example, if the taxonomy is {{animal, {horse, cow}}, {vehicle, {bus, motorbike}}}, then the loss for misclassifying a 'cow' with 'horse' will be 2 whereas the loss for mis-classification between 'cow' and 'motorbike' will be 4. Thus, the number of possible loss values is $\mathcal{O}(\log c)$, where c is the number of class labels. It should be noted that usually $c \ll n$,where n is the number of training samples.

The joint feature map, ϕ used in this work, is the standard one used in multi-class and taxonomic prediction [15,16]. This is given by $\phi(x_i, y_i) = \lambda(y_i) \otimes x_i$. $\lambda(y_i) \in \mathcal{R}^c$ is the class attribute vector, which is defined as: $\lambda_j(y_i) = 1$, if $j = y_i$, zero otherwise. $x_i \in \mathcal{R}^d$ is the ith image represented as a d-dimensional feature vector. Here $\otimes$ denotes a Kronecker product, thus $\phi(x_i, y_i) \in \mathcal{R}^{d \cdot c}$. The ordinal constraints of (2) therefore enforce that the scores of the classes are ordered in proportion to their distance in the taxonomic tree to a ground truth class.

Evaluation Measure. The performance is evaluated using the cumulative taxonomic loss [15]. This is computed by accumulating the taxonomic loss over the top scoring t classes for a given image, where $t \in [1..C]$. The results are reported (Section 6) as the mean cumulative taxonomic loss which is obtained by averaging the cumulative taxonomic loss for different ranks over all the test images. The ImageNet challenge [17] also uses a hierarchical cost as an evaluation criteria.

We test how well structured ranking performs compared to other methods for the following two datasets:

Indoor Scene Database. The indoor scene database [18] consists of 15620 images for 67 different indoor categories. The categories are further grouped into 5 scene groups which defines a two level taxonomy. The dataset is partitioned into the training set and the test set by choosing 80 and 20 images from each of the classes, respectively.

PASCAL VOC 2007 Classification Dataset. The PASCAL VOC 2007 classification dataset [2] is comprised of 5011 images in the combined training and validation set and 4952 images in the test set. Each image may contain multiple objects and the images are annotated for 20 different object categories. A taxonomy is defined with these 20 classes by the organizers [2], which we use for our experiments.

4.1 Implementation Details

Image Descriptors. SIFT descriptors [19] are extracted with a spatial stride of 5 pixels, and at four scales, defined by setting the width of the SIFT spatial bins to 4, 6, 8 and 10 pixels respectively. For the indoor scene database experiments, the features are quantised into a visual vocabulary of size 1000. A 2-level spatial pyramid model [20] is obtained by dividing the image in 1×1 and 2×2 grids, for a total of 5 regions. For the experiments on the VOC 2007 dataset, the visual vocabulary used is of size 10000, and the quantized descriptors are encoded using locality-constraint linear encoding (LLC) [21]. The spatial regions are obtained by dividing the image in 1×1, 3×1 and 2×2 grids, for a total of 8 regions.

Learning Methods. SVM and SVM-rank classifiers are trained by minimizing the 0/1 loss and are learned in a 1 vs. all fashion. SOSVM and structured ranking SVM algorithms minimize the taxonomic loss and are modelled using the joint feature map.

5 Person Layout

In the person layout competition of the VOC challenge [2], a bounding box (refered to hereafter as a human ROI) is provided for each 'person' object in a test image. The job is then to predict the presence or absence of parts (head/hands/feet), and the bounding boxes of those parts. The prediction for a person layout should be output with an associated real-valued confidence of the layout. This confidence score is then used to compute the precision-recall (PR) curve and AP (area under the PR curve) for each of the parts. The mean AP across all the parts is considered as the AP for the person. A submission is evaluated by the AP for individual parts and also by its summary for the person. Therefore, in order to win the competition, it is imperative to perform well on each of the individual parts categories.

Current layout detection methods tend to model the human body as a pictorial structure, and to predict the pose/layout of the person by maximising the posterior of the joint configuration of the body parts [22,23]. However, these methods suffer from a common curse of pictorial structures, the inability to model occlusion of parts and the over-counting of confidence from a given pixel location. In the experiments, we show that unmodified pictorial structure models are not suited to this setting.

Another approach to solve the person layout problem could be to apply individual part detectors and then combine their outputs in some fashion. There are two caveats here: (i) the task needs the confidence score for the whole layout, not the individual parts; (ii) detection of parts is performed independently, which may lead to sub-optimal performance unless some kind of co-occurrence information is introduced into the framework.

The method we implement here proceeds in two stages, (i) part candidates are generated using individual detectors, (ii) candidates for individual parts are combined and the joint output space is optimized and ranked using the structured output ranking approach. We note that feet are not detected in the current experiments as the training set size is not sufficient to reliably estimate the wide range of appearance in the test set (The AP of the best performing foot detection method for the PASCAL VOC 2010 competition was 1.2%).

Experiments are performed using the PASCAL VOC 2011 [24] person layout dataset. There are 609 images in both the training and validation sets having 850 human ROIs. The results are reported as the mean AP and standard deviation (Section 6).

5.1 Part Candidates Generation

The candidates for heads and hands are generated using individual part detectors. Head candidates are generated using a part-based detector of the human head [25]. For the generation of hand candidates, the hand detector available from [26] is used. The output of both the detectors is a bounding box around the part (refered to as ROI hereafter) with a confidence value. The candidates for the parts so obtained are rescored using separate linear SVM classifiers. This is done to include local image information such as positional and scale attributes of the candidates, relative to the human ROI in the image.

The linear SVM classifier for head candidates is trained over a feature vector (Φ_{head}) formed by concatenating: (i) confidence score from the detector, (ii) relative size of head and human ROIs, (iii) fraction of area of head ROI in human ROI. The intuition behind using these features is to suppress any bounding box which either has an abnormal height with respect to the size of the image, or which does not fully lie within the given bounding box of the person. For every human ROI the top scoring head candidate is returned as the detected head.

The linear classifier for the hand is trained in a similar fashion. The feature vector (Φ_{hand}) consists of: (i) confidence score of the detector, (ii) position within human ROI, (iii) relative position of hand and head ROIs within human ROI, (iv) relative size of hand and head ROIs, (v) overlap score of head and hand ROIs, (vi) fraction of area of hand ROI in human ROI. A head can be detected more reliably in an image compared to a hand. Therefore, the information about the head position is utilized for the detection of hands. The scores of hand candidates are thresholded to give 75% recall on the training set. For every person a maximum of top two scoring hand bounding boxes are returned as the detected hands (zero or one hand may be returned if no image regions score above the threshold).

5.2 Joint Learning Using Structured Ranking

We obtain confidence score for the person layout from a ranking function which is learned by jointly optimizing the output spaces of the two parts using structured output ranking. We also compare our results with naïve techniques for combining the confidences of different parts. However, they do not optimise the AP for all parts jointly and as we will show tend to benefit one of the parts at the expense of others.

We define the loss value (Δ) for a human layout as 1 - precision. This defines a limited number of loss values corresponding to the fraction of hypothesized part detections that are incorrect. For example, if all parts are hypothesized to be present, then the set of possible loss values is: $\{0, \frac{1}{3}, \frac{2}{3}, 1\}$. The numbers in the bracket correspond to the losses when {all, two, one, none} of the hypothesized body parts are correct. The ranking objective function is trained on the feature vector formed by concatenating the features used earlier for rescoring of parts (i.e., by concatenating the feature vectors of head and all the hands). Thus, $\phi(x_i, y_i) = [\Phi_{head}\,(\Phi_{hand})^h]$, where h is the number of hands in the ith image, therefore, $\phi(x_i, y_i) \in \mathcal{R}^{3+6h}$.

Table 1. Mean cumulative taxonomic loss at different ranks. The cumulative loss is computed as explained in Section 4. 'Obj loss' is the loss that is minimized by the respective learning method, where 'tax' stands for the taxonomic loss. 'Min loss' is the theoretically possible minimum taxonomic loss which is obtained by optimally ordering the class labels. The minimum loss is zero for the top result as the taxonomic loss is zero for correctly labeling an image. For the top two ranked classes, the minimum cumulative loss is the lowest taxonomic loss of a second category. This measure differentiates methods that correctly order multiple predictions by their taxonomic loss. The mean cumulative taxonomic loss for the structured output ranking method is lowest among all the learning methods.

		Indoor			VOC 2007		
Method	Obj Loss	1	5	10	1	5	10
SVM	0/1	2.75	16.18	33.51	2.83	17.09	39.84
SVM-struct	tax	3.71	18.50	36.97	3.98	20.71	45.19
SVM-rank	0/1	3.14	15.93	32.11	3.02	17.04	39.29
Struct rank	tax	**2.62**	**14.75**	**30.29**	**2.54**	**15.07**	**36.07**
Min loss		0.00	8.00	18.00	0.00	11.70	33.35

6 Experimental Results

In this section we show that using structured ranking SVM a significant improvement is achieved for both the applications. Due to the space constraints, results for slack rescaled versions of structured SVMs are reported. We also experimented with margin rescaled version and found that it performs slightly worse than slack rescaled version, but the difference was negligible.

6.1 Taxonomic Multi-class Prediction

In the following experiments, we compare our approach with binary SVM, SOSVM (SVM-struct) and ordinal regression (SVM-rank). For experiments on the indoor scene database, we train our model using the training set and test it on the test set. For the VOC 2007 dataset, training is done using the training-validation set and testing on the test set following the competition protocol. A validation step was employed to set the C parameter. For all formulations linear kernels were used.

Table 1 gives the numbers for cumulative loss for the top 1, 5 and 10 ranks for the different methods. It can be seen that the cumulative taxonomic loss decreases for ranking algorithms and it reduces even further by using structured ranking algorithms. Some qualitative results are shown in Figure 3.

The performance is evaluated over taxonomic loss, therefore, an objective function minimizing taxonomic loss is supposed to give the optimal performance. However, SOSVM (labelled 'SVM-struct') performs *worse* on these data sets than a binary SVM even when it optimizes taxonomic loss. A SVM optimizing ordinal regression with binary loss (SVM-rank) tends to perform worse than a

	Indoor			VOC 2007		

SVM	airport, restaurant, mall	bath, elevator, cloister	deli, museum, studio	person, chair, tv	train, cow, bus	car, bus, tv
SVM struct	salon, audi, bowling	deli, florist, mall	church, florist, studio	cat, car, bus	sheep, horse, cat	chair, sofa, sheep
SVM rank	video, grocery, bookstore	cellar, corridor, childroom	locker, pool, prison	sofa, chair, table	train, bus, cycle	table, tv, plant
Struct rank	mall, grocery, bookstore	elevator, waiting, pool	museum, locker, church	chair, sofa, plant	train, plane, boat	person, plane, tv

Fig. 3. Sample results for the indoor scene and the VOC 2007 classification test datasets. The top three labels (in order) predicted by each method are shown for several test images. More semantically meaningful labels are retrieved by structured ranking than the other methods.

binary SVM when few labels are returned, but improves over the binary SVM when more labels are returned. However, structured output ranking dominates the performance of all other learning variants. This shows that structured output ranking is the optimal way of optimizing taxonomic loss for the given scenario. The mean cumulative taxonomic loss for the structured output ranking method is closer to the minimum loss for the VOC 2007 dataset than the indoor scene database. This may be because the VOC 2007 dataset has a deeper taxonomy.

6.2 Person Layout

For all the following experiments, 5-fold cross-validation is performed using the training and validation set of the PASCAL VOC 2011 [24] person layout dataset.

Part Candidates Generation. After rescoring the head and hand candidates using linear SVM classifiers, AP for the head part increases from (68.59±3.14) to (81.04±1.7) and for hands from (23.97±2.24) to (28.32±2.12). It shows that the modeling of dependencies between parts improves detection performance. In general, this can be thought of as a (directed) graphical model that encodes the dependencies between parts. On the same images Yang et al.'s method [23] gives (37.71±1.73) AP for head and (0.27±0.02) AP for hand. Their system was designed using a stickman for person layout (i.e., one line segment indicating location, size and orientation for each part). To evaluate their detections using the PASCAL criteria, we estimate the bounding boxes from the stickman. The height is given by length of the stickman line segments and the width is fixed by cross-validation. The hand bounding box is detected by extrapolating along the orientation of the arm from the detected wrist end-point. The poor performance

Table 2. AP for different scoring methods. The confidence score for the person layout prediction is computed by combining parts scores in different ways. The last column is the mean of head and hand APs, which is the metric to be maximized. Experiments were performed on train-val set of the VOC 2011 layout dataset.

Ordering by	**Head AP%**	**Hand AP%**	**Mean**
Head score	81.04±1.77	20.98±2.21	51.01±1.23
Max-hand score	74.95±3.16	26.16±2.49	50.55±1.55
Mean-hand score	75.61±2.33	28.32±2.12	51.96±1.15
Mean head, hands	79.77±2.20	22.90±2.27	51.33±1.10
Max head, hands	79.49±2.00	21.53±2.30	50.51±1.25

Table 3. (a) AP scores resulting from different learning techniques. The last two rows are different variants of the proposed method. They differ only slightly, but improve substantially over the SVM. The dataset used for the experiments was train-val set of the VOC 2011 layout dataset. **(b) AP for the VOC 2010 person layout test dataset.** We train our method on the train-val portion of the VOC 2010 layout dataset. The evaluation was computed on the competition server. The results for the other methods are as reported on the competition website [27]. Our result for hand detection is even better than [26], which reports AP of 23.18 for the same dataset.

(a)

Method	**Head**	**Hand**	**Mean**
SVM linear	73.92±3.15	20.29±1.76	47.1±1.87
Rank linear	79.32±2.77	27.88±1.75	53.6±1.28
Rank RBF	79.55±2.88	28.22±2.25	**53.9±1.29**

(b)

Method	**Head**	**Hand**	**Mean**
Our Method	72.85	26.7	**49.8**
BCNPCL	74.4	3.3	38.8
OXFORD	52.7	10.4	31.5

of Yang et al.'s method shows that unmodified pictorial structure approaches do not successfully solve the current problem.

Joint Learning Using Structured Ranking. For the experiments, both linear and non-linear kernels were explored. The C parameter and the σ parameter of the Gaussian RBF kernel are optimized by a validation step.

Table 2 shows the inherent tradeoff between the confidences of various parts. While naïve combination schemes can be employed to compute a joint detection score based on the individual part scores, such a strategy will likely choose a suboptimal score. By directly optimizing a loss computed over the combination of parts, the structured output ranking objective can better balance the performance of each part detection. Table 3(a) shows the improved performance when an appropriate joint scoring objective is applied. We see that the ranking objectives (c.f. Section 2) perform substantially better than a binary SVM (first row) and improves the AP for both head and hands.

Comparison with PASCAL VOC 2010 Results. Table 3(b) compares our results with the best performing results in the PASCAL VOC 2010 layout detection competition. We achieve a substantial improvement over the wining entries using our method. For the comparison, we trained the model on train-val set of the VOC 2010 layout dataset. Figure 1 shows some sample results for person layout.

Thus, the person layout experiments show both the effects of the prediction architecture and feature design, as well as the benefits of using a structured output ranking formulation.

Time Analysis. Run-time is measured for training on train-val set of the PASCAL VOC 2011 layout dataset. Our method takes on average about $1/80^{th}$ of a second whereas a normal $\mathcal{O}(n^2)$ implementation takes around 0.5 seconds (i.e., takes 40 times more time) per cutting plane iteration for a linear kernel training.

7 Conclusions

The experiments in Section 6 lead to several broad conclusions. There is a consistent improvement when using structured output ranking over structured output SVMs and ordinal regression. This indicates that structured output ranking is able to encapsulate the benefits of both approaches, leading to better overall performance. Furthermore, the training of structured output ranking is no more computationally expensive than that of binary SVMs or ordinal regression (c.f. Section 3). Using our method we also achieve state-of-the art results for the PASCAL VOC human layout problem.

The efficient linear time training algorithm for structured output ranking can be used whenever the number of loss values is small and independent of the number of training samples. This is true for a large variety of practical problems. In this work, we have demonstrated this to be the case for taxonomic multi-class prediction and person layout. As such diverse applications as scene layout, object layout, multi-class and multi-label prediction are characterized by small numbers of loss values, and also methods that rank learning from continuous loss values such as [28] can simply be discretized into a small number of losses, we expect that the methods proposed here will find wide application across learning based computer vision.

Acknowledgements. We thank Ken Chateld and Mayank Juneja for providing us with SIFT descriptors for the experiments. We are grateful for financial support from ERC grant VisRec no. 228180, ERC grant no. 259112, ONR MURI N00014-07-1-0182 and PASCAL2 Network of Excellence.

References

1. Bengio, S., Weston, J., Grangier, D.: Label embedding trees for large multi-class tasks. In: NIPS (2010)
2. Everingham, M., Van Gool, L., Williams, C.K.I., Winn, J., Zisserman, A.: The PASCAL Visual Object Classes (VOC) challenge. IJCV (2010)
3. Tsochantaridis, I., Hofmann, T., Joachims, T., Altun, Y.: Support vector machine learning for interdependent and structured output spaces. In: Proc. ICML (2004)

4. Joachims, T., Finley, T., Yu, C.N.J.: Cutting-plane training of structural SVMs. Machine Learning (2009)
5. Li, Y., Huttenlocher, D.P.: Learning for stereo vision using the structured support vector machine. In: Proc. CVPR (2008)
6. Blaschko, M.B., Lampert, C.H.: Learning to Localize Objects with Structured Output Regression. In: Forsyth, D., Torr, P., Zisserman, A. (eds.) ECCV 2008, Part I. LNCS, vol. 5302, pp. 2–15. Springer, Heidelberg (2008)
7. Szummer, M., Kohli, P., Hoiem, D.: Learning CRFs Using Graph Cuts. In: Forsyth, D., Torr, P., Zisserman, A. (eds.) ECCV 2008, Part II. LNCS, vol. 5303, pp. 582–595. Springer, Heidelberg (2008)
8. Blaschko, M.B., Vedaldi, A., Zisserman, A.: Simultaneous object detection and ranking with weak supervision. In: NIPS (2010)
9. Rahtu, E., Kannala, J., Blaschko, M.B.: Learning a category independent object detection cascade. In: Proc. ICCV (2011)
10. Zhang, Z., Warrell, J., Torr, P.H.S.: Proposal generation for object detection using cascaded ranking SVMs. In: Proc. CVPR (2011)
11. Huang, J.C., Frey, B.J.: Structured ranking learning using cumulative distribution networks. In: NIPS (2008)
12. Herbrich, R., Graepel, T., Obermayer, K.: Large margin rank boundaries for ordinal regression. In: Advances in Large Margin Classifiers (2000)
13. Joachims, T.: Training linear SVMs in linear time. In: KDD (2006)
14. Deng, J., Berg, A.C., Li, K., Fei-Fei, L.: What Does Classifying More Than 10,000 Image Categories Tell Us? In: Daniilidis, K., Maragos, P., Paragios, N. (eds.) ECCV 2010, Part V. LNCS, vol. 6315, pp. 71–84. Springer, Heidelberg (2010)
15. Binder, A., Müller, K.R., Kawanabe, M.: On taxonomies for multi-class image categorization. IJCV (2011)
16. Cai, L., Hofmann, T.: Exploiting known taxonomies in learning overlapping concepts. In: IJCAI (2007)
17. Imagenet: `http://www.image-net.org/`
18. Quattoni, A., Torralba, A.: Recognizing indoor scenes. In: Proc. CVPR (2009)
19. Lowe, D.: Distinctive image features from scale-invariant keypoints. IJCV (2004)
20. Lazebnik, S., Schmid, C., Ponce, J.: Beyond Bags of Features: Spatial Pyramid Matching for Recognizing Natural Scene Categories. In: Proc. CVPR (2006)
21. Wang, J., Yang, J., Yu, K., Lv, F., Huang, T., Gong, Y.: Locality-constrained linear coding for image classification. In: Proc. CVPR (2010)
22. Eichner, M., Ferrari, V.: Better appearance models for pictorial structures. In: Proc. BMVC (2009)
23. Yang, Y., Ramanan, D.: Articulated pose estimation with flexible mixtures-of-parts. In: Proc. CVPR (2011)
24. Everingham, M., Van Gool, L., Williams, C.K.I., Winn, J., Zisserman, A.: The PASCAL Visual Object Classes Challenge 2011, VOC 2011 (2011), `http://www.pascal-network.org/challenges/VOC/voc2011/`
25. Marin-Jimenez, M., Zisserman, A., Ferrari, V.: Heres looking at you, kid. detecting people looking at each other in videos. In: Proc. BMVC (2011)
26. Mittal, A., Zisserman, A., Torr, P.H.S.: Hand detection using multiple proposals. In: Proc. BMVC (2011)
27. VOC2010-Results: `http://pascallin.ecs.soton.ac.uk/challenges/voc/voc2010/results/`
28. Li, F., Carreira, J., Sminchisescu, C.: Object recognition as ranking holistic figure-ground hypotheses. In: Proc. CVPR (2010)

Robust Point Matching Revisited: A Concave Optimization Approach

Wei Lian[1] and Lei Zhang[2,⋆]

[1] Dept. of Computer Science, Changzhi University, Changzhi, 046011, Shanxi, China
lianwei3@gmail.com
[2] Dept. of Computing, The Hong Kong Polytechnic University
cslzhang@comp.polyu.edu.hk

Abstract. The well-known robust point matching (RPM) method uses deterministic annealing for optimization, and it has two problems. First, it cannot guarantee the global optimality of the solution and tends to align the centers of two point sets. Second, deformation needs to be regularized to avoid the generation of undesirable results. To address these problems, in this paper we first show that the energy function of RPM can be reduced to a concave function with very few non-rigid terms after eliminating the transformation variables and applying linear transformation; we then propose to use concave optimization technique to minimize the resulting energy function. The proposed method scales well with problem size, achieves the globally optimal solution, and does not need regularization for simple transformations such as similarity transform. Experiments on synthetic and real data validate the advantages of our method in comparison with state-of-the-art methods.

1 Introduction

Point matching is a fundamental yet challenging problem in computer vision, pattern recognition and medical image analysis. Many methods [1,2,3,4,5,6,7] have been proposed to solve the problem. Among them, the robust point matching (RPM) method [3] is very popular because of its robustness to many types of disturbances such as deformation, noise and outliers. Several variants [4,7,6] of RPM were later proposed.

In its basic form, RPM models point matching as a linear assignment−least square problem, where the energy function takes the following form:

$$E(P,\theta) = \sum_{i,j} p_{ij} \|y_j - T(x_i|\theta)\|^2 + g(\theta) \qquad (1)$$

Here x_i and y_j denote the model point i and data point j, respectively. $P = \{p_{ij}\}$ denotes the correspondence matrix with $p_{ij} = 1$ indicating that there is a correspondence between x_i and y_j and $p_{ij} = 0$ otherwise. $T(\cdot|\theta)$ denotes the transformation with parameters θ. g denotes the regularization term used to

⋆ Corresponding author.

A. Fitzgibbon et al. (Eds.): ECCV 2012, Part II, LNCS 7573, pp. 259–272, 2012.

regularize the value of θ. To minimize (1), RPM relaxes P to be continuously valued and employs deterministic annealing (DA) for optimization. Although RPM performs well in practice, it cannot guarantee the global optimality of the solution and tends to align the centers of two point sets. Besides, regularization g is always needed to avoid the generation of undesirable results.

In this paper, we are interested in minimizing energy function (1) using global optimization techniques, instead of heuristic schemes such as DA. After eliminating the transformation variables, it can be observed that the minimization problem is reduced to a concave quadratic program, which facilitates the use of concave optimization techniques for global optimality. In contrast, RPM does not possess such property. Unfortunately, it is known that general concave optimization techniques are only suitable for small scale problems, whereas the number of variables in our problem is the product of the cardinalities of two point sets to be matched, which is quite large. Fortunately, after applying the eigen decomposition based linear transformation to our problem, the number of quadratic terms shrinks to be the number of transformation parameters, which is generally very small. It becomes a concave optimization problem where the number of variables in the linear part is much greater than the number of variables in the concave part. For this type of problems, there exist efficient optimization techniques [8]. Consequently, the proposed method scales well with problem size. Another advantage of our method over RPM lies in that it does not need regularization when simple transformations such as similarity transform is employed. In contrast, RPM always needs regularization to avoid the generation of undesirable results.

The rest of the paper is organized as follows. Section 2 reviews related work. Section 3 discusses the proposed energy function. Section 4 presents the optimization algorithm. Section 5 presents the experimental results. Finally, Section 6 concludes the paper.

2 Related Work

Point Matching. The iterative closest point (ICP) method [1] iterates between finding point correspondence based on nearest neighbor relationship and updating transformation as a least square problem. However, ICP is not robust because of the discrete nature of point correspondence. To address the problem, RPM [3] relaxes point correspondence to be continuously valued and employs DA for optimization. Nonetheless, the optimization scheme of RPM is quite complex. To address the problem, the coherent point drift (CPD) method [4] models point matching under the probabilistic framework and uses the expectation-maximization (EM) technique for optimization. The methods in [5,6] view a point set as the result of sampling from an unknown distribution and convert point matching into the problem of matching corresponding distributions. The covariance driven correspondence method [7] uses the covariance of the transformation to guide the determination of point correspondences, but the method can only handle rigid transformations. The above methods are all heuristic schemes and therefore they can not guarantee the global optimality of the solution.

Concave Optimization. Concave optimization was used in [9] to solve the correspondence problems arising from computer vision, but the techniques employed there are only suitable for small scale problems. In contrast, our method scales well with problem size because of its special structure of optimization, which facilitates the use of large scale optimization techniques.

Branch-and-Bound (B&B). B&B is a popular technique for solving difficult nonlinear optimization problems. It was used in [10] to solve the rigid registration problem, where the correspondences between planes, lines or points are assumed to be known, and hence only the transformation needs to be solved, which involves a small number of variables. However, both point correspondence and transformation are not known in our problem, which makes the optimization much harder. In [11], two B&B methods were proposed to minimize the energy function of RPM. The first method is based on branching in the correspondence variable. But because of the high dimensionality of the correspondence variable, this method is only suitable for small scale problems. In contrast, our method works in the transformed variable space instead of the original correspondence variable space, and the number of variables to be branched equals the number of deformation parameters, which is generally very small. Therefore, our method has reasonable running time and scales well with problem size. The second method in [11] is based on branching in the transformation variable. Due to lack of properties such as concavity by the energy function, the lower bound of this method is not tight, and its convergence speed is slow.

3 Derivation of the Energy Function

Suppose that there are two point sets in $d-$dimensional space to be matched: the model point set $\mathscr{X} = \{x_i, i = 1, \ldots, m\}$, where point $x_i = \left[x_i^1, \cdots, x_i^d\right]^T$, and the data point set $\mathscr{Y} = \{y_j, j = 1, \ldots, n\}$, where point $y_j = \left[y_j^1, \cdots, y_j^d\right]^T$.

To make our problem tractable, we assumes that the transformation $T(x_i|\theta)$ is linear with respect to its parameters θ, i.e., $T(x_i|\theta) = J(x_i)\theta$, where $J(x_i)$ is called the Jacobian matrix (examples include Eq. (13) and (14) in section 5). We consider the following form of regularization in this paper: $g(\theta) = (\theta - \theta_0)^T H(\theta - \theta_0)$, i.e., θ is required to be close to a constant vector θ_0. Here H is a positive semidefinite matrix whose elements represent the weights assigned to elements of θ.

With the above consideration, the energy function (1) takes the following form:

$$E(P, \theta) = \sum_{i,j} p_{ij} \|y_j - J(x_i)\theta\|^2 + (\theta - \theta_0)^T H(\theta - \theta_0) \tag{2}$$

The correspondence matrix P satisfies the two way normalization constraint:

$$P1_n = 1_m, \quad 1_m^T P \leq 1_n, \quad P \geq 0 \tag{3}$$

Here we require $P1_n = 1_m$, i.e., every point in $\mathscr{X}$ has a counterpart in $\mathscr{Y}$. This assumption is essential in simplifying formulas (see Eq. (4) and (5)) in the sequel. This assumption is commonly used in point matching literature [3].

E is apparently a convex quadratic function of θ. Therefore, by letting $\frac{\partial E}{\partial \theta} = 0$, we can get the optimal solution of θ as:

$$\hat{\theta} = (J^T J + H)^{-1} \left[J^T (P \otimes I_d) Y + H\theta_0 \right] \tag{4}$$

where $J \triangleq \left[J^T(x_1), \dots, J^T(x_m) \right]^T$ and $Y \triangleq \left[y_1^T, \dots, y_n^T \right]^T$. Symbol $\otimes$ denotes the Kronecker product operator.

By substituting (4) into (2), the variable θ is eliminated and we arrive at an energy function only in P:

$$\begin{aligned} E(P) =& 1_m^T PZ - \left[Y^T (P \otimes I_d)^T J + \theta_0^T H \right] (J^T J + H)^{-1} \\ & \cdot \left[J^T (P \otimes I_d) Y + H\theta_0 \right] + \theta_0^T H \theta_0 \end{aligned} \tag{5}$$

where $Z \triangleq \left[\|y_1\|_2^2, \dots, \|y_n\|_2^2 \right]^T$. By eliminating the constant terms in (5), we get an equivalent optimization problem where the energy function is:

$$\begin{aligned} E'(P) =& 1_m^T PZ - 2\theta_0^T H (J^T J + H)^{-1} J^T (P \otimes I_d) Y \\ & - Y^T (P \otimes I_d)^T J (J^T J + H)^{-1} J^T (P \otimes I_d) Y \end{aligned} \tag{6}$$

Let the Cholesky factorization [12] of the positive definite matrix $(J^T J + H)^{-1}$ be

$$U^T U = (J^T J + H)^{-1} \tag{7}$$

where U is an upper triangular matrix. Then we have

$$E'(P) = 1_m^T PZ - 2\theta_0^T H (J^T J + H)^{-1} J^T (P \otimes I_d) Y - \|U J^T (P \otimes I_d) Y\|_2^2 \tag{8}$$

It's apparent that E' is a concave quadratic function of P. We have the following proposition.

Proposition 1. *There exists an optimal integer solution of E'.*

Proof. The constraint on P in Eq. (3) satisfies the total unimodularity property [13], hence the vertices of the polytope (i.e., bounded polyhedron) determined by Eq. (3) will be integer valued. It's well known that the minimum solution of a concave function over a polytope can be obtained at its vertices. Therefore there exists an optimal integer solution of E'.

Based on the above Proposition 1, the output of our method will be binary point correspondences if simplex-like optimization algorithms are adopted, as in contrast to [14] where post-processing is needed to convert point correspondences to binary values. For the convenience of discussion in the sequel, we define the vectorization of matrix P as the concatenation of its rows:

$$\text{vec}(P) = [p_{11}, \dots, p_{1n}, p_{21}, \dots, p_{2n}, \dots, p_{m1}, \dots, p_{mn}]^T$$

Let $p = \text{vec}(P)$, E' becomes

$$\begin{aligned} E'(p) =& \left\{ 1_m^T \otimes Z^T - 2 \left[\left(\theta_0^T H (J^T J + H)^{-1} J^T \right) \otimes Y^T \right] W \right\} p \\ & - \| \left[(U J^T) \otimes Y^T \right] W p \|_2^2 \end{aligned} \tag{9}$$

Here the $mnd \times mn$ matrix $W \triangleq I_m \otimes \left[I_n \otimes e_d^1, \ldots, I_n \otimes e_d^d\right]^T$ satisfies $\text{vec}(P \otimes I_d) = W\text{vec}(P)$, where e_d^i is a $d-$dimensional column vector with the ith element being 1 and the rest elements being 0s. W is a large but sparse matrix and can be implemented using function *peye* in Matlab.

4 Optimization of the Energy Function

It is well known that a quadratic function can be converted into a separable form via linear transformation. It is also known that the convex envelope (i.e., the tightest convex underestimator) of a separable function over a rectangle is the sum of the convex envelope of each component of the function over the corresponding interval [8]. Based on these facts, the normal rectangular algorithm [8], which is specifically designed to minimize separable functions, is adopted in this paper to minimize the energy function (9). To this end, we first transform (9) into a separable form via eigen decomposition, and then derive the convex envelope of the resulting function over a rectangular region. We finally use the B&B technique [8] for optimization.

4.1 Eigen Decomposition

A quadratic function can be transformed into a separable function by a linear transformation of its variables, and the choice of the linear transformation is based on the eigen decomposition of the quadratic part of the function. Therefore, in this subsection, we focus on the eigen decomposition of the quadratic part of (9).

Let us define the $\#\theta \times mn$ matrix $A = \left[(UJ^T) \otimes Y^T\right] W$, where $\#\theta$ denotes the dimensionality of θ. Then the quadratic part of (9) is $-p^T A^T Ap$. Since $A^T A$ has dimension $mn \times mn$, which is very high, directly applying eigen decomposition to $A^T A$ is impractical. In the following, we propose an efficient way of finding the nonzero eigenvalues and eigenvectors of $A^T A$. Let the QR factorization of A^T be:

$$QR = A^T$$

where R is an upper triangular matrix. The columns of Q are mutually orthogonal and have a unity norm.

It's apparent that

$$A^T A = QRR^T Q^T$$

Denote the eigenvalues and eigenvectors of RR^T as λ_i and u_i^R, $i = 1, \cdots, \#\theta$, respectively. Then the nonzero eigenvalues and eigenvectors of $A^T A$ are λ_i and $u_i = Qu_i^R$, $i = 1, \cdots, \#\theta$, respectively. Therefore we can get the separable form of the quadratic part of (9) as:

$$-\|Ap\|_2^2 = -\sum_{i=1}^{\#\theta} \lambda_i (u_i^T p)^2 \tag{10}$$

4.2 Convex Envelope of the Energy Function over a Rectangle

With Eq. (10), E' now takes the following separable form:

$$E'(p) = b^T p - \sum_{i=1}^{\#\theta} \lambda_i (u_i^T p)^2 \tag{11}$$

where $b \triangleq 1_m^T \otimes Z^T - 2\left[\left(\theta_0^T H(J^T J + H)^{-1} J^T\right) \otimes Y^T\right] W$.

For a separable function over a rectangle, its convex envelope can be readily obtained based on the following proposition [8]:

Proposition 2. *The convex envelope of a separable function* $\sum_{i=1}^{l} f_i(t_i)$ *over a rectangle* $M = \{t_i | r_i \leq t_i \leq s_i, i = 1 \ldots, l\}$ *equals the sum of the convex envelopes of components* $f_i(t_i)$ *over intervals* $[r_i, s_i], i = 1, \ldots, l$.

It's apparent that the convex envelope of $f(t) = -t^2$ over an interval $[r, s]$ is an affine function that agrees with f at the endpoints of this interval: $f_M(t) = -(r+s)t + rs$, as illustrated in Fig. 1. Based on this fact and the above proposition, we can get the convex envelope of function (11) over a rectangle $M = \{p | r_i \leq u_i^T p \leq s_i, i = 1, \ldots, \#\theta\}$ as

$$E'_M(p) = b^T p - \sum_{i=1}^{\#\theta} \lambda_i (r_i + s_i) u_i^T p + \sum_{i=1}^{\#\theta} \lambda_i r_i s_i \tag{12}$$

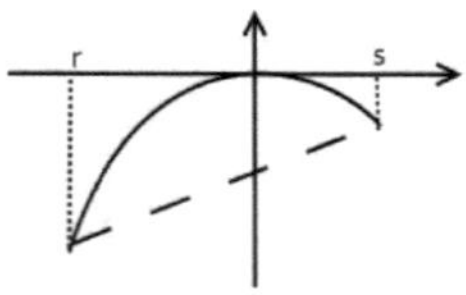

Fig. 1. The convex envelope (dashed line) of function $-t^2$ (solid line) over an interval $[r, s]$

4.3 Bisection of a Rectangle

We use the B&B algorithm [8] to find the global $\epsilon-$optimal solution of E', i.e., a solution with function value no larger than ϵ from the global optimal value of E'. In the branching phase, a rectangle $M = \{p | r_i \leq u_i^T p \leq s_i, i = 1, \ldots, \#\theta\}$ is partitioned into two subrectangles. There are two issues to be addressed: 1) deciding the dimension along which to split the rectangle, and 2) along a chosen dimension where to split the rectangle. We use the bisection scheme [8] to solve these issues for its simplicity and effectiveness. For bisection, the second issue is addressed by choosing the midpoint as the splitting location, and the first issue is addressed based on the following fact: the difference between $f(t) = -t^2$ and its convex envelope $f_M(t) = -(r+s)t + rs$ over an interval $[r, s]$ satisfies:

$$\max\{f(t) - f_M(t), r \leq t \leq s\} = \frac{1}{4}(s - r)^2$$

Based on this fact, we can see that the dimension along which to split a rectangle should be chosen as $j \in \arg\max_i \frac{1}{4}\lambda_i(s_i - r_i)^2$. Given the optimal splitting dimension j, bisection results in two subrectangles: $M_1 = \{p \in M | u_j^T p \le \frac{1}{2}(r_j + s_j)\}$ and $M_2 = \{p \in M | u_j^T p \ge \frac{1}{2}(r_j + s_j)\}$. It can be proved [8] that bisection leads to a B&B algorithm which is convergent.

4.4 Algorithm

We use the normal rectangular algorithm [8], a B&B approach specifically designed for separable functions, to optimize (11). During initialization, the bounding rectangle (i.e., the smallest rectangle containing the solution space) is computed. Then in each iteration of the algorithm, the rectangle yielding the lowest lower bound among all the rectangles is further subdivided so as to improve the global lower bound of the problem. Meanwhile, the upper bound is updated by evaluating the energy function with solutions of the linear programs used to compute the lower bound. The pseudo-code of the algorithm is summarized as follows.

Initialization

Select tolerance error $\epsilon > 0$.
Solve the $2\#\theta$ linear programs

$$\min_{p \in D} u_i^T p, \quad \max_{p \in D} u_i^T p$$

to obtain the basic optimal solutions $p^{0i}, \bar{p}^{0i}$ and the optimal values $\eta_i, \bar{\eta}_i$. Here D denotes the solution space of p, as determined by Eq. (3). Clearly, $D \subset M_0 = \{p | \eta_i \le u_i^T p \le \bar{\eta}_i, i = 1, \dots, \#\theta\}$. Set $\mathscr{M}_1 = \mathscr{N}_1 = \{M_0\}$, where $\mathscr{M}_1$ is the collection of all rectangles and $\mathscr{N}_1$ is the collection of active rectangles. Let $p^0 = \arg\min\{E'(p^{0i}), E'(\bar{p}^{0i}), i = 1, \dots, \#\theta\}$.

Iteration $k = 1, 2, \dots$

1. For each rectangle $M \in \mathscr{N}_k$, construct the convex envelope $E'_M(p)$ according to Eq. (12), and solve the linear program

$$\begin{aligned} &\min E'_M(p) \\ &s.t. \quad p \in D \cap M \end{aligned}$$

   to obtain a basic optimal solution $\omega(M)$ and the optimal value $\beta(M)$. $\beta(M)$ is the lower bound for region $D \cap M$.
2. Let p^k equal to the best among all feasible solutions so far encountered: p^{k-1} and all $\omega(M), M \in \mathscr{N}_k$. Delete all rectangles $M \in \mathscr{M}_k$ such that $\beta(M) \ge E'(p^k) - \epsilon$. Let $\mathscr{R}_k$ be the remaining collection of rectangles.
3. If $\mathscr{R}_k = \emptyset$, terminate: p^k is the global ϵ−minimal solution. Otherwise, go to Step 4.
4. Select the rectangle to be divided: $M_k = \{p | r_i^k \le u_i^T p \le s_i^k, i = 1, \dots, \#\theta\} \in \arg\min\{\beta(M) | M \in \mathscr{R}_k\}$.

5. Let $i_k \in \arg\max_i\{\frac{1}{4}\lambda_i(s_i^k - r_i^k)^2\}$. Divide M_k along dimension i_k to get two subrectangles M_{k1} and M_{k2}.
6. Let $\mathscr{N}_{k+1} = \{M_{k1}, M_{k2}\}$, $\mathscr{M}_{k+1} = (\mathscr{R}_k\backslash\{M_k\}) \cup \mathscr{N}_{k+1}$. Set $k \leftarrow k+1$ and return to Step 1.

Since the time complexity of the B&B algorithm is exponential in the worst case, the worst case time complexity of our algorithm is also exponential.

5 Experimental Results

We implement all the competing methods in Matlab R2010 on a PC with 2.4GHz CPU. Since all the competing methods output point correspondences, we use the correspondences computed by a method to find the best affine transformation between the two point sets, and define the error as the mean of the Euclidean distances between the affinely transformed model points and their ground truth data points. To get a complete picture of the performance of our method, in the following experiments we consider two cases for our method: θ is not regularized (i.e., $H = 0$) and θ is regularized. In the former case, our method becomes invariant to the corresponding transformation. The Matlab source code of this paper is available at: `http://www4.comp.polyu.edu.hk/~cslzhang/code.htm`.

5.1 Case One: θ Is Not Regularized

When θ is not regularized, with the increase of $\#\theta$, more degree of transformation freedom is allowed, and the matching results become less predictable. Our experimental results showed that for 2-D point matching, similarity transformation is a good trade-off between transformation flexibility and predictability of the matching results. For 2-D similarity transformation with parameters $\theta = [a, b, c, d]^T$, where $[c, d]^T$ is translation and $a = s\cos(\phi)$, $b = s\sin(\phi)$ with s being scale and ϕ being rotation angle, the Jacobian matrix is

$$J(x_i) = \begin{bmatrix} x_i^1 & -x_i^2 & 1 & 0 \\ x_i^2 & x_i^1 & 0 & 1 \end{bmatrix} \tag{13}$$

Assuming that the data point set is unit sized, we set the tolerance error $\epsilon = 1$. Since the worst case complexity of our algorithm is exponential, we set the maximum search depth as 3 to make a good trade-off between running time and matching accuracy. We compare our method with 4 state-of-the-art methods: the unified graphical (UG) method [15] where similarity transformation is chosen, the fan-shaped triangulation (FST) method [16], the Viterbi algorithm (VA) based method [17] and the linear programming (LP) based method [14]. These methods can guarantee globally optimal or sub-optimal (for LP) solutions and some of them (UG and FST) are also rotation invariant, making them good candidates for comparison. For LP, we use shape context [18] as the feature descriptor. Since VA and LP are not rotation invariant, we render them rotation invariant by evaluating them on 8 evenly quantized angles and choosing the result with the minimum cost.

Experiments on the Chui-Rangarajan Synthesized Data Sets. Synthetic data are often used to quantitatively evaluate specific aspects of an algorithm. In this subsection, we use the Chui-Rangarajan synthesized data sets [3] to test the 5 competing methods' robustness against non-rigid deformation, noise in position and outliers. In each test, the model shape is subject to first random rotation and then one of the above distortions to generate a data point set. The model shapes (a tropical fish and a Chinese character) and examples of data point sets in the 3 categories of tests are shown in Fig. 2.

Fig. 2. For every 4 columns, from left to right: the model point set and examples of data point set in the deformation, noise and outlier tests, respectively

The matching errors of the methods are shown in Fig. 3. It can be seen that for the deformation and noise tests, our method outperforms other methods, demonstrating its robustness to deformation and noise. For the outlier test, our method performs in average compared with other methods for the fish test while slightly worse than other methods for the Chinese character test. Part of the reason is that all the other methods except for UG employ the shape context feature descriptor for matching, which can much increase their robustness to

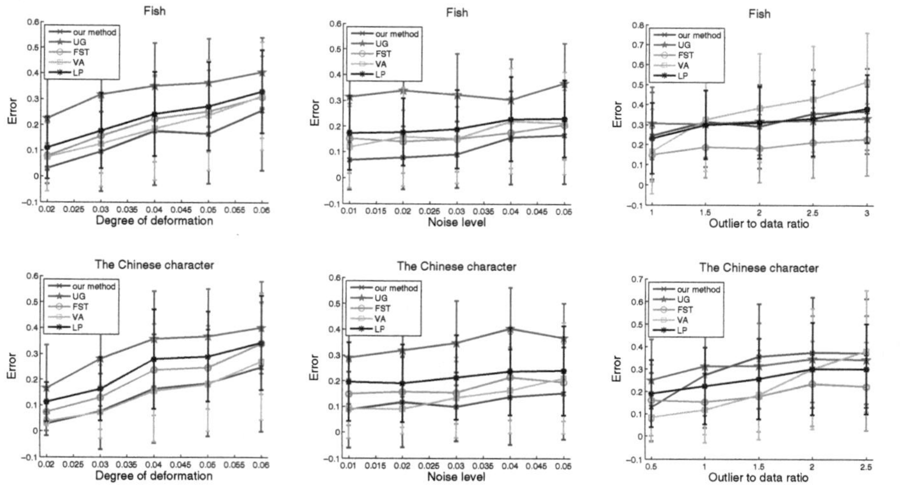

Fig. 3. Matching errors by the 5 competing methods on the Chui-Rangarajan synthesized data sets. The error bars indicate the standard deviation of the error over 100 random trials.

outliers. In comparison, our method and UG only use the information of point positions for matching.

The average running time of the 5 competing methods are listed in Table 1. The proposed method is the slowest among them. This is because linear programming needs to be performed at each iteration of our method. Nonetheless, the high running time is the price for the global optimality of the proposed scheme. It can also be seen that the running time of our method is acceptable when the number of points is not big. When the number of points becomes large (e.g., in the case of outliers), the running time of our method increases much.

Table 1. Average running time (in seconds)

	Deformation	Noise	Outliers
our method	23.4567	23.9379	162.6343
UG	10.6118	10.4448	157.1455
FST	7.8901	8.8471	46.3078
VA	4.0145	4.0323	14.3741
LP	19.5272	18.4779	31.3505

Experiments on Image Sequences. We then test the 5 competing methods by using the CMU hotel and house sequences (CMU Image Database: `http://vasc.ri.cmu.edu/idb/html/motion/`) and two other image sequences from [19]. Similar to the experimental set up in [20], for each image sequence, we select 30 feature points and manually track them over the image sequence to generate a sequence of point sets. For two images separated by different sequence gap, the associated pair of point sets are used for matching, as illustrated in the 1st and 3rd columns of Fig. 4 and Fig. 5, respectively. The matching accuracy (fraction of correct correspondences) by the competing methods are shown in the 2nd and 4th columns of Fig. 4 and Fig. 5, respectively. It can be seen that our method has higher matching accuracy than other methods. In particular, it achieves almost 100% accuracy on the CMU sequence tests over a wide range

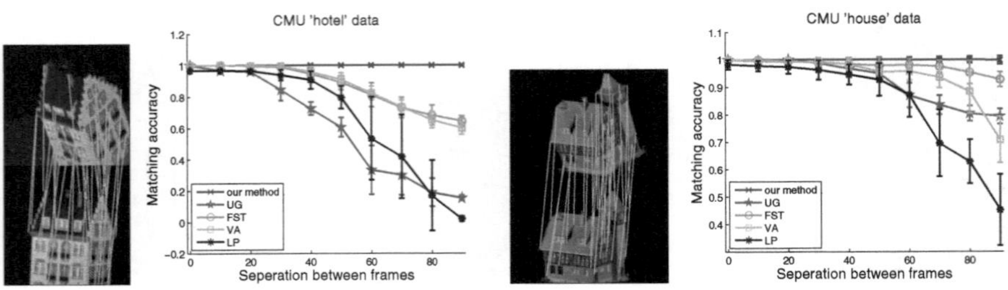

Fig. 4. 1st and 3rd columns: examples of input image pair and ground truth point correspondences; 2nd and 4th columns: average matching accuracy by the 5 competing methods. The error bars indicate the standard deviation of the error.

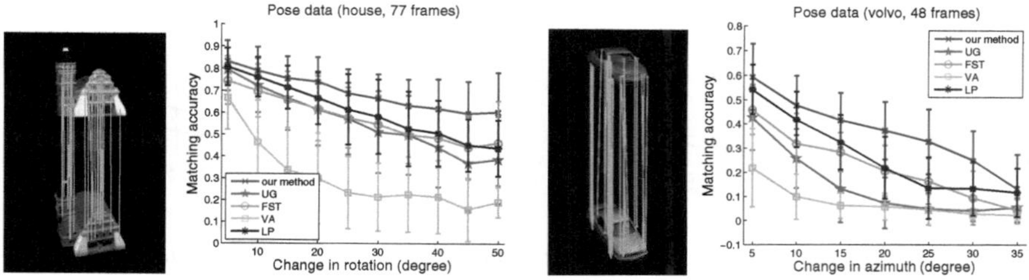

Fig. 5. 1st and 3rd columns: examples of input image pair and ground truth point correspondences; 2nd and 4th columns: average matching accuracy by the 5 competing methods. The error bars indicate the standard deviation of the error.

of frame intervals. For the other 2 sequences, our method outperforms other methods by a large margin (see Fig. 5).

5.2 Case Two: θ is Regularized

When θ is regularized, our method becomes transformation variant, but the benefit is that our method's matching accuracy and robustness to disturbances can be improved.

We use affine transformation in our method as it is the simplest non-rigid transformation and the number of parameters is small (note that our method's running time depends on the number of transformation parameters). For 2-D affine transformation with parameters $\theta = \left[a, b, c, d, e, f\right]^T$, where $[a, b, c, d]^T$ is the linear part of the transformation and $[e, f]^T$ is translation, the Jacobian matrix is

$$J(x_i) = \begin{bmatrix} x_i^1 & x_i^2 & 0 & 0 & 1 & 0 \\ 0 & 0 & x_i^1 & x_i^2 & 0 & 1 \end{bmatrix} \tag{14}$$

We choose the weighting matrix as $H = diag([1\ 1\ 1\ 1\ 0\ 0])$, i.e., we only regularize the linear part of the transformation. We choose $\theta_0 = [1\ 0\ 0\ 1\ 0\ 0]^T$, i.e., the linear part of the transformation should be close to the identity transformation (please refer to Eq. (2)).

The tolerance error is set as $\epsilon = 0.06m$, i.e., proportional to the number of model points. We compare our method with 3 methods: RPM [3], CPD [4] and the local neighborhood structure preserving (LNSP) method [21]. These 3 methods are very popular and represent state-of-the-art. Affine transformation is used for RPM and CPD.

First, we use the Chui-Rangarajan synthesized data sets to test the 4 competing methods' robustness against non-rigid deformation and noise (outlier is not tested; instead, it is replaced by a more challenging clutter test in the following). The experimental set up is similar to that in section 5.1 except that there is no rotation between two point sets. Performances of the 4 methods are shown in Fig. 6. It can be seen that our method has the lowest error among all the methods.

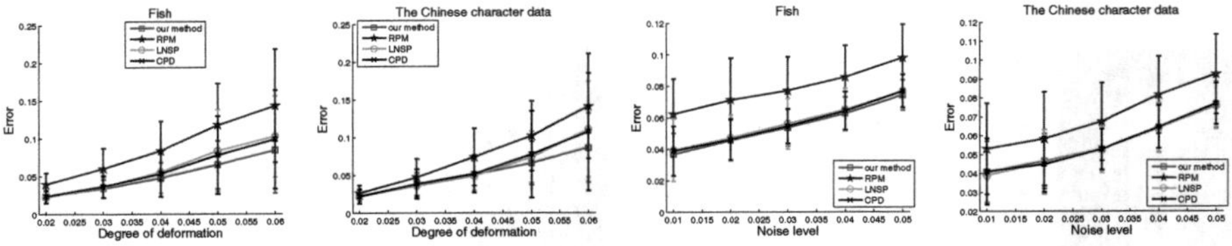

Fig. 6. Matching errors by the 4 competing methods on the Chui-Rangarajan synthesized data sets. The error bars indicate the standard deviation of the error over 100 random trials.

Second, we test the robustness of the 4 methods against clutter. The experimental set up is as follows. For a shape which is represented as a point set, we first obtain its shortest Hamiltonian cycle by solving a traveling salesman problem. Then a segment of the cycle starting at a random point and with different length is chosen as the model point set (the remaining points correspond to clutter). The moderately non-rigidly deformed version of the original shape is chosen as the data point set. The two shapes, the tropical fish and the Chinese character, as shown in the 1st and 5th columns of Fig. 2, are used in the experiments. Examples of model and data point sets are shown in the top row of Fig. 7.

Fig. 7. Top row: examples of model (1st and 3rd columns) and data (2nd and 4th columns) point sets used in the clutter tests. Bottom row: examples of matching results by our method (1st and 3rd columns) and RPM (2nd and 4th columns), where the affinely transformed model points are shown as red $*$ and point correspondences are indicated by black line segments.

Performances of the 4 methods are shown in Fig. 8. It can be seen that our method is less sensitive to clutter and its error keeps almost unchanged when clutter becomes severe. In contrast, for other methods the errors increase quickly with the increase of the severity of clutter. This demonstrates the robustness of our method against clutter. Examples of matching results by our method and RPM are shown in the bottom row of Fig. 7.

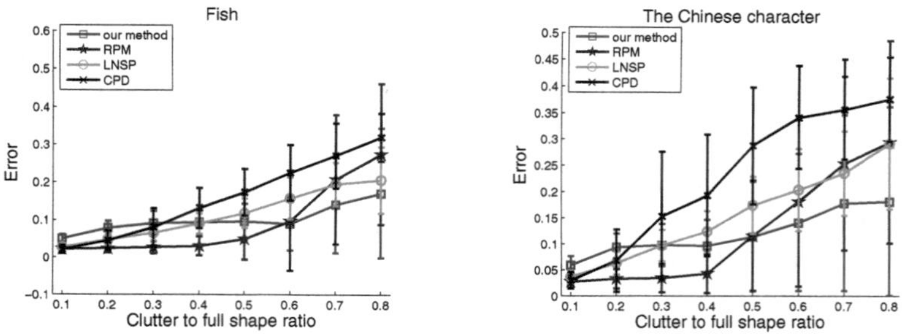

Fig. 8. Matching errors by the 4 competing methods on the test of clutter. The error bars indicate the standard deviation of the error over 100 random trials.

6 Conclusion

We proposed a new approach to minimizing the energy function of the classical RPM method. After eliminating the transformation variable, we reduced the energy function to a concave quadratic program, which can be efficiently solved by large scale concave optimization techniques. Our method can guarantee the global optimality of the solution, and does not need to regularize deformation for simple transformations such as similarity transform. Our method also scales well with problem size due to the special structure of its optimization problem. Extensive experimental results demonstrated that the proposed method has high matching accuracy and high robustness to disturbances, such as clutter, in comparison with state-of-the-art methods.

Acknowledgement. This work is supported by the Natural Science Foundation for Young Scientists of Shanxi Province, China (Grant No. 2012021015-2).

References

1. Besl, P.J., McKay, N.D.: A method for registration of 3-d shapes. IEEE Trans. Pattern Analysis and Machine Intelligence 14, 239–256 (1992)
2. Zhang, Z.: Iterative point matching for registration of free-form curves and surfaces. International Journal of Computer Vision 13, 119–152 (1994)
3. Chui, H., Rangarajan, A.: A new point matching algorithm for non-rigid registration. Computer Vision and Image Understanding 89, 114–141 (2003)
4. Myronenko, A., Song, X.: Point set registration: Coherent point drift. IEEE Transactions on Pattern Analysis and Machine Intelligence 32, 2262–2275 (2010)
5. Tsin, Y., Kanade, T.: A Correlation-Based Approach to Robust Point Set Registration. In: Pajdla, T., Matas, J(G.) (eds.) ECCV 2004. LNCS, vol. 3023, pp. 558–569. Springer, Heidelberg (2004)
6. Jian, B., Vemuri, B.C.: A robust algorithm for point set registration using mixture of gaussians. In: IEEE International Conference on Computer Vision, vol. 2, pp. 1246–1251 (2005)

7. Sofka, M., Yang, G., Stewart, C.V.: Simultaneous covariance driven correspondence (cdc) and transformation estimation in the expectation maximization framework. In: IEEE Conf. Computer Vision and Pattern Recognition, pp. 1–8 (2007)
8. Horst, R., Tuy, H.: Global Optimization, Deterministic Approaches. Springer (1996)
9. Maciel, J., Costeira, J.: A global solution to sparse correspondence problems. IEEE Trans. Pattern Analysis and Machine Intelligence 25, 187–199 (2003)
10. Olsson, C., Kahl, F., Oskarsson, M.: Branch-and-bound methods for euclidean registration problems. IEEE Transactions on Pattern Analysis and Machine Intelligence 31, 783–794 (2009)
11. Pfeuffer, F., Stiglmayr, M., Klamroth, K.: Discrete and geometric branch and bound algorithms for medical image registration. Annals of Operations Research 196, 737–765 (2012)
12. Golub, G.H., Loan, C.F.V.: Matrix computations. The Johns Hopkins University Press (1996)
13. Papadimitriou, C.H., Steiglitz, K.: Combinatorial optimization: algorithms and complexity. Dover Publications, Inc., New York (1998)
14. Jiang, H., Drew, M.S., Li, Z.-N.: Matching by linear programming and successive convexification. IEEE Trans. Pattern Analysis and Machine Intelligence 29, 959–975 (2007)
15. Caetano, T.S., Caelli, T.: A unified formulation of invariant point pattern matching. In: 18th International Conference on Pattern Recognition (ICPR 2006), vol. 3, pp. 121–124 (2006)
16. Lian, W., Zhang, L.: Rotation Invariant Non-rigid Shape Matching in Cluttered Scenes. In: Daniilidis, K., Maragos, P., Paragios, N. (eds.) ECCV 2010, Part V. LNCS, vol. 6315, pp. 506–518. Springer, Heidelberg (2010)
17. Thayananthan, A., Stenger, B., Torr, P.H.S., Cipolla, R.: Shape context and chamfer matching in cluttered scenes. In: IEEE Conf. Computer Vision and Pattern Recognition, vol. 1, pp. 127–133 (2003)
18. Belongie, S., Malik, J., Puzicha, J.: Shape matching and object recognition using shape contexts. IEEE Trans. Pattern Analysis and Machine Intelligence 24(4), 509–522 (2002)
19. Vikstén, F., Forssén, P.E., Johansson, B., Moe, A.: Comparison of local image descriptors for full 6 degree-of-freedom pose estimation. In: IEEE International Conference on Robotics and Automation, pp. 2779–2786 (2009)
20. Caetano, T.S., Caelli, T., Schuurmans, D., Barone, D.A.C.: Graphical models and point pattern matching. IEEE Trans. Pattern Analysis and Machine Intelligence 28(10), 1646–1663 (2006)
21. Zheng, Y., Doermann, D.: Robust point matching for nonrigid shapes by preserving local neighborhood structures. IEEE Trans. Pattern Analysis and Machine Intelligence 28, 643–649 (2006)

Learning Discriminative Spatial Relations for Detector Dictionaries: An Application to Pedestrian Detection

Enver Sangineto, Marco Cristani, Alessio Del Bue, and Vittorio Murino

Pattern Analysis and Computer Vision (PAVIS), Istituto Italiano di Tecnologia (IIT)
Via Morego 30, 16163, Genova, Italy

Abstract. The recent availability of large scale training sets in conjunction with accurate classifiers (e.g., SVMs) makes it possible to build large sets of "simple" object detectors and to develop new classification approaches in which dictionaries of visual features are substituted by dictionaries of object detectors. The responses of this collection of detectors can then be used as a high-level image representation. In this work, we propose to go a step further in this direction by modeling spatial relations among different detector responses. We use Random Forests in order to discriminatively select spatial relations which represent frequent co-occurrences of detector responses. We demonstrate our idea in the specific people detection framework, which is a challenging classification task due to the variability of the human body articulations and appearance, and we use the recently proposed *poselets* as our basic object dictionary. The use of poselets is not the only possible, actually the proposed method can be applied more in general since few assumptions are made on the basic object detector. The results obtained show sharp improvements with respect to both the original poselet-based people detection method and to other state-of-the-art approaches on two difficult benchmark datasets.

1 Introduction

A new trend in high-level computer vision is the use of large object detector dictionaries to represent images. A battery of a few hundreds of relatively simple detectors is applied to the input image. The response of these detectors provides a powerful image representation which is then further analyzed for detection or classification purposes. Pioneering works in this direction were the papers of Torresani et al. [1] and Li-Jia Li et al. [2]. In [2] an image is represented by means of an *object bank*, i.e., the response of a few hundreds object detectors for common objects (e.g., tables, cars, humans, etc.). A somehow similar approach is the work of Bourdev and Malik on *poselets* [3–5], where a poselet denotes an object part (e.g., a human body part in a people detection task) corresponding to a tight cluster in both the configuration and the appearance space. In this approach, a few hundreds SVM-trained object detectors have been built, each one specific to a given poselet. These are run to the analyzed image giving a set

A. Fitzgibbon et al. (Eds.): ECCV 2012, Part II, LNCS 7573, pp. 273–286, 2012.

of *poselet activations* (positive detector responses), which are finally clustered (see Sec. 2) to get the complete object recognition.

In this paper, we propose a people detection method which takes as input the responses of an object detector dictionary and exploits spatial information among positive detections in order to recognize human bodies. We assume that the dictionary is composed of basic detectors, each one independently searching for different parts of the human body. More specifically, we adopt the poselet dictionary developed in [4], where each poselet detector is specialized in searching for specific body segments. These segments do not necessarily correspond to anatomically salient parts. For instance, a poselet detector may be specialized in "half of a frontal face and a left shoulder" or can represent the whole body as well [3]. As proven by the success of the poselet method, the redundancy of a battery of simple detectors compensates the lack of robustness of each single detector. As mentioned above, our image representation is not based on image features but on the response of a detector dictionary. How the basic detectors are built and what internal image representation they use is independent of what our system does: we only assume the availability of a redundant set of detectors for different parts of the same object (the human body in our case).

Assembling independent object detection responses using spatial information is clearly not a new idea. It is widely exploited especially for *articulated* object detection. For instance, part-based approaches [6–14] to human body detection are very common. Particularly noticeable are the Pictorial Structures [6] and their numerous variants [7–10]. Pictorial Structures are a hierarchical representation of the human body describing the spatial relations between pairs of adjacent body components. Several other part-based approaches exploit the idea of separately searching for every object component in the image and then assembling the rigid detection results [11–14]. However, our proposal differs from the standard part-based paradigm in several aspects.

The first new contribution is that we use a discriminative approach in learning the "most successful" spatial relations, where success is judged by the ability of the selected relations to discriminate between class-specific and uninformative co-occurrences of basic detector responses. Pictorial Structures and other common part-based approaches usually learn spatial relations among basic components using a generative framework, in which positive samples of human bodies, labeled with the positions of the selected components, are used to create a statistical model of the spatial distributions. The drawback of this framework is that the use of only positive samples prevents the inclusion in the model of knowledge about what spatial relations are *not* valid because of false positive occurrences. In fact, false detections of the object components wrongly recognized in the input image (e.g., limbs detected on the background) are one of the most frequent failure reasons in the component clustering process [15]. Conversely, in our approach, we use both positive *and* negative object training samples in order to learn those spatial relations which are less likely to happen by chance.

The second novelty of this work is the use of Random Forests (RFs) to perform informative spatial relation selection. Specifically, we build a battery of

RFs, one forest for each basic object detector type. RFs [16] are ensembles of Decision Trees (DTs) with different degrees of randomness in the training process and which have been proven to be robust to overfitting both from a theoretical [16] and an empirical [17, 18] point of view. The DTs forming our RFs are in turn based on spatial tests between the relative positions of positive basic detector responses (i.e., poselet activations). We select the most informative tests among a huge set of possible combinations by randomly generating tests on each node of the tree and choosing the one which best discriminates between positive and negative samples. Each RF is then a "wrapper", i.e., a classifier which also performs "feature" selection [19], where the feature pool in our case is the set of all possible pairwise spatial relationships among pairs of poselet types (see Sec. 3.3).

The rest of this article is organized as follows. Sec. 2 briefly describes the related literature. Sec. 3 begins with an overview of our approach, followed by details on the learning and the testing phases. In Sec. 4 we report experiments on different people detection benchmarks and we draw conclusions in Sec. 5.

2 Related Work

In the object bank proposal [2], spatial information among objects is represented using spatial pyramids, i.e., histograms of the detector outputs computed using different resolution grids. However, that work is mainly oriented to *scene classification*, which makes the spatial arrangement of the positive detections less important than in the *object detection* task addressed in this paper.

Poselet activations are assembled by Bourdev and Malik using different techniques. In [3] they use a Hough-like voting approach. In [4] the same authors discuss the methodological and experimental limitations of using the Generalized Hough Transform for poselet activation clustering and propose an agglomerative clustering algorithm based on spatial *consistency*. Poselet activations consistency is measured by comparing the spatial distributions of a set of keypoints associated with each poselet type. Finally, in [5] they propose an *activation vector*, which is a histogram of the poselet activations over a specific sliding window. We use the pre-trained poselet detector dictionary provided by the authors as our base detector dictionary and we empirically compare the results of our system with their clustering strategies in Sec. 4, showing a sharp improvement with respect to the poselet people detector system on two challenging benchmarks.

In [20] RFs are combined with Conditional Random Fields (CRFs) in order to learn pairwise dependencies between variables for image labeling. The main difference between the approach proposed here and [20] is that their (pre-fixed) CRF structure determines the topology and the exact disposition of the involved spatial relations. Conversely, in our case, RFs are used to *automatically select* the number and the spatial layout of the model's pairwise relations as well as the pairs of depending variables (i.e. poselet types). Moreover, inference in the CRF framework is computationally expensive [20].

Besides the works mentioned in this and in the previous section, the approaches to people detection and the more general object detection problem are so numerous that cannot be extensively described in a few lines. They vary from Part Based methods [6–14] to Boosting techniques [21–24], SVM methods [25, 26], Hough and chamfer-based transforms [18, 27–29], constellation models [30], covariance matrices [31, 32] and many others. We refer the reader to the interesting survey on pedestrian detection [33] for a more exhaustive review of the most recent and successfully object detection methods specifically applied to the challenging task of human body detection.

3 The Proposed Approach

3.1 Overview of the Method

The poselet dictionary we used is composed of 150 different detectors [4]. We typically get a few hundreds positive responses ("poselet activations") by running this detector dictionary on an input image using a sliding window procedure. For instance, the number of poselet activations (of any type) obtained on the 825×698 image of Fig. 1(a) is 604. Most of these poselet activations are indeed false positives. Fig. 1(b) shows a detail of the same image, where the red rectangle represents the *person* bounding box of a (false positive) detection performed by the system presented in [4]. Moreover, the blue and the white rectangles represents the bounding boxes of two specific poselet activations, roughly corresponding to a whole body and a lower body poselet type respectively (the relative average silhouettes are shown as well). These and other poselet activations have (wrongly) been clustered together possibly because their spatial proximity is sufficiently consistent [4]. However, their mutual scale and positions can potentially be used to reject this assembling hypothesis because it cannot actually correspond to a real human body. Our idea is to automatically learn the parameters of spatial relations among neighboring poselet activations which can either reject or confirm a given poselet activation using its context.

The set of all the poselet activations of a given image is our high-level image representation. Our goal is to prune the huge number of false positives to (hopefully) get only those activations corresponding to true positives. To this aim, we classify each poselet activation using RFs. The poselet activation classified as positives by our classifier are then used to predict the whole person bounding box by means of a simple linear regression on the poselet activation's coordinates. Finally, standard Non Maxima Suppression (NMS) is applied on all the obtained bounding boxes to get the final results. In the following we show the details of this strategy and we begin by introducing some useful terminology.

We call $D_1, ..., D_n$ the basic poselet detectors composing our dictionary (V) and the index $i \in [1, n]$ indicates the poselet *type*. Given an image I, the set of *poselet activations* obtained using V is $\{A_1, ..., A_m\}$, where m is variable and it also depends on the image size. Each $A_i = (b_i, j)$ is associated with a bounding box b_i representing its position and scale in I and a type j, corresponding to the detector D_j which has produced the activation.

(a) (b) (c)

Fig. 1. (a) An example of input image. (b) An example of outcome of the poselet-based people detector presented in [4]. The red rectangle represents the predicted person bounding box, while the other rectangles represent poselet activation bounding boxes b_i. The associated poselet silhouettes give a visual representation of each poselet's "average shape". (c) The final person bounding boxes predicted by our system.

At training time are given two sets T_{Pos} and T_{Neg} of, respectively, positive and negative images. T_{Neg} is a set of images not containing people (e.g., images showing animals, common objects, landscapes, etc.). Let us call N the set of all the poselet activations obtained running $D_1, ..., D_n$ on all the images in T_{Neg} (negative samples). Moreover, each image I in T_{Pos} is annotated using a set of bounding boxes representing the persons in I. All the poselet activations $A_i = (b_i, j)$ in I whose bounding box b_i overlaps with at least one ground truth person bounding box is considered to be a positive sample and it is collected in the set P (in more detail: we require that the value of the intersection over union of b_i with the ground truth bounding box is larger than 0.5). Finally, for each A_i in P we store the image I and the ground truth bounding box g from which it has been extracted. Note that usually more than one poselet activation in P is associated with the same pair (I, g) and this means that they (very probably) represent different parts of *the same person*.

3.2 Learning Discriminative Spatial Information

We want to learn a set of pairwise spatial relations holding between different poselet types. For this reason, we first collect statistics concerning the average disposition of a poselet activation of type j with respect to an activation of type i. They will be used later to define our spatial tests. This step is done using only the positive samples in P. In more detail, let us consider two poselet activations $A_1 = (b_1, j_1)$ and $A_2 = (b_2, j_2)$ associated with the same image and ground truth bounding box pair (I, g). Assuming that $b_1 = (x_1, y_1, w_1, h_1)$ and $b_2 = (x_2, y_2, w_2, h_2)$, we can compute the scale ratio as:

$$s = \frac{w_2}{w_1} \tag{1}$$

and a scale normalized offset vector δ such that:

$$\delta = \begin{pmatrix} dx \\ dy \end{pmatrix} = \frac{1}{w_1} \begin{pmatrix} x_2 - x_1 \\ y_2 - y_1 \end{pmatrix}. \tag{2}$$

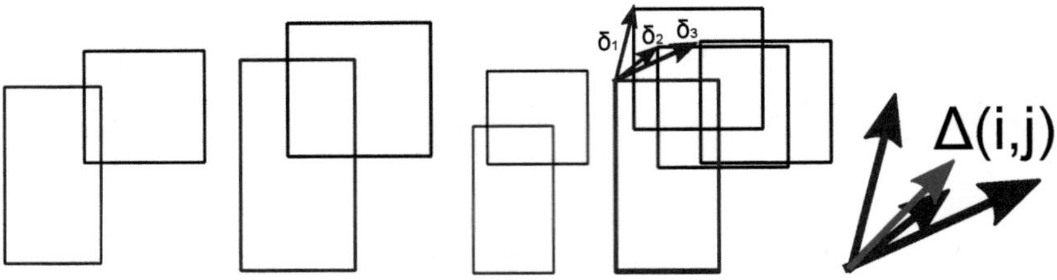

(a) (b) (c)

Fig. 2. A schematic representation of $\Delta(i, j)$. (a) For each pair of poselet types i (blue) and j (black) we collect corresponding poselet activation pairs from different positive image samples. (b) For each pair, a corresponding *normalized* offset δ is computed using Eq. (2). (c) Finally, $\Delta(i, j)$ is obtained by averaging these normalized offsets.

Scanning the whole set of positive samples P and using Eqs (1)-(2) we compute the average displacements of different poselet activation types referring to a same person. Let $S(i, j)$ be the mean scale ratio between type i and type j poselets computed by averaging the value in Eq. (1) for all the activations A_1 and A_2 in P which are associated with the same pair (I, g). Similarly, let $\Delta(i, j)$ be the average displacement vector computed using the values δ defined in Eq. (2). The vector $\Delta(i, j)$ is the average position of poselet j with respect to poselet i (see Fig. 2). Finally, we also compute the standard deviation $\sigma(i, j)$ of all the scale values s which have contributed in computing $S(i, j)$.

Note that this pairwise displacement information is similar to what is usually used in common part-based approaches in order to describe mutual spatial relations between object components. However, we use $S(i, j)$, $\Delta(i, j)$ and $\sigma(i, j)$ as a base to discriminatively build spatial tests which implicitly embed our final spatial model.

In more detail, given a poselet activation $A = (b, i)$ extracted from image I with $b = (x, y, w, h)$, we define a parametric spatial test as follows:

$$t_\theta(A, I) = \begin{cases} true & \text{if } \exists A' = (b', j) \text{ in } I \text{ s.t. } p(b, b') \\ false\ otherwise, \end{cases} \tag{3}$$

where $p(b, b')$ is a predicate defined as below:

$$p(b, b') = \begin{cases} true & \text{if } |s - S(i, j)| \leq 3\sigma(i, j) \\ & \text{and } ||\delta - \Delta(i, j)||_2 \leq \tau \\ false\ otherwise. \end{cases} \tag{4}$$

In Eq. (4) s is the scale ratio between the two compared poselet activation bounding boxes b and b', computed using Eq. (1). If $|s - S(i, j)|$ is greater than

3 times the standard deviation between the poselet types i and j, then $p(b, b')$ is false. Moreover, δ is the normalized bounding box distance computed as in Eq. (2) and it is compared with the average disposition $\Delta(i, j)$. If the distance between δ and $\Delta(i, j)$ is greater than a threshold τ, then $p(b, b')$ is false (Fig. 3). The test $t_\theta()$ is defined by specifying the types i and j and the threshold τ: $\theta = (i, j, \tau)$.

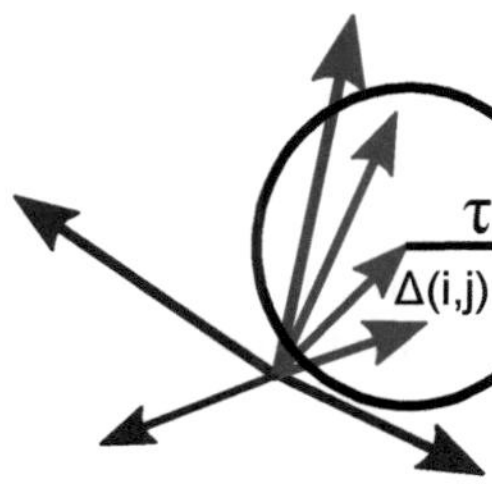

Fig. 3. A schematic representation of a parametric test. The average distance $\Delta(i, j)$ between poselt types i and j is represented by the red vector. Poselet activations whose distance from $\Delta(i, j)$ is greater than τ (violet vectors) correspond to $false$ values of the test, while activations closer than τ (green vectors) obtain $true$.

For each poselet type i we want to select a set of parametric tests $t_{(i,*,*)}()$ which will allow our classifier to discriminate between true positive and false positive activations of type i. For this reason, *for each type* i we separately build a random forest composed of k DTs. Let P_i be the subset of all the positive poselet activation samples of type i extracted from P and let N_i be the corresponding subset of N. We further split P_i and N_i in k different sets $P_i^1, ..., P_i^k$ and $N_i^1, ..., N_i^k$ in order to have a pair (P_i^h, N_i^h) for each tree. This split is performed by randomly partitioning each P_i and N_i without sample replacement. We are now ready to build our DT in a standard way (e.g., see [17]). Let $Q = P_i^h \cup N_i^h$. The h-th DT DT_i^h of type i is constructed as follows.

1. Randomly propose a set of splitting candidate tests $C = \{t_\theta\}$.
2. For each $t_\theta \in C$, partition Q into left and right subsets:
$$Q_l(\theta) = \{A \in Q | t_\theta(A, I) = true\}, \tag{5}$$
$$Q_r(\theta) = Q \setminus Q_l(\theta), \tag{6}$$
where I in Eq. (5) is the image from which A has been extracted.
3. Compute θ^* giving the largest information gain:
$$\theta^* = \arg\max_\theta G(\theta), \tag{7}$$
$$G(\theta) = H(Q) - \sum_{z \in \{l,r\}} \frac{|Q_z(\theta)|}{|Q|} H(Q_z(\theta)), \tag{8}$$
where $H(Q)$ is the Shannon entropy.

4. Recursively split both left and right subsets $Q_l(\theta)$ and $Q_r(\theta)$ unless the stopping criteria are satisfied.

Splitting is stopped when *at least one* of the following criteria is satisfied:

- All the samples in Q belong to the same class.
- The depth of the current tree branch has reached a fixed maximum value.
- The number of training samples in Q is less than a fixed value M or the number of samples in either Q_l or Q_r is less than $M/2$ (note that these two conditions are not equivalent).

Candidates tests in C (Step 1) are chosen with a mixed deterministic and random method. While the value i of the first poselet type is fixed for all the current forest, the value j is chosen at random by uniform sampling over all the types $1, ..., n$. However, we discard types j whose number of co-occurences with i in P is low[1].

On the other hand, the threshold τ is selected deterministically by maximizing the information gain $G(i, j, \tau^*)$ with the following procedure. Once j has been fixed, for a given $A_1 \in Q$ ($A_1 = (b, i)$) we analyze all the poselet activations $A_1', A_2', ...$ associated with the same image I of A_1 and whose type is j. We discard those poselet activations whose bounding box scale ratio with respect to A_1 is not compatible with the expected value in $S(i, j)$ (see Eq. (4)). For each pair (A_1, A_z') we compute δ_z using Eq. (2). Then, we associate A_1 with the value:

$$\lambda_1 = \min_{\delta_z} ||\delta_z - \Delta(i, j)||_2. \tag{9}$$

Note that λ_1 can be ∞ in case no sample A_z' was found in I which satisfies both the scale and the type conditions. We then repeat this process for all the elements $A_2, ..., A_m$ in Q, obtaining the set of distances $\Lambda = \{\lambda_1, ..., \lambda_m\}$. The value of τ is searched for in the discrete set Λ. We order Λ in an ascending order and, for each value $\tau = \lambda_q \in \Lambda$, we compute $G(i, j, \tau)$ using Eq. (8) choosing the one giving the largest G value. This method is inspired by the threshold selection procedure for "stump" weak classifiers in Boosting techniques [34]. Note that the reason for which we can associate the poselet activation sample A_1 with only the minimum possible distance λ_1 from $\Delta(i, j)$ in Eq. (9) is due to the fact that the parametric tests are based on *existential* quantifications (Eq. (3)), thus $\lambda_1 \leq \tau$ implies $||\delta - \Delta(i, j)||_2 \leq \tau$ for some valid δ.

Finally, each leaf L of the tree is associated with a posterior probability distribution $p(L) = P(person|A)$, computed as the ratio of the positive samples on the negative samples reaching L. This posterior will be used at testing time to estimate the probability of an input poselet activation to be a true positive, as shown in the next section.

[1] We do not take into account j if there are only few poselet activations A_1 and A_2 in P, respectively A_1 type i and A_2 type j, which are associated with the same image-ground truth pair (I, g).

3.3 Discussion

While the parameter τ in Eq. (4) is optimized in every node of the tree, we adopted a fixed constraint on the scale values ($3\sigma(i,j)$). In fact we empirically observed that the distribution of the scale ratios between poselets of a fixed pair type, activated on the same person (I, g), is mono-modal and highly peaked around the mean. Thus, optimization in this case is not necessary and we can save computation time during training using the standard deviation $\sigma(i,j)$ to select consistent scale poselet activations in a given image.

Conversely, the δ values distribution is much more variable and probably multi-modal. A relatively simple extension of the technique proposed above would be using different values $\Delta_1(i,j), \Delta_2(i,j), ...$ (e.g., the centroids of pre-computed clusters) and choosing the reference $\Delta_z(i,j)$ in Eq. (4) either at random or deterministically selecting the value associated with the largest information gain. This extension has not been investigated yet and the results presented here assume the simple mean $\Delta(i,j)$ as reference. Another possible extension concerns n-ary spatial relations (as opposite to the pairwise relations (i,j) taken into account here). However, training time would probably increase. Still another possible extension is the inclusion of the confidence threshold of the dictionary detectors in the selection process performed at each node. This has not been tested. However, besides efficiency issues, the increasing of the number of features to be automatically selected in the learning phase can lead to overfitting problems, especially given a limited number of training samples.

Finally, we emphasize the importance of using RFs instead of other more common classifiers (e.g., SVMs, etc.). The main reason for adopting the RF paradigm is the need to perform feature selection simultaneously to the classifier construction. In our case a "feature" is a parametric test determined by the poselet types i and j and by the distance threshold τ. It is worth noticing that most of the standard classifiers usually assume as input a feature vector of fixed dimensions. Even if in principle for every poselet activation sample and every poselet type we could compute all the pairwise distances and build corresponding fixed dimension feature vectors to train a SVM, such learning process will be influenced by *all* the features. Anyway, most of the poselet distances are uninformative because only a minor subset of poselet types are correlated (e.g. a sideview of the legs should not influence a front view of an upper body). When we select the parametric test to associate with a node of one of our DTs, we choose the poselet type which is the most informative with respect to the current tree type and the current training set inherited by the node. Hence, we simultaneously build a classifier (the RF) *and* perform feature selection. It is important to note that the feature selection process is not only useful for computational issues (only a subset of poselet distances will be tested once the tree is built) but mainly to avoid the learning process being influenced by noisy features.

3.4 Person Detection Using the Random Forests

In Sec. 3.2 we have shown how we build a battery of RFs $F_1, ..., F_n$, one forest for each poselet type. At testing time, given an input image I, we run all the poselet detectors of our dictionary V to get a set of poselet activations $\{A_1, A_2, ...\}$. Given a test activation $A = (b, i)$, we use the corresponding forest F_i to classify A. For each tree DT_i^h of F_i, we compute a confidence value using the posteriors associated with the leaves of DT_i^h. In fact A is passed down DT_i^h until it reaches a leaf node L. By averaging on all the trees DT_i^h of F_i we obtain a confidence value for A. If this confidence is greater than 0.5, A is a positive detection. Different threshold values on the final confidence can be used to obtain different points on the ROC curve. Alternatively, ROC curve points can be computed by thresholding the confidence of the clusters obtained after NMS (see below).

Since a poselet typically represents a part of the human body, we need to estimate the position of the whole person from the bounding box b of each positive detection. This problem can be solved using a simple linear regression separately applied to each element of b. At training time, for each poselet type i we use the corresponding poselet activation samples $A = (b, i) \in P$ to compute the average person bounding box B_i. This B_i can be easily calculated by averaging the values of the ground truth bounding boxes corresponding to each A.

Finally, standard NMS is applied to all the predicted person rectangles in order to cluster highly intersecting hypotheses. Fig. 1(c) shows the final detection outcome obtained from the image in Fig. 1(a).

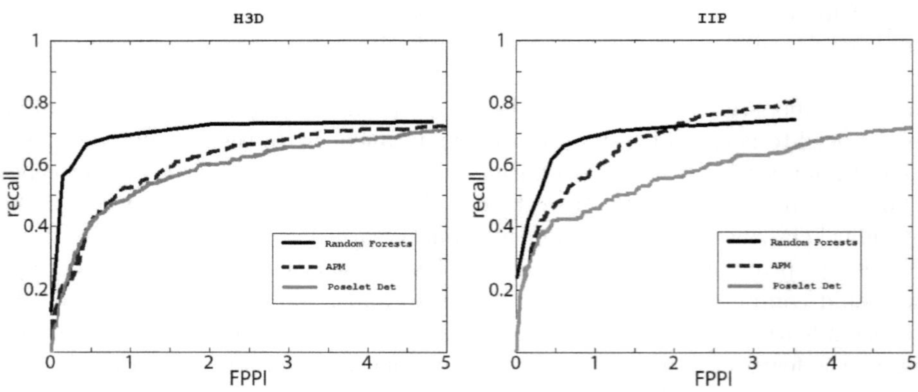

Fig. 4. Experimental comparison of our system (Random Forests) with the original Poselet People Detector (Poselet Det) [4] and the Articulated Part-based Model system (APM) [35] on the H3D test set [4] (left) and the IIP test set [9] (right)

4 Experiments

The results shown in this section were obtained by building a RF for each poselet type associated with at least 200 (positive + negative) poselet activation samples in the training set. The final number of forests depends on the training set magnitude and varies between 40 and 70.

In all the experiments the maximum number of tests per node was fixed to 20 and the maximum depth to 15 (this depth has never been reached by our DTs). The longest training time obtained for the whole set of 70 RFs was only about 2 minutes on a common PC with non-optimized and non-parallelized C++ code. At testing time, an image is classified in a few milliseconds. These computation times do not include the time necessary to compute poselet activations (usually, a few seconds per image). Our method is extremely efficient because a parametric test can be computed in time linear in m, being m the number of poselet activations of type j in I (typically a few dozens). Given a poselet activation of type i, the average computational complexity for its classification is $O(kdm)$, where k is the number of trees of the i-th forest ($k = 10$ in all our experiments) and d is the average depth of each tree (typically less than 10). Given an image I with N poselet activations, the average computational time for classifying all the activations is $O(Nkdm)$, which must be summed with the time necessary to compute NMS.

In the first experiment we used the same protocol adopted in [35], training our system with the positive images from the H3D dataset [3] and negative images from the INRIA dataset [25] (note that in [35] negative images were taken from PASCAL'07 [36], while in [3, 4] the source dataset for negative samples is not specified). Fig. 4 shows the results obtained on, respectively, the H3D [3] and the Iterative Image Parsing (IIP) [9] test sets (a few sample images are shown in Fig. 6). The latter is a challenging benchmark containing sport images with human bodies in atypical poses. No sample of the IIP training set was used in our training. The plots in Fig. 4 compare our system with the original poselet-based people detector [4] and with the recent work on Articulated Part-based Model (APM) [35]. In both test sets our system significantly outperforms the other methods.

In the second experiment we followed the protocol adopted in [4] for a "torso" detection task. We recomputed the regression parameters for estimating the final bounding box given the current poselet activation (Sec. 3.4) in order to predict the torso position, leaving all the rest unchanged. Results are shown in Fig. 5(a).

In the last experiment we followed the protocol proposed in [33] by training our system with the positive and negative samples of the INRIA training set. Fig. 5(b) shows a comparison of some of the best state-of-the-art pedestrian detector systems on the INRIA test set (Fig. 6, bottom) performed in [33]. In black we have superimposed our results obtained on the same benchmark. To make the comparison possible, we adopted the FPPI (False Positive Per Image) criterion suggested in [33] rather than the FPPW (False Positive Per Window) approach used in [25]. As remarked in [33], FPPI is more suitable for assessing the performance of a *detection* system in which multiple local classifications must be clustered (e.g., using NMS) to obtain a reasonable result on a complete image. The plots in Fig. 5(b) show that, for values lower than 10^0 FPPI, our method is comparable with the best performing systems on this very common benchmark. For larger values the obtained recall is inferior to the best performing systems but it is still close to the medium ranking techniques. The reason why

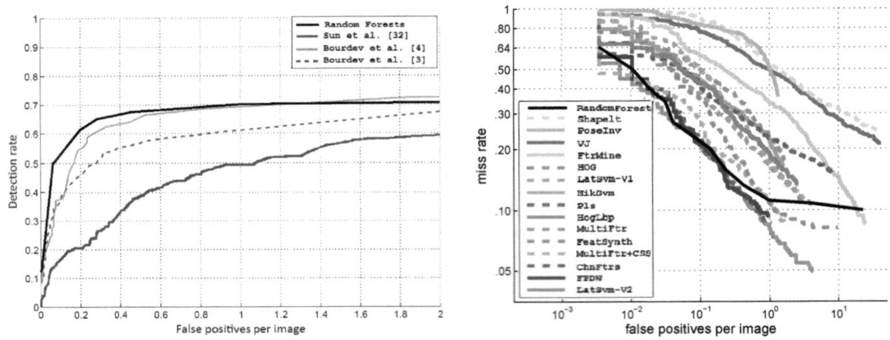

(a) (b)

Fig. 5. (a) Human torso detection results on the H3D test set. (b) Pedestrian Detection results on the INRIA dataset [25]. Figure (b) is courtesy of Piotr Dollár: we have superimposed our results (black line) on the results obtained in [33]. We refer to [33] for the details on the specific methods and the evaluation protocol.

Fig. 6. Some output examples. Blue bounding boxes show the system's predictions, while white and black rectangles show false negatives and false positives respectively. First column: IIP dataset [9]. Second column: H3D dataset [4]. Last column: INRIA dataset [25].

the miss rate of our method decreases very slowly after 10^0 FPPI is probably due to false negatives given by the initial detections with the dictionary (the SVM poselet detectors in the experiments performed here) which cannot be recovered by our approach. In other words, if none or very few poselect activations "hit" the region of the input image covered by a human body, our method based on checking spatial configurations among poselet activations cannot detect that person. However, for applications in which a low false positive rate is necessary, our approach is clearly competitive with the state-of-the-art systems.

5 Conclusions

In this paper we addressed the problem of modeling spatial information among the positive responses of an object detector dictionary. Specifically, we assume to have a pre-built set of basic detectors (poselets, in the case presented here) specialized in detecting different parts of the same object (e.g., the human body). The spatial co-occurrence of these parts on a given image naturally leads to a corresponding co-occurrence of different detector types activations. However, rather than modeling such spatial relations using a classic generative part-based approach, we have explored a discriminative method in which spatial tests are automatically selected in order to minimize the probability of random co-occurrences. The discriminative framework adopted is based on RFs and spatial test selection is performed at training time during the tree construction.

The experimental results on different benchmarks gave a significant improvement with respect to [4] and a competitive accuracy with respect to other state-of-the-art pedestrian detector systems. Finally, since no specific assumption was made on the characteristics of the detector dictionary's components, we believe that our approach can be used as well with other types of basic detectors.

References

1. Torresani, L., Szummer, M., Fitzgibbon, A.: Efficient Object Category Recognition Using Classemes. In: Daniilidis, K., Maragos, P., Paragios, N. (eds.) ECCV 2010, Part I. LNCS, vol. 6311, pp. 776–789. Springer, Heidelberg (2010)
2. Li, L.J., Su, H., Xing, E.P., Fei-Fei, L.: Object bank: A high-level image representation for scene classification and semantic feature sparsification. In: NIPS (2010)
3. Bourdev, L., Malik, J.: Poselets: Body part detectors trained using 3D human pose annotations. In: ICCV (2009)
4. Bourdev, L., Maji, S., Brox, T., Malik, J.: Detecting People Using Mutually Consistent Poselet Activations. In: Daniilidis, K., Maragos, P., Paragios, N. (eds.) ECCV 2010, Part VI. LNCS, vol. 6316, pp. 168–181. Springer, Heidelberg (2010)
5. Maji, S., Bourdev, L., Malik, J.: Action recognition from a distributed representation of pose and appearance. In: CVPR (2011)
6. Felzenszwalb, P.F., Huttenlocher, D.P.: Pictorial structures for object recognition. Int. J. of Computer Vision 61, 55–79 (2005)
7. Ferrari, V., Marín-Jiménez, M.J., Zisserman, A.: Progressive search space reduction for human pose estimation. In: CVPR (2008)
8. Andriluka, M., Roth, S., Schiele, B.: Pictorial Structures Revisited: People Detection and Articulated Pose Estimation. In: CVPR, pp. 1014–1021 (2009)
9. Ramanan, D.: Learning to parse images of articulated bodies. In: Advanced in Neural Information Processing Systems (2006)
10. Yang, Y., Ramanan, D.: Articulated pose estimation using flexible mixtures of parts. In: CVPR (2011)
11. Felzenszwalb, P.F., Huttenlocher, D.P.: Efficient matching of pictorial structures. In: CVPR (2000)
12. Forsyth, D.A., Fleck, M.M.: Body plans. In: CVPR, pp. 678–683 (1997)
13. Ramanan, D., Forsyth, D.A.: Finding and tracking people from the bottom up. In: CVPR (2003)

14. Sigal, L., Bhatia, S., Roth, S., Black, M.J., Isard, M.: Tracking loose-limbed people. In: CVPR, pp. 421–428 (2004)
15. Eichner, M., Ferrari, V.: Better appearance models for pictorial structures. In: BMVC (2009)
16. Breiman, L.: Random forests. Machine Learning 45 (2001)
17. Shotton, J., Fitzgibbon, A., Cook, M., Sharp, T., Finocchio, M., Moore, R., Kipman, A., Blake, A.: Real-time human pose recognition in parts from single depth images. In: CVPR (2011)
18. Gall, J., Lempitsky, V.: Class-specific Hough forests for object detection. In: CVPR (2009)
19. Hall, M.A., Smith, L.A.: Feature selection for machine learning: Comparing a correlation-based filter approach to the wrapper. In: FLAIRS, pp. 235–239 (1999)
20. Nowozin, S., Rother, C., Bagon, S., Sharp, T., Yao, B., Kohli, P.: Decision tree fields. In: ICCV, pp. 1668–1675 (2011)
21. Viola, P., Jones, M., Snow, D.: Detecting pedestrians using patterns of motion and appearance. Int. J. of Computer Vision 63, 153–161 (2005)
22. Chen, Y.T., Chen, C.S., Hung, Y.P., Chang, K.Y.: Multi-class multi-instance boosting for part-based human detection. In: 9th IEEE International Workshop on Visual Surveillance (2009)
23. Chen, Y.T., Chen, C.S.: Fast human detection using a novel boosted cascading structure with meta stages. IEEE Trans. on Image Processing 17, 1452–1464 (2008)
24. Wachs, J.P., Kolsch, M., Goshorn, D.: Human posture recognition for intelligent vehicles. J. of Real Time Image Processing 5, 231–244 (2010)
25. Dalal, N., Triggs, B.: Histograms of oriented gradients for human detection. In: CVPR, pp. 886–893 (2005)
26. Felzenszwalb, P.F., Girshick, R.B., McAllester, D.A., Ramanan, D.: Object detection with discriminatively trained part-based models. IEEE Trans. on PAMI 32, 1627–1645 (2010)
27. Leibe, B., Leonardis, A., Schiele, B.: Combined object categorization and segmentation with an implicit shape model. In: ECCV (2004)
28. Leibe, B., Seemann, E., Schiele, B.: Pedestrian detection in crowded scenes. In: CVPR, pp. 878–885 (2005)
29. Gavrila, D.M.: Pedestrian Detection from a Moving Vehicle. In: Vernon, D. (ed.) ECCV 2000. LNCS, vol. 1843, pp. 37–49. Springer, Heidelberg (2000)
30. Fergus, R., Perona, P., Zisserman, A.: Object class recognition by unsupervised scale-invariant learning. In: CVPR, pp. 264–271 (2003)
31. Tuzel, O., Porikli, F., Meer, P.: Pedestrian Detection via Classification on Riemannian Manifolds. IEEE Trans. on PAMI, 1713–1727 (2008)
32. Tosato, D., Farenzena, M., Cristani, M., Spera, M., Murino, V.: Multi-class Classification on Riemannian Manifolds for Video Surveillance. In: Daniilidis, K., Maragos, P., Paragios, N. (eds.) ECCV 2010, Part II. LNCS, vol. 6312, pp. 378–391. Springer, Heidelberg (2010)
33. Dollár, P., Wojek, C., Schiele, B., Perona, P.: Pedestrian detection: An evaluation of the state of the art. IEEE Trans. on PAMI 34, 743–761 (2012)
34. Viola, P., Jones, M.: Rapid object detection using a boosted cascade of simple features. In: CVPR, pp. 511–518 (2001)
35. Sun, M., Savarese, S.: Articulated part-based model for joint object detection and pose estimation. In: ICCV (2011)
36. Everingham, M., Van Gool, L., Williams, C.K.I., Winn, J., Zisserman, A.: (The PASCAL Visual Object Classes Challenge 2007 (VOC 2007) Results)

Learning Deformations with Parallel Transport

Donglai Wei, Dahua Lin, and John Fisher III

CSAIL, MIT

Abstract. Many vision problems, such as object recognition and image synthesis, are greatly impacted by deformation of objects. In this paper, we develop a deformation model based on Lie algebraic analysis. This work aims to provide a generative model that explicitly decouples deformation from appearance, which is fundamentally different from the prior work that focuses on deformation-resilient features or metrics. Specifically, the deformation group for each object can be characterized by a set of Lie algebraic basis. Such basis for different objects are related via parallel transport. Exploiting the parallel transport relations, we formulate an optimization problem, and derive an algorithm that jointly estimates the deformation basis for a class of objects, given a set of images resulted from the action of the deformations. We test the proposed model empirically on both character recognition and face synthesis.

1 Introduction

The changes in shapes of objects, often referred to as *deformations*, are widely observed in computer vision data. In many problems, such as object recognition, the performance can be greatly influenced by deformations. Whereas past decades have seen tremendous efforts devoted to developing features and classifiers that are resilient to shape variations, the modeling of deformations has not been extensively explored. In this paper, we focus on modeling deformations, aiming to develop a method that can decouple deformation from object appearance.

We provide a brief review of existing approaches to deformation analysis in next section. Careful examination of these approaches suggests that they are limited in several aspects: (1) Manifold-based methods [1,2] are popular in image modeling. Such methods, though partly capturing shape variations, are usually not very effective in modeling deformations. The key issue here is the lack of a mechanism that can decouple the effects of deformations and other factors that contribute to the variations of appearance. (2) The methods for deformation-resilient metrics [3,4] aim to suppress the influence of deformation on discriminative performance, which again does not offer an explicit deformation model. (3) Other work that explicitly takes deformations into consideration [5,6,7] has a narrow focus on individual local tangent spaces, neglecting the relations between them. As we will show, there are significant dependencies between the different tangent spaces of the deformation manifolds, which, if appropriately exploited, contribute greatly to learning a model of deformation.

A. Fitzgibbon et al. (Eds.): ECCV 2012, Part II, LNCS 7573, pp. 287–300, 2012.

In this paper, we propose a new approach to deformation modeling, where each observed image is considered to be generated by deforming an object template. In typical images, the deformation of an object usually exhibit some regular patterns. This observation leads to the belief that deformations of an object can be approximated by a low-dimensional Lie group. In general, a Lie group is uniquely associated with a vector space, called the Lie algebra, which can be characterized by a set of bases. Intuitively, each base vector in this space can be considered as a base deformation pattern, and any deformation in the group can be expressed as a linear combination of these bases with the Lie algebraic characterization. Generally, a different Lie algebra is associated with a different object template. For object templates that represent different poses of an object, the associated Lie algebras are related to each other via the parallel transport property. Specifically, the Lie algebra for one object template is a transported version of the one for others. The fact that parallel transport is covariant with geometric transformation ensures the consistency of this relation.

Consequently, with the Lie algebraic characterization, the problem of learning deformations reduce to the one of estimating the deformation bases for different object templates. Here, we formulate an optimization problem for estimating these bases from a given set of observed images. In this formulation, two levels of relations are exploited:

1. Observed images are closed to the deformation orbits, *i.e.* the manifold is comprised of all deformed versions of the templates.
2. The bases associated with different templates are constrained by the parallel transport relations.

The use of the first relation, which explicitly incorporates deformation into the generative process of an image, clearly sets this work apart from the large amount of prior work (*e.g.* those on image manifold learning) that directly model the image space. Additionally, the use of the parallel transport relation further distinguishes the proposed approach from the methods which focus on local neighborhoods only.

The remainder of this paper is organized as follows. Section 3 reviews existing theoretical results on deformations. The emphasis is particularly placed on the Lie algebraic characterization and parallel transport. Section 4 formulates the optimization algorithm for estimating the deformation model from observed images. Empirical results are presented in section 5, where we compare the proposed method with related methods on character recognition and synthesis, as well as face reconstruction. Discussion of the method and results is provided in section 6.

2 Related Work

We first briefly review previous work on deformations, which roughly fall into two categories. The first category of methods focuses on estimating global affine transformation. Frey and Jojic [8,9,10] proposes a mixture model, where the space of affine transforms is discretized, and an indicator is used to choose a specific transform in generating each image. Miller *et. al* [11] proposed a non-parametric probabilistic model, which estimates the global affine transforms by gradually aligning the images, using a gradient descent method referred to as "congealing".

The second category takes into account non-rigid deformations that can lead to changes in shapes. Cootes *et. al* [12,13] proposed the active appearance model for object alignment, where the deformation is represented via the displacement of pre-specified control points. In addition, approaches by directly matching local descriptors are also widely used. Belongie et al. [3] developed a direct matching method using local shape context based on statistics of edges. Keyser et al. [4] developed an Image Distortion Model (IDM) [4], which pursues a dense match of local patches between two images as a representation of the deformation. Though simple, this method leads to substantial improvement on character recognition, providing significant evidence as to the important role of local deformations in object recognition. The pioneering work by Tenenbaum etal [1] and Roweis and Saul [2] initiated a large amount of work that directly models the image manifold via embeddings it into local low-dimensional spaces.

While deformation information is made use of in building object metrics in the work mentioned above, these methods do not establish an explicit model of deformations. Recently, new models have been proposed to address this issue. Simard et al. [5] considered the manifold of deformations, approximating it via local tangent spaces. In this work, the basis of these tangent spaces are hand-crafted, with some apparent deformation patterns taken into account (*e.g.* rotation and changes of thickness). However, some subtle variations of shapes are difficult to capture via manually devised patterns. Another drawback of this method lies in the introduction of tangent spaces for all training samples, incurring unnecessary computational costs in both training and testing phases when the samples are dense. Hastie and Simard [6,7] improve upon this method by grouping nearby samples into clusters and deriving the tangent basis via learning. However, learning is performed independently for each tangent space, utilizing only the samples within a local neighborhood. This makes it potentially difficult to obtain reliable estimations.

3 The Theory of Deformation

Generally, the shape and size of an non-rigid object can change over time. Such a change is often referred to as a *deformation*, which is ubiquitous in vision problems. In this paper, we focus on the two-dimensional image space, where a deformation can be formalized as a *diffeomorphic transform* on the image plane.

3.1 Lie Group and Lie Algebra

Deformations typically observed in vision problems are a subset of all diffeomorphic transforms, which we assume constitute a Lie group of dimension K. A

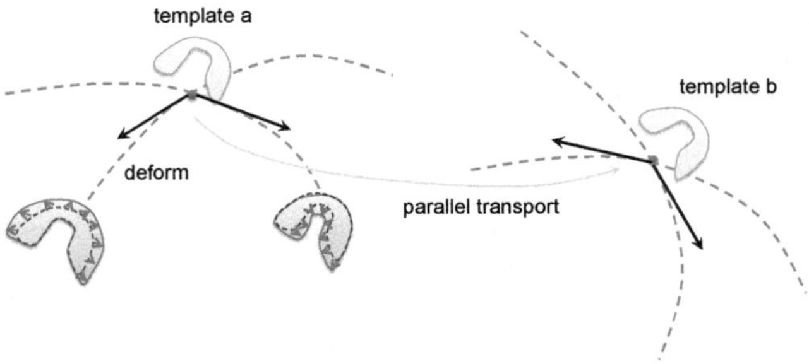

Fig. 1. This figure illustrates the Lie algebraic characterization of deformation groups. Here, starting from an object template, a deformed image can be generated following a velocity field, which can be expressed as a linear combination of some basic patterns (captured by the Lie algebraic basis). The basis associated with different object templates are related by parallel transport.

Lie group G is a finite-dimensional manifold with an algebraic group structure, meaning that it has the following properties:

1. The identity transform is in G.
2. If T_1 and T_2 are both in G, then the composition $T_1 \circ T_2$ is also in G.
3. For each transform $T \in G$, the inverse transform T^{-1} also exists in G.

The Lie group G is associated with a Lie algebra $\mathfrak{g}$, a vector space of dimension K. Each vector $V \in \mathfrak{g}$ is a velocity field and corresponds uniquely to a transform $T \in G$ via the exponentiation mapping as below

$$T = \exp(V). \tag{1}$$

Here, V is called the *Lie algebraic representation* of T.

The relations between a Lie group G and its associated Lie algebra $\mathfrak{g}$ can be described through the construction of a continuous transformation process. Let $V \in \mathfrak{g}$, then for every $t > 0$, $T_t = \exp(tV)$ is a transform. Hence, the function below defines a trajectory on the image plane.

$$\mathbf{x}(t) = T_t \mathbf{x}_0 = \exp(tV)\mathbf{x}_0. \tag{2}$$

Intuitively, this trajectory can be generated through a continuous transformation process described as follows. Consider a particle starting from $\mathbf{x}_0$. If the particle travels across the image plane, passing through each location $\mathbf{x}(t)$ with velocity $V(\mathbf{x}(t))$, the resultant trajectory is then given by

$$\mathbf{x}(t) = \mathbf{x}_0 + \int_{\tau=0}^{t} V(\mathbf{x}(\tau)) d\tau. \tag{3}$$

This provides a detailed characterization of the trajectory defined in Eq.(2), namely $\exp(tV)\mathbf{x}_0$. Therefore, the transform $\exp(tV)$ can be understood as an operation that sends each point to move for time t, following the velocity field V. Equivalently, the trajectory is characterized by the differential equation below

$$\frac{d\mathbf{x}(t)}{dt} = V(\mathbf{x}(t)). \tag{4}$$

Given a basis of $\mathfrak{g}$, denoted by $\mathcal{B} = (B_1, \ldots, B_K)$, each Lie algebraic vector $V \in \mathfrak{g}$ can be expressed as a linear combination as $V = \sum_{k=1}^{K} \alpha^k B_k$. As illustrated by Figure 1, each base vector of $\mathfrak{g}$ reflects a basic deformation pattern, and all deformations in G are combinations of such base patterns. The Lie algebraic characterization provides a representation, where such combinations can be done via linear operations, great simplifying the modeling and estimation.

3.2 The Action on Images

A deformation $T \in G$ can act on an image by moving the locations of its pixels. Let I be an image. Applying T to I results in an deformed image $T \circ I$, given by

$$(T \circ I)(\mathbf{x}) = I(T^{-1}\mathbf{x}). \tag{5}$$

This means that the pixel value of $T \circ I$ at $\mathbf{x}$ equals that of I at $T^{-1}\mathbf{x}$. Let $V \in \mathfrak{g}$. Applying a continuous transform process $\exp(tV)$ to the image I yields a continuous sequence of images, as

$$I_t(\mathbf{x}) = (\exp(tV) \circ I)(\mathbf{x}) = I(\exp(-tV)\mathbf{x}). \tag{6}$$

Taking the derivative *w.r.t.* t, we get

$$\left.\frac{dI_t(\mathbf{x})}{dt}\right|_{t=0} = -V(\mathbf{x})^T \nabla I(\mathbf{x}) \triangleq (V \circ I)(\mathbf{x}). \tag{7}$$

Here, $V \circ I$ denotes the *action of* V *on* I, which produces a scalar map, whose value at $\mathbf{x}$ equals the negated inner product between the velocity $V(\mathbf{x})$ and the image gradient $\nabla I(\mathbf{x})$. Clearly, the action of V is a linear operation on I.

Given a basis $\mathcal{B}$, we can write V in form of a linear combination as $V = \sum_{k=1}^{K} \alpha^k B_k$. Consequently, we can rewrite Eq.(7) into

$$\left.\frac{dI_t(\mathbf{x})}{dt}\right|_{t=0} = \sum_{k=1}^{K} \alpha^k (B_k \circ I)(\mathbf{x}). \tag{8}$$

This equation establishes the linear isomorphism between the Lie algebraic representation and the image changes due to deformation. Specifically, the infinitesimal changes generated by a deformation $V = \sum_{k=1}^{K} \alpha^k B_k$ can be expressed as a linear combination of the "base changes" – those generated by the base deformations – with the same set of coefficients $\alpha_1, \ldots, \alpha_K$.

3.3 Parallel Transport

In general, a deformation group is associated with a specific object, which can not be directly applied to a different object (*e.g.* a transformed version of the object). However, one can adapt a deformation group via the *parallel transport* of the associated Lie algebra, enabling its application to different objects.

Consider an object being deformed, which are observed from two different views. The point at $\mathbf{x}$ from the first view is transformed to $\mathbf{x}' = T\mathbf{x}$ from the second view. Suppose this point has velocity $\mathbf{v}$ at $t = 0$ from the first view, then *what is the velocity of the corresponding point, i.e.* $T\mathbf{x}$*, from the second view?* The derivation below shows the answer:

$$\mathbf{v}' := \lim_{\delta t \to 0} \frac{T(\mathbf{x} + \mathbf{v}\delta t) - T(\mathbf{x})}{\delta t} = \mathbf{J}_T(\mathbf{x})\mathbf{v}. \tag{9}$$

Here, $\mathbf{J}_T(\mathbf{x})$ is the Jacobian matrix of T at $\mathbf{x}$. Here $\mathbf{v}'$ is called the *parallel transport* of $\mathbf{v}$ *w.r.t.* the transform T. The parallel transport can be applied to an entire velocity field V, resulting in a new velocity field $T \bullet V$, given by

$$(T \bullet V)(T\mathbf{x}) = \mathbf{J}_T(\mathbf{x})V(\mathbf{x}). \tag{10}$$

The parallel transports are *covariant* with the inducing transforms, meaning that they satisfy two properties below: (1) the parallel transport induced by an identity transform in itself is an identity, and (2) the parallel transport induced by a composition of two transforms equals the composition of the transports respectively induced, as $(T_2T_1) \bullet V = T_2 \bullet (T_1 \bullet V)$.

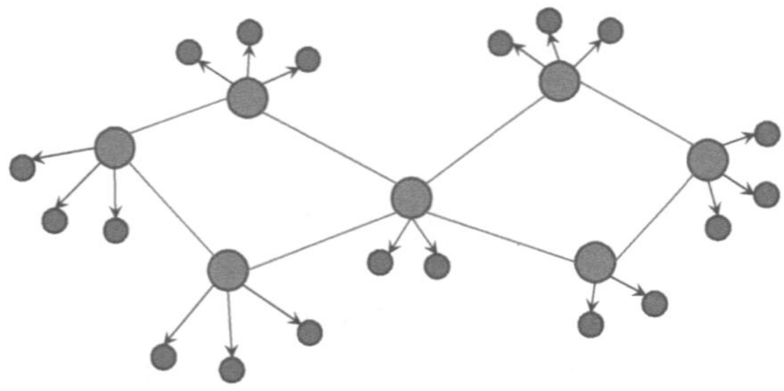

Fig. 2. This figure shows the two-level formulation of the proposed optimization formulation. At the first level, each center image (depicted by blue circles) are connected to all its neighbors (red circles) within the same cluster, and at the second level, different centers are connected via parallel transport constraints.

4 Model Estimation Algorithm

In this section, we formulate an optimization problem to estimate the deformation groups for a specific class of objects, given a set of images, and thereon derive an algorithm that jointly solves the basis of the deformation groups and the Lie algebraic coefficients for the training samples.

4.1 Two-Level Formulation

Given a set of n images, we first group them into m clusters, using K-medoid, where each cluster has a *center image.* The number of clusters m is chosen via cross validation, such that all samples within a cluster are close enough to the corresponding center. Suppose the i-th cluster contains n_i samples. For this cluster, we use $I_{i,0}$ to denote the center image of this, and $I_{i,j}$ (with $j = 1, \ldots, n_i$) to the j-th non-center image. Here, we consider each center image as the representation of the canonical shape of an object, and other images in the same cluster as generated by deforming the center image.

As discussed in previous section, a deformation group can be characterized by a Lie algebra. With the Lie algebraic characterization the problem of learning the deformation groups reduces to the one of estimating the Lie algebraic basis for each cluster. Here, we denote the basis for the i-th cluster by $\mathcal{B}_i = (B_{i,1}, \ldots, B_{i,K})$. To estimate these basis, we formulate an optimization problem, of which the objective function comprises two levels of terms, as shown in Figure 2.

Within-Cluster Level. Applying the deformation group characterized by the Lie algebraic basis $\mathcal{B}_i$ to the image $I_{i,0}$ yields a K-dimensional manifold comprised of all the deformed images, denoted by $G(\mathcal{B}_i) \circ I_{i,0}$, as

$$G(\mathcal{B}_i) \circ I_{i,0} \triangleq \{\exp(V) \circ I_{i,0} : V \in \mathfrak{g}(\mathcal{B}_i)\}. \tag{11}$$

Here, $\mathfrak{g}(\mathcal{B}_i)$ denotes the Lie algebraic space spanned by $\mathcal{B}_i$. With the assumption that $I_{i,j}$ is generated by deforming $I_{i,0}$, we expect that the $I_{i,j}$ is close to $G(\mathcal{B}_i) \circ I_{i,0}$. Particularly, the distance from $I_{i,j}$ to $G(\mathcal{B}_i) \circ I_{i,0}$ is given by

$$\operatorname{dist}(I_{i,j}, G(\mathcal{B}_i) \circ I_{i,0}) = \min_{\boldsymbol{\alpha}} \left\| I_{i,j} - \exp\left(\sum_{k=1}^{K} \alpha^k B_{i,k}\right) \circ I_{i,0} \right\|. \tag{12}$$

When the deformed image $I_{i,j}$ is close to the center $I_{i,0}$, the coefficients are small. Consequently, by Eq.(8), we can approximately write

$$\exp\left(\sum_{k=1}^{K} \alpha^k B_{i,k}\right) \circ I_{i,0} \simeq I_{i,0} + \sum_{k=1}^{K} \alpha^k (B_{i,k} \circ I_{i,0}). \tag{13}$$

As a result, we have

$$\begin{aligned}
\operatorname{dist}(I_{i,j}, G(\mathcal{B}_i) \circ I_{i,0})^2 &\simeq \min_{\boldsymbol{\alpha}} \left\| (I_{i,j} - I_{i,0}) - \sum_{k=1}^{K} \alpha^k (B_{i,k} \circ I_{i,0}) \right\|^2 \\
&= \min_{\boldsymbol{\alpha}} \sum_{\mathbf{x} \in \mathcal{D}} \left((I_{i,j}(\mathbf{x}) - I_{i,0}(\mathbf{x})) + \sum_{k=1}^{K} \alpha^k B_{i,k}(\mathbf{x})^T \nabla I_{i,0}(\mathbf{x}) \right)^2 .
\end{aligned} \tag{14}$$

Here, $\mathcal{D}$ is the set of all observable pixel locations. For convenience, we define

$$Q_{ij}(\mathcal{B}_i, \boldsymbol{\alpha}_{i,j}) = \left\| (I_{i,j} - I_{i,0}) - \sum_{k=1}^{K} \alpha_{i,j}^k (B_{i,k} \circ I_{i,0}) \right\|^2 . \tag{15}$$

Note that Q_{ij} is quadratic *w.r.t.* $\boldsymbol{\alpha}_{i,j}$. Hence, the optimal coefficients that yield the minimum (approximate) distance can be readily solved, given $\mathcal{B}_i$.

Inter-cluster Level. The basis associated with different groups are related to each other via parallel transport. Specifically, we establish a higher-level network between cluster centers, where each center image is connected to several *neighboring centers*, *i.e.* other centers that are not too far from it, such that the optical flow between them can be reliably estimated.

For each pair of neighboring centers $I_{i,0}$ and $I_{i',0}$, we estimate the dense correspondence between them $T_{ii'}$ and $T_{i'i}$, using an optical flow algorithm [14]. Ideally, we would expect the basis $\mathcal{B}_i$ to be the transported version of $\mathcal{B}_{i'}$ *w.r.t.* the transform $T_{i'i} = T_{ii'}^{-1}$, *i.e.* $B_{i,k} = T_{ii'}^{-1} \bullet B_{i',k}$, and vice versa. As some errors may arise in optical flow estimation, we use the quadratic term as follows to penalize the deviation from this relation:

$$H_{ii'}(\mathcal{B}_i, \mathcal{B}_{i'}) = \sum_{k=1}^{K} \| B_{ik} - T_{ii'}^{-1} \bullet B_{i',k} \|^2 \tag{16}$$

Here, we have

$$\| B_{ik} - T_{ii'}^{-1} \bullet B_{i,k} \|^2 = \sum_{\mathbf{x} \in \mathcal{D} \cap T_{ii'}(\mathcal{D})} \| B_{ik}(\mathbf{x}) - \mathbf{J}_{T_{ii'}}(T_{ii'}(\mathbf{x})) B_{i'k}(T_{ii'}(\mathbf{x})) \|. \tag{17}$$

Here, $T_{ii'}(\mathbf{x})$ is the location of the pixel on $I_{i',0}$ that corresponds to the pixel at $\mathbf{x}$ of $I_{i,0}$. In general, $T_{ii'}(\mathbf{x})$ does not yield integer coordinates. Under such circumstances, linear interpolation can be used to derive the values of $\mathbf{J}_{T_{ii'}}(T_{ii'}(\mathbf{x}))$ and $B_{ik}(T_{ii'}(\mathbf{x}))$. In addition, $\mathbf{x} \notin T_{ii'}(\mathcal{D})$ indicates that the pixel at $\mathbf{x}$ of $I_{i,0}$ is transformed outside of the observable region, and thus the corresponding term is not included.

Joint Formulation. Integrating the terms at both levels, we derive the joint objective function as follows.

$$L(\mathcal{B}) = \sum_{i=1}^{m} \sum_{j=1}^{n_i} \min_{\boldsymbol{\alpha}} Q_{ij}(\mathcal{B}_i, \boldsymbol{\alpha}) + \gamma \sum_{i=1}^{m} \sum_{i' \in \mathcal{N}_i} H_{ii'}(\mathcal{B}_i, \mathcal{B}'_i). \tag{18}$$

Here, $\mathcal{N}_i$ is a set consisting of the indices of $I_{i,0}$'s neighboring centers, and γ is a positive weight that controls the contribution of the parallel transport constraints. To minimize this function, we introduce an auxiliary function that involves $\boldsymbol{\alpha}_{i,j}$ as arguments:

$$L_{aux}(\mathcal{B}, \boldsymbol{\alpha}) = \sum_{i=1}^{m} \sum_{j=1}^{n_i} Q_{ij}(\mathcal{B}_i, \boldsymbol{\alpha}_{i,j}) + \gamma \sum_{i=1}^{m} \sum_{i' \in \mathcal{N}_i} H_{ii'}(\mathcal{B}_i, \mathcal{B}'_i). \tag{19}$$

Obviously, L_{aux} gives an upper bound of L and has

$$L(\mathcal{B}) = \min_{\alpha} L_{aux}(\mathcal{B}, \boldsymbol{\alpha}). \tag{20}$$

Consequently, $L(\mathcal{B})$ can be optimized by alternating the updates of $\boldsymbol{\alpha}$ and $\mathcal{B}$:

$$\hat{\boldsymbol{\alpha}}_{i,j}^{(t)} \leftarrow \underset{\boldsymbol{\alpha}}{\operatorname{argmin}}\ Q_{ij}(\mathcal{B}_i^{(t-1)}, \boldsymbol{\alpha}), \tag{21}$$

$$\hat{\mathcal{B}}_i^{(t)} \leftarrow \underset{\mathcal{B}}{\operatorname{argmin}}\ \sum_{j=1}^{n_i} Q_{ij}(\mathcal{B}, \boldsymbol{\alpha}_{i,j}^{(t)}) + \gamma \sum_{i' \in \mathcal{N}_i} H_{ii'}(\mathcal{B}_i, \mathcal{B}_{i'}). \tag{22}$$

Note that the value of $L_{aux}(\mathcal{B}, \boldsymbol{\alpha})$ decreases with each updating step. Particularly, the values of L and L_{aux} become equal each time when $\boldsymbol{\alpha}$ is updated to the optima, *i.e.* $L(\mathcal{B}^{(t)}) = L_{aux}(\mathcal{B}^{(t)}, \boldsymbol{\alpha}^{(t+1)})$.

4.2 Initialization

While L_{aux} is convex *w.r.t.* $\mathcal{B}$ and $\boldsymbol{\alpha}$ respectively, this is not a convex optimization problem jointly. Hence, appropriate initialization is crucial as to obtaining a reasonably good solution. Here, we describe a simple yet effective scheme to initialize the the basis $\mathcal{B}$.

We choose a particular cluster as the "standard cluster", and compute the optical flow [14] from the center of this standard cluster to the centers of other clusters. With these optical flows, we can warp the images in other clusters towards the standard one. For example, suppose $I_{1,0}$ is selected as the standard, and the optical flow from $I_{1,0}$ to $I_{2,0}$ is T_{12}, then we warp each image in the second cluster as $I'_{2,j} = T_{12}^{-1}(I_{2,j})$ for $j = 0, 1, \ldots, n_2$. In this way, for each non-standard cluster, we acquire a warped center as well as a set of warped images, which are considered as generated by deforming the warped center.

At the initialization stage, we assume that the standard cluster and the warped clusters share the same basis. To estimate this basis, we compute the optical flow fields from the standard center to other images in the standard cluster, and those from each warped center to other images in the corresponding cluster. All these flow fields can be roughly considered as residing near the space spanned by the shared basis. Therefore, the basis can be estimated by applying principal component analysis (PCA) to these optical flow fields pooled together. After the basis associated with the standard cluster is initialized, the bases for other clusters can be readily obtained via parallel transport.

5 Experiments

Given the learned prototypes and deformation bases, we now have a generative model for images. In this section, we apply our deformation model to two vision tasks: (1) handwritten character recognition with training sets of varying sizes, and (2) synthesis of digits and human faces. These experiments demonstrate the utility of the proposed method on both discriminative and generative tasks.

5.1 Handwritten Digit Recognition

On the popular MNIST [15] dataset, state-of-the-art algorithms can achieve very high accuracy (with error rates less than 0.5%). However, these methods usually rely on a large training set that densely cover all possible variations of each character. Actually, in such a training set, one can find very close matches to most testing samples. Consequently, a simple K-Nearest Neighbor (KNN) method [4] with a properly chosen metric suffices to achieve a very low error rate. However, a large data set is often cumbersome in practice, and methods relying on dense data set are difficult to generalize. In this experiment, we compare the proposed approach with several widely used algorithms in handwritten digit recognition. As we will see, the results obtained on training sets of varying sizes show that a structured deformation model can improve generalizability, making it possible to maintain an comparably effective model with much smaller number of prototypes. We compare four methods in the experiments:

1. **L2**: Find the nearest sample in terms of Euclidean distance in the feature space, and classify the testing sample to the resultant sample's class.
2. **TD**: Construct a tangent space for each training sample using a set of pre-defined bases, and find the closest tangent spaces to a given testing sample. This method is known as *Tangent Distance* [5].
3. **IDM**: This is a well-known method proposed by Keysers *et al.* [4], which was the best-performing method on MNIST. The basic idea is to divide an image into small patches, with each patch matched to the closest patch in a training image. The patch is allowed to move within a small window during the matching.
4. **DL-PT**: Use the proposed deformation model. With a learned model, a tangent space is associated with each prototype. The bases for different prototypes are different, but they are related through *parallel transport.*

In addition, two image features are considered: *pixel intensities (pix)* and *Sobel gradients (sob).*

For each method, the training is performed on a training set of varying sizes, with the purpose of testing their generalizability. In particular, for our deformation model, the prototypes are found by K-medoid clustering, while the associated bases are jointly learned with the parallel transport relations taken into account. Here, the dimension of each tangent space (*i.e.* the size of the basis) is determined empirically (through PCA with 90% of the variation preserved in the principal subspace). Note that our focus here is to test the effectiveness of the deformation model instead of comparing classifiers. Hence, we use best-match strategy for each method. However, one can adapt more powerful classifiers, such as Support Vector Machine (SVM) and Convolutional Networks to further improve the recognition accuracy.

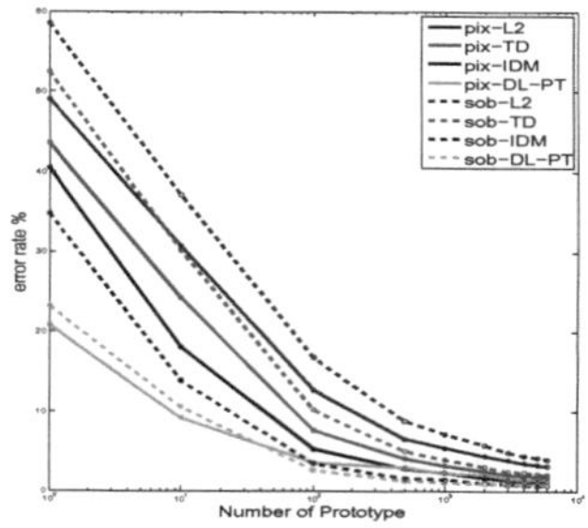

Fig. 3. Filled Line: Recognition error on MNIST dataset with pixel intensity as the feature; Dashed Line: Recognition error on MNIST dataset with Sobel gradients as the feature

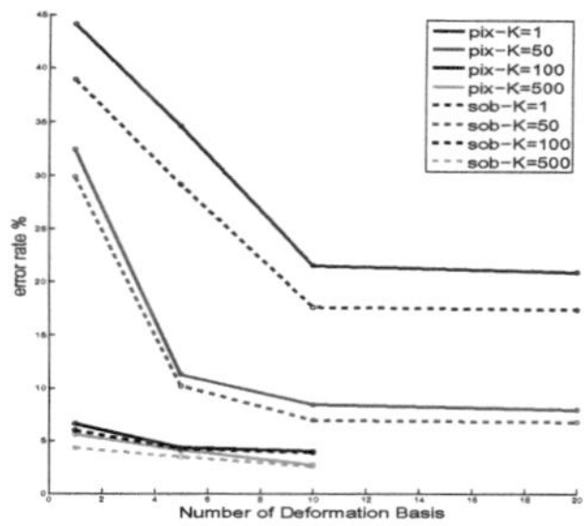

Fig. 4. Filled Line: Recognition error on MNIST dataset with pixel intensity as the feature; Dashed Line: Recognition error on MNIST dataset with Sobel gradients as the feature

Figure 3 shows that when the training set is small, all methods make a considerable amount of errors, and the error rates decrease as the training set grows. We can see that with a structured deformation model, the error rate yielded by the proposed method clearly drops faster than that by other methods. This is partly ascribed to the fact that statistical strength is shared among local models via parallel transport constraints.

In the second experiment, we vary both the number of prototypes and the number of deformation basis to investigate their influence in classification performance. In Figure 4, each colored curve corresponds to the error rate for a given number of prototypes and the x-axis of each point on the curve represents the number of deformation basis selected for each digit. As expected, increasing the number of local components (*i.e.* a prototype together with its tangent space) and the tangent space dimension generally leads to better classification performance. In addition, we notice that the performance becomes stable as the number of local components increases beyond a threshold (about 500), which is clearly much smaller than the size of the entire training set.

5.2 Image Synthesis

While many image synthesis experiments are designed to demonstrate super resolution results which are appealing from a human perceptual standpoint, our primary purpose is different. We instead wish to show that the learned basis, which is shared across the manifold, are meaningful from a geometric perspective.

Digit Synthesis. Given the digit manifold learned from MNIST dataset, we synthesize new images of digits by generating samples from a randomly selected local component with random Lie algebraic coefficients. In particular, given a

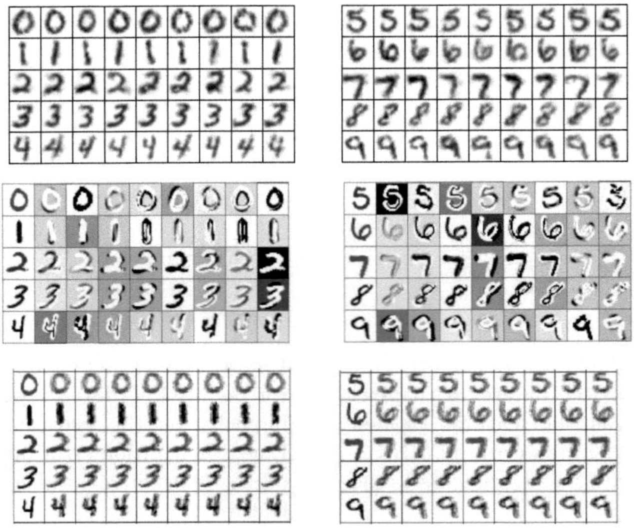

Fig. 5. Synthesized digits from the learned digit deformation manifold. The first digit in the row is the prototype; the rest are locally deformed from the prototype with a random coefficients of the learned basis

coefficient vector, a sample can be generated through integration along a geodesic on the learned manifold.

The top row of Figure 5 shows the sampled prototype of each digit in the first column and synthesized new digit images in the rest of each row. One can see that the synthesized images reflect local variations which the global affine transforms are not able to explain. For example, for digit "2", we can see that there are some basis related to the size of the lower left circle of the digit. For comparison, we plot the synthesis results using Tangent Distance (TD) [5] (whose bases are pre-defined rather than being learned) in the middle row and that using IDM (averaging over the randomly shifted patches of the image)

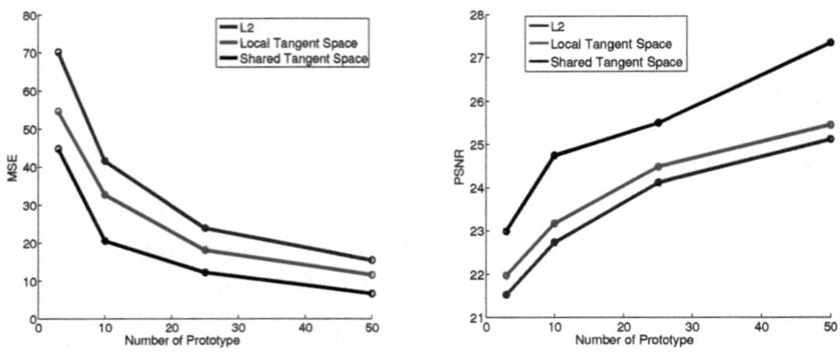

Fig. 6. Comparison of reconstruction performance on face synthesis

in the bottom row. Note that TD makes a combination of rigid transformation, hyperbolic deformations and intensity deformations to the prototype, while IDM only changes the detail of the prototype.

Face Synthesis. In addition, we learn a face manifold using the face dataset of Brendan Frey, containing around $2,000$ grayscale images of size 20×28 in different expressions and angles of view. For this experiment, we first learn the commonly shared basis to construct the manifold from $1,000$ sampled images. Then, for a separate set of randomly sampled 500 testing images, we try to see how close they can be projected onto the manifold. We tested three different algorithms for reconstruction: nearest training image in Euclidean metric, closest projection onto tangent spaces and closest projection onto our connected deformation manifold with shared basis. Again, we test our results with a varying number of prototypes. Figure 6 shows that, in terms of both Euclidean distance and PSNR ratio, the reconstruction from the manifold with a learned shared basis is consistently better than those learned independently from training examples. Note that the images are small and many reconstruction errors are not obviously perceivable. Consequently, we feel that a quantitative evaluation is more appropriate than showing the reconstructed faces.

6 Conclusion

We have presented a new method for manifold learning over images. The method is distinct from previous approaches in that the model explicitly incorporates a local Lie algebraic representation of deformations combined with a consistency relation derived from the parallel transport property. While previous methods consider local tangent spaces parameterized by a deformation basis, the methods of which we are aware utilize a hand crafted basis in contrast to the presented method which learns the basis. This process was enabled by exploiting the parallel transport property which imposes geometric consistency across local tangent spaces and effectively leverages the full training set (rather than local clusters) for learning properties of the deformation manifold. An efficient coordinate descent algorithm was presented along with a suggested initialization procedure. Empirical results demonstrating the utility of the methodology were presnted for hand written character recognition and synthesis as well as human face reconstruction.

Acknowledgement. D. Wei was partially supported by ONR MURI grant N00014-09-1-1051. D. Lin was partially supported by the Office of Naval Research Multidisciplinary Research Initiative (MURI) program, award N000141110688. J. Fisher was partially supported by DARPA award FA8650-11-1-7154.

References

1. Tenenbaum, J., Silva, V., Langford, J.: A global geometric framework for nonlinear dimensionality reduction. Science 290, 2319 (2000)
2. Roweis, S., Saul, L.: Nonlinear dimensionality reduction by locally linear embedding. Science 290, 2323 (2000)
3. Belongie, S., Malik, J., Puzicha, J.: Shape context: A new descriptor for shape matching and object recognition. In: Advances in Neural Information Processing Systems, pp. 831–837 (2001)
4. Keysers, D., Deselaers, T., Gollan, C., Ney, H.: Deformation models for image recognition. IEEE Trans. on Pattern Analysis and Machine Intelligence 29, 1422–1435 (2007)
5. Simard, P., Cun, Y.L., Denker, J., Victorri, B.: Transformation invariance in pattern recognition: Tangent distance and tangent propagation. International Journal of Imaging Systems and Technology 11, 181–197 (2000)
6. Hastie, T., Simard, P.: Metrics and models for handwritten character recognition. Statistical Science, 54–65 (1998)
7. Keysers, D., Macherey, W., Ney, H., Dahmen, J.: Adaptation in statistical pattern recognition using tangent vectors. IEEE Transactions on Pattern Analysis and Machine Intelligence 26, 269–274 (2004)
8. Frey, B., Jojic, N.: Transformed component analysis: Joint estimation of spatial transformations and image components. In: The Proceedings of the Seventh IEEE International Conference on Computer Vision, vol. 2, pp. 1190–1196. IEEE (1999)
9. Frey, B., Jojic, N.: Estimating mixture models of images and inferring spatial transformations using the em algorithm. In: IEEE Computer Society Conference on Computer Vision and Pattern Recognition, vol. 1. IEEE (1999)
10. Frey, B., Jojic, N.: Transformation-invariant clustering using the em algorithm. IEEE Transactions on Pattern Analysis and Machine Intelligence 25, 1–17 (2003)
11. Miller, E., Matsakis, N., Viola, P.: Learning from one example through shared densities on transforms. In: Proceedings of the IEEE Conference on Computer Vision and Pattern Recognition, vol. 1, pp. 464–471. IEEE (2000)
12. Cootes, T., Edwards, G., Taylor, C.: Active appearance models. IEEE Transactions on Pattern Analysis and Machine Intelligence 23, 681–685 (2001)
13. Jones, M., Poggio, T.: Multidimensional morphable models: A framework for representing and matching object classes. International Journal of Computer Vision 29, 107–131 (1998)
14. Bruhn, A., Weickert, J., Schnörr, C.: Lucas/kanade meets horn/schunck: Combining local and global optic flow methods. International Journal of Computer Vision 61, 211–231 (2005)
15. LeCun, Y.: Mnist handwritten digit database. AT&T Labs (Online) (1998), `http://yann.lecun.com/exdb/mnist`

Multi-channel Shape-Flow Kernel Descriptors for Robust Video Event Detection and Retrieval

Pradeep Natarajan, Shuang Wu, Shiv Vitaladevuni, Xiaodan Zhuang, Unsang Park, Rohit Prasad, and Premkumar Natarajan

Speech, Language and Multimedia Business Unit,
Raytheon BBN Technologies, Cambridge, MA 02138
{pradeepn,swu,svitalad,xzhuang,upark,rprasad,pnatarajan}@bbn.com

Abstract. Despite the success of spatio-temporal visual features, they are hand-designed and aggregate image or flow gradients using a pre-specified, uniform set of orientation bins. Kernel descriptors [1] generalize such orientation histograms by defining match kernels over image patches, and have shown superior performance for visual object and scene recognition. In our work, we make two contributions: first, we extend kernel descriptors to the spatio-temporal domain to model salient flow, gradient and texture patterns in video. Further, we apply our kernel descriptors to extract features from different color channels. Second, we present a fast algorithm for kernel descriptor computation of $O(1)$ complexity for each pixel in each video patch, producing two orders of magnitude speedup over conventional kernel descriptors and other popular motion features. Our evaluation results on TRECVID MED 2011 dataset indicate that the proposed multi-channel shape-flow kernel descriptors outperform several other features including SIFT, SURF, STIP and Color SIFT.

Keywords: Kernel Descriptor, Multi-channel, Low Level Feature, Video Event Detection, TRECVID.

1 Introduction

The widespread availability of cheap hand-held cameras and video sharing websites such as YouTube has resulted in massive amounts of video content online. The ability to rapidly analyze and summarize content from such videos entails a wide range of applications. Significant effort has been made in recent literature to develop such techniques [2][3][4][5]. However, the sheer volume of such content as well as the challenges in analyzing videos introduce significant scalability challenges in applying successful bag-of-words approaches [6] used in image retrieval.

Features such as STIP [7] and HoG3D [8] that extend image level features to the spatio-temporal domain have shown promise in recognizing actions from unstructured videos [8][9]. These features discretize the gradient or optical flow

A. Fitzgibbon et al. (Eds.): ECCV 2012, Part II, LNCS 7573, pp. 301–314, 2012.

orientations into a d-dimensional indicator vector $\delta(z)$=$[\delta_1(z),\ldots,\delta_d(z)]$ with

$$\delta_i(z) = \begin{cases} 1 & \text{if } \lfloor \frac{d\theta(z)}{2\pi} \rfloor = i - 1 \\ 0 & \text{otherwise} \end{cases} \tag{1}$$

Despite their success, these features are hand designed and do not utilize full information available in measuring patch similarity. In recent work, several efforts have been made to develop principled approaches to design and learn such low-level features. In [10], a convolutional GRBM method was proposed to extract spatio-temporal features using a multi-stage architecture. In [11], a convolutional independent subspace analysis (ISA) network was proposed to extract patch level features from pixel attributes.

These deep learning approaches are in effect mapping pixel attributes into patch level features using a hierarchical architecture. In [12], a two layer hierarchical sparse coding scheme is used for learning image representations at the pixel level. The orientation histogram in (1) in effect uses a pre-defined d-dimensional codebook that divides the θ space into uniform bins, and uses hard quantization for projecting pixel gradients. In contrast [12] allows data driven learning of pixel level dictionaries, and the pixel features are projected to the learnt dictionary using sparse coding to get a vector $W(z)$=$(w_1(z),\ldots,w_d(z))$. After pooling such pixel level projections within local regions, the first layer codes are passed to the second layer for jointly encoding signals in the region. The orientation histograms and hierarchical sparse coding in effect define the following kernel for measuring the similarity between two patches P and Q:

$$K(P,Q) = F_h(P)^\top F_h(Q) = \sum_{z \in P} \sum_{z' \in Q} \tilde{m}(z)\tilde{m}(z')\Phi(z)^\top \Phi(z') \tag{2}$$

where

- $F_h(P)$=$\sum_{z \in P} \tilde{m}(z)\Phi(z)$ is the patch sum
- $\tilde{m}(z)$=$m(z)/\sqrt{\sum_{z \in P} m(z)^2 + \epsilon_g}$ is the normalized gradient magnitude with ϵ_g a small constant, and
- $\Phi(z)$=$\delta(z)$ for HoG and $\Phi(z)$=$W(z)$ for hierarchical sparse coding.

The kernel descriptors proposed in [1] generalize these approaches by replacing the product $\Phi(z)^\top \Phi(z')$ in equation (2) with a match kernel $k(z,z')$ and allows us to induce arbitrary feature spaces $\Phi(z)$ (including infinite dimensional) from pixel level attributes. This provides a powerful framework for designing rich low-level features and has shown state-of-the-art results for image and object recognition [1][13].

A crucial limitation of kernel descriptors is that kernel computations are costly and hence it is slow to extract them from densely sampled video patches. In our work, we present a fast algorithm for kernel descriptor computation that takes $O(1)$ operations per pixel in each patch, based on pre-computed kernel values. This speeds up the kernel descriptor features under consideration, to levels that are comparable with D-SIFT[14] and color SIFT[15], and two orders of magnitude faster than STIP[16] and HoG3D[8]. In contrast, the kernel descriptor computation in [1] is 4× and 10×slower than SIFT, for gradient and LBP based kernel descriptors respectively. Furthermore, we apply kernel descriptors to extract gradient, flow and texture based features for video analysis. We test our approach on a large database of internet videos used in the TRECVID MED 2011 evaluations, and compare the proposed kernel descriptors with a large set of image and motion based features. Our flow based kernel descriptors are up to two orders of magnitude faster than STIP and HoG3D, and also produce significant performance improvements. Further, using features from multiple color planes produces small but consistent gains.

The rest of the paper is organized as follows - we provide an overview of kernel descriptors in section 2, describe video specific features we extract in our experiments in section 3, present a fast feature computation algorithm in section 4, describe feature representation and early and late fusion techniques we use in section 5, and present experimental results in section 6.

2 Kernel Descriptors

Kernel descriptors [1] provide a unified framework for turning pixel level attributes such as gradients into patch level features, by highlighting the kernel view of orientation histogram features such as SIFT and HoG. Feature extraction using kernel descriptors involves three steps: (1) designing kernels for matching patches using pixel attributes; (2) learning a compact set of basis vectors using kernel principal component analysis (KPCA); (3) constructing kernel descriptors by projecting the infinite-dimensional feature vectors induced by pixel attributes to the learned basis vectors.

Following the notations in [1], the gradient match kernel $K_{grad}(P, Q)$ measures the similarity between patches P and Q based on the pixel gradient attribute:

$$K_{grad}(P, Q) = \sum_{z \in P} \sum_{z' \in Q} \tilde{m}(z)\tilde{m}(z')k_o(\tilde{\theta}_z, \tilde{\theta}_{z'})k_p(z, z') \tag{3}$$

where z denotes the 2D position of a pixel in an image patch normalized to [0,1] and $\tilde{\theta}_z$ is the normalized gradient vector defined as:

$$\tilde{\theta}_z = [sin(\theta(z)), cos(\theta(z))] \tag{4}$$

The position kernel k_p and orientation kernel k_o are defined using Gaussian kernels as:

$$\begin{aligned} k_p(z, z') &= e^{-\gamma_p ||z-z'||^2} \\ k_o(\tilde{\theta}_z, \tilde{\theta}_{z'}) &= e^{-\gamma_o ||\tilde{\theta}(z) - \tilde{\theta}(z')||^2} \end{aligned} \tag{5}$$

Based on the patch similarity kernel defined in equation (3), kernel descriptors extract compact low-dimensional features by sampling sufficient basis vectors uniformly and densely from each pixel attribute's support region, and then learning compact basis vectors using KPCA. Thus, the gradient kernel descriptor for a patch P will have the form:

$$F^t_{grad}(P) = \sum_{i=1}^{d_o}\sum_{j=1}^{d_p} \alpha^t_{ij}\left\{\sum_{z\in P}\tilde{m}(z)k_o(\tilde{\theta}(z),x_i)k_p(z,y_j)\right\} \quad (6)$$

where $\{x_i\}_{i=1}^{d_o}$ and $\{y_j\}_{j=1}^{d_p}$ are uniformly sampled from the corresponding support regions and d_o and d_p are the sizes of the basis vectors for the orientation and position kernels respectively. Similarly, a match kernel based on local binary pattern (LBP)[17] is defined in [1] as:

$$F^t_{LBP}(P) = \sum_{i=1}^{d_l}\sum_{j=1}^{d_p} \alpha^t_{ij}\left\{\sum_{z\in P}\tilde{s}(z)k_l(b(z),x_i)k_p(z,y_j)\right\} \quad (7)$$

where $\tilde{s}(z){=}s(z)/\sqrt{\sum_{z\in P}s(z)^2+\epsilon_s}$ is the standard deviation of the pixel values in the $3{\times}3$ neighborhood of z, ϵ_s is a small constant and $b(z)$ is the 8-dimensional LBP vector at z as defined in [17]. The set of all possible $2^8{=}256$ LBP vectors is chosen as the basis vector set and k_l is defined using an RBF kernel similar to 5.

The coefficients α^t_{ij} are learned through kernel principal component analysis as follows:

$$\begin{aligned}\mathbf{K}_{ijst} &= k_o(x_i,x_j)k_p(y_s,y_t)\\ \mathbf{K}_c &= \mathbf{K} - \mathbf{1}_N\mathbf{K} - \mathbf{K}\mathbf{1}_N + \mathbf{1}_N\mathbf{K}\mathbf{1}_N\\ \mathbf{K}_c\alpha^t &= \lambda^t\alpha^t\end{aligned} \quad (8)$$

where $\mathbf{K}$ is the kernel matrix, $\mathbf{K}_c$ is the centered kernel matrix, and 1_N denotes a $N{\times}N$ matrix with each element taking value $1/N$. Thus, α^t correspond to the eigenvectors of the centered kernel matrix $\mathbf{K}_c$.

3 Multi-channel Gradient Flow Kernel Descriptors

We extract kernel descriptors using image and optical flow gradients from a dense grid of spatio-temporal patches. In our experiments we consider the following six features.

Grayscale Gradient Descriptors (Gray KDES-G): These features are extracted from the gradients L_x and L_y computed along the x and y directions, on gray scale image frames sampled from a video. We extract kernel descriptors based on equation (6) for each patch.

Grayscale Flow Descriptors (Gray KDES-F): These features are extracted from the optical flow fields F_x and F_y computed from adjacent frames in different temporal locations of the video. F_x and F_y are then used to estimate orientations θ at different pixel locations for computing the gradient kernel descriptors.

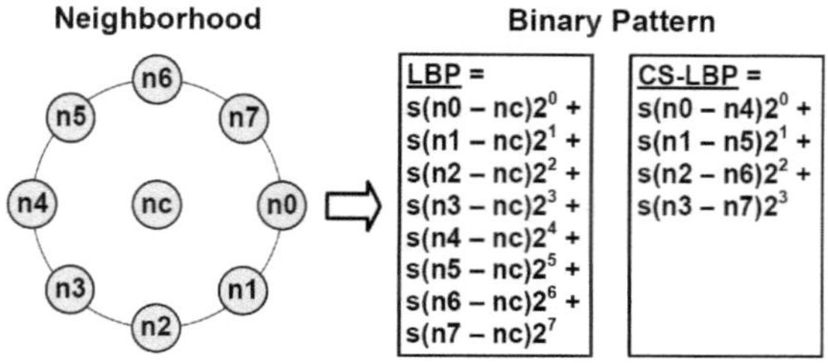

Fig. 1. Schematic comparing LBP and CS-LBP [18]

Grayscale Gradient+Flow Descriptors (Gray KDES-FG): These features combine gradient and flow information, by concatenating the Gray KDES-G and Gray KDES-F descriptors at each video patch.

Grayscale LBP Descriptors (Gray KDES-L): We extracted LBP features [17] from the intensity values of grayscale frames and used them within the kernel descriptor framework as described in [1].

Grayscale Center Surround LBP Descriptors (Gray KDES-CL): The number of basis vectors for the joint LBP-position kernel in equation (7) is $256\times25=6400$. Applying KPCA on the joint set results in too many components that slows down feature extraction, while using a fixed, small number of components (such as 200 in [1]) results in poor approximation of the space. In our work we used a variant of LBP called center-symmetric LBP (CS-LBP)[18] that extracts a 4-dimensional binary vector from a pixel's neighborhood (See Figure 1.). This space has $16\times25=400$ dimensions and KPCA produces better approximation of the space with fewer principal components.

Color Gradient Descriptors (Color KDES-G): We first split the frame images sampled from video to constituent color planes. In our experiments we used the (R,G,B) planes, but we can use other color channels too. We then extract KDES-G features from the gradients computed on each plane. For each patch, we concatenate the KDES-G features from the different color planes.

Color Flow Descriptors (Color KDES-F): We compute these features from the optical flow fields computed in each color plane and then concatenate the KDES-F features from different color planes for each video patch.

Color Gradient+Flow Descriptors (Color KDES-FG): For these features we concatenate the Color KDES-G and Color KDES-F features for each video patch.

Color LBP Descriptors (Color KDES-L): These features extract KDES-L features from each of the (R,G,B) channels.

Color Center Surround LBP Descriptors (Color KDES-CL): These features are similar to Gray KDES-CL, but are extracted from each of the (R,G,B) channels.

For our experiments, we uniformly sample every 50 frames from each video, and compute the descriptors from patches of size $16\times16\times1$, $25\times25\times1$ and $31\times31\times1$ on an evenly spaced grid of 8 pixels.

4 Fast Computation of Kernel Descriptors

The major bottleneck in computing kernel descriptors is in evaluating the kernel function $k_o k_p$ in equation (6). The naive approach of computing the product for each (x_i, y_j) would cost $d_o d_p$ kernel computations. We can minimize the number of calls to costly kernel computation functions by computing the two kernel values separately at cost $d_o + d_p$, but computation of the sum in equation (6) still costs $O(d_o d_p)$ for each pixel $z \in P$. In this section we will describe our approach to compute the kernel sum at each pixel in $O(1)$ time.

Let $\mathbf{K}_o$ and $\mathbf{K}_p$ be the kernel matrices defined over the orientation and position basis vectors respectively:

$$\mathbf{K}_{o,ij} = k_o(x_i, x_j) \quad \mathbf{K}_{p,st} = k_p(y_s, y_t) \tag{9}$$

Let $\mathbf{K}_{o,c}$ and $\mathbf{K}_{p,c}$ denote the corresponding centered orientation and position kernel matrices. Then from the definitions in (8) and (9) we have

$$\mathbf{K}_{o,c} \otimes \mathbf{K}_{p,c} \alpha^t = \lambda^t \alpha^t \tag{10}$$

where $\otimes$ denotes the Kronecker product. Since the kernel matrices $\mathbf{K}_{o,c}$ and $\mathbf{K}_{p,c}$ are symmetric positive definite, we have

$$\begin{aligned} \mathbf{K}_{o,c} \otimes \mathbf{K}_{p,c} &= [U_{o,c}^\top S_{o,c} U_{o,c}] \otimes [U_{p,c}^\top S_{p,c} U_{p,c}] \\ &= [U_{o,c} \otimes U_{p,c}]^\top [S_{o,c} \otimes S_{p,c}][U_{o,c} \otimes U_{p,c}] \end{aligned} \tag{11}$$

This indicates that the eigenvectors of $\mathbf{K}_{o,c} \otimes \mathbf{K}_{p,c}$ can be computed from the Kronecker product of the eigenvectors of $\mathbf{K}_{o,c}$ and $\mathbf{K}_{p,c}$ and the eigenvalues of $\mathbf{K}_{o,c} \otimes \mathbf{K}_{p,c}$ are the product of the eigenvalues of $\mathbf{K}_{o,c}$ and $\mathbf{K}_{p,c}$.

This factorization was used in [13] for fast computation of the eigenvectors of the Kronecker product of kernel matrices. We utilize the same factorization in the sum in equation (6) for fast computation of the kernel descriptors. Here each eigenvector α^t in equation (8) can be written as the Kronecker product of corresponding orientation and position eigenvectors $\alpha^t = \alpha_o^t \otimes \alpha_p^t$, and each coefficient α_{ij}^t in (6) can be represented by the product $\alpha_{o,i}^t \alpha_{p,j}^t$. Substituting in (6) we have:

$$F_{grad}^t(P) = \sum_{i=1}^{d_o} \sum_{j=1}^{d_p} \alpha_{o,i}^t \alpha_{p,j}^t \left\{ \sum_{z \in P} \tilde{m}(z) k_o(\tilde{\theta}(z), x_i) k_p(z, y_j) \right\} \tag{12}$$

Rearranging, we get

$$F_{grad}^t(P) = \sum_{z \in P} \tilde{m}(z) \left\{ \sum_{i=1}^{d_o} \alpha_{o,i}^t k_o(\tilde{\theta}(z), x_i) \right\} \left\{ \sum_{j=1}^{d_p} \alpha_{p,j}^t k_p(z, y_j) \right\} \tag{13}$$

With this factorization, we can compute the inner sums over x_i and y_j separately at cost $d_o + d_p$ per pixel, in each patch P. We can achieve further speed up by pre-computing the inner sums for a large number of orientation and position values and storing them in look-up tables T_o^t and T_p^t respectively, for each KPCA component t. Given an orientation $\theta(z)$ and position z, we can simply retrieve from T_o^t and T_p^t, the values corresponding to the nearest pre-computed orientation and position:

$$F_{grad}^t(P) = \sum_{z \in P} \tilde{m}(z) T_o^t(\theta(z)) T_p^t(z) \tag{14}$$

This takes $O(1)$ for each pixel z in patch P. In our experiments, we use 25 basis vectors x_i for the orientation, and sample the position basis vectors using a 5×5 grid. Thus the fast kernel descriptor computation in (14) produces a 625× speed-up over the naive computation in (6) and 50× speedup over the factorized sum computation in (13). We pre-compute orientation sums for n_o=1000 $\theta(z)$ values in the range $[0, 2\pi]$, n_l=16 possible values for CS-LBP vectors and n_p=1000 points for $z \in [0,1] \times [0,1]$.

5 Feature Representation and Fusion

We use the popular bag-of-words framework to represent the information from different feature descriptors. This is done in two steps - in the first *coding* step the descriptors are projected to a pre-trained codebook of descriptor vectors, and then in the *pooling* step the projections are aggregated to a fixed length feature vector. We use both spatial [19] and spatio-temporal [7] pooling. From these features, we further employ kernel based fusion and score level fusion to achieve more robust performance.

5.1 Coding and Pooling Strategies

Formally, we present a video by a set of low-level descriptors, x_i, where $i \in \{1..N\}$ is the set of locations. Let M denote the different spatial/spatio-temporal regions of interest, and N_m denote the number of descriptors extracted within region m. Let f and g denote the coding and pooling operators respectively. Then, the vector z representing the entire video is obtained by sequentially coding and pooling over all regions and concatenating:

$$\alpha_i = f(x_i), \quad i = 1..N \tag{15}$$

$$\mathbf{h}_m = g(\{\alpha_i\}_{i \in N_m}), \quad m = 1, ..., M \tag{16}$$

$$\mathbf{z}^T = [h_1^T ... h_M^T] \tag{17}$$

Coding: For the coding step, we first learn a codebook using k-means or a similar unsupervised clustering algorithm from a sample set of feature vectors. In hard quantization, we assign each feature vector x_i to the nearest codeword from the codebook as

$$\alpha_i \in \{0,1\}^K, \quad \alpha_{i,j} = 1 \Leftrightarrow j = \arg\min_{k \leq K} ||x_i - c_k||^2 \tag{18}$$

where c_k is the kth codeword. In soft quantization [20], the assignment of the feature vectors to codewords is distributed as

$$\alpha_{i,j} = \frac{\exp\left(-\beta||x_i - c_j||^2\right)}{\sum_{k=1}^{K} \exp\left(-\beta||x_i - c_k||^2\right)} \tag{19}$$

where β controls the soft assignment. In our experiments we find soft quantization to consistently outperform hard quantization.

Pooling: The two most popular pooling strategies are average and max. In average pooling, we take the average of the α_i assigned to different codewords for different feature vectors as $\mathbf{h} = 1/N \sum_{i=1}^{N} \alpha_i$. In max pooling, we take the maximum of the α_i's as $\mathbf{h} = \max_{i=1..N} \alpha_i$. In our work, we find average pooling to consistently outperform max pooling for video retrieval. Further spatial pooling with 1×1+2×2+1×3 partition of the (x, y) space has consistently superior performance for all the features considered. This is similar to previous results that show improvements with spatial [19] and spatio-temporal [7] feature pooling.

5.2 Kernel-Based Feature Fusion

We combine multiple features in an early fusion framework by using p-norm Multiple Kernel Learning (MKL)[21], with p>1. For each feature, we first compute exponential χ^2 kernels, defined by $K(\mathbf{x}, \mathbf{y}) = e^{-\rho \sum_i \frac{(x_i - y_i)^2}{x_i + y_i}}$ for each pair of samples $\mathbf{x}$ and $\mathbf{y}$ in the training set. Then, given a set of kernels $\{K_k\}$ for individual features, we learn a linear combination $K = \sum_k d_k K_k$ of the base kernels. The primal of this problem can be formulated as

$$\begin{aligned} &\min_{w,b,\xi\geq 0,d\geq 0} \frac{1}{2} \sum_k \mathbf{w}_k^t \mathbf{w}_k + C \sum \xi_i + \frac{\lambda}{2} (\sum_k d_k^p)^{\frac{2}{p}} \\ &\quad \text{s.t. } y_i (\sum_k \sqrt{d_k} \mathbf{w}_k^t \phi_k(x_i) + b) \geq 1 - \xi_i \end{aligned} \tag{20}$$

The convex form of (20) is obtained by substituting w_k for $\sqrt{d_k} w_k$. To solve (20) efficiently, we use Sequential Minimal Optimization (SMO) [22]. This is possible by first computing the Lagrangian

$$\begin{aligned} L = &\frac{1}{2} \sum_k \mathbf{w}_k^t \mathbf{w}_k / d_k + \sum (C - \beta_i) \xi_i + \frac{\lambda}{2} (\sum_k d_k^p)^{\frac{2}{p}} \\ &- \sum_i \alpha_i [y_i (\sum_k \mathbf{w}_k^t \phi_k(x_i) + b) - 1 + \xi_i] \end{aligned} \tag{21}$$

and then computing the l_p-MKL dual as

$$D = \max_{\alpha \in A} \mathbf{1}^t \alpha - \frac{1}{8\lambda} (\sum_k (\alpha^t H_k \alpha)^q)^{\frac{2}{q}} \tag{22}$$

where $\frac{1}{p} + \frac{1}{q} = 1$, $A = \{\alpha \mid 0 \leq \alpha \leq C\mathbf{1},\ \mathbf{1}^t Y\alpha = 0\}$, $H_k = YK_kY$, and Y is a diagonal matrix with labels on the diagonal. The kernel weights can then be computed as

$$d_k = \frac{1}{2\lambda}\left(\sum_k (\alpha^t H_k \alpha)^q\right)^{\frac{1}{q}-\frac{1}{p}} (\alpha^t H_k \alpha)^{\frac{q}{p}} \tag{23}$$

Since the dual objective (22) is differentiable with respect to α, the SMO algorithm can be applied by selecting two variables at a time and optimizing until convergence.

5.3 Score Level Late Fusion

We adopted a weighted average fusion strategy that assigns video specific weights based on each system's detection threshold. This is based on the intuition that a system has low confidence when its score for a particular video is close to the detection threshold, and high confidence when the scores are significantly different from the threshold. Given the confidence score p_i from system i for a particular video, the weight for that system and video is computed as:

$$w_i = \begin{cases} \frac{Th_i - p_i}{Th_i} & \text{if } p_i < Th_i \\ \frac{p_i - Th_i}{1 - Th_i} & \text{else} \end{cases} \tag{24}$$

where Th_i is the detection threshold. The final score P for a video is computed as $P = \sum_i w_i p_i / \sum_i w_i$. In our experiments, this approach consistently improved performance over any individual system.

6 Experimental Results

For our experiments, we used the dataset released as part of the TRECVID MED 11 evaluations (http://www.nist.gov/itl/iad/mig/med11.cfm). This set includes event kits containing ≈100-200 videos for each of the 10 test events of interest, and the DEV-T set containing 10723 background videos. The 10 events of interest include the following - *birthday party (BP), changing a vehicle tire (CT), flash mob gathering (FM), getting a vehicle unstuck (GV), grooming an animal (GA), making a sandwich (MS), parade (PA), parkour (PK), repairing an appliance (RA), working on a sewing project (WS)*. Figure 2 shows sample frames from each of the events of interest.

A key challenge in web video retrieval is the large imbalance in the available training data for positive and negative examples. In our experiments on the TRECVID MED11 dataset, the ratio of positive to negative examples is about 1:49. Since the MKL optimization function in equation (20) optimizes for accuracy, the solution often converges to the trivial classifier that declares all examples as negative, which has 98% accuracy in our case. To address this, we train models for combining multiple features by performing an extensive grid search over C and p. At each parameter setting, we perform a k-fold validation on the available training data and estimate a threshold that minimizes the Normalized Detection Cost (NDC) score that is defined as:

$$f = \min_{Th} \{w_{MD}P_{MD}(Th) + w_{FA}P_{FA}(Th)\}, \quad P_{MD}(Th) < 0.75 \qquad (25)$$

where Th is the detection threshold, $P_{MD}(Th)$ and $P_{FA}(Th)$ are the missed detection and false alarm rates at the detection threshold, and w_{MD}, w_{FA} are the relative weights for missed detections and false alarms. For the TRECVID MED dataset, different systems are compared with $w_{MD} = 1.0$, $w_{FA} = 12.49$. A similar training regime can also be used to minimize other metrics such as the area under curve (AUC), and mean average precision (MAP).

We compared the performance of KDES (Kernel Descriptor) features with a large set of image, color and flow based features. For image gradient based features, we compared with SURF[23], SIFT[24], D-SIFT[14], and CHoG[25]. For color features, we considered RGB-SIFT and C-SIFT[15]. For motion based features, we compared with STIP[7], HoGHoF3D[8] and ISA[11]. Table 1 compares the performance of the KDES features with different state-of-the-art features, for each of 10 events of interest. The proposed KDES features are the single best features for 7 of the 10 classes.

The Gray KDES-FG features that extract pixel level flow and gradient information similar to STIP and HoGHoF3D significantly outperform these features, and are also 2 orders of magnitude faster. Further, KDES-FG also outperforms the ISA features, which learn spatio-temporal patch features from pixel attributes using deep learning. The color KDES-G features outperform the RGB-SIFT and C-SIFT features that also extract gradient patterns from different color planes. The grayscale KDES-G features perform similarly to D-SIFT at approximately the same speed. The KDES-L features have weaker performance, primarily due to the small number of principal components chosen during KPCA out of the 6400 dimensional basis vector space. However, the KDES-CL features based on the more compact CS-LBP features produce comparable performance to KDES-G features. We see improved performance with KDES features over a range of missed detection and false alarm rate operating points on the DET

Fig. 2. Example video frames from each of the 10 test events

Table 1. Comparative Performance of KDES Features (using NDC score), and speed (fps) measured on 640×360 pixel resolution video, for each patch size at which features are extracted

	BP	CT	FM	GV	GA	MS	PA	PK	RA	WS	Mean	Speed
SURF[23]	0.98	**0.77**	0.44	0.85	1.04	1.34	0.87	0.82	0.81	0.79	0.91	0.600
SIFT[24]	1.07	0.90	0.51	0.95	0.91	1.57	0.89	0.79	0.73	0.93	0.93	0.530
D-SIFT[14]	0.84	0.82	0.45	0.82	0.98	1.30	0.91	0.78	0.73	0.67	0.83	0.250
CHoG[25]	1.01	0.92	0.43	0.91	1.39	1.57	0.91	0.87	0.76	0.97	0.97	0.177
RGB-SIFT[15]	0.80	0.81	0.40	0.85	1.09	1.51	0.91	0.75	0.75	0.80	0.87	0.019
C-SIFT[15]	0.90	1.02	0.44	0.88	1.16	1.11	0.92	0.79	0.67	0.83	0.87	0.019
STIP[7]	1.16	1.14	0.48	1.06	1.18	1.27	**0.84**	0.77	0.64	**0.54**	0.91	0.008
HoGHoF3D[8]	1.09	1.14	0.48	1.30	1.14	1.43	0.92	0.76	0.58	0.76	0.96	0.002
ISA[11]	1.42	1.04	0.64	0.99	1.18	1.40	0.99	1.02	0.64	1.17	1.05	0.001
Gray KDES-F	1.11	0.94	0.45	1.05	1.15	1.41	0.86	0.89	0.66	0.71	0.92	0.230
Gray KDES-G	0.90	0.90	0.41	0.78	0.90	1.25	0.92	0.76	0.67	0.76	0.83	0.240
Gray KDES-FG	0.88	0.88	0.39	0.83	0.96	**1.07**	0.93	**0.72**	0.62	0.64	**0.79**	0.120
Gray KDES-L	0.88	1.02	0.47	1.08	1.35	1.39	0.93	0.84	0.80	0.84	0.96	0.180
Gray KDES-CL	0.90	0.89	0.38	0.85	0.91	1.36	0.89	0.80	0.71	0.68	0.84	0.180
Color KDES-F	1.20	0.99	0.45	1.15	0.96	1.22	0.95	0.83	**0.54**	0.84	0.91	0.072
Color KDES-G	0.80	0.85	0.41	**0.73**	**0.83**	1.41	0.93	0.76	0.69	0.66	0.81	0.084
Color KDES-FG	**0.78**	0.86	0.40	0.80	0.95	1.2	0.87	0.73	0.66	0.66	**0.79**	0.036
Color KDES-L	0.96	0.97	0.44	0.98	1.21	1.23	1.05	0.88	0.71	0.73	0.92	0.060
Color KDES-CL	0.89	0.89	**0.36**	0.89	0.96	1.43	0.88	0.83	0.67	0.62	0.84	0.060

curve. This is illustrated in figures 3 and 4 for two of the events considered. The processing speed is also comparable with conventional features (Shown in the last column of Table 1).

Fusion Experiments: We next experimented with different combinations of KDES features. We combined the KDES-F and KDES-G that extract pixel level information from flow and gradient patterns, and with KDES-FG that extracts pixel level information jointly from flow and gradients. We also tested the performance of including KDES-CL features for fusion. We considered feature fusion using both early fusion (MKL) and score level fusion. Table 2 summarizes the results of our fusion experiments. KDES-F+KDES-G fusion produces comparable performance to KDES-FG. Combining all the features produces better performance for both grayscale and color features. In addition, combining grayscale

Table 2. Comparison of different fusion strategies of KDES features (using NDC score)

	Individual KDES Features				MKL			Score Fusion		
	F	G	FG	CL	F+G	F+G+FG	F+G+FG+CL	F+G	F+G+FG	F+G+FG+CL
Gray	0.9238	0.8262	0.7927	0.8362	0.8238	0.7852	0.7871	0.7758	0.7554	0.7623
Color	0.9123	0.8077	0.7908	0.8413	0.7809	0.7860	0.7863	0.7822	0.7490	0.7459
Combined						0.7787	0.7904		0.7379	**0.7374**

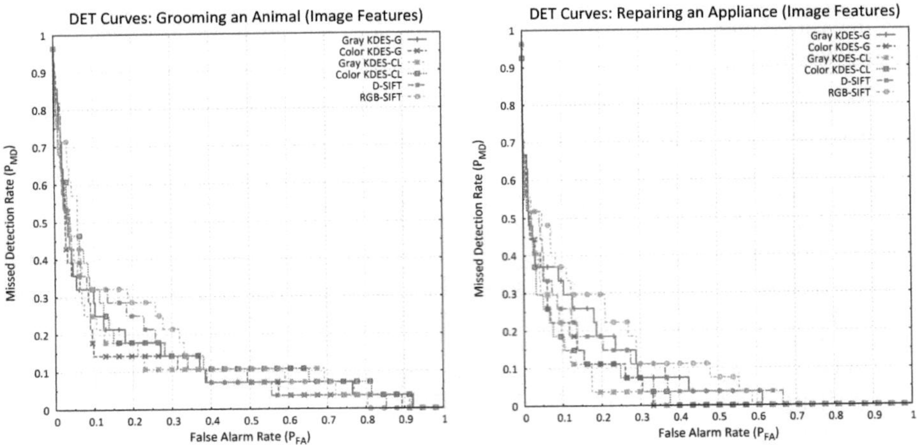

Fig. 3. DET curves comparing image features for classes "Grooming an animal" and "Repair an appliance"

Table 3. Fusion of KDES features with standard features

Feature Combination	NDC
D-SIFT+RGB-SIFT+STIP+HoGHoF3D	0.7539
All Individual KDES	0.7374
All Individual KDES+D-SIFT+RGB-SIFT+ STIP+HoGHoF3D	**0.7148**

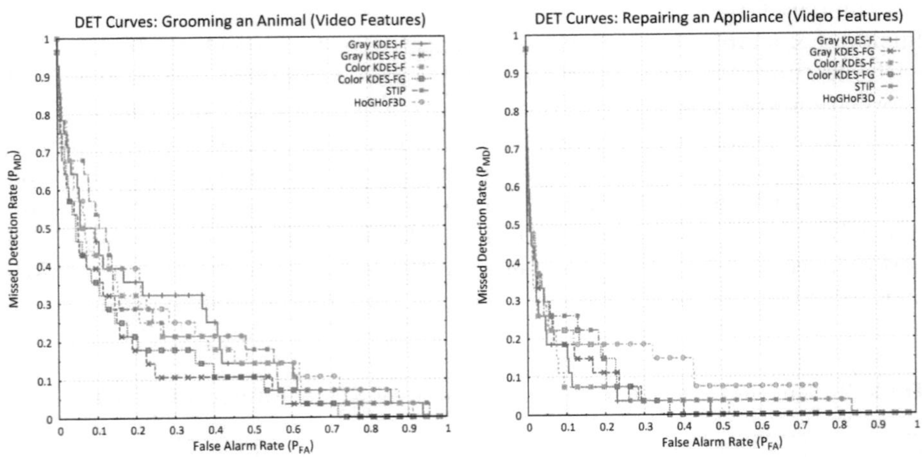

Fig. 4. DET curves comparing motion features for classes "Grooming an animal" and "Repair an appliance"

and color features produces further gains indicating presence of complementary information in the two types of features. Further, score level fusion generally yields better performance than MKL for the different combinations considered.

Next, we combined our KDES features with a set of standard features. We chose D-SIFT, RGB-SIFT, STIP and HoGHoF3D since they extract information similar to Gray KDES-G, Color KDES-G and Gray KDES-FG features. Table 3 compares the performance of different combinations. The KDES feature combination outperforms the D-SIFT+RGB-SIFT+STIP+HoGHoF3D system, while combining all the KDES and standard features produces additional gains, indicating presence of complementary information from the KDES features on top of the standard feature set.

7 Conclusion

We present a set of features that extend kernel descriptors for analyzing videos, and present an efficient algorithm for rapid computation of such features in videos. Together, this allows us to define a rich set of pixel level spatio-temporal features for robust video analysis. We rigorously analyzed their performance on large benchmark video event detection dataset used in the TRECVID MED 2011 evaluations. Our results indicate that kernel descriptors significantly outperform popular motion features such as STIP, HoGHoF3D and the recently developed ISA features. Furthermore, incorporating color information produces small performance improvements at the cost of increased computation. In the future, within the kernel descriptor framework, we aim to explore a larger set of pixel attributes as well as develop hierarchical architectures for learning video level features.

Acknowledgment. This work was supported by the Intelligence Advanced Research Projects Activity (IARPA) via the Department of Interior National Business Center contract number D11PC20071. The U.S. Government is authorized to reproduce and distribute reprints for Governmental purposes notwithstanding any copyright annotation thereon. The views and conclusions contained herein are those of the authors and should not be interpreted as necessarily representing the official policies or endorsements, either expressed or implied, of IARPA, DoI/NBC or the U.S. Government.

References

1. Bo, L., Ren, X., Fox, D.: Kernel descriptors for visual recognition. In: NIPS, pp. 244–252 (2010)
2. Zanetti, S., Zelnik Manor, L., Perona, P.: A walk through the web's video clips. In: InterNet, pp. 1–8 (2008)
3. Song, Y., Zhao, M., Yagnik, J., Wu, X.: Taxonomic classification for web-based videos. In: CVPR, pp. 871–878 (2010)
4. Wang, Z., Zhao, M., Song, Y., Kumar, S., Li, B.: Youtubecat: Learning to categorize wild web videos. In: CVPR, pp. 879–886 (2010)

5. Toderici, G., Aradhye, H., Pasca, M., Sbaiz, L., Yagnik, J.: Finding meaning on youtube: Tag recommendation and category discovery. In: CVPR, pp. 3447–3454 (2010)
6. Csurka, G., Dance, C.R., Fan, L., Willamowski, J., Bray, C.: Visual categorization with bags of keypoints. In: Workshop on Statistical Learning in Computer Vision, ECCV, pp. 1–22 (2004)
7. Laptev, I., Marszalek, M., Schmid, C., Rozenfeld, B.: Learning realistic human actions from movies. In: CVPR, pp. 1–8 (2008)
8. Wang, H., Ullah, M.M., Kläser, A., Laptev, I., Schmid, C.: Evaluation of local spatio-temporal features for action recognition. In: BMVC (2009)
9. Liu, J., Luo, J., Shah, M.: Recognizing realistic actions from videos in the wild. In: CVPR (2009)
10. Taylor, G.W., Fergus, R., LeCun, Y., Bregler, C.: Convolutional Learning of Spatio-temporal Features. In: Daniilidis, K., Maragos, P., Paragios, N. (eds.) ECCV 2010, Part VI. LNCS, vol. 6316, pp. 140–153. Springer, Heidelberg (2010)
11. Le, Q.V., Zou, W.Y., Yeung, S.Y., Ng, A.Y.: Learning hierarchical invariant spatio-temporal features for action recognition with independent subspace analysis. In: CVPR, pp. 3361–3368 (2011)
12. Yu, K., Lin, Y., Lafferty, J.D.: Learning image representations from the pixel level via hierarchical sparse coding. In: CVPR, pp. 1713–1720 (2011)
13. Bo, L., Lai, K., Ren, X., Fox, D.: Object recognition with hierarchical kernel descriptors. In: CVPR, pp. 1729–1736 (2011)
14. Boureau, Y., Bach, F., Le Cun, Y., Ponce, J.: Learning mid-level features for recognition. In: CVPR, pp. 2559–2566 (2010)
15. van de Sande, K.E.A., Gevers, T., Snoek, C.G.M.: Evaluating color descriptors for object and scene recognition. IEEE Transactions on Pattern Analysis and Machine Intelligence 32, 1582–1596 (2010)
16. Laptev, I.: On space-time interest points. International Journal of Computer Vision 64, 107–123 (2005)
17. Ojala, T., Pietikainen, M., Maenpa, T.: Multiresolution gray-scale and rotation invariant texture classification with local binary patterns. PAMI 24, 971–987 (2002)
18. Heikkilä, M., Pietikäinen, M., Schmid, C.: Description of Interest Regions with Center-Symmetric Local Binary Patterns. In: Kalra, P.K., Peleg, S. (eds.) ICVGIP 2006. LNCS, vol. 4338, pp. 58–69. Springer, Heidelberg (2006)
19. Lazebnik, S., Schmid, C., Ponce, J.: Beyond bags of features: Spatial pyramid matching for recognizing natural scene categories. In: CVPR, vol. II, pp. 2169–2178 (2006)
20. van Gemert, J.C., Veenman, C.J., Smeulders, A.W.M., Geusebroek, J.M.: Visfual word ambiguity. PAMI 32(7), 1271–1283 (2010)
21. Kloft, M., Brefeld, U., Sonnenburg, S., Zien, A.: l_p-norm multiple kernel learning. Journal of Machine Learning Research 12, 953–997 (2011)
22. Platt, J.C.: Fast training of support vector machines using sequential minimal optimization, pp. 185–208. MIT Press (1999)
23. Bay, H., Ess, A., Tuytelaars, T., Gool, L.V.: Surf: Speeded up robust features. CVIU 110, 346–359 (2008)
24. Lowe, D.G.: Distinctive image features from scale-invariant keypoints. IJCV 60, 91–110 (2004)
25. Chandrasekhar, V., Takacs, G., Chen, D.M., Tsai, S.S., Grzeszczuk, R., Girod, B.: Chog: Compressed histogram of gradients a low bit-rate feature descriptor. In: CVPR, pp. 2504–2511 (2009)

Tracking Using Motion Patterns for Very Crowded Scenes

Xuemei Zhao, Dian Gong, and Gérard Medioni

Institute for Robotics and Intelligent Systems,
University of Southern California Los Angeles, CA, 90089
{xuemeiz,diangong,medioni}@usc.edu

Abstract. This paper proposes Motion Structure Tracker (MST) to solve the problem of tracking in very crowded structured scenes. It combines visual tracking, motion pattern learning and multi-target tracking. Tracking in crowded scenes is very challenging due to hundreds of similar objects, cluttered background, small object size, and occlusions. However, structured crowded scenes exhibit clear motion pattern(s), which provides rich prior information. In MST, tracking and detection are performed *jointly*, and motion pattern information is integrated in both steps to enforce scene structure constraint. MST is initially used to track a single target, and further extended to solve a simplified version of the multi-target tracking problem. Experiments are performed on real-world challenging sequences, and MST gives promising results. Our method significantly outperforms several state-of-the-art methods both in terms of track ratio and accuracy.

Keywords: motion pattern, tracking, very crowded scenes.

1 Introduction

Object tracking has been of broad interest in several applications for decades, such as security and surveillance, human-computer interaction and traffic control. Specifically, tracking in crowded scenes gets more and more attention as it pushes the limit of traditional tracking algorithms.

Crowded scenes can be divided into two categories, structured and unstructured, depending on whether there are clear motion patterns in the scene. The definition is different from [1], in which the authors distinguish between the two based on whether each spatial location supports only one dominant crowd behavior or more. For instance, Fig. 1(d) shows a scene of Italian police riders putting on a motorbike display. Two groups of riders ride in the opposite directions. Due to occlusions, one location may have two opposite velocities which correspond to two groups of coordinated movements. The scene is structured because the two groups of movements form two clear motion patterns.

In this paper, we focus on the problem of single and multiple target tracking in structured crowded scenes (examples are shown in Fig. 1), and we want to track objects in general, instead of specific ones, such as pedestrians. The first

A. Fitzgibbon et al. (Eds.): ECCV 2012, Part II, LNCS 7573, pp. 315–328, 2012.

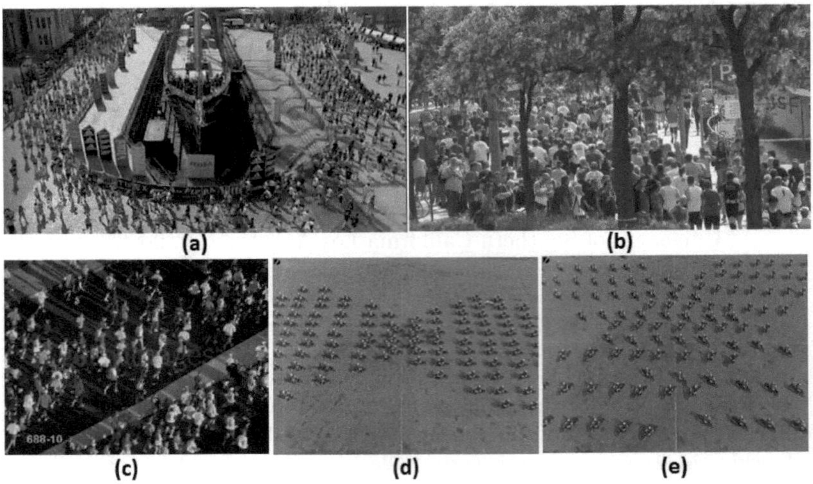

Fig. 1. Examples of structured crowded scenes. (a)(b)(c): Marathon sequences. (d)(e): Italian motorbike display sequences

issue is to solve the motion pattern problem. In very crowded scenes, tracking is difficult for many reasons: the size of a target is usually small; there is a large number of similar objects in the scene; partial and full object occlusions. Furthermore, the "detect and track" paradigm fails here. However, the most salient characteristic of structured scenes is, objects do not move randomly, but follow a pattern instead. Several efforts have been devoted to studying motion patterns, and some of them [2, 3] are successfully used in crowded scene tracking.

The second issue is single vs multi-target tracking. The fundamental difference between the two is whether targets are tracked individually or jointly. In single object tracking, a target is labeled in the first one or several frame(s), and matching is used for detection in the following frames. In multi-target tracking, targets are detected and associated in each frame. Two commonly used methods for detection are appearance based detector, and background modeling based motion blob detector, but neither of them works (as shown in Fig. 2) in very crowded scenes due to the small size, high density and the general object requirement. Thus, in both single and multiple object tracking, we require user labeling in the first frame as input. In multi-target tracking, supervised learning is used for detection. A supervised learning method requires a large number of samples from each kind of object for training. To save a user from tedious work, we only ask to label one example. After tracking the examplar for a few frames to train a detector, we go back to the first frame and use the learned detector to detect similar objects, then track. As an extension of previous work, our approach (Fig. 3) incorporates motion pattern learning results in both the detection and tracking stages, and extends the motion pattern based tracker from single target tracking to a simplified version of multiple target tracking.

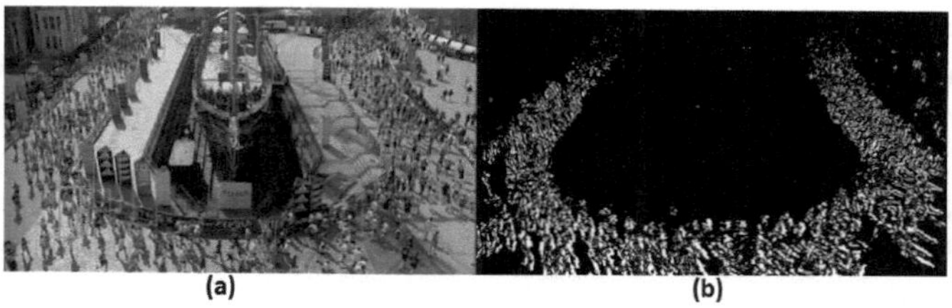

Fig. 2. The commonly used detection methods fail in very crowded scenes. (a) Pedestrian detection results by [4]. (b) Foreground extraction results by MoG

In summary, MST has several advantages compared to existing methods:

–**Better tag and track:** to track a single object in very crowded scenes, MST combines tracking and detection, in both of which motion pattern information is used as prior knowledge, and outperforms state-of-the-art trackers.
–**Improved multi-target tracking:** although it is almost impossible to track all objects in very crowded scenes, we partially address this by proposing a simplified version and solving it by MST.
–**Online:** the proposed algorithm can sequentially process both temporally stationary and non-stationary scenes, infer motion patterns, and use them in both single and multiple object tracking.

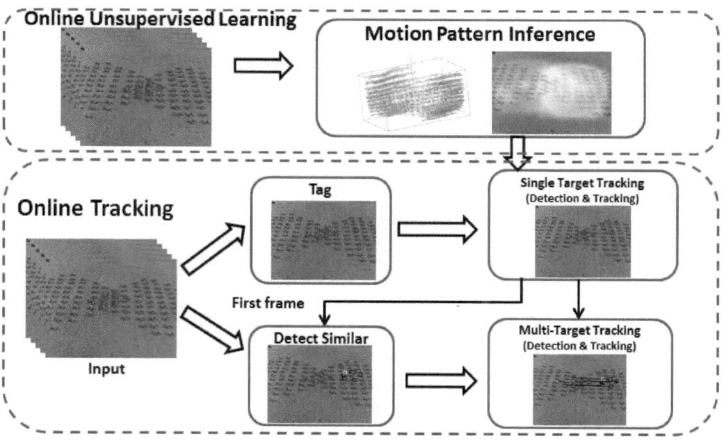

Fig. 3. An overview of Motion Structure Tracker

2 Related Work

Tracking has been a major focus of research in computer vision. Interested readers are referred to a survey [5] for a review. In this section, we give a brief review from several aspects, (1) visual tracking, (2) motion pattern, (3) tracking in crowded scenes, and (4) multiple target tracking.

Visual tracking addresses the problem of tracking a specific object labeled in the first frame or first few frames by a user, and it faces several challenges, such as abrupt motion. IVT Tracker [6] presents a method that incrementally learns a representation, efficiently adapting online to changes in the appearance of the target. P-N Tracker [7] addresses these problems by exploring the structure of unlabeled data, which are positive and negative structures. Single object tracking in a structured crowded scene is similar to visual tracking, but some differences exist. 1) Due to the high density constraint, objects in crowded scene move smoothly, and abrupt motion is rare. 2) The size of a target in crowded scenes is small, thus advanced appearance model based matching is not so helpful. 3) The scale of targets is relatively stable in crowded scenes. 4) Many objects look similar to the target. 5) Although crowded scenes may have cluttered background, it rarely suffers from big change. Fortunately, some of these characteristics contribute to solve the difficult problem of tracking in crowded scenes. For example, due to the smooth movement constraint, a search area can be assumed as in [8, 9]. Thus, we solve single object tracking in crowded scene based on the techniques in state-of-the-art visual tracker, with special constraints from the application.

Motion patterns are the most salient feature in structured crowded scenes. They convey rich information such as how the objects move, and how they interact with each other. From the point of view of what input to learn motion patterns, [10–12] use optical flow, [13] uses object tracking results, and [14] uses keypoints tracking results. These methods have their pros and cons. In the application of crowded scenes, optical flow is too noisy, and object tracking is impossible to get and use as input (and it's just the problem we want to solve). Therefore, keypoints tracking is chosen. From the application point of view, motion patterns have been used to understand scenes [11, 14], improve tracking [13, 15], detect anomalous events [16, 17], and learn traffic rules [18].

Tracking in crowded scenes catches a lot of attention in recent years, and most related works directly or indirectly use motion pattern information. [1–3] all propose novel algorithms and get promising results. Specifically, [1] focuses on unstructured scenes. [2, 3] use motion patterns to assist tracking. The seminal work [2] proposes static floor field, dynamic floor field and boundary floor field to determine the probability of moving from one location to another. [3] presents an elegant framework by training a Hidden Markov model to capture spatio-temporal motion patterns to describe pedestrian movement at each space-time location. [19] proposes a ground breaking idea to first learn a set of crowd behavior priors off-line, then match crowd patches in testing to the database to get priors. Compared to the previous work, we combine tracking and detection, and integrate motion pattern knowledge into both stages in an online fashion.

Multiple target tracking(MTT) is a well studied problem that has received considerable attention [20–23]. Besides the same issues encountered in classic tracking, it deals with additional challenges, e.g., unknown number of targets and the interactions among them. To handle these, jointly optimization of data association is the key, and progress has been made. However, MTT in crowded scenes is seldom successful. Detecting objects in each frame is a challenge, let alone associating them. [24] addresses the problem of person detection and tracking in crowded scenes, by exploring constraints imposed by crowd density to localize individual people. That's a major improvement of MTT in crowded scenes, but it's not for general objects (human heads specifically), and it requires a large training dataset. In this paper, we look into the problem from another viewpoint, and attempt to solve a simpler problem of MTT: once a user labels a target in the first frame, we try to find similar objects and track all of them.

3 Motion Pattern Inference

As observed in [13], tracklet points form manifold structures which correspond to motion patterns in (x, y, θ) space, where (x, y) is spatial position and θ stands for velocity direction. However, in [13], tracklets are obtained by extracting motion blobs and associating them, making velocity magnitude unreliable. In very crowded scenes, we use KLT keypoint tracker [25] to get short tracklets, making velocity magnitude more reliable. Since magnitude conveys important information of how objects move, we embed tracklet points into (x, y, v_x, v_y) space. After normalizing (v_x, v_y) to the same scale as (x, y), manifold structures emerge. Two examples of the projection in (x, y, v_x) space are shown in Fig. 4. To explore manifold property, Tensor Voting is performed to learn the local geometric structure. Then outliers are filtered out, again using Tensor Voting. As a result, a motion pattern is represented by a set of points $\boldsymbol{q_l} = (x_l, y_l, v_{xl}, v_{yl}),\ l = 1, 2, ..., n$.

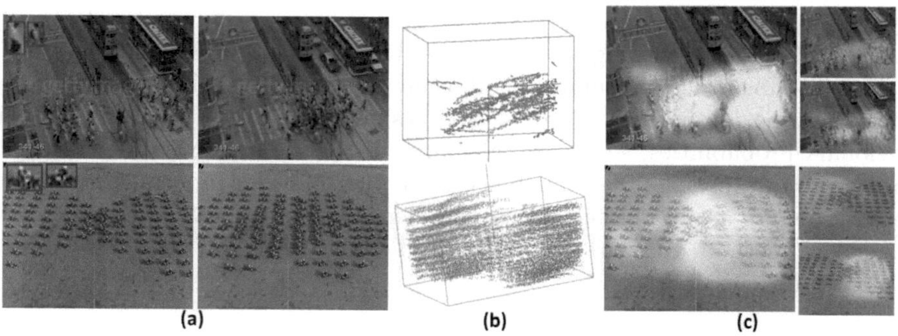

Fig. 4. Temporally non-stationary scenes. First row: Hongkong. Second row: Motorbike. (a) Input sequences and examples of targets. (b) The visualization of motion patterns learning results projected in (x, y, v_x) space. (c) The visualization of motion patterns learning results in image space

3.1 *N*D Tensor Voting

Tensor Voting [26] is a perceptual organization method to analyze the local structures at input points in ND space. Instead of a global estimation for the entire input, local learning results enable us to learn geometric structure and estimate dimensionality, and furthermore to measure geodesic distance and perform nonlinear interpolation for input with outliers and intersections.

The geometric information at each ND point is represented by a second order, symmetric, and non-negative tensor $\boldsymbol{T}$, corresponding to an $N \times N$ matrix and an ellipsoid in ND space. $\boldsymbol{T}$ represents the manifold structure going through the point by encoding the manifold's normals and tengents as eigenvectors corresponding to $\boldsymbol{T}$'s non-zero and zero eigenvalues respectively. Any such tensor is decomposed as $\boldsymbol{T} = \sum_{d=1}^{N} \lambda_d \boldsymbol{e_d} \boldsymbol{e_d}^T$, where $\{\lambda_d\}$ are the eigenvalues in descending order of magnitude and $\{\boldsymbol{e_d}\}$ are the corresponding eigenvectors. By analyzing the eigen-system of $\boldsymbol{T}$, normals and tangents can be calculated. Also, the confidence, or saliency, of the structure which has d normals is encoded as $\lambda_d - \lambda_{d+1}$, or λ_N for the ball tensor.Therefore, the local structure that the point is assumed to belong to is corresponding to the one with the largest saliency.

Inputs are encoded with tensors, propagate their information to their neighbors' tensors, and collect information from them, in a voting process. The local geometric information of each point can be obtained by examining its tensor.

3.2 Outlier Filtering

Tracklet extraction results are inaccurate due to many reasons, such as low resolution of image, occlusions, illumination change, etc. Therefore, velocities calculated from tracklets are noisy and bring in outliers in (x, y, v_x, v_y) space, making outlier filtering a necessary step. In practice, we use λ_1 as inlier degree measure. Intuitively, λ_1 can be viewed as the sum of the probabilities for all manifolds (a point's local geometric structures) with different intrinsic dimensionalities. By ranking all points according to their λ_1, outliers can be filtered out.

This filtering process is similar to diffusion process [27] in spirit. Conceptually, ranking all the data points according to λ_1 is similar to ranking according to their stationary probabilities, which are calculated from the random walk model built on the data graph [28]. The difference is, in the diffusion process, the weights between points are calculated from a pre-defined kernel, e.g., Gaussian kernel, but in our method, they are calculated from the Tensor Voting process, which is more robust to outliers.

4 Motion Structure Tracker

To track object(s) in crowded scenes, we combine visual tracker, learning-detection [7], and motion pattern learning together, and propose Motion Structure Tracker(MST), which utilizes motion pattern information in both detection and tracking stages.

4.1 Exploiting Motion Pattern in Detection

Objects in structured crowded scenes move smoothly by following some patterns. To establish an object correspondence in the next frame, we search in a window within which the largest corresponding velocity is no higher than twice the largest velocity found in motion pattern prior. The search space is thus greatly reduced.

The detection probability $Pr_{\boldsymbol{f},\boldsymbol{m}} = Pr(y = 1|\boldsymbol{f}, \boldsymbol{m})$ in MST is calculated as,

$$Pr(y = 1|\boldsymbol{f}, \boldsymbol{m}) \propto Pr(y = 1|\boldsymbol{f}) \times Pr(y = 1|\boldsymbol{m}) \tag{1}$$

where $y = 1$ denotes a detection is positive, $\boldsymbol{f}$ denotes the appearance feature vector used to judge a detection, and $\boldsymbol{m}$ denotes the motion structure information in (x, y, v_x, v_y) space used to judge a detection. In particular, $Pr(y = 1|\boldsymbol{f})$ indicates the appearance based detection probability and $Pr(y = 1|\boldsymbol{m})$ indicates motion detection probability. Eq. 1 approximately holds based on the assumption that the two marginal probabilities with $\boldsymbol{f}$ and $\boldsymbol{m}$ are independent.

Appearance Detection Probability. Random ferns [29] are proposed to speed up random forest. Random fern classifiers have proven to be efficient and effective in tasks such as tracking [7], image classification [30], and action recognition [31]. Thus, we use a random fern classifier for detection, and as in [7], explore the structure of unlabeled data, i.e. the positive and negative structures. Given a video, in the first frame, image patches close to the target are used as positive training examples, and those far from it are used as negative training examples. In the following frames, once the target is validated, corresponding examples (positive and negative) are extracted and used to update the detector.

The detector contains a set of ferns. Once a patch is given, each fern evaluates it independently, by taking a set of measurements in feature vector $\boldsymbol{f}$. At the leaf node that $\boldsymbol{f}$ points to, the posterior probability of whether the patch is positive $(y = 1)$ is calculated based on how many positive (s^+) and negative (s^-) samples are already recorded by that leaf, $s^+/(s^+ + s^-)$. And $Pr(y = 1|\boldsymbol{f})$ is an average of the posterior probabilities from all the ferns.

Motion Detection Probability. Moreover, each candidate patch is examined to test whether it is consistent with motion pattern prior knowledge. For a target centered at (x_i, y_i) in frame t, possible correspondences with displacements $(v_{xij}, v_{y_{ij}}), (j = 1, ..., m)$ in frame $t + 1$ produces a set of points $\boldsymbol{p_{ij}} = (x_i, y_i, v_{xij}, v_{y_{ij}})$. Intuitively, we want to check whether these points get support from motion pattern prior. Thus, each point $\boldsymbol{q_l} = (x_l, y_l, v_{xl}, v_{y_l}), (l = 1, 2, ..., n)$ from motion pattern learning votes for $\boldsymbol{p_{ij}}$, and the sum of all the votes is,

$$vote_{ij} = \sum_{l=1}^{n} e^{-||\boldsymbol{q_l} - \boldsymbol{p_{ij}}||^2/\sigma_1^2} \tag{2}$$

We normalize the votes as follows:

$$Pr(y = 1|\boldsymbol{m}) = \frac{vote_{ij}}{\sum_{j=1}^{m} vote_{ij}} \tag{3}$$

By combining $Pr(y = 1|\boldsymbol{f})$ and $Pr(y = 1|\boldsymbol{m})$, the final MST detection probability not only captures the object appearance feature but also incorporates the motion structure, which is important to detect objects in crowded scenes.

4.2 Exploiting Motion Pattern in Tracking

In addition to detecting correspondence of a target, we also track the target directly by selecting keypoints on it, and find their correspondences in the next frame. However, crowded scenes have low resolution and cluttered background, making optical flow results unreliable. To solve the problem, we propose a motion structure based optical flow, i.e., Structure Flow (SF), by generalized Tikhonov regularization. Structure flow is a Bayesian extension of optical flow, since motion pattern information gives some prior knowledge about the movement.

Formally, by using the prior knowledge as regularization term, the structure flow $\boldsymbol{v} = (v_x, v_y)$ is optimized by minimizing the following loss function,

$$\mathcal{L}_{SF}(\boldsymbol{v}) = \mathcal{L}_{AF}(\boldsymbol{v}) + \lambda \mathcal{L}_{MP}(\boldsymbol{v}) \tag{4}$$

where $\mathcal{L}_{AF}(\boldsymbol{v})$ stands for the loss based on the appearance features and $\mathcal{L}_{MP}(\boldsymbol{v})$ stands for the loss based on motion pattern prior. λ is the regularization parameter to control the impact of priors. These two items are described as follows.

$\mathcal{L}_{AF}(\boldsymbol{v})$: Recall the Lucas-Kanade [32] method. To calculate the velocity (v_x, v_y) of a point $q = (x, y)$, we consider K points $(\{p_i = (x_i, y_i)\}, i = 1, 2, ..., K)$ in q's neighborhood. Let $\boldsymbol{I_x}(p_i)$, $\boldsymbol{I_y}(p_i)$ and $\boldsymbol{I_t}(p_i)$ represent the partial derivatives of the image $\boldsymbol{I}$ with respect to position x, y and time t, evaluated at the point p_i. Based on LK assumptions, (v_x, v_y) must satisfy

$$\boldsymbol{I_x}(p_i)v_x + \boldsymbol{I_y}(p_i)v_y + \boldsymbol{I_t}(p_i) = 0 \tag{5}$$

Let

$$\boldsymbol{A} = \begin{pmatrix} \boldsymbol{I_x}(p_1) & \boldsymbol{I_y}(p_1) \\ \boldsymbol{I_x}(p_2) & \boldsymbol{I_y}(p_2) \\ \cdots & \cdots \\ \boldsymbol{I_x}(p_K) & \boldsymbol{I_y}(p_K) \end{pmatrix}, \boldsymbol{v} = \begin{pmatrix} v_x \\ v_y \end{pmatrix}, \boldsymbol{b} = \begin{pmatrix} \boldsymbol{I_t}(p_1) \\ \boldsymbol{I_t}(p_2) \\ \cdots \\ \boldsymbol{I_t}(p_K) \end{pmatrix}$$

Then the K points satisfy $\boldsymbol{Av} = \boldsymbol{b}$ ideally. However, usually the points do not move in the same way, so this does not hold in practice. Thus, we can have the following loss function,

$$\mathcal{L}_{AF}(\boldsymbol{v}) = ||\boldsymbol{Av} - \boldsymbol{b}||^2 \tag{6}$$

where eq. 6 itself can also be viewed as an over-determined system if $K > 2$.

$\mathcal{L}_{MP}(\boldsymbol{v})$: We use motion pattern information in (x, y, v_x, v_y) space as prior. For a point $\boldsymbol{x} = (x, y)$, consider a $W \times W$ area around it. It collects the information from each point $\boldsymbol{x_i} = (x_i, y_i), (i = 1, 2, ..., L)$ in the area with a correspondence $(x_i, y_i, v_{ix}, v_{iy})$ in the motion pattern prior. We weigh the impact as $w_i = e^{-||\boldsymbol{x}-\boldsymbol{x_i}||^2/\sigma_2^2}$, and normalize it as $\overline{w_i} = \frac{w_i}{\sum_{j=1}^{L} w_i}$. Then the weighted sum of velocity is used as an estimation of the expected velocity $\boldsymbol{v_0} = (v_{0x}, v_{0y})^T$, and the covariance matrix Σ_v can also be derived. Based on the estimations of mean and co-variance matrix, we design the following loss function,

$$\mathcal{L}_{MP}(\boldsymbol{v}) = (\boldsymbol{v} - \boldsymbol{v_0})^T \Sigma_v^{-1} (\boldsymbol{v} - \boldsymbol{v_0}) \tag{7}$$

Essentially, eq. 7 can be viewed as a multivariate Gaussian probabilistic framework to model the prior of structure flow.

$\mathcal{L}_{SF}(\boldsymbol{v})$: By replacing the two proposed loss functions into eq. 4, structure flow $\boldsymbol{v}$ is estimated by minimizing

$$\mathcal{L}_{SF}(\boldsymbol{v}) = ||\boldsymbol{A}\boldsymbol{v} - \boldsymbol{b}||^2 + \lambda||\boldsymbol{v} - \boldsymbol{v}_0||^2_{\Sigma_v^{-1}} \tag{8}$$

where $||\boldsymbol{v} - \boldsymbol{v}_0||^2_{\Sigma_v^{-1}}$ stands for the Mahalanobis distance $(\boldsymbol{v} - \boldsymbol{v}_0)^T \Sigma_v^{-1}(\boldsymbol{v} - \boldsymbol{v}_0)$.

According to the generalized Tikhonov regularization, the closed-form solution is

$$\boldsymbol{v} = \boldsymbol{v}_0 + (\boldsymbol{A}^T\boldsymbol{A} + \lambda(\Sigma_v)^{-1})^{-1}\boldsymbol{A}^T(b - \boldsymbol{A}\boldsymbol{v}_0) \tag{9}$$

Thus, for each keypoint on the target, a velocity estimation $\boldsymbol{v}$ incorporating motion structure information is generated. The target position can be estimated.

It is worth noting that, as $\lambda \to 0$, eq. 9 degenerates to $(\boldsymbol{A}^T\boldsymbol{A})^{-1}\boldsymbol{A}^T\boldsymbol{b}$, which is the standard Lucas-Kanade optical flow. This is because no regularization is used in $\mathcal{L}_{SF}(\boldsymbol{v})$. On the other hand, as $\lambda \to \infty$, eq. 9 degenerates to $\boldsymbol{v}_0$, which means we fully trust the motion pattern priors.

Fig. 5. Temporally stationary scenes and examples of targets. (a) Marathon-1. (b) Marathon-2. (c) Marathon-3

4.3 Simplified Multiple Target Tracking in Structured Crowded Scenes

In crowded scenes, tracking many similar objects is extremely challenging. One of the difficulties is how to detect multiple targets. Due to the small target size and large intra class variance caused by viewpoint and occlusion of objects, an object detector does not provide satisfying results (an example of pedestrian detection results by state-of-the-art detector [4] is given in Fig. 2). Therefore, we step back to solve a simpler problem: once a user labels a target in the first frame, find similar objects and track all of them.

We track the user labeled object for a few frames, and in parallel train our detector. Then we go back to the first frame, detect the top n_1 (user input) similar objects by the detector. Motion structure tracker tracks multiple targets in a way similar to single target tracking. Specifically, we treat each of the $n_1 + 1$ objects as a single object to track. If the tracking results in frame t are good (measured by confidence scores from detector and structure flow tracker), we move to frame $t+1$. If not, we consider a window of size L, from frame t to frame $t+L-1$, and locate candidates by detector and structure flow tracker based on frame t. Then association is formulated as inference in a set of Bayesian networks [22]. Confidence score is the driving force behind finding the MAP data association estimate. Then we move forward to frame $t+1$ and repeat the process.

5 Experimental Validation

We apply Motion Structure Tracker(MST) in four sets of experiments. The video sequences we use can be divided into two groups: *temporally stationary* and *temporally non-stationary* scenes, depending on whether the motion patterns change with time. Fig. 5 shows three examples of Marathon sequences (from [2, 15] and YouTube), in which motion patterns are the same from the beginning to the end. For such sequences, we only need to learn motion patterns in the first few frames, and then use them for the whole sequence. On the contrary, the HongKong sequence [15] and the Italian motorbike sequence (from Youtube) have changing motion patterns, making it necessary to online update motion pattern learning results. Besides, the task performed in each sequence can also be divided into two groups: single target tracking and multiple target tracking. Therefore, four sets of experiments are designed for the four combinations. In all the experiments, we use 10 ferns and 13 features per fern, and we fix $\sigma_1 = 10$, $\sigma_2 = 5$, $\lambda = 2$. Results are robust to a certain range of these parameters. In outlier filtering step, the points whose λ_1 is smaller than 0.02 of the median of the λ_1 of all the points are filtered out. The appearance similarity between the target and candidate is calculated by normalized cross correlation(NCC) at the gray-level. Our single target tracking results are compared with IVT Tracker [6], P-N Tracker [7] and CTM [1].

1. Single target tracking results in temporally stationary scenes.
The three Marathon sequences (Fig. 5) capture athletes from static overhead cameras. They are challenging real-world scenes due to the existence of hundreds of similar small-size objects, and occlusions from time to time. The three have 343, 249 and 143 frames respectively, and resolutions are 720×404, 1280×720 and 480×360 respectively. In each experiment, we manually select a rectangular region around a target in the first frame. In each sequence, the first 50 frames are used to learn motion patterns, and 10 targets (whole body or upper body in Marathon-1 and Marathon-3, and heads in Marathon-2) are randomly selected to test, with an average size of target as 15×21, 21×26 and 17×29 pixels respectively. In the Matlab application provided by [1], bounding box size is fixed, and only target center is the input. Since target size varies in different sequences, we resize the input images of every sequence to the most proper size.

Ground truth is manually labeled for each target in each frame. Two criteria are used to compare the tracking results between different trackers. (1) Average Center Location Error (ACLE), which measures the pixel difference between tracked object center and the ground truth. (2) Average Track Ratio (ATR), which is calculated as successfully tracked frames divided by total number of frames in which a target is in FOV. The results are presented in Table 1. It can be seen that our tracker outperforms other state-of-the-art, and we get low ACLE because even if our tracker shifts to a wrong object, it is still following motion pattern, thus close to the target. The best results are on Marathon-3 sequence, since it contains relatively large-size targets with clear appearance. In Marathon-1, runner size is small, and there is viewpoint change as runners run through the U-shape street. In Marathon-2, we only track heads of runners, thus the discrimination power is weak. Also, trees in Marathon-2 cause occlusion, which is a major source of errors. An example of tracking results is shown in the first row of Fig. 6.

Table 1. Tracking evaluation results of single target in temporally stationary scenes

Method	Marathon-1		Marathon-2		Marathon-3	
	ATR	ACLE	ATR	ACLE	ATR	ACLE
IVT Tracker [6]	35.21%	62.8	33.47%	86.5	40.03%	64.1
P-N Tracker [7]	56.16%	35.1	68.60%	56.4	69.16%	33.9
CTM [1]	52.35%	38.8	65.72%	62.8	71.69%	30.5
Ours	**81.40%**	**6.7**	**73.12%**	**28.5**	**91.08%**	**4.8**

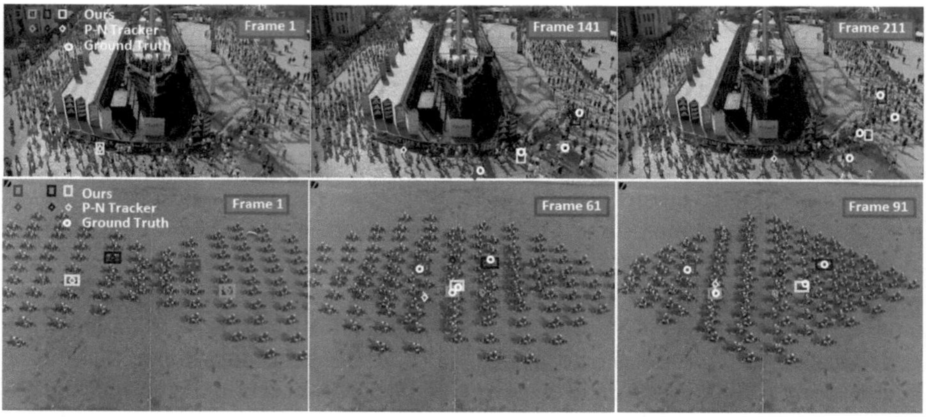

Fig. 6. Examples of tracking results comparison. First row: temporally stationary scenes. Second row: temporally non-stationary scenes.

2. Single target tracking results in temporally non-stationary scenes. To capture changing motion patterns, an online motion pattern learning and tracking framework is built. Each time, we consider a fixed-length window of size 40 in time, extract motion pattern information in the window and utilize it to assist tracking. Then the window shifts 40 frames to deal with the next 40 frames (or less in the last window), and so on.

The Hongkong sequence (first row in Fig. 4) and Motorbike sequence (second row in Fig. 4) have 248 frames and 100 frames respectively. In each sequence, 10 targets are randomly selected, with an average size of 15×24 and 30×22 pixels respectively. Since each of the two sequences contains two motion patterns, we divide motion pattern points in (x, y, v_x, v_y) space into two groups by k-means. To calculate $\mathcal{L}_{MP}(\boldsymbol{v})$, we first decide which motion pattern the point (or the object it's from) belongs to by the vote from the object's past trajectory.

The motion pattern learning results for the two whole sequences are shown in Fig. 4. Fig. 4 (b) shows the visualization of projection in (x, y, v_x) space, and Fig. 4 (c) shows the projection on images. Tracking results comparison are presented in Table 2. An example is shown in the second row of Fig. 6. Our tracker still significantly outperforms the others. In Motorbike sequence, a large number of similar objects exist, and motion pattern prior effectively reduces drift. The Hongkong sequence is the most challenging one, since motion patterns are not as clear as others.

Table 2. Tracking evaluation of single target in temporally non-stationary scenes

Method	Hongkong		Motorbike	
	ATR	ACLE	ATR	ACLE
IVT Tracker [6]	27.63%	58.9	31.56%	69.7
P-N Tracker [7]	39.58%	42.3	47.22%	55.4
CTM [1]	52.17%	35.2	42.35%	58.3
Ours	**62.31%**	**28.5**	**88.75%**	**5.6**

3. Multi-target tracking results in temporally stationary scenes.
In each experiment, we manually select a rectangular region around a target in the first frame. We track the target for 10 frames to train our detector. Going back to the first frame, we use the detector to detect $n_1 = 6$ similar objects. Window size L is fixed as 8. If the tracking result for each target (by detector and structure flow tracker) has confidence ([0,1]) larger than 0.8, we move to the next frame. Otherwise use the $L = 8$ window to jointly optimize. The detection and tracking results are shown in Fig. 7(a). A red rectangle denotes the user labeled target, a blue rectangle denotes true positive detection of similar objects, and a yellow rectangle denotes false positive detection in the first frame. As we increase n_1, more false positives are brought in.

4. Multi-target tracking results in temporally non-stationary scenes.
Settings are the same as before. Online motion pattern learning is performed in the same setting as in Section 5.2. Detection and tracking results are shown in Fig. 7(b). It shows that tracking helps us remove some false alarms, and correct some others. For example, the false positive on the right in Fig. 7(b) detects two people in the first frame, but the tracker gradually moves to one target, so the detection is kept in tracking results.

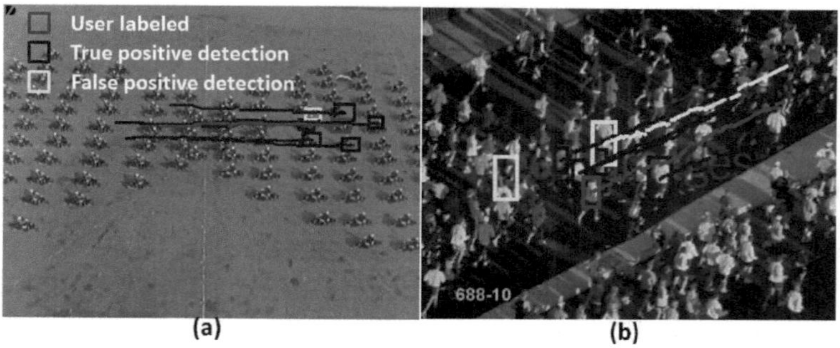

Fig. 7. Simplified multi-target detection and tracking results in temporally (a) stationary and (b) non-stationary scenes respectively. Red rectangle denotes the user labeled target. Blue rectangles denote the similar objects detected by the learned detector

6 Conclusion

This paper addresses the problem of tracking single and multiple targets in structured crowded scenes by Motion Structure Tracker, which combines several research topics: visual tracking, motion pattern learning, and multiple target tracking. Although each topic has been intensively studied, they are not jointly considered before. The experimental results on several challenging sequences and the comparison with state-of-the-art methods demonstrate the effectiveness of motion structure tracker. In the future, we will generalize our tracker to tracking in unstructured crowded scenes, and go further in multiple-target tracking.

Acknowledgments. This work was supported in part by grant DE-FG52-08NA28775 from the U.S. Department of Energy and NIH Grant EY016093.

References

1. Rodriguez, M., Ali, S., Kanade, T.: Tracking in unstructured crowded scenes. In: ICCV, pp. 1389–1396 (2009)
2. Ali, S., Shah, M.: Floor Fields for Tracking in High Density Crowd Scenes. In: Forsyth, D., Torr, P., Zisserman, A. (eds.) ECCV 2008, Part II. LNCS, vol. 5303, pp. 1–14. Springer, Heidelberg (2008)
3. Kratz, L., Nishino, K.: Tracking with local spatio-temporal motion patterns in extremely crowded scenes. In: CVPR, pp. 693–700 (2010)
4. Huang, C., Nevatia, R.: High performance object detection by collaborative learning of joint ranking of granules features. In: CVPR, pp. 41–48 (2010)
5. Yilmax, A., Javed, O., Shah, M.: Object tracking: A survey. ACM Journal of Computing Surveys 38 (2006)
6. Ross, D., Lim, J., Lin, R., Yang, M.: Incremental learning for robust visual tracking. In: IJCV, pp. 125–141 (2008)
7. Kalal, Z., Matas, J., Mikolajczyk, K.: P-n learning: Bootstrapping binary classifiers by structural constraints. In: CVPR, pp. 49–56 (2010)

8. Babenko, B., Yang, M.H., Belongie, S.: Visual tracking with online multiple instance learning. In: CVPR, pp. 983–990 (2009)
9. Grabner, H., Leistner, C., Bischof, H.: Semi-supervised On-Line Boosting for Robust Tracking. In: Forsyth, D., Torr, P., Zisserman, A. (eds.) ECCV 2008, Part I. LNCS, vol. 5302, pp. 234–247. Springer, Heidelberg (2008)
10. Mehran, R., Moore, B., Shah, M.: A streakline representation of flow in crowded scenes. In: ECCV, pp. 439–452 (2010)
11. Saleemi, I., Hartung, L., Shah, M.: Scene understanding by statistical modeling of motion patterns. In: CVPR, pp. 2069–2076 (2010)
12. Hu, M., Ali, S., Shah, M.: Learning motion patterns in crowded scenes using motion flow field. In: ICPR, pp. 1–5 (2011)
13. Zhao, X., Medioni, G.: Robust unsupervised motion pattern inference from video and applications. In: ICCV, pp. 715–722 (2011)
14. Zhou, B., Wang, X., Tang, X.: Random field topic model for semantic region analysis in crowded scenes from tracklets. In: CVPR, pp. 3441–3448 (2011)
15. Ali, S., Shah, M.: A lagrangian particle dynamics approach for crowd flow segmentation and stability analysis. In: CVPR, pp. 1–6 (2007)
16. Hu, W., Xiao, X., Fu, Z., Xie, D., Tan, T., Maybank, S.: A system for learning statistical motion patterns. In: PAMI, pp. 1450–1464 (2006)
17. Wang, X., Ma, X., Grimson, E.: Unsupervised activity perceptionby hierarchical bayesian models. In: CVPR, pp. 1–8 (2007)
18. Kuettel, D., Breitenstein, M.D., Gool, L.V., Ferrari, V.: What's going on? discovering spatio-temporal dependencies in dynamic scenes. In: CVPR, pp. 1951–1958 (2010)
19. Rodriguez, M., Sivic, J., Laptev, I., Audibert, J.: Data-driven crowd analysis in videos. In: ICCV, pp. 1235–1242 (2011)
20. Andriluka, M., Roth, S., Schiele, B.: People-tracking-by-detection and people-detection-by-tracking. In: CVPR, pp. 1–8 (2008)
21. Huang, C., Wu, B., Nevatia, R.: Robust Object Tracking by Hierarchical Association of Detection Responses. In: Forsyth, D., Torr, P., Zisserman, A. (eds.) ECCV 2008, Part II. LNCS, vol. 5303, pp. 788–801. Springer, Heidelberg (2008)
22. Prokaj, J., Medioni, G.: Inferring tracklets for multi-object tracking. In: Workshop of Aerial Video Processing Joint with IEEE CVPR, pp. 37–44 (2011)
23. Zhang, L., Li, Y., Nevatia, R.: Global data association for multi-object tracking using network flows. In: CVPR, pp. 1–8 (2008)
24. Rodriguez, M., Sivic, J., Laptev, I., Audibert, J.: Density-aware person detection and tracking in crowds. In: ICCV, pp. 2423–2430 (2011)
25. Tomasi, C., Kanade, T.: Detection and tracking of point features. In: IJCV (1991)
26. Mordohai, P., Medioni, G.: Dimensionality estimation, manifold learning and function approximation using tensor voting. JMLR 11, 411–450 (2010)
27. Coifman, R.R., Lafon, S., Lee, A., Maggioni, M., Nadler, B., Warner, F., Zucker, S.: Geometric diffusion as a tool for harmonic analysis and structure definition of data, part i: Diffusion maps. The National Academy of Sciences (2005)
28. Zhou, D., Weston, J., Gretton, A., Bousquet, O., Schölkopf, B.: Ranking on data manifolds. In: NIPS (2004)
29. Ozuysal, M., Calonder, M., Lepetit, V., Fua, P.: Fast keypoint recognition using random ferns. In: PAMI, pp. 448–461 (2010)
30. Bosch, A., Zisserman, A., Munoz, X.: Image classification using random forests and ferns. In: ICCV, pp. 1–8 (2007)
31. Oshin, O., Gilbert, A., Illingworth, J., Bowden, R.: Action recognition using randomised ferns. In: ICCV, pp. 530–537 (2009)
32. Lucas, B., Kanade, T.: An iterative image registration technique with an application to stereo vision. IJCAI, 674–679 (1981)

Long-Range Spatio-Temporal Modeling of Video with Application to Fire Detection

Avinash Ravichandran and Stefano Soatto

Vision Lab, University of California, Los Angeles,
Los Angeles, CA, 90095

Abstract. We describe a methodology for modeling backgrounds subject to significant variability over time-scales ranging from days to years, where the events of interest exhibit subtle variability relative to the normal mode. The motivating application is fire monitoring from remote stations, where illumination changes spanning the day and the season, meteorological phenomena resembling smoke, and the absence of sufficient training data for the two classes make out-of-the-box classification algorithms ineffective. We exploit low-level descriptors, incorporate explicit modeling of nuisance variability, and learn the residual normal-model variability. Our algorithm achieves state-of-the-art performance not only compared to other anomaly detection schemes, but also compared to human performance, both for untrained and trained operators.

1 Introduction

We are motivated by outdoor fire detection from remote video monitoring stations. While every serious fire is detected *eventually*, the longer the lag between onset and detection, the more difficult the fire is to manage. So, we are interested in detecting fires with *minimum latency*. Although this is a standard binary classification problem, where each video frame must be labeled as positive (fire alarm) or negative, a fire may manifest itself in a large variety of fashions depending on the time of the day, the season, weather conditions, landscape, pose of the camera, vegetation type, etc. Such *nuisance variability* cannot be easily "learned away", for a balanced training set would require multiple instances of fire in different locations, against different landscapes, different weather, season, etc. Even learning the *normal mode*, and detecting fire as a violation of the null hypothesis, requires long training, as the photometric conditions change during the entire year, and one would need sufficient sampling of weather conditions. Clouds look similar to smoke, so one can expect significant overlap between the class-conditional distributions.

In this manuscript, we *explore the tradeoff between modeling and learning, when the underlying data exhibits nuisance variability over multiple time-scales.* Our paper can be interpreted as dealing with background subtraction when the background exhibits fine-grained long-range variability over long time-scales. We describe a process whereby long-range temporal variability is partly modeled, partly learned, and report state of the art results in fire detection, even when

A. Fitzgibbon et al. (Eds.): ECCV 2012, Part II, LNCS 7573, pp. 329–342, 2012.

compared to trained humans. While fire detection is our driving application, our method can be extended to other cases where there is significant photometric variability over long time scales.

1.1 Related Work

Prior work on fire monitoring [1,2,3,4] relies on color and/or background subtraction to detect either flames or smoke. A variety of descriptors are then computed in these regions and fed to a classifier together with negative samples from surrounding regions. Such methods require training for both the null and the alternate hypothesis; given the lack of positive samples, authors generate synthetic ones or create ad-hoc footage of fire devoid from the context. These methods generally fail outdoors, where the photometric signatures of smoke and fire are shared by clouds, ground, and sun.

Other methods frame the problem as anomaly or fault detection, thus modeling the null hypothesis without requiring positive examples of fire. Most work on background subtraction falls in this category, e.g. [5,6]; [7,8] use optical flow, [9] mixtures of dynamic textures, [10] dictionaries, and [11] spatio-temporal energies. Some methods [10,8,11] incrementally update the normal models; Zhao et al [10] extract spatiotemporal interest points using sliding windows and then learn a dictionary for these volumes. Anomalies are then defined as regions that have a high reconstruction error based on the learnt dictionary. Kim et al [8] define a spatial grid and learn histograms of optical flow in each spatiotemporal volume. Anomalies are detected by comparing new observations with the learnt model using a markov random field. Similarly, [11] also learn histograms in spatiotemporal volumes. These methods work for video sequences that are a few hours long, but fail when the nuisance variability (due to weather and season) trumps the change due to an onset of fire.

There has been increasing interest in outdoor fire monitoring since the 2007 Station Fire obliterated 70% of the Angeles National Forest. That was attributed to a long delay in detection due to the dismantling of manned stations, to the point where the fire had become uncontrollable. Since then, a large number of unmanned stations have been set up, providing large scale video databases, for instance [12]. Large temporal scale has been addressed by [13,14], who summarized data using PCA [13] or Fast Subset PCA [14]. Such approaches require a large set of data such as the AMOS [15] database to learn the basis and assume that all normal variations are available. Modeling based approaches such as [16] on the other hand rely on exploiting meta information such as latitude, longitude and time of the day to calculate the position of the sun and use a sky appearance model [17] to obtain the appearance of the sky. This information is then mapped to the images using camera calibration as well as the inverse transfer function of the camera. While such methods alleviate the need for a large set of exemplars, they suffer from issues such as drift in the calibration over long periods. Also, any change in imaging parameters would require a recalibration.

Our goal is to develop methods that can be deployed on a newly installed monitoring station, without the need for careful calibration, without explicit knowledge of mapping of the landscape, and without the need for long training over the course of several months or years.

2 Methodology

We denote an image by $I : D \subset \mathbb{R}^2 \times \mathbb{R}_+ \to \mathbb{R}^3_+;\ (\mathbf{x}, t) \mapsto I_t(\mathbf{x})$. We call $\lambda_t(\mathbf{x}) \in \{0, 1\}$ the decision variable, with $\lambda_t(\mathbf{x}) = 0$ being the null hypothesis (normal mode) and $\lambda_t(\mathbf{x}) = 1$ being an alarm (alternate hypothesis/anomaly detected at position $\mathbf{x}$ at time t). We are interested in obtaining $\lambda_t(\mathbf{x})$, given a video sequence up to time t.

2.1 Change Detection

We first tackle the short time-scale to discard regions of temporally adjacent images, I_t and I_{t+dt}, where no changes occur. From a static camera in the absence of memory this is just frame differencing. When memory is available, one can learn a background model as in standard background subtraction. Changes are then detected as deviations from the background model. However, when nuisance variability is present, for instance due to motion of the sun, clouds and vegetation, a large number of false alarms is generated. To enable local insensitivity to changes in contrast and small motion from vegetation, we employ gradient orientation histograms, a' la SIFT [18] and compute dense displacement optical flow. Let $u : D \times \mathbb{R}_+ \to \mathbb{R}^2; (\mathbf{x}, t) \mapsto u_t(\mathbf{x})$ denote the optical flow that maps $I_t(\mathbf{x})$ into $I_{t+dt}(\mathbf{x})$, $C : D \times \mathbb{R}_+ \to \{0, 1\}; (\mathbf{x}, t) \mapsto C_t(\mathbf{x})$ denote the presence/absence of a change at $(\mathbf{x}, t)$ and $\mu : D \times \mathbb{R}_+ \to \mathbb{R}^{128}; (\mathbf{x}, t) \mapsto \mu_t(\mathbf{x})$ denote the SIFT descriptor at $(\mathbf{x}, t)$. We would like to compute $P(C_t(\mathbf{x}) = 1)$, given $I_t(\mathbf{x})$ and $I_{t+dt}(\mathbf{x})$, by combining the complementary descriptive characteristics of gradient orientation histograms (that can detect changes in homogeneous regions) and optical flow (that can explain photometrically consistent motion between adjacent images):

$$P(C_t(\mathbf{x}) = 1) = w_1 P_S(C_t(\mathbf{x}) = 1) + w_2 P_F(C_t(\mathbf{x}) = 1), \tag{1}$$

where

$$P_S(C_t(\mathbf{x}) = 1) = e^{-\gamma_1 \|\mu_{t+dt}(\mathbf{x}) - \mu_t(\mathbf{x})\|_2}, \tag{2}$$

$$P_F(C_t(\mathbf{x}) = 1) = e^{-\gamma_2 \|u_t(\mathbf{x})\|_2}. \tag{3}$$

The weights γ_1 and γ_2 are determined as the mean of the differences over the image and $w_1 = w_2 = 0.5$.

2.2 Nuisance Maps

Our next step is to model the variability due to the interaction of the geometry of the scene and the light source, specifically the location of the sun and of cast shadows. To this end, we introduce *nuisance maps*, $N : D \times \mathbb{R}_+ \to [0, 1]$; $(\mathbf{x}, t) \mapsto N_t(\mathbf{x})$, where $N_t(\mathbf{x})$ denotes the probability of nuisance variability occurring at $(\mathbf{x}, t)$. For a scene, several such nuisance maps $\{N^i\}_{i=1}^m$ might be available, for instance "sun," "shadow," "roadway," etc. Nuisance maps discount the probability of an alarm in their corresponding region. If $N(\mathbf{x}, t) = 1$, changes in that location are discarded entirely. Otherwise, their relevance is weighted by their probability

$$P(C_t(\mathbf{x}) = 1, N_t^1(\mathbf{x}) = 0, \ldots, N_t^m(\mathbf{x}) = 0) \tag{4}$$

$$= P(C_t(\mathbf{x}) = 1) \prod_{i=1}^{m} \left[1 - P(N_t^i(\mathbf{x}) = 1)\right]. \tag{5}$$

The regions of interest can then be defined as

$$a_t^L(\mathbf{x}) = \mathbb{1}\left[P(C = 1, N^1 = 0, \ldots, N^m = 0) \geq \theta\right], \tag{6}$$

where $\mathbb{1}[\cdot]$ is the indicator function of the event in brackets.

2.3 Classifier

Once static regions and nuisance maps are taken into account, we are left with learning the residual variability. The most significant for the case of fire detection is due to weather conditions. We learn this variability using features and their distributions. The image is divided into a regular grid of spatial patches. Features in each patch are aggregated and a model is learnt for them.

When learning the normal mode, we need to account for seasonal changes that affect the length of the day, sunset and sunrise times. Consequently, the same normal-mode occurs at different time instants during the year e.g. sunrise. We address this issue by *canonizing* the time scale [19]. The canonized time is defined as $t_c = \frac{t - t_0}{t_1 - t_0}$, where t is the time in the day and t_1 and t_0 are the sunrise and sunset times for that particular day. This ensures that the length of the days in a year, the sunrise times and sunset times are the same.

As photometric and texture cues are shared by the normal-mode and the anomaly (fire), at pixels where there is change i.e. $a_t^L(\mathbf{x}) = 1$, we use the following feature

$$\mathbf{F}_t(\mathbf{x}) = \left[\phi_t(\mathbf{x}) \; t_c\right]^\top \in \mathbb{R}^2, \tag{7}$$

where $\phi_t(\mathbf{x})$ is the flow angle at $(\mathbf{x}, t)$, t_c is the canonized time. A key difference between existing anomaly detection methods and our algorithm is that we explicitly parameterize our features with time as opposed to learning histograms of features independent of time. This is necessary since outdoor videos do not exhibit stationary statistics, but are instead cyclo-stationary in canonized time, with significant variability across the time scale.

We learn the feature distribution in each patch using a kernel density estimator (KDE) with gaussian kernels. Given the set of features $\mathcal{F}_i = \{F_t(\mathbf{x}) | t \in [1, T], \mathbf{x} \in$

$\Omega_i\}$, where $\Omega_i \subset D$ is a fixed size rectangular image patch such that $\Omega_i \cap \Omega_j = \emptyset, i \neq j$ and $\cup_i \Omega_i = D$, the features distribution is represented as

$$P(F_t(\mathbf{x})) = \sum_{F_j \in \mathcal{F}_i} w_j K_{\Sigma_{F_j}}(F_t(\mathbf{x}) - F_j), \tag{8}$$

where $K_\Sigma(F) = \frac{1}{2\pi|\Sigma|^{1/2}} e^{-\frac{1}{2}(F^\top \Sigma^{-1} F)}$. The challenge with such an approach is estimating the width of the kernel at each point and removing redundant data points from the KDE. We use the approach proposed in [20], which allows us to adaptively estimate the kernel bandwidth in an online fashion, and remove redundant points from the model. Consequently, the learning is incremental and updates the model as new data becomes available. This removes the need for a large amount of data for learning the classifier, and for archiving data, allowing for a small storage footprint.

Given the model M_i learnt over the patch Ω_i, a new observation at $\mathbf{x} \in \Omega_i$ is considered an anomaly as follows

$$a_t^C(\mathbf{x}) = \mathbb{1}[P(F_t(\mathbf{x}) \in M_i) \leq \beta_i], \tag{9}$$

where β_i is the minimum probability of the normal data under M_i. β_i is updated as the minimum between the current β_i and the new β_i calculated on the current data under the new model. Hence, we do not need to recalculate the probabilities of old data when we update the model and can update this threshold using the current data and the updated model.

2.4 Context Priors

Our method so far has exploited visual information present in the image sequences and proposed a generic framework for detecting any anomaly in outdoor scenes. However, given a specific anomaly of interest, we would like to exploit non-visual characteristics that can be leveraged into our framework. One such candidate is *context* information e.g. flooding is restricted to the ground, flying objects are restricted to the sky and fires originate from the ground (although its effects can be measured against the sky). Furthermore, when visual and motion cues are ambiguous in discriminating between the normal-mode and the anomaly, context can help to disambiguate them. For example, clouds and fire looks very similar and prevailing winds influence the direction of both clouds and fire. However, from the context perspective clouds are higher up when compared to fires. The context information is incorporated using a context prior $P(\lambda(\mathbf{x}) = 1)$ that indicates the probability of an anomaly occurring at a given pixel location $\mathbf{x}$. The context prior is incorporated with the classifier response as $a_t^P(\mathbf{x}) = P(\lambda(\mathbf{x}) = 1) \cdot a_t^C(\mathbf{x})$, which we will temporally integrate in §2.5.

2.5 Temporal Integration

The decision of whether there is an anomaly present in an image is obtained using a short temporal scale ($[t, t+1]$). To aggregate this information over longer temporal scales ($[1, t]$), we consider a_t^P and integrate it as follows:

$$S_t^P(\mathbf{x}) = a_t^P(\mathbf{x}) + \gamma S_{t-1}^P(b_t(\mathbf{x})), \tag{10}$$

where $S_1^P(\mathbf{x}) = a_1^C(\mathbf{x})$, γ is a forgetting factor that weights the observations up to $t-1$ and $b_t(\mathbf{x})$ is the pixel location in I_{t-1} that gets mapped to $\mathbf{x}$ in I_t via optical flow. This gives a score at each pixel and anomalies are detected as $\lambda_t^P(\mathbf{x}) = \mathbb{1}\left[S_t^P(\mathbf{x}) \geq \alpha\right]$.

For the purpose of analysis, we could also temporally integrate the *low-level* mask a_t^L (change detection + nuisance maps) or the *classifier* mask a_t^C (change detection + nuisance map + classifier) as shown in Eq. (10). Anomalies can then be detected as $\lambda_t^L(\mathbf{x}) = \mathbb{1}\left[S_t^L(\mathbf{x}) \geq \alpha\right]$ and $\lambda_t^C(\mathbf{x}) = \mathbb{1}\left[S_t^C(\mathbf{x}) \geq \alpha\right]$. In §3, we refer to $S_t^L(\mathbf{x})$, $S_t^C(\mathbf{x})$ and $S_t^P(\mathbf{x})$ as the low-level, the classifier and the context component respectively. We will show results not only using our entire pipeline i.e. $S_t^P(\mathbf{x})$ but also $S_t^C(\mathbf{x})$ and $S_t^L(\mathbf{x})$ to show the contribution of each step in our framework.

3 Experiments

Our data consists of time lapse images obtained from the publicly available repository maintained by the Applied Network Research Center, San Diego. From this set, we chose cameras that contain recent and archived fire incidents. Specifically, the East facing camera at Lyons Peak[1], the North East facing camera at Volcan mountain[2] and the South East facing camera at red mountain[3]. The cameras are static and capture images at the rate of 1 frame/2 mins. Sample frames from the fire sequences are shown in Fig. 1 where the fire location is indicated by a black rectangle.

The test data comprises of 96 hours of video with equal distribution of normal and fire sequences, under a variety of weather from clear/sunny to clouds and fog. The training data comprises of 3 days of data for each camera, chosen at random within the data repository. The initial classifier is learnt using data from one day in batch mode and then incrementally updated with data from each frame for the next 2 days. We compare our method to the state-of-the-art in anomaly detection [10] which outperforms [8]. The training and testing conditions are identical to our approach.

In our approach, we used the same parameters for all the cameras and did not optimize them. We used a patch size of 20×20 for learning the classifiers with $\gamma = 0.9, \theta = 0.5$. The optical flow is calculated using the large-displacement method [21]. The shadow map was obtained by converting the color image to YCrCb and the nuisance map for the shadow is defined as $\frac{1}{2}\frac{Y+1}{Cr+1}$. The nuisance map for the sun was obtained using one third of the L_2-norm of the normalized color intensity at each pixel. By construction, the nuisance maps lie between 0 and 1.

[1] `http://anr.ucsd.edu/cameras/LyonsPeak.html`
[2] `http://anr.ucsd.edu/cameras/SantaYsabel.html`
[3] `http://anr.ucsd.edu/cameras/RedMtn.html`

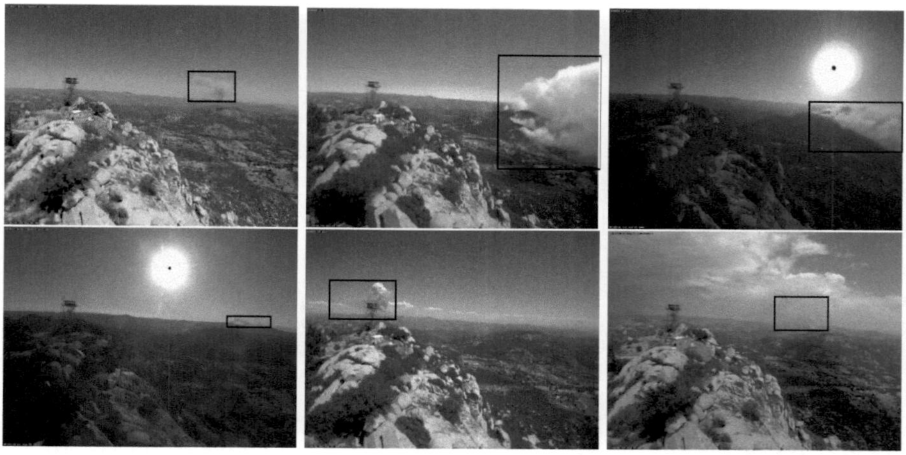

Fig. 1. Sample frames from sequences of fire from the Lyons Peak Camera. Fire regions are denoted by a black bounding box.

The context prior is a simple weight. Given the horizon (marked manually) in the image, the context prior is set to one below the horizon and exponentially decays to 0 at the top of the image. We compare the performance of each component of our framework as defined in §2.5 namely the low-level method, the classifier method and the context method.

3.1 Qualitative Results

Qualitative results are shown in Fig. 2 for a single frame. This figure shows the video frame with the score maps overlaid and the ground truth shown as a black box. From this figure we see that the low-level component of our algorithm is able to suppress the known nuisances i.e. the shadow and the sun. However, there are multiple false alarms. In the red mountain camera, there are anomalies detected at the top of the image due to vignetting. The classifier is able to learn such artifacts and reduces the number of false positives. There is only a slight difference between the detections by the classifier component and that of the context prior component. This is because these sequences do not have weather phenomena such as clouds.

Additional qualitative results in Fig. 3 show the effect of the context prior in our method. The setup of this figure is identical to Fig. 2. The first row shows an image with severe clouds. This sequence is extremely challenging as there are several weather phenomena such as heavy clouds and rain. In this case, the context prior significantly reduces the number of false positives. While the localization is not perfect, we are able to detect the anomaly with fewer false positives. The second row in Fig. 3 shows an image with a large fire. Here, the context prior reduces the localization support. However, it still maintains a high precision.

(a) Frame (I_t) (b) Low Level (S_t^L) (c) Classifier (S_t^C) (d) Context (S_t^P)

Fig. 2. Qualitative results. Each column shows the performance of different components of our method. The results are shown by overlaying the temporal integrated score over the gray scale frame and the ground truth is shown as a black box. The first row corresponds to a sequence from the Lyons Peak camera, the second row corresponds to a sequence from the Red Mountain camera and the last row corresponds to a sequence from the Volcan Mountain Camera. These are easy samples; for difficult ones, see the next figure.

3.2 Quantitative Results

To evaluate our algorithm, we compute detection performance, localization performance and detection lag.

Detection Performance. Detection performance is calculated on a per-frame basis. A frame is marked as anomalous even if a single pixel in that frame is classified as an anomaly. We can then compare this with the ground truth and calculate the different metrics. Detection performance is evaluated using the receiver operating characteristic (ROC) curves which show the true positive rate vs the false positive rate. The true positive rate is defined as $TPR = \frac{TP}{TP+FN}$, where TP is the number of true positive and FN is the number of false negatives. Similarly, the false positive rate is defined as $FPR = \frac{FP}{FP+TN}$, where TN is the number of true negatives. We report the ROC curve for both the normal as well as anomalous videos.

The ROC curves obtained by varying the score threshold α for each camera are shown in Fig. 4. The different curves illustrate the different components of our framework. We also report the equal error rate (EER), i.e. the performance when the FPR is equal to the false negative rate $(1 - TPR)$ in Table 1. This figure shows that the best performance is achieved after including the context prior

(a) Frame (I_t) (b) Low Level (S_t^L) (c) Classifier (S_t^C) (d) Context (S_t^P)

Fig. 3. Qualitative results showing the effect of the context prior. Each column shows the performance of different components of our method. The results are shown by overlaying the temporal integrated score over the gray scale frame and the ground truth is shown as a black box.

and the classification step improves upon our low-level detection step across all cameras. For the Lyons Peak camera, the gain in the performance as compared to the low-level framework is not significant. This can be attributed to the fact that the test data for this camera is several years apart from the training data. Furthermore, we have extremely challenging sequences both for the normal case as well as the fire case for this camera. The low-level curve for the Red mountain camera does not intersect the EER line. This is due to the false positives present on the top of the image as shown in Fig. 2. Hence increasing the threshold only retains these detections and is reflected in the precision curves in Fig. 5(b).

Also shown in this figure is the detection performance of [10] in purple. For all cameras, the performance of the context component of the algorithm is much

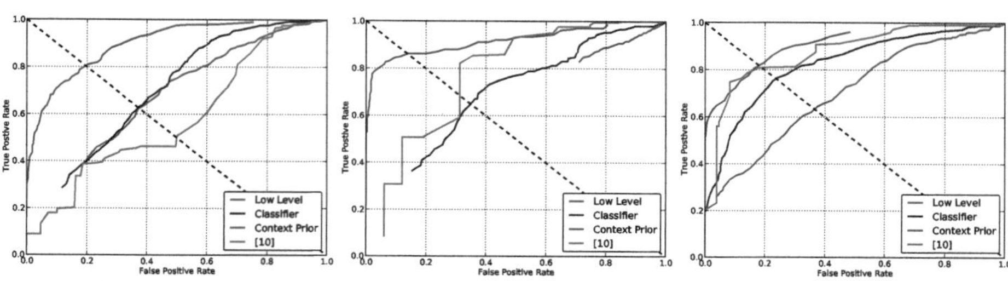

(a) Lyons Peak (b) Red Mountain (c) Volcan Mountain

Fig. 4. Frame level detection performance. Each plot show the TPR vs the FPR for different components in our algorithm for a particular camera. In addition, we also show the performance of the baseline [10]. The curve is calculated by varying the score threshold α for both normal and anomalous sequences. The intersection of the curves with the dashed black line indicates the EER performance.

better than the baseline. In the case of the Red mountain and the Volcan mountain cameras, the classifier components perform worse than the baseline. However, for the Lyons Peak camera, even the low-level component is better than the baseline. Unfortunately, the detection performance of the baseline in several cases relies on false positives and this becomes evident when we calculate the localization performance.

Localization Performance. Since detection performance is evaluated at the frame level, there is a chance that false positives contribute to the frame being tagged as an anomaly. This is the case for the baseline method. Hence, we also evaluate the localization performance by manually annotating sequences that contain anomalies. Since annotating the exact contour of the fire in every frame of the sequence is extremely taxing, we instead mark a bounding box around the fire in each frame and use this annotation as our ground truth. Fig. 5 shows the precision of the anomaly detection as a function of the threshold of each method. Here the precision of each sequence that contains anomalies is evaluated and then averaged over all the sequences for each camera. The solid line shows the mean performance, while the shaded area shows the region within one standard deviation. The maximum mean precision of the baseline is shown as a black dashed line. This was obtained by varying the threshold for the baseline and computing the maximum mean precision across the sequences. We use precision as a metric to report the performance as opposed to the precision recall graph as our ground truth is based on bounding boxes. Hence, even in the case that the fire is perfectly detected, we always return false negatives. Therefore, we feel that reporting precision is a more appropriate metric.

From this figure, we notice that the context component has the best precision rate followed by the classification component and finally the low-level. The standard deviation also decreases as we move from the low-level component to the context component. As discussed earlier, the low-level performance for the Red Mountain camera decreases as we increase the threshold. While the opposite should occur, this can be attributed to the fact that the high scoring anomalies are due to the vignetting effect on the top of the image as shown in Fig. 2. When these normal modes are learnt using the classifier, the precision increases as we increase the threshold.

Also shown in this figure is the performance of the baseline. We see that for the Lyons peak camera, the maximum localization performance of the baseline is worse than the minimum performance of the low-level component. For the Red Mountain and the Volcan Mountain cameras, the baseline performance outperforms the low-level component but does not outperforms the classifier component. This is different from the trend in the detection performance where the baseline outperformed the low-level and the classifier component. This shows that the baseline algorithm generates a large number of false positive which influence the detection performance.

For normal sequences, there are no true positives. Hence precision cannot be reported for these sequences. Instead, we report the accuracy for the normal sequences. Fig. 6 shows the accuracy for each camera. The plot is similar to the

Table 1. Equal error rate for different cameras

Method	Lyons Peak	Volcan Mountain	Red Mountain
Low-Level	37.38	36.50	-
Classifier	37.18	23.67	34.93
Context	19.47	17.97	13.81
[10]	50.06	19.0	31.23

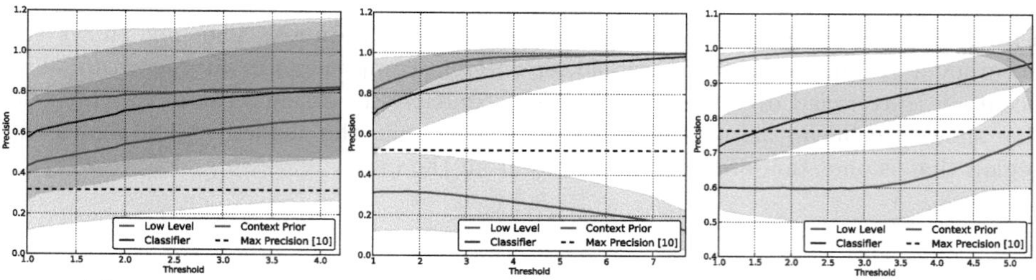

(a) Lyons Peak (b) Red Mountain (c) Volcan Mountain

Fig. 5. Localization performance for sequences containing anomalies. The plot shows the precision rate as a function of the threshold for different components in our algorithm. The solid line shows the mean across the videos that contain anomaly while the shaded region shows the region that is one standard deviation away from the mean. The dashed line shows the maximum precision obtained by [10].

precision plots for the anomalous sequences. The solid lines shows the mean over all the normal sequences and the shaded regions represent the region which is one standard deviation away from the mean. These figures show that the trend is the same as that of the sequences that contain anomalies. The context component of our method has the best mean performance followed by the classifier and then the low-level component. The standard deviation also changes correspondingly. Notice that the context component of our method starts with a very high accuracy for even a low threshold. We do not report the accuracy of [10] as we have shown that this method is not adequate for our task.

Comparison with Human Performance. We have collected experimental data from 10 subjects, of which 5 were trained on random subsets of the annotated data – and 5 were untrained, having seen just a single fire sequence before the onset of the experiment. The performance metric chosen is the *detection lag*, i.e. the time from the onset of the fire to when it is detected. Since the evidence of fire grows over time, and eventually becomes obvious, precision measured on an entire time-series is not a meaningful performance metric. Eventually, any algorithm achieves 100% correct detection. What matters instead is how long it takes before an alarm is called. The longer the detection lag, the more difficult it is to control the fire.

Subjects were presented with 32 videos taken from 3 different stations. Of these, 16 contained a fire commencing at a random instant distributed uniformly

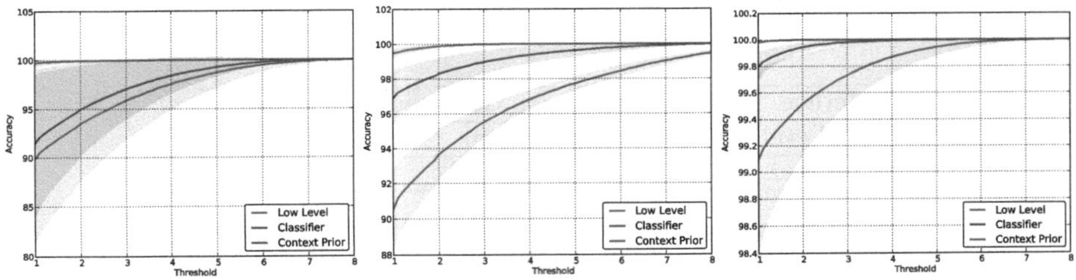

(a) Lyons Peak (b) Red Mountain (c) Volcan Mountain

Fig. 6. Localization performance for normal sequences. The plot shows the accuracy as a function of the threshold for different components in our algorithm. The accuracy is averaged over the normal video sequences for a single cameras. The solid line shows the mean across the video sequences while the shaded region shows the region that is one standard deviation away from the mean.

in the duration of the sequence; 16 contained no fire. Subjects were not told the ratio between sequences with and without a fire. They had control on when to advance to the next frame (to ensure they had sufficient time for inspection) and were allowed to browse frames backwards in time. When they sounded an alarm (report fire), the time corresponding to the current frame was recorded.

For our algorithm, the detection lag is the delay between the ground truth onset of fire and the instant when localization precision exceeds 0.9 over all possible values of threshold. This ensures that we not only detect the fire, but we detect it in the correct place. Table 2 shows the mean and the median detection lag of our algorithm compared with the human subjects, both trained and untrained. The detection lag of our algorithm, averaged over the dataset, had a median of 4.0min and a mean of 5.75min. It significantly outperforms both untrained (best performer had 9.0min median and 19.38min mean) and trained subject (best performer had 10.0min median and 13.12mins mean).

Time Complexity. We implemented our algorithm in MATLAB on an 8-core Intel Xeon 2.66GHz processor machine. However, we only used one CPU for running our method. Our algorithm took on average 11.57 mins to train on 3 hrs of data. Our testing procedure took about 0.48 seconds per frame. Additional results of our algorithm can be found at `vision.ucla.edu/fire/`.

Table 2. Detection lag for human subjects compared with our algorithm. T denotes trained subjects and U denotes untrained subjects.

	Our Algorithm	T 1	T 2	T 3	T 4	T 5	U 1	U 2	U 3	U 4	U 5
Median (in mins)	4.0	13.0	11.0	18.0	10.0	9.0	9.0	21.0	9.0	8.0	12.0
Mean (in mins)	5.8	24.4	20.4	33.2	13.1	15.9	19.4	30.8	22.4	20.2	30.0

4 Discussion

We have presented a methodology to detect anomalies in long video sequences, where the phenomenology of the event exhibits significant nuisance variability, that overlaps with normal-mode variability. This is the case for outdoor fire detection from monitoring stations, where illumination variability at the scale of one day, seasonal variability at the scale of one year, and unpredictable weather variability are hard to "learn away." As a result, we have chosen to combine generic priors from short time-scale (like photometric and dynamic homogeneity from gradient orientation histograms and optical flow), explicit modeling of nuisance maps for known distractors (such as the sun and cast shadows), and learning for the residual normal-mode variability using optical flow features. Alarms are generated as a violation of the null hypothesis. Our method outperforms humans in detection lag, that is the critical measure of performance in a fire monitoring system. While there are still false alarms, this system outperforms the state-of-the-art anomaly detection method that we tested.

Fire detection is an important societal application, with urbanization encroaching wild forest, and with insufficient funds to maintain manned monitoring stations. Disaster management costs are increasing rapidly, and this is an area where Computer Vision can make a difference.

Acknowledgments. This work was supported with funds from NSF CCF-0969032, ARO W911NF-11-1-0391 and ONR N000141110863.

References

1. Liu, C.B., Ahuja, N.: Vision based fire detection. In: ICPR (2004)
2. Kolesov, I., Karasev, P., Tannenbaum, A., Haber, E.: Fire and smoke detection in video with optimal mass transport based optical flow and neural networks. In: ICIP (2010)
3. Habiboglu, Y., Gunay, O., Cetin, A.: Flame detection method in video using covariance descriptors. In: ICCASP (2011)
4. Toreyin, B., Cetin, A.: Online detection of fire in video. In: CVPR (2007)
5. Stauffer, C., Grimson, W.: Learning patterns of activity using real-time tracking. PAMI 22(8), 747–757 (2000)
6. Basharat, A., Gritai, A., Shah, M.: Learning object motion patterns for anomaly detection and improved object detection. In: CVPR (2008)
7. Wang, X., Ma, X., Grimson, E.: Unsupervised activity perception by hierarchical bayesian models. In: CVPR (2007)
8. Kim, J., Grauman, K.: Observe locally, infer globally: A space-time mrf for detecting abnormal activities with incremental updates. In: CVPR (2009)
9. Mahadevan, V., Li, W., Bhalodia, V., Vasconcelos, N.: Anomaly detection in crowded scenes. In: CVPR (2010)
10. Zhao, B., Fei-Fei, L., Xing, E.: Online detection of unusual events in videos via dynamic sparse coding. In: CVPR (2011)

11. Zaharescu, A., Wildes, R.: Anomalous Behaviour Detection Using Spatiotemporal Oriented Energies, Subset Inclusion Histogram Comparison and Event-Driven Processing. In: Daniilidis, K., Maragos, P., Paragios, N. (eds.) ECCV 2010, Part I. LNCS, vol. 6311, pp. 563–576. Springer, Heidelberg (2010)
12. Applied Research Network, `http://anr.ucsd.edu/cameras/`
13. Jacobs, N., Burgin, W., Speyer, R., Ross, D., Pless, R.: Adventures in archiving and using three years of webcam images. In: CVPR Workshops (2009)
14. Abrams, A., Feder, E., Pless, R.: Exploratory analysis of time-lapse imagery with fast subset PCA. In: WACV (2011)
15. Jacobs, N., Roman, N., Pless, R.: Consistent temporal variations in many outdoor scenes. In: CVPR (2007)
16. Lalonde, J.F., Narasimhan, S.G., Efros, A.A.: What do the sun and the sky tell us about the camera? IJCV 88(1), 24–51 (2010)
17. Perez, R., Seals, R., Michalsky, J.: All-weather model for sky luminance distribution - preliminary configuration and validation. Solar Energy 50(3), 235–245 (1993)
18. Lowe, D.: Distinctive image features from scale-invariant keypoints. IJCV 20, 91–110 (2004)
19. Soatto, S.: On the distance between non-stationary time series. In: Modeling, Estimation and Control. Springer (2007)
20. Kristan, M., Leonardis, A., Skočaj, D.: Multivariate online kernel density estimation with gaussian kernels. Pattern Recognition 44(10-11), 2630–2642 (2011)
21. Brox, T., Bregler, C., Malik, J.: Large displacement optical flow. In: CVPR (June 2009)

GMCP-Tracker: Global Multi-object Tracking Using Generalized Minimum Clique Graphs

Amir Roshan Zamir, Afshin Dehghan, and Mubarak Shah

UCF Computer Vision Lab, Orlando, FL 32816, USA

Abstract. Data association is an essential component of any human tracking system. The majority of current methods, such as bipartite matching, incorporate a limited-temporal-locality of the sequence into the data association problem, which makes them inherently prone to ID-switches and difficulties caused by long-term occlusion, cluttered background, and crowded scenes. We propose an approach to data association which incorporates both motion and appearance in a global manner. Unlike limited-temporal-locality methods which incorporate a few frames into the data association problem, we incorporate the whole temporal span and solve the data association problem for one object at a time, while implicitly incorporating the rest of the objects. In order to achieve this, we utilize Generalized Minimum Clique Graphs to solve the optimization problem of our data association method. Our proposed method yields a better formulated approach to data association which is supported by our superior results. Experiments show the proposed method makes significant improvements in tracking in the diverse sequences of Town Center [1], TUD-crossing [2], TUD-Stadtmitte [2], PETS2009 [3], and a new sequence called Parking Lot compared to the state of the art methods.

Keywords: Data Association, Human Tracking, Generalized Graphs, GMCP, Generalized Minimum Clique Problem.

1 Introduction

In the context of tracking, data association is the problem of finding the detections corresponding to one particular object in different frames of a video. The input to the data association problem in a sequence can ideally be represented by a graph in which all the detections in each frame are connected to all the other detections in the other frames, regardless of their closeness in time. Similarly, the output can be ideally represented by several subgraphs of the input in which the detections belonging to common entities are connected.

Finding the ideal subgraphs which represent the exact solution to data association requires solving an optimization problem which remains unsolved to date due to its extreme complexity. Therefore, approximation methods are employed in order to simplify the conditions and find an acceptable solution. The natural, and probably the simplest, approximation is considering a limited-temporal-locality, e.g. two or few frames of the input graph, and solving the optimization

A. Fitzgibbon et al. (Eds.): ECCV 2012, Part II, LNCS 7573, pp. 343–356, 2012.

problem for the smaller, less complex subgraph. This natural approximation forms one main category of data association methods which has been investigated thoroughly in literature. Best known examples of such methods are bipartite matching (considering only two frames) and its extensions [4,5], which use an extended, yet limited, number of frames. In [4], an approach based on k-partite matching in an extended temporal window is proposed. However, the complexity of their method is proportional to the size of the temporal window (the number of frames), which makes their method impractical for a window size larger than 5-10 frames. The approach in [6] first generates low level tracklets and then employs heuristics in order to merge tracklets into trajectories. The authors of [7,8,9] use a similar approach; however the motion models are improved by incorporating social interaction using a social force model. Despite good complexity performance of the aforementioned methods, their approximation assumption makes them inherently prone to ID-switches and difficulties caused by long-term occlusions, complex motion scenarios, inaccurate bounding boxes, background domination, etc.

Several methods, generally termed *global*, have recently been proposed that make an effort to reduce or remove the limited-temporal-locality assumption. The common point among all of these methods is that they consider the whole temporal span of the sequence rather than limiting it to a number of frames. Zhang et al. [10] define a graph similar to [4] and solve the data association problem by optimizing the cost flow network in order to find the globally optimal trajectories. Brendel et al. [11] use Maximum Weight Independent Set to merge short tracks of size 2 into full trajectories. Berclaz et al. [12] use a grid of potential spatial locations and formulate their data association problem using the K-Shortest Path algorithm. However, their method does not actively incorporate appearance features into the data association process, which makes their approach prone to ID-switches in complicated scenarios. In contrast, Horesh et al. [13] address this limitation by exploiting the global appearance constraints in a similar framework.

In this paper, we propose a method for data association which incorporates both appearance and motion in a global way. In the proposed framework, we incorporate the whole temporal span of the sequence into the data association problem, but we focus on one object at time rather than addressing all of them simultaneously. This is to avoid dealing with an extremely complex optimization problem. Although we focus on solving the data association problem for one object at time, we also incorporate all the other objects implicity. Therefore, our approximation in the object-domain is significantly less restrictive than those used by other approximate methods, such as limited-temporal-locality. This is because the limited-temporal-locality methods are literally *blind* to the information outside of the temporal neighborhood they are focused on, while the proposed method incorporates the whole approximation domain, i.e. all objects, implicitly. We argue that this fundamental difference, along with our proposed framework, yields a better formulation of the data association problem which is supported by our superior results.

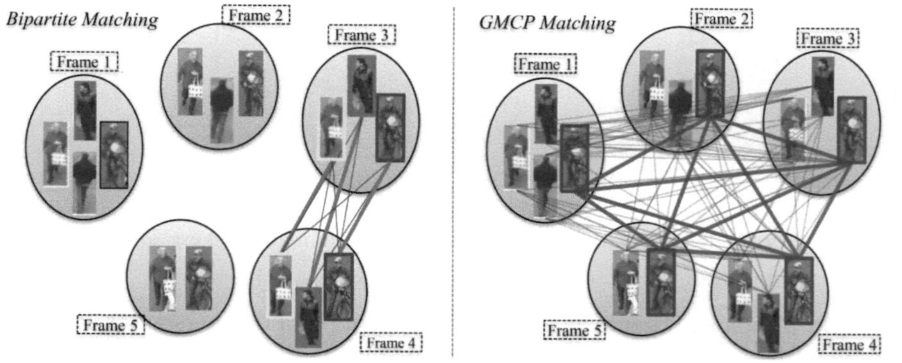

Fig. 1. Bi-partite vs. GMCP matching. Gray and colored edges represent the input graph and optimized subgraph, respectively. Bi-partite matches all objects in a limited temporal window. On the other hand, the proposed method matches one object at a time across full temporal span, while incorporating the rest of the objects implicitly.

The proposed method and bi-partite matching are both shown schematically in Fig. 1 for a sequence of 6 frames. The gray edges show the input graph for the data assosiation for one iteration of the algorithms. The colored thick edges show the optimized subgraph representing the results of that iteration. As shown in the right, the resultant subgraph of our method determines the detections of one person over the whole temporal span, while keeping a notion of other pedestrians in the optimization process. In contrast, the limited-locality-methods do not carry the information out of their current locality (i.e. no edges to or from the frames other than 3 and 4).

The proposed framework is composed of detecting humans in frames[14], calculating tracklets in video segments (subsec. 2.1) and merging them into trajectories(subsec. 2.2). We utilize Generalized Minimum Clique Graphs to solve our data association problem (subsec. 2.1). We tested the proposed method on the diverse sequences of Town Center [1], TUD-corssing [2], TUD-Stadtmitte [2], PETS2009 [3], and a new sequence called Parking Lot, all with promising results.

2 GMCP-Tracker

The block diagram of the proposed global data association algorithm is shown in Fig. 2. The first step is to detect the humans in each frame. We used Felzenszwalb et al.'s [14] part-based human detector. However, any other detector could be used. Next, we divide the input video into a number of segments and find the tracklet of pedestrians within each segment using the proposed global method for tracklet generation utilizing GMCP. In the last step, we merge the tracklets found in all of the segments to form the trajectory of each person over the course of the whole video.

Despite the appearance of the pedestrians remaining rather consistent throughout a video, the pattern of motion tends to differ significantly in short and long

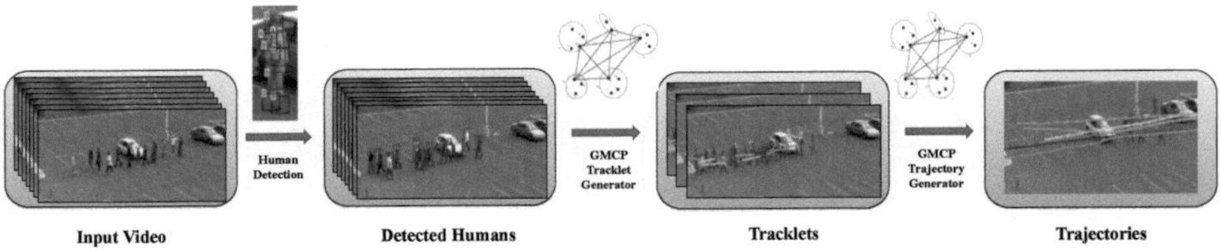

Fig. 2. The block diagram of the proposed human tracking method

term. In principle, it's difficult to model the motion of one person for a long duration without having the knowledge of the destination, structure of the scene, interactions between people, etc. However, the motion can be modeled sufficiently using constant velocity or acceleration models over a short period of time. Therefore, the way motion is incorporated into the global data association process should be different in short and long terms. This motivated us to employ the hierarchical approach, i.e. finding tracklets first and then merging them into full trajectories.

The rest of this section is organized as follows: 2.1 explains the proposed method for finding tracklets along with an overview of Generalized Minimum Clique Problem, our global motion-cost model and occlusion handling method. Merging the tracklets to form global trajectories is explained in 2.2.

2.1 Finding Tracklets Using GMCP

We divide a video into s segments of f frames each. We propose a data association method for finding tracklets which are globally consistent in terms of motion and appearance over the course of a segment. The input to our data association problem for finding tracklets is a graph $G = (\boldsymbol{V}, E, w)$, where $\boldsymbol{V}$, E and w denote the set of nodes, set of edges and weights of edges, respectively. $\boldsymbol{V}$ is divided into f disjoint clusters. Each represents one frame, and the nodes therein represent the human detections in that particular frame. Let C_i, where $i \in \mathbb{Z} : 1 \leq i \leq f$, denote the frame (≡cluster) i, and v^i_m denote the mth detection (≡node) in the ith frame. Therefore $\boldsymbol{C}_i = \{v^i_1, v^i_2, v^i_3, ...\}$. The edges of the graph are defined as $E = \{(v^i_m, v^j_n)|i \neq j\}$ which signifies that all the nodes in G are connected as long as they do not belong to the same cluster. A node, v^i_m, is associated with a location feature, $\boldsymbol{x}^i_m$, which is the 2-dimensional spatial coordinates of the center of the corresponding detection and appearance features, $\underset{l}{\boldsymbol{\phi}^i_m}$, which represents the color histogram of the lth body part of the detection v^i_m. The weight of an edge between two nodes, $w : E \rightarrow \mathbb{R}^+$, represents the similarity between the two corresponding detections:

$$w(v^i_m, v^j_n) = \sum_{l=1}^{8} k(\underset{l}{\boldsymbol{\phi}^i_m}, \underset{l}{\boldsymbol{\phi}^j_n}), \tag{1}$$

where k represents histogram intersection kernel.

The task of finding the tracklet of one particular person in a segment requires identifying the detections of that person in each frame. Therefore, a feasible solution to this problem can be represented by a subgraph of G in which one node (≡detection) is selected from each cluster(≡frame). We call this subgraph which represents a feasible solution $G_s = (\boldsymbol{V}_s, E_s, w_s)$. Therefore, G_s contains a set of nodes which includes the general form $\boldsymbol{V}_s = \{v_a^1, v_b^2, v_c^3, ...\}$ which means the ath node from 1st cluster, bth one from 2nd cluster, and so on are selected to be in $\boldsymbol{V}_s$. By definition, $E_s = \{E(p,q)|p \in \boldsymbol{V}_s, q \in \boldsymbol{V}_s\}$ and $w_s = \{w(p,q)|p \in \boldsymbol{V}_s, q \in \boldsymbol{V}_s\}$. Bear in mind that the feasible solution G_s represents the tracklet of *one person* and not all the people visible in the segment. Fig 3 (a) shows the human detections in a small segment of 6 frames along with the graph G they form in (b). (d) shows a feasible solution G_s with the tracklet it forms in (c). Since the set of nodes $\boldsymbol{V}_s$ is enough to form G_s, we use $\boldsymbol{V}_s$ to denote a feasible solution hereafter.

We define the appearance cost of the feasible solution V_s as:

$$\gamma_{appearance}(\boldsymbol{V}_s) = \frac{1}{2}(\sum_{i=1}^{f} \sum_{j=1, j \neq i}^{f} w(\boldsymbol{V}_s(i), \boldsymbol{V}_s(j))), \quad (2)$$

which is the cost of the complete graph induced by the nodes in $\boldsymbol{V}_s$. Eq. 2 is a global cost function since it is based on comparing all pairs of detection in a feasible solution no matter how close they are temporally. This is based on the assumption that the appearance of people does not change drastically in a segment. Overlapping bounding boxes, occlusion, noisy descriptors, background domination, etc in part of a trajectory can potentially cause an ID-switch in the majority of current methods, in particular the limited-temporal-locality ones. The formulation defined in eq. 2 minimizes the chance of such cases of ID-switches as all possible pairs of detections are compared regardless of their temporal order.

By finding the feasible solution with the minimum appearance cost, i.e. $\underset{\boldsymbol{V}_s}{\text{argmin}}(\gamma_{appearance}(\boldsymbol{V}_s))$, the tracklet of the person with the most stable color histogram features in the segment will be found. In the following subsection, we explain that Generalized Minimum Clique Graph is a perfect fit for our problem, and can be used for solving the aforementioned optimization task for finding tracklets.

Generalized Minimum Clique Problem (GMCP). Generalized Graph Problems, more formally known as Generalized Network Design Problems [15], are a class of problems which are commonly built on generalizing the standard subgraph problems. The generalization is commonly done by expanding the definition of a node to a cluster of nodes. For instance, the objective in the standard Traveling Salesman Problem (TSP) is to find the minimal Hamiltonian cycle which visits all the nodes of the input graph exactly once. In the *Generalized* Traveling Salesman Problem, the nodes of the input graph are grouped into disjoint clusters, and the objective is to find the minimal Hamiltonian cycle which visits all the clusters of the input graph exactly once. From each cluster, exactly one node should be visited.

Fig. 3. Finding a tracklet for a small segment of 6 frames. The left column shows the detections in each frame along with graph G they induce. The middle column shows the feasible solution with minimal cost along with the tracklet it forms, *without* adding hypothetical nodes. The right column shows the feasible solution with minimal cost *with* hypothetical nodes added for handling occlusion, along with the tracklet it forms.

Similarly, in the Generalized Minimum Clique Problem (GMCP) the nodes of the input graph are grouped into disjoint clusters. The objective is to find a subset of the nodes that include exactly one node from each cluster while requiring the minimum cost for the complete graph they produce [15]. Recently, GMCP has been used in the fields of biology and telecommunications [15]. However, its potential applications in Computer Vision have not been studied to date.

In order to have a more formal definition for GMCP, assume a graph $G = (\boldsymbol{V}, E, w)$ exists, where G is undirected and weighted, $\boldsymbol{V}$ is the set of all nodes, E is the set of edges, and $w : E \rightarrow \mathbb{R}^+$ is the weight of a given edge. The set of nodes V is divided into f clusters $\boldsymbol{C}_1, \boldsymbol{C}_2, \ldots, \boldsymbol{C}_f$ such that all of the clusters are completely disjoint: $\boldsymbol{C}_1 \cup \boldsymbol{C}_2 \cup \ldots \cup \boldsymbol{C}_f = V$ and $\boldsymbol{C}_1 \cap \boldsymbol{C}_j = \emptyset$ $(1 \leq i \neq j \leq k)$. A feasible solution of the GMCP instance is a subgraph $G_s = (\boldsymbol{V}_s, E_s, w_s)$, where $\boldsymbol{V}_s$ is a subset of $\boldsymbol{V}$ which encompasses only one node from a given cluster. E_s is a subset of E which includes the nodes V_s induces, and w_s is their corresponding weights from w. The goal of the GMCP is to find the feasible solution with the minimal cost, where the cost is defined to be the sum of all the weights along the solution subgraph.

In this formulation, there exists an edge in E for all possible pairs of nodes of $\boldsymbol{V}$, as long as they do not belong to the same cluster. Therefore, the subgraph G_s is essentially complete, which makes any feasible solution of GMCP a clique.

As can be seen from the formulation of our data association problem explained in 2.1, GMCP essentially solves the same optimization problem we need to solve for finding a tracklet if the input graph G is formed as explained in 2.1. Therefore, by solving GMCP for the graph G, the optimal solution which corresponds to the feasible solution with the most consistency in appearance features over the course of the segment, i.e. $\underset{\boldsymbol{V}_s}{\operatorname{argmin}}(\gamma_{appearance}(\boldsymbol{V}_s))$, is found. More details about solving GMCP will be discussed in section 3.

In order to incorporate motion, as well as appearance, into the data association problem, we add one more term to the cost function and define our global data association task as the following optimization problem:

$$\hat{\boldsymbol{V}}_s = \underset{\boldsymbol{V}_s}{\operatorname{argmin}}(\gamma_{appearance}(\boldsymbol{V}_s) + \alpha.\gamma_{motion}(\boldsymbol{V}_s)), \tag{3}$$

where $\hat{\boldsymbol{V}}_s$ is the optimal solution to determine the data association for *one* tracklet, and α is the mixture constant which balances the contribution of appearance and motion.

Finding $\hat{\boldsymbol{V}}_s$ by solving eq. 3 yields the tracklet of *one* person in the segment. Therefore, in order to find the tracklets of all the pedestrians in the segment, the optimization problem of eq. 3 has to be solved several times. The first time eq. 3 is solved, the algorithm finds the tracklet which has the lowest total cost, i.e. the most stable appearance features and most consistent motion with the model. Then, the vertices selected in $\hat{\boldsymbol{V}}_s$ are excluded from G and the above optimization process is repeated to find the tracklet for the next person, and so on. This process is repeated until zero or few nodes remains in G.

Since the algorithm finds the tracklets in order of how stable and consistent their appearance and motion features are, the tracklets which are less likely to be confused are calculated and excluded from G first. Therefore, our method does not lower the chance of successful extraction for the tracklets found at the last iterations. Our global motion-cost model, which defines the term $\gamma_{motion}(\boldsymbol{V}_s)$, is explained in the next subsection.

Tracklet-global Motion Cost Model. In order to incorporate motion into the optimization process of eq. 3, we need to calculate a cost for the feasible solution $\boldsymbol{V}_s$ based on motion. The spatial velocity vector for the feasible solution $\boldsymbol{V}_s$ is defined as: $\dot{\boldsymbol{X}}_s(i) = \boldsymbol{X}(i+1) - \boldsymbol{X}(i)$, where $1 \leq i \leq (f-1)$. One common approach to computing the motion cost is to calculate the deviation from a presumed model, such as constant velocity. This can be done by using each velocity vector to predict the spatial location of the detection immediately after it, and summing up the errors between the predicted locations and corresponding locations in the feasible solution. This piecewise approach is mainly used in bipartite matching and similar approaches [4,5]. However, in our global framework, one feasible solution is meant to represent one tracklet over the course of the whole segment; therefore we can calculate the motion cost in a more effective way, which assures both piecewise and global consistency within the model. We assume the constant velocity model for the motion of pedestrians in one segment and calculate the motion cost as:

$$\gamma_{motion}(\boldsymbol{V}_s) = \sum_{i=1}^{s}\sum_{j=1}^{s-1} \overbrace{|\boldsymbol{X}_s(i) - \underbrace{[\boldsymbol{X}_s(j) + \dot{\boldsymbol{X}}_s(j).(i-j)]}_{prediction}|}^{deviation}, \tag{4}$$

where the term in brackets in eq. 4 is the predicted location for the node $\boldsymbol{V}_s(i)$ using $\dot{\boldsymbol{X}}_s(j)$. In eq. 4, we assumed a person moves at a constant velocity manner in one segment, and each element of $\dot{\boldsymbol{X}}_s$ vector is used to predict the location of all other nodes in the feasible solution $\boldsymbol{V}_s$.

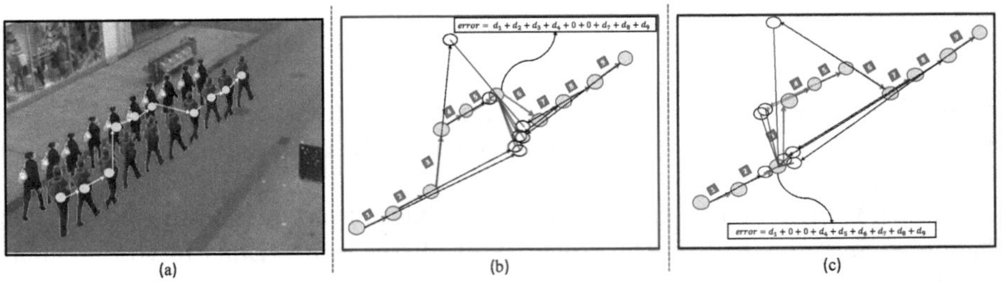

Fig. 4. Tracklet-Global motion cost. (a) shows the tracklet of a feasible solution with three outliers. (b) and (c) show the cost for an outlier and inlier, respectively.

Fig. 4 shows this in more detail. Fig. 4 (a) shows a feasible solution which is being generated for the person with the red boundary. However, three detections of another person are mistakenly selected in the feasible solution. Therefore, we expect the three wrong selections to add a large value to the motion cost, while the rest of the selected nodes, which are consistent, to add low cost values. The value of eq. 4 is shown for two nodes of $i = 6$ and $i = 3$ in parts (b) and (c), respectively. The black circles show the predicted locations for the node i. The red lines depict the distance between the predicted locations and $\boldsymbol{X}_s(i)$, which shows the deviation from the model. The value node i, which adds to the motion cost, is the sum of these distances. As can be seen, the node $i = 6$, which is not consistent with the majority of the tracklet, adds a large value to the cost, while $i = 3$ adds a lower value.

Therefore, in contrast to the piecewise motion models, the motion cost in eq. 4 is calculated by measuring the deviation from the constant velocity model in a tracklet in a global manner, because all nodes are contributing to the cost of the other nodes. Although we use the constant velocity model in eq. 4, the extension to the constant acceleration and higher order models for more complicated scenarios is straightforward.

Handling Occlusion Using Hypothetical Nodes. In some cases, a given frame may not include a detection for a particular person due to occlusion, missed detection, etc. In order to cope with this issue, we add a Hypothetical Node to each cluster, thus if one frame does not include an appropriate detection, the hypothetical node is selected.

We need to define appearance and motion features for the hypothetical nodes, as each node in G has these two features. Solving the optimization problem of eq. 3 is an iterative process. In each iteration these two features for the Hypothetical Nodes are re-estimated using the method explained in the rest of this subsection and the hypothetical nodes are updated.

$\boldsymbol{V}_s$ is expected to include the detections for one person (inliers), along with other detections (outliers) for the frames, which do not include a detection for that particular person. Due to the short temporal span of one segment, we assume a person moves at a constant velocity in a segment and use this assumption in order to identify inliers and outliers in $\boldsymbol{V}_s$. According to 2-dimensional constant velocity motion, the spatial location of the detections can be modeled using $\boldsymbol{X}_s(i) = \boldsymbol{a_1} i + \boldsymbol{a_o}$, where $\boldsymbol{a_1}$ and $\boldsymbol{a_0}$ are 2-dimensional constant vectors. Therefore, we identify the inliers and outliers to the constant velocity model determined by $\boldsymbol{a_1}$ and $\boldsymbol{a_0}$ using:

$$\boldsymbol{V}_s^{inliers} = \{\boldsymbol{V}_s(i) : |\boldsymbol{a_1} i + \boldsymbol{a_0} - \boldsymbol{X}_s(i)| < \delta\}, \tag{5}$$

where δ is the fitting tolerance. The best parameters of the tracklet's constant velocity model are the ones which maximize the number of inliers:

$$\hat{\boldsymbol{a_1}}, \hat{\boldsymbol{a_0}} = \underset{\boldsymbol{a_1}, \boldsymbol{a_0}}{argmax}(\#\{\boldsymbol{V}_s^{inliers}\}), \tag{6}$$

where # represents the cardinality of the set. Since V_s is composed of inliers and outliers, we employ *RANSAC*, which is a robust estimation method, to compute $\boldsymbol{a_1}$ and $\boldsymbol{a_0}$ in eq. 6 with the error criterion of eq. 5

The inlier nodes in V_s are those which survive the criterion of eq. 5 using $\hat{\boldsymbol{a_1}}$ and $\hat{\boldsymbol{a_0}}$. The spatial coordinates of the hypothetical nodes are computed using the estimated model $\boldsymbol{x}_H^i = \hat{\boldsymbol{a_1}} i + \hat{\boldsymbol{a_0}}$, where $\boldsymbol{x}_H^i$ denotes the spatial location of the hypothetical node of cluster i. The appearance feature of the hypothetical nodes is the average appearance of the inlier nodes' appearances (mean of their color histograms). However, a constant penalty is added to the weights of the edges connected to the hypothetical nodes in G, in order to avoid selecting the hypothetical node if the frame includes a proper detection.

As mentioned earlier, the hypothetical nodes are updated at the end of each iteration when solving the optimization problem of eq. 3. In the first few iterations, hypothetical nodes are not likely to be selected as the algorithm is still selecting the existing detections. However, as the optimization process progresses, the clusters which include correct detections are exhausted and the hypothetical nodes will start to contribute until the algorithm converges to the final solution $\hat{V_s}$. Fig. 3 (f) shows $\hat{\boldsymbol{V}}_s$ two hypothetical nodes selected for the frames with occlusion. The trajectory $\hat{\boldsymbol{V}}_s$ forms is shown in (e).

2.2 Merging Tracklets into Trajectories Using GMCP

As explained earlier, we divide the video into s segments and find the tracklets of all the pedestrians in each segment using the method described in subsection 2.1. In order to generate a trajectory of a person over the course of the full video, we need to merge the tracklets belonging to each person. This is a data association problem for which we can use any available data association method, such as bipartite matching[5,4]. However, in order to have a fully global framework, we use the same GMCP-based data association method we used for finding tracklets to merge them. Therefore, the clusters and nodes in G' now represent segments and tracklets, respectively (vs. representing frames and human detections in 2.1)[1]. The appearance feature of a node, which represents one tracklet, is defined as the average appearance of the human detections in the tracklet (the mean of their color histograms), and its spatial location, $\boldsymbol{x'}^i_m$, is defined as the spatial location of the middle point of the tracklet. Fig. 5 (a) shows six consecutive segments with their tracklets, along with the complete graph their representative nodes induce in (b). Only four tracklets out of fifteen are shown to avoid cluttering of the plots.

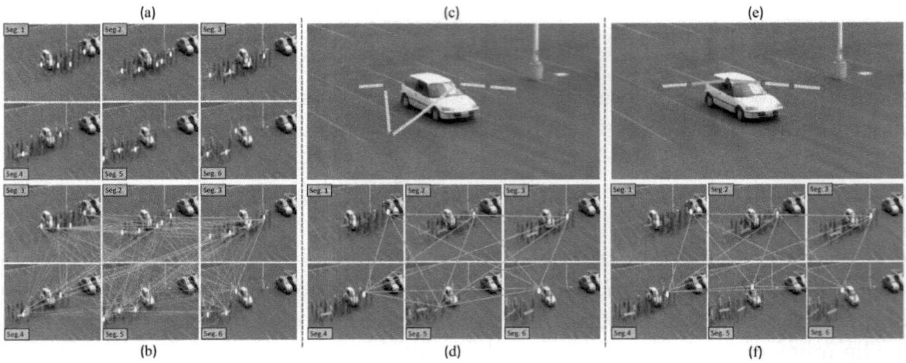

Fig. 5. Merging tracklets into trajectories. The left column shows six consecutive segments with four tracklets in each, along with $\boldsymbol{G'}$. The middle column shows a feasible solution without adding the hypothetical nodes to handle tracklet-occlusion. The right column shows the converged solution, $\hat{\boldsymbol{V}}'_s$, along with the generated full trajectory.

Note that the data association at the track level is fundamentally different from the one used for finding tracklets; there we assumed a pedestrian moves at a constant velocity within one segment, but modeling the human motion over long periods of time in a track becomes extremely difficult. Generally, it's difficult to model the motion of pedestrians for a long duration without the knowledge of scene structure, intentions, destination, social interaction, etc. This major difference prevents us from using the global motion cost model explained in subsection 2.1 and the hypothetical node feature estimation described in subsection 2.1. However, the full trajectory is expected to be temporally smooth. Therefore, at this level, it is essential to change the method for computing the motion cost and estimating hypothetical nodes to piecewise, rather than global, as follows.

Motion-Cost: In order to compute the motion cost for a feasible solution $\boldsymbol{V}'_s$, we use the piecewise extension of the velocity vector immediately preceding each node:

$$\gamma'_{motion}(\boldsymbol{V}'_s) = \sum_{i=3}^{s} |\boldsymbol{X}'_s(i) - [\boldsymbol{X}'_s(i-2) + 2\dot{\boldsymbol{X}}'_s(i-2)]|. \tag{7}$$

[1] We show the notations related to tracklet merging level with prime ($'$) to preserve their correspondence to the ones in tracklet generation level, yet not confuse them.

Compared to the global approach of eq. 4, the second summation in eq. 4 is omitted, so that only the preceding piece of the trajectory contributes to the motion cost, because of this eq. 7 represents a piecewise extension.

Handling occluded tracklets by hypothetical nodes: Short term occlusions and missed detections are already handled at the tracklet level by introducing hypothetical nodes. However, if a pedestrian remains occluded for a period longer than the temporal span of a segment, e.g. over 50 frames, then he/she will not have a tracklet in the corresponding segment, which leads to the *tracklet occlusion.* In order to handle such cases, we add hypothetical nodes to the clusters of the tracklet association input graph G' with piecewise prediction for computing their spatial location:

$$\boldsymbol{x}'^{i}_{Hf} = |\boldsymbol{X}'_s(i-2) + 2\dot{\boldsymbol{X}}'_s(i-2)|. \tag{8}$$

In eq. 8, only the preceding piece of the trajectory is used to compute the spatial location of the hypothetical node, rather than using the global method of subsection 2.1 which incorporated all the nodes.

At the tracklet association level, we add two hypothetical nodes to each cluster rather than one: The *Forward* hypothetical node, denoted by Hf, in which the preceding piece of trajectory is used for prediction, and the *backward* hypothetical node, denoted by Hb, for which the following piece of the trajectory is leveraged for prediction. The backward hypothetical node is necessary for the cases where the tracklets at the beginning of the trajectory are occluded. That way, since there does not exist any tracklet before the beginning of the trajectory to be used to predict the location of the hypothetical nodes of the missing tracklets, the backward hypothetical nodes are added. They use the tail of the trajectory to predict the location of the hypothetical nodes for the missing tracklets at the beginning of the trajectory. Therefore, the spatial location of the backward hypothetical node is computed using $\boldsymbol{x}'^{i}_{Hb} = |\boldsymbol{X}'_s(i+2) + 2\dot{\boldsymbol{X}}'_s(i+1)|$.

The appearance feature of the forward and backward hypothetical nodes are the same as the nodes, which were used to predict the spatial location, i.e. $\boldsymbol{V}'_s(i-2)$ for the forward and $\boldsymbol{V}'_s(i+2)$ for the backward ones. The hypothetical nodes added at the level of tracklet association are useful for solving the problem of entry/ exit as well. For instance, if one pedestrian exits the field of

Fig. 6. Left: The tracklets of six sample consecutive segments from Parking Lot sequence. Right: The trajectories resulting from associating tracklets of all the segments.

view before the end of the video, or enters the view later than the beginning of the video, there will be some segments in which they won't have a tracklet. The optimization process will select hypothetical nodes for those segments. However, the computed spatial location of such hypothetical nodes will be out of the view of the frame as they correspond to the time before the pedestrian enters the view or after exiting.

3 Experimental Results and Discussion

We evaluated our method on four publicly available sequences, which provide a wide range of significant challenges: TUD-Crossing [16], TUD-Stadtmitte [17], Town Center [1], and sequence S2L1 from VS-PET2009 benchmark [3]. We also present experimental results on a new data set called Parking Lot. We set δ to 5 in eq. 5 for all the test sequences. We normalize appearance and motion cost values in eq. 3 in order to make them comparable. A typical value for α in eq. 3 is one which assigns equal weights to appearance and motion in the overall cost. However, based on our experiments, the appearance features are more informative than motion in our formulation. In fact, in many cases using appearance features only is sufficient for finding the appropriate tracklets.

Standard CLEAR MOT [18] are used as evaluation metrics. False positives, false negatives and ID-Switches are measured by MOTA. MOTP is defined as the average distance between the ground truth and estimated targets locations. MOTP shows the ability of the tracker in estimating the precise location of the object, regardless of its accuracy at recognizing object configurations, keeping consistent trajectories, and so forth. Therefore, MOTA has been widely accepted in the literature as the main gauge of performance of tracking methods.

Town Center [1]: The sequence consists of 4500 frames. The size of each segment is 50 frames in this experiment. The quantitative results of the competitive methods for this sequence are presented in [8] and shown in Table 1. Our precision and recall values for this sequence are 92.65% and 81.64% respectively.

Table 1. Tracking results on Town Center sequence

	MOTA	MOTP	MODP	MODA
Benfold et al. [1]	64.9	80.4	80.5	64.8
Zhang et al. [10]	65.7	71.5	71.5	66.1
Pellegrini et al. [9]	63.4	70.7	70.8	64.1
Yamaguchi et al. [7]	63.3	70.9	71.1	64.0
Leal-Taixe et al. [8]	67.3	71.5	71.6	67.6
Ours/GMCP	**75.59**	**71.93**	**72.01**	**75.71**

Table 3. Tracking results on Parking Lot sequence

	MOTA	MOTP	Prec.	Rec.
Shu et al. [5]	74.1	79.3	91.3	81.7
Ours/GMCP	**90.43**	**74.1**	**98.2**	**85.3**

Table 2. Tracking results on TUD and PETS 09 sequences

Dataset	MOTA	MOTP	Prec.	Rec.	IDsw
TUD-Crossing. [20]	84.3	71.0	85.1	98.6	2
TUD-Crossing. [11]	85.9	73.0	89.2	98.8	2
TUD-Crossing-Ours	**91.63**	**75.6**	**98.6**	**92.83**	**0**
TUD-Stadtmitte. [2]	60.5	65.8	-	-	7
TUD-Stadtmitte-Ours	**77.7**	**63.4**	**95.6**	**81.4**	**0**
PET2009-View1. [12]	80.00	58.00	81.00	60.00	28
PET2009-View1. [13]	81.46	58.38	90.66	90.81	19
PET2009-View1. [2]	81.84	73.93	96.28	85.13	15
PET2009-View1. [19]	84.77	68.742	92.40	94.03	10
PET2009-View1-Ours	**90.3**	**69.02**	**93.64**	**96.45**	**8**

PET2009-S2L1-View One [3]: The sequence consists of 800 frames. In sec. 2.1, we assumed the motion of pedestrians in one segment is near constant velocity in order to identify the outliers and estimate the location of hypothetical nodes. Therefore, segment size should be set in a way that this assumption is not severely violated. Otherwise, the location of hypothetical nodes will be inaccurate which results in a misplaced tracklet. Typically, the segment size is determined with regard to the frame rate of the video. Therefore, regarding the low frame rate of PET2009-S2L1, we chose a smaller segment size of 15 frames. The quantitative comparison is provided in Table 2. All reported results are calculated using original tracking outputs provided by the authors [12,13,2,19] with the same overlap threshold for CLEAR MOT metrics.

TUD Data Set [2]: TUD-Crossing and TUD-Stadtmitte are two sequences in this data set with low camera angle and frequent occlusions. Crossing and Stadtmitte include 201 and 179 frames respectively. Due to the short length of these sequences, we divided each one into three segments. Quantitative results are provided in Table 2 [11,20].

Parking Lot: This sequence consists of 1,000 frames of a relatively crowded scene with up to 14 pedestrians walking in parallel. It includes frequent occlusions, missed detections, and parallel motion with similar appearances. Quantitative results are shown in Table 3. No ID-switch was observed in our results. Six sample segments and the merging results are shown in fig. 6.

As can be see in Tables 1, 2 and 3, the proposed method constantly outperforms the state of the art on all the standard sequences.

Several application-oriented methods for solving GMCP, such as branch-and-cut algorithm and multi-greedy heuristics [15], have been proposed to date. Inspired by the solutions proposed for the other generalized graph problems, such as GMST [15], we employ Tabu-search to solve our optimization problem of eq. 3. The size of the search neighborhood is changed at each iteration in order to make the optimization process faster and avoid becoming stuck in suboptimal regions. The main contributing factors to the complexity of GMCP are the number of clusters and number of nodes within each cluster. Regarding the small size of GMCP instances we need to solve in our tracking problem, one instance of the optimization problem of eq. 3 is typically solved in the negligible time of a fraction of a second. For a segment of 50 frames with approximately 15 pedestrians, processing a frame using the full proposed framework, excluding human detection, takes an average time of 4.4 seconds on a 4core 2.4 GHz machine running non-optimized Matlab code. Using an optimized parallel implementation in C, the algorithm is likely to work in real time.

4 Conclusion

We propose a global framework for data association. We utilized Generalized Minimum Clique Problem to solve the formulated optimization problem. Our method is based on shifting the approximation from the temporal domain to the

[1] This work was partially supported by Pacific Northwest National Laboratory, WA.

object domain while keeping a notion of the full object domain implicitly. We argue that this framework yields a better developed approach to data association. A two level method, i.e. finding tracklets first and forming full trajectories later, is employed to cope with different characteristics of human motion in the short and long term. Also, we utilize a global approach to compute the motion cost at the tracklet level. Experiments show superior results over the state of the art.

References

1. Benfold, B., Reid, I.: Stable multi-target tracking in real time surveillance video. In: CVPR (2011)
2. Andriyenko, A., Schindler, K.: Multi-target tracking by continuous energy minimization. In: CVPR (2011)
3. Ferryman, J., Shahrokni, A.: Pets2009: Dataset and challenge. In: International Workshop on Performance Evaluation of Tracking and Surveillance (2009)
4. Shafique, K., Shah, M.: A noniterative greedy algorithm formultiframe point correspondence. In: PAMI (2005)
5. Shu, G., Dehghan, A., Oreifej, O., Hand, E., Shah, M.: Part-based multiple-person tracking with partial occlusion handling. In: CVPR (2012)
6. Leibe, B., Schindler, K., Gool, L.V.: Coupled detection and trajectory estimation for multi-object tracking. In: ICCV (2007)
7. Yamaguchi, K., Berg, A., Ortiz, L., Berg, T.: Who are you with and where are you going? In: CVPR (2011)
8. Leal-Taixe, L., et al.: Everybody needs somebody: Modeling social and grouping behavior on a linear programming multiple people tracker. In: ICCV 2011 Workshops (2011)
9. Pellegrini, S., Ess, A., Van Gool, L.: Improving Data Association by Joint Modeling of Pedestrian Trajectories and Groupings. In: Daniilidis, K., Maragos, P., Paragios, N. (eds.) ECCV 2010, Part I. LNCS, vol. 6311, pp. 452–465. Springer, Heidelberg (2010)
10. Zhang, L., Li, Y., Nevatia, R.: Global data association for multi-object tracking using network flows. In: CVPR (2008)
11. Brendel, W., Amer, M., Todorovic, S.: Multiobject tracking as maximumweight independent set. In: CVPR (2011)
12. Berclaz, J., Fleuret, F., Turetken, E., Fua, P.: Multiple object tracking using k-shortest paths optimization. In: PAMI (2011)
13. Shitrit, H.B., Berclaz, J., Fleuret, F., Fua, P.: Tracking multiple people under global appearance constraints. In: ICCV (2011)
14. Felzenszwalb, P., Girshick, R., McAllester, D., Ramanan, D.: Object detection with discriminatively trained part based models. In: PAMI (2010)
15. Feremans, C., Labbe, M., Laporte, G.: Generalized network design problems. In: EJOR (2003)
16. Andriluka, M., Roth, S., Schiele, B.: People-tracking-by-detection and people-detection-by-tracking. In: CVPR (2008)
17. Andriluka, M., Roth, S., Schiele, B.: Monocular 3d pose estimation and tracking by detection. In: CVPR (2010)
18. Kasturi, R., et al.: Framework for performance evaluation of face, text, and vehicle detection and tracking in video: Data, metrics, and protocol. In: PAMI (2009)
19. Henriques, J.F., Caseiro, R., Batista, J.: Globally optimal solution to multi-object tracking with merged measurements. In: ICCV (2011)
20. Breitenstein, M., Reichlin, F., Leibe, B., Koller-Meier, E., Gool, L.V.: Robust tracking-by-detection using a detector confidence particle filter. In: ICCV (2009)

Heliometric Stereo: Shape from Sun Position

Austin Abrams, Christopher Hawley, and Robert Pless

Washington University in St. Louis
St. Louis, USA

Abstract. In this work, we present a method to uncover shape from webcams "in the wild." We present a variant of photometric stereo which uses the sun as a distant light source, so that lighting direction can be computed from known GPS and timestamps. We propose an iterative, non-linear optimization process that optimizes the error in reproducing all images from an extended time-lapse with an image formation model that accounts for ambient lighting, shadows, changing light color, dense surface normal maps, radiometric calibration, and exposure. Unlike many approaches to uncalibrated outdoor image analysis, this procedure is automatic, and we report quantitative results by comparing extracted surface normals to Google Earth 3D models. We evaluate this procedure on data from a varied set of scenes and emphasize the advantages of including imagery from many months.

Keywords: Photometric stereo, webcams, camera response.

1 Introduction

This paper presents an approach to heliometric stereo — using the sun as a moving light source to recover surface normals of objects in an outdoor scene. This is a classic application of photometric stereo because the position of the sun is known very accurately, but made challenging because of variations in lighting and weather. Additionally, most long term imagery is captured by webcams that may not share geometric or radiometric calibration information. Thus, we explore what it would take to fully automate the solution to the photometric stereo problem for uncalibrated, outdoor cameras.

Our approach is to optimize the similarity between long term time-lapse imagery and an image formation model that includes the surface normal and albedo for each pixel in the scene, color and intensity of the ambient and direct lighting terms in each frame, and a shadow mask in each frame. This optimization results in estimates of all these parameters of the scene structure, albedo, lighting and camera properties. Although the WILD database [1] has sparked a rich recent literature in algorithms to understand outdoor image time-lapses, this paper is unique in tractably computing explicit, geo-referenced surface normals without any user interaction.

Alternative approaches without user interaction parameterize pixels with respect to time-series basis functions which have an unknown, non-linear relationship to surface normals [2], or cluster pixels groups that have approximately the

A. Fitzgibbon et al. (Eds.): ECCV 2012, Part II, LNCS 7573, pp. 357–370, 2012.

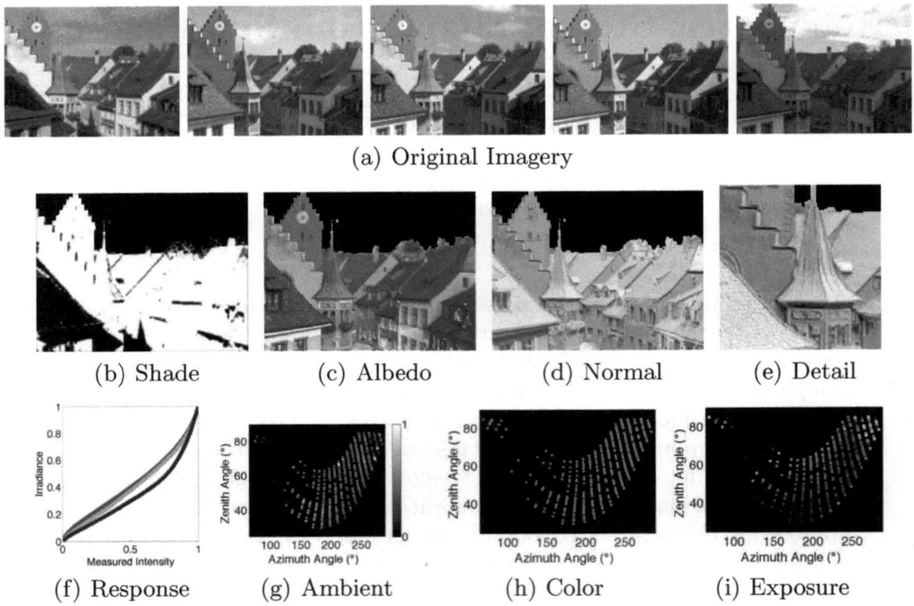

Fig. 1. Given a sequence of geo-located, timestamped imagery taken over the span of several months (a), we recover a shadow mask for each image (b) (here shown as the mask for the leftmost original image), albedo (c), a dense normal map represented in East-North-Up Coordinates (d) (detail image shown in (e), and colormap described in Figure 2), nonlinear camera response (f), and for each image, measures of ambient lighting (g), light color (h), and exposure (i). We show the temporal variables (g)-(i) as a function of the image's solar azimuth and zenith angle. Best viewed in color.

same, but unknown surface normals [3]. Approaches that compute metric surface normals require user interaction to identify three pixel locations on orthogonal surfaces [4], and all these approaches result in surface normals in the coordinate system of the camera, not a geo-referenced coordinate system.

Thus, our approach is appropriate to deploy on very large webcam archives [2,5] in order to extract quantitative remote sensing measurements without human input. Despite the allure of using already emplaced webcams for environmental monitoring, the few published uses of uncalibrated webcams are limited to simple color changes [6,7]. We hope that our approach to automatically estimate scene shape, scene lighting and surface reflectance will support a larger range of environmental measurement uses of these webcam archives.

There are three major contributions of this work. First, we adapt the photometric stereo algorithm [8] to work for outdoor scenes by integrating a richer image formation model. We present a gradient descent approach and methods for initialization and regularization of this optimization. Second, we test this across a variety of types and scales of natural scenes and highlight the ability to capture very small scale surface structure. We report surface normals geo-referenced to an "East-North-Up" coordinate system, and we are the first to offer quantita-

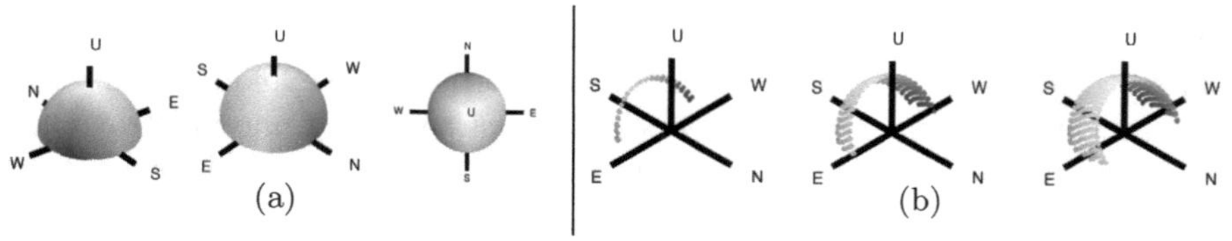

Fig. 2. (a) The colormap used for all normals in this paper. Notice that the normals are represented in an absolute, East-North-Up reference frame, rather than with respect to the camera's optical axis. (b) Input solar lighting directions for one camera, using progressively longer spans of time (1 month, 3 months, and 6 months, from left to right). The longer the input sequence, the richer the set of lighting directions.

tive comparisons between our results and 3D geometry from Google Earth. These highlight both the accuracy of our results and limitations in the completeness and resolution of the ground truth.

Third, we characterize performance under which this approach gives good results. This emphasizes the importance of using imagery from many months, because over the course of one day or one week, the solar path does not give sufficient constraints to recover surface normals (see Figure 2(b)).

2 Background and Related Work

The original constraints for photometric stereo [8] assumed multiple images of scenes with known lighting directions captured with a calibrated camera. While there is immense literature on variations of this problem, in this review we consider only those most relevant to our problem domain of long term, outdoor, webcam imagery. Specifically, our imagery is captured with known lighting directions because the primary light source is the sun whose direction can be computed given a timestamp and geolocation of the camera. However, lighting may vary due to weather conditions, and the camera may perform some unknown nonlinear radiometric distortion before publishing the image.

Papers that address uncalibrated photometric stereo have primarily concentrated on indoor scenes lit by unknown lights. One approach clusters pixels into groups with the same albedo and surface normal to provide constraints to solve for the unknown radiometric response and the generalized bas-relief ambiguity [9]. Another works with constant albedo objects and uses non-linear optimization to solve for the radiometric response, lighting directions, and surface normals [10]. Because these focus on indoor images (in a dark room), they have relatively noise-free images and no ambient light term.

There is less work on outdoor, uncalibrated photometric stereo. Shen and Tan [11] explored the solution for photometric stereo from unstructured internet imagery, combining multi-view stereo to register images from different viewpoints. Assuming the surface albedo and surface normals are constant at a scene location between images, an optimization was used in order to estimate the lighting parameters and therefore infer the weather of each image.

A related approach [12] focused on a photometric stereo variant for recovering surface orientation from webcam images. This method also exploited multi-view stereo to solve for scene geometry, which was then used in a photometric stereo by example approach, which transfers normals from locations with known surface normals to the rest of the scene. Our approach does not require or use such an example, and is applicable to time-lapse captured from a single location.

In [13], Sunkavalli et al. factor a time-lapse sequence of images taken from a single day into several meaningful components, including shadows, albedo, and a one-dimensional surface normal projection. We follow this work towards a more flexible model that accounts for solar variations over the span of a year, which uncovers the full three-dimensional normal field. In addition, we incorporate the effects of nonlinear camera response.

Kim et al. [14] present an approach to take a series of images taken through the span of a day and use changing light to infer radiometric calibration and exposure values for each image. Using a PCA basis for camera response functions introduced by Grossberg and Nayar [15], Kim et al. recover the response function that is most consistent with a Lambertian assumption. We take a similar approach toward solving the exposure and radiometric curves, but we simultaneously solve for surface normals in the process.

Recently, Ackermann et al. [16] describe an approach to perform photometric stereo on outdoor webcams. While they use a richer reflectance model to explicitly handle specularities, we offer a model which allows a trackable optimization, giving our algorithm an 8x speedup. We also perform a more rigorous evaluation, by comparing surface normals to Google Earth models and producing 3D shapes, and use a shadow estimation procedure appropriate for months of imagery.

Given a sequence of images taken under partly-cloudy conditions and an estimate of wind direction and speed, Jacobs et al. [17] provide an algorithm to extract shape based on cues derived from observing cloud shadows through time. While Jacobs et al. focus on time-lapse sequences on the scale of minutes or hours, we take advantage of the changing position of the sun over the span of many months. This increased timespan relaxes the assumption that the image was taken under specific meteorological conditions, and solves for surface normals rather than depth.

3 Method

This section presents our outdoor image formation model, and our methods for solving for the parameters of that model. The inputs to this model are timestamped images, and the direction to the sun computed from the timestamp and geolocation. Our algorithm extracts several components of our image formation model, including surface normals and photometric properties of the camera.

3.1 Model

The input consists of n images $I_1, \ldots, I_i, \ldots, I_n$, each represented as a p-pixel vector in $[0, 255]^p$. Given the latitude and longitude of the camera, as well as the timestamps from each image, we use [18] to determine the sun direction for each image $L_1, \ldots, L_n$, represented as a 3-vector in the East-North-Up coordinate frame. To keep consistent notation, temporally-indexed variables are annotated with the subscript i from 1 to n, and spatially-indexed variables with the subscript $\mathbf{x}$ from 1 to p.

The Lambertian lighting model assumes that the intensity of a pixel $\mathbf{x}$ in image i is a function of the surface normal $N_\mathbf{x} \in \mathbb{R}^3$, the albedo $\rho_\mathbf{x} \in \mathbb{R}$, and lighting direction $L_i \in \mathbb{R}^3$. More formally, the intensity of image i at pixel $\mathbf{x}$ is given by the linear model $\rho_\mathbf{x} L_i^\top N_\mathbf{x}$.

Webcam imagery from real scenes is also affected by ambient lighting conditions, which we model by including $a_i \in [0, 1]$ for each image i in sequence. Natural scenes also include both cast shadows, such as a tree shadow on a road, and attached shadows such as the side of a building that is not illuminated. This is modeled with a per-pixel-per-image shadow volume $S_{i,\mathbf{x}} \in [0, 1]$, that models how much light is received from the sun at each time at each pixel.

$$\rho_\mathbf{x}(L_i^\top N_\mathbf{x} S_{i,\mathbf{x}} + a_i) \tag{1}$$

The reported pixel intensity of a camera also depends on the radiometric camera calibration. Webcams rarely publish results in RAW format, rarely include meta-data describing their radiometric response, and may not be accessible to allow radiometric calibration using images of known calibration objects. Thus, we must solve for, and include in our model, an unknown, monotonic, nonlinear photometric response function $f : [0, 255] \to [0, 255]$, which we assume to be fixed through all the images in sequence, and we modulate each image by an exposure value $e_i \in \mathbb{R}$:

$$I_{i,\mathbf{x}} = f(e_i \rho_\mathbf{x}(L_i^\top N_\mathbf{x} S_{i,\mathbf{x}} + a_i)) \tag{2}$$

Here, we take advantage of the invertibility of f and rewrite the above as

$$f^{-1}(I_{i,\mathbf{x}}) = e_i \rho_\mathbf{x}(L_i^\top N_\mathbf{x} S_{i,\mathbf{x}} + a_i). \tag{3}$$

To make the estimation of f tractable, we use the Empirical Model of Response introduced by Grossberg and Nayar [15]. This is a PCA basis for typical camera response functions, which models the nonlinear response function f^{-1} as a linear composition of nonlinear bases:

$$f_v^{-1}(x) = f_0^{-1}(x) + \sum_{j=1}^{b} f_j^{-1}(x) v_j \tag{4}$$

where f_0^{-1} is the mean inverse response curve, $f_1^{-1}, \ldots, f_b^{-1}$ are the set of basis curves, v_j are the unknown, camera-specific coefficients that implicitly describe the shape of the nonlinear function, and b is the number of bases used (in our experiments, we use $b = 5$). We use f_v^{-1} as notation to define the radiometric response defined by a vector of coefficients v.

Color. To incorporate color, we largely use the above model independently on each color channel. Allowing different exposures for each color channel can be interpreted as modeling the color and intensity of the sunlight for each image. For each image we have a single term for ambient intensity a_i, which models the ambient light as the same color as the direct light, but allows variation in its intensity. We also have a single normal $N_{\mathbf{x}}$ for each pixel, and a single shadow volume $S_{i,\mathbf{x}}$. Unless otherwise specified, we do not denote each color channel individually, and in a slight abuse of notation, treat Equation 3 as an equality over a three-element vector.

3.2 Optimization

Given a set of images and their lighting directions, we wish to extract each component of the lighting model. Our algorithm is a simple gradient-descent procedure that minimizes the following loss function:

$$\underset{v,e,\rho,N,a}{\operatorname{argmin}} \ \frac{1}{pn} \sum_{\mathbf{x}=1}^{p} \sum_{i=1}^{n} ||f_v^{-1}(I_{i,\mathbf{x}}) - e_i \rho_{\mathbf{x}} (L_i^\top N_{\mathbf{x}} S_{i,\mathbf{x}} + a_i)||^2. \tag{5}$$

Notice that we do not solve for the shadow volume $S_{i,\mathbf{x}}$. Similar to Sunkavalli et al. [13], we first estimate a shadow volume and leave it fixed for the remainder of the optimization. See Section 3.3 for our shadow estimation approach.

To enforce a physically-based lighting model, we impose additional constraints on the variables in Equation 5. We constrain that the albedo and ambient lighting are bounded between 0 and 1, that the normals are unit length, that the exposures are all non-negative, and that the response function is monotonic (which can be expressed as a linear inequality constraint over v; see [15]).

To prevent overfitting the response curve, we employ a smoothness regularization term on the response function that penalizes large changes across intensity bins:

$$R_v = \sum_{i=1}^{255} \left|\left|f_v^{-1}(i) - f_v^{-1}(i-1)\right|\right|^2, \tag{6}$$

which is expressed as a system of linear equations over the curve coefficients v.

The overall optimization is therefore

$$\underset{v,e,\rho,N,a}{\operatorname{argmin}} \frac{1-\lambda}{pn} \sum_{\mathbf{x}=1}^{p} \sum_{i=1}^{n} ||f_v^{-1}(I_{i,\mathbf{x}}) - e_i \rho_{\mathbf{x}} (L_i^\top N_{\mathbf{x}} S_{i,\mathbf{x}} + a_i)||^2 + \frac{\lambda}{255} R_v \tag{7}$$

subject to the constraints listed above. Here, λ is a regularization constant that defines the weight of satisfying the data term versus the smoothness term.

To make this optimization tractable, we take an alternating minimization strategy, which minimizes the normals and albedos in one step, then all other variables in another step, and repeats until convergence:

$$\underset{\rho,N}{\text{argmin}}\frac{1-\lambda}{pn}\sum_{\mathbf{x}=1}^{p}\sum_{i=1}^{n}||f_v^{-1}(I_{i,\mathbf{x}})-e_i\rho_{\mathbf{x}}(L_i^\top N_{\mathbf{x}}S_{i,\mathbf{x}}+a_i)||^2 \tag{8}$$

$$\underset{v,e,a}{\text{argmin}}\frac{1}{pn}\sum_{\mathbf{x}=1}^{p}\sum_{i=1}^{n}||f_v^{-1}(I_{i,\mathbf{x}})-e_i\rho_{\mathbf{x}}(L_i^\top N_{\mathbf{x}}S_{i,\mathbf{x}}+a_i)||^2 \quad +\frac{\lambda}{255}R_v \tag{9}$$

This formulation has substantially smaller computational overhead, because Equation 8 can be broken into p independent subproblems, one for each pixel. Although neither of these subproblems are convex, there are immediate linear approximations to each of these problems which can be solved by least squares.

Linear Approximation to Equation 8. We cannot simultaneously solve for ρ and N and achieve a convex solution, because the surface normal N must be unit length. We can rewrite the lighting model from Equation 3 as:

$$f^{-1}(I_{i,\mathbf{x}})-e_i\rho_{\mathbf{x}}a_i=e_iL_i^\top(\rho_{\mathbf{x}}N_{\mathbf{x}})S_{i,\mathbf{x}}. \tag{10}$$

Therefore, we approximate a solution by fixing the $\rho_{\mathbf{x}}$ on the left-hand side of the above equation as the last iteration's approximation for the albedo, then solve for the unconstrained 3-element vector $\rho_{\mathbf{x}}N_{\mathbf{x}}$ on the right hand side via least squares for each color channel, where the magnitude of the resulting variable is the albedo. Since this allows a surface normal for each color channel, we repeat this optimization by fixing the albedo and solving for the single best normal over all color channels via least squares, and then scaling the albedos so that each normal is unit length. Since Equation 8 is independent for each pixel, this optimization can be done for each pixel in parallel.

The above method makes the assumption that the albedo does not change dramatically from iteration to iteration. Therefore, when we minimize Equation 8, we make use of a learning rate that encourages a slow change in the albedo and normal. If ρ' and N' are the solution to the linear approximation, then we update the estimates of the albedo and normal for the next iteration as:

$$\rho\leftarrow\rho'\tau+\rho(1-\tau) \tag{11}$$

$$N\leftarrow\frac{N'\tau+N(1-\tau)}{||N'\tau+N(1-\tau)||}. \tag{12}$$

Each time we minimize Equation 8, we repeat the solve-and-update procedure 20 times, using a learning rate of $\tau=0.1$.

Linear Approximation to Equation 9. Because the ambient lighting term is single-channel, Equation 9 is nonconvex. However, if we separate the ambient lighting into three channels, then we can solve for the radiometric parameters v, the ambient light in each channel a, and the exposure e. An auxiliary variable

$\hat{e}_i = e_i a_i$ transforms Equation 9 into a linear system with respect to unknowns $v, e_i, \hat{e}_i$:

$$f_0^{-1}(I_{i,\mathbf{x}}) + \sum_{j=1}^{b} f_j^{-1}(I_{i,\mathbf{x}})v_j = e_i \rho_{\mathbf{x}} L_i^\top N_{\mathbf{x}} S_{i,\mathbf{x}} + \hat{e}_i \rho_{\mathbf{x}}. \tag{13}$$

Notice that we can keep the constraint $a_i \leq 1$ by use of the linear constraint over the auxiliary variable as $\hat{e}_i \leq e_i$.

This solves for an independent ambient lighting term for each color channel. However, after fixing all other terms, the optimal single-channel a can be found through a simple closed-form solution.

The full algorithm therefore initializes its albedo, normals, ambient light, exposures, and nonlinear response and iterates between the two linear approximations until convergence.

Ambiguity. As presented, there is an ambiguity between the exposures and albedo, in that we can double the exposure and halve the albedo image, and keep the same reconstruction. We fix this ambiguity by scaling each term so that the mean exposure is 255.

3.3 Shadow Estimation

To initialize the shadow volume, we initially tried the shadow estimation algorithm from Sunkavalli et al. [13], which uses a per-pixel threshold to define at which times that pixel is in shadow. This threshold is defined as the median of the bottom 20% of intensities ever seen by that pixel, multiplied by some constant (Sunkavalli et al. use 1.5).

While this approach works well for one day's worth of video, over the span of a year, pixel intensities vary drastically as the position and intensity of the sun change; a shadowed pixel when the sun is highest in the sky may have the same intensity as a directly-lit pixel at the opposite time of year, and so there usually is not a single correct threshold.

We modify this thresholding technique by introducing an adaptive, per-pixel threshold which changes over time. For each pixel $\mathbf{x}$, we use two centroids $s_{\mathbf{x}}$ and $l_{\mathbf{x}}$ that model the intensity of that pixel in shade and direct sunlight, respectively. We initialize $s_{\mathbf{x}}$ and $l_{\mathbf{x}}$ similarly to Sunkavalli et al., where $l_{\mathbf{x}}$ is the median of the top 5% of pixels, and $s_{\mathbf{x}}$ is the median of the bottom 5% of pixels. Then, for each image i in chronological order, we compute whether the original image pixel $I_{i,\mathbf{x}}$ is closer to $s_{\mathbf{x}}$ or $l_{\mathbf{x}}$, set its corresponding pixel in the shadow volume, and update that threshold as $s_{\mathbf{x}} \leftarrow 0.8 s_{\mathbf{x}} + 0.2 I_{i,\mathbf{x}}$ or $l_{\mathbf{x}} \leftarrow 0.8 l_{\mathbf{x}} + 0.2 I_{i,\mathbf{x}}$. In this way, as we loop over all times i, from 1 to n, the values of $l_{\mathbf{x}}$ and $s_{\mathbf{x}}$ rise and fall as needed. Figure 3 shows that this method produces better shadow volumes than Sunkavalli et al. when working over the span of many months. As in [13], we perform bilateral filtering [19] to smooth the shadow images.

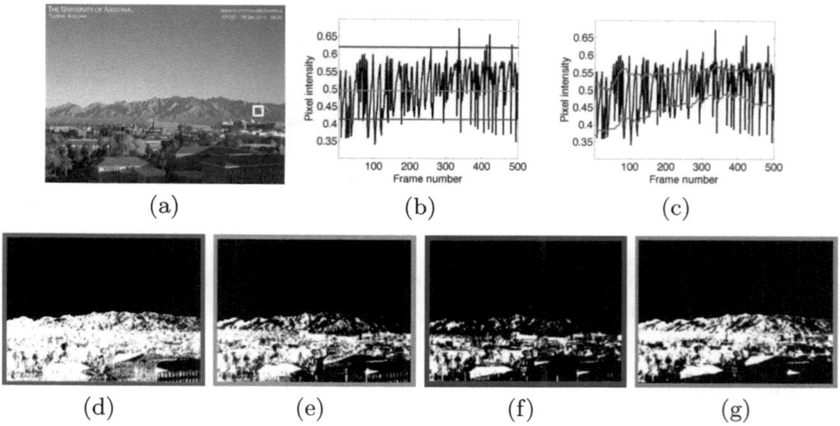

Fig. 3. (a) An example image. The pixel trajectory for the pixel centered in the white box is shown in (b), along with three scalar multiples of the threshold generated by the shadow estimation method of Sunkavalli et al. [13]. The blue line is the threshold suggested in [13]. (c) The centroids used in our adaptive approach. (d)-(g) The resulting shadow images from each approach for the image in (a), where the color of the border indicates which thresholding technique was used.

3.4 Implementation

Although we can decompose our optimization into a sequence of convex steps, the overall optimization is nonconvex and is subject to initialization. We initialize our variables rather simply: the normals begin as the all-up vector, the ambient intensity is 1 for all images, the exposure is 255 for each color channel, the response function is linear (i.e., we choose the v so that $f_v^{-1}(x) = x$), and we initialize the albedo as the mean in-shade image.

In all of the experiments used in this paper, we use $n = 500$ images. When selecting images, it's important to select from a wide range of lighting angles, but not to include any times of day when the sun is in view, producing lens flare effects in the image. Furthermore, we aim to select images that are the least overcast or hazy. Therefore, we begin by sampling 1000 lighting directions uniformly from the set of sun illumination directions the camera observes.

Because many cameras experience large numbers of cloudy days, and direct sunlight is important to constrain surface normals, we use a heuristic to encourage selection of sunny images. For each of the 1000 target lighting directions, we consider all images whose lighting direction is within 3 degrees of that target, and select the image with the largest saturation. From these 1000 candidate images that span the observed lighting directions, we select the 500 most-saturated images, in order to remove times of day which are consistently hazy, cloudy, or when the sun is in view.

For all experiments, we manually mask off the sky, timestamps, streets, bodies of water, pathways, or other areas prone to transient objects. Optimization is performed only on the remaining pixels. We use $\lambda = 0.9$ in Equation 9.

(a) 1 month (b) $1\frac{1}{2}$ months (c) 2 months (d) 4 months

Fig. 4. The normal maps recovered from our algorithm as the duration of original imagery ranges from 1 to 4 months.

Runtime depends on the size of the image and number of pixels, but we report timing for the results in Figure 1. On a machine with dual 2.66GHz processors with 6 cores each and 12GB of RAM, the entire inference process from loading imagery to completion takes 62 minutes on a sequence with 500 images and 224,052 non-sky pixels using our MATLAB implementation. We perform 10 iterations of alternating descent for each experiment. The main bottleneck is in solving for albedo and normals, which takes about four and a half minutes.

We emphasize that this data comprises 500 images captured over many months, so our algorithm is substantially faster than real-time.

4 Results

As discussed briefly in the introduction, photometric stereo requires lighting to come from a diverse set of directions. To evaluate its importance, we ran our algorithm on one camera and progressively increased the duration of the input sequence from one week to a few months, starting in August 2011. Figure 4 shows that only once we have about six weeks of imagery can we begin to uncover three-dimensional normals, and the quality of the normals increases as more imagery is included. Depending on the times of year used, even longer lengths of time may be required to reliably extract usable normals (i.e., a week near an equinox produces a larger solar cover than a week at a solstice).

Figure 5 shows the results of our algorithm on real-world cameras. We reliably recover shadows, response functions, and surface normals for a variety of scenes from the AMOS dataset [2].

4.1 Evaluation

To evaluate our approach, we compare our surface normals to the normals from Google Earth models. Using the interface from [20], we geo-calibrated two webcams and generated normals from the surrounding Google Earth geometry.

Figure 6 shows a quantitative evaluation of our approach, by measuring the angular difference between our normals and the normals from Google Earth. These histograms show that many locations in the image have substantial angular error. However, the colored squares help parse this difference, and show that

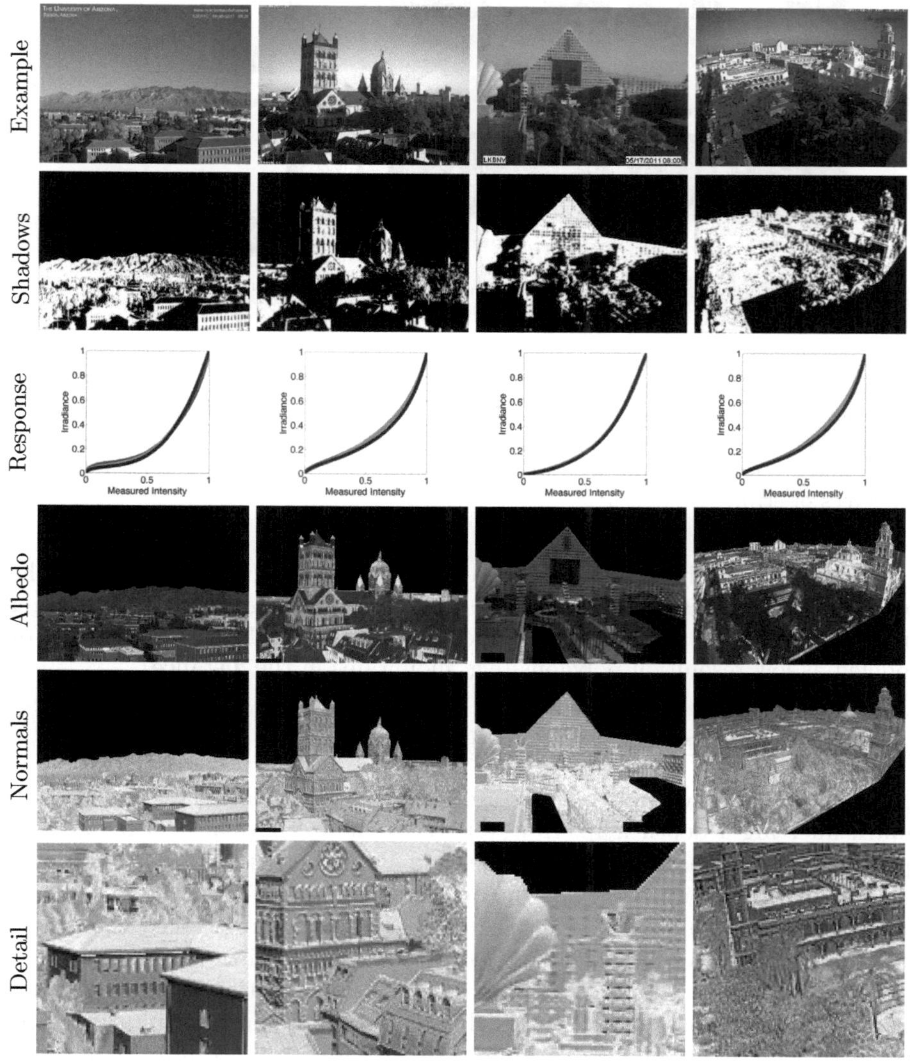

Fig. 5. Results on a variety of cameras. From top to bottom, we show an example image, the recovered shadow mask for that image, nonlinear camera response curves, albedo, surface normals, and a crop of the surface normal image to show detail. Notice that the shadow mask accurately captures large-scale shadows as well as small-scale details. We reliably recover physically-meaningful, nonlinear response curves, yet our model is flexible enough to allow variety of real-world responses. Because we allow each pixel a unique normal, we produce high-fidelity normals that capture the tiny changes in surface orientation due to windows and the detailed geometry of trees.

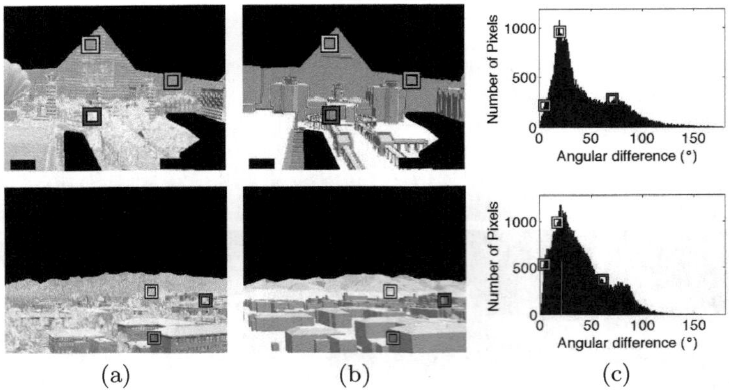

Fig. 6. Comparing our results to the models from Google Earth. (a) Our recovered surface normals. (b) The surface normals from Google Earth. (c) A histogram of the angular difference, in degrees, between our model and the Google model. The green, yellow, and red squares show locations on the images and histograms with 5, 20, and 70 degrees of error.

in locations where the Google Earth geometry is an accurate reflection of the scene geometry, the angular error is on the order of 5 degrees, and that larger angular errors occur on objects not modeled by Google Earth (e.g. trees), or modeled as low resolution polygons (e.g. mountains in the distance).

4.2 Depth from Normal Field Integration

The normals from photometric stereo are often computed as an intermediate step toward inferring a depth map. However, the standard normal field integration equations make the assumption that the normals are represented in a coordinate frame relative to the camera (i.e., the optical axis is the Z-axis).

Since our algorithm returns surface normals in a geo-referenced coordinate system, we perform a search over pan and tilt angles of possible camera rotations, choosing the rotation that yields the best resulting integration error; see [21] for a more detailed discussion on normal field integration. Example results for image regions that consist of objects with interesting shapes are shown in Figure 7.

5 Conclusions and Future Work

We have presented an image formation model rich enough to capture variations in outdoor webcam imagery over long time periods. We acknowledge that there are many additional components that affect outdoor imagery, many of which we could add within our formation model and optimization. Over long time periods, both the surface normal and the albedos can change (buildings may undergo construction, snow may fall, trees may change color) and this could be captured by solving for normal maps or albedos with constraints on how they

Fig. 7. 3D reconstructions of objects from webcams in the wild. In each example, we show an original image, and two novel views of the reconstructed object. The shape of the seashell in (a) is captured nicely (and shown from a very different viewpoint), and the rooftop of the building in the other scene is accurately reconstructed with a right angle when viewed from overhead in the top right of (b).

vary through time. The lighting model could be extended to include haze or non-uniform ambient light. The surface reflectance model can be modified to explicitly include a specular component [16], or we could use estimators for the surface normal that are robust to non-Lambertian effects [22].

Understanding how to incorporate additional terms within a tractable optimization scheme is something that we look forward to pursuing. We believe that this current work offers one step in that direction, by being the first to tractably return real-world surface reflectance properties from uncalibrated images, which could be used toward more reasoned environmental monitoring.

To facilitate future comparative studies, our data, code, and ground truth are available at `research.engineering.wustl.edu/~abramsa/heliometric`.

References

1. Narasimhan, S.G., Wang, C., Nayar, S.K.: All the Images of an Outdoor Scene. In: Heyden, A., Sparr, G., Nielsen, M., Johansen, P. (eds.) ECCV 2002, Part III. LNCS, vol. 2352, pp. 148–162. Springer, Heidelberg (2002)
2. Jacobs, N., Roman, N., Pless, R.: Consistent temporal variations in many outdoor scenes. In: Proc. IEEE Conference on Computer Vision and Pattern Recognition (2007)
3. Koppal, S.J., Narasimhan, S.G.: Clustering appearance for scene analysis. In: Proc. IEEE Conference on Computer Vision and Pattern Recognition (2006)
4. Sunkavalli, K., Romeiro, F., Matusik, W., Zickler, T., Pfister, H.: What do color changes reveal about an outdoor scene? In: Proc. IEEE Conference on Computer Vision and Pattern Recognition (2008)
5. Lalonde, J.F., Efros, A.A., Narasimhan, S.G.: Webcam clip art: Appearance and illuminant transfer from time-lapse sequences. ACM Transactions on Graphics (SIGGRAPH Asia 2009) 28 (2009)

6. Jacobs, N., Burgin, W., Fridrich, N., Abrams, A., Miskell, K., Braswell, B.H., Richardson, A.D., Pless, R.: The global network of outdoor webcams: Properties and applications. In: Proc. ACM International Conference on Advances in Geographic Information Systems (SIGSPATIAL GIS) (2009)
7. Riordan, E., Graham, E., Yuen, E., Estrin, D., Rundel, P.: Utilizing public internet-connected cameras for a cross- continental plant phenology monitoring system. In: 2010 IEEE International Geoscience and Remote Sensing Symposium (IGARSS), pp. 1501–1504 (2010)
8. Woodham, R.J.: Photometric method for determining surface orientation from multiple images. Optical Engineerings I, 139–144 (1980)
9. Shi, B., Matsushita, Y., Wei, Y., Xu, C., Tan, P.: Self-calibrating photometric stereo. In: Proc. IEEE Conference on Computer Vision and Pattern Recognition, pp. 1118–1125 (2010)
10. Mongkulmann, W., Okabe, T., Sato, Y.: Photometric stereo with auto-radiometric calibration. In: ICCV Workshops, pp. 753–758 (2011)
11. Shen, L., Tan, P.: Photometric stereo and weather estimation using internet images. In: Proc. IEEE Conference on Computer Vision and Pattern Recognition (2009)
12. Ackermann, J., Ritz, M., Stork, A., Goesele, M.: Removing the example from example-based photometric stereo. In: ECCV Workshop on Reconstruction and Modeling of LargeScale 3D Virtual Environments (2010)
13. Sunkavalli, K., Matusik, W., Pfister, H., Rusinkiewicz, S.: Factored time-lapse video. In: Proc. ACM Conference on Computer Graphics and Interactive Techniques (SIGGRAPH), vol. 26, pp. 101–111 (2007)
14. Kim, S.J., Frahm, J.M., Pollefeys, M.: Radiometric calibration with illumination change for outdoor scene analysis. In: Proc. IEEE Conference on Computer Vision and Pattern Recognition (2008)
15. Grossberg, M.D., Nayar, S.K.: What is the space of camera response functions? In: IEEE Conference on Computer Vision and Pattern Recognition (CVPR), vol. II, pp. 602–609 (2003)
16. Ackermann, J., Langguth, F., Fuhrmann, S., Goesele, M.: Photometric stereo for outdoor webcams. In: Proc. IEEE Conference on Computer Vision and Pattern Recognition (2012)
17. Jacobs, N., Bies, B., Pless, R.: Using cloud shadows to infer scene structure and camera calibration. In: Proc. IEEE Conference on Computer Vision and Pattern Recognition (2010)
18. Reda, I., Andreas, A.: Solar position algorithm for solar radiation applications. In: NREL Report No. TP-560-34302 (2003)
19. Tomasi, C., Manduchi, R.: Bilateral filtering for gray and color images. In: Proc. IEEE International Conference on Computer Vision (1998)
20. Abrams, A., Pless, R.: Webcams in context: Web interfaces to create live 3D environments. In: Proc. ACM SIGMM International Conference on Multimedia (ACMMM), pp. 331–340 (2010)
21. Zhang, L., Curless, B., Hertzmann, A., Seitz, S.M.: Shape and motion under varying illumination: Unifying structure from motion, photometric stereo, and multi-view stereo. In: Proc. IEEE International Conference on Computer Vision (2003)
22. Wu, L., Ganesh, A., Shi, B., Matsushita, Y., Wang, Y., Ma, Y.: Robust Photometric Stereo via Low-Rank Matrix Completion and Recovery. In: Kimmel, R., Klette, R., Sugimoto, A. (eds.) ACCV 2010, Part III. LNCS, vol. 6494, pp. 703–717. Springer, Heidelberg (2011)

Shape from Single Scattering for Translucent Objects

Chika Inoshita[1], Yasuhiro Mukaigawa[1], Yasuyuki Matsushita[2], and Yasushi Yagi[1]

[1] Osaka University
[2] Microsoft Research Asia

Abstract. Translucent objects strongly scatter incident light. Scattering makes the problem of estimating shape of translucent objects difficult, because reflective or transmitted light cannot be reliably extracted from the scattering. In this paper, we propose a new shape estimation method by directly utilizing scattering measurements. Although volumetric scattering is a complex phenomenon, single scattering can be relatively easily modeled because it is a simple one-bounce collision of light to a particle in a medium. Based on this observation, our method determines the shape of objects from the observed intensities of the single scattering and its attenuation. We develop a solution method that simultaneously determines scattering parameters and the shape based on energy minimization. We demonstrate the effectiveness of the proposed approach by extensive experiments using synthetic and real data.

1 Introduction

In real-world scenes, there are many translucent objects around us, such as wax, plastic products, and precious stones. Inside a translucent object, incident light scatters and randomly travels. Although vision-based shape estimation techniques are maturing, it is still difficult to estimate the shape of translucent objects. Passive approaches based on triangulation require a target objects to be well-textured, and active methods tend to fail due to strong scattering of the incident light. As pointed out by Godin *et al.* [1], the incident light shows the brightest observation off the object surface for translucent materials due to scattering. Methods based on refractive or transmitted light cannot be directly applied to translucent media where strong scattering exists. Figure 1 shows an example of a failure mode for measuring translucent objects using a commercial 3D laser scanner, Konica-Minolta Vivid 9i. While it works well for human skin, the shape of translucent objects is not accurately estimated due to strong scattering. Shape estimation of translucent objects is still a wide open problem.

While scattering is well studied in computer graphics, it is less discussed in computer vision because the complexity of light interactions renders inverse problems intractable. Therefore, for vision applications, scattering has been regarded as a nuisance and eliminated by various approaches, *e.g.*, polarization [2], coating with diffuse powder [3], and phase-shift measurements [4]. In contrast

A. Fitzgibbon et al. (Eds.): ECCV 2012, Part II, LNCS 7573, pp. 371–384, 2012.

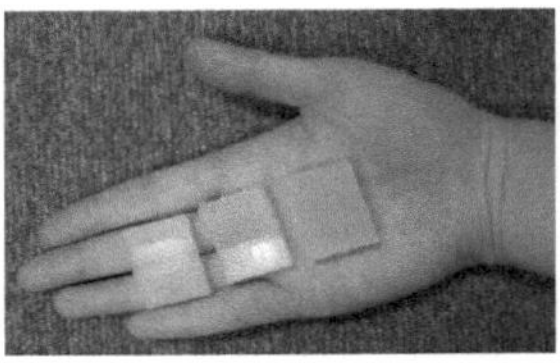

(a) Translucent blocks on the hand

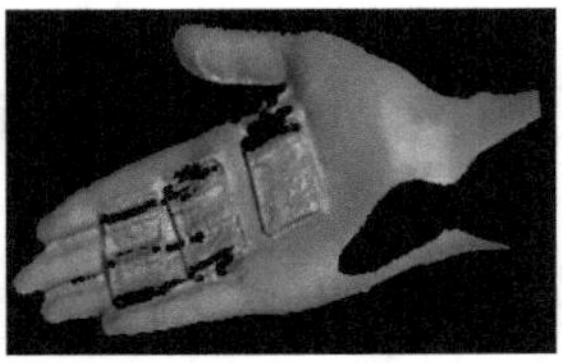

(b) Shape measurement result by a laser range finder

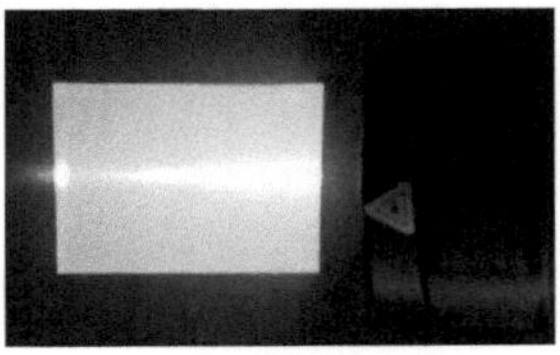

(c) Strong scattering in translucent object

Fig. 1. Failure mode of shape measurement of translucent objects using a 3D laser scanner

to these approaches, we propose a new shape estimation method based on the observed scattering itself. In particular, we develop a method that uses the observation of single scattering, which occurs via a one-bounce collision of light to a particle, and its attenuation along the light path. We derive a solution method from a scattering model that takes into account the refraction, an extinction coefficient, and a phase function.

The primary contributions of our work are as follows. We propose a new shape estimation technique for translucent objects. It introduces the use of scattering as a beneficial signal for determining shape. The proposed method is effective when the target object shows strong scattering where other shape estimation approaches cannot be applied. In fact, since there exist various objects in our daily life that exhibit strong scattering, our method has wide applicability. This work is the first attempt to directly use the observed intensities of single scattering for shape measurement. In addition, we develop an effective solution method based on energy minimization for simultaneously estimating shape and scattering parameters.

2 Related Work

Shape-from-intensity is a generic framework for shape measurement based on observed intensities. Various optical phenomena, such as diffuse [5,6] or specular reflection [7,8], have been used as cues for shape estimation. Liao *et al.* [9] estimate object's shape from light attenuation, which is inversely proportional to the square of distance. Our method is related to Liao *et al.*'s method because we also use the attenuation of the light although the setting is different.

Refractive lights have been used to measure the shape of transparent objects, because most incident lights to the surface are transmitted inside. Miyazaki and Ikeuchi [10] estimate the object surface by analyzing multiple interreflections in the object by a polarization ray-tracing method. Huynh *et al.* [11] use multi-spectral polarization for obtaining surface normals. Kutulakos and Steger's method [12] performs triangulation from the analyzed transmitted light path. Wetzstein *et al.* [13] use a light field probe to analyze the transmitted light path. Trifonov *et al.*'s method [14] immerses target objects in fluid whose refractive index is the same as the target and applies tomography for obtaining shape. Hullin *et al.* [15] use a scan-line illumination for transparent objects immersed in fluorescent fluid. While these methods use refracted light, Morris and Kutulakos [16] propose scatter-trace photography focusing on the transparent object that reflects some of the incident light. While these methods are effective, it is not straightforward to apply them to translucent objects due to strong scattering.

Shape measurement methods for objects in scattering media have been also proposed. Narasimhan *et al.* [17] measure the shape of target objects in scattering media by light stripe scanning and photometric stereo. Kim *et al.* [18] remove scattering light by angular filtering and estimate the shape by tomography. Treibitz and Schechner [19] not only remove backscattering in an underwater scene, but also estimate the scene depth based on backscattering falloff. Florescu *et al.* [20] apply the optical tomography using observed single scattering based on a radiative transfer equation and reconstruct the attenuation parameter of the 3D volume. While these are related, these cannot be directly applied to estimate the shape of translucent objects. More recently, characteristics of scattering media have been actively studied. Mukaigawa *et al.* [21] propose a method for separating single and multiple scatterings and analyze the light transport. Narasimhan *et al.* [22] dilute scattering media to reduce multiple scattering for estimating scattering parameters. The spatial distribution of scattering media, such as smoke or milk drops, has also been studied [23,24]. We develop our method based on these studies on the characteristics of scattering.

Scattering has similar properties to interreflections. In fact, scattering can be regarded as interreflections of light in a medium. In the study of shape estimation with the existence of interreflections, there are three major approaches:

1. Elimination of the interreflections: Nayar *et al.* [25] show a method to remove interreflections using high frequency illumination. After the elimination of interreflections, a classic technique, such as Lambertian photometric stereo, can be well applied.
2. Modeling of interreflections: Nayar *et al.* [26] iteratively estimate the shape of concave surface by explicitly modeling the interreflection based on radiosity.
3. Use of the interreflection itself: Liu *et al.* [27] show that the light transport of the interreflections can be used as a cue for shape estimation.

Thus, similar approaches may be applicable for shape measurement of a translucent object. Our approach is close to the third approach where we wish to recover shape from scattering itself.

3 Shape from Single Scattering

3.1 Background

When light travels through a translucent medium, the light scatters in the medium due to collisions with particles. Single scattering is a type of scattering, in which light scatters at only once in the medium before reaching a viewer. Figure 2(a) shows a parametric scattering model. In scattering media, the incident

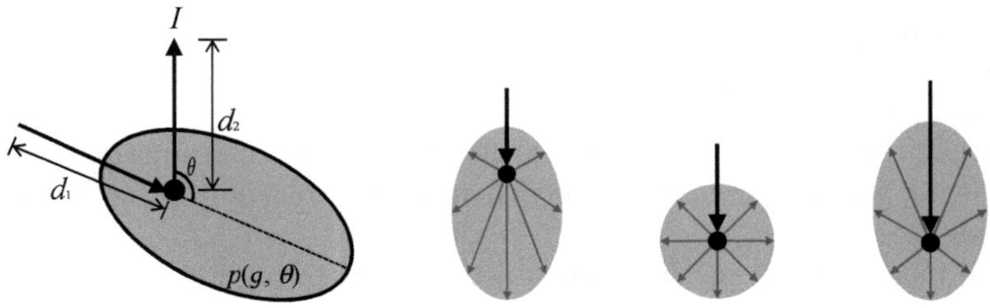

(a) Scattering model (b) $g > 0$ (c) $g = 0$ (d) $g < 0$

Fig. 2. Illustration of the scattering model and examples of distribution profiles with a varying phase function

light exponentially attenuates with the length of light path by the Lambert-Beer law [28]. It also scatters in the media, and a Henyey-Greenstein phase function [29] is known as a good approximation for the phenomenon. With this phase function, the observed intensity I of single scattering is described as [21,22]

$$I = sp(g, \theta)e^{-\sigma_t(d_1+d_2)}, \tag{1}$$

$$p(g, \theta) = \frac{1}{4\pi}\frac{1-g^2}{(1+g^2-2g\cos\theta)^{\frac{3}{2}}}, \tag{2}$$

where s is a scaling constant that includes the intensity of the incident light and scattering coefficient, σ_t is an extinction coefficient, $(d_1 + d_2)$ represents the length of the light path in the medium, and $p(g, \theta)$ is the phase function. The phase function represents the scattering distribution, and the distribution profile is controlled by a parameter g $(-1 \leq g \leq 1)$. Figures 2(b), (c), and (d) show examples of the distribution profiles produced by varying g.

3.2 Formulation

We formulate the relationship between observed intensities of single scattering and the shape of translucent target. Figure 3 shows our setting for the shape measurement. A translucent object is illuminated from one side and observed from the top. We assume a homogeneous material as a target object and orthographic projection for both illumination and observation. In addition, we ignore multiple scattering for now, but a method for handling it will be explained in later sections.

Figure 4 illustrates a light path of single scattering in a medium. The incident ray $\mathbf{i}_x$ scatters at scattering point (x', y'), and reaches to surface point (x, y). $\mathbf{n}(x, y)$ represents the surface normal and $\mathbf{i}_x = [1, 0, 0]^T$ and $\mathbf{i}_z = [0, 0, 1]^T$ are incident and exitant light vectors, respectively. $\mathbf{r}(x, y)$ is a unit scattering vector pointing from the scattering point (x', y') to the surface point (x, y). The angle between the incident vector $\mathbf{i}_x$ and the scattering vector $\mathbf{r}(x, y)$ is denoted as θ_p. θ_r represents the projected angle of θ_p on the plane spanned by $\mathbf{r}(x, y)$ and $\mathbf{i}_z$. Our purpose is to estimate the height of the translucent object $h(x, y)$ from the

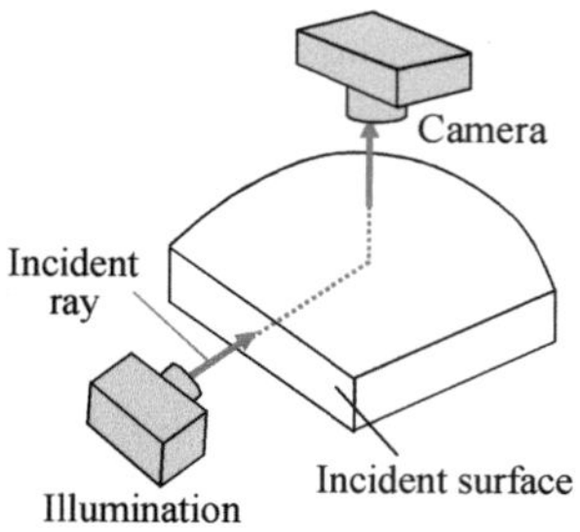

Fig. 3. Setting for shape estimation. A translucent object is illuminated from the side and observed from the top.

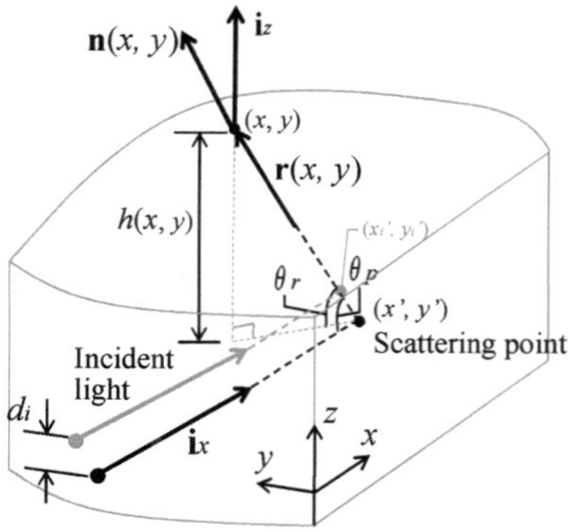

Fig. 4. Light path in the target object. The incident plane is almost planer, and incident light is assumed parallel to x-axis. The illuminated ray reaches to surface point (x, y) changing the travel direction at the scattering point (x', y').

observed intensities $I(x, y)$ at the surface point (x, y) on the surface, where the height of the incident ray is $z = 0$. Scattered incident ray $\mathbf{i}_x$ is finally refracted at the object surface. The angle of refraction obeys Snell's law represented as

$$\mathbf{n}(x, y) \times \mathbf{i}_z = \eta \mathbf{n}(x, y) \times \mathbf{r}(x, y), \tag{3}$$

where η is a refractive index, $\times$ represents a cross-product operator. The total length of the light path becomes the sum of x', which corresponds to the distance from the incident point to scattering point and the distance from the scattering point to the surface point, $h(x, y)/\sin\theta_r$. Since the intensity of single scattering is modeled as Eq. (1), the observed intensity is represented by

$$I(x, y) = sF_t^{in} F_t^{out}(x, y) p(g, \theta_p) e^{-\sigma_t \left(x' + \frac{h(x,y)}{\sin\theta_r}\right)}, \tag{4}$$

where s is a scaling constant, $F_t^{out}(x, y)$ represents the Fresnel transmittance on the surface point (x, y), and F_t^{in} is the constant Fresnel transmittance on the incident point because the incident light is perpendicular to the incident plane. Equation (4) shows that the observed intensity depends on both the geometric shape and scattering parameters including extinction parameter σ_t, refractive index η, and phase function parameter g. Given these scattering parameters, the height of the translucent object is determined up to an unknown offset due to s by

$$h(x, y) = \frac{\sin\theta_r}{\sigma_t} \left(\log s + \log F_t^{in} + \log F_t^{out}(x, y) + \log p(g, \theta_p) - \log I(x, y)\right) \\ - x' \sin\theta_r. \tag{5}$$

4 Solution Method

In the previous section, we described a basic theory of the shape from single scattering. However, in reality, we cannot directly estimate the object height $h(x, y)$ by Eq. (5) due to the unknown parameters. In addition, the observed intensities include the contributions not only from single scattering but also from multiple scattering. In this section, we discuss a solution method for these problems. In our method, we assume that the refractive index η is known because it can be directly measured using a refractometer.

In our method, we employ an energy minimization approach for simultaneously determining both the shape and scattering parameters. When the unknown parameters and height are correctly estimated, Eq. (4) should produce the intensity that becomes equivalent to the observed intensity $I(x, y)$. Although we can estimate the unknown parameters by seeking parameters, which generate the observed intensity, parameter estimation tends to be unstable due to a larger number of unknowns than the captured intensity. To reliably derive a solution to this problem, we use multiple $n(2 \leq n)$ images that are captured by changing the height of the incident ray. Namely, we record multiple intensities $I_i(x, y)$ with varying heights of the incident rays $z = d_i \quad (i = 1, \ldots, n)$ as shown in Fig. 4. Now we have n intensity observations per scene point $I_i(x, y)$ as

$$I_i(x, y) = sF_t^{in} F_t^{out}(x, y)p(g, \theta_p)e^{-\sigma_t(x'_i + \frac{h(x,y)-d_i}{\sin\theta_r})}, \quad i = 1, \ldots, n. \tag{6}$$

We also take into account the signal-to-noise ratio of the observed intensities; the darker observations suffer more from image noise while the brighter observations are more reliable. We incorporate this as a weighting factor w_i when determining the unknown parameters. Based on these, we define an energy function for computing heights $h(x, y)$ and scattering parameters s, g, σ_t as

$$E(h(x, y), s, g, \sigma_t) = \sum_i w_i \sum_{x,y} \left(I_i(x, y) - I_i^{gen}(h(x, y), s, g, \sigma_t)\right)^2, \tag{7}$$

where I_i^{gen} is the generated intensity based on Eq. (6), and w_i is a weighting factor for reducing the effect of noise. We define the weighting factor w_i as

$$w_i = \frac{\sum_{x,y} I_i(x, y)}{\sum_{k=1}^{n} \sum_{x,y} I_k(x, y)}. \tag{8}$$

The energy function E evaluates the closeness between observed intensity and generated intensity based on Eq. (6). The minimizer of the energy function E gives us estimates of the height $h(x, y)$ per-pixel and scattering parameters s, g and σ_t as

$$\{h(x, y), s, g, \sigma_t\} = \underset{h(x,y),s,g,\sigma_t}{\operatorname{argmin}} \; E(h(x, y), s, g, \sigma_t). \tag{9}$$

We describe the optimization method in the following section.

4.1 Implementation

This section describes the implementation details of the solution method. Our method uses a non-linear optimization because of the non-convexity of Eq. (7) with respect to the unknown parameters. We now describe the computation method of the initial guess of the height $h(x,y)$ and the following optimization strategy.

Estimation of Initial Shape. To obtain an initial guess of the estimated parameters, we use the initial shape $h^0(x,y)$ that can be computed by ignoring refraction ($\eta = 1$). When $\eta = 1$, the scattering vector coincides with the output vector $\mathbf{i}_z$, the 2D projection of the scattering point (x', y') becomes identical with the surface point (x,y), and Fresnel transmittance $F_t^{out}(x,y)$ is constant because the refraction is disregarded. Since the angle θ_p equals to $\pi/2$, phase function $p(g, \theta_p)$ becomes constant. Therefore, the intensity generated from initial height $h^0(x,y)$ is described as

$$I_i^0(x,y) = Se^{-\sigma_t(h^0(x,y)+x-d_i)}, \quad S = sF_t^{in}F_t^{out}p\left(g, \frac{\pi}{2}\right). \tag{10}$$

Here, unknown parameters are the height $h^0(x,y)$, scaling constant S, and extinction coefficient σ_t. Using a pair of intensity observations $I_i(x,y)$ and $I_j(x,y)$ taken by different heights of incident rays d_i and d_j, the extinction coefficient is calculated as

$$\sigma_t = \frac{\log I_i(x,y) - \log I_j(x,y)}{d_i - d_j} \quad (d_i \neq d_j). \tag{11}$$

In practice, we take the average as the estimate of σ_t using all the pairs of d_i and d_j. We employ an intensity at the incident point as the initial scaling constant S as the scaling without attenuation. The initial guess of the height $h^0(x,y)$ is therefore described as

$$h^0(x,y) = \frac{1}{\sigma_t}(\log S - \log I_i(x,y)) - x + d_i, \tag{12}$$

and is estimated using the parameters σ_t and S. We use this initial guess as an input to the optimization: $h(x,y) \leftarrow h^0(x,y)$.

Optimization. Now we estimate the shape and parameters by minimizing Eq. (9) using h^0 as the initial guess of the shape. The unknowns to be estimated are per-pixel height $h(x,y)$ and scattering parameters s, g, and σ_t. To efficiently avoid local minima, we use a two-step approach for the optimization. Namely, we first apply the Particle Swarm optimization [30] for limiting the search range in a coarse manner, and then use the Nelder-Mead method [31] for finding the optimal parameter set in a fine scale.

Extraction of Single Scattering. As discussed above, actual observations consist of both single and multiple scatterings as shown in Fig. 1(c). To separate the single scattering component from multiple scattering, we utilize a separation method [21] which uses projector as a light source as shown in Fig. 3. The extracted single scattering component is used as input for our method. Readers are referred to [21] for the details of the separation method.

5 Experiments

We assess the effectiveness of the proposed method using both synthetic and real-world scenes. With the synthetic scenes, we assess the accuracy of the proposed method by comparing with the ground truth. For the real-world scenes, we prepare two objects where the ground truth shape is available while the scattering parameters are unknown.

5.1 Synthetic Scenes

For the synthetic scene experiment, we used one 1-D curved surface, one 1-D discontinuous surface, and one 2-D discontinuous surface $h(x)$ as the scenes; Scenes A, B, and C. For each scene, we simulated intensity observations $I_i(x)$ with varying heights of incident rays $d_i = 0.2 \times i[\mathrm{mm}]$, $i = 0, \cdots, 9$ using the scattering model of Eq. (6). We added Gaussian noise to the intensity observations at 5 levels ($\mu = 0$ and $\sigma = 0, 5, 10, 15, 20$). The optical parameters are consistently set to $\eta = 1.2$, $g = 0.1$, $\sigma_t = 15$, and $s = 50000$.

Figure 5(a) shows Scene A and (b) shows simulated intensity observation in the case of Gaussian noise $\sigma = 10$. From this intensity, we estimate the object shape. Figure 5(c) shows the estimated result of Scene A. The initial height is globally skewed due to the inaccurate assumption of the refractive index $\eta = 1$ and local deformations due to observation noise. Especially, when Gaussian noise levels are $\sigma = 15$ and 20, estimated shapes become noisier as the length of light paths are greater because of the low S/N ratio. However, the optimized results consistently agree well with the ground truth except for some fluctuations. Figure 5(d) shows RMSE of the estimated height at each noise level. Although the RMSE increases according to the noise amplitude, the overall errors are small and show the accuracy of the method. Estimated scattering parameters and the RMSE values are summarized in Table 1. With small noise, the scaling parameter s and extinction coefficient σ_t are almost correct. The scattering parameter g has a larger deviation from its ground truth. Although g controls the scattering distribution, it effects to both intensity scale and intensity attenuation depending to object shape. Thus, estimating g becomes more difficult than estimating other parameters.

Other experimental results using synthetic 1-D stepped shape (Scene B) and 2-D pyramid like shape (Scene C). The ground truth and the estimated result in the case of Gaussian noise $\sigma = 10$ are shown in Fig. 6(a) and Fig. 7(b). For these asymmetric and discontinuous scenes as well, the estimation well converges near to the ground truth.

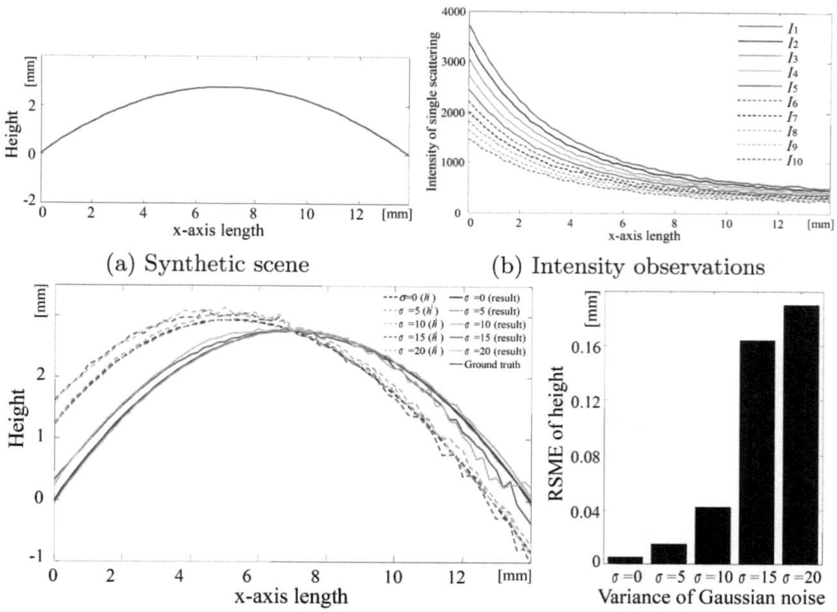

(a) Synthetic scene (b) Intensity observations

(c) Estimated result at each noise level (d) RMSE of height at each noise level

Fig. 5. Estimated heights of Scene A

Table 1. Estimated parameters and RMSE of estimated height at each noise level

	Scaling constant s	Parameter g	Extinction coefficient σ_t [mm^{-1}]	RMSE of height [mm]
Ground truth	5.0×10^4	0.1	1.5	-
$\sigma = 0$	5.08×10^4	0.069	15.0	0.05×10^{-1}
$\sigma = 5$	4.95×10^4	0.007	15.0	0.15×10^{-1}
$\sigma = 10$	4.95×10^4	0.002	15.0	0.42×10^{-1}
$\sigma = 15$	6.09×10^4	-0.002	16.0	1.64×10^{-1}
$\sigma = 20$	6.33×10^4	0.003	16.1	1.90×10^{-1}

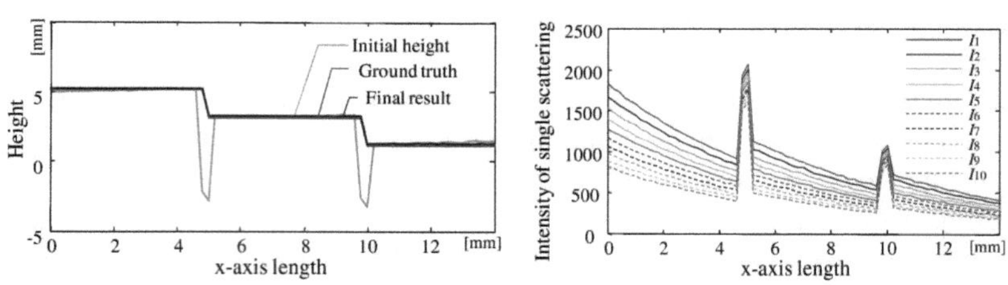

(a) Scene B and estimation result (b) Intensity observations

Fig. 6. Estimated heights of discontinuous Scene B

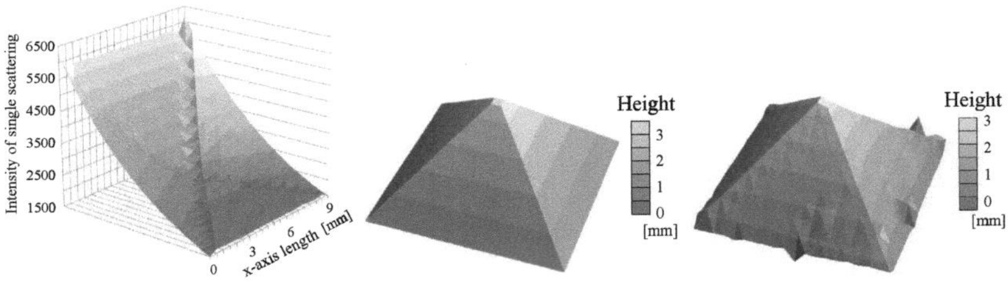

(a) Intensity observations (b) Scene C (c) Estimation result

Fig. 7. Estimated heights of discontinuous Scene C

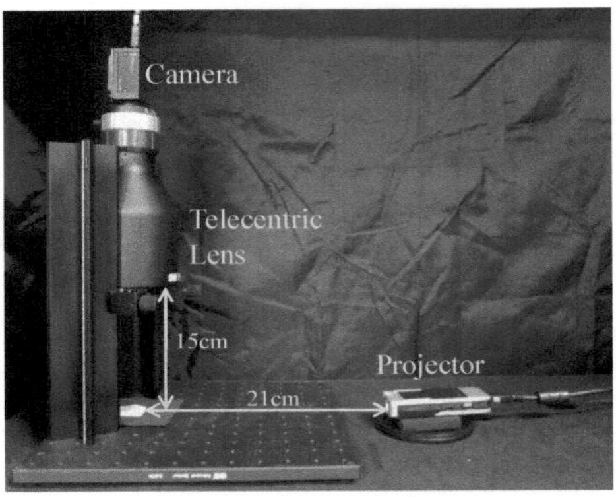

Fig. 8. Experimental setting. A projector is placed on the side of the object, and a camera is vertically placed, we used a telecentric lens for orthographic projection.

5.2 Real Scenes

We also applied the proposed method to real-world scenes. Figure 8 shows the experimental setting. A 3M MPro110 projector is placed on the side of the target object, and a Point Grey Grasshopper camera which has a linear response sensor is vertically placed to obtain a top view. To avoid the perspective effect of the imaging system, we use an Edmund optics telecentric lens for approximating an orthographic projection. To perform a comprehensive analysis, we use two different shapes of translucent objects; one is concave, and the other is convex. We made concave object using same material as shown in Fig. 1 (b) and convex object using a colored gelatin. The ground truth of these objects are known for performing a quantitative evaluation. We set the refractive index η as 1.3. We captured intensities of single scattering $I_i(x, y)$ ($d_i = 0.25 \times i$[mm], $i = 0, \cdots, 9$) with shifting height of incident light.

Figure 9(a) shows the concave object. The object is illuminated by a projector from its side plane. Figures 9(a) and (b) show the decomposition of the scattering components. The red, green, and blue plots show the intensities of single scattering, multiple scattering, and observed scattering, respectively. It can be

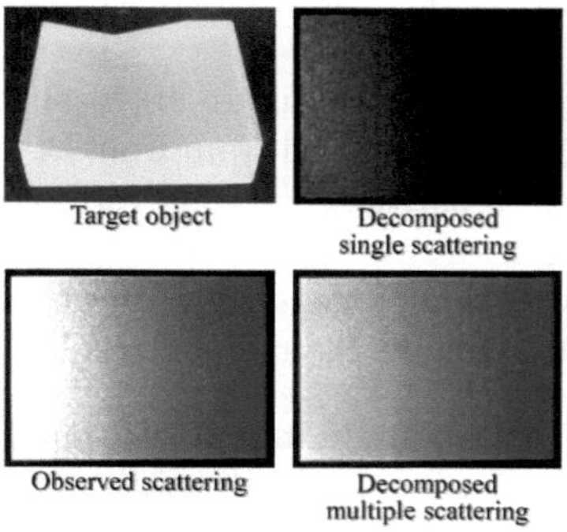

(a) Target object and decomposition results

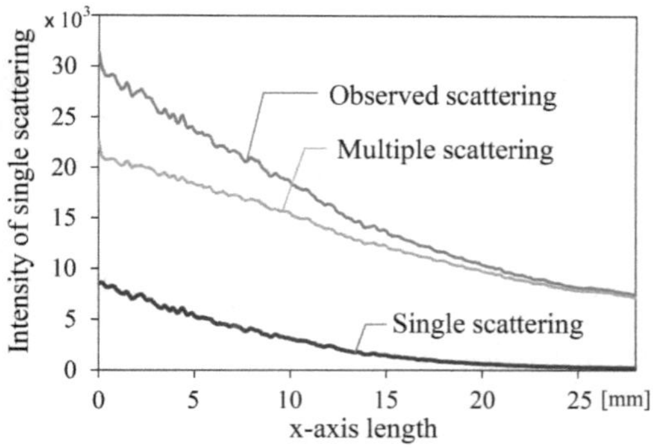

(b) Decomposition of the scattering components

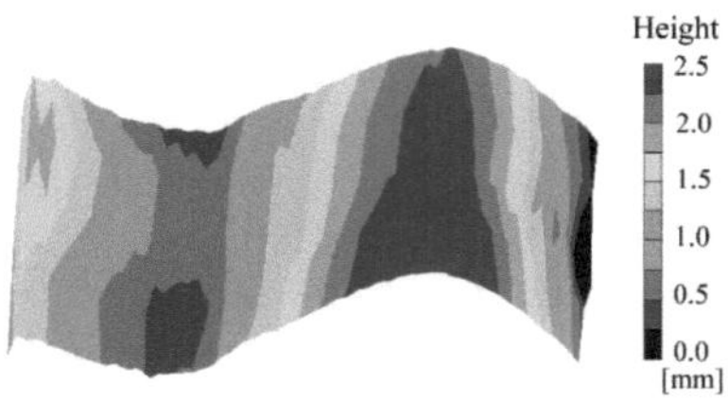

(c) 3D plot of the result

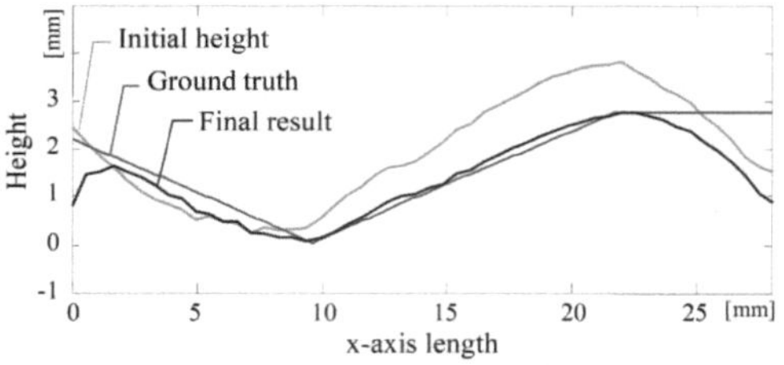

(d) Estimation result

Fig. 9. Experimental result using a concave scene

(a) Target object

(b) 3D plot of the merged result

Fig. 10. Experimental results using a asymmetric convex scene. (b) shows the 3D plot of the merged result.

seen that single scattering is almost exponentially attenuated with the increased distance from the incident point. Figure 9(c) shows the shape estimation result plotted as a 3D surface. We can see that our method is able to estimate the overall shape of the target except for the flat region. A possible reason for the incorrect estimation is insufficient intensities of single scattering for shape estimation because the light paths are longer for observing this region. In addition, the shape nearby the incident plane did not match the ground truth well due to the bright observation at the incident point and its glare. Estimated scattering parameters are $s = 12118$, $g = 0.042$, and $\sigma_t = 13.244$.

We also show the result of the convex scene in Fig. 10. Figure 10(b) shows the reconstruction result given by single scattering illuminated from front of the target object. Because of insufficient intensities of single scattering, estimated height has large error in back area. To reduce the error, we capture the intensities of single scattering by illuminating from the other side of the target object, and merge the two reconstruction results. Figure 10(c) shows the merged result.

Computation Time. In this experiment, it takes about 15 minutes to capture images (6 images for extracting single scattering at each of 10 different depths), and it takes about a few hours to compute the shape with an unoptimized Matlab implementation. We compute estimates on Intel Core 2 Duo CPU (3.00 GHz) and 3GB RAM. The size of problem is 74 (71 points for $h(x)$, s, g, and σ_t) in synthetic data, 259 (256 points for $h(x, y)$, s, g, and σ_t) in symmetric real data, and 873 (870 points for $h(x, y)$, s, g, and σ_t) in asymmetric real data.

6 Discussions

In this paper, we proposed a method for estimating the shape of translucent objects based on the attenuation of single scattering. We showed synthetic and real-world results that our method has a potential for accurate modeling of translucent objects, which has been difficult with other appearance-based methods. While the method works well for various translucent objects, the accuracy suffers from low-intensity measurements and high signal-to-noise ratio when optically dense objects are measured, in which multiple scattering dominate the appearance. Another issue of the current approach is its high computational cost. We are interested in looking into more in these aspects for making the approach more practical.

Limitations. There are a few limitations in the current method. These limitations will be removed in our future work.

Object Shape: Our current formulation requires that the incident plane is planer and incident light in target object is parallel to the x-axis for extracting single scattering using high frequency projection. When projected patterns interfere each other, single scattering cannot be extracted. This assumption needs to be relaxed when it is applied to a more general shape.

Single Scattering in An Inhomogeneous Material: Since our method uses single scattering which exponentially attenuates with constant scattering parameters, we cannot estimate shape of an inhomogeneous material.

Acknowledgment. This work is partially supported by the Japan Society for Promotion of Science (JSPS) through "Funding Program for Next Generation World-Leading Researchers (NEXT Program)," initiated by the Council for Science and Technology Policy (CSTP).

References

1. Godin, G., Rioux, M., Beraldin, J.A.: An assessment of laser range measurement on marble surfaces. In: Conference on Optical 3D Measurement Techniques (2001)
2. Chen, T., Lensch, H.P.A., Fuchs, C., Seidel, H.P.: Polarization and phase-shifting for 3d scanning of translucent objects. In: Proc. of IEEE Conference on Computer Vision and Pattern Recognition, CVPR (2007)
3. Goesele, M., Lensch, H.P.A., Lang, J., Fuchs, C., Seidel, H.P.: Disco - acquisition of translucent objects. In: Proc. ACM SIGGRAPH, pp. 835–844 (2004)
4. Gupta, M., Agrawal, A., Veeraraghavan, A., Narasimhan, S.: Structured light 3d scanning in the presence of global illumination. In: Proc. of IEEE Conference on Computer Vision and Pattern Recognition, CVPR (2011)
5. Horn, B.K.P.: Shape from shading: A method for obtaining the shape of a smooth opaque object from one view. Technical report, Massachusetts Institute of Technology (1970)
6. Woodham, R.J.: Photometric method for determining surface orientation from multiple images. Optical Engineering 19, 139–144 (1980)
7. Healey, G., Binford, T.O.: Local shape from specularity. Computer Vision, Graphics, and Image Processing 42, 62–86 (1987)
8. Sankaranarayanan, A.C., Veeraraghavan, A., Tuzel, O., Agrawal, A.: Specular surface reconstruction from sparse reflection correspondences. In: Proc. of IEEE Conference on Computer Vision and Pattern Recognition, CVPR (2010)
9. Liao, M., Wang, L., Yang, R., Gong, M.: Light fall-off stereo. In: Proc. of IEEE Conference on Computer Vision and Pattern Recognition, CVPR (2007)
10. Miyazaki, D., Ikeuchi, K.: Shape estimation of transparent objects by using inverse polarization raytracing. IEEE Trans. Pattern Analysis and Machine Intelligence (PAMI) 29, 2018–2030 (2007)
11. Huynh, C.P., Robles-Kelly, A., Hancock, E.: Shape and refractive index recovery from single-view polarisation images. In: Proc. of IEEE Conference on Computer Vision and Pattern Recognition, CVPR (2010)
12. Kutulakos, K.N., Steger, E.: A theory of refractive and specular 3d shape by light-path triangulation. In: Proc. of International Conference on Computer Vision, ICCV (2005)
13. Wetzstein, G., Roodnick, D., Heidrich, W., Raskar, R.: Refractive shape from light field distortion. In: Proc. of International Conference on Computer Vision, ICCV (2011)
14. Trifonov, B., Bradley, D., Heidrich, W.: Tomographic reconstruction of transparent objects. In: Proc. of Eurographics Symposium on Rendering (2006)
15. Hullin, M.B., Fuchs, M., Ihrke, I., Seidel, H.P., Lensch, H.P.A.: Fluorescent immersion range scanning. ACM Trans. on Graph (ToG) 27, article no. 87 (2008)
16. Morris, N.J., Kutulakos, K.N.: Reconstructing the surface of inhomogeneous transparent scenes by scatter trace photography. In: Proc. of International Conference on Computer Vision, ICCV (2007)
17. Narasimhan, S.G., Nayar, S.K., Sun, B., Koppal, S.J.: Structured light in scattering media. In: Proc. of International Conference on Computer Vision, ICCV (2005)
18. Kim, J., Lanman, D., Mukaigawa, Y., Raskar, R.: Descattering Transmission via Angular Filtering. In: Daniilidis, K., Maragos, P., Paragios, N. (eds.) ECCV 2010, Part I. LNCS, vol. 6311, pp. 86–99. Springer, Heidelberg (2010)
19. Treibitz, T., Schechner, Y.Y.: Instant 3descatter. In: Proc. of IEEE Conference on Computer Vision and Pattern Recognition, CVPR (2006)

20. Florescu, L., Schotland, J.C., Markel, V.A.: Single-scattering optical tomography. Physical Review E 79, 036607 (2009)
21. Mukaigawa, Y., Yagi, Y., Raskar, R.: Analysis of light transport in scattering media. In: Proc. of IEEE Conference on Computer Vision and Pattern Recognition, CVPR (2010)
22. Narasimhan, S.G., Gupta, M., Donner, C., Ramamoorthi, R., Nayar, S.K., Jensen, H.W.: Acquiring scattering properties of participating media by dilution. In: Proc. ACM SIGGRAPH, pp. 1003–1012 (2006)
23. Hawkins, T., Einarsson, P., Debevec, P.: Acquisition of time-varying participating media. ACM Trans. on Graph (ToG) 24, 812–815 (2005)
24. Gu, J., Nayar, S.K., Grinspun, E., Belhumeur, P.N., Ramamoorthi, R.: Compressive Structured Light for Recovering Inhomogeneous Participating Media. In: Forsyth, D., Torr, P., Zisserman, A. (eds.) ECCV 2008, Part IV. LNCS, vol. 5305, pp. 845–858. Springer, Heidelberg (2008)
25. Nayar, S.K., Krishnan, G., Grossberg, M.D., Raskar, R.: Fast separation of direct and global components of a scene using high frequency illumination. In: Proc. ACM SIGGRAPH, vol. 25, pp. 935–944 (2006)
26. Nayar, S.K., Ikeuchi, K., Kanade, T.: Shape from interreflections. International Journal of Computer Vision (IJCV) 6, 173–195 (1991)
27. Liu, S., Ng, T.-T., Matsushita, Y.: Shape from Second-Bounce of Light Transport. In: Daniilidis, K., Maragos, P., Paragios, N. (eds.) ECCV 2010, Part II. LNCS, vol. 6312, pp. 280–293. Springer, Heidelberg (2010)
28. Beer, A.: Bestimmung der absorption des rothen lichts in farbigen flussigkeiten. Annalen der Physik und Chemie 86, 78–88 (1852)
29. Henyey, L.G., Greenstein, J.L.: Diffuse radiation in the galaxy. Astrophysical Journal 93, 70–83 (1941)
30. Kennedy, J., Eberhart, R.C.: Particle swarm optimization. In: IEEE International Conference on Neural Networks (1995)
31. Nelder, J.A., Mead, R.: A simplex method for function minimization. The Computer Journal 7, 308–313 (1965)

Scale Invariant Optical Flow

Li Xu, Zhenlong Dai, and Jiaya Jia

Department of Computer Science and Engineering
The Chinese University of Hong Kong
{xuli,zldai,leojia}@cse.cuhk.edu.hk

Abstract. Scale variation commonly arises in images/videos, which cannot be naturally dealt with by optical flow. Invariant feature matching, on the contrary, provides sparse matching and could fail for regions without conspicuous structures. We aim to establish dense correspondence between frames containing objects in different scales and contribute a new framework taking pixel-wise scales into consideration in optical flow estimation. We propose an effective numerical scheme, which iteratively optimizes discrete scale variables and continuous flow ones. This scheme notably expands the practicality of optical flow in natural scenes containing various types of object motion.

1 Introduction

Optical flow estimation, which captures per-pixel 2D apparent motion between two or more images, can be applied to many computer vision tasks, including tracking, video editing, view interpolation and scene understanding. Traditional methods handle small motion while recent development in this field begins to tackle the more challenging large-displacement estimation problem [1,2,3,4,5]. These effective methods, however, still do not consider large and non-uniform scale variation, which is ubiquitous when images are sparsely captured or objects quickly move towards or away from the camera.

The inherent difficulty of existing optical flow models to handle scale-variant images is explainable. On the one hand, dense pixel correspondence establishment between two regions or objects with scale variation turns flow estimation to the problem of finding one-to-many or many-to-one mapping because multiple pixels, after scaling down, could become one, as shown in Fig. 1(b). On the other hand, spatial regularization commonly enforced in optical flow estimation favors piece-wise constant flow. But scale-varied regions get flow vectors pointing either outwards to the higher-resolution view (illustrated in Fig. 1(a)) or inwards to the lower-resolution one.

We show one example in Fig. 2. For the input images in (a)-(b) that contain pixels at different scales, the result of [6], shown in (c), is not sufficiently accurate when inspecting the warped image (d) based on the computed flow. Scale invariant features, such as SIFT and SURF [10,11], can only produce sparsely matched points. SIFT flow [7] uses patches of the same size to compute descriptors for pixels. So it also does not address scale variation in matching. Its flow

A. Fitzgibbon et al. (Eds.): ECCV 2012, Part II, LNCS 7573, pp. 385–399, 2012.

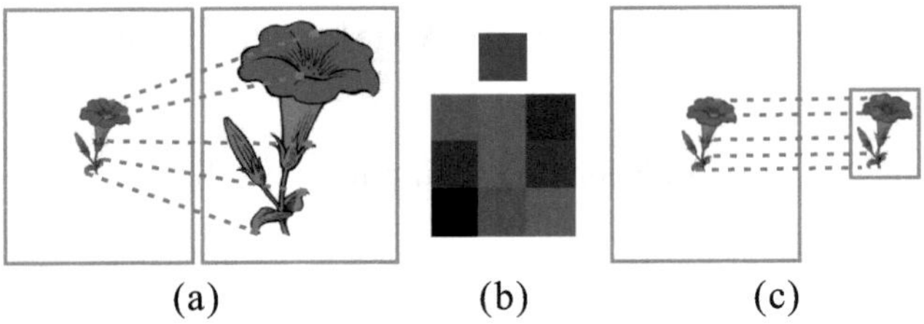

Fig. 1. Scale difference in optical flow. (a) Two inputs containing objects at different scales. Displacement vectors are not piece-wise constant. (b) One pixel in the small object mapping to a patch in the large one, making optical flow estimation suffer from color mixing. (c) Matching at the same scale does not have these problems.

Fig. 2. Scale variation causes big trouble in optical flow estimation. (a)-(b) Two frames containing pixels at different scales. (c)-(d) Optical flow and warping results of [6]. (e)-(f) SIFT flow [7] and its warping results. (g)-(h) Generalized Patch Matching [8] and the warping result. Flow vectors are visualized with the color coding of [9].

and the warping results are shown in (e) and (f). The generalized PatchMatch [8] reconstructs the image through search, as shown in (h). But it cannot guarantee the motion correctness as shown in (g). It is therefore notable that non-uniform scale variation for optical flow estimation is a real challenge. As change of scale is a common occurrence for low-frame-rate videos, photos taken in burst mode, and general scenes, its inappropriate handling could affect a variety of tasks in computer vision.

In this paper, we present a new optical flow estimation framework and explicitly introduce a scale variable for each pixel in the objective function to establish dense correspondences between images. Although this type of change greatly complicates the model, we derive an effective numerical solver. We jointly optimize the discrete scale variables and continuous flow ones in an Expectation-Maximization procedure. The system, with our flow initialization and update in a coarse-to-fine framework, makes full use of visual cues from different scales and can be applied to challenging scenarios where scale variation is inevitable.

Experiments show that our method can properly address the *non-uniform-scaling dense matching* problem.

2 Related Work

Optical flow estimation methods were developed quickly with the establishment of the Middlebury optical flow benchmark dataset [9]. The variational framework of [12] has been extensively studied in [6,13,14,15,4,16] where improvements were made to enhance robustness against illumination change and other outliers [17,6,13,16], or to avoid over-smoothing [6,14,18,15,19,16]. Segmentation [20], layer [21], and temporal constraints [21,22] were introduced to regularize flow computation.

Optical flow estimation becomes more difficult when two frames are not sampled densely in time or rapidly-moving objects exist. It leads to the large displacement problem. Brox *et al.* [3] integrated rich descriptors into the variational framework. This method is quick through a GPU acceleration [5]. Steinbrücker *et al.* [2] proposed not involving the coarse-to-fine warping scheme in order to avoid local minima. Xu *et al.* [4] proposed using sparse descriptor matching to improve optical flow initialization in the variational setting. It reduces the excessive reliance on the coarse-to-fine warping scheme.

All the above methods cannot handle images when large scale variation exists, as detailed in the Sec. 3. The parametric affine motion model [17,23,20] has 6 degrees of freedom, but is still not suitable because the one-to-many and many-to-one relationship is not dealt with. The affine flow is, thus, typically used to describe region-wise or segment-wise rigid motion in order to regularize flow vectors. In general image matching, SIFT and SURF [10,11] are distinctive sparse feature points. Generalized patch matching [8] involves an extra scale space when performing the randomized nearest-neighbor search. Its result generally does not correspond to underlying motion, due to the lack of spatial constraints.

In [24], Seitz and Baker proposed a new optical framework where each pixel is associated with a filter. By setting different filters for corresponding pixels at the two frames, the model is capable of handling color mixture caused by blurriness. Note that automatic filter selection is still an open problem. Essentially different from all these methods, we explicitly introduce spatially varying parameters for general non-uniform scale variation and propose an effective framework to estimate them.

3 Optical Flow Model with Scale Variables

The commonly employed variational optical flow model can be expressed as

$$\int \phi(|\mathbf{I}_2(\mathbf{x}+\mathbf{u}) - \mathbf{I}_1(\mathbf{x})|^2) + \alpha\phi(|\nabla u|^2 + |\nabla v|^2)d\mathbf{x}, \tag{1}$$

where $\mathbf{x} = (x, y)$ indexes the 2D coordinates. $\mathbf{I}_1$ and $\mathbf{I}_2$ are input image pairs. $\mathbf{u} = (u, v)$ is the unknown optical flow field. $\phi(a^2) = \sqrt{a^2 + \epsilon^2}$ is the robust function to deal with outliers [6]. α is a weight.

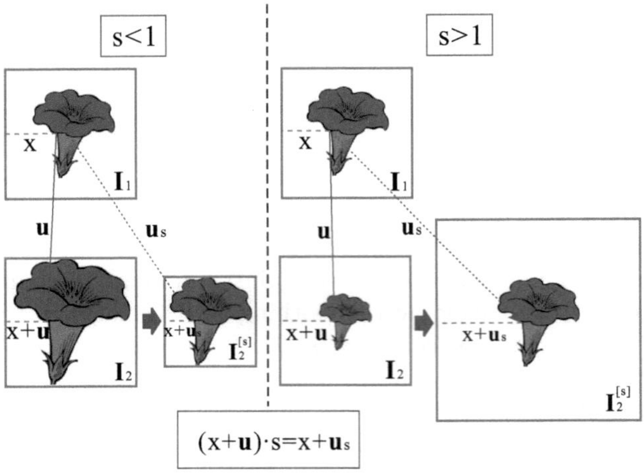

Fig. 3. Illustration of coordinate correspondence between images with different scales

$\phi(|\mathbf{I}_2(\mathbf{x}+\mathbf{u}) - \mathbf{I}_1(\mathbf{x})|^2)$ is the data term. As discussed in Sec. 1, for points at different scales, it cannot describe correct matching because a point may correspond to a region. The regularization term $\phi(|\nabla u|^2 + |\nabla v|^2)$ raises penalty if motion varies locally, undesirable for optical flow with scale change.

Our solution is to set scale as a variable for each pixel in optical flow estimation. We regard the first image $\mathbf{I}_1$ as the reference. For correspondence establishment for each pixel, we also denote the relative scale between $\mathbf{I}_1$ and $\mathbf{I}_2$ as s, and introduce the new data term

$$\phi(|\mathbf{I}_2^{[s]}(\mathbf{x}+\mathbf{u}_s(\mathbf{x})) - \mathbf{I}_1^{[s]}(\mathbf{x})|^2), \tag{2}$$

where $\mathbf{I}_2^{[s]}$ and $\mathbf{I}_1^{[s]}$ are variations of $\mathbf{I}_2$ and $\mathbf{I}_1$ counting in scale difference.

We now discuss two cases, illustrated in Fig. 3. If $s < 1$, $\mathbf{x}$ in $\mathbf{I}_1$ corresponds to the color blended version of more than one pixel in $\mathbf{I}_2$. We build the correspondence by locally smoothing $\mathbf{I}_2$ by a Gaussian filter with standard deviation $\sigma = (1/s - 1)$ and downsampling it with scale $1/s$. It yields $\mathbf{I}_2^{[s]}$. So the correspondence $\mathbf{x} + \mathbf{u}_s(\mathbf{x})$ in the downsampled $\mathbf{I}_2^{[s]}$ is actually a scaled version of $\mathbf{x} + \mathbf{u}(\mathbf{x})$ in the original $\mathbf{I}_2$. Their relationship can be expressed as

$$\mathbf{x} + \mathbf{u}_s(\mathbf{x}) = (\mathbf{x} + \mathbf{u}(\mathbf{x})) \cdot s. \tag{3}$$

Contrarily, if $s > 1$, a region around $\mathbf{x}$ corresponds to a pixel in $\mathbf{I}_2$. We thus need to locally Gaussian filter $\mathbf{I}_1$ and then match $\mathbf{x}$ to a pixel in an upsampled version of $\mathbf{I}_2$ with scale s, i.e., $\mathbf{I}_2^{[s]}$. In this case, Eq. (3) still holds.

This type of scale-involved correspondences enables mapping a pixel to a region or the other way around. In fact, we do not need to physically resize $\mathbf{I}_1$ – for points with $s > 1$, we Gaussian filter it – and only impose scaling on $\mathbf{I}_2$, as shown in Fig. 3. With the x and y coordinates, Eq. (3) is decomposed to

$$\begin{cases} (x + u(x,y)) \cdot s = x + u_s(x,y) \\ (y + v(x,y)) \cdot s = y + v_s(x,y) \end{cases} \tag{4}$$

Eq. (2) thus only involves the target motion variable $\mathbf{u}$ defined at the original resolution:

$$\phi_d(\mathbf{u}, s) = \phi(|\mathbf{I}_2^{[s]}(((\mathbf{x} + \mathbf{u}(\mathbf{x})) \cdot s) - \mathbf{I}_1^{[s]}(\mathbf{x})|^2), \tag{5}$$

where $\mathbf{I}_2^{[s]}$ is a scaled version of $\mathbf{I}_2$ when $s \neq 1$ while $\mathbf{I}_1^{[s]}$ is the Gaussian smoothed $\mathbf{I}_1$ when $s > 1$.

Also, for a specific s, the gradient term $|\nabla u_s|^2$ can be expressed as $|s \cdot u_x + (s-1)|^2 + |s \cdot u_y|^2$, given the difference between u_s and u in different image spaces. Note that the magnitude of $\mathbf{u}_s$ could vary with respect to s, as $\mathbf{u}_s$ indicates a mapping towards a scaled image $\mathbf{I}_2^{[s]}$. It consequently affects the gradients according to the expansion $|\nabla u_s|^2 = |s \cdot u_x + (s-1)|^2 + |s \cdot u_y|^2$, where a small s possibly receives a small penalty for large u_y. This is *not* desirable.

To address this issue, we define our regularization term on a normalized gradient $|\nabla u_s/s|^2$, so that the magnitudes of ∇u_s for different s are quantitatively comparable, which yields

$$\begin{aligned}\phi_s(\mathbf{u}, s) &= \phi(|\nabla u_s/s|^2 + |\nabla v_s/s|^2) \\ &= \phi(|u_x + (s-1)/s|^2 + |u_y|^2 + |v_x|^2 + |v_y + (s-1)/s|^2),\end{aligned} \tag{6}$$

where u_x, v_x, u_y, and v_y denote the partial derivatives of the flow in the x and y directions, respectively. Eq. (6) is obtained by taking the equations in Eq. (4) into (5).

The regularization term encourages flow to be locally constant only when the points are at the same scale, complying with our observation. When $s < 1$, which indicates the object size is growing, u_x and v_y are encouraged to be positive for outward pointing flow vectors. Similarly, when $s > 1$, Eq. (6) reaches a minimum for inward flow.

The new function for optical flow estimation from $\mathbf{I}_1$ to $\mathbf{I}_2$ with respect to scale variable s for each pixel is given by

$$E(\mathbf{u}, s) = \int \phi_d(\mathbf{u}, s) + \alpha\phi_s(\mathbf{u}, s)\mathrm{d}\mathbf{x}. \tag{7}$$

Number of Scales. As described above, for each scale s, to establish correct correspondence, filtering and resizing of images are needed. So it is not feasible to estimate s continuously. We discretize s also because optical flow estimation moderately tolerates small scale variation.

To determine a sampling rate for s, we run the optical flow method [6] that does not consider scale variance on a sequence that is shown in Fig. 4. It contains a car moving away from the camera. The frame in the middle is the reference. Optical flow is computed followed by frame warping to the reference. It yields different levels of root-mean-square errors in the car region, highlighted in Fig. 4. We exclude surrounding pixels in this experiment to only evaluate scale change.

The errors are plotted in the bottom row of Fig. 4, indicating scale change larger than $2^{0.5}$ cannot be dealt with properly. We have also conducted experiments using the same configuration on another 10+ synthetic and real examples

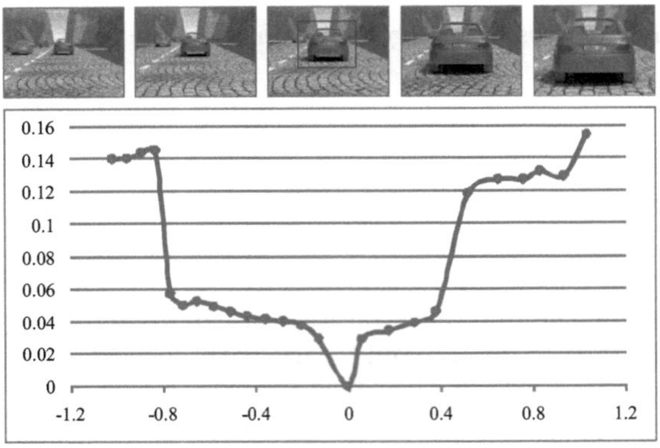

Fig. 4. Warping errors based on the optical flow estimate (y-axis) v.s. scale variation in the logarithm domain (x-axis). The reference frame is the middle one. The car is highlighted in the red rectangle. Warping error raises quickly when the scale difference increases.

and found existing optical flow methods fail when $s < 0.7$ or $s > 1.5$. So in our algorithm, for safety's sake, we consider scale interval $\sqrt{2}$. In the range of $[1/2, 2]$, for example, s can be with 5 different values, i.e.,

$$s \in S = \{1/2, 1/\sqrt{2}, 1, \sqrt{2}, 2\}. \tag{8}$$

Note that the range can be different in practice. But this 5-value configuration is generally enough for many examples.

To avail following optimization, we introduce a 5-dimensional vector $\mathbf{z}$ for each pixel. Only one element in each $\mathbf{z}$ can be 1 while all others are zeros to indicate the suitable scale for matching. Element $z_i = 1$ means scale value s_i is selected for the current pixel. Introducing $\mathbf{z}$ modifies Eq. (7) to

$$E(\mathbf{u}, \mathbf{z}) = \int \sum_{i=1}^{5} z_i \cdot (\phi_d(\mathbf{u}, s_i) + \alpha \phi_s(\mathbf{u}, s_i)) \mathrm{d}\mathbf{x}. \tag{9}$$

This function is similar to common variational optical flow models, except for the involvement of the extra variable $\mathbf{z}$.

4 Optimization

Our optimization grounds on a probabilistic inference. The energy in Eq. (9) can be linked to a corresponding posterior distribution

$$\begin{aligned} p(\mathbf{u}, \mathbf{z}|\mathbf{I}) &\propto p(\mathbf{u}, \mathbf{z}, \mathbf{I}) \\ &= \frac{1}{M} \prod_{\mathbf{x}} \prod_{i} \exp\left\{-\beta \left(\phi_d(\mathbf{u}, s_i) + \alpha \phi_s(\mathbf{u}, s_i)\right)\right\}^{z_i}, \end{aligned} \tag{10}$$

where the integral over x becomes multiplication. β is the temperature and M is the partition function to form a probability distribution. z_i is the binary indicator. Taking negative logarithm in Eq. (10) results in Eq. (9).

To estimate flow field $\mathbf{u}$, it is natural to integrate $\mathbf{z}$ by summing over all possible configurations. However, the resulting distribution is a mixture model that is hard to optimize. We instead resort to optimizing the expected log posterior

$$\mathbb{E}_{\mathbf{z}}[-\ln p(\mathbf{u},\mathbf{z}|\mathbf{I})] \propto \sum_{\mathbf{x}} \sum_{i} \mathbb{E}[z_i](\phi_d(\mathbf{u},s_i) + \alpha\phi_s(\mathbf{u},s_i)). \tag{11}$$

It leads to the following optimization steps, which alternate between computing the expected value of indicator z_i and optimizing optical flow $\mathbf{u}$ given z_i in an Expectation-Maximization (EM) framework.

4.1 Computing $\mathbb{E}[z_i]$

By Bayes' rule, $p(\mathbf{z}|\mathbf{I},\mathbf{u}=\mathbf{u}^{t-1}) \propto p(\mathbf{z},\mathbf{I},\mathbf{u}=\mathbf{u}^{t-1})$ due to variable independence, where $\mathbf{u}^{t-1}$ is the flow estimate in iteration $t-1$. Eq. (10) also implies the probability independence for different z_i. The expected z_i thus can be computed as

$$\begin{aligned} \bar{z}_i &:= \mathbb{E}(z_i) = p(z_i = 1|\mathbf{I},\mathbf{u}^{t-1}) \\ &= \frac{\exp\left\{-\beta\left(\phi_d(\mathbf{u}^{t-1},s_i) + \alpha\phi_s(\mathbf{u}^{t-1},s_i)\right)\right\}}{\sum_i \exp\left\{-\beta\left(\phi_d(\mathbf{u}^{t-1},s_i) + \alpha\phi_s(\mathbf{u}^{t-1},s_i)\right)\right\}}, \end{aligned} \tag{12}$$

where $\bar{z}_i$ is the expectation of z_i.

4.2 Minimizing Optical Flow Energy

With $\bar{z}_i$ estimation, the objective function in Eq. (9) can be updated to

$$E(\mathbf{u}) = \int \sum_i \bar{z}_i(\phi_d(\mathbf{u},s_i) + \alpha\phi_s(\mathbf{u},s_i))\mathrm{d}\mathbf{x} \tag{13}$$

in iteration t. Eq. (12) guarantees $\sum_i \bar{z}_i = 1$, which is important in selecting the correct scale for matching for each pixel. Here, the spatially continuous formulation can ease derivation of the numerical solver using the variational framework. Note that discrete MRF [15] can also be employed.

We optimize Eq. (13) by minimizing the corresponding Euler-Lagrange (EL) equations. The flow vectors $\mathbf{u}$ are estimated in a coarse-to-fine warping scheme [6] and hence are in an incremental fashion. At each image level, the flow field is $\mathbf{u} = \mathbf{u}_0 + \mathrm{d}\mathbf{u}$, where $\mathbf{u}_0$ is the initialization from the coarser level or from previous warping iterations. Taylor expansion is performed given the current estimate. The linearization step needs to involve s_i, and is written as

$$\begin{aligned} \mathbf{I}_2^{[s_i]}(s_i\cdot(\mathbf{x}+\mathbf{u})) \approx \mathbf{I}_2^{[s_i]}(s_i\cdot(\mathbf{x}+\mathbf{u}_0)) &+ \\ \mathbf{I}_{2x}^{[s_i]}(s_i\cdot(\mathbf{x}+\mathbf{u}_0))s_i du &+ \mathbf{I}_{2y}^{[s_i]}(s_i\cdot(\mathbf{x}+\mathbf{u}_0))s_i dv \end{aligned} \tag{14}$$

after a few algebraic operations, where $\mathbf{I}_{2x}^{[s]}$ and $\mathbf{I}_{2y}^{[s]}$ are the partial derivatives of $\mathbf{I}_2^{[s]}$ in two directions. We further define

$$\mathbf{I}_\nabla^{s_i} := \left[\mathbf{I}_{2x}^{[s_i]}(s_i\cdot(\mathbf{x}+\mathbf{u}_0))\cdot s_i, \mathbf{I}_{2y}^{[s_i]}(s_i\cdot(\mathbf{x}+\mathbf{u}_0))\cdot s_i, \mathbf{I}_2^{[s_i]}(s_i\cdot(\mathbf{x}+\mathbf{u}_0)) - \mathbf{I}_1^{[s_i]}(\mathbf{x})\right]^T$$

Algorithm 1. SIOF Framework

input: A pair of frames ($\mathbf{I}_1$, $\mathbf{I}_2$)
initialization: $\bar{z}_i \leftarrow 1/|S|$
repeat
  construct two image pyramids;
  for each level in the pyramids **do**
    flow initialization;
    optical flow $\mathbf{u}$ estimation using nested fixed point iteration (Eqs. (15) and (16));
    flow boundary filtering;
  end for
  compute $\bar{z}_i = \mathbb{E}[z_i]$ given $\mathbf{u}$ using Eq. (12);
until $\|\mathbf{z} - \mathbf{z}^{old}\|^2 < \epsilon$ or the maximum iteration number is reached
output: optical flow field $\mathbf{u}$ and expectation $\bar{z}_i$ for each pixel i.

Then the 3×3 symmetric motion tensor is obtained as $J^{s_i} = \mathbf{I}_\nabla^{s_i} \mathbf{I}_\nabla^{s_i\,T}$. The Euler-Lagrange equations are written as

$$\sum_i \bar{z}_i \left\{\phi'_d \cdot (J_{11}^{s_i} du + J_{12}^{s_i} dv + J_{13}^{s_i}) - \alpha \mathrm{div}(\mathbf{w}_u)\right\} = 0, \tag{15}$$

$$\sum_i \bar{z}_i \left\{\phi'_d \cdot (J_{21}^{s_i} du + J_{22}^{s_i} dv + J_{23}^{s_i}) - \alpha \mathrm{div}(\mathbf{w}_v)\right\} = 0, \tag{16}$$

where $\mathbf{w}_u$ and $\mathbf{w}_v$ are two vectors counting in discrepancy of the smoothing term for flow vectors in different directions caused by scale, expressed as

$$\mathbf{w}_u = (\phi'_s \cdot ((u+du)_x + (s_i - 1)/s_i), \phi'_s \cdot (u+du)_y)^T,$$
$$\mathbf{w}_v = (\phi'_s \cdot (v+dv)_x, \phi'_s \cdot ((v+dv)_y + (s_i - 1)/s_i))^T.$$

ϕ'_d and ϕ'_s are defined as

$$\phi'_d = \phi'(|(du, dv, 1) \cdot \mathbf{I}_\nabla^{s_i}|^2),$$
$$\phi'_s = \phi'(|u_x + (s_i - 1)/s_i|^2 + |u_y|^2 + |v_x|^2 + |v_y + (s_i - 1)/s_i|^2).$$

Here $u_x = (u_0 + du)_x$ and $u_y = (u_0 + du)_y$. Non-linearity of Eqs. (15) and (16) exists in ϕ'_d and ϕ'_s. We adopt the nested fixed point iteration to tackle it, which uses the flow estimate from the previous iteration to compute ϕ'_d and ϕ'_s. The resulting equation system is linear w.r.t. du and dv, and accordingly can be solved using standard linear solvers. In our implementation, we use Successive Over Relaxation (SOR) with relaxation factor 1.98.

4.3 Overall Computation Framework

Flow Initialization. Our method handles scale variation between frames during optical flow estimation. To further equip it with the ability to estimate large displacements, we cannot solely rely on the coarse-to-fine scheme, according to the explanation in [4]. Instead, in flow initialization in each level, we introduce descriptor matching based on SIFT features and use these matches to ameliorate problematic or missing flow vectors, following the extended initialization method of Xu *et al.* [4]. We note it is not a compulsory step for scale-aware flow estimation. It is used only for capturing very large motion.

Flow Discontinuity Filtering. Flow vectors near motion discontinuity are usually problematic due to occlusion and over-smoothing. We improve them by detecting boundary pixels using the criterion $|\mathbf{u}_x|^2 > \delta$, and then dilating the detected regions using a 5×5 mask. For each pixel $\mathbf{x}_i$ in the region, we perform a robust weighted median [15] with weight

$$w_{i,j} \propto \exp\left(-\frac{(\mathbf{x}_i - \mathbf{x}_j)^2}{2\sigma_s^2} - \frac{(\mathbf{I}_1(\mathbf{x}_i) - \mathbf{I}_1(\mathbf{x}_j))^2}{2\sigma_r^2}\right)\frac{w_d(j)}{w_d(i)}. \tag{17}$$

$w_{i,j}$ represents the importance of flow at pixel x_j when updating that at x_i. It counts in the spatial and range distance, as well as the weight to indicate whether it is around motion discontinuity or not. We set $w_d = 0.3$ for pixels in the detected boundary regions and $w_d = 1$ for all others. σ_s and σ_r are with values 7 and 0.07, respectively.

Overall Framework. We present our framework in Algorithm 1. In each iteration, we first initialize expectation $\bar{z}$ as $1/|S|$, where $|S|$ is the number of scales used, defined in Eq. (8), and estimate optical flow in a coarse-to-fine strategy by solving the Euler-Lagrange equations in Eqs. (15) and (16). After getting the flow field, we compute new $\bar{z}_i$ with Eq. (12) and use it to update flow again. The maximum iteration number is set to 5 empirically. We also stop the algorithm if the average $\|\mathbf{z} - \mathbf{z}^{old}\|^2 < 0.01$, where $\mathbf{z}$ and $\mathbf{z}^{old}$ are sets of scales in the current and previous iterations. The running time for a pair of 640×480 images is about 5 minutes on a standard desktop PC equipped with a Core i3 CPU at 3.10GHz and 4G memory.

5 Experiments

We extensively evaluate our method on image pairs and provide comparisons with other state-of-the-arts. In all experiments, parameter β is set to 0.2 and $\alpha \in [10, 30]$, depending on the noise level. The main results in the following figures are optical flow $\mathbf{u}$ between frames $\mathbf{I}_1$ and $\mathbf{I}_2$ and the backward warping result $\mathbf{I}_1'(\mathbf{x}) = \mathbf{I}_2(\mathbf{x} + \mathbf{u})$, where bilinear interpolation is applied to sub-pixels. To visualize vector $\bar{z}$, we show the expected value $\bar{i} = \sum_i i \cdot \bar{z}_i$ representing the scales. $\bar{i}$ is linearly scaled for visualization in gray, where value 128 indicates no scale change; brighter pixels are with scale $s > 1$ and darker ones are with $s < 1$. We, in what follows, call $\bar{i}$ the *pseudo scale map*.

5.1 Evaluation of Our Model to Handle Scales

Fig. 5(a) and (b) show two images, in which a butterfly undergoes a large scaling. The ground truth optical flow is visualized in (c). We optimize scales in range $[2^{-\frac{3}{2}}, 2^{\frac{3}{2}}]$ in this example due to the very large scale variation.

Our optical flow and warping results are shown in Fig. 5(h) and (d). Note that both the butterfly and background textures are reasonably recovered. Pseudo scale maps $\bar{i}$ for our estimates in the first two iterations and in the last (5th) iteration are shown in (e)-(g). One iteration can already reasonably shape our scale estimate, which is further improved with more of them. We plot the average end point errors w.r.t. the number of iterations in Fig. 8. They fall sharply at the first two iterations and decrease slightly in the following ones, indicating stable scale estimation.

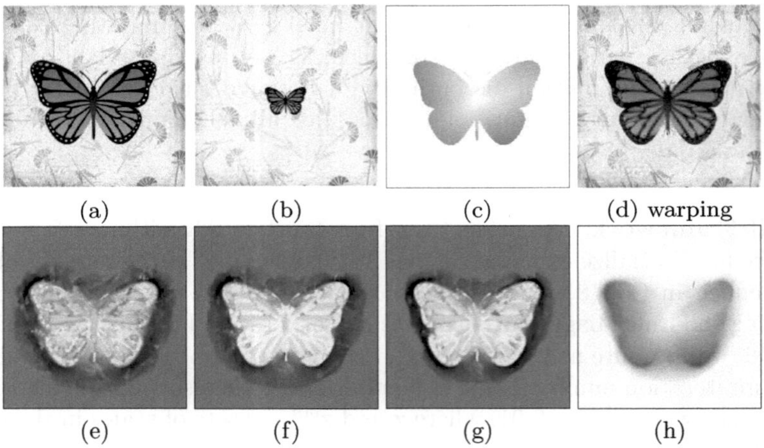

Fig. 5. Scale handling. (a) and (b) show an image pair with ground truth flow in (c). Pseudo scale maps in iterations 1, 2, and 5 are shown in (e)-(g). The final optical flow result is shown in (h) with its warping result in (d).

5.2 Comparison with Other Optical Flow Methods

We now compare our method with other optical flow estimation approaches. Fig. 6(a) shows two frames used in [25], where the camera is mounted on a moving car. There is another car moving faster. Fig. 6(b) shows the result of Brox *et al.* [6], which can compute flow without scale variation. So the background motion estimate is accurate. However, the motion estimate of the foreground car is problematic, manifesting the general scale limitation of conventional optical flow models.

We also run the large displacement optical flow methods of [4,3]. The results in Fig. 6(c)-(d) are better, but still with noticeable errors. The regularization on flow gradients adversely affects the estimation process, even with sparse feature matching. The result of SIFT flow [7] is shown in (e). The inaccuracy is still due to not handling the scale problem, as discussed in Sec. 1.

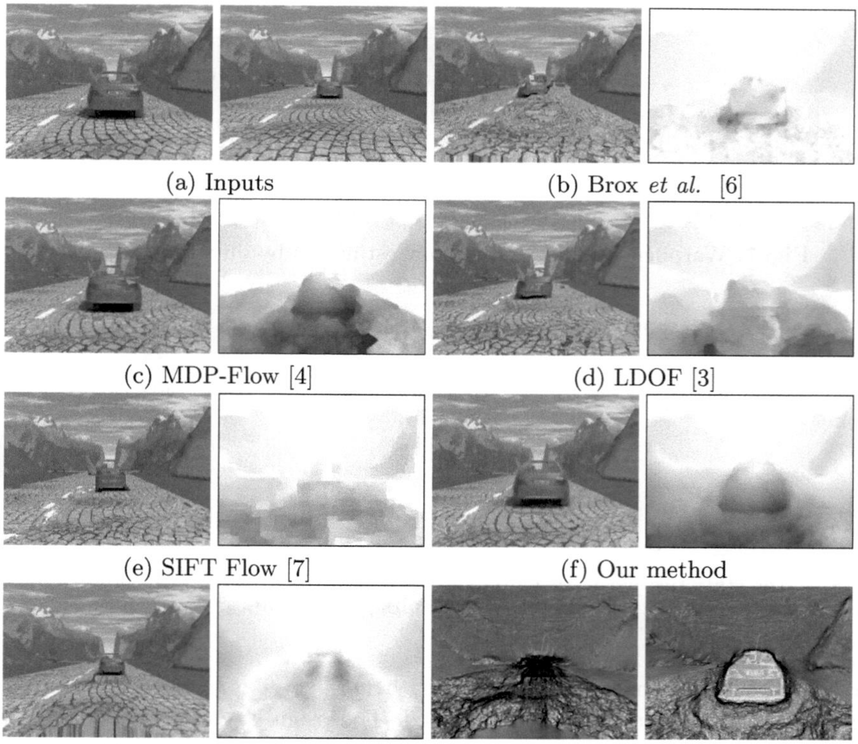

(a) Inputs (b) Brox *et al.* [6]

(c) MDP-Flow [4] (d) LDOF [3]

(e) SIFT Flow [7] (f) Our method

(g) Our backward flow (h) The pseudo scale map

Fig. 6. Comparison with other methods. In each result pair, the warping result is on the left, which ideally should be similar to the left image in (a). Color coded optical flow result is on the right.

Our result is shown in Fig. 6(f). No extended initialization is applied for this example. Motion of the car, however, can still be well recovered. The estimated pseudo scale map, shown on the right of (h), is primarily correct. Bright pixels indicate $s > 1$, complying with the fact that the car is moving away. The background mountain, on the contrary, does not present much scale variation and thus is labeled in gray. As the camera is also rapidly moving forward, the road is partly occluded and moves out of the frame.

Table 1. End Point Errors (EPEs) and Warping Errors (WEs) of different optical flow methods on the "butterfly" example

Methods	Brox *et al.* [6]	LDOF	Sun *et al.* [15]	Ours
EPE	8.84	3.79	25.70	3.31
WE	0.44	0.23	0.46	0.11

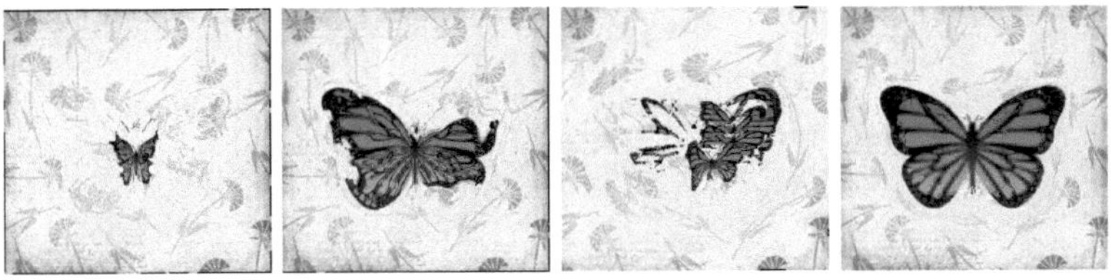

(a) [6] (b) [3] (c) [15] (d) Ours

Fig. 7. Warping results based on flow estimated by different methods

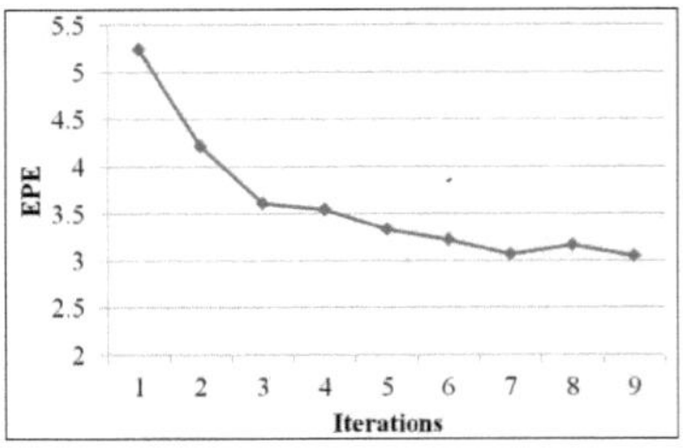

Fig. 8. Error statistics w.r.t. the number of iterations

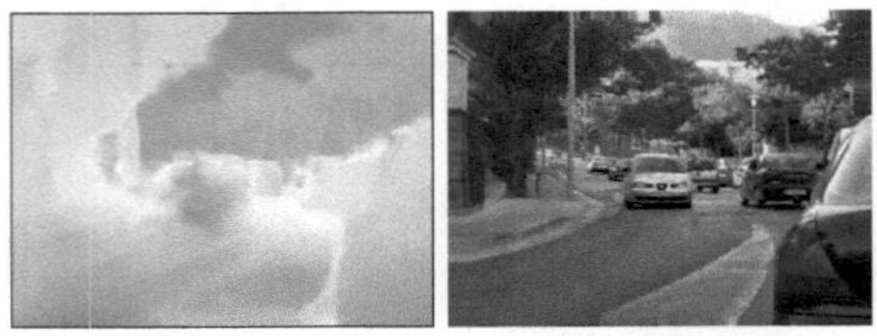

(a) (b)

Fig. 9. Our optical flow and warping results given inputs [26] shown in Fig. 2

We also show the backward flow in (g), where the car in this case is getting larger. Its motion is successfully estimated. The pseudo scale map is on the left of (h), with the car correctly labeled in black.

We quantitatively compare our method with others using the "butterfly" example in Fig. 5. The end point and warping errors are listed in Table 1 with warping results shown in Fig. 7. Another example is included in Fig. 9 with inputs in Fig. 2. Compared with other results in Fig. 2, the scale variation of the car is best captured in our framework.

5.3 Comparison with Sparse Feature Matching

Sparse feature matching, such as SIFT [10], is robust against scale variation. In these methods, a discrete scale space is constructed so that features are selected associating with their scales. However, only sparse matching can be obtained. Our result, in contrast, can be much denser. Our method also differs from sparse feature matching in the way to select scales. It is noteworthy that in SIFT and other feature matching methods, scales are determined in a single image, while our method finds the scale ratio using information from an image pair.

Fig. 10 gives a comparison with SIFT feature matching using an example presented in [27], which was originally used to test feature matching under scale variation. (a) and (b) show the two inputs. The SIFT feature matching results are shown in (d) and (g), where matched pixels are marked by circles. Their radiuses correspond to the scales. To establish robust correspondence, we perform optical flow estimation bidirectionally, and use cross-check to reject matching outliers. If a flow vector satisfies $\|\mathbf{u}^+(\mathbf{x}) + \mathbf{u}^-(\mathbf{x} + \mathbf{u}^+(\mathbf{x}))\| < 2$, we treat it as a reliable

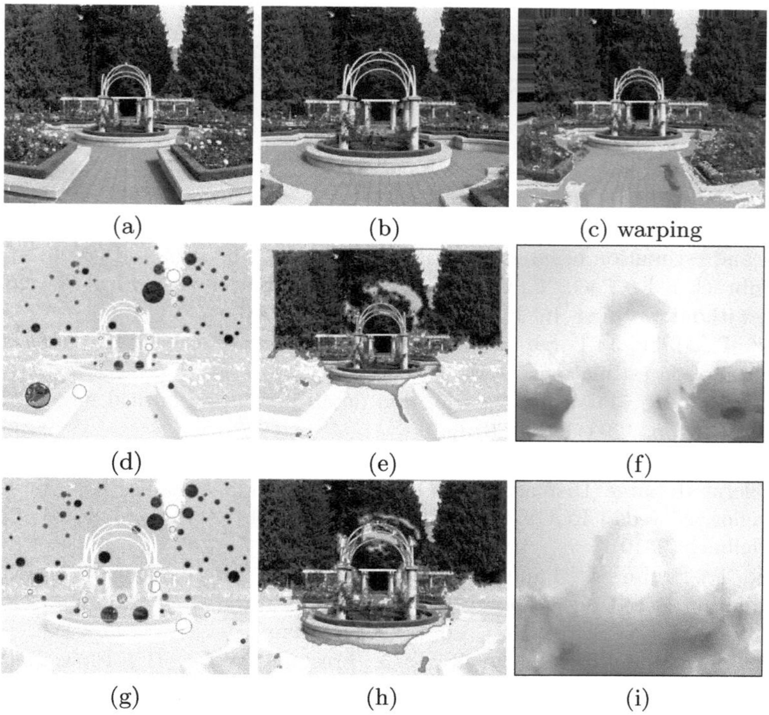

Fig. 10. Comparison with SIFT feature matching. (a) and (b) are two inputs. (c) shows our backward warping result using the flow shown in (f). (d) and (g) are the results of SIFT feature matching. Sparse correspondences are built. (e) and (h) are our matching results. There are much more correctly matched pixels. The corresponding bidirectional flow is visualized in (f) and (i).

matching. $\mathbf{u}^+$ and $\mathbf{u}^-$ are used to denote the forward and backward flow fields, shown in (f) and (i). Our matching results are shown in (e) and (h) where matching outliers are masked. Our method yields dense correspondences.

More evaluations and results on the Middlebury Dataset are included in the project website[1].

6 Concluding Remarks

We have presented a new framework to address the scale variant optical flow estimation problem. We show ignoring pixel scale variation is an inherent limitation of traditional models and propose incorporating scale parameters explicitly in the variational framework. We also propose the numerical solver using Expectation Maximization. The established dense matching across frames can be used widely in many applications. Future work includes integrating advanced occlusion models and method speedup.

[1] `http://www.cse.cuhk.edu.hk/%7eleojia/projects/siof/`.

Acknowledgements. The work described in this paper was supported by a grant from the Research Grants Council of the Hong Kong Special Administrative Region (Project No. 412911).

References

1. Wills, J., Agarwal, S., Belongie, S.: A feature-based approach for dense segmentation and estimation of large disparity motion. IJCV 68, 125–143 (2006)
2. Steinbrücker, F., Pock, T., Cremers, D.: Large displacement optical flow computation without warping. In: ICCV, pp. 1609–1614 (2009)
3. Brox, T., Malik, J.: Large displacement optical flow: descriptor matching in variational motion estimation. PAMI 33, 500–513 (2011)
4. Xu, L., Jia, J., Matsushita, Y.: Motion detail preserving optical flow estimation. In: CVPR, pp. 1293–1300 (2010)
5. Sundaram, N., Brox, T., Keutzer, K.: Dense Point Trajectories by GPU-Accelerated Large Displacement Optical Flow. In: Daniilidis, K., Maragos, P., Paragios, N. (eds.) ECCV 2010, Part I. LNCS, vol. 6311, pp. 438–451. Springer, Heidelberg (2010)
6. Brox, T., Bruhn, A., Papenberg, N., Weickert, J.: High Accuracy Optical Flow Estimation Based on a Theory for Warping. In: Pajdla, T., Matas, J(G.) (eds.) ECCV 2004. LNCS, vol. 3024, pp. 25–36. Springer, Heidelberg (2004)
7. Liu, C., Yuen, J., Torralba, A., Sivic, J., Freeman, W.T.: SIFT Flow: Dense Correspondence across Different Scenes. In: Forsyth, D., Torr, P., Zisserman, A. (eds.) ECCV 2008, Part III. LNCS, vol. 5304, pp. 28–42. Springer, Heidelberg (2008)
8. Barnes, C., Shechtman, E., Goldman, D.B., Finkelstein, A.: The generalized patchmatch correspondence algorithm. In: ECCV (3), pp. 29–43 (2010)
9. Baker, S., Scharstein, D., Lewis, J.P., Roth, S., Black, M.J., Szeliski, R.: A database and evaluation methodology for optical flow. IJCV 92, 1–31 (2011)
10. Lowe, D.G.: Distinctive image features from scale-invariant keypoints. IJCV 60, 91–110 (2004)
11. Bay, H., Tuytelaars, T., Van Gool, L.: SURF: Speeded Up Robust Features. In: Leonardis, A., Bischof, H., Pinz, A. (eds.) ECCV 2006. LNCS, vol. 3951, pp. 404–417. Springer, Heidelberg (2006)
12. Horn, B.K.P., Schunck, B.G.: Determining optical flow. Artif. Intell. 17, 185–203 (1981)
13. Bruhn, A., Weickert, J.: Towards ultimate motion estimation: Combining highest accuracy with real-time performance. In: ICCV, pp. 749–755 (2005)
14. Werlberger, M., Trobin, W., Pock, T., Wedel, A., Cremers, D., Bischof, H.: Anisotropic Huber-L1 optical flow. In: BMVC (2009)
15. Sun, D., Roth, S., Black, M.J.: Secrets of optical flow estimation and their principles. In: CVPR, pp. 2432–2439 (2010)
16. Zimmer, H., Bruhn, A., Weickert, J.: Optic flow in harmony. IJCV 93, 368–388 (2011)
17. Black, M.J., Anandan, P.: The robust estimation of multiple motions: Parametric and piecewise-smooth flow fields. CVIU 63, 75–104 (1996)
18. Wedel, A., Cremers, D., Pock, T., Bischof, H.: Structure- and motion-adaptive regularization for high accuracy optic flow. In: ICCV, pp. 1663–1668 (2009)
19. Werlberger, M., Pock, T., Bischof, H.: Motion estimation with non-local total variation regularization. In: CVPR, pp. 2464–2471 (2010)

20. Xu, L., Chen, J., Jia, J.: A Segmentation Based Variational Model for Accurate Optical Flow Estimation. In: Forsyth, D., Torr, P., Zisserman, A. (eds.) ECCV 2008, Part I. LNCS, vol. 5302, pp. 671–684. Springer, Heidelberg (2008)
21. Sun, D., Sudderth, E.B., Black, M.J.: SURF: Speeded Up Robust Features. In: NIPS, pp. 2226–2234 (2010)
22. Volz, S., Bruhn, A., Valgaerts, L., Zimmer, H.: Modeling temporal coherence for optical flow. In: ICCV (2011)
23. Ju, S.X., Black, M.J., Jepson, A.D.: Skin and bones: Multi-layer, locally affine, optical flow and regularization with transparency. In: CVPR, pp. 307–314 (1996)
24. Seitz, S.M., Baker, S.: Filter flow. In: ICCV, pp. 143–150 (2009)
25. Vaudrey, T., Rabe, C., Klette, R., Milburn, J.: Differences between stereo and motion behavior on synthetic and real-world stereo sequences. In: Intl. Conf. of Image and Vision Computing New Zealand (IVCNZ), pp. 1–6 (2008)
26. Liu, C., Freeman, W.T., Adelson, E.H., Weiss, Y.: Human-assisted motion annotation. In: CVPR (2008)
27. Brown, M., Lowe, D.G.: Invariant features from interest point groups. In: BMVC (2002)

Structured Image Segmentation Using Kernelized Features

Aurélien Lucchi[1], Yunpeng Li[1], Kevin Smith[2], and Pascal Fua[1,*]

[1] Computer Vision Laboratory, EPFL, Lausanne
[2] Light Microscopy Center, ETHZ, Zurich

Abstract. Most state-of-the-art approaches to image segmentation formulate the problem using Conditional Random Fields. These models typically include a unary term and a pairwise term, whose parameters must be carefully chosen for optimal performance. Recently, structured learning approaches such as Structured SVMs (SSVM) have made it possible to jointly learn these model parameters. However, they have been limited to linear kernels, since more powerful non-linear kernels cause the learning to become prohibitively expensive. In this paper, we introduce an approach to "kernelize" the features so that a linear SSVM framework can leverage the power of non-linear kernels without incurring the high computational cost. We demonstrate the advantages of this approach in a series of image segmentation experiments on the MSRC data set as well as 2D and 3D datasets containing imagery of neural tissue acquired with electron microscopes.

1 Introduction

Conditional random fields (CRFs) are a class of powerful graphical models that have been highly successful in image segmentation. In the CRF framework, the solution is typically obtained by minimizing an energy function that is the sum of *unary* and *pairwise* terms [1]. The unary term encodes the likelihood that a particular label should be assigned to a pixel based on local image features[2]. The pairwise term encodes the tendency of neighboring pixels or superpixels to share the same label, thus enforcing spatial regularity.

In recent years, machine learning techniques have increasingly been used to derive these terms in favor of simpler traditional models. However, this is usually done separately for each term: the unary term is optimized for labeling individual pixels while the pairwise term is optimized for labeling pixel pairs. As a result, the two terms can often be incommensurate, and an *ad hoc* weighting step is required to balance their relative influences. Instead, the parameters of the unary and pairwise terms should be learned jointly to infer the optimal labeling. This can be done using the recent structured-SVM (SSVM) framework [1]. It involves learning the unary and pairwise terms jointly through an iterative cutting-plane scheme that provably minimizes an upper bound on the empirical loss and the model complexity. Currently, SSVMs can be of practical use

* This work was supported in part by the MicroNano ERC project.

1 Higher order terms are also possible in theory, though less commonly used in practice due to higher computational cost. The unary term is also referred to as the data term.

2 Alternatively, groups of pixels or superpixels can be used in order to speed up computation.

A. Fitzgibbon et al. (Eds.): ECCV 2012, Part II, LNCS 7573, pp. 400–413, 2012.

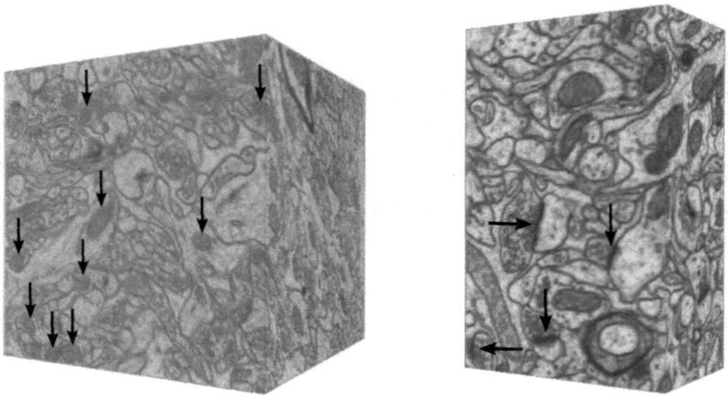

(a) mitochondria (b) synapses

Fig. 1. Two nearly isotropic stacks of neural tissue acquired using EM microscopy annotated for training and testing. *(a)* This stack contains 1000 images of 1024×1024 pixels, and was used for the task of segmenting mitochondria, indicated by arrows. *(b)* This stack contains 250 images of 655×429 pixels and was used to segment synaptic gaps, indicated by arrows.

only in conjunction with terms that are linear functions of the input features. This is because introducing non-linear terms would result in quadratic times for learning iterations, which quickly becomes unmanageable for regular-size 2D images and even more so for 3D data. Thus, it is usually not practical to use non-linear kernels in an SSVM framework, though they are often more powerful than their linear counterparts.

In this paper, we overcome this limitation through a two-step learning approach. We first use a regular non-linear SVM to create kernel-transformed feature vectors, each of which consists of kernel products between the input feature vector and a set of basis vectors that may not be orthogonal to each other. We then train a linear SSVM on the transformed features. This approach combines the power of non-linear kernels for individual pixel classification in the unary term with the regularizing effect of the pairwise term, while enforcing consistency between the two. This yields both improved segmentation performance and computational efficiency.

This line of research was primarily motivated by the need to more accurately segment synapses and mitochondria in electron microscopy (EM) stacks, such as those of Fig. 1. In this kind of data, unlike in popular segmentation benchmarks such as MSRC [2], global features that predict whether or not a type of object appears anywhere in the image are not useful. This is because it is known that synapses and mitochondria always appear in EM stacks, whereas it is not known if a cow or bird will appear in a particular image from a standard benchmark dataset such as MSRC. Thus, for EM applications, the CRF must rely solely on unary evidence and spatial smoothness. We demonstrate on all three datasets that our approach indeed boosts the performance of the learned CRF. Furthermore, it outperforms the previous state-of-the-art in our target applications: synapse and mitochondria segmentation.

2 Related Work

For tasks such as segmentation, consistent labeling of highly-correlated neighboring pixels is of great importance. Structured prediction has emerged as a powerful tool to take into account such correlations. In this section, we first discuss current approaches to structured prediction and the computational complexity issues that restrict them from use in conjunction with non-linear kernels. We then consider kernel approximation techniques that can be used to address these issues. Finally, we discuss structural kernels which, like our approach, rely on kernel functions in a structured prediction framework. But unlike our approach, they do so over the entire output space, which carries certain disadvantages.

Structured Prediction. Structured prediction methods such as conditional random fields (CRFs) [3] have been widely applied to problems with structured outputs. While traditional classifiers, such as decision trees and SVMs independently map each data instance to a single label, structured prediction methods take into account the statistical correlations between labels. This is critical for tasks such as image segmentation, where such correlations are strong between nearby pixels. Learning CRF models using large-margin methods has rapidly gained popularity in recent years. This is because they are more objective-driven and do not involve the daunting partition function that can render maximum-likelihood approaches intractable in CRFs with loopy graph structures. Compared with earlier approaches including the max-margin Markov network [4], the structured support vector machine (SSVM) [1] is especially appealing, and has since been successfully applied to many computer vision tasks, such as in [5,6,7], among others. The SSVM's appeal is due, in part, to its ability to take into account a variety of *loss functions*.

Computational Complexity. SSVMs, however, require the CRF energy function to be linear, which in turn places the same restriction on all the unary and spatial terms due to the additive nature of CRF energies. While, in principle, the linear function can be defined in some high dimensional or possibly infinite-dimensional space, reproducing this kernel Hilbert space through the use of non-linear kernels is often infeasible in practice given that the number of kernel evaluations grows quadratically with the model size and must be optimized in the dual space. Though SSVM learning techniques based on sampled cuts [8,9] have alleviated this problem to some extent, they do have to sacrifice some performance for speed and, even with this trade-off, are still generally much slower than linear SSVMs [8]. Moreover, earlier implementations of these techniques were intended for use in conjunction with the cutting-plane method to speed up training of regular non-linear SVMs. This results in a *multivariate* output space in the SSVM formulation, analogous to a CRF without edges, which is considerably less useful for image segmentation.

Kernel Approximation. Kernel Approximation is another way to improve SSVM training efficiency by seeking a lower, finite-dimensional representation of the kernel-induced feature map that lies in a higher or infinite dimensional space. This can be achieved by random sampling from the typically infinite-dimensional feature map [10,11] whose analytical form can be obtained using Fourier analysis when the kernel is homogeneous or stationary [12]. While promising results have been shown for specific additive kernels [13,12], it is less clear how this approach generalizes to non-additive kernels, such as the Gaussian RBF that is more difficult to approximate. Alternatively, the recently proposed *locally* linear SVM [14] can be used to simulate a non-linear decision boundary. However, this does not yield a *globally* linear function and, thus, does not fit into the SSVM framework. Moreover kernel approximation typically introduces additional tuning parameters such as the number of samples, which often present a performance-speed trade-off for which well-defined tuning criteria are lacking.

Structural Kernels. Finally, it is worth pointing out the difference between our approach and the recently proposed *structural kernels*, which also perform structured prediction using non-linear kernels, but in a very different setting. In [9,15], the kernels are defined on the overall output space, that is, the entire CRF, to exploit image-level "structural" information such as shape and color. While this serves to bias local labels and is useful for segmenting large dominant objects from the background, it often requires training data that completely characterizes the possible object configurations, such as binary masks. Multiple objects, or objects whose pose are not represented in the trained model will cause the approach to fail. Our approach, on the other hand, uses regular kernels defined as products between a set of basis vectors and the feature vectors extracted from individual nodes (i.e. pixels or superpixels). This has the effect of making it more "local", and robust to such failures.

3 Learning a CRF with Kernelized Features

We begin by describing our CRF model for segmentation in Sec. 3.1. We then discuss how to learn its parameters using an SSVM framework in Sec. 3.2, with specific details on how to express the CRF model in the required linear form in Sec. 3.3. In Sec. 4, we introduce a technique to create "kernelized" features, enabling us to leverage the power of non-linear kernels while the SSVM remains linear. Fig. 2 outlines our approach.

3.1 CRF for Segmentation

As a standard preprocessing step, we perform a preliminary over-segmentation of our input image into superpixels [3] using SLIC [16]. The CRF $\mathcal{G} = (\mathcal{V}, \mathcal{E})$ is thus defined so that each node $i \in \mathcal{V}$ corresponds to a superpixel and there is an edge $(i, j) \in \mathcal{E}$ between two nodes i and j if the corresponding superpixels are adjacent in the image. Let $Y = \{y_i\}$ for $i \in \mathcal{V}$ denote the labeling of the CRF which assigns a class label y_i to each node i. Its energy function can then be written as

$$E_{\mathbf{w}}(Y) = \sum_{i \in \mathcal{V}} D_i(y_i) + \sum_{(i,j) \in \mathcal{E}} V_{ij}(y_i, y_j), \quad (1)$$

where D_i is the unary term and V_{ij} is the pairwise term. Both D_i and V_{ij} depend on the observed data and the CRF parameters $\mathbf{w}$, in addition to the labeling Y. The energy is

[3] Or supervoxels in the case of volumetric data.

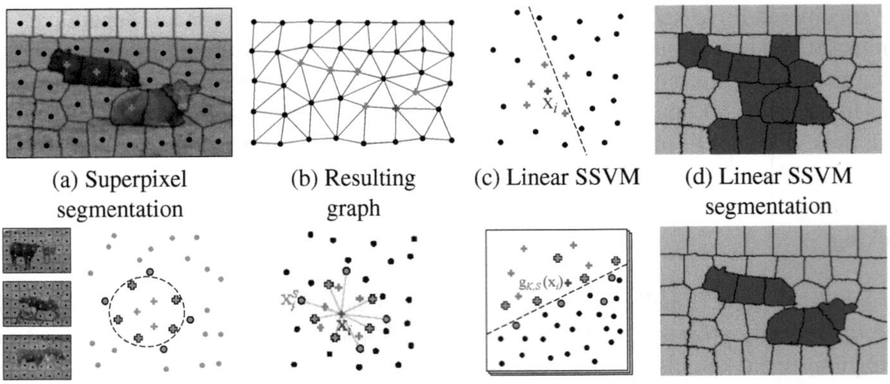

(a) Superpixel segmentation
(b) Resulting graph
(c) Linear SSVM
(d) Linear SSVM segmentation
(e) Standard RBF SVM trained with individual superpixels
(f) Kernel transform
(g) "Kernelized" SSVM
(h) "Kernelized" SSVM segmentation

Fig. 2. Our approach. *(a)* A superpixel over-segmentation of an image where each superpixel center is marked (+/• denotes foreground/background). *(b)* The superpixel graph used to construct the CRF, where each node corresponds to a superpixel, and edges indicate adjacency in the image. *(c)* An illustration of the feature space. Each point represents a feature vector extracted from a superpixel. Because it is not linearly separable, the standard SSVM gives a poor segmentation result in *(d)*. *(e)* To address this, we train a non-structured kernel SVM on individual superpixels to obtain a set of support vectors S, indicated by outlined points. *(f)* Kernel-transformed features $\mathbf{g}_{K,S}(\mathbf{x}_i)$ are obtained for each feature vector x_i from the kernel products of x_i and S. *(g)* Data in the $|S|$-dimensional "kernelized" feature space is linearly separable, and can be used to train a linear SSVM. *(h)* The improved segmentation result.

also commonly referred to as the "cost" in the literature and we will use the two terms interchangeably. The inferred optimal labeling is simply the one that minimizes it, that is, $Y^* = \arg\min_{Y \in \mathcal{Y}} E_{\mathbf{w}}(Y)$, where $\mathcal{Y}$ denotes the set of all possible labelings. While the exact minimization of the energy function is generally intractable on loopy CRFs, good approximate solutions can be found efficiently using techniques such as graph cuts [17] and belief propagation [18]. In our case, we use graph cuts when the energy function is submodular [19] and belief propagation otherwise.

3.2 Learning the CRF Using SSVM

Structured SVM (SSVM) is a large-margin method for learning the parameters of models with structured outputs, such as the CRF model we use for segmentation. The SSVM uses the ground truth training data to learn the CRF parameters so that the inferred labeling of the CRF is "close" to that of the training data, defined as yielding a low *loss*. More specifically, given a set of N training examples with ground truth labelings $(Y^{(1)}, \ldots, Y^{(N)})$, the SSVM [4] optimizes a quadratic objective function of the parameters $\mathbf{w}$ subject to a set of linear soft margin constraints

[4] Here, we use the margin-rescaling variant of SSVM [1].

$$\min_{\mathbf{w},\boldsymbol{\xi}\geq\mathbf{0}} \frac{1}{2}\|\mathbf{w}\|_2^2 + \frac{C}{N}\sum_{n=1}^{N}\xi_n \qquad (2)$$
$$\text{s.t. } \forall n, Y \in \mathcal{Y}_n \backslash Y^{(n)} : \delta E_{\mathbf{w}}(Y) \geq \Delta(Y^{(n)}, Y) - \xi_n$$

where $\mathcal{Y}_n$ is the set of all possible labelings for example n, ξ_n are the slack variables, and $\delta E_{\mathbf{w}}(Y)$ is shorthand for $E_{\mathbf{w}}(Y) - E_{\mathbf{w}}(Y^{(n)})$. The constant C controls the trade-off between margin and training error, and the loss function Δ measures the closeness of a labeling Y to the ground truth $Y^{(n)}$.

A natural choice for Δ is the per-superpixel 0-1 loss $\Delta(Y^{(n)}, Y) = \sum_{i\in\mathcal{V}} \Delta(y_i^{(n)}, y_i)$ with $\Delta(y_i^{(n)}, y_i) = I(y_i \neq y_i^{(n)})$, which penalizes all errors equally. However, in image segmentation, it is common for certain classes to occur much more frequently than others. To ensure good performance across all classes, we adopt a loss function that weighs errors for a given class inversely proportional to the frequency with which it appears in the training data

$$\Delta(y_i^{(n)}, y_i) = \begin{cases} \frac{1}{\text{frequency}(y_i^{(n)})} & \text{, if } y_i \neq y_i^{(n)} \\ 0 & \text{, otherwise.} \end{cases} \qquad (3)$$

Since the total number of constraints grows exponentially with the CRF size, they cannot be exhaustively enumerated in most cases. The SSVM solves this by employing an iterative cutting-plane algorithm, which finds the most violated constraint for each example n

$$\hat{Y} = \arg\min_{Y\in\mathcal{Y}_n} E_{\mathbf{w}}(Y) - \Delta(Y^{(n)}, Y) \qquad (4)$$

at every iteration and adds it to the working set of constraints. As with inferring the optimal labeling, finding the most violated constraint is intractable on loopy CRFs. However, the approximate most violated constraints can be found efficiently using the same kind of energy minimization techniques as in inference, and this approach has proven effective in practice [20,5].

3.3 Linearizing the CRF Energy Function

Since the SSVM operates by solving a quadratic program (QP), all the constraints in Equation 2 must be linear [1]. This requires that the energy function $E_{\mathbf{w}}$ be expressible as an inner product between the parameter vector and a feature map. Since the energy is the sum of individual unary and pairwise terms, this implies that D_i and V_{ij} also must be expressible as

$$D_i(y_i) = \langle \mathbf{w}^D, \psi_i^D(y_i) \rangle \qquad (5)$$

and

$$V_{ij}(y_i, y_j) = \langle \mathbf{w}^V, \psi_{ij}^V(y_i, y_j) \rangle , \qquad (6)$$

where $\psi_i^D(y_i)$ and $\psi_{ij}^V(y_i, y_j)$ are feature maps dependent on both the observed data and the labels, and where

$$\mathbf{w} = ((\mathbf{w}^D)^T, (\mathbf{w}^V)^T)^T \qquad (7)$$

is the vector of parameters that define the functions D_i and V_{ij} respectively.

If we let $\Psi^D(Y) = \sum_{i \in \mathcal{V}} \psi_i^D(y_i)$ and $\Psi^V(Y) = \sum_{(i,j) \in \mathcal{E}} \psi_{ij}^V(y_i, y_j)$, then $\Psi(Y) = (\Psi^D(Y)^T, \Psi^V(Y)^T)^T$. allowing the CRF energy to now be written linearly as

$$E_{\mathbf{w}}(Y) = \langle \mathbf{w}, \Psi(Y) \rangle . \tag{8}$$

Let $\mathbf{x}_i$ be a feature vector associated with node i extracted from the observed data. We can define the data feature map as

$$\psi_i^D(y_i) = (I(y_i = 1)\mathbf{x}_i^T, \ldots, I(y_i = K)\mathbf{x}_i^T)^T , \tag{9}$$

where K is the number of possible labels, i.e., $y_i \in \{1, \ldots, K\}$. If we write $\mathbf{w}^D = (\mathbf{w}_1^D, \ldots, \mathbf{w}_K^D)^T$, the unary term becomes the inner product

$$D_i(y_i) = \left\langle \mathbf{w}_{y_i}^D, \mathbf{x}_i \right\rangle , \tag{10}$$

which represents the energy of node i taking on label y_i. Similarly, if we define the pairwise feature map as

$$\psi_{ij}^V(y_i, y_j) = (I(y_i = a, y_j = b))_{(a,b) \in \{1,\ldots,K\}^2} \tag{11}$$

with the corresponding parameters $\mathbf{w}^V = (w_{ab})_{(a,b) \in \{1,\ldots,K\}^2}$, then the pairwise term

$$V_{ij}(y_i, y_j) = w_{y_i y_j} \tag{12}$$

reflects the transition cost between nodes i and j from label y_i to label y_j. Although the above definition depends only on the labels y_i and y_j, the pairwise term can, in fact, be made data-aware (as in [2,7]). For instance, it can be made gradient-adaptive by including parameters for each discretized gradient level. In a similar fashion, it can be made to consider geometric relationships such as "sky should appear above grass"[5].

4 Kernel-Transformed Features

As shown in the previous section, standard SSVMs require an energy function that is linear in the parameters and features. Since unary terms based on non-linear SVMs are often more powerful and produce better results [21,7], this constitutes a major limitation. It should be possible, in principle, to learn non-linear unary terms within the SSVM framework by implicitly defining $\mathbf{w}$ and $\mathbf{x}_i$ of Eq. 10 in a high-dimensional space through kernels. In practice, however, these kernels are very high- or even infinite-dimensional, making such an approach computationally intractable.

Our approach aims at circumventing this problem. It starts from the observation that a non-linear binary (+1/-1 label) SVM classifier always takes the form

$$\text{Score}(\mathbf{x}) = \sum_j \alpha_j y_j^S K(\mathbf{x}_j^S, \mathbf{x}) , \tag{13}$$

[5] We incorporate both geometric and gradient context in our model. They are omitted from the notation for brevity, as the extension follows naturally from above.

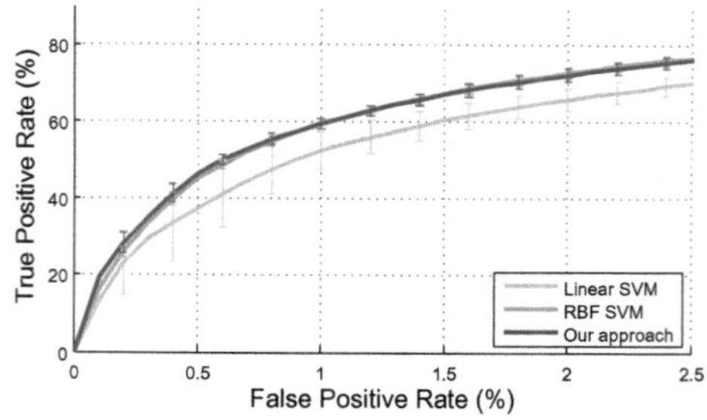

Fig. 3. Comparison of a linear SVM, RBF-SVM, and a linear SVM trained on feature vectors kernelized using the support vectors of the RBF-SVM. For classification of individual superpixels (ignoring structure), training a linear SVM on kernelized feature vectors yields a similar performance to a standard RBF-SVM. Error bars indicate standard deviation over 10 experiments

where $\mathbf{x}_j^S \in S$ are the support vectors with corresponding labels y_j^S. Extended to multi-class labels ($y_i \in \{1, \ldots, K\}$) for a general unary term, it becomes

$$D_i(y_i) = -\sum_j \alpha_j c(y_j^S, y_i) K(\mathbf{x}_j^S, \mathbf{x}_i) , \tag{14}$$

where $c(y_j^S, y_i)$ is 1 if $y_i = y_j^S$ and -1 otherwise. Note that, although the function is non-linear in the input features $\mathbf{x}_i$, because of the non-linear kernel K, it is linear in the kernel products $K(\mathbf{x}_j^S, \mathbf{x}_i)$.

If we define $\mathbf{g}_{K,S}(\mathbf{x}_i)$ as the vector of kernel products

$$\mathbf{g}_{K,S}(\mathbf{x}_i) = (K(\mathbf{x}_1^S, \mathbf{x}_i), \ldots, K(\mathbf{x}_{|S|}^S, \mathbf{x}_i))^T , \tag{15}$$

and $\mathbf{w'}_{y_i}$ as their coefficients

$$\mathbf{w'}_{y_i} = (-\alpha_1 c(y_1^S, y_i), \cdots, -\alpha_{|S|} c(y_{|S|}^S, y_i))^T , \tag{16}$$

then the unary term can be re-expressed as

$$D_i(y_i) = \langle \mathbf{w'}_{y_i}, \mathbf{g}_{K,S}(\mathbf{x}_i) \rangle , \tag{17}$$

which is of the finite-dimensional linear form needed for learning within the SSVM framework, as discussed in the previous section.

This suggests a simple, 2-step learning approach to incorporate kernels into an SSVM, illustrated in Fig. 2. First, we train a standard non-structured non-linear kernel SVM using feature vectors extracted from individual superpixels to obtain a set of support vectors S. S are then used as *basis vectors* to create a set of *kernel-transformed* (or "kernelized") feature vectors $\mathbf{g}_{K,S}(\mathbf{x}_i)$, which are provided to train the linear SSVM.

Although our formulation is not equivalent to a non-linear kernel SSVM[6], nor can it be shown to approximate a non-linear SSVM as kernel approximation methods

[6] The parameters $\mathbf{w}'$ now correspond to the primal variables of a linear SSVM instead of the dual variables of a non-linear SSVM.

do [10,13,12], it does produce models with the same functional form as those learned using a kernel SSVM and, importantly, performs well in practice. To demonstrate the principle that a linear SVM trained using kernel-transformed features performs similarly to a non-linear SVM that uses the same kernel, we conducted a simple experiment. The goal was to classify individual superpixels, ignoring structure. We compare the performance of a standard linear SVM, an SVM trained with an RBF kernel, and a simplification of our approach in which feature vectors kernelized using the support vectors obtained from the RBF-SVM are used to train a standard linear SVM. The results appearing in Fig. 3 support our intuition – so long as we transform the original feature vector using the right set of basis vectors, learning the new coefficients under a different objective function (i.e., as primal instead of dual variables) yields performance similar to a non-linear kernel SVM.

5 Results

Our primary motivation for developing the technique presented here was to segment synaptic gaps and mitochondria from images acquired with an electron microscope, such as the ones depicted in Fig. 1. For such data, it is known *a priori* that particular cellular structures will appear in the image. Consequently, the use of global features and/or priors which has proved to be essential when the presence of a particular category is uncertain, as is the case for segmentation benchmarks such as MSRC [2], is of no particular benefit. Because EM segmentation methods can not use such global features, they have to more heavily rely on smoothness terms. Nevertheless, we demonstrate that our approach boosts performance of the learned CRF model on the MSRC dataset as well as the EM data. In subsection 5.2 we are able to match state-of-the-art results on the MSRC dataset by incorporating global features. For the EM data in subsections 5.3 and 5.4, our approach significantly outperforms the state-of-the-art.

5.1 Competing Methods

To highlight the relative importance of the various components of our approach, we compare against the following variations which we treat as baselines.

- **Linear SVM** – A standard linear SVM trained on the original feature vectors x_i. Each superpixel is classified independently (i.e., without CRF).
- **Linear SSVM/CRF** – As described in Sec. 3.2, a linear SSVM on the original features is used to learn the parameters of a CRF, which is used for segmentation.
- **RBF SVM** – A non-linear SVM trained on the original feature vectors using an RBF kernel. Each superpixel is classified independently.
- **RBF+SSVM/CRF** – Instead of being kernelized versions of the original feature vectors as in our approach, transformed feature vectors contain the per-class scores of an RBF SVM trained on the original features. A linear SSVM learns the parameters of a CRF using the transformed features.
- **Codebook SVM** – The original feature vectors are transformed using a "kernel codebook" approach inspired by [22]. It relies on k-means clustering to create a set of basis vectors (codewords) instead of discriminatively learned SVM support vectors. We used as many codewords as support vectors for all our experiments. The resulting features are classified independently with a linear SVM.

Table 1. MSRC segmentation results. We follow the standard reporting procedure. For each category, the pixel-wise classification rate is provided. Global pixel-wise accuracy and average per-category scores provide measures for overall performance. The first part of the table shows baseline methods that ignore global information, while the second part compares our approach to state-of-the-art methods that consider global information. Bold entries are used for each part separately to indicate best performance.

	building	grass	tree	cow	sheep	sky	airplane	water	face	car	bicycle	flower	sign	bird	book	chair	road	cat	dog	body	boat	**Global**	**Average**
Linear SVM	**59**	79	78	60	63	70	78	61	46	61	76	57	64	59	58	63	70	52	55	68	31	68	62
RBF SVM	47	83	**80**	83	62	76	74	62	72	55	73	59	**86**	40	54	62	73	66	34	60	34	70	64
Linear SSVM/CRF	53	81	74	76	72	73	85	63	59	60	81	54	77	62	68	72	76	66	**68**	**71**	6	71	65
RBF+SSVM/CRF	54	**84**	70	75	69	80	86	**66**	69	**77**	87	46	74	**66**	65	69	65	77	58	68	18	71	68
Kernelized SSVM/CRF	41	77	79	**87**	**91**	**86**	**92**	65	**86**	65	**89**	**61**	76	48	**77**	**91**	**77**	**82**	32	48	**39**	**73**	**70**
G-Kernelized SSVM/CRF	59	90	**92**	82	83	94	91	80	85	**88**	96	89	73	48	96	62	81	87	33	44	30	82	76
Shotton et al. [23]	49	88	79	**97**	**97**	78	82	54	**87**	74	72	74	36	24	93	51	78	75	35	**66**	18	72	67
Ladicky et al. [24]	**80**	**96**	86	74	87	**99**	74	**87**	86	87	82	**97**	**95**	30	86	31	**95**	51	**69**	**66**	09	**86**	75
Gonfaus et al. [21]	60	78	77	91	68	88	87	76	73	77	**93**	**97**	73	**57**	95	**81**	76	81	46	56	46	77	75
Lucchi et al. [7]	50	83	87	81	84	90	**97**	72	75	79	90	95	79	52	**97**	**81**	80	**89**	51	64	**60**	79	**78**

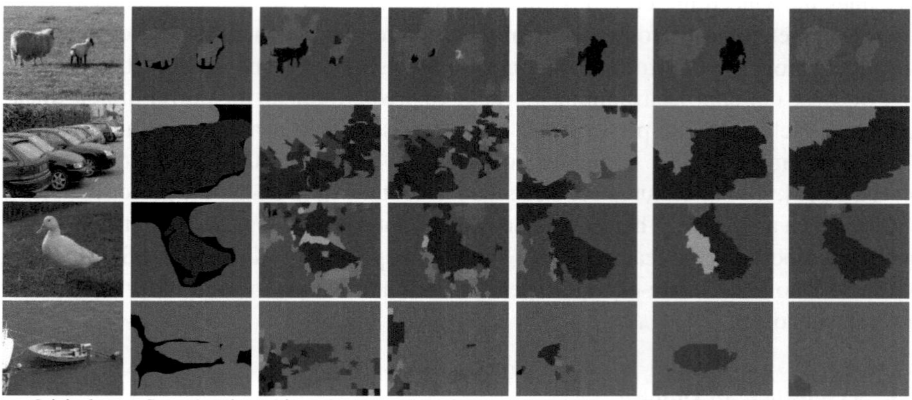

Original | Ground truth | Linear SVM | RBF-SVM | Linear SSVM/CRF | RBF+SSVM/CRF | Kernelized SSVM/CRF

Fig. 4. Example segmentations from the MSRC dataset

- **Codebook SSVM/CRF** – Features are constructed in the same manner as for Codebook SVM, but a linear SSVM is used to learn a CRF for structured prediction.
- **Kernelized SSVM/CRF** – Our method. A linear SSVM learns the parameters of a CRF for structured prediction, using kernel-transformed features $\mathbf{g}_{K,S}(\mathbf{x}_i)$, as described in Sec. 4.

In addition to these, we also compare to state-of-the-art methods, [23,24,21,7] for MSRC and [25] for the EM dataset. All SSVM methods used Joachims' *SVM-struct* software [1] for training.

5.2 MSRC Dataset

The MSRC-21 dataset is a popular multi-class object segmentation benchmark dataset which contains 591 images with objects from 21 categories.

We extract feature vectors from each image by first over-segmenting the image using SLIC superpixels [16]. We then extract SIFT descriptors and color histograms from image patches surrounding each superpixel centroid. We also include location information as in [24]. This information is converted to a bag-of-words descriptor using a nearest-neighbor search[7]. The resulting descriptor serves as the feature vector x_i used to train the various methods. Training and testing is done using the standard split of the dataset [2]. Note that the Codebook SVM and Codebook SSVM methods are not reported since x_i already contains a bag-of-words descriptor. In addition to the baseline methods described above, we compare state-of-the-art approaches [23,24,21,7] to our approach incorporating global features:

- **G-Kernelized SSVM/CRF** – Our method as described in Sec. 4 using an augmented feature vector. In addition to SIFT descriptors and color histograms, the feature vector contains the global features described in [21].

Table 1 summarizes the segmentation performance of the various approaches and example segmentations appear in Fig. 4. The top of Table 1 compares our method to the baselines introduced in Sec. 5.1, demonstrating that structured learning tends to yield higher segmentation performance than unstructured approaches. It is also clear that non-linear models outperform linear ones for both structured and instance-based learning. Because our approach combines structured prediction with the power of non-linear kernels, it yields superior performance over the baselines in nearly every category.

The bottom of Table 1 compares our approach to state-of-the-art methods. As observed in [7], global features are necessary to obtain state-of-the-art performance on datasets such as MSRC. Therefore, when we do not use them our performance is lower but by incorporating the features of [21] into our approach (G-Kernelized SSVM/CRF), we are able to match state-of-the-art performance and out-perform all other methods in several categories.

5.3 Synaptic Gap Dataset

Segmenting the synaptic gaps from EM images of neural tissue shown in Fig. 1*(b)* is challenging due to the large amount of clutter including vesicles, mitochondria, and various cellular membranes that exhibit a variety of distracting shapes and textures. The dataset of Fig. 1*(b)* contains 250 images of 655×429 pixels and a total of 24 synapses. Each pixel was labeled by an expert as either synaptic or non-synaptic. The dataset was then split into 2 parts for training and testing.

We begin by over-segmenting each image using SLIC superpixels [16]. Each image contained an average of 4000 superpixels and 11400 edges. At the location of each superpixel we extract a feature vector consisting of intensity histograms and steerable filter responses. The later is computed by convolving a patch extracted at the center of each superpixel with a set of steerable filters at 3 different scales ($\sigma = \{2, 5, 6\}$). An SVM with an RBF kernel trained on 40K randomly sampled superpixels provides the support vectors for the kernel transform in our approach.

[7] A dictionary containing 1,000 words for SIFT features and 400 words for color histograms is constructed using k-means on extracted features.

Table 2. Segmentation results for the synaptic gap EM dataset. We measure segmentation performance using the *Jaccard index*, the ratio of the correctly segmented area to the union of the segmentation and the ground truth.

Linear SVM	Linear SSVM/CRF	RBF SVM	RBF+ SSVM/CRF	Codebook SVM	Codebook SSVM/CRF	**Kernelized SSVM/CRF**
58%	60%	61%	64%	60%	63%	**66%**

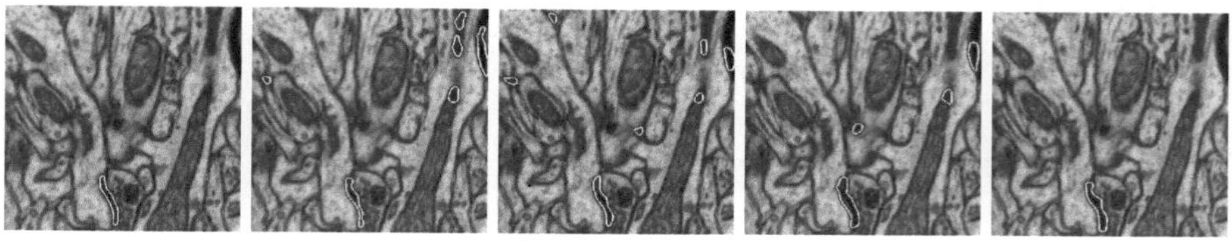

Fig. 5. Segmentation results on the synaptic gap dataset. The kernelized SSVM correctly segments the synapse in this example, while the baseline methods include spurious segments.

A summary of the segmentation performance is provided in Table 2, and examples appear in Fig. 5. As with the MSRC baselines, we observe a trend in which structured learning yields higher segmentation performance than unstructured approaches and non-linear models outperform linear models. Our approach, which combines structured learning with non-linear models outperforms all other methods.

5.4 Mitochondria Dataset

Here, we perform mitochondria segmentation in 3D using large image stacks from Fig. 1*(a)*. This greatly increases the scale of the problem since the image stacks are orders of magnitude larger than most 2D images.

We begin by over-segmenting the volume using SLIC supervoxels [16]. For each supervoxel, we extract a feature vector that captures local shape and texture information using Ray descriptors [27,25] and intensity histograms. Those feature vectors x_i are used to train each baseline methods, as well as our model. Due to the high cost of labeling such large volumes, our experiments are restricted to two subvolumes containing $1024 \times 768 \times 165$ voxels. The first subvolume, containing 42 mitochondria, was used to train the various methods; the second, containing 45 mitochondria, was used for testing. Each subvolume contains $\sim$13K supervoxels. The resulting graphs have $\sim$91K edges. An SVM with an RBF kernel trained on 4K randomly sampled supervoxels provides the support vectors for the kernel transform in our approach.

A summary of the segmentation performance is provided in Table 3. Example segmentations are provided in Fig. 6. Once again, we observe the trend in which structured learning yields higher performance than unstructured approaches and non-linear models outperform linear models. Comparing to [25], we can see that our approach of jointly learning the data and pairwise parameters in an SSVM framework is superior to learning them independently and then using CRF energy minimization for inference.

Table 3. Segmentation results for the mitochondria EM dataset. We measure segmentation performance using the *Jaccard index*.

Linear SVM	Linear SSVM/CRF	RBF SVM	RBF+ SSVM/CRF	Codebook SVM	Codebook SSVM/CRF	Lucchi et al. [25]	**Kernelized SSVM/CRF**
73%	79%	75%	80%	75%	80%	80%	**84%**

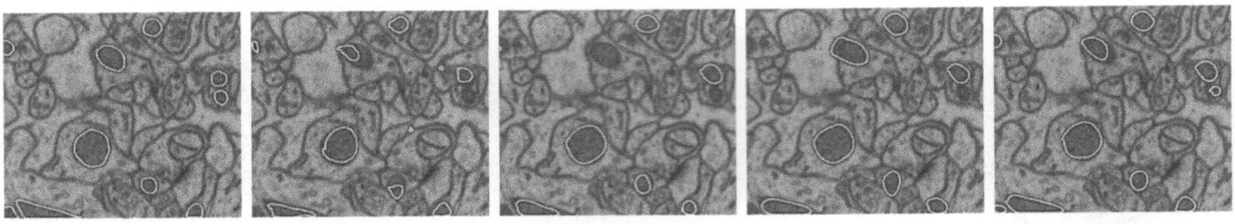

Ground truth Linear SVM RBF SVM Codebook SSVM/CRF Kernelized SSVM/CRF

Fig. 6. Segmentation results on the EM dataset. The kernelized SSVM correctly segments all mitochondria in this example, while other methods fail to detect some mitochondria, poorly delineate certain boundaries, or erroneously insert extra regions. Note that the data and segmentations are 3-dimensional – the images above correspond to slices through the test volume.

5.5 Discussion

The expense of training is an important consideration for any classification-based approach. As previously noted, an SSVM can, in principle, be trained using a non-linear kernel. However, this is not feasible in practice as the number of kernel evaluations grows quadratically with the size of the graph. We keep the cost linear by applying a kernel-transform to the features. But to do so, we must first train a standard non-linear SVM to obtain the support vectors used in the kernel transform. The training time of this step could be a potential cause for concern, as it incurs the same quadratic cost. Fortunately, it can be kept in check using known techniques such as randomly sampling the data or iteratively mining for hard examples [26]. However, these techniques cannot be applied to directly speed up the SSVM because they disregard the structure of the graph, which is essential for learning. Note that while we only used Gaussian radial basis functions in our experiments, they are not required by design and one could easily substitute them with other kernels such as Polynomial or Hyperbolic tangent.

6 Conclusion

In this work, we introduced a technique to leverage the power of non-linear kernels in a structured prediction framework by applying a kernel transform to the feature vectors. Results on three different datasets demonstrate the advantages of our approach. Although this work focuses on segmentation, the concept should generalize to other structured prediction problems such as gene sequencing and natural language parsing.

References

1. Tsochantaridis, I., Hofmann, T., Joachims, T., Altun, Y.: Support vector machine learning for interdependent and structured output spaces. In: ICML (2004)

2. Shotton, J., Winn, J., Rother, C., Criminisi, A.: Textonboost for Image Understanding: Multi-Class Object Recognition and Segmentation by Jointly Modeling Texture, Layout, and Context. IJCV 81 (2009)
3. Lafferty, J., McCallum, A., Pereira, F.: Conditional random fields: Probabilistic models for segmenting and labeling sequence data. In: ICML (2001)
4. Taskar, B., Guestrin, C., Koller, D.: Max-margin Markov networks. In: NIPS (2003)
5. Szummer, M., Kohli, P., Hoiem, D.: Learning CRFs Using Graph Cuts. In: Forsyth, D., Torr, P., Zisserman, A. (eds.) ECCV 2008, Part II. LNCS, vol. 5303, pp. 582–595. Springer, Heidelberg (2008)
6. Nowozin, S., Gehler, P.V., Lampert, C.H.: On Parameter Learning in CRF-Based Approaches to Object Class Image Segmentation. In: Daniilidis, K., Maragos, P., Paragios, N. (eds.) ECCV 2010, Part VI. LNCS, vol. 6316, pp. 98–111. Springer, Heidelberg (2010)
7. Lucchi, A., Li, Y., Boix, X., Smith, K., Fua, P.: Are Spatial and Global Constraints Really Necessary for Segmentation? In: ICCV (2011)
8. Yu, C.N.J., Joachims, T.: Training structural svms with kernels using sampled cuts. In: KDD (2008)
9. Aliaksei, M., Severyn, A.: Fast support vector machines for structural kernels. In: ECML (2011)
10. Rahimi, A., Recht, B.: Random features for large-scale kernel machines. In: NIPS (2007)
11. Balcan, M.F., Blum, A., Vempala, S.: Kernels as features: On kernels, margins, and low-dimensional mappings. Mach. Learn. 65, 79–94 (2006)
12. Vedaldi, A., Zisserman, A.: Efficient additive kernels via explicit feature maps. In: PAMI (2011)
13. Maji, S., Berg, A.: Max-Margin Additive Classifiers for Detection. In: ICCV (2009)
14. Ladicky, L., Torr, P.: Locally Linear Support Vector Machines. In: ICML (2011)
15. Bertelli, L., Yu, T., Vu, D., Gokturk, B.: Kernelized Structural Svm Learning for Supervised Object Segmentation. In: CVPR (2011)
16. Achanta, R., Shaji, A., Smith, K., Lucchi, A., Fua, P., Suesstrunk, S.: SLIC Superpixels Compared to State-of-the-art Superpixel Methods. PAMI (in press, 2012)
17. Boykov, Y., Veksler, O., Zabih, R.: Fast Approximate Energy Minimization via Graph Cuts. PAMI 23 (2001)
18. Murphy, K.: Bayesian Map Learning in Dynamic Environments. In: NIPS, pp. 1015–1021 (1999)
19. Kolmogorov, V., Zabih, R.: What Energy Functions Can Be Minimized via Graph Cuts? PAMI 26, 147–159 (2004)
20. Finley, T., Joachims, T.: Training structural SVMs when exact inference is intractable. In: ICML (2008)
21. Gonfaus, J., Boix, X., Weijer, J., Bagdanov, A., Serrat, J., Gonzalez, J.: Harmony Potentials for Joint Classification and Segmentation. In: CVPR, pp. 3280–3287 (2010)
22. van Gemert, J.C., Geusebroek, J.-M., Veenman, C.J., Smeulders, A.W.M.: Kernel Codebooks for Scene Categorization. In: Forsyth, D., Torr, P., Zisserman, A. (eds.) ECCV 2008, Part III. LNCS, vol. 5304, pp. 696–709. Springer, Heidelberg (2008)
23. Shotton, J., Johnson, M., Cipolla, P.: Semantic Texton Forests for Image Categorization and Segmentation. In: CVPR (2008)
24. Ladicky, L., Russell, C., Kohli, P., Torr, P.H.S.: Associative Hierarchical CRFs for Object Class Image Segmentation. In: ICCV (2009)
25. Lucchi, A., Smith, K., Achanta, R., Knott, G., Fua, P.: Supervoxel-Based Segmentation of Mitochondria in Em Image Stacks with Learned Shape Features. TMI 31, 474–486 (2011)
26. Felzenszwalb, P., Mcallester, D., Ramanan, D.: A Discriminatively Trained, Multiscale, Deformable Part Model. In: CVPR (2008)
27. Smith, K., Carleton, A., Lepetit, V.: Fast Ray Features for Learning Irregular Shapes. In: ICCV, pp. 397–404 (2009)

Salient Object Detection: A Benchmark

Ali Borji, Dicky N. Sihite, and Laurent Itti

Department of Computer Science, University of Southern California
http://ilab.usc.edu/~borji

Abstract. Several salient object detection approaches have been published which have been assessed using different evaluation scores and datasets resulting in discrepancy in model comparison. This calls for a methodological framework to compare existing models and evaluate their pros and cons. We analyze benchmark datasets and scoring techniques and, for the first time, provide a quantitative comparison of 35 state-of-the-art saliency detection models. We find that some models perform consistently better than the others. Saliency models that intend to predict eye fixations perform lower on segmentation datasets compared to salient object detection algorithms. Further, we propose combined models which show that integration of the few best models outperforms all models over other datasets. By analyzing the consistency among the best models and among humans for each scene, we identify the scenes where models or humans fail to detect the most salient object. We highlight the current issues and propose future research directions.

1 Introduction

Visual saliency is the ability of a vision system (human or machine) to select a certain subset of visual information for further processing. This mechanism serves as a filter to select only the *interesting* information related to current behaviors or tasks to be processed while ignoring irrelevant information.

Recently, salient object detection has attracted a lot of interest in computer vision as it provides fast solutions to several complex processes. Firstly, it detects the most salient and attention-grabbing object in a scene, and then it segments the whole extent of that object. The output usually is a map where the intensity of each pixel represents the probability of that pixel belonging to the salient object. This problem in its essence is a segmentation problem but slightly differs from the traditional general image segmentation. While salient object detection models segment only the salient foreground object from the background, general segmentation algorithms partition an image into regions of coherent properties. Salient object detection methods also differ from other saliency models that aim to predict scene locations where a human observer may fixate. Since saliency models, whether they address segmentation or fixation prediction, both generate saliency maps; they are interchangeably applicable.

The value of saliency detection methods lies in their applications in many fields including: object detection and recognition [30][9], image compression [59], video

A. Fitzgibbon et al. (Eds.): ECCV 2012, Part II, LNCS 7573, pp. 414–429, 2012.

summarization [60], and photo collage [20][17]. A comparison of some image retargeting techniques (some based on salient object detection [13][35]) is available at: `http://people.csail.mit.edu/mrub/retargetme/`.

Some work has been published on quantitative evaluation of general segmentation algorithms [44][48][1]. To the authors' best knowledge, such attempt for benchmarking salient object segmentation methods has not been reported. Unfortunately, these methods have often been evaluated on different datasets, which in some cases are small and not easily accessible. The lack of published benchmarks causes discrepancy in quantitative comparison of competing models. Not only does a benchmark allow researchers to compare their models with other algorithms, but it also helps identify the chief factors affecting performance. This could result in an even faster performance improvement.

2 Related Works

Here we provide a short summary of the main trends in saliency detection. The interested reader can refer to the extensive reviews for more details [67][61].

As a pioneer, Itti *et al.* [2] derived bottom-up visual saliency using center-surround differences across multi-scale image features. Ma and Zhang [51] proposed an alternative local contrast method using a fuzzy growth model. Harel *et al.* [3] used graph algorithms and a measure of dissimilarity to achieve efficient saliency computation with their Graph Based Visual Saliency (GBVS) model. Liu *et al.* [33] used conditional random field to learn regions of interest using three features: multi-scale contrast, center-surround histogram, and color spatial-distribution. More recently, Goferman *et al.* [15] simultaneously modeled local low-level clues, global considerations, visual organization rules, and high-level features to highlight salient objects along with their contexts. Zhai and Shah [12] defined pixel-level saliency by contrast to all other pixels. However, for efficiency they used only luminance information, thus ignoring distinctive clues in other channels. Achanta *et al.* [16] proposed a frequency-tuned method that directly defines pixel saliency using the color differences from the average image color. Visual saliency is equated to discrimination in [62] and extended to bottom-up mechanism in the pre-attentive biological vision. Spectral components in an image have been explored to detect visual saliency [5][34][56]. In Hou and Zhang [5], the gist of the scene is represented with the average Fourier envelope and the differential spectral components are used to extract salient regions. This is replaced by the phase spectrum of the Fourier transform in [34] because it is more effective and computationally efficient. Some researchers including Bruce and Tsotsos [4] and Zhang *et al.* [10] attempted to define visual saliency based on information theory. Some others have further used graph-cut or grab-cub algorithms to refine borders of their saliency maps and count for salient object contours [23][13]. While some methods define visual saliency in a local way (e.g., Itti *et al.* [2], SEO [8], GBVS [3], AWS [7], and DAKlein [25]),

[1] `http://www.wisdom.weizmann.ac.il/$\sim$vision/Seg_Evaluation_DB`

some others are based on global rarity of image regions over the entire scene (e.g., AIM [4], SUN [10], HouNIPS [6], HouCVPR [5], and RC [13]).

Object-based theories of attention propose that humans attend to objects and high-level concepts. Inspired by these cognitive findings, some models (e.g., Judd *et al.* [1]) have used object detectors such as faces, humans, animals, and text to detect salient locations. Some models address saliency detection in the spatio-temporal domain by employing motion, flicker, optical flow (e.g., [65]), or interest points learned from the image regions at fixated locations (e.g., [63]). Since the research in this area is rather new and the few existing models are in their early phases, thus we leave their quantitative evaluation for the future.

Recently a new trend called *active visual segmentation* has emerged with the intention to segment a region that contains a fixation point (Mishra *et al.* [49]). Their framework combines monocular cues (color/intensity/texture) with stereo and/or motion, in a cue-independent manner. Similarly, Siagian and Koch [50] also proposed a new approach for active segmentation by combining boundary and region information. We consider adding them to promote this new trend.

3 The Salient Object Detection Benchmark

Saliency Detection Models. In this work, as the initial seed, we focus on those models that are easily accessible, attained good accuracies, or have been highly referred. Software for some models was already available online. For others, we contacted their creators for the code; the authors then either sent us the source code to compile or the executables. Some authors, however, preferred to run their models on our stimuli and hence send us back the saliency maps. In order to achieve a thorough model comparison, we intend to open an online challenge where modelers could contribute by submitting their results.

We compare three categories of models: 1) those aiming to detect and segment the most salient object in a scene (emphasized more here), 2) active segmentation approaches, and 3) models that address fixation prediction. Table 1 shows the list of models from the first two categories, and table 2 shows category 3.

Datasets. We choose 5 benchmark datasets based on the following criteria: 1) being widely-used, 2) having size and stimulus variety, and 3) containing different biases such as number of annotators, number of salient objects, and center-bias. Due to specialty of various datasets, it is likely that model rankings may differ across datasets. Hence, to come up with a fair comparison, it is recommended to run models over several datasets and draw objective conclusions. A model is considered to be good, if it performs well over almost all datasets.

Fig. 1 provides explanation of the 5 datasets used here as well as sample images of the five smallest and largest objects from each. Fig. 2 shows *Mean Annotation Position*: $MAP = (1/UV) \sum_{u=1}^{U} \sum_{v=1}^{V} s_{uv}$ averaged over U images and annotated bounding boxes of V subjects (s_{uv}). There is a strong center-bias in the single-object datasets, most probably due to the tendency of photographers to frame interesting objects at the image center [11]. Similarly, there are two peaks (at the left and the right) in the images with two salient objects

Table 1. Compared salient object detection models (checked) sorted chronologically. Abbreviations: {M: Matlab, C: C/C++, S: Sent saliency maps}. w and h: image width/height. DB shows the datasets that we have results over them. JiaLiSal is applied to 100 and 1000 images of ASD and MSRA, respectively. *max X*: Preserve the aspect ratio while resizing the bigger dimension to X.

#	**Acronym** (Model)	**Ref.**	**Pub/Year**	**Code**	**Resolution**	**DB**	Avl.
1	**IO**: Inter-observer model	-	-	M	$w \times h$	All	✓
2	**MAP**: Mean Annotation Position	-	-	M	500×500	All	✓
3	**MZ**: Ma and Zhang	[51]	ACM-M/2003	S	$w \times h$	ASD	✓
4	**LC**: Zhai and Shah	[18]	ACM-M/2006	C	$w \times h$	All	✓
5	**salLiu**: Liu *et al.*	[33]	CVPR/2007	M	max 200	All	✓
6	**AC**: Achanta *et al.*	[14]	ICVS/2008	M	$w \times h$	All	✓
7	**MSSS**: Achanta and Sußstrunk	[55]	ICIP/2009	M	$w \times h$	All	✓
8	**FTS**: Achanta *et al.*	[16]	CVPR/2009	M	$w \times h$	All	✓
9	**EDS**: Rosin	[19]	PR/2009	C	$w \times h$	All	✓
10	Gopalakrishnan *et al.*	[34]	CVPR/2009	-	-	-	-
11	Marchesotti *et al.*	[35]	ICCV/2009	-	-	-	-
12	**Valenti**: Valenti *et al.*	[40]	ICCV/2009	S	$w \times h$	ASD/MSRA	✓
13	**Goferman**: Goferman *et al.*	[15]	CVPR/2010	M	max 250	All	✓
14	**PMehrani**: Mehrani and Veksler	[23]	BMVC/2010	S	$w \times h$	ASD/SED1	✓
15	Rahtu *et al.*	[29]	ECCV/2010	-	-	-	-
16	Khuwuthyakorn *et al.*	[28]	ECCV/2010	-	-	-	-
17	Zhang *et al.*	[21]	IEEE TOM/2010	-	-	-	-
18	**JiaLiSal**: Jia Li *et al.*	[36]	IJCV/2010	S	$[w\ h]/16$	ASD/MSRA	✓
19	**LiuICIP**: Liu *et al.*	[53]	ICIP/2010	S	$w \times h$	ASD	✓
20	**MichalGazit**: Gazit *et al.*	[37]	ECCV-W/2010	M	$w \times h$	All	✓
21	**DAKlein**: Klein and Frintrop	[25]	ICCV/2011	S	$w \times h$	All	✓
22	**MengW**: M. Wang *et al.*	[18]	CVPR/2011	S	$w \times h$	ASD	✓
23	Feng *et al.*	[22]	ICCV/2011	-	-	-	-
24	Deng and Luo	[39]	OE/2011	-	-	-	-
25	Lu *et al.*	[24]	ICCV/2011	-	-	-	-
26	L. Wang *et al.*	[26]	ICCV/2011	-	-	-	-
27	**SVO**: Chang *et al.*	[27]	ICCV/2011	M	$w \times h$	All	✓
28	**CBsal**: Jiang *et al.*	[31]	BMVC/2011	M	$w \times h$	All	✓
29	**RC**: M.M. Cheng *et al.*	[13]	CVPR/2011	C	$w \times h$	All	✓
30	**HC**: M.M. Cheng *et al.*	[13]	CVPR/2011	C	$w \times h$	All	✓
31	**Materias**: Li *et al.*	[36]	BMVC/2011	M	$w \times h$	All	✓
32	**LiuIETIP**: Liu *et al.*	[42]	IEEE TIP/2011	S	$w \times h$	ASD	✓
33	**Mishra**: Mishra *et al.*	[49]	PAMI/2011	C	$w \times h$	All	✓
34	**SRS1**: Siagian and Koch	[50]	Submitted.	C	$w \times h$	All	✓

Table 2. Compared saliency models originally developed for eye fixation prediction

#	**Acronym** (Model)	**Ref.**	**Pub/Year**	**Code**	**Resolution**	**DB**	Avl.
1	**ITTI**: Itti *et al.*	[2]	PAMI/1998	C	$w/16 \times h/16$	All	✓
2	**ITTI98**: Itti *et al.* (maxNorm)	[2]	PAMI/1998	C	$w/16 \times h/16$	All	✓
3	**AIM**: Bruce and Tsotsos	[4]	NIPS/2005	M	$w/2 \times h/2$	All	✓
4	**GBVS**: Harel *et al.*	[3]	NIPS/2006	M	$w \times h$	All	✓
5	**HouCVPR**: Hou and Zhang	[5]	CVPR/2007	M	64×64	All	✓
6	**HouNIPS**: Hou and Zhang	[6]	NIPS/2008	M	$w \times h$	All	✓
7	**SUN**: Zhang *et al.*	[10]	JOV/2008	M	$w/2 \times h/2$	All	✓
8	**PQFT**: Guo and Zhang	[56]	TIP/2009	M	400×400	All	✓
9	**SEO**: Seo and Milanfar	[8]	JOV/2009	M	$w \times h$	All	✓
10	**AWS**: Diaz *et al.*	[7]	ACIVS/2009	M	$w/2 \times h/2$	All	✓
11	**Judd**: Judd *et al.*	[1]	ICCV/2009	M	$w \times h$	All	✓

(SED2). Fig. 2.a shows entropy of images. ASD and MSRA contain more cluttered scenes. Histogram of normalized object sizes (object size/image size) is plotted in Fig. 2.b. It shows there are few images with large objects in these datasets. Objects usually range from small to medium size, about 30% of the whole image (with MSRA containing larger objects on average). Fig. 2.c shows subject agreement for an image which is defined as:

$$r = \frac{2}{n(n-1)} \sum_{i=1}^{n-1} \sum_{j=i+1}^{n} \frac{|s_i \cap s_j|}{|s_i \cup s_j|} \tag{1}$$

where s_i and s_j are annotations of the $i-th$ and $j-th$ subjects (of n subjects). Above score has the well-defined lower bound of 0 when there is no overlap in segmentations of users and upper-bound of 1 when they have perfect overlap. As Fig. 2 shows, subjects have higher agreement over MSRA, SED1, and SED2 datasets (about 70% of r values are above 0.9) compared to the SOD dataset.

Proposed Combined Models. Since different models are based on different hypotheses and algorithms, it is likely that combining evidences from them may enhance the saliency detection accuracy. Here, we investigate such an idea. Let $p(x_f)$ represent the probability of an image pixel x being part of the salient foreground object (i.e., 2D normalized saliency map [0 1]). Let $p(x_f|M_i)$ be such evidence from the $i-th$ model. Assuming independence among models (i.e., $p(x_f|M_i, M_j) \propto p(x_f|M_i)p(x_f|M_j)$), then a Naive Bayesian evidence accumulation would be:

$$p(x_f|M_1, M_2, \cdots, M_K) \propto \frac{1}{Z} \prod_{k=1}^{K} p(x_f|M_k) \tag{2}$$

where K is the number of models and Z is chosen in a way that the final map is a probability density function (pdf). Since, a very small value by only a single model suppresses all evidences from the other models in the multiplication case (Eq. 2), we also consider another combination scheme using linear summation:

$$p(x_f|M_1, M_2, \cdots, M_K) \propto \frac{1}{Z} \sum_{k=1}^{K} \mathcal{G}(p(x_f|M_k)) \tag{3}$$

where $\mathcal{G}(x)$ is one of three combination functions: 1) *identity* (*i.e.*, $\mathcal{G}(x) = x$), 2) $exp(x)$, and 3) $-1/log(x)$. We chose *exp* and $-1/log$ functions to avoid negative values and weigh the highly salient regions more, assuming that models are more accurate at the peaks of their saliency maps.

Evaluation Scores. Similar to [16], we calculate the precision-recall (*PR*) curve by varying a threshold on the intensity values [0:0.05:1] and generating a binary saliency map. Since MSRA dataset has bounding boxes, we first fit a rectangle to the thresholded saliency map, fill it, and then calculate scores using bounding boxes. We also report the F-Measure defined as: $F_\beta = \frac{(1+\beta^2) Precision \times Recall}{\beta^2 Precision + Recall}$.

Here, as in [16] and [13], we use $\beta^2 = 0.3$ to weigh precision more than recall. We also calculate the ROC and AUC (Area Under ROC Curve) results from *true positive rates* and *false positive rates* obtained during the calculation of PR.

4 Experiments and Results

Baseline Models. We implemented two simple yet powerful baseline models: 1) MAP explained in Sec. 3 and Fig. 2, and 2) Human Inter-observer (IO) 'model' which is the aggregated map of annotations by other subjects (excluding the one under test) for each image. The IO model provides an upper bound for other models since humans usually agree in annotating the most salient object.

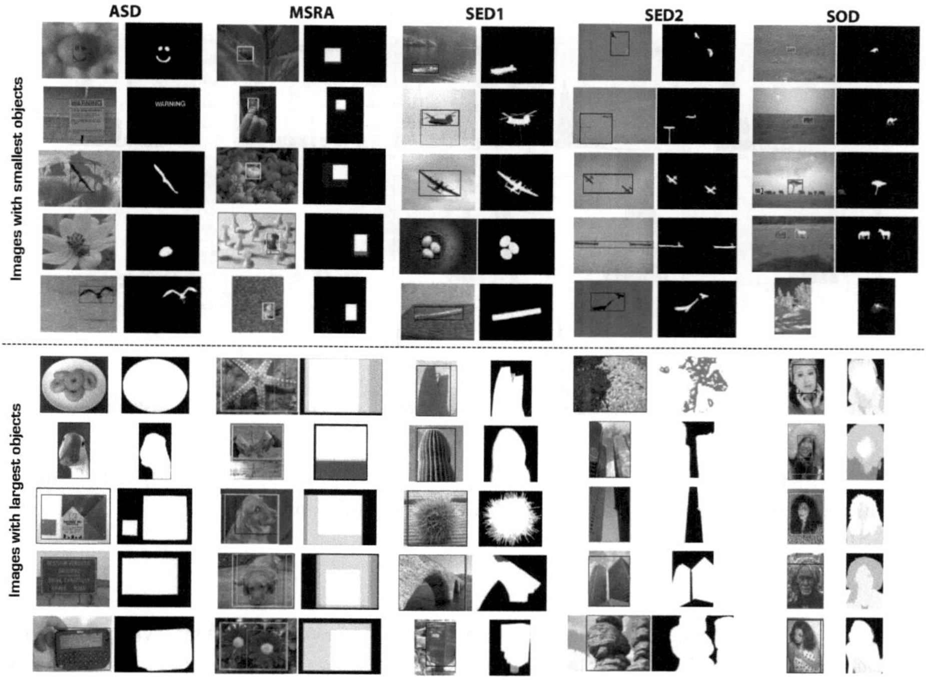

Fig. 1. Sample images from the datasets. Top row shows the five smallest objects and bottom row shows the five largest objects from each dataset. 1) **ASD** [16]: This dataset contains 1,000 images from the MSRA dataset. Authors have manually segmented the salient object (contour) within the user-drawn rectangle to obtain binary masks. Link: `http://ivrgwww.epfl.ch/$\sim$achanta/`. 2) **MSRA** [33]: This dataset (part B of the original dataset) includes 5,000 images containing labeled rectangles from nine users drawing a rectangular shape around what they consider the most salient object. There is a large variation among images including natural scenes, animals, indoor, outdoor, resolution, etc. Link: `http://research.microsoft.com/en-us/um/people/jiansun/SalientObject/salient_object.htm` . 3) **SED** [47]: This dataset contains two parts. The first one, *single object database*(**SED1**), has 100 images containing only one salient object similar to the ASD. But in the second one, *two objects database*(**SED2**), there are two salient objects in each image (100 images). Our purpose in employing this dataset is to evaluate the accuracy of models when there is more than one object in a scene is to evaluate accuracy of models over more complex stimuli. It is still not clear how the models developed over single-object datasets will scale up in more general cases. Each of one-object and two-object datasets contain 100 images. Link: `http://www.wisdom.weizmann.ac.il/$\sim$vision/Seg_Evaluation_DB`. 4) **SOD** [46]: This dataset is a collection of salient object boundaries based on the Berkeley Segmentation Dataset (BSD). Seven subjects are asked to choose the salient object(s) in 300 images. This dataset contains many images with several objects making it challenging for models. Link: `http://elderlab.yorku.ca/$\sim$vida/SOD/index.html`. Another interesting dataset called *Imgsal* contains both human fixations and tagging of objects with different sizes. Link: `http://www.cim.mcgill.ca/$\sim$lijian/database.htm`.

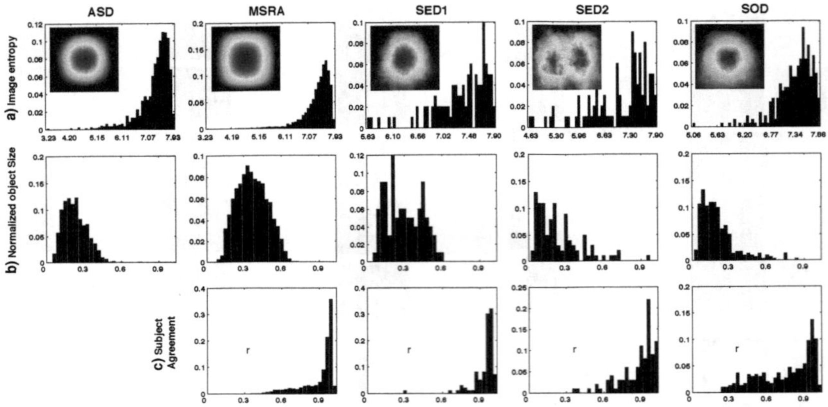

Fig. 2. a) histogram of image entropy (inset: location prior MAP), b) distribution of normalized object sizes, c) distribution of annotators agreement ($0 \leqslant r \leqslant 1$). Note that the ASD dataset has only one annotator.

Fig. 3 shows precision-recall, F-measure, ROC curves, and AUC values for all models over five datasets. Model rankings using F-measure usually do not match with the other scores (although very similar). Therefore, we focus on drawing conclusions based on ROC, AUC, and PR scores as they are more consistent.

Accuracy of Baseline Models. There is still a large gap between existing models and the IO over all datasets which indicates room for improvement. The IO model performs lower on the SOD. This also could be verified from Fig. 2 where subjects show less agreement since there is no unique salient object in many images. MAP model stands somewhere in the middle, better than some models indicating that a simple center-biased model could capture a lot of salient regions. MAP performs the lowest on the SED2 because two objects do not always happen at exact locations of the two left and right peaks of the MAP model. Random predictor, a map with the value for each pixel taken uniformly random from the range [0 1], scores 0.5 on AUC and provides a theoretical lower-bound for models. All models perform above chance level in all cases.

Model Rankings. Table 3 shows the best four models from salient object detection and fixations prediction categories over 5 datasets. Based on average rankings using AUC, SVO, Goferman, CBsal, and RC rank as the top four in order. For fixation prediction, on average the four best models are: GBVS, AIM, HouNIPS, and AWS. Among salient object detection models, SRS1, MichalGazit, Mishra, and EDS usually rank at the bottom over datasets. LC and AC models also perform poorly using AUC and PR. SalLiu is a good model in terms of AUC score and F-measure but not PR. This might be due to the binary nature of its saliency maps. Goferman is usually good using AUC but not as good using PR. Low performance of MichalGazit is probably due to its very sparse maps. MAP model does well over SOD dataset indicating existence of center-bias. Our results show that SOD is the most difficult dataset for models (they perform

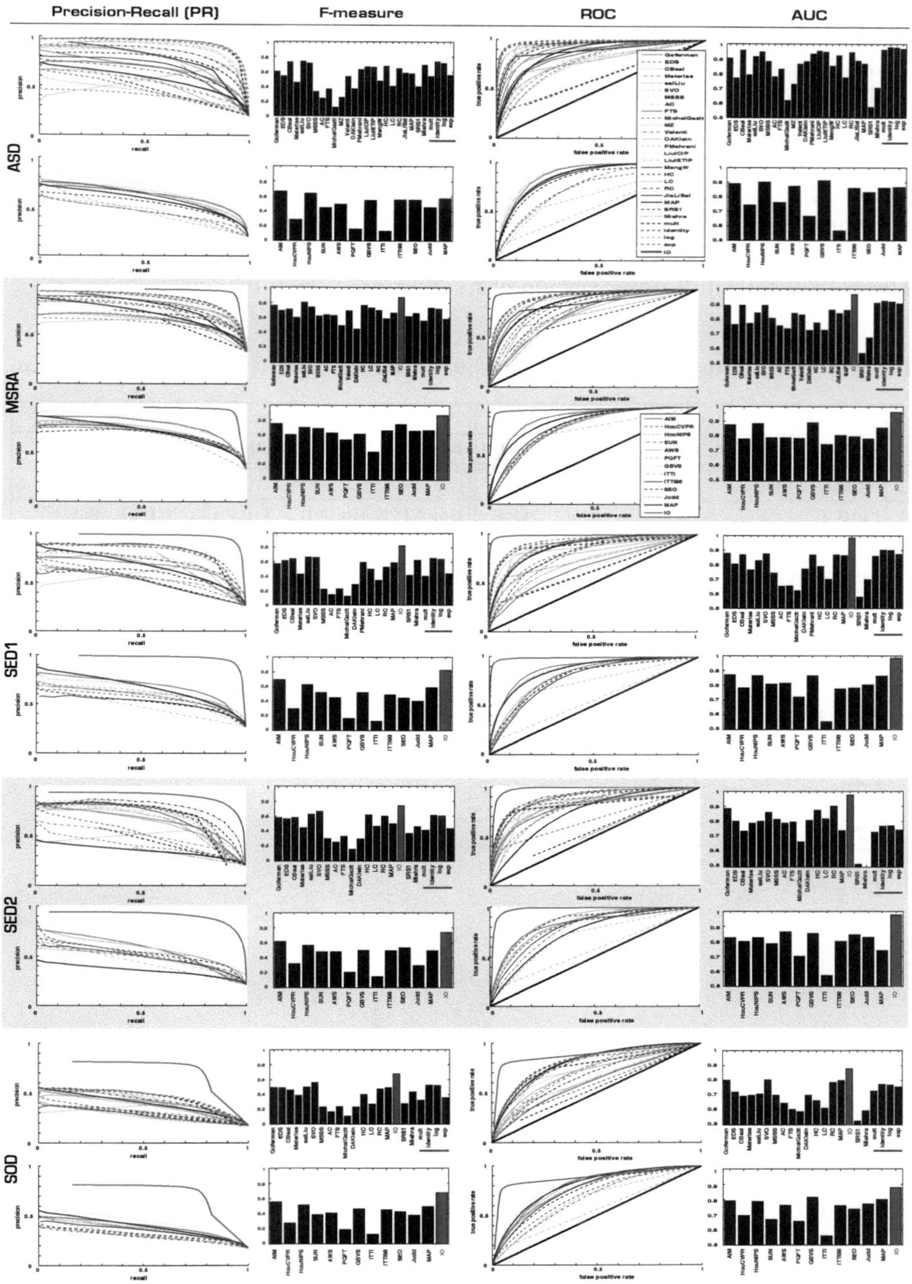

Fig. 3. PR, F-measure, ROC, and AUC scores of saliency models: Top row for each dataset shows saliency segmentation and bottom row shows fixation prediction models. *mult* indicates multiplication of models, and *identity*, *log*, *exp* indicate linear summation of identity, logarithmic, and exponential functions, respectively (see text).

poorly and score on a narrow band) while ASD and MSRA (the biggest dataset with rectangular annotations) datasets are the easiest ones.

MAP model ranks in the middle among fixation prediction models. On SOD, MAP model works very well, right below the best model, repeatedly indicating high center bias in this dataset (Fig. 2). Using F-measure AIM consistently ranks above other models. ITTI and PQFT rank at the bottom over all datasets. The ITTI98 model is based on the same principles of the ITTI model but uses *maxNorm* normalization: For each feature map, find the global max M and the average m of all other local maxima. Then, weigh the map by $(M-m)^2$. Please refer to [67] for a full investigation of fixation prediction models.

Table 3. Model rankings over categories and datasets using AUC. Gof. = Goferman.

#	Salient object detection models					Fixation prediction models				
	ASD	**MSRA**	**SED1**	**SED2**	**SOD**	**ASD**	**MSRA**	**SED1**	**SED2**	**SOD**
1	CBsal	CBsal	Gof.	RC	SVO	GBVS	GBVS	AIM	AWS	GBVS
2	LiuICIP	SVO	SVO	Gof.	Gof.	HouNIPS	HouNIPS	GBVS	GBVS	MAP
3	SVO	Gof.	CBsal	HC	MAP	AIM	AIM	MAP	SEO	AIM
4	LiuIETIP	RC	PMehrani	SVO	RC	AWS	MAP	HouNIPS	AIM	HouNIPS

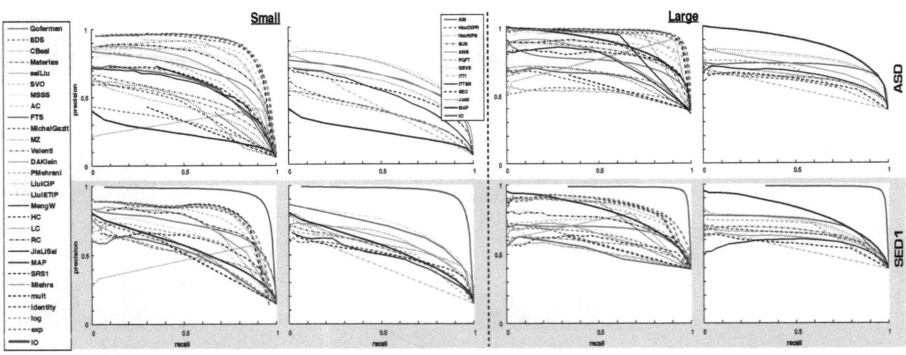

Fig. 4. Accuracy of models over small and large objects from ASD and SED1 datasets

Models built originally for fixation prediction, on average, perform lower than models specifically built to detect and segment the most salient object in a scene. Best fixation prediction models perform better than poor saliency detection models. Why does performance accuracy of the two categories of approaches differ over segmentation datasets? The reason lies on the amount of true positives vs. false positives. Segmentation approaches try to generate white salient regions to capture more of the true positives. On the other hand, fixation prediction models are very selective and generate few false positives (there are not many fixations on the image). In a separate study, we noticed that fixation prediction models perform better than the saliency detection models over eye fixation datasets (for fixation prediction) [67]. Active segmentation algorithms score consistently below the other two categories. The main reason is the dependency of these models on the initial seed which sometimes may not happen on the most salient object due to the spatial outliers in the image.

Accuracy of Combined Models. Our combined models (using CBsal, SVO, and RC) score the highest in many cases supporting our claim in evidence integration. Overall, our combined models rank the best in the following order: *identity*, *log*, *exp*, and *mult*. Over **SED2** and **SOD** datasets, combined models perform lower compared to single object datasets but still outperform many models. According precision-recall curves, our models stand on top (except SED2). This is because of CBsal model perform poorly on these datasets causing the performance to drop for combined models. Note that our selection of which models to combine was purely based on the ASD dataset and not by over-fitting results to all datasets. It is possible that combining best models over each dataset will outperform all models over that dataset. We found that the combination of the best two models (CBsal and SVO) still works as good as (slightly below) combining the three best models (supplement).

The Role of Object Size. It is more challenging to obtain high precision-recall for small objects than large objects [16][25]: an algorithm that selects the whole image obtains 80% precision with 100% recall if an object occupies 80% of the image. We compare accuracy of models over 100 images of ASD (50 for SED1) with the smallest and 100 (50 for SED1) images with the largest objects (Fig. 1 shows samples). On average, the object occupied 6.2% (15% for SED1), 38.2% (39% for SED1) of the image area, respectively for small and large objects. The resulting PR curves for ASD and SED1 datasets are shown in Fig. 4 (see supplement for other DBs). Models (specially MAP) score higher on large objects. IO scores higher on large objects thus showing higher subject agreement. Combined models still perform higher than other models in both cases (difference is more pronounced over small objects). Good models (e.g., CBsal, SVO, and LiuIETIP) still perform well with the exception of SVO that shows a noticeable performance drop over large objects. Fixation prediction model rankings differ over both cases. While GBVS is the best over small objects, HouNIPS (over ASD) and AIM (over SED1) are the best over large objects. MAP model outperforms all fixation prediction models over large objects.

The Role of Annotation Consistency. To check whether annotation consistency affects accuracy, we selected (according to Eq. 1) 100 most and 100 least consistent images (50 for SED datasets) of all datasets and calculated the scores shown in Fig. 6. As expected, IO and MAP models perform very high over most consistent images (on average for all other models). Combined models are at the top in both cases (except SED2 in the least consistent case).

Easy/Difficult Stimuli for Models. Here, we study the easiest and most difficult scenes for 11 models that did well in all cases. For each model, we sorted the stimuli based on their AUC score and chose the top (easiest) and bottom (hardest) five images (supplement). We noticed that models have many easy and difficult scenes in common (Fig. 7). The top five stimuli usually have one

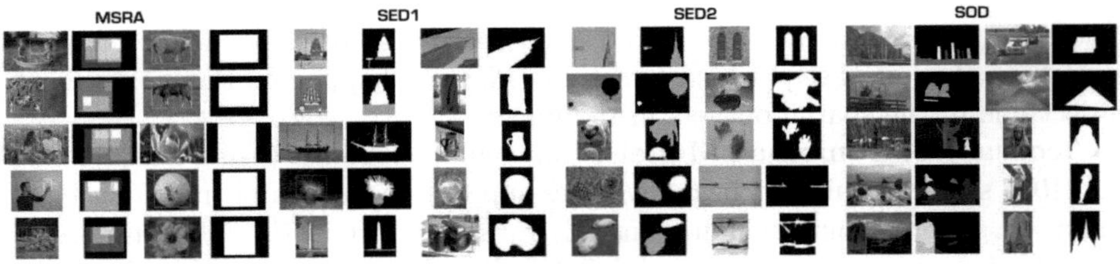

Fig. 5. Five images with least (and most) annotation consistency from datasets

vivid salient object at the center with a distinctive color from the background. The bottom five stimuli often contain objects in a textured background, objects composed of several different parts, or objects that attract top-down attention (e.g., text, faces, human, social interactions, gaze direction, or animals).

Analysis of Map Smoothing and Center-Bias. Here, we investigate the role of map smoothing (blurring) as it has been shown to affect scoring for fixation prediction in the past [10]. We convolve saliency maps of models with variable-sized Gaussian kernels and calculate the scores. We also add (separately) central Gaussian kernels to the saliency maps. AUC scores are shown in Fig. 8. With smoothing, scores slightly change but qualitative trends and model rankings stay the same, hence not affecting our conclusions. The reason why smoothing changes fixation prediction but not salient object detection accuracy is because: 1) there is uncertainty in fixations such that they often do not land on the exact intended locations, and 2) in salient object detection, scores are calculated using image regions while in fixation prediction, they are calculated by sampling maps from eye positions. Shown in Fig. 2, all datasets have center-bias similar to the eye movement datasets ([67][11]). From Fig. 8 (right side), we conclude that adding center-bias raises the accuracy of low-performing models while it decreases the accuracy of good models. However, this change in accuracy is not significant and does not alter model rankings.

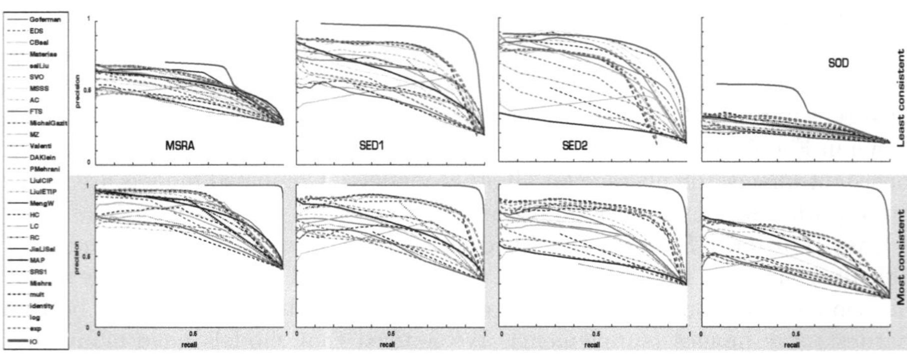

Fig. 6. Accuracy of saliency detection models over least and most consistent images

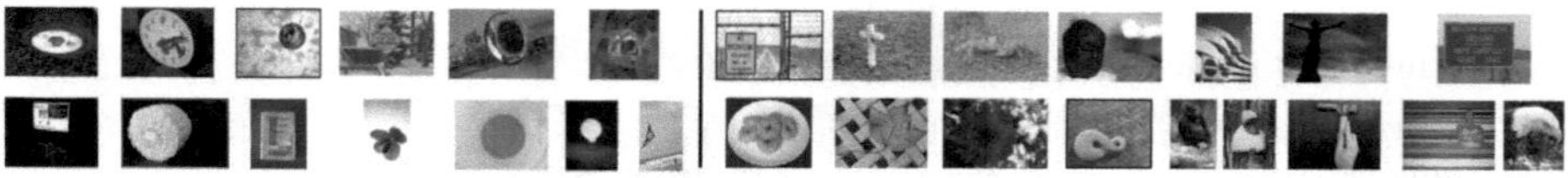

Fig. 7. Left) Easiest stimuli for 11 best models (Fig. 3), Right) Most difficult stimuli

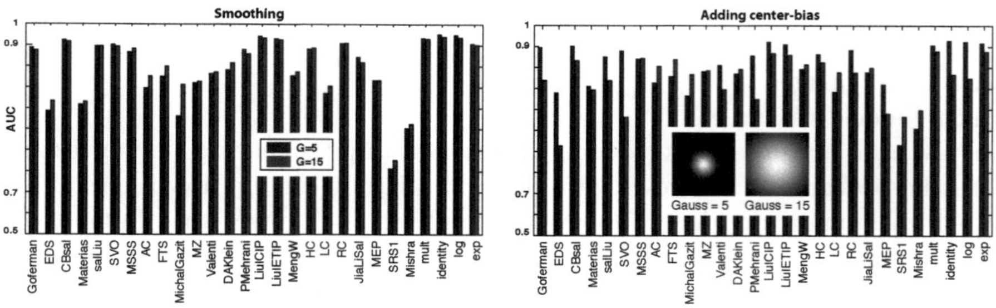

Fig. 8. Left: scores of models for maps smoothed with 2 Gaussian kernel sizes over ASD dataset. Right: model accuracy by adding Gaussian center-bias to center of a map.

Analysis of Model Similarity. Following Judd [64], here we measure the similarity among salient object detection models. We build a similarity matrix Q with the element ij measured as follows. For each image of a dataset, calculate the correlation coefficients (CC) of saliency maps between models i and j. Then the q_{ij} will be the average of all CCs over all images. Over the ASD dataset, (HC, RC), (LiuICIP, LiuIETIP), (MSSS, FTS), (SVO, Goferman, Valenti, AWS), (HouNIPS, AIM, GBVS) are the most similar ones to each other. We calculate dissimilarity as 1 minus similarity (thus ranging between [-1 0]), and use multi-dimensional scaling (MDS) analysis to represent models in a 2D space (Fig. 9 for ASD). AC, MZ, ITTI, and SRS1 models are most different from the others (see supplement).

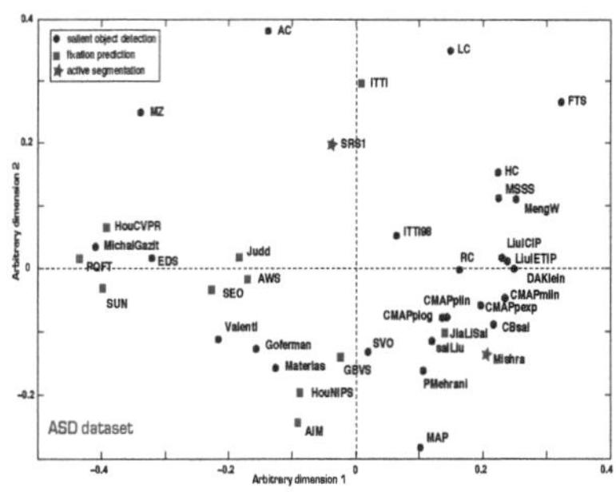

Fig. 9. Measuring model similarities

Analysis of Human-Model Agreement. Finally, over the MSRA dataset, we plot in Fig. 10 human vs. model agreement (5 best models including: CBsal, SVO, LiuICIP, LiuIETIP, and Goferman) for each image. Aligning with Fig. 2, most of the subjects show annotation consistency while models are less consistent. We inspect cases of agreement/disagreement between and within humans and models: 1) Images that both humans and models agree, usually have one clear object with different features from the background rendering them bottom-up salient. 2) Images that humans and models disagree (within the same group), usually are not easy to define the most salient object. Salient objects have several parts in a crowded background. The most interesting case is when humans (within) disagree with models agree (and vice versa). 3) Images for which models disagree usually have textured backgrounds with salient objects sharing similar features with the background. However, this does not disrupt the top-down mechanisms by which humans decide the most salient object. 4) Images that humans disagree but models agree, usually contain salient objects with multiple parts and different features from the background. This makes detecting the salient object with several parts easy for models but difficult for humans. Overall, there are not many cases for which humans disagree.

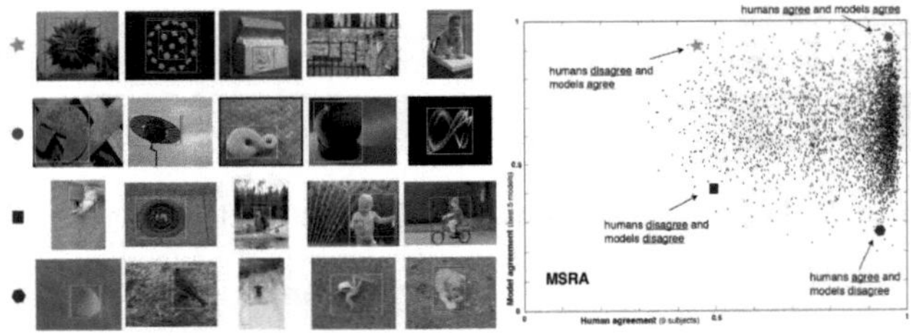

Fig. 10. Analysis of human model agreement over MSRA dataset

5 Conclusions

Based on the extensive experiments over 5 datasets, we conclude that SVO [27], Goferman [15], CBsal [31], RC [13], and Liu *et al.* [53][52] (LiuICIP and LiuIETIP) work better than the others overall. Salient object detection models (Table 1) perform better than fixation prediction models (Table 2). Map smoothing is not a big challenge to scoring as opposed to the fixation prediction. SOD has 300 images and is the hardest dataset for models which encourages further effort in the future. Many models share the easiest and the most difficult stimuli. Although model rankings remain the same over small and large objects, model accuracy is higher over large objects. Further, models work better on the most consistent images. Scenes containing objects in textured and cluttered backgrounds are challenging for many models. There are cases where the level of agreement on salient object is low among humans but high for the models. Analysis of model similarity shows that some models use different saliency detection mechanisms. Focusing on these models may inspire further development.

We showed that a simple integration scheme generalizes well across datasets. It suggests using more sophisticated combination techniques (e.g., by selecting and combining different models) which may enhance accuracies. While most of the models try to correctly segment the object regions, only recently researchers (e.g., [46]) have started to account for image boundary. Contemporary saliency detection datasets suffer from the drawback that they contain images with few (oftentimes one) close-up objects. Future work should investigate collecting datasets with more variety including cluttered scenes with multiple objects. Majority of existing models are only applicable to static images. Further research is needed to scale up current models or build new models in the spatio-temporal domain. Models have different implementation languages (C++, Matlab) which makes analysis of computational complexity challenging. While previous progress is promising, further work is needed to bridge the existing gap among current models and human performance. To ease this process and initiate a collaborative effort, we share our results, data, and software in our website.

References

1. Judd, T., Ehinger, K., Durand, F.: Learning to predict where humans look. In: ICCV (2009)
2. Itti, L., Koch, C., Niebur, E.: A model of saliency-based visual attention for rapid scene analysis. IEEE Trans. PAMI 20(11), 1254–1259 (1998)
3. Harel, J., Koch, C., Perona, P.: Graph-based visual saliency. In: NIPS (2006)
4. Bruce, N.D.B., Tsotsos, J.K.: Saliency based on information maximization. In: NIPS (2005)
5. Hou, X., Zhang, L.: Saliency detection: A spectral residual approach. In: CVPR (2007)
6. Hou, X., Zhang, L.: Dynamic attention: Searching for coding length increments. In: NIPS (2008)
7. Garcia-Diaz, A., Fdez-Vidal, X.R., Pardo, X.M., Dosil, R.: Decorrelation and Distinctiveness Provide with Human-Like Saliency. In: Blanc-Talon, J., Philips, W., Popescu, D., Scheunders, P. (eds.) ACIVS 2009. LNCS, vol. 5807, pp. 343–354. Springer, Heidelberg (2009)
8. Seo, H.J., Milanfar, P.: Static and space-time visual saliency detection by self-resemblance. Journal of Vision 9, 1–27 (2009)
9. Walther, D., Koch, C.: Modeling attention to salient proto-objects. Neural Net. (2006)
10. Zhang, L., Tong, M.H., Marks, T.K., Shan, H., Cottrell, G.W.: SUN: A Bayesian framework for saliency using natural statistics. JOV (2008)
11. Tatler, B.W.: The central fixation bias in scene viewing: selecting an optimal viewing position independently of motor bases and image feature distributions. J. Vision 14(7) (2007)
12. Zhai, Y., Shah, M.: Visual attention detection in video sequences using spatiotemporal cues. ACM Multimedia (2006)
13. Cheng, M.M., Zhang, G.X., Mitra, N.J., Huang, X., Hu, S.M.: Global contrast based salient region detection. In: CVPR (2011)
14. Achanta, R., Estrada, F.J., Wils, P., Süsstrunk, S.: Salient Region Detection and Segmentation. In: Gasteratos, A., Vincze, M., Tsotsos, J.K. (eds.) ICVS 2008. LNCS, vol. 5008, pp. 66–75. Springer, Heidelberg (2008)
15. Goferman, S., Zelnik-Manor, L., Tal, A.: Context-aware saliency detection. In: CVPR (2010)
16. Achanta, R., Hemami, S., Estrada, F., Süsstrunk, S.: Frequency-tuned salient region detection. In: CVPR (2009)
17. Wang, J., Sun, J., Quan, L., Tang, X., Shum, H.Y.: Picture collage. In: CVPR (2006)
18. Wang, M., Konrad, J., Ishwar, P., Jing, Y., Rowley, H.: Image saliency: from intrinsic to extrinsic context. In: CVPR (2011)
19. Rosin, P.L.: A simple method for detecting salient regions. Pattern Rec. (2009)

20. Goferman, S., Tal, A., Zelnik-Manor, L.: Puzzle-like collage. In: EuroGraphics (2010)
21. Zhang, W., Wu, Q.M.J., Wang, G., Yin, H.: An adaptive computational model for salient object detection. IEEE Trans. on Multimedia 12(4) (2010)
22. Feng, J., Wei, Y., Tao, L., Zhang, C., Sun, J.: Salient object detection by composition. In: ICCV (2011)
23. Mehrani, P., Veksler, O.: Saliency segmentation based on learning and graph cut. In: BMVC (2010)
24. Lu, Y., Zhang, W., Lu, H., Xue, X.: Salient object detection using concavity context. In: ICCV (2011)
25. Klein, D.A., Frintrop, S.: Center-surround divergence of feature statistics for salient object detection. In: ICCV (2011)
26. Wang, L., Xue, J., Zheng, N., Hua, G.: Automatic Salient object extraction with contextual cue. In: ICCV (2011)
27. Chang, K.Y., Liu, T.L., Chen, H.T., Lai, S.H.: Fusing generic objectness and visual saliency for salient object detection. In: ICCV (2011)
28. Khuwuthyakorn, P., Robles-Kelly, A., Zhou, J.: Object of Interest Detection by Saliency Learning. In: Daniilidis, K., Maragos, P., Paragios, N. (eds.) ECCV 2010, Part II. LNCS, vol. 6312, pp. 636–649. Springer, Heidelberg (2010)
29. Rahtu, E., Kannala, J., Salo, M., Heikkilä, J.: Segmenting Salient Objects from Images and Videos. In: Daniilidis, K., Maragos, P., Paragios, N. (eds.) ECCV 2010, Part V. LNCS, vol. 6315, pp. 366–379. Springer, Heidelberg (2010)
30. Kanan, C., Cottrell, G.: Robust classification of objects, faces, and flowers using natural image. In: CVPR (2010)
31. Jiang, H., Wang, J., Yuan, Z., Liu, T., Zheng, N., Li, S.: Automatic salient object segmentation based on context and shape prior. In: BMVC (2011)
32. Li, J., Tian, Y., Huang, T., Gao, W.: A dataset and evaluation methodology for visual saliency in video. In: Int. Conf. on Multimedia and Expo., pp. 442–445 (2009)
33. Liu, T., Sun, J., Zheng, N., Tang, X., Shum, H.: Learning to detect a salient object. In: CVPR (2007)
34. Gopalakrishnan, V., Hu, Y., Rajan, D.: Random walks on graphs to model saliency in images. In: CVPR (2009)
35. Marchesotti, L., Cifarelli, C., Csurka, G.: A framework for visual saliency detection with applications to image thumbnailing. In: ICCV (2009)
36. Li, J., Levine, M.D., An, X., He, H.: Saliency detection based on frequency and spatial domain analysis. In: BMVC (2011)
37. Holtzman-Gazit, M., Zelnik-Manor, L., Yavneh, I.: Salient edges: A multi scale approach. In: ECCV, Workshop on Vision for Cognitive Tasks (2010)
38. Luo, Y., Yuan, J., Xue, P., Tian, Q.: Saliency Density Maximization for Object Detection and Localization. In: Kimmel, R., Klette, R., Sugimoto, A. (eds.) ACCV 2010, Part III. LNCS, vol. 6494, pp. 396–408. Springer, Heidelberg (2011)
39. Deng, Q., Luo, Y.: Edge-based method for detecting salient objects. Opt. Eng. 50 (2011)
40. Valenti, R., Sebe, N., Gevers, T.: Image saliency by isocentric curvedness and color. In: ICCV (2009)
41. Zhang, Q., Liu, H., Shen, J., Gu, G., Xiao, H.: An improved computational approach for salient region detection. Journal of Computers (2010)
42. Li, H., Ngan, K.N.: A co-saliency model of image pairs. IEEE Trans. Image Process (2011)
43. Ge, F., Wang, S.: New benchmark for image segmentation evaluation. Journal of Electronic Imaging 16(3) (2007)

44. Estrada, F.J., Jepson, A.D.: Benchmarking image segmentation algorithms. IJCV (2009)
45. Ancuti, C.O., Ancuti, C., Bekaert, P.: CVPR (2011)
46. Movahedi, V., Elder, J.H.: Design and perceptual validation of performance measures for salient object segmentation. In: POCV (2010)
47. Alpert, S., Galun, M., Basri, R., Brandt, A.: Image segmentation by probabilistic bottom-up aggregation and cue integration. In: CVPR (2007)
48. Ge, F., Wang, S., Liu, T.: Image-segmentation evaluation from the perspective of salient object extraction. In: CVPR (2006)
49. Mishra, A.K., Aloimonos, Y., Fah, C.L., Kassim, A.: Active visual segmentation. IEEE Trans. PAMI (2011)
50. Siagian, C., Koch, C.: Salient segmentation using contours and region growing (submitted)
51. Ma, Y.F., Zhang, H.J.: Contrast-based image attention analysis by using fuzzy growing. ACM Multimedia, 374–381 (2003)
52. Liu, Z., Xue, Y., Yan, H., Zhang, Z.: Efficient saliency detection based on Gaussian models. IET Image Processing 5(2), 122–131 (2011)
53. Liu, Z., Xue, Y., Shen, L., Zhang, Z.: Nonparametric saliency detection using kernel density estimation. In: ICIP, pp. 253–256 (2010)
54. Li, J., Tian, Y., Huang, T., Gao, W.: Probabilistic multi-task learning for visual saliency estimation in video. IJCV 90(2), 150–165 (2010)
55. Achanta, R., Susstrunk, S.: Saliency detection for content-aware image resizing. In: ICIP (2009)
56. Guo, C., Zhang, L.: A novel multiresolution spatiotemporal saliency detection model and Its applications in image and video compression. IEEE Trans. on Image Processing (2010)
57. Huang, T.H., Cheng, K.Y., Chuang, Y.Y.: A collaborative benchmark for region of interest detection algorithms. In: CVPR (2009)
58. Masciocchi, C.M., Mihalas, S., Parkhurst, D., Niebur, E.: Everyone knows what is interesting: salient locations which should be fixated. Journal of Vision (2009)
59. Itti, L.: Automatic Foveation for Video Compression using a neurobiological model of visual attention. IEEE Trans. Image Process (2004)
60. Ma, Y., Hua, X., Lu, L., Zhang, H.: A generic framework of user aattention model and its application in video summarization. IEEE Trans. Multimedia (2005)
61. Borji, A., Itti, L.: State-of-the-art in visual attention modeling. IEEE Trans. Pattern Anal. Mach. Intell (2012)
62. Gao, D., Vasconcelos, N.: Discriminant saliency for visual recognition from cluttered scenes. In: NIPS (2004)
63. Kienzle, W., Franz, M.O., Schölkopf, B., Wichmann, F.A.: Center-surround patterns emerge as optimal predictors for human saccade targets. J. Vision (2009)
64. Judd, T.: Understanding and predicting where people look. Phd Thesis, MIT (2011)
65. Itti, L., Dhavale, N., Pighin, F.: SPIE (2003)
66. Koehler, K., Guo, F., Zhang, S., Eckstein, M.: Vision Science Society (2011)
67. Borji, A., Sihite, D.N., Itti, L.: Quantitative analysis of human-model agreement in visual saliency modeling: a comparative study. IEEE Trans. Image Processing (2012)

Automatic Segmentation of Unknown Objects, with Application to Baggage Security

Leo Grady[1], Vivek Singh[2], Timo Kohlberger[2], Christopher Alvino[3], and Claus Bahlmann[2]

[1] HeartFlow, Inc., Redwood City, CA, USA
[2] Imaging and Computer Vision, Siemens Corporation, Corporate Research and Technology, Princeton, NJ, USA
[3] American Science and Engineering, Billerica, MA, USA

Abstract. Computed tomography (CT) is used widely to image patients for medical diagnosis and to scan baggage for threatening materials. Automated reading of these images can be used to reduce the costs of a human operator, extract quantitative information from the images or support the judgements of a human operator. Object quantification requires an image segmentation to make measurements about object size, material composition and morphology. Medical applications mostly require the segmentation of prespecified objects, such as specific organs or lesions, which allows the use of customized algorithms that take advantage of training data to provide orientation and anatomical context of the segmentation targets. In contrast, baggage screening requires the segmentation algorithm to provide segmentation of an unspecified number of objects with enormous variability in size, shape, appearance and spatial context. Furthermore, security systems demand 3D segmentation algorithms that can quickly and reliably detect threats. To address this problem, we present a segmentation algorithm for 3D CT images that makes no assumptions on the number of objects in the image or on the composition of these objects. The algorithm features a new Automatic QUality Measure (AQUA) model that measures the segmentation confidence for any single object (from any segmentation method) and uses this confidence measure to both control splitting and to optimize the segmentation parameters at runtime for each dataset. The algorithm is tested on 27 bags that were packed with a large variety of different objects.

1 Introduction

Image segmentation is a core problem in computer vision that can be used to assess material and morphological properties of the objects being imaged. Classically, the unsupervised image segmentation problem has been posed as the localization of contiguous regions in an image that satisfy some measure of appearance homogeneity and/or some shape regularity. Classical methods to perform unsupervised image segmentation include watershed [1], mean shift [2] and normalized cuts [3]. More recent work has focused on addressing the homogeneity of complex appearances (e.g., textures) and operation across scales (e.g., [4]).

A. Fitzgibbon et al. (Eds.): ECCV 2012, Part II, LNCS 7573, pp. 430–444, 2012.

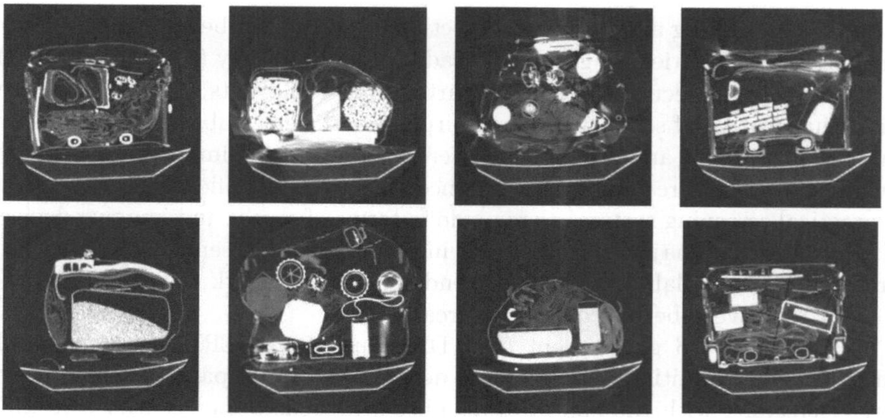

Fig. 1. A sample of 2D cross-sectional images in our 3D baggage screening dataset. Each bag contained objects with a large variety in size, shape, homogeneity and luggage exterior.

The established methods have proven effective for the creation of "superpixels" that can be used to drive further analysis by calculating and comparing localized region properties in the image (e.g., [5]). However, when considered from the standpoint of object segmentation (e.g., one segment label per object) these established methods tend to create oversegmentations that split each object into many pieces, requiring a further local merging step to reassemble the objects. This merging step is challenging to perform since the merging criterion is usually described at a global scale (e.g., to look like an "object") but the merging choices are made at a local level of assembling two adjacent superpixels. Furthermore, the results of the merging process is highly dependent on the order in which potential merges are evaluated.

To overcome these problems of the classical approach to unsupervised object segmentation, we propose a new algorithm consisting of three main steps:

1. Identification of all "object" voxels (as opposed to"background" voxels).
2. Creation of candidate splits into individual objects based on a partitioning method with global criteria.
3. Evaluation of these candidate splits using a novel Automatic QUality Assessment (AQUA) module that is trained on a wide variety of objects to recognize "good" objects in the candidate splits. Note that the AQUA module proposed here is different from the work in [6,7] which apply strictly to 2D images only and depend on having color/texture information available.

To validate the proposed approach we chose the application of security screening, more specifically the segmentation of objects in 3D CT scans of luggage. The role of security screening systems is to inspect checked and hand baggage, cargo and containers for dangerous content, such as, explosives, improvised explosive devices (IEDs), firearms, contraband, drugs, etc. These screening systems play a key role in the US Homeland Defense/Security strategy for increased safety of airports, air and sea traffic.

Security screening and explosive detection systems have been studied for several decades by a variety of groups in academia and industry (see [8] for review). A new decade for security screening started after the events of Sept. 11th, creating an elevation of security levels at airports and other hubs of mobility. Government investment and commercial interest increased the importance of highly sensitive security screening systems. Since that time, significant improvements to practical screening systems were made in terms of sensor and imaging devices [9]. However, the majority of research in the security screening area was performed in national labs and scanner vendors, and this work was kept classified in order to prevent better concealed threats.

Recently, the US government (i.e., DHS and the ALERT center of excellence[1]) began an initiative to promote academic and 3rd party research in security screening with the aim of developing next generation security screening systems. These efforts were accompanied by a series of workshops, where the latest (unclassified) state-of-the-art in security screening has been published [10]. The work described in this paper is a response to the ALERT initiative, which established the infrastructure and released appropriate security screening data to the unclassified domain.

Today's systems for CT based explosive detection [11] involve the following steps: First, during automatic screening, CT scan data is obtained and volumetric data is reconstructed, providing pseudocolor volumes that encode the main material properties such as density or, in case of dual energy scans, the effective atomic number Z_{eff}. Then, contiguous objects are segmented and physical properties such as density, Z_{eff} and volume are computed. If the combination of density, mass, and Z_{eff} are considered critical, suspicious regions are flagged and scheduled for operator inspection. The wide range of objects, sizes and appearances that can appear in baggage screening is illustrated in Figure 1. Our method for volumetric CT object segmentation is motivated by this application due to the difficulty of the problem but our algorithm could be applied to any unsupervised CT object segmentation problem.

2 Method

3D segmentation of CT images is challenging due to the unknown number of objects, variety of object sizes/shapes, objects consisting of multiple distinct parts, inhomogeneous internal density distribution (appearance) of some objects and the presence of artifacts. Segmentation in the context of baggage screening is particularly challenging due to the fact that metal is common (causing strong streaking artifacts) and the objects are packed tightly.

Each of the challenges listed above is addressed in our algorithm. To correct artifacts and identify "object" voxels, we utilize a Mumford-Shah algorithm to reduce noise. Separation of touching objects is performed using a global splitting algorithm (the isoperimetric algorithm [12,13]). Finally, we develop our

[1] `http://www.northeastern.edu/alert/`

Automatic QUality Assessment (AQUA) system to learn "good" object segments based on a large training database.

Our algorithm consists of three steps: 1) Identification of "object" voxels, 2) Generating candidate splits using a global partitioning criterion, 3) Evaluation of the candidate splits for good "objectness" using our novel AQUA method. These steps will now be described in detail.

2.1 Identification of Object Voxels

In the context of security screening with CT, objects of interest are ideally identified as consisting of voxels above a certain threshold. However, the identification of "object" voxels in this application is not quite so simple since artifacts and noise can disrupt CT imagery by creating false separations within objects or by merging nearby objects. These disruptions can be ameliorated by reducing artifacts and image denoising. In our application we do both by first applying the metal artifact reduction of Tuy [14] and then applying a version of the Mumford-Shah algorithm to perform denoising. The Mumford-Shah functional [15,16,17] is a core model in computer vision, for which variants can be used for image denoising, image segmentation and many other problems. We take advantage of the speed and robustness of recent advances in combinatorial optimization by applying the Mumford-Shah algorithm described in [18] to the artifact-reduced image in order to quickly identify all "object" voxels. Since this optimization is nonconvex it requires an initialization, which we provided in our application using the idealized target threshold for an object of interest (-500HU).

Following the artifact reduction and application of the Mumford-Shah technique in [18], each voxel in the image is labeled as either "object" or "background". We now describe how the "object" voxels can be split into candidate objects for evaluation with the AQUA.

2.2 Object Splitting with the Isoperimetric Algorithm

The output of the previous stage is to label each voxel as object or background. If each object in the image were spatially isolated, then it would be possible to simply return each connected component as a different object and conclude the segmentation. Unfortunately, real images often contain objects which are significantly touching each other. The problem of touching objects is particularly acute in the baggage screening application in which objects are deliberately packed tightly to conserve space. Consequently, it is necessary to adopt an algorithm that can be used to split touching objects by using a global criterion.

One global algorithm, the isoperimetric algorithm [12,13], was adapted to operate in linear time by operating on a *subgraph* (the *distance tree*) of the lattice graph representing a connected component [19]. The isoperimetric method searches for a split within a component, $\mathcal{M} \subseteq \mathcal{V}$ for the set of voxels $\mathcal{V}$ that minimizes

$$E(\mathcal{S}, \bar{\mathcal{S}}) = \frac{\text{cut}(\mathcal{S}, \bar{\mathcal{S}})}{\min(\text{Volume}(\mathcal{S}), \text{Volume}(\bar{\mathcal{S}}))}, \tag{1}$$

where $\mathcal{S} \subset \mathcal{M}$ and $\bar{\mathcal{S}} = \mathcal{M} - \mathcal{S}$. Due to the low overhead in speed and memory, we applied this isoperimetric distance tree algorithm [19] to find object separations in each connected component of the objects. This algorithm was applied recursively on each connected component until it was unable to find a high quality separation (or the component was too small) at which point the algorithm terminated. Taking advantage of the speed of the isoperimetric distance tree method, we ran it several times to produce candidate splits by using randomly chosen reference nodes in the connected component (see [19]). These splits were evaluated and the best split was chosen to continue the recursion if the split produced objects that were considered to have sufficiently high quality. The accurate assessment of a "high quality" object is key to the successful termination of this method and the avoidance of over- or under-segmentations. Our novel approach to this problem is detailed in the next section.

2.3 Automated QUality Assessment

We developed a novel confidence measure to automatically compute the quality of an image segmentation without *a priori* knowledge of the object being segmented. Such an **Automated QUality Assessment (AQUA)** is of great significance to the image segmentation problem, since it can be used to compare different segmentations and autonomously select the best one. Furthermore, such a measure can be used within a segmentation algorithm to iteratively improve the overall segmentation. An AQUA can also be used to flag the user of an automatic segmentation algorithm that the solution needs to be visually examined and fixed before the segmentation results should be used.

To obtain the confidence measure, we identified 92 good object segments (both ground truth and algorithm-generated) and employed a data-driven approach for model learning. A key challenge is to design or select appropriate features to allow us to learn which segments are "high quality". We determined these features by considering a set of features inspired by the literature on global methods for object segmentation. Effectively, we took each objective function as a feature and applied machine learning to create a model of "high quality".

Features. The main motivation behind the choice of our 42 features was to use a variety of segmentation metrics as indicators about whether a segmentation is correct. The purpose of this variety was to remain agnostic about which feature choices worked well for the final classifier in any given situation. The features we used can be broken down into major categories: (weighted or unweighted) geometric features, intensity features, gradient features, and ratio features.

Before beginning our exposition of the features, note that all weights in these descriptions refer to the Cauchy distribution function applied to the appropriate image intensities differences, i.e.,

$$w(i,j) = \frac{1}{1+\beta\left(\frac{I_i - I_j}{\rho}\right)^2}, \tag{2}$$

where I_i and I_j are image intensities of neighboring voxels, where I_i and I_j are image intensities of neighboring voxels, v_i and v_j, β, which was set to 10^4 for all feature computations, is intended to control the sensitivity of the weight to intensity difference, and $\rho = \max_{(x,y)\in\mathcal{M}} \|\nabla I(x,y)\|_1$ was the maximum L1 norm of all intensity gradients within the segmentation mask, $\mathcal{M} \subseteq \mathcal{V}$. The purpose of ρ is to normalize the weights. Similarly, we define $w_-(I_i, I_j) = 1$ when $I_i > I_j$ and $w_-(I_i, I_j) = w(I_i, I_j)$ otherwise.

We used geometric features to capture some measure of size and regularity of the segmentation mask $\mathcal{M} \subset \mathcal{V}$, a concept dating back to some of the earliest works on image segmentation [20,15,21]. Of these, we chose:

$$\text{Volume}(\mathcal{M}) = |\mathcal{M}|, \quad \text{Surface Area}(\mathcal{M}) = \sum_{i,j:v_i\in\mathcal{M},v_j\in\bar{\mathcal{M}}} 1,$$

$$\text{Total Curvature}(\mathcal{M}) = \sum_{i,j:v_i\in\mathcal{M},v_j\in\bar{\mathcal{M}}} H(i,j),$$

where $H(i,j)$ is the discretely computed mean curvature on the surface of $\mathcal{M}$, which was locally computed as in [22].

Weighted geometric features are similar to the geometric features, but the geometric measures are locally emphasized when intensity values were similar to each other and suppressed when dissimilar. This concept that has been pervasive in image segmentation since the work of Caselles *et al.* [23] and has been seen in many other recent works [3,24,25]. The weighted geometric features we used were

$$\text{Weighted Volume}(\mathcal{M}) = \sum_{i,j:v_i\in\mathcal{M},v_j\in\mathcal{M}} w(i,j), \tag{3}$$

$$\text{Weighted Cut}(\mathcal{M}) = \sum_{i,j:v_i\in\mathcal{M},v_j\in\bar{\mathcal{M}}} w(i,j), \tag{4}$$

$$\text{Total Weighted Curvature}(\mathcal{M}) = \sum_{i,j:v_i\in\mathcal{M},v_j\in\bar{\mathcal{M}}} w(i,j)H(i,j), \tag{5}$$

$$\text{Low-High Weighted Cut}(\mathcal{M}) = \sum_{i,j:i\in\mathcal{M},j\in\bar{\mathcal{M}}} w_+(I_i, I_j), \tag{6}$$

$$\text{High-Low Weighted Cut}(\mathcal{M}) = \sum_{i,j:i\in\mathcal{M},j\in\bar{\mathcal{M}}} w_-(I_i, I_j). \tag{7}$$

Our intensity features employed various measures of the direct image intensities. These features were either intended to measure absolute intensity or intensity spread. Without exception, only intensities inside the segmentation mask $\mathcal{M}$ were included. Of these, we chose Mean Intensity($\mathcal{M}$)= $\frac{1}{|\mathcal{M}|}\sum_{v_i\in\mathcal{M}} I_i$; Median Intensity($\mathcal{M}$)= median($\{I_i : v_i \in \mathcal{M}\}$); Total Intensity($\mathcal{M}$)= $\sum_{v_i\in\mathcal{M}} I_i$; Minimum Intensity($\mathcal{M}$)= $\min_{v_i\in\mathcal{M}} I_i$; Maximum Intensity($\mathcal{M}$)= $\max_{v_i\in\mathcal{M}} I_i$; and Standard Deviation ($\mathcal{M}$)= $\frac{1}{|\mathcal{M}|-1}\sum_{v_i\in\mathcal{M}} (I_i - \text{Mean Intensity}(\mathcal{M}))^2$; Interquartile Distance, defined as half of the difference between the 75th percentile and the 25th percentile values of intensities;

Gradient features used various measures of the intensity gradients (local intensity changes). All intensity derivatives comprising these gradients were computed via central differences. Of these, we chose: Total L1 Gradient Norm($\mathcal{M}$)= $\sum_{v_i \in \mathcal{M}} \|\nabla I(v_i)\|_1$; Total L2 Gradient Norm($\mathcal{M}$)= $\sum_{v_i \in \mathcal{M}} \|\nabla I(v_i)\|_2$; Mean L1 Gradient Norm($\mathcal{M}$)= $\frac{1}{|\mathcal{M}|} \sum_{v_i \in \mathcal{M}} \|\nabla I(v_i)\|_1$; Mean L2 Gradient Norm($\mathcal{M}$) = $\frac{1}{|\mathcal{M}|} \sum_{v_i \in \mathcal{M}} \|\nabla I(v_i)\|_2$; Median L2 Gradient Norm($\mathcal{M}$) = median($\{\|\nabla I(v_i)\|_1 : v_i \in \mathcal{M}\}$); Min L1 Gradient Norm($\mathcal{M}$)= $\min_{v_i \in \mathcal{M}} \|\nabla I(v_i)\|_1$; Max L1 Gradient Norm($\mathcal{M}$)= $\max_{v_i \in \mathcal{M}} \|\nabla I(v_i)\|_1$; L1 Norm Interquartile Distance($\mathcal{M}$); L1 Norm Standard Deviation($\mathcal{M}$); and L2 Norm Standard Deviation($\mathcal{M}$).

We opted to explicitly include a selection of features that were ratios of our other features. The intent was not to be completely comprehensive, but rather to use domain knowledge of segmentation problems to explicitly choose combinations that the literature and our experience told us would be good indicators of segmentation performance. The ratio features were simply the ratio of two features above. Several fall into the category of cut divided by volume, a concept that has appeared in various forms [3,13,12]. Of these, we chose: *all four weighted and unweighted combinations of cut divided by volume*; *all four combinations of low-high weighted cut or high-low weighted cut divided by unweighted or weighted volume*; *weighted cut divided by unweighted cut*; *all four combinations of low-high weighted cut or high-low weighted cut divided by unweighted or weighted cut*; *blur index* defined as *sum the L2 norms of the gradients* divided by *sum of the L1 norms of the gradients*; *normalized cut* as defined in [3]; *curvature over unweighted cut*; and *weighted curvature over unweighted cut.*

We note that some of the features, such as the geometric features and most of the intensity-based features, were not meant to be discriminative alone. Rather, they were intended to lend context about the expected values for some of the other more discriminative features for a given candidate segmentation. All features mentioned above are both translation and rotation invariant.

Model Learning. We used a data-driven approach to model learning by annotating a number of "high quality" object segments and fitting a generative model over these segments in the feature space. A generative model for "high quality" segments was chosen over a discriminative model due to our expectation that the variability in feature space of "low quality" segmentations is much higher than the variability for "high quality" segmentations. Specifically we used a Gaussian mixture model (GMM) to approximate the distribution of the good segments in the feature space which we fit via Expectation Maximization. Prior to fitting the GMM model, we normalized each feature by subtracting the mean (over all segments) and dividing by the standard deviation.

We used Principal Component Analysis (PCA) to reduce the dimensionality of the data. This step is essential since the number of features is large compared to the size of the training set. Consequently, the distribution of the "high quality" object segments in the training set may be too sparse in the original feature space. Furthermore, the features are likely to be highly correlated and therefore redundant. The number of PCA dimensions was chosen based on the performance on a validation set. We fit the GMM model (using eight Gaussians) over the PCA coefficients of all the segments in the training set using the EM algorithm.

We define the AQUA of an object segment $\mathcal{S} \subseteq \mathcal{V}$ as

$$\text{AQUA}_{\text{seg}}(\mathcal{S}) = \sum_{i=1}^{8} w_i \mathcal{N}(f(\mathcal{S}); \mu_i, \boldsymbol{\Sigma}_i) \tag{8}$$

where $f(\mathcal{S})$ is the PCA projected feature vector for segment $\mathcal{S}$ and w, μ, σ are GMM parameters of the ith Gaussian in the mixture.

We also define the AQUA of the cut of a connected component mask $\mathcal{M}$ and a component object $\mathcal{R} \subset \mathcal{M}$ as

$$\text{AQUA}_{\text{cut}}(\mathcal{R}, \mathcal{M}) = \max\left(\text{AQUA}_{\text{seg}}(\mathcal{R}), \text{AQUA}_{\text{seg}}(\mathcal{M} - \mathcal{R})\right). \tag{9}$$

One challenge in using the AQUA derived from a GMM is that it is often the case that initial connected components may contain many objects which are fused together. Splitting a connected component with many fused objects into two pieces may create two components which are each individually composed of several fused objects. Since the AQUA is trained to recognize individual objects, a split of several fused objects into two smaller sets of fused objects may be rejected as “poor quality”. Since we want intermediate stages of the recursion to split an aggregate of fused objects into two smaller aggregates of fused objects, we use a combination of the AQUA and the isoperimetric ratio of the cut [13]. More formally:

$$\text{SP}(\mathcal{R}, \mathcal{M}) > \text{SP}(\mathcal{S}, \mathcal{M}) \equiv \begin{cases} \text{AQUA}(\mathcal{R}, \mathcal{M}) > \text{AQUA}(\mathcal{S}, \mathcal{M}) & \text{if AQUA}(x, \mathcal{M}) > \gamma, \\ \text{ISO}(\mathcal{R}, \mathcal{M}) < \text{ISO}(\mathcal{S}, \mathcal{M}) & \text{otherwise}, \end{cases} \tag{10}$$

where $x \in \mathcal{R}, \mathcal{M}$, $\text{ISO}(\mathcal{R}, \mathcal{M})$ is the isoperimetric ratio of split $\text{SP}(\mathcal{R}, \mathcal{M})$ (see [13]) and γ is a free parameter set to determine if the AQUA score of the split indicates that one piece of the split represents an object.

AQUA Usage. The AQUA is used in two stages of the algorithm: First, to assess the quality of the candidate splits from the isoperimetric distance tree method using randomized reference points (to determine whether to continue recursion) and second, to select the best segmentation result obtained by running the complete segmentation algorithm at three different parameter settings.

To guide our segmentation, we use the AQUA in the splitting phase of our segmentation algorithm. Recall from Section 2.2 that the splitting method iteratively splits under-segmented objects into two segments by considering multiple splits (derived from different reference voxels) and selects the best split using (10). Moreover, the recursive splitting also stops if one of three conditions are met: 1) The original mask has a very large probability of being a single object (as determined by the AQUA), 2) None of the multiple splits has a sufficiently high AQUA (greater than a threshold γ), 3) The original mask is too small. The first condition is derived from the fact that the GMM was trained to recognize that an object is high quality, so when the GMM registers an object as being very high quality we assume that no further splitting is required. In the context of the baggage screening application we selected a 50mL size as "too small" to continue recursion.

The AQUA can also be used to evaluate an overall segmentation of the entire image by averaging the AQUA of each individual segmented object. This overall AQUA can be used generally to compare different segmentation results obtained using different parameter settings of a segmentation algorithm, or quite possibly a different segmentation algorithm altogether. In this work, we use the overall image AQUA to evaluate the segmentations obtained using our segmentation algorithm at different parameter settings and then selected the segmentation with the greatest overall AQUA to be the final segmentation. Specifically, we experimented with α (a free parameter in the edge weight function in isoperimetric segmentation [12]) and γ in (10); a lower value of α and/or higher value of γ encourages further splitting and avoids undersegmentation. Based on several experiments on 4 baggage datasets, we selected the following parameter sets to yield the best performance: $(\alpha, \gamma) \in \{(100, -250), (100, -350), (10, -350)\}$. For validation, we compared the selected best segmentation with other segmentation results by visual inspection.

2.4 Summary

Our segmentation algorithm of a CT volume is comprised of the following steps:

1. Metal artifact reduction using [14].
2. Applying the Mumford-Shah method in [18] to identify all object voxels.
3. For each connected component, recursively apply the isoperimetric distance tree algorithm with several randomly chosen reference voxels and use (10) to determine the best split. End the recursion as determined by comparing the AQUA of the best split, (8) to parameter γ.

To improve the execution speed, we applied the algorithm with a coarse-to-fine segmentation, using the segmentation from the previous level as the initial masks for further splitting. This entire pipeline running single-threaded code requires about 4 minutes per parameter set on an Intel Core 2 Duo 2.8GHz machine. Therefore, we can change the two parameters and re-run the entire pipeline, or run them in parallel processes, several times and select the segmentation with the best average AQUA for all objects. Note that this algorithm would be applied to checked baggage, so 4 minutes is acceptable.

3 Results

We evaluate our algorithm on the challenging problem of baggage screening. The data was generated to mimic a real baggage screening application by creating 27

Fig. 2. Left: Histogram showing the number of segments placed into each bin of the AQUA. Red bars represent "bad" segmentations and blue bars represent "good" segmentations. Note that the good and bad segmentations are completely separable by thresholding the AQUA. Top: Examples of object segments labeled "good" (blue) and object segments labeled "bad" (red). Right: A variety of object segments and the corresponding AQUA score.

baggage scans using a medical CT scanner. Each scan contained a single piece of luggage, such as backpacks, duffel bags and soft-shell suitcases. Within each piece of luggage, nine to twenty different objects were packed that had a large variability in size, shape, orientation and material (appearance) composition. Some objects consisted of several parts (e.g., a large model car with clearly defined wheels and battery). The produced images had resolution 0.98mm $\times$ 0.98mm $\times$ 1.2mm. Depending on the size of the suitcase, the number of slices ranged from 665 to 953 and each slice consisted of 512×512 voxels. For each scan, almost all objects inside a luggage piece were manually segmented by baggage screening experts to provide a ground truth. Figure 1 shows several examples of the data that we used for evaluation, which illustrates the difficulty in segmenting these datasets in meaningful objects.

Our experiments are aimed at answering the following questions: 1) Does the AQUA qualitatively match our intuitive conception of a "good" object segment? 2) Does the AQUA quantitatively allow us to discriminate high quality segmented objects from poor quality segmented objects? 3) Does the overall segmentation algorithm produce segmentations that qualitatively agree with our conception of high quality segmentations? 4) How does the overall segmentation algorithm quantitatively match the manual (ground truth) segmentations? 5) How much improvement is gained by using our AQUA to end recursion as opposed to using the conventional isoperimetric ratio from [12]?

3.1 AQUA Evaluation

In this section, we perform an experiment to evaluate the quantitative and qualitative accuracy of the AQUA. We collected 60 object segments from the

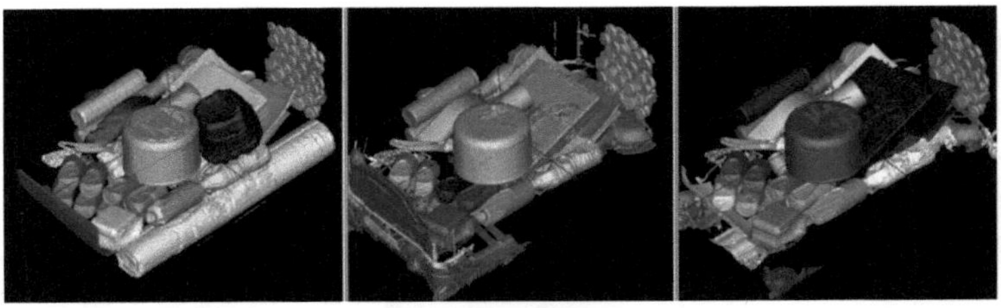

Fig. 3. Segmentation of a luggage CT Scan. Segments with different labels are rendered in different colors. (left) Ground truth segmentation, (middle) segmentation obtained using iso-ratio, and (right) segmentation obtained using AQUA.

intermediate and final results of the segmentation algorithm and labeled each "high quality" or "poor quality". Some of the poor quality object segmentations were undersegmented and others were oversegmented. Our AQUA was applied to each object. Figure 2 shows a histogram for the AQUA and the number of "high quality" and "low quality" objects that were placed into each AQUA bin. The figure also gives several examples of object segments that were labeled "high quality" or "low quality" and the values of the AQUA for a range of object segments (good and bad) that we tested on. Since perfect discrimination was achieved by the AQUA for segments of "high quality" and "low quality", we can conclude that the AQUA is accurately evaluating the quality of each object segment.

It is somewhat surprising that the AQUA performs so well for such a large variety of objects. However, the features describing each object were derived from the objective functions that have been optimized in the literature for different segmentation algorithms. The assumption behind each of these algorithms is that the best segmented object in an image is the segmented object that optimizes the criterion established by the objective function. Although these segmentation algorithms were all intended for general-purpose image segmentation, we are not aware of any previous examination of whether the values of the objective function for an object can be used to *discriminate* "good" object segmentations from "bad" object segmentations across images and application domains. Our experiment demonstrates that using these objective function evaluations as features for a generative GMM model does allow us to identify "good" segmentations.

3.2 Segmentation of the Baggage Datasets

A qualitative result from our segmentation system is given by Figure 3. In order to quantify the segmentation quality we developed error metrics that are based on mutual overlaps between ground truth (manual segmentations) and the segments produced by our algorithm. In our evaluation, we assumed that each computed label/segment is assigned to exactly one ground truth label/segment and vice-versa. Therefore, even if a computed segment overlaps with more than one ground truth segment the overlap is compared with only one of the ground truth segments, and not compared with any of the other ones. Conversely, if one ground truth segment overlaps with several computed segments, the overlap

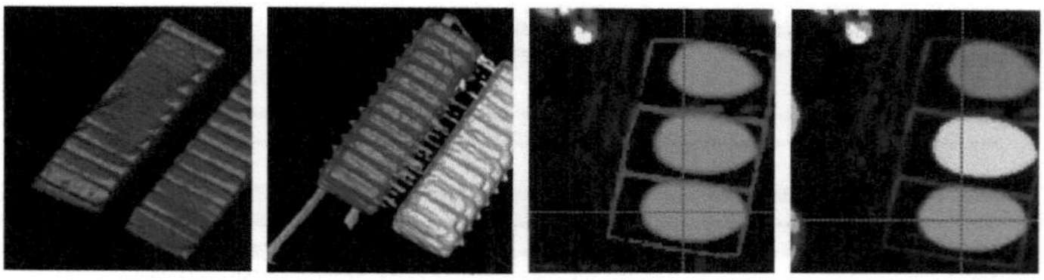

Fig. 4. Oversegmentations relative to ground truth. The ground truth annotations of the battery pack (left) and the soaps (right) assigned a single label to the whole package. However, the segmentation algorithm assigned several labels to sub-components, i.e., the two separate groups of batteries and the three soaps, respectively. Consequently, our overlap measure was poor for these objects, even though our segmentations could be considered to simply represent different notions of the target object.

with only one of them is compared and all of the others were ignored. Therefore, differences in object definition between the ground truth and the segmentation can sometimes appear as a segmentation having a very poor score using this evaluation method. Figure 4 illustrates this situation.

The one-to-one assignments of ground truth segments to computed segments was determined automatically and such that the total sum of all overlaps (in voxels) was maximal. Since this problem is equivalent to the matching of two independent graphs with equal or differing number of nodes, here we were able to employ the Hungarian algorithm to find the optimal matching. Technically, this matching is realized by first computing the mutual overlaps (in voxels) between all ground truth and all computed segments, which results in an overlap matrix whose row index the list of ground truth labels and whose column index the list of computed labels. The Hungarian algorithm then finds the optimal assignment that maximizes the total overlap.

Based on this optimal matching of ground truth segments/labels to computed segments/labels, we computed the relative overlap per ground truth segment by dividing its overlap with the assigned computed segment (in voxels) by the size of the individual ground truth label (in voxels). The resulting overlap percentages are then plotted for each ground truth label. The overlap measures for each object in one dataset is shown in Figure 5. Both quantitatively and qualitatively, the use of our AQUA system to perform quality assessment significantly improved the quality of the segmentation (per-object and overall) as compared to the conventional use of the isoperimetric ratio from [12] to end recursion.

Besides these per-ground truth segment measures, as overall overlap metric we computed the average overlap percentage per dataset. The mean of the average overlap percentage over all 27 datasets with ground truth was 54% ($\sigma = 10$) when using AQUA in the splitting algorithm, and only 44% ($\sigma = 12$) when using just the isoperimetric ratio. As noted previously, this score appears worse than it is as a result of differences in "object philosophy" between the algorithm and the ground truth (see Figure 4).

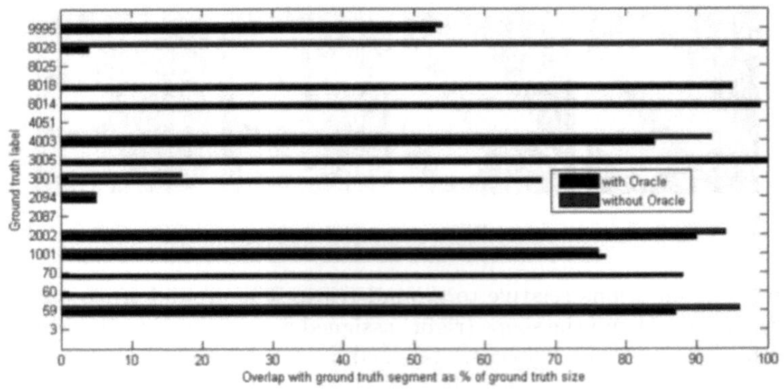

Fig. 5. Relative overlaps for one dataset. Average overlap percentage: 53% (with AQUA) and 31% (with isoperimetric ratio). Red: Overlap using isoperimetric ratio. Blue: Overlap using AQUA. Using AQUA to end recursion is a major improvement over using the isoperimetric ratio of [12] to end recursion. Note that most of the low object scores were due to partial matches that resulted from a different "object philosophy" between the algorithm and ground truth (see Figure 4).

4 Conclusion

We presented a new algorithm for unsupervised image segmentation that introduces a novel Automatic QUality Assessment (AQUA) module which is trained as a generative model (for "good" object segments) using a combination of different objective functions dispersed in the literature. The AQUA is then used both iteratively to end the splitting recursion (and choose between candidate splits) and at the end to assess the overall quality of the segmentation.

Our segmentation algorithm was applied to the challenging and important application of the unsupervised segmentation of baggage screening images acquired from 3D computed tomography scans. The challenge of image segmentation in these images is a product of the unknown number of objects, significant imaging artifacts, the wide variety of shapes and sizes, inhomogeneity and the tight packing of the objects against each other. General segmentation algorithms into superpixels of region homogeneity are unsuited for these images in which the goal is to make measurements about total object composition. A further challenge of segmenting these images is their large size and the speed requirements necessary for an algorithm to be useful.

We tested our algorithm on a novel dataset designed to mimic a real baggage screening data application. The evaluation demonstrated that our new AQUA can accurately determine the quality of an object segment *even for objects that were not in the training set.* Furthermore, our overall algorithm could be used to match a manually-derived ground truth for these 27 images. These experiments demonstrate the suitability and future prospects for applying this algorithm to improve the baggage security screening capabilities of today's airports.

Acknowlegement. This material is based upon work supported by the U.S. Department of Homeland Security under Task Order Number HSHQDC-10-J-00396. The views and conclusions contained in this document are those of the authors and should not be interpreted as necessarily representing the official policies, either expressed or implied, of the U.S. Department of Homeland Security. Datasets owned and provided by ALERT DHS Center of Excellence, Northeastern University, Boston MA.

References

1. Vincent, L., Soille, P.: Watersheds in digital spaces: An efficient algorithm based on immersion simulations. IEEE PAMI 13(6), 583–598 (1991)
2. Comaniciu, D., Meer, P.: Mean shift: A robust approach toward feature space analysis. IEEE PAMI 24(5), 603–619 (2002)
3. Shi, J., Malik, J.: Normalized cuts and image segmentation. IEEE PAMI 22(8), 888–905 (2000)
4. Arbelaez, P., Maire, M., Fowlkes, C., Malik, J.: Contour detection and hierarchical image segmentation. IEEE PAMI 33(5), 898–916 (2011)
5. Li, Y., Sun, J., Tang, C., Shum, H.: Lazy snapping. In: Proc. of ACM SIGGRAPH 2004, pp. 303–308 (April 2004)
6. Endres, I., Hoiem, D.: Category Independent Object Proposals. In: Daniilidis, K., Maragos, P., Paragios, N. (eds.) ECCV 2010, Part V. LNCS, vol. 6315, pp. 575–588. Springer, Heidelberg (2010)
7. Carreira, J., Sminchisescu, C.: Cpmc: Automatic object segmentation using constrained parametric min-cuts. IEEE PAMI 34, 1312–1328 (2012)
8. Singh, S., Singh, M.: Explosives detection systems (EDS) for aviation security: A review. Signal Process 83(1), 31–55 (2003)
9. Smith, R., Connelly, J.: CT technologies (chapter 7). In: Aspects of Explosives Detection, pp. 131–145. Elsevier (2009)
10. ALERT (Awareness and Localization of Explosives-Related Threats), Northeastern University, ed.: Algorithm Development for Security Applications (ADSA) Workshops 1-6 (2008–2011)
11. Martz Jr., H.E., Crawford, C.: Overview of deployed EDS technologies. Technical report, LLNL-TR-417232, Lawrence Livermore National Laboratory (September 2009)
12. Grady, L., Schwartz, E.L.: Isoperimetric graph partitioning for image segmentation. IEEE PAMI 28(3), 469–475 (2006)
13. Grady, L., Schwartz, E.L.: Isoperimetric partitioning: A new algorithm for graph partitioning. SIAM J. on Scientific Computing 27(6), 1844–1866 (2006)
14. Tuy, H.K.: A post-processing algorithm to reduce metallic clip artifacts in CT images. Eur. Radiol. 3, 129–134 (1993)
15. Mumford, D., Shah, J.: Optimal approximations by piecewise smooth functions and associated variational problems. Comm. PAM 42, 577–685 (1989)
16. Tsai, A., Yezzi, A., Willsky, A.: Curve evolution implementation of the Mumford-Shah functional for image segmentation, denoising, interpolation, and magnification. IEEE Trans. on Image Proc. 10(8), 1169–1186 (2001)
17. Chan, T., Vese, L.: A level set algorithm for minimizing the Mumford-Shah functional in image processing. In: Workshop on VLSM, pp. 161–168. IEEE (2001)

18. Grady, L., Alvino, C.: The piecewise smooth Mumford-Shah functional on an arbitrary graph. IEEE TIP 18(11), 2547–2561 (2009)
19. Grady, L.: Fast, Quality, Segmentation of Large Volumes – Isoperimetric Distance Trees. In: Leonardis, A., Bischof, H., Pinz, A. (eds.) ECCV 2006. LNCS, vol. 3953, pp. 449–462. Springer, Heidelberg (2006)
20. Blake, A., Zisserman, A.: Visual Reconstruction. MIT Press (1987)
21. Caselles, V., Kimmel, R., Sapiro, G., Sbert, C.: Minimal surfaces based object segmentation. IEEE Trans. on PAMI 19(4), 394–398 (1997)
22. El-Zehiry, N., Grady, L.: Fast global optimization of curvature. In: Proc. of CVPR. IEEE Computer Society, IEEE (2010)
23. Caselles, V., Kimmel, R., Sapiro, G.: Geodesic active contours. International Journal of Computer Vision 22, 61–79 (1997)
24. Boykov, Y., Jolly, M.P.: Interactive graph cuts for optimal boundary & region segmentation of objects in N-D images. In: Proc. of ICCV, pp. 105–112 (2001)
25. Grady, L.: Random walks for image segmentation. IEEE PAMI 28(11), 1768–1783 (2006)

Multi-scale Clustering of Frame-to-Frame Correspondences for Motion Segmentation

Ralf Dragon, Bodo Rosenhahn, and Jörn Ostermann

Institut für Informationsverarbeitung
Leibniz Universität Hannover, Germany

Abstract. We present an approach for motion segmentation using independently detected keypoints instead of commonly used tracklets or trajectories. This allows us to establish correspondences over non-consecutive frames, thus we are able to handle multiple object occlusions consistently. On a frame-to-frame level, we extend the classical split-and-merge algorithm for fast and precise motion segmentation. Globally, we cluster multiple of these segmentations of different time scales with an accurate estimation of the number of motions. On the standard benchmarks, our approach performs best in comparison to all algorithms which are able to handle unconstrained missing data. We further show that it works on benchmark data with more than 98% of the input data missing. Finally, the performance is evaluated on a mobile-phone-recorded sequence with multiple objects occluded at the same time.

1 Introduction

Motion is a key element for image understanding. Many animals can easily get fooled by prey standing still for long times. In computer vision, the most-known exploit of motion is to learn 3D shapes of rigid objects by structure-from-motion. Furthermore, recent image segmentation approaches [1,2,3] make use of long-time motion observation as prior for image segmentation. To determine motion, trajectories are established, e.g. from dense optical flow [4] or from tracking feature points like KLT. The trajectories are compared and classified according to their motion, which may be generic 2D or 3D motion or specialized motion templates as used in [5]. For higher discriminativity, it is of advantage to observe long-time trajectories like [6]. However in many real-world applications, trajectories

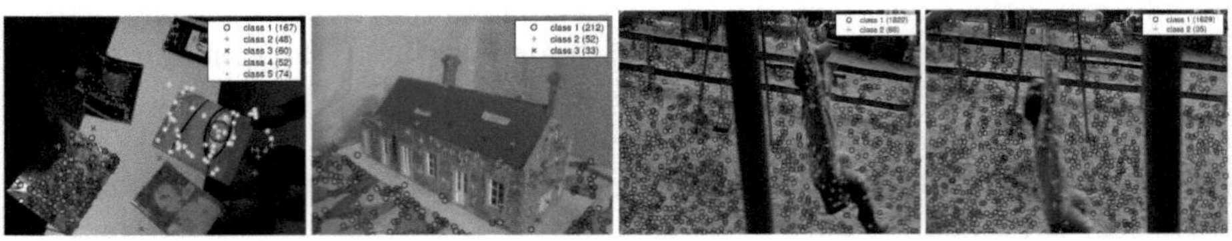

Fig. 1. Results of our multi-scale motion segmentation with automatic class number assignment using SIFT correspondences between pairs of images as input

A. Fitzgibbon et al. (Eds.): ECCV 2012, Part II, LNCS 7573, pp. 445–458, 2012.

are not only incomplete (data is missing at the beginning and at the end) but split by one or several gaps into different parts. Repairing trajectories [7,8] is only tractable as long as the gap is small and it bears the risk of introducing falsely-connected trajectories.

In our approach, we use correspondences from keypoints like SIFT [9] as input for motion segmentation which, e.g., allows learning object appearance from motion. In contrast to *tracked* features, keypoints are detected independently in different frames. On the one hand, comparing keypoint descriptors allows establishing correspondences over missing trajectory elements. On the other hand, although the redetection rate for keypoints in similar images is quite high, it is still far lower than for tracked features. So by gaining the possibility of matching over multiple frames, we loose trajectory length. In this paper, we show that by building a bottom-up frame-to-frame motion segmentation framework on multiple time scales, we can have the advantages of both tracked features *and* keypoints. Due to this, we are able to accurately segment motions of objects which are temporarily or spatially not visible, for example as they are occluded or leave the field of view. Furthermore, our approach is robust to outliers which are explicitly taken into account during the frame-to-frame motion segmentation. Our contributions are

- the motion-split-and-merge (MSAM) algorithm[1] with keypoint correspondences as input, performing fast motion segmentation on a frame-to-frame basis,
- the multi-scale motion clustering (MSMC) approach[1], which combines frame-to-frame-results of multiple frames *and* scales,
- and a metric to robustly and accurately determine the number of motion classes even under very high missing data percentages.

Related Work. Motion segmentation approaches can be characterized using the terms *subspace*- and *affinity*-based. In both methods, a certain time window is observed and trajectories of points are assigned to one of several objects.

In *subspace*-based methods, all trajectory points are combined in a data matrix $\mathbf{W}$. Under the affine camera model, trajectories from rigid objects form linear subspaces in $\mathbf{W}$, which can be extracted using algebraic transformations and rank constraints. [10] shows a closed form solution. However, most approaches cannot handle missing data (e.g. [10,11,12] with good results besides this). To allow incomplete trajectories, the following subspace techniques have been proposed: In [13] the power factorization, which allows the decomposition of matrices with missing data, is used for matrix decomposition of the generalized PCA (GPCA) of $\mathbf{W}$. The agglomerative lossy compression (ALC) approach [14] tries to segment $\mathbf{W}$ by minimizing the number of bits needed to represent $\mathbf{W}$. However reconstructing missing data is only possible as long as at least one complete trajectory is available. As it can be seen in Fig. 4, such an assumption does not hold here since no object is visible throughout the whole sequence.

[1] Code available on `www.tnt.uni-hannover.de/staff/dragon`

Our approach belongs to *affinity*-based methods. Here, pair-wise affinities between trajectories are computed. They form the affinity matrix **A** which is analyzed during a final clustering step. In contrast to *subspace*-based methods, the affinity metric does not depend on complete data. [4] use spectral clustering [15] with affinities from spatial trajectory distances combined with their similarity of translational motion. [16] propose affine motion similarity as basis for affinities which are clustered by J-linkage [17]. Both approaches build **A** from motions of consecutive frames only. Thus, slowly-drifting motions still have high affinity. This effect is solved by spatial terms in **A**, but only if the trajectory density is homogeneous and if the trajectories have high overlap. In [7] the trajectory features speed and direction are decomposed using non-negative matrix factorization. The resulting weights are used as affinities for spectral clustering. However, the factorization cannot handle noisy data or outliers.

Outstanding results were received by combining both *subspace*- and *affinity*-based methods: In [18], a sparse representation is estimated from **W** and used as affinity for spectral clustering. However, justification for handling missing data is only given as long as there is at least one trajectory with complete data. Despite this, the computational complexity for the sparse representation does not allow a high number of trajectories (> 6000 in Section 4.3). In our approach, we also combine the advantages of *affinity*-based methods with a long-term optimization like in *subspace*-methods. But our multi-scale motion clustering has low complexity and no constraints how the missing data is formed.

The rest of this paper is structured as follows: In Section 2, we explain our frame-to-frame motion-split-and-merge algorithm (MSAM). In Section 3, we derive our multi-scale motion clustering (MSMC) approach which combines frame-to-frame segmentations of multiple frames and scales. Section 4 shows experimental results and in Section 5, we give a conclusion.

2 Frame-to-Frame Motion Segmentation

A set $\{\boldsymbol{y}_1, \boldsymbol{y}_2, \ldots\}$ of given point correspondences $\boldsymbol{y}_i$ between two frames is to be partitioned into n subsets $\mathcal{F}_k$, called segments here, s.t. $\mathcal{F}_k$ and underlying motion coincide. Furthermore, the number of segments n is to be estimated. Let $\boldsymbol{y}_i = (\boldsymbol{x}_i^{(1)\top}, \boldsymbol{x}_i^{(2)\top})^\top$ be the data vector consisting of the corresponding points $\boldsymbol{x}_i^{(1)}$ and $\boldsymbol{x}_i^{(2)}$. The motion of $\mathcal{F}_k$ is parametrized by the vector $\boldsymbol{p}_k$, in this paper the 8 parameters of a homography.

Since block-wise segmentation for video coding or motion segmentation of dense optical flow denote different problems, there is only [19] as application tackling a similar problem. It consists of J-linkage and many post-processing steps preventing fast runtimes. Since the segmentation is carried out very often in our global framework, we introduce MSAM as fast and precise approach.

2.1 Motion-Split-And-Merge (MSAM)

The inspiration of our approach is the classical top-down split and merge algorithm [20, pp 96–104] for image segmentation, where image segments are split until they are consistent and then merged with neighboring segments until convergence. *Consistency* in our case means that all correspondences $\boldsymbol{y}_i$ from a segment $\mathcal{F}_k$ are inlier according to

$$d^2(\boldsymbol{y}_i \mid \boldsymbol{p}_k) < \epsilon^2 \,, \tag{1}$$

where $d^2(\boldsymbol{y}_i \mid \boldsymbol{p}_k)$ is the model distance metric for the data $\boldsymbol{y}_i$ using the model parameters $\boldsymbol{p}_k$ of $\mathcal{F}_k$, here the symmetric squared error. ϵ^2 is a threshold in this metric. However, motion parameters $\boldsymbol{p}_k$ have to be estimated from $\mathcal{F}_k$ which is problematic if $\mathcal{F}_k$ consists of multiple underlying models. Furthermore, combining *neighboring* segments in terms of similar parameters will not work if one of the segments is too small for the estimation step. Thus, we formulate motion-split-and-merge in a way we avoid too much splitting. It consists of advanced split and merge operations and explicit outlier handling.

Initially, we assume all correspondences to be in one segment. At each iteration, the following operations are performed:

1. Split segments: For each segment $\mathcal{F}_k$, RANSAC [21] estimates parameters $\boldsymbol{p}_k$. Outliers according to Eq. (1) are assigned to an outlier segment. If however the inlier ratio is smaller than θ_s, we believe that RANSAC could not estimate a valid motion because of too much perturbation from outliers or from multiple models inside the segment. Thus, we split the segment into two by the approach explained in Section 2.3.
2. Merge segments: For each pair of segments $(\mathcal{F}_k, \mathcal{F}_l)$, the inlier ratio τ of the smaller segment $\mathcal{F}_l$ is determined using parameters $\boldsymbol{p}_k$. The intention is that the parameters of the bigger segment are more stable and accurate. Besides, the inliers of the smaller segment can be computed faster. Like in regular split-and-merge, the segments are merged if τ is bigger than a threshold θ_m.
3. Split outlier segment: All outliers are put into one segment which is split like in step 1. If one of both parts contains enough inliers, it is added as a new segment.
4. Merge outlier segment: Each correspondence $\boldsymbol{y}_i$ from the outlier segment is assigned to a segment $\mathcal{F}_k$ if it is inlier according to its parameters $\boldsymbol{p}_k$.

The algorithm ends if no operation was performed during an iteration. Please note that by the outlier handling, we cannot guarantee convergence but to our experience, MSAM converges quickly if the underlying motions are parameterizable under the given ϵ. If not, MSAM is stopped after a cutoff iteration count experimentally found in Section 4.1. In order to disallow repeated splits and merges, a neccessary constraint for θ_s and θ_m is

$$1 + \theta_m \geq 2 \cdot \theta_s \,. \tag{2}$$

A high θ_s allows RANSAC with only few samplings in step 1 (cf. Eq. (7)), but on the other hand may result in too small segments from many splits and few merges by θ_m being too high. Thus, optimal thresholds depend on outlier percentages and the desired granularity of the segmentation. Since an over-segmentation will not harm the on-top multi-frame motion clustering, we empirically found

$$\theta_m = 0.9, \quad \theta_s = 0.95 \tag{3}$$

as biggest parameters usable for SIFT and KLT correspondences.

2.2 J-Linkage

As the splitting step from Section 2.3 is based on concepts used in J-linkage [17], we briefly repeat it using our notation. J-linkage belongs to the field of model selection, where data vectors $\boldsymbol{y}$ (not necessarily correspondences) are to be assigned to one of several underlying segments having different parameters $\boldsymbol{p}_k$. J-linkage consists of a sampling and a clustering step. In the sampling step, M model parameter vectors $\boldsymbol{p}$ are estimated from M varying randomly-selected minimal data sets. To increase the probability of drawing samples with the same underlying parameters, samples with similar $\boldsymbol{y}$ are drawn with higher probability.

After the sampling, for each correspondence $\boldsymbol{y}_i$ the set of its preferred parameters $\mathcal{P}(\boldsymbol{y}_i)$, or short $\mathcal{P}_i$, is found containing all parameter vectors $\boldsymbol{p}$ to which it is inlier (cf. Eq. (1)):

$$\boldsymbol{p} \in \mathcal{P}_i \quad \Leftrightarrow \quad d(\boldsymbol{y}_i \mid \boldsymbol{p}) < \epsilon \,. \tag{4}$$

In the clustering step segments are found using bottom-up agglomerative clustering, starting with many segments $\mathcal{F}_k = \{\boldsymbol{y}_k\}$ each containing one data vector. For further explanation, let the model preference set $\mathcal{M}_k$ of a segment $\mathcal{F}_k$ contain the common preferred parameter vectors of all its data

$$\mathcal{M}_k := \bigcap_{\boldsymbol{y}_i \in \mathcal{F}_k} \mathcal{P}(\boldsymbol{y}_i) \,. \tag{5}$$

In J-linkage, iteratively the two segments $\mathcal{F}_k$ and $\mathcal{F}_l$ with lowest Jaccard distance $J(\mathcal{M}_k, \mathcal{M}_l)$ between their model preference sets are combined. The Jaccard distance for two sets $\mathcal{A}$ and $\mathcal{B}$ is defined as

$$J(\mathcal{A}, \mathcal{B}) = \begin{cases} \frac{|\mathcal{A} \cup \mathcal{B}| - |\mathcal{A} \cap \mathcal{B}|}{|\mathcal{A} \cup \mathcal{B}|} & \mathcal{A} \cup B \neq \emptyset \\ 1 & \text{otherwise} \,. \end{cases} \tag{6}$$

The second case may occur if both $\mathcal{F}_k$ and $\mathcal{F}_l$ have empty preference sets since they are outliers to all estimated parameter vectors. The clustering ends if all pairs $(\mathcal{F}_k, \mathcal{F}_l)$ have disjoint $\mathcal{M}_k$ and $\mathcal{M}_l$ and thus $J(\mathcal{M}_k, \mathcal{M}_l) = 1$. Last, small clusters are combined to an outlier segment.

Although the clustering stop criterion sounds reasonable, the agglomerative clustering suffers from local optima by combining wrong segments (e.g. of ambiguous correspondences or outliers). This leads to over-segmentation as these partitions cannot be merged because the model preference sets $\mathcal{M}_k$ become too sparse. Furthermore, the parameters for the clustering are inaccurate as they have always been found from local minimal sampling sets. These problems could be overcome (cf. Fig. 2) by a motion validation which is performed by our MSAM approach. Thus the idea is to use a simplified and sped up version of J-linkage in step 1 of MSAM which is described in the following.

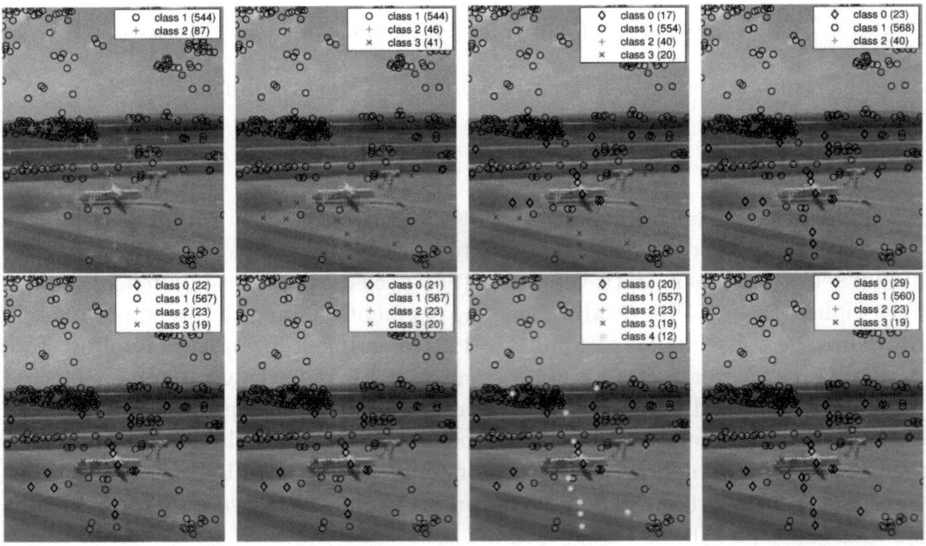

Fig. 2. The segmentation of a turning airplane using (upper row) our MSAM approach after 1, 2, 4 and 6 of 6 iterations, and using (lower row) J-linkage [17] with optimized parameters and 2500, 5000, 7500 and 10000 samplings. The motion model and the outlier threshold from Eq. (4) are the same. Using MSAM, the airplane is correctly segmented after 6 iterations. Motion class 3 is split in iterations 2 and 4. One of the split parts gets merged with the background such that the outliers (class 0) are increasingly detected. After convergence, all 23 outliers were detected correctly and the airplane as well as the background class are motion consistent. Using J-linkage, the correspondences are still oversegmented and not all outliers are detected. More iterations seem not to give better results.

2.3 MSAM Split Operation

The goal of this operation is to split the correspondences of a non-consistent segment $\mathcal{F}_k$ into motion consistent partitions. As further splits as well as merges may follow this operation, we may assume that we have to split $\mathcal{F}_k$ into two parts. This allows sampling preferred parameters $\mathcal{P}_i$ using a far lower number of parameter estimation sets M as in J-linkage. Here we chose $M = 10$. Furthermore, we enhance the parameter vector $\boldsymbol{p}$ in inlier count and precision by using the best RANSAC result of r samplings. r is chosen such that the parameters are estimated from true inliers with more than $p = 50\%$, assuming we have at least $w = 50\%$ model inliers. From [21], we know that

$$r \geq \frac{\log(1-p)}{\log(1-w^s)} \approx 11\,, \tag{7}$$

where $s = 4$ is the size of a minimal sampling set.

After this sampling step, the Jaccard distance $J(\mathcal{P}_i, \mathcal{P}_j)$ is computed according to Eq. (6), in contrast to J-linkage between the preferred parameter sets of *all* pairs of correspondences $\boldsymbol{y}_i, \boldsymbol{y}_j \in \mathcal{F}_k$. In order to include spatial constraints, we combine the Jaccard distance with the Mahalanobis distance M_k:

$$M_k(\boldsymbol{x}_i, \boldsymbol{x}_j) = \sqrt{(\boldsymbol{x}_i - \boldsymbol{x}_j)^\intercal \mathbf{C}_{\boldsymbol{x}}^{-1} (\boldsymbol{x}_i - \boldsymbol{x}_j)} \quad \wedge \quad \boldsymbol{x} \in \mathcal{F}_k\,, \tag{8}$$

where $\boldsymbol{x}$ is wlog. the destination point of correspondence $\boldsymbol{y}$ and $\mathbf{C}_{\boldsymbol{x}}$ is the covariance matrix of $\boldsymbol{x}$. To combine J and M_k, the affinity matrix $\mathbf{A}$ is defined:

$$A_{i,j} = 1 - J(\mathcal{P}_i, \mathcal{P}_j) \cdot \min\{M_k(\boldsymbol{x}_i, \boldsymbol{x}_j), 1.0\}\,. \tag{9}$$

The distances J and M_k are combined multiplicatively in order to cluster correspondences which are spatially *or* by common model parameters near to each other. To give both the same weight, M is saturated to the value range $[0, 1]$. By this, clustering of isolated correspondences randomly moving together is inhibited while elongated or discontinuous clusters remain possible. Finally, the columns of $\mathbf{A}$ and by this $\mathcal{F}_k$ is split into two segments using k-Means.

2.4 Runtime and Precision Considerations

Comparing our motion segmentation with J-linkage as strongest other approach, there are three main reasons for speedups and three for enhanced precision which justify using MSAM for frame-to-frame motion segmentation: In total, we have to perform less samplings for parameter estimation, most samplings are used for splitting classes containing only a fraction of all correspondences, and the clustering method may be simpler since further parameter validations are possible. On our equipment (cf. Section 4), the segmentations of 631 correspondences in Fig. 2 took 0.7 s for MSAM, where J-linkage with just 2500 samplings took 20.1 s (just the clustering took 16.6 s), both on compiler-optimized C code.

Since MSAM's parameters are estimated using *all* correspondences from a segment (and not minimal sampling sets), they are more precise. Second, because J-linkage draws samples spatially close to each other, its parameters become prone to imprecise feature localization, while MSAM incorporates spatial knowledge during the clustering when parameters are already estimated. Furthermore, because of the explicit outlier handling, all segments are motion consistent if MSAM terminates regularly. As it is displayed in Fig. 2, MSAM finds the true solution whereas J-linkage with the same outlier distance and optimized parameters performs an over-segmentation containing outliers in all classes.

3 Global Multi-scale Optimization

3.1 Global Motion Segmentation Using Successive Frames

To combine the results from multiple frame-to-frame motion segmentations in a time-consistent way, linked frame-to-frame inlier correspondences $(\boldsymbol{x}_i^{(1)}, \boldsymbol{x}_i^{(2)})$, $(\boldsymbol{x}_i^{(2)}, \boldsymbol{x}_i^{(3)})$, ... are assigned to trajectories T_i. In contrast to the clustering in Section 2, we now cluster the set of all T_i according to multiple frame-to-frame

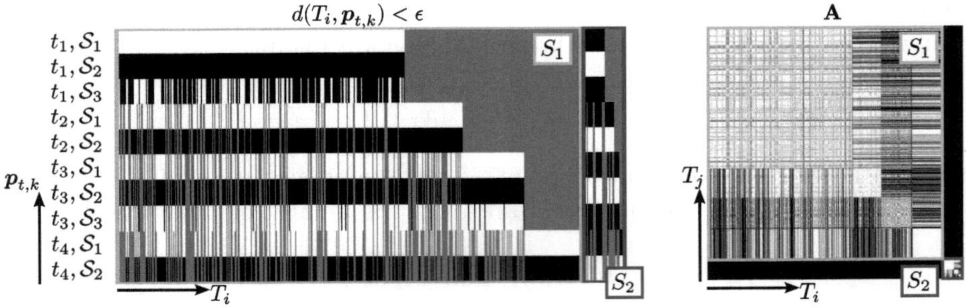

Fig. 3. Left: Preferred motion parameters $\boldsymbol{p}_{t,k}$ of trajectory T_i, clustered by motions $\mathcal{S}_1$ (yellow) and $\mathcal{S}_2$ (red). White denotes inliers, black outliers and green missing data (no observation of T_i at frame t). Right: Corresponding affinity matrix $\mathbf{A}$ of the affinity between trajectories T_i and T_j.

motions. Let $\mathcal{F}_{t,k}$ be a segment of a frame-to-frame segmentation of correspondences $\boldsymbol{y}^{(t)} = (\boldsymbol{x}^{(t)\intercal}, \boldsymbol{x}^{(t+1)\intercal})^\intercal$, and accordingly let $\boldsymbol{p}_{t,k}$ be its parameter vector.

Similar to Eq. (4), we define the preferred parameter set $\mathcal{H}(T_i)$, or short $\mathcal{H}_i$, of trajectory T_i containing the parameters $\boldsymbol{p}_{t,k}$ from different frames t and different motions k, to which T_i is inlier (cf. Fig. 3):

$$\boldsymbol{p}_{t,k} \in \mathcal{H}_i \quad \Leftrightarrow \quad \boldsymbol{y}_i^{(t)} \in T_i \quad \wedge \quad d(\boldsymbol{y}_i^{(t)} \mid \boldsymbol{p}_{t,k}) < \epsilon\,. \tag{10}$$

To segment all trajectories into n spatio-temporal motion clusters $\mathcal{S}_u$, we use spectral clustering [15]. Its affinity matrix $\mathbf{A}$ which contains pairwise affinities $A_{i,j}$ between two trajectories T_i and T_j, is defined using Eq. (10):

$$A_{i,j} = 1 - J(\mathcal{H}_i, \mathcal{H}_j)\,. \tag{11}$$

By this, we allow clustering trajectories with missing data without any constraints how the missing data is formed.

3.2 Multi-scale Motion Clustering (MSMC)

In contrast to the approaches of [4,16], our presented trajectory clustering allows combining independent frame-to-frame segmentations over arbitrary time scales h_Δ. By this, slow or randomly coinciding motions can be segmented. To combine the results of different scales, linked inlier correspondences are merged and treated as part of the same trajectory. The indices t, k from Section 3.1 become t, Δ, k denoting motion k from frame t to frame $t + \Delta$. Eq. (10) becomes the definition of the preferred motion parameter set $\mathcal{H}'(T_i)$ over multiple scales:

$$\boldsymbol{p}_{t,\Delta,k} \in \mathcal{H}'_i \quad \Leftrightarrow \quad \boldsymbol{y}_i^{(t,\Delta)} \in T_i \ \wedge \ d(\boldsymbol{y}_i^{(t,\Delta)} \mid \boldsymbol{p}_{t,\Delta,k}) < \epsilon\,, \tag{12}$$

where $\boldsymbol{y}_i^{(t,\Delta)} = (\boldsymbol{x}_i^{(t)\intercal}, \boldsymbol{x}_i^{(t+\Delta)\intercal})^\intercal$. Using $\mathcal{H}'_i$ instead of $\mathcal{H}_i$ for the affinities of the spectral clustering of trajectories T_i in Eq. (11), correspondences over *all scales* and *all frames* are clustered in one step (cf. Fig. 4).

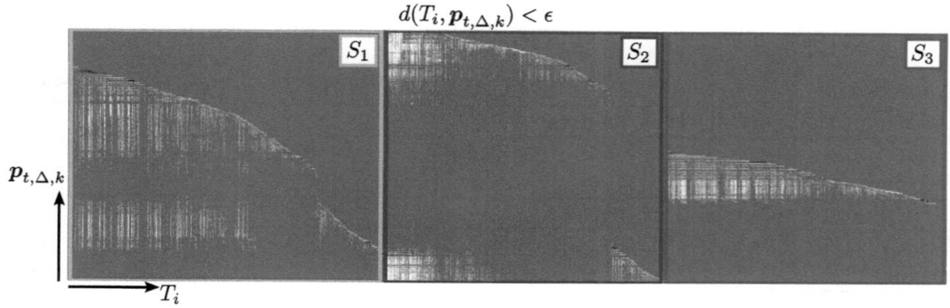

Fig. 4. Preferred motion parameters $\boldsymbol{p}_{t,\Delta,k}$ of 6795 trajectories and 768 frame-to-frame motions from the bookstack sequence (Section 4.3). Several objects are occluded at the same time. White denotes inliers, black outliers and green missing data (98.5%), e.g. due to occlusion. $\mathcal{S}_2$ corresponds to the lowest book and $\mathcal{S}_3$ to the topmost (cf. Fig. 8).

3.3 Estimation of the Number of Motion Classes

In the following we present a simple yet powerful method to determine the number of motions n by comparing the results of clusterings having different motion counts ξ. For each ξ, the $\xi \times \xi$ class similarity matrix $\mathbf{B}(\xi)$ is established. Element $B_{u,v}(\xi)$ contains the sum of affinities of all trajectories $T_i \in \mathcal{S}_u$ and $T_j \in \mathcal{S}_v$, normalized by the total overlap between $\mathcal{S}_u$ and $\mathcal{S}_v$:

$$B_{u,v} = \frac{\sum_{T_i \in \mathcal{S}_u} \sum_{T_j \in \mathcal{S}_v} (1 - J(\mathcal{H}'(T_i), \mathcal{H}'(T_j)))}{\sum_{T_i \in \mathcal{S}_u} \sum_{T_j \in \mathcal{S}_v} |T_i \cap T_j|} \,. \tag{13}$$

If there is no overlap between trajectories from $\mathcal{S}_u$ and $\mathcal{S}_v$, we set $B_{u,v} = 0$.

Since different motions $\mathcal{S}_u \neq \mathcal{S}_v$ should have a low similarity $B_{u,v}$ and the self-similarity $B_{u,u}$ should be high, we find the optimal number of classes n by a worst case minimization:

$$n = \arg\min_{\xi} \left(\max_{u \neq v} B_{u,v}(\xi) - \min_{u} B_{u,u}(\xi) \right) \,. \tag{14}$$

Minimizing only the first $B_{u,v}$- or the second $B_{u,u}$-term results in an under- or oversegmentation, respectively. As we will show in the experiments, the combination of both terms result in a quite accurate and robust estimation of n.

4 Experiments

4.1 Complete Data

We start analyzing the segmentation performance using complete trajectories from the Hopkins 155 benchmark [22]. We use the non-synthetic *Articulated* and the *Traffic* data set, each separated into two- and three-motion sequences. In all experiments, we use three scales h_1 (frame-to-frame tracking), h_5 (to close gaps)

Table 1. Classification error rates and recall in the Hopkins data set without missing data. The CPU times are collected from different papers with comparable systems.

Approach	ALC[14]	GPCA[22]	NNMF[7]	VLS[16]	**MSMC**
Articulated, 2 motions, 11 sequences					
Error	10.70%	2.88%	10.00%	5.38%	6.03%
Recall	1	1	1	1	0.963
Articulated, 3 motions, 2 sequences					
Error	21.08%	16.85%	15.00%	20.41%	8.27%
Recall	1	1	1	1	0.974
Traffic, 2 motions, 31 sequences					
Error	1.75%	1.41%	0.10%	1.92%	0.66%
Recall	1	1	1	1	0.979
Traffic, 3 motions, 7 sequences					
Error	8.86%	19.83%	0.10%	4.89%	0.17%
Recall	1	1	1	1	0.987
All 51 sequences					
Error	**5.41%**	**4.86%**	**2.82%**	**3.80%**	**2.05%**
Recall	1	1	1	1	0.977
CPU time/sequence	261.3s	0.3s	3.0s	5.7s	13.8s

and h_{25} (long-time motion analysis). To demonstrate MSAM converges even under very small outlier thresholds ϵ (cf. Eq. (4)), it was set to $\epsilon = 0.5$ pel. First, we use the provided number of classes for the segmentation. Since RANSAC and k-Means introduce a fluctuation of the results, we average over 10 repetitions.

The convergence of MSAM over all sequences and repetitions is displayed in Fig. 7 (b): More than 90% of all segmentations converge with less than 10, and 99% with less than 20 iterations. The rest is likely to contain motions not parameterizable by homographies, so we terminate MSAM after 20 iterations.

Next we compare our MSMC to all existing approaches which can handle missing data without completeness constraints (which [14,18] have, cf. Section 1): subspace-based GPCA ([13], results from [22]), and the affinity-based approaches from [7] (NNMF) and [16] (various life span – VLS). We further add ALC [14] since we will refer to it in Section 4.2. Traditionally, all trajectory elements are assigned to motion segments and classification errors are reported. As our approach may not only result in such true (tp) and false positives (fp), but also in false negatives (fn), we evaluate

$$\text{precision} = {}^{\text{tp}}/_{\text{tp+fp}}, \quad \text{and recall} = {}^{\text{tp}}/_{\text{tp+fn}}. \tag{15}$$

error = 1 − precision equals the usual benchmark performance metric [22].

The results in terms of average error rate and recall are displayed in Table 1. It can be observed that we receive the best overall error rate at a recall very close to 1 and reasonable runtime on a 3.0 GHz quadcore standard desktop PC. Using the metric from Section 3.3, the number of motions could be estimated with an accuracy of 78.4%, which is the best result reported so far: [23] received an accuracy of 63.4% and [24] 74.8% (including the synthetic sequences).

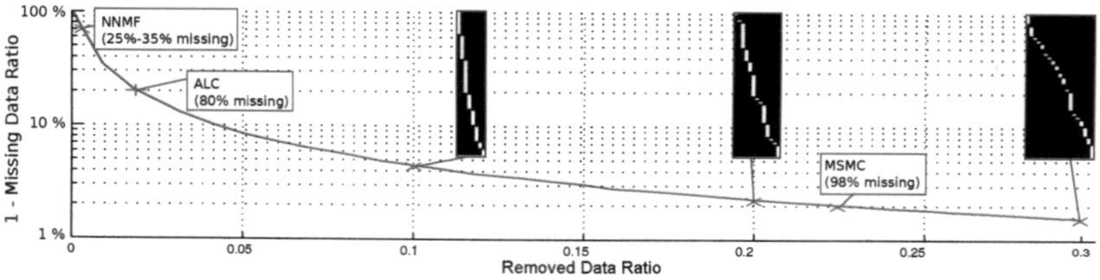

Fig. 5. Simulation how *removed* data affects *missing* data. The three binary images are examples of the result of one trajectory getting split because of gaps from 10%, 20%, and 30% *removed* data. The images show if data is known (white) or missing (black) for different resulting trajectories (columns) over time (rows).

4.2 Missing Data

Starting with the complete data, we randomly remove data from the trajectories as it occurs when features are not detected. By such gaps, trajectories become separated. For realistic evaluation, a trajectory with a gap is treated as two different disjoint trajectories, one ending before the gap and one starting after it. We use the term *removed data* for the amount of gaps introduced and *missing data* for the amount of resulting missing trajectory data given to the algorithm. When trajectory points are only removed at the ends as in [7], both terms coincide. However if, e.g., one trajectory element is removed in the middle of f frames, the removed data ratio is $1/f$ whereas the missing data ratio is $\rho = 0.5 + 2/f$ for the two resulting trajectories (cf. Fig. 5). By this, the clustering of trajectories becomes much more complex. Our approach reduces the complexity by merging trajectories on different scales as long as the motion segmentation does not fail (e.g. because of too little available data). Using this procedure, we randomly *remove* up to 30% data, which results in up to 98,5% *missing* data. As a comparison: In the trajectory recovery of [14] (ALC), by removing complete trajectories, up to 80% data was *missing* which corresponds to $\rho \approx 2\%$ *removed* data here. The masks used to simulate missing data in [7] (NNMF) contained 25%-35% missing data at beginning and ends of trajectories corresponding to $\rho < 1\%$ (cf. Fig. 5). We evaluate precision, recall and accuracy of class number estimations over removed data using the setup from Section 4.1.

Fig. 6 displays the results with [7] as comparison. It can be observed that our approach is very robust with respect to missing data in terms of precision, recall and class estimation accuracy. The outcomes are reasonable even if more than 20% of the data is *removed*, corresponding more than 98% *missing* data. This justifies that we can use MSMC with keypoint correspondences as input.

4.3 Multi-scale SIFT Motion Clustering

In this experiment, keypoint correspondences from SIFT features [9] are used for motion segmentation. For fast computation of features and correspondences, we use the GPU approach from [25]. We demonstrate our multi-scale approach

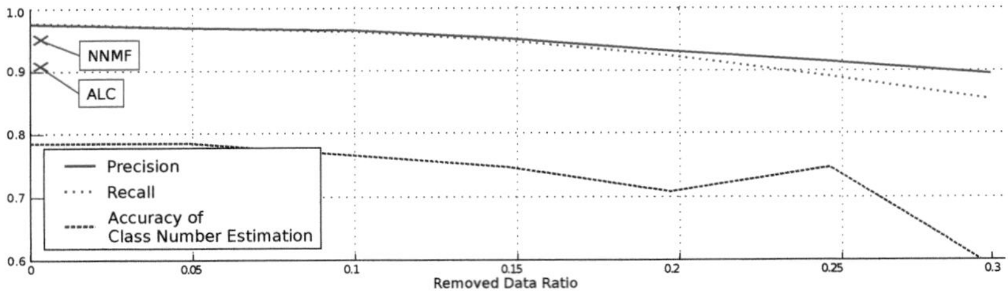

Fig. 6. Average precision, recall and class number estimation accuracy from Section 4.2 over the ratio of removed data. The precisions from ALC and NNMF are extracted from [7].

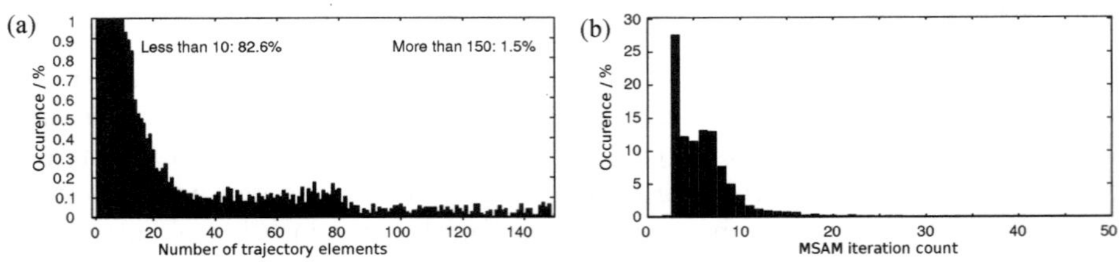

Fig. 7. (a) Histogram of the number of known trajectory elements for the bookstack sequence (Section 4.3). (b) Histogram of MSAM iteration count of all frames, scales and sequences of the experiment in Section 4.1.

on the bookstack video sequence (225 frames, $840 \times 480\,\text{pel}^2$, Fig. 8) which was taken with a regular mobile phone camera. Thus, the captured video contains motion blur and artifacts from compression and rolling shutter. The books occlude each other in the first half of the sequence and get uncovered later. The background intentionally was left blank to give the algorithm no information about the motion of the lowest book. We used three objects to demonstrate that multiple objects may become occluded at the same time. If only one object is occluded and the number of motions is given, an occlusion would be solved by assigning disjoint classes the same motion. With the following exceptions, the parameters remained the same as in previous experiments. To be able to segment consistently through the long-time occlusion, we added scales h_{100} and h_{200}. Further, to reduce computational complexity because of too many frame-to-frame motions segments, the outlier threshold from Eq. (4) was set to $\epsilon = 3\,\text{pel}$. As baseline for comparison, we input the sequence into the approach of [4] which is based on dense trajectories from optical flow.

The preferred parameter sets for 768 frame-to-frame motion segments and 6795 trajectories, containing 67103 SIFT inliers, is displayed in Fig. 4, the histogram of trajectory lengths in Fig. 7 (a), and images with classified features are shown in Fig. 8. It can be observed that MSMC allows very high precision under full occlusions, high image perturbation and very high missing trajectory

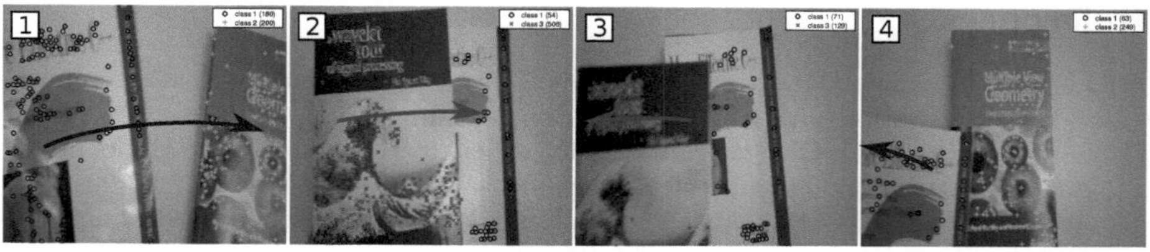

Fig. 8. Images from the bookstack sequence with the segmentation result: The green-labeled book becomes occluded by the blue-labeled book at $t = 1$ which in turn becomes occluded by the red-labeled book at $t = 2$. The books are assigned consistently again.

data rates (here 98.5%). The number of motions was correctly estimated as 3, corresponding to the three books. The precision, measured every 10 frames, is at 98.2%. The baseline approach of course fails in re-assigning the books. But even when taking only the stacking of the books into account, it results in severe oversegmentation such that the precision is only 61.9%. Further, with a frame rate of 4.1 s for motion segmentation plus 30.2 s for the optical flow, the baseline approach is by far slower than MSMC with an overall rate (including SIFT extraction and matching) of 1.1 s per frame. We think that by introducing mechanisms to feed back the result of one frame-to-frame segmentation as initialization for others, realtime performance can be reached.

5 Conclusion

We presented a bottom-up approach for motion segmentation using correspondences from multiple scales. On a frame-to-frame level, they are segmented into different motions using our fast and precise motion-split-and-merge (MSAM) approach. These frame-to-frame correspondences of multiple frames and scales are merged to trajectories. The motion of such trajectories with various lengths, time spans and missing data is segmented by multi-scale motion clustering (MSMC), a single spectral clustering step with Jaccard distances of preferred trajectory motion parameter sets as input. Last, an accurate estimator of the number of motions was presented.

Using complete trajectories from the Hopkins data set as input, the overall error rate was better than any other current state-of-the-art motion segmentation approach which is able to handle missing data without constraints. Furthermore, we estimated the number of motion classes with best precision reported so far. We showed that our approach allows more than 98% data of the input trajectories missing. In a challenging real-world example with low-quality image data and multi-object occlusions, we demonstrated that our algorithm allows fast and accurate motion segmentation of SIFT correspondences on multiple scales.

Acknowledgement. This work was funded by the German Federal Ministry of Education and Research, BMBF project ASEV.

References

1. Lezama, J., Alahari, K., Sivic, J., Laptev, I.: Track to the future: Spatio-temporal video segmentation with long-range motion cues. In: CVPR, pp. 3369–3376 (2011)
2. Ochs, P., Brox, T.: Object segmentation in video: A hierarchical variational approach for turning point trajectories into dense regions. In: Proc. ICCV (2011)
3. Sheikh, Y., Javed, O., Kanade, T.: Background subtraction for freely moving cameras. In: Proc. ICCV, pp. 1219–1225 (2009)
4. Brox, T., Malik, J.: Object Segmentation by Long Term Analysis of Point Trajectories. In: Daniilidis, K., Maragos, P., Paragios, N. (eds.) ECCV 2010, Part V. LNCS, vol. 6315, pp. 282–295. Springer, Heidelberg (2010)
5. Cifuentes, C.G., Sturzel, M., Jurie, F., Brostow, G.J.: Motion models that only work sometimes. In: Proc. BMVC (2012)
6. Sand, P., Teller, S.: Particle video: Long-range motion estimation using point trajectories. IJCV 80, 72–91 (2008)
7. Cheriyadat, A., Radke, R.: Non-negative matrix factorization of partial track data for motion segmentation. In: Proc. ICCV, pp. 865–872 (October 2009)
8. Sivic, J., Schaffalitzky, F., Zisserman, A.: Object level grouping for video shots. IJCV 67(2), 189–210 (2006)
9. Lowe, D.G.: Distinctive image features from scale-invariant keypoints. IJCV 60, 91–110 (2004)
10. Favaro, P., Vidal, R., Ravichandran, A.: A closed form solution to robust subspace estimation and clustering. In: Proc. CVPR, pp. 1801–1807 (2011)
11. Chen, G., Lerman, G.: Motion segmentation by scc on the hopkins 155 database. In: Proc. ICCV Workshop on Dynamical Vision (2009)
12. Yu, J., Chin, T.J., Suter, D.: A global optimization approach to robust multi-model fitting. In: Proc. CVPR (2011)
13. Vidal, R., Hartley, R.: Motion segmentation with missing data using powerfactorization and gpca. In: Proc. CVPR, pp. 310–316 (2004)
14. Rao, S., Tron, R., Vidal, R., Ma, Y.: Motion segmentation in the presence of outlying, incomplete, or corrupted trajectories. TPAMI 32, 1832–1845 (2010)
15. Ng, A.Y., Jordan, M.I., Weiss, Y.: On spectral clustering: Analysis and an algorithm. In: Proc. NIPS, pp. 849–856 (2001)
16. Fradet, M., Robert, P., Perez, P.: Clustering point trajectories with various lifespans. In: Proc. CVMP, pp. 7–14 (2009)
17. Toldo, R., Fusiello, A.: Robust Multiple Structures Estimation with J-Linkage. In: Forsyth, D., Torr, P., Zisserman, A. (eds.) ECCV 2008, Part I. LNCS, vol. 5302, pp. 537–547. Springer, Heidelberg (2008)
18. Elhamifar, E., Vidal, R.: Sparse subspace clustering. In: Proc. CVPR, pp. 2790–2797 (2009)
19. Fouhey, D.F., Scharstein, D., Briggs, A.J.: Multiple plane detection in image pairs using j-linkage. In: Proc. ICPR (2010)
20. Jain, R., Kasturi, R., Schunck, B.G.: Machine Vision. McGraw-Hill (1995)
21. Fischler, M.A., Bolles, R.C.: Random sample consensus. CACM 24, 381–395 (1981)
22. Tron, R., Vidal, R.: A benchmark for the comparison of 3-d motion segmentation algorithms. In: Proc. CVPR (2007)
23. Chin, T.J., Wang, H., Suter, D.: The ordered residual kernel for robust motion subspace clustering. In: Proc. NIPS, pp. 333–341 (2009)
24. Chin, T.J., Suter, D., Wang, H.: Multi-structure model selection via kernel optimisation. In: Proc. CVPR, pp. 3586–3593 (2010)
25. Wu, C.: SiftGPU: A GPU implementation of scale invariant feature transform (SIFT) (2007), http://cs.unc.edu/~ccwu/siftgpu

Fourier Kernel Learning

Eduard Gabriel Băzăvan[1], Fuxin Li[2], and Cristian Sminchisescu[3,1]

[1] Institute of Mathematics of the Romanian Academy
[2] College of Computing, Georgia Institute of Technology
[3] Faculty of Mathematics and Natural Science, University of Bonn
eduard.bazavan@imar.ro, fli@cc.gatech.edu,
cristian.sminchisescu@ins.uni-bonn.de

Abstract. Approximations based on random Fourier embeddings have recently emerged as an efficient and formally consistent methodology to design large-scale kernel machines [23]. By expressing the kernel as a Fourier expansion, features are generated based on a finite set of random basis projections, sampled from the Fourier transform of the kernel, with inner products that are Monte Carlo approximations of the original non-linear model. Based on the observation that different kernel-induced Fourier sampling distributions correspond to different kernel parameters, we show that a scalable optimization process in the Fourier domain can be used to identify the different frequency bands that are useful for prediction on training data. This approach allows us to design a family of linear prediction models where we can learn the hyper-parameters of the kernel together with the weights of the feature vectors jointly. Under this methodology, we recover efficient and scalable linear reformulations for both single and multiple kernel learning. Experiments show that our linear models produce fast and accurate predictors for complex datasets such as the Visual Object Challenge 2011 and ImageNet ILSVRC 2011.

1 Introduction

The proper choice of kernel function and its hyper-parameters are crucial to the success of kernel methods in practical applications. These selections span a number of different problems, from choosing a single width parameter in radial basis kernels, scaling feature dimensions with different weights [6], to learning a linear or a non-linear combination of multiple kernels (MKL) [17]. In complicated practical problems such as computer vision, sometimes the need of multiple kernels arises naturally [32]. Images can be represented using descriptors based on shape, color and texture, and these descriptors have different roles in classifying different visual categories. In such situations it is, in principle, easy to design a classifier where each kernel operates on one of the descriptors or feature channels and the classifier is obtained as a combination of kernels with category dependent learnt weights.

A natural difficulty in kernel learning is scalability. Kernel methods scale with an already mediocre time complexity of at least $O(N^{2.3})$ with respect to the size

A. Fitzgibbon et al. (Eds.): ECCV 2012, Part II, LNCS 7573, pp. 459–473, 2012.

N of the training set, but combining multiple kernels or learning the hyper-parameters of a single kernel significantly slows down training. Some speed-ups apply to specific kernels, but only in limited scenarios [22]. As a consequence, some of the standard kernel learning approaches can only handle a few thousand training examples at most. This is insufficient for the current age of massive datasets, such as the 11 million images ImageNet, or the 19 million articles within Wikipedia.

An emerging technique that can in principle speed up the costly kernel method while at the same time preserving its non-linear predictive power is the random Fourier feature methodology (RFF) [23,33,19]. By sampling components from the frequency space of the kernel using Monte Carlo methods, RFF obtains a bounded, approximate representation of a kernel embedding, even for non-linear models that may span an infinite-dimensional space. Many operations are simplified once such a representation is available, the most notable being that any kernel learning algorithm would now scale as $O(N)$, where N is the number of examples. This opens path for applying kernel methods to the realm of massive datasets.

In the seminal work on random Fourier approximations [23], the methodology was developed primarily for radial basis kernels. Recent work [33,19,25] focused on extending this technique to other useful kernels defined on histogram features (empirical estimates of multinomial distributions), such as the χ^2 and the histogram intersection measures. However, the potential of the linear Fourier methodology for *kernel learning* remains largely unexplored. In this paper we develop the methodology for learning both single kernel and for multiple kernel combinations in the Fourier domain and show that these models produce accurate and efficient predictors. We conduct experiments in the visual object recognition domain, using both the PASCAL Visual Object Challenges 2011 and the ImageNet ILSVRC 2011 datasets, to illustrate the performance of the proposed Fourier kernel learning methodology. We also compare against non-linear learning algorithms, designed to operate in the original kernel space and show significant speedups at comparable accuracy.

2 Related Work

Approaches to kernel learning can be broadly classified into methods that estimate the hyper-parameters of a single kernel[6,15] and methods that estimate the weights of a linear combination of kernels and possibly their hyper-parameters – the multiple kernel learning framework, MKL[2,16,34].

A popular approach for single kernel learning is the gradient-based method pursued by Chapelle et al. [6,15]. Keerthi et al. [15] give an efficient algorithm that alternates between learning an SVM and optimizing the feature weights. Cortes et al. [8] propose a two-stage method based on the modification of a kernel alignment [9] metric and prove a number of learning bounds. Approaches to single kernel learning under a kernel prior have been pursued both as semi-definite programs[17] and within unconstrained optimization formulations[12], although in both cases the optimization is fairly involved and the complexity remains an issue. More recent methods attempt to track the entire regularization path in the non-linear case [20].

Multiple kernel learning provides a powerful conceptual framework for both model combination and model selection and has attracted significant research recently. Initial approaches, originating with work by Lanckriet et al. [17] estimated a linear combination of kernels using semi-definite programming. This was reformulated by Bachet al. [3] as block-norm regularization, reducing the optimization problem to a second order cone program applicable to medium scale problems. More recent methods [7] learn a polynomial combination of kernels. A number of approaches have pursued different l_p-norms for kernel selection [16,34]. Hierarchical kernel learning approaches like (HKL) [2] perform feature selection combinatorially, by choosing kernel combinations obtained by mapping to a directed acyclic graph. The search for such combinations can then be performed in polynomial time.

A difficulty with many single or multiple kernel learning formulations is their relatively unfavorable scaling properties. When kernels are used, such methods usually scale at least quadratically in the number of examples. Sometimes scaling in the combined number of kernel parameters and number of kernel models can also become an issue. A formulation of kernel learning within a linear Fourier framework, as pursued in this paper, carries the promise of better scalability and wider applicability to large datasets, while at the same time preserving the non-linear predictive power that makes kernel methods attractive.

3 Learning Kernels in the Random Fourier Domain

3.1 Random Fourier Approximations

Kernels offer substantial power and flexibility to predictive models. Central to their use is the 'kernel trick' which allows the design of algorithms that depend only on the inner product of their arguments. This is based on the property of positive definite kernels $k(\cdot,\cdot)$ to define a lifting ϕ so that the inner product between lifted data points can be efficiently computed as $\phi(\mathbf{x})^\top\phi(\mathbf{y}) = k(\mathbf{x},\mathbf{y})$, without having to explicitly construct $\phi(\mathbf{x})$. Algorithms become linear in a complex feature space induced by ϕ, but access the data only through evaluations of the kernel k in input space. This makes possible to handle complex or infinite dimensional feature space mappings ϕ, and indeed these usually give the best results in visual recognition datasets [14,18]. However the very advantage that make kernel methods popular – the kernel trick, requires the manipulation of matrices of pairwise examples. For large datasets, the scaling of kernel methods is at least quadratic in the number of examples. This makes their direct usage impractical beyond datasets of 10^4 elements. The methodology we pursue is to approximate the kernel function linearly using random feature maps.

Key to the random Fourier methodology is Bochner's theorem, that connects positive definite kernels and their Fourier transforms [26,23,19]. For positive definite translation-invariant kernels $k(\mathbf{x},\mathbf{y}) = k(\mathbf{x}-\mathbf{y})$ on $\mathbb{R}^m$, Bochner's theorem

Table 1. Examples of kernels that can be efficiently optimized within our framework, given for the unidimensional case. In the multidimensional case, the Fourier methodology decomposes, hence it requires a simple multiplication of parameters corresponding to each dimension. Above, the random variable ω is drawn from the uniform distribution.

kernel	parametric form (k_σ)	probability distribution $\mu_k(\gamma)$	quantile $\sigma h(\omega)$
Gaussian	$\frac{1}{\sigma\sqrt{2\pi}}e^{-\frac{\|x-y\|^2}{2\sigma^2}}$	$\frac{\sigma}{\sqrt{2\pi}}e^{-\frac{\sigma^2\gamma}{2}}$	$\sigma\sqrt{2}\mathrm{erf}^{-1}(2\omega-1)$
Skewed $-\chi_2$	$\frac{2(x+c)^\sigma(y+c)^\sigma}{(x+c)^{2\sigma}+(y+c)^{2\sigma}}$	$\frac{1}{2\sigma}\mathrm{sech}\left(\frac{\pi\gamma}{2\sigma}\right)$	$\sigma\frac{2}{\pi}\log\left(\tan\left(\frac{\pi}{2}\omega\right)\right)$
Skewed Intersection	$\min\left\{\frac{(x+c)^\sigma}{(y+c)^\sigma},\frac{(y+c)^\sigma}{(x+c)^\sigma}\right\}$	$\frac{1}{\pi}\frac{\sigma}{\sigma^2+\gamma^2}$	$\sigma\tan\left(\pi(\omega-\frac{1}{2})\right)$

guarantees that every kernel is the inverse Fourier transform of a proper probability distribution μ_k. Defining $\zeta(\mathbf{x}) = e^{j\gamma^\top \mathbf{x}}$ (with j the imaginary unit), the following equality holds:

$$k_{\boldsymbol{\sigma}}(\mathbf{x},\mathbf{y}) = \int_{\mathbb{R}^m} e^{j\gamma^\top(\mathbf{x}-\mathbf{y})}\mu_k(\gamma)d\gamma = \mathbf{E}_{\mu_k}[\zeta_\gamma(\mathbf{x})\zeta_\gamma(\mathbf{y})^*] \approx \psi_{\boldsymbol{\Gamma}}(\mathbf{x})^\top\psi_{\boldsymbol{\Gamma}}(\mathbf{y}) \quad (1)$$

where $*$ is the (complex) conjugate, and

$$\psi_{\boldsymbol{\Gamma}}(\mathbf{x}) = \sqrt{\frac{2}{d}}\left[\cos\left(\gamma_i^\top\mathbf{x}+2\pi b_i\right)\right]_{i=1,d} \in \mathbb{R}^{d\times 1} \quad (2)$$

is the random feature map at samples $\boldsymbol{\Gamma} = \{\gamma_1,\ldots,\gamma_d\}$ drawn from μ_k and $b \sim \mathrm{U}[0,1]$, the uniform distribution in the interval $[0,1]$. We approximate the expectation $\mathbf{E}_{\mu_k}[\zeta_\gamma(\mathbf{x})\zeta_\gamma(\mathbf{y})^*]$ by means of a Monte-Carlo sample drawn from the distribution μ_k. This is an operation on linear functions with explicit features. The algorithm for the change of representation has two steps: i) Generate d random samples Γ from the distribution μ_k; ii) Compute the random projection $\psi_{\boldsymbol{\Gamma}}$ using (2), for all training examples. The approximation has the convergence rate of Monte Carlo methods, $O(d^{-1/2})$, dependent on the random sample size, but independent of the input dimension. One usually needs up to a few thousand dimensions to approximate the original kernel accurately.

Our kernel learning approach is based on the observation that manipulating the sampling distribution μ_k in an optimization process identifies the different frequency bands that are useful for prediction on training data. This effectively leads to a posterior frequency distribution, given μ_k as a prior. Generating samples from this posterior and optimizing with respect to their expectation on the training set gives a direct way of learning the parameters of the kernel in the Fourier domain. However, as the kernel hyper-parameters $\boldsymbol{\sigma}$ change, $\boldsymbol{\Gamma}$ (the distribution induced by the kernel) changes and needs to be re-sampled. Although this is feasible, changing the sampling distribution introduces conceptual difficulties during optimization as sampling introduces noise, high-variance and non-smoothness in the optimization cost. Importance sampling can be used to avoid resampling at each step, but if the parameterized frequency distribution

μ_k drifts far away from the initial kernel-induced distribution, the original samples will have little importance weights, and resampling would potentially be necessary for convergence. Such difficulties can be overcome for several interesting kernels that belong to a class of functions where μ_k has an explicit quantile which is linear in the kernel parameters. Assuming the quantile of μ_k has the form $\boldsymbol{\gamma} = \boldsymbol{\sigma} \odot h(\boldsymbol{\omega})$ where h is a nonlinear function, and $\odot$ is the Hadamard product of two vectors then we can draw the required samples $\boldsymbol{\Gamma}$ from μ_k using the following procedure: *(i)* draw d vectors $\boldsymbol{\omega}_i$ of the same dimensionality as the input vectors $\mathbf{x}$ from the uniform distribution; *(ii)* pass each $\boldsymbol{\omega}_i$ through the nonlinearity h, and *(iii)* multiply each dimension of the resulting $h(\boldsymbol{\omega}_i)$ with the corresponding σ_i. The desired samples are obtained as

$$\gamma_i = \boldsymbol{\sigma} \odot h(\boldsymbol{\omega}_i) \tag{3}$$

Notice that when changing the kernel parameters $\boldsymbol{\sigma}$ we no longer have to resample $\boldsymbol{\omega}_i$. Throughout the entire optimization process, sampling needs to be done only once from the uniform distribution for each $\boldsymbol{\omega}_i$. When $\boldsymbol{\sigma}$ is changed, samples from the new distribution are generated automatically from the stored values of $h(\boldsymbol{\omega}_i)$. In the sequel, we consider the case of anisotropic input scaling. In this case we have $\gamma_i = [\sigma_1 h(\boldsymbol{\omega}_{i,1}), \ldots, \sigma_r h(\boldsymbol{\omega}_{i,r})]$, and the Fourier embedding can be written as

$$\psi_{\boldsymbol{\sigma}}(\mathbf{x}) = \sqrt{\frac{2}{d}} \left[\cos \left(\sum_{j=1}^{r} \sigma_j h(\boldsymbol{\omega}_{i,j})^\top \mathbf{x}_j + 2\pi b_i \right) \right]_{i=1,d} \in \mathbb{R}^{d \times 1} \tag{4}$$

where $\mathbf{x}_j$ is the block from the input data $\mathbf{x}$ that corresponds to σ_i, and r is the number of blocks $\mathbf{x}$ is split into. Examples of kernels that can be learned using this procedure are the Gaussian, the generalized Skewed-χ_2 and the generalized Skewed Intersection[19] (see Table 1).

3.2 General Learning Model

We express our kernel learning model as a general cost optimization problem where we jointly learn the kernel parameters $\boldsymbol{\sigma}$ and the weights $\mathbf{w}$ of a linear predictor operating on the new Fourier representation. In the sequel we denote $\mathbf{X}$ and $\mathbf{y}$ the matrix of inputs or covariates $\mathbf{x}$ (column-wise organized) and $\mathbf{y}$ the vector of targets on the training set, respectively. We define $\psi_{\boldsymbol{\sigma}}(\mathbf{X}) \in \mathbb{R}^{d \times n}$, where n is the number of inputs, to be the feature map applied to all inputs(columns) of matrix $\mathbf{X} \in \mathbb{R}^{m \times n}$. The general form of the error function we wish to minimize can be written as

$$f(\boldsymbol{\sigma}, \mathbf{w}) = l(\psi_{\boldsymbol{\sigma}}(\mathbf{X})^\top \mathbf{w}, \mathbf{y}) + \nu(\mathbf{w}) + \eta(\boldsymbol{\sigma}) \tag{5}$$

where $\psi_{\boldsymbol{\sigma}}(\mathbf{x})$ is the Fourier embedding of an input data $\mathbf{x}$, $l(\bar{\mathbf{y}}, \mathbf{y})$ is the loss function which measures how close the predicted labels $\bar{\mathbf{y}} = \psi_{\boldsymbol{\sigma}}(\mathbf{X})^\top \mathbf{w}$ are to the ground truth $\mathbf{y}$, $\nu(\mathbf{w})$ is a regularizer on the linear parameters $\mathbf{w}$ and $\eta(\boldsymbol{\sigma})$ is a regularizer on the kernel hyper-parameters $\boldsymbol{\sigma}$.

Optimizing the parameters in equation (5) depends on the different design decisions made for the model. In Table 2 we show different choices of loss functions and regularization terms. If f is smooth in both $\boldsymbol{\sigma}$ and $\mathbf{w}$ and we choose to jointly optimize all parameters, we will need to compute the gradient of f with respect to these parameters. The following derivatives are completely general, based on the model (5)

$$\frac{\partial f(\boldsymbol{\sigma}, \mathbf{w})}{\partial \boldsymbol{\sigma}} = \left(\frac{\partial l\left(\psi_{\boldsymbol{\sigma}}(\mathbf{X})^\top \mathbf{w}, \mathbf{y}\right)}{\partial \psi_{\boldsymbol{\sigma}}(\mathbf{X})^\top \mathbf{w}} \right)^\top \frac{\partial \psi_{\boldsymbol{\sigma}}(\mathbf{X})^\top}{\partial \boldsymbol{\sigma}} \mathbf{w} + \frac{\partial \eta(\boldsymbol{\sigma})}{\partial \boldsymbol{\sigma}} \tag{6}$$

$$\frac{\partial f(\boldsymbol{\sigma}, \mathbf{w})}{\partial \mathbf{w}} = \left(\frac{\partial l\left(\psi_{\boldsymbol{\sigma}}(\mathbf{X})^\top \mathbf{w}, \mathbf{y}\right)}{\partial \psi_{\boldsymbol{\sigma}}(\mathbf{X})^\top \mathbf{w}} \right)^\top \psi_{\boldsymbol{\sigma}}(\mathbf{X}) + \frac{\partial \nu(\mathbf{w})}{\partial \mathbf{w}} \tag{7}$$

In the above equations, the derivative of the loss with respect to the linear predictor $\psi_{\boldsymbol{\sigma}}(\mathbf{X})^\top \mathbf{w}$, as well as the derivatives of the regularizers are usually easy to compute. A key quantity is the derivative of the random Fourier map with respect to the parameters $\frac{\partial \psi_{\boldsymbol{\sigma}}(\mathbf{X})^\top}{\partial \boldsymbol{\sigma}}$, *e.g.* (11).

The number of parameters for the joint optimization can be large (up to thousands) which indicates that a limited memory quasi Newton algorithm, such as `l-bfgs` is appropriate. When f is not smooth because of specific choices of regularization, *e.g.* l_1 norms, it is possible to use methods based on projection onto the constraint set instead [21]. In such cases, we only need to provide the derivative of l with respect to $\boldsymbol{\sigma}$ and $\mathbf{w}$.

There are situations when, given $\boldsymbol{\sigma}$, there is a closed form solution for $\mathbf{w}$. Then we can follow an optimization scheme for $\boldsymbol{\sigma}$, and at each gradient step provide the solution for $\mathbf{w}$. In such sitations, we might also have to provide a derivative of $\mathbf{w}$ with respect to $\boldsymbol{\sigma}$. Denote by $\mathbf{w}_{\boldsymbol{\sigma}}$ the $\mathbf{w}$ that minimizes f given a fixed $\boldsymbol{\sigma}$. Then we have to provide the following gradient

$$\frac{\partial f(\boldsymbol{\sigma})}{\partial \boldsymbol{\sigma}} = \left(\frac{\partial l\left(\psi_{\boldsymbol{\sigma}}(\mathbf{X})^\top \mathbf{w}_{\boldsymbol{\sigma}}, \mathbf{y}\right)}{\partial \psi_{\boldsymbol{\sigma}}(\mathbf{X})^\top \mathbf{w}_{\boldsymbol{\sigma}}} \right)^\top \left(\frac{\partial \psi_{\boldsymbol{\sigma}}(\mathbf{X})^\top}{\partial \boldsymbol{\sigma}} \mathbf{w}_{\boldsymbol{\sigma}} + \psi_{\boldsymbol{\sigma}}(\mathbf{X})^\top \frac{\partial \mathbf{w}_{\boldsymbol{\sigma}}}{\partial \boldsymbol{\sigma}} \right) + \left(\frac{\partial \nu(\mathbf{w}_{\boldsymbol{\sigma}})}{\partial \mathbf{w}_{\boldsymbol{\sigma}}} \right)^\top \frac{\partial \mathbf{w}_{\boldsymbol{\sigma}}}{\partial \boldsymbol{\sigma}} + \frac{\partial \eta(\boldsymbol{\sigma})}{\partial \boldsymbol{\sigma}} \tag{8}$$

Such methods are applicable not only for random Fourier feature maps, but for any other embeddings where it is easy to compute the gradient of the map $\frac{\partial \psi_{\boldsymbol{\sigma}}(\mathbf{X})}{\partial \boldsymbol{\sigma}}$ with respect to the parameters.

In the next sections we present two models that we find particularly effective for visual applications. Each one has an equivalent non-approximated counterpart which scales quadratically in the number of training samples, whereas our Fourier reformulations have linear complexity.

3.3 Single Kernel Learning

First we consider the case of single kernel learning. We use the Fourier embedding $\psi_{\boldsymbol{\sigma}}$, introduced earlier (4) as our approximation of the kernel lifting. This model

Table 2. Different loss functions and regularizations for the parameters. These could be combined in many ways. For each combination, different derivations are needed, but all will require the derivatives of the Fourier feature map with respect to the kernel parameters, *e.g.* (11).

$l(\bar{\mathbf{y}}, \mathbf{y})$		$\nu(\mathbf{w})$		$\eta(\boldsymbol{\sigma})$
square loss:	$\Vert\bar{\mathbf{y}} - \mathbf{y}\Vert_2^2$	l_2:	$\lambda\Vert\mathbf{w}\Vert_2^2$	l_2: $\nu\Vert\boldsymbol{\sigma}\Vert_2^2$
hinge loss:	$\sum_i \max(\bar{y}_i - y_i, 0)$	l_1:	$\lambda\Vert\mathbf{w}\Vert_1$	l_1: $\nu\Vert\boldsymbol{\sigma}\Vert_1$
logistic loss:	$\sum_i \log(1 + \exp(-y_i\bar{y}_i))$	$l_{2,1}$:	$\lambda\sum_j \Vert\mathbf{w}_j\Vert_2$	

uses a quadratic loss function and a quadratic regularizer on both $\mathbf{w}$ and $\boldsymbol{\sigma}$. The instantiation of the error function in (5) is

$$f(\boldsymbol{\sigma}, \mathbf{w}) = \frac{1}{2}\left\Vert \psi_{\boldsymbol{\sigma}}(\mathbf{X})^\top \mathbf{w} - \mathbf{y}\right\Vert_2^2 + \lambda \Vert\mathbf{w}\Vert_2^2 + \rho\Vert\boldsymbol{\sigma}\Vert_2^2 \quad (9)$$

For fixed $\boldsymbol{\sigma}$ there is a closed form solution for $\mathbf{w}$, as this becomes a ridge regression problem

$$\mathbf{w}_{\boldsymbol{\sigma}} = \left(\psi_{\boldsymbol{\sigma}}(\mathbf{X})\psi_{\boldsymbol{\sigma}}(\mathbf{X})^\top + \lambda\mathbf{I}\right)^{-1} \psi_{\boldsymbol{\sigma}}(\mathbf{X})\mathbf{y} \quad (10)$$

We further need to compute the gradients $\frac{\partial\psi_{\boldsymbol{\sigma}}(\mathbf{X})}{\partial\boldsymbol{\sigma}}$ and $\frac{\partial\mathbf{w}_{\boldsymbol{\sigma}}}{\partial\boldsymbol{\sigma}}$, of (8). We give gradients for a single training input $\mathbf{x}$, being easy to extrapolate for the entire matrix

$$\frac{\partial\psi_{\boldsymbol{\sigma}}(\mathbf{x})}{\partial\sigma_j} = \left[-\sqrt{\frac{2}{d}} h(\boldsymbol{\omega}_{i,j})^\top \mathbf{x}_j \sin\left(\sum_{j=1}^{r} \sigma_j h(\boldsymbol{\omega}_{i,j})^\top \mathbf{x}_j + 2\pi b_i\right)\right]_{i=1,d} \quad (11)$$

Let $\mathbf{Q} = \psi_{\boldsymbol{\sigma}}(\mathbf{X})\psi_{\boldsymbol{\sigma}}(\mathbf{X})^\top + \lambda\mathbf{I}$, and using a standard result, $\frac{\partial\mathbf{Q}^{-1}}{\partial\sigma} = -\mathbf{Q}^{-1}\frac{\partial\mathbf{Q}}{\partial\sigma}\mathbf{Q}^{-1}$, we obtain

$$\frac{\partial\mathbf{w}_{\boldsymbol{\sigma}}}{\partial\sigma_j} = -\mathbf{Q}^{-1}\frac{\partial\mathbf{Q}}{\partial\sigma_j}\mathbf{Q}^{-1}\psi_{\boldsymbol{\sigma}}(\mathbf{X})\mathbf{y} + \mathbf{Q}^{-1}\frac{\partial\psi_{\boldsymbol{\sigma}}(\mathbf{X})}{\partial\sigma_j}\mathbf{y}$$

The gradient of $\mathbf{Q}$ with respect to σ_j can be obtained as

$$\frac{\partial\mathbf{Q}}{\partial\sigma_j} = \frac{\partial\psi_{\boldsymbol{\sigma}}(\mathbf{X})}{\partial\sigma_j}\psi_{\boldsymbol{\sigma}}(\mathbf{X})^\top + \psi_{\boldsymbol{\sigma}}(\mathbf{X})\frac{\partial\psi_{\boldsymbol{\sigma}}(\mathbf{X})^\top}{\partial\sigma_j}. \quad (12)$$

The overall cost we employ bears a certain similarity to the objective introduced in [6] where the authors use a gradient descent learning technique for kernel ridge regression based on the exact kernel matrix. It also relates to the multiple learning technique for products of kernels introduced in [30]. However, besides the technical differences introduced by the usage of a Fourier map, an important advantage of our methodology is that we do not have to store the kernel matrices in memory, which takes $O(N^2)$ space. Our memory requirement is just $O(Nd + d^2)$ where d is the size of the Fourier embedding. The computational complexity of the method is dominated by $O(i_{skl}(Nd^2+d^3+rNd))$ where d is the size of the random Fourier features, N is the number of training samples, r is the number of kernel hyper-parameters and i_{skl} is the number of iterations to convergence. $O(Nd^2+d^3)$ is the cost of computing the matrix $\mathbf{Q}$ and inverting it.

3.4 Multiple Kernel Learning

We propose a multiple kernel learning formulation where the feature channels are initially transformed using random Fourier embeddings and concatenated within an optimization framework based on block l_1 norm regularizer (RFF-MKL). We prove that this new formulation is equivalent to an l_1 regularized multiple kernel learning formulation introduced in [30] (GMKL) and then compare the two methodologies. Experiments show that both approaches have similar performance. In contrast, the block l_1 regularized MKL method based on random Fourier maps runs faster and scales better since we do not need to compute or store the Gram matrices associated with the input features.

In this case, the Fourier embedding has the following concatenated form $\psi_{\boldsymbol{\sigma}}(\mathbf{X}) = \left[\psi_{\sigma_1}(\mathbf{X}_1)^\top, \ldots, \psi_{\sigma_r}(\mathbf{X}_r)^\top\right]^\top$ where we have split row-wise the input matrix $\mathbf{X}$ into r different input matrices $\{\mathbf{X}_1, \ldots, \mathbf{X}_r\}$, one corresponding to each feature channel. We have a different embedding for each descriptor

$$\psi_{\sigma_j}(\mathbf{X}_j) = \left[\sqrt{\frac{2}{d}}\cos\left(\sigma_j h(\boldsymbol{\omega}_{i,j})^\top \mathbf{X}_j + 2\pi b_i\right)\right]_{i=1,d} \in \mathbb{R}^{d\times n} \tag{13}$$

and for different input samples $\mathbf{u}$ and $\mathbf{v}$ on which the same anisotropic scaling is applied we have $\psi_{\boldsymbol{\sigma}}(\mathbf{u})^\top\psi_{\boldsymbol{\sigma}}(\mathbf{v}) = \sum_{i=1}^r \psi_{\sigma_i}(\mathbf{u}_i)^\top\psi_{\sigma_i}(\mathbf{v}_i) \approx \sum_{i=1}^r k_{\sigma_i}(\mathbf{u}_i, \mathbf{v}_i)$. This corresponds to the sum of kernels for the different feature channels.

We now show that the l_1 regularized GMKL is equivalent, as an optimization procedure, with RFF-MKL. For GMKL, we have the following primal problem[30]

$$\min_{\mathbf{w},\mathbf{d}} \frac{1}{2}\mathbf{w}^\top\mathbf{w} + Cl(\phi(\mathbf{X})^\top\mathbf{w}, \mathbf{y}) + \sum_{j=1}^r d_j, \text{ subject to } \mathbf{d} \geq 0 \tag{14}$$

where l is the ϵ-insensitive hinge loss used for svm regression and

$$\phi(\mathbf{X}) = [\sqrt{d_1}\phi_1(\mathbf{X}_1)^\top, \ldots, \sqrt{d_r}\phi_r(\mathbf{X}_r)^\top]^\top, \tag{15}$$

with $\phi_j(\mathbf{X}_j)$ the lifting associated to kernel k_j, which is applied on the feature channel $\mathbf{X}_j$. From the Representer Theorem [27] we know that the solution for $\mathbf{w}$ will be a linear combination of basis functions

$$\mathbf{w} = \sum \boldsymbol{\alpha}_{\mathbf{x}}\phi(\mathbf{x}) = \left[\sqrt{d_1}\mathbf{w}_1^\top, \ldots, \sqrt{d_r}\mathbf{w}_r^\top\right]^\top \tag{16}$$

where we have summed over all input data $\mathbf{x}$ and dropped the bias term for simplicity. We can then rewrite the above equation (14) as

$$\min_{\mathbf{w},\mathbf{d}} \sum_{j=1}^r \frac{d_j}{2}\|\mathbf{w}_j\|_2^2 + Cl(\sum_{j=1}^r d_j\phi_j(\mathbf{X}_j)^\top\mathbf{w}_j, \mathbf{y}) + \sum_{j=1}^r d_j, \text{ subject to } \mathbf{d} \geq 0 \tag{17}$$

Following a standard trick from the multiple kernel learning literature[1] we make the substitution $d_j \mathbf{w}_j \rightarrow \mathbf{w}_j$ to obtain the optimization problem

$$\min_{\mathbf{w},\mathbf{d}} \sum_{j=1}^{r} \frac{\|\mathbf{w}_j\|_2^2}{2d_j} + Cl(\sum_{j=1}^{r} \phi_j(\mathbf{X}_j)^\top \mathbf{w}_j, \mathbf{y}) + \sum_{j=1}^{r} d_j, \text{ subject to } \mathbf{d} \geq 0 \quad (18)$$

It can easily be shown that $\frac{1}{2}\frac{\|\mathbf{w}_j\|_2^2}{d_j} + d_j \geq \sqrt{2}\|\mathbf{w}_j\|_2$, and we observe that the loss function no longer depends on $\mathbf{d}$. Replacing the lifting ϕ by our Fourier embedding $\psi_{\boldsymbol{\sigma}}$ and the ϵ-insensitive hinge loss with an approximate smooth loss[10,24], the primal multiple kernel learning formulation is equivalent to the following $l_{2,1}$ norm optimization formulation

$$\min_{\mathbf{w}} l(\psi_{\boldsymbol{\sigma}}(\mathbf{X})^\top \mathbf{w}, \mathbf{y}) + \lambda \sum_{j=1}^{r} \|\mathbf{w}_j\|_2 \quad (19)$$

where we set $\lambda = \frac{\sqrt{2}}{C}$. The equality holds when $d_j = \frac{1}{\sqrt{2}}\|\mathbf{w}_j\|_2$. We see this is a particular case of the general model (5) where $\boldsymbol{\sigma}$ is fixed and we have to optimize for $\mathbf{w}$ with an $l_{2,1}$ regularizer. The loss function we use to approximate the ϵ-insensitive loss (ϵ-IL) used in standard support vector regression is the ϵ-insensitive γ logistic loss (ϵ-IGLL) function[10,24](see Fig. 1) defined as

$$l_{\gamma,\epsilon}(\bar{\mathbf{y}}, \mathbf{y}) = \frac{1}{\gamma} \sum_{i=1}^{N} \left[\log\left(1 + e^{\gamma(\bar{y}_i - y_i - \epsilon)}\right) + \log\left(1 + e^{\gamma(-\bar{y}_i + y_i - \epsilon)}\right) - 2\log(1 + e^{-\gamma\epsilon})\right]$$

where N is the number of input samples, $\bar{\mathbf{y}} = \psi_{\boldsymbol{\sigma}}(\mathbf{X})^\top \mathbf{w}$ and we have to provide the gradient $\frac{\partial l_{\gamma,\epsilon}(\psi_{\boldsymbol{\sigma}}(\mathbf{X})^\top \mathbf{w}, \mathbf{y})}{\partial \mathbf{w}}$. We give the gradient for a single input $\mathbf{x}$, and the first term in $l_{\gamma,\epsilon}$. It can be easily extended to the entire matrix $\mathbf{X}$, and to the other two terms of $l_{\gamma,\epsilon}$

$$\frac{\partial \log(1 + e^{\gamma(\psi_{\boldsymbol{\sigma}}(\mathbf{x})^\top \mathbf{w} - \mathbf{y} - \epsilon)})}{\partial \mathbf{w}} = \gamma \frac{e^{\gamma(\psi_{\boldsymbol{\sigma}}(\mathbf{x})^\top \mathbf{w} - \mathbf{y} - \epsilon)}}{1 + e^{\gamma(\psi_{\boldsymbol{\sigma}}(\mathbf{x})^\top \mathbf{w} - \mathbf{y} - \epsilon)}} \psi_{\boldsymbol{\sigma}}(\mathbf{x}) \quad (20)$$

In an associated technical report[36] we discuss the computational and memory complexities and conclude that RFF-MKL scales linearly, while GMKL is quadratic.

4 Experiments

We present experiments for single kernel learning and multiple kernel learning, comparing the random linear Fourier methodology with its non-linear kernel counterparts both in terms of running times and in terms of accuracy.

In a first set of experiments, we have evaluated the methods in the PASCAL VOC2011[35] segmentation challenge. This consists of 2223 images for training with ground truth split into halves for training and validation. Another 1111 images are given for testing without ground truth. Following the standard procedure we have trained the methods on the training set (further split, internally into training and validation for kernel hyper-parameter learning) and tested on the PASCAL VOC2011 validation set. We have used the methodology presented in Li et al. [18] and relied on the publicly available CPMC segmentation algorithm from Carreira and Sminchisescu [4] to filter the initial pool of segments to around 100 segments per image. For each of these segments we extracted 7 types of features among which two bag of visual words for color SIFT [29] and two dense gray scale SIFT descriptors, one on each segment and one on the background of each segment and three types of phog descriptors, two on the Pb edges given by [13] computed at different scales, one on the contour and one on the foreground. The third phog descriptor does not use Pb. Because the number of segments (around 10^5) was still too large for any kernel support vector based algorithm to cope with, we have chosen up to 10^4 segments for each class. The segments were chosen based on their individual scores and we balanced the examples to have a fair split between positives and negatives. More detail on how the scores are defined and computed can be found in [18].

Single Kernel Learning. We run a set of experiments for our single kernel learning technique based on random Fourier features (RFF-SKL) and compare in terms of accuracy with the single kernel learning technique introduced by Chapelle et al. [6] (KRR-GD). We want to predict the class for more than 10^5 segments. We expect RFF-SKL to give comparable results in terms of accuracy to KRR-GD. Results are shown in Table 3. We vary the size of the training set from 10^3 to 10^5 and measure both the running times of RFF-SKL and the accuracy. In Fig. 1 we show how the accuracy depends on the size of the training data and the average time required for RFF-SKL and KRR-GD to run on one class. We observe that RFF-SKL running time scales linearly in the number of examples. The number of random Fourier samples we have chosen was $d = 3000$. This is consistent with our computational complexity discussed in Section 3.3. We are able to tune the hyper-parameters of a Fourier model trained with more than 10^5 samples, each with 3000 attributes in less than 15 minutes.

Table 3. Accuracy of RFF-SKL versus KRR-GD. For a large number of training samples the nonlinear method could not be run due to memory limits.

Samples	$2.5 \cdot 10^3$	$5 \cdot 10^3$	$7.5 \cdot 10^4$	10^4	$2 \cdot 10^4$	$6 \cdot 10^4$
RFF-SKL	0.21	0.25	0.28	0.29	0.31	0.32
KRR-GD	0.24	0.29	0.31	0.32	*	*

Multiple Kernel Learning. We also report experiments for multiple kernel learning. For GMKL we have evaluated an exponentiated χ^2 kernel for each image feature. We set the scaling parameter to be the mean of the chi-square distance matrix following the procedure from [14]. Gram matrices were created for each class since for different classes we had to select different representative samples. For our multiple kernel learning based on random Fourier features

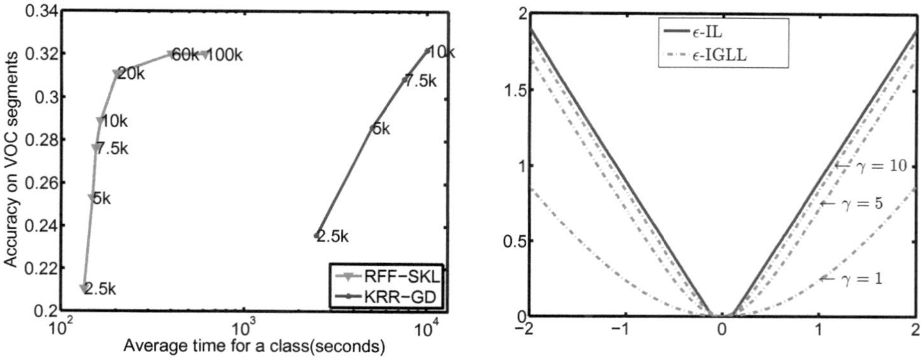

Fig. 1. On the left, we plot time versus accuracy for classifying the VOC segments for RFF-SKL and KRR-GD. We varied the number of training points from 10^3 up to 10^5 and measured the average time for a class, for 20 classes. For KRR-GD it was not feasible to go beyond 10^4 training samples (horizontal axis, log scale). On the right we show that an ϵ-insensitive γ loss function we use for optimization provides a good approximation to the exact ϵ-insensitive loss. Here we show values for $\epsilon = 0.1$ and $\gamma = 1, 5, 10$.

within the l_1 block regularizer (RFF-MKL) we have approximated the kernel as in [28] using the recommended settings. In Fig. 2 we compare the accuracy of predicting the correct class of segments and we show the average running time per class. We see that for a small number of training samples GMKL is slightly superior, but RFF-MKL catches up eventually due to its better scalability. Notice that RFF-MKL scales linearly and GMKL scales quadratically. Working with kernel matrices larger than 10^4 was not feasible for GMKL. We also conducted experiments on the Skewed χ_2 kernel and evaluated performance as we varied the dimension d of the Fourier embedding. For each dimension we trained a different model and compared to GMKL. Results are shown on Fig. 3. To build the regularization path we traced the parameter λ in equation (19).

We have experimented on the ImageNet[11] ILSVRC2011 dataset as well. We first considered 12 classes taken from the ILSVRC2011, each having 1300 images and split them into a train and test sets of 1000 and 300, respectively. For each image we extracted three types of feature channels: two types of phog descriptors at 3 pyramid levels each and at 20, respectively 40 orientations, and a phow[31] feature channel extracted over three pyramid levels. We converted all the features in the Fourier domain using the procedure from [28]. We used this data to compare two joint models with their corresponding average models. In the joint models both $\boldsymbol{\sigma}$ and $\mathbf{w}$ are learned, whereas for the average models $\boldsymbol{\sigma}$ is fixed and only $\mathbf{w}$ is learned. First, we compared a multiple kernel learning joint model with a square loss and a $l_{2,1}$ regularizer with its average model, identified as RFF-SQL-MKL-JOINT and RFF-SQL-MKL respectively. Then we compared a single kernel learning joint model with a square loss and a quadratic regularizer with its average model, identified as RFF-SQL-SKL-JOINT and RFF-SQL-SKL respectively. Results are presented in Fig. 3.

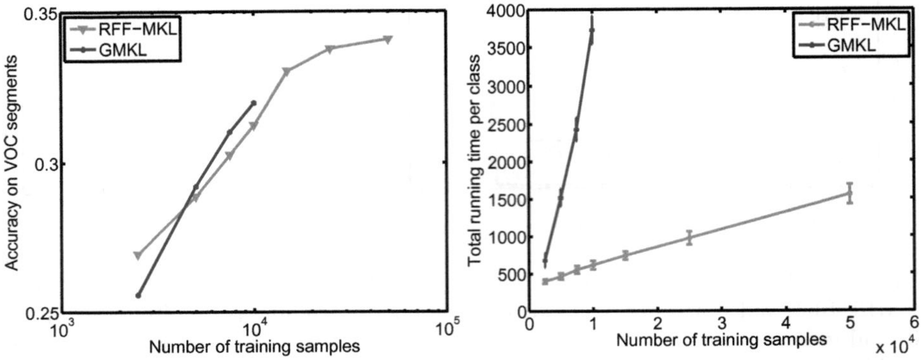

Fig. 2. On the left, we show the accuracy for classifying the VOC segments for RFF-MKL and GMKL, as a function of the number of training examples. RFF-MKL scales significantly better than GMKL. On the right, we show running times expressed in seconds for RFF-MKL and GMKL. Notice that RFF-MKL scales linearly whereas GMKL scales quadratically. Error-bars are obtained by averaging over the number of classes (20 in this case).

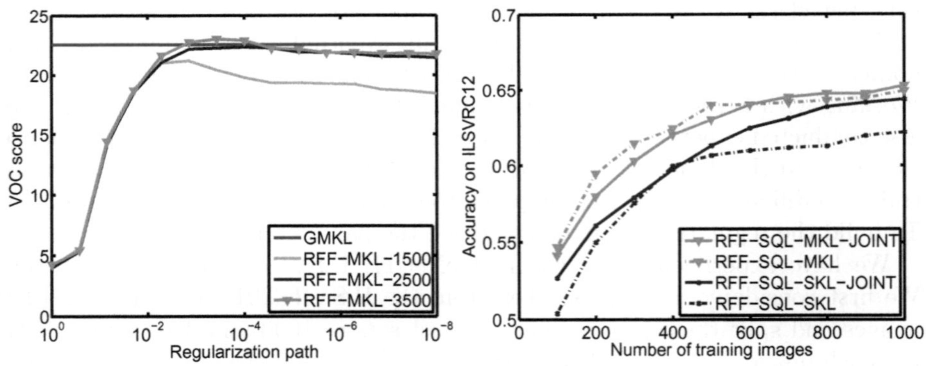

Fig. 3. On the left, we show the VOC score for three choices of dimensionality of Fourier embeddings, as well as the GMKL. On the right, we plot the accuracy of the joint and the average models on ILSVRC12. Notice that given enough training data, the joint models give better performance.

Table 4. Accuracy on the ILSVRC2011 dataset and average training time per class. $l_{2,1}$ regularizers are more effective than l_2 norms in this case. The single kernel learning model is indeed faster, but the multiple kernel learning models give better performance.

Method	RFF-SQL-MKL	RFF-SQL-SQR-MKL	RFF-SQL-SKL
Accuracy	**18.5%**	**12.3%**	**10%**
Time	196±42s	101±41s	27±13s

We then extracted the same feature channels for all the 1000 classes of the ILSVRC2011 dataset. We trained in the Fourier domain RFF-SQL-MKL, RFF-SQL-SKL and a third multiple kernel learning model with l_2 loss and l_2 regularizer, identified as RFF-SQL-SQR-MKL, on the entire dataset. We tested on the 50,000 images validation set, since the ground truth for the test set is not publicly available. Results are shown in Table 4. We observe that our results match the accuracy levels reported for Imagenet baselines [5]. While better features and kernels can certainly improve performance, we appreciate that fast, yet generic approximate non-linear learning methods like the ones we propose, have potential for such large datasets.

5 Conclusions

The Fourier methodology provides a powerful and formally consistent class of linear approximations for non-linear kernel machines, carrying the promise of both good model scalability and non-linear prediction power. This has motivated research in extending the class of useful kernels that can be approximated, *e.g.* χ^2 [33,19,25], but leaves ample space for reformulating standard problems like single or multiple kernel learning in the linear Fourier domain. In this paper, we have developed gradient-based methods for single and multiple-kernel learning in the Fourier domain and showed that these are efficient and produce accurate results on complex computer vision datasets like VOC2011 and ILSVRC2011. In future work we plan to explore alternative kernel map approximations, feature selection and non-convex optimization techniques for learning.

Acknowledgements. This work was supported by CNCS-UEFICSDI, under PNII RU-RC-2/2009, PCE-2011-3-0438, and CT-ERC-2012-1.

References

1. Bach, F.: Consistency of the group Lasso and multiple kernel learning. JMLR 9, 1179–1225 (2008)
2. Bach, F.: Exploring Large Feature Spaces with Hierarchical Multiple Kernel Learning. In: NIPS (2009)
3. Bach, F., Lanckriet, G.R.G., Jordan, M.I.: Multiple kernel learning, conic duality, and the SMO algorithm. In: ICML (2004)

4. Carreira, J., Sminchisescu, C.: Constrained Parametric Min-Cuts for Automatic Object Segmentation. In: CVPR (2010)
5. ILSVRC (2011), http://www.image-net.org/challenges/LSVRC/2011/index
6. Chapelle, O., Vapnik, V., Bousquet, O., Mukherjee, S.: Choosing Multiple Parameters for Support Vector Machines. Machine Learning 46, 131–159 (2002)
7. Cortes, C., Mohri, M., Rostamizadeh, A.: Learning Non-linear Combinations of Kernels. In: NIPS (2009)
8. Cortes, C., Mohri, M., Rostamizadeh, A.: Two-Stage Learning Kernel Algorithms. In: ICML (2010)
9. Cristianini, N., Kandola, J., Elisseeff, A., Shawe-Taylor, J.: On Kernel-Target Alignment. In: NIPS (2002)
10. Dekel, O., Shalev-Shwartz, S., Singer, Y.: Smooth epsilon-Insensitive Regression by Loss Symmetrization (2003)
11. Deng, J., Dong, W., Socher, R., Li, L.J., Li, K., Fei-Fei, L.: ImageNet: A Large-Scale Hierarchical Image Database. In: CVPR (2009)
12. Li, F., Fu, Y., Dai, Y.H., Sminchisescu, C., Wang, J.: Kernel learning by unconstrained optimization. In: AISTATS (2009)
13. Maire, M., Arbelaez, P., Fowlkes, C., Malik, J.: Using Contours to Detect and Localize Junctions in Natural Images. In: CVPR (2008)
14. Gehler, P., Nowozin, S.: On Feature Combination for Multiclass Object Classification. In: ICCV (2009)
15. Keerthi, S., Sindhwani, V., Chapelle, O.: An Efficient Method for Gradient-Based Adaptation of Hyperparameters in SVM Models. In: NIPS (2007)
16. Kloft. M., Brefeld, U., Sonnenburg, S., Laskov, P., Müller, K. R., Zien, A.: Efficient and Accurate Lp-Norm Multiple Kernel Learning. In: NIPS (2009)
17. Lanckriet, G.R.G., Cristianini, N., Bartlett, P., El Ghaoui, L., Jordan, M.I.: Learning the Kernel Matrix with Semidefinite Programming. JMLR 5, 27–72 (2004)
18. Li, F., Carreira, J., Sminchisescu, C.: Object Recognition as Ranking Holistic Figure-Ground Hypotheses. In: CVPR (2010)
19. Li, F., Ionescu, C., Sminchisescu, C.: Random Fourier Approximations for Skewed Multiplicative Histogram Kernels. In: Goesele, M., Roth, S., Kuijper, A., Schiele, B., Schindler, K. (eds.) DAGM 2010. LNCS, vol. 6376, pp. 262–271. Springer, Heidelberg (2010)
20. Li, F., Sminchisescu, C.: The Feature Selection Path in Kernel Methods. In: AISTATS (2010)
21. Schmidt, M., van den Berg, E., Friedlander, M.P., Murphy, K.: Optimizing Costly Functions with Simple Constraints: A Limited-Memory Projected Quasi-Newton Algorithm. In: AISTATS (2009)
22. Maji, S., Berg, A.C., Malik, J.: Classification using Intersection Kernel Support Vector Machines is Efficient. In: CVPR (2008)
23. Rahimi, A., Recht, B.: Random features for large-scale kernel machines. In: NIPS (2007)
24. Jason, D.M.R.: Maximum-Margin Logistic Regression (2004), http://people.csail.mit.edu/jrennie/writing
25. Li, F., Lebanon, G., Sminchisescu, C.: Chebyshev Approximations to the Histogram χ^2 Kernel. In: ICCV (2012)
26. Rudin, W.: Fourier Analysis on Groups. Wiley Interscience (1990)
27. Schölkopf, B., Smola, A.: Learning with kernels: support vector machines, regularization, optimization, and beyond. MIT Press (2002)
28. Sreekanth, V., Vedaldi, A., Jawahar, C.V., Zisserman, A.: Generalized RBF feature maps for efficient detection. In: BMVC (2010)

29. van de Sande, K.E.A., Gevers, T., Snoek, C.G.M.: Evaluating Color Descriptors for Object and Scene Recognition. PAMI 9, 1582–1596 (2010)
30. Varma, M., Babu, B.R.: More Generality in Efficient Multiple Kernel Learning. In: ICML (2009)
31. Vedaldi, A., Fulkerson, B.: VLFeat – An open and portable library of computer vision algorithms. In: ACM International Conference on Multimedia (2010)
32. Vedaldi, A., Gulshan, V., Varma, M., Zisserman, A.: Multiple Kernels for Object Detection. In: ICCV (2009)
33. Vedaldi, A., Zisserman, A.: Efficient Additive Kernels via Explicit Feature Maps. In: CVPR (2010)
34. Visnwanathan, S.V.N., Sun, Z., Theera-Ampornpunt, N., Varma, M.: Multiple Kernel Learning and the SMO Algorithm. In: NIPS (2010)
35. Everingham, M., Gool, L.V., Williams, C.K.I., Winn, J., Zisserman, A.: The PASCAL Visual Object Classes Challenge, VOC 2011 (2011)
36. Bazavan, E., Li, F., Sminchisescu, C.: Learning Kernels in Fourier Space. Technical Report, Romanian Academy of Sciences and University of Bonn (July 2012)

Efficient Optimization for Low-Rank Integrated Bilinear Classifiers

Takumi Kobayashi and Nobuyuki Otsu

National Institute of Advanced Industrial Science and Technology,
1-1-1, Umezono, Tsukuba, Japan
{takumi.kobayashi,otsu.n}@aist.go.jp

Abstract. In pattern classification, it is needed to efficiently treat two-way data (feature matrices) while preserving the two-way structure such as spatio-temporal relationships, *etc*. The classifier for the feature matrix is generally formulated by multiple bilinear forms which result in a matrix. The rank of the matrix, *i.e.*, the number of bilinear forms, should be low from the viewpoint of generalization performance and computational cost. For that purpose, we propose a low-rank bilinear classifier based on the efficient optimization. In the proposed method, the classifier is optimized by minimizing the trace norm of the classifier (matrix), which contributes to the rank reduction for an efficient classifier without any hard constraint on the rank. We formulate the optimization problem in a tractable convex form and propose the procedure to solve it efficiently with the global optimum. In addition, by considering a kernel-based extension of the bilinear method, we induce a novel multiple kernel learning (MKL), called heterogeneous MKL. The method combines both inter kernels between heterogeneous types of features and the ordinary kernels within homogeneous features into a new discriminative kernel in a unified manner using the bilinear model. In the experiments on various classification problems using feature arrays, co-occurrence feature matrices, and multiple kernels, the proposed method exhibits favorable performances compared to the other methods.

1 Introduction

Classification problems are usually addressed to the tasks to classify feature vectors extracted from the target domain such as images [1,2] and motion sequences [3,4]. The features are often to be represented in a *vector* form (one-way) such as by concatenation, whereas it is inherently defined in a *matrix* form (two-way). For example, the matrix forms are found in image pixels, arrays of (local) feature vectors extracted at spatio-temporal (grid) points such as in HOG [1], and co-occurrence features (Fig. 1). The dimensionality of the concatenated feature vector is the product of two-way's dimensions, resulting in high dimensionality, and the inherent structure of the two-way features is unfortunately collapsed [5].

There are some recent works to directly deal with the features in a matrix form; 2DPCA [6] and 2DLDA [7] are extended from PCA and LDA to matrix-based formulations for dimensionality reduction, and the methods in [8,9] are

A. Fitzgibbon et al. (Eds.): ECCV 2012, Part II, LNCS 7573, pp. 474–487, 2012.

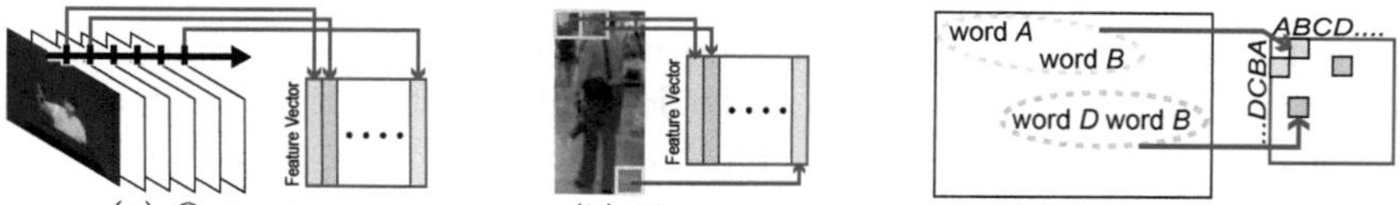

(a) One-way (b) Two-way (c) Co-occurrence

Fig. 1. Examples of feature matrices. Arrays of feature vectors extracted from one-way (a) and two-way data (b) and co-occurrence features (c) are defined in a matrix form.

also proposed to factorize the feature matrix. Those methods are formulated mainly to learn effective image representations in a matrix form and are not intended for classification problems in a supervised framework.

For classification, significant research efforts have been made on constructing linear classifiers for feature vectors, *e.g.*, SVM [10] and L_1-SVM [11] in the maximum-margin framework [12], which can be further extended to kernel-based methods [13]. On the other hand, the classifier to deal with feature matrices is naturally defined as a *bilinear* model comprising two kinds (row and column) of weights [5], which forms a matrix in general. Along with the advances of the linear classifiers, some bilinear classifiers have been recently proposed [14,15]. The main concern in the bilinear methods is to construct the bilinear classifier (matrix) of low rank in a manner similar to the maximum-margin framework; The VC-dimension of the low-rank bilinear model is proven to be less than that of the concatenated linear models [15]. In those methods, the approximated optimization approaches are usually employed, resulting in local minima, since the optimization problems are formulated as a biconvex (non-convex) formulations and semi-definite programming (SDP) which is computationally less efficient. In addition, the constraint regarding to the rank is explicitly introduced as a free parameter; that is, users are required to determine the classifier rank in advance.

In this paper, we propose a novel method to optimize the efficient bilinear classifier which results in low rank. Without approximations nor hard constraints on the rank, the proposed method automatically produces the optimal low-rank classifier by minimizing the trace norm of the classifier matrix, while reducing the classification errors.

The contributions of this paper are 1) to formulate a tractable convex optimization problem and propose an efficient optimization procedure to provide the global minimum, and 2) by considering a kernel extension of the bilinear classifier, to apply the proposed method to multiple kernel learning (MKL) [16] and induce a novel MKL, called *heterogeneous MKL*. In the heterogeneous MKL, by using the bilinear model, we can integrate both inter kernels between heterogeneous types of features and the ordinary kernels within homogeneous features into a new discriminative kernel in a unified manner.

2 Bilinear Classifier

Let $\boldsymbol{X}$ be a feature matrix whose dimensions are denoted by h and w ($\boldsymbol{X} \in \mathbb{R}^{h \times w}$). For example, $\boldsymbol{X}$ is regarded as the array of the h-dimensional feature vectors extracted at w points, such as in xy-coordinates for images or along t-axis for time-series signals, as shown in Fig. 1. To deal with the feature matrix, a bilinear classifier is simply formulated as $\hat{y}=\boldsymbol{w}_h^\top \boldsymbol{X}\boldsymbol{w}_w+b$ where $\boldsymbol{w}_h\in\mathbb{R}^h$, $\boldsymbol{w}_w\in\mathbb{R}^w$. This is regarded as a '1-rank' classifier, and by integrating multiple such classifiers, the general bilinear classifier is defined by

$$\hat{y} = \mathrm{tr}(\boldsymbol{W}_h^\top \boldsymbol{X}\boldsymbol{W}_w) + b = \mathrm{tr}(\boldsymbol{W}^\top \boldsymbol{X}) + b, \tag{1}$$

where b is the bias and $\boldsymbol{W} = \boldsymbol{W}_h\boldsymbol{W}_w^\top \in \mathbb{R}^{h\times w}$ is the classifier matrix ($\boldsymbol{W}_h \in \mathbb{R}^{h\times r}$, $\boldsymbol{W}_w\in\mathbb{R}^{w\times r}$ where $r\leq \min[w,h]$). For simplicity, we consider a two-class classification problem, given n samples $\{\boldsymbol{X}_i, y_i\}_{i=1}^n$ where y_i is the class label ($y_i\in\{+1,-1\}$) of the i-th sample. As in the maximum-margin framework [12], we measure the margin of the bilinear classifier in (1) by the matrix trace norm, *i.e.*, sum of singular values, for minimizing the matrix rank, which results in the following optimization problem:

$$\min_{\boldsymbol{W},b} \ ||\boldsymbol{W}||_\Sigma + C\sum_{i=1}^n \max\big[0, 1-y_i\{\mathrm{tr}(\boldsymbol{W}^\top \boldsymbol{X}_i) + b\}\big], \tag{2}$$

where $||\boldsymbol{W}||_\Sigma$ indicates the trace norm of $\boldsymbol{W}$. Let the singular values of $\boldsymbol{W}$ be denoted by $\boldsymbol{\sigma} \in \mathbb{R}^r$. The trace norm is represented by $||\boldsymbol{W}||_\Sigma = ||\boldsymbol{\sigma}||_1$, while the rank is measured by $\mathrm{rank}(\boldsymbol{W})=||\boldsymbol{\sigma}||_0$. Thus, in the formulation (2), the L_1 norm (trace norm) in the objective cost is regarded as a relaxation of the L_0 norm which directly minimizes the rank. Such L_1-norm minimization induces sparsity [11] in the singular values, thereby minimizing the rank. In the followings, we reformulate (2) to the tractable convex problem (10) and propose the procedure to solve it efficiently.

2.1 SDP Problem

We begin with rewriting (2) to semi-definite programming (SDP) [17]. By introducing the augmented variables,

$$\tilde{\boldsymbol{X}}_i = \begin{bmatrix} \boldsymbol{0} & \boldsymbol{X}_i \\ \boldsymbol{X}_i^\top & \boldsymbol{0} \end{bmatrix}, \quad \tilde{\boldsymbol{W}} = \begin{bmatrix} \boldsymbol{W}_h \\ \boldsymbol{W}_w \end{bmatrix}\begin{bmatrix} \boldsymbol{W}_h \\ \boldsymbol{W}_w \end{bmatrix}^\top = \begin{bmatrix} \boldsymbol{W}_h\boldsymbol{W}_h^\top & \boldsymbol{W} \\ \boldsymbol{W}^\top & \boldsymbol{W}_w\boldsymbol{W}_w^\top \end{bmatrix},$$

the formulation (2) results in

$$\min_{\tilde{\boldsymbol{W}}\succcurlyeq 0,b} \frac{1}{2}\mathrm{tr}(\tilde{\boldsymbol{W}}) + C\sum_i \max\Big[0, 1-y_i\Big\{\frac{1}{2}\mathrm{tr}(\tilde{\boldsymbol{W}}^\top \tilde{\boldsymbol{X}}_i)+b\Big\}\Big], \tag{3}$$

where we replace $||\boldsymbol{W}||_\Sigma$ by $\mathrm{tr}(\tilde{\boldsymbol{W}})$ as in [17]. In the convex problem (3), the global optimum is obtained by SDP [18], but it requires significant computational costs, which makes it infeasible for large-scaled samples.

2.2 Efficient Convex Problem

Considering $\tilde{\boldsymbol{W}}=\begin{bmatrix} \boldsymbol{W}_h \\ \boldsymbol{W}_w \end{bmatrix}\begin{bmatrix} \boldsymbol{W}_h \\ \boldsymbol{W}_w \end{bmatrix}^\top$, we further rewrite (3) to

$$\min_{\boldsymbol{W}_w}\Big[\frac{1}{2}\mathrm{tr}(\boldsymbol{W}_w\boldsymbol{W}_w^\top) + \underline{\min_{\boldsymbol{W}_h,b}\Big\{\frac{1}{2}\mathrm{tr}(\boldsymbol{W}_h\boldsymbol{W}_h^\top)+C\sum_i \max\big[0, 1-y_i\{\mathrm{tr}(\boldsymbol{W}_h^\top\boldsymbol{X}_i\boldsymbol{W}_w)+b\}\big]\Big\}}\Big]. \tag{4}$$

The formulation (4) is biconvex (non-convex) or bilevel [19], and the iterative approach which optimizes either of $\boldsymbol{W}_h$ or $\boldsymbol{W}_w$ in an alternating manner is applicable as in [14]. Such an approach is tractable in contrast to SDP, but it results in local minima. In this study, we reformulate (4) to a tractable convex problem and propose a procedure to produce the global optimum efficiently.

Here, we suppose the column size is smaller than the row size, $h > w$, without loss of generality. The inner optimization (underlined term) in (4) is regarded as the standard SVM problem with respect to $\boldsymbol{W}_h, b$, and thus it has the dual:

$$\max_{\boldsymbol{\alpha}\in\Theta_{\boldsymbol{y}}} \sum_i \alpha_i - \frac{1}{2}\sum_{i,j}\alpha_i\alpha_j y_i y_j K_{ij}, \tag{5}$$

$$\text{where } \Theta_{\boldsymbol{y}} = \left\{\boldsymbol{\alpha} \mid \forall i,\ 0 \le \alpha_i \le C,\ \textstyle\sum_i y_i\alpha_i = 0\right\}, \tag{6}$$

$$K_{ij} = \mathrm{tr}\{(\boldsymbol{X}_i\boldsymbol{W}_w)^\top(\boldsymbol{X}_j\boldsymbol{W}_w)\} = \mathrm{tr}(\boldsymbol{W}_w\boldsymbol{W}_w^\top\boldsymbol{X}_i^\top\boldsymbol{X}_j). \tag{7}$$

Thereby, given the optimum $\boldsymbol{W}_w^*$, we get the optimum bilinear classifier as

$$\boldsymbol{W}_h^* = \sum_i \alpha_i^* y_i \boldsymbol{X}_i \boldsymbol{W}_w^*, \quad \hat{y} = \mathrm{tr}(\boldsymbol{W}_w^*\boldsymbol{W}_w^{*\top}\sum_i \alpha_i^* y_i \boldsymbol{X}_i^\top \boldsymbol{X}), \tag{8}$$

where α_i^* are the optimizers in (5). In the forms (4-8), we can see that the key variable is $\boldsymbol{\Sigma}_w \triangleq \boldsymbol{W}_w\boldsymbol{W}_w^\top \succcurlyeq 0$ rather than $\boldsymbol{W}_w$ itself. Since the inner optimization in (4) can be replaced with its dual (5) due to the string duality [20,21], the optimization (4) is reformulated into

$$\min_{\boldsymbol{\Sigma}_w\succcurlyeq 0}\left[\frac{1}{2}\mathrm{tr}(\boldsymbol{\Sigma}_w) + \max_{\boldsymbol{\alpha}\in\Theta_{\boldsymbol{y}}}\left\{\sum_i\alpha_i - \frac{1}{2}\sum_{i,j}\alpha_i\alpha_j y_i y_j K_{ij(\boldsymbol{\Sigma}_w)}\right\}\right],$$

$$\text{where } K_{ij(\boldsymbol{\Sigma}_w)} = \mathrm{tr}(\boldsymbol{\Sigma}_w\boldsymbol{X}_i^\top\boldsymbol{X}_j). \tag{9}$$

This is still one form of bilevel optimization [19], but by using the *unique* optimizer $\boldsymbol{\alpha}^*$ in (5), we finally obtain our proposed formulation from (2) as

$$\min_{\boldsymbol{\Sigma}_w\succcurlyeq 0}\left[J(\boldsymbol{\Sigma}_w) \triangleq \frac{1}{2}\mathrm{tr}(\boldsymbol{\Sigma}_w) + \sum_i \alpha^*_{i(\boldsymbol{\Sigma}_w)} - \frac{1}{2}\sum_{i,j}\alpha^*_{i(\boldsymbol{\Sigma}_w)}\alpha^*_{j(\boldsymbol{\Sigma}_w)} y_i y_j K_{ij(\boldsymbol{\Sigma}_w)}\right], \tag{10}$$

$$\text{where } \boldsymbol{\alpha}^*_{(\boldsymbol{\Sigma}_w)} = \arg\max_{\boldsymbol{\alpha}\in\Theta_{\boldsymbol{y}}} \sum_i\alpha_i - \frac{1}{2}\sum_{i,j}\alpha_i\alpha_j y_i y_j K_{ij(\boldsymbol{\Sigma}_w)}. \tag{11}$$

The optimization problem (10) is a single-level form by $\boldsymbol{\Sigma}_w$ and is *convex* (refer to supplementary material for the proof). Thus, we can obtain the global optimum $\boldsymbol{\Sigma}_w^*$, instead of $\boldsymbol{W}_w^*$, by means of the following gradient-descent approach.

By using Lemma 2 in [22] (see supplementary material for the detail), the derivative of J is given, as if $\boldsymbol{\alpha}^*_{(\boldsymbol{\Sigma}_w)}$ do not depend on $\boldsymbol{\Sigma}_w$, by

$$\frac{\partial J}{\partial\boldsymbol{\Sigma}_w} = \frac{1}{2}\left\{\boldsymbol{I} - \sum_{ij}\alpha^*_{i(\boldsymbol{\Sigma}_w)}\alpha^*_{j(\boldsymbol{\Sigma}_w)} y_i y_j \boldsymbol{X}_i^\top\boldsymbol{X}_j\right\}.$$

For optimization of (10), to ensure the positive semi-definiteness of $\boldsymbol{\Sigma}_w$, the projected gradient descent [20,21] is applied via the eigen decomposition of $\boldsymbol{\Sigma}_w - \eta\frac{\partial J}{\partial\boldsymbol{\Sigma}_w}$ and cutting off the negative eigenvalues and their eigenvectors:

$$\boldsymbol{\Sigma}_w^{old} - \eta\frac{\partial J}{\partial\boldsymbol{\Sigma}_w} = \boldsymbol{V}\boldsymbol{\Lambda}\boldsymbol{V}^\top = \sum_{i=1}^{w}\lambda_i\boldsymbol{v}_i\boldsymbol{v}_i^\top, \quad \boldsymbol{\Sigma}_w^{new} \leftarrow \sum_{i|\lambda_i>0}\lambda_i\boldsymbol{v}_i\boldsymbol{v}_i^\top = \boldsymbol{V}_+\boldsymbol{\Lambda}_+\boldsymbol{V}_+^\top, \tag{12}$$

where η is the step size determined by the line search [23] and $\lambda_i, \boldsymbol{v}_i$ are the i-th eigenvalue and eigenvector, respectively. The variables $\boldsymbol{W}_w, \boldsymbol{W}_h$ are easily retrieved by using those positive eigenvalues and eigenvectors: $\boldsymbol{W}_w = \boldsymbol{V}_+ \boldsymbol{\Lambda}_+^{\frac{1}{2}}$, and $\boldsymbol{W}_h = \sum_i \alpha_i^* (\boldsymbol{V}_+ \boldsymbol{\Lambda}_+ \boldsymbol{V}_+^\top) y_i \boldsymbol{X}_i \boldsymbol{V}_+ \boldsymbol{\Lambda}_+^{\frac{1}{2}}$.

The essential rank of the classifier $\boldsymbol{W} = \boldsymbol{W}_h \boldsymbol{W}_w^\top$ is usually less than r, and the redundant ranks are eventually eliminated by assigning zero singular values through the optimization in (10) which corresponds to minimization of the trace norm $||\boldsymbol{W}_h \boldsymbol{W}_w^\top||_\Sigma$, even if starting with the full rank $\boldsymbol{\Sigma}_w$.

In the proposed formulation (10), the dimensionality of the variable $\boldsymbol{\Sigma}_w$, $O(w^2)$, is much smaller than that of $\tilde{\boldsymbol{W}}$, $O((h+w)^2)$, in SDP (3). The computational complexity of the above optimization procedure is solely dependent on that of the quadratic programming (QP) in (11). For solving the QP, we can apply the efficient off-the-shelf SVM solver, such as libsvm [24]. The computationally exhaustive step other than the QP is the eigen decomposition in (12). In practice, however, either the dimension h, w is low; e.g., high-dimensional features are extracted at a few points ($h \gg w$), or either of the dimensionalities can be reduced such as by applying PCA in advance. Thus, the computational cost of the eigen decomposition is negligible compared to those of QP in most cases.

2.3 Comparison to Related Works

The formulation of the linear SVM [10] is actually regarded as the minimization of the Frobenius norm $\|\boldsymbol{W}\|_F = \mathrm{tr}(\boldsymbol{W}^\top \boldsymbol{W})$, but it usually results in a full rank classifier. The Frobenius norm corresponds to the L_2 norm of the singular values $\boldsymbol{\sigma}$ and the obtained classifier tends to have dense singular values, resulting in the full-rank classifier, unlike the trace norm (the L_1 norm of $\boldsymbol{\sigma}$). Therefore, to achieve low-rank SVM, Wolf *et al.* [15] and Pirsiavash *et al.* [14] additionally introduced a hard constraint on the rank, $\mathrm{rank}(\boldsymbol{W}) \le k$, into the formulation using $\|\boldsymbol{W}\|_F$. Those methods, however, usually produce the classifier of the maximum rank under that constraint, *i.e.*, $\mathrm{rank}(\boldsymbol{W}) = k$, since the objective cost $\|\boldsymbol{W}\|_F$ is the same as in the SVM, and it is difficult to determine the optimal rank k in advance.

The bilinear models are also addressed in the literature of the collaborative filtering [17,25,26]. In those methods, the trace norm $||\boldsymbol{W}||_\Sigma$ was employed as the objective cost, but the authors also mentioned that the resulting SDP is exhaustive and difficult to solve for large-scale samples. Thus, Loeff and Farhadi [26] and Rennie and Srebro [25] applied the approximated optimization approaches, though resulting in local minima.

Compared to the above methods, in terms of optimization, our contribution is to formulate the bilinear classification problem in the tractable convex form (10) and to propose the computationally efficient optimization procedure to solve it. Without any hard constraint on the rank, the proposed method can automatically produce the bilinear classifier of the optimal low rank.

3 Extensions of Bilinear Classification

3.1 Smoothing Regularization

Either or both of the bilinear weights, $\boldsymbol{W}_h, \boldsymbol{W}_w$, are occasionally connected to physical properties; *e.g.*, $\boldsymbol{W}_w$ works as weights on spatio-temporal positions, while $\boldsymbol{W}_h$ is for the feature vector. In such cases, it is useful to take into account the (physical) relationships between the weight components in terms of regularization for improving the generalization performance. For that purpose, we introduce the smoothing regularization. In the case of time-series, the extracted features are not independently drawn but naturally have *continuity* between adjacent features, which expects the smooth weights $\boldsymbol{W}_w$. The smoothing regularization is expressed by using the quadratic form derived from Laplacian of the weights, and the formulation results in

$$\min_{\boldsymbol{W}_w, \boldsymbol{W}_h, b} \frac{1}{2}\mathrm{tr}(\boldsymbol{W}_w \boldsymbol{W}_w^\top) + \frac{1}{2}\mathrm{tr}(\boldsymbol{W}_h \boldsymbol{W}_h^\top) + \frac{1}{2}C_w \mathrm{tr}(\boldsymbol{W}_w^\top \boldsymbol{L}_w \boldsymbol{W}_w) + \frac{1}{2}C_h \mathrm{tr}(\boldsymbol{W}_h^\top \boldsymbol{L}_h \boldsymbol{W}_h)$$
$$+ C\sum_i \max\left[0, 1 - y_i\{\mathrm{tr}(\boldsymbol{W}_h^\top \boldsymbol{X}_i \boldsymbol{W}_w) + b\}\right],$$

where $\boldsymbol{L}_w, \boldsymbol{L}_h$ are the matrices measuring the smoothness and C_w, C_h are regularization parameters. For time-series (one-way), the matrix $\boldsymbol{L}_w$ is determined based on $\mathrm{tr}(\boldsymbol{W}_w^\top \boldsymbol{L}_w \boldsymbol{W}_w) = \sum_t \| - \boldsymbol{w}_{w,t-1} + 2\boldsymbol{w}_{w,t} - \boldsymbol{w}_{w,t+1}\|^2$. In this study, the regularization parameter C_w is set so as to equally balance the two spectral matrix norms of $\boldsymbol{I}$ and $\boldsymbol{L}_w$ by $C_w = 1/||\boldsymbol{L}_w||_s$, ($C_h = 1/\|\boldsymbol{L}_h\|_s$ for $\boldsymbol{L}_h$), where $\|\boldsymbol{L}_w\|_s$ indicates the spectral matrix norm (the maximum singular value) of $\boldsymbol{L}_w$. Then, the above formulation is rewritten to the following form similar to (4):

$$\min_{\bar{\boldsymbol{W}}_w, \bar{\boldsymbol{W}}_h, b} \frac{1}{2}\mathrm{tr}(\bar{\boldsymbol{W}}_w \bar{\boldsymbol{W}}_w^\top) + \frac{1}{2}\mathrm{tr}(\bar{\boldsymbol{W}}_h \bar{\boldsymbol{W}}_h^\top) + C\sum_i \max\left[0, 1 - y_i\{\mathrm{tr}(\bar{\boldsymbol{W}}_h^\top \bar{\boldsymbol{X}}_i \bar{\boldsymbol{W}}_w) + b\}\right],$$
$$\text{where } \bar{\boldsymbol{X}}_i = (\boldsymbol{I} + C_h \boldsymbol{L}_h)^{-\frac{1}{2}} \boldsymbol{X}_i (\boldsymbol{I} + C_w \boldsymbol{L}_w)^{-\frac{1}{2}}.$$

The optimization procedure in Sec.2.2 is applicable to it and we obtain the smoothed classifier weights $\boldsymbol{W}_h = (\boldsymbol{I} + C_h \boldsymbol{L}_h)^{-\frac{1}{2}} \bar{\boldsymbol{W}}_h$, $\boldsymbol{W}_w = (\boldsymbol{I} + C_h \boldsymbol{L}_w)^{-\frac{1}{2}} \bar{\boldsymbol{W}}_w$.

3.2 Heterogeneous Multiple Kernel Learning

By considering a kernel-based extension of the bilinear classifier, we naturally apply the proposed method to multiple kernel learning (MKL) [16], which induces a novel MKL, called *heterogeneous multiple kernel learning.*

For kernelization, we employ the kernels for $\boldsymbol{R}^{ij} \triangleq \boldsymbol{X}_i^\top \boldsymbol{X}_j \in \mathbb{R}^{w \times w}$ in (9). In this case, the optimized $\boldsymbol{\Sigma}_w$ works as weights for the multiple ($w \times w$ types) kernels in $\boldsymbol{R}^{ij}$ to produce a new composite kernel in (9), which is closely related to MKL [16]. In the followings, we consider the column feature vectors $\boldsymbol{x}_{ic}$ ($c=1, \cdots, w$) in $\boldsymbol{X}_i = [\boldsymbol{x}_{i1}, \cdots, \boldsymbol{x}_{iw}]$. When the feature vectors $\boldsymbol{x}_{ic}$ are all homogeneous, an identical kernel function is simply applied as $R^{ij}_{cd} = k(\boldsymbol{x}_{ic}, \boldsymbol{x}_{jd})$. The proposed bilinear model can also deal with multiple types of kernels (features), which induces heterogeneous MKL (hMKL), as follows. Given respective types of kernels k_c, the main concern in the hMKL is to construct kernels, especially for the off-diagonal elements of $\boldsymbol{R}^{ij}$; those are inter kernels between heterogeneous types of kernels (features), which is a novel concept in this paper. We propose the following form of the kernels for $\boldsymbol{R}^{ij}$,

$$R^{ij}_{cd} = \boldsymbol{k}_{ic}^\top \boldsymbol{K}_c^{-\frac{1}{2}} \boldsymbol{K}_d^{-\frac{1}{2}} \boldsymbol{k}_{id}, \tag{13}$$

where $\boldsymbol{K}_c$ is the c-th type of kernel Gram matrix, $\boldsymbol{K}_c = \{k_c(\boldsymbol{x}_{ic}, \boldsymbol{x}_{jc})\}_{i=1,..,n}^{j=1,..,n} \in \mathbb{R}^{n\times n}$, and the kernel feature vector $\boldsymbol{k}_{ic} = [k_c(\boldsymbol{x}_{ic}, \boldsymbol{x}_{1c}), \cdots, k_c(\boldsymbol{x}_{ic}, \boldsymbol{x}_{nc})]^\top \in \mathbb{R}^n$ (the i-th column vector of $\boldsymbol{K}_c$). We give an interpretation to this formulation of the kernel (13) as follows.

For the intra kernels between homogeneous types of kernels, each type of feature vector $\boldsymbol{\phi}_{ic}$ associated with $\boldsymbol{x}_{ic}$ in the reproducing kernel Hilbert space (RKHS) is projected into the subspace by PCA [13],

$$R^{ij}_{cc} = \boldsymbol{k}_{ic}^\top \boldsymbol{K}_c^{-\frac{1}{2}} \boldsymbol{K}_c^{-\frac{1}{2}} \boldsymbol{k}_{jc} = \boldsymbol{\phi}_{ic}^\top \boldsymbol{V}_c \boldsymbol{V}_c^\top \boldsymbol{\phi}_{jc},$$

where $\boldsymbol{\Phi}_c = [\boldsymbol{\phi}_{1c}, \cdots, \boldsymbol{\phi}_{nc}] = \boldsymbol{V}_c \boldsymbol{\Lambda}_c \boldsymbol{U}_c^\top$ (SVD), and $\boldsymbol{k}_{ic} = \boldsymbol{\Phi}_c^\top \boldsymbol{\phi}_{ic}$. Note that $\boldsymbol{K}_c = \boldsymbol{U}_c \boldsymbol{\Lambda}_c^2 \boldsymbol{U}_c^\top$ and $\boldsymbol{V}_c$ is the projection matrix by PCA in RKHS. Especially, for the training samples, the diagonal elements of $\boldsymbol{R}^{ij}$ are identical to the original kernels; $R^{ij}_{cc} = k_c(\boldsymbol{x}_{ic}, \boldsymbol{x}_{jc})$. When dealing with only the diagonal matrix of R^{ij}_{cc}, the proposed bilinear method (10) corresponds to the MKL method of [21].

On the other hand, the inter kernels between heterogeneous types of kernels are represented by

$$R^{ij}_{cd} = \boldsymbol{k}_{ic}^\top \boldsymbol{K}_c^{-\frac{1}{2}} \boldsymbol{K}_d^{-\frac{1}{2}} \boldsymbol{k}_{jd} = \boldsymbol{\phi}_{ic}^\top \boldsymbol{V}_c \boldsymbol{U}_c^\top \boldsymbol{U}_d \boldsymbol{V}_d^\top \boldsymbol{\phi}_{jd}. \tag{14}$$

In this form, the consistency between the different types of kernels is ensured via canonical correlation analysis (CCA). The CCA provides the projections $\boldsymbol{A}, \boldsymbol{B}$ for the two types of features $\boldsymbol{\Phi}_c, \boldsymbol{\Phi}_d$ in RKHS so as to maximize the correlation coefficient, by solving the following eigenvalue problem:

$$\begin{bmatrix} \boldsymbol{0} & \boldsymbol{\Phi}_c\boldsymbol{\Phi}_d^\top \\ \boldsymbol{\Phi}_d\boldsymbol{\Phi}_c^\top & \boldsymbol{0} \end{bmatrix} \begin{bmatrix} \boldsymbol{A} \\ \boldsymbol{B} \end{bmatrix} = \begin{bmatrix} \boldsymbol{\Phi}_c\boldsymbol{\Phi}_c^\top & \boldsymbol{0} \\ \boldsymbol{0} & \boldsymbol{\Phi}_d\boldsymbol{\Phi}_d^\top \end{bmatrix} \begin{bmatrix} \boldsymbol{A} \\ \boldsymbol{B} \end{bmatrix} \boldsymbol{\Omega}, \ \ \therefore \boldsymbol{A} = \boldsymbol{V}_c \boldsymbol{\Lambda}_c^{-1} \boldsymbol{P}, \ \boldsymbol{B} = \boldsymbol{V}_d \boldsymbol{\Lambda}_d^{-1} \boldsymbol{Q},$$

where $\boldsymbol{U}_c^\top \boldsymbol{U}_d = \boldsymbol{P}\boldsymbol{\Omega}\boldsymbol{Q}^\top$ (SVD). In the CCA, the feature vectors $\boldsymbol{\phi}_{ic}, \boldsymbol{\phi}_{jd}$ are first whitened by $\boldsymbol{V}_c\boldsymbol{\Lambda}_c^{-1}, \boldsymbol{V}_d\boldsymbol{\Lambda}_d^{-1}$ via PCA, and then the PCA axes are rotated by $\boldsymbol{P}, \boldsymbol{Q}$ so as to ensure the consistency and to maximize the correlation coefficient. By using these notations, (14) is rewritten to

$$R^{ij}_{cd} = \boldsymbol{\phi}_{ic}^\top \boldsymbol{V}_c \boldsymbol{P} \boldsymbol{\Omega}^{\frac{1}{2}} \boldsymbol{\Omega}^{\frac{1}{2}} \boldsymbol{Q}^\top \boldsymbol{V}_d^\top \boldsymbol{\phi}_{jd}.$$

This is quite similar to the CCA projection; The feature vectors $\boldsymbol{\phi}_{ic}, \boldsymbol{\phi}_{jd}$ are projected into PCA subspaces by $\boldsymbol{V}_c, \boldsymbol{V}_d$, and then they are rotated by the CCA rotation matrices $\boldsymbol{P}, \boldsymbol{Q}$ with weighting the CCA axes by the correlation coefficients $\boldsymbol{\Omega}^{\frac{1}{2}}$. The differences from the CCA projections are that 1) we use the orthogonal PCA projection, not whitening, for preserving the magnitude (norm) of $\boldsymbol{\phi}_{ic}, \boldsymbol{\phi}_{jd}$ and then 2) we use the weighting by the correlation coefficients $\boldsymbol{\Omega}$ which measure consistency between the heterogeneous kernels.

As a result, in hMKL, we deal with the feature matrix which is explicitly represented by the following form;

$$\boldsymbol{X} = [\boldsymbol{K}_1^{-\frac{1}{2}} \boldsymbol{k}_1, \cdots, \boldsymbol{K}_w^{-\frac{1}{2}} \boldsymbol{k}_w] \in \mathbb{R}^{n\times w}, \ \ \boldsymbol{k}_c = [k_c(\boldsymbol{x}_c, \boldsymbol{x}_{1c}), \cdots, k_c(\boldsymbol{x}_c, \boldsymbol{x}_{nc})]^\top \in \mathbb{R}^n.$$

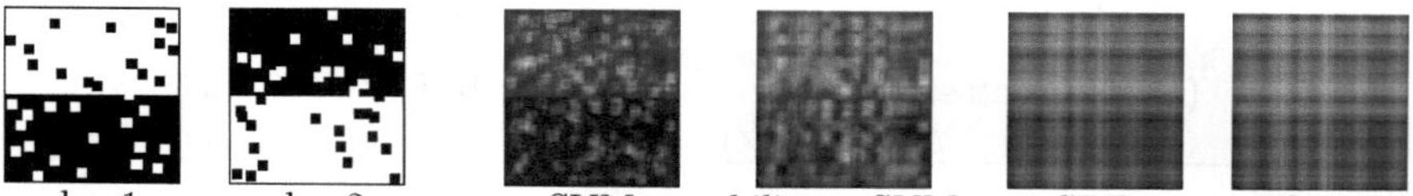

Fig. 2. Classifier weights on toy data. Negative and positive weights are shown by pseudo colors from blue to red.

Thus, the resultant bilinear classifier is also represented in the bilinear form (1) and the proposed optimization procedure (Sec.2.2) is directly applicable even to this hMKL. It should be noted again that $\boldsymbol{\Sigma}_w = \boldsymbol{W}_w \boldsymbol{W}_w^\top$ is regarded as the weights on both the intra and inter kernels.

4 Experimental Results

We applied the proposed bilinear classification method to various classification problems using feature arrays, co-occurrence features and multiple kernels.

For comparison, we also applied linear SVM [10] to the concatenated feature vectors and bilinear SVM [14] to the feature matrices except in multiple kernel learning. The bilinear SVM [14] includes an rank parameter for rank($\boldsymbol{W}$) $\leq k$ which is determined based on two-fold cross validations from $k \in \{5, 10\}$ as in [14]. In all the methods, to cope with multi-class problems, the one-vs-rest approach is employed. All the methods were implemented by MATLAB with libsvm [24] on 3.33GHz PC.

4.1 Toy Example

First, by using toy data, we intuitively demonstrate how the proposed method works on feature matrices. For two-class classification, two types of binary images (100×100) are used as feature matrices ($\boldsymbol{X} \in \mathbb{R}^{100 \times 100}$), as shown in Fig. 2; the images have basically one rank with salt and pepper noise of size 5×5, and there are 100 samples in each type (class). The obtained classifier ($\boldsymbol{W}$) is shown in Fig. 2, compared to those by the other method including SDP (3) which is feasible in such a small dataset by using SeDuMi solver. In the linear SVM, the concatenated linear classifier (vector) is folded into the intrinsic matrix form and its rank is also measured. The proposed method favorably produces the one-rank classifier which is the same as the global optimum one by SDP, while the classifiers by the methods of linear SVM and bilinear SVM [14] are overly fitted to the data with higher (full) rank. Without any hard constraint about the rank, the proposed method recovers the essential rank in data with a low computational cost (0.4 sec) compared to the exhaustive SDP method (14.0 sec).

4.2 Feature Array

Next, we conducted the practical experiments on motion classification using RWC gesture dataset [3] and image classification (detection) using INRIA person

Table 1. Classification performances for feature arrays

(a) RWC dataset

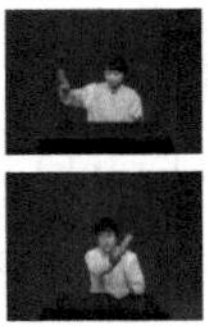

Method	Rank	Err. (%)
SVM	50	2.11
bilinear SVM [14]	5.59	1.41
Ours	3.27	**0.98**
Ours (smooth)	3.25	1.01
[4]	-	1.9
[3]	-	4.14

(b) INRIA dataset

Method	Rank	EER (%)
SVM	32	0.55
bilinear SVM [14]	10	0.71
Ours	12	0.62
Ours (smooth)	12	**0.53**
[27]	-	0.58
[1]	-	2.25

dataset [1]. In these experiments, the array of the feature vectors extracted at temporal/spatial points forms the feature matrix $\boldsymbol{X}$ as shown in Fig. 1ab.

RWC Gesture Dataset [3] contains 17 types of human gesture as shown in Table 1a. Each of these gestures is performed four times by 48 subjects (23 men and 25 women). We extract 751-dimensional CHLAC motion feature vector [3] at every frame with multiple correlation intervals $\Delta r \in \{1, 3, 5\}$; for details of this feature, refer to [3]. Since the numbers of frames are different across the motion image sequences, we subsample those frame-based features by bilinear interpolation into 50-frame feature vectors. As a result, the feature matrix is formed as feature-vs-time; $\boldsymbol{X} \in \mathbb{R}^{751 \times 50}$ (Fig. 1a). The performance is evaluated by three-fold cross validation, and both the error rates and the ranks of the classifiers averaged across classes are shown in Table 1a. The proposed method produces the favorable performance compared to the other methods of SVM and bilinear SVM [14] and the prior works [4,3]. While the rank of the SVM classifier is 50, the proposed classifier has around only three rank, improving the efficiency of information compression and also the generalization performance. In this case, the smoothed classifier (Sec.3.1) that imposes the smoothing regularization on the temporal weight $\boldsymbol{W}_w$ produces slightly inferior performance. This is because the feature matrices are already smoothed by the subsampling procedure and such further smoothing slightly degrades the performance.

In **INRIA Person Dataset** [1], we used 2,416 person and 12,180 person-free images (64×128) for training, and 1,132 person and 13,590 person-free images for test as shown in Table 1b. The image is divided into 4×8 subregions and 324-dimensional GLAC feature vectors [27] are extracted from each region with the same parameter settings as in [27]. Thereby, the feature matrix is formed as feature-vs-space (positions); $\boldsymbol{X} \in \mathbb{R}^{324 \times 32}$ (Fig. 1b). The performance results are shown in Table 1b. In the proposed method, the smoothed classifier that imposes the regularization on the (two-way) spatial positions $\boldsymbol{W}_w$ slightly improves the performance. The performance is comparable to SVM and is superior to the prior works [27,1]. It should be noted that the proposed classifier of low rank ($=12$) significantly reduces the computational cost in the detection stage since our low-rank classifier is decomposed into a few separable filters which require $O(\text{rank}(\boldsymbol{W}) \times \max(h, w))$ compared to $O(hw)$ of the full rank SVM classifier.

4.3 Co-occurrence Feature

The bilinear classifier can also directly deal with the co-occurrence features which are inherently formed as a matrix (Fig. 1c). In the bag-of-features [2], the local features, such as HOG [1], are assigned with (visual) words via clustering, and the simple occurrence of the words are counted to produce the final histogram-based feature vector. The occurrence features are extended to the co-occurrence features of the words in local neighborhoods in the bag-of-features framework [28]. For motion recognition, we follow the framework used in [4] which extracts frame-based motion features at every 10 frames and applies k-means to cluster the features into motion words in Fisher discriminant space; refer to [4] for more details. In these experiments, we count the co-occurrence of the motion words along the time axis, as follows. Given w motion words, the frame-based feature at time t is assigned with multiple motion words of which weights form a vector $\boldsymbol{f}(t) \in \mathbb{R}^w$ [4]. The co-occurrence features are extracted by $\boldsymbol{F}(\Delta t) = \sum_t \boldsymbol{f}(t)\boldsymbol{f}(t+\Delta t)^\top$, in which Δt denotes the interval along the t axis, say $\Delta t \in \{0, 20\}$ in these experiments, and those features are concatenated into the final feature matrix $\boldsymbol{X} = [\boldsymbol{F}(0), \boldsymbol{F}(20)]^\top \in \mathbb{R}^{2w \times w}$. The number of words is simply determined by $w = 10 \times \#\text{class}$. We conducted the motion classification experiments by using UCF sport action dataset [29] and Cambridge hand gesture dataset [30]. In the smoothed classifier (Sec.3.1), the matrices $\boldsymbol{L}_h, \boldsymbol{L}_w$ are set as the graph Laplacian [31] for which the similarities between words are measured by 10 nearest neighbors of word centers.

UCF Sport Action Dataset [29] contains nine types of sport actions as shown in Table 2a. Each action is performed by several (about 17) players, and the total number of sequence is 150. To enlarge the training size, the number of training samples are doubled by adding horizontal mirror images. For evaluation, three-fold cross validation is applied and the averaged error rates across action classes are reported in Table 2a. The performances reported in the prior works [29,14], which are measured in a slightly different protocol (slightly different number of action classes), are also shown as a reference. The proposed methods exhibit superior performances to the other methods, and in particular, the smoothed bilinear classifier improves the performance with quite low rank. In Fig. 3a, we show the performances by increasing the number of words to evaluate the robustness of the methods. In the proposed method, due to the appropriate low rank, the performances are stably high even for larger number of words, while the other methods degrade their performances.

Cambridge Hand Gesture Dataset [30] contains nine hand gestures defined by three primitive hand shapes and three primitive motions, which are performed ten times by two subjects under five different illumination conditions, as shown in Table 2b. We used the sequences acquired under the plain illumination condition for training and those under the remaining four conditions for test. The averaged error rates across all gesture classes over the four test conditions are reported in Table 2b. The proposed method produces superior performances to the others including the prior works [4,30]; the smoothed classifier is the most favorable. Fig. 3b also shows the performances for various numbers of words, demonstrating the robustness of the proposed method as is the case with UCF dataset.

These experimental results show that the proposed method robustly produces high performances, requiring users only to set sufficiently large number of words

Table 2. Classification performances for co-occurrence features

(a) UCF dataset

Method	Rank	Err. (%)
SVM	246.67	28.80
bilinear SVM [14]	9.63	27.87
Ours	1.15	24.19
Ours (smooth)	1.11	**23.73**
[29]	-	35.2
[14]	-	30.8

(b) Cambridge dataset

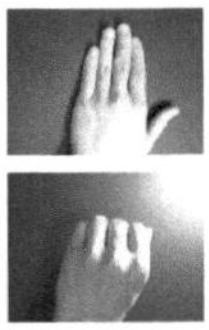

Method	Rank	Err. (%)
SVM	251	14.03
bilinear SVM [14]	10	14.17
Ours	1.22	9.17
Ours (smooth)	1.33	**9.03**
[4]	-	11
[30]	-	18

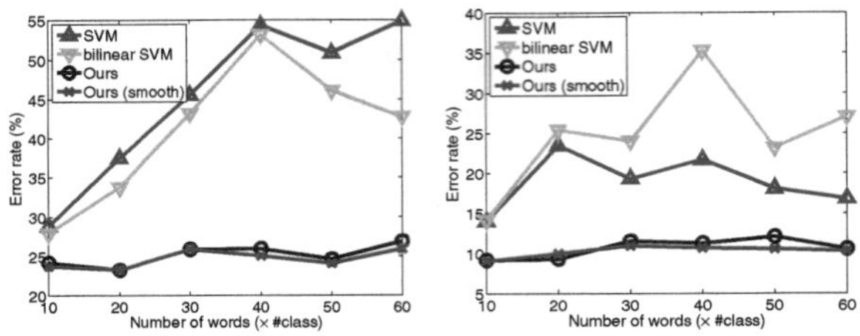

(a) UCF dataset (b) Cambridge dataset

Fig. 3. Performances for various numbers of words

without carefully tuning the number of words nor the rank of the classifier for classifying the co-occurrence features.

4.4 Multiple Kernels

At the last, we applied the proposed method to classification using multiple kernels (Sec.3.2) and compared the performance to those of the other MKL methods: simpleMKL [20] and the method of [21]. It should be noted again that the proposed method dealing with only diagonal matrix of $R^{ij}_{cc} = k_c(\boldsymbol{x}_{ic}, \boldsymbol{x}_{jc})$ corresponds to the MKL method [21] and it is denoted by "diagonal ([21])".

To demonstrate the effectiveness of the proposed kernel (13), we conducted the comparative experiment using **PASCAL VOC 2007 dataset**[1] which contains 5,011 images for training and 4,952 images for test in 20 object categories. We used 15 types of precomputed features provided in the website[2] of the authors [32] (for deals of the features, refer to [32]), and employed the RBF kernels of those features as $k_c(\boldsymbol{x}_{ic}, \boldsymbol{x}_{jc}) = \exp(-||\boldsymbol{x}_{ic} - \boldsymbol{x}_{jc}||^2/\gamma)$ where γ is the mean of pairwise distances. The following alternative forms to the proposed kernel (13) are conceivable.

$$\textit{Product: } R^{ij}_{cd} = \boldsymbol{k}_{ic}^\top \boldsymbol{k}_{jd},$$
$$\textit{PCA: } R^{ij}_{cd} = \boldsymbol{k}_{ic}^\top \boldsymbol{U}_c \boldsymbol{\Lambda}_c^{-1} \boldsymbol{\Lambda}_d^{-1} \boldsymbol{U}_d^\top \boldsymbol{k}_{jd} = \boldsymbol{\phi}_{ic}^\top \boldsymbol{V}_c \boldsymbol{V}_d^\top \boldsymbol{\phi}_{jd},$$
$$\textit{Inverse: } R^{ij}_{cd} = \boldsymbol{k}_{ic}^\top \boldsymbol{K}_c^{-1} \boldsymbol{K}_d^{-1} \boldsymbol{k}_{jd} = \boldsymbol{\phi}_{ic}^\top \boldsymbol{V}_c \boldsymbol{\Lambda}_c^{-1} \boldsymbol{U}_c^\top \boldsymbol{U}_d \boldsymbol{\Lambda}_d^{-1} \boldsymbol{V}_d^\top \boldsymbol{\phi}_{jd}.$$

Compared to (13, 14), the *PCA* kernel loses the CCA rotation matrix derived from $\boldsymbol{U}_c$, while the *inverse* kernel additionally introduces the whitening by $\boldsymbol{\Lambda}_c^{-1}$

[1] `http://www.pascal-network.org/challenges/VOC/voc2007/workshop/index.html`
[2] `http://lear.inrialpes.fr/people/guillaumin/data.php`

Table 3. PASCAL VOC 2007

(a) Kernel types

Kernel	mAP (%)
Product	42.30
PCA	45.60
Inverse	37.88
Proposed	**48.64**

(b) Comparison

Method	mAP (%)
simpleMKL [20]	48.04
diagonal ([21])	45.83
Ours	**48.64**

Table 4. Flower dataset

Method	Acc. (%)
simpleMKL [20]	81.08
simpleMKL (multiclass) [20]	82.55
diagonal ([21])	85.10
[33]	85.5
Ours	**86.47**

Table 5. Butterfly dataset

Method	Acc. (%)
simpleMKL [20]	69.60
simpleMKL (multiclass) [20]	67.95
diagonal ([21])	74.42
Ours	**76.54**

Table 6. Bird dataset

Method	Acc. (%)
simpleMKL [20]	69.21
simpleMKL (multiclass) [20]	68.71
diagonal ([21])	72.85
Ours	**74.50**

to normalize the magnitudes (norms) of features. Table 3a shows the mean of average precision rates (mAP) across the categories. The proposed kernel (13) is superior to the other types of kernels, showing that both the rotation matrix by CCA and magnitude preserving by PCA are effective for classifications. Table 3b shows that the proposed method produces the favorable performance compared to the others.

We further conducted the MKL experiments using Oxford flower dataset [34], Butterfly dataset [35] and Bird dataset [36]. We used the RBF kernel in the same manner as described above. The **Oxford flower dataset** [34] is composed of 80 images of 17 flower categories. We used the seven types of precomputed pairwise distances provided in the website[3] of the authors [37]; for the details of the distances, refer to [34,37]. Table 4 shows the performances evaluated by three-fold cross validations using the same predefined splits as in [34]. For comparison, the performance of the method [33] which uses the same features and cross validation splits is also shown. The **Butterfly dataset** [35] has 619 images of seven butterfly classes, and the **Bird dataset** [36] contains six bird classes with 100 images per class. In these datasets, we used the three types of precomputed pairwise distances provided in the website[4] of the authors [38]; for the details of the distances, refer to [38]. The classification accuracies are evaluated by three-fold cross validations and are shown in Table 5 and Table 6. In those three datasets, the proposed method produces superior performances to the others. Especially, in comparison to diagonal [21], the inter kernels between heterogeneous kernels effectively contribute to improve the performances.

As shown in above experimental results, the proposed heterogeneous MKL method, which combines both intra (diagonal) and inter (off-diagonal) kernels by using the bilinear model, is effective compared to the standard MKL methods.

[3] http://www.robots.ox.ac.uk/~vgg/research/flowers/index.html

[4] http://www.eecs.berkeley.edu/Research/Projects/CS/vision/shape/msorec/

5 Conclusion

We have proposed an efficient method to optimize a bilinear classifier for feature matrices which results in low rank without any hard constraint on the rank. The classifier is optimized by minimizing the trace norm of the classifier matrix, which contributes to the rank reduction. The optimization is formulated in a tractable convex form and an computationally efficient optimization procedure is proposed. In addition, by considering a kernel-based extension of the bilinear method, a novel multiple kernel learning, called heterogeneous multiple kernel learning (hMKL), is induced. In the hMKL, we can combine not only the ordinary kernels of homogeneous kernels (features) but also the inter kernels between heterogeneous kernels (features) into a new composite kernel by using the bilinear model. In the experiments on various classification problems using feature arrays, co-occurrence feature matrices and multiple kernels, the proposed method exhibited favorable performances compared to the other methods.

References

1. Dalal, N., Triggs, B.: Histograms of oriented gradients for human detection. In: CVPR (2005)
2. Csurka, G., Bray, C., Dance, C., Fan, L.: Visual categorization with bags of keypoints. In: ECCV Workshop on Statistical Learning in Computer Vision (2004)
3. Kobayashi, T., Otsu, N.: A three-way auto-correlation based approach to motion recognition. Pattern Recognition Letters 30, 185–192 (2009)
4. Kobayashi, T., Otsu, N.: Motion recognition using local auto-correlation of space-time gradients. Pattern Recognition Letters 33, 1188–1195 (2012)
5. Tenenbaum, J.B., Freeman, W.T.: Separating style and content with bilinear models. Neural Computation 12, 1247–1283 (2000)
6. Yang, J., Zhang, D., Frangi, A.F., Yang, J.: Two-dimensional pca: A new approach to appearance-based face representation and recognition. IEEE Trans. on Pattern Analysis and Machine Intelligence 26, 131–137 (2004)
7. Ye, J., Janardan, R., Li, Q.: Two-dimensional linear discriminant analysis. In: Advances in Neural Information Processing System, vol. 17, pp. 1569–1576 (2005)
8. Lee, D.D., Seung, H.S.: Learning the parts of objects by non-negative matrix factorization. Nature 401, 788–791 (1999)
9. Eriksson, A., van den Hengel, A.: Efficient computation of robust low-rank matrix approximations in the presence of missing data using the l_1 norm. In: CVPR (2010)
10. Vapnik, V.N.: Statistical Learning Theory. Wiley (1998)
11. Graepel, T., Herbrich, R., Schölkopf, B., Smola, A., Bartlett, P., Muüller, K.-R., Obermayer, K., Williamson, R.: Classification on proximity data with lp-machines. In: ICANN (1999)
12. Bartlett, P.J., Schölkopf, B., Schuurmans, D., Smola, A.J.: Advances in Large-Margin Classifiers. MIT Press (2000)
13. Schölkopf, B., Smola, A.J.: Learning with Kernels. MIT Press (2001)
14. Pirsiavash, H., Ramanan, D., Fowlkes, C.: Bilinear classifiers for visual recognition. In: Advances in Neural Information Processing Systems (2009)
15. Wolf, L., Jhuang, H., Hazan, T.: Modeling appearances with low-rank svm. In: CVPR (2007)

16. Lanckriet, G., Cristianini, N., Bartlett, P., Ghaoui, L.E., Jordan, M.I.: Learning the kernel matrix with semidefinite programming. Journal of Machine Learning Research 5, 27–72 (2004)
17. Srebro, N., Rennie, J.D.M., Jaakkola, T.S.: Maximum-margin matrix factorization. In: Advances in Neural Information Processing Systems, vol. 17, pp. 1329–1336 (2005)
18. Boyd, S.P., Vandenberghe, L.: Convex optimization. Cambridge university press, Cambridge (2004)
19. Dempe, S.: Foundations of Bilevel Programming. Kluwer Academic Publishers (2002)
20. Rakotomamonjy, A., Bach, F.R., Canu, S., Grandvalet, Y.: SimpleMKL. Journal of Machine Learning Research 9, 2491–2521 (2008)
21. Varma, M., Ray, D.: Learning the discriminative power-invariance trade-off. In: ICCV (2007)
22. Chapelle, O., Vapnik, V., Bousquet, O., Mukherjee, S.: Choosing multiple parameters for support vector machines. Machine Learning 46, 131–159 (2002)
23. Nocedal, J., Wright, S.J.: Numerical optimization. Springer, New York (1999)
24. Chang, C.C., Lin, C.J.: LIBSVM: a library for support vector machines (2001)
25. Rennie, J.D.M., Srebro, N.: Fast maximum margin matrix factorization for collaborative prediction. In: ICML (2005)
26. Loeff, N., Farhadi, A.: Scene Discovery by Matrix Factorization. In: Forsyth, D., Torr, P., Zisserman, A. (eds.) ECCV 2008, Part IV. LNCS, vol. 5305, pp. 451–464. Springer, Heidelberg (2008)
27. Kobayashi, T., Otsu, N.: Image Feature Extraction Using Gradient Local Auto-Correlations. In: Forsyth, D., Torr, P., Zisserman, A. (eds.) ECCV 2008, Part I. LNCS, vol. 5302, pp. 346–358. Springer, Heidelberg (2008)
28. Ling, H., Soatto, S.: Proximity distribution kernels for geometric context in category recognition. In: ICCV (2007)
29. Rodriguez, M.D., Ahmed, J., Shah, M.: Action mach a spatio-temporal maximum average correlation height filter for action recognition. In: CVPR (2008)
30. Kim, T.-K., Wong, S.-F., Cipolla, R.: Tensor canonical correlation analysis for action classification. In: CVPR (2007)
31. Belkin, M., Niyogi, P.: Laplacian eigenmaps for dimensionality reduction and data representation. Neural Computation 15, 1373–1396 (2003)
32. Guillaumin, M., Verbeek, J., Schmid, C.: Multimodal semi-supervised learning for image classification. In: CVPR (2010)
33. Gehler, P., Nowozin, S.: On feature combination for multiclass object classification. In: ICCV (2009)
34. Nilsback, M.E., Zisserman, A.: A visual vocabulary for flower classification. In: CVPR (2006)
35. Lazebnik, S., Schmid, C., Ponce, J.: Semi-local affine parts for object recognition. In: BMVC (2004)
36. Lazebnik, S., Schmid, C., Ponce, J.: A maximum entropy framework for part-based texture and object recognition. In: CVPR (2005)
37. Nilsback, M.E., Zisserman, A.: Automated flower classification over a large number of classes. In: ICVGIP (2008)
38. Mario Christoudias, C., Urtasun, R., Salzmann, M., Darrell, T.: Learning to Recognize Objects from Unseen Modalities. In: Daniilidis, K., Maragos, P., Paragios, N. (eds.) ECCV 2010, Part I. LNCS, vol. 6311, pp. 677–691. Springer, Heidelberg (2010)

Metric Learning for Large Scale Image Classification: Generalizing to New Classes at Near-Zero Cost

Thomas Mensink[1,2], Jakob Verbeek[1], Florent Perronnin[2], and Gabriela Csurka[2]

[1] LEAR, INRIA Grenoble, 655 Avenue de l'Europe, 38330 Montbonnot, France
firstname.lastname@inria.fr

[2] TVPA, Xerox Research Centre Europe, 6 chemin de Maupertuis, 38240 Meylan, France
firstname.lastname@xrce.xerox.com

Abstract. We are interested in large-scale image classification and especially in the setting where images corresponding to new or existing classes are continuously added to the training set. Our goal is to devise classifiers which can incorporate such images and classes on-the-fly at (near) zero cost. We cast this problem into one of learning a metric which is shared across all classes and explore k-nearest neighbor (k-NN) and nearest class mean (NCM) classifiers. We learn metrics on the ImageNet 2010 challenge data set, which contains more than 1.2M training images of 1K classes. Surprisingly, the NCM classifier compares favorably to the more flexible k-NN classifier, and has comparable performance to linear SVMs. We also study the generalization performance, among others by using the learned metric on the ImageNet-10K dataset, and we obtain competitive performance. Finally, we explore zero-shot classification, and show how the zero-shot model can be combined very effectively with small training datasets.

1 Introduction

In the last decade we have witnessed an explosion in the amount of images and videos that are digitally available, *e.g.* in broadcasting archives or social media sharing websites. Only a small fraction of this data is consistently annotated and thus scalable methods are needed for annotation and retrieval to efficiently access this huge volume of data. This need has been recognized in the computer vision research community and large-scale methods have become an active topic of research in recent years, see among others [1,2,3,4,5,6,7,8,9,10]. The introduction of the ImageNet dataset [1], which contains more than 14M manually labeled images of 22K classes, has provided an important benchmark for large-scale image classification and annotation algorithms.

In this paper we focus on the problem of large-scale image annotation, where the goal is to assign automatically a set of relevant labels to an image, *e.g.* names of objects appearing in the image. The predominant approach to this problem is to treat it as a classification problem. To ensure scalability, often linear classifiers such as SVMs are used [8,10], sometimes in combination with dimension reduction techniques to speed-up the classification [7]. Recently, impressive results have been reported on 10,000 or more classes [3,7,8,11]. A drawback of these methods, however, is that when images of new categories become available, new classifiers have to be trained at a relatively high computational cost.

A. Fitzgibbon et al. (Eds.): ECCV 2012, Part II, LNCS 7573, pp. 488–501, 2012.

Many real-life large-scale datasets are open-ended and dynamic: new classes appear over time and new photos/videos are continuously added to existing classes. Therefore, the main objective of our work is to propose and study approaches which enable the addition of new classes and new images to existing classes at (near) zero cost. We explore two techniques to do so. The first is k-NN classification, where images of new classes are added in the database, and can be used for classification without further processing. This is a highly non-linear and non-parametric classifier that has shown competitive performance for image annotation [3,7,12]. Its main drawback is that the nearest neighbor search for classification is computationally demanding for large and high-dimensional datasets. The second is the nearest class mean classifier (NCM), where classes are represented by their mean feature vector [13,14,15]. The cost of computing the mean can be neglected with respect to the cost of feature extraction and this operation does not require accessing images of other classes. Contrary to the k-NN classifier, this is a linear classifier which leads to efficient classification. The complete distribution of the training data of a class is, however, only characterized by its mean and it is therefore unclear whether this is sufficient for competitive performance.

The success of both methods critically depends on the metric which is used to compute the distance between an image and other images (for k-NN) or class means (for NCM), see Figure 1 for an illustration. Metric learning has received much attention in the machine learning and computer vision communities recently, and has been shown to significantly increase the performance of distance-based classifiers. Therefore, we cast our classifier learning problem as one of learning a metric which is shared across all classes. For k-NN classification, we use the Large Margin Nearest Neighbor (LMNN) framework [16] and propose a variation that significantly improves its performance. For the NCM classifier, we propose a novel metric learning algorithm based on multi-class logistic discrimination. A sample from a given class is enforced to be closer to its class mean than to any other class mean in the projected space. To apply these metric learning techniques on large-scale datasets, we employ stochastic gradient descend (SGD) algorithms, which access only a small fraction of the training data at each iteration [17]. To allow metric learning on high-dimensional image features of large scale datasets that are too large to fit in memory, we in addition use product quantization [18], a data compression technique that was recently used with success for large-scale image retrieval [6] and classifier training [8].

We report experiments on the ImageNet Large Scale Visual Recognition Challenge 2010 (ILSVRC'10) dataset, which consists of 1.2M train images of 1,000 classes. As a baseline approach, we use the setup of the winning entry in the 2011 edition of the challenge [8]: Fisher vector image representations [19] are used to describe images and one-vs-rest linear SVM classifiers are learned independently for each class. Surprisingly, we find that the NCM classifier outperforms the more flexible k-NN classifier. Moreover, the NCM classifier performs on par with the SVM baseline. We also consider the generalization performance to new classes. In a first experiment, we train the metric on a subset of classes of ILSVRC'10 and include the held-out classes at test time. We only observe a small drop in performance compared to the experiment where the metric is learned with all classes. In a second experiment, we train the metric on ILSVRC'10 and apply it to a larger set of 10K ImageNet classes. Once the metric is

Fig. 1. The nearest classes for three reference classes using the the ℓ_2 and Mahalanobis metric learned for the NCM classifier. Class probabilities are given for a simulated image signature that equals the mean of the reference class, see Section 4.3 for details.

learned, we can learn the 10K classifiers (*i.e.* compute their means) on 64K dimensional features in less than an hour on a single CPU, while learning one-vs-rest linear SVMs on the same data takes on the order of 280 CPU days. Finally, we explore a zero-shot setting where the class mean of novel classes are estimated based on related classes in the ImageNet hierarchy. We show that the zero-shot class mean can be effectively combined with the empirical mean of a small number of training images. This provides an approach that smoothly transitions from settings without training data to ones with abundant training data.

The rest of the paper is organized as follows. In Section 2 we discuss a selection of related work which is most relevant to this paper. In Section 3 we present the metric learning techniques we explored for the k-NN and NCM classifiers. We then present extensive experimental results in Section 4, followed by our conclusions in Section 5.

2 Related Work

In this section we discuss some of the most relevant work on large-scale image annotation, metric learning, and transfer learning.

Large-Scale Image Annotation. The ImageNet dataset [1] has been a catalyst for research on large-scale image annotation. The current state-of-the-art [8,10] uses efficient linear SVM classifiers trained in a one-vs-rest manner in combination with high-dimensional bag-of-word [20] or Fisher vector representations [19]. Besides one-vs-rest training, large-scale ranking-based formulations have also been explored in [7]. Interestingly, this approach performs joint classifier learning and dimensionality reduction of the image features. Operating in a lower-dimensional space acts as a regularization during learning and reduces the cost of classifier evaluation at test time. The proposed NCM approach also learns low-dimensional projection matrices but the weight vectors are constrained to be the class means. This allows the efficient addition of novel classes.

In [3,7] k-NN classifiers were found to be competitive with linear SVM classifiers in a very large-scale setting involving 10,000 or more classes. The drawback of k-NN classifiers, however, is that they are expensive in storage and computation, since in principle all training data needs to be kept in memory and accessed to classify new images. The storage issue is also encountered when SVM classifiers are trained since all training data needs to be processed in multiple passes. Product quantization (PQ) was introduced in [6] as a lossy compression mechanism for local SIFT descriptors in a bag-of-features image retrieval system. It has been subsequently used to compress bag-of-word and Fisher vector image representations in the context of image retrieval [9] and classifier training [8]. We also exploit PQ in our work to compress high-dimensional image signatures when learning our metrics.

Metric Learning. Here, we only discuss methods that learn metrics for image classification problems. Other methods aim at learning metrics for verification problems and essentially learn binary classifiers that threshold the learned distance to decide whether two images belong to the same class or not, see *e.g.* [21].

Among those methods that learn metrics for classification, the Large Margin Nearest Neighbor (LMNN) approach of [16] is specifically designed to support k-NN classification. It tries to ensure that for each image its predefined set of target neighbors from the same class are closer than samples from other classes. Since the cost function is defined over triplets of points —that can be sampled in an SGD training procedure— this method can scale to large datasets. In [16] the set of target neighbors is chosen and fixed using the ℓ_2 metric in the original space, that can be problematic as this distance is far from being ideal, see *e.g.* Figure 1. Therefore, we propose two variants of LMNN that avoid using such a pre-defined set of target neighbors, both leading to significant improvements.

The large margin nearest local mean classifier [22] assigns a test image to a class based on its distance to the mean of its nearest neighbors in each class. This method was reported to outperform LMNN but requires computing all pairwise distances between training instances and therefore does not scale well to large datasets. Similarly, TagProp [12] suffers from the same problem. It consists in assigning weights to training samples based on their distance to the test instance and in computing the class prediction by the total weight of samples of each class in a neighborhood. Because of their poor scaling properties, we do not consider these methods in our experiments.

Closely related to our metric learning approach for the NCM classifier is the LESS model of [14]. They learn a diagonal scaling matrix to modify the ℓ_2 distance by rescaling the data dimensions, and include an ℓ_1 penalty on the weights to perform feature selection. However, in their case, NCM is used to address small sample size problems in binary classification, *i.e.* cases where there are fewer training points (tens to hundreds) than features (thousands). Our approach differs significantly in that (i) we work in a multi-class setting and (ii) we learn a low-dimensional projection which allows efficiency in large-scale. The method of [15] is also related to our method since they use a NCM classifier and an ℓ_2 distance in a subspace that is orthogonal to the subspace with maximum within-class variance. However, their technique involves computing the first eigenvectors of the within-class covariance matrix, which has a computational cost between $O(D^2)$ and $O(D^3)$, which again is undesirable for high-dimensional feature vectors. Moreover, this metric is heuristically obtained, rather than directly optimized for maximum classification performance.

Transfer Learning. The term transfer learning is used to refer to methods that share information across classes during learning. Examples include the use of part-based or attribute class representations. Part-based object recognition models [23] define an object as a spatial constellation of parts, and share the part detectors across different classes. Attribute-based models [24] characterize a category (*e.g.* animal) by a combination of attributes (*e.g.* yellow, stripes, carnivore), and share the attribute classifiers across classes. Other approaches include biasing the weight vector learned for a new class towards the weight vectors of classes that have already been trained [25]. Zero-shot learning [26] is an extreme case of transfer learning where for a new class no training instances are available but a description is provided in terms of parts, attributes, or other relations to already seen classes. In [5] various transfer learning methods were evaluated in a large-scale setting using the ILSVRC'10 dataset. They found transfer learning methods to have little added value when training images are available for all classes. In contrast, transfer learning was found to be effective in a zero-shot learning setting, where classifiers were trained for 800 classes, and performance was tested in a 200-way classification across the held-out classes.

In this paper we also aim at transfer learning, in the sense that we allow only a trivial amount of processing on the data of new classes (storing in a database, or averaging), and rely on a metric that was trained on other classes to recognize the new ones. In contrast to most work on transfer learning, we do not use any intermediate representation in terms of parts or attributes, nor do we train classifiers for the new classes. While also considering zero-shot learning, we further evaluate performance when combining a zero-shot model inspired by [5] with progressively more training images per class, from one up to thousands. We find that the zero-shot model provides an effective prior when a small amount of training data is available.

3 Learning Metrics to Generalize to New Categories

In this section we discuss metric learning for the k-NN and NCM classifiers. We learn Mahalanobis distances of the form $(x - x')^\top M(x - x')$ to improve classification accuracy, where $x \in \mathbb{R}^D$. We focus on low-rank metrics with $M = W^\top W$ and $W \in \mathbb{R}^{d \times D}$, where $d \leq D$ acts as regularizer and improves efficiency for computation and storage. The Mahalanobis distance induced by W is equivalent to the ℓ_2 distance after projection:

$$\| x - x' \|_W^2 = (x - x')^\top W^\top W(x - x') = \| Wx - Wx' \|^2 . \tag{1}$$

3.1 Metric Learning for k-NN Classification

K-NN classification is essentially a ranking problem, which is reflected in the metric learning approach of LMNN [16]. Their learning objective is based on triplets of images, where the distance between a query image q and a target image p of the same class should be smaller than the distance to a negative image n of a different class. The 0/1-loss for such a triplet is upper-bounded by the hinge-loss on the distance difference:

$$L_{qpn} = \left[1 + \| x_q - x_p \|_W^2 - \| x_q - x_n \|_W^2 \right]_+, \tag{2}$$

which is zero if the negative image n is at least one distance unit farther from the query q than the positive image p, and positive otherwise. The sum of the per-triplet loss is the final learning criterion:

$$L = \sum_{q=1}^{N} \sum_{p \in P_q} \sum_{n \in N_q} L_{qpn}, \tag{3}$$

where P_q and N_q denote the set of positive and negative images for a query image x_q. The sub-gradient of the loss is obtained as:

$$\nabla_W L = \sum_{q=1}^{N} \sum_{p \in P_q} \sum_{n \in N_q} \nabla_W L_{qpn}, \tag{4}$$

$$\nabla_W L_{qpn} = [\![L_{qpn} > 0]\!] 2W \Big((x_q - x_p)(x_q - x_p)^\top - (x_q - x_n)(x_q - x_n)^\top \Big), \tag{5}$$

where we use Iversons bracket notation $[\![\cdot]\!]$ that equals one if its argument is true, and zero otherwise.

In LMNN the set of targets P_q for a query q is set to the query's k nearest neighbors from the same class, using the ℓ_2 distance. The rationale is the following one: if we can ensure that these targets are closer than the instances of the other classes, then the k-NN classification will succeed. In practice, however, it is not always possible to achieve this situation with a given set of target neighbors, since it implicitly assumes that the ℓ_2 distance in the original space is a good similarity measure. Therefore, we consider two alternatives to using a fixed set of target neighbors:

- First, we can set P_q to contain all images with the same class label as q. This is similar to [2] where the same type of loss was used to learn image similarity defined as the scalar product between images after a learned linear projection.
- Second, we can define P_q dynamically to contain the k images of the same class that are closest to q using the current metric. This option corresponds to minimizing the loss function also with respect to the choice of P_q. Hence, different target neighbors can be selected, that are closer than the original ones according to the current metric. A similar approach has been proposed in [16], where every T iterations P_q is redefined using target neighbors according to the current metric.

Since the number of possible triplets tends to be large for any of these strategies[1], at each SGD iteration we generate triplets from a limited set of $m \ll N$ images.

3.2 Metric Learning for the Nearest Class Mean Classifier

We formulate the NCM classifier using multi-class logistic regression and define the probability for a class c given an image feature vector x as:

$$p(c|x) = \frac{\exp - \parallel \mu_c - x \parallel_W^2}{\sum_{c'=1}^{C} \exp - \parallel \mu_{c'} - x \parallel_W^2}, \tag{6}$$

where μ_c is the mean for class $c \in \{1, \ldots, C\}$. Our objective is to minimize the negative log-likelihood of the ground-truth class labels $y_i \in \{1, \ldots, C\}$ of the training images:

$$\mathcal{L} = -\frac{1}{N} \sum_{i=1}^{N} \ln p(y_i|x_i). \tag{7}$$

The gradient of this objective function is easily verified to be:

$$\nabla_W \mathcal{L} = \frac{2}{N} \sum_{i=1}^{N} \sum_{c=1}^{C} \Big([\![y_i = c]\!] - p(c|x) \Big) W (\mu_c - x_i)(\mu_c - x_i)^\top. \tag{8}$$

To learn the projection matrix W, we use SGD training and sample at each iteration a fixed number of m training images to estimate the gradient.

Note that the NCM classifier is linear in x since we assign an image x to the class c^* with minimum distance:

$$c^* = \arg\min_c \{ \parallel x - \mu_c \parallel_W^2 \} = \arg\min_c \{ \parallel W\mu_c \parallel^2 - 2\mu_c^\top (W^\top W) x \}. \tag{9}$$

This observation shows that our classifier can be related to the WSABIE method of [7]. In the latter paper, a class c is scored using $f_c(x) = v_c^\top W x$, where W projects the image into a lower-dimensional space, and v_c is a class specific weight vector learned from data. However, we enforce that $v_c = W\mu_c$, which allows us to add new classes without the need to learn v_c from labeled data and therefore at almost zero cost.

Note that our classifier can also be related to the solution of ridge-regression, or regularized linear least-squares regression. Let $f_c(x_i) = b_c + w_c^\top x_i$ and let $y_{ic} = 1$, if x_i belongs to class c, and $y_{ic} = 0$ otherwise. The ridge-regression loss function, $\frac{1}{N}\sum_i (f_c(x_i) - y_{ic})^2 + \lambda \parallel w_c \parallel^2$, can be minimized in closed form and leads to $f_c(x) = \frac{n_c}{N}(1 + \mu_c^\top (\Sigma + \lambda I)^{-1} x)$, where Σ is the (class-independent) data covariance matrix, and n_c denotes the number of images in class c. If n_c is equal for all classes, then the score function is equivalent to $\mu_c^\top (\Sigma + \lambda I)^{-1} x$ up to additive and multiplicative constants. This is similar to our NCM classifier if we set W such that $W^\top W = (\Sigma + \lambda I)^{-1}$, see Eq. (9). Moreover, just like the NCM classifier, the ridge-regression function for a new class can also be found from the class mean μ_c and count n_c, once the data covariance matrix has been estimated.

[1] Even if we disregard the set of target neighbors, each query image is paired with all images of other classes. Thus, if we have N training images evenly distributed among C classes, this would yield already $N(N - \frac{N}{C})$ pairs. For ILSVRC'10, we have $N \approx 10^6$ and $C = 10^3$ which leads to roughly 10^{12} pairs, and to even more triplets.

4 Experimental Evaluation

In this section we first describe the dataset and evaluation measures used in our experiments. Then, we present our results for metric learning using k-NN classification in Section 4.2, and those using NCM classification in Section 4.3. Finally, in Section 4.4, we present results for transfer learning, where we apply metrics trained on some classes to novel ones, and assess performance as a function of the number of training images.

4.1 Experimental Setup and Baseline Approach

Dataset. In most of our experiments we use the dataset of the ImageNet Large Scale Visual Recognition 2010 challenge (ILSVRC'10). This dataset contains 1.2M training images of 1,000 object classes (with between 660 to 3047 images per class), an evaluation set of 50K images, and a test set of 150K images.

Features. We represent each image, with a Fisher vector (FV) [19] computed over densely extracted SIFT descriptors and local color features, both projected with PCA to 64 dimensions. FVs are extracted and normalized separately for both channels and then combined by concatenating the two feature vectors. We do not make use of spatial pyramids. In our experiments we use FVs extracted using a vocabulary of either 16 or 256 Gaussians. For 16 Gaussians, this leads to a 4K dimensional feature vector, which requires about 20GB for the 1.2M training set (using 4-byte floating point arithmetic). This fits into the RAM of our 32GB servers.

For 256 Gaussians, the FVs are 16 times larger, *i.e.* 64K dimensional, which would require 320GB of memory. Hence, we compress the feature vectors using product quantization [18]. In a nutshell, it consists in splitting the high-dimensional vector into small sub-vectors, and vector quantizing each sub-vector independently. We compress the dataset to approximately 10GB using 8-dimensional sub-vectors and 256 centroids per sub-quantizer, which allows storing each sub-quantizer index in a single byte. In each iteration of SGD learning, we decompress the features of a limited number of images, and use these (lossy) reconstructions for the gradient computation.

Evaluation Measures. We report the average top-1 and top-5 flat error used in the ILSVRC'10 challenge. The flat error is one if the ground-truth label does not correspond to the top-1 label with highest score (or any of the top-5 labels), and zero otherwise. Unless specified otherwise, we report the top-5 flat error on the test set using the 4K dimensional features; we use the validation set for parameter tuning only. In tables, we highlight the best result per row in bold, and do so for each feature set if several are used. Additionally, the baseline performance is also highlighted if it is best.

Baseline Approach. For our baseline, we follow the state-of-the-art approach of [8] and learn 1,000 one-vs-rest SVMs with SGD. The results of the baseline can be found in Table 2. We see that the 64K dimensional features lead to significantly better results than the 4K ones, despite the lossy PQ compression. The performance using the 64K features is slightly better than the ILSVRC'10 challenge winners [10] (28.0 vs. 28.2 flat top-5 error), and very close to the results of [8] (25.7 flat top-5 error). Note that there a much higher dimensional representation was used of more than 1M features.

Table 1. k-NN classification performance with 4K dimensional features. For all methods, except those indicated by 'Full', the data is projected to a 128 dimensional space.

	SVM	ℓ_2	ℓ_2	k-NN classifiers				
				LMNN		All	Dynamic	
	Full	Full	+ PCA	10	20		10	20
Flat top-1 error	**60.2**	75.0	76.3	72.9	72.8	67.9	**65.1**	66.0
Flat top-5 error	**38.2**	55.9	57.3	50.6	50.4	44.2	**39.8**	40.7

SGD Training and Early Stopping. To learn the projection matrix W, we use SGD training, sampling at each iteration a fixed number of training images to estimate the gradient. Following [27], we use a fixed learning rate and use the projection dimension $d \leq D$ as well as the number of iterations as an implicit form of regularization. We run SGD for 750K-4M iterations, and the performance is validated every 10K (NCM) or 50K (k-NN) iterations. The metric which yields the lowest top-5 error is selected. Similarly, all hyper-parameters, like the value of k for the k-NN classifiers, are validated in this way. Unless stated otherwise, training is performed using the ILSVRC'10 training set, and validation on the provided 50K validation set.

4.2 k-NN Metric Learning Results

We start with an assessment of k-NN classifiers using metrics learned with the methods described in Section 3.1. Given the cost of k-NN classifiers, we focus our experiments on the 4K features. We consider the impact of the different choices for the set of target images P_q as described in Section 3.1, and the influence of the projection dimensionality. We initialize W as a PCA projection, the optimal k is typically 100 or 250.

Target selection for k-NN metric learning. In the first experiment we compare the three different options of Section 3.1 to define the set of target images P_q, while learning projections to 128 dimensions. For LMNN and dynamic targets, we experimented with various numbers of targets on the validation set and found that using 10 to 20 targets yields the best results.

The results in Table 1 show that all methods lead to metrics that are better than the ℓ_2 metric in the original space, or after a PCA projection to 128 dimensions. Furthermore, we can improve over LMNN by using all within-class images as targets, or even further by using dynamic targets. The success of the dynamic target selection can be explained by the fact that among the three alternatives, it is the most closely related to the k-NN classifier objective. The best performance on the flat top-5 error of 39.8 using 10 dynamic targets is, however, slightly worse than the 38.2 error rate of the SVM baseline.

Impact of Projection Dimension on k-NN Classification. Next, we evaluate the influence of the projection dimensionality, by varying it between 32 and 1024. We only show results using 10 dynamic targets, since this performed best among the evaluated k-NN methods. From the results in Table 2 we see that a projection to 256 dimensions yields the lowest error of 39.0, still somewhat inferior of those of the SVM baseline.

Table 2. Performance of k-NN and NCM classifiers, as well as baselines, using the 4K and 64K dimensional features, for various projection dimensions, see text for details

	4K dimensional features							64K dimensional features			
Projection dim.	32	64	128	256	512	1024	Full	128	256	512	Full
SVM baseline							**38.2**				**28.0**
k-NN, dynamic 10	47.2	42.2	39.8	**39.0**	39.1	40.4					
NCM, learned metric	49.1	42.7	39.0	37.4	**37.0**	**37.0**		31.7	31.0	**30.7**	
NCM, PCA+ℓ_2	78.7	74.6	71.7	69.9	68.8	68.2	**68.0**				**63.2**
NCM, PCA+inv.cov.	75.5	67.7	60.6	54.5	49.3	46.1	**43.8**				
PCA+Ridge-regress.	86.3	80.3	73.9	68.1	62.8	58.9	**54.6**				
WSABIE [7]	51.9	45.1	41.2	39.4	38.7	**38.5**		32.2	30.1	**29.2**	

4.3 Nearest Class Mean Classification Results

We now consider the performance of NCM classifiers and the related methods described in Section 3.2. In Table 2 we show the results for various projection dimensionalities.

We first consider the results for the 4K dimensional features. Our first, unexpected, observation is that our NCM classifier (37.0) outperforms the more flexible k-NN classifier (39.0), and even slightly outperforms the SVM baseline (38.2) when projecting to 256 dimensions or more. Interestingly, using the ℓ_2 instead of a learned metric, the situation is reversed and the k-NN classifier is better (55.9, see Table 1) than the NCM classifier (68.0). WSABIE scores slightly worse (38.5) than the baseline and our NCM classifier, and does not generalize to new classes without retraining. Like the NCM classifier, ridge-regression does allow generalization to new classes, but leads to significantly worse results (54.6) and pre-processing the data with PCA further degrades its performance.

We also consider two variants of the NCM classifier where we use PCA to reduce the dimensionality. In one case we use the ℓ_2 metric after PCA. In the other, inspired by ridge-regression, we use the metric generated by the inverse of the regularized covariance matrix, see Section 3.2. We tuned the regularization parameter λ on the validation set, as was also done for ridge-regression. From these results we can conclude that, just like for k-NN, the ℓ_2 metric with or without PCA leads to poor results as compared to a learned metric. Second, the feature whitening implemented by the inverse covariance metric, leads to results that are better than using the ℓ_2 metric, and also substantially better than ridge-regression. The results are however significantly worse than using our learned metric, in particular when using low-dimensional projections.

When we use the 64K dimensional features, the results of the NCM classifier (30.7) are somewhat worse than the SVM baseline (28.0); again the learned metric is better than using ℓ_2 (63.2). WSABIE obtains an error of 29.2, in between the SVM and NCM.

In Figure 1 we illustrate the difference between the ℓ_2 and the Mahalanobis metric induced by a learned projection from 64K to 512 dimensions. For three reference classes we show the five nearest classes, based on the distance between class means. We also show the probabilities on the reference class and its five neighbor classes according to

Table 3. Performance of 1,000-way classification among test images of 200 classes not used for metric learning, and control setting with metric learning using all classes. Left column denotes the number of training classes used, and "plain" denotes k-NN or NCM using the ℓ_2 distance.

	4K dimensional features									64K dimensional features				
	SVM	k-NN			NCM					SVM	NCM			
	Full	128	256	Full	128	256	512	1024	Full	Full	128	256	512	Full
Plain				54.2					66.6					61.9
1000	37.6	39.1	38.4		38.6	36.8	**36.4**	36.5		**27.7**	31.7	30.8	**30.6**	
800		42.2	42.4		42.5	40.4	39.9	**39.6**			39.3	37.7	**37.1**	

Eq. (6). The feature vector x is set as the mean of the reference class, *i.e.* a simulated perfectly typical image of this class. For the ℓ_2 metric, we used our metric learning algorithm to learn a scaling of the ℓ_2 metric to minimize Eq. (7). This does not change the ordering of classes, but ensures that we can compare probabilities computed using both metrics. We find that, as expected, the learned metric has more semantically related class neighbors. Moreover, we see that using the learned metric most of the probability mass is assigned to the reference class, whereas the ℓ_2 metric leads to rather uncertain classifications.

4.4 Generalization to New Classes and Using Few Samples

Given the encouraging classification accuracy of the NCM classifier observed above —and its superior efficiency as compared to the k-NN classifier— we now explore its ability to generalize to novel classes. We also consider its performance as a function of the number of training images available to estimate the mean of novel classes.

Generalization to novel classes not seen during training. In this experiment we use approximately 1M images corresponding to 800 random classes to learn metrics, and evaluate the error of a 1,000-way classification across all classes. We report the error computed over the 30K images in the test set of the held-out 200 classes. Performance among test images of the 800 train classes changes only marginally and would obscure the changes among the test images of the 200 held-out classes.

In Table 3 we show the performance of NCM and k-NN classifiers for several projection dimensions, and compare it to two control settings, training on all 1,000 classes, and using the ℓ_2 distance. The results show that both classifiers generalize remarkably well to new classes. In particular for 1024 dimensional projections of the 4K features, the NCM classifier achieves an error of 39.6 over classes not seen during training, as compared to 36.5 when using all classes for training. For the 64K dimensional features the drop in performance is larger, but it is still surprisingly good considering that training for the novel classes consists only in computing the mean.

To further demonstrate the generalization ability of the NCM classifier using learned metrics, we also compare it against the SVM baseline on the ImageNet-10K dataset. This dataset, introduced in [3], consists of 4.5M training images of 10,184 classes, and a test set of another 4.5M images. We use projections learned on the ILSVRC'10

Table 4. Average per-class performance of the NCM classifier on the ImageNet-10K dataset, using metrics learned on the ILSVRC'10 dataset, and comparison to previously published results

	4K dimensional features					64K dimensional features				21K	128K	128K
Proj. dim.	128	256	512	1024	SVM	128	256	512	SVM	[3]	[8]	[11]
Flat top-1	91.8	90.7	90.5	**90.4**	**86.0**	87.1	86.3	**86.1**	**78.1**	93.6	83.3	81.9
Flat top-5	80.7	78.9	**78.6**	**78.6**	**72.4**	71.7	70.5	**70.1**	**60.9**			

dataset, and only compute the means of the 10K classes. The results in Table 4 show that even in this extremely challenging setting the NCM classifier performs remarkably well compared to [3,8,11] and our baseline, all of which require training 10K classifiers. We note that, to the best of our knowledge, our baseline results exceed the previous known state-of-the-art [3,8,11] on this dataset. Training our SVM baseline system took 9 and 280 CPU days respectively for the 4K and 64K features, while the computation of the means for the NCM classifier took approximately 3 and 48 CPU minutes respectively. This represents roughly a 8,500 fold speed-up as compared to the baseline, without counting the time to learn the projection matrix.

Accuracy as a Function of the Number of Training Images of Novel Classes. In our last experiment we consider the error as a function of the number of images that are used to compute the means of novel classes. We also include results of a zero-shot learning experiment, where we use the ImageNet hierarchy to estimate the mean of novel classes from the means of related training classes. We follow ideas of [5] and estimate the mean of a novel class as the average of the means associated with all ancestor nodes in the ILSVRC'10 class hierarchy. The means of internal nodes are computed as the average of the means of all descendant training classes. If we view the estimation of a class mean as the estimation of the mean of a Gaussian distribution, then the sample average μ_s corresponds to the Maximum Likelihood (ML) estimate and the zero-shot estimate μ_z can be thought of as a prior. We can combine this prior with the ML estimate to obtain a maximum a-posteriori (MAP) estimate μ_p on the class mean. The MAP estimate of the mean of a Gaussian is obtained as the ML estimate weighted by the number n of images that were used to compute it, plus the prior mean which has a weight m determined on the validation set [28], *i.e.* $\mu_p = (n\mu_s + m\mu_z)/(n + m)$.

In Figure 2 we analyze the performance of the NCM classifier trained on the images of the same 800 classes used above, with a learned projection from 64K to 512 dimensions. We again report the error among test images of the held-out classes, both in a 1,000-way classification as above, and in a 200-way classification as in [5]. We repeat the experiment 10 times, and show error-bars at three times standard deviation. For the error to stabilize we only need approximately 100 images to estimate the class means. The results also show that the prior leads to zero-shot performance of 64.3, which is comparable to the result of 65.2 reported in [5], even though they used a different set of 200 test classes. More importantly, we show that the zero-shot prior can be effectively combined with the empirical mean to provide a smooth transition from the zero-shot setting to a setting with many training examples. Inclusion of the zero-shot prior leads to a significant error reduction in the regime where ten images or less are available.

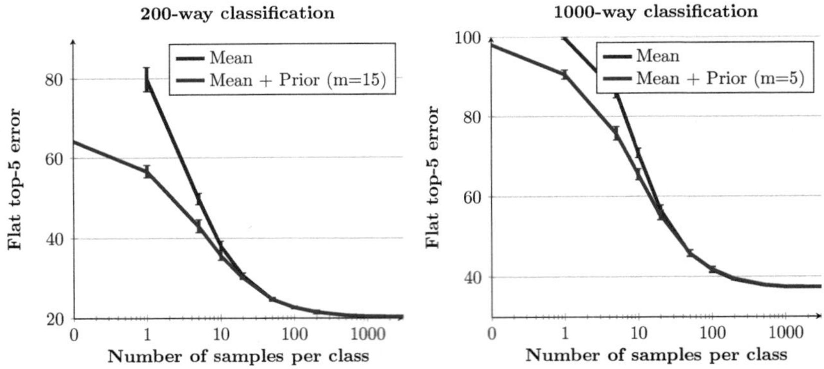

Fig. 2. Performance of NCM as a function of the number of images used to compute the means for classes not used during training, with and without the zero-shot prior. See text for details.

5 Conclusions

We have evaluated metric learning techniques to support k-NN and NCM classifiers, which can be applied on large scale dynamic and open-ended image datasets, and allow extensions at (near) zero cost to new classes not used for training. Surprisingly we found that the NCM classifier outperforms the more flexible k-NN approach. Moreover, using a learned metric, the performance of the NCM classifier is comparable to that of SVM classifiers, while projecting the data to only 256 dimensions. Our learned metrics generalize well to unseen classes, as shown in experiments where the metric is learned on a subset of the classes, and further corroborated by our experiments on the ImageNet-10K dataset. In addition, we have shown that our NCM classifiers can be used in a zero-shot setting where no training images are available for novel classes, and that the zero-shot model significantly boosts performance when combined with a class mean estimated from a limited amount of training images.

In the proposed NCM classifiers each class is represented only by its mean, while this has the advantage of obtaining fast linear classifiers at test time, this representation is also rather restrictive. In ongoing work we extend this class representation, for example by using a representation based on a set of class centroids, to obtain more flexible and non-linear classifiers.

Interestingly, query-by-example image retrieval can be seen as a classification problem where a single positive sample is provided. In such a case, the class mean simplifies to the query which shows that the proposed NCM provides a unified way to treat classification and retrieval problems. This is a direction that we will explore in future work.

References

1. Deng, J., Dong, W., Socher, R., Li, L.-J., Li, K., Fei-Fei, L.: ImageNet: A large-scale hierarchical image database. In: CVPR (2009)
2. Checkik, G., Sharma, V., Shalit, U., Bengio, S.: Large scale online learning of image similarity through ranking. Journal of Machine Learning Research 11, 1109–1135 (2010)
3. Deng, J., Berg, A.C., Li, K., Fei-Fei, L.: What Does Classifying More Than 10,000 Image Categories Tell Us? In: Daniilidis, K., Maragos, P., Paragios, N. (eds.) ECCV 2010, Part V. LNCS, vol. 6315, pp. 71–84. Springer, Heidelberg (2010)

4. Vedaldi, A., Zisserman, A.: Efficient additive kernels via explicit feature maps. In: CVPR (2010)
5. Rohrbach, M., Stark, M., Schiele, B.: Evaluating knowledge transfer and zero-shot learning in a large-scale setting. In: CVPR (2011)
6. Jégou, H., Douze, M., Schmid, C.: Product quantization for nearest neighbor search. IEEE Trans. PAMI 33, 117–128 (2011)
7. Weston, J., Bengio, S., Usunier, N.: WSABIE: Scaling up to large vocabulary image annotation. In: IJCAI (2011)
8. Sánchez, J., Perronnin, F.: High-dimensional signature compression for large-scale image classification. In: CVPR (2011)
9. Jégou, H., Perronnin, F., Douze, M., Sánchez, J., Pérez, P., Schmid, C.: Aggregating local image descriptors into compact codes. IEEE Trans. PAMI (to appear, 2012)
10. Lin, Y., Lv, F., Zhu, S., Yang, M., Cour, T., Yu, K., Cao, L., Huang, T.: Large-scale image classification: Fast feature extraction and SVM training. In: CVPR (2011)
11. Perronnin, F., Akata, Z., Harchaoui, Z., Schmid, C.: Towards good practice in large-scale learning for image classification. In: CVPR (2012)
12. Guillaumin, M., Mensink, T., Verbeek, J., Schmid, C.: Tagprop: Discriminative metric learning in nearest neighbor models for image auto-annotation. In: ICCV (2009)
13. Webb, A.R.: Statistical pattern recognition. Wiley, New-York (2002)
14. Veenman, C., Tax, D.: LESS: a model-based classifier for sparse subspaces. IEEE Trans. PAMI 27, 1496–1500 (2005)
15. Zhou, X., Zhang, X., Yan, Z., Chang, S.-F., Hasegawa-Johnson, M., Huang, T.: SIFT-Bag kernel for video event analysis. In: ACM Multimedia (2008)
16. Weinberger, K., Saul, L.: Distance metric learning for large margin nearest neighbor classification. Journal of Machine Learning Research 10, 207–244 (2009)
17. Bottou, L.: Large-scale machine learning with stochastic gradient descent. In: COMPSTAT (2010)
18. Gray, R., Neuhoff, D.: Quantization. IEEE Trans. Information Theory 44, 2325–2383 (1998)
19. Perronnin, F., Sánchez, J., Mensink, T.: Improving the Fisher Kernel for Large-Scale Image Classification. In: Daniilidis, K., Maragos, P., Paragios, N. (eds.) ECCV 2010, Part IV. LNCS, vol. 6314, pp. 143–156. Springer, Heidelberg (2010)
20. Zhang, J., Marszałek, M., Lazebnik, S., Schmid, C.: Local features and kernels for classification of texture and object categories: a comprehensive study. IJCV 73, 213–238 (2007)
21. Nowak, E., Jurie, F.: Learning visual similarity measures for comparing never seen objects. In: CVPR (2007)
22. Chai, J., Liua, H., Chenb, B., Baoa, Z.: Large margin nearest local mean classifier. Signal Processing 90, 236–248 (2010)
23. Fei-Fei, L., Fergus, R., Perona, P.: One-shot learning of object categories. IEEE Trans. PAMI 28, 594–611 (2006)
24. Lampert, C., Nickisch, H., Harmeling, S.: Learning to detect unseen object classes by between-class attribute transfer. In: CVPR (2009)
25. Tommasi, T., Caputo, B.: The more you know, the less you learn: from knowledge transfer to one-shot learning of object categories. In: BMVC (2009)
26. Larochelle, H., Erhan, D., Bengio, Y.: Zero-data learning of new tasks. In: AAAI Conference on Artificial Intelligence (2008)
27. Bai, B., Weston, J., Grangier, D., Collobert, R., Qi, Y., Sadamasa, K., Chapelle, O., Weinberger, K.: Learning to rank with (a lot of) word features. Information Retrieval – Special Issue on Learning to Rank 13, 291–314 (2010)
28. Gauvain, J.L., Lee, C.H.: Maximum a posteriori estimation for multivariate Gaussian mixture observations of Markov chains. IEEE Trans. Speech and Audio Proc. 2, 291–298 (1994)

Leafsnap: A Computer Vision System for Automatic Plant Species Identification

Neeraj Kumar[1], Peter N. Belhumeur[2], Arijit Biswas[3], David W. Jacobs[3], W. John Kress[4], Ida C. Lopez[4], and João V.B. Soares[3]

[1] University of Washington, Seattle WA
[2] Columbia University, New York NY
[3] University of Maryland, College Park MD
[4] National Museum of Natural History, Smithsonian Institution, Washington DC

Abstract. We describe the first mobile app for identifying plant species using automatic visual recognition. The system – called Leafsnap – identifies tree species from photographs of their leaves. Key to this system are computer vision components for discarding non-leaf images, segmenting the leaf from an untextured background, extracting features representing the curvature of the leaf's contour over multiple scales, and identifying the species from a dataset of the 184 trees in the Northeastern United States. Our system obtains state-of-the-art performance on the real-world images from the new Leafsnap Dataset – the largest of its kind. Throughout the paper, we document many of the practical steps needed to produce a computer vision system such as ours, which currently has nearly a million users.

1 Introduction

In this work, we describe a visual recognition system for automatic plant species identification. The system, called Leafsnap, is a mobile app that helps users identify trees from photographs of their leaves (see Fig. 1). The current version of Leafsnap has coverage for all of the 184 tree species of the Northeastern United States. To date, nearly one million copies of Leafsnap have been installed on iPhones and iPads. It is now being used by scientists, ecologists, foresters, urban planners, amateur botanists, gardening clubs, landscape architects, citizen scientists, educators, and even school children in classes across the United States.

Leafsnap was developed to greatly speed up the manual process of plant species identification, collection, and monitoring. Without visual recognition tools such as Leafsnap, a dichotomous key (decision tree) must be manually navigated to search the many branches and seemingly endless nodes of the taxonomic tree. Identifying a single species using this process – by answering dozens of often-ambiguous questions, such as, "are the leaves flat and thin?" – may take several minutes or even hours. This is difficult for experts, and exceedingly so (or even impossible) for amateurs.

In this work, we show how computer vision can be used to significantly simplify the plant species identification problem. Our automatic system requires that a

A. Fitzgibbon et al. (Eds.): ECCV 2012, Part II, LNCS 7573, pp. 502–516, 2012.

(a) Home (b) Recognition (c) Nearby Species

Fig. 1. Screenshots of the iPad version of Leafsnap. (a) The Home screen, with an image of a flower from the Redbud tree (*Cercis canadensis*). (b) A user's collection (left) and recognition results for a leaf (right), with the image and corresponding segmentation at the top and ranked species results below. (c) The Nearby Species screen, with pins denoting trees recently labeled by Leafsnap users around New York City.

single leaf specimen is photographed on a solid light-colored background. The recognition process consists of:

Classifying whether the image is of a valid leaf, to decide if it is worth processing further, using a binary classifier applied to gist features [1]. (Section 2)

Segmenting the image to obtain a binary image separating the leaf from the background. We do this by estimating foreground and background color distributions in the saturation-value space of the HSV colorspace. (Section 3)

Extracting curvature features from the binarized image for compactly and discriminatively representing the shape of the leaf. We robustly compute histograms of curvature over multiple scales using integral measures of curvature. (Section 4)

Comparing the features to those from a labeled database of leaf images and returning the species with the closest matches. Due to the discriminative power of the features and the size of our labeled dataset, we use a simple nearest neighbor approach with histogram intersection as the distance metric. (Section 5)

All computation is completed in about 5 seconds, and can be trivially parallelized across many machines. Users are then shown the top matches and make the final identification themselves, by examining additional content present in the app, such as high-quality images of the species and textual descriptions of their characteristics. The complete Leafsnap system is discussed in Sec. 6.

Automatic species identification has been an area of recent but growing interest in computer vision. [2] describes a system that combines human input with computer vision results to assist in the identification of birds. In the plant world, [3] describes a system that can automatically identify plant species using images of flowers. While this system shows impressive results, its concerns are largely complementary to ours. Identification of species (or varietals) from flowers is of great interest to gardeners and flower enthusiasts. However, flowers are of limited value in systems used in biodiversity studies or for identifying local trees, because flowers are not present throughout most of the year. A summary of recent work on algorithms for plant identification and as well as detailed evaluations are described in the CLEF 2011 plant images classification task [4].

The work described here is most closely related to [5,6], which describe a much earlier version of the current Leafsnap system. (Other related works on plant identification can be found in those references.) Apart from the basic approach of using a color-based segmentation algorithm, all aspects of our work are completely new. In particular: the use of a pre-filter on input images; numerous speedups and additional post-processing within the segmentation algorithm; the use of a simpler and more efficient curvature-based recognition algorithm instead of Inner Distance Shape Context (IDSC) [7]; a much larger dataset of images, including over 5,000 taken using mobile phones; and the creation and deployment of an interactive system for use by non-expert users.

More generally, our system is an example of fine-grained visual categorization: the discrimination of instances into classes that are more specific than basic level categorization (*e.g.*, leaves or animals) yet not as specific as the identification of individuals (*e.g.*, face recognition). This is a rapidly growing area of computer vision. To spur further related research, we have publicly released our large dataset of real-world leaf images, as well as optimized source code for both the segmentation and feature extraction algorithms[1].

2 Leaf/Non-leaf Classification

Untrained users initially try to take photos of leaves *in-situ*, with multiple leaves present amid clutter, often with severe lighting and blur artifacts, resulting in images that we cannot handle (usually due to segmentation failures). In addition, many users also take photos of objects that are not leaves. We address both of these issues by first running a binary leaf/non-leaf classifier on all input images. If this classifier detects that an input image is not valid – of a single leaf, placed on a light, untextured background with no other clutter – we inform the user of this fact and instruct them on how to take an appropriate image. We found this simple procedure very helpful for training users without the need for long tutorials or help pages, which often go unread. It also greatly reduces the computational load on our server, as images that fail this classification (about 37.1%) are discarded from further processing.

We implement this classifier using gist features [1] computed on the image, which are fed into a Support Vector Machine (SVM) [8] with an RBF kernel as the classification function. To ensure that the gist values are scale-invariant, we resize the input image to 300×400 (rotating it by $90°$ if it has the wrong aspect ratio). We use the libsvm [9] implementation of SVMs and the LEAR [10] implementation of gist. The classifier was trained on 5,972 manually labeled

[1] `http://leafsnap.com/dataset/` and `http://leafsnap.com/code/`

images and takes 1.4 seconds to run per image. We have found the classifier to be extremely effective, with very few invalid images slipping through, and the occasional false negatives addressed by the user simply taking another photo.

3 Color-Based Segmentation

Our system uses the distinctive shapes of leaves as the sole recognition cue. Other features such as the color of the leaf, its venation pattern, or images of the flowers are not suitable for various reasons – they are either too highly variable across different leaves of the same species, undetectable due to the poor imaging capabilities of most mobile phone cameras, or only present at limited times of year. Reliable leaf segmentation is thus crucial in order to obtain shape descriptions that are sufficiently accurate for recognition. We require that users photograph leaves against a light, untextured background; however, even with this requirement, segmentation is challenging due to shadows, blur, fine-scale structures on leaves (such as serrations and thin stems), and specular reflections.

We segment images by estimating foreground and background color distributions and using these to independently classify each pixel. This initial segmentation, solved using Expectation-Maximization (Sec. 3.1), is then post-processed to remove false positive regions (Sec. 3.2) and the leaf stem (Sec. 3.3). Our color-based segmentation has several advantages compared to other approaches. Leaves vary greatly in shape. Some species of leaves are compound (consisting of small leaflets); others are found grouped into clusters (*e.g.*, pine needles). This gives rise to complex segmentation boundaries that are difficult to handle for edge-based methods, or region-based methods that bias towards compact shapes. Our color-based pixelwise approach works much better. In addition, by not making absolute assumptions about the color distributions, our clustering approach is able to adapt to major sources of color variability such as lighting changes and natural variations in leaf color (*i.e.*, although many leaves are a deep green, others have yellowish or brownish hues). Finally, our approach is very fast, suitable for use in an interactive application.

3.1 Initial Segmentation via Expectation-Maximization

We experimented with different color spaces and noted that both the saturation and value of the HSV space were consistently useful to distinguish leaf pixels from the background (see Fig. 2). Hue is not useful because the background often has a greenish tinge due to reflections from the leaf or surrounding foliage. Pixel clustering is thus performed in the saturation-value space.

The probability distribution of a pixel $\boldsymbol{x}$, represented by its saturation and value, is modeled as the sum of two Gaussians:

$$p(\boldsymbol{x}|\boldsymbol{\Theta}) = \sum_{k=1}^{2} \frac{1}{2} p(\boldsymbol{x}|\boldsymbol{\mu}_k, \boldsymbol{\Sigma}), \tag{1}$$

(a) (b) (c) (d)

Fig. 2. A leaf image (a) in original RGB, (b) converted to saturation-value space, and (c) segmented using EM (before any post-processing). (d) The distribution of leaf and background pixels in saturation-value space. The outlined lower-right portion of the space tends to contain leaf pixels. During EM, pixels that fall inside this region are weighted such that their sum matches that of pixels outside it.

where each $p(\boldsymbol{x}|\boldsymbol{\mu}_k, \boldsymbol{\Sigma})$ is a Gaussian with mean $\boldsymbol{\mu}_k$ and a common shared covariance $\boldsymbol{\Sigma}$. The set of model parameters is $\boldsymbol{\Theta} = \{\boldsymbol{\mu}_1, \boldsymbol{\mu}_2, \boldsymbol{\Sigma}\}$. Note that we have assigned each Gaussian an equal weight of 1/2 for now.

We initialize each of the two Gaussians near the expected center of their respective distributions, so that they converge to the corresponding clusters when provided with pixel data from a new image. It is also important that the covariance matrix be initialized to a value near the expected final values to quickly converge to appropriate solutions. We found that a scaled identity matrix worked well. The segmentation is done via EM, by alternating between independently estimating probabilities of each pixel using the current parameters, and updating the parameters using current pixel probabilities.

Straightforward application of the above method works well in general, but has some difficulty with pine leaves, in which the leaf comprises only a tiny fraction of the image. The problem is caused by the model assuming the same weight for each of the two Gaussians, in effect biasing the result towards clusters that are assigned equal numbers of pixels. We resolve this by pixel weighting. We manually define a rectangular region in saturation-value space that tends to contain leaf pixels (see Fig. 2). Then, prior to running EM, we assign different weights to pixels inside and outside this region, such that each set of pixels has equal total weight. This greatly improves segmentation performance on pines without significantly affecting performance for other leaves.

We have optimized our implementation for speed, allowing it to handle reasonably large images. First, the fact that the covariance matrix is shared between the two Gaussians brings a significant speed advantage. In the two-class case, the posterior function defining cluster memberships takes on a linear logistic form [11], which can be efficiently computed. Specifically, if we denote the label of pixel $\boldsymbol{x}$ as $z \in \{1, 2\}$, then we can write

$$p(z = 1|\boldsymbol{x}) = 1/[1 + \exp(\beta_0 + \boldsymbol{\beta}^T \boldsymbol{x})], \text{ where} \tag{2}$$

$$\boldsymbol{\beta} \equiv (\boldsymbol{\mu}_2 - \boldsymbol{\mu}_1)^T \boldsymbol{\Sigma}^{-1}, \text{ and} \tag{3}$$

$$\beta_0 \equiv -\frac{1}{2} (\boldsymbol{\mu}_2^T \boldsymbol{\Sigma}^{-1} \boldsymbol{\mu}_2 - \boldsymbol{\mu}_1^T \boldsymbol{\Sigma}^{-1} \boldsymbol{\mu}_1). \tag{4}$$

After computing Equation 2 for each pixel $\boldsymbol{x}$, we can quickly obtain $p(z = 2|\boldsymbol{x}) = 1 - p(z = 1|\boldsymbol{x})$. A second optimization is that it is possible to obtain reliable estimates of the Gaussian parameters using only a fraction of the pixels in an image. We thus use a downsampled version of the original image during EM. Once the procedure has converged, the labels for each pixel can be quickly computed over the complete original image using only Equation 2. Using these optimizations, segmentation runs on average in 0.062 seconds on a 700×525 image using 25% of pixels during EM, converging in 6.6 iterations on average.

3.2 Removing False Positive Regions

After the EM procedure, each pixel is assigned to leaf or background based on its membership to either of the two Gaussians. This results in an initial segmentation that sometimes contains false positive regions, caused by uneven backgrounds, shadows, or extraneous objects in the picture. Another type of false positive region can appear at the outer border of the image. Most users place the leaf on a white sheet of paper when taking the picture. It is common to find that some parts of the image border lay outside the piece of paper, potentially giving rise to falsely detected regions (see Fig. 3, rows 2-3).

Our post-processing procedure aims to remove such false positive regions. We first compute connected components on a dilated version of the segmentation. Any connected component that has a large boundary on the image border (relative to its area) is then excluded, which eliminates regions that have fallen outside the white background. The largest of the remaining components is then taken to be the leaf. This step takes 0.006 seconds for a 700×525 image.

3.3 Removing the Stem

At this point, the stem of the leaf may or may not be present in the segmentation. The original leaf might not have had a stem to begin with, or it might have been lost during segmentation, which may occur when the stem has a lighter color than the leaf. Even when the stem is correctly segmented, it may vary in length depending on how the user picked the leaf. To standardize the shape, we remove the stems from all segmentations through a series of morphological operations.

First, the set of all thin structures that protrude from the leaf is determined. This is done by taking the top-hat transformation of the segmentation [12], using as structuring element a disc with diameter larger than the width of any potential stem. For a binary image B and structuring element s, the top-hat is

$$T_{\text{hat}}(B) = B - B \circ s, \tag{5}$$

where $\circ$ denotes the opening operation: an erosion followed by a dilation.

Next, we determine which of these candidate structures is most likely to be the stem. First, we note that removing the stem should not change the number of connected components in the segmented leaf or in the background; thus, only such candidates are considered as possible stems. Of the possible stem candidates, we only consider those of appropriate size, and finally remove the one

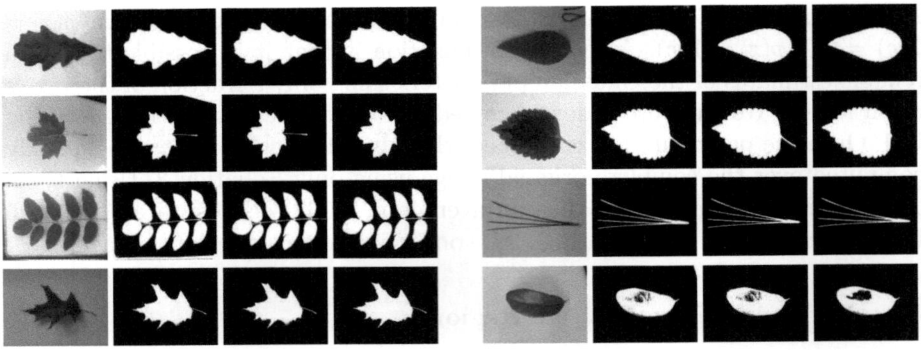

Fig. 3. Segmentation results. (l-r): input image, initial segmentation, results after removing false positive regions, final result after stem removal. The last row shows typical failure cases, due to shadows (left) and specular highlights (right).

that is most elongated (*i.e.*, with the highest ratio of the two principal moments). This step takes 0.036 seconds for a 700×525 image.

3.4 Segmentation Results

Segmentation results are shown in Fig. 3. In general, segmentation succeeds on the vast majority of valid input images (those that pass the initial leaf classifier). We have observed that the most frequent segmentation errors are caused either by shadows cast by the leaf onto the background, which show up as false positives (*e.g.*, bottom row, left), or by specularities present in certain shiny leaves, which show up as false negatives (*e.g.*, bottom row, right). We have also experimented with other, more sophisticated segmentation methods, but found that these are generally too slow, and/or do not perform adequately on more complex images, such as compound leaves or pines. A forthcoming journal article evaluates various segmentation approaches on leaves, showing the efficacy of our method.

4 Curvature-Based Shape Features

Leaf shape can be effectively represented using multiscale curvature measures. Fig. 4a shows a diagrammatic example with segmented images of four different leaf species, and histograms of curvature along the boundary for each shape, computed at two different scales – coarse (large radius) on top, and fine (small radius) on bottom. The pair of images in each row share the same general shape, but the images on the left have a smooth boundary, and the ones on the right have a serrated boundary. Thus, the histograms of coarse-scale values differ for each *row*, while the histograms of fine-scale values differ for each *column*. By using both histograms together, we can distinguish these shapes from each other. We expand upon this basic idea to extract our features.

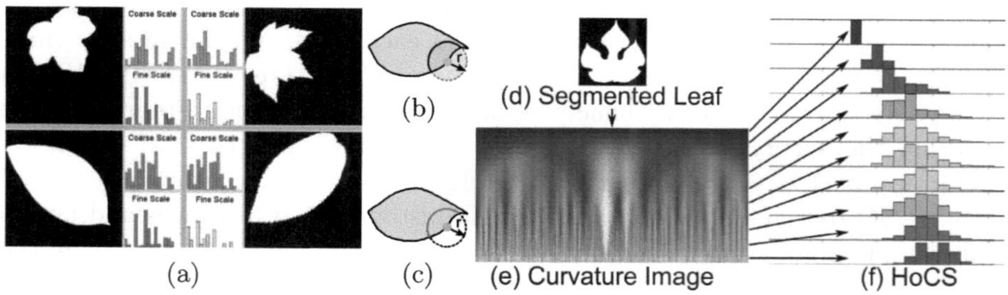

Fig. 4. (a) Histograms of curvature at two different scales are sufficient to distinguish these leaves of four different species. By computing these features over many scales, we can reliably distinguish between hundreds of species. Curvature values can be robustly computed using either (b) the area measure, the fraction of the circle's area contained inside the object (shown in pink); or (c) the arclength measure, the fraction of the circle's perimeter contained inside the object (shown in red). The scale is determined by the radius r of the circle. Using these measures, we take (d) the segmented leaf's contour and extract (e) a curvature image, which shows curvatures for each contour point along the x-axis and at different scales along the y-axis. (f) By taking histograms along each row, we create the *Histograms of Curvature over Scale* (HoCS) feature.

Curvature is a fundamental property of shape and has thus attracted much attention from the vision community; however, when dealing with images on discrete pixel grids, the elegant mathematical definitions of curvature are tricky to implement in a stable manner. Typically, curvatures are computed using differential techniques, which amplify noise, are sensitive to the orientation and scale of captured images, and are difficult to measure at multiple scales. Instead, we can use *integral measures* to compute functions of the curvature at a boundary point [13,14,15]. One such measure in 2D is the area of intersection of a disk centered at a contour point and the inside of the contour (see Fig. 4b). For straight, concave, and convex boundaries, the fraction of the disk intersected will be $=$, $>$, or < 0.5, respectively. Another measure uses the arclength: the fraction of the disk's perimeter inside the contour (Fig. 4c). Furthermore, these representations naturally capture scale by the radius of the disk – perturbations much smaller than the disk radius are ignored. Thus, a serrated boundary will show large, alternating curvatures at a fine scale, but a uniform curvature at a coarse scale. Unlike their differential counterparts, integral measures are fast and easy to compute for images on discrete grids, invariant to rotation, insensitive to small segmentation and discretization errors, independent of the topological complexity, and straightforward to extend to 3D [15].

Given this reliable method for computing curvatures, how should one construct a feature vector suitable for classification? Manay *et al.* [14] concatenated integral measures of curvature along the contour of the object into a single feature vector. But this has several disadvantages in our domain: different contours will have different lengths, making them difficult to compare; contours must be aligned to have the same starting point, otherwise they will not match; minor changes in topology or orientation can cause huge changes in the feature vector;

and there is no straightforward way to handle multiple contours. Instead, we compute histograms of the curvature values at each scale, and concatenate these histograms together to form the Histograms of Curvature over Scale (HoCS) feature. Histograms have the benefit of being compact, simple to represent, not requiring alignment, and fast to compare using metrics such as L_1.

Our approach is very different from the IDSC-based [7] recognition described in [5]. IDSC represents shape implicitly via histograms of distances and angles from sample points on the contour to all other points, along a path inside the leaf shape. This is significantly more expensive to compute ($O(N^3)$ vs $O(N)$ in the number of sample points), requires a complex matching algorithm comparing sets of points ($O(N^2)$) rather than simple histogram intersection ($O(N)$), and harder to reason about than curvature, which is well understood. In addition, IDSC may be more sensitive to segmentation errors.

4.1 Computing Histograms of Curvature over Scale

To get the most accurate results, we implement the integral measures of curvature carefully and efficiently. To remove problems caused by "holes" in the shape (*e.g.*, due to segmentation drop-outs), we completely fill-in the contours obtained from the segmented images prior to curvature extraction. For scale invariance, we resize these filled-in images to a common area before extracting curvatures from the boundaries. To reduce histogramming artifacts, we use bilinear interpolation to do soft-binning of curvature values.

The simplicity of these measures also allows for new speed optimizations. When computing the area measure, the change in intersected area from one contour point to the next can be computed by simply checking the crescent-shaped boundaries of the circle in the direction of the shift. Since the change in position is limited to 4 or 8 different translations (depending on the connectedness of the contour points) and our set of radii are fixed, we precompute the offset coordinates. This results in approximately $2\pi r$ pixels to check for each contour point, *i.e.*, only those that have changed from the last location of the disk, resulting in an order of magnitude improvement over a naive $4r^2$ check over the whole disk. For the arclength measure, we first find the points on the segmented shape contour that intersect the disk edge. The contour is represented as an array of contiguous point locations, and so we search along the contour in both directions away from the current point (the center of the disk), initially jumping r points away from the current point, since the disk has radius r. Once we find the appropriate points, we go along the disk edge (whose coordinates have been precomputed) and simply check each pixel's segmentation value in the image.

From a given contour, we extract a *curvature image* as shown in Fig. 4e. Each row in this image contains the integral measures of curvature values computed along the contour at a given scale; each column contains the curvature measures at all scales for a single contour point. Finally, we compute histograms of curvature values at each scale (*i.e.*, from each row of the curvature image, as in Fig. 4f) and then concatenate these histograms to form the HoCS feature. The complete feature extraction process takes on average 0.11 seconds per image.

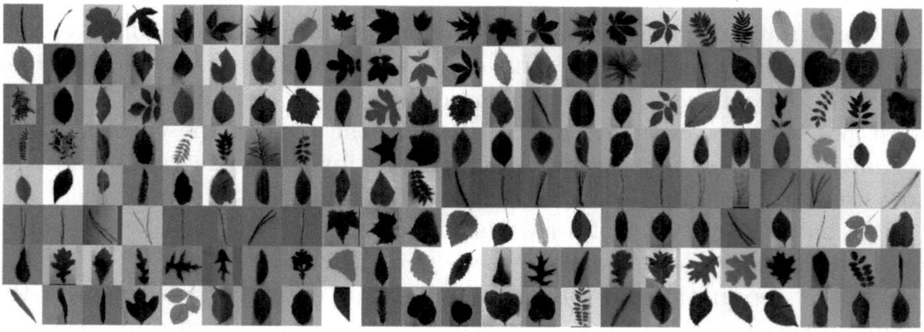

(a) Thumbnails of all 184 tree species from the Northeastern United States

(b) Images of *Broussonettia papyrifera*

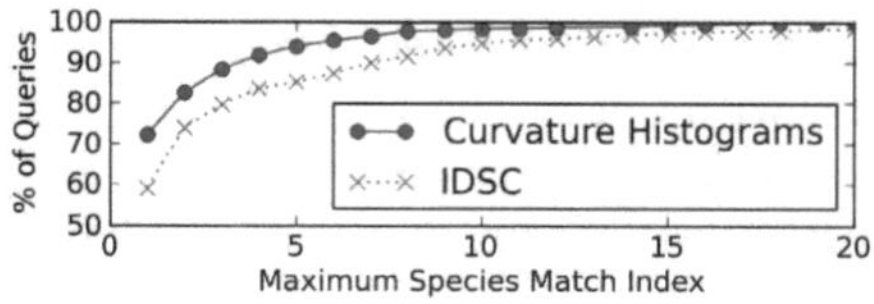

(c) Recognition accuracy

Fig. 5. (a) A single image from all 184 species in our database. Compare the often small inter-species variation against the (b) large intra-species variation for *Broussonettia papyrifera*. (c) Plot showing the percentage of queries with the correct species appearing in the top N results returned. The correct match is within the top 5 results for 96.8% of queries using curvature histograms, compared to only 85.1% using IDSC [7].

5 Species Identification Using Nearest Neighbors

Identification is done by running a nearest neighbors search using the HoCS feature extracted from the input image as the query. The search database consists of features extracted from 23,915 "clean" lab images of pressed leaves (captured using a high-quality camera) and 5,192 field images taken by mobile devices. The field images contain varying amounts of blur and were photographed with different viewpoints and illumination. A single image from each of the 184 species in our dataset can be seen in Fig. 5a. The difficulty of the problem can be seen, *e.g.*, by comparing the often small inter-species variation against the large intra-species variation shown in Fig. 5b for leaves of the *Broussonettia papyrifera*.

The feature dimensionality is $N = 25$ scales $\times$ $B = 21$ bins per scale $= 525$ values for histograms of the area and arclength measures (each). Histograms are compared using the histogram intersection distance, defined as:

$$d(\mathbf{a}, \mathbf{b}) = N - \sum_{i}^{B} min(a_i, b_i), \tag{6}$$

where the histogram at each scale has been normalized to unit length. (Other metrics – including L_1, L_2, Bhattacharyya distance, and χ^2 – did not perform as well.) Retrieval takes 0.31 seconds using a linear scan of the database. The top 25 results are presented to the user for final identification.

To quantitatively measure recognition performance, we perform leave-one-image-out species identification, using only the field images as queries, matching against all other images in the recognition database. The goal is to have the lowest possible *species match rank*, defined as the rank of the correct *species* (not *image*). This is the most appropriate metric for our application because we show users only the list of matched species, not images. So even if there are, *e.g.*, 20 matches to images of a particular incorrect species, those will count as only a single species error from the user's point of view.

A plot of recognition rates on a subset of our data[2], as a function of the maximum species match rank, is shown in Fig. 5c. Performance for IDSC [7] (used in [5]) is shown as the dotted blue line, and for our curvature histogram features as the solid red line. 96.8% of queries have a species match rank of 5 or lower with our method, *i.e.*, within the top 5 results shown to the user, which is substantially better than IDSC's 85.1%. This vast improvement highlights the effectiveness of our approach for shape retrieval on real-world images.

6 The Leafsnap System

To allow the general public to use the results of this research, we have implemented a complete end-to-end recognition system and packaged it as an electronic field guide called Leafsnap. The recognition engine consists of a backend server that accepts input images from various front-end clients. Currently, we have front-end apps for the iPhone and iPad devices, with work on Android devices in progress. The Leafsnap app contains high-quality photographs (taken by the non-profit group *Finding Species*) and botanist-curated descriptions of all the 184 tree species of the Northeastern United States. This already represents a significant step up from a traditional field guide: as a software application, operations such as browsing, sorting, and textual searching are trivial. Our automatic visual recognition system further improves on this by providing the user with the most likely candidate species for a given query input image. The user makes the final classification decision by visually comparing the actual plant to the high-quality photographs in the app, which span all aspects of the species – the leaf, flower, fruit, petiole, bark, *etc.*

Figures 1 and 6 show screenshots from the iPad and iPhone apps, respectively. For the latter, in scanline order: (a) the home screen, with a randomly-chosen image cycling every few seconds and access to educational games, (b) the browse screen, with a sortable and searchable list of all the species contained in the system, (c) the search functionality for finding particular species by scientific or common name, (d) the detail view for a particular species, showing the different images available for viewing, (e) the Snap It! screen, for performing automatic identification, (f) the returned identification results, in sorted order, (g-i) the manual verification stage as the user explores the images and textual descriptions of one of the results to confirm it as the correct match, (j) labeling the correct

[2] IDSC [7] was too slow to run a test on the entire dataset.

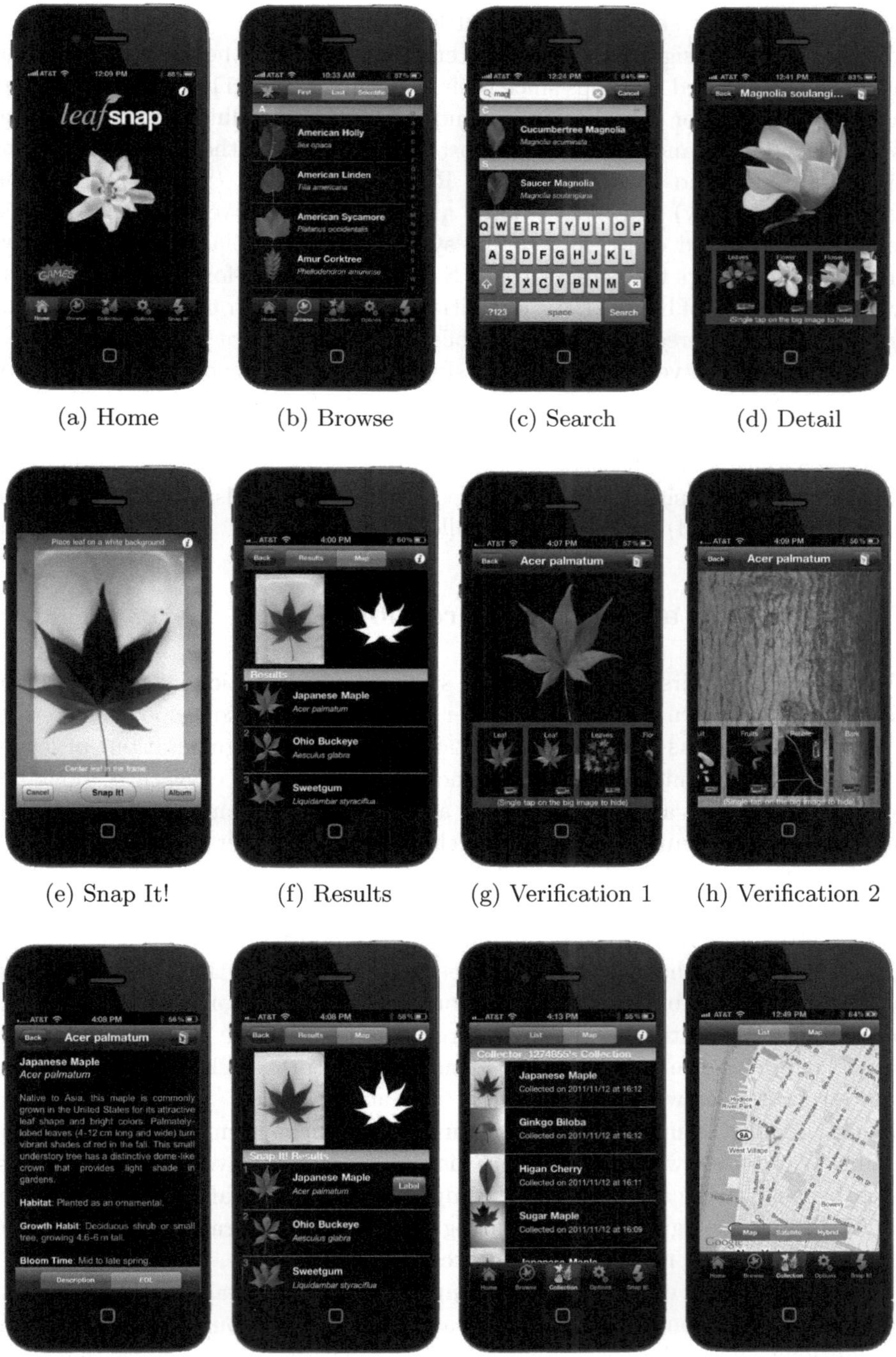

(a) Home (b) Browse (c) Search (d) Detail

(e) Snap It! (f) Results (g) Verification 1 (h) Verification 2

(i) Verification 3 (j) Label (k) Collection (l) Map

Fig. 6. Tour of the iPhone version of Leafsnap. See text for details match, (k) the addition of that leaf to the user's collection for future reference, and (l) a map view showing where that leaf was collected.

There has been significant public interest in Leafsnap – nearly a million people have downloaded the apps since their launch in May 2011. We received press coverage from major news outlets around the world, including newspapers (The New York Times and Washington Post), wire services (the Associated Press and Reuters), radio (National Public Radio), magazines (Science), television (The Tonight Show) and blogs (Wired and Techcrunch). We have also received requests to use and contribute to the system by urban planners in local governments, educators throughout the U.S. and abroad, not-for-profit institutions working on issues of biodiversity, and citizen scientists eager to map and monitor the flora of their street, backyard, or local park.

The backend server is currently a single Intel Xeon machine with 2 quad-core processors running at 2.33 Ghz each, and 16 GB of RAM. Aside from high-resolution versions of some images, which are served via Amazon's Simple Storage Service (S3), all other operations are handled by our server. The total time for serving a single recognition request is 5.4 seconds (not including the initial image upload) and is easily parallelizable.

7 Discussion and Future Directions

We have built the first computer vision system for automatic plant species identification. Our system relies on computer vision for several key aspects, including classifying images as leaves or not, obtaining fine-scale segmentations of leaves from their backgrounds, efficiently extracting histograms of curvatures along the contour of the leaf at multiple scales, and retrieving the most similar species matches using a nearest neighbors search on a large dataset of labeled images.

All steps of our algorithm have been carefully designed to excel on our task of plant species identification; however, we feel that there are many practical lessons for others in the vision community. The effectiveness of our initial leaf classifier suggests that such simple expedients can greatly improve the overall performance of a public system. Our color-based segmentation outperforms other published segmentation methods, in large part because the constraints for this task – requiring the preservation of fine-scale features such as serrations and thin structures, as well as operating at interactive speeds – are more stringent than commonly assumed in the literature, yet frequent in many application domains. We have shown that curvature histograms are effective shape descriptors, both because they can be robustly computed using integral measures, and because they can be aggregated into histograms at multiple scales, which make for efficient and simple retrieval using nearest neighbors.

The high level of engagement with our Leafsnap system allows for many possible future directions. We are looking at ways of crowd-sourcing the collection of additional species for the system, as well as the verification of labels that users mark in the app. The latter also poses interesting machine learning questions, such as how to automatically determine the trustworthiness of particular users or labels without requiring (extensive) expert supervision. Since our apps save the GPS coordinates and timestamp of each photo, we also hope to be able to map the biodiversity of a region over space and time. Finally, we would like to further explore the educational aspects of this project. This includes adding more collaborative features in the apps, *i.e.*, for entire classrooms to use together, as well as studying the efficacy of the app in teaching children (and adults) about plants. We believe that the tight feedback loop the app provides via its games and the visual recognition feature are ideal mechanisms for training people to recognize plants themselves and would like to quantify this effect.

The strong response to Leafsnap shows the potential for widespread adoption of computer vision technology, when appropriately packaged and distributed.

Acknowledgments. This work was supported by National Science Foundation grants #0968546, #0325867, and #1116631, as well as funding from Google.

References

1. Oliva, A., Torralba, A.: Modeling the shape of the scene: A holistic representation of the spatial envelope. IJCV 42, 145–175 (2001)
2. Branson, S., Wah, C., Schroff, F., Babenko, B., Welinder, P., Perona, P., Belongie, S.: Visual Recognition with Humans in the Loop. In: Daniilidis, K., Maragos, P., Paragios, N. (eds.) ECCV 2010, Part IV. LNCS, vol. 6314, pp. 438–451. Springer, Heidelberg (2010)
3. Nilsback, M., Zisserman, A.: Automated flower classification over a large number of classes. In: Indian Conference on Computer Vision, Graphics and Image Processing (2008)
4. Goëau, H., Bonnet, P., Joly, A., Boujemaa, N., Barthelemy, D., Molino, J.F., Birnbaum, P., Mouysset, E., Picard, M.: The clef 2011 plant images classification task. In: CLEF (Notebook Papers/Labs/Workshop) (2011)
5. Belhumeur, P.N., Chen, D., Feiner, S.K., Jacobs, D.W., Kress, W.J., Ling, H., Lopez, I., Ramamoorthi, R., Sheorey, S., White, S., Zhang, L.: Searching the World's Herbaria: A System for Visual Identification of Plant Species. In: Forsyth, D., Torr, P., Zisserman, A. (eds.) ECCV 2008, Part IV. LNCS, vol. 5305, pp. 116–129. Springer, Heidelberg (2008)
6. Agarwal, G., Belhumeur, P., Feiner, S., Jacobs, D., Kress, W.J., Ramamoorthi, R., Bourg, N.A., Dixit, N., Ling, H., Mahajan, D., Russell, R., Shirdhonkar, S., Sunkavalli, K., White, S.: First steps toward an electronic field guide for plants. Taxon 55, 597–610 (2006)
7. Ling, H., Jacobs, D.: Shape classification using the inner-distance. TPAMI 29, 286–299 (2007)
8. Cortes, C., Vapnik, V.: Support-vector networks. Machine Learning 20 (1995)
9. Chang, C.C., Lin, C.J.: LIBSVM: A library for support vector machines. ACM Transactions on Intelligent Systems and Technology 2, 27:1–27:27 (2011)
10. Douze, M., Jégou, H., Sandhawalia, H., Amsaleg, L., Schmid, C.: Evaluation of gist descriptors for web-scale image search. In: International Conference on Image and Video Retrieval (2009)
11. Efron, B.: The efficiency of logistic regression compared to normal discriminant analysis. Journal of the American Statistical Association 70, 892–898 (1975)

12. Gonzalez, R., Woods, R.: Digital image processing. Pearson/Prentice Hall (2008)
13. Connolly, M.L.: Measurement of protein surface shape by solid angles. Journal of Molecular Graphics 4, 3–6 (1986)
14. Manay, S., Cremers, D., Hong, B.W., Yezzi, A.J., Soatto, S.: Integral invariants for shape matching. TPAMI 28, 1602–1618 (2006)
15. Pottmann, H., Wallner, J., Huang, Q.X., Yang, Y.L.: Integral invariants for robust geometry processing. Computer Aided Geometric Design 26, 37–60 (2009)

Large Scale Visual Geo-Localization of Images in Mountainous Terrain

Georges Baatz, Olivier Saurer, Kevin Köser, and Marc Pollefeys

Department of Computer Science, ETH Zurich, Switzerland
{gbaatz,saurero,kevin.koeser,marc.pollefeys}@inf.ethz.ch

Abstract. Given a picture taken somewhere in the world, automatic geo-localization of that image is a task that would be extremely useful e.g. for historical and forensic sciences, documentation purposes, organization of the world's photo material and also intelligence applications. While tremendous progress has been made over the last years in visual location recognition within a single city, localization in natural environments is much more difficult, since vegetation, illumination, seasonal changes make appearance-only approaches impractical. In this work, we target mountainous terrain and use digital elevation models to extract representations for fast visual database lookup. We propose an automated approach for very large scale visual localization that can efficiently exploit visual information (contours) and geometric constraints (consistent orientation) at the same time. We validate the system on the scale of a whole country (Switzerland, 40 000km^2) using a new dataset of more than 200 landscape query pictures with ground truth.

1 Introduction and Previous Work

In intelligence and forensic scenarios as well as for searching archives and organising photo collections, automatic image-based location recognition is a challenging task that would however be extremely useful when solved. In such applications GPS tags are typically not available in the images requiring a fully image-based approach for geo-localization. During the last years progress has been made in urban scenarios, in particular with stable man-made structures that persist over time. However, for recognizing the camera location in natural environments the problem is substantially more challenging since vegetation changes rapidly during the seasons, and lighting and weather conditions (e.g. snow lines) make the use of appearance-based techniques (e.g. using patch-based local image features [1,2]) very difficult. Additionally, dense street-level data commonly used is limited to cities and major roads, and for the mountains or countryside only aerial footage exists that is much harder to relate with terrestrial imagery.

This paper targets camera geo-localization in natural environments. In particular we focus on recognizing the skyline in a query image, given a digital elevation model (DEM) of a country — or ultimately, the world. In contrast to previous work of matching e.g. a peak in the image to a set of mountains known to be nearby, we aggregate shape information across the whole skyline (not only

A. Fitzgibbon et al. (Eds.): ECCV 2012, Part II, LNCS 7573, pp. 517–530, 2012.

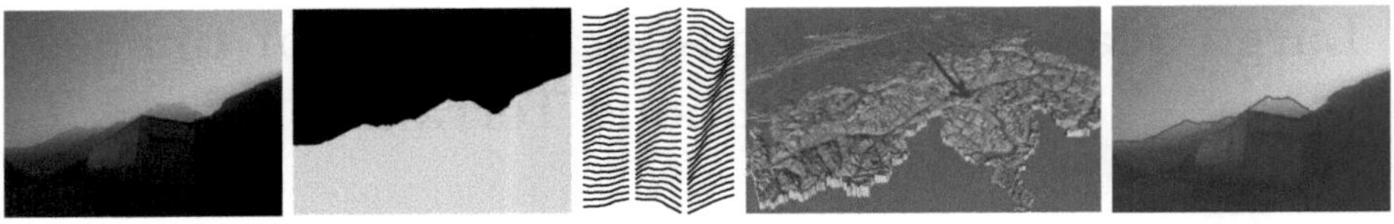

(a) (b) (c) (d) (e)

Fig. 1. Different stages in the proposed pipeline: (a) Query image somewhere in Switzerland, (b) sky segmentation, (c) sample set of extracted 10° contourlets, (d) recognized geo-location in digital elevation model, (e) overlaid visible horizon at estimated position

the peaks) and search for a similar configuration of basic shapes in a large scale database that is organized to allow for query images of largely different fields of view. The method is based on sky segmentation (either automatic or easily supported by an operator for challenging pictures such as those with reflection, occlusion or taken from inside a cable car).

Contributions. The main contributions are a novel method for robust contour encoding as well as two different voting schemes to solve the large scale camera pose recognition from contours. The first scheme operates only in descriptor space (it checks where in the model a panoramic skyline is most likely to *contain* the current query picture) while the second one is a combined vote in descriptor and rotation space. We validate the whole approach using a public digital elevation model of Switzerland that covers more than 40 000km^2 and a set of more than 200 images from different sources with ground truth information that is published along with the paper. In particular we show the improvements of all novel contributions compared to a baseline implementation motivated by classical bag-of-words [3] based techniques like [2]. Also, we demonstrate that the horizon is highly informative and can be used effectively for localization.

Previous Work. To the best of our knowledge there has never been a similar attempt at large-scale localization of a photo based on a digital elevation model before. The closest works to ours are smaller scale navigation and localization in robotics [4,5], and building/location recognition in cities [1,6,2] or with respect to community photo collections of popular landmarks [7]. These, however, do not apply to landscape scenes of changing weather, vegetation, snowlines, or changing lighting conditions. The robotics community has considered the problem of robot navigation and robot localization using digital elevation models for quite some time. Talluri et al. [8] reason about intersection of known viewing ray directions (north, east, south, west) with the skyline and relies thus on the availability of 360° panoramic query contours and the knowledge of vehicle orientation (i.e. north direction). Thompson et al. [9] suggest general concepts of how to estimate pose and propose a hypothesize and verify scheme. They also rely on known view orientation and match viewpoint-independent features (peaks, saddle points, ...) from a DEM to features found in the image, this way ignoring much of the skyline information. In [10], computer vision techniques are used to extract mountain peaks which are matched to a database of nearby mountains to support a remote operator in navigation. However, we believe that their approach of considering relative positions of absolute peaks detected in a DEM is too restrictive and would not scale to our orders of magnitude larger problem, in particular with respect to less discriminative locations. [11] proposes to first match three features of a contour to a digital elevation model and estimate an initial pose from that before a non-linear refinement. Also here the first step of finding three good correspondences is again not easily possible in larger databases. [5] assumes panoramic query data with known heading, and computes super-segments on a polygon fit, however descriptiveness/robustness is not evaluated on a bigger database, while [12] introduces a probabilistic formulation for a similar setting. The key point is that going from tens of potential locations to millions of locations requires a conceptually different approach, since exhaustive image comparison or trying all "mountain peaks" simply does not scale to a large-scale geo-localization problem. Similarly, for urban localization, in [13] an upward looking 180° field of view fisheye is used for navigation in urban canyons. The authors render untextured city models near the predicted pose and extract contours for comparison with a query image. Also this is meant as a local method for navigation. Most recently, in [14] the authors optimize the camera orientation given the exact position, i.e. they estimate the viewing direction given a good GPS tag. None of the above systems considered large scale recognition.

On the earth scale, the authors of [15] source photo collections and aim at learning location probability based on color, texture, and other image-based statistics. Conceptually, this is not meant to find an exact pose based on geometric considerations but rather discriminates landscapes or cities with different (appearance) characteristics on a global scale. The authors of [16] exploit the position of the sun (given the time) for geo-localization. In the same work it is also shown that identifying a large piece of clear sky without haze provides information about the camera pose (although impressive given the data, still more than 100km average localization error is reported). Both approaches are appealing for excluding large parts of the earth from further search but do not aim at exactly localizing the camera within a few hundred meters.

Besides attacking the DEM-based, large scale geo-localization problem we propose new techniques that might also be transferred to bag-of-words approaches based on local image patches (e.g. [3,1,2]). Those approaches typically rely on pure occurrence-based statistics (visual word histogram) to generate a first list of hypotheses and only for the top candidates geometric consistency of matches is checked. Such a strategy fails in cases where pure feature coocurrence is not discriminative but where the relative locations of the features are important. Here, we propose to do a (weak) geometric verification already in the histogram distance phase. Furthermore, we show also a representation that tolerates largely different document sizes (allowing to compare a panorama in the database to an image with an order of magnitude smaller field of view).

2 Mountain Recognition Approach

The location recognition problem in its general form is six-dimensional since three position and three orientation parameters have to be estimated. We make the assumption that the photo has been taken not too far from the ground and use the fact that people rarely twist the camera relative to the horizon [17] (i.e. small roll). We will propose a method to solve that problem using the outlines of mountains against the sky (a skyline), which we call the **visible horizon**. For the visual database we seek a representation that is robust with respect to tilt of the camera which means that we are effectively left with estimating the 2D position on our height model (latitude and longitude) and the viewing direction of the camera. The visible horizon of the DEM is extracted offline at regular grid positions (360° at each position) and represented by a collection of vector-quantized local contourlets (contour words, similar in spirit to visual words obtained from quantized image patch descriptors [3]). In contrast to visual word based approaches, additionally an individual viewing angle α_d ($\alpha_d \in [0; 2\pi]$) relative to north direction is stored. At query time, a sky segmentation technique is applied that copes with the often present haze. Subsequently the extracted contour is robustly described by a set of local contourlets plus their relative angular distance α_q with respect to the optical axis of the camera. Then, we use an inverted file system for the contour words to find the most promising location and simultaneously vote for the viewing direction, which is an integrated geometric verification already during the bag-of-words search.

2.1 Processing the Query Image

Sky Segmentation. The estimation of the visible horizon can be cast as a foreground-background segmentation problem. Virtually any good segmentation method could be used here and the focus of this paper is on the recognition, not on the segmentation part. Consequently, due to space limitations in the following we can only sketch our implementation roughly:

Since sky and mountains have different local statistics with respect to color, gradient and other cues' distribution, we decided to follow a standard approach based on unary data costs [18,19] for a pixel being assigned sky or ground and smoothness costs along the visible horizon that depend also on the local image structure [20]. As we assume almost no camera roll and since overhanging structures are extremely rare, finding the highest foreground pixel (foreground height) for each image column provides an excellent approximation, at the same time allowing for a dynamic programming solution (as suggested already in e.g. [21]). To obtain the data term for a candidate height in a column we sum all foreground costs below the candidate contour and sky costs above the contour, where we have trained a pixel's color and gradient likelihoods for ground and sky. Furthermore, we dehaze the image according to [22] and exploit the (continuous) relative depth information (obtained from dehazing and normalized to maximum depth 1) to steer the smoothness term similar to [20]. The intuition is that when running along the visible horizon from one candidate height in

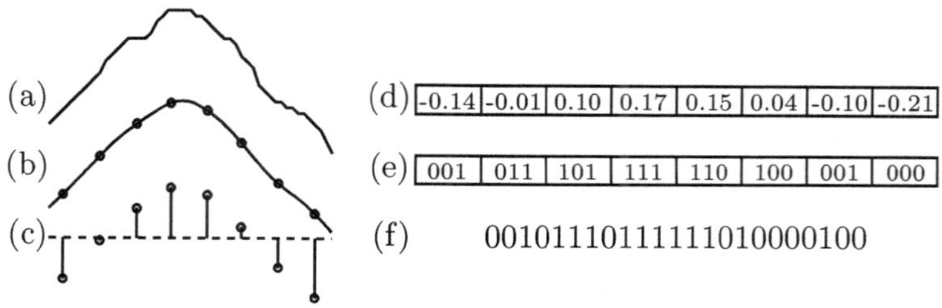

Fig. 2. Contour word computation: (a) raw contour, (b) smoothed contour with n sampled points, (c) sampled points after normalization, (d) contourlet as numeric vector, (e) each dimension quantized to 3 bits, (f) contour word as 24-bit integer

one column to a candidate height in the next column, there should be local evidence in terms of an orthogonal depth gradient on the connection line. We train weights and foreground/sky likelihoods on a manually labelled offline data set. Further, we add interaction capabilities for a potential user where simple strokes can mark foreground or sky in the query picture forcing these pixels and all below or above to these labels. This provides a simple and effective means to correct very challenging situations (e.g. reflections in picture from inside a cable car, power lines or people corrupting the skyline) or previously unseen colors (e.g. picture at sunset or night).

Contourlet Extraction. In the field of shape recognition, there are many shape description techniques that deal with closed contours, e.g. [23]. However, recognition based on partial contours is still a largely unsolved problem, because it is difficult to find representations invariant to viewpoint. For the sake of robustness to occlusion, to noise and systematic errors (inaccurate focal length estimate or tilt angle), we decided to use local representations of the visible horizon curve (compare also [24] for an overview on shape features).

To describe the contour, we consider overlapping curvelets of width w (imagine a sliding window, see Fig. 1). These curvelets are then sampled at n equally spaced points, yielding each an n-dimensional vector $\tilde{y}_1, \ldots, \tilde{y}_n$ (before sampling, we low-pass filter the horizon to avoid aliasing). The final descriptor is obtained by subtracting the mean and dividing by the feature width (see Fig. 2(a)–(d)):

$$y_i = \frac{\tilde{y}_i - \bar{y}}{w} \text{ for } i = 1, \ldots, n \qquad \text{where} \qquad \bar{y} = \frac{1}{n} \sum_{j=1}^{n} \tilde{y}_j \tag{1}$$

Mean subtraction makes the descriptor invariant w.r.t. vertical image location (and therefore robust against camera tilt). Scaling ensures that the y_i's have roughly the same magnitude, independently of the feature width w.

The next step is vector quantisation (Fig. 2(e)–(f)). Since our features are very low-dimensional compared to traditional patch-based feature descriptors like SIFT [25], we choose not to use a vocabulary tree. Instead, we directly quantize each dimension of the descriptor *separately*, which is both faster and much more memory-efficient compared to a vocabulary tree and the best bin is guaranteed to be found. Each y_i falls into one bin and the n associated bin numbers are concatenated into a single integer (contour word). For each descriptor, we also make note of the viewing direction α_q (relative to the camera's optical axis) where the feature was observed, which can be calculated using the camera's intrinsics. We have verified that an approximate focal length estimate is enough. In case the focal length is completely unknown, it is possible to sample several tentative values (see evaluation in Section 3).

2.2 Visual Database Creation

The digital elevation model we use for validation is available from the Swiss Federal Office of Topography, and similar data sets exist also for the US and other countries. There is one sample point per 2 square meters and the height quality varies from 0.5m (flat regions) to 3m-8m (above 2000m elevation) average error[1]. This data is converted to a triangulated surface model with level-of-detail support in a scene graph representation[2]. At each position on a regular grid on the surface (every 0.001° in N-S direction and 0.0015° in E-W direction, i.e. 111m and 115m respectively) and from 1.80m above the surface[3], we render a cubemap of the textureless DEM (face resolution 1024×1024) and extract the visible horizon by checking for the rendered sky color. Overall, we generate 3.5 million cubemaps. Similar to the query image, we extract contourlets, but this time with *absolute* viewing direction. We organize the contourlets in an index to allow for fast retrieval. In image search, inverted files have been used very successfully for this task [3]. We extend this idea by also taking into account the viewing direction, so that we can perform rough geometric verification on-the-fly. For each word we maintain a list that stores for every occurrence the panorama ID and the azimuth α_d of the contourlet.

2.3 Recognition and Verification

Baseline. The baseline for comparison is an approach borrowed from patch based systems (e.g. [26,1,2]) based on the (potentially weighted) L1-norm between normalized visual word frequency vectors:

$$D^E(\tilde{\mathbf{q}}, \tilde{\mathbf{d}}) = \|\tilde{\mathbf{q}} - \tilde{\mathbf{d}}\|_1 = \sum_i |\tilde{q}_i - \tilde{d}_i| \quad \text{or} \quad D^{E_w}(\tilde{\mathbf{q}}, \tilde{\mathbf{d}}) = \sum_i w_i |\tilde{q}_i - \tilde{d}_i| \tag{2}$$

$$\text{with} \quad \tilde{\mathbf{q}} = \frac{\mathbf{q}}{\|\mathbf{q}\|_1} \quad \text{and} \quad \tilde{\mathbf{d}} = \frac{\mathbf{d}}{\|\mathbf{d}\|_1} \tag{3}$$

[1] `http://www.swisstopo.admin.ch/internet/swisstopo/en/home`
[2] `http://openscenegraph.org`
[3] Synthetic experiments verified that taking the photo from ten or fifty meters above the ground does not degrade recognition besides very special cases like standing very close to a small wall.

Where q_i and d_i is the number of times visual word i appears in the query or database image respectively, and $\tilde{q}_i$, $\tilde{d}_i$ are their normalized counterparts. w_i is the weight of visual word i (e.g. as obtained by the term frequency - inverse document frequency (tf-idf) scheme). This gives an ideal score of 0 when both images contain the same visual words at the same proportions, which means that the L1-norm favors images that are *equal* to the query.

[26] suggested transforming the weighted L1-norm like this

$$D^{E_w}(\tilde{\mathbf{q}}, \tilde{\mathbf{d}}) = \sum_i w_i \tilde{q}_i + \sum_i w_i \tilde{d}_i - 2 \sum_{i \in Q} w_i \min(\tilde{q}_i, \tilde{d}_i) \tag{4}$$

in order to enable an efficient method for evaluating it by iterating only over the visual words present in the query image and updating only the scores of database images containing the given visual word.

"Contains"-Semantics. In our setting, we are comparing 10°–70° views to 360° panoramas, which means that we are facing a 5×–36× difference of magnitude. Therefore, it seems ill-advised to implement an "equals"-semantics, but rather one should use a "contains"-semantics. We modify the weighted L1-norm as follows:

$$D^C(\mathbf{q}, \mathbf{d}) = \sum_i w_i \max(q_i - d_i, 0) \tag{5}$$

The difference is that we are using the raw contour word frequencies, q_i and d_i without scaling and we replace the absolute value $|\cdot|$ by $\max(\cdot, 0)$. Therefore, one only penalizes contour words that occur in the query image, but not in the database image (or more often in the query image than in the database image). An ideal score of 0 is obtained by a database image that contains every contour word at least as often as the query image, plus any number of other contour words. If the proposed metric is transformed as follows, it can be evaluated just as efficiently as the baseline:

$$D^C(\mathbf{q}, \mathbf{d}) = \sum_{i \in Q} w_i q_i - \sum_{i \in Q} w_i \min(q_i, d_i) \tag{6}$$

This subtle change makes a huge difference, see Fig. 5(a) and Table 1: (B) versus (C). Note that this might also be applicable to other cases where a "contains"-semantics is desirable.

Location and Direction. We further refine retrieval by taking geometric information into account already during the voting stage. Earlier bag-of-words approaches accumulate evidence purely based on the frequency of visual words. Voting usually returns a short-list of the top n candidates, which are reranked using geometric verification (typically using the number of geometric inliers). For performance reasons, n has to be chosen relatively small (e.g. $n = 50$). If the correct answer already fails to be in this short-list, then no amount of reordering

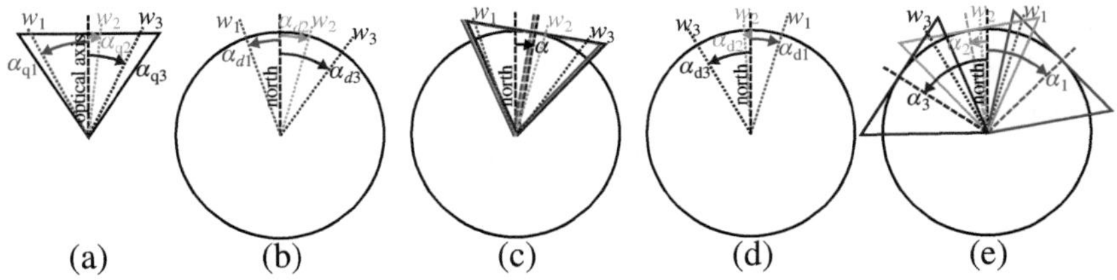

Fig. 3. Voting for a direction is illustrated using a simple example: We have a query image (a) with contour words w_i and associated angles α_{qi}. We consider a panorama (b) with contour words in the same *relative* positions α_{di} as the query image. Since the contour words appear in the same order, they all vote for the same viewing direction α (c). In contrast, we consider a second panorama (d) with contour words in a different order. Even though the contour words occur in close proximity they each vote for a different direction α_i, so that none of the directions gets a high score (e).

can bring it back. Instead, we check for geometric consistency already at the voting stage, so that fewer good candidates get lost prematurely. Not only does this increase the quality of the short-list, it also provides an estimated viewing direction, which can be used as an initial guess for the full geometric verification. Since this enables a significant speedup, we can afford to use a longer short-list, which further reduces the risk of missing the correct answer.

If the same contour word appears in the database image at angle α_d (relative to north) and in the query image at angle α_q (relative to the camera's optical axis), the camera's azimuth can be calculated as $\alpha = \alpha_d - \alpha_q$. Weighted votes are accumulated using soft binning and the most promising viewing direction(s) are passed on to full geometric verification. This way, panoramas containing the contour words in the right order get many votes for a single direction, ensuring a high score. For panoramas containing only the right mix of contour words, but in random order, the votes are divided among many different directions, so that none of them gets a good score (see Fig. 3). Note that this is different from merely dividing the panoramas into smaller sections and voting for these sections: Our approach effectively requires that the order of contour words in the panorama matches the order in the query image. As an additional benefit, we do not need to build the inverted file for any specific field-of-view of the query image.

Geometric Verification. We verify the top 1000 candidates with a geometric check. Verification consists in calculating an optimal alignment of the two visible horizons using iterative closest points (ICP). While we consider in the voting stage only one angle (azimuth), ICP determines a full 3D rotation. First, we sample all possible values for azimuth and keep the two other angles at zero. The most promising one is used as initialization for ICP. In the variants that already vote for a direction, we try only a few values around the highest ranked ones. The average alignment error is used as a score for re-ranking the candidates.

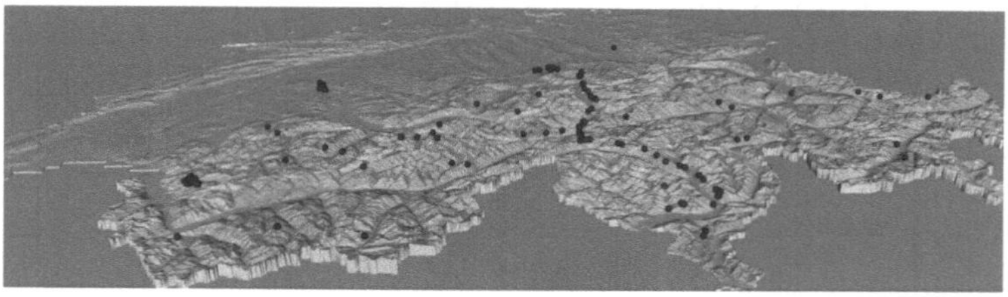

Fig. 4. Oblique view onto Switzerland model (40 000km^2). Spheres indicate the 213 query images' ground truth coordinates (size reflects 1km tolerance radius). Source of DEM data: Bundesamt für Landestopografie swisstopo (Art. 30 GeoIV): 5704 000 000

3 Evaluation

Query Set. In order to evaluate the approaches we assembled a set of photos from different sources such as internet photo collections and on site. For all of the photos, we verified the GPS tag or location estimate by comparing the skyline to the surface model. For a large part the information is consistent, only for a small fraction the position did not match the digital elevation model view. This can be explained by a bad cell phone GPS tag, because of bad/no GPS reception at the time the photo was taken. For these cases, we use dense geometric verification (on each 111×115m grid position up to a 10km radius around the tagged position) to generate hypotheses for the correct GPS tag. We verify this by visual inspection and remove the image in case of no agreement. The whole set of query images is available at the project website[4] and the distribution of pictures on the map is displayed in Fig. 4. For all of the query images FoV information is available (e.g. from EXIF tag). However, we have verified experimentally that also in case of fully unknown focal length the system can be applied by sampling over this parameter (see Fig. 8 for an example).

Parameter Selection. The features need to be clearly smaller than the images' field-of-view, but wide enough to capture the geometry rather than just discretization noise. We consider descriptors of width $w = 10°$ and $w = 2.5°$. The number of sample points n should not be so small that it is uninformative (e.g. $n = 3$ would only distinguish concave/convex), but not much bigger than that otherwise it risks being overly specific, so we choose $n = 8$. The curve is smoothed by a Gaussian with $\sigma = \frac{w}{2n}$, i.e. half the distance between consecutive sample points. Descriptors are extracted every σ degrees.

Each dimension of the descriptor is quantized into k bins of width 0.375, the first and last bin extending to infinity. We chose k as a power of 2 that results in roughly 1 million contour words, i.e. $k = 8$. This maps each y_i to 3 bits, producing contour words that are 24 bit integers. Out of the 2^{24} potential contour words, only 300k–500k (depending on w) remain after discarding words that occur too often (more than a million) or not at all.

[4] `http://cvg.ethz.ch/research/mountain-localization`

Table 1. Overview of tested recognition pipelines

	Voting scheme	Descriptor width	Dir. bin size	Geo. ver.	Top 1 correct
(A)	random	N/A	N/A	no	0.008%
(B)	"equals"	10°	N/A	no	8%
(C)	"contains"	10°	N/A	no	30%
(D)	loc.&dir.	10°	2°	no	45%
(E)	loc.&dir.	10°	3°	no	44%
(F)	loc.&dir.	10°	5°	no	46%
(G)	loc.&dir.	10°	10°	no	42%
(H)	loc.&dir.	10°	20°	no	38%
(I)	loc.&dir.	2.5°	3°	no	30%
(J)	loc.&dir.	10°&2.5°	3°	no	62%
(K)	loc.&dir.	10°&2.5°	3°	yes	88%

Recognition Performance. All of the tested recognition pipelines (see Table 1) return a ranked list of candidates. We evaluate them as follows: For every $n = 1, \ldots, 100$, we count the fraction of query images that have at least one correct answer among the top n candidates. We consider an answer correct if it is within 1km of the ground truth position (see Fig. 4).

In Fig. 5(a), we compare different voting schemes: (B) voting for location only, using the traditional approach with normalized visual word vectors and L1-norm ("equals"-semantics); (C) voting for location only, with our proposed metric ("contains"-semantics); (E) voting for location and direction simultaneously (i.e. taking order into account). All variants use 10° descriptors. For comparison, we also show (A) the probability of hitting a correct panorama by random guessing

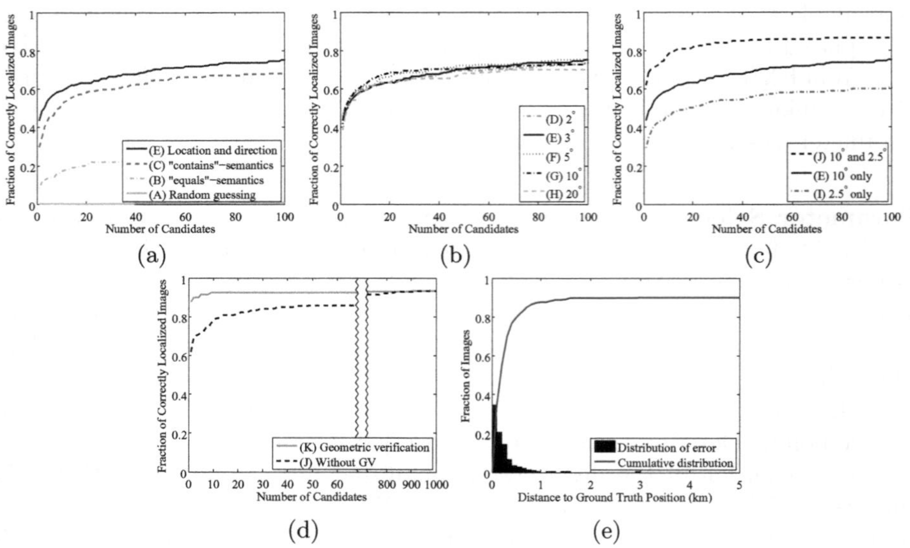

Fig. 5. Retrieval performance for different: (a) voting schemes, (b) bin sizes in direction voting, (c) descriptor sizes. (d) Retrieval performance before and after geometric verification. (e) Fraction of queries having (at most) a given distance to the ground truth position. Not shown: 21 images (9.9%) with an error between 7 and 217km.

(the probability of a correct guess is extremely small, which shows that the tolerance of 1km is not overly generous). Our proposed "contains"-semantics alone already outperforms the baseline ("equals"-semantics) by far, but voting for a direction is even better!

In Fig. 5(b), we analyze how different bin sizes for direction voting affects results. (D)–(H) correspond to bin sizes of $2°, 3°, 5°, 10°, 20°$ respectively. While there are small differences, none of the settings outperforms an other consistently: Our method is quite insensitive over a large range of this parameter.

In Fig. 5(c), we study the impact of different descriptor sizes: (E) only 10° descriptors; (I) only 2.5° descriptors; (J) both 10° and 2.5° descriptors combined. All variants vote for location and direction simultaneously. While 10° descriptors outperforms 2.5° descriptors, the combination of both is better than either descriptor size alone. This demonstrates that different scales capture different information, which complement each other.

In Fig. 5(d), we show the effect of geometric verification by aligning the full countours using ICP: (J) 10° and 2.5° descriptors voting for location and direction, without verification; (K) same as (J) but with geometric verification. We see that ICP based reranking is quite effective at moving the best candidate(s) to the beginning of the short list: With probability 88%, the top-ranked candidate is within a radius of 1km from the ground truth position. See Fig. 5(e) for other radii. In computer assisted search scenarios, an operator would choose an image from a small list which would further increase the percentage of correctly recovered pictures. Besides that, from geometric verification we not only obtain an estimate for the viewing direction but the full camera orientation which can be used for augmented reality. Fig. 6&7 show successful and unsuccessful examples.

We also ran the experiment after artificially adding tilt to the queries and determined that recognition performance is largely unaffected up to 20° tilt.

Fig. 6. Sample Results: Input Image (top row), depth image from dehazing (second row), segmentation (third row) and augmentation of retrieved contour from database onto bright version of original image (bottom row). The images in the third and the two right-most columns have been segmented with the help of user interaction.

Fig. 7. Some incorrectly localized images. This usually happens to images with a relatively smooth horizon and only few distinctive features. The pipeline finds a contour that fits somewhat well, even if the location is completely off.

Field-of-View. Fig. 8 illustrates the effect of inaccurate or unknown field-of-view (FoV). For one query image, we run the localization pipeline (K) assuming that the FoV is 11° and record the results. Then we run it again assuming that the FoV is 12° etc, up to 70°. Fig. 8 shows how the alignment error and estimated position depend on the assumed FoV.

In principle, it is possible to compensate a wrong FoV by moving forward or backward. This holds only approximately if the scene is not perfectly planar. In addition, the effect has hard limits because moving too far will cause objects to move in or out of view, changing the visible horizon. Between these limits, changing the FoV causes both the alignment error and the position to change smoothly. Outside of this stable range, the error is higher, fluctuates more and the position jumps around wildly.

This has two consequences: First, if the FoV obtained from the image's meta-data is inaccurate it is usually not a disaster, the retrieved position will simply be slightly inaccurate as well, but not completely wrong. Second, if the FoV is completely unknown, one can get a rough estimate by choosing the minimum error and/or looking for a range where the retrieved position is most stable.

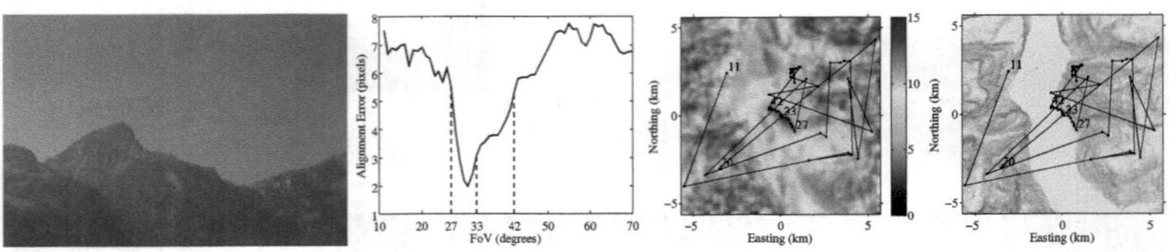

(a) (b) (c) (d)

Fig. 8. (a) Query image. (b) Alignment error of the best position for a given FoV. Dashed lines indicate the limits of the stable region and the FoV from the image's EXIF tag. (c) Alignment error of the best FoV for a given position. For an animated version, see `http://cvg.ethz.ch/research/mountain-localization`. (d) Shaded terrain model. The overlaid curve in (c) and (d) starts from the best location assuming 11° FoV and continues to the best location assuming 12°, 13°, etc. Numbers next to the markers indicate corresponding FoV.

Runtime. We implemented the algorithm partly in C/C++ and partly in Matlab. On the evaluation dataset 51% of the images were segmented completely automatically, 42% required small user interaction, such as correcting for occlusions and 7% needed more intensive manual labeling i.e. correcting for small snow fields and reflections etc. After segmentation, one image takes 10 seconds to find the camera's position and rotation in an area of 40 000km^2 (Exhaustively computing an optimal alignment between the query image and each of the 3.5M panoramas would take on the order of several days). For comparison, the authors of [14] use a GPU implementation and report 2 minutes for determining rotation alone (assuming that the camera position is already given).

4 Conclusion and Future Work

We have presented a system for large scale location recognition based on digital elevation models. This is very valuable for geo-localization of pictures when no GPS information is available (for virtually all video or DSLR cameras, archive pictures, in intelligence and military scenarios). We extract the sky and represent the visible horizon by a set of contour words, where each contour word is represented together with its offset angle from the optical axis. This way, we can do a bag-of-words like approach with integrated geometric verification, i.e. we are looking for the panorama (portion) that has a similar frequency of contour words with a consistent direction. We show that our representation is very discriminative and the full system allows for excellent recognition rates close to 90% on our challenging dataset including different seasons, landscapes and altitudes. We believe that this is a step towards the ultimate goal of being able to geo-localize images taken anywhere on the planet, but for this also other additional cues of natural environments have to be combined with the given approach. This will be the subject of future research.

Acknowledgements. This work has been supported through SNF grant 127224 by the Swiss National Science Foundation. We would also like to thank Simon Wenner for his help with rendering the DEMs.

References

1. Schindler, G., Brown, M., Szeliski, R.: City-scale location recognition. In: Computer Vision and Pattern Recognition, CVPR 2007, pp. 1–7 (2007)
2. Chen, D., Baatz, G., Köser, K., Tsai, S., Vedantham, R., Pylvanainen, T., Roimela, K., Chen, X., Bach, J., Pollefeys, M., Girod, B., Grzeszczuk, R.: City-scale landmark identification on mobile devices. In: CVPR (2011)
3. Sivic, J., Zisserman, A.: Video Google: A text retrieval approach to object matching in videos. In: Proc. ICCV 2003, vol. 2, pp. 1470–1477 (2003)
4. Woo, J., Son, K., Li, T., Kim, G.S., Kweon, I.S.: Vision-based uav navigation in mountain area. In: MVA, pp. 236–239 (2007)

5. Stein, F., Medioni, G.: Map-based localization using the panoramic horizon. IEEE Transactions on Robotics and Automation 11, 892–896 (1995)
6. Baatz, G., Köser, K., Chen, D., Grzeszczuk, R., Pollefeys, M.: Leveraging 3d city models for rotation invariant place-of-interest recognition. IJCV, Special Issue on Mobile Vision 96 (2012)
7. Li, Y., Snavely, N., Huttenlocher, D.P.: Location Recognition Using Prioritized Feature Matching. In: Daniilidis, K., Maragos, P., Paragios, N. (eds.) ECCV 2010, Part II. LNCS, vol. 6312, pp. 791–804. Springer, Heidelberg (2010)
8. Talluri, R., Aggarwal, J.: Position estimation for an autonomous mobile robot in an outdoor environment. Transact. Robotics and Automation 8, 573–584 (1992)
9. Thompson, W.B., Henderson, T.C., Colvin, T.L., Dick, L.B., Valiquette, C.M.: Vision-based localization. In: Image Understanding Workshop, pp. 491–498 (1993)
10. Cozman, F., Krotkov, E.: Position estimation from outdoor visual landmarks for teleoperation of lunar rovers. In: WACV 1996, pp. 156–161 (1996)
11. Naval, P.C., Mukunoki, M., Minoh, M., Ikeda, K.: Estimating camera position and orientation from geographical map and mountain image. In: 38th Pattern Sensing Group Research Meeting, Soc. of Instrument and Control Engineers, pp. 9–16 (1997)
12. Cozman, F.: Decision Making Based on Convex Sets of Probability Distributions: Quasi-Bayesian Networks and Outdoor Visual Position Estimation. PhD thesis, Robotics Institute, Carnegie Mellon University, Pittsburgh, PA (1997)
13. Ramalingam, S., Bouaziz, S., Sturm, P., Brand, M.: Skyline2gps: Localization in urban canyons using omni-skylines. In: IROS 2010, pp. 3816–3823 (2010)
14. Baboud, L., Cadík, M., Eisemann, E., Seidel, H.P.: Automatic photo-to-terrain alignment for the annotation of mountain pictures. In: CVPR, pp. 41–48 (2011)
15. Hays, J., Efros, A.A.: im2gps: estimating geographic information from a single image. In: Proceedings of CVPR 2008 (2008)
16. Lalonde, J.F., Narasimhan, S.G., Efros, A.A.: What do the sun and the sky tell us about the camera? International Journal on Computer Vision 88, 24–51 (2010)
17. Brown, M., Lowe, D.G.: Automatic panoramic image stitching using invariant features. Int. J. Comput. Vision 74, 59–73 (2007)
18. Luo, J., Etz, S.: A physics-motivated approach to detecting sky in photographs. In: Proc. ICPR., vol. 1, pp. 155–158 (2002)
19. Martin, D.R., Fowlkes, C.C., Malik, J.: Learning to detect natural image boundaries using local brightness, color, and texture cues. PAMI 2004 26, 530–549 (2004)
20. Blake, A., Rother, C., Brown, M., Perez, P., Torr, P.: Interactive Image Segmentation Using an Adaptive GMMRF Model. In: Pajdla, T., Matas, J(G.) (eds.) ECCV 2004. LNCS, vol. 3021, pp. 428–441. Springer, Heidelberg (2004)
21. Lie, W.N., Lin, T.C.I., Lin, T.C., Hung, K.S.: A robust dynamic programming algorithm to extract skyline in images for navigation. Pattern Recognition Letters 26, 221–230 (2005)
22. He, K., Sun, J., Tang, X.: Single image haze removal using dark channel prior. In: Computer Vision and Pattern Recognition, pp. 1956–1963 (2009)
23. Manay, S., Cremers, D., Hong, B.W., Yezzi, A., Soatto, S.: Integral invariants for shape matching. Pattern Analysis and Machine Intelligence (2006)
24. Yang, M., Kpalma, K., Ronsin, J.: A Survey of Shape Feature Extraction Techniques. In: Yin, P.Y. (ed.) Pattern Recognition, pp. 43–90. IN-TECH (2008)
25. Lowe, D.G.: Distinctive Image Features from Scale-Invariant Keypoints. International Journal of Computer Vision 60, 91–110 (2004)
26. Nistér, D., Stewénius, H.: Scalable recognition with a vocabulary tree. In: CVPR (2), pp. 2161–2168. IEEE Computer Society (2006)

Manifold Statistics for Essential Matrices

Gijs Dubbelman[1], Leo Dorst[2], and Henk Pijls[2]

[1] Carnegie Mellon University, The Robotics Institute, Pittsburgh, USA
gijsdubb@cs.cmu.edu
[2] University of Amsterdam, Faculty of Science, Amsterdam, The Netherlands
{L.Dorst,H.G.J.Pijls}@uva.nl

Abstract. Riemannian geometry allows for the generalization of statistics designed for Euclidean vector spaces to Riemannian manifolds. It has recently gained popularity within computer vision as many relevant parameter spaces have such a Riemannian manifold structure. Approaches which exploit this have been shown to exhibit improved efficiency and accuracy. The Riemannian logarithmic and exponential mappings are at the core of these approaches.

In this contribution we review recently proposed Riemannian mappings for essential matrices and prove that they lead to sub-optimal manifold statistics. We introduce correct Riemannian mappings by utilizing a multiple-geodesic approach and show experimentally that they provide optimal statistics.

1 Introduction

Statistical inference on a set of samples is at the basis of many computer vision algorithms. These algorithms typically require a metric to be expressed in the parameter space in which the samples reside. The most often used metrics are the Euclidean distance or one of its generalizations such as the Mahalanobis distance. All are based on the usual dot product between vectors and assume that the parameter space is a Euclidean vector space. Recent work in computer vision has pointed out that many parameter spaces are *differentiable manifolds*, i.e. they are differentiable subsets of Euclidean spaces. Neglecting the manifold structure of parameter spaces within statistics typically leads to reduced accuracy and efficiency, as one is optimizing over, and measuring distances through, irrelevant degrees of freedom.

Improved accuracy and efficiency can be obtained by restricting computations to the meaningful degrees of freedom, i.e. those of the manifold. This can be achieved by exploiting the paradigm of *manifold statistics* based on *metric charts*. A metric chart is a local linearization (or flattening) of the manifold for one particular point on the manifold, called the *charting point*, such that distances over the manifold with respect to this point can be computed using the Euclidean distance formula in this chart. Algorithms using metric charts to compute statistical properties of samples residing on manifolds are also referred to as *intrinsic statistical* algorithms and usually are iterative in nature. Crucial to this approach are *charting functions* which define the metric charts for each point on a particular manifold. They can be used to transfer samples residing in the manifold to the metric charts and back. Riemannian geometry provides the theory and tools to develop such charting functions (where they are called logarithmic and exponential mappings) and is discussed in Sec. 2.

A. Fitzgibbon et al. (Eds.): ECCV 2012, Part II, LNCS 7573, pp. 531–544, 2012.

The use of Riemannian geometry to disclose statistical information on manifolds can be traced back to [1]. This methodology has recently received considerable attention from the computer vision research community. For a theoretical overview see [2, 3] and the references therein. An example of a statistical algorithm that was generalized to certain manifolds is mean-shift [4, 5]. In [6] it was used for robust pose estimation, in [7] for robust essential matrix estimation and in [8] for simultaneous multiple motion estimation. In [9] a Riemannian approach was taken to estimate the dimension and entropy of shape spaces, particularly the shape space of handwritten digits. Riemannian geometry has also been used to estimate statistical properties of diffusion tensor data [10, 11]. In [12] Riemannian geometry was used to estimate properties from image point configurations. A Riemannian clustering approach was proposed in [13] and applied to 2D motion segmentation and to diffusion tensor segmentation. In [14] a Riemannian clustering approach was proposed for pedestrian detection from image data.

This work focuses on *epipolar configurations*, i.e. *scale-free* Euclidean motions, which are encoded by *essential matrices*. In Sec. 3 we develop our charting functions for essential matrices by using methods from Riemannian geometry. They are inspired by mappings proposed earlier in [15, 16, 17]. As is explained in Sec. 2 and in Sec. 3 the mappings in [15, 16, 17] are designed for manifold optimization (estimating essential matrices from image point correspondences) and cannot be used *as is* within manifold statistics. This was already pointed out in [5, 7] which introduced alternative mappings. In Sec. 3.2 it is proven that the mappings in [5, 7] are, strictly speaking, mathematically incorrect and in Sec. 4 it is shown that they result in sub-optimal statistics. This stands in contrast to our mappings for which it is shown that they lead to optimal statistics. Although our focus is mostly theoretical, the broader relevance of our findings is demonstrated by showing that *state-of-the-art* robust estimators based on the RANSAC [18, 19, 20] paradigm can potentially benefit from incorporating our mappings. Our conclusion are summarized in Sec. 5.

2 Riemannian Geometry and Manifold Statistics

Manifold statistics conceptually requires a distance metric for every point pair on the manifold. In Riemannian geometry the distance $d(\mathbf{p}, \mathbf{u})$ between two points $\mathbf{p}$ and $\mathbf{u}$ residing on a differentiable manifold $\mathcal{M}$ is defined as the length of the shortest curve over the manifold connecting the two points, i.e.

$$d(\mathbf{p}, \mathbf{u}) = \min_{\gamma \in \Gamma} l_{\mathbf{p}}^{\mathbf{u}}(\gamma), \tag{1}$$

where Γ is the set of all possible curves residing on the manifold joining $\mathbf{p}$ and $\mathbf{u}$ and $l_{\mathbf{p}}^{\mathbf{u}}(\gamma)$ is the length of one such curve between these two points. Under this definition $d(\ ,\ )$ is a metric [21] and obeys to all its axioms, i.e. *positive definiteness*, *identity of indiscernibles*, *symmetry* and the *triangle inequality*. Curves which provided paths of least distance over manifolds are often called *geodesics*.

Just as in Euclidean spaces, the length of a curve γ in $\mathcal{M}$ is the integral of all the local contributions of all points on the curve. Let the curve γ pass through the point $\mathbf{p}$ at $\gamma(0)$ and pass through the point $\mathbf{u}$ at $\gamma(1)$, then the length of the curve segment between $\mathbf{p}$ and $\mathbf{u}$ is defined as

$$l_{\mathbf{p}}^{\mathbf{u}}(\gamma) = \int_0^1 \sqrt{\langle \frac{d\gamma}{dt}, \frac{d\gamma}{dt} \rangle_{\gamma(t)}} dt. \tag{2}$$

Each local contribution $\langle \frac{d\gamma}{dt}, \frac{d\gamma}{dt} \rangle_{\gamma(t)}$ is computed by the *Riemannian metric* $\langle\ ,\ \rangle$ which is an inner product defined on *tangent vectors* of $\mathcal{M}$. A differentiable manifold equipped with a Riemannian metric is called a *Riemannian manifold*. As the Riemannian metric can vary over the manifold, the subscript $\gamma(t)$ denotes the point on the curve at which the Riemannian metric is computed and $\frac{d\gamma}{dt}$ is the tangent vector of the curve at this point. Note that the locally defined Riemannian metric should not be confused with the globally defined Riemannian distance $d(\mathbf{p}, \mathbf{u})$.

Fortunately, we need not work with these equations as for certain manifolds, including that of essential matrices, the globally defined metric $d(\mathbf{p}, \mathbf{u})$ can be computed efficiently through a construct known as the *Riemannian logarithmic map*. The Riemannian logarithmic map $\text{Log}_{\mathbf{p}}(\mathbf{u}) = \mathfrak{u}$ takes the point $\mathbf{u}$ on the manifold to the *tangent space* at $\mathbf{p}$, i.e. $T_{\mathbf{p}}\mathcal{M}$, producing the tangent vector $\mathfrak{u}$. $T_{\mathbf{p}}\mathcal{M}$ is the collection of all tangent vectors of the manifold at $\mathbf{p}$, we denote its elements in gothic font. The Riemannian logarithmic map does so such that

$$d(\mathbf{p}, \mathbf{u}) = \sqrt{\text{Log}_{\mathbf{p}}(\mathbf{u})^{\top} \text{Log}_{\mathbf{p}}(\mathbf{u})} = \|\mathfrak{u}\|, \tag{3}$$

i.e. the distance over the manifold can be computed as the Euclidean length of the tangent vector $\mathfrak{u}$ produced by $\text{Log}_{\mathbf{p}}(\mathbf{u})$. It is clear that the tangent spaces constructed by the logarithmic map are the metric charts of Sec. 1. Note that only for specific manifolds Eq. 3 holds globally for all $\mathbf{u}$, given $\mathbf{p}$. In general, it only holds for $\mathbf{u}$ sufficiently close to $\mathbf{p}$ on the manifold.

The Riemannian logarithmic map is differentiable and invertible. Its inverse, the *Riemannian exponential map*, takes the tangent vector $\mathfrak{u}$ defined in the tangent space (or metric chart) at $\mathbf{p}$ back to the manifold such that $\text{Log}_{\text{Exp}_{\mathbf{p}}(\mathfrak{u})}(-\mathfrak{u}) = \mathbf{p}$.

By using the direct product between Riemannian manifolds one can combine existing manifolds into new manifolds. Under the direct product points on the manifold $\mathcal{M} = \mathcal{M}_1 \times \mathcal{M}_2$ are ordered pairs of points on $\mathcal{M}_1$ and points on $\mathcal{M}_2$, i.e. $\mathbf{p} = (\mathbf{p}_1, \mathbf{p}_2)$ with $\mathbf{p}_1 \in \mathcal{M}_1$ and $\mathbf{p}_2 \in \mathcal{M}_2$. The exponential and logarithmic mappings of the direct product manifold are simply the combination of the individual mappings of each sub-manifold, i.e.

$$\begin{aligned} \text{Log}_{\mathbf{p}}(\mathbf{u}) &= (\text{Log}_{\mathbf{p}_1}(\mathbf{u}_1), \text{Log}_{\mathbf{p}_2}(\mathbf{u}_2)) \qquad \text{and} \\ \text{Exp}_{\mathbf{p}}(\mathfrak{u}) &= (\text{Exp}_{\mathbf{p}_1}(\mathfrak{u}_1), \text{Exp}_{\mathbf{p}_2}(\mathfrak{u}_2)). \end{aligned} \tag{4}$$

Every property of the sub-manifolds $\mathcal{M}_1$ and $\mathcal{M}_2$ are automatically transferred to the direct product manifold $\mathcal{M}$. The intrinsic distance between $\mathbf{p}$ and $\mathbf{u}$ over the direct product manifold $\mathcal{M}$ is defined as

$$\begin{aligned} d(\mathbf{p}, \mathbf{u}) &= \sqrt{d(\mathbf{p}_1, \mathbf{u}_1)^2 + d(\mathbf{p}_2, \mathbf{u}_2)^2} \\ &= \sqrt{\|\text{Log}_{\mathbf{p}_1}(\mathbf{u}_1)\|^2 + \|\text{Log}_{\mathbf{p}_2}(\mathbf{u}_2)\|^2}, \end{aligned} \tag{5}$$

it is the square root of the sum of the squared lengths of the individual minimal length curves. Such a definition is called a *multiple geodesics* or a *product metric* approach [21, 22] and automatically obeys the axioms for metrics.

When the mappings of Eq. 4 are available for all combinations of $\mathbf{p}$ and $\mathbf{u}$ of interest to the statistical algorithm, the Riemannian logarithmic map can be used to generalize statistical algorithms based on the Euclidean distance formula. This generalization is performed by applying the substitution

$$(\mathbf{u}-\mathbf{p})^{\top}\Sigma^{-1}(\mathbf{u}-\mathbf{p}) \;\rightarrow\; \mathrm{Log}_{\mathbf{p}}(\mathbf{u})^{\top}\Sigma^{-1}\mathrm{Log}_{\mathbf{p}}(\mathbf{u}), \tag{6}$$

to a statistical objective function. It assures that all statistical calculations are performed in the metric charts of the manifold and therefore are constrained to the actual degrees of freedom of this manifold. The manifold statistical objective functions in [2, 3, 4, 5, 6, 7] are all expressed similarly in terms of a logarithmic map, whereas the manifold optimization methods in [15, 16, 17] only require the exponential map. The required logarithmic mappings for essential matrices are also not provided in [15, 16, 17].

3 Riemann Mappings for Essential Matrices

The essential matrix $\mathbf{E}$ [23] is a 3×3 matrix which algebraically describes the *epipolar geometry* between two calibrated cameras. Let $\mathbf{x}$ and $\mathbf{x}'$ be the homogeneous normalized projections of the same world point on the imaging planes of the first and the second camera respectively. The essential matrix is then defined algebraically as the matrix that satisfies

$$\mathbf{x}'^{\top}\mathbf{E}\mathbf{x} = \mathbf{0} \tag{7}$$

for all such correspondences $\mathbf{x}$ and $\mathbf{x}'$.

The epipolar geometry of a normalized camera setup is defined by the translation $\mathbf{t}$ and rotation $\mathbf{R}$ between the two cameras. Given this translation and rotation a geometric composition of the essential matrix is $\mathbf{E} = [\mathbf{t}]_{\times}\mathbf{R}$, realizing that it can only be determined up to a global scale ambiguity from corresponding image points. The nine values in $\mathbf{E}$ have five degrees of freedom, 3 for rotation and 2 for translation modulo global scale. Due to this scale ambiguity the length of the translation vector can be normalized to have unit length $\|\mathbf{t}\| = 1$ without loss of information. The normalized essential matrix is therefore defined as

$$\mathbf{E} = [\mathbf{t}]_{\times}\mathbf{R}\,, \quad \text{with } \|\mathbf{t}\| = 1. \tag{8}$$

This definition allows us to specify the parameter space of normalized essential matrices as the direct product space $\mathrm{S}^2 \times \mathrm{SO}(3)$ [16, 17]. Both S^2 and $\mathrm{SO}(3)$ are well known Riemannian manifolds and so is their direct product space $\mathrm{S}^2 \times \mathrm{SO}(3)$. We call points on $\mathrm{S}^2 \times \mathrm{SO}(3)$ *epipolar configurations*. The challenge of this parametrization is that $\mathrm{S}^2 \times \mathrm{SO}(3)$ is a four-fold covering of the space of essential matrices, every essential matrix maps to four epipolar configurations. This is a well known ambiguity which is of less concern to manifold optimization than it is to manifold statistics.

Manifold optimization methods like those in [15, 16, 17] are only concerned with estimating a single essential matrix at a time. For any particular essential matrix one can randomly pick any of its four epipolar configurations and start optimizing from there. The challenge is to parametrize $S^2 \times SO(3)$ (at each iteration of the optimizer) such that it cannot jump between epipolar configurations which all are related to the same essential matrix and hence all have the same *summed squared error* (sse).

In manifold statistics we typically have an empirical distribution consisting of several hundred essential matrices. When each of them is randomly mapped to one of its four epipolar configurations, almost all statistical information of the distribution is lost. This is demonstrated in Sec. 4.1. One creates a situation where the distance between two essential matrices depends purely on a random choice and is no longer related to the epipolar configurations that they encode. The challenge for manifold statistics is therefore to make a consistent choice when mapping each essential matrix to a point on $S^2 \times SO(3)$. As pointed out in [5, 7] the mappings in [15, 16, 17] do themselves not provide mechanism to perform this mapping consistently for multiple essential matrices as is required.

3.1 The Normalized Essential Manifold $S^2 \times SO(3)$

We start with the normalized essential manifold $S^2 \times SO(3)$ of [16, 17]. In this direct product space the sphere S^2 is related to normalized translations, which we will call *directions*, and $SO(3)$ is related to rotations in 3D. When considering the *unit quaternion* representation of rotations, then it is clear that rotational sub-space $SO(3)$ has the shape of a unit hyper-sphere S^3.

Each essential matrix must be taken to a unique point on this manifold $S^2 \times S^3$ in a differentiable and invertible fashion. This requires resolving the *four-fold ambiguity* and can be performed efficiently by enforcing the *positive depth constraint* [24]. In contrast to the remarks in [5, 7] we found that this can be done efficiently and robustly, we come back to this in Sec. 4. The image data and the *positive depth constraint* together with Eq. 8 provide an invertible and differentiable mapping between essential matrices and points in $S^2 \times S^3$. Conceptually speaking, the knowledge that the observed image data is a projection of a Euclidean space allows for 'lifting' the essential matrix from a projective entity to an epipolar configuration. The ability to do so is the main difference between a computer vision approach, where image data is always available, and a pure mathematical approach like [15].

Each essential matrix $\mathbf{E}$ can be represented uniquely by a seven dimensional vector $\mathbf{E} \equiv (\mathbf{d}, \mathbf{q}) = (d_x, d_y, d_z, q, q_i, q_j, q_k)^\top$ with $\mathbf{d} \in S^2$ (modeling directions) and $\mathbf{q} \in S^3$ (modeling rotations by unit quaternions). Due to the fact that $\|\mathbf{d}\| = 1$ and $\|\mathbf{q}\| = 1$ there are only five degrees of freedom as desired. Using a multiple geodesic approach on $S^2 \times S^3$ results in the Riemannian logarithmic and exponential mappings

$$\begin{aligned} \mathfrak{e}_2 &= \mathrm{Log}_{\mathbf{E}_1}(\mathbf{E}_2) = (\mathrm{Log}_{\mathbf{d}_1}(\mathbf{d}_2), \mathrm{Log}_{\mathbf{q}_1}(\mathbf{q}_2)) \quad \text{and} \\ \mathbf{E}_2 &= \mathrm{Exp}_{\mathbf{E}_1}(\mathfrak{e}_2) = (\mathrm{Exp}_{\mathbf{d}_1}(\mathfrak{d}_2), \mathrm{Exp}_{\mathbf{q}_1}(\mathfrak{q}_2)). \end{aligned} \tag{9}$$

The Riemannian distance between two essential matrices can then be computed with $\|\mathrm{Log}_{\mathrm{E}_1}(\mathrm{E}_2)\|$. These mappings are all that is required to generalize statistical algorithms according to the substitution of Eq. 6. Our contribution is providing explicit and efficient functions for these mappings.

For S^3 we choose the quaternion identity $(1,0,0,0)^\top$ as the origin. For this choice the Riemannian exponential map wrt. the origin is

$$\mathbf{q} = \mathrm{Exp}(\mathfrak{q}) = \begin{cases} (\cos(\|\mathfrak{q}\|)\ ,\ \sin(\|\mathfrak{q}\|)\ \frac{\mathfrak{q}}{\|\mathfrak{q}\|})\ , & \|\mathfrak{q}\| \neq 0 \\ (1,0,0,0) & , \|\mathfrak{q}\| = 0 \end{cases} . \quad (10)$$

For S^2 we take $(1,0,0)^\top$ as the origin which gives

$$\mathbf{d} = \mathrm{Exp}(\mathfrak{d}) \equiv \begin{cases} (\cos(\|\mathfrak{d}\|), \sin(\|\mathfrak{d}\|)\ \frac{\mathfrak{d}}{\|\mathfrak{d}\|})\ , & \|\mathfrak{d}\| \neq 0 \\ (1,\ 0,\ 0) & , \|\mathfrak{d}\| = 0 \end{cases} . \quad (11)$$

These mappings are well known [25] and very similar to that of [16, 17] except that we choose to use S^3 (unit quaternions) instead of of $SO(3)$ (rotation matrices).

In contrast to [15, 16, 17] we also require the logarithmic mappings of S^3 and S^2. At the origin of S^3 with $\mathbf{q} = (q, q_i, q_j, q_k)^\top$ it is provided by

$$\mathfrak{q} = \mathrm{Log}(\mathbf{q}) = \begin{cases} \underline{\arccos}(q)\frac{(q_i,q_j,q_k)}{\|(q_i,q_j,q_k)\|}\ , & q \neq 1 \\ (0,\ 0,\ 0) & , q = 1 \end{cases} \quad \text{with } \underline{\arccos}(q) = \begin{cases} \arccos(q) - \pi\ , & q < 0 \\ \arccos(q) & , 0 \leq q \end{cases} \quad (12)$$

and at the origin of S^2 with $\mathbf{d} = (d_x, d_y, d_z)^\top$ it is

$$\mathfrak{d} = \mathrm{Log}(\mathbf{d}) \equiv \begin{cases} \arccos(d_x)\frac{(d_y,d_z)}{\|(d_y,d_z)\|}, & d_x \neq 1 \\ (0,\ 0)\ , & d_x = 1 \end{cases} . \quad (13)$$

Note that $\underline{\arccos}$ assures that antipodal quaternions $\mathbf{q}$ and $-\mathbf{q}$ are mapped to the same point in the tangent space such that $d(\mathbf{q}, -\mathbf{q}) = 0$. This is required as S^3 is a double cover of $SO(3)$, i.e. $\mathbf{q}$ and $-\mathbf{q}$ both represent the same rotation. Apart from $\underline{\arccos}$, these mappings are again well known [25].

The next step is to express these mappings wrt. general points on the manifolds S^3 and S^2 and not only wrt. to their origins. For S^3 this can be performed by exploiting the Lie group structure of unit quaternions [3]. The general logarithmic and exponential mappings for S^3 are defined by:

$$\begin{aligned} \mathfrak{q}_2 &= \mathrm{Log}_{\mathbf{q}_1}(\mathbf{q}_2) = \mathrm{Log}(\mathbf{q}_1^{-1} \star \mathbf{q}_2) \quad \text{and} \\ \mathbf{q}_2 &= \mathrm{Exp}_{\mathbf{q}_1}(\mathfrak{q}_2) = \mathbf{q}_1 \star \mathrm{Exp}(\mathfrak{q}_2). \end{aligned} \quad (14)$$

The Special Case S^2: It is well known that S^2 does not allow for a Lie group structure [26] which makes obtaining the general mappings significantly more challenging. Correct manifold statistics requires that all tangent space bases of all points on S^2, except that of the antipodal of $(1,0,0)^\top$ which is $(-1,0,0)^\top$, are smoothly aligned with the tangent space basis at $(1,0,0)^\top$ such that minimal length curves originating from $(1,0,0)^\top$ are geodesics (i.e. it requires a torsion-free metric alignment related to the *Levi-Civita* connection[21] of S^2). This is because manifold statistics must simultaneously handle multiple empirical distributions on S^2 consisting out of multiple points and therefore requires a globally consistent approach to relate all tangent space bases and all minimal length curves of all these points to each other.

In manifold optimization this is not required as it is concerned with the exponential map of one point at a time. As such, [16, 17] can use a Gram-Schmidth process to define the bases of tangent spaces at each iteration. Their approach does not provide the required alignment of tangent space bases, does not provide a general logarithmic map such that $\mathrm{Log}_{\mathrm{Exp}_{\mathbf{d}_1}(\mathfrak{d}_2)}(-\mathfrak{d}_2) = \mathbf{d}_1$ with $d(\mathbf{d}_1, \mathbf{d}_2) = \|\mathrm{Log}_{\mathbf{d}_1}(\mathbf{d}_2)\|$ and therefore cannot be used *as is* for manifold statistics. The same holds for the approach in [15].

Our main theoretical contribution is that we provide a product structure on S^2 such that its general Riemannian mappings can be expressed as

$$\begin{aligned} \mathfrak{d}_2 &= \mathrm{Log}_{\mathbf{d}_1}(\mathbf{d}_2) = \mathrm{Log}(\mathbf{d}_1^{-1} \star \mathbf{d}_2) \quad \text{and} \\ \mathbf{d}_2 &= \mathrm{Exp}_{\mathbf{d}_1}(\mathfrak{d}_2) = \mathbf{d}_1 \star \mathrm{Exp}(\mathfrak{d}_2). \end{aligned} \tag{15}$$

Our product structure coincides with the torsion-free metric alignment of S^2 at $\mathbf{e}$, see Fig. 1. Similarly to the quaternion product, its purpose is to provide an invertible map between geodesics originating from general points on S^2 to geodesics originating at $\mathbf{e}$ by *parallel transport*[21]. The existence of such a product structure is often contributed to a Lie group structure which S^2 does not allow [26]. Still we show that S^2 has many useful *Lie-group-like* properties similar to that of the Lie group of unit quaternions. Our product structure for S^2 is provided in Theorem 1.

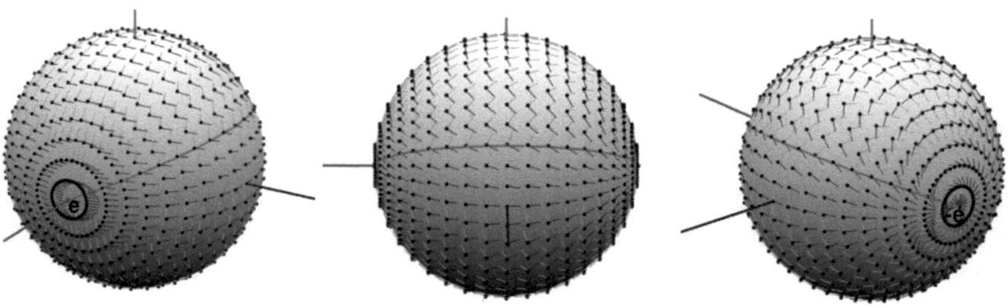

(a) (b) (c)

Fig. 1. The alignment of tangent space bases on S^2 enforced by our product with $\mathbf{e} = (1,0,0)^\top$. Only at $-\mathbf{e} = (-1,0,0)$ it has a discontinuity for all other points it is smooth. A minimal length curve through $\mathbf{e}$ is plotted in magenta. Note that it does not change direction with respect to the tangent space bases of all points except that of $-\mathbf{e}$, i.e. the antipodal and *cut locus* of $\mathbf{e}$. Therefore, it is a geodesics everywhere except at $-\mathbf{e}$. The same holds for any other geodesic starting at $\mathbf{e}$.

Theorem 1: The product $\star$ between general points $\mathbf{d}_1 \in \mathrm{S}^2$ and $\mathbf{d}_2 \in \mathrm{S}^2$ is

$$\star:\ \mathrm{S}^2 \times \mathrm{S}^2 \to \mathrm{S}^2, \quad \mathbf{d}_1 \star \mathbf{d}_2 = \mathrm{R}_{\mathbf{d}_1}\mathrm{R}_{\mathbf{d}_2}(1,0,0)^\top \tag{16}$$

where $\mathrm{R}_{\mathbf{d}} = \mathrm{I}$ when $\mathbf{d} = (1,0,0)^\top$ and $\mathrm{R}_{\mathbf{d}} = -\mathrm{I}$ when $\mathbf{d} = (-1,0,0)^\top$ and for all other $\mathbf{d} \in \mathrm{S}^2,\ \mathbf{d} \notin \{(1,0,0)^\top, (-1,0,0)^\top\}$,

$$\mathrm{R}_{\mathbf{d}} = \mathbf{I} + \sin(\theta_{\mathbf{d}})\,[\mathbf{r}_{\mathbf{d}}]_\times + (1 - \cos(\theta_{\mathbf{d}}))\,[\mathbf{r}_{\mathbf{d}}]_\times^2 \tag{17}$$

with

$$\mathbf{r_d} = \frac{(0, -d_z, d_y)^\top}{\sqrt{d_y^2 + d_z^2}} \quad \text{and} \quad \theta_\mathbf{d} = \arccos(d_x). \tag{18}$$

The identity element $\mathbf{e}$ belonging to this product is $(1, 0, 0)^\top$ and inversion of an element $\mathbf{d}$ is provided by $\mathbf{d}^{-1} = \mathrm{R}_\mathbf{d}^{-1}\mathbf{e}$. We define the product to be *left associative*, i.e. $\mathbf{d}_1 \star \mathbf{d}_2 \star \mathbf{d}_3 = (\mathbf{d}_1 \star \mathbf{d}_2) \star \mathbf{d}_3$.

Proof: First note that we defined $\mathrm{R}_\mathbf{d}$ such that $\mathbf{d} = \mathrm{R}_\mathbf{d}\mathbf{e}$ for all $\mathbf{d} \in \mathrm{S}^2$. The axiom of *closure* is satisfied as both rotation matrices and $\pm\mathrm{I}$ map points on S^2 onto S^2. The axiom of *identity* follows from $\mathbf{d} \star \mathbf{e} = \mathrm{R}_\mathbf{d}\mathrm{I}\mathbf{e} = \mathrm{R}_\mathbf{d}\mathbf{e} = \mathbf{d}$ and $\mathbf{e} \star \mathbf{d} = \mathrm{I}\mathrm{R}_\mathbf{d}\mathbf{e} = \mathbf{d}$. The axiom of *invertibility* is guaranteed by $\mathbf{d} \star \mathbf{d}^{-1} = \mathrm{R}_\mathbf{d}\mathrm{R}_\mathbf{d}^{-1}\mathbf{e} = \mathrm{I}\mathbf{e} = \mathbf{e}$ and $\mathbf{d}^{-1} \star \mathbf{d} = \mathrm{R}_\mathbf{d}^{-1}\mathrm{R}_\mathbf{d}\mathbf{e} = \mathrm{I}\mathbf{e} = \mathbf{e}$. □

The profound relation between minimal length curves starting at $\mathbf{e}$, the exponential map at $\mathbf{e}$ and our product structure is best illustrated by Theorem 2.

Theorem 2: The product structure of Theorem 1 is related to the exponential map of S^2 at $\mathbf{e}$, which traces out minimal length curves with $\mathrm{Exp}(t\mathfrak{d})$, by the Taylor series of the exponential function, i.e.

$$e^{\mathfrak{d}} \equiv \sum_{n=0}^{\infty} \frac{\mathfrak{d}^n}{n!} = (\cos(\|\mathfrak{d}\|), \sin(\|\mathfrak{d}\|)\frac{\mathfrak{d}}{\|\mathfrak{d}\|}) \tag{19}$$

where $\mathfrak{d} \in T_\mathbf{e}\mathcal{M}$ and $0 < \|\mathfrak{d}\|$.

Proof: In order to evaluate $\mathfrak{d}^n$, with $n \in \{0, \mathbb{Z}^+\}$, the product structure must be expressed on tangent vectors in $\mathfrak{d} \in T_\mathbf{e}\mathcal{M}$ for which $0 < \|\mathfrak{d}\|$. We can do so by defining the map $\mathcal{S} : T_\mathbf{e}\mathcal{M} \to \mathrm{S}^2$, $\mathcal{S}(\mathfrak{d}) = (0, \frac{\mathfrak{d}}{\|\mathfrak{d}\|})$. For $n = 0$ the power is then defined by $\mathfrak{d}^0 = \mathbf{e}$ and for $0 < n$ it is defined by $\mathfrak{d}^n = \|\mathfrak{d}\|(\mathfrak{d}^{n-1} \star \mathcal{S}(\mathfrak{d}))$. The powers of order 1 and higher evaluate to

$$\begin{array}{llll} \mathfrak{d}^1 = \|\mathfrak{d}\|(0, \frac{\mathfrak{d}}{\|\mathfrak{d}\|}), & \mathfrak{d}^2 = -\|\mathfrak{d}\|^2\mathbf{e}, & \mathfrak{d}^3 = -\|\mathfrak{d}\|^3(0, \frac{\mathfrak{d}}{\|\mathfrak{d}\|}), & \mathfrak{d}^4 = \|\mathfrak{d}\|^4\mathbf{e}, \\ \mathfrak{d}^5 = \|\mathfrak{d}\|^5(0, \frac{\mathfrak{d}}{\|\mathfrak{d}\|}), & \mathfrak{d}^6 = -\|\mathfrak{d}\|^6\mathbf{e}, & \mathfrak{d}^7 = -\|\mathfrak{d}\|^7(0, \frac{\mathfrak{d}}{\|\mathfrak{d}\|}), & \ldots \end{array} \tag{20}$$

In geometric terms, every power $\mathfrak{d}^n$ rotates $(0, \frac{\mathfrak{d}}{\|\mathfrak{d}\|})$ over its geodesic, which starts at $\mathbf{e}$ and goes through $(0, \frac{\mathfrak{d}}{\|\mathfrak{d}\|})$, with angle $\frac{(n-1)}{2}\pi$. From the equalities in Eq. 20 it follows that

$$\begin{aligned} e^{\mathfrak{d}} &\equiv \textstyle\sum_{n=0}^{\infty} \frac{\mathfrak{d}^n}{n!} \\ &= \mathbf{e} + \mathfrak{d} - \frac{\|\mathfrak{d}\|^2}{2!}\mathbf{e} - \frac{\|\mathfrak{d}\|^3}{3!}(0, \frac{\mathfrak{d}}{\|\mathfrak{d}\|}) + \frac{\|\mathfrak{d}\|^4}{4!}\mathbf{e} + \frac{\|\mathfrak{d}\|^5}{5!}(0, \frac{\mathfrak{d}}{\|\mathfrak{d}\|}) - \frac{\|\mathfrak{d}\|^6}{6!}\mathbf{e} - \ldots \\ &= (1 - \frac{\|\mathfrak{d}\|^2}{2!} + \frac{\|\mathfrak{d}\|^4}{4!} - \frac{\|\mathfrak{d}\|^6}{6!} + \ldots)\mathbf{e} + (\|\mathfrak{d}\| - \frac{\|\mathfrak{d}\|^3}{3!} + \frac{\|\mathfrak{d}\|^5}{5!} - \ldots)(0, \frac{\mathfrak{d}}{\|\mathfrak{d}\|}) \\ &= \cos(\|\mathfrak{d}\|)\mathbf{e} + \sin\|\mathfrak{d}\|(0, \frac{\mathfrak{d}}{\|\mathfrak{d}\|}) \\ &= (\cos(\|\mathfrak{d}\|), \sin(\|\mathfrak{d}\|)\frac{\mathfrak{d}}{\|\mathfrak{d}\|}). \end{aligned} \tag{21}$$

□

Similar proofs are well known for the unit circle and for unit quaternions and many other useful Lie groups [27]. We have extended this to include the *non-Lie-group* S^2. The deeper mathematical foundations (i.e. the Levi-Civita connection [21] of S^2) related to our product on S^2 are beyond the scope of this text. Our purpose here is to prove that such a product exists and that it has useful applications to manifold statistics.

3.2 Alternative Approach

Alternative Riemannian mappings for essential matrices were proposed earlier in [5, 7] within the context of manifold statistics. In this section we prove that their Riemannian mappings are incorrect as they are ambiguous, i.e. they do not map essential matrices which represent the same epipolar configuration to a unique point on the manifold.

Performing a singular value decomposition on an essential matrix results in $\mathrm{E} = \mathrm{U}\Sigma\mathrm{V}^\top$. The first two singular values of Σ are identical elements of $\mathbb{R}^+$ and the last one is zero [24]. Since an essential matrix is a projective entity, it is not affected by scaling, hence Σ can be set to $\Sigma_1 = \mathrm{diag}\{1, 1, 0\}$. When $\det(\mathrm{U}) = \det(\mathrm{V}) = 1$ the four possible epipolar configurations on $S^2 \times SO(3)$ belonging to the essential matrix $\mathrm{E} = \mathrm{U}\Sigma\mathrm{V}^\top$ are $(+\mathbf{u}_3, \mathrm{UWV}^\top)$, $(+\mathbf{u}_3, \mathrm{UW}^\top\mathrm{V}^\top)$, $(-\mathbf{u}_3, \mathrm{UWV}^\top)$ and $(-\mathbf{u}_3, \mathrm{UW}^\top\mathrm{V}^\top)$ where $\mathrm{W} = \begin{bmatrix} 0 & -1 & 0 \\ 1 & 0 & 0 \\ 0 & 0 & 1 \end{bmatrix}$ and $\mathbf{u}_3$ is the last column of U[24]. As pointed out in [24] performing a rotation around the z-axis by an angle γ, denoted as $\mathrm{R}_z(\gamma)$, does not change the essential matrix. Furthermore, due to its projective nature the essential matrices E and −E both relate to the same epipolar configurations. This equivalence relation is denoted as $\mathrm{E} =_{\mathrm{H}} -\mathrm{E}$. For the SVD of E we thus have the equality

$$\mathrm{U}\,\mathrm{R}_z(\gamma)\,\Sigma_1\,(\mathrm{V}\,\mathrm{R}_z(\gamma + k\pi))^\top \;=\; (-1)^k\,\mathrm{U}\Sigma_1\mathrm{V}^\top \;=_{\mathrm{H}}\; \pm\mathrm{E}, \tag{22}$$

with $k \in \mathbb{Z}$. This shows that there is a more general equivalence class of essential matrices, denoted as $\mathcal{R}_z$, which all encode the same epipolar configuration. The claim in [5, 7] is that they can map all elements of $\mathcal{R}_z$ to a single point on a Riemannian manifold without using image data or the positive-depth constraint. We now prove that their claim is incorrect pointing out an unavoidable ambiguity in their mappings.

Consider that when computing the SVD there is an arbitrariness in the choice for the basis vectors being used. For a 3×3 matrix there are 8 such choices. The choice being made often depends on considerations driven by numerical stability but it could just as well be random. This arbitrary choice results in the following equality

$$\mathrm{E} = \mathrm{UB}\Sigma(\mathrm{V}(\pm\mathrm{B}))^\top = \pm\mathrm{U}\Sigma\mathrm{V}^\top =_{\mathrm{H}} \pm\mathrm{E} \tag{23}$$

where $\mathrm{B} = \mathrm{diag}\{\pm1, \pm1, \pm1\}$. In [24] it is implicitly assumed that $\det(\mathrm{U}) = \det(\mathrm{V}) = 1$ i.e. U and V are both elements of SO(3). Due to B both U and V are merely orthogonal transformations, i.e. they are combinations of rotations and reflections. Since the last singular value of Σ is zero, the last column of both U and V can be multiplied by −1 such that their determinants become positive without changing the essential matrix. This ensures that U and V become elements of SO(3) and ensures that retrieving the correct epipolar configuration by using the positive-depth constraint is unaffected by B. This is not true for the approach in [5, 7].

The task in [5, 7] is to take the essential matrix E_2 (with SVD $\mathrm{U}_2\mathrm{diag}\{1,1,0\}\mathrm{V}_2^\top$), to a unique point in the tangent space of E_1 (with SVD $\mathrm{U}_1\mathrm{diag}\{1,1,0\}\mathrm{V}_1^\top$). The general form of their logarithmic map is

$$\mathrm{Log}_{\mathrm{E}_1}(\mathrm{E}_2) = (\mathrm{Log}(\mathrm{U}_1^\top \mathrm{U}_2), \mathrm{Log}(\mathrm{V}_1^\top \mathrm{V}_2)) = (\mathfrak{u}, \mathfrak{v}) \tag{24}$$

where Log on the right side of the equality denotes the Riemannian logarithmic map on SO(3) and $(\mathfrak{u}, \mathfrak{v}) \in \mathfrak{so}(3) \times \mathfrak{so}(3)$. The exponential map of the SM method is defined as

$$\mathrm{Exp}_{\mathrm{E}_1}((\mathfrak{u}, \mathfrak{v})) = (\mathrm{U}_1\mathrm{Exp}(\mathfrak{u}), \mathrm{V}_1\mathrm{Exp}(\mathfrak{v})) \tag{25}$$

where Exp on the right side of the equality denotes the Riemannian exponential map on $\mathfrak{so}(3)$. This is conceptually similar to a multiple geodesic approach of two copies of SO(3). The challenge is that both E_1 and E_2 are general elements of their own equivalence classes but the logarithmic map must return the same tangent vector for all combinations consistently.

In [5, 7] the equivalence class $\mathcal{R}_z$ is resolved by enforcing $\log_{\mathrm{E}_1}(\mathrm{E}_2)$ to have the form $[u_x, u_y, z, v_x, v_y, -z]^\top$. It does so by an initialization procedure followed by iteratively updating the development point according to $\mathrm{E}_1 = \exp_{\mathrm{E}_1}([0, 0, \delta, 0, 0, \delta])$ for some δ. This basically applies z-axis rotations which assure that all essential matrices in $\mathcal{R}_z$ are mapped to a single point. The resulting tangent vector $[u_x, u_y, z, v_x, v_y, -z]^\top$ has the same number of degrees of freedom as an essential matrix, i.e. five, and therefore provides a minimal representation. This representation is not unique however.

The focus is on B related to choice of basis when computing the SVD. If the claim in [5, 7] is correct, then every choice for B must result in the same point on their manifold. By ensuring a positive unit determinant of U and V the four choices for B related to reflections, i.e. $\mathrm{diag}\{-1,-1,-1\}$, $\mathrm{diag}\{-1,1,1\}$, $\mathrm{diag}\{1,-1,1\}$ and $\mathrm{diag}\{1,1,-1\}$, are mapped to $\mathrm{diag}\{-1,-1,1\}$, $\mathrm{diag}\{-1,1,-1\}$, $\mathrm{diag}\{1,-1,-1\}$ and $\mathrm{diag}\{1,1,1\}$ respectively. Note that the identity $\mathrm{I} = \mathrm{diag}\{1,1,1\}$ and $\mathrm{diag}\{-1,-1,1\}$ are both elements of $\mathcal{R}_z$ and can therefore be resolved to I. The remaining two elements of $\mathcal{B}$, i.e. $\mathrm{diag}\{1,-1,-1\} = \mathrm{R}_x(\pm\pi)$ and $\mathrm{diag}\{-1,1,-1\} = \mathrm{R}_y(\pm\pi)$, relate to rotations by an angle $\pm\pi$ around respectively the *x*-axis and *y*-axis. They are not elements of $\mathcal{R}_z$. Indeed, $\mathrm{R}_x(\pm\pi)\ \mathrm{R}_z(\pm\pi) = \mathrm{R}_y(\pm\pi)$ and therefore the initialization procedure in [5, 7] should ideally be able to map both to a single element, e.g. $\mathrm{R}_y(\pm\pi)$ (but [5, 7] provide no control over which one). When nevertheless assuming that $\mathrm{R}_x(\pm\pi)$ is mapped to $\mathrm{R}_y(\pm\pi)$ consistently, then there are still two choices for B. They are: I and $\mathrm{R}_y(\pm\pi)$. They clearly do not differ by a *z*-axis rotation. Therefore, both will be mapped to tangents of the form $[u_x, u_y, z, v_x, v_y, -z]^\top$ but these tangent vectors will not be equal. Hence, there remains at least a twofold ambiguity in the approach of [5, 7].

Instead of trying to resolve the four-fold ambiguity algebraically as in [5, 7], we exploit the positive-depth constraint before applying our mappings.

4 Experimental Evaluation

Our novel Riemannian mappings and those in [5, 7] are evaluated by incorporating them into two intrinsic statistical algorithms. One algorithm computes the intrinsic mean [3] the other computes the dominant mode by using intrinsic mean-shift [4, 5, 6, 7, 8]. When reporting results of our mappings we use the prefix *Our* and for the mappings in [5, 7] we use the prefix *SM* (Subbarao and Meer). The mappings in [15, 16, 17] are not evaluated as they cannot be used *as is* for manifold statistics.

4.1 Maximum Likelihood Lower Bound

Artificial image data is generated by projecting 3D world points onto two camera planes. The poses between the cameras are randomly generated with translation directions uniformly distributed over the unit sphere, translation distance varying uniformly between 1 m and 10 m and rotation yaw, pitch and roll parameters distributed uniformly in the interval $\pm 45^\circ$. Gaussian image noise with $\sigma = 0.2$ pixel is added to the projections. Essential matrices are estimated on minimal subsets, i.e. of size 5 point correspondences.

Fig.2(a,d) depicts the results (on a logarithmic scale) of computing the intrinsic mean on an increasing number of essential matrices. For this experiment the essential matrices are obtained using an ML estimator which minimizes reprojection errors.

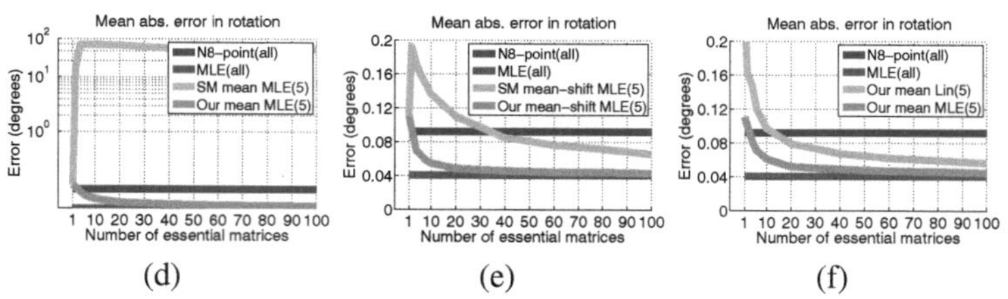

Fig. 2. Result averaged over 500 poses. Errors in translation direction are visualized in the top row and rotational errors in the bottom row. See Sec. 4.1 for details.

It can clearly be seen that when using our mappings, the accuracy asymptotically reaches the ML lower bound, i.e. the accuracy of an ML estimator on all image points. For reference, the accuracy of the normalized 8-point algorithm on all image points is also shown. When using the mappings of [5, 7], the mean does not produce a useable result. This is because all essential matrices, which only differ by a small random perturbation from the ground truth, are mapped to two clusters far apart from each other instead of to one. This is due to the two-fold ambiguity in their mappings. Computing the mean on these two clusters will result in a point in between the two clusters which does not correspond to the ground truth. This experiment clearly illustrates our theoretical findings of Sec. 3.2.

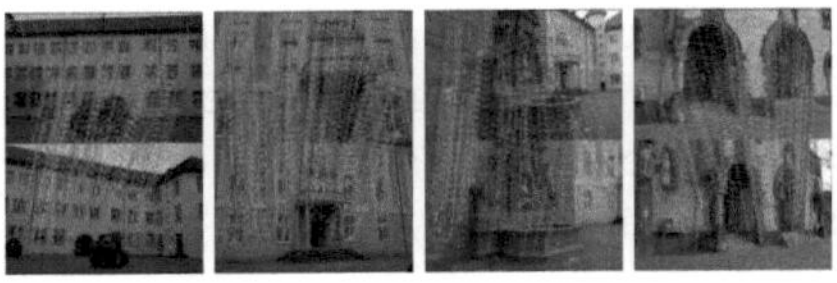

(a) (b) (c) (d)

Fig. 3. Example image pairs from the benchmark images provided by [28]

	Max. subset	Tra. dir.	Rot.
Cov-RANSAC	14	0.39°	0.13°
LO-RANSAC	all inliers	0.27°	0.08°
Our mean-shift	5	1.21°	0.43°
SM mean-shift	5	1.47°	0.77°
Our top10-mean	5	**0.26°**	**0.07°**
SM top10-mean	5	24.9°	28.4°

Table 1. Absolute error averaged over 10 runs on 44 benchmark images of [28]

The experimental evaluation in [5, 7] did not reveal this because the statistical algorithm used in [5, 7] is mean-shift. In Fig.2(b,e) we therefore show the result obtained when using mean-shift. When using the mappings in [5, 7] accuracy converges but results are still factors less accurate than when using our mappings. This is because mean-shift with the mappings in [5, 7] converges to the mode of the most dominant of two clusters and ignores the other cluster. It will therefore not use all available statistical information, though it will produce a result. Also note that its error on two essential matrices is larger than that of a single essential matrix. This is because for two essential matrices, there can be no dominant cluster. Our mappings do not exhibit this behavior.

In Fig.2(c,f) we show the result of our method when using a linear estimator (5-point algorithm) to generate the essential matrices. Again we see that the mean converges to satisfactory accuracy. Its rotational estimate even becomes more accurate than that of the normalized 8-point algorithm on all image points. Resolving the four-fold ambiguity is taken care of within our ML estimator, but for the 5-point algorithm we have to do it explicitly before applying our Riemannian mappings. We do this efficiently by immediately rejecting a configuration as soon as one point from the minimal subset is behind a camera. We found that there is practically no difference in the computation time between this approach and the iterative approach of [5, 7].

4.2 Robust Pose Clustering and RANSAC

We now show the practical relevance of our theoretical work by comparing against dominant state-of-the-art robust estimators, i.e. Cov-RANSAC[19] and LO-RANSAC[20]. We evaluate on 44 benchmark images of [28], see Fig. 3, which are accompanied by ground-truth pose information. All approaches use ML estimators for improved accuracy and extensive parameters sweeps are performed to assure that their accuracy is not limited by sub-optimal parameter settings.

The satisfactory accuracy of Cov-RANSAC and LO-RANSAC averaged over ten runs (i.e. 440 image pairs) is depicted in the top two rows of Table 1. Note the favorable accuracy of LO-RANSAC as it computes inner ML estimates on all inliers. This however counterbalances its reduction in the number of iterations which causes this LO-RANSAC approach to be around 1.5 times slower than regular RANSAC while our Cov-RANCAC implementation is around 2.5 times faster. The outlier percentage of the data sets estimated by these methods is 70%. The next two rows in Table 1 are of mean-shift applied to models obtained from regular RANSAC as in [5, 7]. These errors are factors higher than those of the state-of-the-art RANSAC methods. However, it can again be observed that when using our Riemannian mappings, improved accuracy is obtained. While mean-shift clearly has great practical relevance, it is no match for Cov-RANSAC and LO-RANSAC in this experimental context.

The final two rows in Table 1 show the accuracy when computing the intrinsic mean on the top-10 ranking RANSAC models, which is a *RANSAC-manifold hybrid* method. It can be observed that when using our Riemannian mappings this obtains optimal accuracy for both directional and rotational estimates. This is because there are typically models estimated on points which are on the boundary of being inliers but are not real outliers either. These models can be identified based on their relative high number of inliers and computing their intrinsic mean can be as accurate as an ML estimate on the union of their subsets. This was demonstrated in Fig.2(a,d,c,f). The hybrid approach has practically the same computation time as regular RANSAC. When using the mappings in [5, 7] to compute the mean, no satisfactory accuracy is obtained.

The purpose of this experiment is to illustrate the advantage of using our mappings in a realistic setting. Their purpose is explicitly not to provide a comparison against all *state-of-the-art* RANSAC methods.

5 Conclusions

We have provided correct Riemannian logarithmic and exponential mappings for essential matrices. They allow the generalization of statistical algorithms designed for Euclidean vector spaces to the manifold of essential matrices. Mapping functions proposed earlier were proven to be incorrect. Using them within statistical calculation leads to sub-optimal or even erroneous results. Our theoretical findings are shown to be relevant to whoever is interested in developing robust statistical algorithms for essential matrices.

References

1. Karcher, H.: Riemannian Center of Mass and Mollifier Smoothing. Communications on Pure and Applied Mathematics 30, 509–541 (1977)
2. Pennec, X., Ayache, N.: Uniform Distribution, Distance and Expectation Problems for Geometric Features Processing. Journal of Mathematical Imaging and Vision 9, 49–67 (1998)
3. Pennec, X.: Intrinsic Statistics on Riemannian Manifolds: Basic Tools for Geometric Measurements. Journal of Mathematical Imaging and Vision 25, 127–154 (2006)
4. Subbarao, R., Meer, P.: Nonlinear Mean Shift for Clustering over Analytic Manifolds. In: IEEE Computer Society Conference on Computer Vision and Pattern Recognition, vol. 1, pp. 1168–1175 (2006)
5. Subbarao, R., Meer, P.: Nonlinear Mean Shift over Riemannian Manifolds. International Journal of Computer Vision 84, 1–20 (2009)
6. Subbarao, R., Genc, Y., Meer, P.: Nonlinear Mean Shift for Robust Pose Estimation. In: IEEE Workshop on Applications of Computer Vision, vol. 6 (2007)
7. Subbarao, R., Genc, Y., Meer, P.: Robust Unambiguous Parametrization of the Essential Manifold. In: IEEE Conference on Computer Vision and Pattern Recognition, pp. 1–8 (2008)

8. Tuzel, O., Subbarao, R., Meer, P.: Simultaneous Multiple 3D Motion Estimation via Mode Finding on Lie Groups. In: Proceedings of the Tenth IEEE International Conference on Computer Vision, vol. 1, pp. 18–25 (2005)
9. Costa, J., Hero, A.O.: Learning I. In: Statistics and Analysis of Shapes, pp. 231–252. Birkhauser, Cambridge (2006)
10. Fletcher, P.T., Joshi, S.: Riemannian Geometry for the Statistical Analysis of Diffusion Tensor Data. Signal Processing 87, 250–262 (2007)
11. Pennec, X., Guttmann, C.R.G., Thirion, J.: Feature-based Registration of Medical Images: Estimation and Validation of the Pose Accuracy. In: Wells, W.M., Colchester, A.C.F., Delp, S.L. (eds.) MICCAI 1998. LNCS, vol. 1496, pp. 1107–1114. Springer, Heidelberg (1998)
12. Begelfor, E., Werman, M.: Affine Invariance Revisited. In: IEEE Computer Society Conference on Computer Vision and Pattern Recognition, pp. 2087–2094 (2006)
13. Goh, A., Vidal, R.: Clustering and Dimensionality Reduction on Riemannian Manifolds. In: IEEE Computer Society Conference on Computer Vision and Pattern Recognition, pp. 1–7 (2008)
14. Tuzel, O., Porikli, F., Meer, P.: Pedestrian Detection via Classification on Riemannian Manifolds. IEEE Transactions on Pattern Analysis and Machine Intelligence 30, 1713–1727 (2008)
15. Helmke, U., Hüper, K., Lee, P.Y., Moore, J.: Essential Matrix Estimation Using Gauss-Newton Iterations on a Manifold. International Journal of Computer Vision 74, 117–136 (2007)
16. Kŏsecká, J., Ma, Y., Sastry, S.S.: Optimization Criteria, Sensitivity and Robustness of Motion and Structure Estimation. In: Triggs, B., Zisserman, A., Szeliski, R. (eds.) ICCV-WS 1999. LNCS, vol. 1883, pp. 166–182. Springer, Heidelberg (2000)
17. Ma, Y., Košecká, J., Sastry, S.: Optimization Criteria and Geometric Algorithms for Motion and Structure Estimation. International Journal of Computer Vision 44, 219–249 (2001)
18. Fischler, M.A., Bolles, R.C.: Random sample consensus: a paradigm for model fitting with applications to image analysis and automated cartography. Communications of the ACM 24, 381–395 (1981)
19. Raguram, R., Frahm, J., Pollefeys, M.: Exploiting Uncertainty in Random Sample Consensus. In: International Conference on Computer Vision (2009)
20. Chum, O., Matas, J., Kittler, J.: Locally Optimized RANSAC. In: Michaelis, B., Krell, G. (eds.) DAGM 2003. LNCS, vol. 2781, pp. 236–243. Springer, Heidelberg (2003)
21. do Carmo, M.P.: Riemannian Geometry, 1st edn. Mathematics: Theory and Applications. Birkhäuser (1992)
22. Cullen, H.F.: Introduction to General Topology, Heath, Boston (1967)
23. Longuet-Higgins, H.C.: A Computer Algorithm for Reconstructing a Scene from Two Projections. Nature 293, 133–135 (1981)
24. Hartley, R.I., Zisserman, A.: Multiple View Geometry in Computer Vision, 2nd edn. Cambridge University Press (2004) ISBN: 0521540518
25. Park, F.C.: Distance Metrics on the Rigid-Body Motions with Applications to Mechanism Design. Transactions of the ASME 117, 48–54 (1995)
26. Eisenberg, M., Guy, R.: A Proof of the Hairy Ball Theorem. The American Mathematical Monthly 86, 571–574 (1979)
27. Selig, J.M.: Geometrical Methods in Robotics. Springer (1996)
28. Strecha, C., von Hansen, W., van Gool, L., Fua, P., Thoennessen, U.: On Benchmarking Camera Calibration and Multi-View Stereo for High Resolution Imagery. In: IEEE Conference on Computer Vision and Pattern Recognition, pp. 1–8 (2008)

Covariance Propagation and Next Best View Planning for 3D Reconstruction

Sebastian Haner and Anders Heyden

Centre for Mathematical Sciences
Lund University, Sweden
{haner,heyden}@maths.lth.se
http://www.maths.lth.se

Abstract. This paper examines the potential benefits of applying next best view planning to sequential 3D reconstruction from unordered image sequences. A standard sequential structure-and-motion pipeline is extended with active selection of the order in which cameras are resectioned. To this end, approximate covariance propagation is implemented throughout the system, providing running estimates of the uncertainties of the reconstruction, while also enhancing robustness and accuracy. Experiments show that the use of expensive global bundle adjustment can be reduced throughout the process, while the additional cost of propagation is essentially linear in the problem size.

Keywords: Structure and motion, covariance propagation, next best view planning.

1 Introduction

Three-dimensional reconstruction from unordered image sequences is a well-studied problem in the computer vision literature, see e.g. [1,2,3,4,5]. Part of the challenge is that little is known about the input data at the outset in terms of scene coverage or camera calibration. Active sensor planning, on the other hand, is the problem of finding the optimal input data to a reconstruction algorithm, given full control over image acquisition (see [6] for an overview). In the photogrammetry literature this is known as the 'camera network design' problem. For example, in [7] a genetic algorithm is used to search a high-dimensional parameter space of camera placements to find the optimal measurement setup, given a limited number of cameras. In a serial acquisition process, the 'next best view' (NBV) problem asks from which viewpoint to capture the next image, given a partial reconstruction, to minimize some objective such as the reconstruction error. NBV planning is most effective when the user has full control over image acquisition, and has been applied to vision metrology using cameras mounted on robotic arms [8,9], and autonomous robot exploration [10,11].

This paper applies view planning to the unordered image reconstruction problem; although we are not free to choose any viewpoint, there is usually a choice between a subset of the images at every step of a sequential algorithm. The

A. Fitzgibbon et al. (Eds.): ECCV 2012, Part II, LNCS 7573, pp. 545–556, 2012.

aim is to choose the image giving the smallest error, which we approximate as the trace of the camera covariance matrix times the reprojection error. To be able to determine the covariance, it is necessary to know the uncertainty of the observed geometry. In the following sections, it is shown how this is achieved by propagating covariances when resectioning cameras and triangulating points, and how as a side effect the algorithms gain robustness and better approximate the maximum likelihood estimate.

2 Estimation from Uncertain Geometry

The cornerstones of sequential structure-and-motion are triangulation and camera pose estimation. Usually, one attempts to find the maximum likelihood solution given noisy image measurements, but assuming that all other parameters are known exactly. This is of course rarely the case, since points and cameras are triangulated and resectioned using noisy data. Below, we derive algorithms that also take the uncertainty of the 3D structure or camera parameters into account.

2.1 Pose Estimation

Consider the problem of camera pose estimation given N 3D point coordinates X and their measured projections in one image, $\tilde{x}$. Assuming there are errors in the image measurements, the problem is to find the maximum likelihood solution, i.e. the camera parameters θ^* satisfying

$$\theta^* = \arg\max_{\theta} \; \mathcal{L}(\theta) \,, \tag{1}$$

where

$$\mathcal{L}(\theta) = \mathcal{L}(\theta \,|\, \tilde{x}, X) = p(\tilde{x} \,|\, \theta, X) \tag{2}$$

is the likelihood function. In this formulation it is assumed that the structure parameters X are precisely known. More generally, given a probability distribution of X, the problem is to maximize

$$\mathcal{L}(\theta) = \int_{\mathbb{R}^{3N}} p(\tilde{x} \,|\, \theta, X) p(X) \, dX \,. \tag{3}$$

We restrict our attention to the case of Gaussian distributions. Then we have

$$\mathcal{L}(\theta) \propto \int_{\mathbb{R}^{3N}} e^{-\|\tilde{x} - f(X,\theta)\|^2_R} \cdot e^{-\|X - \bar{X}\|^2_Q} \, dX \,, \tag{4}$$

where $f(X, \theta)$ is the projection of the points X using camera parameters θ, R the measurement error covariance, Q and $\bar{X}$ are the covariance matrix and mean of the distribution of X and $\|y\|^2_{\Sigma} = y^{\top} \Sigma^{-1} y$ the squared Mahalanobis distance. Next, we project the distribution of X onto the image plane, by integrating along the light rays. Formally, for a given θ we parametrize each 3D point by its image projection $x = f(X, \theta)$ and depth ρ, so that

$$\mathcal{L}(\theta) \propto \int_{\mathbb{R}^{2N}} e^{-\|\tilde{x}-x\|_R^2} \left(\int_{\mathbb{R}^N} e^{-\|(x,\rho)-\bar{X}\|_Q^2} \, d\rho \right) dx \,. \tag{5}$$

The right-hand factor is a distribution on the $2N$-dimensional generalized image plane, and may be seen as the projection of a random variable, i.e. $f\big(\mathcal{N}(\bar{X}, Q), \theta\big)$. By Taylor expansion about $\bar{X}$, f can be approximated by $\tilde{f}(X, \theta) = f(\bar{X}, \theta) + J(X - \bar{X})$, and for affine functions $\tilde{f}\big(\mathcal{N}(\mu, \Sigma), \theta\big) = \mathcal{N}\big(\tilde{f}(\mu, \theta), J_X \Sigma J_X^\top\big)$ with $J_X = \frac{\partial f}{\partial X}\big|_\theta$. We now have

$$\mathcal{L}(\theta) \underset{\sim}{\propto} \int_{\mathbb{R}^{2N}} e^{-\|\tilde{x}-x\|_R^2} \cdot e^{-\|f(\bar{X},\theta)-x\|_{JQJ^\top}^2} \, dx \,, \tag{6}$$

which is just the convolution $\mathcal{N}(\tilde{x}, R) * \mathcal{N}(0, JQJ^\top) = \mathcal{N}(\tilde{x}, R + JQJ^\top)$. Maximizing

$$\mathcal{L}(\theta) \underset{\sim}{\propto} e^{-\|\tilde{x}-f(\bar{X},\theta)\|_{R+JQJ^\top}^2} \tag{7}$$

is then equivalent to minimizing

$$-\log \mathcal{L}(\theta) \underset{\sim}{\propto} \|\tilde{x} - f(\bar{X}, \theta)\|_{R+JQJ^\top}^2 \,, \tag{8}$$

which can be solved using an iteratively reweighted nonlinear least-squares algorithm. In fact, only a minor modification to a standard algorithm for minimizing the reprojection error is required. For example, a Levenberg-Marquardt optimization loop would be modified to

while not converged **do**
  ...
  $W \leftarrow (R + J_X Q J_X^\top)^{-1}$
  $\delta\theta \leftarrow (J_\theta^\top W J_\theta + \lambda I)^{-1} J_\theta^\top W b$
  ...
end while

where $J_\theta = \frac{\partial f}{\partial \theta}\big|_\theta$ and J_X as above. After convergence, the covariance matrix of the recovered camera parameters θ^* can be estimated by the inverse of the Hessian matrix evaluated at the minimum, $\Sigma_\theta \approx (J_{\theta^*} W^* J_{\theta^*}^\top)^{-1}$ [12,13].

Of course, a good initial guess is required to start the iterative algorithm, and can be obtained using standard minimal or linear solvers. The general effect of taking the distribution of X into account is to give more weight to well-determined 3D points than uncertain ones when finding the camera pose.

2.2 Triangulation

Handling uncertainty in camera parameters when triangulating 3D structure is completely analogous to the pose estimation case. The linearized problem formulation is to find

$$\theta^* = \arg\min_\theta \|\tilde{x} - f(\theta, \bar{P})\|_{R+JSJ^\top}^2 \,, \tag{9}$$

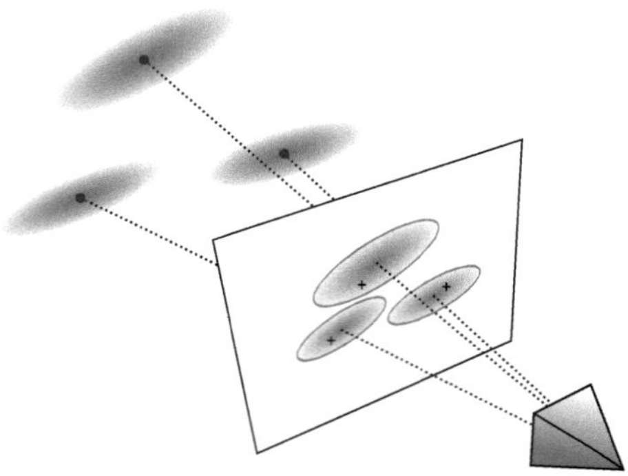

Fig. 1. Resectioning: the uncertainties of the 3D points are projected onto the image plane and convolved with the image measurement uncertainty giving the reprojection error metric. Note that the projections are not necessarily independent; however, in this work inter-point covariances are discarded for computational reasons.

where θ now represents the 3D structure, $\bar{P}$ is the mean of the distribution of the cameras with covariance S and $J = \frac{\partial f}{\partial P}\big|_\theta$.

2.3 Complexity

The introduction of the weight matrix W in the algorithms above inevitably incurs extra computational costs. In particular, if the input variables are correlated, W will be a full matrix and the natural sparsity of the problems is lost. To mitigate this, we will assume no correlation between pairs of cameras or points, so that W is block diagonal. Such simplification is also necessary since the full covariance matrix of even a moderately sized reconstruction problem would occupy hundreds of gigabytes of memory. Furthermore, it may not be necessary to recompute W every iteration, since the projection is not expected to change significantly given a good initialization.

3 Covariance Propagation

The proposed algorithms open the possibility of covariance propagation throughout the reconstruction process. Uncertainties in 3D points are transferred to uncertainty in resectioned cameras, which in turn transfer uncertainty to triangulated points, and so on. In this manner, a rough estimate of the covariances is available at any time and can be used, for example, to improve reconstruction accuracy and for next best view planning, which we exploit to reduce error accumulation.

Below we detail a system for 3D reconstruction from unordered image sequences and show the benefits that can be gained.

3.1 Selecting the Seed

In choosing the set of images on which to initialize the reconstruction, we strive for the following: the initial reconstruction should be stable, contain many structure points and it should be near the center of the camera graph (the graph with each camera a vertex and edges between cameras observing common features). The latter is motivated by the fact that error accumulation is a function of the distance from the seed; if the 'degrees of separation' from the seed is kept low, error accumulation can be minimized. We therefore wish to minimize the distance of every camera to the seed. For our purposes we define the center as any vertex of the camera connectivity graph with minimal *farness*, the sum of shortest distances from the node to all others. We define the edge weights of the graph as $1/\max(0, n_c - 4)$, where n_c is the number of observed points common to both cameras. This heuristic, while ignoring the actual two-view geometry, is based on the assumption that cameras sharing many observed points are well-determined relative to each other. The maximum imposes a 5 point overlap threshold, needed to determine relative motion between views. Now, all shortest paths in the graph can be computed and summed for each camera, the k lowest scoring yielding a set of candidate images. For each candidate, an adjacent view with a balance between many common image points and good parallax is selected as in [1], i.e. each pairing is scored according to the proportion of outliers to a homography fit. The top-scoring pair is selected, and standard two-view reconstruction is performed, followed by bundle adjustment.

In experiments, the effect of choosing a seed near the center of the graph turns out to be relatively small, so this step is not essential.

3.2 Fixing the Gauge

Reconstruction from image measurements only is subject to global translation, rotation and scale ambiguity. Unlike [14], which measured pairwise covariances in local coordinate systems, we need globally referenced covariances and so must compute these for the seed reconstruction. For the covariances to be defined we must fix the gauge, especially the scale, since the dimension of the nullspace of the Hessian matches the number of degrees of freedom of the system. From a theoretical standpoint, taking the pseudoinverse of the unconstrained Hessian is the most satisfying solution [12,13], however it can be computationally very expensive if the seed views share many points (i.e. > 1000). An alternative approach is to constrain the parameters of the system by adding penalties to the cost function, making the Hessian full rank so it can be inverted without finding an SVD. Different constraints lead to somewhat different estimates of the covariance; one way is to lock the first camera and impose a distance constraint on the mean of the structure points, as was done in [14], or one can simply fix the distance between the first and second camera. The first prior gives results closer to the pseudoinverse, but also destroys the sparsity of the Hessian matrix making inversion more expensive. In cases where the pseudoinverse is too expensive we choose the second option which preserves sparsity.

After fixing the scale, there is still a difficulty in quantifying just how large an uncertainty is, since it must be put in relation to the overall size of the reconstruction. The scale is unknown in the beginning, since there is no guarantee that the distance between the seed cameras is representative of the whole scene. This has implications for the various outlier rejection thresholds used in the reconstruction pipeline.

4 Next Best View Planning

View planning in a sequential reconstruction process aims to actively choose the most favorable sensor configuration (i.e. camera position and orientation) to achieve a certain goal, in this case geometric accuracy. In each iteration, we can choose which camera to resection among those observing a sufficient number of triangulated points. Usually, the camera observing the largest number of triangulated points is chosen first. However, if the geometry is such that the pose is poorly determined, triangulations using the image will have larger errors, propagating to subsequently resectioned cameras, etc. It therefore makes sense to minimize the error accumulation in every step. To this end, we propose to select the camera with lowest estimated reconstruction error, by exhaustive search among candidate images. The covariance is computed by first resectioning the camera using a linear or minimal solver and taking the inverse of the Hessian, $\Sigma_{\text{cam}} \approx (J_\theta W J_\theta^\top)^{-1}$ as defined in section 3. As a scalar measure of reconstruction error we use $\text{trace}(\Sigma_{\text{cam}}) \cdot \epsilon_{\text{rp}}$, where ϵ_{rp} is the mean reprojection error. This turns out to give better results than the covariance alone; a small estimated covariance does not necessarily imply a low reprojection error, and a well-determined camera should ideally have both. Note that the score can be cached for each camera between iterations and need only be recomputed if more points in the camera's view have been triangulated. While the number of views that need to be resectioned in each iteration is dependent on the particular data set and could theoretically grow with the number of triangulated points, in practice this number is found to be approximately constant throughout the reconstruction process and typically between 10 and 50.

5 Reconstruction Pipeline

We apply NBV planning and covariance propagation to the problem of reconstruction from unordered image collections. We will assume that matching and tracking of image features has been performed and is outlier free. If not, the proposed method is easily integrated with outlier detection schemes such as RANSAC. The algorithm is mainly standard fare:

1. Find initial seed views (section 3.1).
2. Reconstruct and bundle adjust the seed geometry.
3. Compute the covariance of the seed (section 3.2).

4. Choose a camera to resect following section 4. Resect using a linear method; if it fails (i.e. large reprojection error or points behind the camera) try an L_∞ formulation [15] instead. If that also fails, choose another camera and try again. Else, refine the camera pose by minimizing (8) and store its covariance.
5. Triangulate all points seen by at least two resectioned cameras using a linear method. Compute an approximate uncertainty by evaluating the Hessian of the standard reprojection error and taking the trace of the inverse. Well-determined points, i.e. with low covariance and reprojection error, as specified by thresholds, are kept and further refined by minimizing (9). Store the covariance derived from this reprojection error.
6. If possible, goto 4) and find the next view, else terminate.

Note that global optimization is only performed on the seed. In real use, bundle adjustment cannot be avoided, but as one aim of this algorithm is to reduce the need for this relatively expensive operation, this step has been left out in the experiments that follow to illustrate the reduction in error accumulation possible with the proposed method.

6 Experiments

Figure 2 shows a simple synthetic example of the dependence on the seed of the propagated covariances. Although the *relative* uncertainties between all cameras remain the same in our linearized Gaussian propagation model, in reality the reconstruction errors depend heavily on the path taken.

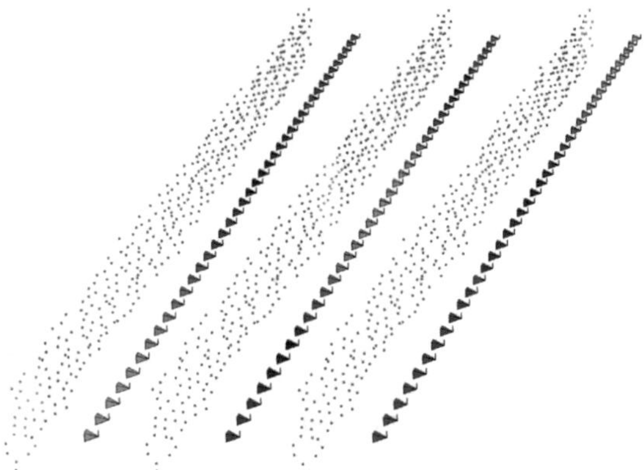

Fig. 2. Toy example of camera array observing a wall illustrating the covariance estimation results depending on which seed is chosen (from left to right, cameras 1 and 2, 19 and 20, 39 and 40). The points and cameras are color coded by the trace of their covariance, with green through blue to red for increasing uncertainty. Choosing the seed in the middle reduces the maximum camera uncertainty with respect to the seed.

Fig. 3. Resulting point cloud reconstruction of the 'Spilled blood' dataset using the proposed algorithm, color coded by estimated covariance. No bundle adjustment has been performed. The dataset has 781 images, 162,521 points and 2,541,736 feature measurements.

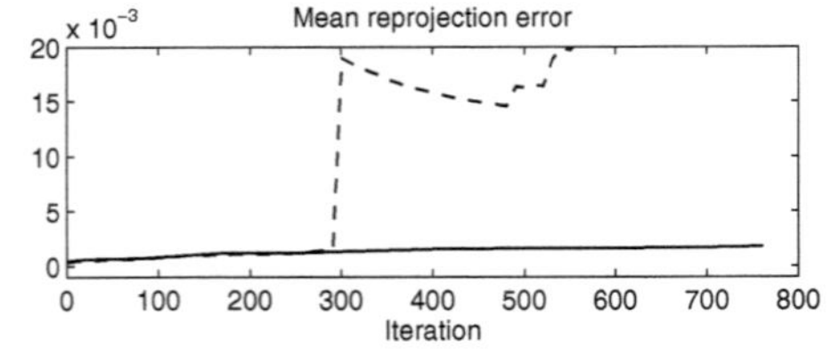

Fig. 4. Comparison between the proposed algorithm and a 'plain' method on the 'Spilled blood' dataset. In the plain method the standard reprojection error is minimized instead, and the next camera is chosen by the maximum overlap principle. Running times were 22 and 13 min respectively. There is no absolute scale on the top graph since it depends on the overall scale of the reconstruction, which is arbitrary.

Next, the algorithm is applied to a dataset extracted from photos of the 'Spilled blood' church in St. Petersburg. The reconstruction and a comparison with a standard method is shown in figures 3 and 4. The comparison shows the mean standard reprojection error and the ground truth deviation, defined

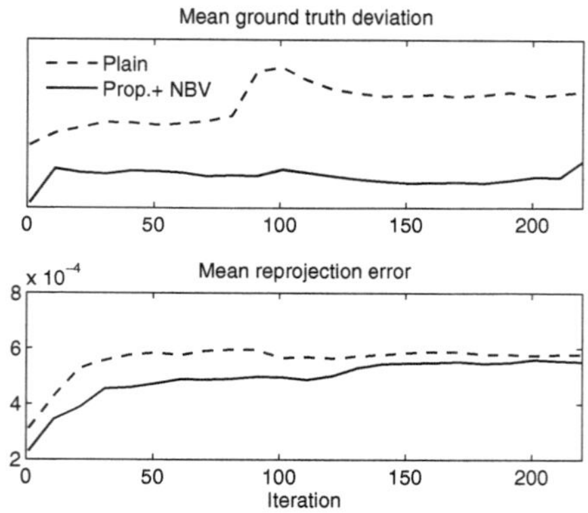

Fig. 5. Results for the Trafalgar dataset (256 images). Running times were 83 and 138 s respectively.

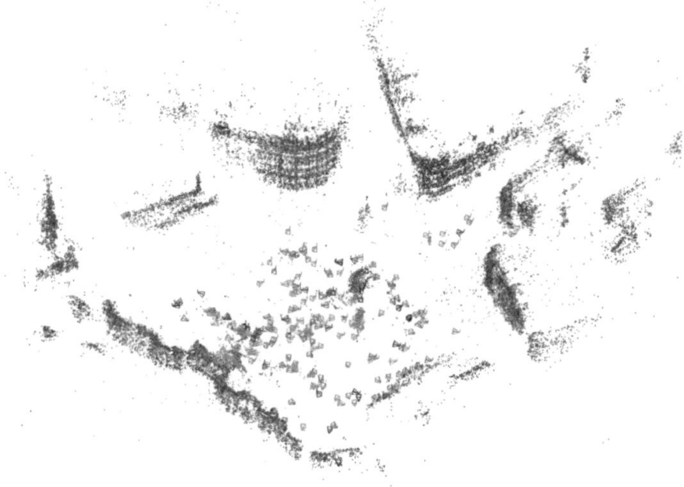

Fig. 6. Resulting point cloud reconstruction of the Trafalgar dataset

as the mean distance of each triangulated point from its ground truth position, after the two point clouds have been aligned using a Procrustes transformation. The 'ground truth' in this case has been obtained from the system described in [4]. The plain method, without covariance propagation or NBV planning, runs into trouble around iteration 300 and does not manage to resection all cameras, whereas the proposed algorithm does and is generally more robust and accurate. A similar comparison is made for the 'Trafalgar' dataset of [16] in figure 5.

Finally, we compare three variants of the proposed algorithm on the Lund Cathedral dataset. The covariance propagation and next best view-planning can be used independently, i.e. the next image can be chosen by maximum overlap while propagating covariances, or the next view can be chosen based on camera uncertainty calculated using zero point covariances, with no propagation. As figure 7 shows, using NBV planning alone doesn't work well at all and the process breaks down, like the plain method. Propagation without planning works almost as well as both combined, and is probably the greatest contributing factor.

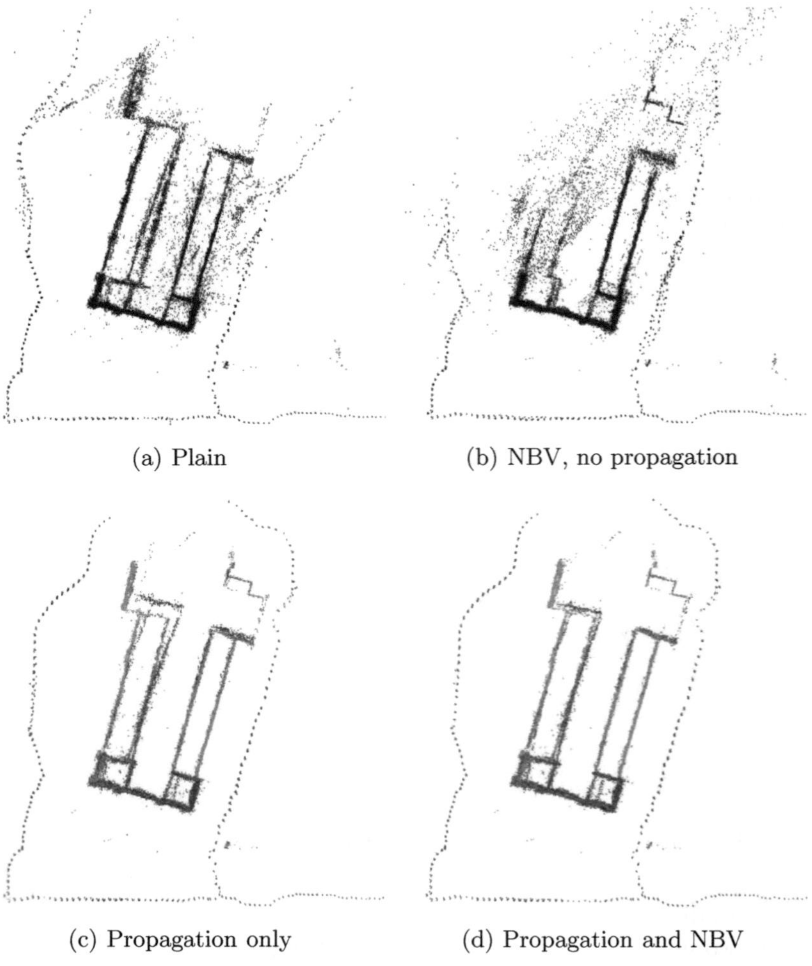

(a) Plain (b) NBV, no propagation

(c) Propagation only (d) Propagation and NBV

Fig. 7. Lund Cathedral dataset (1060 images, 45770 points, 408625 projections) reconstructed using the baseline algorithm, next best view-planning only without propagating covariances, propagating covariances but using the maximum overlap principle, and the proposed algorithm, using both NBV planning and propagation

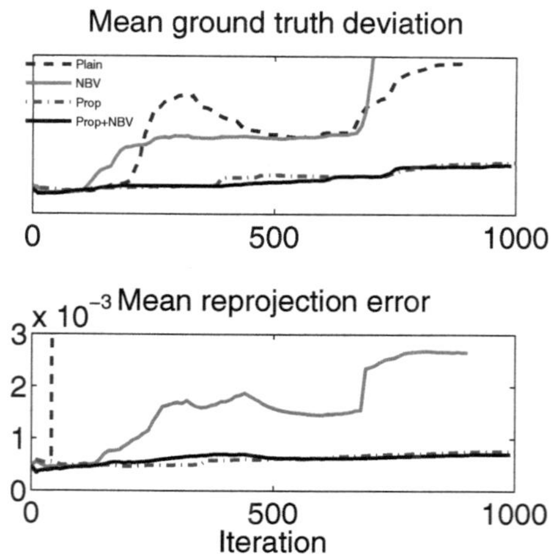

Fig. 8. Error plots for the Lund Cathedral dataset

6.1 Bundle Adjustment

In real use, bundle adjustment would be performed locally and/or globally at regular intervals during the reconstruction process. Unfortunately, after bundling the estimated covariances are no longer valid and need to be updated. Inverting the whole BA Hessian matrix is infeasible, but it is possible to compute only the block diagonal of the inverse quite efficiently, given the full covariance of only the camera parameters. The dominating cost is computing this as the inverse of the Schur complement of the camera block of the Hessian, a cost cubic in the number of cameras. As more cameras are resectioned, updating the covariances this way eventually becomes time-consuming and thus pointless.

Preliminary results indicate that the proposed algorithm still outperforms the standard method on datasets with outliers, where regular local bundle adjustment with a robust cost function and outlier removal is applied, even without updating the covariances at all. Nevertheless, an efficient mechanism for computing the new covariances is still needed and is the subject of future research.

7 Conclusion

The proposed method increases robustness to errors such as poorly resectioned cameras and poorly triangulated points, reduces error accumulation and also provides estimates of reconstruction accuracy which could be further processed for outlier detection etc. This comes at a cost of up to a twofold increase in running time. However, this cost is practically linear in the problem size, whereas iterated bundle adjustment costs between $\mathcal{O}(n^3)$ and $\mathcal{O}(n^4)$, depending on problem structure. Thus, trading less frequent bundling for covariance propagation and next best view planning should pay off for large problems.

References

1. Snavely, N., Seitz, S.M., Szeliski, R.: Modeling the World from Internet Photo Collections. International Journal of Computer Vision 80, 189–210 (2007)
2. Agarwal, S., Snavely, N., Simon, I., Seitz, S.M., Szeliski, R.: Building rome in a day. In: ICCV, pp. 70–79 (2009)
3. Frahm, J.-M., Fite-Georgel, P., Gallup, D., Johnson, T., Raguram, R., Wu, C., Jen, Y.-H., Dunn, E., Clipp, B., Lazebnik, S., Pollefeys, M.: Building Rome on a Cloudless Day. In: Daniilidis, K., Maragos, P., Paragios, N. (eds.) ECCV 2010, Part IV. LNCS, vol. 6314, pp. 368–381. Springer, Heidelberg (2010)
4. Olsson, C., Enqvist, O.: Stable Structure from Motion for Unordered Image Collections. In: Heyden, A., Kahl, F. (eds.) SCIA 2011. LNCS, vol. 6688, pp. 524–535. Springer, Heidelberg (2011)
5. Crandall, D., Owens, A., Snavely, N., Huttenlocher, D.P.: Discrete-Continuous Optimization for Large-Scale Structure from Motion. In: Proc. IEEE Conf. on Computer Vision and Pattern Recognition, pp. 3001–3008. IEEE (2011)
6. Chen, S., Li, Y.F., Zhang, J., Wang, W.: Active Sensor Planning for Multiview Vision Tasks, 1st edn. Springer Publishing Company, Incorporated (2008)
7. Dunn, E., Olague, G., Lutton, E.: Parisian camera placement for vision metrology. Pattern Recognition Letters 27, 1209–1219 (2006)
8. Wenhardt, S., Deutsch, B., Hornegger, J., Niemann, H., Denzler, J.: An Information Theoretic Approach for Next Best View Planning in 3-D Reconstruction. In: Proc. International Conference on Pattern Recognition (ICPR 2006), vol. 1, pp. 103–106. IEEE Computer Society (2006)
9. Trummer, M., Munkelt, C., Denzler, J.: Online Next-Best-View Planning for Accuracy Optimization Using an Extended E-Criterion. In: Proc. International Conference on Pattern Recognition (ICPR 2010), pp. 1642–1645. IEEE Computer Society (2010)
10. Dunn, E., van den Berg, J., Frahm, J.M.: Developing visual sensing strategies through next best view planning. In: IEEE/RSJ International Conference on Intelligent Robots and Systems, IROS 2009, pp. 4001–4008 (2009)
11. Haner, S., Heyden, A.: Optimal View Path Planning for Visual SLAM. In: Heyden, A., Kahl, F. (eds.) SCIA 2011. LNCS, vol. 6688, pp. 370–380. Springer, Heidelberg (2011)
12. Hartley, R., Zisserman, A.: Multiple View Geometry. Cambridge University Press (2003)
13. Morris, D.D.: Gauge Freedoms and Uncertainty Modeling for 3D Computer Vision. PhD thesis, Carnegie Mellon University (2001)
14. Snavely, N., Seitz, S.S.M., Szeliski, R.: Skeletal graphs for efficient structure from motion. In: IEEE Conference on Computer Vision and Pattern Recognition, CVPR 2008, pp. 1–8. IEEE (2008)
15. Kahl, F., Hartley, R.: Multiple View Geometry Under the L_∞ Norm. IEEE Transactions on Pattern Analysis and Machine Intelligence 30, 1603–1617 (2008)
16. Agarwal, S., Snavely, N., Seitz, S.M., Szeliski, R.: Bundle Adjustment in the Large. In: Daniilidis, K., Maragos, P., Paragios, N. (eds.) ECCV 2010, Part II. LNCS, vol. 6312, pp. 29–42. Springer, Heidelberg (2010)

Dilated Divergence Based Scale-Space Representation for Curve Analysis

Max W.K. Law[1,2,⋆], KengYeow Tay[2,3], Andrew Leung[2,3], Gregory J. Garvin[2,4], and Shuo Li[1,2]

[1] GE Healthcare, Canada
[2] University of Western Ontario, London, Canada
[3] London Health Sciences Centre, London, Canada
[4] St. Joseph's Health Care London, London, Canada
max.w.k.law@gmail.com

Abstract. This study proposes the novel dilated divergence scale-space representation for multidimensional curve-like image structure analysis. In the proposed framework, image structures are modeled as curves with arbitrary thickness. The dilated divergence analyzes the structure boundaries along the curve normal space in a multi-scale fashion. The dilated divergence based detection is formulated so as to 1) sustain the disturbance introduced by neighboring objects, 2) recognize the curve normal and tangent spaces. The latter enables the innovative formulation of structure eccentricity analysis and curve tangent space-based structure motion analysis, which have been scarcely investigated in literature. The proposed method is validated using 2D, 3D and 4D images. The structure principal direction estimation accuracies, structure scale detection accuracies and detection stabilities are quantified and compared against two scale-space approaches, showing a competitive performance of the proposed approach, under the disturbance introduced by image noise and neighboring objects. Moreover, as an application example employing the dilated divergence detection responses, an automated approach is tailored for spinal cord centerline extraction. The proposed method is shown to be versatile to well suit a wide range of applications.

1 Introduction

Scale-space theory [1,2,3,4,5,6,7,8,9] has been actively studied for decades for the recognition and detection of blob-like, curvilinear and planar local image structures. The conventional scale-space detection is performed by invoking a diffusion process for the analysis of an image signal. The duration of the diffusion process implicitly defines the detection scale. In this regard, scale-space approaches are mainly designed to manipulate the diffusion tensor or post-process the resultant image of the diffusion process to perform detection. During the analysis at a particular scale-level, undersized image details and structures are generally suppressed. Nonetheless, the intensity variation in the vicinity of structures is

⋆ Corresponding author.

A. Fitzgibbon et al. (Eds.): ECCV 2012, Part II, LNCS 7573, pp. 557–571, 2012.

possibly independent to the structure. For instance, the widths of the separation between bones and the attached soft tissue in medical images are small and do not scale according to the sizes of the adjacent interested objects. These narrow object separations can be annihilated at a coarse detection level for recognizing large objects. In addition, for eccentric curves, such as ellipsoid or elliptical curvilinear structures, the disagreement of object scales along different orientations is unconsidered in the aforementioned conventional scale-space techniques.

In this study, a dilated divergence based scale-space framework is proposed. It is formulated to precisely capture thin edges of large structure and simultaneously avoid the disturbance introduced by other closely positioned objects. The proposed method is designed to handle curves in multi-dimensional images. The curve structures such as spherical, curvilinear, and planar or some volumetric structures can be generally modeled as curves with arbitrary thickness[1]. Along the curve tangent space, intensity changes of the curves are minimal, while abrupt intensity changes are observed across the structure boundary along the curve normal space. The proposed method is devised to capture these abrupt intensity changes. Object scales are estimated according to the responses acquired in various scales. Furthermore, identifying the curve normal and tangent spaces enables the analysis of structure eccentricity to recognize the structure geometry, and the analysis of structure motion based on spatial-temporal curve tangent space.

Distinct to the linear scale-space methods [1,3,6,8,9], the proposed method considers fine image details for recognizing large structures. It is non-diffusion based and hereby utilizes no expensive iterative computation as most of the non-linear scale-space methods [2,4,5,7] require. At each detection scale, the detection responses are acquired as a set of linear image filtering responses. It well handles the curve eccentricity and is also helpful for low level curve motion estimation. It is beneficial to a wide range of image processing application, such as road (1D curves in 2D images) extraction, intracranial vein or spinal cord (eccentric 1D curves in 3D images) segmentation, and coronary artery or trachea motion (2D curves in 4D images) analysis.

2 Dilated Divergence

The divergence of a vector field $\boldsymbol{f}(\boldsymbol{x})$ is defined as

$$\mathrm{div}(\boldsymbol{f}(\boldsymbol{x})) \equiv |\delta C(\boldsymbol{x})|^{-1} \lim_{C(\boldsymbol{x})\to 0} \int_{\delta C(\boldsymbol{x})} \boldsymbol{f}(\boldsymbol{x}+\boldsymbol{y}) \cdot \boldsymbol{da}, \tag{1}$$

where $C(\boldsymbol{x})$ is an infinitesimal region centered at $\boldsymbol{x}$, $\boldsymbol{y}$ is the position vector inside C, $\boldsymbol{da}$ is the outward normal of the region surface and its magnitude is the infinitesimal area on δC. The divergence operator falls into the category of second order derivatives operation. The scale-space methods in this category

[1] E.g. blob-like, curvilinear and planar structures are zero-dimensional curves, one-dimensional curves and two-dimensional curves respectively.

mainly serve the detection of curve structures based on diffusion based image smoothing, such as curvilinear structure analysis [7,9,10].

The dilated divergence of $\boldsymbol{f}$ is defined as $\mathcal{D}^r(\boldsymbol{f}) = -|\delta S_r|^{-1} \int_{\delta S_r} \boldsymbol{f} \cdot \boldsymbol{da}$, where S_r is a n-ball of radius r and n is the dimensionality of $\boldsymbol{f}$. The sign of the operator is reverted in order that bright structures produce positive responses. For simplicity of discussion, the position vector $\boldsymbol{x}$ is omitted hereafter. Distinct to the diffusion based scale-space approaches, the detection scale of the proposed framework is governed by the detection radius r.

The above dilated divergence is general to process any vector field $\boldsymbol{f}$ in any dimension. In this study, the image gradient is employed to form the dilated divergence descriptor $\mathcal{D}^r(\nabla I)$. Employing the image gradient, this descriptor aims at capturing information about the intensity changes occurring across object boundaries. The descriptor is designed to convey a strong detection response at the center of a curve structure, when the hypersphere radius coincides with the structure semi-thickness. This situation implies that the boundary of the curve structure touches the hypersurface, where the image gradient at the contact positions is aligned with $\boldsymbol{da}$ and S_r is centered at the center of the object. For the hypersurfaces of other concentric hyperspheres associated with different radii, dilated divergence produces low or no responses. It is because undersized hypersphere cannot reach the object boundary while when a hypersurface overshoots the object boundary, $\boldsymbol{da}$ is not parallel to the image gradient that penalizes the response.

2.1 Anisotropic Dilated Divergence

Distinct to 0D curves which yield significant intensity variations along all directions, the higher-dimensional curves exhibit low or no intensity changes in one or more directions. Detection of these structures requires an orientation sensitive descriptor. Given an arbitrary detection direction $\hat{\nu}$, an anisotropic dilated divergence is obtained as $\mathcal{D}^r((\nabla I \cdot \hat{\nu})\hat{\nu})$. On the one hand, a well adjusted detection direction helps selectively capture intensity changes along the curve normal directions. On the other hand, through inspecting the anisotropic dilated divergence responses along various directions, structure orientations are computed. The anisotropy of this descriptor subsequently enables the detection of object scales along different principal directions, thereby yielding the analysis of structure eccentricity. By generalized Stroke's theorem, the anisotropic dilated divergence operator is rewritten as,

$$\mathcal{D}^r((\nabla I \cdot \hat{\nu})\hat{\nu}) = \hat{\nu}^T \left[\frac{1}{|\delta S_r|} \int_{S_r} \mathcal{H}(I) dv \right] \hat{\nu}, \tag{2}$$

where $\mathcal{H}$ is the Hessian matrix of the image. This equation allows the anisotropic dilated divergence responses to be synthesized based on tensor $\frac{1}{|\delta S_r|} \int_{S_r} \mathcal{H}(I) dv$. Denoting this tensor by $\mathcal{T}^r(I)$, it can be computed efficiently by applying the Fourier transform,

$$\mathcal{T}^r(I) = -\frac{4\Gamma(\frac{n+1}{2})}{r^{\frac{n}{2}} \pi^{\frac{n-3}{2}}} \mathcal{F}^{-1} \left(\mathcal{F}(I) ||\boldsymbol{\omega}||^{-\frac{n}{2}} \boldsymbol{\omega}\boldsymbol{\omega}^T B_{\frac{n}{2}}(2\pi r ||\boldsymbol{\omega}||) \right), \tag{3}$$

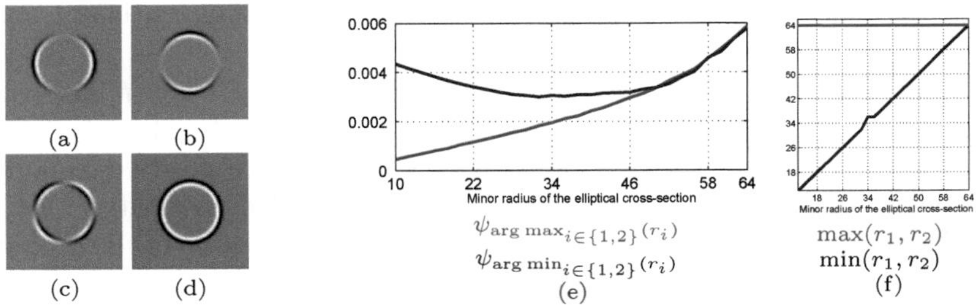

Fig. 1. (a-d) The anisotropic dilated divergence obtained based on a 2-D dirac image function δ, $j = 0$, $r = 16$ and $\sigma = 2$. (a, b) The diagonal elements of $\mathcal{T}^{r,j}$ that are equivalent of the responses of $\mathcal{D}^r((\nabla\delta \cdot \hat{\nu})\hat{\nu})$ where $\hat{\nu}$ is the horizontal direction in (a), and the vertical direction in (b). (c) The image of the off-diagonal elements of $\mathcal{T}^{r,j}(\delta)$. (d) The image of $\mathrm{Tr}(\mathcal{T}^{r,j}(\delta))$, which is equivalent to the sum of the images shown in (a) and (b). (e, f) Different responses obtained at the center of a 1D curve with elliptical cross-section (major radius=64 unit-length) in a 3D image.

where $\mathcal{F}$ and $\mathcal{F}^{-1}$ are respectively the multidimensional Fourier transform and inverse Fourier transform operators, $\boldsymbol{\omega}$ is the frequency domain position vector in cycle-per-unit-length, Γ is the Gamma function and B_k is the kth order Bessel function of the first kind. The tensor based computation allows an analytical form estimation of the most contributive detection direction, i.e.

$$\arg\max_{\hat{\nu}} |\mathcal{D}^r((\nabla I \cdot \hat{\nu})\hat{\nu})| = \arg\max_{\hat{\nu}} |\hat{\nu}^T \mathcal{T}^r(I)\hat{\nu}|.$$

This optimization procedure results in an eigen-decomposition at each local position. In which, the most contributive detection directions are the eigenvectors of $\mathcal{T}^r(I)$ associated with the largest absolute value of the eigenvalues.

2.2 Multi-scale Detection and Scale Selection

For curve analysis, the dilated divergence response is induced from the intersecting space between the hypersuface and object boundaries. In discrete image analysis, the intersection is an n dimensional space. The dilated divergence responses are normalized according to the hypervolume of the intersection. Denote σ is the voxel-length of an image, the image gradient can be regarded as piecewise constant within an interval of σ. From this perspective, the scale normalization is elaborated in Appendix A.

Meanwhile, applying the band-unlimited dilated divergence operator to the band-limited discrete signal causes aliasing artifacts. This is overcome by a Gaussian smoothing with a scale factor equal to σ in the dilated divergence operation. With the Gaussian smoothing and the curve dimensionality based scale normalization, the final anisotropic dilated divergence tensor is calculated as,

$$\mathcal{T}^{r,j} = -\left(\frac{r}{\sqrt{2r\sigma - \sigma^2}}\right)^j \frac{4\Gamma(\frac{n+1}{2})}{r^{\frac{n}{2}}\pi^{\frac{n-3}{2}}} \mathcal{F}^{-1}\left(\mathcal{F}(I)e^{-2\pi\sigma^2||\boldsymbol{\omega}||^2}||\boldsymbol{\omega}||^{-\frac{n}{2}}\boldsymbol{\omega}\boldsymbol{\omega}^T B_{\frac{n}{2}}(2\pi r||\boldsymbol{\omega}||)\right), \tag{4}$$

where j is the dimensionality of the curve, which is defined beforehand depending on the types of the desired curves. This tensor is symmetric and has $n \times n$ entries which contains $\sum_{i=1}^{n} i$ independent channels. For $n = 2$, Figs. 1a-c illustrate the three independent channels of $\mathcal{T}^{r,j}$ and Fig. 1d exemplifies the trace of $\mathcal{T}^{r,j}$. As multiplication in the frequency domain is equivalent to convolution in the spatial domain, $\mathcal{T}^{r,j}(\delta)$ can be regarded as a group of image filters capturing the intensity changes occurring at the interested scale defined by r. The scale-normalized dilated divergence is capable of performing multi-scale analysis using a set of pre-defined radius set. The maximum radius and radius-interval of the radius set are respectively suggested to be the semi-thickness of the largest target structure in the image, and 0.5σ according to the Nyquist rate. The best detection scale at each local position is chosen by comparing the responses obtained across different scales.

During the scale selection, at each scale, the dilated divergence responses influenced by descending and ascending intensity edges are assessed separately. In the n eigenvalues of $\mathcal{T}^{r,j}$, the positive and negative ones are produced by descending and ascending intensity transitions respectively. Denote the largest-magnitude eigenvalue and its eigenvector at the scale r are γ_1^r and $\hat{\varphi}_1^r$,

$$\lambda_1^r = \max\left\{ \max_{\delta \in \{\sigma, 1.5\sigma, 2\sigma \dots r\}} \left(\gamma_1^\delta\right), 0 \right\} + \min\left\{ \min_{\delta \in \{\sigma, 1.5\sigma, 2\sigma \dots r\}} \left(\gamma_1^\delta\right), 0 \right\}. \quad (5)$$

This measure is formulated using the competition between the largest ascending intensity change and the descending counterparts. It penalizes the responses obtained from oversized scales, of which the detection hyperspheres overshoot the object boundary and reach adjacent one exhibiting opposite intensity changes. The optimal detection scale is selected based on the strongest detection responses obtained over multiple scales up to the maximum detectable scale to be $\mathbf{R}$,

$$r_1 = \min\left(\arg \max_{r \in \{1.5\sigma, 2\sigma, 2.5\sigma \dots \mathbf{R}\}} |\lambda_1^r| \right), \psi_1 = \lambda_1^{r_1}, \hat{e}_1 = \hat{\varphi}_1^{r_1}. \quad (6)$$

The scale selection omits the smallest scale σ because at which the competition is always disabled. This selection procedure searches for a scale where the response magnitude first attains its maxima. It gives strongest responses at object centers, while the signs of the detection responses are reverted across the object boundaries analogous to other second derivatives based approaches.

2.3 Eccentricity Analysis and Structure Orientation

The curves which exhibit a 2 or higher dimensional normal space can possess eccentric intensity patterns (e.g. 2D ellipse and tubular structures with elliptical cross-sections) and yield different object scales along various directions. In eccentricity analysis, the procedures to extract detection responses, the optimal detection orientation and scale selection are reiterated at all principal directions of the curve normal space to capture the possibly disagreed object scales along different direction. Given the analysis of the first $m-1$ basis of the normal space is completed, the mth basis is acquired by performing eigen-decomposition on,

$$(Q_m)^T T^{r,j} Q_m, \tag{7}$$

where $Q_m = \text{IDTY} - \sum_{i=1}^{m-1} \hat{e}_i(\hat{e}_i)^T$, and IDTY is an identity matrix. This produces at most $n-m$ non-zeros eigenvalues. Denote the largest-magnitude eigenvalue and the corresponding eigenvector are γ_m^r and $\hat{\varphi}_m^r$ respectively, the response at scale r is obtained based on the competition between the descending and ascending intensity transition responses, analogous to Eq. 5,

$$\lambda_m^r = \max\left\{\max_{\delta\in\{\sigma,1.5\sigma,2\sigma...r\}}\left(\gamma_m^\delta\right),0\right\} + \min\left\{\min_{\delta\in\{\sigma,1.5\sigma,2\sigma...r\}}\left(\gamma_m^\delta\right),0\right\}. \tag{8}$$

Saddle points on the intensity surface at which the detection responses possess different signs are not the focus of this study. The scale selection of eccentricity analysis prefers the responses showing the same response sign as ψ_1. The desired scale level r_m, response ψ_m and basis $\hat{e}_m$ are,

$$r_m = \min\left(\arg\max_{r\in\{1.5\sigma,2\sigma,2.5\sigma...\mathbf{R}\}}\left(sign(\psi_1)\lambda_m^r\right)\right), \psi_m = \lambda_m^{r_m}, \hat{e}_m = \hat{\varphi}_m^{r_m}. \tag{9}$$

An example of the responses and scales delivered by this eccentricity analysis is given in Figs. 1e and f. Finally, the curve tangent space is the orientations along which the object possesses minimal intensity variation. The orthogonal basis of the curve tangent space is the non-singular eigenvectors of $\text{IDTY} - \sum_{i=1}^{n-j} \hat{e}_i(\hat{e}_i)^T$.

2.4 Spatial-temporal Curve Based Spatial Curve Motion Estimation

Structure motions can be assessed based on image sequences. In an nD image sequence, a moving jD curve yields a $(j+1)$D curve in the $(n+1)$D spatial-temporal image. This interpretation allows an intuitive estimation of the low level curve motion without prior segmentation of the structures. The low level curve motion assumes that the curve structure center translation across adjacent time frame is small compared to the semi-thickness of the curve. As such, the structure motion fields are piecewise linear inside the structure and the geometry of a local segment of the curve is unaltered across adjacent time frames. This suits the tracking of deformation induced curve movement, such as extracting the motion of the aorta in image sequences [11].

To formulate the spatial-temporal curve detection, the spatial-temporal voxel length along the time dimension is suggested to be less than or equal to 2σ.Define a $(n+1)$-by-n matrix $\mathbf{C}$ of which the first n rows form an identity matrix and the $(n+1)$th row is zero, and let $\hat{u}_1, \hat{u}_2, ..., \hat{u}_j$ the curve tangent space orthogonal basis. In the spatial-temporal image, the $(j+1)$D curve tangent space basis are $\mathbf{C}\hat{u}_1, \mathbf{C}\hat{u}_2, ..., \mathbf{C}\hat{u}_j$ and an additional basis denoted as $\hat{\tau}$. Given the piecewise linear assumption, after the time elapsed by Δt, the curve tangent space basis can be expressed as $\hat{u}_i + \Delta t \frac{1}{\hat{\tau}\cdot\hat{T}} \left(\mathbf{C}^T \hat{\tau}\right)$ and thus, the spatial curve motion is,

$$\frac{1}{\hat{\tau}\cdot\hat{T}}\mathbf{C}^T\hat{\tau}. \tag{10}$$

3 Evaluation and Discussion

The proposed method is evaluated based on various criteria in three synthetic and one clinical experiments. The synthetic experiments employ 2D, 3D and 4D images respectively, followed by spinal cord centerline extraction experiment which involves 15 clinical image volumes. In the synthetic images, the interested objects have an intensity value 1 and the background intensity is zero. The images are Gaussian-smoothed with a scale factor of 1 unit-length prior to analysis. The proposed method is compared against two approaches, multi-dimensional $\gamma-$Normalized Hessian method [3,9] and the three-dimensional optimally oriented flux method [12], referred to as HESSIAN and OOF respectively hereafter. These methods, including the proposed method are stemmed from second order techniques. Nonetheless, distinct from the proposed method, HESSIAN omits image details during the analysis of sizable structures, while OOF is developed only for non-eccentric curves embedded in 3D images. The image features extracted from HESSIAN and OOF resemble those from the proposed method in three aspects: they are low level detection approaches that convey general-purpose features for possible subsequent application-specific analysis; they provide scalar "curveness" detection responses and corresponding principal directions; and they are grounded on multi-scale analysis. The scale sets used by the optimally oriented flux and the proposed method are identical, from 1 unit-length to 20 unit-length, with a 0.5 unit-length interval. They both employ a pre-Gaussian smoothing with a 1 unit length scale factor (i.e. $\sigma = 1$ unit-length for the proposed method). The scale set used by the Hessian method contains the same number of scales and dynamic range, but with a fixed geometric step.

3.1 Multi-scale Detection and Scale Selection

The first experiment concerns a single-layer spiral (Fig. 2a). The semi-width of this structure gradually increases from 9 unit-length at the inner end to 10.125 unit-length at the outer end. Two sections of this structure are closely located and their boundaries are in a distance of 1.5 unit-length apart. Fig. 2b demonstrates the response computed from this structure. The anisotropic dilated divergence produces positive responses inside the structure and forms a ridge at the structure centerline. It returns negative responses in the vicinity of the structure. The response pattern inside the structure at the optimal scale is consistent regardless of the curve width change and the disturbance the adjacent segment. In Figs. 2c and d, the response profiles along two different positions of the structure are visualized. Inside the structure, the response ridges show a bifurcation-like

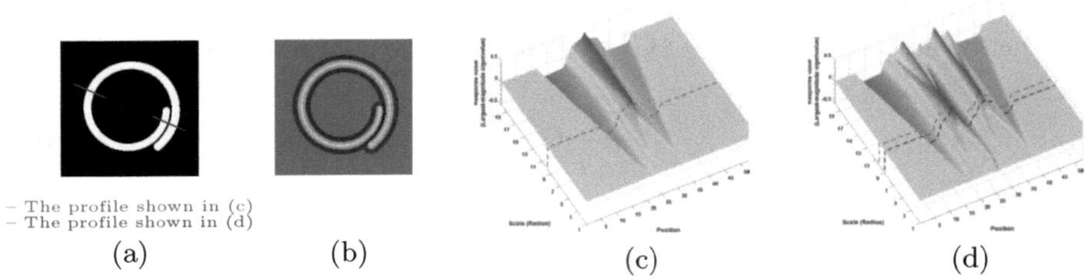

Fig. 2. A 1D curve in a 2D image with a unit pixel size. (a) The original image. (b) The detection response image ψ_1. (c, d) The intermediate multi-scale responses λ_1^r obtained at the highlighted positions shown in (a). The dotted lines illustrate the selected scales based on Eq. 6 which coincide with the ground-truth scale (object semi-width).

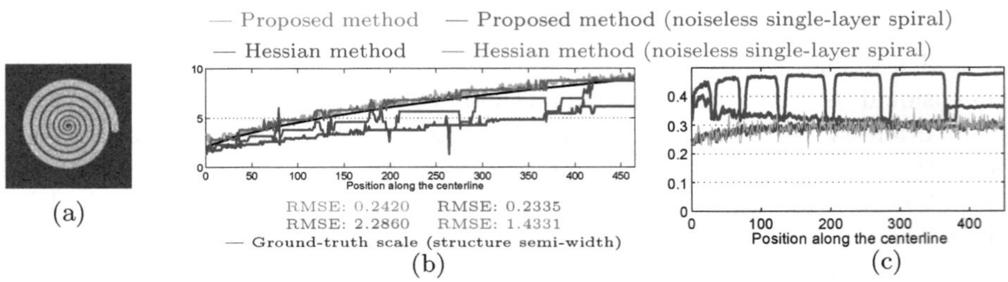

Fig. 3. An experiment of a noise corrupted spiral (1D curve) in a 2D image with a unit pixel size. The radius of the spiral gradually increases from 2 to 10 unit-length. (a) The Gaussian noise (0.2 standard deviation) corrupted spiral. (b) The estimated scales based on the proposed method and the Hessian method. (c) The detection responses based on the proposed method and the Hessian method.

pattern over various scales. The response ridge pair at undersized scales is induced from the boundaries at two opposite sides of the structure. The ridge pair intersects at the structure center when the scale coincides to the structure semi-width and yield a sharp response peak. In Fig. 2c, the response peak sustains in the oversized scales when no neighboring object interfere the detection. When a neighboring object presents, the responses reported at oversized scales are attenuated as evidenced in Fig. 2d. These attenuated responses are consequently eliminated in the scale selection procedures (Eqs. 6 and 9).

Furthermore, a comparison between the proposed method and HESSIAN concerning the multi-scale detection performance is conducted. It involves two set of images - the noise corrupted spiral image (Fig. 3a) and seven noiseless single-layer spiral images. The noiseless single-layer spirals are acquired by partitioning the noiseless spiral into seven single-layer spirals. The study is performed along the spiral centerline in the noisy spiral image and the corresponding single-layer spiral images. Each single-layer spiral is further revolved outward by an angular distance of $\frac{\pi}{8}$ radian (see Fig. 2a for the outermost single-layer spiral). The extended portions of the spirals serve as neighboring objects which possibly interfere the detection. These two sets of images offer three distinct testing conditions - noisy and with neighboring objects, noiseless and without neighboring objects, and noiseless and with neighboring objects. For HESSIAN, the largest-magnitude eigenvalue is used as the response at each scale and the final responses are chosen according to the maximum magnitude responses over scales. The resultant scales of HESSIAN shows large discrepancies to the ground-truth in various cases (compare the purple and red curves against the black curve, and see the corresponding root-mean-square errors (RMSEs) in Fig. 3b). In the noiseless single-layer spiral tests (the purple curve in Fig. 3b), HESSIAN underestimates structure scales at the beginning of each layer. It is because the further revolved portion of the spiral interferes the detection. These underestimated scales resemble the scales estimated from the noisy spiral (see the overlaps between the red curve and the lower envelop of the purple curve in Fig. 3b).

On the contrary, the scales estimated by the proposed method are accurate (see the largely overlapped cyan, teal and black curves and the small RMSEs in Fig. 3b) regardless of the presence of image noise and closely located objects. This figure illustrates that the proposed method exhibits superior performance over the Hessian method for scale estimation when neighboring objects exist. Similar observation is found in the detection response values shown in Fig. 3c. The proposed method delivers consistent and similar detection responses among the noisy spiral and the noiseless single-layer spiral cases. When neighboring object does not exist, HESSIAN gives a consistent responses despite of the scale changes (see the upper envelop of the purple curve in Fig. 3c), analogous to the proposed method. The response values of both methods are slightly reduced at the thinnest part of the spiral because of the high structure curvature. Nonetheless, when neighboring objects exist, HESSIAN responses drop significantly (the red curve and the lower envelop of the purple curve in Fig. 3c).

3.2 Eccentricity Analysis and Structure Orientation

The eccentricity analysis experiment focuses on the accuracies of estimating object principal axes and the object scales along the axes. It employs a noise corrupted 3D spiral with elliptical cross-section (Figs. 4a and b). The proposed method is compared against HESSIAN and OOF. This image has an anisotropic voxel size that commonly exists in practical 3D image scans. Sinc interpolation [9] is applied for HESSIAN and OOF method to produce isotropic voxels. The responses of these methods at each scale level are the arithmetic mean of the two largest magnitude eigenvalues [9,12]. Their optimal scales are chosen as the maximum magnitude response over scales. At the optimal scales, the structure orientations, major and minor axes are acquired as the eigenvectors associated with the smallest, medium and largest magnitude eigenvalues respectively.

Along the centerline of the spiral, there are three local orientations - the structure orientation, the major and minor axes. In addition, two object scales - major and minor radii are involved. In Fig. 4c, the accuracies of the estimated orientations of various axes based on different methods are shown. In all cases, the proposed method yields significantly lower discrepancies to the ground-truth than HESSIAN and OOF do. Theoretically, the eigenvalue ratios

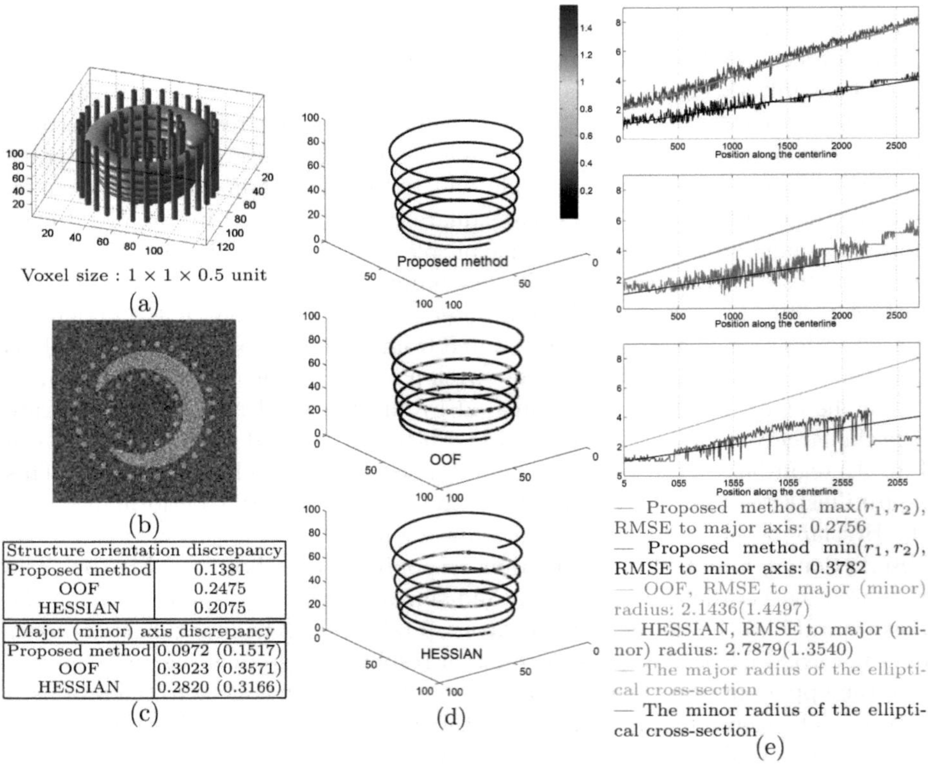

Structure orientation discrepancy	
Proposed method	0.1381
OOF	0.2475
HESSIAN	0.2075

Major (minor) axis discrepancy	
Proposed method	0.0972 (0.1517)
OOF	0.3023 (0.3571)
HESSIAN	0.2820 (0.3166)

(c)

Fig. 4. The experiment on an anisotropic voxel-sized volume. The spiral major and minor radii are 2 and 1 unit-length at the bottom and gradually increase to 8 and 4 at the top. The separation between layers is 1 unit-length. (a) The isosurface of the spiral and its neighboring objects. (b) The $z = 70$ slice of the image volume corrupted by additive Gaussian noise with a 0.3 standard deviation. (c) The mean acute angular discrepancies (in radian) of different local axes measured along the centerline. (d) The acute angular discrepancies (in radian) of the structure orientation estimated along the centerline. (e) The optimal scales extracted by different methods.

of HESSIAN hint the structure eccentricity [13]. However, the disturbance introduced by neighboring objects prohibits the eigenvalues from being extracted at the desired scale. In addition, the circular cross-section assumption imposed by OOF deviates from the elliptical cross-section of this spiral. Their estimation of the structure orientation, the major and minor axes are therefore less accurate. Fig. 4d depicts the profiles of the angular discrepancies of structure orientation estimation based on different approaches. The large discrepancy cases of HESSIAN and OOF are observed in the entire spiral. It suggests that the estimation error is independent to object scales. In Fig. 4e, the estimated object scales for the spiral cross-section are presented. The scales estimated by HESSIAN and OOF fluctuate in between the major and minor radii. In contrast, the proposed method precisely estimates both minor and major radii and shows promising accuracies with RMSEs less than one scale step (0.5 unit-length).

3.3 Spatial-temporal Curve Based Spatial Curve Motion Estimation

In this experiment, a randomly deformed spiral (Fig. 5a) is used for studying the accuracy of the structure centerline motion estimated by the spatial-temporal curve analysis (Eq. 10). During the experiment, Frame-1 and Frame-7 are replicated twice and padded to the volumetric sequence to handle the wrap-around effect of the frequency domain based computation of Eq. 7. Based on Eq. 10, the centerline motion of the Frames-2, 3, 4, 5, 6 are retrieved. The motion vector in the Frame-t is employed to predict the centerline position based on the given position in the Frame-$(t-1)$. Denote q, Δq, $\boldsymbol{c}(q)$, $\boldsymbol{m}(q)$ are time, time interval between adjacent frames, ground-truth centerline positions and the estimated motions at $\boldsymbol{c}(q)$. The predicted positions at the time $q+\Delta q$ are given as $\boldsymbol{c}(q-\Delta q)+2\Delta q\boldsymbol{m}(q)$. The Euclidean distances (error) between the predicted positions and the ground-truth positions are visualized in Fig. 5b. To help assess the prediction results, Euclidean distances of the ground-truth centerline movement is shown. Towards the end of the sequence, more cases of high curvature positions appear and reduce the accuracy of the estimated curve motion.

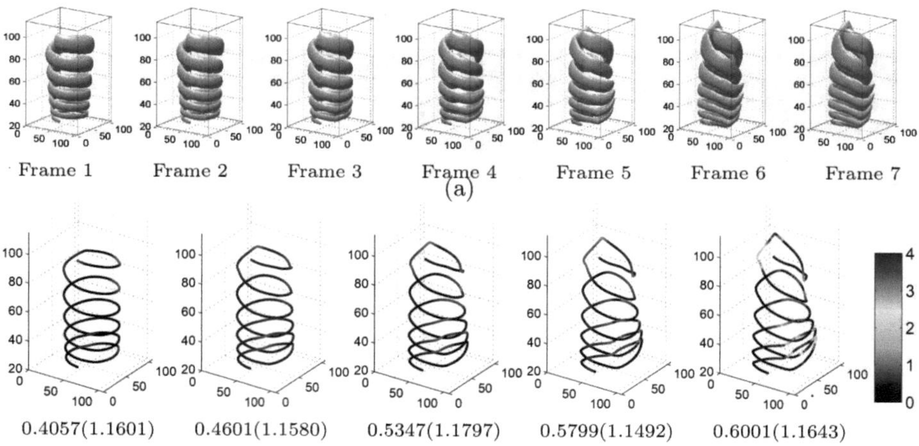

(a)

(b)

Fig. 5. Motion analysis experiment based on a Gaussian noise (with a 0.2 standard deviation) corrupted, randomly deformed 3D spiral. The major and minor radii are 2 and 1 unit-length at the bottom of the spiral and gradually increase to 8 and 4 at the top of the spiral. The spatial-temporal voxel size is $0.5 \times 0.5 \times 1 \times 2$ unit. (a) The isosurface of the deforming spiral in different time frames. In Frames-3, 5 and 7, the spiral is deformed by randomly (according to the uniform distribution) offsetting 64 control points in a range of $[-0.15\times$image-length, $0.15\times$image-length$]$ along each dimension. These control point positions are linearly interpolated for Frames-2, 4 and 6. Voxel intensity is determined by using bicubic interpolation. (b) The discrepancies between the estimated position and the true position of the spiral centerlines, numbers are shown as "Average centerline displacement compared to the ground-truth".

3.4 Application Example

In the final experiment, 15 volumetric T2-weighted magnetic resonance images (T2-MRI) from the cervical and thoracic spinal regions are employed (Fig. 6). In T2-MRIs, the cord is comprised of a grey center (grey matter) and a dark border (white matter). The spinal cord is surrounded by a bright layer (cerebrospinal fluid), which exhibits varying thickness, and voxel intensity significantly drops and fluctuates outside this layer. In addition, the intensity contrast across the spinal cord boundary declines towards the bottom slice of an image due to dispersal of the low intensity white matter. Thus, the intensity pattern of the spinal cord is inconsistent, thereby leading to disturbance for spinal cord analysis. As such, spinal cord analysis is extremely challenging.

In our dataset, the spinal cords are approximately vertically aligned 1D eccentric curves (elliptical curvilinear structures) which traverse every slice of the volumetric images, having minor and major radii ranged from 6 to 15 unit-length. In this experiment, the dilated divergence measures ψ_1 and ψ_2 are aggregated as $-\min(\psi_1, 0) - \min(\psi_2, 0)$ to contribute a speed field for shortest-path extraction [14]. The multi-scale selection results based on the sum of the two largest-magnitude eigenvalues of HESSIAN [9] and OOF [12] are employed as

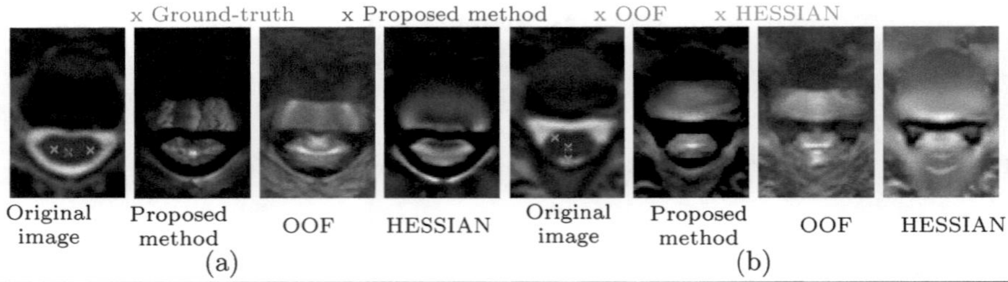

	The proposed method	OOF	HESSIAN
Error (Mean ± S.D. in unit-length)	1.7959 ± 0.2573	13.1076 ± 15.2215	14.6881 ± 13.0967

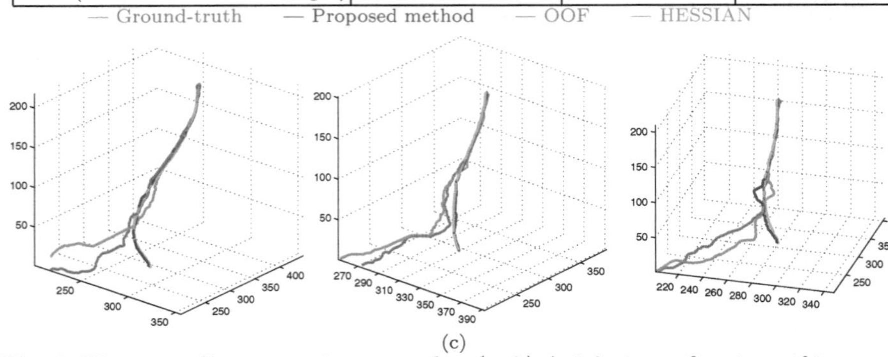

Fig. 6. Five centerline extraction examples. (a, b) Axial views of regions-of-interest of two cases, the original images and the speed fields computed by different methods. (c) The quantitative centerline extraction result, and three examples of extracted centerlines based on different methods. Errors are measured as the average distance between extracted centerline point samples and the closest ground-truth centerline points.

the speed field for centerline extraction comparison. Subsequent to the construction of the speed fields, two additional slices filled with an infinity speed value are padded beyond the top and bottom slices of the speed fields. The shortest-path source and destination are positioned at the corners of these two slices respectively, constituting a fully automatic spinal cord centerline extraction algorithm. This experiment concerns two aspects, handling eccentric curves surrounded by structure possessing inconsistent intensity pattern; and finding the path corresponding to the target curve in a large volumetric image ($512 \times 512 \times 200$ voxels, voxelsize $1 \times 1 \times 2.1157$ unit, 1 unit-length = 0.4727mm in this experiment), i.e. reporting distinguishable and strong responses inside the curves as compared to those inside irrelevant structures. Spinal cord-specific knowledge is excluded from the formulation of the speed fields of all methods. Therefore, the experimental results generally reflect the performance of the examined methods on handling different eccentric curves.

In Figs. 6a and b, the proposed method gives strong detection responses at the centerline of the spinal cord, while OOF and HESSIAN supply strong responses close to the boundary of the cord and lead to incorrect extraction. The significant HESSIAN response difference between the cases shown in Figs. 6a and b suggests that HESSIAN is extremely sensitive to the intensity fluctuation outside the curve. Meanwhile, OOF is solely developed for circular curvilinear 1D curve. It reports strong responses in multiple positions on the curve cross-section (Figs. 6a and b, OOF) and results in erroneous centerline extraction. In addition, the largely overlapped cyan and red lines and crosses in Figs. 6a-c illustrate the accurate centerlines extracted by the proposed method. On the contrary, OOF and HESSIAN result in large disagreements in the extraction result. Furthermore, the extracted centerlines of OOF and HESSIAN are driven away from the spinal cords towards the tracking source points located at the origin. It manifests that OOF and HESSIAN cannot supply distinguishable responses inside curve structures. Finally, the centerline extraction errors shown in Fig. 6c further evidences the very accurate and stable centerline extraction based on the proposed method, compared to those based on OOF and HESSIAN.

4 Conclusion

This paper proposes the novel dilated divergence based scale-space representation for curve analysis. The proposed scale-space framework is non-diffusion based. Its computation is grounded on linear filters and therefore, it is efficient and parallelizable. The proposed method is studied and validated in three aspects - scale selection, eccentricity analysis and spatial-temporal curve analysis. In particular, the dilated divergence addresses analysis of structure eccentricity and spatial-temporal curve tangent space which have been scarcely studied.

In the experiments, the proposed method is shown to be capable of sustaining the disturbance introduced by closely positioned objects. It outperforms conventional scale-space approaches in the comparison. The formulation of the proposed framework is general to serve a wide range of applications. Investigation of the dilated divergence framework for detection of saddle points on intensity surface for corner and junction recognition, structure centerline extraction, 0D curve based-salient feature detection, curve segmentation and curve motion tracking, particularly for high dimensional curves are the future direction of this research.

Acknowledgement. This work was supported by the Mitacs-Accelerate fellowship (App. Ref. IT00716) granted to the first author of this paper.

References

1. Mikolajczyk, K., Schmidt, C.: Scale & affine invariant interest point detectors. IJCV 60, 63–86 (2004)
2. Weickert, J.: A review of nonlinear diffusion filtering. In: Scale-Space, pp. 3–28 (1997)
3. Lindeberg, T.: Edge detection and ridge detection with automatic scale selection. IJCV 30, 117–156 (1998)
4. Perona, P., Malik, J.: Scale-space and edge detection using anisotropic diffusion. PAMI 12, 629–639 (1990)
5. Okada, K., Comaniciu, D., Krishnan, A.: Scale selection for anisotropic scale-space: application to volumetric tumor characterization. In: CVPR, vol. 1, pp. 594–601 (2004)
6. Lowe, D.: Distinctive image features from scale-invariant keypoints. IJCV 60, 91–110 (2004)
7. Manniesing, R., Viergever, M., Niessen, W.: Vessel enhancing diffusion a scale space representation of vessel structures. MedIA 10, 815–825 (2006)
8. Deng, H., Zhang, W., Mortensen, E., Dietterich, T., Shapiro, L.: Principal curvature-based region detector for object recognition. In: CVPR, pp. 1–8 (2007)
9. Sato, Y., Nakajima, S., Shiraga, N., Atsumi, H., Yoshida, S., Koller, T., Gerig, G., Kikinis, R.: Three-dimensional multi-scale line filter for segmentation and visualization of curvilinear structures in medical images. MedIA 2, 143–168 (1998)
10. Krissian, K.: Flux-based anisotropic diffusion applied to enhancement of 3-D angiogram. TMI 21, 1440–1442 (2002)
11. Biesdorf, A., Wörz, S., Müller, T., Weber, T.F., Heye, T., Hosch, W., von Tengg-Kobligk, H., Rohr, K.: Model-Based Segmentation and Motion Analysis of the Thoracic Aorta from 4D ECG-Gated CTA Images. In: Fichtinger, G., Martel, A., Peters, T. (eds.) MICCAI 2011, Part I. LNCS, vol. 6891, pp. 589–596. Springer, Heidelberg (2011)
12. Law, M.W.K., Chung, A.C.S.: Three Dimensional Curvilinear Structure Detection Using Optimally Oriented Flux. In: Forsyth, D., Torr, P., Zisserman, A. (eds.) ECCV 2008, Part IV. LNCS, vol. 5305, pp. 368–382. Springer, Heidelberg (2008)
13. Frangi, A.F., Niessen, W.J., Vincken, K.L., Viergever, M.A.: Multiscale Vessel Enhancement Filtering. In: Wells, W.M., Colchester, A.C.F., Delp, S.L. (eds.) MICCAI 1998. LNCS, vol. 1496, pp. 130–137. Springer, Heidelberg (1998)
14. Sethian, J., Vladimirsky, A.: Fast methods for the eikonal and related hamilton-jacobi equations on unstructured meshes. PNAS 97, 5699–5703 (2000)

A Appendix - Scale Normalization

Given a 1D curve in a 2D image where $\boldsymbol{\nu}$ is the curve 1D-normal space, σ is the edge diffuseness, which is analyzed by a circular region (S_r in Eq. 2) represented as $y = \sqrt{R^2 - x^2}$, $\sigma < R$ and image gradient has a unit magnitude within the edge and is null anywhere else, the anisotropic dilated divergence response is,

$$\frac{1}{\pi R}\int_{R-\sigma}^{R}\frac{x}{R}\int_{-\sqrt{R^2-x^2}}^{\sqrt{R^2-x^2}} dydx = \frac{2}{\pi R}\sqrt{2R\sigma - \sigma^2}.$$

An appropriate normalization is $\frac{\pi R}{2}\sqrt{2R\sigma - \sigma^2}$. Without loss of generality, define an nD image patch $J(\boldsymbol{x})$, which consists of a jD curve centered at the local position $\boldsymbol{x}$. Denote $\hat{u}_1, ..., \hat{u}_j$ and $\hat{u}_{j+1}, ..., \hat{u}_n$ are the orthogonal basis of the curve normal space and the curve tangent space respectively. Eq. 2, the dilated divergence for J can be re-written as, $\hat{\nu}^T \left[\frac{1}{|\delta S_r|}\int_{S_r}\mathcal{H}(J)\left(\int_{S_r} d\hat{u}_1...d\hat{u}_j\right) d\hat{j+1}_1...d\hat{u}_n\right]\hat{\nu}$. The inner integral is independent to the image term (analogous to $\int_{-\sqrt{R^2-x^2}}^{\sqrt{R^2-x^2}} dy$ in the above 2D image example). The nested integrals along the tangent space become a multiplicative factor to the outer integrals operated along the normal space. As such, given $\hat{\nu}$ is one of the principal directions in the curve normal space and r equals to the structure semi-thickness along $\hat{\nu}$,

$$\mathcal{D}^r((\nabla I \cdot \hat{\nu})\hat{\nu}) \propto \left(\frac{r}{\sqrt{2r\sigma - \sigma^2}}\right)^j. \qquad (11)$$

A Parameterless Line Segment and Elliptical Arc Detector with Enhanced Ellipse Fitting

Viorica Pătrăucean[1,2], Pierre Gurdjos[1], and Rafael Grompone von Gioi[3]

[1] IRIT-ENSEEIHT*, Toulouse, France
[2] Military Technical Academy of Bucharest, Romania
[3] CMLA, ENS Cachan, France
{viorica.patraucean,pierre.gurdjos}@enseeiht.fr,
grompone@cmla.ens-cachan.fr

Abstract. We propose a combined line segment and elliptical arc detector, which formally guarantees the control of the number of false positives and requires no parameter tuning. The accuracy of the detected elliptical features is improved by using a novel non-iterative ellipse fitting technique, which merges the algebraic distance with the gradient orientation. The performance of the detector is evaluated on computer-generated images and on natural images.

Keywords: ellipse detection, *a contrario* approach, ellipse fitting.

1 Introduction

The automatic detection of elementary geometric features (line segments, elliptical arcs) in images, is as old as computer vision itself [11], being often a prerequisite for high-level procedures, e.g. see [10]. The task is far from trivial and many research works addressed it over the decades. Nonetheless, the problem is not completely settled. Most of the existing detectors, despite the parameter tuning they demand, provide no control of false detections. Theoretical tools that guard against false detections exist in the literature [18,3] and efficient implementations for line segment detection were proposed [3,8]. The purpose of this paper is to put in such a theoretical framework the simultaneous detection of line segments and elliptical arcs, in order to obtain a low-level detector that requires no parameter tuning, and produces reliable results when applied on any kind of image, regardless of its size, content, or source.

Existing geometric feature detectors can be roughly classified into two categories: *Hough-based* and *edge chaining* methods. Most of them rely on an edge detector, e.g. like [1]. The Hough-based algorithms [21] implement variants of the Hough transform (HT) [11] together with some detection thresholds. HT accumulates in an array the votes granted by the edge points to each potential feature. Array points that exceed the threshold become detections. The critical

* The authors wish to thank Géraldine Morin and Vincent Charvillat from IRIT-ENSEEIHT for their helpful input and comments on this work.

A. Fitzgibbon et al. (Eds.): ECCV 2012, Part II, LNCS 7573, pp. 572–585, 2012.

parameters involved are the detection thresholds and the quantisation precision of the accumulator array. Their values –usually empirically tuned– have direct impact on the number of false detections: too permissive detection thresholds or too coarse quantisation step introduce false positives, whilst over-restraining detection thresholds or too fine quantisation step cause false negatives.

A second class of detection methods relies on edge chaining techniques, which use extensively the geometric properties of the sought features, such as straightness criteria for line segments or curvature properties for ellipses [5,20]. Usually, these algorithms begin with a seed pixel (or a group of pixels), and subsequently, other pixels are added, provided they obey some geometric properties of the sought feature. At the end, a line (or an ellipse) is fitted on the gathered pixels, using either some deterministic fitting techniques (e.g. based on least-squares [6]), or randomised robust RANSAC-like approaches [13]. Although efficient in execution time (as opposed to Hough-based methods), these algorithms have difficulties in handling noisy edge maps, reporting an important number of false detections [5,2], caused by inappropriate detection thresholds.

A few works have tried to address the detection thresholds issue. In the Hough class, the *progressive probabilistic* HT (PPHT), introduced by Matas et al., stops the voting procedure for a particular feature when an excess is observed in the accumulator that could not have appeared by accident [14]. The *non-accidentalness* is assessed by using as detection threshold, a cut-off value on the probability that the observed excess occurred by chance in a noise image. This reasoning allows the rejection of false positives. Nonetheless, PPHT lacks scalability: the cut-off values are set for a predefined image size, and the guard against false positives is not ensured when larger images are analysed [8]. Similar reasonings are present in the edge chaining class, based generally on Lowe's criterion of significance [12,20]. Albeit parameter-free, Lowe's criterion does not assess the *overall* non-accidentalness, which causes an incomplete guard against false detections. The ellipse detector proposed by Chia et al. [2] tackles this problem by learning detection threshold values on computer-generated images. Although their results are improved comparing to existing works, their detector is still dependent on critical parameters: e.g. the learned detection thresholds favour complete ellipses; they are not able to reject small complete ellipses reported on parasite contours, while falsely rejecting some valid incomplete ellipses.

The formalisation of the false detections control within the feature detection problem was addressed by some authors: e.g. MINPRAN, proposed by Stewart for 3D alignment detection [18], but it still needs a parameter tuning.

A successful parameterless approach was introduced by Desolneux et al. [3], and it is known as the *a contrario* approach. It provides an efficient technique for the automatic computation of the detection thresholds based on what they call Helmholtz's perception principle; informally, it states that there is no perception in white noise. This comes basically to the non-accidentalness principle, used also by PPHT and Lowe's criterion. The major difference is that the *a contrario* statistical framework controls the overall number of false detections. Accordingly, the detection thresholds are self-tuning, guarding efficiently against false positives. Moreover, in the spirit of the parameter-free quest, Desolneux et al.'s approach detects geometric features taking as input the original image, without a previous edge detection step. Using this framework, Grompone von Gioi et al. proposed an efficient parameterless line segment detector (LSD) [8].

The key contribution of our work is to describe a parameter-free combined line segment and elliptical arc detector, based on the *a contrario* approach, which focuses on the control of false detections. The detector obeys a 3-step scheme: candidate selection, candidate validation, and model selection. The latter two are formally sound, being grounded on statistical foundations. Only the candidate selection is heuristic, for efficiency reasons. Our second contribution is related to the candidate selection step, where the proposed detector requires the use of an ellipse fitting operator. We propose a non-iterative fitting technique, which exhibits improved performance on incomplete data, due to the efficient merge of the geometric and photometric information available in images.

The remaining paper is organised as follows. Section 2 details the stages of the proposed feature detector ELSD (Ellipse and Line Segment Detector). Section 3 presents the ellipse fitting technique used by ELSD and compares it with other fitting operators. Section 4 reflects experimentally the efficiency and the robustness of the proposed detector, and section 5 concludes the paper.

2 ELSD – Ellipse and Line Segment Detector

The ELSD algorithm is a three-stage process: (1) first feature candidates are identified using a heuristic; (2) then each candidate has to pass a validation phase. Owing to the multiple families of features addressed, (3) a model selection step is required to choose the best geometric interpretation. The candidate selection step is based on a greedy (heuristic) approach, in the same spirit as in LSD. Ideally, to avoid heuristics at this step, all possible candidates should be considered; but this is impossible in practice, due to time constraints. Therefore we consider a heuristic free of critical parameters and as permissive as possible, which does not alter the quality of the result. In contrast, the validation step is formally sound, being grounded on the probabilistic *a contrario* approach proposed by Desolneux et al. [3], which ensures an efficient guard against false positives. Equally, the model selection step is based on a selection criterion that follows the principles of the model selection theory. Algorithm 1 gives the main steps of ELSD.

2.1 Candidate Selection

Due to the *a contrario* validation, the guard against false positives is ensured. The false negatives, however, are strictly due to an over-restrictive candidate selection procedure, i.e. there exist candidates which do not even get the chance to arrive to the validation phase. Any of the existing feature detectors could carry out this step. But they usually operate on edge maps and no reliable parameterless edge detector is yet available. The main feature of the proposed candidate selection is to be free of critical parameters and as permissive as possible, in order to avoid introducing false negatives.

Algorithm 1. ELSD

Input: Gray-level image x, **parameters**: none
Output: $\mathcal{L}_f$ – list of valid features (line segments, circular arcs, elliptical arcs).

$grad \leftarrow$ compute_gradient(x);
foreach *pixel* p_i *in* x **do**
    $R \leftarrow$ region_grow(p_i, $grad$);
    $C \leftarrow$ curve_grow(R, $grad$);
    $line \leftarrow$ fit_rectangle(R);
    $circle \leftarrow$ fit_circular_ring(C);
    $ellipse \leftarrow$ fit_elliptical_ring(C);
    $(\text{NFA}_{line}, \text{NFA}_{circle}, \text{NFA}_{ellipse}) = \text{NFA}(line, circle, ellipse)$;
    $\text{NFA}_{min} \leftarrow \min(\text{NFA}_{line}, \text{NFA}_{circle}, \text{NFA}_{ellipse})$;
    if $\text{NFA}_{min} \leq 1$ **then**
        add feature corresponding to NFA_{min} in $\mathcal{L}_f$;
    end
end

For the line segment part, we use the heuristic proposed for LSD [8], i.e. starting from seed pixels, a *region growing* process recursively groups pixels into connected regions sharing the same gradient orientation up to a given precision (see figure 1, first row). For the circular and elliptical arcs, we propose a *curve growing* procedure that adds a second level of grouping compared to the LSD approach, by simply alternating region growing and region chaining operations. The ends of the rectangle given by region growing are used as seed pixels, p_{s_r} and p_{s_l}, for subsequent region growing procedures. In LSD, the region growing chains pixels sharing the same orientation; in ELSD, the curve growing chains neighbour regions produced by region growing, provided they obey some loose, elementary constraints, which characterise the elliptical shapes. Namely, we impose that the contour described by the chained regions be *convex* and *roughly*

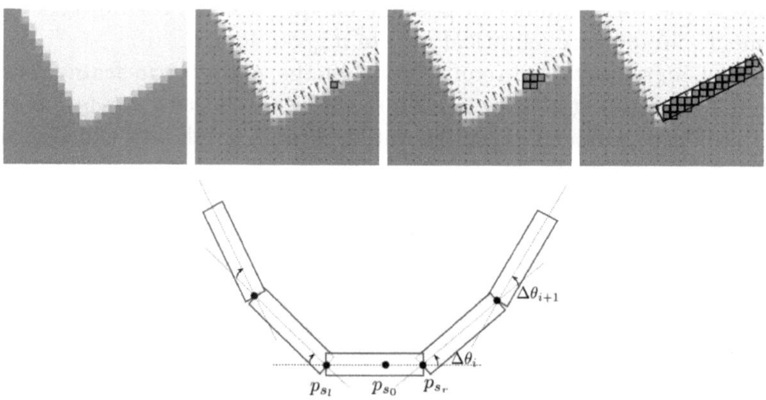

Fig. 1. First row: Region growing. Second row: Curve growing.

smooth (figure 1, second row). The **convexity rule** imposes that consecutive pairs of rectangles turn in the same direction; thus $\Delta\theta_i$ and $\Delta\theta_{i+1}$ have the same sign. The **smoothness rule** is roughly imposed by chaining only regions whose orientations differ by less than $\pi/2$.

The curve growing yields a polygonal approximation of the curve through a recursive scheme. When no more regions can be added, we compute the five parameters of the ellipse that fits the gathered pixels, using the technique detailed in section 3, as well as the three additional parameters of the elliptical ring that covers the pixels, namely the delimiting angles and the ring width. The delimiting angles are computed by sorting the gathered pixels according to their angular coordinate and taking the extremes, whilst the width is computed by summing the distances[1] of the points that are the farthest from the ellipse towards the exterior and the interior respectively. Additionally, a circle is fitted as well, together with the delimiting parameters of the circular ring. This redundancy is justified by the poor accuracy of ellipse fitting techniques when input data are sampled only along small arcs. In these cases, the curve, even if part of an ellipse, can be fairly approximated by a circular arc [17].

At the end of this stage, we are in possession of three candidates: the initial rectangle obtained after the region growing, and the circular and elliptical rings covering the pixels gathered by curve growing.

2.2 Validation

The main idea in the *a contrario* validation technique is to automatically compute the detection thresholds in a way that rejects candidates whose presence might be accidental. We remind the generic validation setup proposed by Desolneux et al. for feature detection [3] and then we state the formulation for circle and ellipse detection.

All along this study, we consider gray-level images of size $m \times n$, defined on a grid $\Gamma = [1, m] \times [1, n] \subset \mathbb{N}^2$, with values in $\mathbb{R}$, and we call *candidate* any region of pixels $c \subset \Gamma$, that might support a sought geometric feature. We will denote by N the total number of possible candidates of a certain type (namely line segment, circular arc, elliptical arc) in a given image.

Two main ingredients are required within the *a contrario* framework: *(i)* a measure function giving a score to each candidate, reflecting its *degree of structuredness*, and *(ii)* a model of unstructured data. A candidate will be validated if it is too structured to be expected in *(ii)*, according to the measure of *(i)*.

For line segment detection, Desolneux et al. give credit to the orientation of the gradient, rather than to its magnitude. Hence, the measure function $k_x(c)$ used to assess the degree of structuredness of the candidate c observed in an image x, is the number of *aligned pixels* that c contains (figure 2, left). A pixel $p \in \Gamma$ is said to be *aligned* with an oriented line segment s up to a precision σ if

$$Angle(\nabla x(p), dir_{\perp}(s)) \leq \sigma\pi, \quad (1)$$

[1] We use Rosin's approximation [17] to compute the Euclidean distance between a point and an ellipse.

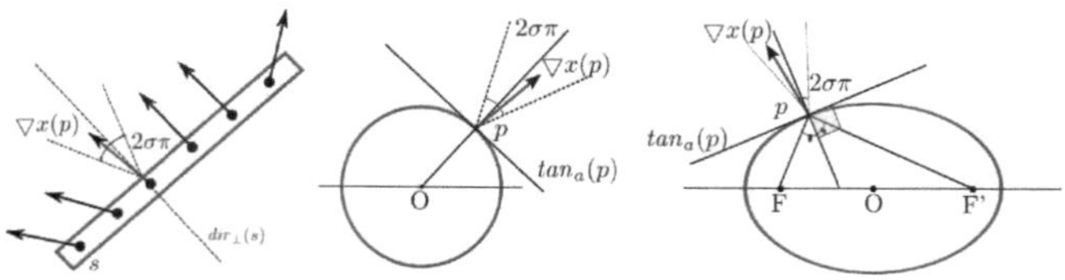

Fig. 2. Left: A segment s containing three σ-aligned pixels. Middle and right: Aligned pixel in circle and ellipse case.

where $\nabla x(p)$ is the gradient of the image x at p and $dir_\perp(s)$ is the direction orthogonal to s [3].

For the proposed algorithm ELSD, additional definitions need to be stated for circle and ellipse (see figure 2, middle and right). A pixel $p \in \Gamma$ is said to be *aligned* with a circular or elliptical arc a up to a precision σ if

$$Angle(\nabla x(p), dir_\perp(tan_a(p))) \leq \sigma\pi, \tag{2}$$

where $\nabla x(p)$ is the gradient of the image x at p and $dir_\perp(tan_a(p))$ is the direction orthogonal to the tangent $tan_a(p)$ to the circle or ellipse in p.

With this choice for assessing the degree of structuredness, a convenient unstructured model, that will be denoted as the *a contrario* $\mathcal{H}_0$ model, is one in which gradient orientations are i.i.d. random variables, i.e.:

1. $\forall p \in \Gamma, Angle(\nabla x(p))$ is uniformly distributed over $[0, 2\pi]$;
2. $\{Angle(\nabla x(p))\}_{p\in\Gamma}$ are independent random variables.

It has been proven by Desolneux et al. that these two assertions hold under certain conditions of subsampling if x is a Gaussian white noise image [3, p. 67]. From now on, x will refer to the analysed image and X to an (unstructured) Gaussian white noise image of the same size as x, drawn from the $\mathcal{H}_0$ model.

The *a contrario* model proposed by Desolneux et al. for line segment detection can be seamlessly applied for ellipse detection as well. Note that $\mathcal{H}_0$ is not meant to model the real noise of images; instead, it is a simple and effective model for unstructured, isotropic zones of the image, where no aligned structures are perceived. This model was thoroughly evaluated in [3] and a convincing agreement was obtained between results of line segment detectors grounded on this model and human perception.

The following *a contrario* definition, used jointly with a result from probability theory (Proposition 1), completes the *a contrario* validation setup.

Definition 1. *Let $\mathcal{Z} = \{Z_1, \ldots, Z_{N_\mathcal{Z}}\}$ be a set of $N_\mathcal{Z}$ integer random variables. Observing a value z_i for Z_i is an ε-meaningful event in $\mathcal{Z}$ if its associated* number of false alarms, *defined by* NFA $= N_\mathcal{Z}\mathbb{P}[Z_i \geq z_i]$, *is less than or equal to ε.*

Proposition 1. *The expected number of ε-meaningful events in $\mathcal{Z}$ is less than or equal to ε.*

Proof. We define the set of thresholds $\kappa_i = \min\{z \in \mathbb{N} \mid N_{\mathcal{Z}}\mathbb{P}[Z_i \geq z] \leq \varepsilon\}$. With this definition, an observed value z_i is ε-meaningful if and only if $z_i \geq \kappa_i$. Then, the subset of elementary ε-meaningful events associated to Z_i is $\{Z_i \geq \kappa_i\}$, and the expected overall number of ε-meaningful events in $\mathcal{Z}$ is given by

$$\mathbb{E}\left[\sum_{i=1}^{N_{\mathcal{Z}}} \mathbb{1}_{\{Z_i \geq \kappa_i\}}\right] = \sum_{i=1}^{N_{\mathcal{Z}}} \mathbb{P}[Z_i \geq \kappa_i] \leq \sum_{i=1}^{N_{\mathcal{Z}}} \frac{\varepsilon}{N_{\mathcal{Z}}} = \varepsilon. \quad \blacksquare$$

In our case, we deal with the events of observing in image x candidates c_i, containing $k_x(c_i)$ aligned pixels. A candidate c_i is considered a valid detection and said to be ε-meaningful, in agreement with Definition 1, when its associated number of false alarms $\text{NFA}(c_i, x) = N\mathbb{P}[k_X(c_i) \geq k_x(c_i)]$ satisfies the *validation test*:

$$\text{NFA}(c_i, x) \leq \varepsilon \, . \tag{3}$$

Thus, the set $\mathcal{Z}$ corresponds to the N random variables $k_X(c_i)$ and NFA reflects the probability of observing in a random image X (of the same size as x) candidates at least as structured as the analysed one. The smaller the NFA, the more unlikely is c_i to appear in an image X drawn from $\mathcal{H}_0$; thus, it is meaningful.

Thanks to Proposition 1, the expected number of candidates in an unstructured image X with *at least* the same degree of structuredness as in the analysed image x is ensured to be (statistically speaking) less than ε. In other words, *if a candidate is accepted as valid detection when the equation* (3) *holds, then the number of accidental detections, which are in fact false positives, is guaranteed to be less than the chosen* ε. This result reflects precisely the formalisation of Helmholtz's perception principle, which states that in an unstructured image, only a very small number of detections should be reported.

In practice, ε can be set as small as desired. As it is proven in [3, p. 77], the threshold values $\kappa_i = \min\{k \in \mathbb{N} \mid N\mathbb{P}[k_X(c_i) \geq k] \leq \varepsilon\}$, such that the candidates c_i are ε-meaningful when $k_x(c_i) \geq \kappa_i$ (using a similar reasoning as in the above proof), have a logarithmic dependence on ε; thus a simple, convenient value can be assigned to ε. The value $\varepsilon = 1$ yielded satisfactory results [8], so it will be kept for the proposed detector as well. With this choice, we assume the risk of accepting on average one false positive per image. Considering the weak dependence on the *unique* detection threshold ε fixed to 1, the approach can be considered as parameterless.

If the angular precision for declaring a pixel as aligned is $\pi\sigma$, then the probability for a pixel to be aligned under the *a contrario* model is $\frac{2\pi\sigma}{2\pi} = \sigma$. Since the gradient orientations are independent under the chosen model, $k_X(c)$ follows a binomial law with parameters $l(c)$, $k_x(c)$, and σ, where $l(c)$ is the total number of pixels in the rectangle or ring. Therefore, we can write $\text{NFA}(c, x) = N\mathcal{B}(l(c), k_x(c), \sigma)$, with $\mathcal{B}(l, k, \sigma) = \sum_{i=k}^{l} \binom{l}{i} \sigma^i (1-\sigma)^{l-i}$ being the binomial tail. For σ we set the value $1/8$, which proved to be satisfactory in practice [8].

Considering a one pixel precision, in the line segment case, the number of potential candidates in an $m \times n$ image is $N_{line} = (mn)^{5/2}$, as each rectangular region has five degrees of freedom: centre (2), length (1), orientation (1), and

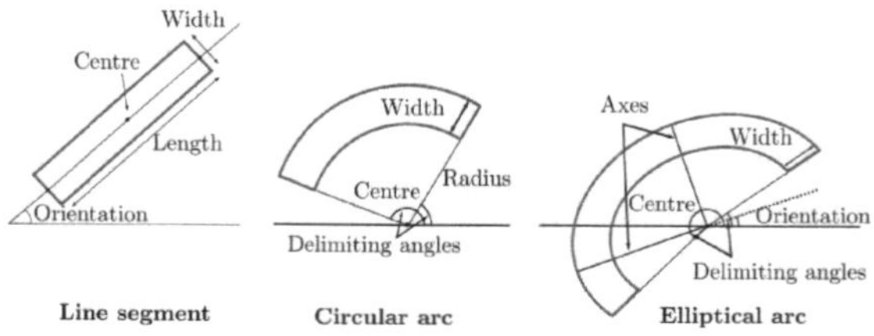

Fig. 3. Degrees of freedom for line segment, circular arc, and elliptical arc

width (1); see figure 3 left. We count $(mn)^{1/2}$ possible values for each degree of freedom. For circular arcs we have $N_{circle} = (mn)^3$ for six degrees of freedom: centre (2), radius (1), width (1), and delimiting angles (2); see figure 3 middle. Finally, elliptical arcs have eight degrees of freedom: centre (2), axes (2), orientation (1), width (1), and delimiting angles (2), thus $N_{ellipse} = (mn)^4$; see figure 3 right. These estimates count roughly all the possible combinations of pixels that could support a feature in the given image and they allow the detection thresholds to adapt to the image size. But in practice, only the candidates proposed by the candidate selection step will be analysed, for efficiency reasons.

All-in-all, with the chosen value for ε and the estimates for the number of candidates, the tests that the feature candidates must pass in order to be considered valid detections are:

$$\begin{aligned} \text{NFA}_{line} &= (mn)^{5/2}\mathcal{B}(l,k,\sigma) \leq 1 \text{ for line segments,} \\ \text{NFA}_{circle} &= (mn)^{3}\mathcal{B}(l,k,\sigma) \leq 1 \text{ for circular arcs,} \\ \text{NFA}_{ellipse} &= (mn)^{4}\mathcal{B}(l,k,\sigma) \leq 1 \text{ for elliptical arcs.} \end{aligned} \tag{4}$$

2.3 Model Selection

The candidates declared meaningful in the validation step compete subsequently in a *model selection* phase for the best interpretation for the given data and the winner is kept as final valid detection. The model selection theory is a central subject in statistical learning and an important number of model selection criteria is available in the literature [4]. The proposed detector ELSD entails a model selection step within a linear regression problem: given a set of pixels in an image, and three fitted models (line, circle, ellipse), decide which model is the most suitable to explain the data. We choose to use the NFA of a candidate as model selection criterion, i.e. the candidate possessing the smallest NFA is considered as most meaningful, and kept as final valid detection. This idea was suggested by Desolneux et al. [3, p. 245], but not carried out. The pertinence of this usage needs a thorough discussion. Due to space limitation, here we only point out that, qualitatively, NFA follows the *Ockham's razor principle* which guides the model selection theory, namely it contains a term illustrating the goodness of fit (the binomial tail) and a term penalising for complexity (the number of candidates N, proportional with the number of free parameters). We refer the reader to [16] for more details on this topic.

3 Conic Fitting Using Gradient Orientations

The candidate selection of ELSD relies on a conic fitting technique, restricted to the cases of circle and ellipse. Addressing circular and elliptical arcs, we seek for a closed-form solution that performs well on those being small or incomplete. Let $\mathcal{C}$ be a general conic represented in homogeneous matrix form by:

$$\tilde{\mathbf{p}}^\top \mathsf{C}_{\boldsymbol{\theta}} \tilde{\mathbf{p}} = 0, \tag{5}$$

where $\mathsf{C}_{\boldsymbol{\theta}}$ is the order-3 symmetrical matrix of conic (homogeneous) coefficients, stacked in the vector $\boldsymbol{\theta}_{6\times 1}$ (six coefficients with five degrees of freedom), and $\tilde{\mathbf{p}} = (x\ y\ 1)^\top$ is the vector of augmented Cartesian coordinates of a point.

Given n points, we consider the problem of fitting to the data an ellipse modeled by an implicit equation of the form (5). The fitting comes to minimising in a least-squares sense the objective function $\mathsf{F} = \sum_{i=1}^{n} \delta^2(\boldsymbol{\theta}, \tilde{\mathbf{p}}_i)$, subject to $h(\boldsymbol{\theta}) = 0$, where $\delta(\boldsymbol{\theta}, \tilde{\mathbf{p}}_i) = \tilde{\mathbf{p}}_i^\top \mathsf{C}_{\boldsymbol{\theta}} \tilde{\mathbf{p}}_i$ is the *error-of-fit* between the input points and the estimated conic, and $h(\cdot)$ models different constraints that need to be imposed on the conic coefficients to avoid the trivial solution or/and to ensure ellipticity [6]. Several authors proposed weighting schemes to improve the performance on incomplete data, where this technique has the tendency to grossly underestimate the eccentricity [19].

A few works have tried to put forward the usefulness of the derivative constraint entailed by the gradient orientation. Förstner and Gulch use exclusively the gradient orientation to accurately locate the centre of a circle, which corresponds to the intersection point (computed in a least-squares sense) of the lines supporting the gradient vectors of the pixels situated on the contour of the circle. This is due to the fact that these lines all converge towards the centre of the circular shape [7]. The radius can be computed subsequently using the positional constraints. Guennebaud and Gross applied Förstner's idea in 3D for sphere fitting, in a computer graphics application [9]. In the ellipse case, this idea cannot be seamlessly applied, as the lines supporting the gradient vectors of the pixels situated on the ellipse contour do not converge towards the ellipse centre. To overcome this, Ouellet and Hebert perform the ellipse fitting in the dual space [15], but their formulation omits useful information, namely the positional constraints. All these methods improve the fitting results while remaining computationally efficient, but they still lack accuracy on incomplete data.

We suggest that the simultaneous usage of the positional and tangential information can further improve the results. Accordingly, the fitting problem writes as: $\min_{\boldsymbol{\theta}} \sum_{i=1}^{n} (\delta^2(\boldsymbol{\theta}, \tilde{\mathbf{p}}_i) + \gamma^2(\boldsymbol{\theta}, \tilde{\mathbf{p}}_i, \mathbf{g}_i))$, subject to $h(\boldsymbol{\theta}) = 0$, where $\gamma(\cdot)$ returns the error-of-fit on the gradient orientation, and $\mathbf{g}_i$ denotes the 2-vector of the image gradient at (x_i, y_i). To obtain the expression of $\gamma(\cdot)$, we make use of the *pole-polar duality*, given by $\mathsf{C}\tilde{\mathbf{p}} \sim \mathbf{l}$, where $\sim$ denotes the projective equality [10]. The point with vector $\tilde{\mathbf{p}}$ is called the pole of the line $\mathbf{l}$ w.r.t. the conic $\mathcal{C}$, and conversely, the line with vector $\mathbf{l}$ is the polar of $\tilde{\mathbf{p}}$. Given a point $\tilde{\mathbf{p}}$ belonging to $\mathcal{C}$ and with gradient vector $\mathbf{g} = (g_1, g_2)^\top$, its polar $\mathbf{l}$ is tangent to $\mathcal{C}$ at $\tilde{\mathbf{p}}$ and is orthogonal to any line with direction $\mathbf{g}$. Thus, the point at infinity (denoted by

$\tilde{\mathbf{g}}_\infty^\perp$) associated to the direction orthogonal to $\mathbf{g}$ lies on $\mathbf{l}$, that is: $\mathbf{l}^\top \tilde{\mathbf{g}}_\infty^\perp = 0$. If one assumes that the camera has square pixels, then $\tilde{\mathbf{g}}_\infty^\perp = (-g_2, g_1, 0)^\top$. Using the pole-polar duality, we obtain a new equation, linear in the elements of $\mathsf{C}_{\boldsymbol{\theta}}$:

$$\tilde{\mathbf{p}}^\top \mathsf{C}_{\boldsymbol{\theta}} \tilde{\mathbf{g}}_\infty^\perp = 0 \,. \tag{6}$$

Together with the positional constraints (5), the linear equation system becomes:

$$\begin{cases} \tilde{\mathbf{p}}_i^\top \mathsf{C}_{\boldsymbol{\theta}} \tilde{\mathbf{p}}_i = 0 \\ \tilde{\mathbf{p}}_i^\top \mathsf{C}_{\boldsymbol{\theta}} \tilde{\mathbf{g}}_{\infty_i}^\perp = 0 \end{cases} \quad i = \{1, \ldots, n\} \,. \tag{7}$$

This way, each point contributes with two independent equations. This technique can be seamlessly applied to both circle and ellipse fitting. To improve the numerical stability, the input data are first normalised as described in [10].

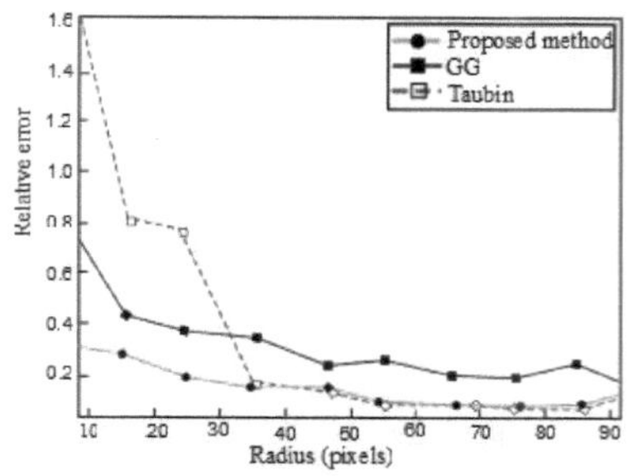

Fig. 4. Mean relative error on the estimated radius for 200 tests performed on real images of printed drawn circles. Input data are sampled along arcs of $\sim$ 45 degrees.

To show the improvement obtained by using simultaneously the positional and the tangential constraints, we compared the proposed method with Taubin's circle fitting operator [19], which uses only positional constraints, and with Guennebaud and Gross's method [9] mentioned above (denoted GG in figure 4). The results of the three methods on incomplete data are shown in figure 4. Table 1 presents a comparison with Ouellet and Hebert's method [15], in fitting ellipses on incomplete data. This comparative study shows that when input data are sampled along incomplete conics, and especially when the features are small, it is crucial to exploit simultaneously all the information they possess.

Table 1. Mean(Max) error on the estimated centre, for 500 tests performed on computer-generated images; input points are sampled along incomplete ellipses generated randomly, with axes values in the range 10 – 100 pixels

Method	75% of contour	50% of contour
Proposed	0.1136(0.4465)	0.5972(4.8615)
Ouellet	0.2018(1.0942)	3.4944(8.3421)

4 Results

The proposed detector was extensively tested on various (computer-generated and natural) images. Its performance is compared with relevant feature detectors available online: Etemadi's detector [5], which addresses the simultaneous detection of line segments and circular arcs, and Hough detectors for circles (HC) [21] and ellipses (HE) [21], respectively. All detectors were tested with their default parameters. The edge maps were obtained using Canny's edge detector available in Matlab, with default parameters. The tests carried out on computer-generated images of overlapping and non-overlapping geometric shapes, analysed the robustness against noise, and the precision at different scales. Figure 5 illustrates the typical behaviour of the above detectors when applied on these test images. Generally, Etemadi's detector is accurate in reporting the correct detections (line segments and circular arcs), but has no ability in eliminating false positives, reported on parasite contours. Equally, its precision at reduced scale is poor. The two Hough-based detectors behave reasonably well as long as the images are noise-free. When noise is present, they encounter serious difficulties and the results are not satisfactory: HC reports an important number of false positives, whereas HE reports no detection. The proposed detector gives reasonable results in all these cases: it is accurate when applied on noise-free images, even at

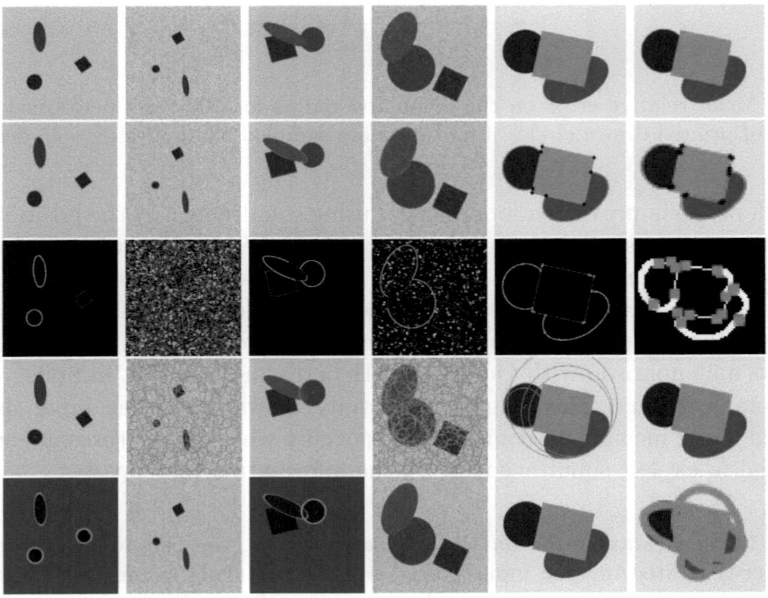

Fig. 5. Results on computer-generated images of geometric shapes (square, circle, ellipse) for different noise types and different scales. From top to bottom: original image, ELSD, Etemadi, HC, HE. From left to right: noise-free image, image altered by Gaussian noise, overlapping shapes, overlapping shapes altered by salt-and-pepper noise, overlapping shapes-normal scale, overlapping shapes-reduced scale.

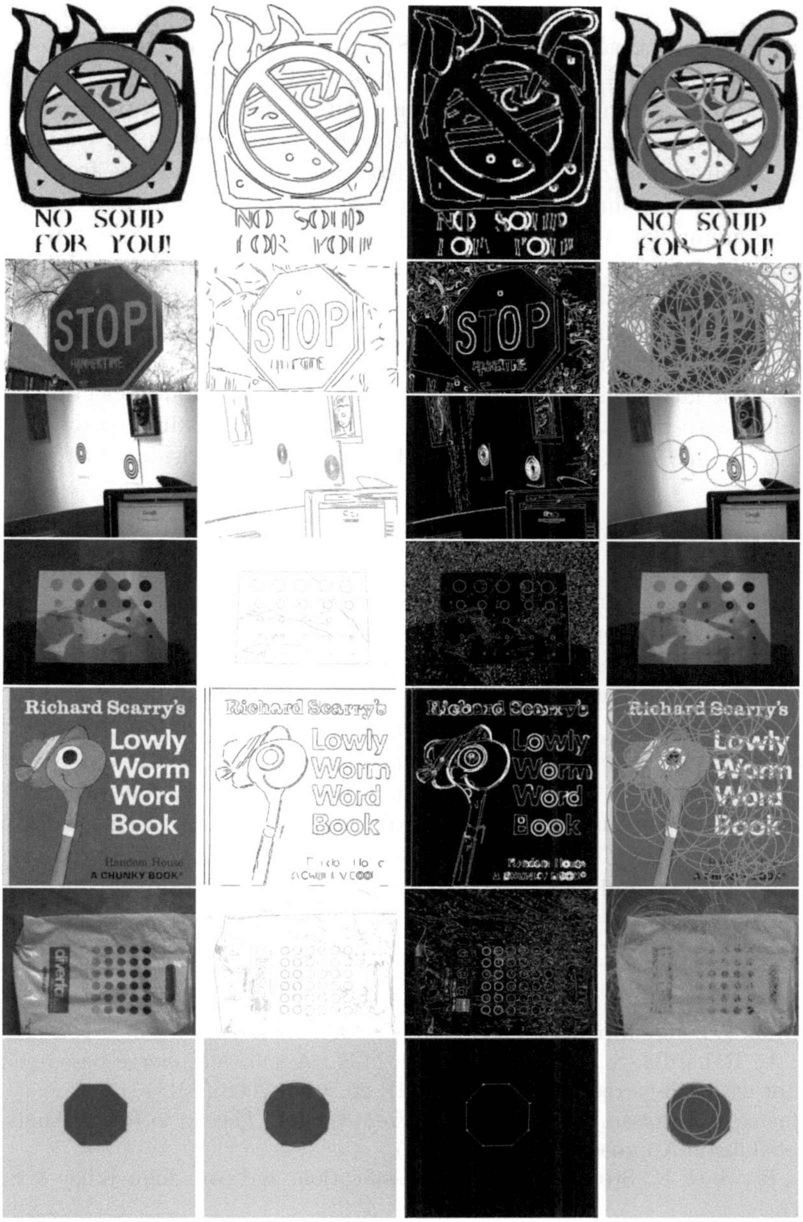

Fig. 6. Results on natural images. 1st column: original image, 2nd column: ELSD, 3rd column: Etemadi, 4th column: HC. HE reported no detection. Image size and ELSD's execution time on a regular machine for each example from top to bottom: 213×279 0.3s, 445×304 1s, 640×480 0.4s, 1600×1200 1.3s, 442×450 0.6s, 1600×1200 3.1s, 612×563 0.1s.

reduced scale, due to the enhanced conic fitting used; the noise (especially salt-and-pepper) provokes an over-segmentation of contours, but no false positive is reported, which reflects the validity of ELSD's theoretical grounds.

In order to assess the behaviour of the proposed detector in real-world applications, we have extensively tested it on natural images. Unfortunately, the literature lacks an appropriate benchmark with labeled images for evaluating geometric feature detectors. We downloaded one thousand images from flickr and used them as test images. Figure 6 gives some relevant results. The source code and an online demo of ELSD, where users can upload images and test the detector, can be found at `http://ubee.enseeiht.fr/vision/ELSD/`. A full description of the detector is given in [16]. The current limitations of ELSD are shown in figure 5, 4th column, and figure 6, last row. For the former case, a merging step should be implemented to overcome the contour over-segmentation due to noise [2]. The latter case illustrates the behaviour of the model selection step, when we deal with polygonal shapes that can be fairly approximated by curves. To improve the accuracy, polygonal candidates should be considered as well.

5 Conclusion

We proposed a parameterless line segment and elliptical arc detector, grounded on the *a contrario* approach, which controls the number of false positives. Addressing multiple feature families (line segments, circular and elliptical arcs), the proposed detector entails a model selection step. The essential quantity of the *a contrario* approach –NFA– is used for both validation and model selection purposes. To improve the accuracy of occluded shapes detection, a non-iterative circle and ellipse fitting technique was introduced; it uses simultaneously the positional and the tangential information of the image pixels. Future work will concentrate on the merging of elliptical arcs to obtain precise ellipses in case of fragmented contours, and on the model selection phase, to improve its accuracy.

References

1. Canny, J.: A computational approach to edge detection. PAMI 8, 679–698 (1986)
2. Chia, A., Rahardja, S., Rajan, D., Leung, M.K.: A split and merge based ellipse detector with self-correcting capability. TIP 20, 1991–2006 (2011)
3. Desolneux, A., Moisan, L., Morel, J.M.: From Gestalt Theory to Image Analysis: A Probabilistic Approach. Springer (2008)
4. Duda, R., Hart, P., Stork, D.: Pattern classification, 2nd edn. John Wiley & Sons (2001)
5. Etemadi, A.: Robust segmentation of edge data. In: Int. Conf. on Image Processing and its Applications, pp. 311–314 (1992)
6. Fitzgibbon, A., Pilu, M., Fisher, R.: Direct least-squares fitting of ellipses. PAMI 21, 476–480 (1999)
7. Forstner, W., Gulch, E.: A fast operator for detection and precise location of distinct points, corners and centres of circular features. In: Intercom. Conf. on Fast Processing of Photogrammetric Data, pp. 281–305 (1987)

8. Grompone von Gioi, R., Jakubowicz, J., Morel, J.M., Randall, G.: LSD: A fast line segment detector with a false detection control. PAMI 32, 722–732 (2010)
9. Guennebaud, G., Gross, M.: Algebraic point set surfaces. ACM Trans. Graph. 26, 231–239 (2007)
10. Hartley, R.I., Zisserman, A.: Multiple View Geometry in Computer Vision. 2nd edn. Cambridge University Press (2004)
11. Hough, P.: Method and means for recognizing complex patterns. U.S. Patent 3069654 (1962)
12. Lowe, D.G.: Perceptual Organization and Visual Recognition. Kluwer Academic Publishers (1985)
13. Mai, F., Hung, Y.S., Zhong, H., Sze, W.F.: A hierarchical approach for fast and robust ellipse extraction. Pattern Recognition 41, 2512–2524 (2008)
14. Matas, J., Galambos, C., Kittler, J.: Progressive probabilistic hough transform. In: BMVC, pp. 256–265 (1998)
15. Ouellet, J., Hebert, P.: Precise ellipse estimation without contour point extraction. Machine Vision and Applications 21, 59–67 (2009)
16. Pătrăucean, V.: Detection and identification of elliptical structure arrangements in images: Theory and algorithms. PhD thesis. University of Toulouse, France, `http://ethesis.inp-toulouse.fr/archive/00001847/`
17. Rosin, P.L.: Ellipse fitting using orthogonal hyperbolae and Stirling's oval. Graphical Models and Image Processing 60, 209–213 (1998)
18. Stewart, C.V.: MINPRAN: A new robust estimator for computer vision. PAMI 17, 925–938 (1995)
19. Taubin, G.: Estimation of planar curves, surfaces, and nonplanar space curves defined by implicit equations with applications to edge and range image segmentation. PAMI 13, 1115–1138 (1991)
20. West, G., Rosin, P.: Multi-stage combined ellipse and line detection. In: BMVC, pp. 197–206 (1992)
21. Xu, L., Oja, E., Kultanen, P.: A new curve detection method: Randomized Hough Transform. Pattern Recogn. Lett. 11, 331–338 (1990)

Detecting and Reconstructing 3D Mirror Symmetric Objects

Sudipta N. Sinha, Krishnan Ramnath, and Richard Szeliski

Microsoft Research, Redmond, WA
{sudipsin,kramnath,szeliski}@microsoft.com

Abstract. We present a system that detects 3D mirror-symmetric objects in images and then reconstructs their visible symmetric parts. Our detection stage is based on matching mirror symmetric feature points and descriptors and then estimating the symmetry direction using RANSAC. We enhance this step by augmenting feature descriptors with their affine-deformed versions and matching these extended sets of descriptors. The reconstruction stage uses a novel edge matching algorithm that matches symmetric pairs of curves that are likely to be counterparts. This allows the algorithm to reconstruct lightly textured objects, which are problematic for traditional feature-based and intensity-based stereo matchers.

Keywords: Symmetry detection, 3D reconstruction, curve matching.

1 Introduction

Mirror (bilaterally) symmetric 3D objects are all around us in the man-made world, and yet most computer vision algorithms do not take advantage of this potential structural regularity. Figure 1 show some of these objects, which often occur in cluttered environments and may also suffer from a dearth of easily matchable keypoint features.

There exists a wide body of literature for detecting skewed planar symmetric shapes [1,2,3,4,5,6]. Techniques have also been developed for reconstructing 3D symmetric scenes [7,8]. However, relatively few algorithms have been developed for reconstructing symmetric 3D objects in cluttered environments. Previously published algorithms either rely on manual intervention [9,10,11], apply photometric stereo to symmetric textureless objects [12], or assume structural regularities, such as piecewise planar surfaces bounded by straight line segments [13].

In this paper, we remove the restrictions found in previous systems and demonstrate the ability to detect and reconstruct a wider range of 3D mirror-symmetric objects in general scenes. We begin by matching pairs of mirrored keypoint descriptors to find the epipolar geometry (vanishing point) corresponding to the direction of symmetry, i.e., the normal of the plane of symmetry (Figure 2a). We enhance the performance of this stage by constructing local affinely deformed versions of each descriptor, which gives us a richer set of potential features to match and better tolerates local foreshortening effects.

A. Fitzgibbon et al. (Eds.): ECCV 2012, Part II, LNCS 7573, pp. 586–600, 2012.

Fig. 1. Some examples of mirror-symmetric 3D objects in cluttered settings

Next, we rectify the input image to obtain a traditional horizontal epipolar geometry (Figure 2b). We then extract edges and curves from the rectified image (Figure 2c) and match these to obtain the disparities (inverse depths) of corresponding points (Figure 2d). Because it uses a different set of features, our curve-based approach to matching is complementary to the feature-based [1,2,3,4,5] and dense pixel-based [7,8] matching approaches used in previous systems and therefore extends the range of applicability of symmetry detection and reconstruction techniques.

The remainder of this paper is structured as follows. We begin with a review of previous work in Section 2. In Section 3, we describe the imaging geometry when viewing a bilaterally symmetric 3D object from both a canonical and general viewpoint. Section 4 describes our RANSAC-based matching algorithm for finding the symmetry direction and our enhanced feature descriptors. Section 5 describes how we rectify each image according to the dominant symmetry direction and determine the likely disparity range. Section 6 describes our curve matching algorithms for finding dense edge correspondences on the symmetric 3D objects. Section 7 summarizes our experiments on a number of challenging scenes and real-world 3D objects. We conclude with a discussion of future work.

2 Previous Work

The computer vision literature on detecting bilateral, point, and translational symmetries is rich and voluminous. Liu *et al.* [1] provide a comprehensive summary and guide to this literature, while [6] summarizes the results presented at the recent Symmetry Detection from Real World Images CVPR 2011 workshop[1].

Among all of the symmetries studied in this field, the most closely related to this paper are *2D bilateral (mirror) skew symmetries*, which are observed when a bilaterally symmetric planar object (e.g., butterfly wings) are observed from an arbitrary perspective camera. Most approaches to detecting such symmetries start by matching affine covariant regions or interest points and then voting for the axis of skew symmetry [2,3,4,5,14].

In this paper, we are interested in detecting and modeling full 3D objects with interesting depth and structure rather than just planar configurations [15].

[1] `http://vision.cse.psu.edu/research/symmComp/workshop/index.shtml`

Fig. 2. Processing pipeline: (a) epipolar geometry from matched points; (b) rectified image with depth range and inlier matches (see text for a longer description); (c) extracted curves; (d) recovered depths for matched curves.

The observation that an object and its image seen in a mirror can be treated as a stereo pair goes back at least two decades. The system described by Mitsumoto *et al.* [9] uses manual correspondences to determine the 3D points from which a wireframe model can be constructed. François *et al.* [10] observe that a mirror-symmetric scene can be similarly treated as a stereo pair; they use the commercial PhotoModeler system to establish manual correspondences in order to create texture-mapped 3D models of objects. Shimshoni *et al.* [12] apply photometric stereo to images of symmetric textureless Lambertian objects.

Jiang *et al.* [11] use orthogonal vanishing points to estimate the camera pose and intrinsics; they then use automated feature detection and matching to estimate a sparse 3D reconstruction, which is then turned into a continuous texture-mapped model with the help of user sketching. Xue *et al.* [13] describe a related system that uses automated straight line segment detection and mapping to produce piecewise-planar models of furniture. The detection of 3D symmetry in range scan data is also an active topic of study in computer graphics [16].

Fully automated methods for dense reconstruction of scenes with extended symmetries have recently been developed. Wu *et al.* [17,7] describe a system for detecting repetitions in architectural scenes and use dense stereo matching to build 3D texture-mapped façade models. Koser *et al.* [8] find the symmetry plane in a bilaterally symmetric architectural interior, façade, or detail using automated feature matching; they then use dense stereo to obtain a depth map.

In this paper, we use similar automated matching techniques to estimate the plane of symmetry, but then use curve matching to reconstruct a sparse 3D object model for objects that lack dense texture. We also demonstrate our results on objects seen in cluttered environments, where determining the epipolar geometry and the extent of the symmetric objects are challenging problems.

3 Problem Formulation

A bilaterally symmetric 3D object has a *plane of symmetry*, where corresponding points are opposite to each other with respect to this plane. Let us call the normal associated with this plane as the *direction of symmetry*.

The simplest case to analyze is when the direction of symmetry is aligned with the x-axis, as in Figure 3a. Under this condition, all corresponding points,

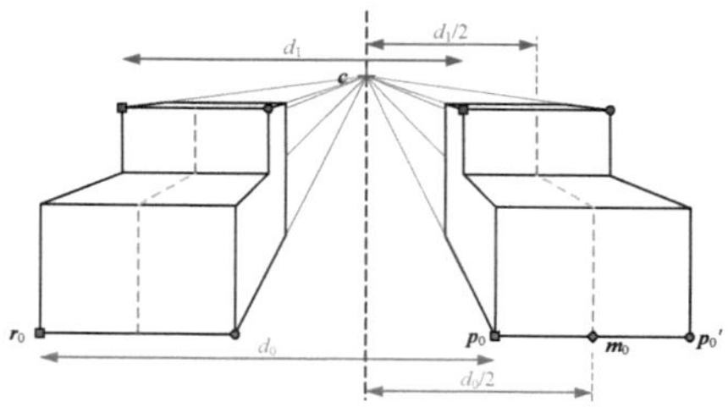

(a)

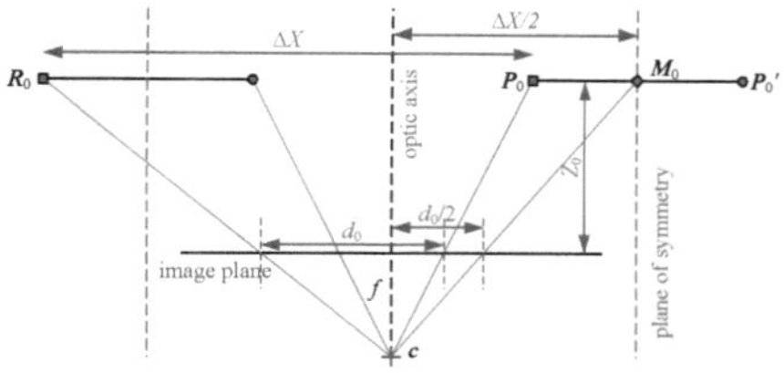

(b)

Fig. 3. Epipolar geometry: (a) In a rectified configuration, the disparity d_0 between a point $\mathbf{p}_0$ matched in an image with its reflected version $\mathbf{r}_0$ is equal to twice the horizontal distance $d_0/2$ between the match midpoint $\mathbf{m}_0$ and the optic center $\mathbf{c}$. Note that in general, objects may have more than one local axis of symmetry per scanline. (b) A top-down view shows the relationship between the 3D horizontal displacement ΔX between corresponding points, between the optic center and the midline $\Delta X/2$, and the pixel horizontal disparity $d_0 = f\Delta X/Z_0$.

e.g., $\mathbf{p}_0$ and $\mathbf{p}_0'$, lie on corresponding scanlines. Furthermore, points that lie at the same depth from the camera have the same *horizontal disparity* $d_0 = \|\mathbf{r}_0 - \mathbf{p}_0\|$, where $\mathbf{r}_0$ is the point in the horizontally reflected image that would end up being matched with $\mathbf{p}_0$ by a traditional stereo matcher.

It is easy to show that the horizontal disparity $d_0 = f\Delta X/Z_0$ is equal to twice the horizontal distance from the optic center to the midpoint $\mathbf{m}_0$ (see Figure 3b). The disparity is linearly related to inverse depth by the scale factor $f\Delta X$, where f is the focal length and ΔX is twice the horizontal distance between the plane of symmetry and the optic axis.[2]

In the case of a camera in a general configuration, the direction of symmetry, i.e., the lines joining all corresponding points, point at a finite epipole $\mathbf{e}$ (Figure 4). By assuming that the camera has orthonormal axes, square pixels and principal point at the center of the image, and by assuming that the focal length f is known[3], we can compute a *rectifying rotation* around the optic center that transforms an arbitrary image into a horizontally rectified one, i.e., where $\mathbf{e}' = (1, 0, 0)$ and all corresponding points lie on corresponding scanlines. Let us denote the rotation between the world coordinate system and the rectified coordinate system using a 3×3 rotation matrix

$$\mathbf{R} = \left[\mathbf{r}_0 \middle| \mathbf{r}_1 \middle| \mathbf{r}_2\right]. \tag{1}$$

$\mathbf{R}$ maps the ideal point $\mathbf{i} = (1, 0, 0)$ to an epipole direction $\mathbf{r}_0 = \mathbf{R}\mathbf{i}$, which then gets projected to the epipole $\mathbf{e}_0 = (e_x, e_y, f)$. We can therefore determine the

[2] This is the same formula as in traditional rectified stereo matching, where $d = fB/Z$ and B is the horizontal baseline between cameras [18].

[3] Modern cameras report their focal lengths in their EXIF tags and mobile vision applications can also assume a calibrated sensor. If such information is missing, additional cues in the image, e.g., orthogonal vanishing points, can be used instead.

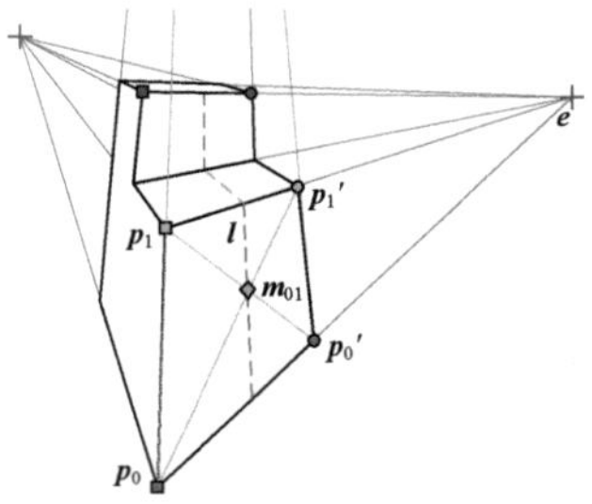

Fig. 4. In a general image configuration (arbitrary camera rotation), lines joining mirror-symmetric points $(\mathbf{p}_i, \mathbf{p}'_i)$ intersect at the vanishing point $\mathbf{e}$ corresponding to the direction of symmetry. Pairs of correspondences delineating a planar surface with bilateral planar symmetry can be used to compute a midline $\mathbf{l}$, which can be made vertical during the rectification stage.

first column of $\mathbf{R}$ by simply normalizing the calibrated epipole coordinates, i.e., $\mathbf{r}_0 = \mathcal{N}(\mathbf{e}_0)$, where $\mathcal{N}(\mathbf{v}) = \mathbf{v}/\|\mathbf{v}\|$ turns a vector into a unit vector.

How can we determine the other entries in $\mathbf{R}$?

One possibility is to minimize the amount of roll around the x axis during the rectification process. This can be achieved by setting

$$\mathbf{r}_1 = \mathcal{N}(\mathbf{k} \times \mathbf{r}_0) \tag{2}$$

$$\mathbf{r}_2 = \mathbf{r}_0 \times \mathbf{r}_1, \tag{3}$$

where $\mathbf{k} = (0, 0, 1)$.

Another possibility is to pick a plane in the image that passes through two matching pairs, say $(\mathbf{p}_0, \mathbf{p}'_0)$ and $(\mathbf{p}_1, \mathbf{p}'_1)$ in Figure 4, and to make this plane orthogonal to the camera in the rectified image. To do this, we first compute the midline $\mathbf{l}$ as the line joining midpoint $\mathbf{m}_{01} = \mathbf{p}_0\mathbf{p}'_1 \times \mathbf{p}_1\mathbf{p}'_0$ and "vanishing point"[4] $\mathbf{v}_{01} = \mathbf{p}_0\mathbf{p}_1 \times \mathbf{p}'_0\mathbf{p}'_1$. We then set

$$\mathbf{r}_1 = \mathcal{N}(\mathbf{l} \times \mathbf{r}_0) \tag{4}$$

$$\mathbf{r}_2 = \mathbf{r}_0 \times \mathbf{r}_1. \tag{5}$$

This choice makes the green midline $\mathbf{l}$ in Figure 4 map to the vertical green midline in Figure 3a.

We have experimented with both of these choices, and found that while the second strategy (which can be implemented using RANSAC and then counting inliers to this plane) does indeed expose the bilateral symmetry on the chosen plane, it also creates larger pixel distortions during the rectification stage. We therefore use the first strategy, which minimizes the amount of distortion while moving the horizontal epipole to infinity.

[4] $\mathbf{v}_{01}$ is not a true vanishing point, since in general $\mathbf{p}_0\mathbf{p}_1$ and $\mathbf{p}'_0\mathbf{p}'_1$ need not be parallel, just bilaterally symmetric.

4 Feature-Based Symmetry Detection

Given this geometric analysis of bilateral 3D symmetry, how can we go about finding corresponding matching points and determining the rectifying transformation? Unlike traditional structure from motion, which requires 5 (calibrated) or 7 or 8 (uncalibrated) correspondences to determine the epipolar geometry [19], we only need to find two sets of corresponding pairs, which makes a RANSAC search for the epipole $\mathbf{e}$ much more efficient.[5]

(a) (b) (c) (d)

Fig. 5. Feature matching results: (a) Hessian-Laplace; (b) FAST-ER; (c) FAST-ER with affine distortions; (d) detected features for FAST-ER+Affine. The blue lines show all feature matches and the green lines show the inliers after finding the best epipole.

The traditional approach to finding such correspondences is to detect scale and affine-covariant features [2,3,4,5,6,7,8] and to then perform nearest neighbor-based matching [20] on the extracted features. In order to compensate for local perspective distortions, affine adaptation of features is used in Hessian-Affine and Harris-Affine detectors [21]. However, performing affine adaptation on the interest points hurts the repeatability, as it increases the likelihood that different features map to the same descriptor.

In order to maintain the repeatability while also allowing for affine distortions, we first run a feature detector with high repeatability. We then extract a bag of features for each interest point location, using an approach similar to the one described in [22]. We sample a set of affine transformations that allow locally distorted patches to match better. However, rather than matching every affine transformed patch in the query image to every patch in the other image, we perform nearest neighbor matching while maintaining the grouping relationship of the features, as described next.

For each query image, given a set of detected keypoints, we compute DAISY descriptors [23] for each of the affinely deformed patches. We then query for nearest neighbor matches using a k-d tree to speed up the search. This gives us a sorted list of neighbors based on descriptor distance. This list can then be scored using the ratio test [20] to find the inlier matches.

This traditional method of scoring, however, does not account for the fact that we have multiple descriptors (affine-transformed patches) per interest point

[5] Note that unlike papers that detect planar skew symmetric configurations [1,2,3,4,5,6], we are looking for a rectifying 3D transformation, since in general we do not expect to find a single bilateral symmetry axis.

location. Performing a k-NN query without considering this grouping can result in repetitive matches, i.e., multiple matching descriptors from the same bag. This prevents us from evaluating potential matches from other bags that did not make it to the k top neighbors list. We adapt our approach by enumerating all neighbors per query descriptor and consider only the best matched pair *per bag* for entry into the ratio test. Hence, each of the k nearest neighbors that are returned are guaranteed to be from unique bags, which results in superior matching performance. A few examples matches using three different interest point variants are shown in Figure 5.

Once we have determined a set of raw correspondences, we use the Random Sample Consensus (RANSAC) algorithm [24] to find the best epipole. For every pair of random correspondences chosen, say $(\mathbf{p}_0, \mathbf{p}'_0)$ and $(\mathbf{p}_1, \mathbf{p}'_1)$, we compute the epipole $\mathbf{e}$ using a cross product of the line equations and then measure the perpendicular distances of each of the endpoints to the line joining its corresponding point to the epipole. We then convert this distance in pixels to a log likelihood assuming a contaminated Gaussian model, where the Gaussian has a standard deviation of $\sigma = 2$ pixels and the outlier probability is $\epsilon = 0.01$. The sum of log likelihoods is then used to score all random samples, and the best sample is used to determine the epipole.

5 Rectification and Disparity Range Estimation

Once we have determined the epipole, we rectify the image (using the first, minimal distortion, heuristic) and re-center the resulting image at the original image center, remembering the true optic center value to later compute disparities.

In order to improve the effectiveness of the edge matching algorithm which is described in the next section, we use the inlier matches from the epipole estimate to compute a set of plausible disparity (inverse depth) values. Recall that in this paper, our aim is to reconstruct compact bilaterally symmetric objects rather than extended scenes. For such objects, we expect some of the feature matches to lie on or near the frontmost visible surface of the object. We also expect the object to be bounded in depth, e.g., to be no more than four times as deep as the distance between the frontmost part and the camera.

In order to compute the disparity range, we compute the disparities (horizontal distances between match midlines and the optic center) for all of the matches that are inliers to the epipolar geometry. We then discard matches whose disparity is on the wrong side of the epipole (and hence have negative depth). From the remaining matches, we find the 80% percentile largest disparity (likely front of the object), and set the disparity range to 25%–130% of this value. This corresponds to the assumptions that the object can be no more that four times as deep as the distance to camera and that it cannot have small protrusions more than one third this distance.

Figure 2b shows an example of the inlier and depth range computation and Figure 8b (and the supplementary materials [30]) show some additional examples. The vertical blue line shows the disparity corresponding to the 80% disparity for all matched epipolar correspondences. The vertical red line shows the

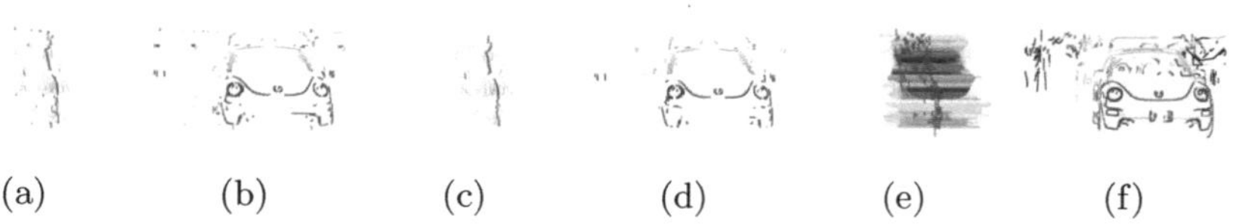

Fig. 6. Curve matching results: (a) cost image generated from all pairs of matching edges with the red line showing the winner on each scanline; (b) the corresponding edge matches, color-coded by depth. (c) the same cost image with the results of vertical dynamic programming with (d) the corresponding edge matches; (e) the cost image associated with running an intra-scanline dynamic program starting inside each inter-edge interval, along with the dynamic programming solution (red) and the midlines (disparities) for all the matches; (f) the corresponding edge matches. Additional examples are included in the supplementary materials [30].

(horizontal) location of the optic center after rectification. The two vertical green lines show the allowable disparity range. Matches whose midpoints fall outside the range defined by the vertical green lines are considered not part of the object. The horizontal match lines for such correspondences are drawn in red, while the "object inlier" correspondences are drawn in green.

6 Curve Matching

Once we have rectified our image and computed a plausible disparity range, we could use various techniques to recover a dense 3D model of the object. The most common approach [7,8] is to use dense pixel-based stereo matching. A lot of our objects, however, have large textureless areas or photometric inconsistencies such as reflections. For this reason, we explore the use of edge and curve-based matching, as a set of techniques complementary to pixel-based stereo.

Over the years, a number of edge-based stereo algorithms have been developed [25]. For example, Ohta and Kanade [26] develop a dynamic programming algorithm that encourages smoothness in disparities both within scanlines and along curves. Collins [27] introduces the notion of a plane sweep and matches binary edges in scenes such as surveillance video. None of these techniques, however, admit a simple mechanism or extension for enforcing that matches are symmetric, which is a fundamental constraint we can exploit in our domain to make our matches more reliable.

Note, however, that occluding contours for rounded symmetric objects need not be symmetric counterparts even though locally they may have similar visual appearance under a mirror transformation. In fact for many symmetric 3D objects, the symmetric counterpart could either be self occluded or may not produce a salient image curve. This inability to accurately reconstruct the occluding contours is a limitation of our method as well as prior methods [7,8].

Recall from Section 3 that the disparity (inverse depth) between a point in our original image and its corresponding point in the mirror-reflected image is twice the horizontal displacement between the midpoint of the equivalent within-image correspondence and the optic center (Figure 3). A simple way to determine correspondences is to have potential matches on each scanline "vote" for their midpoint and to then pick the midpoint with the highest score as indicating the desired disparity.

Finding potential matches: We first split all detected image curves to generate y-monotone segments to ensure that each segment intersects a scanline at most once. We then match all pairs of curves after pruning pairs whose scanline intervals do not overlap or overlap very little. Since the image is rectified, pixels where matching curves meet each scanline must correspond. We perform two simple tests to check the plausibility of curve matches under bilateral symmetry. We check whether under symmetry, the polarity of the intensities around the matching edge (or ridge) pixels agree and also whether the local gradient orientation of the 2D curves at these pixels are similar. A curve pair is assigned a matching score equal to the number of pixels where both conditions are satisfied. Using these scores, we then compute $K = 10$ nearest neighbors for every curve in the image and retain the reciprocal matches, i.e., any match between curves c_0 and c_1 where c_0 is c_1's neighbor and vice versa. The set of filtered curve correspondences specifies a set of potential pixel correspondences, each of which can vote for their midpoints on the respective scanlines.

Figure 6a shows the resulting cost image for each scanline, where darker colors indicate more votes and the red pixel in each row indicates the winning disparity. This process is analogous to the techniques that vote for axes of symmetry in determining bilateral planar skew symmetry [1,2,3,4,5].

If we use this disparity to select matches on each scanline, we can reconstruct a sparse "ribbon-like" 3D model of the object, where the depths at each scanline are restricted to a small range (Figure 6b). We can improve the quality of the results by running a dynamic programming algorithm (DP) vertically across the scanlines, which has the effect of smoothing out the computed midline and hence removing smaller isolated errors (Figure 6c–d). While this approach works for some objects, it often fails to match all of the corresponding curves.

An alternative to the simple voting scheme is to run a two-stage dynamic programming (DP) algorithm, which we describe next. First an intra-scanline DP step is performed to estimate smooth disparity variation within each scanline while enforcing both ordering as well as uniqueness constraint amongst its pixels. The second stage performs DP across scanlines to encourage the continuity of curve-to-curve correspondences across scanlines.

Intra-scanline Dynamic Programming: For a horizontal scanline, we wish to compute an optimal set of correspondences that satisfies the ordering and uniqueness constraints under mirror symmetry. We formulate this as a best path problem on a directed acyclic weighted graph, which can be efficiently computed using dynamic programming. Unlike prior DP-based stereo matching methods that match scanlines, we need to both match the left and right parts of the scanline and simultaneously compute the best point to partition the scanline. We consider all pixel correspondences for the scanline that agrees with the estimated disparity range and find all horizontal intervals generated by these pixels on the scanline. By picking an arbitrary partition point P within one of the intervals,

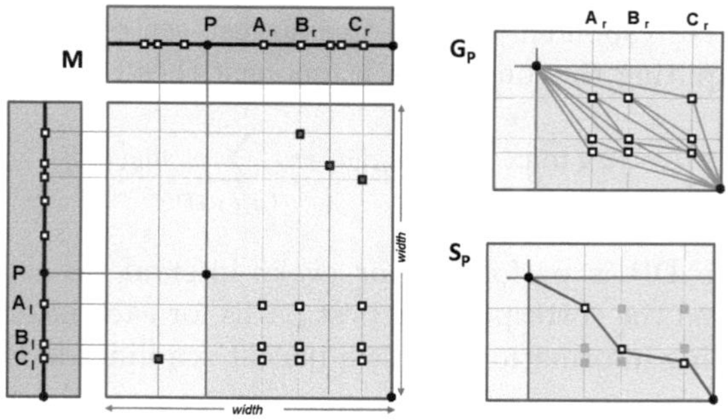

(a) (b)

Fig. 7. Intra-scanline DP for a particular scanline: (a) For a partition point P, all potential correspondences are visualized on a 2D grid M. In this figure, (A_l,A_r), (B_l,B_r) and (C_l,C_r) are true correspondences. All the white nodes in M are admissible given the point P whereas the red nodes are not admissible because both pixels lie on the same side of P on the scanline. (b) A directed acyclic weighted graph G_P is constructed (see text for details) and an optimal path is computed from the vertex corresponding to P to the bottom right point of the grid M in order to choose the most likely set of correspondences under the uniqueness and ordering constraint with respect to P.

we construct a directed acyclic graph corresponding to this interval, which we denote as G_P. The corresponding best path in G_P is denoted as S_P.

The graph $G_P(V, E)$ is constructed as follows. Each of its nodes in V correspond to those potential pixel correspondences (x_l,x_r) on the scanline where $x_l < P.x$ and $x_r > P.x$. Here $P.x$ refers to the x-coordinate of P and the subscripts l and r indicate which of the two corresponding pixels is on the left (and right) on the scanline. The graph G_P has an embedding M on a 2D square grid whose dimensions equal the length of the scanline, as shown in Figure 7. The correspondences that do not fall within the bottom right quadrant of M as shown in Figure 7(a) do not have to be considered. Directed edges are created from a node u to every other node $v \in V$, as long as the following conditions hold true. First, $u.x_r < v.x_r$ and $v.x_l < u.x_l$, i.e., u must be encountered before v when traversing outwards on the scanline starting from P. Second, no vertex w should exist between u and v that satisfies the condition $u.x_r < w.x_r < v.x_r$ and $v.x_l < w.x_l < u.x_l$. This condition amounts to saying that u and v will be connected if their 2D bounding box in M has no third vertex w lying strictly inside it. Intuitively, as we move outwards from P, we consider the next pair of pixels encountered or skip one or both of them. Each edge ($u \rightarrow v$) has a weight

$$w_e(u, v) = \max(0, (\Delta(x)_{\max} - |(v.x_r - u.x_r) - (u.x_l - v.x_r)|)). \quad (6)$$

This choice of edge weights favors paths that are most parallel to the main diagonal of M along which all edge weights attain a maximum value. Each node u in V also has a positive weight $w_s(u)$ assigned to the matching score of the corresponding pixel pairs, which is equal to the matching score of their associated curves. Any path $\mathcal{P}$ in this graph from P to the bottom right corner of M gives a set of feasible correspondences and the largest set of likely candidates are extracted by computing the longest path amongst these.

$$S_P = \arg\max_{\mathcal{P}} \big[\sum_{u \in \mathcal{P}} w_n(u) + \sum_{(u,v) \in \mathcal{P}} w_e(u,v) \big]. \tag{7}$$

The intra-scanline DP is performed for every interval on each scanline. The maximum score and the corresponding best paths for each interval is stored and used for propagating information across adjacent scanlines in the next stage.

Dynamic Programming Across Scanlines: Each interval for which an intra-scanline DP problem was solved previously, now serves as a node in a new weighted directed acyclic graph. All intervals on a scanline are connected to intervals on the scanline below it via directed (top-down) edges. Each node is given a unary weight equal to the corresponding interval's score computed previously during the intra-scanline DP stage. For each edge between nodes j and k, we set the edge weight as $w_{jk} = \max(0, 1 - \frac{n_{jk}}{\kappa})$, where n_{jk} is the number of curve-pairs present in both intervals corresponding to j and k. We set the parameter $\kappa = 5$. This favor selecting interval pairs on adjacent scanlines having many curve pairs in common. For interval pairs that do not share common curve pairs, the weight is set inversely proportional to the x-displacement of the midpoints of the two intervals. This encourages similar disparity changes across scanlines. Finally, the longest path between nodes corresponding to the top and bottom scanline is computed and this produces the final set of curve matches.

Figure 6e shows the cost values computed for each scanline interval in this two-staged algorithm. The red lines overlaid on each scanline are the mid-lines corresponding to matched edges. The associated depth map shown in Figure 6f indicates that the new algorithm matches more edges in the curved regions of the car than the simpler one-pass algorithm.

7 Experimental Results

To determine the best feature detector for our application, we evaluated a variety of popular feature detectors (MSER, Laplace, Harris, FAST-ER, Hessian, Hessian-Laplace, Hessian-Affine, and Edge Foci) [21,28,29]. For detectors that do not estimate a characteristic scale, we computed features at different levels of an image pyramid. As noted in Section 4, we found that affine adaptation of the interest points hurts the repeatability of Hessian-Affine points. MSER, Edge Foci and the Laplace variants produced middle of the pack results while FAST-ER produced the most repeatable interest points.

In order to account for local affine distortions, we generated affine transformed versions [22] of the FAST-ER [28] interest point patches. This produced the best performance in terms of epipolar inliers. The affine transformations can be characterized by ellipses with varying tilt angles and scales. In our experiments, we sampled four different scalings of the ellipse along the horizontal axis in increments of 0.25 to generate the affine distortions. Since most of the images

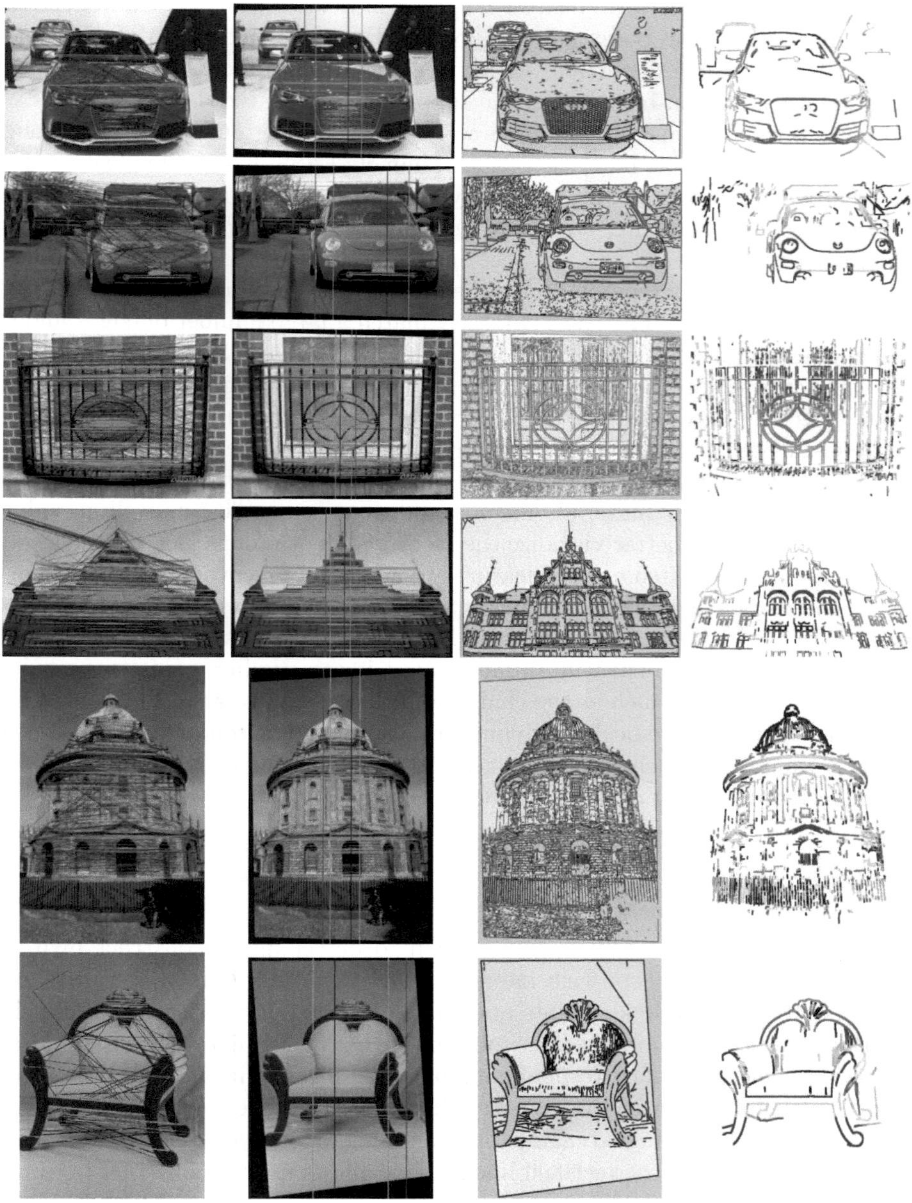
(a) (b) (c) (d)

Fig. 8. Some additional results: (a) epipolar geometry from matched points; (b) rectified image with depth range and inlier matches; (c) extracted curves; (d) recovered depths for matched curves. See the supplementary materials [30] for even more results and some 3D animations.

were upright, varying the tilt angles did not provide much benefit. After interest point extraction, we perform nearest-neighbor matching, as described in Section 4. Figure 5 shows the point matches for the Hessian-Laplace, FAST-ER, and FAST-ER with affine distortions, along with the results for FAST-ER+Affine. Additional results can be found in the supplementary material [30].

Figure 8 shows some of the images we used for testing our algorithms along with the results of using our best variants, namely FAST-ER+Affine feature detector and descriptor, the inlier disparity range computation, and the two-stage DP (intra-scanline and inter-scanline) algorithm used to compute matching edges and their disparities. As you can see, our algorithms successfully estimate the direction of symmetry (epipole) for these images along with reasonable disparity ranges for the objects. They also correctly match a large number of edges under challenging conditions that include textureless regions and background clutter. For well textured scenes, such as for the fourth row in Figure 8, dense pixel-based matching may work better [8]. However, our technique is complementary to theirs and can compute a sparse set of matches more reliably which is important when the photometric cues are less reliable as in our example images.

The supplementary materials include additional examples, as well as video animations that can better visualize the recovered depth maps [30]. Our method sometimes fails to match enough features to accurately recover the axis of symmetry and can have difficulty dealing with highly repetitive patterns which may overwhelm the curve matcher. Although the ordering constraint in our curve matching approach is beneficial in most cases, it can produce erroneous results for certain 3D objects such as the chair shown in the sixth row in Figure 8. Also as discussed earlier, the occluding contours for symmetric rounded objects need not be symmetric and in such cases, the depths computed by our method at pixels on the occluding contour can be inaccurate.

8 Conclusions

In this paper, we have developed a system to detect and reconstruct bilaterally symmetric 3D objects with interesting 3D structure. Our system first extracts highly repeatable keypoints and then generates descriptors from affinely deformed patches around these keypoints. It then determines the direction of symmetry using pairs of corresponding points, rectifies the image, and then computes a plausible disparity range based on the spatial extent of the inliers. We then use a novel two-stage dynamic programming algorithm to match extended curves extracted from the rectified image. This allows us to reconstruct textureless, specular objects which are traditionally problematic for pixel-based stereo. In the future, we would like to combine curve-based matching with pixel-level matching and also explore foreground segmentation and the use of the recovered sparse 3D geometry to aid the recognition of 3D symmetric objects.

References

1. Liu, Y., Hel-Or, H., Kaplan, C.S., Gool, L.V.: Computational symmetry in computer vision and computer graphics. FnT CGCV 5, 1–195 (2010)
2. Tuytelaars, T., Turina, A., Van Gool, L.: Noncombinatorial detection of regular repetitions under perspective skew. IEEE PAMI 25, 418–432 (2003)
3. Loy, G., Eklundh, J.-O.: Detecting Symmetry and Symmetric Constellations of Features. In: Leonardis, A., Bischof, H., Pinz, A. (eds.) ECCV 2006. LNCS, vol. 3952, pp. 508–521. Springer, Heidelberg (2006)
4. Cornelius, H., Perďoch, M., Matas, J(G.), Loy, G.: Efficient Symmetry Detection Using Local Affine Frames. In: Ersbøll, B.K., Pedersen, K.S. (eds.) SCIA 2007. LNCS, vol. 4522, pp. 152–161. Springer, Heidelberg (2007)
5. Cho, M., Lee, K.M.: Bilateral symmetry detection and segmentation via symmetry-growing. In: BMVC 2009, pp. 4.1–4.1. BMVA Press (2009)
6. Rauschert, I., Brocklehurst, K., Kashyap, S., Liu, J., Liu, Y.: First symmetry detection competition: Summary and results. Technical Report CSE11-012, Department of Computer Science and Engineering, The Pennsylvania State University (2011)
7. Wu, C., Frahm, J.M., Pollefeys, M.: Repetition-based dense single-view reconstruction. In: CVPR, pp. 3113–3120 (2011)
8. Köser, K., Zach, C., Pollefeys, M.: Dense 3D Reconstruction of Symmetric Scenes from a Single Image. In: Mester, R., Felsberg, M. (eds.) DAGM 2011. LNCS, vol. 6835, pp. 266–275. Springer, Heidelberg (2011)
9. Mitsumoto, H., et al.: 3-D reconstruction using mirror images based on a plane symmetry recovering method. IEEE PAMI 14, 941–946 (1992)
10. François, A.R.J., Medioni, G.G., Waupotitsch, R.: Mirror symmetry $\Rightarrow$ 2-view stereo geometry. IVC 21, 137–143 (2003)
11. Jiang, N., Tan, P., Cheong, L.-H.: Symmetric architecture modeling with a single image. ACM Transactions on Graphics 28 (2009)
12. Shimshoni, I., Moses, Y., Lindenbaum, M.: Shape Reconstruction of 3D Bilaterally Symmetric Surfaces. IJCV 39, 97–110 (2004)
13. Xue, T., Liu, J.: Symmetric piecewise planar object reconstruction from a single image. In: CVPR, pp. 2577–2584 (2011)
14. Sun, Y., Bhanu, B.: Reflection symmetry integrated image segmentation. IEEE PAMI (2011)
15. Hong, W., Yang, A.Y., Huang, K., Ma, Y.: On symmetry and multiple-view geometry: Structure, pose, and calibration from a single image. IJCV 60, 241–265 (2004)
16. Mitra, N.J., Guibas, L.J., Pauly, M.: Partial and approximate symmetry detection for 3D geometry. ACM Transactions on Graphics 25, 560–568 (2006)
17. Wu, C., Frahm, J.-M., Pollefeys, M.: Detecting Large Repetitive Structures with Salient Boundaries. In: Daniilidis, K., Maragos, P., Paragios, N. (eds.) ECCV 2010, Part II. LNCS, vol. 6312, pp. 142–155. Springer, Heidelberg (2010)
18. Okutomi, M., Kanade, T.: A multiple baseline stereo. IEEE PAMI 15, 353–363 (1993)
19. Hartley, R.I., Zisserman, A.: Multiple View Geometry. Cambridge University Press, Cambridge (2004)
20. Lowe, D.G.: Distinctive image features from scale-invariant keypoints. IJCV 60, 91–110 (2004)
21. Mikolajczyk, K., Schmid, C.: Scale & affine invariant interest point detectors. IJCV 60, 63–86 (2004)

22. Morel, J.M., Yu, G.: ASIFT: A new framework for fully affine invariant image comparison. SIAM J. Imaging Sciences 2, 438–469 (2009)
23. Brown, M., Hua, G., Winder, S.: Discriminative learning of local image descriptors. IEEE PAMI 33, 43–57 (2011)
24. Fischler, M.A., Bolles, R.C.: Random sample consensus: A paradigm for model fitting with applications to image analysis and automated cartography. Communications of the ACM 24, 381–395 (1981)
25. Scharstein, D., Szeliski, R.: A taxonomy and evaluation of dense two-frame stereo correspondence algorithms. IJCV 47, 7–42 (2002)
26. Ohta, Y., Kanade, T.: Stereo by intra- and inter-scanline search using dynamic programming. IEEE PAMI PAMI-7, 139–154 (1985)
27. Collins, R.T.: A space-sweep approach to true multi-image matching. In: CVPR, pp. 358–363 (1996)
28. Rosten, E., Porter, R., Drummond, T.: Faster and better: A machine learning approach to corner detection. IEEE PAMI 32, 105–119 (2010)
29. Zitnick, C.L., Ramnath, K.: Edge foci interest points. In: ICCV, pp. 359–366 (2011)
30. `http://research.microsoft.com/en-us/um/redmond/groups/ivm/SymmRecon3D`

3D Reconstruction of Dynamic Scenes with Multiple Handheld Cameras

Hanqing Jiang[1,2], Haomin Liu[1], Ping Tan[2], Guofeng Zhang[1,⋆], and Hujun Bao[1,⋆]

[1] State Key Lab of CAD&CG, Zhejiang University
[2] National University of Singapore
zhangguofeng@cad.zju.edu.cn

Abstract. Accurate dense 3D reconstruction of dynamic scenes from natural images is still very challenging. Most previous methods rely on a large number of fixed cameras to obtain good results. Some of these methods further require separation of static and dynamic points, which are usually restricted to scenes with known background. We propose a novel dense depth estimation method which can automatically recover accurate and consistent depth maps from the synchronized video sequences taken by a few handheld cameras. Unlike fixed camera arrays, our data capturing setup is much more flexible and easier to use. Our algorithm simultaneously solves bilayer segmentation and depth estimation in a unified energy minimization framework, which combines different spatio-temporal constraints for effective depth optimization and segmentation of static and dynamic points. A variety of examples demonstrate the effectiveness of the proposed framework.

Keywords: multi-view stereo, depth recovery, dynamic scene, spatio-temporal optimization.

1 Introduction

Many 3D reconstruction algorithms such as [11,20] have been proposed for a static scene. However, the real world is full of dynamic objects. The reconstruction of a dynamic scene is often required in many applications, but is also much more challenging. Most works on dynamic scene reconstruction such as [23,8,9] require an array of fixed cameras with relatively narrow baselines to minimize occlusion problems. Further, some of these, such as [23,8,9] require a large number of cameras (usually more than eight) to ensure good results. These requirements on data capturing limit their applications and are typically applied to data carefully captured in laboratories. There are recent non-rigid structure-from-motion algorithms such as [14], which reconstruct dynamic scenes with a single moving camera. Though data capturing is simplified, their accuracy and robustness are rather limited at this moment.

We study dense 3D reconstruction of dynamic scenes from multiple handheld cameras. We allow cameras to move freely and independently so that data

⋆ Corresponding authors.

A. Fitzgibbon et al. (Eds.): ECCV 2012, Part II, LNCS 7573, pp. 601–615, 2012.

Fig. 1. Dynamic 3D reconstruction results of 'Three-Pedestrian' example. (a-b) Two synchronous frames from the two source videos. (c) The recovered depth map of (a). (d) The magnified regions of (a) and (c). (e) The texture-mapped 3D scene visualized from a novel viewpoint.

capturing is much more flexible. Further, we require as few as $2 \sim 3$ cameras to facilitate many applications. An example is shown in Fig. 1, which contains three pedestrians. Our method faithfully recovers the depths in both static and dynamic regions. Compared with previous methods with a fixed camera array, our approach achieves both flexible data capturing and accurate 3D reconstruction.

Most previous works on dynamic scene reconstruction [12,8,15] treated moving objects in the same way as static ones. Some methods such as [5,6,19] segmented pixels into static and dynamic ones while estimating their depths. These methods require exact bilayer segmentation, which itself is a difficult problem. In comparison, we propose a unified global optimization framework to solve dense depth recovery and static/dynamic segmentation simultaneously. Unlike previous methods such as [5,6,19], our segmentation is optimized for better depth estimation. A pixel is classified to "static" or "dynamic" depending on which kind of spatio-temporal constraint models it better. Hence, our method does not require an exact static/dynamic segmentation and is more robust to segmentation errors in challenging scenes like Fig. 6.

2 Related Work

There are many methods such as [22,12,23] to reconstruct a dynamic scene from multiple fixed cameras. They typically applied stereo algorithms to synchronized video frames of different cameras and smoothed the estimated disparities of corresponding pixels in the temporal domain. Here, we only briefly review some of the recent works. In [8], temporal consistency between consecutive frames in multiple cameras was enforced by an enhanced belief propagation algorithm. Aguiar et al. [1] captured temporal coherent human performances with a circular camera array. Lei et al. [9] recovered spacetime-consistent depth maps by a region-tree based stereo approach. Recently, Yang et al. [15] extended the powerful bundle optimization framework [20] to handle dynamic scenes with a novel temporal coherence constraint. This constraint is similar to our spatio-temporal constraint for dynamic points. However, [15] only used one preceding time instance for depth optimization, and is rather sensitive to optical flow errors and occlusions. Hence, their method required more cameras with relative small baselines to ensure robust results. In comparison, our spatio-temporal optimization can effectively utilize more temporal neighboring frames and robustly handle occlusions. As a result, we require only a few cameras and allow cameras to move freely with larger baselines to significantly simplify data capturing.

Bilayer segmentation is an important cue for dynamic scene reconstruction. Zhang et al. [19] proposed a robust bilayer segmentation by dense depth and motion estimation. Although the segmentation and depth/motion estimation are incorporated into an energy function, they are separately solved which may result in a solution that is only locally optimal. In addition, their method requires a manual preprocessing for foreground color distribution learning. Goldlücke and Magnor [5] performed bilayer segmentation and 3D reconstruction for static scenes with fixed cameras, where background images have been recorded from each camera beforehand. Guillemaut et al. [6] used multi-layer segmentation to achieve 3D reconstruction and free-viewpoint video of sports videos captured by multiple broadcast cameras, where the planar background color and depth are also known. Both methods used joint labeling to simultaneously estimate depths and segmentation, which is similar to our work. Nevertheless, both of these approaches require strong prior knowledge on the background scene to facilitate segmentation. Further, their depth estimation and segmentation terms were weakly coupled in the optimization formulation, making these methods easy to get stuck in a local minimum. In comparison, our depth recovery and bilayer segmentation are tightly integrated, and do not require prior background knowledge. Recently, Zhang et al. [18] used a similar expanded labeling formulation for simultaneous stereo and segmentation, but was limited to rigid objects.

There are other works with similar data capturing setup, but targeting different applications. Ballan et al.[2] addressed the video based rendering problem with multiple freely moving cameras, where dynamic objects are only segmented but not reconstructed. Hasler et al.[7] used multiple freely moving cameras for markerless motion capture. Most recently, Yang et al. [16] proposed a dense depth recovery method for a trinocular sequence. In their capture setup, the relative camera poses are constant and the baselines between neighboring cameras should be not large (8∼20cm). To the best of our knowledge, our work is the first to recover dense depth maps for dynamic scenes by multiple handheld cameras.

3 Notation and System Summary

Given a set of synchronized video sequences $\hat{I} = \{\hat{I}_m | m = 1, ..., M\}$ taken by M moving cameras, in which each $\hat{I}_m$ has N frames denoted as $\hat{I}_m = \{I_m^t | t = 1, ..., N\}$, our goal is to recover a set of corresponding depth map sequences

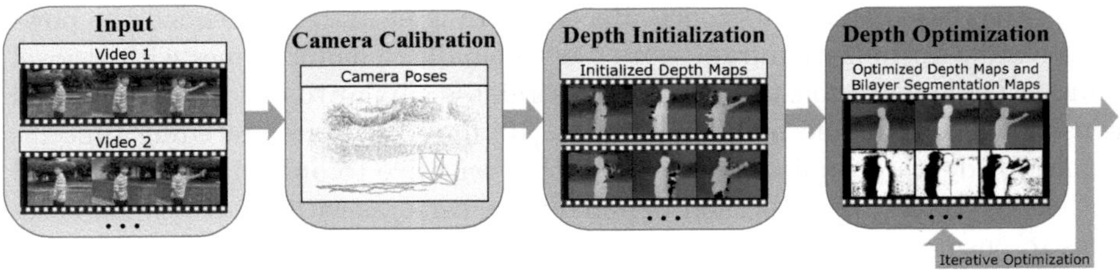

Fig. 2. This figure shows the overview of our system

$\hat{Z} = \{Z_m^t | m = 1, ..., M; t = 1, ..., N\}$. We use $I_m^t(\mathbf{x})$, $Z_m^t(\mathbf{x})$, $D_m^t(\mathbf{x}) = 1/Z_m^t(\mathbf{x})$ to represent the color, depth and disparity at pixel $\mathbf{x}$ in frame t of sequence m, respectively. For clarity, we sometimes use $\mathbf{x}_m^t$ to denote pixel $\mathbf{x}$ in frame (m, t).

The camera parameters for frame t of video sequence m is denoted by $\mathbf{C}_m^t = \{\mathbf{K}_m^t, \mathbf{R}_m^t, \mathbf{T}_m^t\}$, where $\mathbf{K}_m^t$ is the intrinsic matrix, $\mathbf{R}_m^t$ is the rotation matrix, and $\mathbf{T}_m^t$ is the translation vector. The camera parameters for all frames in all sequences are estimated beforehand. Specifically, we use the method in [17] to track feature points in the videos and then use the SFM method proposed in [21] to recover the camera poses. To ensure system robustness, camera intrinsics are pre-calibrated and fixed during data capturing.

The system overview is shown in Fig. 2. We initialize the disparity maps $\{D_m^t | m = 1, ..., M\}$ for each time t using the synchronized images $\{I_m^t | m = 1, ..., M\}$ across M cameras (see Section 4). Then we jointly perform spatio-temporal disparity optimization and bilayer segmentation (see Section 5) so that a set of high-quality depth maps are finally obtained.

4 Depth Initialization

We first estimate the depth maps at time t using the images from different cameras at that time. Denoting the disparity range as $[d_{\min}, d_{\max}]$, we equally quantize the disparity into k levels, such that the ith level $d_i = (k-i)/(k-1) \cdot d_{\min} + (i-1)/(k-1) \cdot d_{\max}$, where $i = 1, \ldots, k$. Specifically, we minimize the following objective energy:

$$E_D(D_m^t; \hat{I}(t)) = E_d(D_m^t; \hat{I}(t)) + E_s(D_m^t), \tag{1}$$

where $\hat{I}(t) = \{I_m^t | m = 1, ..., M\}$ represents all frames captured at time t. E_d is the data term, and E_s is the smoothness term.

The smoothness term E_s measures the smoothness of neighboring disparities, and is simply defined as:

$$E_s(D_m^t) = \lambda \sum_{\mathbf{x}} \sum_{\mathbf{y} \in N(\mathbf{x})} \min\{|D_m^t(\mathbf{x}) - D_m^t(\mathbf{y})|, \eta\}, \tag{2}$$

where $N(\mathbf{x})$ denotes the set of neighbors of pixel $\mathbf{x}$, λ is the smoothness weight, and η is a truncation value for robust estimation. In our experiments, $\lambda = 0.8/(d_{\max} - d_{\min})$ and $\eta = 0.03(d_{\max} - d_{\min})$.

Fig. 3. Illustration of disparity initialization. (a-b) Two synchronous source frames from the 'Boy' data. (c) The estimated disparity map of (a) using the data term defined in Eq. (4), incorporating DAISY descriptors. (d) The visibility map estimated from the disparity maps of (a) and (b). (e) The refined disparity map after occlusion handling. The disparities in the occluded regions are improved. (f) The further refined disparity map after plane fitting.

For conventional stereo algorithms, the data term E_d mainly uses pixel-wise or window-based color similarity. In our examples, baselines between cameras are often large, as shown in Fig. 3(a-b). Due to the foreshortening and occlusions, a simple color similarity measure is insufficient to generate good disparities. To better solve this problem, we use DAISY [13] in the data term. DAISY is an efficient local descriptor for robust wide baseline stereo matching. We define a disparity cost function based on the similarity of DAISY descriptor as:

$$L_{\mathcal{D}}(\mathbf{x}_m^t, d_i; I_m^t, I_{m'}^t) = ||\mathcal{D}(\mathbf{x}_m^t) - \mathcal{D}(\mathbf{x}_{m'}^t)||_2, \tag{3}$$

where $\mathcal{D}(\mathbf{x})$ is the DAISY descriptor at $\mathbf{x}$. The term $\mathbf{x}_{m'}^t = l_{m\to m'}^t(\mathbf{x}_m^t, d_i)$ is the corresponding pixel of $\mathbf{x}_m^t$ by projecting $\mathbf{x}_m^t$ to $I_{m'}^t$ according to the candidate disparity value d_i and camera parameters.

We then define the data term E_d as:

$$E_d(D_m^t; \hat{I}(t)) = \sum_{\mathbf{x}_m^t} \frac{\sum_{m'\neq m} L_{\mathcal{D}}(\mathbf{x}_m^t, D_m^t(\mathbf{x}_m^t); I_m^t, I_{m'}^t)}{M-1}. \tag{4}$$

Basically, we use all the synchronous views in other cameras to initialize the disparity D_m^t. Loopy belief propagation algorithm [4] is used to solve Eq. (1). Fig. 3(c) shows an estimated depth map. There are still visible problems in the occluded regions. In the next subsection, we estimate a visibility map for each pair of synchronous images in cameras m and m' to further handle occlusions.

4.1 Disparity Inference of Occluded Pixels

If a point is visible in both cameras m and m', its depth in both images should be consistent (i.e. corresponding to the same 3D point). Hence, we define the visibility map of camera m with respect to m' as:

$$V^t_{m\to m'}(\mathbf{x}^t_m) = \begin{cases} 1 & |1/Z^t_{m\to m'}(\mathbf{x}^t_m) - D^t_{m'}(\mathbf{x}^t_{m'})| \le \delta_d \\ 0 & |1/Z^t_{m\to m'}(\mathbf{x}^t_m) - D^t_{m'}(\mathbf{x}^t_{m'})| > \delta_d \end{cases}, \tag{5}$$

where $V^t_{m\to m'}(\mathbf{x}^t_m)$ denotes whether the pixel $\mathbf{x}^t_m$ in I^t_m is visible in $I^t_{m'}$ (1 for visible and 0 for invisible). Here, δ_d is a threshold determined empirically as $0.02(d_{\max} - d_{\min})$. The term $Z^t_{m\to m'}(\mathbf{x}^t_m)$ denotes the depth of $\mathbf{x}^t_m$ in m'. It is determined by casting $\mathbf{x}^t_m$ to 3D space according to its disparity $D^t_m(\mathbf{x}^t_m)$ from the camera m, and then projecting it to the camera m'. We define $\hat{V}^t_m(\mathbf{x}^t_m)$ as the total visibility of pixel $\mathbf{x}^t_m$. It is equal to 0, if $\mathbf{x}^t_m$ is invisible in all the other cameras. Otherwise, it is equal to 1. Fig. 3(d) shows the estimated visibility map.

The disparities can be well initialized only at pixels which are visible in at least one reference camera. For a pixels with total visibility $\hat{V}^t_m(\mathbf{x}) = 0$, Eq. (4) does not capture its data cost well. Hence, we estimate their disparities using the traditional photo-consistency constraint from neighboring temporal frames.

Given a candidate disparity d_i and a reference frame t' in camera m', We define a disparity likelihood based on the color similarity measure between I^t_m and $I^{t'}_{m'}$ as follows:

$$L_c(\mathbf{x}^t_m, d_i; I^t_m, I^{t'}_{m'}) = p_c(\mathbf{x}^t_m, \mathbf{x}^{t'}_{m'}), \tag{6}$$

where p_c measures the color similarity of $\mathbf{x}^t_m$ and $\mathbf{x}^{t'}_{m'}$, and is similarly defined as in [20]:

$$p_c(\mathbf{x}^t_m, \mathbf{x}^{t'}_{m'}) = \frac{\sigma_c}{\sigma_c + \left\| I^t_m(\mathbf{x}^t_m) - I^{t'}_{m'}(\mathbf{x}^{t'}_{m'}) \right\|_1}. \tag{7}$$

The parameter σ_c controls the sensitivity of color difference. The term $\mathbf{x}^{t'}_{m'}$ is the projection pixel of $\mathbf{x}^t_m$ to $I^{t'}_{m'}$ according to disparity d_i and camera parameters.

We accumulate the disparity likelihood with all the cameras at nearby time instances (20 nearest frames in our experiments), and compute the data term of the totally invisible pixels as:

$$E_d(D^t_m; \hat{I}) = \sum_{\mathbf{x}^t_m} 1 - \frac{\sum_{m'=1}^{M} \sum_{t' \in N(t)} L_c(\mathbf{x}^t_m, D^t_m(\mathbf{x}^t_m); I^t_m, I^{t'}_{m'})}{M|N(t)|}, \tag{8}$$

where $N(t)$ denotes the set of nearby frames.

By incorporating the above data cost, we can obtain a refined disparity map, as in Fig. 3(e). To better handle textureless regions and disparity noise, we incorporate segmentation information into the disparity initialization. We use Mean-shift [3] to segment the image and consider each segment as a 3D plane with parameters $[a, b, c]$, which are fit to the computed data costs in the segment as in [20]. Disparities of pixels in the segment can be recomputed as $d_{\mathbf{x}} = ax + by + c$. Fig. 3(f) shows the further refined disparity map after plane fitting.

5 Spatio-temporal Optimization

In principle, static and dynamic pixels require different coherence constraints for disparity optimization. A straightforward solution is to perform explicit bilayer segmentation by estimating the background information using methods such as [19] and reconstruct static and dynamic pixels with different strategies. However, accurate background estimation is difficult for many cases, especially when a dynamic object moves slightly such that the background is almost occluded in all frames.

We propose to solve depth optimization and bilayer segmentation in a unified framework. For each pixel, we not only estimate its depth but also infer whether it is static or dynamic. Therefore, each pixel $\mathbf{x}_m^t$ has two variables to be inferred – one is its disparity value $D_m^t(\mathbf{x}_m^t)$ and the other is its static/dynamic label $S_m^t(\mathbf{x}_m^t) \in \{0, 1\}$ (0 for static and 1 for dynamic). Iteratively inferring these two variables might easily get stuck in local minimum. Instead, we formulate these two variables in an expanded labeling set, which is defined as:

$$\mathcal{L} = \{l_1^0, l_2^0, \ldots, l_k^0, l_1^1, l_2^1, \ldots, l_k^1\}.$$

Each label l_i^s naturally encodes a static/dynamic label $s \in \{0, 1\}$ and a candidate disparity value d_i, where $i = 1, 2, \ldots, k$. With this compact representation, we can now estimate a joint labeling map $\mathbf{L}_m^t$ ($\mathbf{L}_m^t(\mathbf{x}_m^t) \in \mathcal{L}$) for each frame I_m^t by minimizing a new energy:

$$E_{\mathbf{L}}(\mathbf{L}_m^t; \hat{I}, \hat{D}) = E_d(\mathbf{L}_m^t; \hat{I}, \hat{D}) + E_s(\mathbf{L}_m^t). \tag{9}$$

Since the spatio-temporal coherence constraints for static and dynamic pixels are different, we use different data cost functions for l_i^0 and l_i^1, which we denote as e_d^0 and e_d^1 respectively.

5.1 Different Spatio-temporal Data Costs on Bilayer Hypotheses

The two different data cost functions are combined for temporal coherence measure on the bilayer hypotheses. Both of them measure the consistency of color and geometry among multiple cameras and multiple temporal frames.

If a pixel $\mathbf{x}_m^t$ is static, we follow the bundle optimization algorithm proposed in [20] to compute its data cost with candidate disparity d_i. Given a reference frame t' in camera m', we can project the pixel $\mathbf{x}_m^t$ to $I_{m'}^{t'}$ by d_i. The projection point is denoted as $\mathbf{x}_{m'}^{t'}$. Similar to [20], we can measure the color and geometry coherence between $\mathbf{x}_m^t$ and $\mathbf{x}_{m'}^{t'}$, and compute a disparity likelihood as

$$L_d(\mathbf{x}_m^t, d_i; I_m^t, I_{m'}^{t'}, D_{m'}^{t'}) = p_c(\mathbf{x}_m^t, \mathbf{x}_{m'}^{t'}) p_v(\mathbf{x}_m^t, \mathbf{x}_{m'}^{t'}), \tag{10}$$

where p_c is the color similarity defined as Eq. (7). p_v is the geometric coherence by computing the backward projection error, which is defined as:

$$p_v(\mathbf{x}_m^t, \mathbf{x}_{m'}^{t'}) = \frac{\sigma_w}{\sigma_w + \left\|\mathbf{x}_m^t - l_{m' \to m}^{t' \to t}(\mathbf{x}_{m'}^{t'}, D_{m'}^{t'}(\mathbf{x}_{m'}^{t'}))\right\|_1}. \tag{11}$$

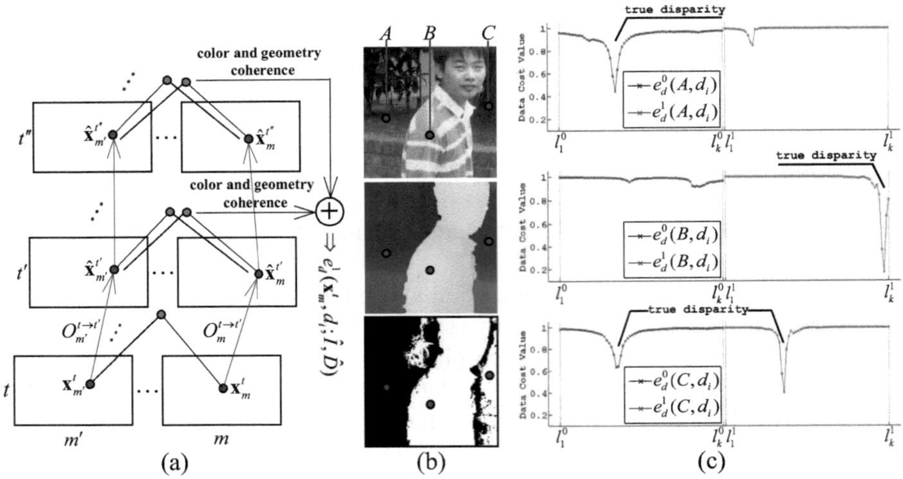

Fig. 4. (a) Illustration of the spatio-temporal coherence constraint on a dynamic-pixel hypothesis. (b) The magnified source frame of Fig. 3(a), its spatio-temporally optimized depth map and the bilayer segmentation map. (c) The data cost values of the three representative pixels A, B and C in (c), computed by e_d^0 and e_d^1, which have a clear minimum to infer the true disparity robustly.

The term $l_{m' \to m}^{t' \to t}(\mathbf{x}_{m'}^{t'}, D_{m'}^{t'}(\mathbf{x}_{m'}^{t'}))$ is the point by projecting $\mathbf{x}_{m'}^{t'}$ to I_m^t as in [20].

We accumulate L_d with all the cameras at nearby time instances (20 nearest frames), and compute the data cost of $\mathbf{x}_m^t$ on the static-pixel hypothesis as:

$$e_d^0(\mathbf{x}_m^t, d_i; \hat{I}, \hat{D}) = 1 - \frac{\sum_{m'=1}^{M} \sum_{t' \in N(t)} L_d(\mathbf{x}_m^t, d_i; I_m^t, I_{m'}^{t'}, D_{m'}^{t'})}{M|N(t)|}. \quad (12)$$

If the pixel $\mathbf{x}_m^t$ is dynamic, the data cost computation is more sophisticated. A straightforward way is to compute its depth among multiple synchronous cameras at time instance t also using bundle optimization as in [20]. However, most of our experimental examples have only $2 \sim 3$ cameras. The small number of synchronous views will significantly degrade the effectiveness of bundle optimization. To address this problem, we incorporate a spatio-temporal coherence measure similar to [15] for dynamic depth optimization. Unlike [15] which only used a preceding time instance for optimization, our data cost combines multiple nearby time instances to enhance the robustness of coherence measures.

Fig. 4(a) illustrates our spatio-temporal constraint for dynamic points. Specifically, given a candidate disparity d_i and a reference camera m', we can project the pixel $\mathbf{x}_m^t$ from camera m to m'. The projection point is denoted as $\mathbf{x}_{m'}^t$. To add its color and geometric coherence constraints from temporal frames at t', we track $\mathbf{x}_m^t$ and $\mathbf{x}_{m'}^t$ to t' by optical flows $O_m^{t \to t'}$ and $O_{m'}^{t \to t'}$ to get the corresponding pixels $\hat{\mathbf{x}}_m^{t'}$ and $\hat{\mathbf{x}}_{m'}^{t'}$. We compute the optical flow maps using the algorithm proposed in [10]. If the optical flows are accurate (i.e., $||O_m^{t \to t'}(\mathbf{x}_m^t) + O_m^{t' \to t}(\hat{\mathbf{x}}_m^{t'})|| < \tau$, and $||O_{m'}^{t \to t'}(\mathbf{x}_{m'}^t) + O_{m'}^{t' \to t}(\hat{\mathbf{x}}_{m'}^{t'})|| < \tau$, where $\tau = 3$ pixels in our experiments), we compute a disparity likelihood $L_g(\hat{\mathbf{x}}_m^{t'}, \hat{\mathbf{x}}_{m'}^{t'})$, by measuring the color and geometry coherence between $\hat{\mathbf{x}}_m^{t'}$ and $\hat{\mathbf{x}}_{m'}^{t'}$ as

$$L_g(\hat{\mathbf{x}}_m^{t'}, \hat{\mathbf{x}}_{m'}^{t'}; I_m^{t'}, I_{m'}^{t'}, D_m^{t'}, D_{m'}^{t'}) = p_c(\hat{\mathbf{x}}_m^{t'}, \hat{\mathbf{x}}_{m'}^{t'}) p_g(\hat{\mathbf{x}}_m^{t'}, \hat{\mathbf{x}}_{m'}^{t'}), \tag{13}$$

where p_g is the geometric coherence defined as:

$$p_g(\hat{\mathbf{x}}_m^{t'}, \hat{\mathbf{x}}_{m'}^{t'}) = \frac{\sigma_w}{\sigma_w + d_g(\hat{\mathbf{x}}_m^{t'}, \hat{\mathbf{x}}_{m'}^{t'}; D_m^{t'}, D_{m'}^{t'})}. \tag{14}$$

The term d_g is the symmetrical projection error. $\hat{\mathbf{x}}_m^{t'}$ is projected to frame $I_{m'}^{t'}$, and calculate its distance to $\hat{\mathbf{x}}_{m'}^{t'}$. Symmetrically, $\hat{\mathbf{x}}_{m'}^{t'}$ is projected to frame $I_m^{t'}$, and calculate its distance to $\mathbf{x}_m^{t'}$. d_g is the RMS of these two distances.

L_g is accumulated with all the reference cameras at nearby time instances (10 nearest frames in our experiments), and the data cost on dynamic-pixel hypothesis is defined as:

$$e_d^1(\mathbf{x}_m^t, d_i; \hat{I}, \hat{D}) = 1 - \frac{\sum\limits_{t' \in N(t)} \sum\limits_{m' \neq m} L_g(\hat{\mathbf{x}}_m^{t'}, \hat{\mathbf{x}}_{m'}^{t'}; I_m^{t'}, I_{m'}^{t'}, D_m^{t'}, D_{m'}^{t'})}{(M-1)|N(t)|}. \tag{15}$$

Now we can redefine the data term in Eq. (9) by combining the two kinds of data cost functions e_d^0 and e_d^1 as:

$$E_d(\mathbf{L}_m^t; \hat{I}, \hat{D}) = \sum_{\mathbf{x}_m^t} e_d(\mathbf{x}_m^t, \mathbf{L}_m^t(\mathbf{x}_m^t); \hat{I}, \hat{D}),$$
$$\text{with } e_d(\mathbf{x}_m^t, l_i^s; \hat{I}, \hat{D}) = \begin{cases} e_d^0(\mathbf{x}_m^t, d_i; \hat{I}, \hat{D}) & s = 0 \\ e_d^1(\mathbf{x}_m^t, d_i; \hat{I}, \hat{D}) & s = 1 \end{cases}. \tag{16}$$

Since L_d and L_g are both multiplication of color and geometry coherence measures in the same form, e_d^0 and e_d^1 can compete fairly to infer the true disparity of each pixel.

5.2 Iterative Optimization

With the redefined data term (16), we iteratively minimize Eq. (9) to jointly refine the disparity maps and infer the static/dynamic labeling (the smoothness term remains the same as Eq. (2), except that the optimized variables are newly defined labels instead of disparities). Since the number of new labels doubles, we typically use 70 disparity levels in our experiments due to memory limitations of BP. The scalability problem can be well addressed by using hierarchical BP as in [18]. While refining $\mathbf{L}_m^t$, we fix the disparity values in all other frames. Each pass of optimization starts from frame 1. One pass completes when the disparity and segmentation maps of all the frames in each camera are optimized. A result is shown at Fig. 5. As shown in Fig. 5(e), after one pass of optimization, the disparity maps are greatly improved in both the static and dynamic regions.

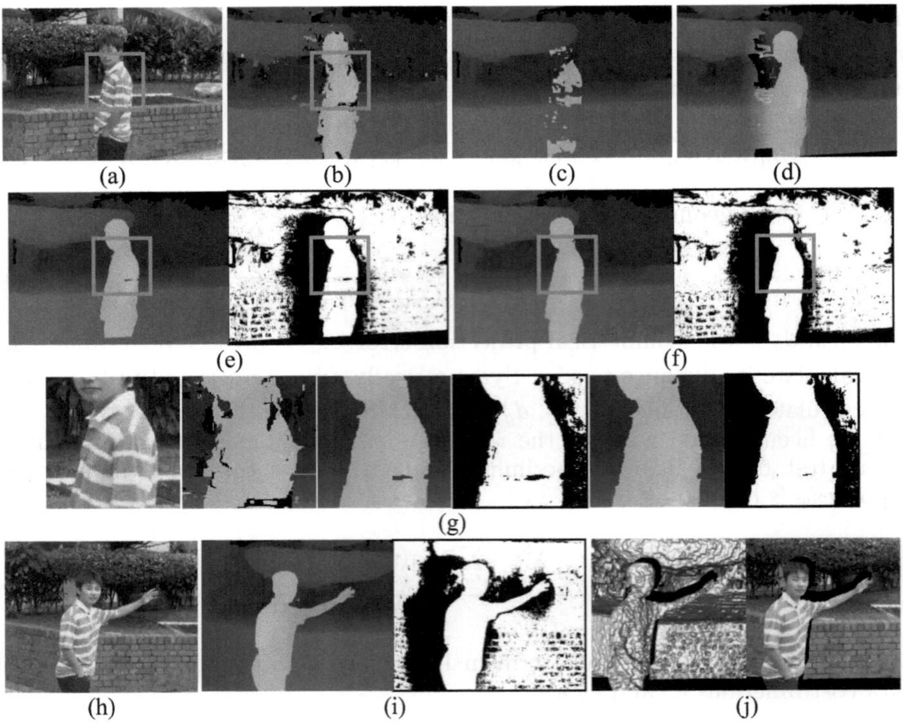

Fig. 5. The results of our spatio-temporal disparity optimization. (a) One source frame. (b) The initialized disparity map. (c) The optimized depth result only using e_d^0 as in [20]. (d) The depth map optimized only using e_d^1 as in [15]. (e) The optimized depth map and bilayer segmentation map by our method after the first iteration, using both e_d^0 and e_d^1. (f) Results after the second iteration of spatio-temporal optimization. (g) Zoomed view of the green rectangles in (a), (b), (e) and (f). (h-i) Another source frame and its spatio-temporal depth optimization result. (j) The 3D surface model reconstructed from the depth map in (i), with texture mapping.

Furthermore, the estimated disparity maps becomes more temporally consistent, as evidenced in our supplementary video [1].

As shown in Fig. 5(c-d), only using e_d^0 or e_d^1 for depth optimization will cause visible problems. In comparison, our combination of both e_d^0 and e_d^1 can robustly infer the true disparity for both static and dynamic pixels (Fig. 5(e)). There are three marked points A, B and C in Fig. 4(b) and their associated data cost values in (c). Pixel A has a clear minimum cost in e_d^0, and has relatively larger cost in e_d^1. Therefore, A has strong preference to be labeled as static. In comparison, pixel B can reach a strong minimum in e_d^1, and has larger cost in e_d^0. Hence, it is labeled as dynamic. Pixel C has low costs in both e_d^0 and e_d^1. In other words,

[1] The supplementary material and video can be downloaded from the corresponding project website under `http://www.cad.zju.edu.cn/home/gfzhang/`

no matter if it is considered as static or dynamic, its disparity can be inferred reliably. This explains why a large number of background static points are labeled as 'dynamic' by our method. Again, our 'bilayer segmentation' only means to select the right data cost function for a pixel. Another interesting phenomena is that the occluded pixels are generally labeled as static and the segmentation are quite accurate around discontinuous foreground boundaries. The reason is that the optical flow estimation is generally difficult for the occluded regions so that the motion-based dynamic data cost e_d^1 will output large values in this case. In contrast, the static data cost e_d^0 is computed by projecting the pixel to temporally neighboring frames with depth, which is robust to occlusions and can output relative small values.

Fig. 5(e) also shows the bilayer segmentation map S_m^t obtained from the optimized $\mathbf{L}_m^t$. As can be seen in Fig. 5(g), most dynamic pixels are correctly labeled and reconstructed except for some outliers. These outliers are generally caused by similar foreground and background colors. Fortunately, we can further improve our depths and segmentation in a second spatio-temporal optimization. Specifically, we check the static/dynamic labels of corresponding pixels in temporal neighboring frames to improve static/dynamic segmentation and depth estimation. We track a pixel by optical flow to its 10 nearest neighboring frames and compute the following dynamic-pixel probability:

$$P_d(\mathbf{x}_m^t) = \frac{\sum_{t' \in N(t)} S_m^{t'}(\mathbf{x}_m^t + O_m^{t \to t'}(\mathbf{x}_m^t))}{|N(t)|}. \tag{17}$$

If the dynamic-pixel probability is large, we tend to believe that $\mathbf{x}_m^t$ is dynamic. Otherwise, it is more likely to be static. We incorporate P_d into the second pass of data cost computation and redefine e_d as:

$$e_d(\mathbf{x}_m^t, l_i^s; \hat{I}, \hat{D}) = \begin{cases} (1 + P_d(\mathbf{x}_m^t))e_d^0(\mathbf{x}_m^t, d_i; \hat{I}, \hat{D}) & s = 0 \\ (2 - P_d(\mathbf{x}_m^t))e_d^1(\mathbf{x}_m^t, d_i; \hat{I}, \hat{D}) & s = 1 \end{cases}. \tag{18}$$

When $P_d < 0.5$, e_d^0 has smaller weight than e_d^1, so that $\mathbf{x}_m^t$ tends to be labeled as static. Otherwise, we tend to label $\mathbf{x}_m^t$ as dynamic. After the second pass,

(a) (b) (c) (d) (e)

Fig. 6. Dynamic 3D reconstruction of the 'Standing' sequences with two input videos. (a) A source frame from the first video. (b-c) The estimated background image and segmentation result by [19]. (d) The refined disparity map based on (c), which contain serious artifacts highlighted in the red rectangles. (e) The refined disparity map by our method, which are accurate in both static and dynamic regions.

the incorrectly estimated disparities and static/dynamic labels are successfully corrected as shown in Fig. 5(f).

6 Experimental Results

We have performed experiments on several examples with source videos taken by 2 $\sim$ 3 handheld cameras. We used Sony HDR-XR550 cameras to capture the videos. Instead of using genlock, we blinked a flashlight when capturing began and then synchronized the videos according to the blinking timestamp. All our experiments are conducted on a desktop PC with Intel 4-Core 2.83GHz CPU. For a sequence with resolution 960×540, depth initialization takes 172 seconds per frame, and disparity optimization requires 81 seconds per frame, which is more efficient than the methods of [9,15]. Fig. 6 shows our results on the 'Standing' sequences, which capture a boy standing and moving slightly. Only part of the body is moving in this example, which makes accurate background estimation and static/dynamic segmentation difficult with the traditional methods such as [19]. As shown in Fig. 6(b), the background is almost occluded in all the frames by the dynamic foreground, and can not be well estimated. Hence, the bilayer segmentation result by [19] is not very accurate as shown in Fig. 6(c). If we use different data cost functions to optimize static and dynamic pixels with this

Fig. 7. Dynamic 3D reconstruction results of the 'Bear' sequences (two videos). Two selected frames from the first video and their depth results.

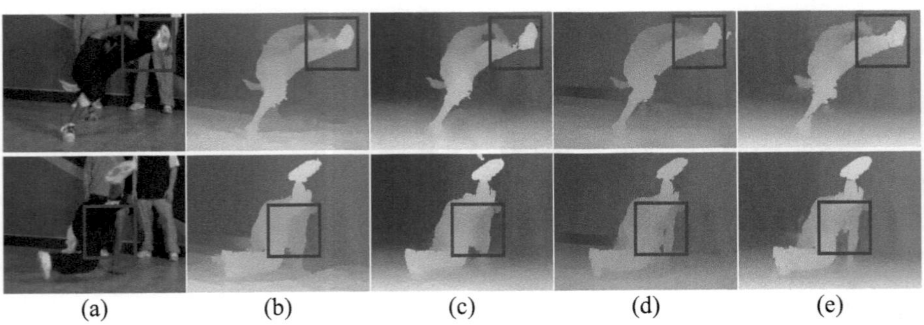

Fig. 8. Comparison of our method to [23], [9] and [15]. (a) Two selected source frames from the third source video of the Microsoft Breakdancing dataset [23]. (b) Microsoft results [23]. (c) The results of [9]. (d) The results of [15]. (e) Our results.

inaccurate segmentation result (e_d^0 for static pixels, and e_d^1 for dynamic ones), the refined depth map will contain serious artifacts as shown in Fig. 6(d). In contrast, our method does not rely on precise bilayer segmentation. By spatio-temporal optimization using two kinds of data cost functions, our method not only achieve high-quality dynamic depth maps for both static and dynamic pixels, but also preserves accurate depth boundaries without explicit bilayer segmentation as shown in Fig. 6(e).

Another challenging example is provided in Fig. 7, capturing a crawling bear. Our method can also handle multiple dynamic objects, as shown in Fig. 1. We also experimented on the Microsoft Research Breakdancing dataset [23]. Fig. 8 shows the comparison of our results with Microsoft results [23], [9] and [15]. The floor reconstructed in [23] and [15] and the body of the dancer reconstructed in [9] both had visible artifacts, as highlighted in the red rectangles. In comparison, our method generated better results. Please refer to our supplementary material and video for the complete frames and more results.

7 Conclusion and Discussion

In this paper, we propose a novel dense depth recovery method for dynamic scenes captured by multiple handheld cameras. We first use the synchronous images in the same time instance from different cameras to compute the initial depth maps. Then, by combining two different kinds of spatio-temporal constraints, depth optimization and bilayer segmentation are performed simultaneously to achieve a high-quality dense depth estimation.

The accuracy of the optical flow will influence the quality of depth recovery, especially when the motions of moving objects are very large. Severely erroneous optical flow estimation will involve incorrect color and geometry coherence constraints in temporal frames, which harms the depth refinement. Fortunately, this problem can be alleviated by backward verification of optical flow error to discard inaccurate optical flow estimation. How to more effectively solve this problem remains to be our future work.

Acknowledgements. We would like to thank Dr. Xun Cao for helping compute the results of Microsoft Breakdancing dataset by running [15]. This work is supported by the 973 program of China (No. 2009CB320802), National Science and Technology Support Plan Project (No. 2012BAH35B02), NSF of China (No. 60903135), the Specialized Research Fund for the Doctoral Program of Higher Education of China (No. 20110101130011), the Fundamental Research Funds for the Central Universities, and the Singapore MOE grant R-263-000-620-112.

References

1. de Aguiar, E., Stoll, C., Theobalt, C., Ahmed, N., Seidel, H.P., Thrun, S.: Performance capture from sparse multi-view video. ACM Transactions on Graphics 27, 98:1–98:10 (2008)

2. Ballan, L., Brostow, G.J., Puwein, J., Pollefeys, M.: Unstructured video-based rendering: interactive exploration of casually captured videos. ACM Transactions on Graphics 29, 87:1–87:11 (2010)
3. Comaniciu, D., Meer, P., Member, S.: Mean shift: A robust approach toward feature space analysis. IEEE Transactions on Pattern Analysis and Machine Intelligence 24, 603–619 (2002)
4. Felzenszwalb, P.F., Huttenlocher, D.P.: Efficient belief propagation for early vision. International Journal of Computer Vision 70(1), 41–54 (2006)
5. Goldlücke, B., Magnor, M.A.: Joint 3D-reconstruction and background separation in multiple views using graph cuts. In: CVPR, vol. 1 (2003)
6. Guillemaut, J.-Y., Kilner, J., Hilton, A.: Robust graph-cut scene segmentation and reconstruction for free-viewpoint video of complex dynamic scenes. In: ICCV, pp. 809–816 (2009)
7. Hasler, N., Rosenhahn, B., Thormählen, T., Wand, M., Gall, J., Seidel, H.-P.: Markerless motion capture with unsynchronized moving cameras. In: CVPR, pp. 224–231 (2009)
8. Larsen, E.S., Mordohai, P., Pollefeys, M., Fuchs, H.: Temporally consistent reconstruction from multiple video streams using enhanced belief propagation. In: ICCV, pp. 1–8 (2007)
9. Lei, C., Da Chen, X., Yang, Y.H.: A new multiview spacetime-consistent depth recovery framework for free viewpoint video rendering. In: ICCV, pp. 1570–1577 (2009)
10. Liu, C.: Beyond pixels: exploring new representations and applications for motion analysis. Ph.D. thesis, Massachusetts Institute of Technology (May 2009)
11. Seitz, S.M., Curless, B., Diebel, J., Scharstein, D., Szeliski, R.: A comparison and evaluation of multi-view stereo reconstruction algorithms. In: CVPR, vol. 1, pp. 519–528 (2006)
12. Tao, H., Sawhney, H.S., Kumar, R.: Dynamic depth recovery from multiple synchronized video streams. In: CVPR, pp. 118–124 (2001)
13. Tola, E., Lepetit, V., Fua, P.: Daisy: An efficient dense descriptor applied to wide-baseline stereo. IEEE Transactions on Pattern Analysis and Machine Intelligence 32(5), 815–830 (2010)
14. Torresani, L., Hertzmann, A., Bregler, C.: Nonrigid structure-from-motion: Estimating shape and motion with hierarchical priors. IEEE Transactions on Pattern Analysis and Machine Intelligence 30(5), 878–892 (2008)
15. Yang, M., Cao, X., Dai, Q.: Multiview video depth estimation with spatial-temporal consistency. In: BMVC (2010)
16. Yang, W., Zhang, G., Bao, H., Kim, J., Lee, H.Y.: Consistent depth maps recovery from a trinocular video sequence. In: CVPR, pp. 1466–1473 (2012)
17. Zhang, G., Dong, Z., Jia, J., Wong, T.-T., Bao, H.: Efficient Non-consecutive Feature Tracking for Structure-from-Motion. In: Daniilidis, K., Maragos, P., Paragios, N. (eds.) ECCV 2010, Part V. LNCS, vol. 6315, pp. 422–435. Springer, Heidelberg (2010)
18. Zhang, G., Jia, J., Bao, H.: Simultaneous multi-body stereo and segmentation. In: ICCV, pp. 826–833 (2011)
19. Zhang, G., Jia, J., Hua, W., Bao, H.: Robust bilayer segmentation and motion/depth estimation with a handheld camera. IEEE Transactions on Pattern Analysis and Machine Intelligence (99), 603–617 (2011)
20. Zhang, G., Jia, J., Wong, T.-T., Bao, H.: Consistent depth maps recovery from a video sequence. IEEE Transactions on Pattern Analysis and Machine Intelligence 31(6), 974–988 (2009)

21. Zhang, G., Qin, X., Hua, W., Wong, T.-T., Heng, P.-A., Bao, H.: Robust metric reconstruction from challenging video sequences. In: CVPR (2007)
22. Zhang, Y., Kambhamettu, C.: Integrated 3D scene flow and structure recovery from multiview image sequences. In: CVPR, vol. 2, pp. 674–681 (2000)
23. Zitnick, C.L., Kang, S.B., Uyttendaele, M., Winder, S., Szeliski, R.: High-quality video view interpolation using a layered representation. ACM Transactions on Graphics 23, 600–608 (2004)

Joint Face Alignment: Rescue Bad Alignments with Good Ones by Regularized Re-fitting

Xiaowei Zhao[1,2], Xiujuan Chai[1], and Shiguang Shan[1]

[1] Key Lab of Intelligent Information Processing of Chinese Academy of Sciences (CAS), Institute of Computing Technology, CAS, Beijing 100190, China
[2] Graduate University of Chinese Academy of Sciences, Beijing 100049, China
mathzxw2002@gmail.com, {chaixiujuan,sgshan}@ict.ac.cn

Abstract. Nowadays, more and more applications need to jointly align a set of facial images from one specific person, which forms the so-called *joint face alignment* problem. To address this problem, in this paper, starting from an initial face alignment results, we propose to enhance the alignments by a fundamentally novel idea: *rescuing the bad alignments with their well-aligned neighbors*. In our method, a discriminative alignment evaluator is well designed to assess the initial face alignments and separate the well-aligned images from the badly-aligned ones. To correct the bad ones, a robust regularized re-fitting algorithm is proposed by exploiting the appearance consistency between the badly-aligned image and its k well-aligned nearest neighbors. Experiments conducted on faces in the wild demonstrate that our method greatly improves the initial face alignment results of an off-the-shelf facial landmark locator. In addition, the effectiveness of our method is validated through comparing with other state-of-the-art methods in joint face alignment under complex conditions.

1 Introduction

In recent years, with the popularity of various digital cameras and the rapid growth of internet-based photo sharing, collecting multiple images of one specific person becomes easier and easier. With the collected multiple facial images for one person, a lot of new applications emerged, e.g., face recognition with image sets [1], face photo album management [2], and person-specific face modeling [3]. These applications appeal for aligning simultaneously the multiple face images of the same person, i.e., the so-called "joint face alignment" problem. Overall speaking, joint face alignment still remains challenging as the appearance of faces can vary a lot due to tremendous variations in pose, expression, occlusion, and low quality imaging, etc.

Joint face alignment problem is initially studied by Learned-Miller's influential congealing procedure, which registers a batch of images by minimizing the entropy of each column of pixels through the image set [4]. Congealing has been proven to work well on simple images, such as binary handwritten digits. Later on, many efforts have been devoted to make congealing more robust to

A. Fitzgibbon et al. (Eds.): ECCV 2012, Part II, LNCS 7573, pp. 616–630, 2012.

complex real-world faces [5,6], which include exploring more robust features for congealing algorithm instead of raw pixels [5] or using least square constrains to estimate warping parameters [6]. Besides these congealing-style methods, Robust Alignment by Sparse and Low-rank Decomposition (RASL) is proposed to make more robust face alignment in the case of occlusions and large lighting changes by minimizing the rank of the image ensemble [7]. However, due to the ignorance of non-rigid transformations, the above methods are restricted from being applied to scenarios which need more accurate face alignment, such as face swapping [8] and face animation [9]. Moreover, the human face information, such as the shape and appearance models of the faces, is not exploited to remove outliers produced in the process of joint face alignment.

Conventional model-based face alignment methods, such as Active Shape Model (ASM) [10] and Active Appearance Model (AAM) [11], are typical non-rigid face alignment techniques, which can also be applied to jointly align a batch of images [12,13]. A straightforward idea is to perform face alignment on each image independently, and jointly align the ensemble of images by registering the facial landmarks of each image with the landmarks of a reference template image. This kind of methods is effective to handle non-rigid pose and shape variations and the incorrect facial landmark configurations can be moderated by exploiting the learned statistical shape or appearance models. However, it is still challenging for these model-based methods to align real-world face images in spite that many efforts have been dedicated to improve the accuracy and efficiency of ASM and AAM (e.g., [14,15,16,17]). In addition, the model-based methods ignore the appearance consistency of the person-specific image ensemble when performing joint face alignment.

More recently, there appeared a few methods that simultaneously consider the human face model and the appearance consistency of image ensemble [18,19]. For example, Zhao et al. perform non-rigid joint face alignment by combining a generic deformable face model (AAM) with RASL [18]. Through the combination, on one hand, RASL is extended from rigid to non-rigid; on the other hand, the generic appearance model (AAM) is regularized to fit adaptively to an unseen face by minimizing the rank of the image ensemble. Tong et al. propose a semi-supervised least-squares congealing algorithm to jointly align an ensemble of facial images [19]. In their method, a small number of images should be manually labeled. During the congealing process, the estimated facial landmark locations are constrained by utilizing an on-line learned non-rigid statistical shape model.

In short, existing joint face alignment methods either depend on an initially labeled image set or regularize the fitting process by minimizing the rank of the whole image set. Different from the above methods, in this paper, we propose a novel method to enhance an initial face alignment results by rescuing the bad alignments with the good ones. Specifically, given a set of facial images from one specific person, we *first* align all the face images in the set with an off-the-shelf model-based facial landmark locator. *Then*, we automatically assess the initial alignments to distinguish the good ones from the bad ones by using

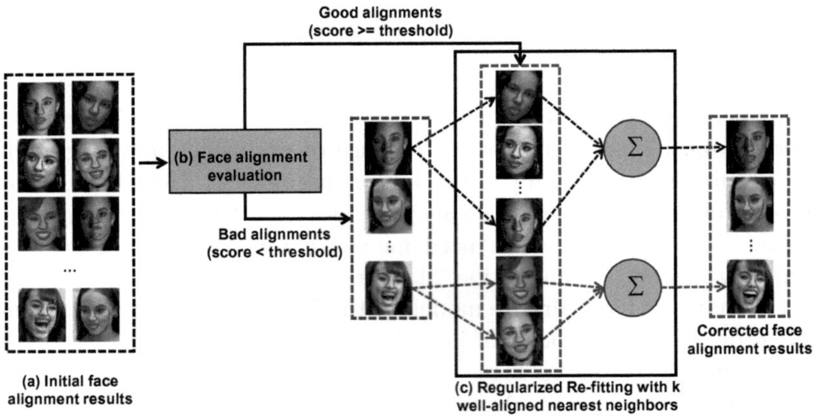

Fig. 1. Overview of the proposed joint face alignment method: (a) initial face alignment results, (b) face alignment evaluation, (c) correcting the bad alignment by regularized re-fitting with k well-aligned nearest neighbors

a simple but robust discriminative face alignment evaluator, which can assign each alignment result a confidence score highly related to the degree of alignment accuracy. *Subsequently*, for each badly-aligned image, we find its k well-aligned nearest neighbors in the image set. *Finally*, through regularizing the shape and appearance space of the badly-aligned image with the selected good neighbors, the facial landmark locations of the badly-aligned image are corrected by our regularized re-fitting algorithm. Experiments conducted on faces in the wild show that our algorithm greatly improves the initial face alignment results. Besides, the effectiveness of our method is also demonstrated through experiments in comparison with competitive methods in joint alignment of complex faces.

Briefly speaking, the main contributions of this paper are: (1) We propose a novel fundamental idea and framework for joint face alignment, i.e., rescuing the bad alignments with their good neighbors. (2) We design a discriminative face alignment evaluator to assess the face alignment. (3) We propose a regularized re-fitting algorithm to correct the bad alignments by the good ones.

The remaining part of this paper is organized as follows. Section 2 gives a brief overview of our joint face alignment method. Section 3 presents more details of our method, including the initialization of face alignments by an off-the-shelf facial landmark locator, the alignment results evaluator, and the regularized re-fitting algorithm. Section 4 reports the experimental results and also the comparisons with the state-of-the-art methods. Section 5 concludes the paper.

2 Method Overview

The basic idea of our method is shown in Fig.1. Simply speaking, our method consists of the following three steps: (1) initialized face alignment, (2) face alignment results evaluation, (3) correcting the bad alignment by regularized re-fitting with k nearest good neighbors.

In the first step, as shown in Fig.1(a), we first perform face alignment on all the images in the set by using an off-the-shelf facial landmark locator. In this study, Gu's method [16] is exploited for this purpose.

In the next step, as shown in Fig.1(b), a pre-learned face alignment evaluator is exploited to assess the initial alignment results for each image in the set. The well-aligned images, i.e., those with high alignment confidence scores, are automatically selected. For convenience, we denote this image subset as **G**.

Then, in the last step, the images with scores less than a threshold, i.e., badly-aligned, are further processed to obtain enhanced alignment results. As illustrated in Fig.1(c), for each badly-aligned image, we find its k nearest neighbor images from **G**, which are then used to correct the bad alignment by regularizing its shape and appearance space. In this study, a better face alignment result is finally obtained by solving an optimization problem. It is worth noting here that, our good alignment set **G** is dynamically updated. In other words, once the alignment score of an image after rescuing is larger than the threshold, it is added to the set **G**. With this strategy, more good alignment samples can be exploited to rescue the remaining bad alignments.

3 Enhance Joint Face Alignment by Regularized Re-fitting

In this section, we will describe the implementation details of our method.

3.1 Initialization with an Off-the-Shelf Model-Based Face Alignment Algorithm

In this paper, Gu's robust face alignment algorithm is implemented as the off-the-shelf facial landmark locator [16] and used to initialize the face alignment results for the image ensemble. Being one of the state-of-the-art methods, this approach produces impressive results on real world images. The robustness of this method comes from the shape regularization model, which incorporates constrained nonlinear shape prior, geometric transformation and likelihood of multiple candidate landmarks in a three-layered generative model [16].

At the bottom layer of the model, multiple candidate points are provided for each facial landmark, and each candidate is assigned a confidence representing its probability. Let $Q = \{Q_{nk}, n = 1, 2, \cdots, N; k = 1, 2, \cdots, K\}$ denotes the whole candidate set, where N is the number of facial landmarks, and K is the number of candidate points. A binary $N \times K$ assignment matrix h is introduced to assign one candidate position to each landmark. $Q\{h\}$ denote the set of positions selected by h.

The global geometric transformation $\theta = \{R, s, t\}$ is modeled by the middle layer, where a noise term is assigned to each facial landmark to measure its fitting error, and the noise level of each facial landmark point is measured by ρ_n.

The top layer models the prior shape distribution as a mixture of constrained Gaussian [20],

$$p(S|b) = \sum_{l} \pi_l \mathcal{N}(\Phi_l b_l + \mu_l; \sigma_l^2 I), \tag{1}$$

where the model parameters associated with each Gaussian component are the mixing rate π_l, the linear principal subspace spanned by the columns of Φ_l, the mean shape μ_l, the isotropic shape noise with zero mean and variance $\sigma^2 I$. $b = \{b_l\}$ denotes the deformation coefficients. A latent component variable z_l is also introduced to stands the mixture component label. Λ_l are eigenvalues for the l-th Gaussian component.

Based on the three-layered generative model, the face alignment problem is formulated as a MAP problem, i.e., finding the optimal deformation parameter b and transformation parameter θ by maximizing the posterior $p(b, \theta|Q)$. EM algorithm is used to solve this MAP problem.

In the E-step, taking the expectation $\langle \cdot \rangle$ of the log of $p(b, \theta, S, h, z|Q)$ over the latent variables S, h, z, we can obtain that:

$$\begin{aligned} \Omega(b, \theta) = \langle \log p(b, \theta, S, h, z|Q) \rangle_{S,h,z} \propto \langle \log p(S|b, z) \rangle \\ + \langle \log p(b) \rangle + \langle \log p(z) \rangle + \langle \log p(Q(h)|S, \theta) \rangle + \langle \log p(h) \rangle. \end{aligned} \tag{2}$$

In the M-step, the updating equations for b and θ can be obtained by taking the derivative of (2), i.e.,

$$\frac{\partial \Omega}{\partial b_l} = -(\Lambda_l^{-1} + \frac{\langle z_l \rangle}{\sigma_l^2}) b_l - \frac{\langle z_l \rangle}{\sigma_l^2} \Phi^{\mathrm{T}} (\mu_l - \bar{S}_l) \tag{3}$$

$$\frac{\partial \Omega}{\partial t} = -\sum_n \frac{1}{\rho_n} (-\sum_k Q_{nk} \sum_l \langle z_l \rangle \langle h_{nk} \rangle) - \sum_n \frac{1}{\rho_n} (sR \sum_l \langle z_l \rangle \bar{S}_{nl} + t) \tag{4}$$

$$\frac{\partial \Omega}{\partial s} = -\sum_n \frac{1}{\rho_n} (-\sum_k Q_{nk}^{\mathrm{T}} R \langle h_{nk} S_n \rangle + t^{\mathrm{T}} R \langle S_n \rangle) - s \sum_n \frac{1}{\rho_n} \langle S_n^{\mathrm{T}} S_n \rangle \tag{5}$$

$$\frac{\partial \Omega}{\partial R} = \sum_n \frac{1}{\rho_n} (\langle S_n \rangle t^{\mathrm{T}} - \sum_k \langle h_{nk} S_n \rangle Q_{nk}^{\mathrm{T}}). \tag{6}$$

In the process of face alignment, Zhao's facial landmark detection algorithm [21] is utilized to automatically detect two eye centers and initialize the facial shape.

3.2 Face Alignment Evaluation with a Discriminative Classifier

In this section, a face alignment evaluator is well designed and developed to automatically assess the quality of the initial face alignment results.

In this paper, it is implemented as a boosting-based discriminative classifier, which consists of a global appearance classifier and multiple component-based classifiers, as shown in Fig.2. Specifically, the discriminative classifier is implemented under the cascaded AdaBoost framework [22] and Real AdaBoost [23]

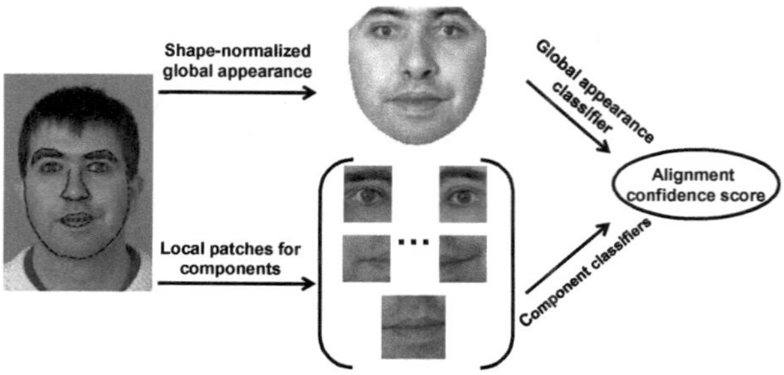

Fig. 2. Illustration of the alignment evaluator, which consists of a global appearance classifier and multiple component-based classifiers

is exploited to assign each alignment result a real-valued confidence score. The alignment confidence score should be correlated with the alignment error. A high score should predict small alignment error and vice visa.

For the global appearance classifier, shape-normalized facial images warped with true alignment are considered as positive class and images warped with perturbed alignment are treated as negative class. Haar-like features are used to characterize the global appearance [22]. This type of global appearance classifier is first used in [14], called Boosted Appearance Model (BAM). However, it shows some limits when being applied to evaluate the face alignment results. As discussed in [15], there is no guarantee that moving along the gradient of BAM's score function will always improve the alignment. It is also verified by our experiments that some alignment results with similar error have very different alignment confidence score, as shown in Section 4.2.

So, in this paper, besides the global appearance classifier, multiple component-based classifiers (e.g., classifiers for eye centers, mouth corners and mouth center) are trained as the compensators to enhance the capability of our face alignment evaluator, as shown in Fig.2. In comparison to the global appearance classifier, the component classifiers characterize more details about the local appearance. For each component classifier, image patches centered at the correct facial landmark location are extracted as positive samples and image patches with several pixels displaced from the true locations are extracted as negative samples.

Given a testing image and its facial landmark locations L, local patches for the components and the shape-normalized global appearance are simultaneously extracted according to L. Then each of them is assigned a confidence value by the corresponding classifier. Finally, the confidence score of L is calculated by the following formula, which is restricted to range $[0, 1]$:

$$f(L) = \frac{1}{1 + \exp\{a[\frac{1}{M}\sum_{i=1}^{M} w_i C_i(L)] + b\}}, \tag{7}$$

where M is the total number of discriminative classifiers, including the global appearance classifier and the component-based classifiers. $C_i(L)$ is the response value of the i-th classifier and w_i is its corresponding weight. Note that in order to unify the dimension of all the cascaded classifiers, we divide the response value of them by the number of cascaded stages. Moreover, in the following experiments, we set $a = -0.5$, $b = 0$, and $w = 1$ respectively.

3.3 Enhancing Bad Alignment by Regularized Re-fitting with *k* Nearest Good Neighbors

Based on the initial face alignment results and their alignment confidence scores, a novel regularized re-fitting algorithm is introduced in this section to rescue the bad alignment with its k nearest good neighbors.

Given a testing image I and its k normalized nearest good neighbors $N_i, i = 1, 2, \cdots, k$, the appearance consistency between them is exploited to regularize the appearance space of I , which is formulated as:

$$\min_{\gamma} \sum_{i=1}^{k} \sum_{x} [I(W(x;\gamma)) - N_i(x)]^2, \tag{8}$$

where γ are the parameters representing the shape of image I , and $W(x;\gamma)$ is a non-rigid piecewise affine warping function for the pixel coordinates x.

Therefore, in our solution, the regularization term in (8) is incorporated into the energy function of the generic model-based fitting algorithm and the initial face alignment result of I is corrected by solving the following optimization problem:

$$\max_{\gamma} E(\gamma) - \lambda \sum_{i=1}^{k} \sum_{x} [I(W(x;\gamma)) - N_i(x)]^2, \tag{9}$$

where $E(\gamma)$ is the objective of the generic model-based fitting algorithm and $\lambda > 0$ is the balance factor for the regularization term. Here, the generic model is mainly used to characterize the general shape or appearance variations of face and the regularization term is exploited to adapt the shape or appearance space to image I.

In order to evaluate the effectiveness of the regularization term, we implement our fitting algorithm based on the energy function of Gu's face alignment algorithm and solve it using the generalized EM algorithm [24]. Note that the energy function is *not restricted to* Gu's algorithm but can be any energy term of a model-based face alignment algorithm.

So, replacing $E(\gamma)$ in equation (9) with Gu's energy function, the problem is formulated as follows:

$$\max_{\gamma=b,\theta} \log[p(\gamma, S, h, z|Q)] - \lambda \sum_{i=1}^{k} \sum_{x} [I(W(x;\gamma)) - N_i(x)]^2. \tag{10}$$

In the E-step, taking the expectation of (10) over the latent variables S, h, z, i.e.,

$$\max_{\gamma=b,\theta} \Omega(\gamma) - \lambda \sum_{i=1}^{k} \sum_{x} [I(W(x;\gamma)) - N_i(x)]^2. \tag{11}$$

In the M-step, because problem (11) remains non-linear with respect to variable γ, a common approach to deal with non-linearity is to make first-order approximation and iteratively solves for increments to the parameters $\Delta\gamma$, i.e., maximize the following equation:

$$\max_{\gamma=b,\theta} \Omega(\gamma) + \frac{\partial \Omega}{\partial \gamma}\Delta\gamma - \lambda \sum_{i=1}^{k}\sum_{x}[I(W(x;\gamma)) + \nabla I \frac{\partial W}{\partial \gamma}\Delta\gamma - N_i(x)]^2 \tag{12}$$

with respect to $\Delta\gamma$ and then update $\gamma = \gamma + \Delta\gamma$. Here, $\nabla I \frac{\partial W}{\partial \gamma}$ is the steepest descent image, ∇I is defined as the gradient of I, and $\frac{\partial W}{\partial \gamma}$ is the Jacobian of the warp parameters evaluated at γ.

Thus, the solution of the equation (12) can be computed below:

$$\Delta\gamma = H^{-1}\frac{\partial \Omega}{\partial \gamma} - 2\lambda H^{-1}\sum_{i=1}^{k}\sum_{x}[\nabla I \frac{\partial W}{\partial \gamma}]^{\mathrm{T}}[I(W(x;\gamma)) - N_i(x)], \tag{13}$$

where H denotes the Gaussian-Newton approximation to the Hessian matrix:

$$H = 2\lambda \sum_{i=1}^{k}\sum_{x}[\nabla I \frac{\partial W}{\partial \gamma}]^{\mathrm{T}}[\nabla I \frac{\partial W}{\partial \gamma}], \tag{14}$$

and the expanded form of $\frac{\partial \Omega}{\partial \gamma}$ is given by equations (3), (4), (5), and (6).

In our implementation, the neighbor samples are determined according to the measurement of the appearance similarity. Here, the simplest Euclidean distance is adopted to characterize the similarity of image intensity. Concretely, the face region is normalized according to positions of the automatically located eye centers. The distance between eye centers is set to 50 pixels.

4 Experiments

In this section, we evaluate the effectiveness of the proposed joint face alignment algorithm through comparing with current state-of-the-art methods. Moreover, the discriminative capability of our face alignment evaluator is also validated in some real world images.

4.1 Data Sets and Evaluation Protocol

In order to quantitatively evaluate the performance of our joint face alignment algorithm and the capability of the discriminative face alignment evaluator, we manually label 3936 images from 20 persons, which are randomly selected from the PubFig [25] database. This database is collected from the internet, which is taken in completely uncontrolled situations with non-cooperative subjects, and covers large variations in pose, expression, lighting and image conditions, etc. For each person, there are about 100~300 images in PubFig database. In our

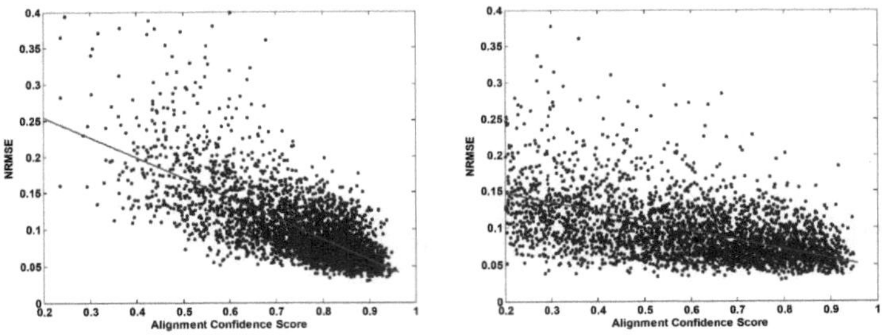

(a) Our face alignment evaluator using combined classifiers (b) Face alignment evaluator just using global appearance classifier

Fig. 3. The correlation between the alignment error (NRMSE) and the alignment confidence score. The red line shows the global trend of alignment error with respect to the confidence score.

experiments, 103 facial landmarks are manually labeled along the boundaries of face contour and facial components.

For our algorithm, the normalized root-mean-squared error (NRMSE) relative to the ground truth is adopted as the error measure for the face alignment. The NRMSE is given as a percentage, computed by dividing the root mean squared error by the distance between the two eye centers. The cumulative distribution function (CDF) of NRMSE is used to evaluate the performance of the face alignment algorithm.

4.2 Performance Evaluation of the Face Alignment Evaluator

In this part, we first describe the training process of the face alignment evaluator. Then its performance is examined through quantitative experimental results and visualized examples.

Training for the Face Alignment Evaluator. To train our discriminative face alignment evaluator, about 7000 facial images are collected from various sources, including the CMU PIE database [26], the FRGC database [27], the FERET database [28], and the CAS-PEAL database [29].

For the global appearance classifier, positive samples are generated by warping images with ground truth landmarks and negative samples are generated by perturbing the shape parameters with independent Gaussian noise with variances multiple of the eigenvalues of the corresponding shape bases. Specifically, for each image, about 100 negative samples are generated by randomly adding perturbations to the first seven shape bases. Here, the first four shape bases represent the global scaling transformation, in-plane rotation and translations in horizontal and vertical directions respectively.

In addition, five component classifiers for eye centers, mouth corners and mouth center are trained in our experiments. Besides the image patches centered

Fig. 4. Example images with the alignment results and the associated confidence scores. Each column shows typical alignment results for the specified score.

at the ground truth position, more synthesized positive samples are generated through transformations, such as shifting by ± 1 pixel, in-plane rotation within 3 degrees. Negative samples are generated by shifting 5~8 pixels away from the manually labeled ground truth position.

Performance of the Face Alignment Evaluator. We first apply Gu's face alignment algorithm to the randomly selected 3936 images, described in Section 4.1. With the alignment results, the alignment error (i.e., NRMSE) and the alignment confidence score are computed separately. Then, the relationship between these two variables is evaluated quantitatively, as shown in Fig.3. A high score should predict small alignment error and vice visa.

In Fig.3(a), the alignment confidence score is assigned by our face alignment evaluator. It shows that our face alignment evaluator is statistically a good indicator of the alignment accuracy. The alignment confidence score is highly correlated with the alignment accuracy (i.e., the Pearson correlation coefficient between them is -0.6989). However, the distinguishing capability of the face alignment evaluator just using the global appearance classifier is not strong. For example, as shown in Fig.3(b), many alignment results with very similar errors have very different confidence scores and the Pearson correlation coefficient is -0.4929.

More visualized results are shown in Fig.4. Each column gives some representative samples with similar alignment confidence score, which further confirm the validity of our face alignment evaluator in selecting the perfect aligned faces.

Especially, Fig.3 shows that the alignment error is less than 10% of eye-to-eye distance (i.e., the alignment is very close to ground truth annotation) with very high probability when the confidence score is larger than 0.9. So, in the following experiments, we set 0.9 as the threshold to distinguish good alignment results from poor alignment results.

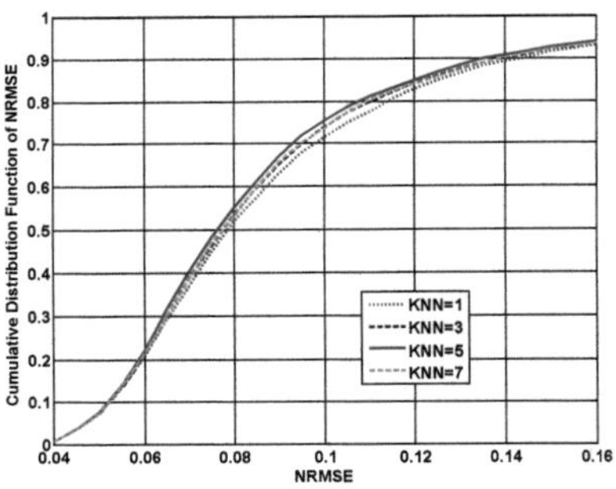

Fig. 5. Performance variation with respect to the number of nearest neighbors

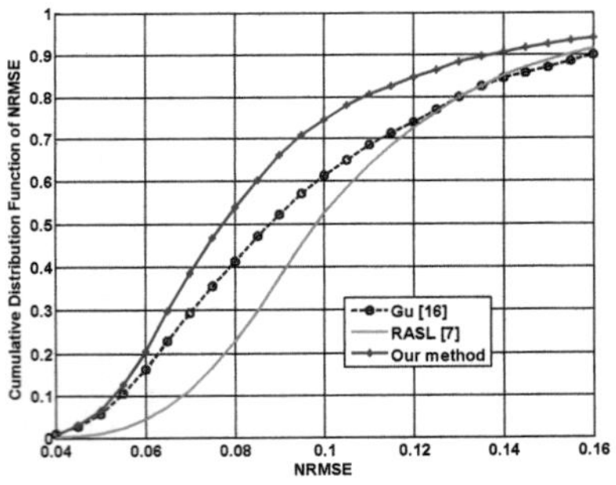

Fig. 6. Comparison with current state-of-the-art methods

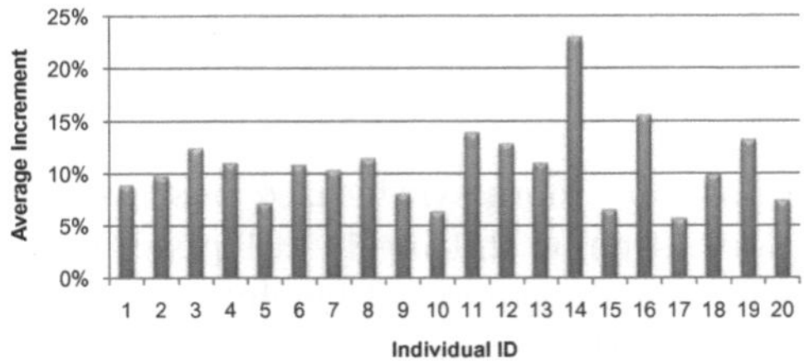

Fig. 7. Alignment accuracy improvement for 20 individuals in comparison with the initial face alignment results

4.3 Performance Evaluation of the Regularized Re-fitting Algorithm

In this section, we evaluate the performance of our method through comparing with Gu's method and RASL, which are state-of-the-art methods for joint face alignment.

It is worth mentioning that, RASL just gives the rigid transformation parameters for each image instead of giving the facial landmark locations. To perform a fair comparison, we first align the image ensemble using RASL. Then, we randomly label five aligned images manually and calculate the mean shape of them. Subsequently, based on the assumption that all aligned images share the same facial landmark configurations, we assign the mean shape to the remaining aligned images. Finally, the facial landmark locations corresponding to the original unaligned images can be calculated by the inverse transformation. Note that, the initial transformation is calculated according to the locations of eye centers.

As for our regularized re-fitting algorithm, the regularization factor λ is set to 1.0. In addition, the alignment performance variation with respect to the number of nearest neighbors is shown in Fig.5. Based on these comparison results, the number of nearest neighbors is set to 5 in the following experiments.

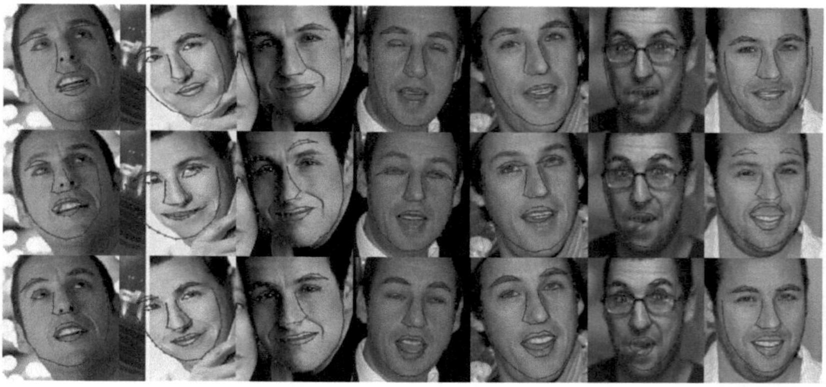

Fig. 8. Alignment results on "Adam Sandler" in comparison with other work. Top row is the alignment results of RASL [7]; second row is the alignment results of Gu's algorithm [16]; the last row is the alignment results of our method.

Our comparison experiments are conducted on the randomly selected 20 image sets, which come from the PubFig database, as described in Section 4.1. The alignment results for these 20 image sets are merged together and the cumulative distribution function of NRMSE is plotted for our method, RASL, and Gu's face alignment algorithm, as shown in Fig.6. It is obvious that our algorithm outperforms the other two kinds of methods significantly. Specifically, our method achieves about 22% higher accuracy than RASL and 13% higher accuracy than Gu's method when the error is less than 10% of eye-to-eye distance.

In addition, the initial face alignment results (i.e., given by Gu's method) for each image set are consistently improved by our regularized re-fitting algorithm. On average, when NRMSE are within $[0.06, 0.14]$, there are about 6%~23% increment of alignment precision for each of the randomly selected individuals, as shown in Fig.7. The mean and standard deviation of the improvements for all 20 individuals are 11% and 4% respectively.

Some example images from comparisons of our method with Gu's method and RASL are shown in Fig.8. More results of our algorithm on some challenging example images are shown in Fig.9.

5 Conclusion and Future Work

Through enhancing the initial face alignment results of an off-the-shelf model-based facial landmark locator, a promising joint face alignment method is introduced in this paper. To automatically identify images with good face alignment results, an effective discriminative face alignment evaluator is developed in our method. Moreover, a robust regularized re-fitting algorithm is proposed to correct alignment results of the badly aligned images. The principal idea of this paper is to constrain the appearance space of the badly-aligned image by exploring its k nearest well-aligned neighbors and regularize the fitting process of

Fig. 9. More face alignment results of our method on some challenging example images

a general model-based face alignment algorithm. Experiments conducted on the PubFig dataset demonstrate that our method greatly improves the initial face alignment results of an off-the-shelf facial landmark locator and impressively outperforms the state-of-the-art methods in joint alignment of complex faces.

Theoretically, our algorithm may work well as long as there are enough good neighbors to constrain the appearance space of testing images, which is not limited to specific person. In future work, we will further validate this idea through experiments on more general face image set. Moreover, other more robust features (e.g., HOG) will be explored to calculate the similarity between facial images.

Acknowledgments. This work is partially supported by National Basic Research Program of China (973 Program) under contract 2009CB320902; Natural Science Foundation of China under contracts Nos. 61173065, 60833013, and 60832004; and Beijing Natural Science Foundation (New Technologies and Methods in Intelligent Video Surveillance for Public Security) under contract No.4111003.

References

1. Wang, R., Shan, S., Chen, X., Gao, W.: Manifold-manifold distance with application to face recognition based on image set. In: CVPR (2008)
2. Zhu, C., Wen, F., Sun, J.: A rank-order distance based clustering algorithm for face tagging. In: CVPR, pp. 481–488 (2011)
3. Kemelmacher-Shlizerman, I., Seitz, S.M.: Face reconstruction in the wild. In: ICCV, pp. 1746–1753 (2011)
4. Learned-Miller, E.: Data driven image models through continuous joint alignment. IEEE T-PAMI 28, 236–250 (2006)
5. Huang, G.B., Jain, V., Learned-Miller, E.: Unsupervised joint alignment of complex images. In: ICCV (2007)

6. Cox, M., Sridharan, S., Lucey, S., Cohn, J.: Least squares congealing for unsupervised alignment of images. In: CVPR (2008)
7. Peng, Y., Ganesh, A., Wright, J., Xu, W.: RASL: Robust alignment by sparse and low-rank decomposition for linearly correlated images. In: CVPR, pp. 763–770 (2010)
8. Bitouk, D., Kumar, N., Dhillon, S., Belhumeur, P.N., Nayar, S.K.: Face Swapping: Automatically replacing faces in photographs. ACM SIGGRAPH (2008)
9. Saragih, J., Lucey, S., Cohn, J.: Real-time avatar animation from a single image. In: FG (2011)
10. Cootes, T.F., Taylor, C.J., Cooper, D.H., Graham, J.: Active shape models: Their training and application. CVIU 61, 38–59 (1995)
11. Cootes, T.F., Edwards, G.J., Taylor, C.J.: Active Appearance Models. In: Burkhardt, H., Neumann, B. (eds.) ECCV 1998. LNCS, vol. 1407, pp. 484–498. Springer, Heidelberg (1998)
12. Cootes, T.F., Marsland, S., Twining, C.J., Smith, K., Taylor, C.J.: Groupwise Diffeomorphic Non-rigid Registration for Automatic Model Building. In: Pajdla, T., Matas, J. (eds.) ECCV 2004. LNCS, vol. 3024, pp. 316–327. Springer, Heidelberg (2004)
13. Cootes, T.F., Twining, C.J., Petrovic, V., Schestowitz, R.: Groupwise construction of appearance models using piece-wise affine deformations. In: BMVC, pp. 879–888 (2005)
14. Liu, X.: Generic face alignment using boosted appearance model. In: CVPR, pp. 1079–1088 (2007)
15. Wu, H., Liu, X., Doretto, G.: Face alignment via boosted ranking model. In: CVPR (2008)
16. Gu, L., Kanade, T.: A Generative Shape Regularization Model for Robust Face Alignment. In: Forsyth, D., Torr, P., Zisserman, A. (eds.) ECCV 2008, Part I. LNCS, vol. 5302, pp. 413–426. Springer, Heidelberg (2008)
17. Liang, L., Xiao, R., Wen, F., Sun, J.: Face Alignment Via Component-Based Discriminative Search. In: Forsyth, D., Torr, P., Zisserman, A. (eds.) ECCV 2008, Part II. LNCS, vol. 5303, pp. 72–85. Springer, Heidelberg (2008)
18. Zhao, C., Cham, W.K., Wang, X.: Joint face alignment with a generic deformable face model. In: CVPR, pp. 561–568 (2011)
19. Tong, Y., Liu, X., Wheeler, F.W., Tu, P.: Automatic facial landmark labeling with minimal supervision. In: CVPR, pp. 2097–2104 (2009)
20. Tipping, M.E., Bishop, C.M.: Mixtures of probabilistic principal component analyzers. Neural Computation 11, 443–482 (1999)
21. Zhao, X., Chai, X., Niu, Z., Heng, C., Shan, S.: Context constrained facial landmark localization based on discontinuous haar-like feature. In: FG, pp. 673–678 (2011)
22. Viola, P., Jones, M.: Rapid object detection using a boosted cascade of simple features. In: CVPR, pp. 511–518 (2001)
23. Friedman, J., Hastie, T., Tibshirani, R.: Additive logistic regression: a statistical view of boosting. The Annals of Statistics 28, 337–407 (2000)
24. Gelman, A., Carlin, J., Stern, H., Rubin, D.: Bayesian data analysis. Chapman Hall, London (1995)
25. Kumar, N., Berg, A.C., Belhumeur, P.N., Nayar, S.K.: Attribute and simile classifiers for face verification. In: ICCV, pp. 365–372 (2009)
26. Sim, T., Baker, S., Bsat, M.: The cmu pose, illumination, and expression (PIE) database. In: FG, pp. 46–51 (2002)

27. Phillips, P.J., Flynn, P.J., Scruggs, T., Bowyer, K.W., Chang, J., Hoffman, K., Marques, J., Min, J., Worek, W.: Overview of the face recognition grand challenge. In: CVPR, pp. 947–954 (2005)
28. Phillips, P.J., Wechsler, H., Huang, J., Rauss, P.J.: The FERET database and evaluation procedure for face-recognition algorithms. IVC 16, 295–306 (1998)
29. Gao, W., Cao, B., Shan, S., Chen, X., Zhou, D., Zhang, X., Zhao, D.: The CAS-PEAL large-scale chinese face database and baseline evaluations. SMC, Part A 38, 149–161 (2008)

Dynamic Facial Expression Recognition Using Longitudinal Facial Expression Atlases

Yimo Guo, Guoying Zhao, and Matti Pietikäinen

Center for Machine Vision Research, Department of Computer Science and Engineering, University of Oulu, Finland
{guoyimo,gyzhao,mkp}@ee.oulu.fi

Abstract. In this paper, we propose a new scheme to formulate the dynamic facial expression recognition problem as a longitudinal atlases construction and deformable groupwise image registration problem. The main contributions of this method include: 1) We model human facial feature changes during the facial expression process by a diffeomorphic image registration framework; 2) The subject-specific longitudinal change information of each facial expression is captured by building an expression growth model; 3) Longitudinal atlases of each facial expression are constructed by performing groupwise registration among all the corresponding expression image sequences of different subjects. The constructed atlases can reflect overall facial feature changes of each expression among the population, and can suppress the bias due to inter-personal variations. The proposed method was extensively evaluated on the Cohn-Kanade, MMI, and Oulu-CASIA VIS dynamic facial expression databases and was compared with several state-of-the-art facial expression recognition approaches. Experimental results demonstrate that our method consistently achieves the highest recognition accuracies among other methods under comparison on all the databases.

1 Introduction

Facial expression recognition plays an important role in computer vision. Its applications include, but not limited to biometrics, human-computer interaction (HCI) systems and psychology. Existing approaches can be categorized into geometric based methods, appearance based methods and combined methods, according to different descriptor types used. Further, facial expression analysis approaches can also be classified into static image based and dynamic based methods.

Over the last decade, facial expression recognition based on the analysis of static images has received lots of attentions [1,2,3]. It mainly consists of two parts: feature extraction and classifier design. For the feature extraction part, Gabor-wavelet features [4] were widely used in the literature. Local binary pattern (LBP) feature [3,5,6] was later introduced and extended to improve recognition performance. Lucey *et al.* [7] used the Active Appearance Model (AAM) to encode both the facial appearance and shape information. For the classifier

A. Fitzgibbon et al. (Eds.): ECCV 2012, Part II, LNCS 7573, pp. 631–644, 2012.

design part, support vector machines (SVM) [8] and KNN classifiers were commonly used.

Recently, facial expression recognition based on the analysis of dynamic image sequences has become an active research topic [9,10] as longitudinal change information of facial features in image sequences can enhance recognition performance. Most approaches follow the same procedures as those of the methods based on static images. For instance, Yang *et al.* [11] extracted dynamic features from image sequences and adopted boosting to construct a classifier. Zhao *et al.* [12] encoded spatial-temporal information in each facial image sequence by using LBP-TOP features [13] and designed a classifier based on AdaBoost algorithm. A more detailed analysis on recent development of dynamic facial expression recognition methods can be found in [14].

Although numerous methods have been proposed, facial expression recognition still remains a challenging task due to large inter-personal variations in facial expressions and non-rigid deformation motions of different expression styles. Motivated by the fact that facial expression is due to diffeomorphic deformation of facial features [15,16], we formulate the dynamic facial expression recognition problem as a groupwise diffeomorphic image registration problem. Here, 'diffeomorphic' means deformation preserves topology of object and is reversible. The proposed method consists of two major stages, namely *longitudinal expression atlases construction stage* and *recognition stage*. During the first stage, longitudinal atlases of each expression are built from training sets. The schematic representation of this stage is illustrated in Figure 1 (a), where both the subject-specific longitudinal information and population information are considered. Specifically, a growth model is constructed for each facial expression image sequence to capture subject-specific longitudinal information. Then, we obtain atlases by estimating the Fréchet mean [17] on the Riemannian manifold with groupwise registration. Thus, atlases can reflect overall facial feature deformable motion among population for each expression and they can suppress inter-personal variations. During the recognition stage, longitudinal atlases of each facial expression are warped to a new facial expression image sequence by diffeomorphic image registration. This facial expression image sequence will be classified to the expression class that has the most similar image appearance with regard to warped atlases. This process is illustrated in Figure 1 (b).

The main contributions of the proposed method lie in the following aspects: 1) Construct atlases for each expression by unbiased groupwise image registration on the whole image, instead of performing pairwise registration based on selected landmarks or detected feature points in images as in [15,16]; 2) Model longitudinal facial expression evolution based on the diffeomorphic distance metric defined on the Riemannian manifold, rather than deriving an expression manifold by embedding image data into a low dimensional subspace as in [18].

The proposed method was extensively evaluated on the Cohn-Kanade, MMI, and Oulu-CASIA VIS dynamic facial expression databases. It was also compared with several state-of-the-art dynamic facial expression recognition methods.

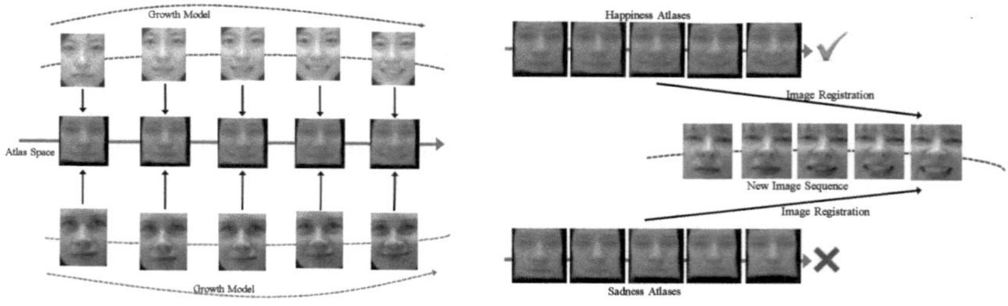

(a) (b)

Fig. 1. (a) Schematic representation of the atlas construction stage, where subject-specific longitudinal information is captured by building a facial expression growth model of each subject (i.e., the dotted line across each subject image sequence). Then, for one expression, a longitudinal atlas is constructed by performing groupwise registration among all subject image sequences. (b) Schematic representation of the recognition stage, where longitudinal atlases of each facial expression are warped to a new image sequence by diffeomorphic image registration. This new image sequence is classified to the type of facial expression with the most similar warped atlases.

Experimental results demonstrate that our method consistently achieves the highest recognition accuracy among other methods under comparison.

2 Longitudinal Facial Expression Atlases Construction

The first stage of the proposed method is to construct longitudinal facial expression atlases of each facial expression. 'Atlases' here means images reconstructed from training subjects to reflect overall trend of the population. Therefore, the aim of this stage is to construct a longitudinal sequence of images (i.e., atlases) of each facial expression. These sequences can reflect overall changes of facial features from the beginning neutral facial expression to the target facial expression among population without bias to any individual facial shape.

Suppose there are K different types of facial expressions of interest. For each type of facial expression l ($l = 1, ..., K$), there are C different subjects, and each subject has n_i ($i = 1, ..., C$) images in his/her dynamic facial expression image sequence. We denote the facial expression image taken from image sequence at the jth time point of subject i as $I_{t_j^i}$. Without loss of generality, we assume that for each facial expression image sequence, it is an evolution process from neutral facial expression at the beginning time point 0 to facial expression type l ($l = 1, ..., K$) at the ending time point 1. Assume there are N different time points t_1,...,t_N, and $t_j \in [0\ 1] (j = 1, ..., N)$, where we intend to construct longitudinal facial expression atlases. Let $T = \{t_1, ..., t_N\}$, and we denote atlas at different time point t as M_t, where $t \in T$. The longitudinal atlas construction procedure can be formulated as an energy minimization problem expressed in Equation 1:

$$E(M_t, \phi^i) = \sum_{t \in T} \sum_{i=1}^{C} \left\{ d(M_t, \phi^i_{(t_0^i \to t)}(I_{t_0^i}))^2 + \lambda_{\phi^i} Reg(\phi^i) \right\}, \qquad (1)$$

where $\phi^i_{(t_0^i \to t)}$ denotes facial expression growth model of subject i which can warp the first time point image $I_{t_0^i}$ of subject i to each time point t in order to construct atlas M_t. ϕ^i is taken as a time-dependent velocity field which can warp $I_{t_0^i}$ to any time point $t_j \in [0\ 1]$. $Reg(\cdot)$ denotes regularization term to ensure the smoothness of growth model, and λ_{ϕ^i} is a parameter trading off the accuracy of image matching and smoothness of growth model. $d(\cdot)$ is the distance metric between two images defined on Riemannian manifold represented by diffeomorphisms [19], which can be expressed by Equation 2:

$$d(I_1, I_2)^2 = \min \left[\int_0^1 ||v_s||_U^2 ds + \frac{1}{\sigma^2} ||I_1(\varphi^{-1}) - I_2||_{L2}^2 \right], \tag{2}$$

where I_1 and I_2 are two input images. $\varphi(\cdot)$ is a diffeomorphic transformation, and v_s is its related velocity field, $||\cdot||_U^2$ denotes Sobolev norm and $||\cdot||_{L2}^2$ denotes $L2$ norm. In this paper, diffeomorphic transformation $\varphi(\cdot)$ is estimated based on the large deformation diffeomorphic metric mapping (LDDMM) settings [19], where the relationship between $\varphi(\cdot)$ and velocity field v_s can be established by Equation 3:

$$\varphi(\boldsymbol{x}) = \boldsymbol{x} + \int_0^1 v_s(\varphi_s(\boldsymbol{x}))ds, \tag{3}$$

where φ_s is displacement vector at pixel position $\boldsymbol{x}$ at time $s \in [0\ 1]$.

The physical meaning of Equation 1 can be interpreted as: First, growth model ϕ^i of each subject i is estimated, which captures subject-specific longitudinal changes during facial expression process. Then, based on the estimated growth model ϕ^i for each subject i, we interpolate facial expression image of subject i at each time point $t \in T$ of interest to build facial expression atlas M_t by warping the first time point image $I_{t_0^i}$ of subject i to time point t (i.e., $\phi^i_{(t_0^i \to t)}(I_{t_0^i})$ in Equation 1). Finally, atlas M_t at each time point t is estimated by performing groupwise diffeomorphic registration among all warp images $\phi^i_{(t_0^i \to t)}(I_{t_0^i})$ $(i = 1, ..., C)$, where C is the number of subjects.

In the following sections, details are provided on how to estimate the optimal variables ϕ^i and M_t to minimize the energy function in Equation 1.

2.1 Subject-Specific Facial Expression Growth Model Estimation

The goal of building facial expression growth model ϕ^i of each subject i is to capture longitudinal geometric changes of facial features during facial expression process of a subject.

In this paper, we obtain ϕ^i for each subject also based on image metric defined in Equation 2. To be specific, suppose subject i has n_i facial expression images in his/her corresponding dynamic facial expression image sequence for some type of facial expression, the growth model ϕ^i and velocity field v_s^i are estimated by minimizing energy function expressed by Equation 4:

$$E(v_s^i, \phi^i) = \int_0^1 ||v_s^i||_U^2 ds + \frac{1}{\sigma^2} \Sigma_{j=0}^{n_i - 1} ||\phi^i_{(t_0^i \to t_j^i)}(I_{t_0^i}) - I_{t_j^i}||_{L2}^2, \tag{4}$$

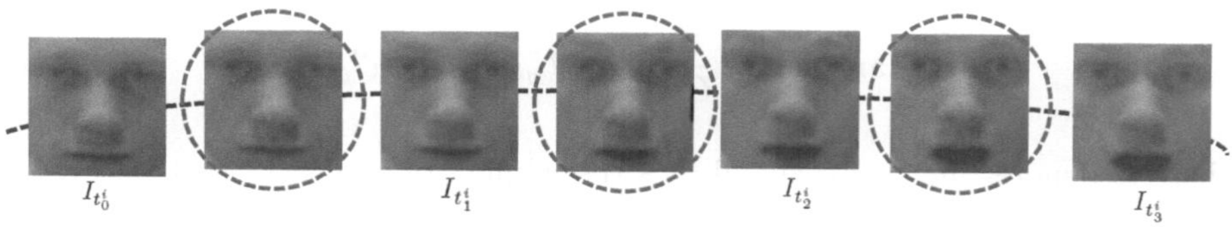

Fig. 2. A typical example illustrating the growth model of subject i. In this example, four images $I_{t_j^i}$ taken at time point t_j^i ($j = 0, ..., 3$) from an input image sequence of facial expression 'surprise' are given. Facial expression images that are interpolated based on the built growth model are highlighted with dotted green circles at time points $(t_j^i + t_{j+1}^i)/2$ ($j = 0, ..., 2$).

which subjects to the constraint:

$$\frac{\partial \phi^i_{(t_0^i \to t_j^i)}(I_{t_0^i})}{\partial s} + \nabla \phi^i_{(t_0^i \to t_j^i)}(I_{t_0^i}) \cdot v_s^i = 0. \tag{5}$$

In Equations 4 and 5, $I_{t_j^i}$ denotes the facial expression image taken at the jth time point from image sequence of subject i. Equation 4 aims to find a growth model ϕ^i, which can be represented as a deformation field so that the deformed images $\phi^i_{(t_0^i \to t_j^i)}(I_{t_0^i})$ match with existing observations $I_{t_j^i}$. Optimization of Equation 4 is implemented by using a Lagrange multiplier based optimization strategy similar to [19].

After obtaining ϕ^i, we can interpolate facial expression images at any time point $t \in [0\ 1]$, with operation $\phi^i_{(t_0^i \to t)}(I_{t_0^i})$, to obtain the state of facial features during facial expression process. Figure 2 shows a typical example, where a growth model is constructed based on the input facial expression image sequence. Facial expression images at different time points are then interpolated based on this growth model. It can be visually observed that interpolated images provide smooth and consistent temporal correspondence among image sequence.

2.2 Atlas Construction by Groupwise Diffeomorphic Image Registration

Given the growth model ϕ^i for each subject i, we then construct longitudinal facial expression atlas M_t at each time point t. By fixing variables ϕ^i, the optimization of Equation 1 with respect to each M_t becomes:

$$J(M_t) = \sum_{i=1}^{C} \left\{ d(M_t, \phi^i_{(t_0^i \to t)}(I_{t_0^i}))^2 \right\}. \tag{6}$$

The optimal solution of M_t can be obtained by Equation 7 with the Fréchet mean principle:

$$M_t = \arg \min_{M_{opt} \in \Omega} \frac{1}{C} \sum_{i=1}^{C} d(M_{opt}, \phi^i_{(t_0^i \to t)}(I_{t_0^i}))^2, \quad (7)$$

where Ω denotes image space and C is the number of subjects.

Different from simple image mean defined in flat Euclidean space, the Fréchet mean estimated in Equation 7 is defined on a Riemannian manifold based on the diffeomorphic image metric $d(\cdot)$ defined in Equation 2. In this paper, we use greedy iterative algorithm similar to [20] to estimate M_t, which is accomplished by performing groupwise image registration among images $\phi^i_{(t_0^i \to t)}(I_{t_0^i})$ of each subject. This process is summarized by Algorithm 1. The schematic representation is illustrated in Figure 3.

Algorithm 1. Construct the atlas M_t at time point t for a specific type of facial expression

Input: Facial expression images $\phi^i_{(t_0^i \to t)}(I_{t_0^i})$ of each subject i ($i = 1, ..., C$) at time point t obtained by the estimated growth model ϕ^i.

Output: The constructed atlas M_t at time point t.

1. Initialize $M_t = \frac{1}{C} \sum_{i=1}^{C} \phi^i_{(t_0^i \to t)}(I_{t_0^i})$.
2. Initialize $\hat{I}_i = \phi^i_{(t_0^i \to t)}(I_{t_0^i})$.
3. FOR $i = 1$ to C
4. Perform diffeomorphic image registration, registering $\hat{I}_i$ to M_t, to minimize the image metric defined in Equation 2 between $\hat{I}_i$ and M_t. Denote the registered images as R_i.
5. END FOR
6. Update $M_t = \frac{1}{C} \sum_{i=1}^{C} R_i$.
7. Repeat Operations 3 to 6 until M_t converges.
8. Return M_t.

Figure 4 shows constructed longitudinal facial expression atlases of expressions 'joy' and 'surprise' at 12 time points on the Cohn-Kanade dynamic facial expression database. It can be visually observed that the constructed atlases satisfactorily reflect overall facial feature changes among the population with respect to each type of expression.

Notably, the proposed atlases construction framework can be generalized to the case that more than one facial expression image sequence are available for a specific facial expression of one subject (i.e., more training samples). In this case, we can treat them separately as if they are belonging to different subjects when build their growth models to estimate atlases. Alternatively, we can first

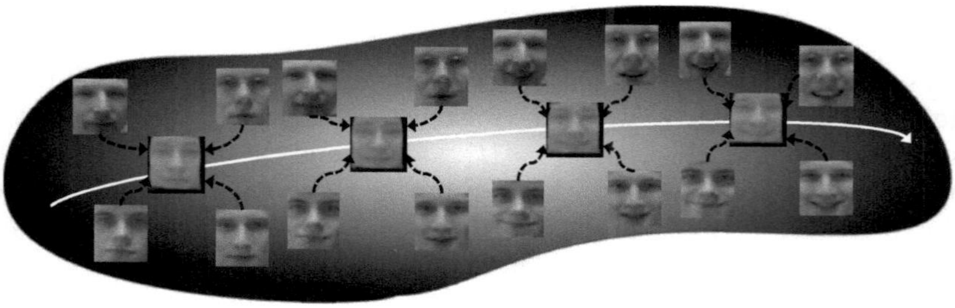

Fig. 3. Schematic representation of constructing longitudinal facial expression atlases, where the atlas space is located on Non-Euclidean Riemannian manifold. The white arrow line indicates the evolution of facial features of atlases at different time points among the population. The dotted black arrow lines indicate groupwise diffeomorphic image registration is performed among facial expression images at each time point of different subjects to build atlas.

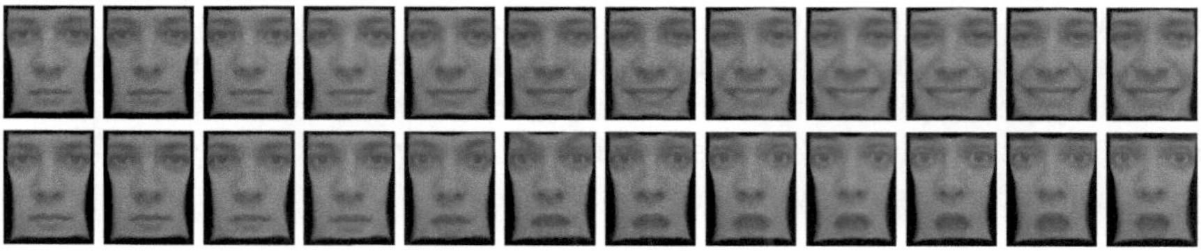

Fig. 4. Longitudinal facial expression atlases constructed on the Cohn-Kanade dynamic facial expression database with respect to the 'joy' (i.e., the first row) and 'surprise' (i.e., the second row) facial expressions at 12 time points

build subject-specific facial expression atlases based on facial expression image sequences that belong to the same subject and the same facial expression; and then use the obtained subject-specific facial expression atlases to build facial expression atlases of the population. In this paper, we assume that only one facial expression image sequence is available for each type of facial expression with respect to each subject, which is a more challenging case.

After constructing longitudinal facial expression atlases of each expression, we are able to recognize expression of a new facial expression image sequence by performing diffeomorphic image registration and matching atlases to the new facial expression image sequence. It is worth pointing out that during the atlas construction stage, training facial expression sequences can be taken in a controlled condition and pre-segmented to ensure that each training facial expression sequence starts from a neutral expression and gradually reaches an apex expression. However, in the recognition stage, a new input facial expression sequence may not follow this condition, that is, it may not start from a neutral expression and end with an apex facial expression as the constructed atlases sequences. Solutions on how to deal with this important issue will be discussed in the next section with regard to the recognition step.

3 Recognition of New Facial Expression Image Sequence

In this section, we give details on the recognition stage of the proposed method. As described in Section 2, we have constructed longitudinal facial expression atlases M_t at time $t \in T$, where $T = \{t_1, ..., t_N\}$, and N is the number of time points of interest to construct atlases. Suppose there are K different types of facial expressions in total, we denote M_t^k $(k = 1, ..., K)$ as the atlas belonging to the kth type of facial expression at time point t.

Given a new facial expression sequence that consists of n_{new} images, we denote them as I_i^{new} $(i = 0, ..., n_{new} - 1)$. Notably, for a new input facial expression sequence to be recognized, it may be taken in an uncontrolled environment, so the beginning frame does not necessarily correspond to the first frame of the constructed atlases sequences. Similar problem also exists for the ending frame (i.e., a new facial expression sequence does not necessarily end with an apex expression corresponding to the last frame of the constructed atlases sequences).

Therefore, the first step in recognition stage is to establish temporal correspondence between an atlas sequence and a new facial expression sequence. More specifically, we find the corresponding time point t_b in atlas space with respect to the beginning frame I_0^{new} of the new facial expression sequence. This is determined by performing diffeomorphic image registration from I_0^{new} to each M_t and selecting the one that is most similar to the warped image of I_0^{new}. This process can be expressed by Equation 8:

$$b = \arg\min_i \left\{ d(M_{t_i}, I_0^{new})^2 \right\}, \tag{8}$$

where $d(\cdot)$ denotes the distance metric. We determine t_e in the same way, which is the corresponding time point in atlas space with respect to the ending frame $I_{n_{new}-1}^{new}$ of the new facial expression sequence, where $e > b$.

We can also estimate the growth model ϕ^{new} of a new facial expression image sequence I_i^{new} $(i = 0, ..., n_{new} - 1)$ similar to the process described in Section 2.1. After obtaining ϕ^{new}, facial expression images at time $t \in \{t_b, t_{b+1}, ..., t_e\}$ are able to be estimated with operation $\phi^{new}_{(t_0^{new} \to t)}(I_0^{new})$, where t_0^{new} is the time point at which the first image of new facial expression image sequence I_0^{new} is taken.

Then label L denoting the type of facial expression of a new facial expression image sequence is determined by Equation 9:

$$L = \arg\min_{L_{opt}} \left\{ \frac{1}{(e-b+1)} \sum_{i=0}^{e-b} d(M_{t_{b+i}}^{L_{opt}}, \phi^{new}_{(t_0^{new} \to t_{b+i})}(I_0^{new}))^2 \right\}, \tag{9}$$

where $L_{opt} \in \{1, ..., K\}$. Therefore, the physical meaning of Equation 9 is to classify a new input facial expression image sequence to the facial expression class which has the most similar registered atlas images within t_b and t_e in terms of image metric $d(\cdot)$.

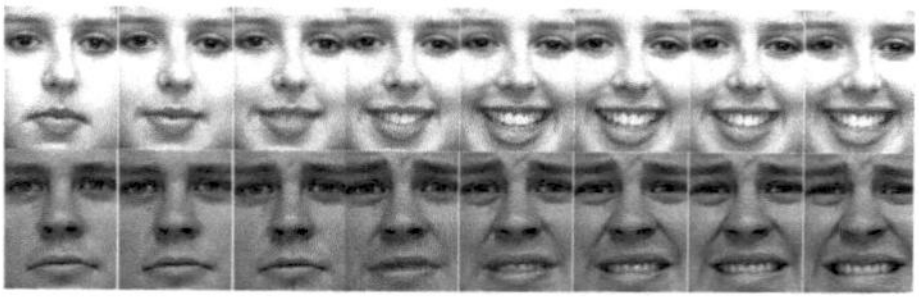

Fig. 5. Exemplar images from the Cohn-Kanade facial expression database

4 Experimental Results

The proposed method is evaluated on the Cohn-Kanade, MMI, and Oulu-CASIA VIS facial expression databases. In all the experiments, we set the number of time points to construct longitudinal facial expression atlases as 12. Notably, the larger the number of time points N used to build the longitudinal atlases, the more detailed and subtle facial feature changes can be represented by atlases. However, larger number of time points will increase the computational burden. Thus, in this paper, we follow the setting of $N = 12$, which is found as a good tradeoff between the representation capability of atlases and computational cost. Experimental results on each database are shown and analyzed in this section.

4.1 Experimental Results on the Cohn-Kanade Database

The Cohn-Kanade (CK) facial expression database [21] consists of 100 university students with ages from 18 to 30 years, among which sixty-five percent were female, fifteen percent were African-American, and three percent were Asian or Latino. Each subject was instructed to perform a series of 23 facial displays, six of which were described by prototypical emotions of anger, disgust, fear, joy, sadness, and surprise. Each facial expression sequence from neutral to the target display was digitized into 640×480 pixel arrays. In this experiment, 374 sequences were selected from the database. The selection criteria was that each selected sequence to be labeled was one of the six basic emotions. The selected sequences were belonging to 97 subjects, with one to six emotions per subject. The positions of two eyes were used for normalization and alignment of the facial images in the preprocessing step. Exemplar images from the CK facial expression database are shown in Figure 5.

The 10-fold cross validation scheme was adopted in this experiment to evaluate the recognition performance of the proposed method. More specifically, all the 97 selected subjects were separated into ten groups, with each group had roughly the same number of subjects. Then, nine groups of subjects were used as training set, while the remaining group served as the testing set. This process was repeated until each group was served as the testing set once.

The confusion matrix obtained by the proposed method is listed in Table 1. It can be observed from Table 1 that the proposed method consistently achieves high recognition rates of each expression (i.e., all above 90%). It was also compared with several state-of-the-art dynamic facial expression recognition

Table 1. Confusion matrix obtained by our method on the Cohn-Kanade database

	Anger (%)	Disgust (%)	Fear (%)	Joy (%)	Sadness (%)	Surprise (%)
Anger	**94.8**	0	0.3	0	4.9	0
Disgust	0.5	**98.4**	0	1.1	0	0
Fear	0	0	**95.3**	3.4	1.3	0
Joy	0	0	0.9	**99.1**	0	0
Sadness	2.8	0	0.7	0	**96.5**	0
Surprise	0	0	0	0	1.1	**98.9**

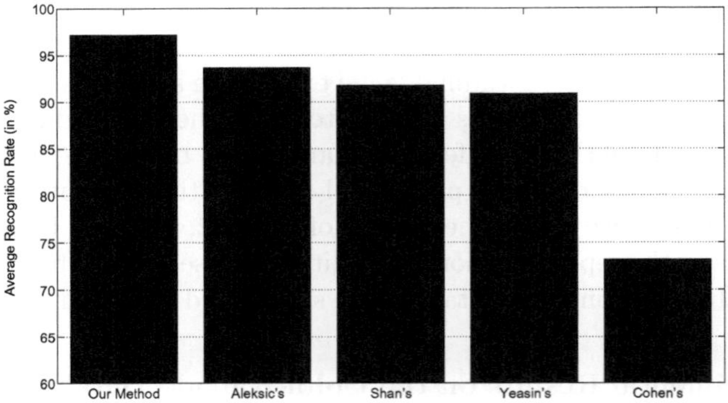

Fig. 6. Comparisons with different approaches of average recognition rates on the Cohn-Kanade facial expression database

approaches proposed by Aleksic *et al.* [22], Shan *et al.* [18], Yeasin *et al.* [23] and Cohen *et al.* [9] on the CK database. The average recognition rates obtained by different approaches are shown in Figure 6. It is shown that our method achieves the best performance among all the methods under comparison, which reflects its effectiveness and robustness. The computation time of the proposed method is 15.7 minutes for the atlases construction step. It takes around 1.4 seconds in the recognition stage for each query sequence (4-core 2.5GHz Processor, 6 GB Memory; Matlab implementation).

4.2 Experimental Results on the MMI Database

In this section, we evaluate the proposed method on the MMI database [24]. 175 facial expression sequences were selected from the MMI database. Similarly to the CK database, the only selection criteria was that for each selected sequence it could be labeled as one of the six basic emotions. The selected sequences were from 35 subjects. Facial images in each sequence were digitized into 720×576 pixels. Exemplar images taken from the MMI database are shown in Figure 7. Similar to Section 4.1, coordinates of two eyes were used for normalization of facial images in the preprocessing step.

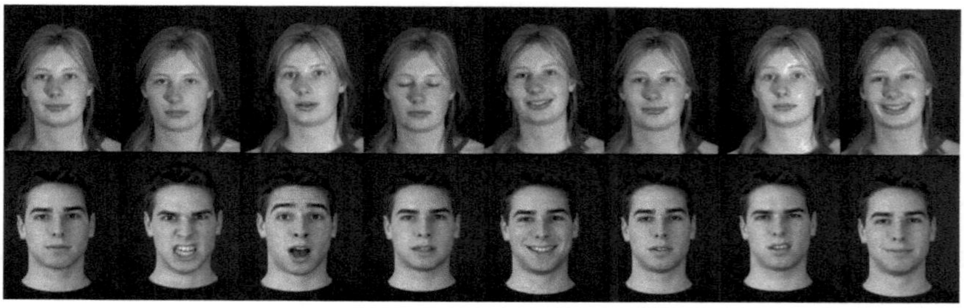

Fig. 7. Exemplar images from the MMI facial expression database

Table 2. Confusion matrix obtained by our method on the MMI database

	Anger (%)	Disgust (%)	Fear (%)	Happiness (%)	Sadness (%)	Surprise (%)
Anger	**92.3**	2.1	0	0	5.6	0
Disgust	1.3	**95.1**	0.9	2.7	0	0
Fear	0	1.6	**93.8**	4.6	0	0
Happiness	0	0.4	2.2	**97.4**	0	0
Sadness	6.3	0	2.0	0	**91.7**	0
Surprise	0	0.8	3.6	1.2	0	**94.4**

The 10-fold cross validation scheme was adopted similar to Section 4.1. The confusion matrix obtained by the proposed method is listed in Table 2 with regard to six basic emotions. It can be observed from Table 2 that the proposed method can still achieve promising recognition accuracies for each facial expression (i.e., all above 90%), which implies its effectiveness. Also, compared to a state-of-the-art facial expression recognition method proposed by Shan *et al.* in [25] which was also evaluated on the MMI database of the six basic emotions, the average recognition rate obtained by the proposed method (i.e., 94.1%) is significantly higher than the one reported in [25] (i.e., 86.9%).

4.3 Experimental Results on the Oulu-CASIA VIS Database

To test the generalizability of the proposed method, the proposed method was evaluated on the Oulu-CASIA VIS database. In this database, six basic emotions (i.e., anger, disgust, fear, happiness, sadness, and surprise) were taken from 80 subjects between 23 and 58 years old, with 73.8% of the subjects are males. All the images were taken under the challenging uncontrolled visible (VIS) light condition. Each image has resolution 320×240 pixels. There are three different illumination conditions from which images were taken: normal, weak, and dark. The normal illumination condition means image sequences were taken under strong and good lighting condition. The weak illumination condition means only computer monitor was on and subject sit in front of the computer during dy-

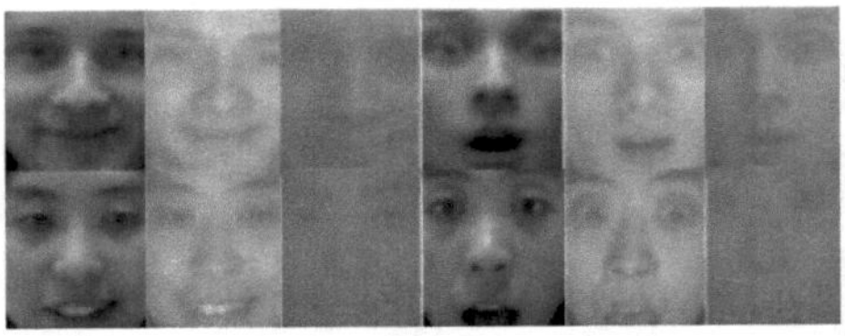

Fig. 8. Exemplar images taken from the Oulu-CASIA VIS facial expression database, where images at each row are belonging to the same subject. The first three columns are images belonging to the happiness facial expression taken under the normal, weak, and dark illumination conditions, respectively. The fourth to the sixth columns are images belonging to the surprise facial expression taken under the normal, weak, and dark illumination conditions, respectively.

namic facial expression process. The dark illumination condition means lighting condition was close to darkness.

The coordinates of two eyes in each image were used to normalize facial images, which is similar to the experiments in Sections 4.1 and 4.2. Figure 8 shows exemplar facial expression images of different subjects under different illumination conditions. We can see that there are large variations among facial expressions across different subjects, and image appearance can be significantly altered due to illumination conditions.

Similar to Sections 4.1 and 4.2, 10-fold cross validation scheme was adopted. Table 3 lists the average recognition rates and corresponding standard deviations obtained by the proposed method under the normal, weak, and dark illumination conditions for each type of facial expression.

Table 3. The average recognition rates and standard deviations (in %) obtained by the proposed method for each type of facial expression under the normal, weak, and dark illumination conditions

	Anger	Disgust	Fear	Happiness	Sadness	Surprise
Normal	79.4 ± 2.2	68.2 ± 1.7	62.9 ± 2.6	85.3 ± 1.8	67.9 ± 1.9	89.4 ± 2.8
Weak	65.0 ± 1.6	50.1 ± 2.0	51.2 ± 2.3	75.4 ± 2.5	44.0 ± 2.4	85.3 ± 1.9
Dark	53.5 ± 3.1	44.9 ± 2.4	49.1 ± 2.6	73.3 ± 1.9	44.2 ± 2.8	81.4 ± 2.4

The proposed method was compared with LBP-TOP method [12] proposed by Zhao *et al.* on this database. The average recognition rates of both the LBP-TOP method and proposed method are shown in Figures 9 (a) to (c) under the normal, weak and dark illumination conditions, respectively. It is observed that recognition rates of the proposed method are consistently higher than those obtained by using LBP-TOP for each type of facial expression and illumination condition. Therefore, the robustness and effectiveness of the proposed method for dynamic facial expression recognition in VIS image sequences is reflected.

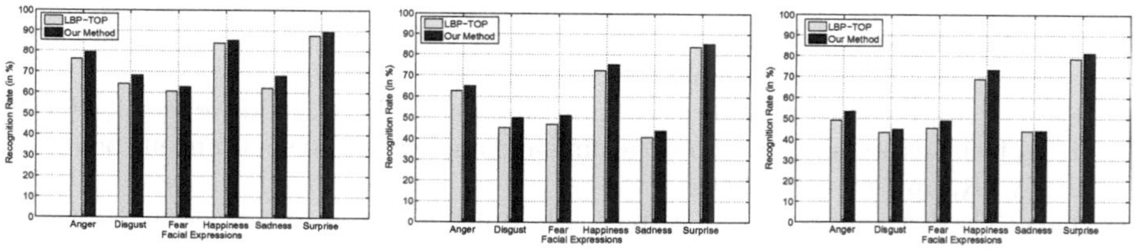

(a) (b) (c)

Fig. 9. Average recognition rates obtained by LBP-TOP [12] method and the proposed method with respect to each type of facial expression under (a) normal, (b) weak, and (c) dark illumination conditions

5 Conclusion

We propose a novel method for dynamic facial expression recognition. The dynamic facial expression recognition problem is formulated as a groupwise diffeomorphic image registration problem. The proposed method has two main stages: longitudinal facial expression atlases construction stage and facial expression recognition stage. During the atlases construction stage, atlases of facial expression are estimated which reflect the overall facial feature appearance among the population. Both the subject-specific longitudinal information and population information are considered in the atlases construction stage. The subject-specific information is captured by estimating growth model of each subject for each facial expression using diffeomorphic image registrations; and the population information is encoded by performing groupwise diffeomorphic image registration among all subject image sequences. In the recognition stage, constructed atlases can be registered to each new facial expression image sequence to determine its type of facial expression by comparing image similarity between each registered facial expression atlas and the new facial expression image sequence. The proposed method was extensively evaluated on the Cohn-Kanade, MMI, and Oulu-CASIA VIS dynamic facial expression databases and was compared with state-of-the-art dynamic facial expression recognition approaches. Experimental results show that the proposed method consistently achieves higher recognition accuracies than the methods under comparison. This method hopefully can inspire new ways of tackling dynamic facial expression recognition problems.

Acknowledgments. The authors wish to acknowledge the financial support from the Infotech Oulu, Academy of Finland and Nokia Foundation.

References

1. Fasel, B., Luettin, J.: Automatic facial expression analysis: a survey. PR 36, 259–275 (2003)
2. Pantic, M., Rothkrantz, L.: Automatic analysis of facial expressions: the state of the art. PAMI 22, 1424–1455 (2000)

3. Feng, X., Pietikainen, M., Hadid, A.: Facial expression recognition with local binary patterns and linear programming. PRIA 15, 546–548 (2005)
4. Bartlett, M., Littlewort, G., Frank, M., Lainscsek, C., Fasel, I., Movellan, J.: Recognizing facial expression: machine learning and application to spontaneous behavior. In: CVPR, pp. 568–573 (2005)
5. Ojala, T., Pietikainen, M., Maenpaa, T.: Multiresolution gray-scale and rotation invariant texture classification with local binary patterns. PAMI 24, 971–987 (2002)
6. Shan, C., Gong, S., McOwan, P.: Robust facial expression recognition using local binary patterns. In: ICIP, pp. 370–373 (2005)
7. Lucey, S., Ashraf, A., Cohn, J.: Investigating spontaneous facial action recognition through aam representations of the face. In: FR, pp. 275–286 (2007)
8. Vapnik, V.: Statistical Learning Theory. Wiley (1998)
9. Cohen, L., Sebe, N., Garg, A., Chen, L., Huang, T.: Facial expression recognition from video sequences: temporal and static modeling. CVIU 91, 160–187 (2003)
10. Zhang, Y., Ji, Q.: Active and dynamic information fusion for facial expression understanding from image sequences. PAMI 27, 699–714 (2005)
11. Yang, P., Liu, Q., Cui, X., Metaxas, D.: Facial expression recognition using encoded dynamic features. In: CVPR, pp. 1–8 (2008)
12. Zhao, G., Huang, X., Taini, M., Li, Z., Pietikainen, M.: Facial expression recognition from near-infrared videos. IVC 29, 607–619 (2011)
13. Zhao, G., Pietikainen, M.: Dynamic texture recognition using local binary patterns with an application to facial expressions. PAMI 29, 915–928 (2007)
14. Zeng, Z., Pantic, M., Roisman, G., Huang, T.: A survey of affect recognition methods: Audio, visual, and spontaneous expressions. PAMI 31, 39–58 (2009)
15. Yousefi, S., Minh, P., Kehtarnavaz, N., Yan, C.: Facial expression recognition based on diffeomorphic matching. In: ICIP, pp. 4549–4552 (2010)
16. Koelstra, S., Pantic, M., Patras, I.: A dynamic texture-based approach to recognition of facial actions and their temporal models. PAMI 32, 1940–1954 (2010)
17. Davis, B., Fletcher, P., Bullitt, E., Joshi, S.: Population shape regression from random design data. IJCV 90, 255–266 (2010)
18. Shan, C., Gong, S., McOwan, P.: Dynamic facial expression recognition using a bayesian temporal manifold model. In: BMVC, pp. 297–306 (2006)
19. Beg, M., Miller, M., Trouve, A., Younes, L.: Computing large deformation metric mappings via geodesic flows of diffeomorphisms. IJCV 61, 139–157 (2005)
20. Joshi, S., Davis, B., Jomier, M., Gerig, G.: Unbiased diffeomorphic atlas construction for computational anatomy. NeuroImage 23, 151–160 (2004)
21. Kanade, T., Cohn, J., Tian, Y.: Comprehensive database for facial expression analysis. In: FG, pp. 46–53 (2000)
22. Aleksic, S., Katsaggelos, K.: Automatic facial expression recognition using facial animation parameters and multi-stream hmms. IEEE IFS 1, 3–11 (2006)
23. Yeasin, M., Bullot, B., Sharma, R.: From facial expression to level of interests: A spatio-temporal approach. In: CVPR, pp. 922–927 (2004)
24. Pantic, M., Valstar, M., Rademaker, R., Maat, L.: Web-based database for facial expression analysis. In: ICME, pp. 317–321 (2005)
25. Shan, C., Gong, S., McOwan, P.: Facial expression recognition based on local binary patterns: a comprehensive study. IVC 27, 803–816 (2009)

Crosstalk Cascades for Frame-Rate Pedestrian Detection

Piotr Dollár[1], Ron Appel[2], and Wolf Kienzle[1]

[1] Microsoft Research Redmond
{pdollar,wkienzle}@microsoft.com
[2] California Institute of Technology
appel@caltech.edu

Abstract. Cascades help make sliding window object detection fast, nevertheless, computational demands remain prohibitive for numerous applications. Currently, evaluation of adjacent windows proceeds independently; this is suboptimal as detector responses at nearby locations and scales are correlated. We propose to exploit these correlations by tightly coupling detector evaluation of nearby windows. We introduce two opposing mechanisms: detector *excitation* of promising neighbors and *inhibition* of inferior neighbors. By enabling neighboring detectors to communicate, *crosstalk cascades* achieve major gains (4-30$\times$ speedup) over cascades evaluated independently at each image location. Combined with recent advances in fast multi-scale feature computation, for which we provide an optimized implementation, our approach runs at 35-65 fps on 640×480 images while attaining state-of-the-art accuracy.

1 Introduction

In many applications, *fast detection* is as important as *accurate detection*. Notable recent efforts for increasing detection speed include work by Felzenszwalb et al. [1] and Pedersoli et al. [2] on cascaded and coarse-to-fine deformable part models, respectively, Lampert et al.'s [3] application of branch and bound search for detection, and Dollár et al.'s [4] and Benenson et al.'s [5] work on the theory and application of fast multi-scale features for detection.

Nevertheless, a majority of detectors remain slow. For most of the 15 pedestrian detectors surveyed in [6], detection time is best measured in seconds per frame (as opposed to frames per second). In this work our goal is to achieve *frame-rate* detection on 640×480 images, i.e. detection at 30 fps or higher. We explicitly avoid the ambiguous phrase *real-time* detection (e.g. a recent paper reported 'real-time' detection rates of under 4 fps on low resolution images).

Detector speed is determined by the speed of both the features and classifier. We provide an optimized implementation of the fast multi-scale features proposed in [4] and introduce a novel framework which couples cascade evaluations at nearby locations. By allowing neighboring detectors to communicate, computational cost is greatly reduced (see Figure 1). The resulting *crosstalk cascades* achieve 4-30 fold reduction in the number of evaluated weak classifiers.

A. Fitzgibbon et al. (Eds.): ECCV 2012, Part II, LNCS 7573, pp. 645–659, 2012.

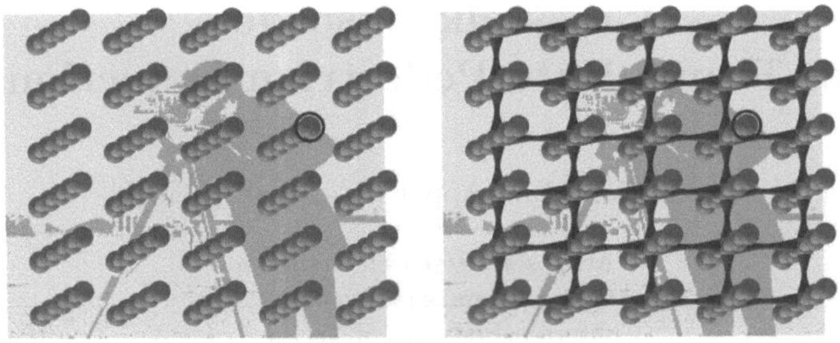

Fig. 1. Each column represents one cascade evaluation, green spheres represent evaluated cascade stages, and the red circles represent locally maximum detector responses. **Left:** In standard cascades, each location is evaluated in isolation. **Right:** Through a combination of *excitation* and *inhibition*, crosstalk cascades can significantly reduce computation, requiring fewer overall weak classifier evaluations.

Crosstalk cascades operate at 45 fps while matching state-of-the-art detection accuracy and 55-65 fps at slightly higher miss rates. These are 6× and greater speedups over [4], the fastest detector surveyed in [6]. Computation of the multi-scale features (with no detector evaluations) runs at 70 fps (~3× speedup over [4]). All reported runtimes are on a single core of a modern PC.

The most competitive approach to our own is [5], whose GPU implementation of [4], along with improved handling of scales, runs at 50 fps on monocular images. The improvements suggested in [5] are orthogonal to our own and could be combined. Other related work can be broken down as follows. A significant body of work exists on optimizing cascades [7,8,9,10,11,12]; however, in all existing work each image window is evaluated independently. Research on fast feature extraction [7,13,4] is complementary to our own. [14,15,16] propose to first compute a sparse set of detector responses and then sample more densely around promising locations; we use similar intuition for *excitation* of promising neighbors, but do so during every stage of detection for greater gains. Finally, research on optimizing other types of classifiers [1,2,3,17,18,19] is of considerable interest, however, such methods have difficulty matching the speed achieved by boosted classifiers.

The rest of this paper is organized as follows. We describe our optimized feature implementation and baseline detector in §2. In §3 we explore lower and upper bounds on the performance of cascades. We describe crosstalk cascades and an unsupervised learning approach for tuning their speed in §4. Finally, in §5, we compare accuracy and speed to existing approaches.

2 Baseline Detector

Channel features [20,4] have state-of-the-art performance and are among the fastest in the literature. Given an input image, several channels (e.g. gradient, color) with the same dimensions are computed. Sums over rectangular channel regions serve as features and can be computed efficiently using integral images

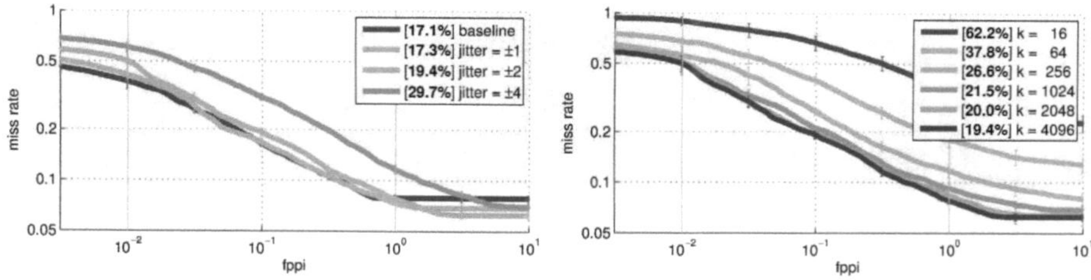

Fig. 2. Left: Our baseline detector (BASELINE) outperforms [20] and the best reported results on INRIA with a log-average miss rate of 17%. Slightly jittering the training data degrades performance slightly but increases detector correlations. **Right:** Increasing the number of weak classifiers k in the detector trained with jitter ± 2 improves performance and using $k = 4096$ is necessary to achieve state of the art accuracy.

[7]. In multi-scale detection, features are typically computed over a dense image pyramid. Instead, [4] showed how to leverage the observation that statistics of natural images follow a power law to accurately approximate features at nearby image scales using channels computed over a sparse image pyramid.

We re-implement the channel features with a focus on low-level optimization. We use the same channels as [4]: gradient magnitude (1 channel), histogram of oriented gradients (6 channels), and LUV color channels (3 channels). For each scale, all 10 channels are downsampled by a factor of 2 for further speed improvements (for details see addendum to [20] available online). The functions make extensive use of SSE instructions but are implemented on a single CPU; further gains could be obtained using multiple cores or a GPU as in [5].

For 640×480 images, computation of sparse feature pyramids with one scale per octave runs at ~**70 fps** on a modern PC (a 4× speedup from [4]). The sparse feature pyramid can be used to obtain detector responses at all scales by 'resampling' a trained detector by up to half an octave as described [4]. In contrast, the traditional approach of computing a dense image pyramid with 8-10 scales per octave is over 4× slower. Benenson et al. [5] describe an extension of [4] that can be used to obtain detector responses at all scales using feature computed at just the original scale, doing so would give a ~25% speedup. Additional speedups of up to 50% are possible by removing gradient normalization, image smoothing, etc., but result in noticeably decreased performance. Our optimized implementation of channel features is available online.

For our baseline detector we use a similar setup to [20]. We apply AdaBoost [21] to train and combine 4096 depth-two trees using a pool of 30,000 random candidate features computed over the channels described above. Training with multiple rounds of bootstrapping takes ~10 minutes (a parallelized implementation of training takes ~3 minutes). The default step size used in the detector is 4 pixels and 8 scales per octave. We closely follow implementation details from [20] for bootstrapping, non-maximum suppression, etc.

Our baseline detector outperforms the best reported results on INRIA [22]. Results are shown in Figure 2 (left). As in [6], we plot miss rate against false

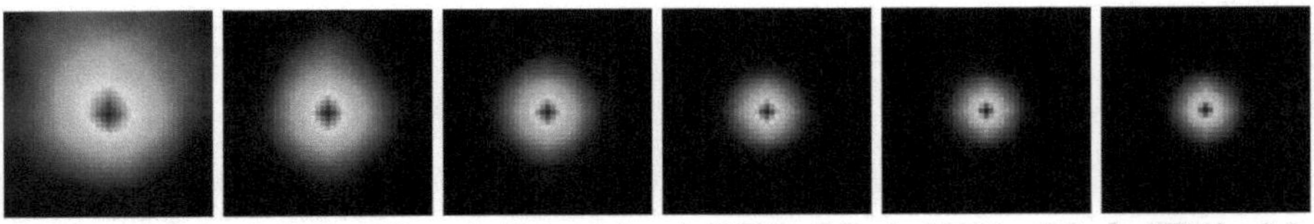

Fig. 3. Region of support (ROS) for our detector trained with jitter for various number of weak classifiers k. Key observations: (1) for every k the ROS has non-negligible extent σ and (2) σ decreases with increasing k. These observations inform our design of crosstalk cascades; in particular we exploit that correlations are strongest in early stages of detection but continue to have non-negligible support for all k.

positives per image (FPPI) and summarize performance using log-average miss rate (MR) between 10^{-2} and 10^{0} FPPI. The MR of our baseline, averaged over the eight random trials, is 17% (MRs for individual trials ranges from 16% to 19%). In comparison, the best reported results in [6] have a MR of 20% for Felzenszwalb et al. [23] and between 21%-22% for the detectors in [20,4].

2.1 Detector Correlations

Detector responses at nearby positions and scales are correlated. In the terminology of [15], every detector has a *region of support* (ROS) which is the neighborhood around a positive location in which the response remains positive. A detector's ROS is determined by the features, discriminability of the classifier, and alignment of the training data. We focus on the latter two factors.

First, we can increase detector correlations by 'jittering' the training data (we replace every positive sample with nine samples offset by $\pm j$ pixels). Performance for the baseline and various j (JITTER $\pm j$) are shown in Figure 2. Using $j = 2$ degrades performance slightly to 19.4% MR but results in stronger detector correlations. We therefore use JITTER ± 2 in all remaining experiments.

We compute the ROS by averaging detector responses across multiple windows whose center contains a locally maximum response and we record the ROS's standard deviation σ. In Figure 3 (top) we show the ROS for the detector for various number of weak classifiers k. For every k the ROS has a non-negligible extent ($\sigma \geq 3$). In previous work [14,15,16] a similar observation for the *complete* detector was used as a basis for fast detection schemes that compute a sparse set of responses and then sample more densely around promising locations.

In this work we exploit that correlations are present at *all* values of k. In fact, *the extent of the detector's ROS decreases with increasing* k. Intuitively this makes sense: we expect the extent of a detector's ROS to be inversely related to its discriminative power, which in this case is determined by k (see Figure 2 (right)). The strong correlation present for every k motivate our approach of allowing neighboring detectors to communicate during classification.

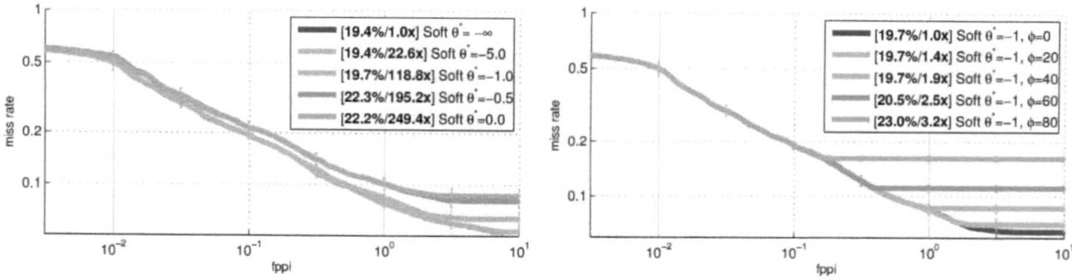

Fig. 4. Left: Soft cascades with thresholds $\theta_k = \theta^*$ for all k. Numbers in brackets indicate MR/speedup. Using $\theta^* = -1$ leaves detection accuracy virtually unchanged (all curves with $\theta^* \leq -1$ overlap nearly perfectly) but results in a ~**120**× speedup. **Right:** Soft cascades with thresholds $\theta_k = \theta^* + \phi k/K$, which are equivalent to *recalibrating* a detector and using constant rejection thresholds (see text). Depending on the desired target recall, ϕ can be set appropriately for additional speedups relative to $\theta_k = \theta^*$.

3 Bounds on Soft Cascades

The seminal work of Viola and Jones [7] popularized cascades for fast detection. A number of subsequent papers have addressed drawbacks of the original cascades [10,11,12]; however, perhaps the simplest and most elegant solution was proposed by Bourdev and Brandt in the form 'soft cascades' [8]. Instead of having multiple distinct cascade stages, a single boosted classifier is trained and only post-training are rejection thresholds set (with one threshold per weak classifier).

A boosted classifier H consisting of K weak classifiers has the form:

$$H(x) = H_K(x) = \sum_{i=1}^{K} \alpha_i h_i(x), \tag{1}$$

where each h_i is a weak classifier (with output -1 or 1) and α_i is its associated weight. x is classified as positive if $H(x) > 0$ and $H(x)$ serves as the confidence. We can define a sequence of score functions $H_k(x)$ for $k < K$ in an analogous manner. During evaluation, a soft cascade tests each $H_k(x)$ against a rejection threshold θ_k, and if $H_k(x) < \theta_k$ computation stops. Various strategies for setting the θ_k have been proposed [8,9], we postpone a discussion to §4.1.

3.1 Constant Rejection Thresholds

We begin by describing a simple heuristic for setting θ_k that will serve as a *lower bound* on the effectiveness of soft cascades: we simply set $\theta_k = \theta^*$ for all k for some $\theta^* \leq 0$. Resulting ROC curves for various choices of θ^* are shown in Figure 4 (left). In the plot legend we report '[MR/speedup]' on INRIA [22] for each method. Setting $\theta^* = -1$ leaves detection accuracy virtually unchanged but results in a ~**120**× speedup. Specifically, on average only 35 weak classifiers are evaluated per classification as opposed to all $k = 4096$ for the original detector.

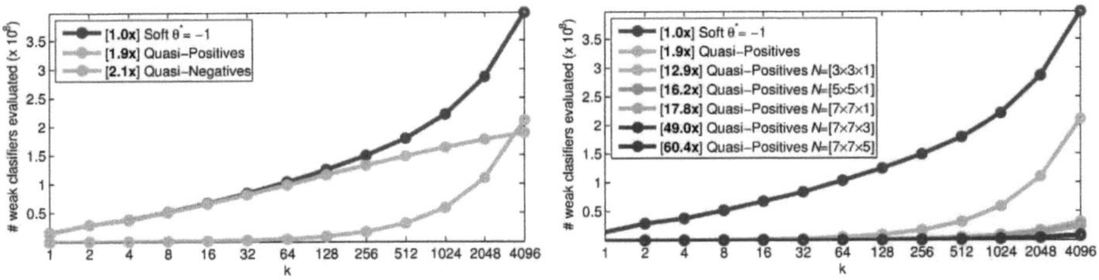

Fig. 5. Left: Cost of evaluating $H(x)$ (with $\theta^* = -1$) on all x and also separately on quasi-positives ($H(x) \geq 0$) and quasi-negatives ($H(x) < 0$). For small k the cost of quasi-negatives dominates; for large k the cost of quasi-positives increases. **Right:** Cost of evaluating $H(x)$ on all x with $z^{\mathcal{N}} = 1$. Evaluating only the x with locally maximum $H(x) > 0$ in fairly small neighborhoods $\mathcal{N}$ results in greatly reduced computation.

Why is setting $\theta_k = \theta^*$ effective? Boosting attempts to train a function H s.t. $H(x) > 0$ if and only if x is positive. However, this observation holds for all intermediate classifiers H_k for $k < K$ (which are trained using an identical procedure to H). In practice, it is rare that $H(x) >> 0$ while $H_k(x) << 0$ for any k. By setting $\theta_k = \theta^* \leq 0$, we are exploiting the fact that if $H(x) > 0$ it is unlikely that $H_k(x) < \theta^*$ (with the likelihood decreasing with decreasing θ^*).

Constant rejection thresholds can be extended to reject all detections such that $H(x) < \phi$ by *recalibrating* H. Let $H'_k(x) = H_k(x) - \phi k/K$ for all k so that $H'_k(x) > 0$ if and only if $H_k(x) > \phi k/K$. Using thresholds $\theta_k = \theta^*$ with H' is equivalent to using $\theta_k = \theta^* + \phi k/K$ with H; ϕ controls the tradeoff between recall and speed. Results for $\theta^* = -1$ and various ϕ are shown in Figure 4 (right). Constant rejection thresholds (with recalibration) will serve as a simple baseline.

3.2 Optimal Soft Cascades

Given a trained classifier $H(x)$, how fast would a hypothetical *optimal* soft cascade be that rejected all $H(x) < 0$ without any computation? Answering this will provide us with intuition and an *upper bound* on soft cascade effectiveness.

We gather a set of detection windows $\mathcal{X}$ by densely sampling windows from 387 images from PASCAL VOC 2007 [24] that contain at least one person. This gives us a validation set with similar statistics to INRIA [22]. Using a step size of 4 pixels and 8 scales per octaves there are ~15 million windows $x_i \in \mathcal{X}$. We assign a label $z_i \in \{\pm 1\}$ to each detection window x_i using our trained detector H according to the sign of $H(x_i)$: $z_i = 1$ if and only if $H(x_i) \geq 0$. We refer to x_i as *quasi-positive* if $z_i = 1$ and *quasi-negative* otherwise (while z_i is correlated with the ground truth label no supervision is needed to obtain z_i).

Over 99.5% of the 15 million $x_i \in \mathcal{X}$ are quasi-negatives. While we may thus expect quasi-negatives to dominate computation, in practice evaluating the small fraction of quasi-positives incurs roughly the same cost. If we compute $H(x_i)$ using rejection thresholds $\theta^* = -1$, evaluating $H(x_i)$ for $z_i = 1$ typically requires evaluating all 4096 weak classifiers but on average only ~18 weak classifiers if $z_i = -1$. Figure 5 (left) shows the total number of weak classifiers that need to be evaluated in order to compute $H_k(x_i)$ over all x_i, x_i with $z_i = 1$, and x_i with $z_i = -1$. Results are averaged over eight trials (see §2).

Observe that even if there existed a cascade that could reject all x_i with $z_i = -1$ without any computation it would **only be ~2**× faster than the soft cascade with $\theta^* = -1$ on this data. Thus, while tuning θ_k can increase speed (see §4.1), we need an alternate approach to achieve greater gains.

If instead of computing each $H(x_i)$ in isolation we consider neighboring x_i jointly, much greater gains are possible. We extend the definition of quasi-positives to include a neighborhood $\mathcal{N}$: $z_i^{\mathcal{N}} = 1$ if $H(x_i) \geq 0$ and $H(x_i) \geq H(x_i')$ $\forall x_i' \in \mathcal{N}(x_i)$. In other words $z_i^{\mathcal{N}} = 1$ if x_i has a locally maximum score $H(x_i) > 0$. Abusing notation we write $\mathcal{N} = [w \times h \times d]$ to denote neighborhoods of width w, height h, and depth d (number of scales) with $\sim whd$ neighbors (our detector uses a step size of 4 pixels so $\mathcal{N} = [w \times h \times d]$ covers a volume of $16whd$ pixels).

In Figure 5 (right) we show the cost of evaluating $H_k(x)$ for all x_i with $z_i^{\mathcal{N}} = 1$ for different neighborhoods sizes. Computing $H(x_i)$ only for x_i with $z_i^{\mathcal{N}} = 1$ for a moderately sized neighborhood $\mathcal{N} = [7 \times 7 \times 3]$ would result in ~**50**× savings. Since typically non-maximum suppression (NMS) is applied to the output of H, returning only x_i that have locally maximum $H(x_i)$ should have little effect on accuracy (especially for small $\mathcal{N}$). We verify this empirically in §5.

A hypothetical soft cascade that could reject all x_i with $z_i^{\mathcal{N}} = -1$ with no computation would improve detection speed by a factor of 10-60× for modest neighborhood sizes $\mathcal{N}$. This gain is an order of magnitude larger than possible for optimal soft cascades that consider each x_i in isolation and motivates our approach of allowing neighboring detectors to communicate during classification.

4 Crosstalk Cascades

In this section we introduce algorithms for constructing four types of cascades:

- **Soft Cascades:** Introduced in §3, a soft cascade rejects a sample x if its score $H_k(x)$ falls below a per-stage *rejection* threshold $\theta_k^R \geq \theta^*$.
- **Excitatory Cascades:** Starting with evaluations over a sparse set of samples x, if for any k the score $H_k(x)$ rises above a per-stage *excitation* threshold $\theta_k^E \geq \theta^*$ evaluation begins on all $x' \in \mathcal{N}(x)$.
- **Inhibitory Cascades:** If the ratio $H_k(x)/H_k(x')$ falls below a per-stage *inhibition* threshold $\theta_k^I < 1$ for some $x' \in \mathcal{N}(x)$ then x is inhibited (rejected).
- **Crosstalk Cascades:** Combines soft, excitatory and inhibitory cascades in a straightforward manner with the goal of computing $H(x_i)$ if and only if $z_i^{\mathcal{N}} = 1$ and rejecting all other x_i with minimal additional computation.

We present an **unsupervised, data-driven framework** for learning the per-stage thresholds for each cascade type that has a **single free parameter** γ controlling tradeoff between speed and accuracy. No data annotation is necessary and only a single parameter γ needs to be selected to tune the cascades.

To keep overhead low we test thresholds only at stages $1 \leq k < K$ where k is a power of 2 (with $K = 4096$ weak classifiers there are 12 such stages).

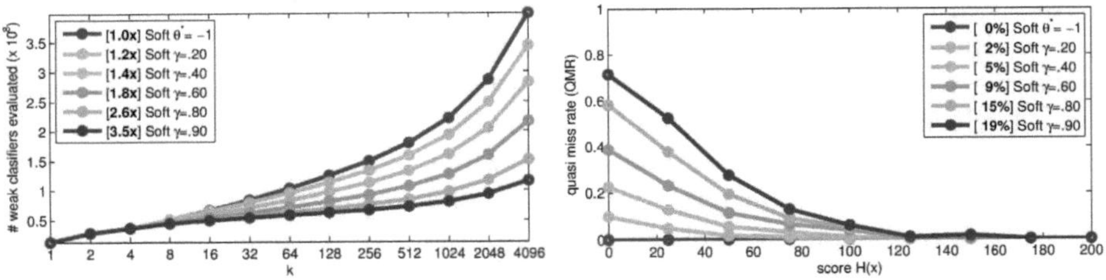

Fig. 6. Soft cascades with per-stage rejection thresholds for various γ. See text.

In all experiments we use windows $x_i \in \mathcal{X}$ sampled from the PASCAL images as described in §3.2. For learning we only require x_i for which $z_i^{\mathcal{N}} = 1$ (i.e. the quasi-positives) that survive a constant rejection cascade with $\theta^* = -1$. Based on experiments in §2.1 and §3.2, we use a neighborhood size of $\mathcal{N} = 7 \times 7 \times 3$.

We next describe each cascade type in detail and show how to learn respective thresholds given γ and a set of quasi-positives. For each cascade type we show two plots (Figures 6-9). **Left**: We plot the breakdown of computational effort versus k using the plot type introduced in §3.2 with overall speedup relative to constant soft cascades given in legend brackets. **Right**: We define the *quasi miss rate* (QMR) as the fraction of quasi-positives with $H_k(x) > \theta^*$ rejected by a cascade. We plot QMR for all x with $H(x) > H_0$ as a function of H_0 and in legend brackets list QMR averaged over $0 \leq H_0 \leq 200$. The QMR is computed in a fully unsupervised manner and serves as a useful estimate of the true MR.

4.1 Soft Cascades

Details for how soft cascades are applied at runtime were given in §3. We now describe our unsupervised approach for setting the rejection thresholds θ_k^R given the boosted classifier H, quasi-positives x_i, and target QMR γ. In practice we only test at rejection stages $k_j = 2^{j-1}$ for $1 \leq j \leq 12$ to keep overhead low, but for notational simplicity we assume testing occurs for every $k \leq K$.

Let $\gamma' = 1 - (1-\gamma)^{1/K}$. If at each rejection stage the QMR is $\leq \gamma'$ the overall QMR of the soft cascade will be $\leq \gamma$. Let $\mathcal{X}_1$ denote the set of quasi-positives and let $\mathcal{H}_1 = \{H_1(x_i) | x_i \in \mathcal{X}_1\}$. We set the first rejection threshold θ_1^R via

$$\theta_1^R = [\mathcal{H}_1]_r - \epsilon \quad \text{where } r = \lfloor \gamma' \cdot |\mathcal{H}_1| \rfloor. \tag{2}$$

Here $[\mathcal{H}]_r$ denotes the rth order statistic of $\mathcal{H}$ (i.e. the rth smallest value in $\mathcal{H}$) and $\epsilon = 10^{-5}$. For each remaining stage $1 < k \leq K$ we let $\mathcal{X}_k = \{x_i \in \mathcal{X}_{k-1} | H_{k-1}(x_i) > \theta_{k-1}^R\}$ and $\mathcal{H}_k = \{H_k(x_i) | x_i \in \mathcal{X}_k\}$ and compute:

$$\theta_k^R = [\mathcal{H}_k]_r - \epsilon \quad \text{where } r = \lfloor \gamma' \cdot |\mathcal{H}_k| \rfloor. \tag{3}$$

Claim: the soft cascade with θ_k^R as defined above has QMR of at most γ. Proof: by construction $|\mathcal{X}_k| \geq |\mathcal{X}_{k-1}| \cdot (1-\gamma')$; therefore $|\mathcal{X}_{K+1}| \geq |\mathcal{X}_1| \cdot (1-\gamma')^K$. The fraction of rejected quasi-positives is therefore at most $1 - (1-\gamma')^K = \gamma$. ■

We can further optimize θ_k^R by performing a second pass with a target QMR $\gamma = 0$ and $\mathcal{X}_{K+1}$ as the initial set of quasi-positives, but doing so has little

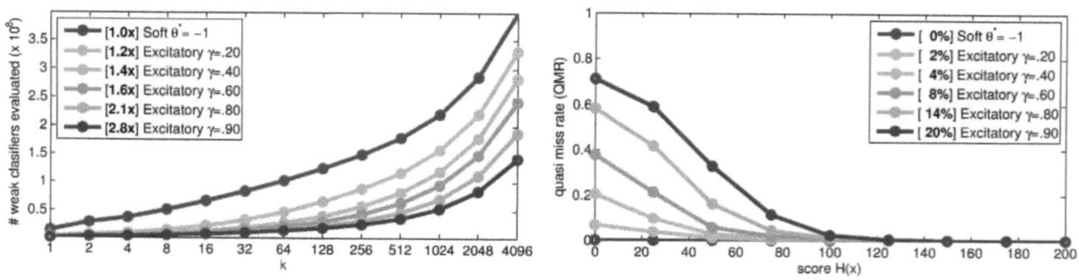

Fig. 7. Excitatory cascades effectively reduce computation for *small* k. See text.

effect in practice. Results for various choices of γ are shown in Figure 6. A value of $\gamma = .60$ results in a $1.8\times$ speedup over using a constant soft cascade, more aggressive settings yield up to a $3.5\times$ speedup but with larger QMR. Note that error decreases for x_i with larger scores $H(x_i)$, meaning high scoring detections are less likely to be rejected.

How does our approach for computing θ_k^R compare with existing methods? Zhang and Viola [9] improved upon the original *fully supervised* method of Bourdev and Brandt [8] by proposing a simple *semi-supervised* approach: their key observation was that if a single sample survives in the neighborhood of a true positive no loss is incurred. Our approach is a natural generalization to the *unsupervised* case, and indeed, the above mechanism shares similarities with [9]; the primary advantage being that no additional labeled data is needed.

4.2 Excitatory Cascades

The goal of excitatory cascades is to generate a set of candidates $\mathcal{X}_c$ that contains every quasi-positive. Let $\mathcal{X}_g$ denote all x sampled in a grid with a step size half the size of $\mathcal{N}$. For $\mathcal{N} = 7 \times 7 \times 3$, the step size is $(3,3,1)$, meaning that one in nine x is in $\mathcal{X}_g$. Initially $\mathcal{X}_c = \emptyset$. Now, for each $x \in \mathcal{X}_g$, computation of $H(x)$ continues until: (1) $H_k(x) < \theta^*$, (2) the maximum excitation stage $k > k^*$ is reached, or (3) $H_k(x) > \theta_k^E$ in which case x and all $x' \in \mathcal{N}(x)$ are added to $\mathcal{X}_c$.

We now describe the unsupervised approach for learning θ_k^E and maximum excitation stage k^* given H, x_i, and target QMR γ. We describe only the 2D case (single scale) and begin with learning θ_k^E for a single excitation stage $k^* = k$. Let $\mathcal{X}_g^o$ denote a sampling grid offset by o relative to x_i. Given a step size (s_x, s_y), there are $s_x s_y$ possible offsets o for $\mathcal{X}_g^o$ (including one case where $x_i \in \mathcal{X}_g^o$). We treat every sampling grid $\mathcal{X}_g^o$ as a separate, equally likely possibility. Let h_i^o be the maximum score $H_k(x_i')$ of all the $x_i' \in \mathcal{N}(x_i) \cap \mathcal{X}_g^o$. Because the step size is half the size of $\mathcal{N}$, at least $n \geq 4$ neighbors of x_i will be in $\mathcal{X}_g^o$ regardless of the offset o, however, the number of neighbors of x_i that survive the soft cascade may be fewer. If all the $x_i' \in \mathcal{N}(x_i) \cap \mathcal{X}_g^o$ were rejected by the soft cascade set $h_i^o = -\infty$, otherwise set $h_i^o = \max(H_k(x_i'))$. Next, compute:

$$\theta_k^E = [\mathcal{H}_k]_r - \epsilon \quad \text{where } r = \lfloor \gamma \cdot |\mathcal{H}_k| \rfloor \text{ and } \mathcal{H}_k = \{h_i^o\}. \tag{4}$$

If $\theta_k^E \neq -\infty$, then by construction on average $1-\gamma$ quasi-positives will end up in $\mathcal{X}_c$. Unfortunately $\theta_k^E = -\infty$ implies no such threshold exists.

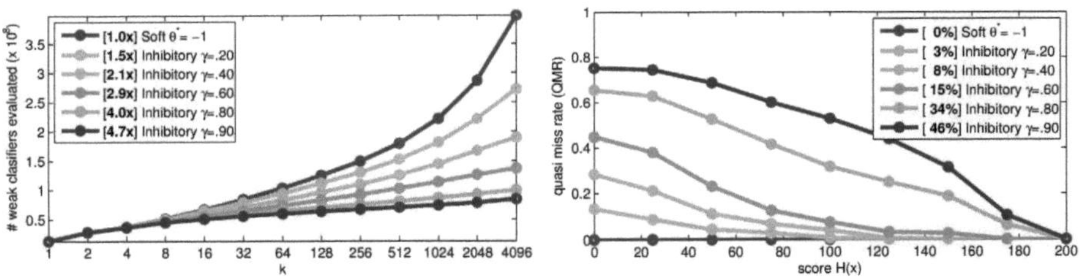

Fig. 8. Inhibitory cascades effectively reduce computation for *large* k. See text.

The above procedure fails if the excitation stage is too late. Recall from §2.1 that a detector's region of support (ROS) decreases with increasing k while its discriminative power increases. This causes a tension between performing excitation early, when discriminability is low, and performing excitation late when the ROS is small. We can find the *last* valid excitation stage by starting with $k = K$ and working backwards until θ_k^E is valid. Finally, θ_k^E for earlier stages are set to the smallest value such that $|\mathcal{X}_c|$ does not increase.

To measure error, we compute the full soft cascade (with $\theta^* = -1$) for all $x \in \mathcal{X}_c$. Results are shown in Figure 7. While overall speedup is modest, computation at early stages k is greatly reduced (a 9× speedup is possible with the given step size). The excitatory cascade effectively deals with quasi-negatives (see Figure 4); to reduce computation for larger k we turn to inhibitory cascades next.

4.3 Inhibitory Cascades

Inhibitory cascades operate on the set of all candidates $x \in \mathcal{X}_1$ in an image. At each stage k we construct the set $\mathcal{X}_{k+1}$ by including $x \in \mathcal{X}_k$ in $\mathcal{X}_{k+1}$ only if $H_k(x) > \theta^*$ and x is not inhibited by any of its neighbors that are still in $\mathcal{X}_k$. Specifically, $x \in \mathcal{X}_k$ is inhibited (not added to $\mathcal{X}_{k+1}$) if for any $x' \in \mathcal{N}(x) \cap \mathcal{X}_k$ with $H_k(x') > \theta^*$ the ratio $H_k(x)/H_k(x') < \theta_k^I$. Observe that previously inhibited x' (i.e. $x' \notin \mathcal{X}_k$) cannot inhibit x (although x' inhibited in the current stage can). To protect against $H_k(x) \leq 0$ we add the constant $\epsilon - \theta^*$ to both $H_k(x)$ and $H_k(x')$ prior to computing $H_k(x)/H_k(x')$. After the last stage $k = K$, the set $\mathcal{X}_{K+1}$ contains all x that survive the inhibitory cascade.

We now describe the approach for learning θ_k^I given H, x_i, and target QMR γ. The procedure bears resemblance to learning soft cascade rejection thresholds (see §4.1). We begin by defining $R_k(x) = \min_{x' \in \mathcal{N}(x)}\{H_k(x)/H_k(x')\}$. Let $\gamma' = 1 - (1-\gamma)^{1/K}$, $\mathcal{X}_k'$ denote the set of surviving quasi-positives in stage k, and $\mathcal{H}_k = \{R_k(x_i) | x_i \in \mathcal{X}_k'\}$. We set θ_k^I via:

$$\theta_k^I = \min\Big\{1, [\mathcal{H}_k]_r/(1+\epsilon)\Big\} \quad \text{where } r = \lfloor \gamma' \cdot |\mathcal{H}_k| \rfloor. \tag{5}$$

$\mathcal{X}_1'$ contains all quasi-positives and we set $\mathcal{X}_k' = \{x_i \in \mathcal{X}_{k-1}' | R_{k-1}(x_i) > \theta_{k-1}^I\}$.

Claim: the inhibitory cascade with θ_k^I as defined above has QMR of at most γ. Proof: it is not hard to see that $\mathcal{X}_k' \subseteq \mathcal{X}_k$ if we run the inhibitory cascade

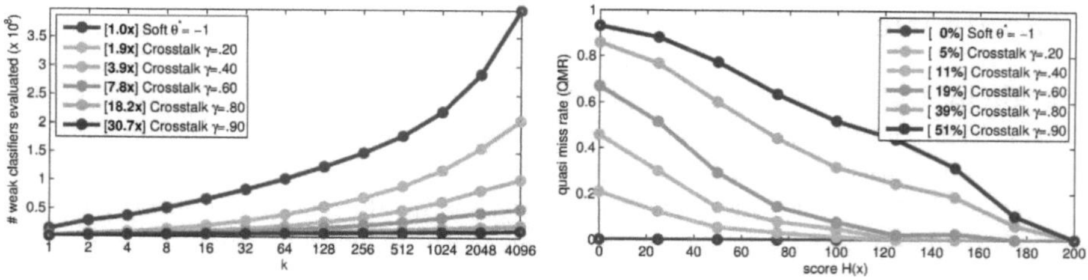

Fig. 9. Crosstalk cascades effectively reduce computation for *all* k by combining soft, excitatory and inhibitory cascades and can achieve dramatic speedups. See text.

with thresholds θ_k^I. However, by construction $|\mathcal{X}'_k| \geq |\mathcal{X}'_{k-1}| \cdot (1 - \gamma')$. Following the proof in §4.1, this implies the QMR is at most γ. ■

Results for various choices of γ are shown in Figure 8. A value of $\gamma = .60$ results in a 2.9× speedup over using a constant soft cascade; larger γ yield bigger speedups but the QMR starts to rise considerably even at higher scores. Nearly all computational savings for inhibitory cascades occur at later stages k.

4.4 Crosstalk Cascades

We now describe the details of how to combine soft, excitatory and inhibitory cascades into *crosstalk cascades*. Excitatory cascades reduce computation for *small* k, inhibitory cascades reduce computation for *large* k, and soft cascades reduce computation across all k. Their combination proves very effective.

Incorporating per-stage rejection thresholds θ_k^R into both excitatory and inhibitory cascades is simple. Both cascade types use θ^* as a rejection criteria, replacing θ^* with θ_k^R in the algorithm definitions is valid and achieves a reduction in computation (but also an increase in error). Combining excitatory and inhibitory cascades is straightforward as well. Excitatory cascades generate a sparse set of candidates $\mathcal{X}_c$ while inhibitory cascades operate on an initial candidate set $\mathcal{X}_1$. We can therefore use the output of excitatory cascades as input to the inhibitory cascades and set $\mathcal{X}_1 = \mathcal{X}_c$. Additionally, evaluations of $H(x)$ used to compute $\mathcal{X}_c$ can be cached and re-used in the inhibitory stage.

To adjust the crosstalk cascade we use a single γ for setting the rejection, excitation, and inhibition thresholds separately. We leave joint optimization of the thresholds for future work.

Results for various choices of γ are shown in Figure 9. Crosstalk cascades achieve dramatic speedups, e.g. for $\gamma = .8$ computation time is reduced by ~**20**× fold (compared to about 2.5×, 2×, and 4× for the individual cascade types). The speedups for crosstalk cascades are close to the product of the individual speedups, especially for lower γ. The QMR is higher, but not drastically so. We examine the true detection accuracy of crosstalk cascades next.

5 Evaluation

We begin by evaluating strategies for setting per-stage rejection thresholds θ_k^R for soft cascades, including our unsupervised approach. We compare three strategies. (1) First, we simply *recalibrate* our trained detector as described in §3.1 by setting $\theta_k^R = \theta^* + \phi k/K$ for various ϕ; this strategy has no data-driven component. (2) Next we utilize a *semi-supervised* approach inspired by the work of Zhang and Viola [9]. For each positive training example x_i, we select the $x_i' \in \mathcal{N}(x_i)$ with maximum scoring response $H(x_i')$, giving us a new set of examples $\mathcal{X}_{semi}$; to set θ_k^R we simply utilize the algorithm in §4.1 but with $\mathcal{X}_{semi}$ in place of the quasi-positives. While not identical to [9], this approach is similar in spirit. (3) Finally we utilize our *unsupervised* approach described in §4.1, varying γ.

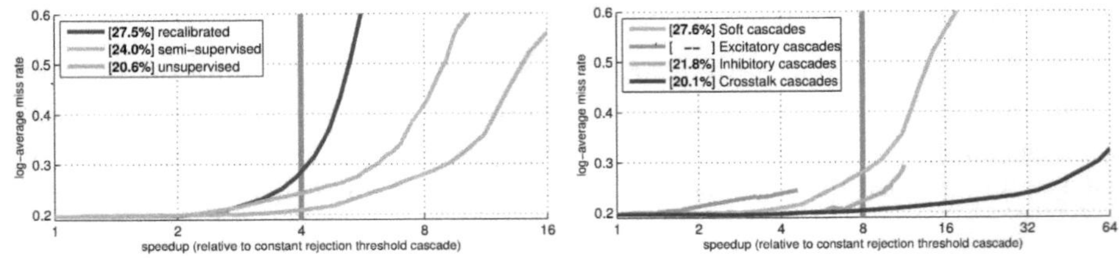

Fig. 10. Left: Effectiveness of strategies for setting per-stage rejection thresholds for soft cascades. For each strategy we sweep over γ (or ϕ) and plot the resulting MR versus relative speedup (legend brackets list MR at 4× speedup). Our *unsupervised* approach to learning soft cascades outperforms other baselines. **Right**: MR versus relative speedup for soft, excitatory, inhibitory, and crosstalk cascades as γ varies (legend lists MR at 8× speedup). In isolation, excitatory and inhibitory cascades provide little benefit, but when coupled the resulting crosstalk cascade achieves dramatic speedups.

Results for soft cascades on INRIA [22] are shown in Figure 10 (left). For each strategy we sweep over γ (or ϕ) and plot the resulting log-average miss rate (MR) versus speedup relative to soft cascades with $\theta_k^R = \theta^*$. Legend brackets list MR at 4× speedup. All approaches achieve a relative speedup of around 2× with no loss in accuracy, but for higher speedups the proposed unsupervised approach to soft cascades has significantly lower error due to its data-driven nature and availability of a large amount of unsupervised data.

Results on INRIA for crosstalk cascades are shown in Figure 10 (right). *Crosstalk cascade achieve large gains, giving a speedup of* **4**× *over the baseline with no loss in accuracy,* **8**× *speedup for a loss under .5% MR, and speedups between* **16 − 32**× *for somewhat larger errors of 2-4%.* Figure 11 shows ROC curves for crosstalk cascades with γ's set to achieve 4-32× speedups and corresponding soft cascades with γ's set to match the error of the crosstalk cascades. The relative speedup of the matching crosstalk cascades is 2-5 times higher.

Using a larger spatial step size can provide additional speedups for soft cascades. We evaluate soft cascades with step sizes that range from 4-12 pixels (the default is 4 pixels). As before, for each variant we sweep over γ and plot MR

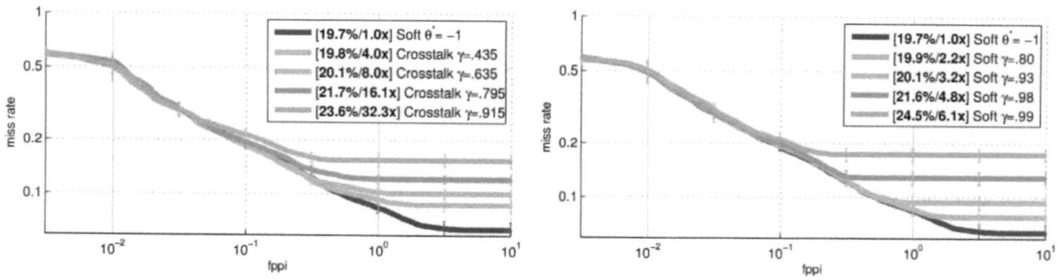

Fig. 11. Left: Crosstalk cascades evaluated on INRIA for multiple settings of γ (MR and speedup given in brackets). Crosstalk cascades achieve a speedup of **4**$\times$ with no loss in performance, **8**$\times$ speedup for a loss under .5% MR, and speedups between **16** $-$ **32**$\times$ if larger errors (2-4%) are acceptable. **Right**: For each soft cascade of approximately equal accuracy (matched by color), the corresponding crosstalk cascade is much faster.

versus relative speedup, see Figure 12. Crosstalk cascades, using the default 4 pixel step size, outperform soft cascade regardless of their spatial step size.

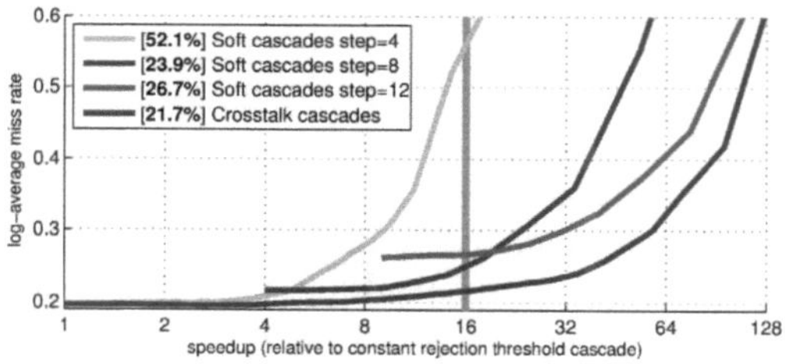

Fig. 12. No setting of the spatial step size and γ for soft cascades can simultaneously match the speed and accuracy of crosstalk cascades (legend lists MR at 16$\times$ speedup).

Crosstalk cascades operate at **45 fps** while matching state-of-the-art detection accuracy and **55-65 fps** at slightly higher MR. Complete results on INRIA along with a comparison to the state of the art are shown in Figure 13. Crosstalk cascades are over 5 times faster than any previously published results. Results on additional pedestrian datasets are shown in Figure 14; on all datasets crosstalk cascade match or outperform the state-of-the-art while running much faster.

6 Discussion

In this paper we: (1) analyzed cascades and experimentally demonstrated lower and upper bounds on their performance, (2) proposed a novel approach to more effectively learn soft cascade rejection thresholds using an unsupervised approach, and (3) introduced crosstalk cascade that enable neighboring detectors to communicate and thereby achieve major computational gains. Our approach is simple and effective and achieves faster than frame-rate detection.

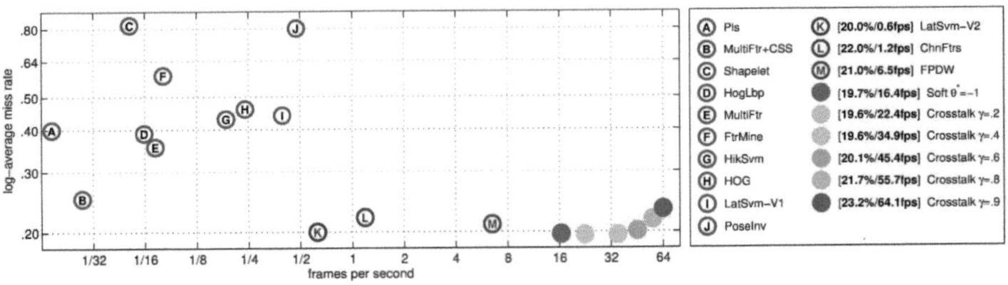

Fig. 13. Log-average miss rate (MR) versus speed (measured in fps) for various detectors on INRIA. Method runtimes were obtained from [6], see also [6] for detector citations. Legend brackets show MR/speedup for select methods. Crosstalk cascades for all setting of γ are much faster than any competing approach. At $\gamma = .6$ **crosstalk cascades have state of the art accuracy while operating at 45 fps.**

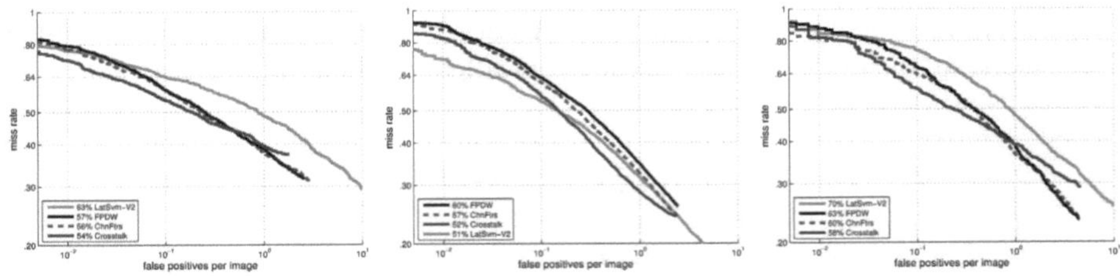

Fig. 14. From left to right: results on the Caltech, ETH, and TUD-Brussels pedestrian datasets (see [6]). Shown competing approaches are ChnFtrs [20], FPDW [4] and LatSvm [23]. On all datasets, crosstalk cascades (with $\gamma = .6$) match or outperform the state-of-the-art (except at high false positives) while running at much higher speeds. Complete results along with comparisons to numerous additional algorithms are available at `www.vision.caltech.edu/Image_Datasets/CaltechPedestrians`.

References

1. Felzenszwalb, P., Girshick, R., McAllester, D.: Cascade object detection with deformable part models. In: CVPR (2010)
2. Pedersoli, M., Vedaldi, A., Gonzalez, J.: A coarse-to-fine approach for fast deformable object detection. In: CVPR (2011)
3. Lampert, C.H., Blaschko, M.B., Hofmann, T.: Efficient subwindow search: A branch and bound framework for object localization. PAMI 31, 2129–2142 (2009)
4. Dollár, P., Belongie, S., Perona, P.: The fastest pedestrian detector in the west. In: BMVC (2010)
5. Benenson, R., Mathias, M., Timofte, R., Van Gool, L.: Pedestrian detection at 100 frames per second. In: CVPR (2012)
6. Dollár, P., Wojek, C., Schiele, B., Perona, P.: Pedestrian detection: An evaluation of the state of the art. PAMI 99 (2011)
7. Viola, P., Jones, M.: Rapid object detection using a boosted cascade of simple features. In: CVPR (2001)
8. Bourdev, L., Brandt, J.: Robust object detection via soft cascade. In: CVPR (2005)
9. Zhang, C., Viola, P.: Multiple-instance pruning for learning efficient cascade detectors. In: NIPS (2007)

10. Xiao, R., Zhu, L., Zhang, H.: Boosting chain learning for object detection. In: ICCV (2003)
11. Šochman, J., Matas, J.: Waldboost - learning for time constrained sequential detection. In: CVPR (2005)
12. Masnadi-Shirazi, H., Vasconcelos, N.: High detection-rate cascades for real-time object detection. In: ICCV (2007)
13. Zhu, Q., Avidan, S., Yeh, M., Cheng, K.: Fast human detection using a cascade of histograms of oriented gradients. In: CVPR (2006)
14. Butko, N., Movellan, J.: Optimal scanning for faster object detection. In: CVPR (2009)
15. Gualdi, G., Prati, A., Cucchiara, R.: Multi-stage Sampling with Boosting Cascades for Pedestrian Detection in Images and Videos. In: Daniilidis, K., Maragos, P., Paragios, N. (eds.) ECCV 2010, Part VI. LNCS, vol. 6316, pp. 196–209. Springer, Heidelberg (2010)
16. Gualdi, G., Prati, A., Cucchiara, R.: A multi-stage pedestrian detection using monolithic classifiers. In: AVSS (2011)
17. Felzenszwalb, P., Huttenlocher, D.: Efficient matching of pictorial structures. In: CVPR (2000)
18. Fleuret, F., Geman, D.: Coarse-to-fine face detection. IJCV 41, 85–107 (2001)
19. Vempati, S., Vedaldi, A., Zisserman, A., Jawahar, C.V.: Generalized RBF feature maps for efficient detection. In: BMVC (2010)
20. Dollár, P., Tu, Z., Perona, P., Belongie, S.: Integral channel features. In: BMVC (2009)
21. Friedman, J., Hastie, T., Tibshirani, R.: Additive logistic regression: a statistical view of boosting. The Annals of Statistics 38, 337–374 (2000)
22. Dalal, N., Triggs, B.: Histograms of oriented gradients for human detection. In: CVPR (2005)
23. Felzenszwalb, P.F., Girshick, R.B., McAllester, D., Ramanan, D.: Object detection with discriminatively trained part based models. PAMI 99 (2009)
24. Everingham, M., Van Gool, L., Williams, C.K.I., Winn, J., Zisserman, A.: The PASCAL visual object classes (VOC) challenge. IJCV 88, 303–338 (2010)

Query Specific Fusion for Image Retrieval

Shaoting Zhang[2], Ming Yang[1],
Timothee Cour[1], Kai Yu[1], and Dimitris N. Metaxas[2]

[1] NEC Laboratories America, Inc.
Cupertino, CA 95014
{myang,timothee,kyu}@sv.nec-labs.com
[2] CS Dept., Rutgers University
Piscataway, NJ 08854
{shaoting,dnm}@cs.rutgers.edu

Abstract. Recent image retrieval algorithms based on local features indexed by a vocabulary tree and holistic features indexed by compact hashing codes both demonstrate excellent scalability. However, their retrieval precision may vary dramatically among queries. This motivates us to investigate how to fuse the ordered retrieval sets given by multiple retrieval methods, to further enhance the retrieval precision. Thus, we propose a graph-based query specific fusion approach where multiple retrieval sets are merged and reranked by conducting a link analysis on a fused graph. The retrieval quality of an individual method is measured by the consistency of the top candidates' nearest neighborhoods. Hence, the proposed method is capable of adaptively integrating the strengths of the retrieval methods using local or holistic features for different queries without any supervision. Extensive experiments demonstrate competitive performance on 4 public datasets, *i.e.*, the *UKbench*, *Corel-5K*, *Holidays* and *San Francisco Landmarks* datasets.

1 Introduction

Image retrieval based on visual features has long been a major research theme due to the many applications such as the web and mobile image search. From the perspective of image representation and methodology, most of the successful scalable image retrieval algorithms fall into two categories: 1) quantized local invariant features [1,2] indexed by a deep vocabulary tree [3]; and 2) holistic features [4,5] indexed by compact hashing codes [6,7]. These two approaches demonstrate *distinct* strengths in finding visually similar images. Vocabulary tree based methods are powerful in identifying near-duplicate images or regions since local features are particularly capable of attending to local image patterns or textures. On the other hand, similar textures may confuse these methods to present some candidates which appear to be irrelevant to a query. By contrast, holistic features such as color histograms or GIST features [4] delineate overall feature distributions in images, thus the retrieved candidates often appear alike at a glance but may be irrelevant. Fig. 1 shows two illustrative cases of a success as well as a failure for either approach. The complementary descriptive capability of local and holistic features naturally raises the question of how to integrate their strengths to yield more satisfactory retrieval results.

A. Fitzgibbon et al. (Eds.): ECCV 2012, Part II, LNCS 7573, pp. 660–673, 2012.

(a) Holistic features yield more satisfactory results than local features.

(b) Local features yield more satisfactory results than holistic feature.

Fig. 1. Retrieval results of two query images (in the green boxes) in the *Corel-5K* dataset, using a holistic feature (GIST) at the first row and in the blue boxes, and BoW of local features (SIFT) at the second row and in the black boxes

Although both lines of retrieval methods have been extensively studied, there is not much research effort focusing on the fusion of image retrieval methods using local and holistic features. This is due to the fact that the feature characteristics and the algorithmic procedures are dramatically different. Generally the fusion can be carried out on the feature or rank levels, *e.g.*, employing the bag-of-words (BoW) representation [2] to combine different types of features in a histogram [8,9], or combining the ordered results from different retrieval methods by rank aggregation [10,11]. However, for a specific query image, it is quite difficult to determine online which features should play a major role in the retrieval. Moreover, it is even possible that there is no intersection among the top candidates retrieved by the local and holistic feature based methods, as shown in Fig. 1. This is very challenging for rank aggregation as it requires voting from multiple rank results. An alternative is to train a classifier to predict the retrieval quality using the similarity scores of top candidates, which is confronted by the issue of being sensitive to different queries and image databases, *e.g.*, the distributions of similarity scores may be quite different for queries with a couple or tens of relevant images. These challenges prompt us to investigate a relatively principled way to evaluate *online* the quality of retrieval results from methods using local or holistic features and fuse them at the rank level in an *unsupervised* way, while preserving the efficiency and scalability of the vocabulary tree structure and compact hashing mechanisms.

Without any supervision or relevance feedback for a retrieval set, we assume that the consensus degree among the top candidates reveals the retrieval quality. Therefore, we propose a graph-based approach to fusing and reranking retrieval results given by different methods, where the retrieval quality of an individual method is measured by the consistency of top candidates' nearest neighborhoods. Given a list of ranked results by one method, *i.e.*, either the vocabulary tree-based method or the hashed holistic features, we first build a weighted graph using the constraints derived from k-reciprocal nearest neighbors [12], described later. Each edge between two nodes, *i.e.*, two candidate images, is assigned a weight based on the Jaccard similarity coefficient [13] of two neighborhoods. Such weights reflect the confidence of including the connected nodes into the retrieval results. Then, multiple graphs from different cues are fused together by appending new nodes or consolidating edge weights of existing nodes. By conducting a link analysis on the resulting graph to search for the PageRank vector [14] or the weighted maximum density subgraph, the candidate images from various retrieval methods are fused and ranked.

The main contribution of the proposed approach is on the *unsupervised* graph-based fusion of retrieval sets given by different methods, which has three merits: 1) the retrieval quality specific to one query is effectively evaluated *online* without requiring any supervision; 2) the fusion favors the candidate images similar to a query in terms of different complementary image representations; and 3) the method can well cope with some singular cases such as little overlap of top candidates from individual cues. We have validated this method of fusing the retrieval sets using the BoW of local features and holistic features on 4 diverse public datasets, the *UKbench*, *Corel-5K*, *Holidays* and the large scale *San Francisco Landmarks* datasets. The evaluation shows our method consistently improves the retrieval precision and compares favorably with the recent state-of-the-art results.

2 Related Work

Most of the scalable image retrieval algorithms fall in two threads: indexing local features by a vocabulary tree and hashing holistic features by binary codes. Their strengths and limitations as well as possible ways to combine them are briefly reviewed below.

Local Features with Vocabulary Trees: Image retrieval based on the BoW of local invariant features [1,2] has been significantly scaled up by using vocabulary trees [3] which contain millions of leaf nodes attached with inverted indexes. This method demonstrates an excellent scalability in computation and precision, although it is memory consuming. It has been further improved by a spatial verification by RANSAC [15]; the query expansion [16]; using Hamming embedding and weak geometry constraints [17]; constructing high-order features [18]; and indexing relative spatial positions [19] or quantized spatial offsets [20] among local features. Since images are essentially delineated by local invariant features, these methods are effective in handling image scaling, rotation, and partial occlusions, leading to a very high precision in near-duplicate image retrieval. However, if no near-duplicate image regions exist in the database, large areas of similar textures may confuse these retrieval methods and lead to irrelevant candidate images and unsatisfactory user experience.

Holistic Features with Compact Hashing: As introduced in [6], holistic features such as color histograms and GIST [4] are indexed by locality sensitive hashing [21], resulting in highly compact binary codes (*e.g.*, 128 bits), which can be efficiently compared with a large database using the Hamming distance. The scalability and performance have been improved by spectral graph partitioning and hashing [7] and incorporating the pairwise semantic similarity and dissimilarity constraints from labeled data [22]. As suggested in [23], a random rotation on the PCA-projected features, which is optimized by iterative quantization, achieves surprisingly good performance. These methods leveraging compact hashing of holistic features are efficient in computation and memory usage. However, holistic features tend to be less invariant than local features, and are in general more sensitive to image transformations induced by illumination changes, scaling and pose variations. In practice, the focus on aggregated image statistics rather than fine details results in images that appear roughly similar but the retrieval precision is often lower compared to local feature based methods.

Fusion of Local and Holistic Feature Based Image Retrieval: For best results, one may want to combine the strengths of complementary cues such as local and holistic features. To our best knowledge, there is little in-depth work addressing how to achieve this properly in the literature, although there have been several attempts combining such cues either at the feature or rank level. Combining local and holistic cues at the feature level makes it hard to preserve the efficiency and scalability induced by the vocabulary tree structure and compact hashing. Rank aggregation [10] is a possible solution to fusing them at the rank level, however, it requires voting from multiple rank lists and is unable to handle two lists with an empty intersection which does occasionally occur for results returned by these two retrieval approaches. In either way, the key issue is how to measure and combine the cues whose effectiveness or importance varies dramatically among different query images. The closest inspiring work to ours includes [12] and [24] which address different problems, *i.e.*, reranking one retrieval result by k-reciprocal nearest neighbors [12] or reranking text-based retrieval results by visual similarities employing the PageRank algorithm [14]. In contrast, we concentrate on how to fuse the retrieval results based on local and holistic features to enhance the precision.

3 Proposed Approach

3.1 Overview

To fuse the ranked retrieval results given by different methods, the critical issue is how to *automatically* measure and compare their quality, since no supervision and user relevance feedbacks are available online. The similarity scores of candidates may vary largely among queries, especially for the vocabulary tree based method, and are not comparable between different retrieval methods. Thus, a reasonable idea is to measure the consistency among the top candidates returned by one retrieval method as the retrieval quality specific to one query. Therefore, for each query image, we construct a weighted undirected graph from the retrieval results of one method, where the retrieval quality or the relevance is modeled by the edge weights using the Jaccard similarity coefficient of two neighborhood image sets. Then we fuse these graphs to one and perform a localized PageRank algorithm or find the weighted maximum density subgraph centered at the query image to rerank the retrieval results. As a result, the fused retrieval results tend to be consistent in terms of different image representations.

3.2 Graph Construction

Denote q the query image, d an image in the database D, and i either the query or a database image. Given a similarity function $S(\cdot,\cdot)$ between images and a retrieval method, we represent retrieval results for a query as a sorted list of candidate images with associated similarity scores $\{(d,s)\}$ where $s = S(q,d)$. We define the neighborhood of an image i as $N_k(i)$ or $N'_\epsilon(i)$, where $N_k(i)$ includes the images that are the top-k retrieved candidates using i as the query and $N'_\epsilon(i)$ includes those with $s > \epsilon$. We further define the reciprocal neighbor relation for i and i' as:

$$R_k(i,i') = i \in N_k(i') \wedge i' \in N_k(i). \tag{1}$$

As discussed in [11,12], being the reciprocal neighbor is a reliable indication that two images are visually similar *w.r.t.* a particular image representation in a retrieval method.

For each set of retrieval results, we construct a weighted undirected graph $G = (V, E, w)$ centered at q where the nodes are the images (q and $d \in D$) and two images i, i' are linked by an edge $(i, i') \in E$ if they satisfy $R_k(i, i')$ as reciprocal neighbors. The attached edge weight w is defined as the Jaccard similarity coefficient $J(i, i')$ between the neighborhoods of i and i':

$$J(i, i') = \frac{|N_k(i) \cap N_k(i')|}{|N_k(i) \cup N_k(i')|} \tag{2}$$

$$w(i, i') = \alpha(q, i, i')J(i, i'), \tag{3}$$

where $|\cdot|$ denotes the cardinality and $\alpha(q, i, i')$ is a decay coefficient related to the number of hops to the query: let $\delta(q, i)$ be the length of the shortest path in G between q and i; we define $\alpha(q, i, i') = \alpha_0^{\max(\delta(q,i),\delta(q,i'))}$, and set $\alpha_0 = 0.8$ in all experiments. The range of edge weights is from 0 to 1, with $J(i, i') = 1$ implying that these two images share exactly the same set of neighbors, in which case we assume the two images are highly likely to be visually similar. The query q's reciprocal neighbors form the first layer in the graph whose reciprocal neighbors are expanded to the second layer *w.r.t.* q, so on so forth. The graph construction continues until either: 1) the number of nodes $|V|$ reaches a given maximum number (*i.e.*, the maximal number of images to retrieve), or 2) no more reciprocal neighbors can be found, or 3) the weights of edges become smaller than a given threshold. An illustrative example is shown in Fig. 2. Note, for holistic feature based retrieval methods, we can also employ the similarity score and the neighborhood $N'_\epsilon(i)$ in place of $N_k(i)$ to define the reciprocal neighbor relation and Jaccard similarity coefficient.

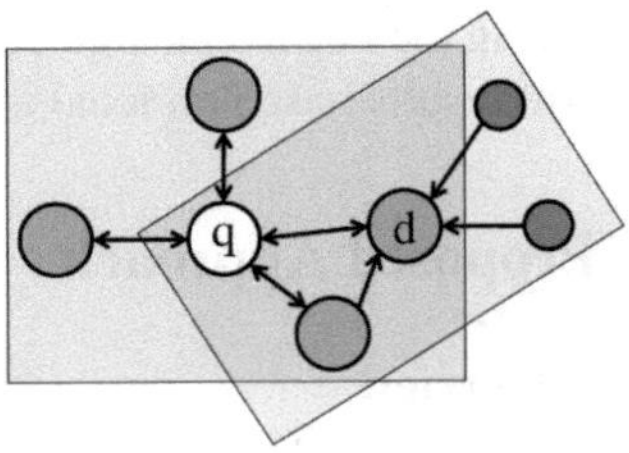

Fig. 2. An example of graph construction, where the query q links to its reciprocal neighbors (*i.e.*, q and the green discs in the green zone). d is a candidate at the first layer with its reciprocal neighbors in the blue zone, whose Jaccard coefficient to q is $3/7$ (# of nodes in the intersection divided by # of nodes in the union of the green and blue zones). The radius of the disc representing a node indicates the influence of decay coefficient α.

3.3 Graph Fusion

After obtaining multiple graphs $G^m = (V^m, E^m, w^m)$ from different retrieval methods, we fuse them together into one graph $G = (V, E, w)$ with $V = \cup_m V^m$, $E = \cup_m E^m$, and $w(i, i') = \sum_m w^m(i, i')$ (with $w^m(i, i') = 0$ for $(i, i') \notin E^m$), see Fig. 3. Though the rank lists or the similarity scores in different methods are not directly comparable, their Jaccard coefficients are comparable as they reflect the consistency of two nearest neighborhoods. Without any prior, here we have to treat multiple retrieval methods equally by simply summing up the edge weights.

3.4 Graph-Based Ranking

Given a graph G (obtained either from a single retrieval method or by fusing multiple ones), the connectivity of a node reflects its visual similarity to others. Thus, we propose two solvers to rerank the candidate images, *i.e.*, by performing the local PageRank algorithm on the edges or finding the weighted maximum density subgraph in G.

Ranking by the PageRank: Since the notion of well-connected nodes in G also reveals the visual consensus degree of images, we conduct a principled link analysis [14] on the whole graph G to rank according to the node connectivity. This graph G is treated as a network. Since this network is built by considering the retrieval relevance, naturally a node is more important or relevant if it has a higher probability to be visited.

We define the $|V| \times |V|$ transition matrix $\mathbf{P}$ as $P_{ii'} = w(i,i')/\deg(i)$ for $(i,i') \in E$, and 0 otherwise. It is row-stochastic, *i.e.*, each row sums to one. Consider the assumption of the *intelligent surfer model* [25], whereby a surfer probabilistically hops from node to node along the edges of G, according to the transition matrix $\mathbf{P}$. Occasionally, with a small probability $1-\beta$, the surfer jumps according to a fixed distribution over nodes π, which we set as $\pi_q = 0.99$ and uniform otherwise, where q is the index of the query node. We denote p_i^t as the probability for the surfer to be at node i at a time t and $p^t = (p_i^t)$. The equilibrium state of p, where a higher probability reflects a higher relevance to the query, is obtained by the query dependent PageRank vector as a stationary point using the power method:

$$p^{t+1} = (1-\beta)\pi + \beta \mathbf{P}^T p^t. \tag{4}$$

Once p has converged, the images are ranked according to their probabilities in p.

Ranking by Maximizing Weighted Density: As the visual similarity of two images in terms of one or more representations has been encoded in the edge weights of G, another natural idea is to search for the subgraph $G' \subset G$ containing q of a weighted maximum density, as follows:

$$G' = \operatorname*{argmax}_{G'=(V',E',w)\subset G:\ q\in V'} \frac{\sum_{(i,i')\in E'} w(i,i')}{|V'|}. \tag{5}$$

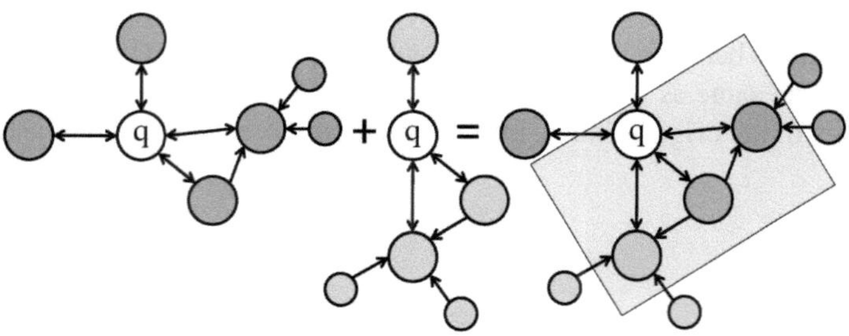

Fig. 3. Fusion of two graphs where the green and yellow graphs are derived from two different retrieval methods.

In other words, we prefer to choose nodes which can contribute more weight to the subgraph. Since edge weights are correlated with the retrieval quality, this approach selects images with potentially a higher visual similarity.

We solve Eq. (5) approximately by a greedy algorithm that grows G' iteratively, starting from $G' = (\{q\}, \emptyset, w)$. We first compute node degrees $\deg(i) = \sum_{i'} w(i, i')$ for each node i linked with q by accumulating weights from its connected edges. Then the node with the largest weight is selected to be incorporated in G'. After that, we consider all nodes connected to the current G', and select the one which can introduce the largest weight to G' (ties broken arbitrarily). Fig. 4 shows one example of determining the candidate nodes of a graph G'. G' is enlarged by applying this procedure iteratively, until a user-specified number of images is retrieved. These nodes are ranked according to their time of insertion into G'. The advantage of this ranking method is its efficiency. The computational complexity mainly depends on the connectivity (*i.e.*, the average valence of all nodes) but not the number of nodes in G, since we only check the nodes connecting to the current G'. Thus this method obtains ranking results within a similar time for different sizes of G. Although this method is not guaranteed to find a global optimum, our experiments in Sec. 4 suggest that this method achieves accurate and consistent ranking.

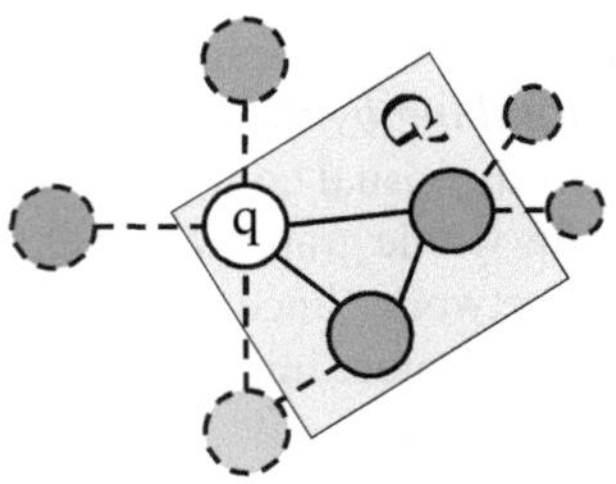

Fig. 4. Illustration of expanding G' (the green zone). Candidate nodes are connected to G', and are denoted by dash lines.

3.5 Complexity and Scalability

The complexity of each power method iteration in the PageRank algorithm is $O(|E|)$. In our experiments, the node valence in G is around 4-10 and the power method converges within 10 iterations. The greedy search for the maximum density subgraph is on average two times faster then the PageRank. The computational cost incurred by the proposed fusion methods is quite small given the top candidates retrieved by different methods. In particular the running time of the proposed fusion is about 1ms regardless of the database size, and the overall query time is less than 1 second for over a million database images in our experiments. The memory overhead is determined by the number of reciprocal neighbors between images in the database, which have to be pre-calculated and stored *offline* the same as [12]. The experiments in Sec. 4 demonstrate the scalability and efficiency of the original image retrieval methods are retained in the fusion method.

4 Experiments

We first describe the datasets (Sec. 4.1) and the methods (Sec. 4.2) compared in the experiments, then present the detailed evaluation results (Sec. 4.3), followed by the discussions about some issues and limitations (Sec. 4.4).

4.1 Datasets

We evaluate the proposed approach on 4 public datasets: the *UKbench*, *Corel-5K*, *Holidays* and *San Francisco Landmarks* (*SFLandmarks*). In the *UKbench* and *Holidays*, relevant images are near-duplicates or the same objects/scenes to the query, while, the *Corel-5K* involves category-level relevant images without any near-duplicate ones. *SFLandmarks* is a realistic large-scale dataset with a variable number of relevant images for different queries. We employ the performance measures from the original papers of these datasets and demonstrate the query specific fusion improves considerably for all these diverse datasets.

UKbench [3] includes 2,550 different objects, and each one has 4 images taken from different viewpoints and illuminations. All 10,200 images are indexed as both database images and queries. The retrieval performance is measured by 4$\times$ recall at the first 4 retrieved images, which is referred as the N-S score (maximum is 4).

Corel-5K [26] consists of 5,000 images that fall in 50 categories, such as beach, bird, jewelry, sunset, *etc.*, each containing 100 images. We use a leave-one-out method to query all 5,000 images, *i.e.*, querying every image with the remaining 4,999 images as the database images. The performance is evaluated by r-precision, *i.e.*, the precision for the top r candidates, averaged over the 5,000 queries.

Holidays [17] contains 1491 personal holiday photos undergoing various transformations. There are 500 image groups where the first image of each group is the query. The performance is measured by mAP in a leave-one-out fashion.

SFLandmarks [27] is a city-scale image database, which contains 1.06M perspective central images (PCIs) and 638K perspective frontal images (PFIs). They are generated from street-view panoramic pictures with building labels. A set of 803 images taken by camera phones is provided as queries. The performance is evaluated by the average recall rate of correct buildings *vs.* the number of candidates.

4.2 Methods

The baseline local and holistic feature based retrieval methods are denoted by the *VOC*, *GIST* and *HSV* (described below), for which we apply our graph construction (Sec. 3.2) on their retrieval results, obtaining G^{VOC}, G^{GIST} and G^{HSV}. The two proposed ranking methods are denoted by ***Graph-PageRank*** and ***Graph-density*** to generate the fused retrieval sets, which are compared with the *rank aggregation*, and a learning based fusion method, referred as *SVM-fusion*. Applying the *Graph-density* to an individual baseline obtains the *VOC-graph*, *GIST-graph* and *HSV-graph*, respectively.

VOC: We employ a variant of vocabulary tree based retrieval [3,28] in which up to 2,500 SIFT features are detected for each image using the VLFeat library [29]. We employ a 7 layer tree with a branch factor 10. The tree is trained on 50K images in the validation set of the *ImageNet* Challenge [30] for *UKbench*, *Corel-5K* and *Holidays*, and on the PCIs and PFIs, respectively, for *SF Landmarks*, following [27].

GIST and HSV: For each image we compute the 960-dimensional GIST [4] descriptor and the 2000-dimensional HSV color histogram (using $20 \times 10 \times 10$ bins for H, S, V components). We then apply a PCA hashing method [23] to compress those to 256 bits. Retrieval is based on exhaustive search using the Hamming distance.

Table 1. Comparison of N-S scores on the *UKbench* dataset with recent retrieval methods and other rank fusion approaches

Jégou *et al.* [11]	Qin *et al.* [12]	*HSV*	*VOC* [28]	*HSV graph*	*VOC graph*	*Rank aggregation*	*SVM fusion*	*Graph PageRank*	*Graph density*
3.68	3.67	3.17	3.54	3.28	3.67	3.31	3.56	3.76	**3.77**

Rank Aggregation: We use the algorithm described in [10] to combine the local and holistic retrieval results.

SVM-Fusion: We train a linear SVM classifier that predicts which retrieval method is most appropriate for a given query, by computing a 20-dimensional input feature consisting of the top-10 normalized similarity scores for two retrieval methods. The SVM outputs binary indications about which method may achieve a higher precision. This is motivated by the observation [12] that a sharp degradation of the similarity scores may imply a confident retrieval and a long tail distribution may imply a less confident one. We employ a 5-fold cross-validation, where at the test time, we output for each query the ranked list of images from the method with a predicted higher quality.

In our graph-based fusion, the main parameter k, determining reciprocal neighborhoods, shall reflect the expected number of relevant images and the database size [12]. We set it to 5 for *UKbench* and *Holidays*, 15 for *Corel-5K*, and 30 for *SFLandmarks*, which is not sensitive to small variations.

4.3 Evaluation

UKbench: We first compare our approach and the baselines with the state-of-the-art methods on this widely used *UKbench* dataset, see Table 1. We consider the fusion of the *VOC* and *HSV* retrievals, as *GIST* yields poor results here (N-S=2.21). Since the relevant images in this dataset undergo severe illumination and pose variations, *VOC* performs substantially better than holistic features. This imbalance limits the performance of rank aggregation and *SVM-fusion*. Moreover, if we employ a cross-dataset *SVM-fusion*, which is learned on the *Corel-5K* and tested on the *UKbench*, the performance (N-S=3.37) is much worse than using *VOC* only, showing that *SVM-fusion* does not generalize well across datasets. The graph-based fusion improves the baselines considerably to N-S=**3.77**, which outperforms the state-of-the-art performance N-S=3.68 in [11]. The rank aggregation was employed to combine 19 vocabulary trees [11] to achieve N-S=3.68, in contrast, we fuse just two types of features. This improvement significantly decreases the relative error rate. Indeed, this excellent performance verifies the power of fusing local and holistic feature based retrieval methods.

The performance of the *Graph-PageRank* and *Graph-density* are close on the *UKbench*. The reason is that on the *UKbench* the graphs are usually well-connected because of the near-duplicate candidates. Thus the PageRank solution by analyzing the whole graph is similar to applying the greedy search. In general, both proposed methods improve the state-of-the-art retrieval precision remarkably on this dataset, even without

Table 2. The top-1 precision (in %) on the *Corel-5K* dataset

VOC	*GIST*	*VOC-graph*	*GIST-graph*	*SVM-fusion*	*Graph-PageRank*	*Graph-density*
46.66	46.16	51.50	50.72	51.34	51.76	**54.62**

requiring a geometrical verification which is both time consuming and makes strong physical assumptions about near duplicates.

Corel-5K: In this dataset, each query is associated with a large number of relevant images (100), and so we report the precision instead of recall for the top r queries, *i.e.*, the corresponding r-precision curves in Fig. 5 and the top-1 precision in Table 2.

We fuse the retrieval results of the *VOC* and *GIST* on this dataset. The top-1 precision 54.62% of the *Graph-density* is about 8% higher than either baseline method. It validates that the Jaccard similarity well reflects the retrieval quality and the graph fusion combines the strength of both baseline methods. *Graph-PageRank* does not achieve such a good precision in the top-3 retrievals. However, it becomes comparable to *Graph-density* after retrieving more images (see Fig. 5), because *Graph-PageRank* pursuits the optimization of the whole graph, while the *Graph-density* greedily finds the most relevant candidate. Thus the latter method may achieve a better performance for the first few retrievals.

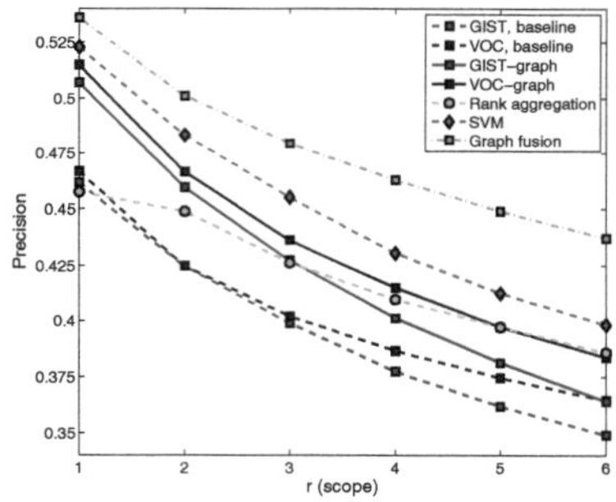

Fig. 5. The scope(r)-precision curves for the *Corel-5K* dataset

The rank aggregation method improves the precision when there are some common retrieved images in both of the top candidate lists, since their ranks are promoted by the voting. However, in some cases the two rank lists may not have any overlap at all (especially for the top-1 candidate), then the aggregation cannot help.

SVM-fusion effectively improves the top-1 precision to 51.34%. However, this performance is kind of too optimistic since the number of relevant images are about the same for all the queries in the *Corel-5K* and both the *VOC* and *GIST* work equally-well, which may not hold for other databases such as the *UKbench.*

Holidays: On the INRIA *Holidays* [17], we observe a consistent performance gain as on the *UKbench*. The *Graph-PageRank* and *Graph-density* improve the mAP of the *VOC* (77.5%) and *HSV* (62.6%) to 84.56% and 84.64% respectively, which are also among the state-of-the-art. In contrast, as shown in Table 3, the rank aggregation and the *SVM-fusion* methods marginally improve over the *VOC* since the mAP of the *HSV* is about 15% lower.

Table 3. Comparison of the mAP (in %) on the *Holidays* dataset with recent retrieval methods and other rank fusion approaches

Jégou *et al.* [17]	Jégou *et al.* [31]	*HSV*	*VOC* [28]	*Rank aggregation*	*SVM fusion*	*Graph PageRank*	*Graph density*
81.3	83.9	62.60	77.50	78.62	79.04	84.56	**84.64**

SFLandmarks: We study the scalability of the proposed fusion on this real-world large-scale dataset. For efficiency, we perform the *VOC* retrieval first, then compute the holistic feature based retrieval using the *GIST* among the top-50 candidates returned by the *VOC*. Since the query is not included in the database, we approximately determine its reciprocal neighbors based on the Jaccard similarity of the top candidates to q. Then, the two graphs of *VOC* and *GIST* are constructed and fused to generate the retrieval results. Please note that although the *GIST* graph is built upon the *VOC* results, by performing the graph fusion and ranking, the method enforces the retrieval results to be consistent in terms of different cues. Thus, this is essentially different from using the *GIST* to rank the *VOC*'s results which actually degrades *VOC*'s performance on the *SFLandmark*. For memory usage, we only store the image id of the top-50 nearest neighbors in the *VOC* for the 1.7M database images which costs 340MB additional memory, a small fraction of the memory requirements for storing the inverted indexes. Although we adopt some approximations for both the *VOC* and *GIST* based retrieval, our experiments show the fusion effectively improves the performance on this large-scale problem. Moreover this is a practical setting that easily integrates with vocabulary tree based retrieval systems.

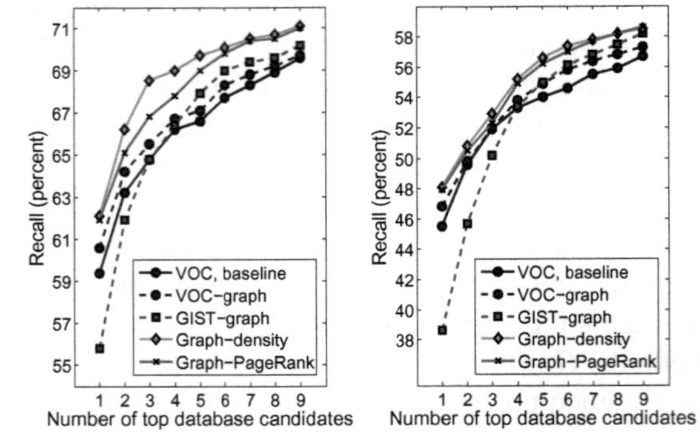

(a) PCIs (b) PFIs

Fig. 6. Retrieval results on the *SFLandmarks*. Recall versus number of top database candidates of (a) query 803 images in the 1.06M PCIs, (b) query 803 images in the 638k PFIs.

Following the same experimental setting as in [27], we report the recall rate averaged over the 803 query images versus the number of candidates on the PCIs and PFIs separately, see Fig. 6. The recall is in terms of retrieving at least once the correct building among the top r candidates, which means multiple correct hits count as a single hit. Using the *GIST-graph* to rerank the top-50 candidates returned by the *VOC* actually adversely affects the accuracy in the top-3 retrievals, which is probably due to the fact that local invariant features are generally more reliable than GIST in finding near-duplicate images under viewpoint changes. However, such holistic features still

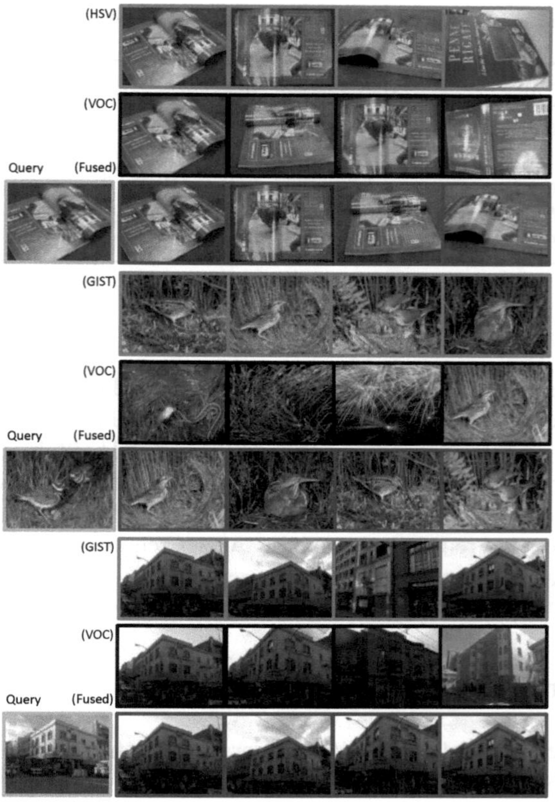

Fig. 7. Three sets of retrieval results from the *UKbench* (top), *Corel-5k* (middle), and *SFLandmarks* (bottom) datasets, respectively. Top-4 candidates are shown for the fusion results (3rd row in the purple boxes) of a query (in a green box on the left), using holistic features (1st row in the blue boxes), and local features (2nd row in the black boxes).

provide complementary information. As shown in Fig. 6, the fusion with the GIST based retrieval improves noticeably upon the *VOC*, leading to top-1 recall rates of **62.14**% for the PCIs and **48.08**% for the PFIs, which compare favorably with the method using oriented local features without GPS in [27] [1]. This validates our proposed approach as a practical retrieval method in a large-scale setting.

The online query in the proposed method is very efficient, since the nearest neighborhoods are pre-computed offline and the Hamming distance matching is optimized by the Intel SSE4.2 assembly. The average query time t_r in millisecond (not including the feature extraction) and the breakdown are reported in Table 4. Illustrative fusion results on three test datasets are shown in Fig. 7, from which we observe that the query specific fusion integrates the strengths of local or holistic features adaptively.

[1] This statement is based on the highest recalls on the green curves in Fig.7(b) and 8(b) in [27].

Table 4. The average query time (in *ms*) and the breakdown on the test datasets

Dataset	# of images	*VOC*	*HSV/GIST*	*Graph-fusion*	t_r *(ms)*
UKbench	10200	85	1	< 1	87
Corel-5K	4999	76	< 1	< 1	78
Holidays	1490	72	< 1	< 1	73
PCI-SFLandmark	1,062,468	645	103	< 1	749
PFI-SFLandmark	638,090	467	64	< 1	532

4.4 Discussion

We discuss implementation issues and limitations here: 1) For certain queries, it is possible neither local nor holistic features are capable of finding relevant candidates, thus no reciprocal neighbors nor any graph can be found and built. In such cases, we just arbitrarily pick up the retrieval results given by the *VOC* or the holistic feature based retrieval without any reranking. 2) As the nearest neighbor information is required, dynamical insertion and removal of database images require some care. One possible solution is to always keep a sufficiently large representative image set to approximate the neighborhood relations, which we leave for the future work.

5 Conclusions

In this paper [2], we proposed a graph-based query specific fusion of retrieval sets based on local and holistic features, where the retrieval quality is measured online by the consistency of the neighborhoods of candidate images. Our approach does not require any supervision, retains the computational efficiency of the vocabulary tree based retrieval, and at the same time considerably improves the image retrieval precision on 4 diverse public datasets. Moreover, this fusion method can be easily reproduced by other researchers and may serve as a plug-in in practical image retrieval systems. These warrant further investigating the fusion of multiple cues for image retrieval.

References

1. Lowe, D.G.: Distinctive image features from scale invariant keypoints. Int'l Journal of Computer Vision 60, 91–110 (2004)
2. Sivic, J., Zisserman, A.: Video google: A text retrieval approach to object matching in videos. In: ICCV (2003)
3. Nistér, D., Stewénius, H.: Scalable recognition with a vocabulary tree. In: CVPR (2006)
4. Oliva, A., Torralba, A.: Modeling the shape of the scene: A holistic representation of the spatial envelope. Int'l Journal of Computer Vision 42, 145–175 (2001)
5. Cai, D., He, X., Han, J.: Spectral regression: a unified subspace learning framework for content-based image retrieval. In: ACM Multimedia (2007)
6. Torralba, A., Fergus, R., Weiss, Y.: Small codes and large image databases for recognition. In: CVPR (2008)

[2] This work was done during the internship of the first author at NEC Laboratories America.

7. Weiss, Y., Torralba, A., Fergus, R.: Spectral hashing. In: NIPS (2008)
8. Gehler, P., Nowozin, S.: On feature combination for multiclass object classification. In: ICCV (2009)
9. Zhang, S., Huang, J., Huang, Y., Yu, Y., Li, H., Metaxas, D.N.: Automatic image annotation using group sparsity. In: CVPR (2010)
10. Fagin, R., Kumar, R., Sivakumar, D.: Efficient similarity search and classification via rank aggregation. In: ACM SIGMOD (2003)
11. Jégou, H., Schmid, C., Harzallah, H., Verbeek, J.: Accurate image search using the contextual dissimilarity measure. IEEE Trans. Pattern Anal. Machine Intell. 32, 2–11 (2010)
12. Qin, D., Gammeter, S., Bossard, L., Quack, T., van Cool, L.: Hello neighbor: accurate object retrieval with k-reciprocal nearest neighbors. In: CVPR (2011)
13. Jaccard, P.: The distribution of the flora in the alpine zone. New Phytologist 11, 37–50 (1912)
14. Page, L., Brin, S., Motwani, R., Winograd, T.: The PageRank citation ranking: Bringing order to the web (1999)
15. Philbin, J., Chum, O., Isard, M., Sivic, J., Zisserman, A.: Object retrieval with large vocabularies and fast spatial matching. In: CVPR (2007)
16. Chum, O., Philbin, J., Sivic, J., Isard, M., Zisserman, A.: Total recall: Automatic query expansion with a generative feature model for object retrieval. In: ICCV (2007)
17. Jégou, H., Douze, M., Schmid, C.: Hamming Embedding and Weak Geometric Consistency for Large Scale Image Search. In: Forsyth, D., Torr, P., Zisserman, A. (eds.) ECCV 2008, Part I. LNCS, vol. 5302, pp. 304–317. Springer, Heidelberg (2008)
18. Wu, Z., Ke, Q., Isard, M., Sun, J.: Bundling feature for large scale partial-duplicated web image search. In: CVPR (2009)
19. Zhou, W., Lu, Y., Li, H., Song, Y., Tian, Q.: Spatial coding for large scale partial-duplicate web image search. In: ACM Multimedia (2010)
20. Zhang, Y., Jia, Z., Chen, T.: Image retrieval with geometry-preserving visual phrases. In: CVPR (2011)
21. Andoni, A., Indyk, P.: Near-optimal hashing algorithms for approximate nearest neighbor in high dimensions. In: Symposium on Foundations of Computer Science, FOCS (2006)
22. Wang, J., Kumar, S., Chang, S.F.: Semi-supervised hashing for scalable image retrieval. In: CVPR (2010)
23. Gong, Y., Lazebnik, S.: Iterative quantization: A procrustean approach to learning binary codes. In: CVPR (2011)
24. Jing, Y., Balujia, S.: VisualRank: Applying PageRank to large-scale image search. In: IEEE Trans. Pattern Anal. Machine Intell., vol. 30, pp. 1877–1890 (2008)
25. Richardson, M., Domingos, P.: The intelligent surfer: Probabilistic combination of link and content information in PageRank. In: NIPS, vol. 14, pp. 1441–1448 (2002)
26. Duygulu, P., Barnard, K., de Freitas, J.F.G., Forsyth, D.: Object Recognition as Machine Translation: Learning a Lexicon for a Fixed Image Vocabulary. In: Heyden, A., Sparr, G., Nielsen, M., Johansen, P. (eds.) ECCV 2002, Part IV. LNCS, vol. 2353, pp. 97–112. Springer, Heidelberg (2002)
27. Chen, D.M., Baatz, G., Köser, K., Tsai, S.S., Vedantham, R., Pylvänäinen, T., Roimela, K., Chen, X., Bach, J., Pollefeys, M., Girod, B., Grzeszczuk, R.: City-scale landmark indentification on mobile devices. In: CVPR (2011)
28. Wang, X., Yang, M., Cour, T., Zhu, S., Yu, K., Han, T.X.: Contextual weighting for vocabulary tree based image retrieval. In: ICCV (2011)
29. Vedaldi, A., Fulkerson, B.: VLFeat: An open and portable library of computer vision algorithms. In: ICME (2010)
30. Deng, J., Dong, W., Socher, R., Li, L.J., Li, K., Fei-Fei, L.: ImageNet: A large-scale hierarchical image database. In: CVPR (2009)
31. Jégou, H., Douze, M., Schmid, C.: On the burstiness of visual elements. In: CVPR (2009)

Size Matters: Exhaustive Geometric Verification for Image Retrieval Accepted for ECCV 2012

Henrik Stewénius, Steinar H. Gunderson, and Julien Pilet

Google Switzerland

Abstract. The overreaching goals in large-scale image retrieval are bigger, better and cheaper. For systems based on local features we show how to get both efficient geometric verification of every match and unprecedented speed for the low sparsity situation.

Large-scale systems based on quantized local features usually process the index one term at a time, forcing two separate scoring steps: First, a scoring step to find candidates with enough matches, and then a geometric verification step where a subset of the candidates are checked.

Our method searches through the index a document at a time, verifying the geometry of every candidate in a single pass. We study the behavior of several algorithms with respect to index density—a key element for large-scale databases. In order to further improve the efficiency we also introduce a new new data structure, called the counting min-tree, which outperforms other approaches when working with low database density, a necessary condition for very large-scale systems.

We demonstrate the effectiveness of our approach with a proof of concept system that can match an image against a database of more than 90 billion images in just a few seconds.

1 Introduction

The growth of content-based image retrieval systems using local features has been driven by better techniques, faster hardware and a knowledge that these systems work well at scale. In this work we only focus on vocabularized local features and ignore the rich literature on other methods. The largest impact on the size growth came from the introduction of visual vocabularies [1], a technique which has been refined in [2–8]. This works aims to further increase the power of this class of systems.

Nowadays, several companies offer large-scale, content-based image retrieval services [9–13]. For example, TinEye [13] reached two billion images in 2011. Unfortunately very little is known about the actual systems.

According to the available literature, a typical vocabulary-based system extracts features from images to produce an inverted index mapping quantized features to a list of images exhibiting the same quantized value—a posting list.

A. Fitzgibbon et al. (Eds.): ECCV 2012, Part II, LNCS 7573, pp. 674–687, 2012.

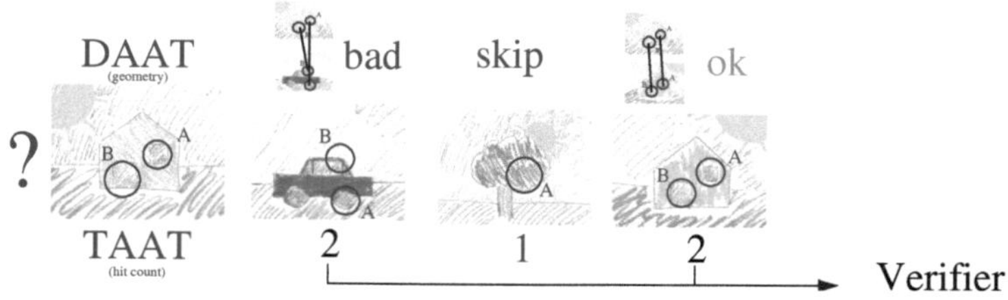

Fig. 1. Features A and B detected in the query image (top) are present in three images. In Term at a Time (TAAT) we first process the posting list for A and then the posting list for B, and accumulate scores. The top candidates are then geometrically verified. In Document at a Time (DAAT) evaluation, posting lists are traversed in parallel, and we do geometric verification for all documents having a sufficient number of matches.

At query time, features are extracted from the query image and quantized. The corresponding posting lists are read, and votes are added for each document in the list, usually using weights computed from features and document statistics. The subset of the documents with the best scores are selected for geometric verification, and a final score is computed, measuring how many and how well query features align with those from the candidate.

We believe that it is important to distinguish systems designed for high quality but where the cost per document is less of a factor, and systems which sacrifice quality in order to go to an extreme scale. One important knob for this is feature counts and vocabulary size.

When scaling such an approach to billions of images, one of two following problems occur, depending on the database density. On one hand, if the feature count per image is high and the vocabulary small, the index density is high and the number of "random" hits in the first stage results in a large number of candidate documents for which the match geometry would ideally be verified. This verification can become expensive, since it typically involves fetching additional data for each tested document. If, on the other hand, the feature count per document is low and the vocabulary size is large, the density is low, and the average number of hits per document will be small, making the vote accumulator very sparse. We show that both low and high densities cause problems for such approaches; in the former case because one has to track many zeroes, and in the latter because the fastest voting structures use too much memory and one has to fall back to sparser, slower ones.

To address these two problems, we propose a novel scoring method that unifies candidate extraction and geometric verification. Our approach efficiently rejects candidates with less than four matches, and validates the geometry of all remaining candidates. The final score is computed in a single step, considering a single document at a time, with the geometry of all its matches, as opposed to pre-scoring with a weighted hit count. In text retrieval, these two approaches are called Document at a Time (DAAT) and Term at a Time (TAAT) [14], or term-ordered evaluation and document-ordered evaluation [15].

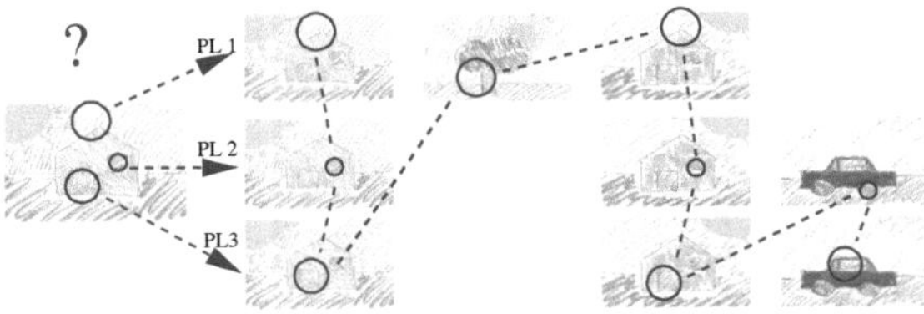

Fig. 2. Document at a Time (DAAT) evaluation: Posting lists are traversed in parallel, the next element is always lowest document identifiers of the remaining documents. Geometric verification can be done for all images with a minimal number of matches.

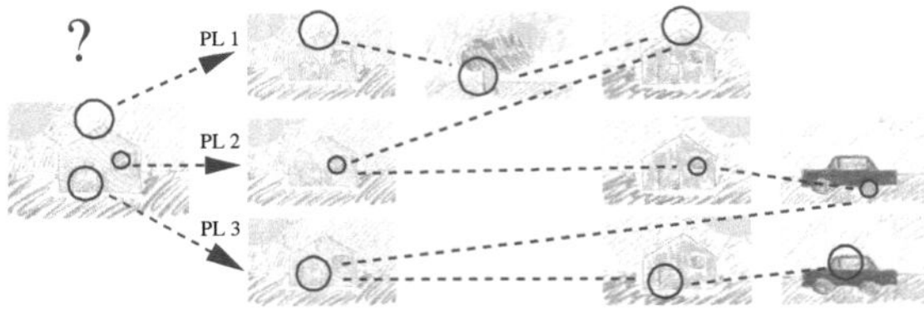

Fig. 3. Term at a Time (TAAT) evaluation: Posting lists are traversed one by one; scores are usually computed by accumulation

To implement our DAAT approach in a computationally efficient manner, we propose a new data structure we call the *counting min-tree* (CMT). It can be used to merge a set of sorted posting lists and count how many lists each document appears in. The counting min-tree allows our DAAT approach to quickly process large databases while extracting the data needed for geometric verification for all remaining candidates.

We compare the performance of TAAT, heap-based DAAT, and CMT-based DAAT under varying database density. We show that our counting min-tree outperforms other approaches.

We validate our approach on a system that quickly retrieves images from an index containing more than 90 billion images. The images were obtained by crawling the web.

2 Related Work

Document at a Time scoring was introduced in 1995[14] for text search and permits retrieval-time checking of the relative position of the query terms in the result. Kaskiel et al. [15] showed that document-ordered query processing is efficient for retrieving text passages. Word positioning in text is the one-dimensional equivalent of geometric consistency testing between images.

Sivic and Zisserman [1] combined the invariance of local features [16] with conventional retrieval techniques applied to vector-quantized SIFT [17] descriptors. The quantization speed and vocabulary size has been significantly improved by using hierarchical k-means [5] or faster search strategies, such as a kd-tree over the k-means trained clusters [6]. Similarly, the introduction of soft assignment [4, 6] has increased matching power, at the expense of additional processing.

Several authors have tried to enforce geometric consistency of the matches using multiple bins during voting [2, 18, 19]. However, the types of geometric constraints which can be enforced this way are relatively limited compared to the exhaustive geometric verification of DAAT.

Jegou et al [2] constructed a local Hamming embedding for each posting list to find the best matches within the posting list at query time. It improves quality and reduces CPU load by scoring fewer images, at the cost of increased memory usage. This approach can be combined with DAAT scoring, and will lower the index density without the drawbacks of a larger vocabulary.

2.1 TAAT scoring variants

TAAT scoring is usually implemented as score accumulation into a vector or a map. It can be implemented using pure counts or by using weights and multiple bins.

Hit Counting: The simplest possible TAAT scoring scheme is hit counting. We will use this scoring variant in the timing experiments on synthetic data.

In order to implement this, we invert the document database to a set of posting lists. At scoring time we then go over the posting lists associated with the features in the query and for each document mentioned in a posting list, we increment the corresponding entry in the accumulator.

TF-IDF Scoring: One way of how to do TF-IDF (Term-Frequency/Inverse Document Frequency) scoring for images is laid out in Section 4 of [5]. Basically, the addition from simple hit counting is that each posting list has a weight and each document a normalizer.

In order to use TF-IDF the document weights have to be kept in memory or be attached to the posting lists. For very large indexes, both options are inconvenient, either due to memory used or a significant increase in posting list sizes.

3 Approach

In this section, we present our approach to large-scale image retrieval.

Feature Detection and Quantization: We believe that the system described will work with any quantized local features framework. Our system considers local maxima of Laplacian of Gaussian as features [20]. It then describes each feature using a descriptor similar to the one presented in [21], where we have removed rotational invariance.

Given a training set of such descriptors, a vocabulary of 5 million vectors for LoG maximums and 5 million vectors for LoG minimums is trained using k-means. At runtime, quantization is achieved using a kd-tree that accelerates the search for the appropriate quantization vector [6].

Indexing: Our indexing process produces an inverted index that allows fast retrieval. First features are extracted and quantized from the database images, yielding sets of quantization value, position and scale. The index is then grouped by quantization value. As a result, each quantization value is linked to a set of entries. Each entry has a document identifier, a normalized image position, and a normalized scale. Within each posting list, entries are sorted by document identifier.

3.1 Retrieval and document at a time scoring

Given a query image, our system extracts and quantizes features. Then, it fetches the posting lists corresponding to these features. The counting min-tree presented in the next paragraph merges the posting lists. It scans the posting lists and groups all matches for each document, one document a time. If an image has fewer than four hits, it is discarded immediately. Otherwise, the geometric consistency of matches is verified, yielding the final score for this image. Then, the counting min-tree provides matches for the next document, and scoring continues.

The system finally sorts results based on their score and returns the best matches.

Our geometric verifier computes a four parameter transformation consisting of stretch and translation along the x- and y-axes, using RANSAC [22] to eliminate outliers, the minimal set for computing such a transformation is two points. The verification uses several rejection criteria: The location and scale of features must match the computed transformation and the transformation must be reasonable. All tests are applied in both transformation directions. Since feature location and scale are embedded in the posting lists, this geometric verification does not require any additional data to be fetched or features to be matched. This makes it very fast, which allows for exhaustive geometric verification.

3.2 Counting Min-Tree

The task of the counting min-tree is to merge the posting lists triggered by the query image. In other words, it groups the information from the posting lists document. The task is made easier by the fact that the posting lists are already sorted by document identifier.

Merging k sorted lists, containing a total of n elements, can be done in $O(n \log(k))$ time by using a binary min-heap. The heap keeps track of which list to take the next element from, as in the merge phase of a merge sort [23].

However, updating a heap for each element is costly in terms of CPU power. Instead, we propose a novel structure called a *counting min-tree*, based on the existing but somewhat lesser-known min-tree structure, sometimes also called a winner tree.

The min-tree, like the min-heap, is realized using a binary tree, but differs from the heap in that it only stores elements in the leaf nodes, of which there is a fixed number—one for each posting list triggered by the query. For simplicity, we use a complete binary tree, so that the number of nodes is always a power of

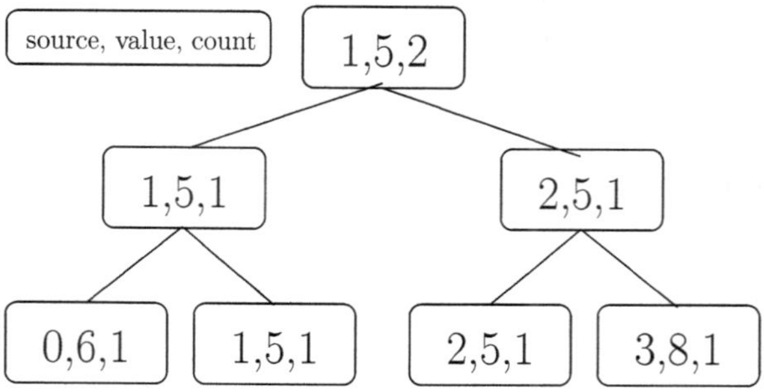

Fig. 4. The counting min-tree maintains a state where each node remembers where its information came from, the value and the count. Every time we remove the element from the root, we step the posting list associated with the current source and propagate the information from the leaf all the way up to the root.

two, with the extra nodes always having a special highest "end-of-file" document identifier.

Each inner node contains the smallest document identifier of its two children, as well as an index into which leaf this document identifier comes from. Therefore, the root element identifies both the least-advanced posting list and its document identifier, allowing for immediate identification of which posting list to step.

We further augment the min-tree into a counting min-tree by including a count in each inner node. The count contains how many leaf nodes below it has the given document identifier; for instance, if an inner node has two leaves below it with document identifiers 100 and 200, its document identifier will be 100 and the count 1, but if the leaves' document identifiers are 100 and 100, the inner node will have a document identifier of 100 and a count of 2.

The count is, like the document identifier, propagated up the tree all the way to the root. The root will then, in turn, not only contain the document identifier of the least-advanced posting lists and its index, but also how many other posting lists point to the same document identifier. Identifying candidates for scoring then simply amounts to looking at the root node; if its count is at least four, we have a candidate for scoring, and if not, we can continue stepping the least-advanced posting list.

The counting min-tree has two main advantages over a heap. First, it is significantly faster, and already at the first hit on a document we know how many hits the document will have. Second, knowing the number of hits without having to advance over all the hits simplifies the logic of collecting geometry data from the posting lists.

4 Scaling Analysis

In this section, we first define a density index. We then study the behavior of several algorithms when this density changes. To do so, we use a synthetic benchmark. We show that, under conditions necessary for large-scale systems, our counting min-tree outperforms other solutions.

4.1 Index Density

In inverted index-based systems, the retrieval computation burden is proportional to the number of posting list entries the system has to process for a given query.

In order to estimate the number of elements scanned during a single query, let N be the number of documents in the database, n_q the number of features in the query image, n_d the average number of features per indexed document, and V the vocabulary size. For simplicity, and without loss of generality, we use in the experiments $n_q = n_d$. We denote the index imbalance factor [2, 24]

$$u = V \sum_{i=1}^{V} p_i^2 , \tag{1}$$

where p_i is the fraction of features quantized to word i. Using Chebyshev's sum inequality, we see that u has a lower bound of 1, reached when $p_i = 1/V$.

We define the index density

$$D = \frac{u n_q n_d}{V} . \tag{2}$$

The number of elements the system has to process for a query is

$$M = N \frac{u n_q n_d}{V} = ND . \tag{3}$$

On average, $M = ND$ is the number of matches between query and indexed features.

The value D can be used to categorize systems as sparse or dense. A high density factor improves retrieval at the cost of a heavier computation and storage burden. A sparse index leads to a lighter system with a potentially lower recall.

The time taken by the retrieval stage is M/r, where r is the number of entries the system processes per second.

In the following, we measure the process rate r of several algorithms, when processing databases of different sizes (N) and densities (D).

4.2 Synthetic Experiment

In order to compare the raw speed of several different scoring strategies, we define a synthetic experiment with a database of N synthesized documents, each with n random features from a vocabulary of size V. The query is a synthesized document with n features drawn from the same uniform distribution. The scoring task is to retrieve from the database all the documents with at least four hits.

We evaluated two DAAT implementations and two TAAT ones:

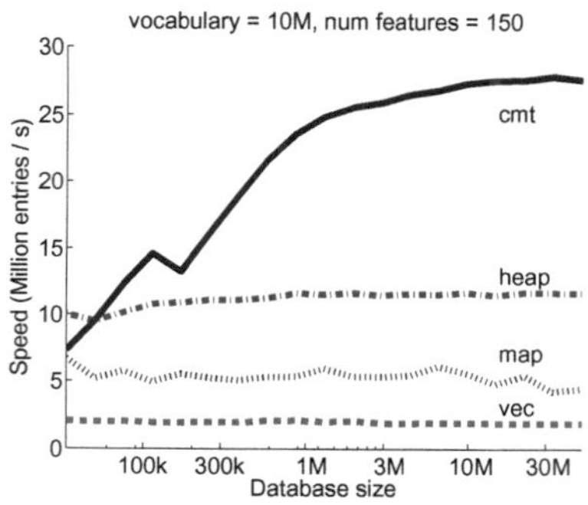

Fig. 5. On synthetic data and a sparse setup with a large vocabulary ($10M$) and a small feature count (150), the advantage of using the counting min tree (CMT) is growing with increased database size

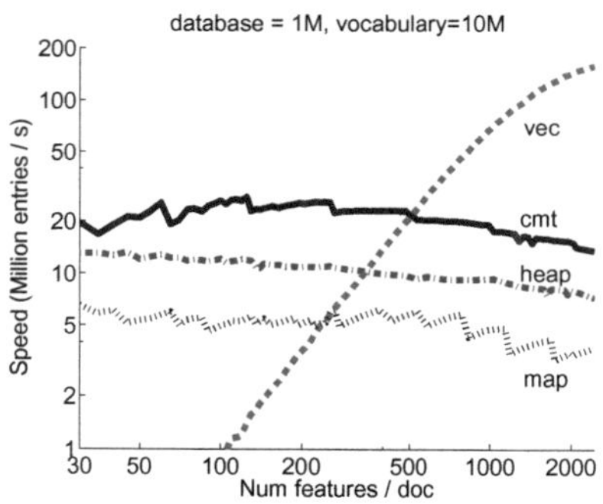

Fig. 6. On synthetic data, the counting min-tree (CMT) is the fastest option for pure hit-counting as long as the problem remains sparse. Above a certain density voting into a vector becomes faster.

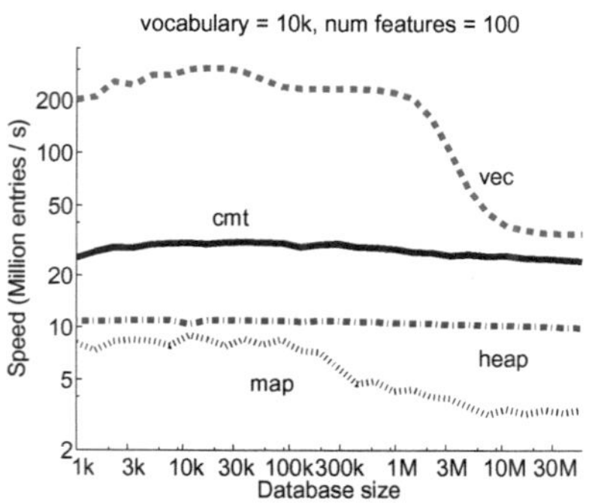

Fig. 7. On synthetic data and very dense setup with a very small vocabulary (10k) and a small feature count (100), the vector based hit counter has a massive advantage in terms of raw speed

CMT DAAT using a counting min-tree.
heap DAAT implemented using a heap.
map TAAT with a sparse vote accumulator, implemented using a hash table [1].
vec TAAT with a dense vote accumulator, implemented using an array of 8-bit integers[2]

For each algorithm, we measure the number r of posting list entries processed per second in dense and sparse scenarios. For both TAAT algorithms, r includes the time required to vote and the time to scan the accumulator for documents with at least four hits. The DAAT algorithms achieve the same task in a single pass.

We compiled our benchmark with GCC 4.4.3, and ran it in 64-bit mode on one core of an Intel E6600 2.4GHz CPU.

The goal of our first experiment is to evaluate how the algorithms behave when database density changes. In this scenario, the database size is $N = 1$ million images. The vocabulary contains 10 million words, as for the real data experiment of Section 5. The number of features per image is equal for both query and reference images: $n_d = n_q = n$. We let n vary from 30 to 2000. By doing so, we change the index density.

Our second experiment concentrates on the sparse case. The vocabulary has 10 million words. The number of features is $n = 150$. This configuration matches the one of our real data experiment.

The third scenario considers a high density case: the vocabulary has 10k words. The number of features per image is set to $n = 100$. This configuration is very costly for large-scale databases, due to the number of entries processed. However, the tested algorithms, exhibit interesting behaviors in these conditions, which are presented next.

4.3 Synthetic Results

The advantage of DAAT scoring over TAAT scoring depends on the sparsity of the problem.

Figure 6 shows how algorithms behaves when the database density changes. When the index is dense, TAAT scoring with a dense accumulator outperforms other methods. When the density is low, as required for large scale databases, the counting min-tree is faster. The counting min-tree is almost always faster than heap-based DAAT which is always faster than TAAT implemented with a hash table. The counting min-tree requires a small, constant time initialization. That explains why its performance degrade compared to other methods when processing extremely short posting lists. The results of this experiment clearly show that one should consider the importance of database density when designing a vocabulary-based image retrieval system.

[1] We use an unordered_map<uint32, int>, which is new for C++11. We found that it outperforms map<uint32, int> and hash_map<uint32, int> in all cases.

[2] For small databases 32-bit integers are slightly faster, but they scale less well.

Figure 5 depicts the sparse database scenario. It shows that the dense accumulator for TAAT is the slowest option. This is because reading out the results and resetting the vector become computationally heavy $O(N)$ compared to traversing the posting lists $O(Nn^2/V)$. A sparse accumulator is a significantly faster option, but it is remains slower than DAAT approaches. The rate at which both TAAT implementations process hits remain roughly constant with respect to the database size. In this sparse database scenario, DAAT scoring outperforms vector based TAAT scoring, since they avoid the $O(N)$ step of finding all elements with a sufficient score in a vector.

Figure 7 shows results of the dense index experiment. In these conditions, TAAT with a dense accumulator outperforms other methods since the $O(N)$ cost of finding the matches in the accumulator is majored by the $O(Nn^2/V)$ cost for processing the posting lists.

By dividing a large problem into smaller sub-problems it is possible to take the highest speed of each method and linearize to larger problems. This also makes it possible to keep the memory requirements of the vector and map based scorers at a reasonable level.

5 Proof of Concept on Real Data

In order to show that this can run at scale we used the method described above build a low invariance index of 94 billion images obtained as part of a large web-crawl. This means that many of the images are small and that there is a high number of near-duplicates in the set, however, the set is still amazingly rich and provides an extraordinary coverage of what is on the internet.

We extracted quantized features for 94 billion images. For each image we extracted (up to) 200 (average 135) non-rotational invariant features and quantized using 10M cells. This gives a total count of $1.3 \cdot 10^{13}$ features, with a feature distribution very close to random which was compressed to $63TB$ with a per feature cost of 5.4 bytes. This feature processing was run integrated with other feature processing on a very large cloud.

We wrote a single posting-list index over these features to a networked file system.

To query against the index, we set up a single machine to which we send the quantized features of the query image. The query is processed in three stages: In the first stage, the posting lists are fetched from the networked storage and decompressed. In the second stage, we advance the posting lists in DAAT-order using a counting min-tree, and documents with at least four hits are scored by geometric consistency. In the last stage, we sort the results by score and return the top 1000 results to the caller.

Unfortunately the time to fetch and decompress is larger than the actual time needed for scoring. For a typical 100 feature query we need to fetch and decompress 65M entries (that is 350MB) which takes just below 2 seconds. The scoring parallelizes very well and runs at around 12.5M entries per core-second on eight cores, for a scoring time of around 0.7 seconds.

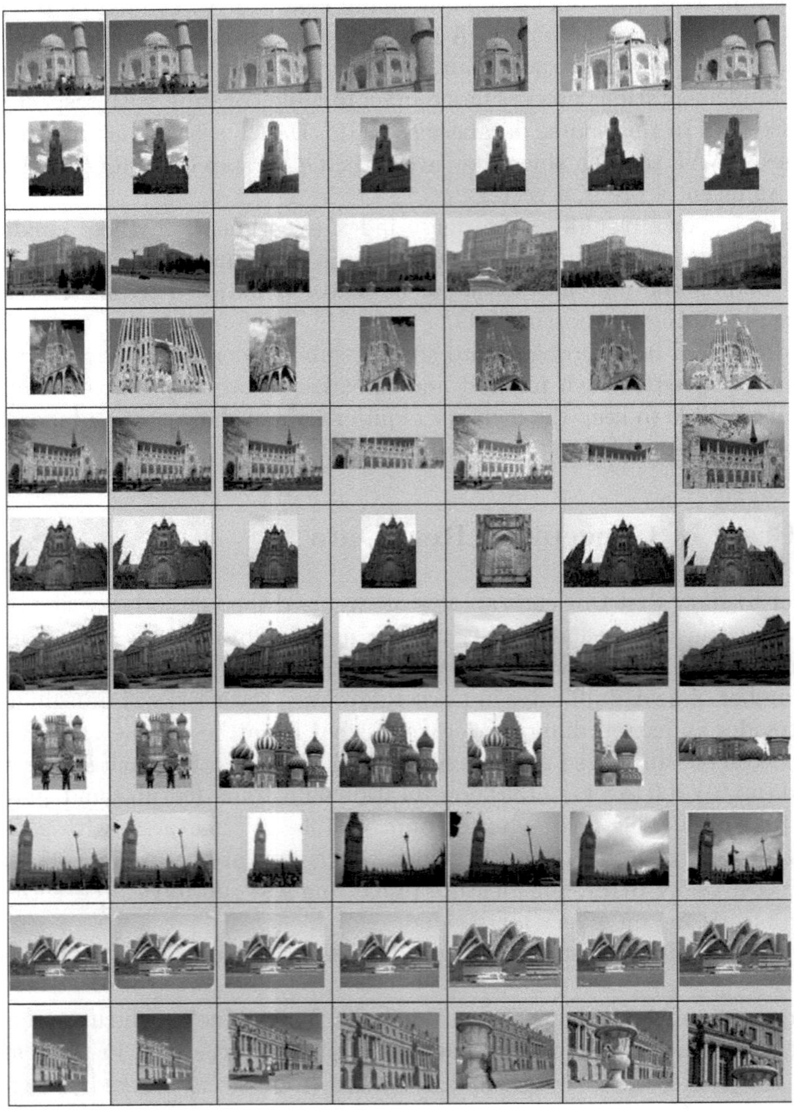

Fig. 8. The query is in the first column; the remaining columns are the first few results in score order. From top to bottom: The Taj Mahal, the Belfry of Bruges, the Palace of the Romanian Parliament, La Sagrada Familia, Notre Dame, St. Vitus Cathedral, the Royal Palace of Brussels, Saint Basil's Cathedral, Big Ben, the Sydney Opera House, and the Versailles. Matching famous landmarks is rather easy since the database contains a very large number of images of these so recall does not have to be perfect.

Fig. 9. Common classes of mismatches. Faces matches other faces, round object match round objects and text matches text.

The difference in scoring speed from the synthetic experiment mainly comes from the fact that in the synthetic experiment the posting lists are zero terminated 32 bit integer arrays while we here deal with more complicated structures which handle 64 bit docids and also hold payloads. Another source of slowdown is that the scoring in the synthetic experiment was simple hit-count scoring while we here do far more complicated scoring. However, since we are considerably much faster than the network, we have demonstrated that we can keep up with the data feed. A system running at 30M entries per core-second would need 160MB/s input per core to stay fed, a rate which would be hard to sustain from any other source than RAM. Already at you need almost 70MB/s per core.

Sharding the system will change the amount of data which needs to be processed per machine but will not change the balance between processing power and io-needs.

The experimental system has considerable amounts of RAM but only requires the memory needed to hold the posting lists relevant for the current query.

Quality Problems Driven By Scale: When running all-against-all on the UKY [5] database, a single false positive corresponds to a pairwise false positive rate of 10^{-8}. With a larger database, this rate corresponds to ten false positives per query per per billion images in the database.

Studying the mismatches on a very large image database is instructive, and most fall into one of four categories: faces, round objects, text and watermarks. In order to prepare Figures 9, we have increased the number of query features in order to make these cases clearer.

If You Have the Images, You Can Index Them: Even though the task of indexing billions of images might sound gigantic, it is worth pointing out that the task of creating an index of this type is in most cases much smaller than the task of collecting the images.

Given a feature detector, descriptor, and quantization pipeline running at 30 images per second, each CPU core can index about three million images per day. The highly parallel nature of the computation and the dropping price of multi-core systems makes it affordable to scale to very large corpora.

6 Conclusions

We have proposed a DAAT approach to image retrieval, efficiently implemented using a counting min-tree. Our method verifies the geometry of every candidate in a single pass. Our proof of concept setup is able to query a database of more than 90 billion images in a few seconds.

By studying the speed of multiple algorithms as a function of the database density, we have shown that our approach efficiently handles the extreme scoring sparsity required to query very large databases, at an acceptable cost.

It was our plan to show a great win from geometric scoring of all possible hits, however, for the hit-density which we have in our proof of concept system there are very few "random" documents with at least four hits and it would have been affordable to fetch these and verify. We suspect that there would be a clear win for a system operating in a denser setting.

It is our hope that this work will have demonstrated that if you can acquire an image collection, then the step to indexing it is not very far.

References

1. Sivic, J., Zisserman, A.: Video Google: A text retrieval approach to object matching in videos. In: ICCV (2003)
2. Jegou, H., Douze, M., Schmid, C.: Hamming Embedding and Weak Geometric Consistency for Large Scale Image Search. In: Forsyth, D., Torr, P., Zisserman, A. (eds.) ECCV 2008, Part I. LNCS, vol. 5302, pp. 304–317. Springer, Heidelberg (2008)
3. Jegou, H., Schmid, C., Harzallah, H., Verbeek, J.: Accurate image search using the contextual dissimilarity measure. PAMI 32, 2–11 (2009)
4. Schindler, G., Brown, M., Szeliski, R.: City-scale location recognition. In: CVPR (2007)
5. Nistér, D., Stewénius, H.: Scalable recognition with a vocabulary tree. In: CVPR (2006)
6. Philbin, J., Chum, O., Isard, M., Sivic, J., Zisserman, A.: Object retrieval with large vocabularies and fast spatial matching. In: CVPR (2007)
7. Philbin, J., Isard, M., Sivic, J., Zisserman, A.: Descriptor learning for efficient retrieval. In: ECCV (2010)
8. Inria, searching for similar images in a database of 10 million images - example queries, `http://bigimbaz.inrialpes.fr/`
9. Google Goggles, `http://www.google.com/mobile/goggles/`
10. Google. Search By Image, `http://www.google.com/insidesearch/searchbyimage.html`
11. Baidu. Search by Image, `http://stu.baidu.com/`
12. Sogou. Search by Image, `http://pic.sogou.com/`
13. TinEye blog, `http://blog.tineye.com/`

14. Turtle, H., Flood, J.: Query evaluation: strategies and optimizations. Information Processing & Management 31, 831–850 (1995)
15. Kaszkiel, M., Zobel, J., Sacks-davis, R.: Efficient passage ranking for document databases. ACM Transactions on Information Systems 17, 406–439 (1999)
16. Matas, J., Chum, O., Urban, M., Pajdla, T.: Robust wide-baseline stereo from maximally stable extremal regions. Image and Vision Computing 22, 761–767 (2004)
17. Lowe, D.: Distinctive image features from scale-invariant keypoints. IJCV 60, 91–110 (2004)
18. Lin, Z., Brandt, J.: A Local Bag-of-Features Model for Large-Scale Object Retrieval. In: Daniilidis, K., Maragos, P., Paragios, N. (eds.) ECCV 2010, Part VI. LNCS, vol. 6316, pp. 294–308. Springer, Heidelberg (2010)
19. Zhang, Y., Jia, Z., Chen, T.: Image retrieval with geometry-preserving visual phrases. In: CVPR (2011)
20. Mikolajczyk, K., Schmid, C.: An Affine Invariant Interest Point Detector. In: Heyden, A., Sparr, G., Nielsen, M., Johansen, P. (eds.) ECCV 2002, Part I. LNCS, vol. 2350, pp. 128–142. Springer, Heidelberg (2002)
21. Zheng, Y.T., Zhao, M., Song, Y., Adam, H., Buddemeier, U., Bissacco, A., Brucher, F., Chua, T.S., Neven, H.: Tour the world: Building a web-scale landmark recognition engine. In: CVPR (2009)
22. Fischler, M., Bolles, R.: Random sample consensus: A paradigm for model fitting with applications to image analysis and automated cartography. Communications of the ACM 24, 381–395 (1981)
23. Knuth, D.E.: The Art of Computer Programming, vol. III: Sorting and Searching, 2nd edn. (1998)
24. Fraundorfer, F., Stewénius, H., Nistér, D.: A binning scheme for fast hard drive based image search. In: CVPR (2007)

Scene Aligned Pooling for Complex Video Recognition

Liangliang Cao[1], Yadong Mu[2], Apostol Natsev[3], Shih-Fu Chang[2], Gang Hua[4], and John R. Smith[1,*]

[1] IBM T. J. Watson Research Center
{liangliang.cao,jsmith}@us.ibm.com
[2] Dept. Electrical Engineering, Columbia University
{muyadong,sfchang}@ee.columbia.edu
[3] Google Research
natsev@google.com
[4] Dept. Computer Science, Stevens Institute of Technology
ghua@stevens.edu

Abstract. Real-world videos often contain dynamic backgrounds and evolving people activities, especially for those web videos generated by users in unconstrained scenarios. This paper proposes a new visual representation, namely scene aligned pooling, for the task of event recognition in complex videos. Based on the observation that a video clip is often composed with shots of different scenes, the key idea of scene aligned pooling is to decompose any video features into concurrent scene components, and to construct classification models adaptive to different scenes. The experiments on two large scale real-world datasets including the TRECVID Multimedia Event Detection 2011 and the Human Motion Recognition Databases (HMDB) show that our new visual representation can consistently improve various kinds of visual features such as different low-level color and texture features, or middle-level histogram of local descriptors such as SIFT, or space-time interest points, and high level semantic model features, by a significant margin. For example, we improve the-state-of-the-art accuracy on HMDB dataset by 20% in terms of accuracy.

1 Introduction

The problem of video event recognition is attracting more and more attention in recent years. This is largely due to two reasons: On one hand, the popularity of video cameras makes it possible for a consumer to record or compose video clips easily. On the other hand, the emergence of social media websites including Youtube, Facebook has aggregated a large amount of online video corpus, which plays a major role in attracting Web users. For example, Youtube hosts more than 100 million videos and serves 1 billion video requests per day. Such a large amount of video data has never been available until today. How to understand the contents of these videos has become an important challenge for computer vision research.

The problem of video event recognition is the key to many applications, including personalized video recommendation, social event mining, and large scale video library

* Gang Hua participated in this project while working for IBM as a visiting researcher. Apostol Natsev was with IBM Watson Research Center when most of this work was performed.

A. Fitzgibbon et al. (Eds.): ECCV 2012, Part II, LNCS 7573, pp. 688–701, 2012.

Fig. 1. Complex videos are usually composed of different scenes. (a) Key frames in a video of wedding ceremony (b) Key frames in a video of parkour activities.

indexing. The definition of "event" generalizes previous studies of simple human actions in a constrained environment [1] [2], or highly distinguishable professional activities in Olympic game or TV channels [3] [4]. In this paper, an event can be either a complicated human activity (e.g., kiss, parade, making a sandwich), or composite multimedia semantics (e.g., birthday party, wedding ceremony). Compared with simple human actions, the events in these complex videos are more attractive, since Web users enjoy those videos with rich semantics but feel bored about simple ones. A real world video often contains heterogeneous backgrounds and different viewpoints, and captures diversified contents or evolving human activities. Fig. 1 illustrates some exemplar videos of complex event (e.g., wedding ceremony and parkour), which are obviously more complicated than simple actions like running or walking.

To study the problem of event recognition in complex videos, we observe that a video clip is composed with shots of different scenes. In this paper we refer "scene" to fine-grained characteristics of video environmental semantics. Both psychological and biological evidences [5] [6] revealed that human vision can easily distinguish different scenes and the results of scene recognition can further help general image understanding. Motivated by these psychological theories, we believe scene information is a good cue to understand complex video events.

The key idea of our method is to use scene information to guide the pooling operation of video features. Traditional pooling is an operation of averaging the feature vectors within a spatial neighborhood of images [7]. In this paper, we aggregate video features into concurrent scene components, and then develop scene-dependent modules for the classification task. Since our new model is designed to capture the visual information in concurrent scenes, we name this new model as *Scene Aligned Pooling* (SAP). The advantages of our scene aligned pooling are four-folds: (1) This new visual representation naturally captures diverse video contents and dynamic semantics based on scene structure. (2) SAP can be applied to various visual features and improve their performance. (3) SAP represents videos as feature vectors of fixed dimensions, and the model is free from the concerns of video length or assumptions on temporal evolvement. (4) We employ a soft weighting strategy named concurrent vector quantization for pooling different scene components, which is not only robust to noise but also able to handle the scenario with overlapped scenes.

2 Related Works

A real world video always conveys rich information, and it is a challenging task to capture such rich information for video event analysis. Existing studies [1] [2] [8] [3] consider human actions in specified scenarios or well-controlled environment. However, there have been not enough studies on recognizing unconstrained video or user generated video from online websites. Compared with traditional human action datasets, these real world videos are more difficult to handle since they contain longer video sequences and diversified scenes. Moreover, when those real world videos contain non-static cluttered background, the popularly used motion-dependent features [9] [10] will not work well since there are a lot of false detections due to the background motion.

Since video event classification is still in its early stage, it is desirable to learn from successful image classification techniques. As argued in [11], a lot of recent progresses in image recognition can be viewed as a combination of alternating series of coding and spatial pooling steps. Average pooling [7] tries to average feature vectors within a spatial neighborhood. Bag-of-words model can be viewed as a special case of average pooling. Max pooling is found to be useful for sparse coding features [12]. Jégou *et al.*developed a new image descriptor called VLAD by pooling local descriptors [13]. Lazebnik *et al.*proposed spatial pyramid matching (SPM) kernel [14], which can be viewed as a pooling method based on the spatial layout of images. This idea is recently generalized in [15], which enlarges the spatial bins with feature space clustering. The difference between this paper and previous image pooling methods is three-fold: (1) [15] uses either hard VQ or sparse coding, which usually requires a large size of codebook. This submission chooses only codebook size =16, using the weights of harmonic average. (2) [15] only pools the coding weights or quantized indices, while we pool the feature vectors. (3) [15] uses either max pooling or average pooling, while we compute the weighted average.

Our work is also motivated by the studies in scene recognition. A number of studies [16] [17] [14] have been carried out to classify natural scenes. Later studies explore various applications of scene recognition. Russell *et al.*[18] employed scene representation for object retrieval. Many research studies show empirical success in learning image representation within similar scenes [19] [18]. Li and Fei-Fei [20] and later Marszalek *et al.*[21] combine scene classifiers to benefit the task of object recognition or activity recognition. However, these approaches treat scene classifiers as an independent component, and require a lot of scene labels to train the scene classifiers. Unlike their method, this paper employs scenes as the pooling context, and only use scene features without the requirement of scene labels.

3 Scene Aligned Pooling

3.1 Model

A video is comprised of a sequence of frames. Following the extensive research in image recognition, we can represent frames with various feature vectors, including color histogram, LBP, texture, or SIFT histogram. Consider a video $X = [x_1, \cdots, x_{Tx}]$, where $1 \leq t \leq Tx$ stands for the index of frames or key frames, x_t corresponds to a feature vector. Note that the number of frames is not consistent across different videos.

According to the representer theorem [22], the classifier will be represented by kernel distances $K(X,Y)$ between two videos X and Y. Since X and Y may contain different number of frames, traditional methods usually compute the kernel by averaging the frame features

$$K(X,Y) = \kappa(\frac{1}{\rho_x}\sum_{t=1}^{Tx} x_t, \frac{1}{\rho_y}\sum_{t=1}^{Ty} y_t), \tag{1}$$

where κ is a kernel function between two vectors, x_t and y_t are the frame level feature vectors, ρ_x and ρ_y are the normalization factors. For example, we can choose $\rho_x = ||\sum_{t=1}^{Tx} x_t||$.

Eq (1) is widely used with different features. In recently years, many systems use bag of words model for video recognition, which fundamentally is to average the histogram features across different frames. The limitation of eq (1) is that it overlooks the diversity of video contents. The learned classification model treats all the frames using the same mechanism. If a video event contains non-uniformed backgrounds, averaging the frame features will inevitably blur the discriminant features and hence reduce the recognition performance.

In this paper, we consider the scenario where a video contains K scenes. Let s_t be the random variable for scene type of frame t, where $1 \leq s_t \leq K$. Note $p^k(x_t) = P(s_t = k|x_t)$ satisfies the constraint $\sum_k p^k(x_t) = 1$. With $p^k(x_t)$ we can redefine the kernel distance between two videos

$$K(X,Y) = \sum_{k=1}^{K} \kappa(\frac{1}{\rho_x^k}\sum_{t=1}^{Tx} p^k(x_t)x_t, \frac{1}{\rho_y^k}\sum_{t=1}^{Ty} p^k(y_t)y_t). \tag{2}$$

To make the representation clearer, we introduce a new variable named *scene component* which combines the outputs of all video frames by

$$s^k = \sum_{t=1}^{Tx} p^k(x_t)x_t, \quad r^k = \sum_{t=1}^{Ty} p^k(y_t)y_t. \tag{3}$$

The kernel becomes

$$K(X,Y) = \sum_{k=1}^{K} \kappa(\frac{1}{||s^k||}s^k, \frac{1}{||r^k||}r^k). \tag{4}$$

This new representation aligned videos of different length by K types of scenes, and we call this method *Scene Aligned Pooling* (SAP). It is easy to see that the average pooling

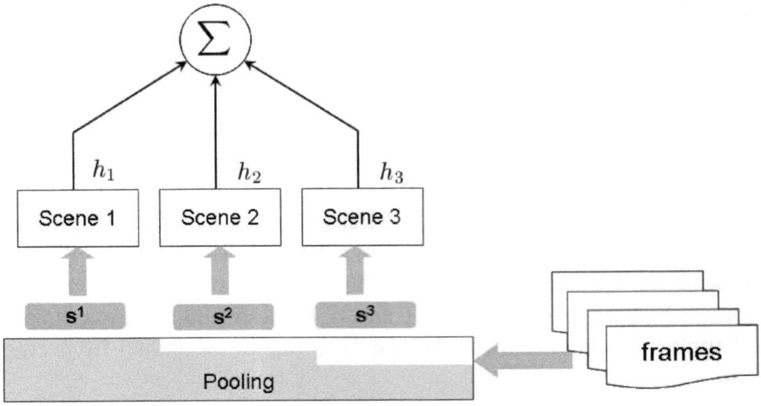

Fig. 2. An practical viewpoint for SAP model

is a special case of SAP with $K = 1$. The motivation of SAP is to employ multiple scenes to represent the diversified video contents.

It is interesting to compare our formulation with Lazebnik *et al.*'s Spatial Pyramid Matching (SPM) [14]. In summary, SAP composes kernels over the domain of semantic scenes, while Lazebnik's SPM builds kernels over spatial grids. However, there are significant differences between SPM and SAP. SAP works in a semantic scene domain with no clear boundaries. SPM works in spatial domain where we can use grids to explicitly separate one image into several parts. As a result, we do not explore the pyramid structures in SAP due to the ambiguous boundaries in video domain. Instead, we choose concurrent vectorization to perform soft weighted assignment, while SPM is based on hard assignments. Table 1 summarizes the differences between SAP and SPM.

Table 1. Comparing SAP with Spatial Pyramid Matching

	Subject	Domain	Grid	Assignment
SAP	video	scene	×	soft
SPM[14]	image	spatial	✓	hard

To provide more insights for the SAP model, we consider the linear classifier corresponding to (4). The linear classifier can be represented as

$$H(X) = \sum_{t=1}^{Tx} \sum_{k=1}^{K} p^k(x_t) w_k^T x_t = \sum_{k=1}^{K} w_k^T s^k \tag{5}$$

It is easy to see that SAP leads to different models for different scene components and combine the estimations from multiple scenes into the final model. Fig. 2 illustrates the idea for SAP classifier.

The biggest advantage of scene component representation is that it makes the training easier. We can first concatenate all the K scene components as a long vector,

$$S = [s^1, s^2, \cdots, s^K]$$

and learn a linear function $H(S) = w^T S + b$. In practice, we enforce $l_2$normalization before training by $S = [\frac{1}{||s^1||_2} s^1, \frac{1}{||s^2||_2} s^2, \cdots, \frac{1}{||s^K||_2} s^K]$. In this way, we obtain the long linear coefficients as a whole. Due to the recent advances in linear model training [23], it has become pretty efficient to learn linear SVMs from high dimensional large scale data, so that training using scene component will not be difficult.

3.2 Implementation

To implement the computation of scene component $s^k = \sum_{t=1}^{T} p^k(x_t)x_t$, in fact what we need to do is to map each frame feature x_t into different scenes

$$x_t \to [p_t^1 x_t, p_t^2 x_t, \cdots, p_t^K x_t], \tag{6}$$

with the constraint $\sum_k p_t^k = 1$. From eqs (3) and (6) we can easily see that our new model is a pooling method. The unique characteristic of our method is that our pooling weights p_t^k are based on scene semantics. That is why we call our method "scene aligned pooling". We will explain how to compute p_t^k in the following.

Our method of modeling p_t^k is very easy to implement. Following the previous studies [16] [18] [24], we use GIST features to represent the scene. Some may argue that we might use the same feature as frame feature vector x to compute the scene, however, as we shown later, the pooling weights are computed based on Euclidean distance, which is not reliable for sparse histogram features like SIFT. As our scene modeling feature, GIST is easy to compute and especially good at describing scenes [16]. Given all the training data, we compute the GIST features and cluster them into K centers using unsupervised K-means. The K center is represented as $g_c^1, g_c^2, \cdots, g_c^K$. To compute the pooling weight $p^k(x_t)$, we extract the GIST feature vector g_t for every frame t. The pooling weight is based on the comparison of $\{g_c^k\}$ and g_t.

The naive way to compute the pooling weight is by vector quantization (VQ), which forces all but one $p^k(x_t)$ to be zero. However, VQ is well-known to be sensitive to noises. Moreover, the hard assignment of VQ cannot capture the overlapping nature of evolving video scenes and hence works poorly. VQ is designed to minimize the quantization error. Suppose G is the set of GIST features, this paper considers a different criteria by

$$C = \sum_{g \in G} HA(g) = \sum_{g \in G} \left(\frac{1}{K} \sum_{k=1}^{K} \frac{1}{||g - g_c^k||} \right)^{-1},$$

where HA denotes the harmonic average proposed by Zhang *et al.*[25]. To study the minimization condition, we let $\frac{\partial}{\partial \mathbf{m}_k} C_2 = \mathbf{0}$, which leads to

$$g_c^k = \sum_{g \in G} w_g^k g, \quad w.t. \quad w_g^k \propto \frac{1}{||g - g_c^k||^3}.$$

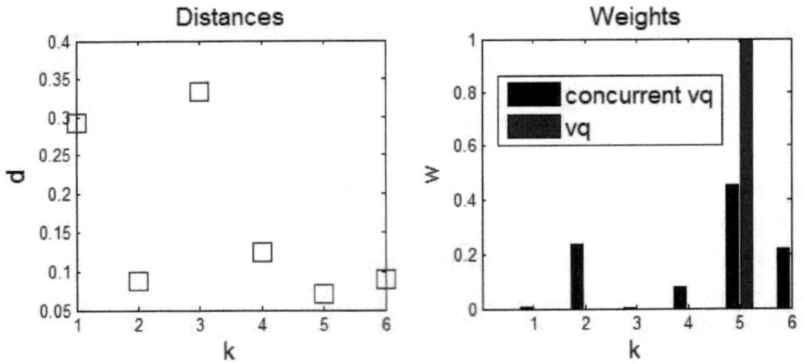

Fig. 3. Differences between concurrent VQ and VQ. Left: an exemplar of $d_t^1, \cdot, d_t^K$ ($K = 6$ in this toy example). Right: the weights from vector quantization and concurrent vector quantization.

To be consistent to the contribution of g_t for harmonic average, we choose our pooling weights as

$$d_k^t = ||g_t - g_c^k||$$
$$p_t^k = \frac{1/(d_t^k)^3}{\sum_{l=1}^K 1/(d_t^l)^3}, \tag{7}$$

It is not difficult to see that our pooling weights satisfy the constraint $\sum_k p_t^k = 1$. Also our pooling weights relies on only GIST feature, with no relations with the event label y. This means we will use the same pooling strategy independent with events. We call the method in eq. (7) as concurrent VQ. Compared with traditional VQ, our new pooling method penalizes the impact of large outliers, and assigns more weights to the center with small distance. Fig. 3 employs a toy example to show the difference between eq. (7) and traditional VQ. In this toy example, the sample is close to three centers ($k = 2, 5, 6$), which can be viewed as a picture with three overlapping scenes. Vector quantization will only pick up $k = 5$, while forcing all the weights to the other centers as zero. In contrast, our new method selects all these three centers with big weights, and hence can handle the scenario of overlapping scenes easily. Moreover, the computation of eq (7) shows that the pooling weights in our method are based on the Euclidian distance d_t^k. For a lot of sparse histogram feature (such as SIFT histogram), their Euclidean distance is not reliable so that they are not as good choices as GIST.

In this paper, we choose an unsupervised way to model scenes. The reasons why unsupervised learning is preferred are as follows: First, unsupervised learning can save the extra labeling efforts. In our model, the goal is not to recognize the exact scene category but to do pooling according to scene context, so supervised learning is not necessary. Moreover, we will explain later that some video frames are associated with overlapping scenes.

In this paper, we use two kinds of κ as kernel function: linear kernel and intersection kernel. When we use linear kernel, we employ liblinear [26] with its default parameter. When we use intersection kernel, we use nonlinear SVM because there is no extra parameter to compute intersection kernel, and the intersection kernel can be computed very efficiently.

One advantage of our scene aligned pooling method is that it can be combined with various features. For example, many low level features have been designed in the image recognition research to represent a single image. To combine these features with scene aligned pooling, we can first identify the scene for each frame, and then aggregate the frame-level representations according to these scenes. For space-time interest point features [10], we can still use scene aligned pooling by aggregating the histogram for short term clips. We can also generalize this approach to multi-modal features, if both visual and audio features are synchronized.

Next we briefly discuss how to select K, the number of scenes. There is no general agreement on how many scenes exist, considering the ambiguity and great complexity contained in real world. Fei-Fei and Perona [17] employed 13 scenes in their experiment, which is later enlarged to 15 scenes by Lazebnik *et al.*[14]. The largest scene collection is recently contributed by Xiao *et al.*[24], which reported a recognition average precision of 34.5% for total 397 scene categories. [24] also conducts an interesting user study, by inviting 7 participants to write down all scene categories they experienced in more than two hundred hours. In this experiments, the participants report 52 different scene categories. In our experiments, we test the performances with different K. Fig. 4 compares results of pooling color histogram features on TRECVID 2011 dataset. We will explain the dataset later in the experiment section. We can see that the performance is similar with $K = 16, 64, 128$. In following section, we will use $K = 16$ for all the experiments, for efficiency.

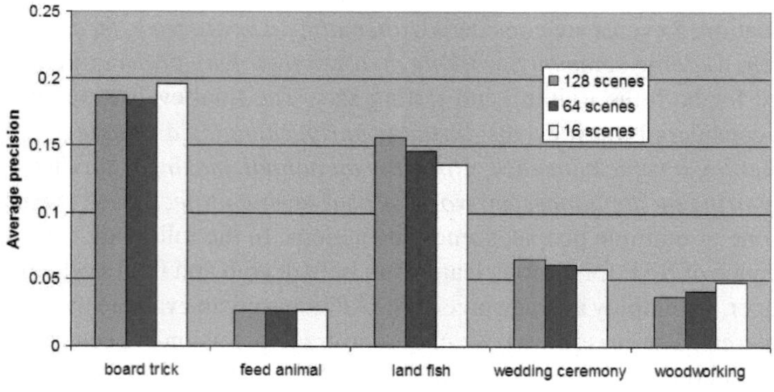

Fig. 4. Comparing the effects of different scene numbers on TRECVID 2011 Dryrun dataset

Algorithm 1 summarizes the workflow of our SAP algorithm.

4 Experiments

In recent years, there has been a proliferation of Web-shared videos, with approximately 48 hours of video uploaded on Youtube every minute, and over 700 billion

Algorithm 1. Scene Aligned Pooling Algorithm

Input: : A video with the set of frame feature vectors $\{x_t\}$, $1 \leq t \leq T$. A codebook with K centers of GIST feature g_c^k, $1 \leq k \leq K$.
Extract GIST descriptor g_t for every frame t.
Compute the pooling weight $p^k(x_t)$ using eq. (7).
Compute scene component s^k using eq. (3).
Normalize s^k and concatenate them into a long vector S.
Train linear SVM or intersection-kernel SVM using S.

videos watched in 2010. In our experiments, we select datasets most similar to real world online videos: TRECVID Multimedia Event Detection (MED) 2011 corpus (http://www.nist.gov/itl/iad/mig/med11.cfm) and the Brown Human Motion Recognition Database(http://serre-lab.clps.brown.edu/resources/HMDB/) (HMDB).

4.1 TRECVID MED Datasets

Trecvid MED 2011 is the largest fully annotated dataset specifically designed to model complex video events. There are about 370 hours of clips in the Event-Kit and Transparent Development (DEV-T) collections, and another 1,200 hours of video clips in the Opaque Development (DEV-O) collection. All these videos are free of editing, accompanied with non-professional recording and variety of illumination, camera motion, and cluttered background. The video duration is similar to the real Youtube video, and the average duration is about 2 to 3 minutes. The evaluation of MED is separated in two test sets: the mid size dryrun evaluation and the large final evaluation set. In the dryrun evaluation, 5 events are considered: *attempting a board trick*, *feeding an animal*, *landing a fish*, *wedding ceremony*, *working on a woodworking project*, for which labels are provided for both the training and testing sets. The final evaluation stage, on the other hand, considers 10 new events: *birthday party*, *changing a vehicle tire*, *flash mob gathering*, *getting a vehicle unstuck*, *grooming an animal*, *making a sandwich*, *parade*, *parkour*, *repairing an appliance*, and *working on a sewing project*. Each event is a combination of one or multiple people, scenes and actions. In the following we will discuss the performance of SAP for various features in both dryrun and final evaluation stage.

In this paper, we employ average precision (AP) measure to evaluate the performance on MED datasets. The reason why we choose average precision is because it is a popular measure in computer vision field and more importantly it is easier to compare the performance of video retrieval using average precision. Suppose the scores are ranked in descending order, the AP of the ranked list is computed by $AP = \sum_{i=1}^{n} p(i)\triangle r(i),$, where $p(i)$ is the precision at i-th position in the ranked list, and $r(i)$ is the recall at i-th position. $\triangle r(i)$ is the change in recall from item $i-1$ and i.

Since the dryrun evaluation is of a relatively small scale, we will try the effectiveness of SAP for different features. We tried the following features: edge histogram (edgehist), color histogram (colorhist), SIFT histogram (SIFT). The details of implementing these features are described in [27]. We compare three pooling methods: max pooling, average pooling, and our SAP. From Table 2 we can see that max pooling works poorly in video recognition. The average pooling works much better than max pooling for video recognition. In the following, we will use average pooling as the default baseline, since it is the standard technique in the field. In our experiments, SAP works consistently best among all the pooling methods for all the features. The improvement over mean AP can be as significantly as $(0.92 - 0.39)/0.39 = 135\%$ for edge histogram, 131% for color histogram, 10% for local binary pattern (LBP), 18% for SIFT features.

Table 2. Comparison of different pooling methods on MED dryrun

Feature	Pooling	Average Precision					
		E1	E2	E3	E4	E5	Mean
edgehist	Max	.027	.024	.051	.024	.016	.029
	Ave	.045	.015	.079	.020	.036	.039
	SAP	.195	.028	.136	.057	.048	.092
colorhist	Max	.023	.024	.036	.078	.028	.038
	Ave	.105	.027	.062	.039	.024	.051
	SAP	.259	.030	.129	.128	.042	.118
LBP	Max	.022	.018	.038	.021	.020	.024
	Ave	.057	.030	.045	.033	.019	.037
	SAP	.067	.028	.046	.041	.020	.041
SIFT	Max	.042	.013	.191	.013	.019	.056
	Ave	.155	.039	.261	.311	.152	.184
	SAP	.166	.044	.252	.432	.190	.217

We also did a few comparison with other pooling techniques. the effects of our concurrent vector quantization and its degenerated case (hard scene assignment). As shown in Table 3, our soft scene assignment strategy is much better than the hard assignment. The only exception is in event 2 (feed an animal), for which neither VQ nor our method does a good job due to the high irregularity and diversity in animal appearance and feeding activities. We also try to use SIFT histogram to compute $p^k(x_t)$, however, the pooling results are very poor since the Euclidian distance of sparse histogram features are not reliable. Another experiment we consider is whether directly combining scene feature and SIFT can improve the result. We extract both GIST and SIFT features for each video frame, and use average pooling to train the classifier. As shown in Table 4, GIST feature is not a good representation for event recognition, so that it bears very low recognition performance. Since GIST feature performs much worse than SIFT, it makes the naive fusion result worse than that of using SIFT only. However, our SAP does not fuse the two features directly but to use scene information as a context to guide the pooling process. As a result, SAP is a much better choice than the naive fusion strategy.

After we finish the dryrun evaluation, we also apply the proposed method on the final evaluation dataset. Since TRECVID has not publicly released the labels for the DEV-O set, we use an internal test set split. The internal test consists of 40 positive video clips per event (400 videos in total) and 5,231 negative videos. The remaining 7,252 videos are used for training. From the dryrun dataset we know that SIFT outperforms many other low-level features so we are especially interested in the performance of average pooling and scene aligned pooling using SIFT feature. As shown in Fig. 5, SAP can

Table 3. Comparing average precision of concurrent vector quantization with vector quantization (soft vs. hard scene assignment) using SIFT feature

	E1	E2	E3	E4	E5	Mean
Our Scene aligned pooling	.166	.044	.252	.432	.190	.217
Pooling using VQ on GIST	.159	.055	.221,	.263	.071	.154
Pooling using VQ on SIFT histogram	.089	.033	0.091	.084	.051	.077

Table 4. Comparison with naive fusion of scene feature with SIFT

Feature	Average Precision				
	E1	E2	E3	E4	E5
GIST	.074	.017	.030	.033	.018
SIFT	.155	.039	.261	.311	.152
GIST + SIFT	.150	.040	.211	.256	.143
SAP + SIFT	.166	.044	.252	.432	.190

significantly improve the average precision in all the ten events. By using SAP, the mean of ap scores can be improved from 0.183 to 0.212.

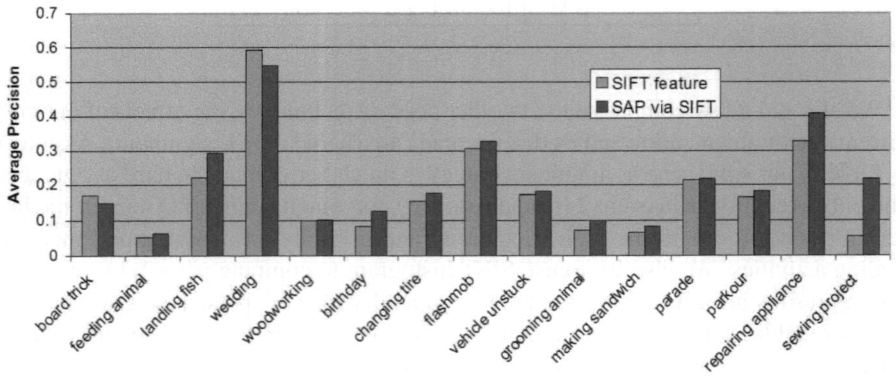

Fig. 5. Results of nonlinear SVM using SAP

Finally, we consider a special feature called semantic model vectors. Our semantic model vector is an intermediate level semantic representation, by evaluating 780 concept classifiers for each frames. The 780 classifiers are trained separately using thousands of labeled web photos. The semantic model vector is complementary to low level features and can be useful in many retrieval and annotation tasks [28] [29]. Our SAP can also significantly improve the semantic model vector. As shown in Fig. 6, SAP improves the performance in 9 of 10 events.

After obtaining the results using different features, we can do a late fusion to get the final classification model. This paper does not focus on fusion techniques but our

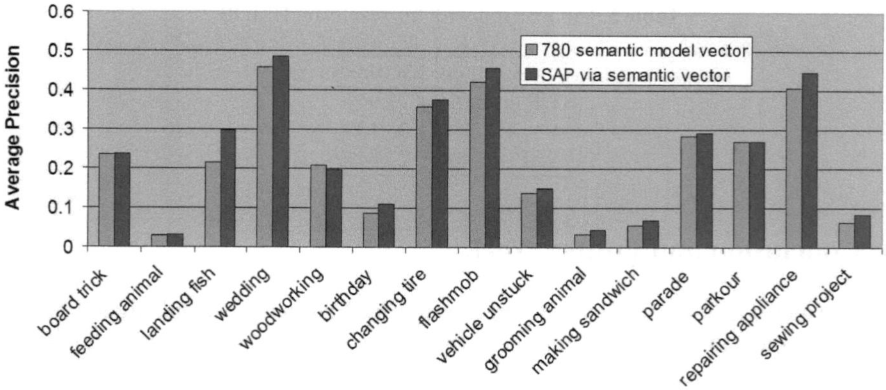

Fig. 6. Results of using SAP for semantic features

simple fusion model can arrive at 0.50 average precision in the dryrun evaluation and 0.45 in the final evaluation (internal test data split).

4.2 HMDB dataset

Very recently, Kuehne *et al.*[30] describe an effort of designing a large video database containing 51 distinct action categories, named the Human Motion DataBase (HMDB), which tries to better capture the richness and complexity of human actions. They argued that the UCF Sports dataset [3] is designed for specific titles on YouTube, in which the actions are usually unambiguous and highly distinguishable from shape cues alone (e.g., the raw positions of the joints or the silhouette extracted from single frames). They collected a new motion dataset, which contains 51 distinct action categories, with at least 101 clips for each category. The final dataset includes a total of 6,766 video clips extracted from a wide range of sources. Each clip was validated by at least two human observers to ensure consistency. Kuehne *et al.*[30] also studied the biological motion perception and recognition technique [31] based on this new dataset.

The HMDB dataset is very challenging. From the reports in [30], the the state-of-the-art's performance is about 23%. It is very interesting to apply our SAP model to this challenging dataset. We use STIP features [10] provided in the dataset webpage, and extract scene features for video frames at every 0.5 seconds. Since the STIP features are only sparsely distributed among video frames, to improve performance we condense the STIP features from nearby half-second video frames when computing on specific target keyframe. The STIP histogram are aggregated together for every 0.5-second clips, and then pooled using SAP model. We compare the performance of SAP with those of STIP histogram, and Kuehne's biological motion system C2. Table 5 compares the recognition accuracy of our SAP with STIP histogram and C2 models. Our model significantly improve the best performance from 23.18% to 27.84%, as a relative 20% increase of accuracy.

Table 5. Comparison with the results on HMDB

Model	Accuracy
STIP histogram	21.96%
C2	23.18%
SAP + STIP	27.84%

5 Conclusion and Future Work

In this paper, we have discussed a new pooling method named scene aligned pooling (SAP). We show that SAP can consistently improve different features (color histogram, SIFT, semantic model vectors) for complex video classification. SAP also significantly improves the state-of-the-art performance on HMDB datasets.

Our future work will focus on generalizing the classification model to more video recognition and annotation tasks. More results will be available on `http://researcher.ibm.com/person/us-liangliang.cao`.

Acknowledgement. This research is supported by Intelligence Advanced Research Projects Activity (IARPA) via Department of Interior National Busyness Center contract number D11PC20070. The U.S. government is authorized to reproduce and distribute reprints for Governmental purposes notwithstanding any copyright thereon. Disclaimer: The views and conclusions contained herein are those of the authors and should not be interpreted as necessarily representing the official policies or endorsements, either expressed or implied, of IARPA, DoI/NBC, or the U.S. Government.

References

1. Schuldt, C., Laptev, I., Caputo, B.: Recognizing human actions: A local SVM approach. In: ICPR (2004)
2. Blank, M., Gorelick, L., Shechtman, E., Irani, M., Basri, R.: Actions as space-time shapes. In: ICCV (2005)
3. Liu, J., Luo, J., Shah, M.: Recognizing realistic actions from videos "in the wild". In: CVPR (2009)
4. Efros, A., Berg, A., Mori, G., Malik, J.: Recognizing action at a distance. In: ICCV, pp. 726–733 (2003)
5. Epstein, R., Kanwisher, N.: A cortical representation of the local visual environment. Nature 392, 598–601 (1998)
6. Friedman, A.: Framing pictures: The role of knowledge in automatized encoding and memory for gist. Journal of Experimental Psychology 108, 316–355 (1979)
7. LeCun, Y., Bottou, L., Bengio, Y., Haffner, P.: Gradient-based learning applied to document recognition. Proceedings of the IEEE 86, 2278–2324 (1998)
8. Niebles, J.C., Wang, H., Fei-Fei, L.: Unsupervised learning of human action categories using spatial-temporal words. IJCV 79, 299–318 (2008)
9. Dollár, P., Rabaud, V., Cottrell, G., Belongie, S.: Behavior recognition via sparse spatio-temporal features. In: IEEE International Workshop on VS-PETS (2005)
10. Laptev, I., Marszalek, M., Schmid, C., Rozenfeld, B.: Learning realistic human actions from movies. In: CVPR (2008)

11. Boureau, Y.L., Bach, F., LeCun, Y., Ponce, J.: Learning mid-level features for recognition. In: CVPR (2010)
12. Yang, J., Yu, K., Gong, Y., Huang, T.: Linear pyramid matching using sparse coding for image classification. In: CVPR (2009)
13. Jégou, H., Douze, M., Schmid, C., Pérez, P.: Aggregating local descriptors into a compact image representation. In: 2010 IEEE Conference on Computer Vision and Pattern Recognition (CVPR), pp. 3304–3311. IEEE (2010)
14. Lazebnik, S., Schmid, C., Ponce, J.: Beyond bags of features: Spatial pyramid matching for recognizing natural scene categories. In: CVPR, vol. 2, pp. 2169–2178 (2006)
15. Boureau, Y., Le Roux, N., Bach, F., Ponce, J., LeCun, Y.: Ask the locals: multi-way local pooling for image recognition. In: ICCV (2011)
16. Oliva, A., Torralba, A.: Modeling the shape of the scene: a holistic representation of the spatial envelope. IJCV 42 (2004)
17. Fei-Fei, L., Perona, P.: A bayesian hierarchy model for learning natural scene categories. In: CVPR (2005)
18. Russell, B., Torralba, A., Liu, C., Fergus, R., Freeman, W.T.: Object recognition by scene alignment. In: NIPS (2007)
19. Boutell, M., Luo, J., Brown, C.M.: Improved semantic region labeling based on scene context. In: ICME (2005)
20. Li, L.J., Fei-Fei, L.: What, where and who? classifying events by scene and object recognition. In: ICCV (2007)
21. Marszalek, M., Laptev, I., Schmid, C.: Actions in context. In: CVPR (2009)
22. Kimeldorf, G., Wahba, G.: Some results on tchebychefan spline functions. Journal of Mathematical Analysis and Applications 33, 82–95 (1971)
23. Yu, H., Hsieh, C., Chang, K., Lin, C.: Large linear classification when data cannot fit in memory. In: Proceedings of ACM SIGKDD, pp. 833–842. ACM (2010)
24. Xiao, J., Haysy, J., Ehinger, K.A., Oliva, A., Torralba, A.: Sun database: Large-scale scene recognition from abbey to zoo. In: CVPR (2010)
25. Zhang, B., Hsu, M., Dayal, U.: K-harmonic means-a data clustering algorithm. Hewlett-Packard Labs Technical Report HPL-1999-124 (1999)
26. Fan, R., Chang, K., Hsieh, C., Wang, X., Lin, C.: Liblinear: A library for large linear classification. The Journal of Machine Learning Research 9, 1871–1874 (2008)
27. Cao, L., Chang, S.F., Codella, N., Cotton, C., Ellis, D., Gong, L., Hill, M., Huang, G., Kender, J., Merler, M., Mu, Y., Natseve, A., Smith, J.R.: Ibm research and columbia university trecvid-2011 multimedia event detection (med) systems. In: NIST TRECVID Workshop (2011)
28. Natsev, A., Naphade, M.R., Smith, J.R.: Semantic representation, search and mining of multimedia content. In: ACM KDD, pp. 641–646 (2004)
29. Merler, M., Bert Huang, L.X., Hua, G., Natsev, A.: Semantic model vectors for complex video event recognition. IEEE Transactions on Multimedia (2011)
30. Kuehne, H., Jhuang, H., Garrote, E., Poggio, T., Serre, T.: Hmdb: A large video database for human motion recognition. In: ICCV (2011)
31. Jhuang, H., Serre, T., Wolf, L., Poggio, T.: A biologically inspired system for action recognition. In: ICCV (2007)

Discovering Latent Domains for Multisource Domain Adaptation

Judy Hoffman[1,2], Brian Kulis[4], Trevor Darrell[1,2], and Kate Saenko[1,2,3]

[1] UC Berkeley EECS, Berkeley, California
[2] ICSI, Berkeley, California
[3] Harvard University, Cambridge, Massachusetts
[4] Ohio State University, Columbus, Ohio
{jhoffman,saenko,trevor}@eecs.berkeley.edu kulis@cse.ohio-state.edu

Abstract. Recent domain adaptation methods successfully learn cross-domain transforms to map points between source and target domains. Yet, these methods are either restricted to a single training domain, or assume that the separation into source domains is known a priori. However, most available training data contains multiple unknown domains. In this paper, we present both a novel domain transform mixture model which outperforms a single transform model when multiple domains are present, and a novel constrained clustering method that successfully discovers latent domains. Our discovery method is based on a novel hierarchical clustering technique that uses available object category information to constrain the set of feasible domain separations. To illustrate the effectiveness of our approach we present experiments on two commonly available image datasets with and without known domain labels: in both cases our method outperforms baseline techniques which use no domain adaptation or domain adaptation methods that presume a single underlying domain shift.

1 Introduction

Despite efforts to the contrary, most image datasets exhibit a clear *dataset bias*: supervised learning on a particular dataset nearly always leads to a significant loss in accuracy when the models are tested in a new domain [1,2]. *Domain Adaptation* methods have been proposed as a solution to dataset bias and are becoming increasingly popular in computer vision. Especially attractive are recent weakly-supervised methods that learn to transform features between domains based on partially labeled data [1,3,4].

A major limitation of these methods is the assumption that the domain/dataset label is provided for each training image. However, in practice, one often has access to large amounts of object labeled data composed of multiple *unknown domains*. For example, images found on the web can be thought of as a collection of many hidden domains. As shown in Figure 1, image search results for "person" and "bicycle" consist of several *types*, such as close-up photos of a face, photos of an entire human figure, group shots, line drawings of a person, etc. Existing

A. Fitzgibbon et al. (Eds.): ECCV 2012, Part II, LNCS 7573, pp. 702–715, 2012.

Fig. 1. Training images for object recognition may contain several unknown domains, such as the line drawings, close-up photos and far-away shots returned by web image search for *person* and *bicycle*

methods have not addressed the problem of separating such data into latent domains for the purpose of domain adaptation.

Even when the separation into source domains is known, the above methods are limited to a single adaptive transform between source and target data, computed by either simply pooling [1,3] or averaging [4] multiple sources into one source domain. Learning a single transform may be sub-optimal in approximating multiple domain shifts. Consider a simple example: two source image datasets, one with *low-resolution*, *color* images and one with *high-resolution*, *grayscale* images. When mapping images from a novel *high-resolution*, *color* domain to each of these source domains, we would like a transform that either discounts the high-resolution details or the color, but not both. Rather than force a single transform to perform both mappings, a richer model with multiple separate transforms is desirable.

The contribution of this paper is two-fold: First, we propose a method that discovers latent domain labels in data which has heterogeneous but unknown domain structure. We use a probabilistic framework to derive a hierarchical constrained assignment algorithm that separates heterogeneous training data into latent clusters, or domains. Our second contribution is an extension of the feature-transform method in [3] to multi-domain adaptation that uses source domain labels to define a mixture-transform model. Tests on standard datasets with known domain labels confirm that our method is more accurate at discovering domain structure than baseline clustering methods, and that our transform mixture model outperforms a single transform approach. When domain labels are unknown, we evaluate the end-to-end recognition performance with no adaptation baseline, baseline adaptation, and transform-mixture adaptation with discovered domain labels (our method). Our experiments on category data from the *Bing* image search dataset confirm improved classification performance using the inferred domains.

2 Related Work

Domain adaptation aims to compensate for covariate shift, i.e. a change in the feature distribution from training to test time, which is a version of the more general dataset shift problem [5].

Several methods have been developed in the NLP community, e.g., structural correspondence learning was proposed for NLP tasks such as sentiment classification [6]. Daume [7] introduced a feature replication method for domain adaptation, which has been applied to both NLP and vision tasks. The basic idea is: given a feature vector $\boldsymbol{x}$, define the augmented feature vector $\tilde{\boldsymbol{x}} = (\boldsymbol{x}; \boldsymbol{x}; \mathbf{0})$ for data points in the source and $\tilde{\boldsymbol{x}} = (\boldsymbol{x}; \mathbf{0}; \boldsymbol{x})$ for data points in the target.

Recently, several authors have developed approaches for vision tasks, and the field is becoming increasingly aware of existing dataset bias [8]. These methods can be roughly categorized as classifier adaptation approaches and feature-transform approaches. The former approach adapts the parameters of each per-category binary classifier, typically a support vector machine, and includes methods like a weighted combination of source and target SVMs; transductive SVMs applied to adaptation in [9]; Adaptive SVM [10], where the parameters are adapted by adding a perturbation function; Domain Transfer SVM [11], which learns a target decision function while reducing the mismatch in the domain distributions; and a related method [12] which utilizes adaptive multiple kernel learning to learn a kernel function based on multiple base kernels. Classifier adaptation approaches are typically supervised, requiring labeled examples for each category in both source and target.

On the other hand, feature transform approaches map or translate the input features directly between domains, and then apply a classifier [1,3,4,13,14]. The advantage of these approaches over the classifier-based ones above is that they are able to transfer the adaptive transformation to novel problems, and even deal with new feature types and dimensionalities. For example, the asymmetric nonlinear transform method [3] learns a domain-independent similarity function between arbitrary feature sets based on class constraints. In this paper we focus on transform learning, as it can be scaled up to many novel object categories and heterogeneous features. Other work on feature-translation has included translating features between camera views to transfer activity models [13], and translating user preferences between text and image domains [14].

Some of the existing methods can accommodate multiple source domains, if they are known. The feature replication method [7] can be easily extended to multiple sources. In methods based on combinations of SVM classifiers, this is done primarily by weighting the classifiers learned on each source domain, either equally, or as in [15], using the maximum mean discrepancy (MMD) criterion, which measures the distance between distributions. The A-MKL [12] learns an optimal weighted combination of the pre-learned classifiers, however, in the evaluation the classifiers came from the same source domain. The unsupervised approach based on Grassman manifolds presented by Gopalan et al. [4] supports multiple sources by first computing the Karcher mean of the sources and then running the single source version of their algorithm.

None of the existing methods address the case of domain adaptation with unknown domain labels, the main focus of our paper. We also present the first multi-domain version of the asymmetric nonlinear transform [3], which so far has been limited to the single domain case.

Our domain discovery method is based on a constrained clustering method, a topic of active research for several years. The most related work to our approach is based on constrained k-means. The method of Wagstaff et al. [16] is the earliest constrained clustering method based on k-means; their algorithm greedily assigns points to the closest cluster which does not violate any constraints. Improvements to this basic algorithm were considered in [17,18]. A variant of constrained k-means was also used recently with soft constraints to learn more discriminative codebooks [19]. In general, the constraints in these approaches are incorporated as additional penalty terms to the k-means objective function (and therefore are not guaranteed to be satisfied), and algorithms are developed to minimize the penalized k-means objective. In contrast to existing work on constrained k-means, our algorithm is guaranteed to find a clustering that satisfies the constraints and provably converges locally under certain assumptions. An overview of recent semi-supervised clustering techniques, including techniques not based on k-means, can be found in [20].

2.1 Single Transform Domain Adaptation

We review the single-transform method of Kulis et al. [3]. Suppose we have a source domain $\mathcal{A}$ containing observations $\boldsymbol{x}_1, ..., \boldsymbol{x}_{n_\mathcal{A}}$. Similarly, let $\mathcal{B}$ be the target domain, containing observations $\boldsymbol{y}_1, ..., \boldsymbol{y}_{n_\mathcal{B}}$. Suppose we are also given a set of labels $l_1^\mathcal{A}, ..., l_{m_\mathcal{A}}^\mathcal{A}$ for the source observations and a partial set of labels $l_1^\mathcal{B}, ..., l_{m_\mathcal{B}}^\mathcal{B}$ for the target observations, with $m_\mathcal{B} < m_\mathcal{A}$ and $l \in \{1, ..., K\}$, where K is the number of categories. The goal of domain transform learning is to estimate a semantic similarity function $sim(\boldsymbol{x}, \boldsymbol{y})$ which outputs high similarity values for pairs of source examples $\boldsymbol{x}$ and novel target examples $\boldsymbol{y}$ if they have the same label, and low similarity values if they have different labels.

Following [3], consider a similarity function between source and target data parametrized by a matrix W, i.e., $sim_W(\boldsymbol{x}, \boldsymbol{y}) = \phi_\mathcal{A}(\boldsymbol{x})^T W \phi_\mathcal{B}(\boldsymbol{y})$, where $\phi_\mathcal{A}$ and $\phi_\mathcal{B}$ map examples from the source and target, respectively, into kernel space. In general, mapping to kernel space makes it possible to learn non-linear similarity mappings in the input space.

The transform W can be learned via a regularized optimization problem with loss functions that depend on sim_W; that is, by optimizing for a matrix W which minimizes $r(W) + \gamma \sum_{i=1}^{C} c_i(\phi_\mathcal{A}(X)^T W \phi_\mathcal{B}(Y))$, where r is a matrix regularizer, C is the number of constraints, $\phi_\mathcal{A}(X)$ is the matrix of source data mapped to kernel space, $\phi_\mathcal{B}(Y)$ is the matrix of target data mapped to kernel space, and c_i are loss functions over the matrix $\phi_\mathcal{A}(X)^T W \phi_\mathcal{B}(Y)$. Though the model can incorporate various constraints/losses, it is customary to focus on constraints that penalize small values of $sim_W(\boldsymbol{x}, \boldsymbol{y})$ when $\boldsymbol{x}$ and $\boldsymbol{y}$ share a class label, and penalize large values of $sim_W(\boldsymbol{x}, \boldsymbol{y})$ when they have different labels. For a particular class of regularizers r, this problem may be efficiently optimized in kernel space; see [3].

3 Multiple Transform Domain Adaptation

We first extend the single source feature transform method [3] to a multi-source algorithm, considering the case of known domain labels, and then in Section 4 we present our main contribution: a method for discovering unknown domain labels.

Transform-based domain adaptation captures category-independent domain shift information, which can be generalized to a held-out category for which no labels are available in a new domain. The single-transform method described in Section 2.1 is sub-optimal when multiple domain shifts are present. We remedy this by constructing a domain transform mixture model as follows.

Suppose we have a set of domains $\mathcal{A}_1, ..., \mathcal{A}_S$ containing observations $\boldsymbol{x}_1, ..., \boldsymbol{x}_n$ and labels $\{\ell_1^{\mathcal{A}}, ..., \ell_n^{\mathcal{A}}\}$. Let $\boldsymbol{a} = \{a_1, ..., a_n\}$ specify the domain of each observation, such that $a_i \in \{1, ..., S\}$.

We start by using the single source feature transform method to learn a transformation W_k for each source $k \in \{1, \ldots, S\}$. Each of the S different object category classifiers outputs a multi-class probability for a given test point, $\boldsymbol{y}$. We denote the output probability over classes, c, of the classifier learned for the kth domain as, $p(c|d = k, \boldsymbol{y})$.

We classify a novel test point from a target domain by considering the domain as a latent variable that is marginalized out as follows:

$$\text{label}(\boldsymbol{y}) = arg \max_{c \in \{1:K\}} p(c|\boldsymbol{y}) \tag{1}$$

$$= arg \max_{c \in \{1:K\}} \sum_{k=1}^{S} p(d = k|\boldsymbol{y}) p(c|d = k, \boldsymbol{y}) \tag{2}$$

Where $p(d|\boldsymbol{y})$ is the output of a domain label classifier and $p(c|d, \boldsymbol{y})$ is the output of a domain specific object model based on the learned transforms. For example, if the domain specific classifier is (kernelized) nearest neighbors, as in our experiments, and we let $\boldsymbol{x}_k^*(\boldsymbol{y})$ be the most similar point in domain k to test point $\boldsymbol{y}$, then our domain specific object category probability can be expressed as:

$$p(c|d = k, \boldsymbol{y}) = \frac{\phi_A(\boldsymbol{x}_k^*(\boldsymbol{y}))^T W_j \phi_B(\boldsymbol{y})}{\sum_{k'=1}^{S} \phi_A(\boldsymbol{x}_{k'}^*(\boldsymbol{y}))^T W_j \phi_B(\boldsymbol{y})} \tag{3}$$

Finally, to obtain $p(d = k|\boldsymbol{y})$ we train an SVM classifier with probabilistic outputs, using known domain labels and source training data. In summary, category classification of a test point $\boldsymbol{y}$ amounts to a weighted sum of the probability of a particular category given that the point is from a particular domain, where the weights are the probability that the test point belongs to each domain.

4 Domain Clustering

For datasets which do not have domain labels, we must infer domain assignments $\hat{\boldsymbol{a}}$ that best approximate the true assignments, $\boldsymbol{a}$. This task is difficult because, in many cases, the data is naturally separated according to semantic categories. That is, a standard clustering method such as k-means or EM for mixtures of Gaussians would tend to return clusters based on the semantic category labels, which is clearly undesirable.

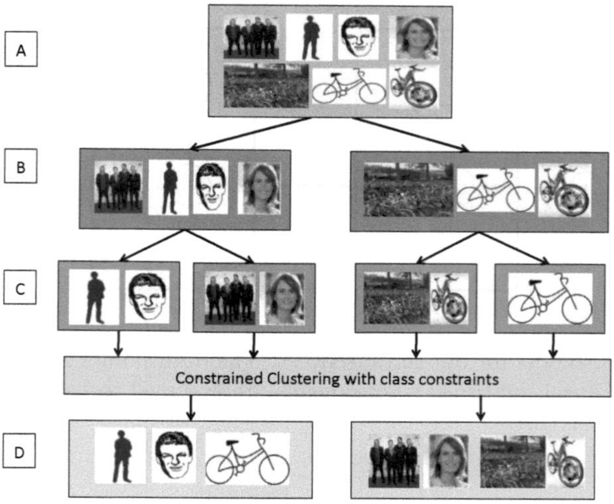

Fig. 2. An illustration of our approach for discovering latent domains: Given input images with unknown domains types (A), we separate examples according to their semantic category labels (B). Then, we cluster the data from each semantic category group to produce local clusters (C), and, finally, use do-not-link constraints between clusters of same category to produce the domain specific clusters (D). This example shows separation of *person* and *bicycle* search results into two domains of line drawing and natural images. Our algorithm iterates between steps (B-D) until convergence.

High-Level Description: We propose a two-stage approach for domain discovery (See Figure 2 for illustration of algorithm). The idea is as follows: if there are K semantic categories and S domains in the data, we will group the data points $\boldsymbol{x}_1, ..., \boldsymbol{x}_n$ into $J = K \cdot S$ *local clusters*—intuitively, each local cluster will contain data points from one domain and one semantic category (step B-C in Figure 2). In the second stage of clustering (*domain clustering*), we will cluster the means of the local clusters, in order to find domains (step C-D in Figure 2). The two stages are iterated to convergence. To make this approach consistent with our goals, we add two crucial constraints to the clustering procedure: a) we require that each local cluster only contains data points from a single category, and b) we constrain each domain cluster to contain only one local cluster from each object category.

Formal Definition: Let us now specify this model more formally. Define a local latent variable $z_{ij}^L \in \{0, 1\}$ to indicate whether observation $\boldsymbol{x}_i$ should be assigned to local cluster j. Let the domain latent variable $z_{jk}^G \in \{0, 1\}$ indicate whether local cluster j is assigned to domain k. Further, let $\boldsymbol{\mu}_j$ be the mean of the observations in local cluster j and $\boldsymbol{m}_k$ be the mean of domain cluster k. Finally, let the mixing weights for the global clusters be given by π_k^G, for $k = 1, ..., S$, and let the mixing weights for the local clusters be given by π_j^L for $j = 1, ..., J$. See Figure 3 for a graphical depiction of our model. Note that,

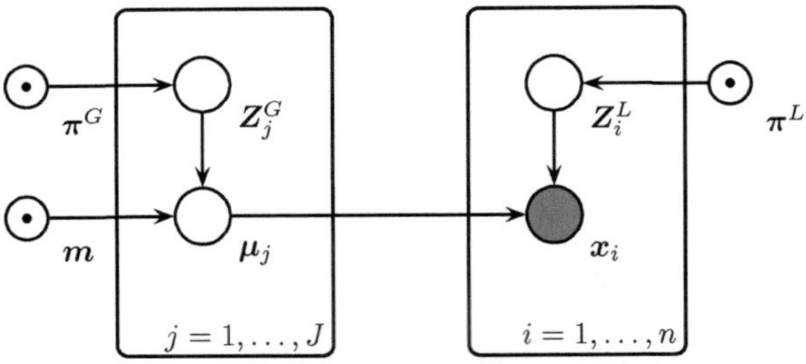

Fig. 3. Graphical model for domain discovery. The data points x_i are generated from category specific local mixtures, whose means are assumed to be drawn from a latent global (*domain*) mixture.

unlike a standard Gaussian mixture model, each cluster mean $\boldsymbol{\mu}_j$ is itself a data point within a mixture model. For simplicity, we are assuming that all clusters have a global covariance of σI—one could easily extend the model to learn the covariances. The conditional probabilities in our graphical model are defined as:

$$p(\boldsymbol{z}_i^L \mid \boldsymbol{\pi}^L) = \prod_{j=1}^{J} (\pi_j^L)^{z_{ij}^L} \qquad p(\boldsymbol{z}_j^G \mid \boldsymbol{\pi}^G) = \prod_{k=1}^{S} (\pi_k^G)^{z_{jk}^G} \tag{4}$$

$$p(\boldsymbol{x}_i \mid \boldsymbol{z}_i^L, \boldsymbol{\mu}) = \prod_{j=1}^{J} \mathcal{N}(\boldsymbol{x}_i \mid \boldsymbol{\mu}_j, \sigma I)^{z_{ij}^L} \tag{5}$$

$$p(\boldsymbol{\mu}_j \mid \boldsymbol{z}_j^G, \boldsymbol{m}) = \prod_{k=1}^{S} \mathcal{N}(\boldsymbol{\mu}_j \mid \boldsymbol{m}_k, \sigma I)^{z_{jk}^G} \tag{6}$$

We may think of this model in a generative manner as follows: for each local cluster $j = 1, ..., J = S \cdot K$, we determine its underlying domain via the $\boldsymbol{\pi}^G$ mixing weights. Given this domain, we generate $\boldsymbol{\mu}_j$, the mean for the local cluster. Then, to generate the data points $\boldsymbol{x}_i$, we first determine which local cluster j the data point belongs to using $\boldsymbol{\pi}^L$, and then we generate the point from the corresponding $\boldsymbol{\mu}_j$.

At this point, we still need to add the constraints discussed above, namely that the local clusters only contain data points from a single category and that domain clusters contain only a single local cluster from each category. Such constraints can be difficult to enforce in a probabilistic model, but are considerably simpler in a hard clustering model. For instance, in semi-supervised clustering there is ample literature on adding constraints to the k-means objective via constraints or penalties [16,18]. Thus, we will utilize a standard asymptotic argument on our probabilistic model to create a corresponding hard clustering model. In particular, if one takes a mixture of Gaussian model with fixed σI covariances across clusters, and lets $\sigma \to 0$, the expected log likelihood approaches the k-means objective, and the EM algorithm approaches the k-means algorithm. In an analogous manner, we will consider the log-likelihood of our model. Let $\boldsymbol{Z}^L = \{\boldsymbol{z}_i^L\}$, $\boldsymbol{Z}^G = \{\boldsymbol{z}_j^G\}$, and $X = [\boldsymbol{x}_1, ..., \boldsymbol{x}_n]$.

$$\ln\left[p(\boldsymbol{Z}^G, \boldsymbol{Z}^L, X \mid \boldsymbol{m}, \boldsymbol{\mu})\right] = \tag{7}$$
$$\sum_{i=1}^{n}\sum_{j=1}^{J}\sum_{k=1}^{S}\left(z_{jk}^G(\ln \pi_k^G + \ln \mathcal{N}(\boldsymbol{\mu}_j \mid \boldsymbol{m}_k, \sigma I)) + z_{ij}^L(\ln \pi_j^L + \ln \mathcal{N}(\boldsymbol{x}_i \mid \boldsymbol{\mu}_j, \sigma I))\right)$$

If we have no prior knowledge about the domains, then we assume the mixing weights π^G and π^L to be uniform. Then to create a hard clustering problem we let σ tend to 0 and taking expectations with respect to $\boldsymbol{Z}^G$ and $\boldsymbol{Z}^L$, we obtain the following hard clustering objective:

$$\min_{\boldsymbol{Z}^G, \boldsymbol{Z}^L, \boldsymbol{\mu}, \boldsymbol{m}} \sum_{i=1}^{n}\sum_{j=1}^{J} \boldsymbol{Z}_{ij}^L(x_i - \mu_j)^2 + \sum_{j=1}^{J}\sum_{k=1}^{S} \boldsymbol{Z}_{jk}^G(\mu_j - \boldsymbol{m}_k)^2 \tag{8}$$
$$\text{subject to: } \forall j,k: \;\; \boldsymbol{Z}_{jk}^G \in \{0,1\}, \quad \forall i,j: \;\; \boldsymbol{Z}_{ij}^L \in \{0,1\} \tag{9}$$
$$\forall j: \; \sum_{k=1}^{S} \boldsymbol{Z}_{jk}^G = 1, \quad \forall i: \; \sum_{j=1}^{J} \boldsymbol{Z}_{ij}^L = 1 \tag{10}$$
$$\tag{11}$$

The constraints above are standard hard assignment constraints, saying that every observation must be assigned to one local cluster and every local cluster must be assigned to only one global cluster. Now that we have transformed the clustering problem into a hard clustering model, we can easily add constraints on the $\boldsymbol{Z}^G$ and $\boldsymbol{Z}^L$ assignments, leading to our final model.

$$\min_{\boldsymbol{Z}^G, \boldsymbol{Z}^L, \boldsymbol{\mu}, \boldsymbol{m}} \sum_{i=1}^{n}\sum_{j=1}^{J} \boldsymbol{Z}_{ij}^L(x_i - \mu_j)^2 + \sum_{j=1}^{J}\sum_{k=1}^{S} \boldsymbol{Z}_{jk}^G(\mu_j - \boldsymbol{m}_k)^2 \tag{12}$$
$$\text{subject to: } \forall j,k: \;\; \boldsymbol{Z}_{jk}^G \in \{0,1\}, \quad \forall i,j: \;\; \boldsymbol{Z}_{ij}^L \in \{0,1\} \tag{13}$$
$$\forall j: \; \sum_{k=1}^{S} \boldsymbol{Z}_{jk}^G = 1, \quad \forall i: \; \sum_{j=1}^{J} \boldsymbol{Z}_{ij}^L = 1 \tag{14}$$
$$\forall j: \; \sum_{i=1}^{n} \delta(l_i \neq l_j)\boldsymbol{Z}_{ij}^L = 0 \tag{15}$$
$$\forall k: \; \sum_{c=1}^{K}\sum_{j=1}^{J} \delta(\text{label}(j) = c)\boldsymbol{Z}_{jk}^G = 1 \tag{16}$$

Equation (15) says that all observations assigned to a single local cluster j must contain the same object category label. Finally, we add the constraint in Equation (16), which says that each global cluster should only contain one local cluster from each object category. Here, we define label(j) to mean the object category label of the observations assigned to the local cluster j. Together the last two constraints restrict the feasible global clustering solutions to be the solutions that contain observations from every object category while placing observations together that are close according to a Euclidean distance.

To solve this optimization problem we formulate an EM style iteration algorithm. We first initialize $\boldsymbol{Z}^G, \mu, \boldsymbol{m}$ and then perform the following updates until convergence (or until the objective doesn't change more than some threshold between iterations):

$\boldsymbol{Z}^L_{ij}$: For each observation $\boldsymbol{x}_i$, set $\boldsymbol{Z}^L_{ij} = 1$ for the particular j that minimizes $(\boldsymbol{x}_i - \mu_j)^2$.

μ_j: For each local cluster j, set $\mu_j = \frac{\sum_i \boldsymbol{Z}^L_{ij}\boldsymbol{x}_i + \sum_k \boldsymbol{Z}^G_{jk}\boldsymbol{m}_k}{\sum_i \boldsymbol{Z}^L_{ij} + \sum_k \boldsymbol{Z}^G_{jk}}$.

$\boldsymbol{Z}^G_{jk}$: For each local cluster j, set $\boldsymbol{Z}^G_{jk} = 1$ for the particular global cluster that minimizes $\boldsymbol{Z}^G_{jk}(\mu_j - \boldsymbol{m}_k)^2$ while satisfying Equation (16). For the case where the number of latent domains is assumed small, we can try all possible assignments of local to global clusters at this stage.

$\boldsymbol{m}_k$: For each global cluster k, set $\boldsymbol{m}_k = \frac{\sum_j \boldsymbol{Z}^G_{jk}\mu_j}{\sum_j \boldsymbol{Z}^G_{jk}}$.

Note, these updates correspond to constrained versions of the EM updates from the probabilistic model as $\sigma \to 0$. In general adding constraints to EM updates can cause the objective to diverge. However, for our problem, when the number of domains, S, is small (which is a practical assumption for many domain adaptation tasks) these updates can be shown to provably converge locally (see supplemental material). In Section 5 we show experimentally that even for large heterogeneous data sources learning to separate into a small number of latent domains is sufficient in practice.

We evaluate absolute domain discovery performance compared against a constrained hard HDP method [21] and a standard unconstrained k-means. The hard HDP seeks to minimize the distance between data points and their local mean plus data points to their assigned global mean, whereas we introduce an intermediate latent variable for the local cluster means. That, combined with the fact that constrained hard HDP can create new global clusters, causes the constrained hard HDP to degenerate to the case where each global cluster contains only one local cluster. In Section 5 we present clustering accuracy experiments that show our method does in fact provide significant benefit over the hard HDP method and a standard k-means baseline.

5 Experiments

We present the following three experiments. First, we evaluate our multidomain mixture model extension of [3] described in Section 3 for the case where the domain labels are known. We compare this to using the single-transform method in [3]. Next, we evaluate the ability of our constrained clustering method to recover domains by mixing datasets and omitting the dataset labels, and compare to two baseline clustering methods. Finally, we evaluate the end-to-end recognition performance on a dataset with unknown domains, compared against methods with no adaptation, baseline adaptation, and our multiple transform adaptation with discovered domain labels.

Datasets: For our experiments we used two different data sets. First we used the *Office* data set created by [1] specifically for object domain adaptation, which we modified to artificially introduce more domains. We use the code provided by the authors to extract features and to implement the single-domain asymmetric transform method. Second, we evaluate on a subset of the *Bing-Caltech256* data set created by [9], using the authors' original image features. The *Bing* dataset is comprised of search results from object label keywords and therefore has many sub-domains without any explicit labels.

The *Office* dataset contains three domains with 31 object categories: Amazon (a), which contains images from amazon.com; Digital SLR (d), and Webcam (w). Webcam and Digital SLR contain images of the same 5 instances for each object category, but vary in pose, lighting, and camera. In addition to these three domains, we also created two more domains which are artificially modified versions of two the the original domains: Webcam-blur (Wb), which contains the blurred version of all webcam data images (using a Gaussian filter of width 5), and Amazon-rotflip (Ar), which contains the result of rotating all amazon images by 10-20 degrees and then creating their mirror image.

Object Classification Using *Office*: For our first object classification experiment, we follow the experimental procedure for semi-supervised learning described in [1,4]: we train the transforms on categories 1-15, with 10 instances per category in each source domain and 5 instances per category in the target domain, and test them using the classifier described in Section 3 on the rest of the categories.

The experiment measures the accuracy of predicting the labels of target data points with no examples of the correct label within the target domain, representing the transform's ability to capture general shifts rather than simply the source shift's effect on a particular object category.

We compared our method to the single-transform method of [3] and the semi-supervised multi-domain version of [4]. The γ parameter of ours and [3] was optimized for the single transform baseline in all experiments. We ran code provided by the authors of [4]; we experimented with over 1000 combinations of the four parameter settings within the ranges specified in the code from the author's website and the paper, but were unable to produce resulting accuracies above the standard KNN with no adaptation baseline for any of the domain shifts presented, and so we omit these results from the following figure.

Figure 4 shows the absolute improvement in accuracy of the supervised multiple-domain method and a single transform method over the KNN classifier using Euclidean distance (i.e., no adaptation) for various domain shifts, averaged over 10 train/test splits for each shift. Overall, the average accuracy gained over KNN was 3.27 for the single source baseline [3] and 5.45 for our domain-supervised method. The average KNN classification accuracy was 28.9, which means these absolute improvements correspond to an 11.3% and 18.9% relative improvement over KNN for each method respectively.

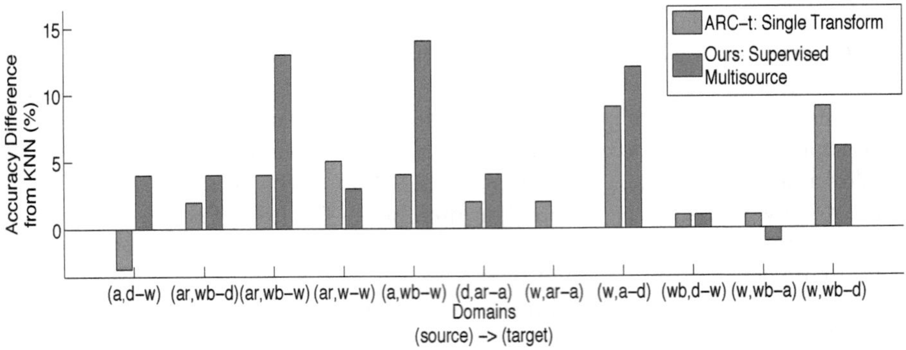

Fig. 4. Classification Accuracy experiment on *Office* dataset with known domain labels. The plot shows the average accuracy improvement of each method over a baseline KNN. Each cluster of bars is the results for a different domain shift, where the domains are indicated on the x-axis. For each of these cases the parameter, γ was set to be the value that maximized the single transform method baseline. The average accuracy gained over KNN across all datasets was 3.27 for the single source baseline [3] and 5.45 for our multisource domain-supervised method. For some datasets our method outperforms [3] significantly, achieving up to a 18.9% relative improvement over KNN.

We notice that shifts where the supervised method achieves the most gains (up to 48% relative gain in accuracy) have higher separability of the source domains via clustering reported below (in Figure 5.)

Clustering: We begin with an analysis of our clustering algorithm on all pairs of the 5 domains in the *Office* dataset, for which we know the ground truth source labels. Figure 5 plots the accuracy improvement over chance between the ground truth domain labels and the cluster labels learned using our constrained clustering algorithm. The results are averaged over 10 runs with different data splits for each run. As baselines, we implemented standard, unconstrained, k-means, as well as, a hard HDP [21] with the same do-not-link class based constraints presented in Section 4.

Our clustering method outperforms these baselines and in general has high accuracy when compared with the ground truth domain labels. The one exception is when clustering the pair (Amazon-rotflip, Amazon). In this case, the domains represented in our feature space are very similar and so there is no adequate separation for the clustering algorithm to find. The last bar in Figure 5 shows the mean clustering accuracy across all domain shifts and shows the significant improvement of using our method to cluster into domains.

Object Classification Using *Bing-Caltech256*: We show the results of running our end-to-end algorithm on the Bing web search and Caltech256 dataset created by [9]. Here we assume the Bing images contain sub-domains. We use the first 30 categories from each of Bing and Caltech, and assume that all points in Bing have strict class labels (in reality, the results of web search are only weakly labeled.) There are no domain labels for the *Bing* source dataset so we present

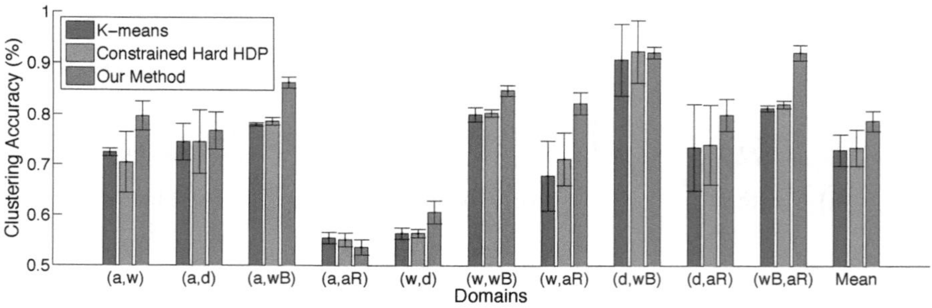

Fig. 5. Clustering quality, measured in terms of accuracy of cluster labels. Each cluster of bars represents a mixed pair of domains from the *Office* dataset, see text. The results are averaged over multiple data splits. Our method significantly outperforms the baselines in 7 out of the 10 datasets.

qualitative clustering results in Figures 6(a-c). The clusters shown represent intuitive domain distinctions, justifying out method: 6(a) cartoon/drawing/synthetic images with limited illumination, 6(b) product images with simple backgrounds and some illumination, 6(c) natural or cluttered scenes.

After clustering, we train the transforms on the first 15 categories in the Caltech256 domain and use categories 16 to 30 for testing, again testing the prediction accuracy of transformed data points into new object categories. We set $S = 2$ and use the SVM-based domain classifier described in Section 3 for the mixture model.

Figure 6 plots the results of running our algorithm with 20 instances per category in the source domain and 10 instances per category in the target domain. Ideally we would cross-validate the learning parameter γ, but due to lack of time we report results over varying γ on the test set. Our method obtains better results for a larger range of γ. The best performance obtained by the baseline is around 40% accuracy, while our method obtains 44% accuracy. This shows the advantage of using our method instead of pooling the data to learn a single transform, and that it is possible to learn domain clusters and to use them to effectively produce a better-adapted object classifier.

6 Conclusion

In this paper we presented a novel constrained clustering algorithm to distinguish unique domains from a large heterogeneous domain. Additionally, we proposed a simple multisource extension to the nonlinear transform-based ARC-t method of [1,3]. Our algorithm provides the ability to separate heterogeneous source data and learn multiple transforms, which creates a more accurate mapping of the source data onto the target domain than a single transform map. Our experiments illustrate that the multiple transformations can be effectively applied to new object categories at test time.

(a) Cluster 1

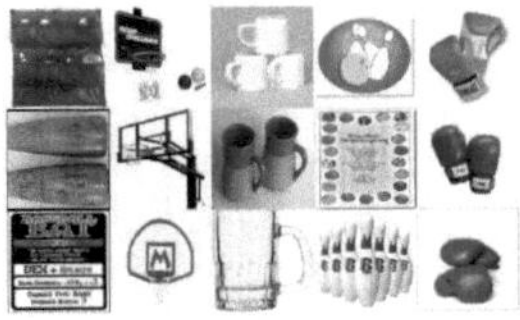

(b) Cluster 2

(c) Cluster 3

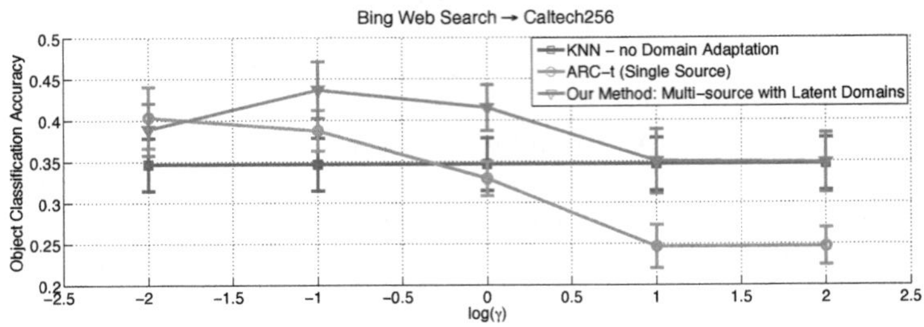

(d) Classification Result

Fig. 6. Results on the *Bing-Caltech256* dataset. (a-c) show example images from clustering the *Bing* dataset into three clusters. For each domain cluster the the three images closest to the domain cluster mean are shown from the categories baseball bat, basketball hoop, beer mug, bowling pin, and boxing glove are shown. The clusters represent intuitive domain definitions: (a) cartoon/drawings/synthetic images with limited illumination, (b) product images with simple backgrounds and some illumination, (c) natural or cluttered scenes. (d) Shows average accuracy versus the log of the learning parameter γ. Our unsupervised multi-domain method outperforms the use of a single learned transform, which falls below the KNN baseline as more weight is put on the constraints in the optimization problem.

Thus far our experiments have focused on the case of multiple domains in the source and only one domain in the target. In future work, we plan to test our algorithm with multiple target domains. This should be a direct extension by clustering the target domain using the method described in Section 4.

References

1. Saenko, K., Kulis, B., Fritz, M., Darrell, T.: Adapting Visual Category Models to New Domains. In: Daniilidis, K., Maragos, P., Paragios, N. (eds.) ECCV 2010, Part IV. LNCS, vol. 6314, pp. 213–226. Springer, Heidelberg (2010)
2. Torralba, A., Efros, A.: Unbiased look at dataset bias. In: IEEE Conference on Computer Vision and Pattern Recognition, CVPR (2011)
3. Kulis, B., Saenko, K., Darrell, T.: What you saw is not what you get: Domain adaptation using asymmetric kernel transforms. In: Proc. CVPR (2011)
4. Gopalan, R., Li, R., Chellappa, R.: Domain adaptation for object recognition: An unsupervised approach. In: 13th International Conference on Computer Vision (2011)

5. Quionero-Candela, J., Sugiyama, M., Schwaighofer, A., Lawrence, N.D.: Dataset Shift in Machine Learning. The MIT Press (2009)
6. Blitzer, J., Dredze, M., Pereira, F.: Biographies, bollywood, boom-boxes and blenders: Domain adaptation for sentiment classification. In: ACL (2007)
7. Daume III, H.: Frustratingly easy domain adaptation. In: ACL (2007)
8. Torralba, A., Efros, A.: Unbiased look at dataset bias. In: IEEE Conference on Computer Vision and Pattern Recognition, CVPR (2011)
9. Bergamo, A., Torresani, L.: Exploiting weakly-labeled web images to improve object classification: a domain adaptation approach. In: Neural Information Processing Systems, NIPS (2010)
10. Yang, J., Yan, R., Hauptmann, A.G.: Cross-domain video concept detection using Adaptive SVMs. ACM Multimedia (2007)
11. Duan, L., Tsang, I.W., Xu, D., Maybank, S.J.: Domain transfer SVM for video concept detection. In: CVPR (2009)
12. Duan, L., Xu, D., Tsang, I., Luo, J.: Visual event recognition in videos by learning from web data. In: Proc. CVPR (2010)
13. Farhadi, A., Tabrizi, M.K.: Learning to Recognize Activities from the Wrong View Point. In: Forsyth, D., Torr, P., Zisserman, A. (eds.) ECCV 2008, Part I. LNCS, vol. 5302, pp. 154–166. Springer, Heidelberg (2008)
14. Dai, W., Chen, Y., Xue, G.R., Yang, Q., Yu, Y.: Translated learning: Transfer learning across different feature spaces. In: Proc. NIPS (2008)
15. Duan, L., Tsang, I.W., Xu, D., Chua, T.S.: Domain adaptation from multiple sources via auxiliary classifiers. In: Proceedings of the 26th Annual International Conference on Machine Learning, ICML 2009 (2009)
16. Wagstaff, K., Cardie, C., Rogers, S., Schroedl, S.: Constrained k-means clustering with background knowledge. In: Proc. ICML (2001)
17. Basu, S., Bilenko, M., Mooney, R.: A probabilistic framework for semi-supervised clustering. In: Proc. 22nd SIGKDD Conference (2004)
18. Kulis, B., Basu, S., Dhillon, I., Mooney, R.: Semi-supervised graph clustering: A kernel approach. In: Proc. ICML (2005)
19. Taralova, E., De la Torre Frade, F., Hebert, M.: Source constrained clustering. In: 13th International Conference on Computer Vision (2011)
20. Basu, S., Davidson, I., Wagstaff, K. (eds.): Constrained Clustering: Advances in Algorithm, Theory, and Applications. CRC Press (2008)
21. Kulis, B., Jordan, M.I.: Revisiting k-means: New algorithms via Bayesian nonparametrics, Arxiv:1111.0352 (2011)

Visual Recognition Using Local Quantized Patterns*

Sibt ul Hussain[1] and Bill Triggs[2]

[1] GREYC, CNRS UMR 6072, Université de Caen, France
[2] Laboratoire Jean Kuntzmann, Grenoble, France
sibt.ul.hussain@gmail.com, bill.triggs@imag.fr

Abstract. Features such as Local Binary Patterns (LBP) and Local Ternary Patterns (LTP) have been very successful in a number of areas including texture analysis, face recognition and object detection. They are based on the idea that small patterns of qualitative local gray-level differences contain a great deal of information about higher-level image content. Current local pattern features use hand-specified codings that are limited to small spatial supports and coarse graylevel comparisons. We introduce Local Quantized Patterns (LQP), a generalization that uses lookup-table-based vector quantization to code larger or deeper patterns. LQP inherits some of the flexibility and power of visual word representations without sacrificing the run-time speed and simplicity of local pattern ones. We show that it outperforms well-established features including HOG, LBP and LTP and their combinations on a range of challenging object detection and texture classification problems.

1 Introduction

"Local pattern" features such as Local Binary Patterns (LBP) [1,2,3], Local Ternary Patterns (LTP) [4] and Weber Law Descriptors (WLD) [5] are based on the idea that small patterns of qualitative local gray-level differences contain a great deal of information about higher-level image content. Despite their extreme simplicity and locality, local patterns have proven very successful in visual recognition tasks ranging from texture classification to face analysis and object detection [3]. For example, [6] shows that LTP outperforms established feature sets such as HOG on the PASCAL VOC2006 object detection challenge, and that combining HOG, LTP and LBP gives even better results.

Local pattern methods associate a discrete "code" with each image pixel – a qualitative gray-value pattern that characterizes the content of the pixel's immediate image neighbourhood – then tally the occurrences of each code value over a suitable set of larger image regions, *e.g.* a grid of rectangular cells overlying the putative object. The resulting histograms are used as visual descriptors for recognition. This strategy is surprisingly effective [3], but current local pattern

* This work was supported by the Higher Education Commission (HEC) of Pakistan and European Commission research project CLASS.

A. Fitzgibbon et al. (Eds.): ECCV 2012, Part II, LNCS 7573, pp. 716–729, 2012.

approaches use hand-specified codings that severely limit the shapes and sizes of neighbourhoods that can be handled and the depths of the gray-value comparisons (typically to simple binary thresholding). It is worth asking whether variants incorporating different neighbourhood shapes such as strips or rectangles of pixels, more pixels, or finer comparisons would be even more effective.

The problem is that the code size (the number of different local patterns that can occur), and hence the size of the cell-level histograms, increases exponentially with the spatial support of the pattern and the number of quantization levels. Specifically, quantizing a group of n gray-level comparisons into k levels gives a code of size k^n. For practical object recognition tasks we would like to limit the histograms to at most a few hundred entries per cell, which limits the size of the local patterns to at most about 8 binary pixel comparisons or 5 ternary ones. For example LBP and LTP neighbourhoods typically sample just 8 pixels on a circle of radius one pixel around the central pixel. LBP [3] then thresholds these at the gray-value of the central pixel to produce a $2^8 = 256$ valued coding, whereas LTP [4] introduces a parameter τ, thresholds at $-\tau$ and τ to generate 3-way comparisons, then splits the resulting ternary codes into "positive" and "negative" binary halves to produce two 256-valued codings. Splitting is introduced because a $3^8 = 6561$ valued code would not be practicable, but despite its heuristic nature it seems to work well in practice [4,6].

Furthermore, in both cases one typically post-processes the output to produce "uniform" codings. Ojala *et al* [1] observed that of the 256 possible LBP code values, the "uniform patterns" – ones that have at most one island of ones and one island of zeros around the sampled circle – both predominate and carry most of the discriminative power. There are 58 of these, and the counts for the remaining patterns are typically pooled into a single additional "non-uniform" bin, giving 59 bin output histograms.

Although the splitting and uniform coding dimensionality reductions are well-established, it should not be forgotten that they are basically palliatives for a more fundamental problem: the exponential growth of codebook size with neighbourhood size and quantization depth. It is unclear how much information is lost during splitting and whether taking positive and negative halves is the best way to organize the split. Similarly, it is unclear how best to generalize uniform coding to non-circular spatial topologies and to ternary or higher-order codes, and even for binary circular ones, the quadratic increase in the number of uniform patterns with circumference limits uniform coding to groups of at most about 20 pixels (and even then, the quality of the coding is likely to suffer as the fraction of the 2^n codes that are uniform rapidly becomes infinitesimal). Nor is it obvious that assigning all of the nonuniform codes to a single histogram bin is the best solution: it might be better to assign each nonuniform code to the "nearest" (in some sense) uniform one. In general it seems likely that such hand-coded reductions are limiting the size and expressiveness of local pattern representations, so it is worthwhile to try to learn more effective reductions from large (*e.g.* k^n bin) input codings to much smaller output codings that can be stored compactly.

The same problem occurs in the popular "visual words" approaches [7,8,9] where (potentially) continuous-valued feature vectors for larger image patches are reduced to a limited set of code values by vector quantization methods such as K-means. These methods could also be applied to local pattern representations, but although they would resolve many of the issues raised above, they would typically be too slow to be practicable. The problem is that they require each incoming sample to be compared to every dictionary element to discover its quantization class, or at very least they require an expensive data structure traversal for each sample at run time. This is already problematic for patch-level descriptors in visual word representations, so it would be much too slow for practical object detectors that need to evaluate the local pattern of every pixel in the image pyramid. To be useable, the cost of run-time code evaluation needs to be reduced to a near-constant-time operation per pixel – *e.g.* a closed form formula or a table lookup[1].

Our Local Quantized Pattern (LQP) approach does just this. We use vector quantization for codebook learning, but choose pattern sizes that allow run-time local pattern coding to be implemented by simple table lookup, thus combining many of the advantages of local pattern and visual word methods in an efficient and practical form that remains well-suited to hardware implementation.

There are other methods that harness quantized local neighbourhood information for visual recognition tasks, and these too suffer from the trade-off between code size and quantization time / code quality that LQP is designed to address. For example, the face recognition method of Cao *et al* [11] takes patches from nine fiducial regions on pre-detected faces and in each samples 24 preprocessed grayvalues on a double ring around each pixel (the same sampling pattern as our Disk_5 descriptors below), converting these to very high (up to 2^{17}) dimensional codes using a random projection tree coder followed by PCA to reduce the output dimensionality. Such a costly projection process is acceptable in Cao's context where descriptors are computed on only a few known patches, but it would be impractical for scanning-window object detection where dense multi-scale evaluation over the whole image is required. Similarly, Calonder *et al* [12] use random pairwise graylevel pixel or smoothed pixel comparisons to produce 128–512 bit binary patch descriptors for keypoint matching. This happens at a patch level and it converts input graylevels to long binary codes (ones much too long to histogram: 2^{128} entry histograms are not practicable), whereas LQP happens at a pixel level and converts moderate-length binary or ternary codes to shorter vector quantized ones.

Our basic LQP approach is sketched in the next section. The subsequent sections give further details and experimental results.

2 Local Quantized Patterns

The essence of LQP is to apply visual word quantization to discrete local patterns, using a precompiled lookup table (LUT) to cache the final coding for

[1] See [10] for a visual word approach with similar motivations.

speed. The main constraint is the size of the lookup table, which must store the output code for every possible input pattern. For example, for a local pattern that includes 24 binary pixel-comparisons the table has $2^{24} = 17$ million entries, while for one including 16 ternary pixel-comparisons it has $3^{16} = 43$ million entries and for one including 10 5-level pixel-comparisons it has $5^{10} = 9.8$ million. These are reasonable upper limits for implementation in hardware, so in practice LQP allows patterns to be about three times the size of existing local pattern methods – going from 8 to 24 pixels for binary coding and from 5 to 16 for direct ternary coding. Alternative data structures may allow these sizes to be increased somewhat, but for simplicity we only test direct table lookup here. Codebooks typically contain only $O(10^2)$–$O(10^3)$ output codes, so $O(10^5)$ input patterns map to each output code.

We will see that the use of larger local pattern neighbourhoods provides a significant increase in discriminative power. LQP also allows a much wider range of neighbourhood shapes, and it adapts the coding to the application, the neighbourhood shape, and the desired output size. Moreover, although we will only test simple L_2 pattern comparison here, LQP's table-lookup structure allows it to handle more sophisticated pattern comparison metrics such as Earth Mover style distances and coding under symmetries such as rotations and reflections [3], all at no additional run-time cost.

The lookup-table architecture also accelerates codebook learning. During learning the codebook-training dataset is scanned once to tally the occurrences of each input code that occurs, storing these in a hash table or index, then these values and counts are passed to the algorithm that actually learns the codebook, *e.g.* a count-weighted version of K-means. This typically makes training fast because most of the possible input codes do not occur at all and for those that do, all occurrences are processed in a single operation. *E.g.* for 24-bit binary vectors over the INRIA Person positive training set, only 671k of the 17M possible input values actually occur and as a result 10 rounds of K-means for a 100 element dictionary takes only 12 minutes.

2.1 Local Pattern Geometry

As mentioned above, within the above size limits (24 pixel-comparisons for binary and split ternary coding, 16 for full ternary coding) LQP allows many different neighbourhood geometries. This flexibility is one of its advantages. Here we test a representative selection of geometries including: horizontal (H), vertical (V), diagonal (D) and antidiagonal (A) strips of pixels; combinations of these like horizontal-vertical (HV), diagonal-antidiagonal (DA) and horizontal-vertical-diagonal-antidiagonal (HVDA); and traditional circular and disk-shaped regions – *c.f.* Figure 1. By default we compare each non-central pixel to the central one, but we also tested "center symmetric" (CS) codes where each pixel is compared to the diametrically opposite one. LQP geometries will be described by notation such as HV_7^3, where HV denotes the neighbourhood shape (here a horizontal-vertical cross), the subscript indicates the neighbourhood diameter (here 7 pixels) and the superscript indicates the quantization level (here native ternary coding – 3^* denotes split ternary coding and 2 binary coding).

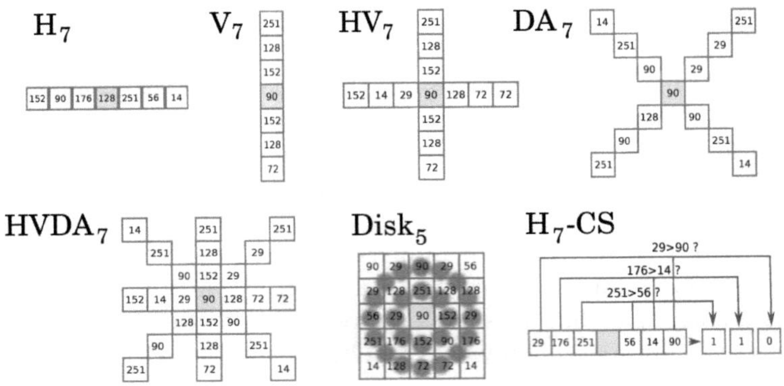

Fig. 1. Some examples of the local pattern geometries that we have tested. The subscript denotes the diameter of the local pattern neighbourhood in pixels. A superscript is added to denote the depth of quantization: 2 for binary coding, 3 for full ternary coding, and 3* for split ternary coding. In each case, pixels are sampled around a central pixel (shaded yellow) and compared with either the central pixel (standard case) or the diametrically opposite one (CS case).

Separate codebooks are learned for the positive and negative halves of split ternary codes. The results below show that when using ternary patterns, it is almost always advantageous to split the code to allow a larger spatial support to be used.

As always, at the cell level simple histogram concatenation can be used to combine the codes from different types of LQP neighbourhoods or from alternative feature sets. This effectively allows neighbourhoods with more pixels to be coded at the cost of ignoring co-occurrences between their different sub-patterns. Also note that elongated LQP's such as the strips H_{25} and V_{25} are typically so wide that they cross several cells, making them difficult to handle owing to boundary effects.

2.2 Codebook Learning

By default we represent input patterns as binary or ternary vectors, using K-means [13] over the standard L_2 inter-vector distance to learn our visual codebooks. Our algorithm counts the number of occurrences of each possible input code on the training set, using the resulting sparse table to run K-means. It is run ten times with different random initializations, taking the codebook from the run that gives the lowest K-means quantization error on the training set. Below we use conventional hard K-means coding. We also tested a soft-coding variant in which the lookup table stored the $c \leq 10$ nearest code centers for each input and the incoming patterns were soft-quantized against all c codes using uniform weighting, but we found that this reduced the accuracy.

For comparison, we also implemented a fast discriminative coding method. We trained random forests of classification trees over raw (unquantized) pixel differences, using them to construct tree-leaf-level output codes in the fashion

Table 1. Texture classification accuracies for various features and datasets. Columns 4-5 show results for our implementations of color and grayscale WLD, while columns 6-7 reproduce grayscale WLD and MWLD results from [5].

	LBP	LTP	Disk_5^{3*}	CWLD	WLD	WLD	MWLD
Brodatz	90.6	95.7	96.9	89.3	89.3	97.1	-
KTH	58.7	60.7	64.2	56.5	59.4	56.4	64.7
CUReT	88.1	88.7	92.2	83.8	82.2	-	-

of [14,15]. To capture the diversity of the datasets, relatively large numbers of relatively shallow trees were used. Although Random Forests do not require a preliminary quantization of the input values, their output codings appear to be less effective than K-means ones as well as being much slower to train and use. This is perhaps because distance-based methods like K-means provide comparatively regular decompositions of the input space, whereas – notwithstanding their discriminative nature and unquantized inputs – Random Forests only provide coarse random partitionings. For instance, anticipating the results below, for the H_7^3+V_7^3 feature combination with single root Latent SVM detectors on the INRIA Person dataset, a K-means coding with 100 centers and hence 200 histogram bins gives an Average Precision of 65.3%, whereas Random Forest codings with 16 trees of respectively 8 leaf nodes (128 bin histograms) and 16 leaf nodes (256 bin histograms) give only 57.7% and 59.0%. For this reason we only present results for K-means in the experiments below.

3 Texture Classification Experiments

We will provide a detailed experimental study of LQP for object detection below, but first we anticipate the settings found there to give some brief results on the simpler problem of texture classification. We test LQP on the Brodatz32 [16,17], CUReT [18][2] and KTH-TIPS-2a [19] datasets. In each case the descriptor is the LQP histogram of the entire unpreprocessed input image. To simplify comparison with previous work we present accuracies for 3-nearest-neighbour classifiers. (SVM classifiers give better results [19] without changing the rankings of the different feature sets). We tested the χ^2 and Normalized Intersection histogram comparison metrics, reporting χ^2. We tested various histogram normalization schemes: unnormalized histograms and L2 normalization gave the equal-best results, so we report results for unnormalized histograms.

We follow the protocols of [5,19,9]. For Brodatz [5], the data for each class is split randomly into equal halves with half used for training and the other half for testing. We report averages over 10 random trials. For KTH [19], three samples of each class are used for training and the fourth for testing. We report averages over four random partitions. For CUReT [9], we split the images of each class into equal parts and use half for training and the remaining half for testing.

Table 1 summarizes the results for the Disk_5^{3*} LQP features. In all three cases, LQP outperforms LTP which in turn outperforms LBP. We also tested against

[2] From `http://www.robots.ox.ac.uk/$\sim$vgg/research/texclass/index.html`

WLD and multi-scale WLD (MWLD, which concatenates WLD histograms from several different spatial supports and scales) [5]. We were not able to reproduce the results of [5] with our grayscale WLD implementation[3], doing worse on Brodatz and better on KTH, so we give figures for both implementations and also for our color WLD to allow comparison with the other features shown. Overall, LQP appears to outperform WLD. A fair comparison with MWLD is more difficult as results for it [5] are available only on KTH and its feature dimension is about 6 times higher than that of LQP.

4 Object Detection Experiments

For object detection we give results on the INRIA Person [20] and PASCAL VOC 2006 and 2007 [21] datasets, using INRIA mainly for parameter setting. We follow VOC2006 protocols for all datasets, reporting Average Precisions (AP's), *i.e.* areas under Precision-Recall curves. Our detectors are based on those of [20,22,6]. For each feature set, we overlay the image with a grid of 8×8 pixel cells, using bilinear spatial interpolation to accumulate votes into the cell-level histograms in order to provide robustness to small spatial displacements. The histograms are gathered into detector-window-level feature vectors and used in Latent SVM sliding window detectors in the manner of [22]. As our principal goal is to evaluate a broad range of LQP configurations, not to get the absolute best possible results on each individual problem, we only test latent detectors without parts. Past experience suggests that including parts would give better results for all of the feature sets tested without significantly changing their relative rankings. The SVM's are trained using densified SVMLight [23,20] (single root case) or LatentSVM [22] (multiple root case).

For HOG we use HOG_{31} features [22] by default – these include both signed and unsigned gradient orientations and dimensionality reduction over the different normalizations of a cell. For LBP and LTP we follow [6]. Circular 8-sample patterns of radius 1 pixel are used, with bilinear interpolation to resample the pixels needed from the unpreprocessed input image. Uniform coding is used, with splitting for LTP. For color images, patterns are evaluated separately on the R, G and B color channels then accumulated into a shared histogram. L_1-Sqrt normalization is used for histograms, *i.e.* they are normalized to sum 1 then square-rooted. Our LQP features use exactly the same approach, simply substituting the LQP code for the LBP/LTP one, without uniform coding but with splitting where indicated.

4.1 INRIA Person Dataset

Strip Layouts. Table 2 shows AP's on the INRIA Person dataset for detectors using LQP features based on single horizontal, vertical or diagonal strips of pixels. These single-strip features turn out to be quite weak, giving significantly lower performance than existing feature sets: LBP, LTP and HOG give

[3] We do not apply the empirical histogram reweighting from [5] as we find that it makes the results much worse, but in either case our results differ from [5].

Table 2. AP's for various detectors trained using single-strip LQP features on the INRIA Person dataset. The missing values correspond to features that have so few input codes that they can be coded directly without using LQP, *e.g.* H^2_7 has $2^7 = 128$ codes in total.

Diameter	H^3	V^3	D^3	H^2	V^2	D^2
7	63.3	61.4	60.5	-	-	-
9	64.9	64.8	61.8	46.4	49.0	47.1
15	67.2	68.4	62.3	54.7	53.8	51.4

Table 3. The effect of different LQP geometries and codebook sizes on the AP's of single root latent detectors on the INRIA Person dataset. Note that for split ('3*') features, the final descriptor size is twice the quoted codebook size.

Codebook Size	50	60	80	100	150	200	300
HV^3_5	76.8	76.4	76.1	77.9	77.0	80.0	79.9
$HVDA^3_5$	77.3	77.0	79.8	78.7	79.9	81.5	82.3
HV^3_7	77.6	77.1	77.8	79.5	79.1	79.6	81.4
DA^3_7	75.1	76.1	76.0	77.0	76.3	78.4	79.1
$HVDA^{3*}_7$	80.1	81.1	80.2	80.9	81.7	82.0	82.6
$Disc^{3*}_5$	79.3	79.9	81.3	81.2	82.2	81.3	81.4

respectively 74.0%, 79.0% and 79.0% AP on this dataset. However it is at least clear that increasing the length of the strip increases the performance, as does replacing binary codes with ternary ones. The corresponding center-symmetric features (which compare each pixel with its diametrically opposite one, not with the center one, thus halving the size of the input code) consistently give much lower performance – *e.g.* H^3-CS and V^3-CS respectively have AP's of 59.3% and 59.1% – so we do not test them further here.

Cross Layouts. Including several complementary strips in the LQP neighbourhood significantly increases the accuracy – *c.f.* Table 3. For instance, for a 100 word dictionary the cross layout HV^3_7 gives 79.5% AP whereas the cell-level concatenation of the 100 word H^3_7 and V^3_7 LQP histograms gives only 74.6%. If split uniform LTP coding is used instead of LQP coding for the H^3_7 and V^3_7 histograms, the results are still worse – 60.4% AP for a $4 \times 33 = 132$ dimensional histogram. It seems that the richer co-occurrence statistics captured by HV^3_7 are more useful than the 100 extra codewords of H^3_7+V^3_7. Despite the inclusion of only two orientations, HV^3_7 is already slightly better than HOG or LTP: both give 79.0% AP on this dataset. In contrast, DA^3_7, which combines diagonal and antidiagonal strips, gives only 77.0% AP: presumably horizontal and vertical slices are more discriminant for people than diagonal ones. Incorporating all four types of strip in a "Union Jack" pattern HVDA further improves the results, although split coding must be used in this case owing to the number of pixels in the pattern.

Disk Layouts. Disk-shaped patterns can do even better. Using 100 word codebooks on the INRIA dataset, the two-ring 24-pixel pattern $Disk^{3*}_5$ (81.2% AP) outperforms both the 16-pixel ($HVDA^3_5$, 78.7% AP) and 24-pixel ($HVDA^{3*}_7$, 80.9% AP) Union Jacks as well as LTP and HOG (both 79.0% AP) – *c.f.* Table 3. The VOC2006 results below confirm that $Disk^{3*}_5$ has slightly better overall performance than $HVDA^{3*}_7$: presumably, dense circular sampling in a compact neighbourhood captures more of the characteristic class structure than sampling a fixed set of rays in the broader neighbourhood covered by $HVDA^{3*}_7$. In fact, $Disk^{3*}_5$ gives better results on the INRIA Person dataset than any previous individual or combined feature set that we are aware of, improving the AP by

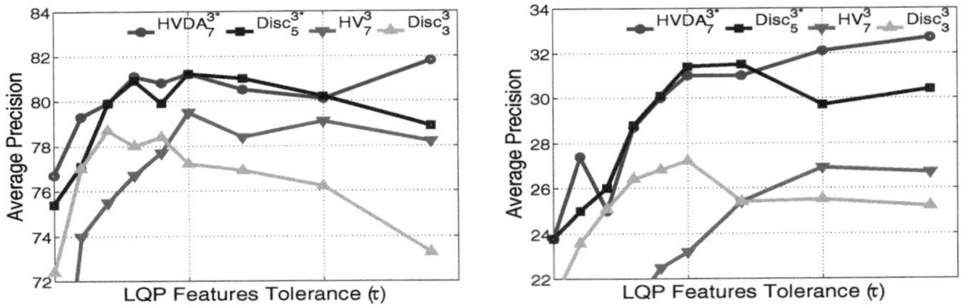

Fig. 2. Average Precisions of LQP features on the INRIA Person (left) and VOC2006 person (right) datasets, for different values of the ternary quantization threshold τ

2.2% (3.2% for the 150 word codebook) relative to the individual feature baselines HOG and LTP and by 0.2% (for the 150 word codebook) relative to the combined feature baseline LBP+LTP+HOG [6].

Haar Layout. To see whether it would be useful to include multiscale information (*c.f.* MWLD [5]), we also tested a Haar wavelet based local pattern. We take 4×4 pixel neighbourhoods around each pixel, apply the Haar wavelet transform, discard the constant term and code the remaining 15 wavelet coefficients using LQP ternary coding. In detail, this involves taking the four 2×2-pixel corner blocks of the neighbourhood and a 2×2 block containing the average of each corner one, and applying 2×2 horizontal, vertical and diagonal Haar filters [24,25] to each block. The resulting Haar LQP features give slightly better results than HOG and LTP: for 100 word codebooks, 80.7% AP versus 79% AP on the INRIA Person set, and 29.4% AP versus 25.1% and 28.9% AP on the VOC2006 person set. However the Haar patterns do not equal the performance of the best Disk and HVDA patterns on these datasets.

Splitting versus LQP. With a 118 word codebook, Disk$^3_3$ (the LQP form of LTP's 8-sample circle of 1 pixel radius) gives identical AP to traditional 118-D split uniform LTP coding. Reducing the LQP codebook size to 88 reduces the AP by only 0.8%. For the 16-sample radius-2 circle Circ$^3_5$ (the largest pattern for which unsplit ternary coding is feasible), split coding with 100 word codebooks (200-D histograms) gives 80.9% AP on INRIA whereas unsplit coding with codebook (and histogram) sizes of 100 and 200 gives respectively 78.8% and 80.5% AP. Similarly, for the VOC2006 person class, split Circ$^{3*}_5$ gives 28.3% AP while unsplit Circ$^3_5$ gives respectively 26.0% and 28.6% AP for 100 and 200 word codebooks. For the VOC2006 car class split Circ$^{3*}_5$ gives 55.0% AP while unsplit Circ$^3_5$ gives 55.2 % and 54.9% AP. These results confirm the quality of the split uniform coding used for LTP. Overall, our results consistently show that splitting causes little loss of discriminative power relative to the equivalent unsplit coding, and that it is beneficial in the sense that it allows larger spatial supports to be used, thus increasing the overall discriminative power.

Ternary Coding Threshold. Figure 2 shows the effect of the ternary coding threshold τ on the APs of various LQP features on the INRIA Person and

VOC2006 person classes. For each feature there is a broad range of τ values that gives similar results, but spatially larger patterns (notably the extended cross layouts) need larger values of τ, presumably because typical gray-level variations increase with increasing spatial separation. Over the full set of classes, $\tau = 5$ is the best value for LTP and both diameters of Disk's, whereas τ in the range of 10–14 is preferred for broad crosses such as HVDA_7^{3*}.

Choice of Codebook. Table 3 shows how codebook size affects the performance of various LQP features. As expected, despite some variability owing to the nonconvexity of K-means learning, larger codebooks usually have better performances. By default we use 100 word codebooks below as they seem to offer a reasonable compromise between descriptor size and performance, but smaller ones offer very respectable performances and larger ones are often better still.

More generally, features can be quantized using either a single codebook (learned from the positives, the negatives, or the complete training set), or several concatenated codebooks – for example ones learned separately on the positive and negative training sets. Moreover, for positive training we can also learn a separate "cell level" codebook for each cell of the detection window, subsequently quantizing the pixels of each cell of the current window using that cell's positive codebook and the global negative one.

Table 4 shows the effect of these different codebook learning schemes on the accuracy of INRIA Person detectors using HV_7^3 features. The single-codebook results are better than the multiple-codebook ones and in the multiple codebook case, learning separate cell-level positive codebooks provides only a small increase in AP so it does not seem to be warranted given its extra complexity. Unsurprisingly, using positives alone for codebook learning is better than using negatives alone – the positive codebooks are trained on structures that are important for characterizing the object class – but, perhaps surprisingly, pooling the positives and negatives during training gives worse results than using either positives or negatives alone. For the binary and split ternary codings, initializing some of the K-means centers at the LBP/LTP uniform patterns to encourage the latter to be well coded does not change the performance. Similarly, for global positive and negative codebooks, learning the negative codebook first and using it to initialize the positive one does not change the performance. By default we therefore use single 100 word codebooks obtained by running K-means on (all of the R, G and B pixels of the annotation windows of) the positive training data.

Combination with HOG Features. On the INRIA Person dataset, the LQP features are so strong that our single root latent SVM classifiers are nearly saturated, so (particularly for strong performers such as Disk_5^{3*}) including additional features such as HOG provides only modest gains in accuracy, *c.f.* Table 5. However the results for VOC2007 below show that (like other local patterns) LQP features complement HOG well on more challenging datasets.

4.2 PASCAL VOC2006

LQP features also give state of the art results on the VOC2006 dataset – *c.f.* Table 6. For instance, HV_7^3 outperforms HOG_{31} on 8 of the 10 classes, increasing

Table 4. The influence of different codebook organizations on the AP's of HV_7^3 detectors on the INRIA Person dataset

Codebook Type	Positive	Negative	Combined	Positive & Negative Cell Based	
Cell Dimension	100	100	100	200	200
HV_7^3	79.5	78.8	77.8	77.0	78.0

Table 5. Average Precisions on the INRIA Person dataset for detectors using classical HOG [20] plus the given ternary LQP features with 100 word codebooks. For comparison, HOG alone gives 79.0%, LTP+HOG gives 81.3% and LBP+LTP+HOG gives 82.0% AP [6].

	HV_7^3	DA_7^3	$HVDA_5^3$	$HVDA_7^{3*}$	$Disk_5^{3*}$	$HVDA_9^3$-CS
LQP	79.5	77.0	78.7	80.9	81.2	78.5
LQP+HOG	81.7	80.5	**82.8**	82.7	**82.8**	81.8

Table 6. Average Precisions of single root latent SVM detectors on the VOC2006 test set using HOG_{31}, LBP, LTP and LQP features. The results for LBP+LTP+HOG are from [6]. Overall, $Disk_5^{3*}$ outperforms all three of HOG, LBP and LTP, and even their combination LBP+LTP+HOG.

LQP Type	CB Size	Desc Size	**Mean**	Bike	Bus	Car	Cat	Cow	Dog	Horse	Mbike	Person	Sheep
HV_7^3	100	100	34.6	55.8	39.8	55.1	16.0	32.8	14.8	21.8	46.9	25.0	38.2
	150	150	35.6	56.4	42.0	54.5	16.1	36.5	15.8	22.2	47.6	25.8	38.9
$HVDA_5^3$	300	300	36.2	52.8	43.5	**56.8**	14.9	35.9	17.3	26.7	48.4	26.8	38.7
$HVDA_7^{3*}$	100	200	38.3	**58.2**	45.9	56.1	14.6	38.0	17.4	27.7	52.4	32.7	39.8
	150	300	39.4	58.0	46.5	56.5	19.0	**39.0**	17.6	28.9	**52.7**	**33.0**	42.6
$Disk_5^{3*}$	100	200	38.8	57.8	46.2	56.1	19.3	37.6	18.8	30.9	50.2	29.9	41.2
	150	300	**39.8**	57.9	**49.0**	56.3	**20.1**	37.7	**18.9**	**32.1**	50.5	31.9	**43.1**
HOG	31	31	31.6	57.2	40.1	55.0	5.0	31.9	5.3	22.0	41.7	25.1	32.2
LBP	59	59	33.2	54.0	39.5	53.8	15.9	33.0	9.2	21.1	44.8	21.8	38.4
LTP	59	118	37.8	56.2	45.2	56.1	17.3	35.8	16.8	29.8	51.4	28.9	40.0
LBP+LTP+HOG	149	208	38.3	57.9	44.4	56.0	18.7	37.0	16.0	29.0	51.2	32.8	39.8

the Mean AP by 4%, and LBP on all 10, increasing the Mean AP by 2.4%. LTP outperforms HV_7^3 on 8 of the 10 classes, but $Disk_5^{3*}$ outperforms LTP on 9 of the 10, increasing the Mean AP by 1.0% (and by 2.0% for 150 word codebooks). $Disk_5^{3*}$ also outperforms $HVDA_7^{3*}$ on 5 of the 10 classes, increasing the Mean AP by 0.4%, and the combination LBP+LTP+HOG [6] on 7 of the 10, increasing the Mean AP by 0.5% despite being lower dimensional. Similarly, for 150 word codebooks $Disk_5^{3*}$ outperforms LBP+LTP+HOG on 7 of the 10 classes, increasing the Mean AP by 1.5%. These improvements occur both for structure-dominated classes like cars and people and texture-dominated ones like cats and dogs, so LQP seems to capture both types of cues well. To the best of our knowledge, the $Disk_5^{3*}$ and $HVDA_7^{3*}$ results surpass those of any previously reported local feature set or combination on INRIA Person and VOC2006, at least for root-

Table 7. Average Precisions for 6-root Latent SVM detectors trained on VOC2007

Class	**Mean**	Aero	Bike	Bird	Boat	Bottle	Bus	Car	Cat	Chair	Cow	Table	Dog	Horse	Mbike	Person	Plant	Sheep	Sofa	Train	TV
HOG	24.1	22.7	51.5	3.2	11.8	16.8	40.1	44.8	8.0	15.6	19.7	10.9	5.7	43.3	38.1	31.6	10.7	14.7	23.7	34.5	34.3
Disk_5^{3*}	28.4	28.8	49.4	5.2	17.0	21.1	44.1	47.0	15.8	19.0	22.5	16.4	**12.7**	53.2	45.0	32.5	**14.1**	23.3	27.0	38.3	35.8
HOG+Disk_5^{3*}	**30.6**	**29.5**	**53.6**	**8.3**	**17.9**	**21.9**	**47.5**	**50.4**	**16.3**	**20.4**	**24.5**	**20.6**	10.1	**55.0**	**47.1**	**37.5**	13.5	**24.2**	**33.0**	**42.1**	**38.7**

only latent detectors without additional context. (The previous records were held respectively by LTP and LBP+LTP+HOG [6]).

Statistical Significance. Treating each class as an independent binomial trial, if a new feature has better AP than an old one on 8, 9, 10 of the ten classes, the hypothesis that the new feature is no better than the old one can be rejected with respectively 94.6%, 98.9%, 99.9% significance, irrespective of the actual differences in the AP's. By this criterion, 100 word and 150 word Disk_5^{3*} outperform LTP at respectively the 98.0% and 98.9% confidence levels and LBP+LTP+HOG at the 82.9% and 96.9% ones on VOC2006. Without multiple trials or paired testing, standard deviation based tests are too weak to establish high levels of significance for the individual classes – VOC2006 has 233–1153 test examples per class giving the estimated AP's binomial-law standard deviations of 1.4–3.3% – but the corresponding Mean AP's have standard deviations of about 0.7% which is enough to establish 95% significance for 150 word Disk_5^{3*} over LTP, and strong suggestiveness for it over LBP+LTP+HOG.

4.3 PASCAL VOC2007

Table 7 illustrates that Disk_5^{3*} LQP features also give state of the art results for multi-root detectors[4] on VOC2007. Disk_5^{3*} outperforms HOG_{31} on 19 of the 20 classes, increasing the Mean AP by 4.3%, while the combination HOG+Disk_5^{3*} outperforms Disk_5^{3*} on 18 of the 20, increasing the Mean AP by 2.2%, most notably on the structure-dominated classes like bicycle and person for which HOG is known to be a strong feature.

5 Discussion

Given the above results, several points seem clear. Firstly, the fact that splitting ternary codes into their two binary halves leads to little performance loss both validates the use of splitting in LTP (and of binary coding in LBP), and suggests that the performance improvements provided by LQP are due mainly to the increased pattern sizes that lookup-table based coding permits, not per se to the absence of splitting or to the replacement of hand-specified codings with adaptive K-means ones. It also suggests that coding orders higher than ternary will give only limited further improvements and that they should be handled by

[4] Our current K-means implementation does not force codebooks to have reflection symmetries, so these results are for detectors with 6 uncoupled roots trained on the regular and reflected examples, not for 3 reflection-symmetric root pairs as in [22].

splitting, but these points remain to be tested. Secondly, in agreement with the forms of existing local pattern features, patterns that sample pixels densely in a compact local neighbourhood around the center seem to give the best performance, so disk-shaped neighbourhoods are likely to be the best choice for many applications. Thirdly, even for large spatial supports, good results are obtained with quite modest codebook sizes – often even smaller than the corresponding LTP code. In any case, LQP itself can handle large codebooks with no loss of speed at run time: the issue is whether the subsequent classifier can handle the large histograms that result.

Despite the extra table lookup, LQP features remain very fast to train and test. For instance on a 3 GHz Pentium 6, HV_7^3, $HVDA_7^{3*}$ and $Disk_5^{3*}$ respectively take about 1.9, 3.1 and 4.5 seconds to scan a VOC2006 image. The extra time for $Disk_5^{3*}$ is due to the need to resample pixels on circles: this takes much longer than the table lookup itself. However replacing the hard-wired table lookup with a conventional best codeword search over a 150 word dictionary makes the $Disk_5^{3*}$ feature computation 15 times slower, and even replacing it with an efficient C++ hash table lookup doubles the LQP run time.

6 Summary

We have presented Local Quantized Patterns (LQP), a generalized form of local pattern feature that replaces the traditional hand-built codebook reduction with vector quantization, using precompiled lookup tables to make coding very fast at run time. LQP inherits some of the flexibility and robustness of visual word representations without sacrificing the efficiency of traditional local pattern ones. It can handle significantly larger patterns than previous local pattern methods (around three times as many pixels), and it easily adapts to different spatial topologies, quantization levels and datasets. These properties allow LQP to outperform traditional local pattern features such as LBP and LTP, and also well-established feature sets like HOG, on a range of challenging texture and object recognition datasets. In practice, patterns with dense sampling over compact spatial supports and split ternary coding work best, with the resulting LQP feature $Disk_5^{3*}$ outperforming LBP, LTP, HOG and even their combination LBP+LTP+HOG on the VOC 2006 and 2007 and INRIA Person datasets. Codebook (and hence descriptor vector) sizes remain modest, and codebook learning is fast owing to the lookup table architecture.

Future Work. So far we have tested only a small selection of the possible LQP configurations, and only on object detection, texture classification and face recognition [26]. LQP should be useful in many other application areas such as semantic segmentation and image classification.

References

1. Ojala, T., Pietikainen, M., Maenpaa, T.: Multiresolution gray-scale and rotation invariant texture classification with local binary patterns. IEEE TPAMI (2002)
2. Ahonen, T., Hadid, A., Pietikainen, M.: Face description with local binary patterns: Application to face recognition. IEEE TPAMI 28 (2006)

3. Pietikäinen, M., Hadid, A., Zhao, G., Ahonen, T.: Computer Vision Using Local Binary Patterns. Springer (2011)
4. Tan, X., Triggs, B.: Enhanced local texture feature sets for face recognition under difficult lighting conditions. IEEE TIP 19, 1635–1650 (2010)
5. Chen, J., Shan, S., He, C., Zhao, G., Pietikainen, M., Chen, X., Gao, W.: WLD: A robust local image descriptor. IEEE TPAMI 32, 1705–1720 (2010)
6. Hussain, S., Triggs, B.: Feature sets and dimensionality reduction for visual object detection. In: BMVC, pp. 112.1–112.10 (2010)
7. Leung, T., Malik, J.: Recognizing surfaces using three-dimensional textons. In: ICCV, pp. 1010–1017 (1999)
8. Csurka, G., Bray, C., Dance, C., Fan, L.: Visual categorization with bags of keypoints. In: Workshop on Statistical Learning in Computer Vision, ECCV (2004)
9. Varma, M., Zisserman, A.: Classifying Images of Materials: Achieving Viewpoint and Illumination Independence. In: Heyden, A., Sparr, G., Nielsen, M., Johansen, P. (eds.) ECCV 2002, Part III. LNCS, vol. 2352, pp. 255–271. Springer, Heidelberg (2002)
10. Tuytelaars, T., Schmid, C.: Vector quantizing feature space with a regular lattice. In: ICCV, pp. 1–8. IEEE (2007)
11. Cao, Z., Yin, Q., Tang, X., Sun, J.: Face recognition with learning-based descriptor. In: CVPR, pp. 2707–2714. IEEE (2010)
12. Calonder, M., Lepetit, V., Strecha, C., Fua, P.: BRIEF: Binary Robust Independent Elementary Features. In: Daniilidis, K., Maragos, P., Paragios, N. (eds.) ECCV 2010, Part IV. LNCS, vol. 6314, pp. 778–792. Springer, Heidelberg (2010)
13. Elkan, C.: Using the triangle inequality to accelerate K-Means. In: ICML, vol. 20, pp. 147–153 (2003)
14. Moosmann, F., Triggs, B., Jurie, F.: Fast discriminative visual codebooks using randomized clustering forests. In: NIPS, vol. 19, p. 985 (2007)
15. Moosmann, F., Nowak, E., Jurie, F.: Randomized clustering forests for image classification. IEEE TPAMI, 1632–1646 (2008)
16. Brodatz, P.: Textures: a photographic album for artists and designers, vol. 66. Dover, New York (1966)
17. Valkealahti, K., Oja, E.: Reduced multidimensional co-occurrence histograms in texture classification. IEEE TPAMI 20, 90–94 (1998)
18. Dana, K., Van Ginneken, B., Nayar, S., Koenderink, J.: Reflectance and texture of real-world surfaces. ACM Transactions on Graphics (TOG) 18, 1–34 (1999)
19. Caputo, B., Hayman, E., Mallikarjuna, P.: Class-specific material categorisation. In: ICCV, pp. 1597–1604. IEEE (2005)
20. Dalal, N., Triggs, B.: Histograms of oriented gradients for human detection. In: CVPR, pp. 886–893 (2005)
21. Everingham, M., Van Gool, L., Williams, C., Winn, J., Zisserman, A.: The PASCAL Visual Object Classes Challenge. IJCV (2010)
22. Felzenszwalb, P., Girshick, R., McAllester, D., Ramanan, D.: Object detection with discriminatively trained part based models. TPAMI (Release 4)
23. Joachims, T.: Making large-scale SVM learning practical. In: Schölkopf, B., Burges, C., Smola, A. (eds.) Advances in Kernel Methods - Support Vector Learning. The MIT Press, Cambridge (1999)
24. Papageorgiou, C., Poggio, T.: A trainable system for object detection. IJCV 38, 15–33 (2000)
25. Viola, P., Jones, M.J.: Robust real-time face detection. IJCV 57, 137–154 (2004)
26. Hussain, S., Napoléon, T., Jurie, F.: Face recognition using local quantized patterns. In: BMVC (2012)

Randomized Spatial Partition for Scene Recognition

Yuning Jiang, Junsong Yuan*, and Gang Yu

School of Electrical and Electronics Engineering
Nanyang Technological University, Singapore 639798
{ynjiang,jsyuan}@ntu.edu.sg, gyu1@e.ntu.edu.sg

Abstract. The spatial layout of images plays a critical role in natural scene analysis. Despite previous work, e.g., spatial pyramid matching, how to design optimal spatial layout for scene classification remains an open problem due to the large variations of scene categories. This paper presents a novel image representation method, with the objective to characterize the image layout by various patterns, in the form of randomized spatial partition (RSP). The RSP-based image representation makes it possible to mine the most descriptive image layout pattern for each category of scenes, and then combine them by training a discriminative classifier, i.e., the proposed ORSP classifier. Besides RSP image representation, another powerful classifier, called the BRSP classifier, is also proposed. By weighting and boosting a sequence of various partition patterns, the BRSP classifier is more robust to the intra-class variations hence leads to a more accurate classification. Both RSP-based classifiers are tested on three publicly available scene datasets. The experimental results highlight the effectiveness of the proposed methods.

Keywords: Random Partition, Spatial Layout, Scene Recognition.

1 Introduction

Images are different from other information carriers such as texts and audios since image patterns convey rich spatial information. Such a difference makes a number of techniques which have been successful in the text-based applications less effectiveness when applied to images, e.g., the popular bag-of-visual-word (BoVW) model [2,3,4,5]. The reason is that the BoVW model ignores the spatial information among the visual primitives in images. A lot of previous work [6,7,8,9,10] has shown that without considering the spatial information, the discriminative power of BoVW model is severely limited. Especially, when the images are composed by several distinguishing components with clear spatial layout, e.g., the natural scenes in Figure 1, the spatial layout information becomes essential in describing these images. Therefore, how to make use of the spatial layout information plays a critical role in natural scene recognition.

The most common way to incorporate the spatial layout information is to quantize the image space. By a pre-defined partition pattern, the two-dimensional image space is divided into several sub-regions, then each visual word is encoded according to the subregions it belongs to. In this way, the spatial layout of the images is characterized by

* This work is supported in part by the Nanyang Assistant Professorship (SUG M58040015) to Dr. Junsong Yuan.

A. Fitzgibbon et al. (Eds.): ECCV 2012, Part II, LNCS 7573, pp. 730–743, 2012.

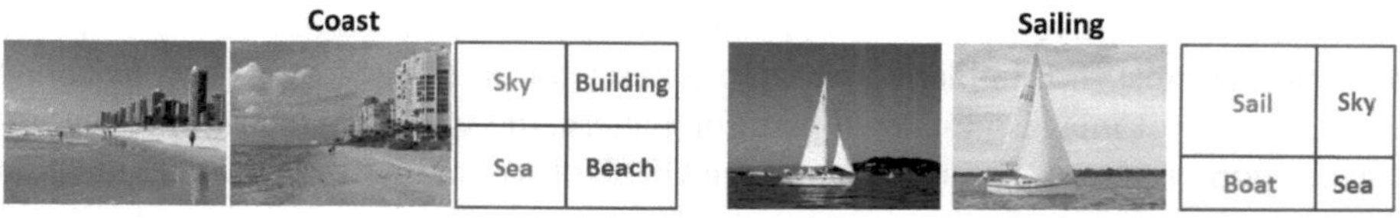

(a)

(b)

Fig. 1. (a) Examples of inter-class variations of the image layout. The left two pictures in each category are the original images while the right one is the optimal partition pattern to describe their spatial layout. We can see that sharing the same partition pattern for all the categories is not an optimal solution; (b) Examples of intra-class variations of the image layout (from 21-land-use dataset [1]). Even for the images containing the same components, their layout may vary quite a lot due to the changes in offset, scale, viewpoint and rotation.

the pre-defined partition pattern. The spatial pyramid matching (SPM) algorithm [11] is one representative of these methods, which symmetrically partitions the image into uniform cells at different levels of resolution. With the help of spatial layout information to improve the discriminative power, the SPM algorithm achieves a significant better performance, and its partition pattern, namely the spatial pyramid, is employed in many other work [1,12].

Despite previous success, the spatial pyramid still has several limitations in capturing the spatial layout information. The first challenge comes from the inter-class variations of the spatial layout of the images. As shown in Figure 1(a), the spatial layout of the images in different scene categories differs a lot from each other, hence sharing one partition pattern for all scene categories is not the optimal solution to characterize the image layout, just as done in [11]. On the contrary, each category should have its own most descriptive partition pattern, in which its spatial layout can be optimally characterized. The second challenge comes from the large intra-class variations of the image layout. From Figure 1(b) we can see that even for the images in the same category that contain the similar components, their spatial layout may vary quite a lot due to the changes in offset, scale, viewpoint and rotation. It means even if we could find one descriptive partition pattern for each category, there will be also many outliers in the same category which cannot be described satisfactorily.

This paper contributes to addressing the two challenges mentioned above: 1) we propose a novel image representation approach based on randomized spatial partition (RSP). Instead of partitioning the images by the pre-defined pattern, e.g., the symmetric spatial pyramid, we randomly partition the images multiple times and obtain a pool of independent partition patterns that can be selected later. By doing so, the image layout can be characterized by various partition patterns; 2) to address the inter-class variations, an effective RSP-based classifier via optimal selection (ORSP) is proposed to mine the most discriminative partition pattern for each category. By representing each category of images in its own partition pattern, the spatial layout of different image categories is better described hence the ORSP classifier improves the classification accuracy; 3) furthermore, a more powerful RSP-based classifier via boosting (BRSP) is proposed, in which a sequence of partition patterns are weighted according to their discriminative abilities and finally boosted into the strong classifier. Since it allows to characterize the spatial layout of one image in multiple patterns, this classifier is more robust to the large intra-class variations of the image layout. We apply both RSP-based classifiers for scene recognition on three publicly available datasets: the 15-scene dataset [13], the 8-event dataset [14], and the 21-land-use dataset [1]. The comparison with the state-of-the-art methods highlights the effectiveness of our RSP-based image classifiers.

2 Related Work

The bag-of-visual-word (BoVW) model [3,4,15,13,14] has been widely adopted in visual recognition although it has an obvious drawback of quantizing high-dimensional descriptors into visual words. In general, there are two ways to address the quantization error incurred by BoVW model. One is to match individual descriptors in the feature space directly, e.g., the Naive-Bayes Nearest Neighbor (NBNN) classifier proposed in [16,17]. However, the NBNN-based algorithms are under the Naive-Bayes assumption that each feature point is independent from the others, therefore they can fail when the assumption is violated. Besides, without considering the spatial information, matching individual features can not provide satisfactory recognition results.

Taking advantage of the spatial information is another way to mitigate the quantization error. By bundling the co-occurred visual words within a constrained spatial distance into a visual phrase or feature group as the basic unit for matching, the spatial context information is incorporated to enhance the discriminative power of visual words and leads to a better performance in object recognition [18,19,20]. Spatial random partition is used in [21,22] for local matching and visual object localization. However, these methods only characterize the relative location of the visual words rather than their absolute location, hence their descriptive abilities are limited on the images which have clear spatial layout, such as natural scenes. As one of the most popular methods in scene recognition, the spatial pyramid matching algorithm [11,1,12] divides the image space into uniform cells at different levels of resolution, and quantizes the continues coordinates of the visual words into discrete cells. In this way, the location of the visual words is encoded and the spatial layout of the images is characterized by the spatial pyramid. However, the pre-defined spatial pyramid could not always be the optimal pattern to describe the image layout of all the categories. In [23], a specific partition pattern is learnt for each category by a series of recursive axis aligned splits of cells, but it is still under the *one-pattern-per-category* restriction, that is, the images in the same category share the only pattern to describe their image layout.

3 Image Representation

In this section, we first briefly describe the original spatial pyramid matching (SPM) algorithm [11], then introduce a novel randomized spatial partition-based (RSP-based) image representation scheme.

3.1 Original SPM Image Representation

Given an image I, we denote by $\{f\}$ all the local features extracted from it. In general each local feature f is represented as $f = (x, y, \mathbf{d})$, where (x, y) is the location coordinates and $\mathbf{d}$ is the continuous high-dimensional descriptor, e.g., 128-dimensional SIFT [24]. Then in the BoVW framework, each local descriptor $\mathbf{d}$ is quantized into a discrete visual word using a vocabulary of V words, while the location coordinates (x, y) are discarded. In this way, each image I can be represented as a histogram with V bins which records its word-occurrence frequency.

In the SPM algorithm, the location coordinates are integrated to enhance the descriptive power of BoVW model, rather than being discarded simply. As in Figure 2, the two-dimensional image space is divided symmetrically into uniform cells at different levels of resolution, namely spatial pyramid. The higher level of the pyramid is, the smaller cells are. Let us consider the current level l $(0 \leq l \leq L-1)$, at which all the local features are assigned to 4^l cells according to their location coordinates. Essentially, for each local feature $f = (x, y, \mathbf{d})$, we quantize its continuous location coordinates (x, y) into these discrete cells, just like quantizing the continuous descriptor $\mathbf{d}$ into discrete visual words. Therefore, the image I can be represented as a histogram h^l with $4^l \times V$ bins at l level, and finally represented as a long histogram with $\sum_{l=0}^{L-1} 4^l V$ bins combining h^l at all levels. Note that the weights associated with different levels are inversely proportional to the cell sizes. Intuitively, the histogram bin associated with a larger cell is penalized because it means a coarser quantization.

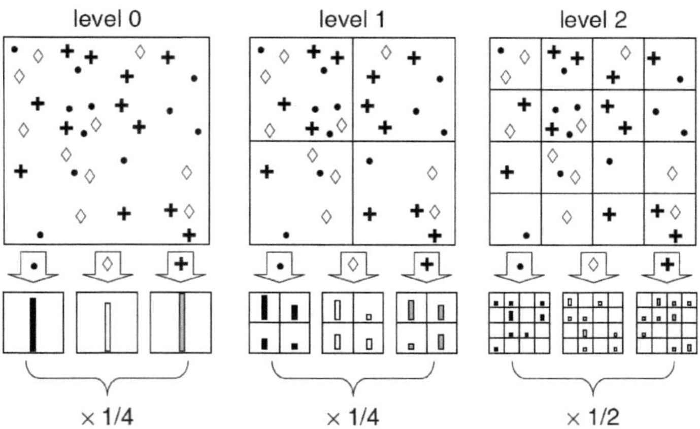

Fig. 2. Toy example of a three-level original SPM image representation method (adapted from [11]). Essentially, the SPM method is a kind of quantization process in the image space, which quantizes the continuous location coordinates (x, y) into discrete cells using the fixed symmetric pattern.

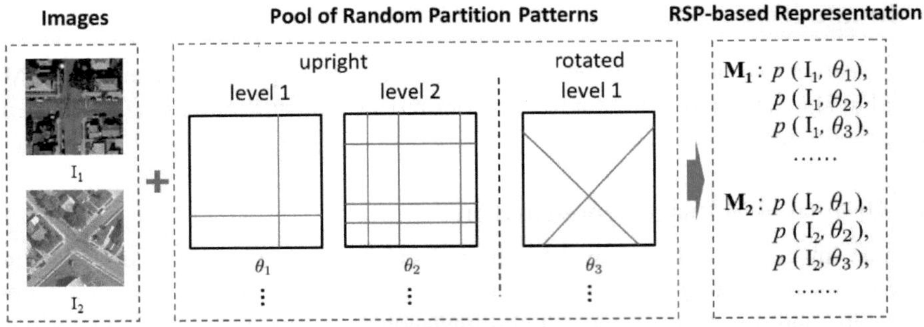

Fig. 3. Illustration of the RSP-based image representation method

3.2 RSP-Based Image Representation

As reported in [11], with the help of spatial layout information the SPM algorithm outperforms the BoVW model. However, quantizing the image space using the pre-defined spatial pyramid is empirical and arbitrary, and in most cases it is not the optimal pattern to describe the spatial layout information of an image. Therefore, here we propose an image representation method based on randomized spatial partition, with the objective to optimally characterize the spatial layout of the images.

Let us consider a single level l first. Instead of symmetrically dividing the image space into uniform cells, we randomly partition the image space into $2^l \times 2^l$ sub-regions of various sizes and shapes by one certain pattern θ. Then such randomized partition is performed for K times independently. In this way, the image space is quantized by these K random patterns, denoted by $\Theta^l = \{\theta^{l,k}\}_{k=1}^{K}$. Now for any an image I_i, it will be partitioned into 4^l image patches by each pattern $\theta^{l,k}$, and be represented as a histogram $h_i^{l,k}$ with $4^l \times V$ bins, denoted as: $h_i^{l,k} = p(I_i, \theta^{l,k})$. Therefore, in total we form a partition pattern pool $\Theta = \bigcup_{l=0}^{L-1} \Theta^l$ combining all levels, by which the image I_i is represented as a histogram collection M_i:

$$M_i = \hat{p}(I_i, \Theta) = \bigcup_{\theta \in \Theta} \{p(I_i, \theta)\}. \tag{1}$$

In this paper we not only use the upright partition patterns as in [11], but also introduce the rotated ones to enrich the variety of our pattern pool. Figure 3 gives an illustration of the RSP-based image representation method.

The motivation of the RSP-based image representation can be understood from two aspects: from the viewpoint of image layout, we perform such randomized spatial partitions with the objective to mine the best patterns which can well separate the distinguishing components of the image; from the viewpoint of local point, both the original SPM algorithm and the proposed RSP-based algorithm are essentially to encode the location coordinates of the local points by quantizing the two-dimensional image space. However, in the SPM algorithm each local point is *hard-quantized* into the unique subregion at each level, and thus the points near the edges of pyramid may be separated from their real nearest neighbors. On the contrary, in the RSP-based method each local point is *soft-quantized* into multiple sub-regions, hence the location coordinates of the point can be better described.

4 Image Classification

Now given a collection of labeled images, denoted by $\Phi = \{(I_i, c_i)\}$, where $c_i \in \{1, 2, \ldots, C\}$ is the category label of the image I_i, and a pool of independent partition patterns Θ, here we propose two approaches to obtain the robust classifier $F(\cdot)$ using the labeled training set.

4.1 RSP-Based Classifier via Optimal Selection

Our intention is straightforward: for each category we seek for an optimal pattern with best discriminative power to separate this category from the others, and then combine these optimal patterns together to train the final classifier. We summarize this procedure in three steps as follows:

Step 1, training and validation. First we divide the entire training set Φ into two subsets Φ_t and Φ_v. Then for each pattern θ, the images in both Φ_t and Φ_v are represented as the corresponding histograms, and C binary classifiers $\{f_\theta^c(\cdot)\}_{c=1}^C$ are trained on Φ_t, which is done with the support vector machine (SVM). After that, the classifier $f_\theta^c(\cdot)$ is validated on Φ_v and its classification error err_θ^c is recorded:

$$err_\theta^c = \sum_{c_v = c} \mathbf{I}(f_\theta^c(I_v) \neq c) + \sum_{c_v \neq c} \mathbf{I}(f_\theta^c(I_v) = c), \tag{2}$$

where (I_v, c_v) is the sample in Φ_v, and $\mathbf{I}(\sigma) = 1$ if σ is true; otherwise $\mathbf{I}(\sigma) = 0$;

Step 2, pattern selection. The best pattern with minimum validation error is selected as the optimal description of spatial layout information for the images of category c:

$$\theta_{best}^c = \arg\min_{\theta \in \Theta} err_\theta^c. \tag{3}$$

In this way, we finally select out C best patterns which are supposed to have strongest discriminative power for each category;

Step 3, classifier recasting. After obtaining the best patterns $\{\theta_{best}^c\}_{l=1}^C$, we re-train the binary classifiers $f_{best}^c(\cdot)$ on the entire set Φ for each θ_{best}^c. Finally the multi-class classification is implemented using the C binary classifiers and taking the majority vote.

Compared with the original SPM algorithm, this approach selects one optimal partition pattern for each category, which can describe this category with the strongest discriminative power, instead of sharing the empirical and fixed partition pattern for all the categories. Therefore, it is more in accord with the fact that each image category has its own characteristics in image layout. Though the idea is straightforward, it contributes to a considerable improvement in classification accuracy in the experiment.

4.2 RSP-Based Classifier via Boosting

In the above, we present how to train a RSP-based classifier via optimal selection (ORSP classifier for short). Despite the advantages in describing spatial layout of each category, the ORSP classifier is still under the *one-pattern-per-category* restriction hence it is not robust to the intra-class variations of image layout. Therefore, in the following we adopt the data-driven weighting strategy to train another RSP-based classifier via boosting (BRSP classifier for short), in which a sequence of patterns are weighted in proportional to their discriminative power and finally boosted together.

Algorithm 1. Training RSP-based Classifier via Boosting

Input:

A collection of labeled images: $\Phi = \{(I_i, c_i)\}_{i=1}^{N}$.
A pool of independent partition patterns: $\Theta = \{\theta\}$.
The target classification accuracy: σ_{target}.

Output:

A robust image classifier $F(\cdot)$. Give an unlabeled image I, we have $c = F(I)$, where $c \in \{1, \ldots, C\}$ is the predicted label of I.

1. **For all** $\theta \in \Theta$:
   - Randomly sample a subset $\Phi_\theta \subset \Phi$, and represent the images in Φ_θ in pattern θ.
   - Train a multi-class classifier $f_\theta(\cdot)$ on the random subset Φ_θ using SVM.
2. Initialize the weight $w_i = \frac{1}{CN_{c_i}}$ for each images I_i, where N_{c_i} is the number of the images with label c_i; the current iteration number $j = 0$; the current accuracy $\sigma^{(0)} = 0$.
3. **While** $(\sigma^{(j)} < \sigma_{target})$
   - $\forall i = 1, \ldots, N, w_i \leftarrow \frac{w_i}{\sum_{i=1}^{N} w_i}; j \leftarrow j + 1.$
   - $\forall \theta \in \Theta$, calculate its classification error on Φ: $err_\theta = \sum_{I_i \in \Phi} w_i \cdot \mathbf{I}(f_\theta(I_i) \neq c_i)$.
   - Select the pattern $\theta^{(j)}$ with minimum error $err^{(j)}$, and then calculate the weight for $\theta^{(j)}$ as:
   $$\alpha^{(j)} = \log \frac{1 - err^{(j)}}{err^{(j)}} + \log(C - 1).$$
   - $\forall i = 1, \ldots, N, w_i \leftarrow w_i \cdot \exp(\alpha^{(j)} \cdot \mathbf{I}(f_{\theta^{(j)}}(I_i) \neq c_i)).$
   - Generate the strong classifier as:
   $$F(I) = \arg\max_c \sum_{m=1}^{j} \alpha^{(m)} \cdot \mathbf{I}(f_{\theta^{(m)}}(I) = c),$$
   and calculate its classification accuracy on Φ: $\sigma^{(j)} = \sum_{I_i \in \Phi} \mathbf{I}(F(I_i) = c_i)/N$.

Since Algorithm 1 has illustrated this algorithm in detail, here we only give some explanations: first, to promote the independence of the weak classifiers, the bootstrapping is adopted in Step 1, i.e., each weak classifier $f_\theta(\cdot)$ is trained on a random subset $\Phi_\theta \subset \Phi$; second, in Step 2, the weight of each image is initialized in inversely proportion to its category size to prevent the problem of unbalanced samples; third, the *SAMME* Adaboost algorithm [25] is employed to address the multi-class cases; in final, we set the stop condition of the loop as a target training accuracy σ_{target}, rather than the number of iterations. The reason is that in the experiment, we find only a few patterns (generally less than 30) will be selected out when it converges. Therefore, to avoid overfitting, we will stop the iterations before the training error becomes 0.

We can see several benefits of the BRSP classifier: first of all, a data-driven weighting strategy is adopted instead of the uniform weighting strategy, that is, the partition patterns are weighted according to their recognition performances on the training dataset; next, it breaks the *one-pattern-per-category* restriction and allows to describe the spatial layout of one image in multiple partition patterns. Therefore, it can better deal with the categories with large intra-class variations; finally, taking the advantages of boosting algorithm, these confusing images which are classified mistakenly will be focused hence the final classifier is more robust to those outliers.

5 Experiment

In this section, we report our experimental results on three publicly available datasets: the 15-scene dataset [13], the 8-event dataset [14], and the 21-land-use dataset [1]. All experiments are repeated 3 times with different randomly selected training and test sets, and the average of recognition rates are recorded as the final results. The SVMs are implemented using the LIBSVM package.[1]

5.1 The 15-Scene Dataset

First, we perform our algorithm for natural scene recognition on the 15-scene datasets, which is one of the most complete scene category datasets collected gradually by several research groups [13,11,26]. The 15-scene dataset is composed of fifteen natural scene categories: *bedroom, suburb, industrial, kitchen, livingroom, coast, forest, highway, insidecity, mountain, opencountry, street, tallbuilding, office* and *store*. Each category has 216 to 400 images with resolution around 300 × 250. As in [11], from each image the dense SIFT descriptors of 16 × 16 pixel patches computed over a grid are extracted with spacing of 8 pixels. And then, 100 images per category, 1500 images in total, are randomly selected out as the training set Φ, while the rest is prepared as testing set. We randomly sample 450 images from the training set Φ, and perform k-means clustering on all the SIFT descriptors of these 450 images to generate a vocabulary with $V = 400$ visual words, by which all the SIFT descriptors from the 15-scene dataset are quantized into discrete words.

We set the randomized spatial partition parameters as follows: the highest level L is set to 3, i.e., $l = 0, 1, 2$. The reason to choose $L = 3$ is that the results in [11] have shown a higher level ($l \geqslant 3$) may lead to a decrease in accuracy due to over subdivision; then for both $l = 1, 2$ levels, the randomized partition number K is set to 100. Specially, for $l = 0$ level the partition number is $K = 1$ since in fact no division is made at this level; to make a fair comparison with the SPM algorithm [11], in which only upright spatial pyramid is used, we do not introduce the rotated partition patterns for this dataset. Therefore, a pool of all upright patterns Θ_u is formed which contains 201 random partition patterns in total.

After the preparation work on image representation, now both the two types of RSP-based classifiers proposed in Section 4 are trained. Linear kernel is incorporated for all SVMs as in [11]. For the ORSP classifier, we set two subsets of the Φ, Φ_t for training and Φ_v for validation, respectively, are in the same size, $|\Phi_t| = |\Phi_v|$. For the BRSP classifier, we also keep $|\Phi_\theta| = 50\% \times |\Phi|$ for all the patterns. The target training error is set as $\sigma_{target} = 98\%$. Table 1 reports the classification accuracy of these two types of RSP-based classifiers and gives a comparison with the results of the SPM algorithm.

The results shown in Table 1 is analyzed as follows: first, by comparing the performance of the original SPM algorithm (2_{nd} column) and the ORSP classifier (3_{rd} column), we can see that the latter leads to a significant increase in classification accuracy while the only difference between these two methods is the way to divide the image space. This comparison supports our point that quantizing the image space by symmetric divisions is not optimal to describe the spatial information, and it can be

[1] `http://www.csie.ntu.edu.tw/ cjlin/libsvm/.`

Table 1. Comparison with SPM at different levels on the 15-scene dataset

level	Original SPM [11]	ORSP Classifier	BRSP Classifier
$l = 0$	74.8%	-	-
$l = 1$	78.8%	80.7%	86.4%
$l = 2$	79.7%	82.6%	87.1%
$l = 0, 1, 2$	81.4%	83.9%	87.2%

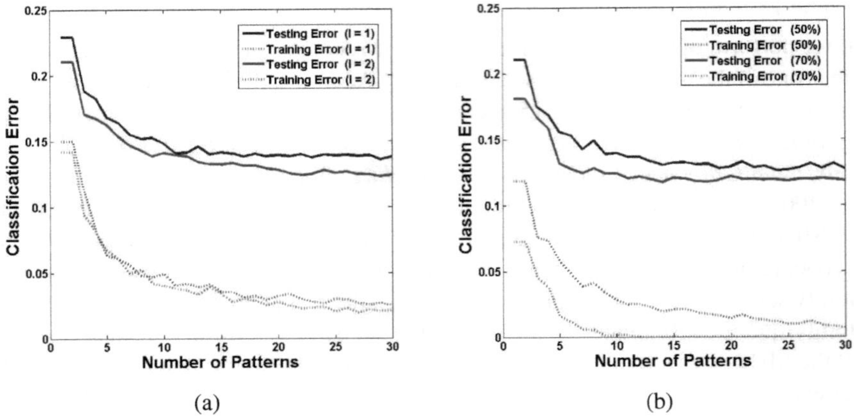

Fig. 4. The curves of training error and testing error of the BRSP classifiers in different conditions, with the number of boosted patterns increasing

done better by the RSP-based image representation; second, compared to the ORSP classifier, the BRSP classifier (4_{th} column) has shown more discriminative power, especially at the low levels (3_{rd} row and 5_{th} row). In fact, it is just the main advantage of the BRSP classifier: the final decision can be made more robustly after combining the votes from several patterns, though sometimes the descriptive power of each single pattern is limited severely.

Next, we study how the number of boosted patterns, as well as the effectiveness of each single weak classifier, affects the overall performance of the final BRSP classifier. Here we change the conditions when training the weak classifiers, and make two pairs of comparison: in the first pair, the weak classifiers are trained using only the level 1 or the level 2 patterns, corresponding to the 3_{rd} and 4_{th} rows in Table 1, respectively; in the second pair, we change the size of the random subset $|\Phi_\theta|$ for weak classifier training, from $50\% \times |\Phi|$ to $70\% \times |\Phi|$, hence obtain weak classifiers with different power. The comparison results are given in Figure 4, in which both of the testing error and training error are plotted with the number of weak classifiers increasing. We can see that in each pair, the gap in discriminative power between the two BRSP classifiers narrows after convergence, despite comparably big difference existing at the very beginning. Moreover, both the graphes show a very sharp decrease in the first ten iterations, nearly 9% in testing error, which means more than 250 initially mis-classified images are corrected by the latter weak classifiers. It once again proves the advantage of the BRSP classifier.

Finally, the proposed algorithms are compared with the state-of-the-art techniques, as shown in Table 2. Though only the simplest SIFT feature and linear-SVM are adopted, the recognition accuracy of our RSP-based algorithms are still better than the best of the previous work [12,27], which validates the effectiveness of the RSP-based image representation method. Also a confusion matrix is given in Figure 5(a). Similar to the results in [11], the top three confusing pairs are: coast/opencounty, bedroom/livingroom and insidecity/industrial. Several mis-classified examples are shown in Figure 5(b).

Table 2. Comparison with the state-of-the-art methods on the 15-scene dataset

Method	Avg. Accuracy
SPM + SIFT with 400 clusters [11]	81.4%
SPM + SIFT with 400 concepts [28]	83.3%
DSP + SIFT with 1000 clusters [23]	80.7%
SP-pLSA + SIFT with 1200 topics [29]	83.7%
CENTRIST + RBF-SVM [12]	83.9%
CENTRIST + LCC + Boosting [27]	87.8%
RSP + Optimal Selection	83.9%
RSP + Boosting ($\lvert\Phi_\theta\rvert/\lvert\Phi\rvert = 50\%$)	87.2%
RSP + Boosting ($\lvert\Phi_\theta\rvert/\lvert\Phi\rvert = 70\%$)	**88.1%**

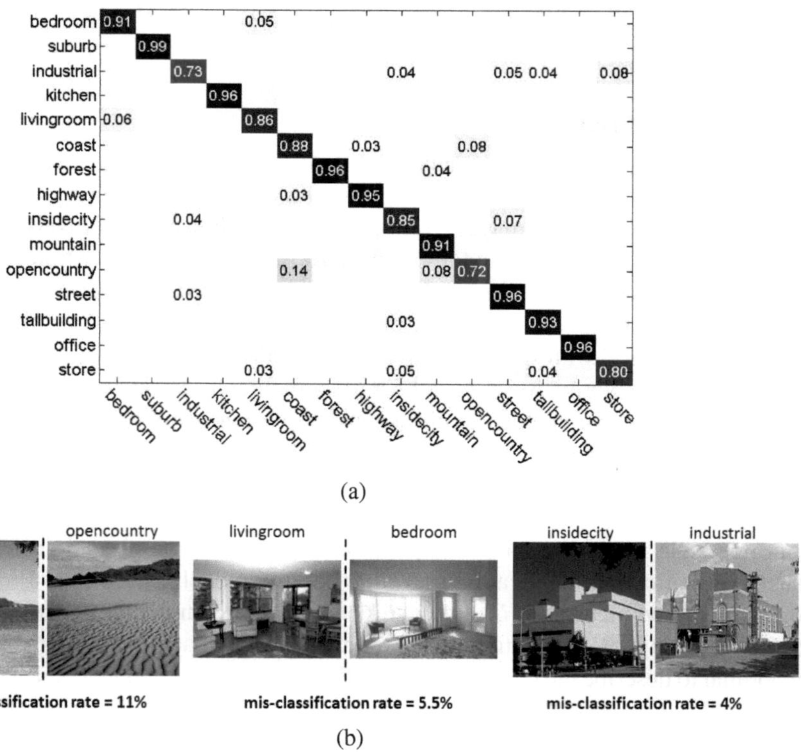

Fig. 5. (a) The confusion matrix of 15-scene recognition by BRSP classifier. Only rates higher than 3% are shown; (b) Examples of the top 3 confusing pairs in the 15-scene dataset.

Fig. 6. Examples of the images in the 8-event dataset

Table 3. Comparison with the state-of-the-art methods on the 8-event dataset

Method	Avg. Accuracy
Scene Model + SIFT [14]	$\approx 60\%$
Scene Model + Object Model + SIFT [14]	73.4%
PACT + RBF-SVM [12]	78.2%
SPM + RBF-SVM	74.0%
RSP + Optimal Selection	77.9%
RSP + Boosting	**79.6%**

5.2 The 8-Event Dataset

The 8-event dataset [14] is composed of eight sport classes: *badminton, bocce, croquet, polo, rock climbing, rowing, sailing, and snowboarding* (see Figure 6). Each class has 137 to 250 high-resolution images (from 800×600 to thousands of pixels per dimension). Following [14,12], we randomly select 70 images per class for training, and 60 for testing. Although more complex PACT features are used in [12], here we only extract the same features as in [14], i.e., the SIFT descriptors of 12×12 pixel patches computed over a grid with spacing of 10 pixels, and then cluster them into a vocabulary of $V = 300$ visual words. As in [12], the RBF kernel replaces the linear kernel in SVM training, and kernel parameters are chosen by a three-fold cross validation on the training set. The other experimental conditions, e.g., the partition parameters, are the same as those in the 15-scene dataset.

Table 3 compares our RSP-based approaches with other state-of-the-art methods. From this table we can see that: 1) spatial layout information plays a critical role in visual recognition. Although a high-level probability model is used in [14] (3_{rd} row), the original SPM algorithm (5_{th} row) still can reach a comparable accuracy with the help of spatial layout information; 2) it once again proves that the symmetric pyramid is not optimal to describe the spatial layout of all the categories of images, since the ORSP classifier (6_{th} row) has a remarkable improvement over the original SPM algorithm, and get a comparable results with [12] in which the complex PACT features are used; 3) the BRSP classifier (7_{th} row) has a more discriminative power than the ORSP classifier, and outperforms all the state-of-the-arts in this dataset.

5.3 The 21-Land-Use Dataset

The 21-land-use dataset [1] contains 21 classes of aerial orthoimagery downloaded from the United States Geological Survey (USGS) National Map: *agricultural, airplane, baseball diamond, beach, buildings, chaparral, dense residential, forest, freeway, golf course, harbor, intersection, medium density residential, mobile home park, overpass, parking lot, river, runway, sparse residential, storage tanks, and tennis courts.* Each class has 100 images with resolution 256×256. SIFT features are computed over the 16×16 patches with an 8-pixel grid spacing. As in [1], a vocabulary of $V = 100$ visual words is generated by applying k-means clustering on a random subset of the feature pool, and then used to label all the SIFT features extracted from this dataset. For each

Table 4. Classification accuracy for the 21-land-use dataset

	BoVW	SPMK [11]	SPCK [1]	SPCK+ [1]	SPCK++ [1]	ORSP	BRSP
Acc.	71.9	74.0	73.1	76.1	77.3	75.5	**77.8**

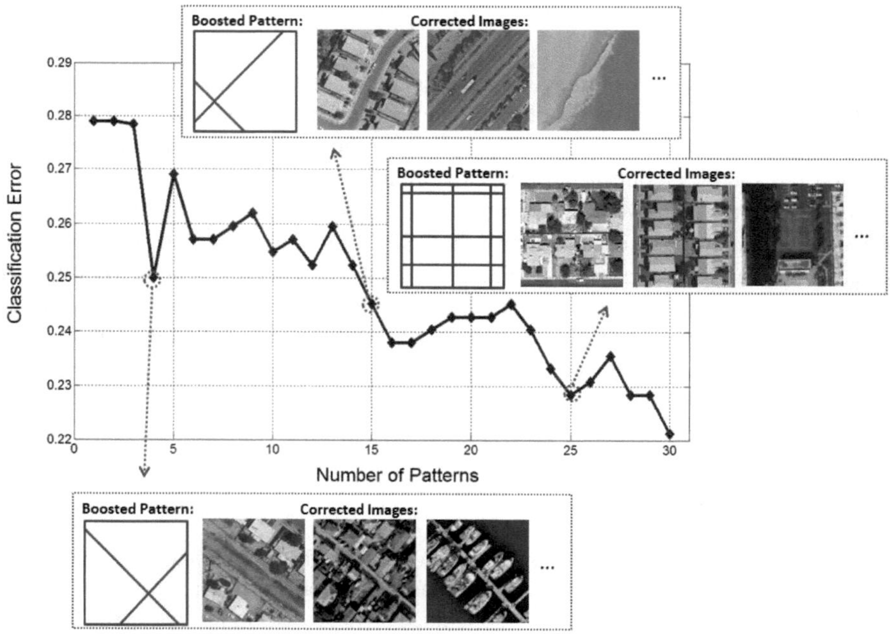

Fig. 7. The classification error curve of the BRSP classifier on the testing set, with the number of boosted patterns increasing. Moreover, we give three examples of the selected patterns and the testing images which are mistakenly classified at the beginning but corrected by the current pattern, as shown in the red boxes. From it we can see that the BRSP classifier can handle the large intra-class variations of image layout (e.g., the *dense residential*) very well by representing the images in multiple partition patterns. Note that although several bad patterns are boosted due to the bias between the training set and testing set, the classification accuracy generally tends to be improved when increasing the number of boosted patterns.

class, we split it into five equal sized sets. Four of the sets are used for training and the held-out set is for testing.

We introduce the rotated partition patterns in this dataset to better describe the spatial layout information of the rotated cases, as shown in Figure 1(b). The rotated partition is performed at $l = 1$ level and repeated independently for $K = 100$ times, which forms a pool of rotated partition patterns Θ_r with 100 random patterns. Therefore, the entire pool we used in this dataset is $\Theta = \Theta_u \cup \Theta_r$ consisting of all upright and rotated patterns. Besides, we set $|\Phi_\theta|/|\Phi| = 75\%$ for training the BRSP classifiers. The other parameters are set the same as the experiments above.

In Table 4 we compare our RSP-based approaches with other methods that use spatial pyramid to characterize the arrangement of visual words, namely spatial pyramid matching kernel (SPMK) in [11], spatial pyramid co-occurrence kernel (SPCK), and its extensions SPCK+ and SPCK++ in [1]. The comparison highlights the effectiveness of our RSP-based approaches. Moreover, Figure 7 provides a very clear impression on how our BRSP classifier can handle the large variations of spatial layout of images, hence achieves a more accurate classification result.

6 Conclusion

This paper presents a novel image representation method based on randomized spatial partition, with the objective to optimally characterize the spatial layout of the images. In contrast to the pre-defined spatial pyramid, in the RSP-based image representation method the spatial layout of the images is characterized by the randomized partition patterns. Furthermore, two discriminative image classifiers, the ORSP classifier and the BRSP classifier, are proposed based on the RSP image representation. The ORSP classifier mines the most descriptive pattern for each category of images to address the inter-class variations of image layout, while the BRSP classifier can handle the large intra-class variations by boosting a sequence of various patterns together. The comparison with the state-of-the-art methods on three publicly available datasets validates the effectiveness of our RSP-based methods.

References

1. Yang, Y., Newsam, S.: Spatial pyramid co-occurrence for image classification. In: ICCV 2011: IEEE International Conference on Computer Vision, Barcelona, Spain (2011)
2. Sivic, J., Zisserman, A.: Efficient visual search of videos cast as text retrieval. IEEE Trans. on Pattern Analysis and Machine Intelligence (2009)
3. Winn, J., Criminisi, A., Minka, T.: Object categorization by learned universal visual dictionary. In: Proc. IEEE Intl. Conf. on Computer Vision (2005)
4. Jurie, F., Triggs, B.: Creating efficient codebooks for visual recognition. In: Proc. IEEE Intl. Conf. on Computer Vision (2005)
5. Grauman, K., Darrel, T.: The pyramid match kernel: Discriminative classification with sets of image features. In: Proc. IEEE Intl. Conf. on Computer Vision (2005)
6. Li, T., Mei, T., Kweon, I., Hua, X.: Contextual bag-of-words for visual categorization. IEEE Transactions on Circuits and Systems for Video Technology (2010)

7. Perdoch, M., Chum, O., Matas, J.: Efficient representation of local geometry for large scale object retrieval. In: Proc. IEEE Conf. on Computer Vision and Pattern Recognition (2009)
8. Wang, X., Yang, M., Cour, T., Zhu, S., Yu, K., Han, T.X.: Contextual weighting for vocabulary tree based image retrieval. In: ICCV 2011: IEEE International Conference on Computer Vision, Barcelona, Spain (2011)
9. Zhang, Y., Jia, Z., Chen, T.: Image retrieval with geometry-preserving visual phrases. In: Proc. IEEE Conf. on Computer Vision and Pattern Recognition (2011)
10. Sivic, J., Russell, B.C., Efros, A.A., Zisserman, A., Freeman, W.T.: Discovering objects and their location in images. In: Proc. IEEE Intl. Conf. on Computer Vision (2005)
11. Lazebnik, S., Schmid, C., Ponce, J.: Beyond bags of features: spatial pyramid matching for recognizing natural scene categories. In: Proc. IEEE Conf. on Computer Vision and Pattern Recognition (2006)
12. Wu, J., Rehg, J.M.: Centrist: A visual descriptor for scene categorization. IEEE Trans. on Pattern Analysis and Machine Intelligence (2011)
13. Fei-Fei, L., Perona, P.: A bayesian hierarchical model for learning natural scene categories. In: Proc. IEEE Conf. on Computer Vision and Pattern Recognition (2005)
14. Li, L.J., Fei-Fei, L.: What, where and who? classifying events by scene and object recognition. In: Proc. IEEE Intl. Conf. on Computer Vision (2007)
15. Csurka, G., Dance, C.R., Fan, L., Willamowski, J., Bra, C.: Visual categorization with bags of keypoints. In: Workshop on Statistical Learning in Computer Vision, ECCV (2004)
16. Behmo, R., Marcombes, P., Dalalyan, A., Prinet, V.: Towards Optimal Naive Bayes Nearest Neighbor. In: Daniilidis, K., Maragos, P., Paragios, N. (eds.) ECCV 2010, Part IV. LNCS, vol. 6314, pp. 171–184. Springer, Heidelberg (2010)
17. Boiman, O., Shechtman, E., Irani, M.: In defense of nearest-neighbor based image classification. In: Proc. IEEE Conf. on Computer Vision and Pattern Recognition (2008)
18. Zhang, S., Tian, Q., Hua, G., Huang, Q., Li, S.: Descriptive visual words and visual phrases for image applications. In: Proc. ACM Multimedia (2009)
19. Zhang, S., Huang, Q., Hua, G., Jiang, S., Gao, W., Tian, Q.: Building contextual visual vocabulary for large-scale image applications. In: Proc. ACM Multimedia (2010)
20. Perina, A., Jojic, N.: Image analysis by counting on a grid. In: Proc. IEEE Conf. on Computer Vision and Pattern Recognition (2011)
21. Yuan, J., Wu, Y.: Spatial random partition for common visual pattern discovery. In: Proc. IEEE Intl. Conf. on Computer Vision (2007)
22. Jiang, Y., Meng, J., Yuan, J.: Randomized visual phrases for object search. In: Proc. IEEE Conf. on Computer Vision and Pattern Recognition (2012)
23. Sharma, G., Jurie, F.: Learning discriminative spatial representation for image classification. In: Proc. of BMVC (2011)
24. Lowe, D.: Distinctive image features from scale-invariant keypoints. Intl. Journal of Computer Vision (2004)
25. Zhu, J., Rosset, S., Zou, H., Hastie, T.: Multi-class adaboost. Technical report, Stanford Univ. (2005), http://www-stat.stanford.edu/hastie/Papers/samme.pdf
26. Oliva, A., Torralba, A.: Modeling the shape of the scene: A holistic representation of the spatial envelope. International Journal of Computer Vision (2001)
27. Yuan, J., Yang, M., Wu, Y.: Mining discriminative co-occurrence patterns for visual recognition. In: Proc. IEEE Conf. on Computer Vision and Pattern Recognition (2011)
28. Li, J., Shah, M.: Scene modeling using co-clustering. In: Proc. IEEE Intl. Conf. on Computer Vision (2007)
29. Bosc, A., Zisserman, A., Munoz, X.: Scene classification using a hybrid generative/discriminative approach. IEEE Trans. on Pattern Analysis and Machine Intelligence (2008)

Nested Sparse Quantization for Efficient Feature Coding

Xavier Boix[1,⋆], Gemma Roig[1,⋆⋆],
Christian Leistner[1], and Luc Van Gool[1,2]

[1] Computer Vision Lab, ETH Zurich, Switzerland
[2] KU Leuven, Belgium
{boxavier,gemmar,vangool}@vision.ee.ethz.ch

Abstract. Many state-of-the-art methods in object recognition extract features from an image and encode them, followed by a pooling step and classification. Within this processing pipeline, often the encoding step is the bottleneck, for both computational efficiency and performance. We present a novel assignment-based encoding formulation. It allows for the fusion of assignment-based encoding and sparse coding into one formulation. We also use this to design a new, very efficient, encoding. At the heart of our formulation lies a quantization into a set of k-sparse vectors, which we denote as sparse quantization. We design the new encoding as two nested, sparse quantizations. Its efficiency stems from leveraging bitwise representations. In a series of experiments on standard recognition benchmarks, namely Caltech 101, PASCAL VOC 07 and ImageNet, we demonstrate that our method achieves results that are competitive with the state-of-the-art, and requires orders of magnitude less time and memory. Our method is able to encode one million images using 4 CPUs in a single day, while maintaining a good performance.

1 Introduction

Recent research has led to important progress in visual object recognition and classification. Many state-of-the-art object recognition schemes consist of a feed-forward architecture, usually divided into feature extraction, feature encoding, spatial pooling, and a classifier [1,2,3]. Recently, sophisticated encoding and pooling schemes have allowed for learning the different blocks in the pipeline [4,5].

Feature encoding is one of the most intriguing blocks in a feed-forward architecture. Encoding aims at partitioning the feature descriptor space into informative regions, in order to both generalize towards intra-class variances and discriminate between different categories. Many authors pointed out the significant influence feature encoding has on object recognition performance, and stressed the need for encodings with better generalization properties [6,7]. The trend has been to introduce refined encodings that certainly generalize better and thus

⋆ Both first authors are the main contributors, and contributed equally.
⋆⋆ Corresponding author.

A. Fitzgibbon et al. (Eds.): ECCV 2012, Part II, LNCS 7573, pp. 744–758, 2012.

achieve higher levels of performance, but that come at the cost of increasing computational complexity. Indeed, feature encoding can be orders of magnitude more demanding than feature extraction and pooling, and it can become the bottleneck of the whole pipeline. For real-time and large scale applications, it is therefore crucial to design efficient feature encoding methods.

In the literature, one finds a plethora of feature encoding techniques. One of the most popular is assignment-based coding (AC). AC encodes a feature by assigning it to one or more codebook entries. When combined with average pooling, this corresponds to Bag-of-Words (BoW) [8,9]. Although simple in principle, it can be computationally demanding, since it requires the calculation of distances between the descriptors and the codebook entries. In particular, its computational cost increases with the size of the codebook and the number of patches [10]. Therefore, several methods were devised to speed up the BoW approach, e.g. [11,12,13].

Sparse coding has emerged as a powerful alternative to AC, showing better results than AC, especially, when combined with max-pooling [2,14,15,16]. In terms of efficiency, however, sparse coding optimizes a convex problem of the size of the codebook length, which makes it comparably slow. Locality-constrained linear encoding (LLC) [17] is an approximation of sparse coding, which speeds it up without a significant loss in performance. The current state-of-the-art in visual classification makes use of super-vector coding [18] and Fisher encoding [19], *cf.* [3]. Yet, both methods are memory-demanding. Using compression methods, *e.g.* [19], the Fisher kernel can be made tractable for large-scale applications, but the need for decompression before classification reduces the efficiency again.

In this paper, we focus on AC because it is a promising compromise in terms of speed and performance [6]. We introduce a new formulation for AC, and from that, we design a new efficient feature encoding scheme. At the heart of our formulation lies a quantization into a set of k-sparse vectors, which we denote as *sparse quantization*. It offers a novel viewpoint of AC, which, although algorithmically equivalent to AC, it allows for the unification of AC and sparse coding. In fact, our formulation allows for the design of a new efficient encoding. We coin it 'Nested Sparse Quantization' (NSQ), which consists of two feature encodings, in a nested architecture. We first encode the features, and the result is then fed to another feature encoder. Both encoders follow the novel formulation of AC. The first one is instantiated in a way that it is very fast to execute, and since it is build from a hard assignment encoder, it yields a binary vector. The second encoder is fed with this binary vector and thus also becomes very efficient to compute.

In the experimental part, we compare NSQ to state-of-the-art methods for object recognition. As we show on various datasets, *i.e.*, Caltech 101, PASCAL VOC 07 and ImageNet, our method demands orders of magnitude less time and memory than those previous approaches, while achieving competitive levels of performance. For instance, it is able to encode one million images in less than 24 hours using one laptop of 4 CPUs and 6GB of disk.

2 Preliminaries

In this section, we introduce the mathematical tools that we use in the rest of the paper, *i.e.*, quantization, sparsity and sparse quantization. All proofs can be found in the Supplementary Material.

Quantization. Let $\mathbf{x} \in \mathbb{R}^q$ be a vector, and $\mathbf{B} \in \mathbb{R}^{q \times m}$ the so called codebook matrix with m entries $\mathbf{b}_i \in \mathbb{R}^q$, *i.e.*, $\mathbf{B} = [\mathbf{b}_1 \ldots \mathbf{b}_m]$.

Definition 1. Quantization *is a mapping of a vector* $\mathbf{x}$ *into its closest vector of the codebook* $\{\mathbf{b}_i | i = 1, \ldots, m\}$, *which we denote as* $\hat{\mathbf{x}}^\star = \arg\min_{\hat{\mathbf{x}} \in \{\mathbf{b}_i\}} \|\hat{\mathbf{x}} - \mathbf{x}\|^2$.

The purpose of quantization is to reduce the cardinality of the representation space. $\mathbf{x}$ has an infinite set of possible values, and when mapped to the codebook, it is restricted to a finite set of possible vectors. In general, the cost of computing a quantization is $\mathcal{O}(m\jmath)$, where $\jmath$ represents the cost of computing a single distance. In practice, the most common used is the squared Euclidean distance, which is expensive since it implies $2q$ float operations, and yields a total cost of $\mathcal{O}(mq)$.

Sparsity. A vector $\boldsymbol{\alpha}$ is k-sparse when it has at most k non-zero entries, *i.e.*, $\|\mathbf{x}\|_0 \leq k$. Let $\mathbb{R}^m_k$ be the space of k-sparse vectors in $\mathbb{R}^m$, which is $\mathbb{R}^m_k = \{\boldsymbol{\alpha} \in \mathbb{R}^m : \|\boldsymbol{\alpha}\|_0 \leq k\}$. Sparsity is a highly non-linear model [20]. Observe that the the sum of two k-sparse vectors does not necessarily result in another k-sparse vector, since their non-zero entries might not coincide. Thus, the result is no longer in $\mathbb{R}^m_k$. We also introduce the subset of binary vectors in $\mathbb{R}^m_k$, which is the set of vectors with k ones and $(m-k)$ zeros. Let $\{0,1\}^m_k = \mathbb{B}^m_k$ be the space of *binary* k-sparse vectors, $\mathbb{B}^m_k = \{\boldsymbol{\alpha} \in \mathbb{B}^m : \|\boldsymbol{\alpha}\|_0 = k\}$, where $\mathbb{B}^m_k$ is a subset of $\mathbb{R}^m_k$, *i.e.*, $\mathbb{B}^m_k \subset \mathbb{R}^m_k$, and it is composed of a finite amount of elements, in particular, its cardinality is $|\mathbb{B}^m_k| = \binom{m}{k}$.

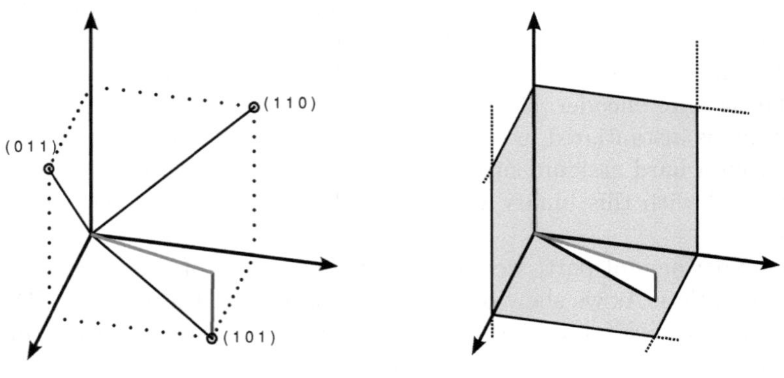

Fig. 1. Representation of $\mathbb{B}^3_2$ (left) and $\mathbb{R}^3_2$ (right) space with the input vector $\mathbf{x}$ in green, and the codification error vector $(\hat{\mathbf{x}} - \mathbf{x})$ in red

Sparse Quantization. We consider the particular case of the quantization when the codebook is the set of k-sparse vectors.

Definition 2. Sparse Quantization *is a quantization into the codebook* $\mathbf{B} = \mathbb{R}^q_k$.

The formulation for the sparse quantization of $\mathbf{x} \in \mathbb{R}^q$ is

$$\hat{\mathbf{x}}^\star = \arg \min_{\hat{\mathbf{x}} \in \mathbb{R}^q_k} \|\hat{\mathbf{x}} - \mathbf{x}\|^2. \tag{1}$$

For brevity, we use the term *Sparse Quantization* (SQ), but to be more precise, it should be called quantization into the codebook $\mathbb{R}^q_k$. Interestingly, sparse quantization can be done in a more efficient way than a quantization into an arbitrary codebook. In the following Proposition, we show that SQ can be achieved with a sorting algorithm, and it does not require the computation of the distances to the codebook entries. The Proposition shows only the case for the codebook $\mathbb{B}^q_k$, which is what we use in our approach. The derivation for sparse quantization in the case where the codebook is the set $\mathbb{R}^q_k$ can be found in the Supplementary Material. We assume that $\mathbf{x} \in \mathbb{R}^q_+$, and that $\mathbf{x}$ is normalized to 1. In all cases where we use the Proposition this is true.

Proposition 1. *Let* $\hat{\mathbf{x}}^\star = \arg\min_{\hat{\mathbf{x}} \in \mathbb{B}^q_k} \|\hat{\mathbf{x}} - \mathbf{x}\|^2$ *be the quantization into* $\mathbb{B}^q_k$ *of* $\mathbf{x} \in \mathbb{R}^q_+$, $\|\mathbf{x}\|^2_2 = 1$. *We can obtain* $\hat{\mathbf{x}}^\star$ *by*

$$\hat{x}^\star_i = \begin{cases} 1 \text{ if } i \in k\text{-Highest}(\mathbf{x}) \\ 0 \text{ otherwise} \end{cases}, \tag{2}$$

where k-Highest$(\mathbf{x})$ is the set of dimensions indices that indicate which are the k highest values in the vector $\mathbf{x}$.

Proposition 1 shows that the sparse quantization can be done with a sorting algorithm of the set $\{x_i\}$, and selecting the k highest values. It has a computational cost of $\mathcal{O}(q)$, in contrast to a general quantization, which has a cost of $\mathcal{O}(mq)$, where in practice $m \gg q$. In Figure 1, we show an example of sparse quantization in $\mathbb{B}^3_2$ and in $\mathbb{R}^3_2$. We plot an input vector $\mathbf{x}$ in green, and the quantization error in red. Also, we show all $\binom{3}{2} = 3$ possible vectors for $\mathbb{B}^3_2$.

3 A New Formulation of Assignment-Based Coding

In this section, we introduce a new framework for Assignment-based Coding (AC), which is based on the principles of sparse quantization. Additionally, we show the relation to Sparse Coding.

3.1 Assignment-Based Coding Revisited

We first review AC and its main variants and identify some common terminology in the literature. This will serve as the basis for our new formulation that we introduce in the subsequent section.

Let $\mathbf{x} \in \mathbb{R}^q_+$ be the vector of a patch descriptor, which has been normalized, and $\mathbf{B} \in \mathbb{R}^{q \times m}$ the codebook matrix with m entries $\mathbf{b}_i \in \mathbb{R}^q$. AC aims at encoding $\mathbf{x}$ by selecting the codebook entries $\mathbf{b}_i$ with minimum distance to $\mathbf{x}$. Such codebook entries are called the k-Nearest Neighbors (k-NN) of $\mathbf{x}$. k is the number of selected codebook entries, and it is a predefined constant.

Vector quantization (VQ) is the simplest AC method. It only selects a single codebook entry, which is the closest to $\mathbf{x}$, with the so called 1-NN. It is in fact a quantization, since it maps $\mathbf{x}$ into a codebook entry. Let $\boldsymbol{\alpha} \in \mathbb{R}^m$ be the vector that encodes the assignment. In VQ, α_i is set to 1 when it is the element of the codebook that is used to quantize $\mathbf{x}$, and the rest is set to 0.

VQ has been extended to the popular hard-assignment (HA), which assigns more than one codebook entry to $\mathbf{x}$, *e.g.* [12]. In this case, there are 1s placed in the elements of $\boldsymbol{\alpha}$ that correspond to the k-NN codebook entries, *i.e.*,

$$\alpha_i = \begin{cases} 1 \text{ if } i \in k\text{-NN}(\mathbf{x}, \mathbf{B}) \\ 0 \text{ otherwise} \end{cases} . \tag{3}$$

k-NN$(\mathbf{x}, \mathbf{B})$ is the set that indicates which k codebook entries are closest to $\mathbf{x}$. According to Definition 1, HA is not a quantization anymore but an assignment, because more than one vector of the codebook is assigned to $\mathbf{x}$. In the case of quantization, $\mathbf{x}$ is always represented with only a single codebook vector.

In HA, $\boldsymbol{\alpha}$ results in a binary vector with k ones and $(m-k)$ zeros. Thus, the $\boldsymbol{\alpha}$'s obtained are k-sparse vectors, which are in $\mathbb{B}^m_k$. In particular, $\boldsymbol{\alpha}$ is in $\mathbb{B}^m_k$ when using HA, and in $\mathbb{B}^m_1$ for VQ.

There exists also the soft version of HA, denoted as soft-assignment (SA) [6][1]. In this case, instead of indicating the k-NN with 1s, $\boldsymbol{\alpha}$ contains some notion of the relative distance to the selected codebook entries, and becomes

$$\alpha_i = \begin{cases} \exp(-\beta d(\mathbf{x}, \mathbf{b}_i)) & \text{if } i \in k\text{-NN}(\mathbf{x}, \mathbf{B}) \\ 0 & \text{otherwise} \end{cases} . \tag{4}$$

$d(\mathbf{x}, \mathbf{y})$ is a given distance function, β a learned constant, and $d(\mathbf{x}, \mathbf{b}_i)$ is the distance between $\mathbf{x}$ and $\mathbf{b}_i$. Thus, SA codifies a patch descriptor $\mathbf{x}$ with a k-sparse $\boldsymbol{\alpha}$ in $\mathbb{R}^m_k$. Note that when $\beta = 0$ we recover HA, and $\boldsymbol{\alpha} \in \mathbb{B}^m_k$.

AC and other codings are usually the computational bottleneck of the patch-based image classification, *cf.* [3]. Typically, the cost of coding scales with the number of visual words, the number of patch descriptors and the dimensionality of these descriptors. This can make the coding an order of magnitude slower than the patch description. The reason is mainly because the encoding requires computing the distances between the patch descriptor and all the codebook entries.

In the following sections, we introduce a new formulation for AC, that also leads up to a very efficient quantization scheme.

[1] In [6], $\boldsymbol{\alpha}$ is normalized such that $\|\boldsymbol{\alpha}\|_2^2 = 1$. In this paper, for the sake of simplicity in the encoding block, we assume it is the pooling stage that normalizes $\boldsymbol{\alpha}$. Note also that in this paper we refer to SA for what [6] calls Localized SA.

3.2 AC as a Sparse Quantization

We now introduce a new view of AC based on a non-linear mapping of $\mathbf{x}$, which we denote as $\phi : \mathbb{R}^q \to \mathbb{R}^m$.

Definition 3. *Let $\phi(\mathbf{x})$ be the following mapping:*

$$\phi(\mathbf{x}) = \frac{1}{Z}[\exp(-\beta d(\mathbf{x}, \mathbf{b}_1)) \ \ldots \ \exp(-\beta d(\mathbf{x}, \mathbf{b}_m))], \tag{5}$$

where β is a learned constant and $d(a, b)$ a given distance. Z normalizes the vector, and $\{\mathbf{b}\}$ parametrize the mapping.

Observe that in AC, $\mathbf{B}$ denotes the codebook matrix, but in our new formulation it is used to parametrize the mapping $\phi(\mathbf{x})$. In the following Proposition, we rewrite HA as a *sparse quantization* of $\phi(\mathbf{x})$ (section 2). We show this fact for SA as well as the proof in the Supplementary Material.

Proposition 2. *Let $\boldsymbol{\alpha}^\star \in \mathbb{B}^m_k$ be the result of Hard Assignment in (3). Then, the same $\boldsymbol{\alpha}^\star$ can be obtained through the following sparse quantization of $\phi(\mathbf{x})$:*

$$\boldsymbol{\alpha}^\star = \arg \min_{\boldsymbol{\alpha} \in \mathbb{B}^m_k} ||\boldsymbol{\alpha} - \phi(\mathbf{x})||_2^2. \tag{6}$$

Proposition 2 shows that HA is a sparse quantization of $\phi(\mathbf{x})$ into the codebook $\mathbb{B}^m_k$. HA is formulated as a non-linear transformation $\phi(\mathbf{x})$, which uses $\mathbf{B}$, and then the resulting vector is quantized into $\mathbb{B}^m_k$. This is in contrast to how HA has been usually interpreted. Previous HA formulations used $\boldsymbol{\alpha}$ in order to indicate to which codebook entries $\mathbf{x}$ is assigned. Both formulations obtain the same coding results, and have the same computational complexity. However, in the next subsection we show that Proposition 2 is able to fuse Assignment-based Coding and Sparse Coding into a single formulation. Also, we show that we can use the new formulation to design a very efficient codification.

3.3 A Formulation for Sparse Coding and AC

When considering AC as a sparse quantization, we can analyze its relation to sparse coding. Sparse coding is the following coding scheme [21]: $\boldsymbol{\alpha}^\star = \arg\min_{\boldsymbol{\alpha} \in \mathbb{R}^m_k} ||\mathbf{C}\boldsymbol{\alpha} - \mathbf{x}||_2^2$, where $\mathbf{C} \in \mathbb{R}^{q \times m}$ is the codebook used in sparse coding. It is usually relaxed in the following way $\boldsymbol{\alpha}^\star = \arg\min_{\boldsymbol{\alpha} \in \mathbb{R}^m} ||\mathbf{C}\boldsymbol{\alpha} - \mathbf{x}||_2^2 + \lambda||\boldsymbol{\alpha}||_1$, where $\lambda||\boldsymbol{\alpha}||_1$ is the convex sparsity regularization term of $\boldsymbol{\alpha} \in \mathbb{R}^m_k$, and it can be tuned to enforce different degrees of sparsity. Note that in [15] it was already shown that Sparse Coding can be seen as an extension of VQ; however, their formulation does not extend to AC in general.

The general formulation for Sparse Coding and Assignment-based Codings is:

$$\boldsymbol{\alpha}^\star = \arg \min_{\boldsymbol{\alpha} \in \mathbb{R}^m_k} ||\mathbf{C}\boldsymbol{\alpha} - \phi(\mathbf{x})||_2^2, \tag{7}$$

where $\phi(\mathbf{x})$ represents a mapping from the original q-dimensional vector $\mathbf{x}$ to a space with a possibly different dimension, such as m in the earlier definition. We now recover Sparse Coding by just setting $\phi(\mathbf{x}) = \mathbf{x}$, and we recover AC by setting $\mathbf{C}$ to be the identity matrix $\mathbf{I}^{m \times m}$.

4 Nested Sparse Quantization

In this section, we introduce an efficient encoding built upon the new formulation of HA in Proposition 2. It consists of two sparse quantizations placed in a nested architecture, coined nested sparse quantization (NSQ). We define NSQ as the following optimization problem:

$$\boldsymbol{\alpha} = \arg\min_{\boldsymbol{\alpha}\in\mathbb{B}^m_k} \|\boldsymbol{\alpha} - \phi(\hat{\mathbf{x}})\|^2, \tag{8}$$

$$\text{where } \hat{\mathbf{x}} = \arg\min_{\hat{\mathbf{x}}\in\mathbb{B}^{m'}_{k'}} \|\hat{\mathbf{x}} - \theta(\mathbf{x})\|^2, \tag{9}$$

where (8) is the *outer* sparse quantization and (9) is the *inner* sparse quantization, respectively. The parameters in the inner quantization are m', k' and the mapping $\theta(\mathbf{x})$, and they are not necessarily the same as in the outer quantization. The inner quantization results in the binary $\hat{\mathbf{x}}$, as a result of the sparse quantization into $\mathbb{B}^m_k$. The mapping in the inner quantization $\theta(\mathbf{x})$ has the real-valued $\mathbf{x}$ as input, whereas the outer mapping $\phi(\hat{\mathbf{x}})$ gets the vector $\hat{\mathbf{x}} \in \mathbb{B}^{m'}_{k'}$ as input, which is a binary vector.

4.1 Implementation Advantages

Observe that the input to the outer quantization has a *finite* amount of possible values, because it receives one of the entries of the inner codebook. This allows to use a look up table for the outer quantization, by memorizing the quantization of all entries of the inner codebook. However, in practice, the cardinality of the inner codebook is huge. In NSQ, the outer quantization is a mapping from a set of $\binom{m'}{k'}$ elements to $\binom{m}{k}$ possible outputs, where in practice $\binom{m'}{k'} \gg \binom{m}{k}$ and they are too high to be memorized in a look up table.

Indeed, the advantage of NSQ results from an appropriately chosen nesting of two different quantizations. The inner quantization turns real-valued vectors $\mathbf{x}$ into one of the $\binom{m'}{k'}$ possible binary vectors $\hat{\mathbf{x}}$, and the non-linear mapping should be simple not to overload the system. The outer quantization starts from a vector in the set $\mathbb{B}^{m'}_{k'}$, which are binary vectors, and can therefore be used to very efficiently deploy a more complex mapping $\phi(\hat{\mathbf{x}})$.

Inner Quantization. For the inner quantization, we use the most efficient and simplistic mapping possible, which is $\theta(\mathbf{x}) = \mathbf{x}$; that is, the mapping $\theta(\mathbf{x})$ does not apply any transformation on $\mathbf{x}$. Thus, the inner quantization in Eq. (9) directly quantizes the input $\mathbf{x}$ into the k'-sparse codebook for that step, without any previous non-linear mapping. It becomes

$$\hat{\mathbf{x}} = \arg\min_{\hat{\mathbf{x}}\in\mathbb{B}^{q}_{k'}} \|\hat{\mathbf{x}} - \mathbf{x}\|^2, \tag{10}$$

where m' is equal to q, and k' is the only parameter to be set. As stated in Proposition 1, optimizing this problem is equivalent to computing the k'-Highest

Algorithm 1. Nested Sparse Quantization

Input: $\mathbf{x} \in \mathbb{R}^q_+$, $\hat{\mathbf{B}} \in \mathbb{B}^{q\times m}_{k'}$
Output: $\boldsymbol{\alpha}$
$\hat{\mathbf{x}} \leftarrow$ Set k' highest values of $\mathbf{x}$ to 1 and the rest to 0
foreach $i = \{1, \ldots, m\}$ **do**
  $\phi_i(\hat{\mathbf{x}}) = \sum_{j=1}^{q}(\hat{x}_j \odot \hat{b}_{ij})$
end
$\boldsymbol{\alpha} \leftarrow$ Set k highest values of $\phi(\hat{\mathbf{x}})$ to 1 and the rest to 0

values in $\{x_i\}$. This implies selecting the k' elements of $\mathbf{x}$ with the highest values, which has a computational cost of $\mathcal{O}(q)$. One could investigate alternatives to $\theta(\mathbf{x}) = \mathbf{x}$ to improve on the classification results, but this would reduce the speed again and is therefore not studied in this paper.

Outer Quantization. The outer quantization now gets the binary output of the inner quantization as its input, which is a vector in $\mathbb{B}^{m'}_{k'}$. The use of binary vectors allows to reduce the complexity by using fast bit-wise comparisons, which most modern CPUs handle with dedicated instructions [22,23]. Thus, we can afford applying a more sophisticated mapping ϕ. Recall that the computational cost of such $\phi(\hat{\mathbf{x}})$ still is $\mathcal{O}(m\jmath)$, with $\jmath$ the cost of computing the distance. We can reduce the cost $\jmath$ by the very fact that $\hat{\mathbf{x}}$ is binary. Thus, the mapping is the same as in (5) but changing the distance function to a Hamming distance, $\hat{d}(\hat{\mathbf{x}}, \hat{\mathbf{b}}_i)$. Recall that the $\hat{\mathbf{b}}_i$ are parameters used in the definition of the non-linear mapping, and do not correspond neither to the codebook vectors of the inner quantization nor to the codebook vectors of the outer quantization. In our case, these are obtained by piping a total of m vectors $\mathbf{b}_i$ through the inner quantization, thus yielding those $\hat{\mathbf{b}}_i$.

Next, the mapping $\phi(\hat{\mathbf{x}})$ can be further simplified by dropping the exponential functions, given the equivalence of $\arg\min_{\boldsymbol{\alpha}}$ with the mapping $\phi(\hat{\mathbf{x}}) = \frac{1}{Z}[\tilde{d}(\hat{\mathbf{x}}, \hat{\mathbf{b}}_1) \;\ldots\; \tilde{d}(\hat{\mathbf{x}}, \hat{\mathbf{b}}_m)]$. Now, suppose we take $\tilde{d}(\hat{\mathbf{x}}, \hat{\mathbf{b}}_i) = \sum_{j=1}^{q}(\hat{x}_j \odot \hat{b}_{ij})$, where $\odot$ is the negation of the exclusive OR operator (*nxor*). It returns 1 if both elements are equal, and 0 otherwise. This is again very efficient to compute.

In Algorithm 1 we depict the implementation of NSQ, which highlights the simplicity and efficiency of the method.

4.2 Discussion

Quantization vs. recognition accuracy At this point the reader may object that NSQ adds an extra quantization step in the feature encoding procedure, and that quantization errors may grow worse, leading to a deteriorated performance. Yet, in recognition, quantization should also allow for sufficient generalization. In the next section, we show that recognition performance is not impaired, but that the speed goes up dramatically.

Relation of the Inner Quantization to Binary Embeddings and Hashing. NSQ is not to be confused with Binary Embeddings or Hashing-based methods. The goal of the inner quantization is a first step of feature encoding, and it is not designed to be a fast nearest neighbor extractor nor a fast distance approximator. In fact, in the experiments we show that NSQ is not a good nearest neighbor approximator. Hashing-based methods tackle fast distance computation rather than feature encoding, and have been typically used to speed up image retrieval in large-scale databases [24,25,26,27]. The binarizations used by these methods range from thresholding linear combinations of input features to solving optimization problems. These have a negligible cost in image retrieval, but not when applied to feature encoding. For example, in Locality Sensing Hashing (LSH) the binary embedding is $h_n(x) = T(\mathbf{r}^T\mathbf{x})$, where $\mathbf{r}$ is a projection vector, and $T(\cdot)$ is a threshold function. Hashing uses L different N-dimensional embedding functions $h(x)$ of an image signature $\mathbf{x}$, and thus, the cost of computing $h(\mathbf{x})$ is $\mathcal{O}(LNq)$. Hashing is typically used in applications where the cost $\mathcal{O}(LNq)$ is negligible compared to the cost of searching the nearest-neighbors, because this search might be among hundreds of thousands of elements. However, in feature encoding, the time of computing $h(\mathbf{x})$ is not negligible anymore, because the nearest neighbor search is only among thousands of elements (the size of the codebook), and in addition, $h(x)$ is computed for each patch. In contrast, the inner quantization of NSQ obtains the binary $\hat{\mathbf{x}}$ at a cheap cost $\mathcal{O}(q)$. Furthermore, the binary embeddings generate each bit independently of the others [26], which is different from NSQ, in which the output bits are dependent since only k of them are 1.

5 Experiments

In this section, we report experiments on different datasets, namely Caltech101 [28], PASCAL VOC 2007 [29] and ImageNet [30]. In none of them we use flipped or blurred images to extend the training set.

Caltech 101. It contains 102 different classes with about 50 images per class. We use 3 random splits of 30 images per class for training and the rest for testing, and evaluate it with the average classification accuracy across all classes. We resize the image to have a maximum of 300 pixels per dimension.

PASCAL VOC 2007. It consists of a total of 9,963 images with 20 different object classes. Half of the dataset is used for training and the other half for testing. The evaluation is based on the mean average precision (mAP) across all classes.

ImageNet. We create a new dataset taking a subset of $1,065,687$ images of ImageNet. This subset contains images of 909 different classes that do not overlap in the synset. We randomly split this subset into two halfs, one for training and one for testing, maintaining the proportion of images per class. For evaluation, we report the average classification accuracy across all classes. Note that we do not use the protocol of taking the 5 highest scores per image and keeping the best. We resize the image to have a maximum of 300 pixels per dimension.

5.1 Implementation Details

Patch Descriptors. We use SIFT [31] extracted from patches on a regular grid, at different scales. In Caltech 101 and ImageNet they are extracted at every 8 pixels and at the scales of 16, 32 and 48 pixels diameter. In VOC07, SIFT is sampled at each 4 pixels and at the scales of 12, 24 and 36 pixels diameter.

Feature Encoding. Apart from comparing NSQ and HA, we also report results with LLC [17] and the Super Vector method [18]. We found that for all settings $k = 5$ is the optimal, except for the combination of HA, max-pooling and linear SVM, which is $k = 10$. In NSQ, $k' = 25$ for the inner quantization (see discussion in 5.2 for those choices).

Codebook Generation. The codebook $\mathbf{B}$ is typically built with a learning algorithm either unsupervised [8,9] or supervised [13]. Recently, Coates and Ng [7] showed that a similar performance can be achieved by randomly picking a set of patches as codebook entries. We compared a codebook obtained using k-means clustering versus building it taking random patches from the training set. Tallying with the observations in [7], compared to k-means clustering, random selection considerably reduces the training time but does not lower the performance for large codebooks. For the methods that are not AC, like LLC or Super Vector, we learned the vocabularies as specified for each of them.

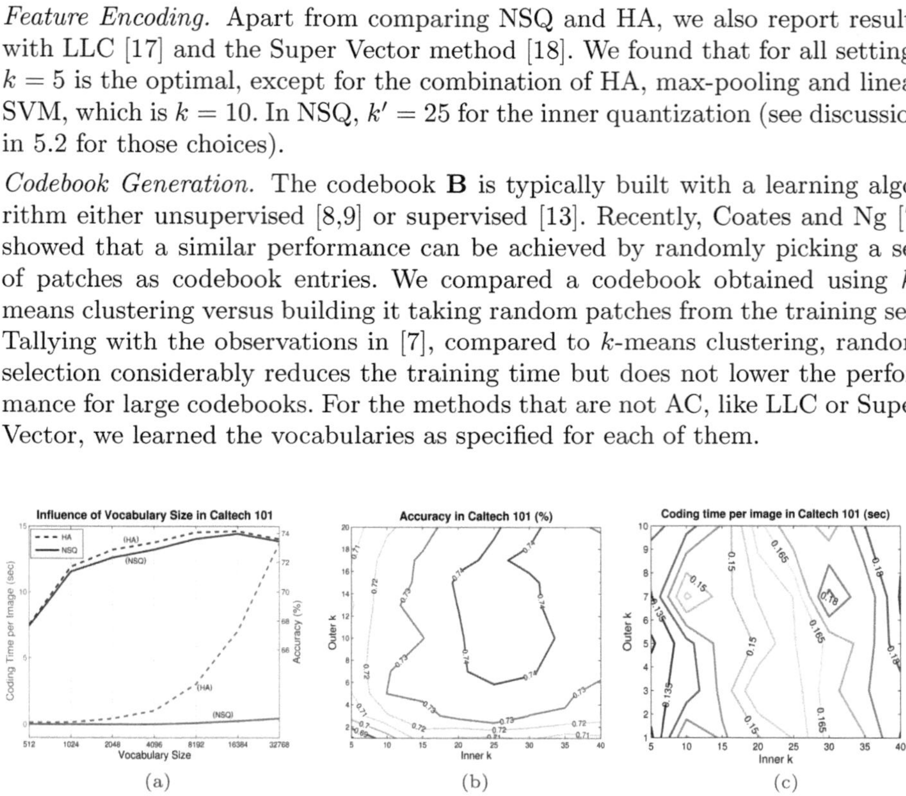

Fig. 2. *Influence of the parameter k and the vocabulary size in Caltech 101.* (a) Comparison of performance and time between NSQ and HA when varying the size of the codebook. (b) Accuracy and (c) Time when varying the inner and outer quantization parameters.

Pooling. We use in all datasets spatial pyramids. In Caltech 101 and ImageNet we divide the image in 4×4, 2×2 and 1×1 regions, yielding 21 different regions, and in VOC07, 3×1, 2×2 and 1×1 regions, yielding 8 regions. We use max-pooling because it has been shown to systematically outperform other types of pooling. In the case of NSQ and HA, the max-pooling results in a binary vector, which is the descriptor of the whole image, which we do not normalize.

Classification. For Caltech 101 and VOC07, we use a linear one versus rest SVM classifier for each class with the parameter C of the SVM set to 1000. In Caltech 101, we also report results using the RB-χ^2 kernel, $\exp\{-\beta\chi^2\}$, setting β to the

Table 1. *Quantitative Results on Caltech 101.* The time and memory measurements are for one image. We refer to $HA_{\{k',k\}}$ for the HA with NSQ, and $HA_{\{k\}}$ for the standard, in which we indicate the k and k' parameters of the outer and inner quantizations, respectively.

	Method				Time per Image 1 CPU *(sec)*			Memory
	Coding	Pool	Kernel	Acc. *(%)*	Feature	Coding	Kernel	*(Bytes)*
NSQ	$HA_{\{25,10\}}$	Max	Linear	$74.2 \pm .7$	$0.27 \pm .11$	$0.17 \pm .05$	–	21K
	$HA_{\{20,5\}}$	Max	Linear	$73.7 \pm .3$	$0.27 \pm .11$	$0.15 \pm .05$	–	21K
	$HA_{\{20,5\}}$	Max	RB-χ^2	$72.0 \pm .6$	$0.27 \pm .11$	$0.15 \pm .05$	.02	21K
	$HA_{\{20,5\}}$	Sum	RB-χ^2	$71.6 \pm .3$	$0.27 \pm .11$	$0.17 \pm .07$	2.10	672K
Standard	$HA_{\{10\}}$	Max	Linear	$74.6 \pm .6$	$0.27 \pm .11$	$2.78 \pm .9$	–	21K
	$HA_{\{5\}}$	Max	Linear	$74.2 \pm .1$	$0.27 \pm .11$	$2.75 \pm .9$	–	21K
	$HA_{\{5\}}$	Max	RB-χ^2	$73.4 \pm .9$	$0.27 \pm .11$	$2.75 \pm .9$	.02	21K
	$HA_{\{5\}}$	Sum	RB-χ^2	$72.1 \pm .4$	$0.27 \pm .11$	$2.78 \pm .9$	2.10	672K
	LLC	Max	Linear	$76.1 \pm .7$	$0.27 \pm .11$	$2.95 \pm .9$	–	672K
	SV	Max	Linear	$76.9 \pm .9$	$0.27 \pm .11$	$1.52 \pm .9$	–	10752K
Other features	HA [6]	Max	Linear	$73.3 \pm .6$	–	–	–	–
	SA [6]	Max	Linear	$74.2 \pm .8$	–	–	–	–
	LLC [17]	Max	Linear	$73.4 \pm -$	–	–	–	–
	FK [3]	Max	Linear	$77.8 \pm .6$	–	–	–	–

mean of the pairwise distances in the training data. Before computing the χ^2 distance, the features are normalized with the ℓ_1-norm. When the image descriptor is binary, the RB-χ^2 kernel can be computed efficiently using dedicated CPU instructions [22,23]. In ImageNet we use as classifier an approximated nearest neighbor that takes a maximum of 400 random examples per class.

Computational Evaluation. We use CPUs at 3.07GHz with the SSE4.1 instruction set, that enables fast popcnt instructions for bit strings.

5.2 Results

Performance Evaluation. In Table 1 we report results in Caltech 101. We show the results for NSQ in combination with different SVM kernels and pooling schemes. We do the same for HA, and we also include a comparison with LLC and Super Vector. We use a codebook of 8,192 entries for all methods except for Super Vector for which we use 1,024, since it achieves the compromise between accuracy and efficiency. LLC and Super Vector perform better than the others, as was reported in previous papers. However, their coding consumes much more memory and time than NSQ. The performance of NSQ is only 2.7% less than the best competing method which is Super Vector, but NSQ requires 500 times less memory than Super Vector and is about 10 times faster, and is 20 times faster than other methods that use the same codebook size. In Table 2 we summarize the results in VOC07. We use a codebook size of 16,258 entries. NSQ obtains a 30 times speed up, while only degrading 2% in performance.

In both tables we also provide the state-of-the-art methods in the literature. Even though they obtain better performance than our method, these techniques come at a far higher computational cost, as seen in the previous comparisons. We did not reproduce results of SA because it was already observed by [6] that

Table 2. *PASCAL VOC 2007 classification results.* The average score provides the per-class average. The time and memory measurements are for one image, using a single CPU.

	Aeroplane	Bicycle	Bird	Boat	Bottle	Bus	Car	Cat	Chair	Cow	Dinning Table	Dog	Horse	Motorbike	Person	Potted Plant	Sheep	Sofa	Train	TV/Monitor	**Average**	**Feature Time**	**Coding Time**	**Memory**
NSQ	67	56	41	66	21	56	72	55	41	48	42	37	71	65	78	21	45	53	71	51	52.87	0.85	0.86	42K
HA	67	56	44	66	22	57	75	56	44	50	43	37	74	69	78	24	46	56	74	51	54.54	0.85	21.22	42K
LLC	69	58	46	70	21	60	74	57	43	52	44	42	73	68	81	24	48	57	72	52	55.56	0.85	23.81	1344K
LLC [17]	75	65	51	71	29	69	79	62	54	49	52	44	77	67	84	31	45	53	79	54	59.30	–	–	–
SV [18]	79	72	55	74	34	72	83	64	57	53	63	49	81	72	85	36	46	60	83	59	64.00	–	–	–

SA only outperforms HA by less than 1%. Also, note that in VOC07 there is a gap between the performance of LCC reported by [17] and the LCC using our descriptors. According to [3], this can be explained by the fact that [17] extend the training set by blurring and flipping the images, and we do not.

Influence of the Parameters. In Figure 2a, we compare time and accuracy when changing the codebook size for NSQ and HA. Up to a certain point, the larger the codebook, the better the accuracy becomes. Interestingly, the computational time for HA explodes when increasing the codebook size, while in NSQ the increase is negligible compared to HA.

We analyze the accuracy and time performance of our method when changing the quantization parameters. We use the first split of Caltech 101 to show the results. In Figures 2b and 2c, we compare the accuracy of our method when changing the k parameter for the inner quantization and the outer quantization, and keeping the codebook size at $8,192$. We see a peak of performance: When the inner k is around 20 and 35 and the outer k is around 10 and 16. In the right plot we analyze the time when changing this parameters, also keeping the codebook at size $8,192$. The lower both k are, the less time classification takes. The best compromise between time and performance is using $k' = 25$ for the inner quantization, and $k = 10$ for the outer.

Influence of the Quantization Error. We analyze the impact of having more quantization error due to the inner quantization. We use Caltech 101 to show results using $8,192$ codebook entries. In Figure 3a, we show that the quantization error of the inner quantization does not have a clear relation with the classification accuracy. The accuracy is maximal for k' at 20 and 35, and the quantization error has its minimum around 45. Moreover, we show the percentage of equal activated elements of $\boldsymbol{\alpha}$ in NSQ and in HA using the same $\mathbf{B}$, in Figure 3b. Around 90% of the nearest neighbors are different. This shows that NSQ is a new encoding and not an approximate nearest-neighbor.

ImageNet in a Laptop in one Day. We introduce a new benchmark to test the efficiency of the encodings. We used ImageNet with restrictions on time and

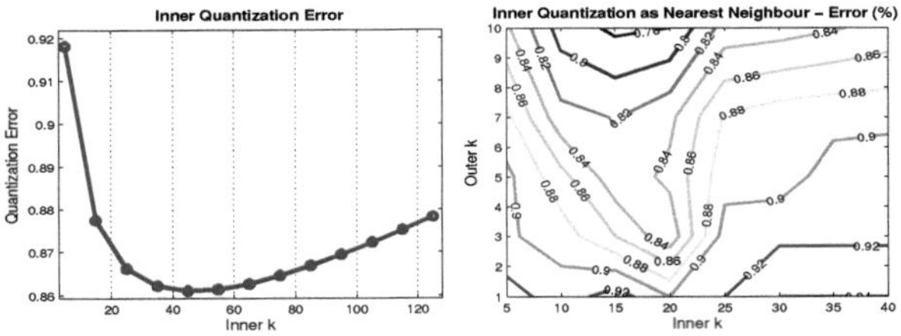

(a) (b)

	NSQ	HA
Time Dataset		
Features	17h 21m	17h 21m
Coding	6h 54m	7h 9m
Total	24h 18m	24h 30m
SizeDataset	5.4GB	700MB
Acc.Top-1	20.01%	16.6%

(c)

Fig. 3. (a) Quantization error of the inner quantization vs k', in Caltech 101. (b) Evaluation of the inner quantization as a nearest neighbor on Caltech 101 changing k and k'. (c) *Quantitative results on ImageNet.* To fulfill the time constraints, NSQ uses a codebook of 2,048 and HA of 256 .

memory, and only let the image encoding algorithms run about 24 hours on a laptop of 4 CPUs. We compared our method with HA with max pooling in which we adjusted the parameters to fulfill the requirements. With NSQ we were able to use a codebook of 2,048 entries, and in HA only of 256. In Figure 3b the results are summarized. In this benchmark, we outperform HA because in the same amount of time NSQ can use a larger codebook, which is crucial to have good classification performance. The reported results are of the same order of magnitude as reported in [32], though a direct comparison is not possible because we use a different subset of ImageNet. The state-of-the-art for this dataset is reported by [33], but the computational effort of this method is huge compared to ours.

6 Conclusion

We investigated efficient encoding schemes for object recognition and presented a novel encoding formulation that allows to fuse sparse coding and assignment-based coding. We proposed a very efficient encoding algorithm called Nested Sparse Quantization (NSQ), which is based on two nested quantizations. The implementation of NSQ is very simple, and can virtually be incorporated everywhere where assignment-based coding schemes are employed, but higher efficiency and more compact representations are demanded, *e.g.* real-time and large scale recognition problems. This potential was corroborated by our experiments on the Caltech 101, PASCAL VOC 07 and ImageNet benchmarks.

Acknowledgments. This work was partially supported by the EU projects FP7-ICT-24314 Interactive Urban Robot (IURO) and FP7-ICT-248873 Robotic ADaptation to Humans Adapting to Robots (RADHAR).

References

1. Boiman, O., Shechtman, E., Irani, M.: In defense of nearest-neighbor based image classification. In: CVPR (2008)

2. Boureau, Y., Bach, F., LeCun, Y., Ponce, J.: Learning mid-level features for recognition. In: CVPR (2010)
3. Chatfield, K., Lempitsky, V., Vedaldi, A., Zisserman, A.: The devil is in the details: An evaluation of recent feature encoding methods. In: BMVC (2011)
4. Zeiler, M.D., Taylor, G.W., Fergus, R.: Adaptive deconvolutional networks for mid and high level feature learning. In: ICCV (2011)
5. Yu, K., Lin, Y., Lafferty, J.: Learning image representations from pixel level via hierarchical sparse coding. In: CVPR (2011)
6. Liu, L., Wang, L., Liu, X.: In defence of soft-assignment coding. In: ICCV (2011)
7. Coates, A., Ng, A.: The importance of encoding versus training with sparse coding and vector quantization. In: ICML (2011)
8. Csurka, G., Dance, C., Fan, L., Willamowski, J., Bray, C.: Visual categorization with bags of keypoints. In: ECCV (2004)
9. Sivic, J., Zisserman, A.: Video google: A text retrieval approach to object matching in videos. In: ICCV (2003)
10. Nowak, E., Jurie, F., Triggs, B.: Sampling Strategies for Bag-of-Features Image Classification. In: Leonardis, A., Bischof, H., Pinz, A. (eds.) ECCV 2006. LNCS, vol. 3954, pp. 490–503. Springer, Heidelberg (2006)
11. Nister, D., Stewenius, H.: Scalable recognition with a vocabulary tree. In: CVPR (2006)
12. Philbin, J., Chum, O., Isard, M., Sivic, J., Zisserman, A.: Lost in quantization: Improving particular object retrieval in large scale image databases. In: CVPR (2008)
13. Moosmann, F., Jurie, F., Triggs, B.: Fast discriminative visual codebooks using randomized clustering forests. In: NIPS (2007)
14. Boureau, Y., Ponce, J., LeCun, Y.: A theoretical analysis of feature pooling in vision algorithms. In: NIPS (2010)
15. Yang, J., Yu, K., Gong, Y., Huang, T.: Linear spatial pyramid matching using sparse coding for image classification. In: CVPR (2009)
16. Benoit, L., Mairal, J., Bach, F., Ponce, J.: Sparse image representation with epitomes. In: CVPR (2011)
17. Wang, J., Yang, J., Yu, K., Lv, F., Huang, T., Gong, Y.: Locality-constrained linear coding for image classification. In: CVPR (2010)
18. Zhou, X., Yu, K., Zhang, T., Huang, T.S.: Image Classification Using Super-Vector Coding of Local Image Descriptors. In: Daniilidis, K., Maragos, P., Paragios, N. (eds.) ECCV 2010, Part V. LNCS, vol. 6315, pp. 141–154. Springer, Heidelberg (2010)
19. Perronnin, F., Sánchez, J., Mensink, T.: Improving the Fisher Kernel for Large-Scale Image Classification. In: Daniilidis, K., Maragos, P., Paragios, N. (eds.) ECCV 2010, Part IV. LNCS, vol. 6314, pp. 143–156. Springer, Heidelberg (2010)
20. DeVore, R.: Nonlinear approximation. Acta Numerica (1998)
21. Olshausen, B., Field, D.J.: Sparse coding with an overcomplete basis set: A strategy employed by v1? Vis. Res. (1997)
22. Shakhnarovich, G.: Learning Task-Specic Similarity. PhD thesis, Massachusetts Institute of Technology (2005)
23. Calonder, M., Lepetit, V., Strecha, C., Fua, P.: BRIEF: Binary Robust Independent Elementary Features. In: Daniilidis, K., Maragos, P., Paragios, N. (eds.) ECCV 2010, Part IV. LNCS, vol. 6314, pp. 778–792. Springer, Heidelberg (2010)
24. Indyk, P., Motwani, R.: Approximate nearest neighbors: towards removing the curse of dimensionality. In: STOC (1998)

25. Weiss, Y., Torralba, A., Fergus, R.: Spectral hashing. In: NIPS (2008)
26. Gordo, A., Perronnin, F.: Asymmetric distances for binary embeddings. In: CVPR (2011)
27. Jégou, H., Matthijs Douze, C.S.: Product quantization for nearest neighbor search. PAMI (2011)
28. Fei-Fei, L., Fergus, R., Perona, P.: One-shot learning of object categories. PAMI (2006)
29. Everingham, M., Van Gool, L., Williams, C.K.I., Winn, J., Zisserman, A.: The PASCAL Visual Object Classes Challenge (VOC 2007) (2007) Results
30. Deng, J., Dong, W., Socher, R., Li, L.J., Li, K., Fei-Fei, L.: ImageNet: A Large-Scale Hierarchical Image Database. In: CVPR 2009 (2009)
31. Lowe, D.: Distinctive image features from scale-invariant keypoints. IJCV (2004)
32. Deng, J., Berg, A.C., Li, K., Fei-Fei, L.: What Does Classifying More Than 10,000 Image Categories Tell Us? In: Daniilidis, K., Maragos, P., Paragios, N. (eds.) ECCV 2010, Part V. LNCS, vol. 6315, pp. 71–84. Springer, Heidelberg (2010)
33. Lin, Y., Lv, F., Zhu, S., Yang, M., Cour, T., Yu, K.: Large-scale image classification: fast feature extraction and svm training. In: CVPR (2011)

Comparative Evaluation of Binary Features

Jared Heinly, Enrique Dunn, and Jan-Michael Frahm

The University of North Carolina at Chapel Hill
{jheinly,dunn,jmf}@cs.unc.edu

Abstract. Performance evaluation of salient features has a long-standing tradition in computer vision. In this paper, we fill the gap of evaluation for the recent wave of binary feature descriptors, which aim to provide robustness while achieving high computational efficiency. We use established metrics to embed our assessment into the body of existing evaluations, allowing us to provide a novel taxonomy unifying both traditional and novel binary features. Moreover, we analyze the performance of different detector and descriptor pairings, which are often used in practice but have been infrequently analyzed. Additionally, we complement existing datasets with novel data testing for illumination change, pure camera rotation, pure scale change, and the variety present in photo-collections. Our performance analysis clearly demonstrates the power of the new class of features. To benefit the community, we also provide a website for the automatic testing of new description methods using our provided metrics and datasets (www.cs.unc.edu/feature-evaluation).

Keywords: binary features, comparison, evaluation.

1 Introduction

Large-scale image registration and recognition in computer vision has led to an explosion in the amount of data being processed in simultaneous localization and mapping [1], reconstruction from photo-collections [2,3], object recognition [4], and panorama stitching [5] applications. With the increasing amount of data in these applications, the complexity of robust features becomes a hindrance. For instance, storing high dimensional descriptors in floating-point representation consumes significant amounts of memory and the time required to compare descriptors within large datasets becomes longer. Another factor is the proliferation of camera-enabled mobile devices (e.g. phones and tablets) that have limited computational power and storage space. This further necessitates features that compute quickly and are compact in their representation.

This new scale of processing has driven several recent works that propose binary feature detectors and descriptors, promising both increased performance as well as compact representation [6,7,8]. Therefore, a comparative analysis of these new, state-of-the-art techniques is required. At the same time, the analysis must embed itself into the large body of existing analyses to allow comparison.

In this paper, we provide such an analysis. We rely on established evaluation metrics and develop a new taxonomy of all features. To evaluate traditional and

A. Fitzgibbon et al. (Eds.): ECCV 2012, Part II, LNCS 7573, pp. 759–773, 2012.

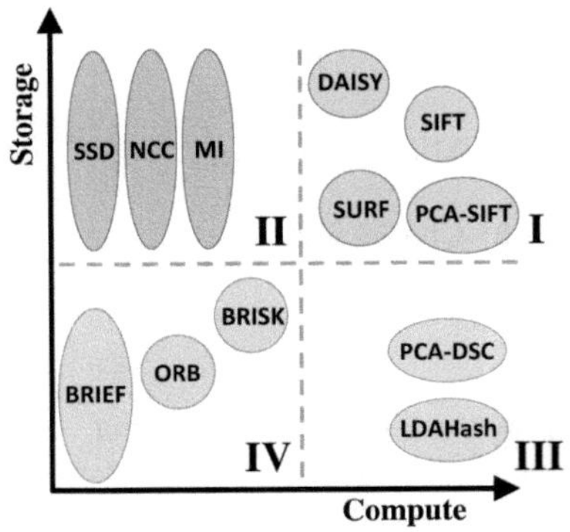

Fig. 1. A taxonomy of descriptors based on their computational and storage requirements: I: Real Value Parameterization [14,19,20,21], II: Patch-Based [17], III: Binarized [22,23], and IV: Binary [6,7,8].

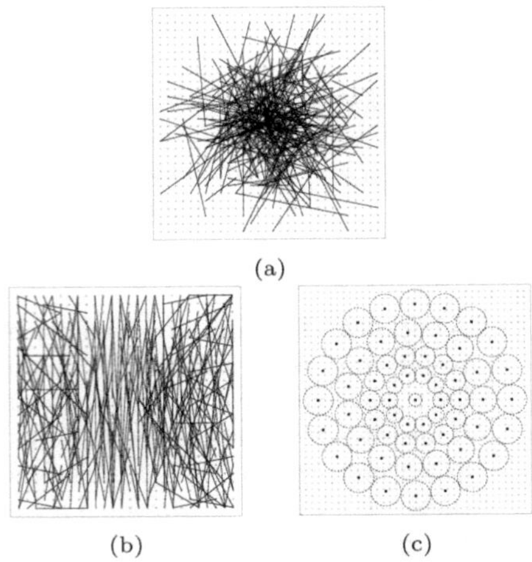

Fig. 2. Example patterns of the (a) BRIEF, (b) ORB, and (c) BRISK descriptors

binary features, we propose a comprehensive set of metrics that also overcomes limitations in the previously performed evaluations. Additionally, when selecting datasets, we chose standard existing image sequences, but supplemented them with our own custom datasets to test for missing aspects. The new complete benchmarking scenes cover a wide variety of challenges including changes in scale, rotation, illumination, viewpoint, image quality, and occlusion due to the change in viewpoint of non-planar geometry. We also decouple the detection and description phases, and evaluate the pairwise combinations of different detectors and descriptors. As a result of our analysis, we provide practical guidelines for the strengths and weaknesses of binary descriptors. Finally, we provide an evaluation website for the automatic benchmarking of novel features (using the results of new detectors and descriptors on the datasets used in our analysis).[1]

2 Related Work

Feature performance (detection, description, and matching) is important to many computer vision applications. In 2005, Mikolajczyk et al. [9] evaluated affine region detectors, and looked to define the repeatability and accuracy of several affine covariant region detectors. They also provided a set of benchmark image sequences (the Oxford dataset) to test the effects of blur, compression, exposure, scale/rotation, and perspective change, which we leverage for compatibility. Also in 2005, Mikolajczyk and Schmid performed an evaluation of local descriptors [10], comparing complex description techniques and several region detectors. It defined two important metrics, *recall* and *1 − precision*. Later,

[1] `www.cs.unc.edu/feature-evaluation`

Moreels and Perona [11] evaluated several popular detectors and descriptors by analyzing their performance on 3D objects. Strecha et al. [12] published a dense 3D dataset, which we use in our evaluation as it provides 3D LIDAR-based geometry and camera poses. Finally, Aanæs et al. [13] evaluated detectors using a large dataset of known camera positions, controlled illumination, and 3D models.

While many evaluations address the performance of a feature, the recent surge in large-scale feature-based applications draws attention to their runtime requirements. We isolate a feature's computation expense (detection, description, or matching) and the amount of memory required (to store and use) to establish a taxonomy for feature classification (see Figure 1).

Small-scale applications can often afford large computational and memory requirements (corresponding to real value parameterization). Techniques in this category rely on a parameterization of an image region, where each dimension is a floating-point type (or a discretization of a float, excluding binary). These techniques, examined in [10], use image gradients, spatial frequencies, etc. to describe the local image patch and to test for similarity by using the L^2 norm, Mahalanobis distance, etc. These descriptors have proven to be effective, and tackle issues such as scale, rotation, viewpoint, or illumination variation. The popular SIFT [14] is in this class. However, increased complexity and robustness comes with an increase in computation and storage requirements. High performance, parallel hardware (e.g. graphics processors) can be used to mitigate higher computational expenses, as shown in [15,16], but even then, descriptor computation can still be the most time-consuming aspect of a system [2].

Therefore, to reduce the computational bottleneck of a system, we address patch-based descriptors. These methods use an image patch surrounding the feature to directly represent it. Distance measures such as sum of squared differences (SSD), normalized cross correlation (NCC), or mutual information (MI) are used to compute pair similarity [17]. The pixels in the patch must be stored, with quadratically increasing requirements for larger patches. However, in large-scale databases (for recognition or reconstruction [18]) the biggest constraints are the matching speed, bandwidth, and the storage required by the descriptor.

The next region in our taxonomy, binarized descriptors, consists of techniques that have high computational but low storage requirements. Binarized descriptors rely on hashing techniques to reduce high-dimensional, real-value parameterizations into compact binary codes [22,23,24,25]. While reducing storage constraints, it also speeds up comparison times through the use of the Hamming distance measure. However, computational requirements are still high as the full real-value parameterization must be computed before the hashing can occur.

The final region in our taxonomy is the binary descriptors. These descriptors have a compact binary representation and limited computational requirements, computing the descriptor directly from pixel-level comparisons. This makes them an attractive solution to many modern applications, especially for mobile platforms where both compute and memory resources are limited.

Table 1. Overview of the basic properties of the binary descriptors

Descriptor	Detector	Rotation Invariant	Scale Invariant
BRIEF	Any	No	No
ORB	FAST	Yes	No
BRISK	AGAST	Yes	Yes

3 Survey of Binary Descriptors

Recent works have focused on providing methods to directly compute binary descriptors from local image patches. We survey these proposed techniques below.

Common Principles: In our analysis, we found that all of the recent binary descriptors possess the same following properties:

- the descriptor is built from a set of pairwise intensity comparisons
- each bit in the descriptor is the result of exactly one comparison
- the sampling pattern is fixed (except for possible scale and rotation)
- Hamming distance is used as a similarity measure

While the binary descriptors use these basic principles, each adds its own unique properties to achieve its design goals. We detail the differences between the binary descriptors (Table 1 highlights their key properties).

BRIEF (Binary Robust Independent Elementary Features) are proposed by Calonder et al. [6], and are the simplest of the methods. It uses a sampling pattern consisting of 128, 256, or 512 comparisons (equating to 128, 256, or 512 bits), with sample points selected randomly from an isotropic Gaussian distribution centered at the feature location (see Figure 2(a). Calonder et al. [6] use the SURF detector negating their computational gain, but BRIEF can be coupled with any other detector. Calonder et al. suggest to use BRIEF with the efficient CenSurE detector [26]. Given its simple construction and compact storage, BRIEF has the lowest compute and storage requirements.

ORB (Oriented FAST and Rotated BRIEF) was proposed by Rublee et al. [7], and overcomes the lack of rotation invariance of BRIEF. ORB computes a local orientation through the use of an intensity centroid [27], which is a weighted averaging of pixel intensities in the local patch assumed not be coincident with the center of the feature. The orientation is the vector between the feature location and the centroid. While this may seem unstable, it is competitive with the single orientation assignment employed in SIFT [28].

The sampling pattern employed in ORB uses 256 pairwise intensity comparisons, but in contrast to BRIEF, is constructed via machine learning, maximizing the descriptor's variance and minimizing the correlation under various orientation changes (see Figure 2(b) for an example).

When using this descriptor, ORB proposes to use the FAST corner detector [29], noting that FAST does not provide a good measure of cornerness and lacks robustness to multi-scale features. In order to combat this, the Harris [30] corner measure is applied at each keypoint location to provide non-maximal suppression

Fig. 3. Example images from the evaluation datasets. From left to right, the datasets are Leuven, Boat, fountain-P11, Herz-Jesu-P8, Reichstag, and Berliner-Dom.

within the image, and a limited image scale pyramid is used to detect keypoints of varying sizes. However, no non-maxima suppression is used between the scales, resulting in potential duplicate detections within different pyramid levels.

BRISK (Binary Robust Invariant Scalable Keypoints) was proposed by Leutenegger et al. [8] and provides both scale and rotation invariance. In order to compute the feature locations, it uses the AGAST corner detector [31], which improves FAST by increasing speed while maintaining the same detection performance. For scale invariance, BRISK detects keypoints in a scale-space pyramid, performing non-maxima suppression and interpolation across all scales.

To describe the features, the authors turn away from the random or learned patterns of BRIEF and ORB, and instead use a symmetric pattern. Sample points are positioned in concentric circles surrounding the feature, with each sample point representing a Gaussian blurring of its surrounding pixels. The standard deviation of this blurring is increased with the distance from the center of the feature (see Figure 2(c) for an illustration). This may seem similar to the DAISY descriptor [20], but the authors point out that DAISY was designed specifically for dense matching, and captures more information than is needed for keypoint description.

To determine orientation, several long-distance sample point comparisons (e.g. on opposite sides of the descriptor pattern) are used. For each long-distance comparison, the vector displacement between the sample points is stored and weighted by the relative difference in intensity. Then, these weighted vectors are averaged to determine the dominant gradient direction of the patch. The sampling pattern is then scaled and rotated, and the descriptor is built up of 512 short-distance sample point comparisons (e.g. a sample point and its closest neighbors) representing the local gradients and shape within the patch.

Overall, BRISK requires significantly more computation and slightly more storage space than either BRIEF or ORB. This places it in the higher compute, higher storage region of the binary descriptor category of our taxonomy.

4 Evaluation

We analyze the performance characteristics of the three recent binary descriptors (BRIEF, ORB, and BRISK), while using state-of-the-art full parametrization descriptors (SIFT and SURF [19]) as a baseline. Besides traditional descriptor performance metrics, we also evaluate the correlation between the detector and descriptor with respect to matching performance. This has received some attention in the past [32], but is important to investigate given its significant practical implications in descriptor post-processing methods (for instance, RANSAC-based estimations [33]). One of the contributions of our comparative analysis is that we test the performance of the studied descriptors with a diverse set of keypoint detectors (Harris, MSER, FAST, ORB, BRISK, SURF, and SIFT).

Datasets: To ensure our work is compatible with existing analyses, we use existing datasets to evaluate the performance of the binary descriptors under various transformations. Specifically, we relied on the Oxford dataset provided and described by Mikolajczyk et al. [9] (for evaluations of the effects of image blur, exposure, JPEG compression, combined scale and rotation, and perspective transformations of planar geometry), and the fountain-P11 and Herz-Jesu-P8 datasets from Strecha et al. [12] (for evaluating the effects of perspective transformations of non-planar geometry). Moreover, we complement the existing datasets with our own to test for pure rotation, pure scaling, illumination changes, and the challenges posed by photo collection datasets such as white balance, auto-exposure, image quality, etc. These various datasets also enable us to isolate the effects of each transformation, or in some cases pairs of transformations.

Performance Metrics: Mikolajczyk et al. [9,10] propose to use the metrics of *recall*, *repeatability*, and *1 − precision*. They describe useful characteristics of a feature's performance, and are widely used as standard measures. However, there are some subtleties to a feature's performance that are missed by only using these measures. For instance, they fail to capture information about the spatial distribution of the features, as well as the frequency of candidate matches.

We wanted to not only use a comprehensive set of metrics that allow us to embed our analysis into the existing body of work, but we also aimed at evaluating parameters relevant to algorithms relying on the features. As such, we propose a set a five different metrics: *putative match ratio*, *precision*, *matching score*, *recall*, and *entropy*.

The putative match ratio, $Putative\ Match\ Ratio = \#\,Putative\ Matches\ /\ \#\,Features$, addresses the selectivity of the descriptor and describes what fraction of the detected features will be initially identified as a match (though potentially incorrect). We define a putative match to be a single pairing of keypoints, where a keypoint cannot be matched to more than one other. Keypoints that are outside of the bounds of the second image (once they are transformed based on the true camera positioning) are not counted.

The value of the putative match ratio is directly influenced by the matching criteria. A less restrictive matching criteria will generate a higher putative match ratio, whereas a criteria that is too restrictive will discard potentially valid matches and will decrease the putative match ratio. Another influencing factor is the distinctiveness of the descriptors under consideration. If many descriptors are highly similar (have small distance values between them), this creates confusion in the matching criteria and can drive down the putative match ratio.

The precision, *Precision* = *# Correct Matches* / *# Putative Matches* [10]), defines the number of correct matches out of the set of putative matches (the inlier ratio). In this equation, the number of correct matches are those putative matches that are geometrically verified based on the known camera positions. The ratio has significant performance consequences for robust estimation modules that use feature matches, such as RANSAC [33], where execution times increase exponentially as the inlier ratio decreases. It is also influenced by many of the same factors that influenced the putative match ratio, but the consequences are different. For instance, while a less restrictive matching criteria will increase the putative match ratio, it will decrease the precision as a higher number of incorrect matches will be generated. Additionally, highly similar descriptors, which drove down the putative match ratio, will also decrease the precision, as confusion in the matching step will also generate a higher number of incorrect matches.

The matching score, *Matching Score* = *# Correct Matches* / *# Features* [10] is equivalent to the multiplication of the putative match ratio and precision. It describes the number of initial features that will result in correct matches, and like the previous two metrics, the matching score can be influenced by indistinct descriptors and the matching criteria. Overall, the matching score describes how well the descriptor is performing and is influenced by the descriptor's robustness to transformations present in the data.

Recall, *Recall* = *# Correct Matches* / *# Correspondences* (defined in [10]), quantifies how many of the possible correct matches were actually found. The correspondences are the matches that should have been identified given the keypoint locations in both images. While this value is dependent on the detector's ability to generate correspondences, recall shares the same influences as the matching score. For instance, a low recall could mean that the descriptors are indistinct, the matching criterion is too strict, or the data is too complex.

The final metric, entropy (used by Zitnick and Ramnath [34]) addresses the influence of the detector on a descriptor. The purpose of this metric is to compute the amount of spread or randomness in the spatial distribution of the keypoints in the image. This is important as too little spread increases the possibility of confusion in the descriptor matching phase due to keypoint clusters.

To compute the entropy, we create a 2D evenly-spaced binning of the feature points. Each point's contribution to a given bin is weighted by a Gaussian relative to its distance to the bin's center. A bin $b(p)$ at position $p = (x, y)$ equals $b(p) = \frac{1}{Z}\sum_{m \in M} G(\|p - m\|)$ where m is a keypoint in the full set M of detected keypoints, and G is a Gaussian. A constant of $1/Z$ is added so that the sum of all bins evaluates to 1. This binning allows us to compute the entropy: $Entropy = \sum_p -b(p) \log b(p)$. Even though entropy is dataset dependent, the relative value of the entropy is useful in identifying detector spatial distribution behaviors such as non-random clustering of keypoint detections (as seen in Figure 4).

We can now quantify how many features were reported as matching (putative match ratio), how many actually matched (precision and matching score), how many were matched out of those possible (recall), and the spread of the detector's keypoints (entropy). Next, we will describe our evaluation framework.

Test Setup: For each dataset, we detect and describe features in each of its images, and use the features in the first image as a reference when matching to all further images in the set. In order to test the detector/descriptor pairings, we had to address several subtleties. For instance, there was a mismatch when a scale invariant descriptor was combined with a detector that was not scale invariant, and vice versa. Additionally, combining detectors and descriptors that were both scale invariant was not trivial, as they typically each use their own method of defining what a feature scale is. In both cases, we simply discarded the scale information, and computed the descriptor at the native image resolution.

In addition, we addressed mismatches in rotation invariance between various detectors and descriptors. We solved this by isolating the orientation computation to the description phase, so that the descriptor overrides any orientation provided by the detector. We next discuss the matching criteria that we use.

Match Criteria: To compute putative matches, we adopt a ratio style test that has proven to be effective [11], [14]. This test compares the ratio of distances between the two best matches for a given keypoint, and rejects the match if the ratio is above a threshold of 0.8 for all tests (the same used in [14]).

To determine the correctness of a match, we use ground truth data to warp keypoints from the first image of the dataset into all remaining images. The warping is achieved either by homographies (provided in the Oxford dataset [9] as well as our non-photo-collection supplemental datasets) or by using ground truth 3D geometry (provided in the Strecha dataset [12]) to project the points into the known cameras. In both cases, match points that are within 2.5 pixels of each other are assumed to be correct. This threshold was chosen empirically as it provided a good balance between pixel-level corner detection (such as Harris [30] and FAST [29]), and the centers of blobs in blob-style detectors (SIFT [14] and SURF [19]). For the photo-collection datasets, we use known camera positions to project points from the first image as epipolar lines in the other images, and once again apply a 2.5 pixel distance threshold test. While we could have used the three camera arrangement test described by Moreels and Perona [11], we opted for the single epipolar line approach as it allowed us to compare only a given pair of images, without the need for a third image to provide correspondences and closely mimics typical uses of features.

5 Analysis and Results

In our analysis we tested the individual effects of various geometric and photometric transformations, as well as several of their combinations to gain a better and more complete understanding of the detectors' and descriptors' performance. Figure 5 provides the results for all tested dataset categories. The individual values making up each measurement (# putative matches, features, etc.) were

Table 2. This table provides statistics for the detectors and descriptors used in our evaluation. For storage, we used a 32 byte BRIEF, and the values in parenthesis for SURF and SIFT are the number of required bytes if the descriptors are stored as floats. For the timings, values in parenthesis are GPU implementations ([15], [16], or our own).

Detector/Descriptor	BRIEF	ORB	BRISK	SURF	SIFT	Harris	MSER	FAST
Avg # Features	n/a	13427	7771	3766	4788	2543	693	8166
Detector Entropy	n/a	12.10	12.33	12.26	12.34	11.84	10.74	12.52
Detector ms/image	n/a	17	43	377(19)	572(25)	78(4.7)	117	2.7
Descriptor μs/feature	4.4(0.4)	4.8	12.9	143(6.6)	314(19)	n/a	n/a	n/a
Storage bytes/feature	16,32,64	32	64	64(256)	128(512)	n/a	n/a	n/a

Fig. 4. This figure shows the distribution of keypoints (for two datasets) from the Harris (left image in the pair) and FAST (right image in the pair) corner detectors. The FAST detector not only detects more keypoints, but has a higher entropy for its detections.

first summed across each pairwise comparison, and one final average was computed.

Detector Performance: As mentioned before, entropy can be used as a measure of the randomness of the keypoint locations, penalizing detectors that spatially cluster their keypoints. In order to compute the entropy across all of the datasets, we perform a weighted average of the individual entropies to account for the different contributions of the datasets (results are in Table 2).

We see several notable attributes. First, FAST has the highest entropy, which can be attributed to its good spread of points and the shear number of detections that occurred. A higher number of keypoints does not necessarily correspond to increased entropy, but it can help if more spatial bins in the entropy equation are populated. The second group of detectors, SIFT, BRISK, and SURF, have the next highest entropies, which is expected as Zitnick's and Ramnath's evaluation [34] noted that a blob-style detector (difference of Gaussian) have high entropies.

On the other end, Harris and MSER reported the lowest two entropy values. The primary reason for this is a lower average number of keypoint detections (especially in the case of MSER), which leads to less spatial bins being populated. While these detectors are still very viable, it is important to note their lower detection rates and potential differences in keypoint distribution (one such example is provided in Figure 4).

Descriptor Performance: One of the most compelling motivations for the use of binary descriptors is their efficiency and compactness. Table 2 shows the timing results for the various detectors and descriptors that we used in our system. The implementations for ORB and BRISK were obtained from the authors, while all others came from OpenCV 2.3 [35]. The code was run on a computer with an Intel Xeon 2.67GHz processor, 12GB of RAM, NVIDIA GTX 285, and Microsoft Windows 7. From the results, we can see that the binary descriptors (and many of their paired detectors) are an order of magnitude faster than the SURF or SIFT alternatives. For mobile devices, while the overall timings would change, a speedup would still be realized as the binary descriptors are algorithmically more efficient. Table 2 also lists the storage requirements for the descriptors. In some cases, the binary descriptors can be constructed such that they are on par with efficient SURF representations, but overall, binary descriptors reduce storage to a half or to a quarter. We are assuming that the real value parameterization descriptors are stored in a quantized form (1 byte per dimension). If instead they are stored as floating-point values, the storage savings of binary features are even more significant.

Figure 5 shows the results for our evaluation of detector and descriptor pairings. Upon a close inspection, several interesting conclusions become apparent.

Non-geometric Transforms: Non-geometric transforms consist of those that are image-capture dependent, and do not rely on the viewpoint (e.g. blur, JPEG compression, exposure, and illumination). Challenges in these datasets involve less-distinct image gradients and changes to the relative difference between pixels due to compression or lighting change.

Upon inspecting the results, BRIEF's performance is very favorable. It outperforms ORB and BRISK in many of the categories (even when compared to SURF or SIFT), though the precision is noticeably lower than ORB or BRISK. The key insight to BRIEF's good performance is that it has a fixed pattern (no scale or rotation invariance), and is designed to accurately represent the underlying gradients of an image patch (which are stable for monotonic color transformations). In regard to the lower precision, as we mentioned before, the precision is decreased when the matching criteria are either less restrictive, or the features are not distinct enough. We enforced the same matching criteria for each descriptor, hence performance differences are due to the lack of distinctiveness. The pattern used by ORB is specifically trained to maximize distinctiveness, and BRISK's descriptor is much more complex (larger number of samples with each sample being a comparison of blurred pixels), which allows it to be much more certain of the matches it generates. Therefore, it is not surprising that BRIEF's precision would suffer slightly compared to ORB or BRISK.

For the choice of detector, both SURF and Harris perform well under these non-geometric transformations. The key is that both are very repeatable in these images. SURF (being a blob detector) does well for the blur dataset, as the smoothing of the gradients negatively impacts corner detectors like Harris. SIFT (also being a blob detector) does not do as well as the accuracy of its keypoint detections decreases as the scale of the blob increases. This is an artifact of the downsampling in the image pyramid, where SURF overcomes this by applying larger filters at the native resolution. For the non-blurred datasets, Harris does well because high gradient change still exists at corners under color changes.

Affine Image Transforms: The affine image transforms that we used in our testing consist of image plane rotation and scaling. Overall, SIFT was the best, but ORB and BRISK still performed well. As is expected, BRIEF performs poorly under large rotation or scale change compared to the other descriptors (as it is not designed to handle those effects). For pure scale change, ORB is better than BRIEF although there is no rotation change in the image. This can be attributed to the limited scale space used by the ORB detector, allowing it to detect FAST corners at several scales. However, of all the binary descriptors, BRISK performs the best, as it is scale invariant.

For pure rotations, the ORB detector/descriptor combination performs better than the BRISK detector/descriptor. However, the FAST detector paired with BRISK is a top performer (as well as the Harris detector paired with ORB), competing on the same level as SIFT. The insight to this result is that both FAST and Harris are not scale invariant, and excel because there is no scale change in the images. The better performances of BRISK and ORB when paired with other detectors are unexpected, but only help to highlight the importance of considering various combinations when deciding on a detector and descriptor.

Finally, when analyzing combined scale and rotation changes, BRISK takes the lead of the binary descriptors. However, SIFT and SURF have competitive matching scores, but significantly higher recalls. This difference in matching score and recall speaks to the performance of the detectors. They detected almost the same percentage of correct matches (the matching score), SURF and SIFT's number of correspondences must have been lower in order for their recall to be higher. This means that for basic scale and rotation combinations, BRISK's detector is more repeatable than SURF or SIFT's.

Turning our attention back to BRIEF, one way to overcome BRIEF's sensitivity to rotation when computing on mobile devices is via inertial sensor-aligned features [36] which aligns a descriptor with the current gravity direction of the mobile device (assuming that the device has an accelerometer), allowing for repeatable detections of the same feature as the device changes orientation.

Perspective Transforms are the result of changes in viewpoint. The biggest issues faced in these sets of images are occlusions due to depth edges, as well as perspective warping. For binary descriptors, BRIEF surprisingly has a slight lead in recall and matching score over ORB and BRISK, given its limited complexity. However, in most of the perspective evaluation datasets, there is no significant change in scale, and the orientation of the images are the same. This is not the case in the photo-collection datasets, which include a higher variety of feature scales. Even then, BRIEF still takes the lead over the other binary descriptors. So, even though there is considerable viewpoint change throughout all of the perspective datasets, the upright nature of all of the images allows the fixed orientation of BRIEF to excel.

(a)

Putative Match Ratio

	BF	OB	BK	SF	ST
H	25	11	11		
MR	19	10	9		
FT	23	10	11		
OB	13	10	8		
BK	20	9	9		
SF	31	15	12	15	
ST	19	8	9		10

Precision

	BF	OB	BK	SF	ST
H	67	78	84		
MR	65	71	69		
FT	68	72	85		
OB	70	78	87		
BK	67	77	73		
SF	72	82	79	71	
ST	63	76	76		73

Matching Score

	BF	OB	BK	SF	ST
H	17	8	9		
MR	12	7	6		
FT	15	7	9		
OB	9	8	7		
BK	13	7	6		
SF	22	12	9	11	
ST	12	6	7		7

Recall

	BF	OB	BK	SF	ST
H	44	22	24		
MR	40	22	19		
FT	39	10	24		
OB	19	16	12		
BK	31	9	14		
SF	55	29	22	28	
ST	38	18	18		24

(b)

Putative Match Ratio

	BF	OB	BK	SF	ST
H	68	54	51		
MR	43	31	29		
FT	50	33	35		
OB	35	36	30		
BK	50	35	33		
SF	59	43	30	47	
ST	35	23	28		29

Precision

	BF	OB	BK	SF	ST
H	95	97	97		
MR	83	88	86		
FT	91	96	97		
OB	95	97	98		
BK	93	97	94		
SF	92	96	94	90	
ST	85	93	94		91

Matching Score

	BF	OB	BK	SF	ST
H	64	53	49		
MR	36	27	25		
FT	46	32	34		
OB	32	35	30		
BK	46	34	32		
SF	54	41	28	42	
ST	30	22	27		26

Recall

	BF	OB	BK	SF	ST
H	80	64	63		
MR	53	40	33		
FT	69	47	54		
OB	47	49	35		
BK	59	43	41		
SF	74	56	39	61	
ST	55	40	40		55

(c)

Putative Match Ratio

	BF	OB	BK	SF	ST
H	39	28	26		
MR	45	31	30		
FT	53	38	39		
OB	36	36	35		
BK	44	32	28		
SF	43	31	25	30	
ST	34	25	29		34

Precision

	BF	OB	BK	SF	ST
H	80	91	93		
MR	76	76	72		
FT	84	93	95		
OB	89	93	96		
BK	81	90	87		
SF	80	88	82	78	
ST	76	88	87		86

Matching Score

	BF	OB	BK	SF	ST
H	31	26	24		
MR	34	24	22		
FT	44	36	37		
OB	32	34	34		
BK	36	29	24		
SF	34	28	21	23	
ST	26	22	25		29

Recall

	BF	OB	BK	SF	ST
H	63	51	52		
MR	63	44	39		
FT	65	51	58		
OB	51	53	45		
BK	55	43	37		
SF	73	58	44	53	
ST	58	48	48		74

(d)

Putative Match Ratio

	BF	OB	BK	SF	ST
H	13	8	7		
MR	15	10	9		
FT	11	7	7		
OB	6	5	5		
BK	9	6	6		
SF	10	5	4	8	
ST	7	5	6		10

Precision

	BF	OB	BK	SF	ST
H	64	76	82		
MR	52	41	36		
FT	71	76	84		
OB	78	80	89		
BK	69	73	79		
SF	57	60	57	37	
ST	49	54	61		55

Matching Score

	BF	OB	BK	SF	ST
H	8	6	5		
MR	8	4	3		
FT	7	5	6		
OB	4	4	4		
BK	6	4	4		
SF	6	3	2	3	
ST	4	3	3		6

Recall

	BF	OB	BK	SF	ST
H	32	23	22		
MR	47	24	18		
FT	25	17	21		
OB	13	13	11		
BK	20	14	15		
SF	35	21	15	19	
ST	24	17	18		40

(e)

Putative Match Ratio

	BF	OB	BK	SF	ST
H	19	10	12		
MR	10	8	9		
FT	15	7	12		
OB	5	21	5		
BK	11	7	40		
SF	15	8	8	56	
ST	14	7	10		57

Precision

	BF	OB	BK	SF	ST
H	80	80	87		
MR	69	48	53		
FT	77	73	89		
OB	79	92	91		
BK	74	73	78		
SF	75	67	70	81	
ST	76	72	82		96

Matching Score

	BF	OB	BK	SF	ST
H	15	8	11		
MR	7	4	5		
FT	11	6	10		
OB	4	19	5		
BK	8	5	31		
SF	11	5	6	45	
ST	11	5	8		54

Recall

	BF	OB	BK	SF	ST
H	24	13	17		
MR	10	6	7		
FT	19	9	17		
OB	6	29	6		
BK	11	7	42		
SF	17	8	8	69	
ST	16	7	10		80

(f)

Putative Match Ratio

	BF	OB	BK	SF	ST
H	3	69	64		
MR	5	44	42		
FT	3	62	68		
OB	1	62	58		
BK	2	52	51		
SF	4	44	38	43	
ST	3	41	50		58

Precision

	BF	OB	BK	SF	ST
H	14	93	88		
MR	18	90	78		
FT	15	91	93		
OB	12	86	94		
BK	12	89	86		
SF	13	88	79	82	
ST	13	93	84		95

Matching Score

	BF	OB	BK	SF	ST
H	0	64	56		
MR	1	40	33		
FT	0	57	64		
OB	0	53	55		
BK	0	46	44		
SF	0	38	30	35	
ST	0	38	42		55

Recall

	BF	OB	BK	SF	ST
H	0	68	62		
MR	1	50	39		
FT	0	63	74		
OB	0	62	53		
BK	0	52	48		
SF	1	57	45	55	
ST	1	50	48		79

(g)

Putative Match Ratio

	BF	OB	BK	SF	ST
H	4	6	6		
MR	6	6	5		
FT	2	4	6		
OB	1	8	4		
BK	2	4	13		
SF	3	4	4	14	
ST	3	4	4		13

Precision

	BF	OB	BK	SF	ST
H	34	65	81		
MR	19	40	35		
FT	23	64	83		
OB	20	83	86		
BK	27	68	84		
SF	20	48	58	68	
ST	18	55	72		84

Matching Score

	BF	OB	BK	SF	ST
H	1	4	5		
MR	1	2	2		
FT	1	3	5		
OB	0	7	3		
BK	0	3	11		
SF	1	2	2	9	
ST	0	2	3		11

Recall

	BF	OB	BK	SF	ST
H	2	6	9		
MR	5	9	8		
FT	1	4	7		
OB	0	8	3		
BK	1	3	14		
SF	1	5	6	25	
ST	1	5	7		30

(h)

Putative Match Ratio

	BF	OB	BK	SF	ST
H	29	14	17		
MR	15	9	9		
FT	25	13	17		
OB	12	15	13		
BK	19	11	13		
SF	18	10	10	15	
ST	18	9	13		24

Precision

	BF	OB	BK	SF	ST
H	88	87	90		
MR	76	68	70		
FT	84	85	89		
OB	89	88	92		
BK	86	83	87		
SF	78	73	75	73	
ST	83	80	81		86

Matching Score

	BF	OB	BK	SF	ST
H	26	13	15		
MR	11	6	6		
FT	21	11	15		
OB	11	13	12		
BK	16	9	11		
SF	14	7	7	11	
ST	15	7	11		20

Recall

	BF	OB	BK	SF	ST
H	36	18	22		
MR	25	13	14		
FT	28	8	21		
OB	13	15	12		
BK	22	7	15		
SF	32	17	17	25	
ST	28	14	17		42

(i)

Putative Match Ratio

	BF	OB	BK	SF	ST
H	22	13	14		
MR	17	11	11		
FT	21	12	15		
OB	9	13	9		
BK	15	9	15		
SF	16	9	9	18	
ST	15	9	13		22

Precision

	BF	OB	BK	SF	ST
H	60	66	73		
MR	55	39	37		
FT	73	73	81		
OB	77	80	85		
BK	63	62	72		
SF	58	54	58	61	
ST	69	68	75		84

Matching Score

	BF	OB	BK	SF	ST
H	13	9	10		
MR	9	4	4		
FT	15	9	12		
OB	7	10	8		
BK	9	5	11		
SF	10	5	5	11	
ST	11	6	10		19

Recall

	BF	OB	BK	SF	ST
H	30	19	23		
MR	32	15	13		
FT	30	17	24		
OB	12	18	11		
BK	19	10	20		
SF	28	14	15	33	
ST	24	13	18		44

(j)

Putative Match Ratio

	BF	OB	BK	SF	ST
H	11	6	6		
MR	11	7	7		
FT	9	5	5		
OB	4	6	4		
BK	7	4	7		
SF	10	6	5	11	
ST	8	4	5		11

Precision

	BF	OB	BK	SF	ST
H	81	78	84		
MR	76	72	63		
FT	84	77	86		
OB	87	84	88		
BK	83	77	86		
SF	79	73	75	79	
ST	76	71	75		83

Matching Score

	BF	OB	BK	SF	ST
H	9	5	5		
MR	8	5	4		
FT	7	4	5		
OB	4	5	3		
BK	6	3	6		
SF	8	4	4	8	
ST	6	3	4		10

Recall

	BF	OB	BK	SF	ST
H	8	5	5		
MR	8	5	4		
FT	7	4	5		
OB	4	5	3		
BK	6	3	5		
SF	8	4	4	9	
ST	6	3	3		10

Fig. 5. Results for (a) blur, (b) JPEG compression, (c) exposure, (d) day-to-night illumination, (e) scale, (f) rotation, (g) scale and rotation, (h) perspective with planar scene, (i) perspective with non-planar scene, (j) photo-collection. Rows are detectors, columns are descriptors: H=Harris, MR=MSER, FT=FAST, BF=BRIEF, OB=ORB, BK=BRISK, SF=SURF, ST=SIFT. Values are in percent (blue 0%, red 100%).

Additionally, it is interesting to note that the Harris corner detector does well when coupled with BRIEF. Harris is not scale invariant, but the nature of corners is that there will be high gradient change even under perspective distortion allowing for repeatable detections.

Another observation is that the precision of BRISK is once again higher than its binary competitors. This points to the descriptiveness of BRISK, allowing it to achieve very high quality matches. Once again, however, SIFT provides the best performance, and proves to be the most robust to changes in perspective.

6 Conclusion

From the analysis of our results, we highlight several pertinent observations, each of which was driven by the metrics used in our evaluation. Moreover, by proposing and integrating a comprehensive set of measures and datasets, we are able to gain insights into the various factors that influence a feature's behavior.

First, consider BRIEF's performance under non-geometric and perspective transforms. In both cases, BRIEF excelled because the images contained similar scales and orientations. This highlights the importance of leveraging any additional knowledge about the data being processed (e.g. similar scales/orientations or orientation from inertial sensors) as it impacts the performance of the binary descriptors. The key idea is that a binary descriptor will suffer in performance when it takes into account a transform not present in the data.

As a result of our evaluation of detector/descriptor pairings, we observed that the best performance did not always correspond to the original authors' recommendations. This leads us to our second observation that by considering the effect a detector has on a descriptor, we enable the educated assignment of detectors to descriptors depending on the expected properties of the data.

Finally, for all datasets except the non-geometric transforms, SIFT was the best. Although achieving a gain in matching rate, some applications using SIFT may unnecessarily forfeit the significant speed gains made possible by binary descriptors (Table 2). This performance tradeoff makes binary features a viable choice whenever the application provides robustness against additional outliers.

Acknowledgments. This work was supported by NSF IIS-0916829 and the Department of Energy under Award DE-FG52-08NA28778.

References

1. Chang, H.J., et al.: P-SLAM: Simultaneous Localization and Mapping With Environmental-Structure Prediction. IEEE Trans. Robot. 23(2), 281–293 (2007)
2. Frahm, J.-M., Fite-Georgel, P., Gallup, D., Johnson, T., Raguram, R., Wu, C., Jen, Y.-H., Dunn, E., Clipp, B., Lazebnik, S., Pollefeys, M.: Building Rome on a Cloudless Day. In: Daniilidis, K., Maragos, P., Paragios, N., et al. (eds.) ECCV 2010, Part IV. LNCS, vol. 6314, pp. 368–381. Springer, Heidelberg (2010)

3. Snavely, N., Seitz, S.M., Szeliski, R.: Photo Tourism: Exploring Photo Collections in 3D. In: SIGGRAPH Conference Proceedings, pp. 835–846 (2006)
4. Nister, D., Stewenius, H.: Scalable Recognition with a Vocabulary Tree. In: CVPR, pp. 2161–2168 (2006)
5. Brown, M., Lowe, D.G.: Recognising Panoramas. In: ICCV, pp. 1218–1225 (2003)
6. Calonder, M., Lepetit, V., Strecha, C., Fua, P.: BRIEF: Binary Robust Independent Elementary Features. In: Daniilidis, K., Maragos, P., Paragios, N. (eds.) ECCV 2010, Part IV. LNCS, vol. 6314, pp. 778–792. Springer, Heidelberg (2010)
7. Rublee, E., Rabaud, V., Konolige, K., Bradski, G.: ORB: An Efficient Alternative to SIFT or SURF. In: ICCV, pp. 2564–2571 (2011)
8. Leutenegger, S., Chli, M., Siegwart, R.: BRISK: Binary Robust Invariant Scalable Keypoints. In: ICCV, pp. 2548–2555 (2011)
9. Mikolajczyk, K., et al.: A Comparison of Affine Region Detectors. IJCV 65(1-2), 43–72 (2005)
10. Mikolajczyk, K., Schmid, C.: A Performance Evaluation of Local Descriptors. IEEE Trans. PAMI 27(10), 1615–1630 (2005)
11. Moreels, P., Perona, P.: Evaluation of Features Detectors and Descriptors based on 3D Objects. IJCV 73(3), 263–284 (2007)
12. Strecha, C., et al.: On Benchmarking Camera Calibration and Multi-View Stereo for High Resolution Imagery. In: CVPR, pp. 1–8 (2008)
13. Aanæs, H., et al.: Interesting Interest Points. IJCV 97(1), 18–35 (2012)
14. Lowe, D.G.: Distinctive image features from scale-invariant keypoints. IJCV 60(2), 91–110 (2004)
15. Wu, C.: SiftGPU (2007), `http://cs.unc.edu/~ccwu/siftgpu`
16. Schulz, A., et al.: CUDA SURF - A real-time implementation for SURF (2010), `http://www.d2.mpi-inf.mpg.de/surf`
17. Hirschmüller, H., Scharstein, D.: Evaluation of Cost Functions for Stereo Matching. In: CVPR, pp. 1–8 (2007)
18. Agarwal, S., et al.: Building Rome in a Day. In: ICCV, pp. 72–79 (2009)
19. Bay, H., et al.: Speeded-Up Robust Features (SURF). Comp. Vis. and Image Understanding 110(3), 346–359 (2008)
20. Tola, E., Lepetit, V., Fua, P.: DAISY: An Efficient Dense Descriptor Applied to Wide Baseline Stereo. IEEE Trans. PAMI 32(5), 815–830 (2010)
21. Ke, Y., Sukthankar, R.: PCA-SIFT: a more distinctive representation for local image descriptors. In: CVPR, pp. 506–513 (2004)
22. Strecha, C., et al.: LDAHash: Improved Matching with Smaller Descriptors. IEEE Trans. PAMI 34(1), 66–78 (2012)
23. Yeo, C., Ahammad, P., Ramchandran, K.: Coding of Image Feature Descriptors for Distributed Rate-efficient Visual Correspondences. IJCV 94(3), 267–281 (2011)
24. Raginsky, M., Lazebnik, S.: Locality-Sensitive Binary Codes from Shift-Invariant Kernels. In: Advances in Neural Info. Processing Systems, pp. 1509–1517 (2009)
25. Gong, Y., Lazebnik, S.: Iterative Quantization: A Procrustean Approach to Learning Binary Codes. In: CVPR, pp. 817–824 (2011)
26. Agrawal, M., Konolige, K., Blas, M.R.: CenSurE: Center Surround Extremas for Realtime Feature Detection and Matching. In: Forsyth, D., Torr, P., Zisserman, A. (eds.) ECCV 2008, Part IV. LNCS, vol. 5305, pp. 102–115. Springer, Heidelberg (2008)
27. Rosin, P.L.: Measuring Corner Properties. Comp. Vis. and Image Understanding, 291–307 (1999)
28. Gauglitz, S., et al.: Improving Keypoint Orientation Assignment. In: BMVC (2011)

29. Rosten, E., Porter, R., Drummond, T.: Faster and Better: A Machine Learning Approach to Corner Detection. IEEE Trans. PAMI 32(1), 105–119 (2010)
30. Harris, C., Stephens, M.: A Combined Corner and Edge Detector. In: Proc. of The Fourth Alvey Vision Conference, pp. 147–151 (1988)
31. Mair, E., Hager, G.D., Burschka, D., Suppa, M., Hirzinger, G.: Adaptive and Generic Corner Detection Based on the Accelerated Segment Test. In: Daniilidis, K., Maragos, P., Paragios, N. (eds.) ECCV 2010, Part II. LNCS, vol. 6312, pp. 183–196. Springer, Heidelberg (2010)
32. Dahl, A.L., Aanæs, H., Pedersen, K.S.: Finding the Best Feature Detector-Descriptor Combination. In: 3DIMPVT, pp. 318–325 (2011)
33. Fischler, M.A., Bolles, R.C.: Random Sample Consensus: A Paradigm for Model Fitting with Applications to Image Analysis and Automated Cartography. Communications of the ACM 24(6), 381–395 (1981)
34. Zitnick, L., Krishnan, R.: Edge Foci Interest Points. In: ICCV, pp. 359–366 (2011)
35. Bradski, G.: The OpenCV Library. Dr. Dobb's Journal of Software Tools (2000)
36. Kurz, D., BenHimane, S.: Inertial sensor-aligned visual feature descriptors. In: CVPR, pp. 161–166 (2011)

Negative Evidences and Co-occurences in Image Retrieval: The Benefit of PCA and Whitening

Hervé Jégou[1] and Ondřej Chum[2]

[1] INRIA Rennes
[2] CMP, Department of Cybernetics, Faculty of EE, CTU in Prague

Abstract. The paper addresses large scale image retrieval with short vector representations. We study dimensionality reduction by Principal Component Analysis (PCA) and propose improvements to its different phases. We show and explicitly exploit relations between i) mean subtraction and the negative evidence, i.e., a visual word that is mutually missing in two descriptions being compared, and ii) the axis de-correlation and the co-occurrences phenomenon. Finally, we propose an effective way to alleviate the quantization artifacts through a joint dimensionality reduction of multiple vocabularies. The proposed techniques are simple, yet significantly and consistently improve over the state of the art on compact image representations. Complementary experiments in image classification show that the methods are generally applicable.

1 Introduction

This paper mainly addresses the problem of large-scale image search and object recognition, as considered by many papers in the literature [1,2,3,4]. More precisely, the task consists of finding images in a large image database that most closely resemble a query image based on their visual similarity. A majority of the papers rely on the bag-of-words (BOW) representation [1,5,2,3] or its derivatives, e.g., [4]. These approaches are limited to search in a few million images on a single machine due to computational or memory constraints. In this paper, we will mainly focus on more scalable approaches in the spirit of recent work on compact images representations [6,7,8], where the image description is a short vector, which is subsequently encoded in compact codes using binarization [6,9] or product quantization techniques [10]. The best performing methods in this context are those that produce the vector representing an image from local features [7,8] such as the Fisher Vectors [11,12,7] or its non probabilistic version, namely the VLAD descriptor [8]. In contrast to global description techniques computed from the pixels [13,6] in a more direct manner, these representations inherit, to some extent, the invariance properties (change in viewpoints, cropping, etc) of the local descriptors from which they are computed.

Methods generating a short code image representation commonly exploit the PCA [14] to perform the dimensionality reduction. It was observed [8] that the performance of BOW is even improved by PCA reduction. In the paper, we study this phenomenon. The PCA can be seen as a two step process (1) centering the

A. Fitzgibbon et al. (Eds.): ECCV 2012, Part II, LNCS 7573, pp. 774–787, 2012.

data, and (2) selecting a de-correlated (orthogonal) basis of a subspace minimizing the dimensionality reduction error. We show that each of the steps has a positive impact on the retrieval, and we provide interpretation of such a behavior. Based on the analysis, we propose simple yet effective techniques to further improve the quality of BOW and VLAD representations. First, we consider the role of *negative evidence*: given two BOW vectors, a visual word jointly missing in both vectors is information that should receive more importance in the similarity measurement. We show relation of the negative evidence to the centering of BOW vectors (mean subtraction). Secondly, both BOW and VLAD representations are further improved by exploiting the de-correlation of the descriptor entries. Two complementary approaches are proposed 1) whitening the vector space, thereby addressing the problem of co-occurrences; and 2) by considering multiple vocabularies with a joint dimensionality reduction. Multiple vocabularies have been considered by prior art, e.g., in the hierarchical k-means [2] or in the rank aggregation technique of [15]. In contrast to those, our method increases the search accuracy for *a fixed size* of the vector describing the image. When querying the indexing structure, the memory and computational complexities are the same as when considering a unique vocabulary.

Albeit simple, the proposed techniques consistently and significantly improve the state-of-the-art image search based on short vectors, as demonstrated by our results on four popular benchmarks. Finally, we will briefly show with experiments on the PASCAL VOC'07 benchmark that the better representation for retrieval also translates to better classification results: Our short vectors obtained from BOW and combined with a linear classifier significantly outperform a soft BOW combined with a Chi-square kernel.

The paper is organized as follows: After introducing the context in Section 2, Section 3 shows the role of co-missing visual words and Section 4 exploits whitening to address the issue arising with co-occurrence over-counting. Section 5 extends it to multiple vocabularies and compares with the state of the art.

2 Background and Datasets

2.1 Image Description Framework

Bag-of-Words. As a baseline, we first consider the regular bag-of-words representation, as proposed by Sivic and Zisserman [1]. This representation extracts a global description vector from an image using the following procedure.

1. Covariant regions of interest are detected [16,17] in the image and described by a local d-dimensional descriptor. We used the Hessian-Affine detector jointly with the SIFT descriptor [18].
2. The resulting descriptors are quantized using a so-called "visual vocabulary", which is learned using k-means algorithm, producing "visual words".
3. The histogram of occurrences of visual words (of size $D = k$) is computed and weighted using inverse document frequency (*idf*) terms.
4. The resulting vector is subsequently normalized. As proposed in [1], we adopt the L2 normalization.

VLAD. The vector of locally aggregated descriptors [8] is a simplification of the Fisher vector [11]. This representation departs from BOW only in the Step 3: instead of producing the histogram of occurrences, VLAD accumulates, in the output vector of size $D = k \times d$, the difference between the descriptors and their respective centroids.

Power-Law Normalization. Both the VLAD and Fisher vector representations are improved [19] by using the so-called *power-law* normalization [7]. This simple method post-processes the output image vector $v = (v_1, ...v_D)$ as $v_i := |v_i|^\beta \times \mathrm{sign}(v_i)$, with $0 \leq \beta < 1$ a fixed constant. The updated vector v is L2-normalized in turn. The impact of this post-processing is argued [19] to reduce the impact of multiple matches and visual bursts [20]. This variant will be considered for $\beta = 0.5$ in the following, denoted by SSR (signed square rooting).

2.2 Efficient PCA

The BOW and VLAD vectors are high dimensional. For instance, typical values of D for BOW ranges from one thousand to one million components, while VLAD vectors are $k \times d$-dimensional, d being the dimensionality of the local descriptor. This means $D = 65,536$ for the typical parameters $d = 128$ and $k = 512$. It is therefore not efficient or even feasible to perform the PCA using the covariance matrix method. However, we only need the first D' first eigenvectors and eigenvalues in Equation 5. By limiting the learning set $\boldsymbol{Y}$ to a reasonable number of vectors (we used the learning image sets introduced in Section 2), one can use the dual gram method (see, e.g., Paragraph 12.1.4 in [14]) to learn the matrix $\boldsymbol{P}$ and eigenvalues λ_1 to $\lambda_{D'}$. This amounts to computing the $n \times n$ gram matrix $\boldsymbol{Y}^\top \boldsymbol{Y}$ instead of the $D \times D$ covariance matrix $\boldsymbol{C}$, and to exploiting the analytical relationship between the eigen-decomposition of these two matrices. The eigenvalue decomposition is performed using the Arnoldi algorithm, which computes the D' desired eigenvectors, i.e., those associated with the largest eigenvalues, using an iterative procedure.

2.3 Datasets

The interest of the proposed techniques is evaluated on a number of popular datasets widely used in the literature.

Oxford5k [21] and Paris6k [22]: These datasets are collections of images from Flickr. The 55 queries correspond to 11 distinct buildings, given by bounding boxes in 55 images from the set. The task is to retrieve all corresponding buildings. The performance is measured by mean average precision (mAP), as defined in [21].

Holidays (+Flickr1M): This dataset contains personal Holiday photos provided by INRIA [4]. The dataset itself contains 1491 images. A subset of 500 images serves as queries. Each query is compared to the other 1490 images in a leave-one-out fashion. To evaluate the performance on a large scale, a distractor dataset of 1 million images downloaded from Flickr is also provided. As for Oxford5k, the performance is measured by mAP.

University of Kentucky Benchmark (UKB). This image set contains 10200 images, corresponding to 2550 distinct objects and scenes (4 images per group). Each image is compared to all the others. The usual performance score is the mean number of images ranked in the first 4 positions.

For the Oxford5k and Paris datasets, we have used to the detector and descriptor used in [23], while the descriptors available online have been used for the other datasets.

Dataset for Learning Stages: We use an independent dataset (no intersection with the test set) to learn the visual vocabularies and for the other learning stages involved in our technique. When evaluating on Holidays, Holidays+Flickr1M and UKB, the independent dataset consists of 10000 images from Flickr. Paris6k is used to learn the meta-data associated with the evaluation on Oxford5k. Note that the *idf* terms do not involve any learning stage and are applied on-the-fly, based on the indexed dataset statistics.

3 Exploiting Evidences from Co-missing Words

Being produced as a weighted histogram of occurrences of visual words, the regular BOW representation contains only non-negative values. Let consider the cosine measure for similarity $s(u, v)$ between BOW vectors u and v, i.e.,

$$s(u, v) = \frac{1}{||u|| \, . \, ||v||} \sum_{i}^{k} u_i \, v_i. \tag{1}$$

If $u_i = 0$, the individual contribution of the visual word with index i is the same if v_i is equal or greater than 0. The difference between these cases is only taken into account by the normalization factor $||v||$. This under-estimates the importance of jointly zero components, which give some limited yet important evidence on visual similarity.

We, therefore, propose a simple way to better take into account this case in BOW vectors. Instead of measuring the angle between points u and v from the origin, we consider an angle between those two points measured at different point m. A good choice for m is a fraction of the mean bag-of-words vector $m = \alpha \cdot \bar{v}$. The novel cosine similarity is computed by Equation (1) on transformed vectors by

$$v := v - \alpha . \bar{v}. \tag{2}$$

The value $\alpha = 1$ corresponds to the case where the mean of the vector (produced from a learning set) is subtracted. Applying such a transformation, the cosine similarity gives a positive contribution for a particular visual word if it is absent (more precisely, if it appeared less than on average) in both the compared images.

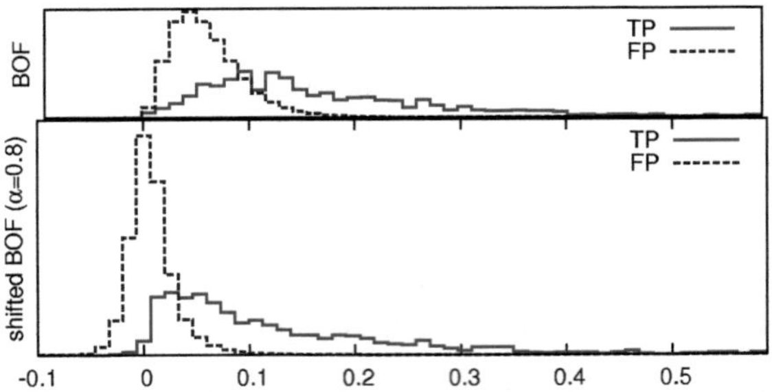

Fig. 1. Empirical distribution (Holidays dataset) of the similarities for true (TP) and false positives (FP) before (regular BOW) and after the proposed correction (shifted BOW). Observe the better separation of true and false positives, which are centered on zero with the shifted BOW.

As a result, the similarity between bag-of-words is improved, as depicted in Figure 1.

Figure 2 shows the impact of this correction as a function of α when measuring the performance on the Holidays and Oxford5K benchmarks. As one can see, the proposed update gives some significant improvement, in particular for smaller vocabulary sizes, and this for a negligible computing and memory cost, as explained below.

Integration within the Inverted File System. The inverted file structure allows for efficient evaluation of the cosine distance for sparse vectors by evaluating only non-negative elements of the product in Equation (1). A naive subtraction of a non-sparse vector m from all sparse vectors in the database has a severe negative effect on both the efficiency of the retrieval and the memory footprint. It is however possible to compute the new similarity measure using the same inverted file structure as for evaluating (1). The cosine distance after the subtraction is expressed as

$$s(u, v) = \frac{1}{\|u - m\| \,.\, \|v - m\|} \sum_i^k (u_i - m_i)(v_i - m_i). \tag{3}$$

For each document v in a database, the normalization factor $\|v - m\|$ is query-independent and therefore pre-computed. Re-writing the similarity as

$$\sum_i^k (u_i - m_i)(v_i - m_i) = u^\top v - v^\top m - u^\top m + \|m\|^2, \tag{4}$$

where the dot product $u^\top v$ is efficiently computed using the original inverted file structure as in (1). The term $v^\top m$ is independent of the query. It is therefore computed and stored when adding a BOW vector to the index. The term $u^\top m$ only depends on the query (computed once per query) and $\|m\|^2$ is a constant. Therefore, although the rest of this paper mainly considers short vector

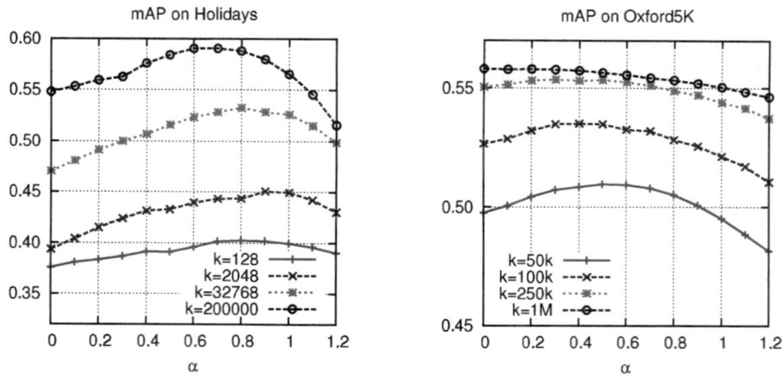

Fig. 2. BOW for Holidays and Oxford5K: mAP performance as a function of α, for different vocabulary sizes k. The optimum values outperform the state-of-the-art for pure-BOW approaches.

representations, we must mention that our shifting approach is effective when considering a regular inverted file implementation [1,2,3], at negligible memory and computational costs.

Discussion. From Fig. 2 it can be seen that the impact of the negative evidence is higher for small vocabularies and diminishes for large vocabularies. This has an intuitive explanation. For large (fine) vocabularies the co-missing visual words become more common event that carries less evidence, while the presence of the same visual words provides a strong evidence. For smaller vocabularies, the relative weights of the positive and negative evidence is changing. This can be observed in Fig. 2 (especially the plot for Oxford 5K dataset), where the optimal value of α (the higher value the higher weight on the negative evidence) is shifting to the left with increasing size of the vocabulary.

4 Co-occurrence Over-Counting: The Benefit of Whitening

An efficient way to obtain a shorter image vector representation consists of applying principal component analysis (PCA) dimensionality reduction directly on the BOW (or VLAD) vector [8]. This, first, performs the implicit centering of the data, therefore taking into account the co-missing visual words and thereby improving the similarity measurement. Second, by concentrating the vector energy of the first components, the similarity between reduced vectors provides a reasonable approximation of the similarity before the projection. We adopt this method to produce short vectors from BOW and VLAD representations.

However, it is worth noticing that an important phenomenon is ignored by such a blind dimensionality reduction, namely the problem of co-occurrences. Chum et al. [24] notice that co-occurrences lead to over-count some visual patterns when comparing two image vector representations. The detector may also introduce some artificial visual word co-occurrences, for instance when an image region is described multiple times for different orientations [25], producing two different but strongly co-occurring descriptors.

Let consider the learning set of image global descriptors (BOW or VLAD), centered according to the mean, and represented by a matrix $\boldsymbol{Y} = [Y_1|\dots|Y_n]$. The D-dimensional covariance matrix is estimated as $\boldsymbol{C} = \boldsymbol{Y} \times \boldsymbol{Y}^\top$. The visual word co-occurrences are captured in this matrix, generating strong responses out of the diagonal and favoring the emergence of an eigenvector associated with a large eigenvalue comprising those values. An efficient way to limit the impact of co-occurrences therefore consists in whitening the data, as done in independent component analysis [26], and as implicitly performed by the Mahalanobis distance.

In our case, this whitening operation is performed jointly with the dimensionality reduction from D to D' components: A given image descriptor X (BOW or VLAD) is first PCA-projected and truncated, and subsequently whitened and re-normalized to a new vector $\hat{X}$ that is our short vector image representation. It is therefore obtained as follows:

$$\hat{X} = \frac{\mathrm{diag}(\lambda_1^{-\frac{1}{2}}, \dots, \lambda_{D'}^{-\frac{1}{2}}) \boldsymbol{P}^\top X}{\left\| \mathrm{diag}(\lambda_1^{-\frac{1}{2}}, \dots, \lambda_{D'}^{-\frac{1}{2}}) \boldsymbol{P}^\top X \right\|}, \tag{5}$$

where the $D \times D'$ matrix $\boldsymbol{P}$ is formed by the largest eigenvectors of the covariance matrix $\boldsymbol{C}$, and where λ_i is the eigenvalue associated with the ith largest eigenvector. Comparing two vectors obtained after this dimensionality reduction with the Euclidean distance is therefore similar to using a Mahalanobis distance, but differs from it in that the vectors are truncated and re-normalized. The comparison is efficiently performed by comparing the reduced vectors using the Cosine similarity. The re-normalization step turns out to be critical for a better comparison metric (up to 10% of mAP of difference on the Holidays dataset).

Impact on Performance. For the sake of consistency, the vector dimensionality is reduced to *D'=128 dimensions* in all the experiments presented in this paper. Figure 3 gives the impact of the dimensionality reduction, of the SSR component-wise normalization, and of our whitening technique, which is shown to provide a large improvement over the BOW baseline.

Remarks:

- The *idf* weighting terms can not be longer applied on-the-fly with the dimensionality reduction, and are therefore be learned on the independent dataset.
- As a side effect of the dimensionality reduction, two ambiguous visual words i and j generate a higher value than for other tuples in the covariance matrix, which favors the projection of these visual words to the same component in the projected vector. This phenomenon can be observed when reconstructing the BOW vector from its PCA projection: The component of the other visual word is "hallucinated".

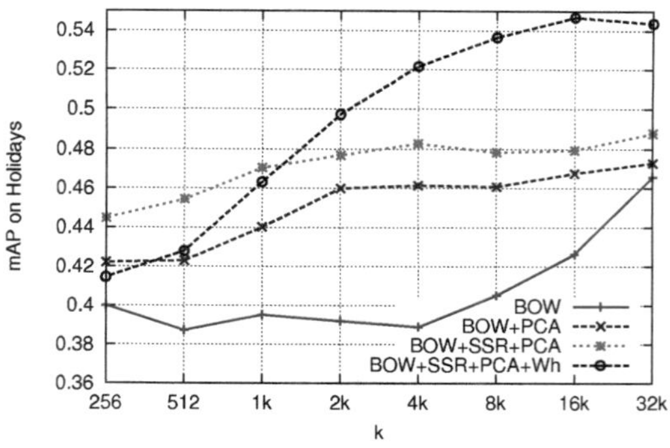

Fig. 3. Impact of the different steps on search accuracy (Holidays) for BOW vectors, as a function of vocabulary size k. The proposed whitening step is denoted by Wh.

– For large values of D', the whitening stage negatively impacts the performance by magnifying the noise on the low-energy components. This issue is addressed by using a robust PCA/whitening method.

5 Joint De-correlation of Multiple Vocabularies

It is well known that the quantization effect have significant impact on the retrieval quality. Different approaches were suggested to overcome the problem, ranging from hierarchical quantization [2], soft assignment [22], to Hamming embedding [4]. We show that the quantization effects are alleviated by multiple quantization. However, straightforward concatenation of the BOW representations not only linearly increases the memory requirements, but improve only marginally the retrieval results, see Fig. 4 or [15]. The different BOW representations are strongly correlated. We show that the PCA removes the correlation, while preserving the additional information from the different quantizations. Results outperforming the state of the art for short image representation are achieved.

5.1 Related Work on Multiple Vocabularies

Some prior art has proposed to use multiple vocabularies to improve the quality of the search, at the cost of reduced efficiency and increased memory usage. For instance, a common and simple strategy consists in simply considering the concatenating of the different BOW vectors as the image representation, as done by Nister et al. [2], who consider a hierarchical quantization method where the intermediate nodes correspond to smaller vocabularies. A late fusion technique based on rank aggregation was also proposed [15], but several inverted files have to be stored and queried in parallel. In addition, those techniques do not take into account the relationship between the vocabularies: their output is processed independently without considering the dependencies between the quantizers.

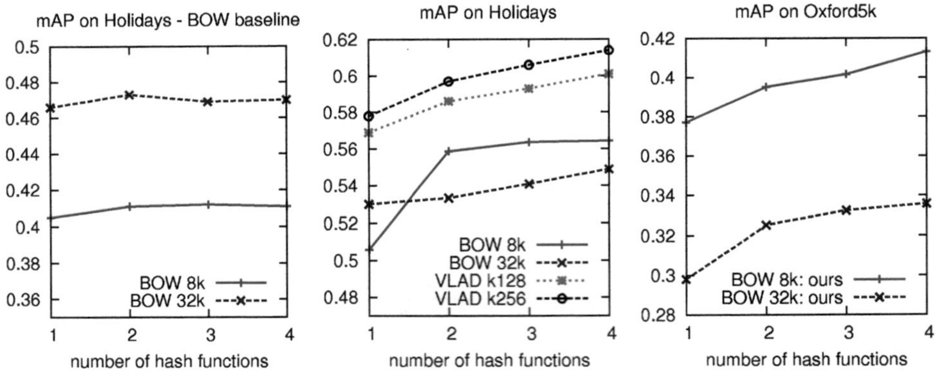

Fig. 4. The leftmost plot gives the BOW baseline when concatenating different numbers of BOW into a single vector (of increasing dimensionality), which provides only a small improvement, while linearly increasing the memory requirements. The middle and right plots show the search accuracy with the proposed joint reduction of the vocabularies to a *fixed* vector size of 128 components. Observe that the improvement brought by the use of several hash functions is comparatively better with our technique than for the concatenation of BOWs, thanks to the joint dimensionality reduction.

A more popular alternative consists of using multiple [15] or soft [22] assignment. This also increases the query time when the search is performed using an inverted file[1]. Since we are more particularly interested by image search in larger databases, taking care of the memory size of the representation is critical in order to keep the indexing structure in memory.

5.2 Joint Reduction of Multiple Vocabularies

The key points of our multiple vocabulary method, which departs from those proposed in the literature, is that it performs *the joint dimensionality reduction* of the BOW vectors produced for the different vocabularies, and apply in turn the whitening technique proposed the previous section to correct the artifacts resulting from the use of multiple vocabularies. Indeed, the different vocabularies are redundant: two descriptors assigned to the same visual word for one vocabulary have higher probability to be assigned to the same visual word for another vocabulary, leading to co-occurrences as those mentioned in Subsection 4.

Another difference with [2] and [27] is that we consider overlapping quantizers. This, jointly with the dimensionality reduction, better addresses the problem of quantization artifacts than these approaches, or of multiple or soft quantization techniques [15,22], as demonstrated later (Table 2) by comparing multiple vocabulary with VLAD (hard assignment) with Fisher Kernel (soft assignment based on a Gaussian mixture model) with a single vocabulary.

We therefore propose the following reduction for multiple vocabularies:

[1] The memory requirement is similarly increased if this assignment is performed in a symmetrical manner on query and database sides.

Table 1. Performance of vocabularies of identical and multiple sizes (Holidays). Complexity: number of vectors comparison per local descriptor when constructing the aggregated representation formed by all BOW vectors. Weighting: see text for details.

Vocabularies	weighting	mAP (%)	complexity
2 × 32k	N/A	53.3	65,536
4 × 16k	N/A	55.8	65,536
8 × 8k	N/A	56.7	65,536
32k+16k+...+128	1	58.5	65,408
32k+16k+...+128	k	54.3	65,408
32k+16k+...+128	log k	58.8	65,408
32k+16k+...+128	*idf*	57.8	65,408

1. The BOW or VLAD vectors are produced independently, using SSR component-wise normalization (see Section 2). The *idf* term is ignored, as it occurs that its influence is limited with multiple vocabularies. The SSR component-wise normalization is applied and the concatenated vector is normalized.
2. The different vectors are jointly reduced and whitened according to the guidelines of Subsection 4.

Figure 4 shows that multiple vocabularies, used jointly with our dimensionality reduction technique, provides an significant improvement for both BOW and VLAD representations, and this for *a fixed output vector size D'*. Larger vocabularies for BOW are not necessarily better than smaller ones: although k=32k provides better results on Holidays with a single vocabulary, we observe the opposite outcome for multiple vocabularies.

5.3 Merging Vocabularies of Different Sizes

The goal of this subsection is to address the trade-off between absolute search quality (for a given vector size), and the quantization cost, and to provide a comparison with similar methods of the literature. The following analysis is mainly intended for BOW, since VLAD typically uses vocabularies of much smaller sizes (*e.g.*, k=256). Although the quantization cost does not depend on the dataset size, it delays the query (jointly with the extraction of the descriptor from the image), which might be critical for some applications. For reference, quantizing 2000 local descriptors of a query image, for 4 vocabularies comprising $k = 8,192$ centroids each, takes 0.45s on 12 cores, using an efficient multi-threaded implementation of exhaustive search (exact). The timings are in this case proportional to k.

To reduce the quantization cost, we consider vocabularies of different sizes, in the spirit of the hierarchical k-means method [2] and of the pyramid match kernel [27]. Vocabularies of different sizes have a different importance, and therefore their respective contribution should be adapted. We compare four different approaches to adjust the contribution of the vocabularies:

Table 2. Comparison against the state of the art on *short* vector image representations. We consider 128-D vectors for all methods (reduced by PCA, including for BOW). Most reference results are extracted from a paper [19] on compact representations.

Method	Vocabulary size(s)	Holidays	Oxford5k	UKB
GIST [13]	N/A	36.5	-	1.64
BOW [1]	k=20k	45.2	19.4	2.95
Improved Fisher [7]	k=64	56.5	30.1	3.33
VLAD [8]	k=64	51.0	-	3.15
VLAD+SSR [19]	k=64	55.7	28.7	3.35
Ours/BOW	4×(8k)	56.7	**41.3**	3.19
Ours/BOW	2×(128+256+...32k)	**60.0**	-	3.28
Ours/VLAD	4×(256)	**61.4**	-	**3.36**

1. The same unit weight is applied for all vocabularies.
2. Similar to [27], the weight of the vocabulary is proportional to its size (to the number of bins).
3. We consider weights proportional to the logarithm of the vocabulary size.
4. Similar to [2], the weights are determined by *idf* after all vocabularies are concatenated.

In the first three approaches (referred to as"1", "k" and "log k"), each descriptor for each vocabulary is first transformed by SSR and L2-normalized, then multiplied by the vocabulary weight. The descriptors of different vocabularies are concatenated and finally, the concatenated vectors are L2-normalized. In the fourth weighing scheme, the *idf* weighting is applied to the vectors after the concatenation of the vocabularies, as proposed in [2].

Table 1 shows the results with when considering multiple vocabularies of fixed and different sizes, and compares the different weighting techniques. For a fixed quantization cost, in this experiment the best choice is to use vocabularies of different sizes and our log weighting technique. Note however that the improvement of this latter is only 1% compared with equal weights for all sizes.

5.4 Comparison with the State-of-the-Art

Table 2 compares our method to the state-of-the-art on short vector representations. The results obtained with the proposed short vector construction are consistently better than reference results. The improvement brought our method is higher when applied to BOW than to VLAD. Compared with BOW of 20k centroids reduced to 128D [19], our method, when applied to BOW with 4 vocabularies of size 8k, increases the mAP of +14.8% on Holidays, +21.9% on Oxford5k. The UKB score is 3.19/4 (BOW reference: 2.95). As a result, the BOW-based representation is competitive, when not better, than the best results reported with PCA-reduced VLAD and Fisher representations, where in [19] these representations are shown to significantly outperform BOW. By applying our method on the VLAD representation, we still obtain an improvement of +5.7% over the state of the art. The improvement is not significant on UKB.

Table 3. Comparison against the state of the art on image representations with short codes on Holidays. The code size is fixed to 16 bytes for all methods.

Method	mAP on Holidays
VLAD [10]	46.0
Fisher vector [19]	50.6
Ours/BOW - 4×(k=8k)	49.8
Ours/VLAD - 4×(k=256)	**53.1**

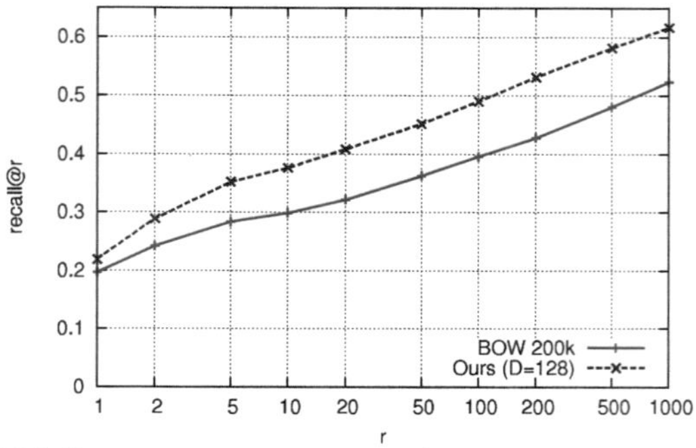

Fig. 5. Holidays+1M distractors: proportion of true positives returned in the first r ranks (recall@r), for BOW with 200k (from [19]) and our method with a 128-D vector

5.5 Encoding Our Short Vectors with Compact Codes

The better results obtained with shorter vectors lead to better results when further coding the vectors using a compressed-domain approximate nearest neighbors search technique [10], as shown by Table 3. With codes of 16 bytes, we increase the mAP of the BOW baseline by +3.6% of mAP on Holidays. with VLAD (4×k=256) on Holidays, we outperform the state-of-the-art coded Fisher Vector [19] by +2.5% of mAP.

5.6 Large Scale Experiments

We have evaluated our approach on one million images, by merging the Holidays dataset with the Flickr1M distractor set, as done in [4,8]. Our method is compared (from curves in [19]) with the BOW representation (k=200k).

The results are presented in Figure 5. Our approach significantly outperforms the baseline, and this by using an image representation which is a 128 dimensional vector only, i.e., using significantly less memory than sparse BOW, which typically requires 4 bytes per encoded local descriptors. The efficiency is also much better than BOW. With an efficient implementation of exhaustive search, querying the whole 500 query images from Holidays takes 3.08 seconds using 12 cores of a 3 Ghz machine, which corresponds to 6 ms per query. This is about two orders of magnitude faster than the timings reported for BOW [4].

5.7 Improving BOW for Classification

Although the primary goal of this paper is to consider image retrieval on a large scale with short vectors, we report some preliminary results showing the interest of our method in a context of classification with very short vectors and efficient linear classifiers. For this purpose, we improve the BOW baseline with our approach (SSR, whitening joint de-correlation of 4 vocabularies) and compare to methods combined with a linear classifier. On Pascal VOC'07 [28], by considering the same protocol as the one proposed in [29], our technique is significantly better than the corresponding BOW: we obtain mAP=46.9% with D'=256 dimensions, instead of 41.4% for BOW with 4k dimensions. The result is approximately the same of the one of spatial pyramid matching (SPM, [30]) with a linear classifier, but with a vector which is 100 times shorter.

6 Conclusion

Different techniques to improve dimensionality reduction by PCA for large scale image retrieval were proposed. First, a solution is proposed for giving more importance to jointly non-occurring visual words, leading to improved image search quality with bag-of-features at a negligible cost in memory and computational complexity. This approach can be also integrated into an inverted file. Then, we considered the problem of co-occurring and correlated visual words, jointly with the dimensionality reduction and the use of multiple vocabularies. This method produces short vectors (128-dimensional, *i.e.*, the size of a *single* SIFT local descriptor) yielding a high retrieval accuracy, as demonstrated by our results on popular image search benchmarks. Finally, it was shown on image classification that the methods are generally applicable.

Acknowledgments. Ondřej Chum was supported by the GACR P103/12/2310 project. Hervé Jégou was supported by the Quaero project, funded by OSEO.

References

1. Sivic, J., Zisserman, A.: Video Google: A text retrieval approach to object matching in videos. In: ICCV (2003)
2. Nistér, D., Stewénius, H.: Scalable recognition with a vocabulary tree. In: CVPR, pp. 2161–2168 (2006)
3. Chum, O., Philbin, J., Sivic, J., Isard, M., Zisserman, A.: Total recall: Automatic query expansion with a generative feature model for object retrieval. In: ICCV (2007)
4. Jégou, H., Douze, M., Schmid, C.: Improving bag-of-features for large scale image search. IJCV 87, 316–336 (2010)
5. Csurka, G., Dance, C., Fan, L., Willamowski, J., Bray, C.: Visual categorization with bags of keypoints. In: ECCV Workshop Statistical Learning in Computer Vision (2004)

6. Torralba, A., Fergus, R., Weiss, Y.: Small codes and large databases for recognition. In: CVPR (2008)
7. Perronnin, F., Liu, Y., Sanchez, J., Poirier, H.: Large-scale image retrieval with compressed Fisher vectors. In: CVPR (2010)
8. Jégou, H., Douze, M., Schmid, C., Pérez, P.: Aggregating local descriptors into a compact image representation. In: CVPR (2010)
9. Weiss, Y., Torralba, A., Fergus, R.: Spectral hashing. In: NIPS (2008)
10. Jégou, H., Douze, M., Schmid, C.: Product quantization for nearest neighbor search. Trans. PAMI 33, 117–128 (2011)
11. Perronnin, F., Dance, C.R.: Fisher kernels on visual vocabularies for image categorization. In: CVPR (2007)
12. Perronnin, F., Sánchez, J., Mensink, T.: Improving the Fisher Kernel for Large-Scale Image Classification. In: Daniilidis, K., Maragos, P., Paragios, N. (eds.) ECCV 2010, Part IV. LNCS, vol. 6314, pp. 143–156. Springer, Heidelberg (2010)
13. Oliva, A., Torralba, A.: Modeling the shape of the scene: a holistic representation of the spatial envelope. IJCV 42, 145–175 (2001)
14. Bishop, C.M.: Pattern Recognition and Machine Learning. Springer (2007)
15. Jégou, H., Schmid, C., Harzallah, H., Verbeek, J.: Accurate image search using the contextual dissimilarity measure. Trans. PAMI 32, 2–11 (2010)
16. Matas, J., Chum, O., Martin, U., Pajdla, T.: Robust wide baseline stereo from maximally stable extremal regions. In: BMVC, pp. 384–393 (2002)
17. Mikolajczyk, K., Schmid, C.: Scale and affine invariant interest point detectors. IJCV 60, 63–86 (2004)
18. Lowe, D.: Distinctive image features from scale-invariant keypoints. IJCV 60, 91–110 (2004)
19. Jégou, H., Perronnin, F., Douze, M., Sánchez, J., Pérez, P., Schmid, C.: Aggregating local descriptors into compact codes. In: Trans. PAMI (2012)
20. Jégou, H., Douze, M., Schmid, C.: On the burstiness of visual elements. In: CVPR (2009)
21. Philbin, J., Chum, O., Isard, M., Sivic, J., Zisserman, A.: Object retrieval with large vocabularies and fast spatial matching. In: CVPR (2007)
22. Philbin, J., Chum, O., Isard, M., Sivic, J., Zisserman, A.: Lost in quantization: Improving particular object retrieval in large scale image databases. In: CVPR (2008)
23. Perdoch, M., Chum, O., Matas, J.: Efficient representation of local geometry for large scale object retrieval. In: CVPR (2009)
24. Chum, O., Matas, J.: Unsupervised discovery of co-occurrence in sparse high dimensional data. In: CVPR (2010)
25. Mikolajczyk, K., Tuytelaars, T., Schmid, C., Zisserman, A., Matas, J., Schaffalitzky, F., Kadir, T., Gool, L.V.: A comparison of affine region detectors. IJCV 65, 43–72 (2005)
26. Comon, P.: Independent component analysis, a new concept? Signal Processing 36 (1994)
27. Grauman, K., Darrell, T.: The pyramid match kernel: Discriminative classification with sets of image features. In: ICCV (2005)
28. Everingham, M., Van Gool, L., Williams, C.K.I., Winn, J., Zisserman, A.: The PASCAL visual object classes (VOC) challenge. IJCV 88, 303–338 (2010)
29. Chatfield, K., Lempitsky, V., Vedaldi, A., Zisserman, A.: The devil is in the details: an evaluation of recent feature encoding methods. In: BMVC (2011)
30. Lazebnik, S., Schmid, C., Ponce, J.: Beyond bags of features: spatial pyramid matching for recognizing natural scene categories. In: CVPR (2006)

WαSH: Weighted α-Shapes for Local Feature Detection

Christos Varytimidis, Konstantinos Rapantzikos, and Yannis Avrithis

National Technical University of Athens
{chrisvar,rap,iavr}@image.ntua.gr

Abstract. Depending on the application, local feature detectors should comply with properties that are often contradictory, *e.g.* distinctiveness vs. robustness. Providing a good balance is a standing problem in the field. In this direction, we propose a novel approach for local feature detection starting from sampled edges. The detector is based on shape stability measures across the *weighted α-filtration*, a computational geometry construction that captures the shape of a non-uniform set of points. The extracted features are blob-like and include non-extremal regions as well as regions determined by cavities of boundary shape. Overall, the approach provides distinctive regions, while achieving high robustness in terms of *repeatability* and *matching score*, as well as competitive performance in a large scale image retrieval application.

1 Introduction

Local features are popular in computer vision tasks due to their invariance to illumination and viewpoint changes. Ideally, local features should comply to a set of properties, namely, *repeatability*, *distinctiveness*, *locality*, *quantity*, *accuracy* and *computational efficiency* [25]. These properties are often contradictory and cannot be satisfied simultaneously, like distinctiveness vs. locality or robustness and quantity vs. computational efficiency. Hence, although several feature detectors have been proposed, there is still a growing need for methods offering better balance between the desired properties.

State-of-the-art methods are based on measures of first- and second-order gray value derivatives (*e.g.* second-moment matrix or Hessian matrix [17]) or on intensity variations [23][14] and—depending on the application—can be considered quite successful. Image edges on the other hand, though bound to naturally stable structures, have not been so successful yet. In this paper, we conjecture that, within a multi-scale representation, a distinctive region approximately maintains its shape across scale, as determined by surrounding edges.

We therefore introduce a detector that groups edge points based on location, gradient strength and local shape. To capture local shape, we employ *α-shapes*, a well-known method in computational geometry introduced by Edelsbrunner *et al.* [8]. In doing so, we devise an efficient way to overcome the main weakness of the method, namely automatic selection of the value of α that best represents

A. Fitzgibbon et al. (Eds.): ECCV 2012, Part II, LNCS 7573, pp. 788–801, 2012.

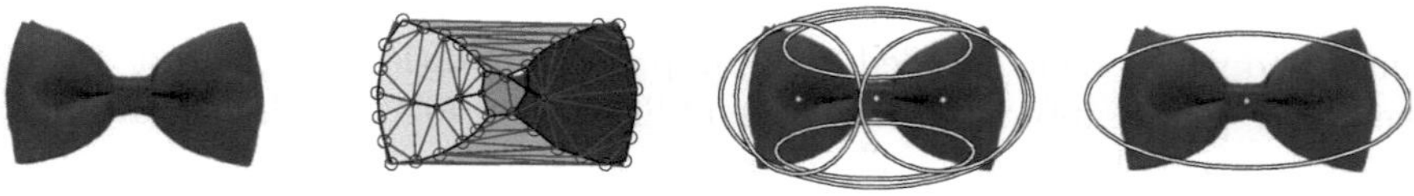

(a) (b) (c) (d)

Fig. 1. Feature detection based on α-shapes. (a) Input image. (b) Edge samples with assigned weights as squared radii (blue) and triangulation. Triangle colors denote distinct connected components of the α-complex. Detected features by: (c) WαSH detector and (d) MSER.

the underlying point set. We also show how noisy points or groupings are automatically filtered out by a shape-based stability measure and how the entire method is controlled by a simple and intuitive parameter. A detection example is given in Fig. 1.

We treat a local feature as a region delineated by a set of points sampled from its contour. Although not critical, we use a roughly uniform sampling scheme along binary edges found by an edge detector and employ α-shapes to capture the evolution of local shape in a multi-scale setting. α-shapes can be thought of as a generalization of the *convex hull*, being parametrized by scalar $\alpha \geq 0$. Starting from the convex hull of the point set for $\alpha = \infty$, they reduce to the set itself at the other extreme, $\alpha = 0$. An α-shape is a *filtration*, a partial ordering of Delaunay simplices (edges and triangles in two dimensions) [27].

Weighted α-shapes [7] provide a richer description of the input. For a single value of α, *i.e.* for a single scale, weighted α-shapes capture different levels of spatial details. The weighted α-filtration is the multi-scale representation we adopt. To capture the evolving topology of local regions in the filtration, we employ a *component tree*, similar to [19]. By applying stability measures on the resulting representation we select distinctive and repeatable local features.

The remaining of the paper is organized as follows: In section 2 we discuss related work, and then describe our detector in detail in section 3. Results are provided in section 4 followed by conclusions and discussion in section 5.

2 Related Work

The literature on local feature detection is rich and since the early work of Beaudet [3] and Harris and Stevens [9], based on the Hessian matrix and the second moment matrix respectively, many detectors have been proposed grounding on similar or novel ideas. In his inspiring work, Lindeberg *et al.* extended detectors by making them scale-invariant [11] and establishing the theoretical foundations for making them affine-invariant [12]. Based on these foundations, Lowe proposed the *scale invariant feature transform* (SIFT) in [13] and Mikolajczyk *et al.* the affine-adapted version of the Harris and Hessian detectors [16], [17].

The *maximally stable extremal regions* (MSER) of Matas *et al.* [14], one of the best performing detectors in [17], detects regions of stable intensity and therefore avoids common problems of gradient-based methods like localization accuracy and noise. The recent trend of achieving a good balance between efficiency and performance has led to a group of computationally efficient detectors like SURF [2], an approximate version of SIFT, and FAST [23], introducing fast corner detection based on an intensity comparison test in a small neighborhood. Recently, BRISK [10] build on FAST detector and provide real-time detection and description of local features with matching performance being comparable to SIFT and SURF.

Although naturally meaningful, image edges have attracted less attention with the reasons being mainly related to the lack of stable edges and the computational inefficiency. One of the earliest attempts, *edge-based region detector* (EBR), starts from corner points and exploits nearby edges by measuring photometric quantities across them. It is suitable for scenes containing intersection of edges (*e.g.* man-made structures like buildings), but not for generic matching, as shown in [17]. Mikolajczyk *et al.* in [18] propose an edge-based detector that combines Canny edge detection with automatic scale selection and use it for object recognition. For efficiency, they start from densely sampled edge points, an approach that we also adopt. Rapantzikos *et al.* compute the binary distance transform of Canny edges and detect regions by grouping its local maxima, guided by the gradient strength of nearby edges [22].

There are also methods that exploit gradient strength directly, without edge detection. Zitnick *et al.* [26] apply an oriented filter bank to the input image and detect *edge foci* (EF), i.e. points that are roughly equidistant from edgels with orientations perpendicular to the points. The idea is quite interesting, but computationally expensive. Avrithis *et al.* compute the weighted medial axis, decompose it into meaningful parts and group regions by taking both contrast and shape into account [1]. *Medial features* (MFD) are then detected based on shape. Although more information is used, gradient strength is more sensitive to lighting and scale variations than binary edges.

Computational geometry is rich in applications based on α-shapes, as opposed to computer vision. One of the earliest applications has been to surface reconstruction from an unorganized set of points [7]. Teichmann *et al.* [24] have used them to reconstruct the shape of point sets and achieve a more accurate separation of surfaces, but they rely heavily on user input. *Conformal α-shapes* and the corresponding filtration, introduced by Cazals *et al.* in [5], are based on a global scale parameter $\hat{\alpha}$ and two local ones, adjusted to some neighborhood of each point. They show interesting results on surface reconstruction of non-uniformly sampled surfaces. In the same direction, Zomorodian *et al.* [27] predict protein structure by employing α-shapes to detect interacting atoms in a protein molecule.

Furthermore, α-shapes have been used for studying *pockets*, defined as regions with limited accessibility from the outside, measuring the surface area and volume of macromolecules, and the packing density of proteins [7]. α-shapes have been also used to reconstruct boundaries of noisy edge maps. Starting from binary edge samples, Meine *et al.* [15] construct the Delaunay triangulation and select a subset of its edges to complete the object boundaries. Their main criteria are triangle size and average color.

Building on edge-based methods, we start from sampled edges like [18]. We use shape as the main selection criterion, a choice that bears similarities to [1], although our geometric representation is entirely different. There are also similarities to MSER [14], in the sense that we employ a hierarchical representation of nested sets. However, we apply this representation on the α-filtration rather than the level sets of image intensity. As a by-product, our method is able to detect gray regions that are adjacent to both brighter and darker ones, as opposed to MSER that can only detect bright or dark extremal regions, as in Fig. 3bc. Furthermore, the proposed detector can handle regions determined by cavities of the boundary shape, as in Fig. 1, bearing similarities to the *pockets* [7], and regions that are not enclosed by complete boundaries like in Fig. 3a.

3 WαSH Detector

3.1 Image Representation

We assume an input (grayscale) image is given as a function f on the plane and that g is its gradient magnitude $\|\nabla f\|$ normalized in interval $[0, 1]$. We apply a binary edge detector on g and sample the resulting edge map E to obtain a discrete set of edge points $P \subseteq \mathbb{R}^2$. Sampling is roughly uniform along edges with a fixed *sampling interval* s, so samples will typically not correspond to key-points like maxima of curvature. Although sparsely sampled along the edges, the points in P capture the shape of the detected boundaries. For each point $p \in P$, we define its *weight* $w(p) \geq 0$ to be multiple of its gradient strength,

$$w(p) = g(p) \left(\frac{s}{2}\right)^2, \tag{1}$$

with $g(p) \in [0, 1]$. The reason for this choice of weight w will be made clear at the end of section 3.2. In practice, the binary edge map is obtained by the *Canny* edge detector [4]. We do not rely on a clear edge map and therefore the high and low hysteresis thresholds of the detector are kept fixed.

3.2 Weighted α-shapes

The definition of α-shapes is based on the Delaunay triangulation. Weighted α-shapes are based on its generalization, the *regular triangulation* formed by replacing the Euclidean distance by the power to weighted points. The discussion given here mostly follows [7], but simplifies for the case of 2 dimensions.

A point $p \in P$ along with its weight $w(p) \geq 0$ makes up a pair $(p, w(p))$ that is called a *weighted point* and can be seen as a *circle* centered at p, with squared radius $w(p)$. We will use the same symbol p for both a circle or weighted point, and will disambiguate as necessary. Given two points $p, q \in P$, define

$$\pi(p, q) = \|p - q\|^2 - w(p) - w(q). \tag{2}$$

Circles p, q intersect at right angles iff $\pi(p, q) = 0$; we then say that p, q are *orthogonal*. Given a subset $T \subseteq P$ of three points, there is a unique circle that is orthogonal to all circles of T. We denote the corresponding weighted point by c_T. The triangle σ_T with vertices given by T is called *regular* if

$$\pi(p, c_T) = 0 \text{ for all } p \in T, \tag{3}$$

$$\pi(p, c_T) > 0 \text{ for all } p \in P \setminus T, \tag{4}$$

where (3) is equivalent to c_T being orthogonal to all points of T. The collection $\mathcal{R}$ of all regular triangles over P is called the *regular triangulation* of P. Observe that, if $w(p) = 0$ for all $p \in T$, the weighted point c_T is the *circumcircle* of triangle σ_T. In this unweighted case, the triangulation reduces to *Delaunay*.

The collection $\mathcal{K}$ of all triangles in $\mathcal{R}$ and their faces (line segments and points) is a *simplicial complex*: each triangle, line segment or point is a 2-, 1-, or 0-simplex respectively, and we will refer to it as *simplex* in general. If we define a *size* $\rho_T \geq 0$ for each simplex $\sigma_T \in \mathcal{K}$, then the *weighted α-complex* of P is the subset of $\mathcal{K}$ containing all simplices up to a given size $\alpha \geq 0$,

$$\mathcal{K}_\alpha = \{\sigma_T \in \mathcal{K} : \rho_T < \alpha\}. \tag{5}$$

Finally, the *weighted α-shape* of P [7] is the union of all such simplices,

$$\mathcal{W}_\alpha = \bigcup_{\sigma \in \mathcal{K}_\alpha} \sigma. \tag{6}$$

Observe that $\mathcal{W}_{+\infty}$ is the *convex hull* of P. It remains to define the *size* ρ_T of a point, line segment or triangle σ_T, when T contains 1, 2 or 3 points of P, respectively. The size of a point $p \in P$ is equal to its weight, $\rho_{\{p\}} = w(p)$. Given a set of two points $T = \{p, q\} \subseteq P$, the size ρ_T of the associated line segment is the squared radius of the unique circle that is orthogonal to circles p, q, whose center is collinear with p, q, as in Fig. 2a. Similarly, given a set of three points $T = \{p, q, r\} \subseteq P$, the size ρ_T of the associated triangle is the squared radius of the unique circle that is orthogonal to circles p, q, r, as in Fig. 2b. From the definition of the weight function in (1) follows that for two points p, q along an image edge, sizes $\rho_{\{p\}}$ and $\rho_{\{q\}}$ take values in $[0, (s/2)^2]$. This ensures that their corresponding circles, as shown in Fig. 2, do not overlap and the line segment $T = \{p, q\}$ has $\rho_T \geq 0$.

3.3 Component Tree

All simplices of $\mathcal{K}$ are typically ordered by ascending size to obtain what is called a *weighted α-filtration* [7]. In this work, we deviate from this standard setting in two ways. First, we only consider *triangles* and their *edges* (line segments) discarding points $p \in P$ themselves. We thus construct complex

$$\mathcal{K}' = \{\sigma_T \in \mathcal{K} : |T| \geq 2\}. \tag{7}$$

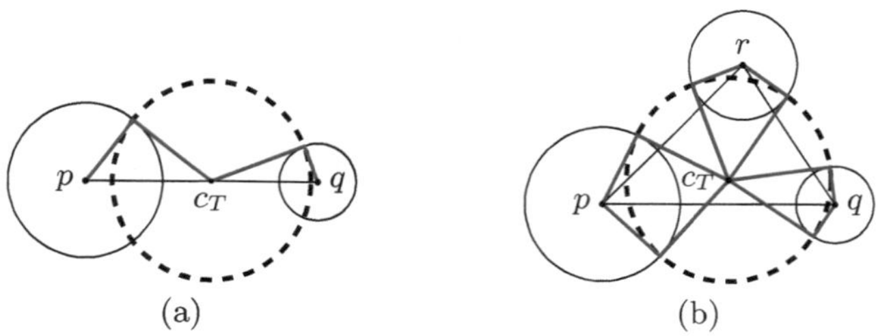

Fig. 2. (a) Size of a 2-point set $\{p, q\}$, as the squared radius of a circle that is orthogonal to p, q. (b) Size of a 3-point set $\{p, q, r\}$, as the squared radius of the circle that is orthogonal to p, q, r.

This is justified because edge size helps control connectivity of triangles, but points do not. Second, contrary to (5), we consider the *upper α-complex*

$$\overline{\mathcal{K}}_\alpha = \mathcal{K}' \setminus \mathcal{K}_\alpha = \{\sigma_T \in \mathcal{K}' : \rho_T \geq \alpha\} \quad (8)$$

ordered by *descending* α. As in [7], we need only consider a finite set of values for α. In particular, we sort all $\sigma_T \in \mathcal{K}'$ by descending size ρ_T to obtain sequence $(\sigma_1, \ldots, \sigma_n)$ where $n = |\mathcal{K}'|$. If ρ_i is the size of σ_i for $i = 1, \ldots, n$, then $\rho_1 \geq \ldots \geq \rho_n$. Now, if $K_i = \{\sigma_1, \ldots, \sigma_i\}$, we obtain the *upper α-filtration*

$$\emptyset = K_0 \subseteq K_1 \subseteq \cdots \subseteq K_n = \mathcal{K}'. \quad (9)$$

Starting from the largest element of size ρ_1 and decreasing the value of α towards ρ_n, the upper α-complex models the growing *cavities* of the original shape. To capture its evolving topology, we construct a *component tree*, similar to [19].

To define *connectedness* on the complex, we specify neighboring relations as follows: the neighbors of each triangle $\sigma_T \in \mathcal{K}'$ (with $|T| = 3$) are its three edges, while, the neighbors of each edge $\sigma_E \in \mathcal{K}'$ (with $|E| = 2$) are the two adjacent triangles in the triangulation. We denote the *neighborhood* of simplex $\sigma \in \mathcal{K}'$ by $N(\sigma)$. Since an edge is not larger than its two adjacent triangles, the intuition is that this edge can keep the two triangles disconnected until it is processed itself. Eventually, this timing depends on image gradient.

Given this neighborhood system, we start off with all simplices in $\mathcal{K}'$ being individual components, and process them in descending order of size, joining them with their neighbors that have already been processed. This process is specified in Algorithm 1.

3.4 Feature Selection

While tracking the evolution of the connected components of the upper α-complex, we measure the significance of changes in its topology so as to decide on stability or distinctiveness of relevant image regions. Whenever a new component arises by joining two adjacent components, these two components are

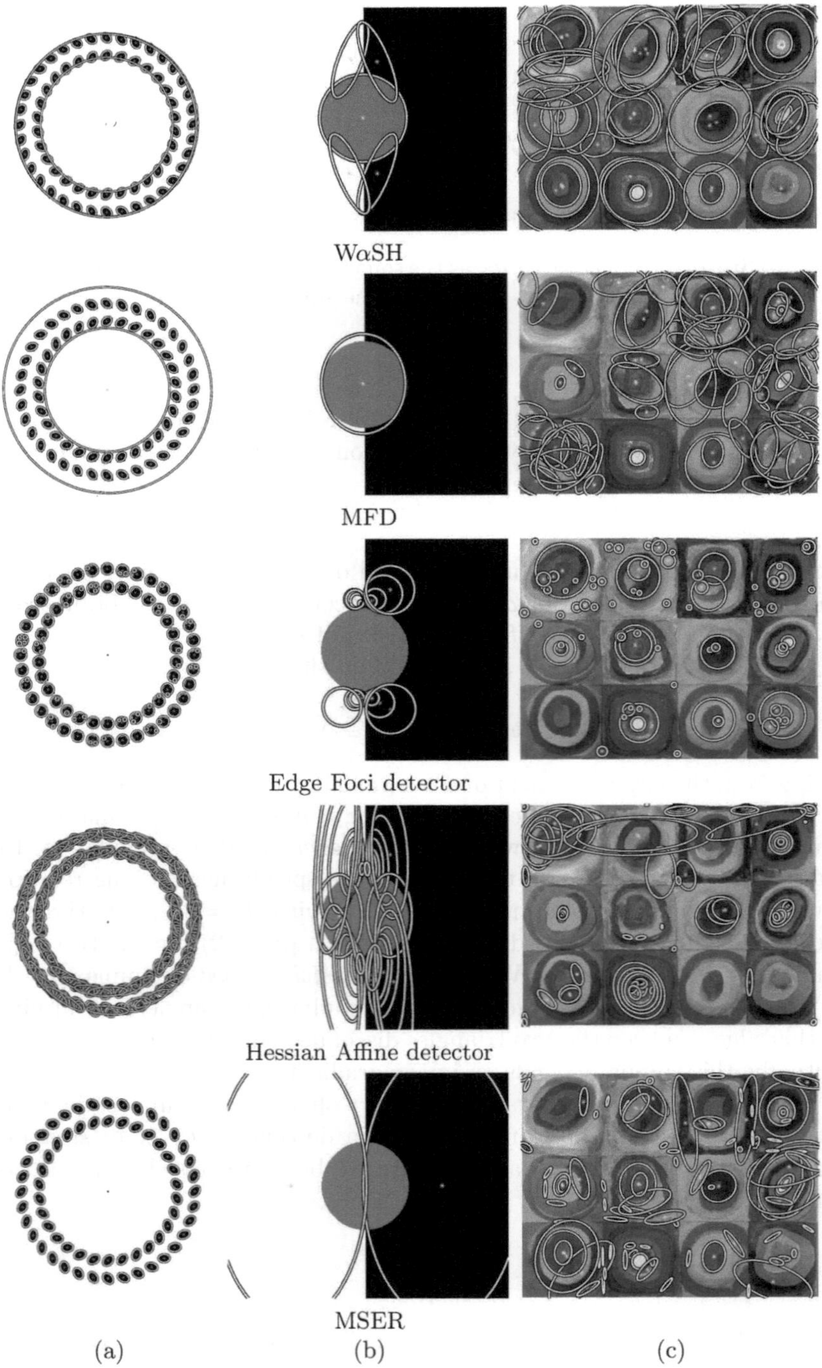

Fig. 3. Detection of (a) incomplete boundaries and (b)(c) non-extremal regions

individually considered as potential *features*. We choose to base the decision on simple measurements requiring minor computational overhead.

In particular, consider component κ_U, which is a set of simplices (edges and triangles) that have been processed. When κ_U is joined through a boundary edge σ_T of size ρ_T to another component, we compute the *strength* of κ_U as the ratio

$$s(\kappa_U) = \frac{a(\kappa_U)}{\rho_T}, \tag{10}$$

where $a(\kappa_U)$ is its total area—precisely, the area of the union of all simplices in κ_U. What remains to do is *select* component κ_U as a feature, if its strength is larger than a fixed threshold τ, and fit a patch over its region support for descriptor extraction. Observe that, since we are processing simplices in descending order of size, ρ_T stands in fact for the largest opening or the weakest gradient strength over the boundary of component κ_U. It follows that strength favors large components with small (or no) openings in their boundary. Since size ρ measures squared length, component strength is a scale invariant quantity.

Some examples are shown in Fig. 3. We can detect regions that are not completely bounded by edges, as the two perceived concentric circles in Fig. 3a, or regions that are not extremal in the intensity domain, in contrast to MSER, as shown in Fig. 3bc.

3.5 Algorithm

The pseudocode for the complete method is given in Algorithm 1. The first steps are straightforward. Function COMPLEX computes complex $\mathcal{K}$ and size map ρ, given the regular triangulation $\mathcal{R}$. Function NEIGHBOR computes the neighborhood map N of a set of edges and triangles, while $\mathcal{K}'$ is as defined in (7). Function AREA computes the area of a triangle given its vertices in point set T, and it returns 0 for an edge.

We use two different tree structures to keep track of connected components, as in [19]. The first is a forest where each simplex serves as the root of a subtree containing all larger simplices in the same component. We maintain a list of children for each simplex, using function ADDCHILD, while all simplices are initially assumed to be leaves. The second is a standard disjoint set forest, with simplices pointing only to their parent, and with functions MAKESET, FIND and UNION having their ordinary meaning [6]. The two structures are interconnected via pointer *root*. The second is used for efficiency, while the first for information access. In particular, for each selected component, we collect its simplices via breadth-first search in the subtree of its root simplex and fit a patch to their convex hull—this is not shown in Algorithm 1.

The computational cost of the regular triangulation is $O(n \log n)$ and the required space is $O(n)$. Hence the cost of weighted α-shape construction is also $O(n \log n)$. The triangulation only needs to be computed once; the remaining part of the algorithm that is based on the component tree is quasi-linear in n [19], that is, linear for all practical purposes.

Algorithm 1. WαSH Feature Detection

```
input : grayscale image f
output: local feature set F

g ← ‖∇f‖/ max{‖∇f‖}                                   // normalized gradient
E ← Canny(g)                                          // edge detection
P ← Sample(E)                                         // edge sampling
R ← Regular(P)                                        // regular triangulation
(K, ρ) ← Complex(R)                                   // simplicial complex + sizes
N ← Neighbor(K')                                      // neighborhood system

F ← ∅
foreach σ_T ∈ K' do                                   // initialize each simplex
    MakeSet(σ_T)                                      // as an individual component
    σ_T.area ← Area(T)                                // with its own area
    σ_T.root ← σ_T

foreach σ_T ∈ K' in descending order of ρ_T do        // current simplex
    κ_T ← Find(σ_T)                                   // current component κ_T
    r_T ← κ_T.root
    foreach σ_U ∈ N(σ_T) such that ρ_U ≥ ρ_T do       // adjacent, processed simplex
        κ_U ← Find(σ_U)                               // adjacent component κ_U
        r_U ← κ_U.root
        if κ_T ≠ κ_U then                             // if different components
            if |U| = 3 ∧ r_U.area/ρ_T > τ then        // if κ_U is triangle & strong
                F ← F ∪ r_U                           // select it
            r_T.AddChild(r_U)                         // add it below κ_T
            r_T.area ← r_T.area + r_U.area            // merge areas
            κ_T ← Union(κ_T, κ_U)                     // and disjoint sets
            κ_T.root ← r_T
```

4 Experiments

We demonstrate the effectiveness of our WαSH detector by measuring *repeatability* and *matching score* on the standard dataset and benchmark of [17], and by carrying out a retrieval experiment on *Oxford Buildings* [20], following the evaluation protocol that has been introduced in [21] and recently used to evaluate detectors in [26] and [1]. The performance of the WαSH detector depends only on the *selection threshold* τ. For all experiments we set $\tau = 100$, which has been set after subjective evaluation on the dataset of [17]. The WαSH detector executable is available online[1].

4.1 Repeatability and Matching Score

We use the publicly available datasets of [17] to test our detector against the state-of-the-art. The sequences evaluate the effect of blur (*bikes*), scale/rotation

[1] `http://image.ntua.gr/iva/research/wash`

Fig. 4. Features detected by WαSH detector for a pair of images from (a)(b) the *bikes* sequence and (c)(d) *Oxford Buildings* (Worcester College)

(*boat*), as well as changes in lighting (*leuven*) and viewpoint (*wall*). Fig. 4ab show a detection example on the first two images of the *bike* sequence. There are not many overlapping detections, while most part of the image is covered.

Fig. 5 shows repeatability and matching score plots for all the detectors included in [17] with the addition of MFD [1] that has proved to have competitive performance to ours (see also Section 4.2). The WαSH detector performs among the best in all cases, while keeping the number of features considerably low; in particular, for the first image of each sequence, *bikes*: 409, *boat*: 365, *leuven*: 299 and *wall*: 782 features. It is quite invariant to scale and blur, which is attributed to the proposed selection criterion on the α-filtration and—naturally—to the stability of image edges across scales. For the same reasons, the detector performs very well under illumination changes.

4.2 Large Scale Image Retrieval

In this section we test the performance of the WαSH detector on an image retrieval task using the *Oxford Buildings* dataset (an example is given in Fig. 4cd). Comparisons are performed against the Hessian-Affine, MSER, SIFT and SURF detectors, plus the recently introduced EF [26] and MFD [1] detectors, follow-

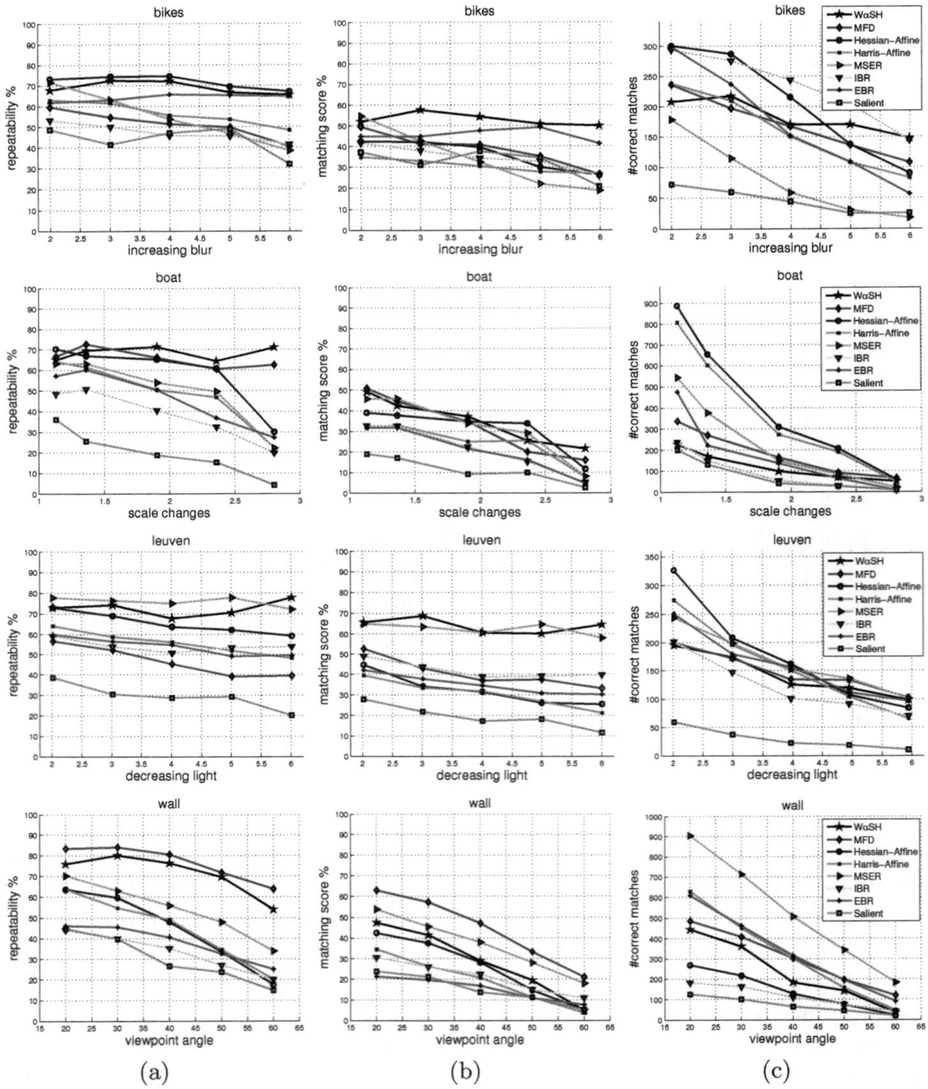

Fig. 5. (a) Repeatability, (b) matching score, and (c) correct matches. Scenes from top to bottom: bikes, boat, leuven, wall

ing their experimental framework. Features are extracted by the corresponding publicly available executables, using default parameters.

We extract SIFT descriptors for all detectors except SURF, for which we use the corresponding descriptor. We then build two visual vocabularies of different sizes for each detector, namely 50K and 200K, by clustering the descriptors using *approximate k-means* [20]. For each vocabulary, we carry out the retrieval experiment using the *bag-of-words* (BoW) model for representation, an *inverted*

Table 1. Results of the retrieval experiment *Oxford Buildings* for all detectors tested and for the 50K and 200K vocabularies. The number of features refers to the entire dataset, while detection time is average per image. Query times are average per query. mAP is measured on the same dataset used for vocabulary training.

Detector		**WαSH**	MFD	EF	HessAff	MSER	SIFT	SURF
Features ($\times 10^6$)		**7.19**	7.64	19.72	29.02	13.33	11.13	6.84
Detection time (s)		**1.32**	2.35	13.51	6.67	4.48	5.29	0.42
Inverted file (MB)	50K	**44.1**	51.9	132.1	116.2	71.2	75.9	47.8
	200K	**49.1**	58.4	146.2	128.8	78.8	84.0	53.5
BoW query (ms)	50K	**0.92**	0.94	3.11	2.71	1.32	1.51	0.88
	200K	**0.75**	0.68	1.81	1.61	0.88	0.95	0.64
FastSM query (s)	50K	**1.43**	2.45	26.01	25.17	6.57	8.35	3.75
	200K	**1.35**	0.93	4.69	6.10	2.20	5.29	3.45
BoW (mAP)	50K	**0.529**	0.531	0.455	0.489	0.489	0.422	0.466
	200K	**0.592**	0.600	0.528	0.578	0.568	0.494	0.575
FastSM (mAP)	50K	**0.541**	0.540	0.500	0.516	0.524	0.446	0.497
	200K	**0.588**	0.600	0.566	0.608	0.593	0.516	0.591

Table 2. mAP measurements for a similar retrieval experiment as in Table 1 for W αSH detector against MFD, with a lower number of detected features, targeting 3×10^6 features for the entire dataset. This time 50K and 100K vocaburaries are built, to avoid overfitting.

Detectors		**WαSH**	MFD
Features ($\times 10^6$)		**3.03**	2.59
BoW (mAP)	50K	**0.530**	0.516
	100K	**0.543**	0.534
FastSM (mAP)	50K	**0.524**	0.517
	100K	**0.539**	0.537

file for indexing, *tf-idf* weighting and *fast spatial matching* (FastSM) [20] for spatial verification. BoW histograms are matched using the histogram intersection following ℓ_1 normalization, while for geometric re-ranking we set the minimum inliers to 7. The evaluation metric is *mean Average Precision* (mAP).

Table 1 summarizes the total number of features, the average detection time per image, average query time and mAP measurements for all detectors. The number of detected features used is critical, since it determines both the amount of memory used for the index and the query time, with FastSM being quadratic in the number of features. The performance of the WαSH detector is at the state-of-the-art, despite using a low number of features (e.g. 1/4 of the Hessian-affine features), hence having a much lower memory footprint. The benefit in terms of query time is also considerable. Increasing the size of the vocabulary boosts the performance of all detectors up to a point.

The performance of MFD is similar to that of the WαSH detector using approximately the same number of features, an observation that has led us to an additional experiment with the detectors tuned to produce a significantly smaller number of regions. Our aim is to test the ability of these detectors to go large scale. By reducing the number of features detected, we have to decrease the size of the vocabulary to prevent overfitting. In this setup, we create vocabularies of 50K and 100K visual words. The performance of the WαSH detector is still high in all cases, especially with the 50K visual vocabulary, as shown in Table 2.

5 Discussion

We have introduced the WαSH detector that relies on grouping edge samples using a shape stability measure on a weighted α-filtration. Weighted α-shapes appear particularly well-suited to model the topology of sampled points, with weights reflecting edge strength. Among our contributions are the use of the α-filtration to represent cavities of boundary shape, the neighboring system of triangles and edges to associate connectedness to boundary strength, the use of the component tree to capture the topology of the α-complex and the feature selection scheme resulting in stable features with minimal computational overhead.

The detected features include cases of salient regions that cannot always be handled by existing detectors, like non-extremal regions or regions that are not enclosed by complete boundaries, and regions determined by cavities of boundary shape. Yet, the detected feature set is typically small, resulting in significant gains in memory and speed in a large-scale image retrieval application without compromising performance. The detection itself is computationally efficient, exploiting regular triangulation and component trees. In the future, we will consider exploiting them for description and propose an integrated method for local features and descriptors.

References

1. Avrithis, Y., Rapantzikos, K.: The medial feature detector: Stable regions from image boundaries. In: International Conference on Computer Vision, ICCV (2011)
2. Bay, H., Ess, A., Tuytelaars, T., Van Gool, L.: Speeded-up robust features (SURF). Computer Vision and Image Understanding (CVIU) 110, 346–359 (2008)
3. Beaudet, P.: Rotationally invariant image operators. In: International Joint Conference on Pattern Recognition (1978)
4. Canny, J.: A computational approach to edge detection. IEEE Transactions on Pattern Analysis and Machine Intelligence (PAMI) 8(6), 679–698 (1986)
5. Cazals, F., Giesen, J., Pauly, M., Zomorodian, A.: Conformal alpha shapes. In: Point-Based Graphics. Eurographics/IEEE VGTC Symposium Proc., (2005)
6. Cormen, T.H., Leiserson, C.E., Rivest, R.L., Stein, C.: Introduction to Algorithms, 3rd edn. MIT Press (2009)
7. Edelsbrunner, H.: Alpha shapes — a survey. In: Tessellations in the Sciences: Virtues, Techniques and Applications of Geometric Tilings. Springer (2010)

8. Edelsbrunner, H., Kirkpatrick, D., Seidel, R.: On the shape of a set of points in the plane. IEEE Transactions on Information Theory 29(4), 551–559 (1983)
9. Harris, C., Stephens, M.: A combined corner and edge detector. In: Alvey Vision Conference (1988)
10. Leutenegger, S., Chli, M., Siegwart, R.: BRISK: Binary Robust Invariant Scalable Keypoints. In: International Conference on Computer Vision (ICCV) (2011)
11. Lindeberg, T.: Feature detection with automatic scale selection. International Journal of Computer Vision (IJCV) 30(2), 79–116 (1998)
12. Lindeberg, T., Garding, J.: Shape-adapted smoothing in estimation of 3-D shape cues from affine deformations of local 2-D brightness structure. Image and Vision Computing 15(6), 415–434 (1997)
13. Lowe, D.: Distinctive image features from scale-invariant keypoints. International Journal of Computer Vision (IJCV) 60(2), 91–110 (2004)
14. Matas, J., Chum, O., Urban, M., Pajdla, T.: Robust wide-baseline stereo from maximally stable extremal regions. Image and Vision Computing 22(10), 761–767 (2004)
15. Meine, H., Köthe, U., Stelldinger, P.: A topological sampling theorem for robust boundary reconstruction and image segmentation. Discrete Applied Mathematics 157(3), 524–541 (2009)
16. Mikolajczyk, K., Schmid, C.: An Affine Invariant Interest Point Detector. In: Heyden, A., Sparr, G., Nielsen, M., Johansen, P. (eds.) ECCV 2002, Part I. LNCS, vol. 2350, pp. 128–142. Springer, Heidelberg (2002)
17. Mikolajczyk, K., Tuytelaars, T., Schmid, C., Zisserman, A., Matas, J., Schaffalitzky, F., Kadir, T., Van Gool, L.: A comparison of affine region detectors. International Journal of Computer Vision (IJCV) 65(1), 43–72 (2005)
18. Mikolajczyk, K., Zisserman, A., Schmid, C.: Shape recognition with edge-based features. In: British Machine Vision Conference (BMVC) (2003)
19. Najman, L., Couprie, M.: Building the component tree in quasi-linear time. IEEE Transactions on Image Processing 15(11), 3531–3539 (2006)
20. Philbin, J., Chum, O., Isard, M., Sivic, J., Zisserman, A.: Object retrieval with large vocabularies and fast spatial matching. In: Computer Vision and Pattern Recognition, CVPR (2007)
21. Philbin, J., Chum, O., Sivic, J., Isard, M., Zisserman, A.: Lost in quantization: Improving particular object retrieval in large scale image databases. In: Computer Vision and Pattern Recognition, CVPR (2008)
22. Rapantzikos, K., Avrithis, Y., Kollias, S.: Detecting regions from single scale edges. In: Intern. Workshop on Sign, Gesture and Activity (SGA), European Conference on Computer Vision (ECCV) (September 2010)
23. Rosten, E., Drummond, T.W.: Machine Learning for High-Speed Corner Detection. In: Leonardis, A., Bischof, H., Pinz, A. (eds.) ECCV 2006. LNCS, vol. 3951, pp. 430–443. Springer, Heidelberg (2006)
24. Teichmann, M., Capps, M.: Surface reconstruction with anisotropic density-scaled alpha shapes. In: IEEE Visualization (1998)
25. Tuytelaars, T., Mikolajczyk, K.: Local invariant feature detectors: A survey. Foundations and Trends in Computer Graphics and Vision 3(3), 177–280 (2008)
26. Zitnick, C., Ramnath, K.: Edge foci interest points. In: International Conference on Computer Vision (ICCV), pp. 359–366 (2011)
27. Zomorodian, A., Guibas, L., Koehl, P.: Geometric filtering of pairwise atomic interactions applied to the design of efficient statistical potentials. Computer-Aided Geometric Design 23(6), 531–544 (2006)

Sparselet Models for Efficient Multiclass Object Detection

Hyun Oh Song[1], Stefan Zickler[2], Tim Althoff[1], Ross Girshick[3], Mario Fritz[4], Christopher Geyer[2], Pedro Felzenszwalb[5], and Trevor Darrell[1]

[1] UC Berkeley
[2] iRobot
[3] University of Chicago
[4] Max Planck Institute for Informatics
[5] Brown University

{song,althoff,darrell}@eecs.berkeley.edu, {szickler,cgeyer}@irobot.com, rbg@cs.uchicago.edu, mfritz@mpi-inf.mpg.de, pff@brown.edu

Abstract. We develop an intermediate representation for deformable part models and show that this representation has favorable performance characteristics for multi-class problems when the number of classes is high. Our model uses sparse coding of part filters to represent each filter as a sparse linear combination of shared dictionary elements. This leads to a universal set of parts that are shared among all object classes. Reconstruction of the original part filter responses via sparse matrix-vector product reduces computation relative to conventional part filter convolutions. Our model is well suited to a parallel implementation, and we report a new GPU DPM implementation that takes advantage of sparse coding of part filters. The speed-up offered by our intermediate representation and parallel computation enable real-time DPM detection of 20 different object classes on a laptop computer.

Keywords: Sparse Coding, Object Detection, Deformable Part Models.

1 Introduction

Scalable category-level recognition is a core requirement for visual competence in everyday environments: domains of modest complexity typically have hundreds to thousands of categories, and as one considers unconstrained search problems, the space of possible categories becomes practically unlimited. As the number of categories grows, individual models are increasingly likely to become redundant. In the case of part-based models this redundancy can be exploited by constructing models with shared parts.

We introduce an intermediate representation into part-based recognition models whereby a fixed set of shared "basis" parts is used to reconstruct category responses and infer detections. We learn the set of basis parts so that reconstructing the response of a target model is extremely efficient: our method decomposes model parameters as sparse linear combinations of the basis elements. With this

A. Fitzgibbon et al. (Eds.): ECCV 2012, Part II, LNCS 7573, pp. 802–815, 2012.

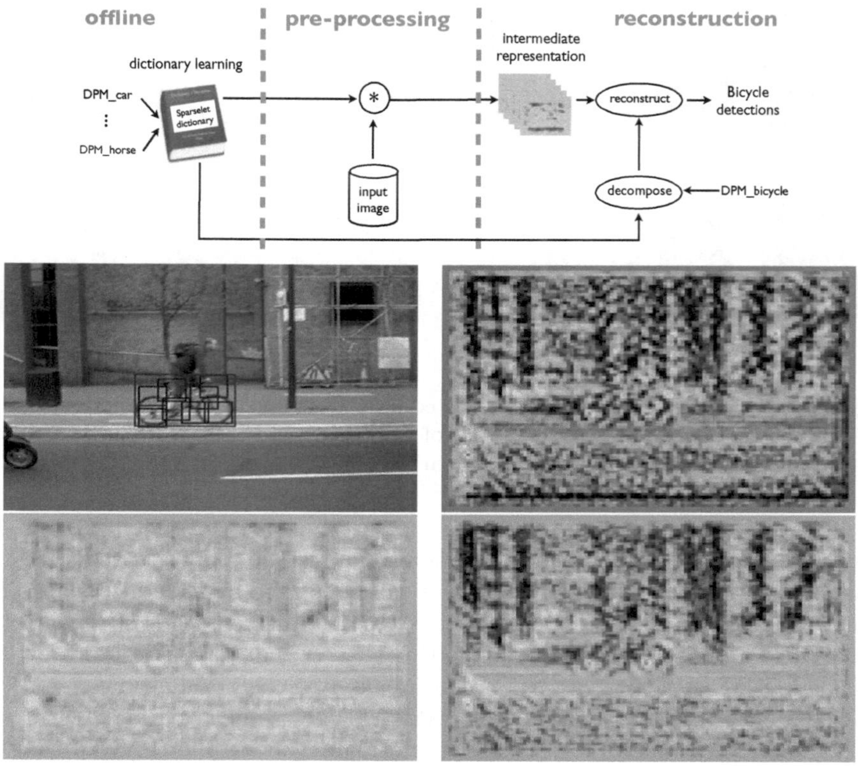

Fig. 1. Top: System concept. Middle row: example bicycle detection and true part filter responses for a wheel part from the bicycle model. Bottom row: reconstructed responses using SVD and sparselets (each using 20 bases). Our method maintains part response specificity (peaked responses at the wheels), while SVD reconstruction fails to maintain the sharpness. Best viewed in color.

representation we can reconstruct approximate part responses using a sparse matrix-vector product instead of exhaustive convolutions.

In contrast to standard applications of sparse coding, where features are encoded as sparse combinations of dictionary elements, we learn a dictionary of *model parameters*, and the models themselves are encoded as sparse combinations of dictionary elements. This leads to a compression of the models that can be exploited to speed-up computation.

As the number of object categories increases the speed-up provided by our "sparselet" model is the ratio of the original part filter size to the average number of non-zero coefficients in the sparse representation. For retrieval of a novel ("post-hoc") category in a large media corpus, low-level features and basis convolutions can be computed in a pre-processing step. For online detection, our representation is especially well-suited to a parallel architecture, where the memory and processor architecture allows for efficient reconstruction in a direct fashion

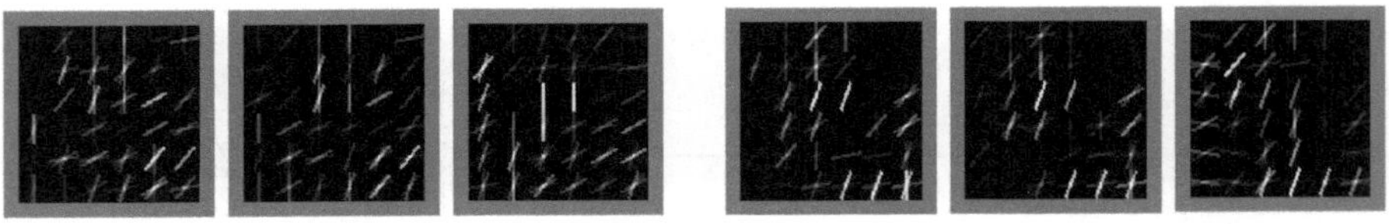

(a) Motorbike part 10 (b) Sofa part 25

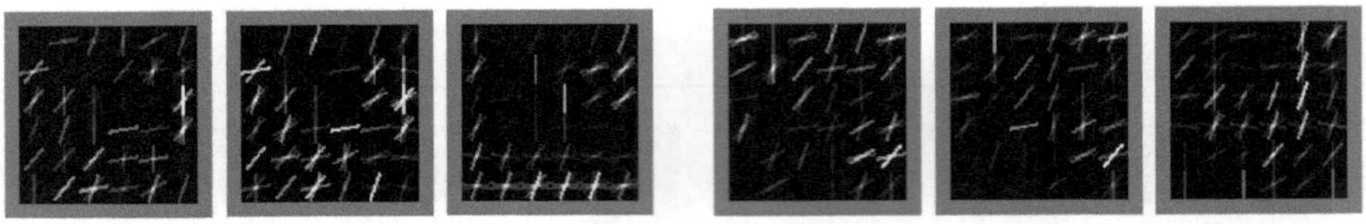

(c) Aeroplane part 27 (d) Cat part 34

Fig. 2. Each block shows a randomly selected part, its sparselet reconstruction, and its SVD reconstruction. In both cases 20 out of 216 bases were used. Note how sparselets preserve filter structure better than singular vectors.

(e.g., without a cascade). The method is also applicable to a cascaded CPU implementation, but the speed improvement can be limited by memory cache issues relative to a GPU implementation. Our CUDA implementation of a sparselet-based DPM model is approximately 35 times faster than the fastest single CPU cascaded DPM implementations on benchmark PASCAL evaluations.

We evaluate our methods using the PASCAL VOC, ImageNet, and TRECVID MED datasets. We show 1) real-time performance on PASCAL VOC using 20 categories on a laptop computer, 2) that sparselets learned on PASCAL can effectively reconstruct detectors trained on the ImageNet dataset, and 3) that post-hoc detectors trained on ImageNet using PASCAL-derived bases can be effective at detecting objects related to TRECVID MED activities.

Although we focus on object and activity recognition, the conceptual contribution of this paper – sparse decomposition of filters – is generally applicable to a variety of multiclass classification settings where linear models are employed.

2 Related Work

Deformable part models have been proven to yield high accuracy on benchmark challenges, yet are computationally demanding. Previous efforts have addressed hypothesis pruning in a cascaded implementation [1], and in coarse-to-fine search schemes [2]. However, relatively little attention has been paid to the problem of scaling such models to detect hundreds or thousands of categories at near real-time speeds, or to quickly search large repositories of media for a category of interest not known a-priori.

Recent work has explored schemes for part sharing, including [3]. Our method implicitly shares part prototypes and can provide a significant improvement in speed by compressing the effective number of parts used in typical DPM models. Other authors have explored group regularization of a prototype representation

[4], and linear manifold [5] and/or topic models [6] over visual classifier parameter spaces, but have not addressed the reconstruction of new models, nor the advantages of sparsity for large-scale detection.

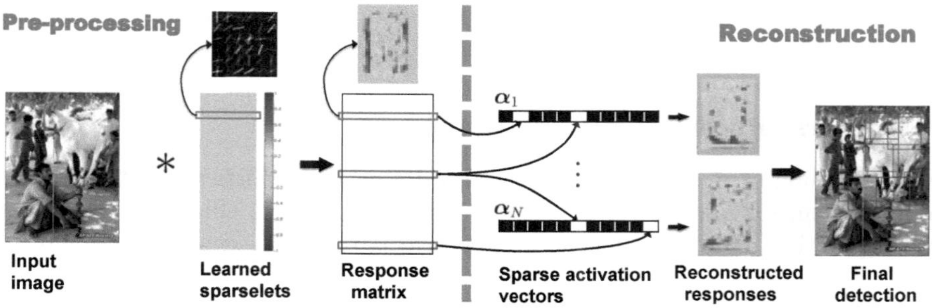

Fig. 3. Overview diagram of the our method. Once we evaluate the image with learned sparselets, the reconstruction phase can be done via efficient sparse matrix vector multiplications

A complementary line of work uses classifier hierarchies to speed up classification by pruning classes while descending the classifier tree. We note a few, focusing on recent works with vision results. Some learn a tree in a top-down fashion [7,8] by spectral clustering on the affinity matrix. Others optimize a discriminative objective [9,10]. [11] builds a taxonomy of object classes based on shared features. These approaches may preemptively discard a correct detection if it falls on the wrong side of a hard decision boundary. Attempts have been made to address this using relaxed hierarchies [12,13]. We note that sparselets may be combined with these approaches to further accelerate them.

3 Sparselets

In this paper we propose and evaluate sparse prototype representations for encoding deformable object models. We use a dictionary of parts learned in a sparse coding framework. This approach, which we term "sparselets", has the advantage of leading not only to fast and accurate multiclass object detection, but also offers an efficient intermediate representation for detecting new object categories. It is important to note that our approach learns a dictionary over *model parameters*, not over observed features, as is the customary application of existing sparse coding methods in the recognition literature.

While sparselets are applicable to a range of settings, we focus in this paper on the star-structured deformable part models (DPM) from [14]. Briefly, a DPM is composed of low-resolution root filters that describe an object category's global appearance and high-resolution part filters that capture local appearance. These filters are weight vectors over HOG [15] style features learned by optimizing a latent SVM [14]. The main computational bottleneck in applying these models is convolving their filters with a HOG feature pyramid. This fact is demonstrated by the cascade algorithm for detection with DPMs [1], which dramatically reduces detection time by computing filter convolutions at a reduced set of locations that is chosen based on learned pruning thresholds. Sparselets offer a complementary, shared-part approach for reducing filter convolution costs when the number of categories becomes large.

3.1 Sparse Reconstruction of Models

Sparse coding of model filters has several desirable properties, most significant among them for our post-hoc scenario being the relative efficiency of a sparse reconstruction at query time. Our objective is to find a generic dictionary of filters $D = \{D_1, D_2, \ldots, D_K\}$, called *sparselets*, that optimally approximates the part filters $P = \{P_1, P_2, \cdots, P_N\}$ pooled from a set of training models, subject to a sparsity constraint. Explicitly, we formulate the optimization problem

$$\begin{aligned} \min_{\alpha_{ij}, D_j} \quad & \sum_{i=1}^{N} ||\text{vec}\,(P_i) - \sum_{j=1}^{K} \alpha_{ij} D_j||_2^2 \\ \text{subject to} \quad & ||\boldsymbol{\alpha}_i||_0 \leq \epsilon \qquad \forall i = 1, ..., N \\ & ||D_j||_2 = 1 \qquad \forall j = 1, ..., K \end{aligned} \tag{1}$$

where $P_i \in \mathbb{R}^{h \times h \times l}$ is a part filter, $D_j \in \mathbb{R}^{lh^2}$ is a dictionary element, $\boldsymbol{\alpha}_i \in \mathbb{R}^K$ is an activation vector, ϵ imposes a cap on the number of activations, h is the filter size (we assume square filters for simplicity), and l is the feature dimension.

Although the above optimization is NP-hard, greedy algorithms such as orthogonal matching pursuit algorithm (OMP) [16,17] can be used to efficiently compute an approximate solution. OMP iteratively estimates the optimal matching projections of the input signal onto the dictionary D. The above optimization problem is convex with respect to D if $\boldsymbol{\alpha}_i$ is fixed, and so we can optimize the objective in a coordinate descent fashion by iterating between updating $\boldsymbol{\alpha}_i$ while fixing D and vice versa. For our experiments we use the online dictionary learning algorithm from [18]. Figure 2 shows randomly chosen part filters from models trained on the PASCAL VOC 2007 [19] dataset and compares our sparselet reconstruction with $\epsilon = 20$ to the SVD-based reconstruction using 20 singular bases out of the full set of 216.

3.2 Precomputation and Efficient Reconstruction

We can precompute convolutions for all sparselets, and by linearity of convolution we can then use the activation vectors estimated for a target object detector to approximate the convolution response we would have obtained from convolution with the original filters. Denoting the feature pyramid of an image as Ψ, we have $\Psi * P_i \approx \Psi * (\sum_j \alpha_{ij} D_j) = \sum_j \alpha_{ij} (\Psi * D_j)$, where $*$ denotes the convolution operator. Concretely, we can recover individual part filter responses via sparse matrix multiplication (or lookups) with the activation vector replacing the heavy convolution operation as shown in Eqn (2):

$$\begin{bmatrix} \text{---}\ \Psi * P_1\ \text{---} \\ \text{---}\ \Psi * P_2\ \text{---} \\ \vdots \\ \vdots \\ \vdots \\ \vdots \\ \text{---}\ \Psi * P_N\ \text{---} \end{bmatrix} \approx \begin{bmatrix} \text{---}\ \boldsymbol{\alpha}_1\ \text{---} \\ \text{---}\ \boldsymbol{\alpha}_2\ \text{---} \\ \vdots \\ \vdots \\ \vdots \\ \vdots \\ \text{---}\ \boldsymbol{\alpha}_N\ \text{---} \end{bmatrix} \begin{bmatrix} \text{---}\ \Psi * D_1\ \text{---} \\ \text{---}\ \Psi * D_2\ \text{---} \\ \vdots \\ \text{---}\ \Psi * D_K\ \text{---} \end{bmatrix} = AM, \qquad (2)$$

where M is a matrix of all sparselet responses, A is the matrix of sparse activation vectors. As the number of classes increases, we amortize the time required to compute the intermediate representation M.

In practice the score of a DPM can be reconstructed as following,

$$\begin{aligned} \text{score}_{\text{recon}}(\omega) &= m_0(\omega) + \sum_{i=1}^{N} \max_{\delta} s_i(\omega+\delta) - d_i(\delta) \\ \text{where } s_i(\omega) &= \sum_{\substack{j=1 \\ \forall \alpha_{ij}\neq 0}}^{K} \alpha_{ij} (\Psi * D_j)[\omega]. \end{aligned} \qquad (3)$$

Here d_i are quadratic deformation costs, δ is a displacement and ω is a position and scale in a feature pyramid. After precomputation, the reconstructed part filter score, $s_i(\omega)$, simplifies to

$$s_i(\omega) = \sum_{\substack{j=1 \\ \forall \alpha_{ij}\neq 0}}^{K} \alpha_{ij} M_j[\omega]. \qquad (4)$$

Note that the summation is only over non-zero elements of the sparse vector $\boldsymbol{\alpha}_i$. Additionally, this could be efficiently implemented as sparse matrix multiplications or lookups. Figure 1 shows a sample reconstruction and Figure 3 summarizes our framework.

For online detection, we convolve the query image with the sparselets and do sparse reconstruction in turn per frame. For dictionary size K, total number of filters N, filter size h and feature dimension l, an exhaustive convolution based detection scheme requires approximately Nlh^2 operations per feature pyramid location. Our scheme requires approximately $Klh^2 + N\mathbb{E}[\,||\boldsymbol{\alpha}_i||_0\,]$ operations. The first term is from convolution with sparselets and the second term is the average activation level from the sparse reconstruction. Note that the convolution time (Klh^2) is not dependent on number of classes or model filters (N) and depends only on the size of sparselet dictionary (K) which is fixed and does not need to grow with the number of classes.

As the number of classes or model filters grows, the convolution time gets amortized and the speedup factor becomes the ratio between the complexity of the convolution kernel and the average activation. Therefore, the sparsity in the sparselet activation vector becomes the key, yielding the speedup

$$\frac{lh^2}{\mathbb{E}[\ ||\boldsymbol{\alpha}_i||_0\ ]}$$

For example, reconstructing response from a 6 by 6 kernel with feature dimension 6 and average activation level of 20, we would get more than an order of magnitude speedup in terms of number of arithmetic operations.

4 Implementation

4.1 CPU Cascaded Sparselets

We first implemented our model using the cascade code of [1], and interleaved sparse reconstruction with the cascaded search. In this implementation we used a sparselet representation for the filters over PCA features as well. We found that a sparse reconstruction model was still successful. We report results in the following section on the ability of sparselet models to reconstruct held-out and/or post-hoc categories; that is, categories which were not used in training the part dictionary model. While reconstruction can be accurate with a small number of bases, as is shown below, the memory cache behavior on a conventional CPU limited the overall speedup of the method, even when the theoretical ratio of the size of the convolution window to the number of sparse bases was relatively large. To address this, we turned to a GPU implementation, described in the following section.

4.2 Vanilla DPM and Sparselets Implementations on GPU

One of our contributions is the highest reported throughput for DPM-based methods, which is due to both the use of GPUs and sparselets. We describe here our CUDA[1] implementation of both a "Vanilla" DPM approach, which follows the classic implementation in [14], as well as sparselets. We expected DPM to benefit from porting to the GPU since a large fraction of the computation time of the original implementation is spent on convolution, HOG computation and distance transforms - all operations that are parallelizable. GPUs offer a massively parallel computing architecture and have been successfully used to speed up similar algorithms, e.g. HOG-based pedestrian detection [15].

[1] Compute Unified Device Architecture (CUDA) is the programming paradigm for Nvidia GPUs. Briefly, the GPU code is specified in kernels written in CUDA - essentially C/C++ with some additional language constructs. Each core executes compiled kernel code in a single thread. See [20] for more information.

The main steps in the GPU implementation are as follows. First, the input image is transferred to the GPU. Second, image pyramids and HOG features are computed as in [14] on the GPU (as are all subsequent operations). Third, filter responses to root, part or part basis filters are computed at each of S scales in the HOG pyramid. For Vanilla DPM, we make SR kernel calls for all R root filter responses, and SN kernel calls for all P part filter responses. A single kernel call instantiates kernel threads for each HOG cell in the given pyramid level. For Sparselets, we make SR kernel calls for the root filters, where each kernel call runs over all HOG pixels in the pyramid level; then, we make S kernel calls for the part bases, where each kernel call runs over each HOG cell in the pyramid level *and* each of the K part bases.To reconstruct all N part responses, we make SN kernel calls, where each part filter is reconstructed from the part bases responses.

We then compute bounded distance transforms (BDT) of the part filter responses. In the cascade implementation of DPM [1], part location offsets are bounded. Furthermore, all deformation penalties learned in training are separable. We therefore employ two one-dimensional BDTs in the horizontal and vertical directions. Each is implemented as a *min* convolution with a length-11 quadratic penalty filter. A total of $2SN$ kernel calls evaluate the horizontal, then vertical, BDT for all scales and parts. Finally, all root filter responses and BDT outputs are summed into a single score via SR kernel calls. Those part locations with scores above threshold are put in a list – added asynchronously by kernel threads and protected by an atomic lock on the GPU. The list of candidate detections is then copied to CPU memory. All remaining operations such as non-maxima suppression are performed on the CPU and follow the original implementation.

4.3 Sparselet Size

In practice we can divide a part filter into smaller subfilters before computing the sparselet representation. The subfilter size (which equals the sparselet size) determines certain runtime and memory tradeoffs. Let F be a $h_F \times w_F \times l$ filter, and let the sparselet size be $h_s \times w_s \times l$. We require that h_s and w_s are divisors of h_F and w_F, respectively, and divide F into an $h_F/h_s \times w_F/w_s$ array of tiled subfilters. We approximate (or "reconstruct") a filter response by summing over approximate subfilter responses.

Given precomputed sparselet responses, reconstructing the response to F requires at most $\epsilon(h_F/h_s)(w_F/w_s)$ operations. Low-cost approximation is essential, so we fix the reconstruction budget for F at $\epsilon(h_F/h_s)(w_F/w_s) \leq B_R$. Within this budget, we can use fewer, smaller sparselets, or more, larger sparselets. We consider two other budget constraints. *Precomputation time* B_P: convolving an input with the entire sparselet dictionary requires $h_s w_s l K$ operations. For a fixed budget $h_s w_s l K \leq B_P$, we can use more, smaller sparselets, or fewer, larger sparselets. *Representation space* B_S: the space required to store the intermediate representation is proportional to the dictionary size K.

Table 1. Reconstruction error for four classes as sparselet parameters are varied. The reconstruction budget (B_R) is fixed for the whole table. The precomputation budget (B_P) is fixed in the top half of the table and varies in the bottom half.

					Reconstruction error			
$h_s \times w_s$	K	$h_s w_s K$	ϵ	$(h_F/h_s)(w_F/w_s)$	**bicycle**	**car**	**cat**	**person**
6×6	128	4608	112	1	1.0645	1.0349	0.8521	1.1939
3×3	512	4608	28	4	0.3116	0.3360	0.2552	0.4573
2×2	1152	4608	13	9	0.2298	0.2706	0.1763	0.4007
1×1	4608	4608	3	36	0.1062	0.1200	0.0820	0.1635
6×6	512	18432	112	1	0.0893	0.0528	0.1134	0.0472
3×3	512	4608	28	4	0.3116	0.3360	0.2552	0.4573
2×2	512	2048	13	9	0.3833	0.5962	0.2561	1.2280
1×1	512	512	3	36	0.3172	0.6599	0.1817	1.8594

For fixed reconstruction and precomputation budgets B_R and B_P, we studied the effect of varying sparselet size. Empirically (Table 1), filter reconstruction error always decreases as we decrease sparselet size.

When there are not too many classes, the precomputation time is not fully amortized and we would like to make B_P small. For a fixed, small B_P we minimize reconstruction error by setting h_s and w_s to small values. However, as we make the sparselets smaller, K grows, possibly making the representation space budget B_S too large. In our GPU experiments, we balance memory usage with sparselet size by setting h_s and w_s to 3.

When precomputation is amortized, minimizing precomputation time is less important. However, in this case we are still concerned with keeping the intermediate representation reasonably small. By fixing the response and representation space budgets, we observe that using more, larger sparselets minimizes reconstruction error (at the expense of requiring a larger precomputation budget). Therefore, in the CPU-based experiments which focused on the offline setting we use larger 6×6 sparselets.

5 Experiments

5.1 Evaluation on Unseen Categories

We performed experiments to analyze the detection performance of reconstructed models for previously unseen categories at a given level of sparsity. We experimented with three datasets: PASCAL VOC 2007 [19], ImageNet [21], and TRECVID [22]. To compute ground truth AP, we ran cascaded deformable part models [1] trained on the held-out category. For a baseline, we extracted singular vectors learned from the training models and estimated the reconstruction

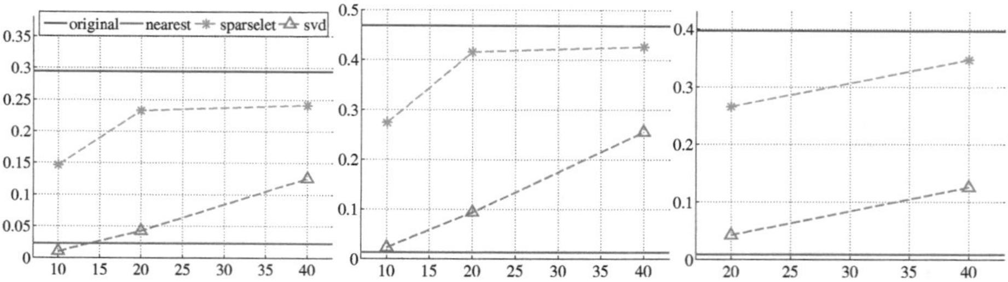

(a) 20 PASCAL categories (b) 9 PASCAL categories (c) 9 ImageNet categories

Fig. 4. Results on held-out evaluation on PASCAL VOC 2007 [19] and ImageNet[21] dataset. Y-axes show class averaged AP. X-axes represent number of bases used in reconstruction for SVD and sparselets.

weight vectors from the previously unseen query category models using a reconstruction from a linear basis of the top-k singular vectors. We also explored a nearest-neighbor-of-parts baseline where the query object model retrieves closest matching part filters (in L2 distance) from the pool of training object models. The global detection threshold was fixed to -1.1 for all object models throughout the experiment for consistency. This number was roughly the saturation threshold for AP evaluation.

To test the reconstruction generalization performance on previously unseen category models we first performed leave one class out evaluation where we used dictionaries and the set of singular vectors that are trained on all other classes.

Figure 4(a) shows the experimental results in AP for all 20 classes from PASCAL VOC 2007 test dataset [19]. Figure 4(b) shows AP for 9 categories that have AP above 0.3. This shows that the reconstruction error is relatively small for well performing models compared to mediocre DPM models. Our intuition is that well performing models have relatively higher classification margin than others and are more tolerant to approximation errors. We can see from Figure 4 that our sparse reconstruction method preserves most of AP on average with only 20 bases while SVD reconstruction does not quite preserve the AP at the same level of reconstruction budget. Although nearest-neighbor-of-parts baseline has poor performance overall, on subset of categories that DPM detector has poor detection performance (e.g. bird, dog and potted plant), it worked as well as or a slightly better than the original held-out query models. Please refer to the supplementary material for full per class AP table.

Next, we investigated whether a part dictionary model trained with PASCAL categories would work on other datasets. We manually selected a set of object categories which are related to events in the 2011 TRECVID MED challenge [22]: sailboat, bread, cake, candle, fish, goat, jeep, scissors, and tire. We trained DPM models using data sampled from ImageNet [21] for these classes. We used the ImageNet bounding boxes for training, and manually annotated 200 additional test images that had at least one instance of the above object categories with bounding boxes. We tested how the dictionary learned from PASCAL models in

Methods	Average Precision
original	0.4853
svd 20	0.0571
svd 40	0.1167
sparselet 20	0.3323
sparselet 40	0.3911

Fig. 5. Left: Example keyframes on TRECVID [22] dataset. Right: Average precision of retrieved examples using models trained with ImageNet training data reconstructed with sparselet representations learned from PASCAL categories. Numbers 20 and 40 represent the number of bases used in the reconstruction.

the previous experiment performed when approximating previously unseen novel categories trained and tested on ImageNet imagery.

Figure 4(c) shows the AP for the 9 categories: the dictionary of parts learned from PASCAL does transfer to novel categories from ImageNet domain. With the domain change however, we can see that SVD reconstruction with 40 bases preserves only about 12% to 15% of the original AP while sparselet reconstruction with 40 bases preserves about 88% to 93% of the AP. Again we can observe the same behavior that well performing DPM models are more tolerant on reconstruction errors than mediocre models. Please refer to the supplementary material for average AP plot of subset of classes which have AP above 0.3.

Finally, we tested how well these classifiers performed and were reconstructed on TRECVID imagery. The contents of TRECVID videos are highly variant, for example, "wedding ceremony" varies from a traditional catholic mass, to a Hindi ceremony, to home-made music videos, so precision is only high at relatively low recall in this model transfer scenario even for the baseline model. Figure 5 shows example frames from the event kit and category averaged precision for top 50 retrieved examples (based on sampled keyframes annotated using AMT [23]). We can see that sparse reconstruction significantly improves the precision as compared to SVD reconstruction for an equivalently compact intermediate representation.

5.2 Runtimes and Performance on the PASCAL VOC 2007 Dataset

In this section we present results of experiments examining runtime, and mean average precision (AP) of *Cascade DPM* [1] on a CPU, *Vanilla DPM* on a GPU, and *Sparselets* on a GPU. Figure 6 (top) plots runtime at 640×480 resolution as a function of the number of objects, where for sparselets we use $(K, \epsilon) = (512, 4)$. Runtimes were measured on a 3.1 GHz Intel Core i5 CPU, and an Nvidia GTX 580 GPU with 512 cores running at 772 MHz. We used the 20-object VOC 2007 dataset [19] to measure runtime, and we repeated VOC 2007 classes to get to

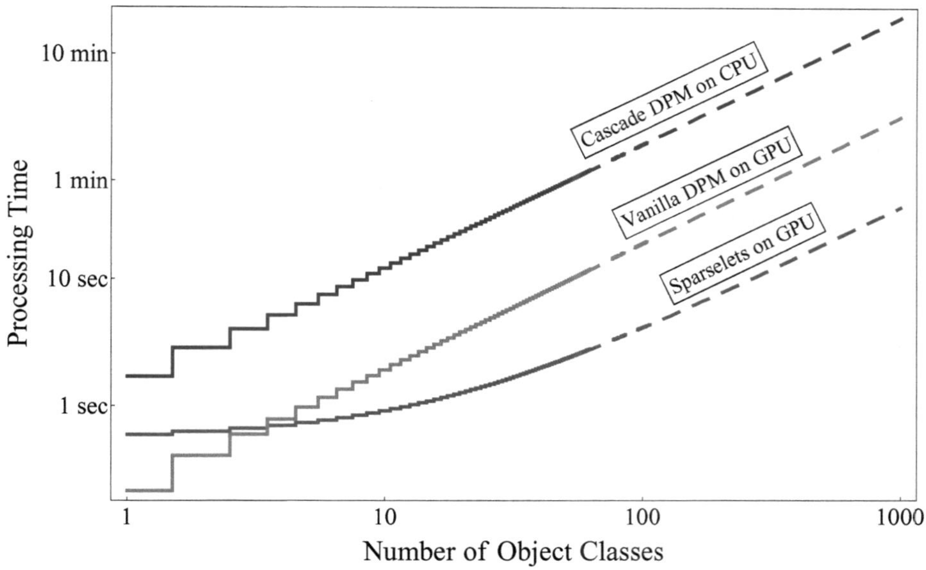

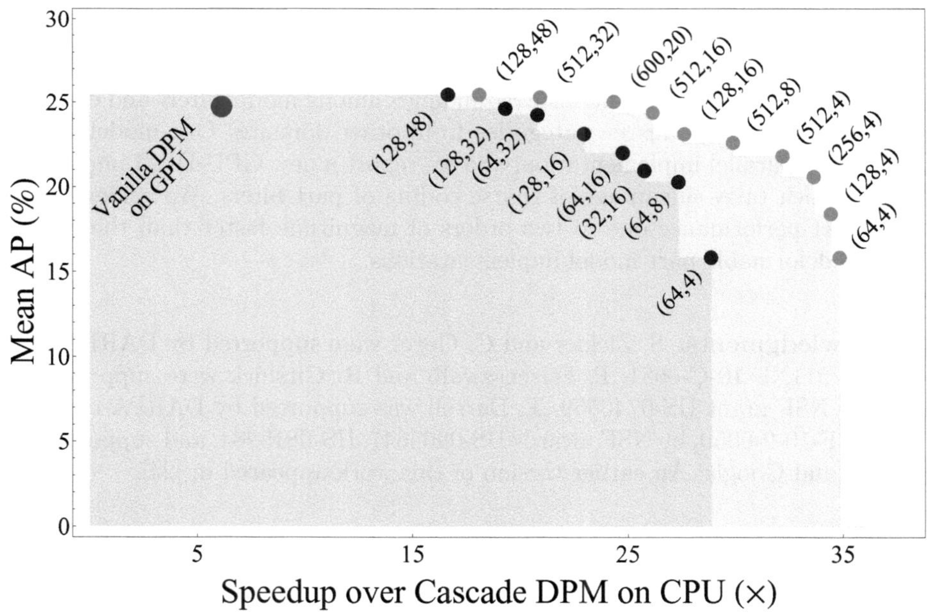

Fig. 6. Top: Comparison of cascade algorithm on CPU vs. vanilla DPM on GPU vs. sparselets accelerated DPM on GPU as number of object classes grows. Sparselet accelerated DPM on GPU offers approximately 35 times faster compared to the cascade implementation on CPU. Frame size used in this experiment was 640 × 480. Bottom: Speedup vs. Mean AP. Blue dots are for "online" results measuring end-to-end time. Orange dots are for "post-hoc" case. The tuple in parenthesis denote (K, ϵ).

60 classes. The dashed portion is an extrapolation based on a linear model of runtime. Overall there is about a 32× speedup of sparselets on a GPU over Cascade DPM on a CPU - equally attributable to the GPU and sparselets.

We also evaluated mean AP for various configurations of (K, ϵ). Figure 6 (bottom) presents mean AP on VOC 2007 vs. speedup over the Cascade DPM on CPU implementation. The lower/blue group of points represent sweet spots in the "online" case and is based on runtimes measured on 20 classes. The upper/orange group is based on the "post-hoc" case where we measure the incremental runtime of a single class only. In both cases we only show those points not dominated by any other configuration - neither AP greater nor runtime faster. In the online case, we achieve speedups up to 25× without significant loss of AP over Vanilla DPM on a GPU. In the post-hoc case where precomputation is not counted, larger K and lower ϵ are favored, only the latter of which counts against per-class runtime, thus achieving even larger speedups - up to 35×.

In the supplemental video we show sparselets detecting 20 PASCAL object classes on video in real time on a laptop computer.

6 Conclusion

We introduced sparse intermediate representations that enable real-time multi-class object detection and efficient post-hoc category retrieval. Our results show that sparselets exploit the intrinsic redundancy among model filters and can generalize to previously unseen categories from other domains. Our model is well suited to a parallel implementation, and we report a new GPU DPM implementation which takes advantage of sparse coding of part filters. We achieve state of the art performance one to two orders of magnitude faster than the fastest current deformable part model implementations.

Acknowledgments. S. Zickler and C. Geyer were supported by DARPA contract W911NF-10-C-0081. P. Felzenszwalb and R. Girshick were supported in part by NSF grant IIS-0746569. T. Darrell was supported by DARPA contract W911NF-10-2-0059, by NSF awards IIS-0905647, IIS-0819984, and support from Toyota and Google. An earlier version of this work appeared in [24].

References

1. Felzenszwalb, P.F., Girshick, R.B., McAllester, D.A.: Cascade object detection with deformable part models. In: CVPR (2010)
2. Pedersoli, M., Vedaldi, A., Gonzàlez, J.: A coarse-to-fine approach for fast deformable object detection. In: CVPR (2011)
3. Ott, P., Everingham, M.: Shared parts for deformable part-based models. In: CVPR, pp. 1513–1520 (2011)
4. Pirsiavash, H., Ramanan, D., Fowlkes, C.: Bilinear classifiers for visual recognition. In: NIPS (2009)

5. Quattoni, A., Collins, M., Darrell, T.: Transfer learning for image classification with sparse prototype representations. In: CVPR (2008)
6. Fritz, M., Schiele, B.: Decomposition, discovery and detection of visual categories using topic models. In: CVPR (2008)
7. Griffin, G., Perona, P.: Learning and using taxonomies for fast visual categorization. In: CVPR (2008)
8. Bengio, S., Weston, J., Grangier, D.: Label embedding trees for large multi-class tasks. In: NIPS (2010)
9. Binder, A., Müller, K.R., Kawanabe, M.: On taxonomies for multi-class image categorization. International Journal of Computer Vision 99(3), 281–301 (2012)
10. Lai, K., Bo, L., Ren, X., Fox, D.: A scalable tree-based approach for joint object and pose recognition. In: Twenty-Fifth Conference on Artificial Intelligence (AAAI) (August 2011)
11. Razavi, N., Gall, J., Gool, L.J.V.: Scalable multi-class object detection. In: CVPR, pp. 1505–1512 (2011)
12. Marszałek, M., Schmid, C.: Constructing Category Hierarchies for Visual Recognition. In: Forsyth, D., Torr, P., Zisserman, A. (eds.) ECCV 2008, Part IV. LNCS, vol. 5305, pp. 479–491. Springer, Heidelberg (2008)
13. Gao, T., Koller, D.: Discriminative learning of relaxed hierarchy for large-scale visual recognition. In: ICCV (2011)
14. Felzenszwalb, P., Girshick, R., McAllester, D., Ramanan, D.: Object detection with discriminatively trained part-based models. IEEE Transactions on Pattern Analysis and Machine Intelligence 32(9), 1627–1645 (2010)
15. Dalal, N., Triggs, B.: Histograms of oriented gradients for human detection. In: CVPR (2005)
16. Cotter, S.F., Rao, B.D., Kreutz-Delgado, K., Adler, J.: Forward sequential algorithms for best basis selection. IEEE Proceedings Vision Image and Signal Processing 146(5), 235 (1999)
17. Mallat, S.G., Zhang, Z.: Matching pursuits with time-frequency dictionaries. IEEE Transactions on Signal Processing 41(12), 3397–3415 (1993)
18. Mairal, J., Bach, F., Ponce, J., Sapiro, G.: Online learning for matrix factorization and sparse coding. Journal of Machine Learning Research 11, 19–60 (2010)
19. Everingham, M., Van Gool, L., Williams, C.K.I., Winn, J., Zisserman, A.: The PASCAL Visual Object Classes Challenge (VOC 2007) Results (2007), `http://www.pascal-network.org/challenges/VOC/voc2007/workshop/index.html`
20. NVIDIA: CUDA Technology, `http://www.nvidia.com/CUDA`
21. Deng, J., Dong, W., Socher, R., Li, L.J., Li, K., Fei-Fei, L.: ImageNet: A Large-Scale Hierarchical Image Database. In: CVPR (2009)
22. Smeaton, A.F., Over, P., Kraaij, W.: Evaluation campaigns and trecvid. In: MIR 2006: Proceedings of the 8th ACM International Workshop on Multimedia Information Retrieval, pp. 321–330. ACM Press, New York (2006)
23. Amazon Mechanical Turk, `http://www.mturk.com`
24. Song, H.O., Fritz, M., Althoff, T., Darrell, T.: Don't look back: Post-hoc category detection via sparse reconstruction. Technical Report UCB/EECS-2012-16, EECS Department, University of California, Berkeley (January 2012)

Nested Pictorial Structures

Steve Gu, Ying Zheng, and Carlo Tomasi

Department of Computer Science,
Duke University, NC, USA 27705
{steve,yuanqi,tomasi}@cs.duke.edu

Abstract. We propose a theoretical construct coined nested pictorial structure to represent an object by parts that are recursively nested. Three innovative ideas are proposed: First, the nested pictorial structure finds a part configuration that is allowed to be deformed in geometric arrangement, while being confined to be topologically nested. Second, we define nested features which lend themselves to better, more detailed accounting of pixel data cost and describe occlusion in a principled way. Third, we develop the concept of constrained distance transform, a variation of the generalized distance transform, to guarantee the topological nesting relations and to further enforce that parts have no overlap with each other. We show that matching an optimal nested pictorial structure of K parts on an image of N pixels takes $O(NK)$ time using dynamic programming and constrained distance transform. In our MATLAB/C++ implementation, it takes less than 0.1 seconds to do the global optimal matching when $K = 10$ and $N = 400 \times 400$. We demonstrate the usefulness of nested pictorial structures in the matching of objects of nested patterns, objects in occlusion, and objects that live in a context.

1 Introduction

We study explicit, visual nesting relations in images. Nested visual patterns are commonly seen in our daily life. To name a few examples: a pupil is contained in an eye contained in a face contained in a person. A portrait is contained in a painting contained in a frame contained in a wall. In general, a *texture* is often contained in a *part* contained in an *object* contained in a *context* contained in a *scene*. In the literature of computer vision, most nesting relations are modeled implicitly. In this paper we present nested pictorial structure to *explicitly* model the nesting relation among textures, parts, objects, and contexts. Figure 1 illustrates that a nested pictorial structure represents parts in a possibly complex topological nesting relation.

1.1 Three New Ideas

To the best of our knowledge, the nesting relation is rarely explicitly modeled in the computer vision literature, and in particular within the context of a pictorial structure. This paper introduces a mathematical and computational model that

A. Fitzgibbon et al. (Eds.): ECCV 2012, Part II, LNCS 7573, pp. 816–827, 2012.

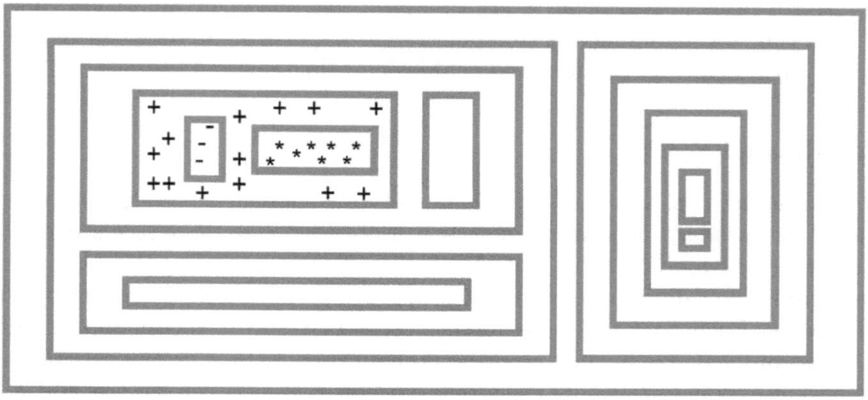

Fig. 1. Each red rectangle represents a part that can be recursively nested. The part arrangement is allowed to deform significantly in the image domain while keeping the nesting relations unchanged. Each part has its own cost function (e.g. $+, -, *$, etc), and a single sliding window without nesting would over-count the data cost. This issue is addressed by nested features in a principled way.

accounts for the *recursive* nesting relations among parts and objects. Three innovative ideas are presented:

First, we define *nested pictorial structure*, a concept that is rooted in the conventional pictorial structure (e.g. [1,2]), but enforces that parts conform to a given topological nesting relation. Moreover, parts are allowed to deform in their geometric arrangement and the matching of a nested pictorial structure is cast as a global optimization on the pixel level. This enriches the common understanding of the pictorial structure framework and suggests possibly new directions and novel computational schemes for the optimal matching.

Second, we define the notion of *nested features*. Nested features provide a better, more detailed accounting of pixel costs when parts are recursively nested. For instance, if part B is contained in part A, the spatial extent of A then needs to exclude the spatial extent of B. The conventional way of using a sliding window for the cost evaluation may involve significant "over-counting" of pixel costs when one part resides within another part (Figure 1 and Figure 2). Consequently, a typical detection algorithm may fail to localize an object under significant occlusion due to the lack of features and to the fact that the visible spatial extent is distributed on the boundaries rather than the interior. Nested features address this problem in an explicit and principled way.

Third, we develop non-overlapping constraints and the *constrained distance transform*, a variation of the generalized distance transform by Felzenszwalb and Huttenlocher [3], for the efficient, global matching of a nested pictorial structure. The constrained distance transform guarantees that no two parts overlap with each other in the deformable template matching. This transform enhances the stability in the geometric part arrangement and rules out the otherwise possible degenerate cases in which parts are collapsed together. Our algorithm runs in $O(NK)$ time for matching a nested pictorial of K parts on an image of N pixels. This is asymptotically optimal and enables real time computation.

1.2 Related Work

Pictorial structures, a.k.a. deformable models or constellation models, have been studied for decades, spanning from early work [1,4,5,6,7] to more recent contributions in recognition [8,9,10,11,12,13,14] and scene understanding [15]. A pictorial structure is typically represented as a graph $\mathcal{G} = \langle \mathcal{V}, \mathcal{E} \rangle$ where $\mathcal{V}$ is a set of symbolic parts. Each part $v \in \mathcal{V}$ is further represented by a rectangular window $W_v \subset \mathbb{Z}^2$ of fixed size in the 2D image domain. Let $f_v(W_v)$ be the cost of placing part v at window W_v. Let the deformation cost between part u and v be $\delta(W_u, W_v)$ that measures the discrepancy between the vector linking u to v and their template configuration. The commonly used objective is to find an optimal part allocation through the following global optimization:

$$\{\hat{W}_v\} = \arg \min_{\{W_v\}_{v \in \mathcal{V}}} \left\{ \underbrace{\sum_{v \in V} f_v(W_v)}_{\text{data cost}} + \lambda \underbrace{\sum_{(u,v) \in \mathcal{E}} \delta(W_u, W_v)}_{\text{deformation cost}} \right\} \tag{1}$$

where λ is a regularization parameter that balances the data cost and deformation cost. The intuition is clear: we want an arrangement of parts that matches a given object template in both appearance (minimizes the data cost) and spatial configuration (minimizes the deformation cost).

The computational challenge is to efficiently compute an optimal matching of a pictorial structure against a template. For instances, in some previous work [6,9], the location of each part is confined to a sparse set of points for practical processing. Felzenszwalb and Huttenlocher [16,2] show that when the spatial constraints form a tree and when the deformation cost δ is in a special form, the optimal allocation of a pictorial structure takes linear time in the size of an image, multiplied by the number of parts. Moreover, the optimization works on the image pixel level. The underlying technique of [2] is coined the generalized distance transform [3], and is equivalent to computing the lower envelope of an array of cones or parabolas. Combined with HoG features [17] and latent SVM, Felzenszwalb et al. [13] demonstrate a state-of-the-art recognition system [18].

Also remotely related are the works in occlusion reasoning [19,20,21] and context or scene recognition [22,23,24]. The nested pictorial structure is expected to be applicable but not limited to these two areas. The notable difference is that instead of detecting occlusion boundaries, the occlusion itself is inherently encoded in the nested model and is therefore enforced in an explicit way. Instead of dividing an image into a spatial grid of cells, nested models represent an image as a foliation of windows, one enclosing another, arranged in a possibly complex inclusion relation. Instead of being rigid, nested parts are allowed to deform

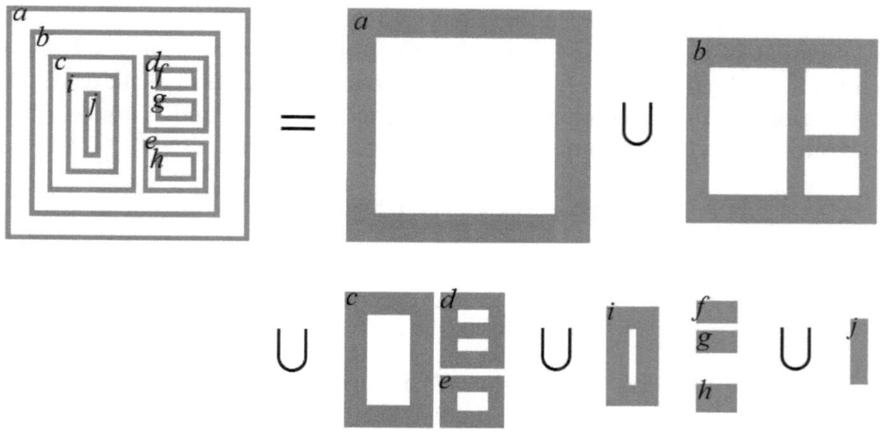

Fig. 2. A nested pictorial structure conformal to a nesting tree. Part a is maximal because it is not contained in any other part. Shaded connected regions are the spatial extent of each part.

significantly in their geometric arrangement. The concept of a nested pictorial structure is new to the best of our knowledge.

2 Nested Pictorial Structures

We use $a \prec b$ to represent that part a is *enforced* to be contained in part b. That is, any window W_a associated to part a must be contained in any window W_b associated to part b: $W_a \subseteq W_b$. We have the following definition:

Definition 1 (Nesting Graph) *Given a set of parts $\mathcal{V}$ and their inclusion relations $\prec$, the nesting graph is represented by $\mathcal{G} = \langle \mathcal{V}, \mathcal{E} \rangle$ where $\mathcal{E}$ is the edge set. Edge $(u, v) \in \mathcal{E}$ if $u \prec v$ and there does not exist $l \in \mathcal{V}$ such that $u \prec l \prec v$. Part u is called maximal if u is not contained in any other part. A window set $\{W_v\}_{v \in \mathcal{V}}$ is said to be conformal to $\mathcal{G}$ if $W_u \subseteq W_v$ for all $(u, v) \in \mathcal{E}$.*

It follows that the constructed graph $\mathcal{G}$ is a forest (a collection of trees) by observing that the graph is acyclic and each child node has at most one parent node by construction. If there is only a single maximal part, $\mathcal{G}$ is reduced to a tree. Figure 2 visualizes each level of a nesting tree. In the figure each connected component represents a single node. The nesting graph encodes topological nesting relations and complements the pairwise spatial relations defined in conventional pictorial structures.

2.1 Nested Features

We describe the visual content of each part using its histogram representation. Applicable descriptors include color histogram, histogram of oriented gradient

(HoG) [17], their possible concatenations and more. The difference is that the spatial extent of each part is inherently nested and the histogram needs to be modified accordingly. Let $h : \Omega \to \mathbb{Z}^L$ be a histogram of L bins calculated in the image region Ω. $h[i]$ is the number of occurrences of i in Ω and is nonnegative. Histograms have an important property that for any $A, B \subseteq \Omega$:

$$h(A \cup B) = h(A) + h(B) - h(A \cap B) \tag{2}$$

A natural consequence is that for $A \subseteq B$,

$$h(B \setminus A) = h(B) - h(A) \tag{3}$$

The subtractive property of Equation (3) is important for computing the histogram of each part in the nested model. Let $C_v \triangleq \{W_u \mid (u, v) \in \mathcal{E}\}$ be the set of child windows of part v. We require that no two child windows overlap with each other, that is, $\bigcap S = \emptyset$ for any $S \subseteq C_v$. This constraint is imposed in the global matching of a pictorial structure (See Section 2.4 for details). The histogram of part v is therefore computed as:

$$h_v(W_v; C_v) \triangleq h(W_v) - \sum_{W \in C_v} h(W) \tag{4}$$

We normalize h_v to $\tilde{h}_v$ by dividing the area of part v:

$$\tilde{h}_v(W_v; C_v) = \frac{h_v(W_v; C_v)}{|W_v \setminus \bigcup C_v|} = \frac{h(W_v) - \sum_{W \in C_v} h(W)}{|W_v| - \sum_{W \in C_v} |W|} \tag{5}$$

so that $\sum_{l=1}^{L} \tilde{h}_v[l] = 1$. $\tilde{h}_v$ may be interpreted as a sample probability distribution (e.g. color distribution) of part v.

2.2 Data Cost

We score each nested part using a linear SVM classifier. Let α_v and β_v be the trained normal vector of the learnt classification boundary and the bias term respectively for part v. We define the data cost of part v as:

$$\varphi_v(W_v; C_v) = \left\langle \alpha_v, \tilde{h}_v(W_v; C_v) \right\rangle + \beta_v \tag{6}$$

Let $\lambda_v = |W_v| - \sum_{W \in C_v} |W|$ be the area of part v. We can further expand Equation (6) by substituting Equation (5):

$$\begin{aligned} \varphi_v(W_v; C_v) &= \frac{1}{\lambda_v} \left\langle \alpha_v, h(W_v) - \sum_{W \in C_v} h(W) \right\rangle + \beta_v \\ &= \frac{1}{\lambda_v} \langle \alpha_v, h(W_v) \rangle - \sum_{W \in C_v} \frac{1}{\lambda_v} \langle \alpha_v, h(W) \rangle + \beta_v \end{aligned} \tag{7}$$

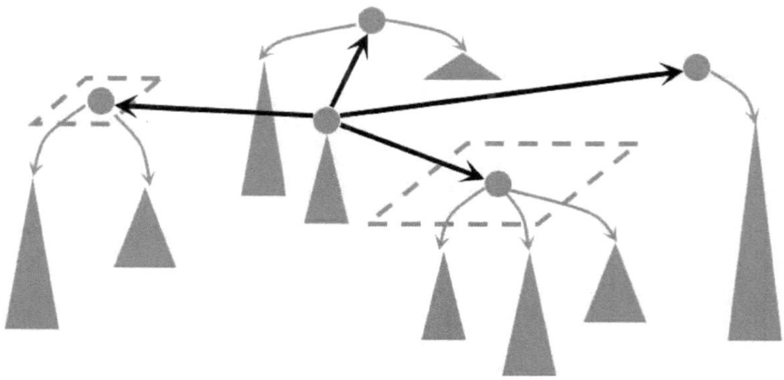

Fig. 3. Additional spatial constraints combine the nesting forest (red) and any spanning tree of the maximal parts (black)

The term $\frac{1}{\lambda_v}\langle\alpha_v, h(W)\rangle$ can be expanded as:

$$\frac{1}{\lambda_v}\langle\alpha_v, h(W)\rangle = \frac{1}{\lambda_v}\sum_{l=1}^{L}\alpha_v[l]h[i] = \sum_{p\in W}\frac{\alpha_v[l[p]]}{\lambda_v} \tag{8}$$

where $l[p]$ is the bin index of pixel p. This way of converting vector dot product to per-pixel computation is also presented in Lampert et al. [25]. We define:

$$\xi_v(p) = \frac{\alpha_v[l[p]]}{\lambda_v} \tag{9}$$

Then, Equation (7) can be rewritten as:

$$\varphi_v(W_v; C_v) = \sum_{p\in W_v}\xi_v(p) - \sum_{W\in C_v}\sum_{p\in W}\xi_v(p) + \beta_v \tag{10}$$

The total data cost of the window set $\{W_v\}_{v\in\mathcal{V}}$ is:

$$\begin{aligned}\varphi\left(\{W_v\}_{v\in\mathcal{V}}\right) &= \sum_{v\in\mathcal{V}}\varphi_v(W_v; C_v)\\ &= \sum_{v\in\mathcal{V}}\left[\underbrace{\sum_{p\in W_v}\xi_v(p)}_{f_v(W_v)} - \sum_{W\in C_v}\underbrace{\sum_{p\in W}\xi_v(p)}_{f_v(W)} + \beta_v\right]\\ &= \sum_{v\in\mathcal{V}}\left[f_v(W_v) - \sum_{W\in C_v}f_v(W)\right] + \text{const.}\end{aligned} \tag{11}$$

where $f_v(W)$ is the summation of all the pixel costs ξ_v within W. We remark that $f_v(W)$ can be evaluated in $O(1)$ time by the use of an integral image

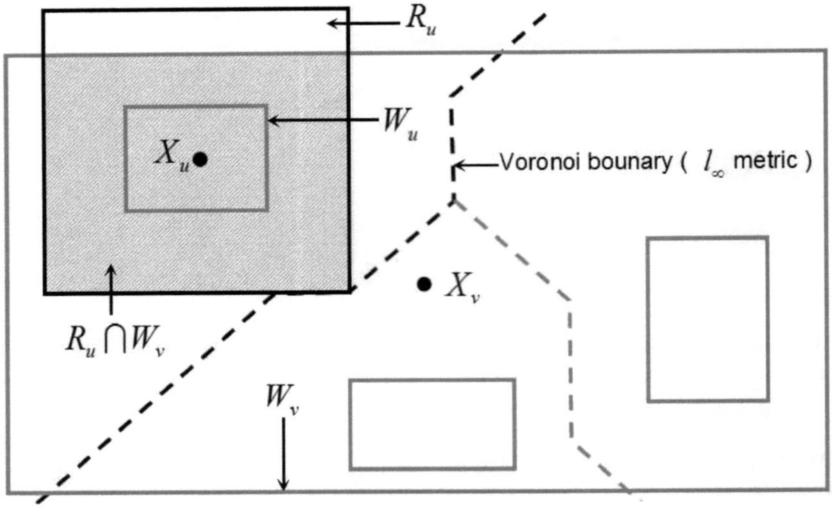

Fig. 4. The shaded region is the intersection of W_v and R_u. W_u is allowed to drift within the shaded region only. Note that the region does not assume a fixed position. It moves with the parent window W_v during deformable template matching.

representation. The constant numbers can be safely removed because they have no effect on the global minimization.

2.3 Deformation Cost

We also model the typical arrangement of a nested pictorial structure. Similar to [13] we connect nested parts by conceptual springs in a tree configuration. In fact, the nesting forest can be directly used for specifying the tree configuration. More spatial constraints are allowed if there are multiple maximal parts. Let $\mathcal{E}'$ be any spanning tree (e.g. minimal spanning tree) of the set of maximal parts. Then, the edge set $\mathcal{E}' \cup \mathcal{E}$ remains a directed tree (Figure 3). Any maximal part can serve as a root node. The deformation cost of a set of windows $\{W_v\}_{v \in \mathcal{V}}$ is:

$$\delta(\{W_v\}_{v\in\mathcal{V}}) = \sum_{(u,v)\in\mathcal{E}\cup\mathcal{E}'} \sum_{(u,v)\in\mathcal{E}\cup\mathcal{E}'} \underbrace{| \, \|(X_u - X_v) - (T_u - T_v)\|_1 \, |}_{\delta(W_u, W_v)} \tag{12}$$

where X_u and X_v are the 2D centroid of W_u and W_v. $T_u - T_v$ is the given template vector linking part u to part v. In the definition we use the L_1 norm although other metrics such as squared Euclidean [3] or its truncation apply equally well and enjoy the same computational complexity.

2.4 Non-Overlapping Constraints

It is important to constrain child parts so as not to overlap, in order to maintain the validity of Equation (4) and to avoid the degeneracies of parts collapsing into a single region. This non-overlapping constraint is also new in the context of pictorial structures. To quantify the range each part is allowed to deform without overlapping, we compute the distance transform spanned by parts' windows under the l_∞ norm in the template image[1]. The rectangle (centered at X_u) that first touches Voronoi boundaries within the Voronoi region of X_u thus bounds the maximal free space of W_u. Let this rectangle be R_u. The non-overlapping constraint can be expressed as $W_u \subseteq R_u$. Note that R_u and W_u share the same centroid by construction. Moreover, since the nesting relation is $W_u \subset W_v$, we can combine both nesting and non-overlapping constraints into a single constraint: $W_u \subseteq R_u \cap W_v$. See Figure 4 for illustration.

2.5 Global Optimization

The inputs to the optimization are: a nesting forest $\mathcal{G} = \langle \mathcal{V}, \mathcal{E} \rangle$, the template vectors $\{T_u\}_{u \in \mathcal{V}}$, the cost functions $\{f_u\}_{u \in \mathcal{V}}$, the spanning tree among maximal parts $\mathcal{E}'$, the range constraints $\{R_u\}_{u \in \mathcal{V}}$ and a regularization parameter λ. The optimal allocation of a nested pictorial structure is:

$$\min_{W_u \subseteq R_u \cap W_v \text{ for each } (u,v) \in \mathcal{E}} \left\{ \sum_{u \in \mathcal{V}} \left[f_u(W_u) - \sum_{W \in C_u} f_u(W) \right] + \lambda \sum_{(u,v) \in \mathcal{E} \cup \mathcal{E}'} \underbrace{\|(X_u - X_v) - (T_u - T_v)\|_1}_{\delta(W_u, W_v)} \right\} \tag{13}$$

The nested pictorial structure is reduced to the conventional one when $f_v = f_u$ for each $(u, v) \in \mathcal{E}$ and when no nesting or overlapping constraints are imposed. In general, the nested model extends the conventional pictorial structure by ensuring that parts conform to a nesting forest and child parts do not overlap in their geometric arrangement.

3 Dynamic Programming

We show that the objective in Equation (13) can be computed in $O(NK)$ time using dynamic programming and a technique called constrained distance transform. Here N is the image size and K is the number of nested parts. Let $O_u(W_u)$ be the optimal cost when part u is placed at window W_u. Then, for each parent node p we derive the following recursive state equation:

[1] In MATLAB, this is easily achieved by the command bwdist(I,'chessboard'). The distance transform is linear in the image size.

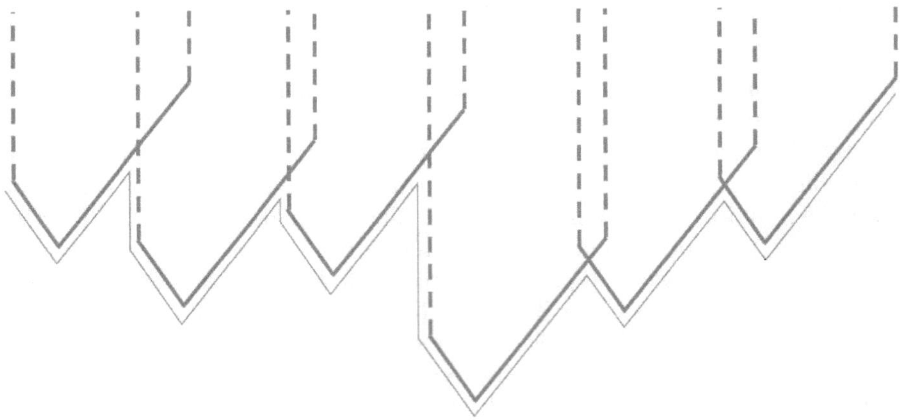

Fig. 5. The lower envelope of cones with sides beyond a range lifted to infinity

$$\Delta_p^c(W_p) = \min_{W_c \subseteq W_p \cap R_c} \{O_c(W_c) - f_p(W_c) + \lambda\delta(W_c, W_p)\} \tag{14}$$

$$F_p^c(W_p) = \min_{W_c} \left\{ O_c(W_c) + \lambda \underbrace{\|(X_p - X_c) - (T_p - T_c)\|}_{\delta(W_c, W_p)} \right\} \tag{15}$$

$$O_p(W_p) = f_p(W_p) + \sum_{c:(c,p)\in\mathcal{E}} \Delta_p^c(W_p) + \sum_{c:(c,p)\in\mathcal{E}'} F_p^c(W_p) \tag{16}$$

Equation (15) can be evaluated in $O(N)$ thanks to the generalized distance transform [3]. Equation (14) can be solved in $O(N)$ time too. Let (x_c, y_c), (x_p, y_p) be the centroid of W_c and W_p. The constraint $W_c \subseteq R_c \cap W_p$ can be conveniently expressed by $B \leq x_c - x_p \leq A$ and $C \leq y_c - y_p \leq D$ where A, B, C, D are constants determined by the size of W_c, R_c and W_p (Figure 4). Equation (14) is equivalent to the following 2D constrained distance transform:

$$g(x, y) = \min_{A \leq x' - x \leq B, C \leq y' - y \leq D} \{f(x', y') + \lambda [|x' - x - E| + |y - y' - F|]\} \tag{17}$$

where E and F are constants. Geometrically the transform is equivalent to the lower envelope of cones with asymmetric sides. The 1D version is shown in Figure 5. Similar to the generalized distance transform of Felzenszwalb and Huttonlocher [3], it is easy to show that 2D constrained distance transform can be computed in $O(N)$ time as well. Therefore, the optimal matching of a nested pictorial structure of K parts takes $O(KN)$ time.

4 Proof of Concept

We demonstrate the usefulness of the proposed nested pictorial structure in localizing highly complex patterns, objects being occluded, and objects in a

Fig. 6. Example matching of nested pictorial structures. We select 12 categories of images from Caltech256, see [26]. Each category is divided into separate sets for training and testing. In the training step, we ask a user to mark a number of nested rectangular windows on each training image, and a linear SVM classifier is trained for each category from both positive and negative samples using nested feature descriptors. The feature descriptor of each part is a concatenation of histogram of gradients and colors in that part, excluding histograms associated to any child parts. In the matching step, the normal vector derived from the trained linear SVM classifier is used to obtain the per-pixel cost of Equation (9). The matching is performed on images from the test set for each category. Similar to the recognition framework of Felzenszwalb et al. [13], we build an image pyramid of 10 levels ranging from twice the size of the original image to half of the original image size. Matching a nested pictorial structure is then performed on each derived image and the one that receives the minimal cost is selected and reshaped back. In some images the rectangles are attached to a single object. In others the rectangles include multiple objects and their surrounding context (e.g. clown fish and anemone, the Sphinx and pyramid, etc).

context. We use a linear SVM as the underlying classifier for training and the testing is similar to what is used in the recognition system of Felzenszwalb et al.[13]. Sample results from the 12 categories of [26] are shown in Figure 6. Some natural applications are: Finding a scene where A is in front of B or Finding an object of particular nested patterns. For instance, we choose the example of matching a surfer against the water, and a clown fish nested in a sea anemone. Our method is also expected to be useful for matching animal or human faces where the nested features are able to separate features associated to eyes, nose, mouth, and features associated to the skin and hair, and other fine scene characteristics. In our MATLAB/MEX implementation it takes less than 0.1 seconds to do the matching in a 400×400 image when the number of parts is less than 10. The running time grows linearly with the number of image pixels and the number of object parts, both asymptotically and experimentally.

5 Conclusions

Nested pictorial structure finds a part arrangement that is flexible in spatial configuration, but confined to be nested accordingly. Moreover, we define nested features which lend themselves to better accounting of pixel data cost, where a sliding window technique may likely over-count. We develop an $O(NK)$ algorithm for the optimal matching of a nested pictorial structure of K parts on an image of N pixels.

Promising but anecdotal results are shown. Many questions remain open. For instance, it is not clear how to automatically construct a reasonable nesting relation from training data. The current nesting relation has to be specified manually in the training data and is therefore difficult for large scale annotation. A deeper study of matching nested patterns is expected to be useful for applications in general recognition, tracking, and instance based query systems.

Acknowledgement: This work is supported by the Army Research Office under Grant No. W911NF-10-1-0387 and by the National Science Foundation under Grant IIS-10-17017.

References

1. Fischler, M., Elschlager, R.: The representation and matching of pictorial structures 22, 67–92 (1973)
2. Felzenszwalb, P., Huttenlocher, D.: Pictorial structures for object recognition. IJCV 61, 55–79 (2005)
3. Felzenszwalb, P., Huttenlocher, D.: Distance transforms of sampled functions. Technical Report TR2004-1963, Cornell Computing and Information Science (2004)
4. Yuille, A., Hallinan, P., Cohen, D.: Feature extraction from faces using deformable templates. IJCV 8, 99–111 (1992)
5. Burl, M.C., Weber, M., Perona, P.: A Probabilistic Approach to Object Recognition Using Local Photometry and Global Geometry. In: Burkhardt, H., Neumann, B. (eds.) ECCV 1998. LNCS, vol. 1407, pp. 628–641. Springer, Heidelberg (1998)

6. Weber, M., Welling, M., Perona, P.: Towards automatic discovery of object categories. In: CVPR, pp. 2101–2108 (2000)
7. Coughlan, J., Yuille, A., English, C., Snow, D.: Efficient deformable template detection and localization without user initialization. Computer Vision and Image Understanding 78, 303–319 (2000)
8. Cootes, T., Edwards, G., Taylor, C.: Active appearance models. IEEE PAMI 23, 681–685 (2001)
9. Fergus, R., Perona, P., Zisserman, A.: Object class recognition by unsupervised scale-invariant learning. In: IEEE CVPR, pp. 264–271 (2003)
10. Crandall, D., Felzenszwalb, P., Huttenlocher, D.: Spatial priors for part-based recognition using statistical models. In: IEEE CVPR, pp. 10–17 (2005)
11. Amit, Y., Trouvé, A.: Pop: Patchwork of parts models for object recognition. IJCV 75, 267–282 (2007)
12. Leibe, B., Leonardis, A., Schiele, B.: Robust object detection with interleaved categorization and segmentation. IJCV 77, 259–289 (2008)
13. Felzenszwalb, P., Girshick, R., McAllester, D., Ramanan, D.: Object detection with discriminatively trained part-based models. IEEE PAMI 32, 1627–1645 (2010)
14. Zhu, L., Chen, Y., Yuille, A., Freeman, W.: Latent hierarchical structural learning for object detection. In: IEEE CVPR, pp. 1062–1069 (2010)
15. Pandey, M., Lazebnik, S.: Scene recognition and weakly supervised object localization with deformable part-based models. In: ICCV (2011)
16. Felzenszwalb, P., Huttenlocher, D.: Efficient matching of pictorial structures. In: IEEE CVPR, pp. 2066–2073 (2000)
17. Dalal, N., Triggs, B.: Histograms of oriented gradients for human detection. In: IEEE CVPR, pp. 886–893 (2005)
18. Everingham, M., Gool, L.V., Williams, C., Winn, J., Zisserman, A.: The PASCAL Visual Object Classes Challenge 2007 (VOC 2007) Results (2007), `http://www.pascal-network.org/challenges/VOC/voc2007/workshop/index.html`
19. Gao, T., Packer, B., Koller, D.: A segmentation-aware object detection model with occlusion handling. In: IEEE CVPR, pp. 1361–1368 (2011)
20. Sundberg, P., Brox, T., Maire, M., Arbelaez, P., Malik, J.: Occlusion boundary detection and figure/ground assignment from optical flow. In: IEEE CVPR, pp. 2233–2240 (2011)
21. Humayun, A., Aodha, O., Brostow, G.: Learning to find occlusion regions. In: IEEE CVPR, pp. 2161–2168 (2011)
22. Woodcock, C., Harward, V.: Nested-hierarchical scene models and image segmentation. Internal Journal of Remote Sensing 13 (1992)
23. Oliva, A., Torralba, A.: Modeling the shape of the scene: A holistic representation of the spatial envelope. IJCV 42, 145–175 (2001)
24. Li, L., Socher, R., Fei-Fei, L.: Towards total scene understanding: Classification, annotation and segmentation in an automatic framework. In: IEEE CVPR, pp. 2036–2043 (2009)
25. Lampert, C., Blaschko, M., Hofmann, T.: Efficient subwindow search: A branch and bound framework for object localization. IEEE PAMI 31, 2129–2142 (2009)
26. Griffin, G., Holub, A., Perona, P.: Caltech-256 object category dataset. Technical Report 7694, California Institute of Technology (2007)

Performance Capture of Interacting Characters with Handheld Kinects

Genzhi Ye[1], Yebin Liu[1], Nils Hasler[2], Xiangyang Ji[1], Qionghai Dai[1], and Christian Theobalt[2]

[1] Department of Automation, Tsinghua Univercity, Beijing, China
[2] Max-Planck Institute for Informatics, Saarbrücken, Germany

Abstract. We present an algorithm for marker-less performance capture of interacting humans using only three hand-held Kinect cameras. Our method reconstructs human skeletal poses, deforming surface geometry and camera poses for every time step of the depth video. Skeletal configurations and camera poses are found by solving a joint energy minimization problem which optimizes the alignment of RGBZ data from all cameras, as well as the alignment of human shape templates to the Kinect data. The energy function is based on a combination of geometric correspondence finding, implicit scene segmentation, and correspondence finding using image features. Only the combination of geometric and photometric correspondences and the integration of human pose and camera pose estimation enables reliable performance capture with only three sensors. As opposed to previous performance capture methods, our algorithm succeeds on general uncontrolled indoor scenes with potentially dynamic background, and it succeeds even if the cameras are moving.

1 Introduction

In recent years, the field of marker-less motion estimation has seen great progress. Two important lines of research have emerged in this domain. On the one side, there are multi-view motion capture approaches that reconstruct skeleton motion, and possibly simple body shape of people in skintight clothing from multi-view video, e.g., [1,2,3,4,5,6]. Even though measurement accuracy has greatly increased in the recent past, these approaches are still limited to largely controlled studio settings, and rely on static frame-synchronized multi-video systems comprising 10 or more cameras. Marker-less *performance capture* approaches take one step further and not only reconstruct a skeletal motion model but also detailed dynamic surface geometry as well as detailed texture, e.g. [7,8,9,10,11,12]. Unlike most skeletal motion capture methods, these approaches can also deal with people in general wide apparel. Recently, performance capture of multiple closely interacting people was also demonstrated [13]. However, performance capture approaches typically require even more strongly controlled studio setups, and often expect an even higher number of video cameras than marker-less motion capture approaches.

A. Fitzgibbon et al. (Eds.): ECCV 2012, Part II, LNCS 7573, pp. 828–841, 2012.

At the other end of the spectrum are methods for marker-less motion capture from a single camera view. Estimation of complex poses from a single video stream is still a very challenging task, in particular if interactive or real-time frame rates are the goal [6]. If additional depth data is available, e.g., obtained by stereo reconstruction, more complex poses and simple human shape representations can be fitted [14,15]. The recent advent of so-called depth cameras, such as time-of-flight sensors [16] and the Microsoft Kinect, has opened up new possibilities. These cameras measure 2.5D depth information at real-time frame rates and, as for the Kinect, video as well. This makes them ideal sensors for pose estimation, but they suffer from significant noise and have at best moderate resolution. Using some form of articulated ICP or body part detection, skeletal poses can be reconstructed from data captured with a single depth sensor [17,18,19]. With such a depth-based local pose optimization scheme, tracking errors more frequently occur due to erroneous local convergence. Monocular depth-based body tracking with improved accuracy at near-real-time is feasible by combination of pose optimization with body part detection [20]. An alternative to model-based pose estimation is real-time joint detection from depth data using a learned decision forest [21]. Recently, this approach has been augmented with a regression method to enable the algorithm to localize joints also under occlusions [22]. As opposed to the model-based pose fitting approaches, these detection methods do not deliver joint angles. To obtain the latter an additional inverse kinematics step is required. Recently it was shown that through a combination of model-based pose optimization with pose detection full joint angles of even complex poses can be captured [23], also at high real-time frame rates [24].

So far it has been difficult to capture 3D models of a complexity and detail comparable to multi-view performance capture results using just a single depth camera. Weiss et al. [25] show an approach to fit a parametric human body model to depth data from a Kinect. However, their method can only capture static models of people in skintight clothing, and the motion of the person is not captured. To capture more detailed performance models one would need more complete, ideally 360 degree, depth data showing the scene from all sides. Earlier work on multi-view image-based 3D reconstruction already hinted at this. These approaches reconstructed dynamic geometry models and skeletal motion models of good quality by fitting a body template to a sequence of shape-from-silhouette reconstructions [26,27,28]. Building up on these ideas from the video domain, Berger et al. [29] use several Kinects to capture simple skeletal body poses based on a shape template.

In this paper, we show a method to do full performance capture of moving humans using just three hand-held, and thus potentially moving, Kinect cameras. Without resorting to any markers in the scene, it reconstructs detailed time-varying surface geometry of humans in general apparel, as well as the motion of the underlying skeleton. It can handle fast and complex motion with many self-occlusions and also captures non-rigid surface deformation, e.g., due to cloth motion. By resorting to depth sensors, our algorithm can be applied to more general uncontrolled indoor scenes and is not limited to studios with controlled lighting and many stationary cameras. Also, our method requires only three hand-held sensors to produce results that rival reconstructions obtained with video-based performance capture methods that require a lot more cameras [13]. To enable this, we developed a method that **a)** tracks the motion of the hand-held cameras and aligns the RGBZ data, and **b)** that simultaneously aligns the surface and skeleton of each tracked performer to the captured RGBZ data. Our algorithm succeeds despite notable sensor noise, and is designed to be insensitive to multi-Kinect interference and occlusions in the scene. Our goal is thus related to the approach by Hasler et al. [30] which enables skeletal motion capture from hand-held video cameras. However, it goes beyond their method by being able to capture motion *and* non-rigid dynamic shape of more than one closely interacting performer from only three camera views.

Similar to the approach by Gall et al. [12] our algorithm deforms a template made of a skeleton and a deforming surface mesh for each performer into the captured RGBZ data. Our algorithm succeeds because of the interplay of several algorithmic contributions: We propose an efficient geometric 3D point-to-vertex assignment strategy to match the Kinect RGBZ data points to the geometric model of each performer. The assignment criterion is stable under missing data due to interference and occlusions between persons. Based on this criterion, a segmentation of the scene into performers, ground plane, and background is implicitly achieved. As a second correspondence criterion, we detect and track SIFT features in the background part of each video frame. Based on these model-to-data assignment criteria, we jointly estimate the pose parameters of the performers and the poses and orientations of the Kinects in a combined optimization framework. Our non-linear objective function can be linearized and effectively minimized through a quasi-Newton method. As we will show, the integration of geometry-based and video-based correspondence estimation is crucial in our setting, as only in this way combined reconstruction of human animation models and camera poses is feasible even in scenes with occlusions, notable sensor noise and moving background. We show results on several challenging single and multi- person motions including dance and martial arts. We also quantitatively prove the accuracy of our reconstruction method by comparing it to video-based performance capture.

2 Data Capture with Handheld Kinects

Our algorithm enables the reconstruction of detailed skeleton models of humans, as well as their deforming surface geometry, in general indoor environments. The method does not expect controlled, i.e., it can handle non-static background and general non-studio lighting. In a typical recording situation, one or more moving humans are recorded by $C = 3$ individuals (camera operators) that stand around the scene. Each of the operators holds a Kinect camera and points it towards the center of the recording volume, Fig. 1(a). Thee operators are free to move the cameras during recording, for instance to get a better view of the action with less occlusions. Our performance capture method can also handle a certain amount of moving scene elements in the background.

Fig. 1. Overview of the processing pipeline. (a) overhead view of typical recording setup: three camera operators (circled in red) film the moving people in the center (blue); (b) input to the algorithm - RGB images and the depth images from three views; (c) 2D illustration of geometric matching of Kinect points to model vertices (Sect. 4.2); (d) segmented RGBZ point cloud - color labels correspond to background, ground plane (green) and interacting humans (red,blue); (e) Registered RGBZ point cloud from all cameras; (f) reconstructed surface models and skeletons.

Exact hardware synchronization of multiple Kinects is impossible, and we thus resort to software synchronization. We connect each Kinect to a notebook computer, and all recording notebooks are connected through WiFi. One computer serves as a master that sends a *start recording* signal to all other computers. The cameras are set to a frame rate of 30fps and with our software solution the captured data of all cameras are frame-synchronized with at most 10ms temporal difference.

The Kinect features two sensors in the same housing, a RGB video camera and an active stereo system to capture depth. The intrinsics of both the depth and the video cameras are calibrated off-line using a checkerboard [31]. Depth and color data are aligned with each other using the OpenNI API[1]

At every time step of video t, each Kinect captures a 640×480 video frame and an aligned depth frame, Fig. 1(b), which yields a combined RGBZ point cloud. For each such RGBZ point p we store a triplet of values $p = \{x_p, n_p, l_p\}$. Here x_p is the 3D position of the point, n_p is the local 3D normal, and l_p is a RGB color triplet. The normal orientations are found by PCA-based plane fitting to local 3D point neighborhoods. Note that the 3D point locations are given with

[1] `http://www.openni.org/`.

respect to each camera's local coordinate system. For performance capture, we need to align the points from all cameras into a global system. Since the Kinects are allowed to move in our setting, we also need to solve for the extrinsic camera parameters Λ_c^t (position and orientation) of each Kinect c at every time step of video t, i.e., solve for the combined extrinsic set $\Lambda^t = \{\Lambda_c^t\}_{c=1}^C$. Fig.1(e) shows the merged point set at time t after solving for the extrinsics using the method later described in this paper. Also, due to occlusions in the scene and interference between several Kinects, 3D points corresponding to some Kinect camera pixels cannot reliably be reconstructed. The joint camera tracking and performance capture method thus needs to be robust against such missing measurements.

3 Scene Models

For each of the $k = 1, \ldots, K$ performers in the scene, a template model is defined. Similar to [12,13] a template model comprises a surface mesh M_k with an embedded kinematic bone skeleton (see Fig. 1(f)). Similar to other model-based performance capture work, we use a laser scanner to get a static surface mesh of the person. Alternatively, image-based reconstruction methods could be used or the mesh could be reconstructed from the aligned Kinect data. We remesh the surface models, such that they have around $N_k = 5000$ vertices. Each vertex is also assigned a color that can change over time as described in Sec. 4.5. Henceforth, the 3D positions of vertices of mesh k with attached colors at time t are denoted by the set $V_k^t = \{v_{k,i}^t\}_{i=1}^{N_k}$. To stabilize simultaneous 3D human shape and Kinect position tracking, we also explicitly model the ground plane as a planar mesh V_0^t with circular boundary. The ground plane model has a fixed radius of 3m and during initialization is centered below the combined center of gravity of the human models (see Fig.1(d)). In total, this yields a combined set of vertex positions $V^t = \{\{V_k^t\}_{k=0}^K\}$ that need to be reconstructed at each time step. This excludes the ground plane vertices as their position is fixed in world space. Its apparent motion is modeled by moving the cameras.

A kinematic skeleton with $n = 31$ degrees of freedom is manually placed into each human mesh and surface skinning weighs are computed using a similar process as [12,13]. Skeleton poses $\chi^t = (\xi^t, \Theta^t) = \left(\theta_0\hat{\xi}, \theta_1, ..., \theta_n\right)$ are parameterized using the twist and exponential maps parameterization [2,12]. $\theta_0\hat{\xi}$ is the twist for the global rigid body transform of the skeleton and Θ^t is the vector of the remaining joint angles. Using linear blend skinning, the configuration of a vertex of human mesh M_k in skeleton pose χ_k^t is then determined by

$$v_i\left(\chi_k^t\right) = \sum_{m=1}^{n} \left(w_i^m \prod_{j=0}^{j_m} \exp\left(\theta_{\psi_m(j)}\hat{\xi}_{\psi_m(j)}\right)\right) v_i. \quad (1)$$

Here, w_i^m is the skinning weight of vertex i with respect to bone m. Further on, j_m is the number of joints in the kinematic chain that influence bone b_m, and $\psi_m(j)$ determines the index of the jth of these joints in the overall skeleton configuration. In addition to $\Lambda^t = \{\Lambda_c^t\}_{c=1}^C$, our performance capture approach thus needs to solve for the joint parameters of all persons at each time step, $\mathrm{X}^t = \{\chi_k^t\}_{k=1}^K$.

4 Simultaneous Performance Capture and Kinect Tracking

Performance capture from 3D point data is only feasible if the RGBZ data from all Kinects are correctly registered. In the beginning, for each time step the correct extrinsics Λ_t are unknown. A traditional approach to track camera extrinsics is structure-from-motion (SfM) performed on the background of the sequence [30]. However, in our recording setting, the moving subjects fill most of the visible area in each video frame. Thus a different approach has to be used. In our setting human pose capture and camera pose estimation are performed simultaneously, leading to more robust results. In other words, the optimization tries to mutually align all point clouds and fit the poses of the actors to the RGBZ data. At the same time, we exploit feature correspondences in the background similarly to SfM since they provide addtional evidence for correct reconstruction. We therefore simultaneously solve for camera and body poses, and regularize the solution to additional feature correspondences found in the video frame.

4.1 Overview

In the first frame of multi-view RGBZ video, camera extrinsics are initialized interactively and the template models are fitted to each person's depth map. The initialization pose in the data sequence is guaranteed to be close to the scanned pose. Thereafter, the algorithm runs in a frame-by-frame manner applying the processing pipeline from Fig. 1(c-f) to each time step. For a time step t the steps are as follows: we first align the Kinect RGBZ point clouds according to the the extrinsics Λ^{t-1} from the previous frame. Starting with the pose parameters X^{t-1} and resulting mesh configurations and vertex colors from the previous frame, a matching algorithm is introduced to match the Kinect point data to the model vertices. During this matching, the RGBZ data are also implicitly segmented into classes for *ground plane*, *background* and one class for each *person*, Sect. 4.2 (Fig. 1(d)). Thereafter, a second set of 3D correspondences is found by matching points from the *ground plane* and the *background* via SIFT features, Sect. 4.3. Based on these correspondences, we simultaneously solve for Kinect and skeleton poses for the current frame, Sect. 4.4. Correspondence finding and reconstruction is iterated several times and the model poses and point cloud alignments are continuously updated (Fig. 1(e)). Non-rigid deformations of the human surface, e.g., due to cloth deformation are not explained by skeleton-driven deformation alone. In a final step we thus non-rigidly deform the meshes M_k into the aligned point clouds via Laplacian deformation and update the vertex colors of the mesh model(s) (Fig. 1(f)). In the following, we explain each step for a specific time t and omit the index t for legibility.

4.2 3D Point Correspondences and Implicit RGBZ Point Cloud Segmentation

As stated above, for finding correct camera and body configurations, we will minimize an error function that measures the alignment of the RGBZ point clouds with the 3D human models, Sect. 4.4. To evaluate this error, for all scene model vertices V, plausible correspondences to the RGBZ points P need to be defined. With these correspondences, we would be able to evaluate an alignment error, as it was also used in video-based performance capture to measure alignment in the image domain [12].

Our matching term ensures that as much as possible of each 3D human template is explained by the point data. Unfortunately, due to mutual occlusions, the Kinect point cloud P will not always sample every part of the body surfaces. Additionally, interference between several Kinects renders some 3D points unreliable. That is, in this scenario, matching model vertices V to Kinect point clouds P tends to be unstable. In contrast, reverse matching is much more robust since all the foreground points physically exist and in theory can all be explained by the model surface, although there is noise and outliers in the captured data. Thus, the closest mesh vertices for all RGBZ points are proposed as matches. Our results show that using this approach tracking is robust even with two performers in the scene.

To this end, we define a distance measure F between Kinect points p and model vertices v that simultaneously measures a color distance and a geometric distance as follows:

$$F\left(v,p\right)=\Delta\left(\left\|l_v-l_p\right\|,\theta_l\right)\Delta\left(\left\|x_v-x_p\right\|,\theta_x\right)\max\left(n_vn_p,0\right) \tag{2}$$

where

$$\Delta\left(x,\theta\right)=\max\left(1-\frac{x}{\theta},0\right) \tag{3}$$

Here, x_p, l_p, n_p and x_v, l_v, n_v denote the position, color, and normal of a Kinect point and a mesh vertex, respectively. The color term enforces color similarity between the mesh vertex and the corresponding Kinect point, the geometry term only matches RGBZ points and vertices that are spatially close and have similar normal orientation. We experimentally choose the maximum color difference $\theta_l = 100$ and the maximum distance a mesh vertex is allowed to move $\theta_x = 100mm$.

For each point p, we first select the vertex v from V to maximize F. If the maximum $F > 0$, according to the label of v, we classify the correspondence (p, v) into a person correspondence set Z_{pv}^k of person k, or into the ground plane correspondence set Z_{pg}. After the correspondences $Z_{pv} = \{Z_{pv}^k\}_{k=1}^K$ and Z_{pg} are established, the RGBZ point cloud is thus implicitly segmented into one class for each *person*, *ground plane*, and *background* for all RGBZ points that were not assigned a corresponding point in V.

4.3 Feature-Based Background Correspondences

As stated in the beginning, our reconstruction error is also based on feature correspondences in the scene background, similar to classical structure-from-motion approaches. The method from Sect. 4.2 provides a classification of background RGBZ points, and thus corresponding RGB pixels in each Kinect video image. We detect SIFT features on the background regions of the RGB images from $t-1$ and t, and convert them into 3D correspondences $Z_s = \{(p', p)\} \mid p' \in P^{t-1}, p \in P^t, (p', p)$ matched via SIFT$\}$ through the available depth. As stated earlier, background correspondences are not always fully-reliable. Measurement accuracy decreases with increasing distance from the camera, and moving objects in the background lead to erroneous correspondences. Thus our error function additionally measures point-to-model correspondences in the foreground. Fig.2(b) shows that alignment based on SIFT features in the background alone will not suffice.

4.4 Optimization of Skeleton and Camera Poses

Given correspondence sets Z_{pv}, Z_{pg}, and Z_s we can define a geometric error function that we minimize in the space of skeleton pose X and camera extrinsics Λ:

$$E(\mathrm{X}, \Lambda) = \underset{\mathrm{X},\Lambda}{\arg\min} \left\{ \sum_{(p,v)\in Z_{pv}} \frac{\|p(\Lambda) - v(\mathrm{X})\|^2}{\|Z_{pv}\|} + \sum_{(p,v)\in Z_{pg}} \frac{\|p(\Lambda) - v\|^2}{\|Z_{pg}\|} + \sum_{(p,p')\in Z_s} \frac{\left\|p(\Lambda) - p'\right\|^2}{\|Z_s\|} \right\} \quad (4)$$

Here $||Z||$ is the number of elements in set Z. We solve this function through linearization within an iterative quasi-Newton minimization. Using Taylor expansion of the exponential map, the transformation of Λ on point p leads to

$$p(\Lambda) = Rp + T = e^{\theta\hat{\xi}}p \approx \left(I + \theta\hat{\xi}\right)p \quad (5)$$

For the body pose a similar expansion can be performed.

We iterate robust correspondence finding and skeleton-camera optimization 20 times. After each iteration, the position and normal of each point p is updated according to the new Λ, while the skeletons and model vertices are updated according to X. Fig.2 shows the comparison of the fused data before pose optimization (a) and after pose optimization (c). Please note that even using state-of-the-art techniques, direct fusion of the point data without the aid of a 3D model is extremely difficult and error prone because of the small overlap region between the different Kinects [32].

4.5 Non-rigid Mesh Deformation and Vertex Color Update

After tracking and skinned deformation of the skeleton-driven model of each character, mesh deformation is performed to refine the surface geometry of the performers and capture non-rigid deformation effects, such as cloth motion. Similar to [8], for each person k, surface deformation is formulated as:

$$\underset{\mathbf{v}}{\arg\min}\{\|L\mathbf{v} - \delta\|_2^2 + \|\mathbf{C}\mathbf{v} - \mathbf{p}\|_2^2\} \quad (6)$$

Here, $\mathbf{v}$ denotes the vector of vertices on human body mesh M_k. L is the cotangent Laplacian matrix and δ is the differential coordinates of the current mesh

Fig. 2. Comparison of RGBZ point data fusion at frame t before and after joint skeleton and Kinect optimization. (a) Fusion using extrinsics from the former time; (b) Fusion based on SIFT features alone fails; (c) Fusion using extrinsics solved by the combined human and camera pose optimization produces much better results.

vertices. C is a diagonal matrix with non-zero entries $c_{jj} = \alpha$ (α=0.1) for vertices in correspondence set Z_{pv}^k. $\mathbf{p}$ is the vector with non-zero position entries for those p in Z_{pv}^k. After non-rigid mesh deformation, the color of each vertex is updated according to a linear interpolation between the previous color and the current color using

$$l_v = \frac{t}{t+1}\widehat{l}_v + \frac{1}{t+1} l_{nn} \tag{7}$$

where $\hat{l}_v$ is the color of v before the update and l_{nn} is the color of the nearest RGBZ neighbor point of v.

5 Results

We recorded 8 test sequences consisting of over 2500 frames. The data was recorded with 3 moving Kinects at a resolution of 640×480 pixels and at a framerate of 30fps. The sequences consist of a wide range of different motions, including dancing, fighting and jumping, see Fig. 5 and the accompanying video. The motions were performed by 5 different persons wearing casual clothing. We also recorded two evaluation sequences where the performer was simultaneously tracked by a multi-view video system. A quantitative evaluation using these data sets is performed in Sect. 5.1. Table 1 shows the capture properties of each sequence.

5.1 Comparison with Multi-view Video Based Tracking

We recorded two sequences captured in a multi-view video studio with 10 calibrated cameras (15fps, 1024×768) and background green screen. The Kinect data were temporally aligned to the multi-view video data at frame-level accuracy using event synchronization. Although the synchronization of the video camera system and the Kinect system is not guaranteed at sub-frame accuracy,

Table 1. Description of the capture sequences

Sequence	Frame rate	Number of performers (K)	Number of Kinects (C)	Kinect status	Comparison with multi-view video
Dancing-walk	30	1	3	Moving	No
Kungfu	30	1	3	Moving	No
Couple-dance	30	2	3	Moving	No
Fight	30	2	3	Moving	No
Hug	30	2	3	Moving	No
Arm-crossing	30	1	3	Static	No
Rolling	15	1	3	Static	Yes
Jump	15	1	3	Static	Yes

the evaluation of the difference between the two results will still give us a conservative performance evaluation of the proposed algorithm.

Since our multi-view video system runs at 15fps, we captured a sequence "Rolling" with slow motion and a sequence "Jump" with fast motion. The Kinect system runs at 30fps, so we subsample the frames for the Kinect based tracking by factor two and compare the performance with multi-view video based tracking (MVT) [12]. We visually compared the results of the two systems by evenly select 4 frames from the "Rolling" sequence (see Fig. 3). Since the MVT tracking requires green screen for clean background subtraction and it thus does not work with extra camera operators in the scene background, we fix the three Kinects in the MVT studio during data capture. With these fixed Kinects, we can validate the proposed algorithm by comparing the optimized Kinect extrinsics in the later frames with that of the first frame. The average distance from the Kinect center in the first frame to the Kinect center of other frames (both "Rolling" and "Jump") for each of the Kinects are 10.66mm, 7.28mm and 6.67mm, respectively. For the slow motion sequence "Rolling", our result closely matches the input images and the result of the MVT system, see Fig. 3. In addition, we quantitatively compare the two results by measuring the differences on the joint centers. The average distance between the corresponding joint positions across all 200 frames of the sequence is 21.42mm with a standard deviation of 27.49mm. This distance also includes the synchronization differences between the two systems. For the fast motion sequences, the MVT even fails despite a much higher number of cameras, while the Kinect based tracking is able to track the whole sequence, see Fig.4.

5.2 Qualitative Evaluation

Our approach enables us to fully-automatically reconstruct skeletal pose and shape of two persons, even if they are as closely interacting as in martial arts fight, hug or while dancing, see Fig. 5 and the accompanying video. Despite notable noise in the captured depth maps, our method successfully captures pose and deforming surface geometry of persons in loose apparel. With a cap-

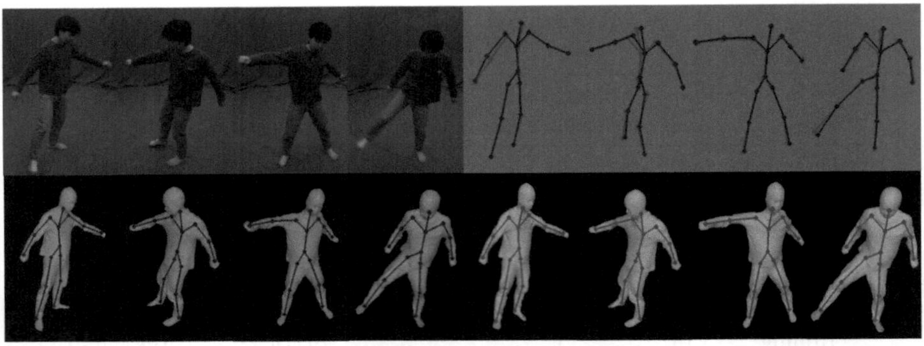

Fig. 3. Comparison with multi-view video tracking (MVT) approach on the "Rolling" sequence. The top left are four input images of the multi-view video sequence. The top right shows the close overlap of the two skeletons tracked with MVT (blue) and our Kinect-based approach (red). The bottom left is the reconstructed surface with the skeleton using MVT and the bottom right is the results from our approach. Quantitative and visual comparisons show that MVT-based and Kinect-based reconstructions are very similar.

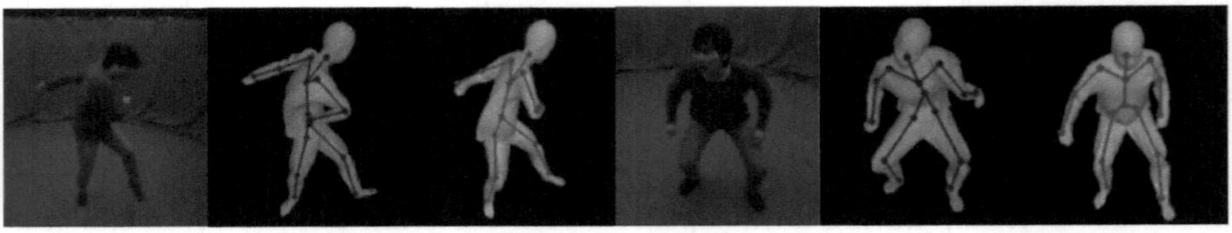

Fig. 4. Comparison with multi-view video tracking (MVT) approach on the "Jump" sequence. The left three and the right three are: input image, result of MVT, result of our Kinect-based approach. On this fast motion Kinect-based tracking succeeds while MVT fails to capture the arm motion.

turing frame rate of only 30fps, the proposed approach can also handle very fast motions, see the jump and kicking motions in Fig. 5. Our system uses local optimization and the complexity of the system mainly depends on the number of captured points. Computational complexity does not starkly depend on the number of subjects in the scene. It takes about 10 seconds for single person tracking of a frame and 12 seconds for the two person tracking on a standard PC using unoptimized code.

5.3 Discussion

We presented a method to capture shape and skeletal motion of one or two characters in fast motion using three handheld depth cameras. Reconstruction accuracy and quality is comparable to multi-view video-based approaches, but our method comes with the additional benefit that it applies also to less controlled

Fig. 5. Performance capture results on a variety of sequences: input image, deformed mesh overlay, and 3D model with estimated skeleton respectively

indoor environments. A key element to the method's success is the integrated estimation of camera and model poses based on geometric and photometric correspondences (see also Fig. 2).

Currently, our approach is designed for setup with multiple synchronized Kinects. An extension to un-synchronized handheld Kinects is feasible and will be investigated in the future. Currently, we do not explicity filter sensor noise and we do not explicitly model multi-Kinect interferences. We will further investigate this in the future. Since the Kinect data is noisy, the mesh deformation is not as effective as the one used in multi-view video systems for the reconstruction of surface details. Noise in the data may thus transfer into the capture meshes. The correspondence finding is implemented as a dense matching between measured points and vertices. More robust deformation in the presence of noise may be achieved by a noise-aware sparse matching algorithm. Similar to multi-view video systems, the tracking of joints on the shoulder may sometimes go error for fast and complex hand motions (e.g., "couple-dancing" sequence in the accompany video). This problem can be solved by adding physical constraints on the shoulders. Since skeleton and Kinect pose optimization can be linearized efficiently, it is also promising to investigate realtime applications in the future. We believe that with the advancement of depth camera techniques, improvement of sensor resolution, sensor quality, portability, and compatibility (between Kinects) will be achieved to allow the efficient production of 3D content in everyday life.

6 Conclusion

In this paper, we proposed a method for simultaneously marker-less performance capture and camera pose estimation with several hand-held Kinects. The tracking approach is based on iterating robust matching of the tracked 3D models and the input Kinect data and a quasi-Newton optimization on Kinect poses and skeleton poses. This joint optimization enables us to reliably and accurately capture shape and pose of multiple performers. The proposed technique removes the common constraint in traditional multi-view motion capture systems that cameras have to be static and scenes need to be filmed in controlled studio settings. Instead, we allow users to hold the Kinects for motion capture and 3D reconstruction of performers. This improves the consumer experience especially with respect to the anticipated introduction of depth cameras in consumer devices like tablets. To our knowledge, this is the first method to fully-automatically perform multi-person performance capture using moving Kinects.

Acknowledgments. This work was supported by the National Basic Research Project (No.2010CB731800) and the Project of NSFC (No.60933006 and No.61073072).

References

1. Deutscher, J., Blake, A., Reid, I.: Articulated body motion capture by annealed particle filtering. In: CVPR, pp. 1144–1149 (2000)
2. Bregler, C., Malik, J., Pullen, K.: Twist based acquisition and tracking of animal and human kinematics. IJCV 56, 179–194 (2004)
3. Sigal, L., Black, M.: Humaneva: Synchronized video and motion capture dataset for evaluation of articulated human motion. Technical Report CS-06-08, Brown University (2006)
4. Balan, A., Sigal, L., Black, M., Davis, J., Haussecker, H.: Detailed human shape and pose from images. In: CVPR (2007)
5. Stoll, C., Hasler, N., Gall, J., Seidel, H.P., Theobalt, C.: Fast articulated motion tracking using a sums of gaussians body model. In: ICCV, pp. 951–958 (2011)
6. Poppe, R.: Vision-based human motion analysis: An overview. CVIU 108, 4–18 (2007)
7. Vlasic, D., Baran, I., Matusik, W., Popović, J.: Articulated mesh animation from multi-view silhouettes. ACM Trans. Graph. 27, 1–9 (2008)
8. De Aguiar, E., Stoll, C., Theobalt, C., Ahmed, N., Seidel, H., Thrun, S.: Performance capture from sparse multi-view video. In: ACM Transactions on Graphics (TOG), vol. 27, Article 98. ACM (2008)
9. Ballan, L., Cortelazzo, G.: Marker-less motion capture of skinned models in a four camera set-up using optical flow and silhouettes. In: 3DPVT (2008)
10. Cagniart, C., Boyer, E., Ilic, S.: Free-form mesh tracking: A patch-based approach. In: CVPR, pp. 1339–1346 (2010)

11. Starck, J., Hilton, A.: Surface capture for performance based animation. IEEE Computer Graphics and Applications 27(3), 21–31 (2007)
12. Gall, J., Stoll, C., De Aguiar, E., Theobalt, C., Rosenhahn, B., Seidel, H.: Motion capture using joint skeleton tracking and surface estimation. In: CVPR, pp. 1746–1753 (2009)
13. Liu, Y., Stoll, C., Gall, J., Seidel, H.P., Theobalt, C.: Markerless motion capture of interacting characters using multi-view image segmentation. In: CVPR, pp. 1249–1256 (2011)
14. Friborg, R., Hauberg, S., Erleben, K.: GPU accelerated likelihoods for stereo-based articulated tracking. In: ECCV Workshops, CVGPU (2010)
15. Plankers, R., Fua, P.: Articulated soft objects for multiview shape and motion capture. TPAMI 25, 1182–1187 (2003)
16. Kolb, A., Barth, E., Koch, R., Larsen, R.: Time-of-flight cameras in computer graphics. Comput. Graph. Forum 29, 141–159 (2010)
17. Knoop, S., Vacek, S., Dillmann, R.: Fusion of 2D and 3D sensor data for articulated body tracking. Robotics and Autonomous Systems 57, 321–329 (2009)
18. Zhu, Y., Dariush, B., Fujimura, K.: Kinematic self retargeting: A framework for human pose estimation. CVIU 114, 1362–1375 (2010)
19. Pekelny, Y., Gotsman, C.: Articulated object reconstruction and markerless motion capture from depth video. CGF 27, 399–408 (2008)
20. Ganapathi, V., Plagemann, C., Koller, D., Thrun, S.: Real time motion capture using a single time-of-flight camera. In: CVPR, pp. 755–762 (2010)
21. Shotton, J., Fitzgibbon, A.W., Cook, M., Sharp, T., Finocchio, M., Moore, R., Kipman, A., Blake, A.: Real-time human pose recognition in parts from single depth images. In: CVPR, pp. 1297–1304 (2011)
22. Girshick, R., Shotton, A., Kohli, P., Criminisi, A., Fitzgibbon, A.: Efficient regression of general-activity human poses from depth images. In: ICCV (2011)
23. Ye, M., Wang, X., Yang, R., Ren, L., Pollefeys, M.: Accurate 3d pose estimation from a single depth image. In: ICCV, pp. 731–738 (2011)
24. Baak, A., Müller, M., Bharaj, G., Seidel, H.P., Theobalt, C.: A data-driven approach for real-time full body pose reconstruction from a depth camera. In: ICCV, pp. 1092–1099 (2011)
25. Weiss, A., Hirshberg, D., Black, M.J.: Home 3d body scans from noisy image and range data. In: ICCV, pp. 1951–1958 (2011)
26. Cheung, K., Kanade, T., Bouguet, J.Y., Holler, M.: A real time system for robust 3D voxel reconstruction of human motions. In: CVPR, pp. 714–720 (2000)
27. Horaud, R., Niskanen, M., Dewaele, G., Boyer, E.: Human motion tracking by registering an articulated surface to 3d points and normals. TPAMI 31, 158–163 (2009)
28. Corazza, S., Mündermann, L., Gambaretto, E., Ferrigno, G., Andriacchi, T.P.: Markerless motion capture through visual hull, articulated icp and subject specific model generation. IJCV 87, 156–169 (2010)
29. Berger, K., Ruhl, K., Schroeder, Y., Bruemmer, C., Scholz, A., Magnor, M.A.: Markerless motion capture using multiple color-depth sensors. In: VMV, pp. 317–324 (2011)
30. Hasler, N., Rosenhahn, B., Thormählen, T., Wand, M., Gall, J., Seidel, H.P.: Markerless motion capture with unsynchronized moving cameras. In: CVPR, pp. 224–231 (2009)
31. Bouguet, J.Y.: (Camera calibration toolbox for matlab)
32. Aiger, D., Mitra, N.J., Cohen-Or, D.: 4-points congruent sets for robust surface registration. ACM Transactions on Graphics 27, #85, 1–10 (2008)

Dynamic Eye Movement Datasets and Learnt Saliency Models for Visual Action Recognition

Stefan Mathe[1,3] and Cristian Sminchisescu[2,1]

[1] Institute of Mathematics of the Romanian Academy (IMAR)
[2] Faculty of Mathematics and Natural Science, University of Bonn, Germany
[3] Department of Computer Science, University of Toronto, Canada

Abstract. Systems based on bag-of-words models operating on image features collected at maxima of sparse interest point operators have been extremely successful for both computer-based visual object and action recognition tasks. While the sparse, interest-point based approach to recognition is not inconsistent with visual processing in biological systems that operate in "saccade and fixate" regimes, the knowledge, methodology, and emphasis in the human and the computer vision communities remains sharply distinct. Here, we make three contributions aiming to bridge this gap. First, we complement existing state-of-the art large-scale dynamic computer vision datasets like Hollywood-2[1] and UCF Sports[2] with human eye movements collected under the ecological constraints of the visual action recognition task. To our knowledge these are the first massive human eye tracking datasets of significant size to be collected for video (497,107 frames, each viewed by 16 subjects), unique in terms of their *(a) large scale and computer vision relevance, (b) dynamic, video stimuli, (c) task control, as opposed to free-viewing*. Second, we introduce novel *dynamic consistency and alignment models*, which underline the remarkable stability of patterns of visual search among subjects. Third, we leverage the massive amounts of collected data in order to pursue studies and build automatic, end-to-end trainable computer vision systems based on human eye movements. Our studies not only shed light on the differences between computer vision spatio-temporal interest point image sampling strategies and human fixations, as well as their impact for visual recognition performance, but also demonstrate that human fixations can be accurately predicted, and when used in an end-to-end *automatic* system, leveraging some of the most advanced computer vision practice, can lead to state of the art results.

1 Motivation

Recent progress in computer-based visual recognition, in particular image classification, object detection and segmentation or action recognition heavily relies on machine learning methods trained on large scale human annotated datasets. The level of annotation varies, spanning a degree of detail from global image or video labels to bounding boxes or precise segmentations of objects[3]. Such annotations have proven invaluable for performance evaluation and have also supported fundamental progress in designing models and algorithms. However, the

A. Fitzgibbon et al. (Eds.): ECCV 2012, Part II, LNCS 7573, pp. 842–856, 2012.

annotations are somewhat subjectively defined, primarily by the high-level visual recognition tasks generally agreed upon by the computer vision community. While such data has made advances in system design and evaluation possible, it does not necessarily provide insights or constraints into those intermediate levels of computation, or deep structure, that are perceived as ultimately necessary in order to design highly reliable computer vision systems. This is noticeable in the accuracy of state of the art systems trained with such annotations, which still lags significantly behind human performance on similar tasks. Nor does existing data make it immediately possible to exploit insights from an existing working system–the human eye–to potentially derive better features, models or algorithms.

The divide is well epitomized by the lack of matching large scale datasets that would record the workings of the human visual system, in the context of a visual recognition task, at different levels of interpretations including neural systems or eye movements. The human eye movement level, defined by image fixations and saccades, is potentially the less controversial to measure and analyze. It is sufficiently 'high-level' or 'behavioral' for the computer vision community to rule-out, to some degree at least, open-ended debates on where and what should one record, as could be the case, for instance with neural systems in different brain areas. It can potentially foster links with the human vision community, in particular researchers developing biologically plausible models of visual attention, who would be able to test and quantitatively analyze their models on common large scale datasets[4, 5].

Apart from linking the human and computer vision communities, human eye movement annotations offer pragmatic potential: fixations provide a sufficiently high-level signal that can be precisely registered with the image stimuli, for testing hypotheses and for training visual feature extractors and recognition models quantitatively. Some of the most successful approaches to action recognition employ bag-of words representations based on descriptors computed at spatial-temporal video locations, obtained at the maxima of an interest point operator biased to fire over non-trivial local structure (space-time 'corners' or spatial-temporal interest points[6]). More sophisticated image representations based on objects and their relations, as well as multiple kernels have been employed with a degree of success[7–9], although it appears still difficult to detect a large variety of useful objects reliably in challenging video footage. The dominant role of sparse spatial-temporal interest point operators as front end in computer vision systems raises the question whether computational insights from a working system like the human visual system can be used to improve performance. The sparse approach to computer visual recognition is actually consistent to the one in biological systems, but the degree of repeatability and the effect of using human fixations in conjunction with computer vision algorithms in the context of action recognition have not been yet explored.

In this paper we make the following contributions:

1. We undertake a significant effort of data recording and analysis of human eye movements in the context of computer vision-based *dynamic visual action*

recognition tasks for two existing computer vision datasets, Hollywood 2[1] and UCF-Sports[2]. This dynamic data, obtained by a significant, capture and processing effort, is made publicly available to the research community at `http://www.imar.ro/clvp/datasets/eyetracking`.
2. We introduce a number of novel consistency models and algorithms, as well as relevance evaluation measures adapted for video. Our findings (see §3) suggest a remarkable degree of dynamic consistency–both spatial and sequential–in the fixation patterns of human subjects but also underline a less extensive influence of task on dynamic fixations than previously believed, at least within the class of the datasets and actions we studied.
3. By using our large-scale training set of human fixations and by leveraging static and dynamic image features based on color, texture, edge distributions (HoG) or motion boundary histograms (MBH), we introduce novel saliency detectors and show that they can be trained effectively to predict human fixations as measured under both average precision (AP), and Kullblack-Leibler spatial comparison measures. See §4.1 and table 1 for results.
4. We show that training an end-to-end automatic visual action recognition system based on our learned saliency interest operator (point 3), and using advanced computer vision descriptors and fusion methods, leads to state of the art results in the Hollywood-2 action dataset. This is, we argue, one of the first demonstrations of a successful symbiosis of computer vision and human vision technology, within the context of a very challenging dynamic visual recognition task. It shows the potential of interest point operators learnt from human fixations for computer vision. We describe models and experiments in §4.3 and give results in table 2.

2 Related Work

Datasets containing human gaze pattern annotations of images have emerged from studies carried out by the human vision community, some of which are publicly available[10, 4, 11, 12] and some that are not[13]. Most of these datasets have been designed for small quantitative studies, consisting of at most a few hundred images or videos, usually recorded under free-viewing, in sharp contrast with the data we provide, which is large-scale, dynamic, and task controlled. These studies[10, 5, 13, 11, 12, 14–16] could however benefit from larger scale natural datasets, and from studies that emphasize the task, as we pursue. See [17] for alternative work, published in this conference, on eye movement data collection and saliency models for action recognition.

The problem of visual attention and the prediction of visual saliency have long been of interest in the human vision community[16, 10, 18]. Recently there was a growing trend of training visual saliency models based on human fixations, mostly in static images (with the notable exception of [13]), and under subject free-viewing conditions[4, 19]. While visual saliency models can be evaluated in isolation under a variety of measures against human fixations, for computer vision, their ultimate test remains the demonstration of relevance within an end-to-end automatic visual recognition pipeline. While such integrated systems are still in their infancy, promising demonstrations have recently emerged for computer vision tasks like scene classification[20] or verifying correlations with object (pedestrian) detection responses[21, 11]. An interesting early biologically inspired recognition system was presented by Kienzle et al.[13], who learn a fixation operator from human eye movements collected under video free-viewing, then learn action classification models for the KTH dataset with promising results.

In contrast, in the field of 'pure' computer vision, interest point detectors have been successfully used in the bag-of-visual-words framework for action classification[6, 1, 7, 22], but a variety of other methods exists, including random field models[23]. Currently the most successful systems remain the ones dominated by complex features extracted at interesting locations, bagged and fused using advanced kernel combination techniques[1, 7].This study is driven, primarily, by our computer vision interests, yet leverages data collection and insights from human vision. While in this paper we focus on bag-of-words spatio-temporal computer-based action recognition pipelines, the scope for study and the structure in the data are far broader. We do not see this investigation as a terminus, but rather as a first step in explaining some of the most advanced data and models that human vision and computer vision can offer at the moment.

3 Human Eye Movement Data Collection in Video. Static and Dynamic Consistency Analysis

An objective of this work is to introduce additional annotations in the form of large-scale eye movement recordings for two popular video datasets for action recognition: Hollywood-2[1] and UCF Sports[2]. The datasets span approximately 21 hours of video (around 500k frames) and cover 12, respectively 9 action classes. Our study includes two subject groups, an active group (12 subjects), asked to perform an action recognition task and a free viewing group (4 subjects), which was simply instructed to watch the video clips. More details on the recording protocol and environment can be found in our companion report[24]. Studies in the human vision community[25, 18] have advocated a high degree of agreement between human gaze patterns for subjects queried under static stimuli. We now investigate whether this effect extends to dynamic data.

Static Consistency Among Subjects: In this section, we investigate how well the regions fixated by human subjects agree on a frame by frame basis, by generalizing the procedure used in [11] for static stimuli to video data.

Evaluation Protocol: For the task of locating people in a static image, one can evaluate how well the regions fixated by a particular subject can be predicted from the regions fixated by the other subjects on the same image[11]. This measure is however not meaningful in itself, as part of the inter-subject agreement is due to bias in the stimulus itself (*e.g.* shooter's bias) or due to the tendency of humans to fixate more often at the center of the screen[18]. One can address this issue by checking how well the fixations of a subject on one simulus can be predicted from those of the other subjects on a different, unrelated, stimulus. We expect fixations to be better predicted on similar compared to different stimuli.

We generalize this protocol for video, by evaluating inter-subject correlation on randomly chosen frames. We consider each subject in turn. For a video frame, a probability distribution is generated by adding a Dirac impulse at each pixel fixated by the other subjects followed by blurring with a Gaussian kernel. The probability at the pixel fixated by the subject is taken as the prediction for its fixation. For our control, we repeat this process for pairs of frames chosen from different videos and predict the fixation of each subject on one frame from the fixations of the other subjects on the other frame. Differently from[11], who consider several fixations per subject for each exposed image, we only consider the single fixation, if any, that our subject made on that frame, since our stimulus is dynamic and the spatial positions of future fixations are influenced by changes in the stimulus itself. We set the width of the Gaussian blur kernel to match a visual angle span of 1.5° and draw 1000 samples for both similar and different stimulus predictions. We disregard the first 200ms from the beginning of each video to remove the bias due to the initial central fixation.

consistency measure	agreement	control
static consistency	94.8%	72.3%
temporal AOI alignment	70.8%	51.8%
AOI Markov Dynamics	70.2%	12.7%

Hollywood2

consistency measure	agreement	control
static consistency	93.2%	69.2%
temporal AOI alignment	65.4%	30.4%
AOI Markov Dynamics	55.5%	12.9%

UCF Sports

(a)

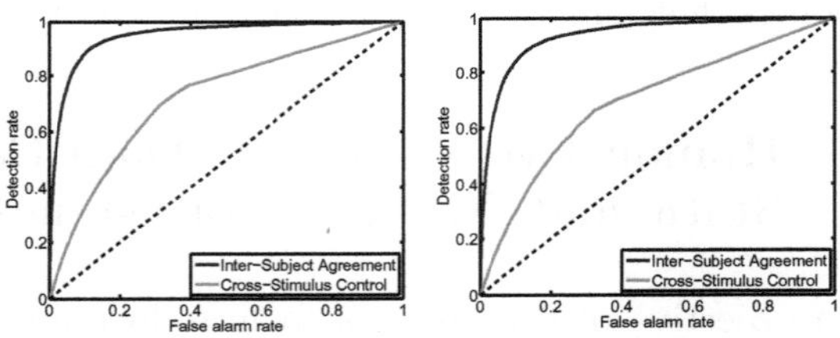

Hollywood2 **UCF Sports**

(b)

Fig. 1. (a) Static and dynamic inter-subject eye movement agreement for the Hollywood-2 and UCF Sports datasets. (b) ROC curves used to evaluate static inter-subject consistency. Fixations of one subject are predicted using data collected from the other subjects on the same video frame (blue) or on a frame coming from a different video (green) randomly selected from the dataset.

Findings: The ROC curves for inter-subject agreement and cross-stimulus control are shown in fig.1b. For the Hollywood-2 dataset, the area under the curve (AUC) is 94.8% for inter-subject agreement and 72.3% for cross-stimulus control. For UCF Sports, we obtain values of 93.2% and 69.2%. These values are consistent with the results reported for static stimuli by [11], with slightly higher cross-stimulus control. This indicates that shooter's bias is stronger in artistic datasets (movies) than in consumer photographs.

The Influence of Task on Eye Movements: Next, we evaluate the impact of task on eye movements from our data. For a given video frame and for each free viewing subject, we compute the p-statistic at the fixated location with respect

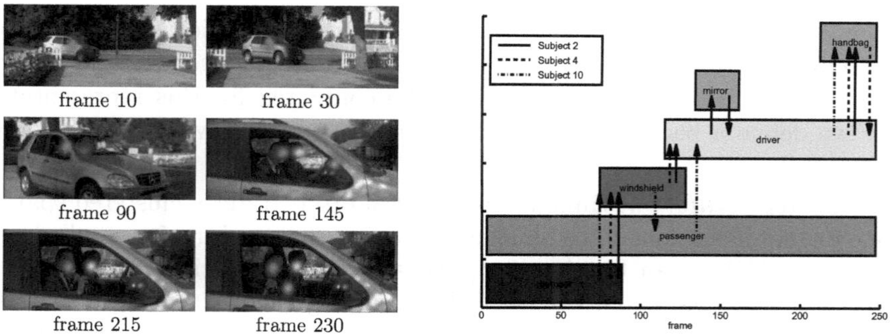

Fig. 2. Illustration for our automatic AOI generation method. Areas of interest are obtained *automatically* by clustering the fixations of subjects. **Left:** Heat maps illustrating the assignments of fixations to AOIs. The colored blobs have been generated by pooling together all fixations belonging to the same AOI and performing a gaussian blur with $\sigma = 1°$ visual angle. **Right:** Scan path through automatically generated AOIs for three subjects. The horizontal axis denotes time. Colored boxes correspond to the AOIs generated by the algorithm. Arrows illustrate saccades which landed in a different AOI than the fixation preceeding them. Drawn according to scale. Semantic labels have been manually assigned, for visualization purposes. This figure illustrates the existence of cognitive routines centered at semantically meaningful objects.

to the probability distribution derived using fixation data from our active subjects. We repeat this process for 1000 randomly sampled frames and compute the average p-value for each subject. Somewhat surprisingly, we find that fixation patterns of our free viewers do not deviate significantly from those of active subjects ($p = 0.65$ for Hollywood-2 and $p = 0.58$ for UCF Sports). Since in the Hollywood-2 dataset several actions can be present in a video, either simultaneously or sequentially, this rules out initial habituation effects and further neglect (free viewing) to some degree.[1]

Dynamic Consistency Among Subjects: Our static inter-subject agreement analysis shows that the spatial distribution of fixations in video is highly consistent across subjects. It does not however reveal whether there is significant consistency in *the order* in which subjects fixate among these locations. To our knowledge, there are no existing agreed upon dynamic consistency measures in the community at the moment. In this section, we propose two metrics that are sensitive to the temporal ordering among fixations and evaluate consistency under these metrics. We first model the scanpath made by each subject as a

[1] Notice that our findings do not assume or imply that free-viewing subjects may not be recognizing actions. However we did not ask them to perform a task, nor where they aware of the purpose of the experiment, or the interface presented to subjects given a task. While this is one approach to analyze task influence, it is not the only possible. For instance, subjects may be asked to focus on different tasks (e.g. actions versus general scene recognition), although this type of setting may induce biases due to habituation with stimuli presented at least twice.

sequence of discrete symbols and show how this representation can be produced *automatically*. We then define two metrics, *AOI Markov dynamics* and *temporal AOI alignment*, and show how they can be computed for this representation. After we define a baseline for our evaluation we conclude with a discussion of the results.

Scanpath Representation: Human fixations tend to be tightly clustered spatially at one or more locations in the image. Assuming that such regions, called *areas of interest* (AOIs), can be identified, the sequence of fixations belonging to a subject can be represented discretely by assigning each fixation to the closest AOI. For example, from the video depicted in fig.2-left, we identify six AOIs: the bumper of the car, its windshield, the passenger and the handbag he carries, the driver and the side mirror. We then trace the scan path of each subject through the AOIs based on spatial proximity, as shown in fig.2-right. Each fixation gets assigned a label. For subject 2 shown in the example, this results in the sequence [*bumper*, *windshield*, *driver*, *mirror*, *driver*, *handbag*]. Notice that AOIs are semantically meaningful and tend to correspond to physical objects. Interestingly, this supports recent computer vision strategies based on object detectors for action recognition[7, 9, 8, 26].

Automatically Finding AOIs: Defining areas of interest manually is labour intensive, especially in the video domain. Therefore, we introduce an *automatic* method for determining their locations based on clustering the fixations of all subjects in a frame. We start by running the k-means algorithm with 1 cluster and we successively increase their number until the sum of squared errors drops below a threshold. We then link centroids from successive frames into tracks, as long as they are closely located spatially. For robustness, we allow for a temporal gap during the track building process. Each resulting track becomes an AOI, and each fixation is assigned to the closest AOI at the time of its initiation.

AOI Markov Dynamics: In order to capture the dynamics of eye movements, we represent the transitions of human visual attention between AOIs by means of a Markov process. We assume that the human visual system transitions to the next AOI conditioned on the previously visited AOIs. Due to data sparsity, we restrict out analysis to a first order Markov process. Given a set of human fixation strings $\mathbf{f}_i$, where the jth fixation of subject i is encoded by the index $f_i^j \in \overline{1, A}$ of the corresponding AOI, we estimate the probability $p(s_t = b \mid s_{t-1} = a)$ of transitioning to AOI b at time t given that AOI a was fixated at time $t-1$ by counting transition frequencies. We regularize the model using Laplace Smoothing to account for data sparsity. The probability of a novel fixation sequence g under this model is $\prod_j p(s_t = g^j \mid s_{t-1} = g^{j-1})$ assuming the first state in the model, the central fixation, has probability 1. We measure the consistency among a set of subjects by considering each subject in turn, computing the probability of his scanpath with respect to the model trained from the fixations of the other subjects and normalizing by the number of fixations in his scanpath. The final consistency score is the average probability over all subjects.

Temporal AOI Alignment: Another way to evaluate dynamic consistency is by measuring how pairs of AOI strings corresponding to different subjects can be globally aligned. Although not modeling transitions explicitly, a sequence alignment has the advantage of being able to handle gaps and missing elements. An efficient algorithm having these properties due to Needleman-Wunsch[24] uses dynamic programming to find the optimal match between two sequences $f^{1:n}$ and $g^{1:m}$, by allowing for the insertion of gaps in either sequence. It recursively computes the alignment score $h_{i,j}$ between subsequences $f^{1:i}$ and $g^{1:j}$ by considering the alternative costs of a match between f^i and g^j versus the insertion of a gap into either sequence. The final consistency metric is the average alignment score over all pairs of distinct subjects, normalized by the length of the longest sequence in each pair. We set the similarity metric to 1 for matching AOI symbols and to 0 otherwise, and assume no penalty is incurred for inserting gaps in either sequence. This setting gives the score a semantic meaning: it is the average percentage of symbols that can be matched when determinig the longest common subsequence of fixations among pairs of subjects.

Baselines: In order to provide a reference for our consistency evaluation, we generate 10 random AOI strings per video and compute the consistency on these strings under our metrics. We note however that the dynamics of the stimulus places constraints on the sampling process. First, a random string must obey the time ordering relations among AOIs (*e.g.* the passenger is not visible until the second half of the video in fig.2). Second, our automatic AOIs are derived from subject fixations and are biased by their gaze preference. The lifespan of an AOI will not be initiated until at least one subject has fixated it, even if the corresponding object is already visible. To remove some of the resulting bias from our evaluation, we extend each AOI both forward and backwards in time, until the image patch at its center has undergone significant appearance changes, and use these extended AOIs when generating our random baselines.

Findings: For the Hollywod-2 dataset, we find that the average transition probability of each subject's fixations under AOI Markov dynamics is 70%, compared to 13% for the random baseline (fig.1a). We also find that, across all videos, 71% of the AOI symbols are successfully aligned, compared to only 52% for the random baseline. We notice similar high gaps in the UCF Sports dataset. These results indicate a high degree of consistency in the dynamics of human eye movements across the two datasets.

4 Learnt Saliency Models for Visual Action Recognition

In this section, we show that it is possible to train an effective human fixation detector on our dataset and present a state-of-the-art end-to-end automatic visual action recognition system based on the saliency maps generated by our detector.

4.1 Human Saliency Map Prediction

We first show that we can effectively predict saliency maps, using several features, both static and motion based. Our analysis includes many features derived directly from low, mid and high level image information. In addition, we train our own detector that fires preferentially at the locations fixated by the subjects, using the vast amount of eye movement data available in the dataset. We evaluate all these features and their combinations on our dataset under two metrics, AUC and KL divergence, and find that our detector gives the best performance under the KL divergence measure, which, we argue, is better suited for recognition.

Human Saliency Map Predictors: We run several saliency map predictors on our dataset, which we describe below.

Baselines: We provide three baselines for saliency map comparison. First, the uniform saliency map, which assigns the same probability to each pixel of the video frame. Second, we consider the center bias (CB) feature, which assigns each pixel with the distance to the center of the frame. This feature is intended to capture both screen and shooter's bias effects. At the other end of the spectrum lies the human saliency predictor, which computes the saliency map derived from the fixations made by half of our human subjects. This predictor is always evaluated with respect to the rest of the subjects, as opposed to the entire group.

Static Features (SF): We consider several features used by the human vision community for saliency prediction in the image domain[4], which can be classified into three categories: low, mid and high-level. The four low level features used are color information, steerable pyramid subbands, the feature maps used as input in[10] and the output of the saliency model described in [27, 28]. We run a Horizon detector[27] as our mid-level feature. Object detectors are used as high level features, which comprise faces[29], persons and cars[30].

Motion Features (MF): We include five novel feature maps, in the context of saliency prediction, which are derived from motion or space-time information.

Flow: We extract optical flow from each frame and compute the magnitude of the flow at each location. We do this in order to investigate whether regions with significant optical changes attract human gaze.

Pb with Flow: We run the Pb edge detector with both image intensity and the flow field as inputs. This detector fires both at intensity boundaries and at motion boundaries, where both image and flow discontinuities arise.

Flow Bimodality: We wish to investigate how often people fixate on motion edges, where the flow field typically has a bimodal distribution. We design a feature that measures optical flow bimodality around each location (for details see[24]).

Harris: This feature encodes the spatio-temporal Harris cornerness measure[6].

HoG-MBH Detector: The models for saliency considered so far access higher level image structure by means of pre-trained object detectors. That approach does not prove effective on our dataset, due to high variability in pose and illumination. On the other hand, our dataset provides a rich set of human fixations. Our analysis suggests that the image regions fixated by human subjects often contain semantically meaningful objects or object parts (see fig.2). Inspired by this insight, we exploit the structure present at these locations and train a detector for human fixations, which uses both static (HoG) and motion (MBH) descriptors centered at fixations. We build a saliency map from the confidence of our HoG-MBH detector when run over each video in a sliding windows fashion.

Feature Combinations: We also linearly combine various subsets of our feature maps in pursuit of better saliency prediction. We investigate the predictive power of static features and motion features alone and in combination, with and without central bias. Details can be found in [24].

Experimental Protocol: When training our HoG-MBH detector, we use 10^6 training examples, half of which are positive and half of which are negative. At each of these locations, we extract spatio-temporal HoG and MBH descriptors, with various grid configurations. These descriptors are concatenated and the resulting vector is lifted into a higher dimensional space by employing an order 3 χ^2 kernel approximation[31]. We train a linear SVM to obtain our detector.

Findings: We first evaluate our saliency predictors under the AUC metric (table 1a), which interprets saliency maps as predictors for separating fixated pixels from the rest. Combining predictors always improves performance under this metric. As a general trend, low-level features are better predictors than high level ones. Low level motion features provide similar performance to static low-level features. On the other hand, our HoG-MBH detector is comparable to the best static feature, the horizon detector.

Table 1. Evaluation of individual feature maps and their combinations for the problem of human saliency prediction. Two metrics are shown, area under the curve (AUC) and KL divergence. Notice that AUC and KL induce different saliency map rankings, but for visual recognition measures that emphasize spatial localization are essential (see also table 2 for action recognition results and [24] for visual illustrations).

feature	AUC (a)	KL divergence (b)
baselines		
uniform baseline	0.500	18.63
central bias (CB)	0.840	15.93
human	0.936	10.12
static features (SF)		
color features [4]	0.644	17.90
subbands [32]	0.634	17.75
Itti&Koch channels [10]	0.598	16.98
saliency map [27]	0.702	17.17
horizon detector [27]	0.741	15.45
face detector [29]	0.579	16.43
car detector [30]	0.500	18.40
person detector [30]	0.566	17.13

feature	AUC (a)	KL divergence (b)
our motion features (MF)		
flow magniture	0.626	18.57
pb edges with flow	0.582	17.74
flow bimodality	0.637	17.63
Harris cornerness	0.619	17.21
HOG-MBH detector	0.743	**14.95**
feature combinations		
SF [4]	0.789	16.16
SF + CB [4]	0.861	15.96
MF	0.762	15.62
MF + CB	0.830	15.97
SF + MF	0.812	15.94
SF + MF + CB	**0.871**	15.89

We also use the Kullback-Leibler (KL) divergence measure for comparing predicted saliency maps to the human ground truth. Interestingly, under this metric, the ranking of the saliency maps changes (table 1) and in this setting the HoG-MBH detector performs best. The only other predictor which performs significantly higher than central bias is the horizon detector. Under KL, the linear combination method does not always improve performance, as it optimizes pixel-level classification accuracy, and is not able to account for the inherent spatial competition due to image-level normalization. We conclude that fusing our

Table 2. Columns a-e: Action recognition performance on the **Hollywood-2** dataset when interest points are sampled randomly across the spatio-temporal volumes of video from various distributions (b-e), with the Harris corner detector as baseline (a). Average precision is shown for the uniform (b), central bias (c) and ground truth (e) distributions, and for the output (d) of our HoG-MBH detector. All pipelines use the same number of interest points per frame. **Columns f-i**: Significant improvements over the state of the art approach[22] (f) can be achieved by augmenting their method with channels derived from the predicted saliency map (g) and ground truth saliency (h), but not when using the classical uniform sampling scheme (e).

	interest points						trajectories + interest points		
action	**Harris corners** (a)	**uniform sampling** (b)	**central bias sampling** (c)	**predicted saliency sampling** (d)	**ground truth saliency sampling** (e)	**trajectories only** (f)	**uniform sampling** (g)	**predicted saliency sampling** (h)	**ground truth saliency sampling** (i)
AnswerPhone	16.4%	21.3%	23.3%	23.7%	**28.1%**	**32.6%**	24.5%	25.0%	32.5%
DriveCar	85.4%	92.2%	92.4%	92.8%	**57.9%**	88.0%	93.6%	93.6%	**96.2%**
Eat	59.1%	59.8%	58.6%	**70.0%**	67.3%	65.2%	69.8%	**75.0%**	73.6%
FightPerson	71.1%	74.3%	76.3%	76.1%	**80.6%**	81.4%	79.2%	78.7%	**83.0%**
GetOutCar	36.1%	47.4%	49.6%	54.9%	**55.1%**	52.7%	55.2%	**60.7%**	59.3%
HandShake	18.2%	25.7%	26.5%	**27.9%**	27.6%	**29.6%**	29.3%	28.3%	26.6%
HugPerson	33.8%	33.3%	34.6%	**39.5%**	37.8%	**54.2%**	44.7%	45.3%	46.1%
Kiss	58.3%	61.2%	62.1%	61.3%	**66.4%**	65.8%	66.2%	66.4%	**69.5%**
Run	73.2%	76.0%	77.8%	82.2%	**85.7%**	82.1%	82.1%	84.2%	**87.2%**
SitDown	54.0%	59.3%	62.1%	**69.0%**	62.5%	62.5%	67.2%	**70.4%**	68.1%
SitUp	26.1%	20.7%	20.9%	29.7%	**30.7%**	20.0%	23.8%	**34.1%**	32.9%
StandUp	57.0%	59.8%	61.3%	**63.9%**	58.2%	65.2%	64.9%	**69.5%**	66.0%
Mean	49.1%	52.6%	53.7%	57.6%	57.9%	58.3%	58.4%	61.0%	**61.7%**

trained HoG-MBH detector with our static and dynamic features gives the best results under AUC metrics, while the HoG-MBH detector is the best predictor of visual saliency from our candidate set, under the probabilistic measure (KL) matching the spatial distribution of human fixations.

4.2 Visual Action Recognition Pipeline

We next present an automatic end-to-end action recognition system based on predicted saliency maps, together with several baselines. Both our recognition system and our baselines use the same processing pipeline, which we will describe upfront. It consists of an interest point operator, descriptor extraction, bag of visual words quantization and an action classifier.

Interest Point Operator: We experiment with various interest point operators, both computer vision based and biologically derived (see §4.3). Each interest point operator takes as input a video and generates a set of spatio-temporal coordinates, with associated spatial and temporal scales.[2]

Descriptors: We obtain features by extracting descriptors at the spatiotemporal locations returned by of our interest point operator. For this purpose, we use the spacetime generalization of the HoG descriptor as well as the MBH descriptor computed from optical flow. We consider 7 grid configurations, fixed throughout

[2] Our studies indicate that the spatial distribution of Harris interest points differs sharply from that of human fixations[24].

our experiments, and extract both types of descriptors for each configuration. We end up with 14 features for classification.

Visual Dictionaries: We cluster the resulting descriptors using k-means into vocabularies of 4000 visual words. For computational reasons, we use only 500k randomly sampled descriptors as input to the clustering step. We then represent each video by the L_1 normalized histogram of its visual words.

Classifiers: From histograms we compute kernel matrices using the RBF-χ^2 kernel and combine them by means of a Multiple Kernel Learning (MKL) framework. We train one classifier for each action label in a one-vs-all fashion. We determine the kernel scaling parameter, the SVM loss parameter C and the regularization parameter σ of the MKL framework by cross-validation. We report the average precision on the test set for each action class, in line with [1, 22].

4.3 Visual Action Recognition Studies

We now configure our action recognition pipeline with an operator that randomly samples interest points from the saliency map predicted by our HoG-MBH detector. We choose this map because it best approximates the ground truth saliency map spatially in a probabilistic sense, *i.e.* under a KL divergence measure. We also provide 4 performance baselines. In order to compare with classical action-recognition approaches, we consider the spatiotemporal Harris corner operator [6] and an operator that randomly chooses interest point locations from the uniform distribution spanning spatio-temporal volume of the video. Our third baseline is an operator that samples interest points using the central bias saliency map, which was also shown to approximate to a reasonable extent human fixations under the less intuitive AOI measure (table 1). Fourth, we consider an operator that samples locations from the ground truth saliency map, computed from human fixations by blurring their locations with a Gaussian spatio-temporal kernel. This last baseline assumes that fixations are available at test time and provides an upper bound on recognition performance. Finally, we also investigate whether our end-to-end recognition system can be combined with the state-of-the-art trajectory approach of [22] for better performance.

Experimental Protocol: We run our HoG-MBH detector over the entire data set and obtain our automatic saliency maps, from which we sample interest points. For our first baseline, we run the Harris corner operator on the input video, while for the other baselines we compute uniform, central bias and ground truth saliency maps from which we randomly sample interest points. All our random sampling operators use the same number of interest points per frame as generated by the Harris corner detector. In a final experiment, we also run the pipeline of [22] and combine the 4 kernel matrices they compute with the ones we obtain for our 14 descriptors, sampled from the saliency maps, using MKL.

Results: We note only a small drop in performance when comparing our automatic pipeline to the one obtained by sampling from ground truth saliency maps (table 2d,e). Average precision is also markedly superior to that of a pipeline sampling interest points uniformly (table 2c). Although central bias is a relatively close approximation of the ground truth saliency map under AOI measures, it performs significantly worse when used for recognition. This further indicates that approximations produced by the HoG-MBH detector are qualitatively different from a central bias distribution, focusing on local image structure that frequently occurs in its training set of fixations, while at the same time being agnostic (as it should be, modulo dataset bias) to image location.

Even though our pipeline is sparse, it achieves near state of the art performance compared to a pipeline that uses dense trajectories. When the sparse descriptors obtained from our automatic pipeline are combined with the kernels associated to the dense trajectory features in [22] using MKL, we are able to go beyond the state-of-the-art. This demonstrates that an end-to-end automatic system incorporating both human and computer vision technology can deliver top performance in a challenging problem such as visual action recognition.

5 Conclusions

We have presented experimental and computational modelling work at the incidence of human visual attention and computer vision, with emphasis on action recognition in video. Inspired by earlier psychophysics and visual attention findings, not validated quantitatively at large scale until now and not pursued for video, we have collected, and made available to the research community, a set of comprehensive human eye-tracking annotations for Hollywood-2 and UCF Sports, some of the most challenging, recently created action recognition datasets in the computer vision community. Besides the collection of large datasets, we have performed quantitative analyses and introduced novel models for evaluating the static and the dynamic consistency of human fixations across different subjects, videos and actions. We have found good inter-subject fixation agreement but, perhaps surprisingly, only moderate evidence of task influence.

We have also presented a large scale analysis of automatic visual saliency models and end-to-end automatic visual action recognition systems. Our studies are performed with particular focus on computer vision techniques and interest point operators and descriptors. In particular we show that accurate saliency operators can be effectively trained based on human fixations. Finally, we show that such automatic saliency predictors can be used within end-to-end computer-based visual action recognition systems to achieve state of the art results in some of the hardest benchmarks in the field.

We hope that our work will foster further communication, benchmarks and methodology sharing between human vision and computer vision, and ultimately lead to improved end-to-end artificial visual action recognition systems.

Acknowledgements. This work was supported by CNCS-UEFICSDI, under PNII RU-RC-2/2009, PCE-2011-3-0438 and CT-ERC-2012-1.

References

1. Marszalek, M., Laptev, I., Schmid, C.: Actions in context. In: CVPR (2009)
2. Rodriguez, M.D., Ahmed, J., Shah, M.: Action mach a spatio-temporal maximum average correlation height filter for action recognition. In: CVPR (2008)
3. Everingham, M., Gool, L.V., Williams, C., Winn, J., Zisserman, A.: The Pascal visual object classes (VOC) challenge. IJCV (2010)
4. Judd, T., Ehinger, K., Durand, F., Torralba, A.: Learning to predict where humans look. In: ICCV (2009)
5. Larochelle, H., Hinton, G.: Learning to combine foveal glimpses with a third-order boltzmann machine. In: NIPS (2010)
6. Laptev, I.: On space-time interest points. In: IJCV (2005)
7. Han, D., Bo, L., Sminchisescu, C.: Selection and context for action recognition. In: ICCV (2009)
8. Prest, A., Schmid, C., Ferrari, V.: Weakly supervised learning of interactions between humans and objects. PAMI (2011)
9. Yao, B., Fei-Fei, L.: Modeling mutual context of object and human pose in human-object interaction activities. In: CVPR (2010)
10. Itti, L., Koch, C.: A saliency-based search mechanism for overt and covert shifts of visual attention. Vision Research 40 (2000)
11. Ehinger, K.A., Sotelo, B., Torralba, A., Oliva, A.: Modeling search for people in 900 scenes: A combined source model of eye guidance. Visual Cognition 17 (2009)
12. Judd, T., Durand, F., Torralba, A.: Fixations on low resolution images. In: ICCV (2009)
13. Kienzle, W., Schölkopf, B., Wichmann, F.A., Franz, M.O.: How to Find Interesting Locations in Video: A Spatiotemporal Interest Point Detector Learned from Human Eye Movements. In: Hamprecht, F.A., Schnörr, C., Jähne, B. (eds.) DAGM 2007. LNCS, vol. 4713, pp. 405–414. Springer, Heidelberg (2007)
14. Fei-Fei, L., Iyer, A., Koch, C., Perona, P.: What do we perceive in a glance of a real-world scene? Journal of Vision (2007)
15. Jhuang, H., Serre, T., Wolf, L., Poggio, T.: A biologically inspired system for action recognition. In: ICCV (2007)
16. Itti, L., Rees, G., Tsotsos, J.K. (eds.): Neurobiology of Attention. Academic Press (2005)
17. Vig, E., Dorr, M., Cox, D.: Space-Variant Descriptor Sampling for Action Recognition Based on Saliency and Eye Movements. In: Fitzgibbon, A., Lazebnik, S., Sato, Y., Schmid, C. (eds.) ECCV 2012, Part VII. LNCS, vol. 7578, pp. 84–97. Springer, Heidelberg (2012)
18. Land, M.F., Tatler, B.W.: Looking and Acting. Oxford University Press (2009)
19. Torralba, A., Oliva, A., Castelhano, M., Henderson, J.: Contextual guidance of eye movements and attention in real-world scenes: The role of global features in object search. Psychological Review 13 (2006)
20. Borji, A., Itti, L.: Scene classification with a sparse set of salient regions. In: ICRA (2011)
21. Elazary, L., Itti, L.: A Bayesian model for efficient visual search and recognition. Vision Research 50 (2010)
22. Wang, H., Klaser, A., Schmid, C.: Liu, C.: Action recognition by dense trajectories. In: CVPR (2011)
23. Li, W., Zhang, Z., Liu, Z.: Expandable data-driven graphical modeling of human actions based on salient postures. In: IEEE TCSVT, vol. 18 (2008)

24. Mathe, S., Sminchisescu, C.: Actions in the eye: dynamic gaze datasets and learnt saliency models for visual recognition. Technical report, Institute of Mathematics of the Romanian Academy and University of Bonn (February 2012)
25. Yarbus, A.: Eye Movements and Vision. Plenum Press, New York (1967)
26. Hwang, A., Wang, H., Pomplun, M.: Semantic guidance of eye movements in real-world scenes. Vision Research (2011)
27. Oliva, A., Torralba, A.: Modeling the shape of the scene: A holistic representation of the spatial envelope. IJCV (42) (2001)
28. Rosenholtz, R.: A simple saliency model predicts a number of motion popout phenomena. Vision Research (39) (1999)
29. Viola, P., Jones, M.: Robust real-time object detection. IJCV (2001)
30. Felzenswalb, P., McAllester, D., Ramanan, D.: A discriminatively trained, multi-scale, deformable part model. In: CVPR (2008)
31. Li, F., Guy, L., Sminchisescu, C.: Chebyshev approximations to the histogram chi-square kernel. In: CVPR (2012)
32. Simocelli, E., Freeman, W.: The steerable pyramid: A flexible architecture for multi-scale derivative computation. In: ICIP (1995)

Coherent Filtering: Detecting Coherent Motions from Crowd Clutters

Bolei Zhou[1], Xiaoou Tang[1,3], and Xiaogang Wang[2,3]

[1] Department of Information Engineering, The Chinese University of Hong Kong
[2] Department of Electronic Engineering, The Chinese University of Hong Kong
[3] Shenzhen Institutes of Advanced Technology, Chinese Academy of Sciences

Abstract. Coherent motions, which describe the collective movements of individuals in crowd, widely exist in physical and biological systems. Understanding their underlying priors and detecting various coherent motion patterns from background clutters have both scientific values and a wide range of practical applications, especially for crowd motion analysis. In this paper, we propose and study a prior of coherent motion called *Coherent Neighbor Invariance*, which characterizes the local spatiotemporal relationships of individuals in coherent motion. Based on the coherent neighbor invariance, a general technique of detecting coherent motion patterns from noisy time-series data called *Coherent Filtering* is proposed. It can be effectively applied to data with different distributions at different scales in various real-world problems, where the environments could be sparse or extremely crowded with heavy noise. Experimental evaluation and comparison on synthetic and real data show the existence of Coherence Neighbor Invariance and the effectiveness of our Coherent Filtering.[1]

1 Introduction

Coherent motion is a universal phenomenon in nature and widely exists in many physical and biological systems. For example, tornadoes, storms, and atmospheric circulation are all caused by the coherent movements of physical particles in the atmosphere. Meanwhile, the collective behaviors of organisms such as swarming ants and schooling fishes have long captured the interests of social and natural scientists [1, 2]. Detecting coherent motions and understanding their underlying principles are related to many important scientific research topics such as self-organization of biological systems [3]. There is also a wide range of practical applications. For example, in video surveillance, detecting coherent motion patterns of pedestrian groups in crowd has important applications to object counting [4, 5], crowd tracking [6], and crowd management [7]. Furthermore, clusters of coherent motions provide a mid-level representation of crowd dynamics, and could be used for high-level semantic analysis such as scene understanding and crowd activity recognition [8–11].

Generally speaking, coherent motion detection can be formulated as finding clusters of dynamic particles with coherent motion from their time-series observation and removing background noise as outliers. Under different scene context, the detected coherent motions may be interpreted as different semantic behaviors. As shown in Figure

[1] Source codes and videos are available from
`http://mmlab.ie.cuhk.edu.hk/coherentfiltering/`

A. Fitzgibbon et al. (Eds.): ECCV 2012, Part II, LNCS 7573, pp. 857–871, 2012.

9, moving keypoints tracked in the scenes exhibit a wide variety of coherent motion patterns, corresponding to individual and group movements, traffic mode, crowd flow *etc*. These examples show that detecting coherent motions from noisy observations is of great importance to crowd behavior analysis and scene understanding.

The goal of this work is to explore the underlying prior in the dynamics of coherent motions and to leverage it for coherent motion detection. We propose a prior called *Coherent Neighbor Invariance*, which exists in the local neighborhoods of individuals in coherent motions, and show that it well distinguishes coherent and incoherent motions. Then we develop a general coherent motion detection technique called *Coherent Filtering* based on such a prior. Experiments show that it can work robustly in online mode for various applications.

1.1 Related Works

Crowd motion analysis has been an active research topic in computer vision. It is closely related to many low-level and high-level computer vision problems in crowded or cluttered environments. For example, Rabaud *et al.* [4] and Brostow *et al.* [5] proposed approaches to detect independent motions in order to count moving objects. Lin *et al.* [12] used Lie algebra of affine transform to learn the global motion patterns of crowds. Ali *et al.* [6] used floor fields from fluid mechanics for the segmentation of crowd flows. Hu *et al.* [13] clustered the single-frame optical flows to learn the motion patterns. Brox *et al.* extended spectral clustering to group long-term dense trajectories for the segmentation of moving objects in video. Meanwhile, the high-level semantic analysis in crowded scenes focuses on modeling scene structures and recognizing crowd behaviors. Wang *et al.* [8, 14] and Zhou *et al.* [10] used hierarchial topic models to learn the models of semantic regions from the co-occurrence of optical flow and tracks. Zhou *et al.* [9] proposed a mixture model of dynamic pedestrian-agents to learn the collective crowd behavior patterns in crowded scenes. In 3D motion segmentation [15], under the assumption of affine transform there are several subspace approaches proposed, such as Generalized Principal Component Analysis (GPCA) [16] and RANSAC [15].

Although these problems are closely related to coherent motions, they were studied separately and had different limited assumptions and solutions in the past literature. For example, the approaches in [4, 5] are specifically designed for object counting and had assumptions on the shape and distribution of coherent motions. The models in [12] and [6] assume the geometric transformation of motion. The clustering methods in [13, 17] are easily affected by noises. GPCA [16] and RANSAC [18] consider the motion trajectories lies on motion subspace and are projected under the affine camera model. Therefore, these approaches cannot be well generalized to other problems related to coherent motions. We develop a general coherent motion technique which can be well applied to the various problems discussed above. It achieves comparable results or even outperforms the state-of-the-arts in different application domains, especially when the background noise is heavy.

2 The Prior: Coherent Neighbor Invariance

Although coherent motions are the macroscopic observations of collective movements of individuals, recent studies [2, 19] show that it actually can be characterized by the

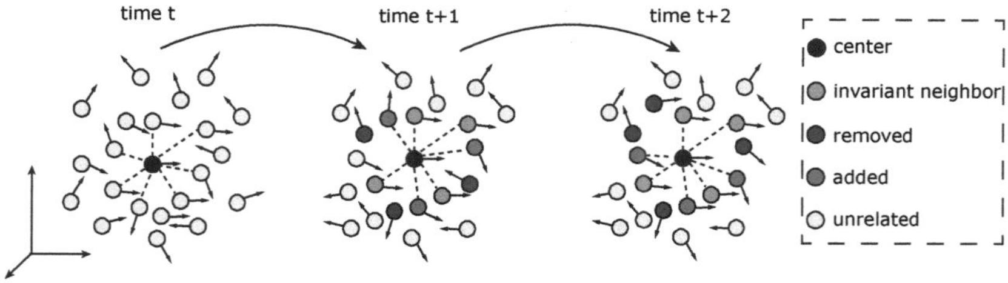

Fig. 1. Illustration of coherent neighbor invariance. The green dots are the invariant K nearest neighbors of the central black dot over time (here $K = 7$). The invariant neighbors have a higher probability to be the dots moving coherently with the central dot, since their local spatiotemporal relationships and velocity correlations with the central dot are inclined to remain invariant over time. The red and blue dots change their neighborship over time (removed or added), so that they have a small probability to move coherently with the central dot.

interactions among individuals within local neighborhoods. Inspired by these observations and results, we propose a prior underlying the dynamics of coherent motion as *Coherent Neighbor Invariance*. There are two key properties of Coherent Neighbor Invariance, which distinguish coherent motions from random motions:

- Invariance of spatiotemporal relationships: the neighborship of individuals with coherent motions tends to remain invariant over time.
- Invariance of velocity correlations: the velocity correlations of neighboring individuals with coherent motions remain high when being averaged over time.

On the contrary, incoherently moving individuals do not have such properties because of the mutual independence of their movements. Coherent neighbor invariance exists in the dynamics of K nearest neighbors of individuals for consecutive time. It reflects the self-organization of coherent motions in neighborship, and explains the formation of global coherent motion patterns from local coordinations of individuals. An illustration of the prior is shown in Figure 1.

To quantitatively analyze this prior, we first define two measurements of Coherent Neighbor Invariance: the coherent neighbor invariance of spatiotemporal relationships (in Section 2.2), and the coherent neighbor invariance of velocity correlations (in Section 2.3). From the following experiments, we show that this prior not only helps reveal the mechanism of coherent motions, but also can be effectively leveraged to separate various coherent motion patterns from background noise using a technique called Coherent Filtering.

2.1 Random Dot Kinematogram

We take Random Dot Kinematogram (RDK) as an example to analyze the coherent neighbor invariance, because it is easy to understand and can be well generalized. RDK is a classic psychophysical stimulus, and is often used for investigating coherent motion perception of visual systems [20]. The stimulus consists of a completely random array of thousands of tiny dots that move either coherently or randomly. An illustration is shown in Figure 2A. Incoherently moving dots(referred as incoherent dots) are

Table 1. Notations used in the paper

$\lvert\cdot\rvert$	The cardinality of a set.
$\cap$	The intersection of two sets.
$\mathcal{F}$	$\mathcal{F}=\{\mathcal{F}_1,...,\mathcal{F}_N\}$. The set of coherent dots.
$\mathcal{B}$	The set of incoherent dots.
$\mathcal{N}_t^i$	$\mathcal{N}_t^i=\{i_t^1,...,i_t^K\}$. The set of the K-NNs of dot i at time t.
$\mathcal{M}_{t\to d}^i$	$\mathcal{M}^i_{t\to d}=\mathcal{N}_t^i\cap\mathcal{N}_{t+1}^i\cap...\cap\mathcal{N}_{t+d}^i$.The dth order invariant neighbor set of i.
$\mathcal{C}^i_{t\to d}$	$\mathcal{C}^i_{t\to d}=\mathcal{M}^i_{t\to d}\cap\mathcal{F}$. The coherent invariant neighbor set of i
$g^{i_k}_{t\to d}$	Averaged velocity correlation between i and i_k from t to $t+d$.
$\mathcal{R}$	$\mathcal{R}=\{(i,i_k)\mid g^{i_k}_{t\to d}>\lambda, i_k\in\mathcal{A}\}$. The set of pairwise connections.
$\mathcal{S}$	$\mathcal{S}=\{s_i\mid i\in\mathcal{I}\}$. The set of the cluster index s_i for each dot i.

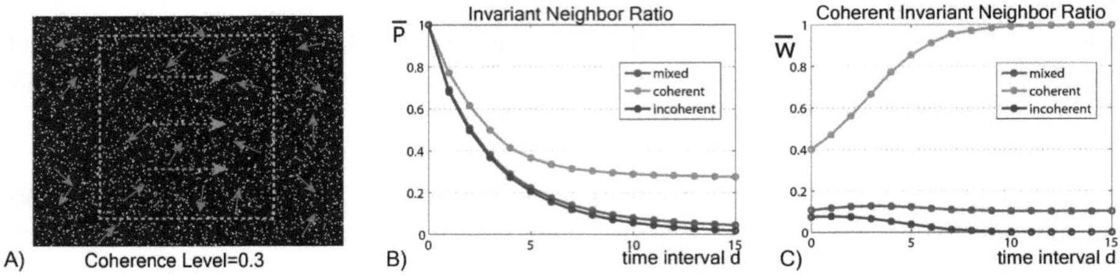

Fig. 2. A) Illustration of random dot kinematogram. Here the number of coherent motion pattern $N=1$. The cyan arrows indicate the random moving directions of some noisy dots with incoherent motions. The green arrows indicate the direction of coherent motion. B) Averaged invariant neighbor ratios $\overline{P}$ with time interval d. C) Averaged coherent invariant neighbor ratios $\overline{W}$ with time interval d. All these measurements are computed and averaged for coherent dots, incoherent dots and all the dots respectively for comparison.

randomly placed over the whole scene and serve as background noise. In the central rectangular area, a group of coherently moving dots(referred as coherent dots) are also randomly placed. The proportion of coherent dots to all the dots in the rectangular area (mixing of coherent dots and incoherent dots) is called the coherence level. In psychophysical study, human subjects are required to identify coherent motions of dots from the background noise. The coherence level determines the difficulty level of the identification task.

Formally, we denote $\mathcal{I}$ as the set of all the dots (mixed dots) in the central rectangular area, $\mathcal{F}$ as the set of coherent dots, and $\mathcal{B}$ as the set of incoherent dots. There could be N different coherent motion patterns which divide $\mathcal{F}$ into subsets $\{\mathcal{F}_1,...,\mathcal{F}_N\}$. Thus the problem of detecting coherent motions from noisy observations of dot movements is formulated as estimating the separation $\mathcal{I}=\{\mathcal{F},\mathcal{B}\}$, and the sub-separation $\mathcal{F}=\{\mathcal{F}_1,...,\mathcal{F}_N\}$. In Sections 2.2 and 2.3, we will analyze two coherent neighbor invariance measurements and study their dynamic behaviors. Table 1 shows the notations used in the paper.

2.2 Invariance of Spatiotemporal Relationships

This subsection analyzes the invariance of spatiotemporal relationships in coherent motions. We first define some related concepts. At time t, the set $\mathcal{N}_t^i$ contains the K nearest neighbors of dot i under Euclidean distance. It evolves into $\mathcal{N}_{t+1}^i$ at time $t+1$[2]. We denote $\mathcal{M}_{t\to 1}^i$ as the 1st order invariant neighbor set, which contains the invariant neighbors among the K nearest neighbors of dot i from time t to $t+1$. Similarly, $\mathcal{M}_{t\to d}^i$ is denoted as the dth order invariant neighbor set which contains the invariant neighbors from time t to $t+d$. We denote $\mathcal{C}_{t\to d}^i$ as the intersection of $\mathcal{M}_{t\to d}^i$ and $\mathcal{F}$, so that it only contains the invariant neighbors with coherent motion. It is called the coherent invariant neighbor set of dot i at d^{th} order .

Two ratios are defined. The first is the invariant neighbor ratio $P_{t\to d}^i$, measuring the proportion of invariant neighbors among the K nearest neighbors during time t to $t+d$. The second is the coherent invariant neighbor ratio $W_{t\to d}^i$, measuring the proportion of coherent dots among the invariant neighbors during time t to $t+d$. Specifically,

$$P_{t\to d}^i = \frac{|\mathcal{M}_{t\to d}^i|}{K}, \quad W_{t\to d}^i = \frac{|\mathcal{C}_{t\to d}^i|}{|\mathcal{M}_{t\to d}^i|},$$

where $P_{t\to d}^i$ and $W_{t\to d}^i \in [0,1]$. Obviously $P_{t\to d}^i$ and $W_{t\to d}^i$ will change with the value of d and they describe the temporal behaviors of dots with coherent and incoherent motions. For an incoherent dot i, since most of the dots in its neighborhood move independently with dot i, its K nearest neighbors would vary greatly over time. Thus $P_{t\to d}^i$ is expected to decrease quickly when d increase, and gradually to 0. On the contrary, for a coherent dot i, dots in its neighborhood, which move coherently with i, would tend to remain in the neighborhood during the whole time interval d because of their consistent movements with i, while other incoherent dots in its neighborhood will easily move out of the neighborship. Thus $P_{t\to d}^i$ is expected to decrease slower than that of incoherent dots and then remains as a constant when d increases further. On the other hand, $W_{t\to d}^i$ measures the proportion of coherent dots in the invariant neighbor set $\mathcal{M}_{t\to d}^i$. Obviously only the dots which move coherently with dot i tend to remain in the neighborhood of i from time t to $t+d$. For an incoherent dot i, because all dots in $\mathcal{M}_{t\to d}^i$ are moving independently with dot i, $W_{t\to d}^i$ is expected to be low over time. For a coherent dot i, since majority of the remaining dots in $\mathcal{M}_{t\to d}^i$ move coherently with i as d increases, $W_{t\to d}^i$ is expected to increase with d.

Since the groundtruth of dots as $\mathcal{F}$ or $\mathcal{B}$ are known in RDK, we can compute and analyze the two ratios for coherent dots, incoherent dots, and mixed dots respectively. We set the coherence level as 0.3, which means there are 30% dots ($\sim$ 800) moving coherently in the central rectangular area of Figure 2A. As shown in Figures 2B and 2C, the experimental results of the two ratios in RDK verify our analysis. We can see that as d increases the averaged invariant neighbor ratios $\overline{P}$ for coherent dots and incoherent dots are clearly separated. Meanwhile, the averaged coherent invariant neighbor ratio $\overline{W}$ for coherent dots increases almost to 1, and that for incoherent dots decreases to 0.

Our analysis and illustrative results in RDK show the invariant neighbor ratio and the coherent invariant neighbor ratio have good discriminability for coherent and incoherent motions. We call this property of coherent motion as *coherent neighbor invariance of spatiotemporal relationships.*

[2] The correspondence of dots over time is assumed.

2.3 Invariance of Velocity Correlations

The other property of coherent motion is the invariance of velocity correlations between neighboring dots. Suppose that dot i_k belongs to the invariant neighbor set of dot i. Their velocity correlation averaged from time t to $t+d$ is

$$g_{t\to d}^{i_k} = \frac{1}{d+1}\sum_{\tau=t}^{t+d}\frac{\mathbf{v}_\tau^i \cdot \mathbf{v}_\tau^{i_k}}{||\mathbf{v}_\tau^i|| \cdot ||\mathbf{v}_\tau^{i_k}||},$$

where $\mathbf{v}_\tau^i$ is the velocity of i at time τ. If dot i_k moves incoherently with dot i, $g_{t\to d}^{i_k}$ would be low as d increases. Otherwise, $g_{t\to d}^{i_k}$ remains high. Therefore, the velocity correlations of coherently moving dots and incoherently moving dots in local regions can be well separated as d increases.

Figure 3 shows the histograms of $g_{t\to d}^{i_k}$ generated from the invariant neighbor set in RDK, with $d = 0, 1, 3, 5, 10$ respectively. The experimental results verify our analysis above. We can see that as d increases, the histogram gradually separates into two modes: one near 0 and the other near 1. This property of coherent motions is called *coherent neighbor invariance of velocity correlations*.

Because of this property, it is simple to remove the incoherent dots i_k from the invariant neighbor set $\mathcal{M}_{t\to d}^i$: setting a threshold λ on the value of $g_{t\to d}^{i_k}$ and then removing i_k from $\mathcal{M}_{t\to d}^i$ if $g_{t\to d}^{i_k} < \lambda$. After thresholding, we can create a set $\mathcal{R}$ containing the thresholded pairwise connections, in which (i, i_k) are connected if i_k still remains in $\mathcal{M}_{t\to d}^i$. Then coherent motions can be easily detected according to $\mathcal{R}$, using the algorithm proposed in Section 3.1.

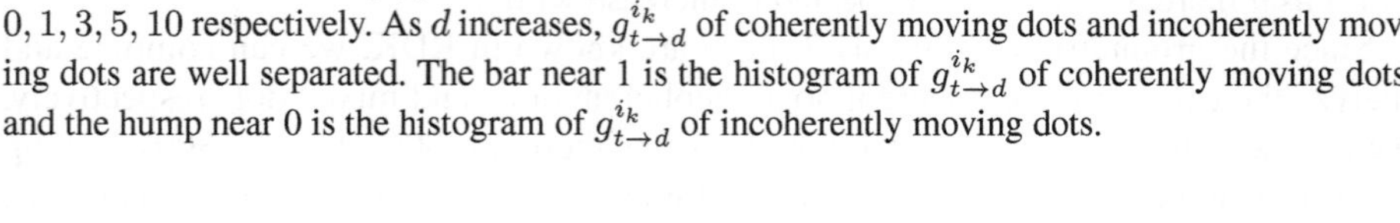

Fig. 3. Histograms of $g_{t\to d}^{i_k}$ generated from the invariant neighbor set in RDK, with $d = 0, 1, 3, 5, 10$ respectively. As d increases, $g_{t\to d}^{i_k}$ of coherently moving dots and incoherently moving dots are well separated. The bar near 1 is the histogram of $g_{t\to d}^{i_k}$ of coherently moving dots, and the hump near 0 is the histogram of $g_{t\to d}^{i_k}$ of incoherently moving dots.

3 Coherent Filtering Using Coherent Neighbor Invariance

Based on Coherent Neighbor Invariance, a clustering technique Coherent Filtering is proposed for coherent motion detection from time-series data. Coherent Filtering consists of two algorithms. The first is to detect coherent motion patterns at one time, the second is to associate detected coherent motion and update existing coherent motion over time. Algorithms are listed in Table 2 and Table 3 respectively.

Coherent Filtering has some important merits. 1) It stems from the coherent neighbor invariance, which is a prior widely observed in coherent motions. Therefore it is a general technique for clustering time-series data and detecting coherent motions in various real-world problems, such as object counting, group movement detection, traffic mode recognition, and crowd flow segmentation. 2) It only relies on local spatiotemporal relationships and velocity correlations without any assumption on the global shape of coherent motion patterns and the distribution of background noise. Therefore it can be robustly applied to data at different scales and distributions without substantial change. 3) In practical applications, it might be difficult to obtain the correspondence of keypoints over a long time, especially in crowded environments. Experiments show that our algorithm only requires correspondence over a short period (normally 4 or 5 frames). This means that it can work robustly in crowded scenes and in an online mode. 4) The cluster number N is automatically decided from data without knowing as *a priori*.

3.1 Algorithm for Detecting Coherent Motions

In Algorithm **CoheFilterDet** we first obtain the invariant neighbor set $\mathcal{M}_{t\to d}^i$ by examining the neighborship in $\mathcal{N}_\tau^i$ from t to $t+d$ for each dot $i \in \mathcal{I}$. According to *coherent neighbor invariance of spatiotemporal relationships*, most dots in $\mathcal{M}_{t\to d}^i$ should be coherent dots. However, it does not guarantee that *all* the dots in $\mathcal{A}$ are coherent dots especially when d is small. Then, according to *the coherent neighbor invariance of velocity correlations*, we set a threshold λ on the averaged velocity correlations to remove incoherent dots and obtain the pairwise connection set $\mathcal{R}$. Finally a connectivity graph is built, where nodes are dots and edges are defined by connection relationships in $\mathcal{R}$. With this graph, incoherent dots $\mathcal{B}$ are identified as isolated nodes and coherent motion clusters $\{\mathcal{F}_1, ..., \mathcal{F}_N\}$ are identified as the connected components of the graph.

Table 2. Algorithm **CoheFilterDet** for detecting coherent motion patterns

FUNCTION $(\mathcal{F}_1, ..., \mathcal{F}_N)$ = **CoheFilterDet**($\mathcal{I}$)

for $\tau = t$ to $t+d$
  search the K nearest neighbor set as $\mathcal{N}_\tau^i$ for each dot $i \in \mathcal{I}$
for each dot $i \in \mathcal{I}$
  search the invariant neighbor set as $\mathcal{M}_{t\to d}^i$
  for each $i_k \in \mathcal{M}_{t\to d}^i$
    compute the averaged velocity correlations $g_{t\to d}^{i_k}$
    include (i, i_k) in $\mathcal{R}$ if $g_{t\to d}^{i_k} > \lambda$.
Build a graph from $\mathcal{R}$. Remove incoherently moving individuals as the isolated nodes and identify coherent motion $\{\mathcal{F}_1, ..., \mathcal{F}_N\}$ as the connected components of the graph.

3.2 Algorithm for Associating Continuous Coherent Motion

Coherent motion clusters will continue and evolve, and new cluster of coherent motion will emerge over time. Based on the temporal overlaps of trajectories we develop another algorithm **CoheFilterAssoci** to associate and update the clusters of coherent motion over consecutive frames.

To associate the clusters of coherent motion over time, we define a variable s_i as the cluster index for each trajectory i. As illustrated in Figure 4A, the algorithm will update

Table 3. Algorithm **CoheFilterAssoci** for associating coherent motions

FUNCTION ($\mathcal{S}^{t+1}$) = **CoheFilterAssoci**($\mathcal{S}^t, \mathcal{I}^{t+1}$)

($\mathcal{F}_1, ..., \mathcal{F}_{N_{t+1}}$) = **CoheFilterDet**($\mathcal{I}^{t+1}$) /**detect new coherent motion at frame* t+1*/
for each $i \in \mathcal{I}^t \bigcap \mathcal{I}^{t+1}$
  $s_i^{t+1} = s_i^t$ /**firstly assume there is no cluster index changing for dot* i*/
M=**max**($\mathcal{S}^t$) /**maximum cluster index value in* $\mathcal{S}^t$*/
for each $\mathcal{F}_{n_{t+1}}$
  S=**mode**($\mathcal{H}$), where $\mathcal{H} = \{s_i^{t+1} | i \in \mathcal{F}_{n_{t+1}}\}$/**get the most frequent value in* $\mathcal{H}$*/
  if S==0 **then** S=M+1 /**add a new cluster index**/
  for each $i \in \mathcal{F}_{n_{t+1}}$ let s_i^{t+1}=S
identify dot $i \in \mathcal{I}^{t+1}$ as foreground and its cluster index as s_i^{t+1} if $s_i^{t+1} > 0$

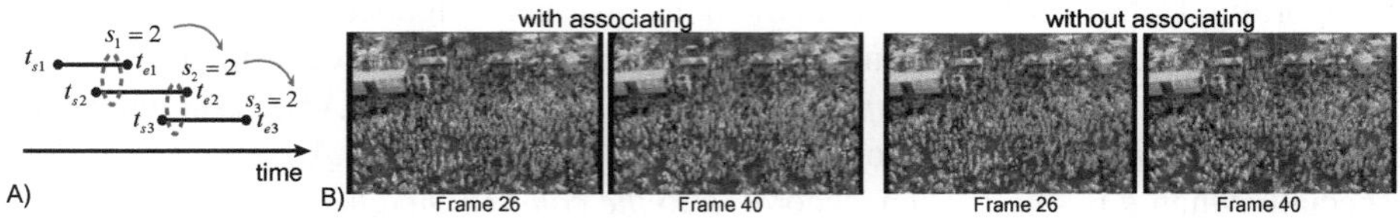

Fig. 4. Illustration of associating continuous coherent motions. A) There are temporal overlaps between trajectory 1 and 2, trajectory 2 and 3. If trajectory 1 and 2 are detected into one coherent motion cluster at one time, and trajectory 2 and 3 are detected into one coherent motion cluster at next time, the index $s_1 = 2$ of trajectory 1 will be transferred to the other two trajectories. Red circles indicate trajectories are detected into one coherent motion cluster, t_{si} and t_{ei} denote the starting and ending time of trajectory i. B) Two representative frames of coherent motion detection result with associating and without associating respectively. Dots in the same color belong to one coherent motion cluster over time and space.

the cluster indice of trajectories by majority voting and keep on detecting new coherent motion cluster over time. The detail of algorithm is listed in Table 3.

4 Experimental Results

In this section, we will evaluate the robustness and effectiveness of Coherent Filtering on complex synthetic data, real 3D motion segmentation database, and crowd videos. On the synthetic data, we test the technique by detecting coherent motion patterns with different dynamics from high-density Brownian motion noise. Then we evaluate the technique on the 3D affine motion segmentation Hopkins155 database [15], and compare it to several baseline methods on the database in the presence of outliers. Lastly we test Coherent Filtering on videos by detecting coherent motion patterns in real scenes with a variety of scales and crowdedness.

4.1 Coherent Motion in Synthetic Data

Figure 5A shows the two synthetic datasets for evaluation. The coherent motion patterns emerging in the datasets vary greatly in scales, shapes, and dynamics. For the 2D

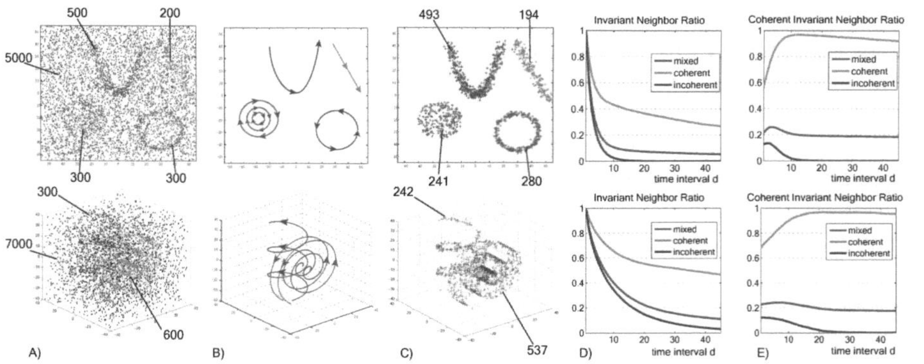

Fig. 5. Coherent motion detection on synthetic 2D and 3D datasets. A) The shapes and the numbers of coherently moving dots (colors indicate different coherent motion patterns) and noisy dots (in blue). B) The traces of each coherent motion patterns. C) The detected coherent motion patterns by Coherent Filtering. D) Invariant neighbor ratios for different types of dots over time. E) Coherent invariant neighbor ratios for different types of dots over time. The algorithm parameters are $K = 15$, $d = 4$ and $\lambda = 0.6$.

	NMI	
	2D	3D
Ncuts	0.28	0.24
K-means	0.21	0.14
Mean-shift	0.20	0.16
Ours	0.89	0.75

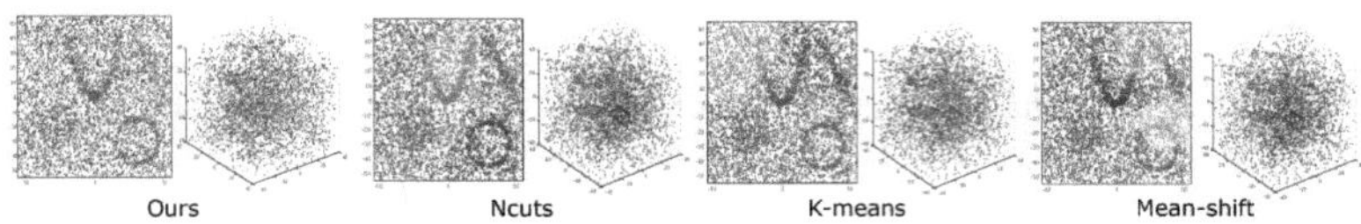

Fig. 6. The qualitative and quantitative results of the four methods for comparison. Colors indicate different clusters. NMI is used to quantitatively evaluate the clustering results. Our technique achieves the best performance.

dataset, the parametric forms of parabola, circle, line, and disk are used to generate four 2D coherent motion patterns. For the 3D dataset, the parametric forms of helix and spiral surface are used to generate two 3D coherent motion patterns. Figure 5B illustrates the traces of the synthetic coherent motion patterns. Initial positions of the coherent dots are randomly sampled from Gaussian distribution along the traces of the coherent motion patterns.

As the detection results shown in Figure 5C, our technique detects well these coherent motion patterns from rather noisy data. The good performance of detecting various coherent motion patterns shows the robustness and generalization ability of our technique. Figures 5D and 5E show that the invariant neighbor ratios and the coherent invariant neighbor ratios for the two datasets. We can see they have good discriminability between coherent dots and incoherent noisy dots. It also verifies the existence of coherent neighbor invariance in the synthetic data.

Three representative clustering methods, *i.e.*, Normalized Cuts (Ncuts) [21], K-means and Mean-shift [22], are selected for comparison. Ncuts, K-means, and Mean-shift are often extended for time-series data clustering [23] and trajectory clustering [24]. By convention, we treat the trajectory of each dot i from time t to $t + d$ as a feature vector

$(x_t^i, y_t^i, v_{x,t}^i, v_{y,t}^i, \cdots, x_{t+d}^i, y_{t+d}^i, v_{x,t+d}^i, v_{y,t+d}^i)$, where (x_τ^i, y_τ^i) and $(v_{x,\tau}^i, v_{y,\tau}^i)$ are the location and velocity of dot i at time τ. Dots are clustered based on the feature vectors. For Ncuts and K-means, the cluster numbers are chosen as 5 and 3 for the two datasets. Mean-shift automatically determines the cluster number. The clustering results are shown in Figure 6. The quantitative result is measured by the Normalized Mutual Information (NMI) [25]. Larger NMI indicates better clustering performance. The time interval d is set as 4, which means that the trajectory of each dot has six samples as the inputs of all the algorithms. Our algorithm achieves the best performance.

4.2 3D Motion Segmentation

There are many potential applications of our Coherent Filtering algorithm in real-world problems. We test it on 3D affine motion segmentation on the Hopkins155 Database [15]. We choose this application because its ground truth is available and it can providequantitative evaluation of our technique. This database consists of 120 video se-

Fig. 7. A) Representative sequences from Hopkins155 database and the segmentation results of Coherent Filtering. B) The first image is one representative frame with groundtruth. There are 2 clusters, one cluster is on the moving object, the other cluster is on the static background objects, which results from moving camera. The second image is the segmentation result of our method. Since Coherent Filtering has no assumption on the number of clusters, it tends to segment some dispersed background cluster into several clusters of separated objects. Yellow + dots are the detected noises.

quences with two motions and 35 video sequences with three motions. Trajectories of feature points on each motion are clustered as ground truth and input for each testing method. The sequences can be categorized into three main groups, checkboard, traffic, and articulated, which contain a variety of motions, such as degenerate and non-degenerate motions, independent motions, and motions from camera movement. Figure 7A shows the representative frames of sequences in the database. For comparison, typical subspace motion segmentation methods, Generalized Principal Component Analysis (GPCA) [16] and RANSAC [15] are taken as the baseline. These approaches utilize the fact that object movements in this database are rigid and under affine transform. However, our method does not need the assumption since it is used to detect motions in more general form. Figure 8A shows the segmentation performance in terms of Normalized Mutual Information and average computation time.[3] Coherent Filtering achieves com-

[3] Codes of comparison methods are downloaded from authors' websites. Average computation time is tested on a computer with 3GHz Core Quad CPU and 4GB RAM with Matlab implementation. Note that since the number of clusters detected by our method may not accurately correspond to the ground truth cluster number, NMI is a more suitable measurement than the misclassification rate reported in [15].

parative performance to these subspace segmentation methods, though it is not specifically designed for 3D affine motion segmentation. The major error of our method comes from that our method has no assumption on the number of motion clusters in the sequence, so that it would tend to segment some dispersed background cluster of ground truth into several small clusters instead of one background cluster, as shown in Figure 7B. This problem is hard to be solved using our method alone without assuming the affine transform since these small clusters are far away to each other in space. Strictly speaking, they do not belong to a single coherent motion, but the database ground truth treats them as one pattern. To further evaluate the robustness of different methods in the

NMI	GPCA	RANSAC	CF
Checkboard	0.699	0.736	0.744
Traffic	0.858	0.829	0.705
Articulated	0.821	0.727	0.748
All sequences	0.748	0.758	0.735
Average Time	1.02s	7.58s	321ms

A)

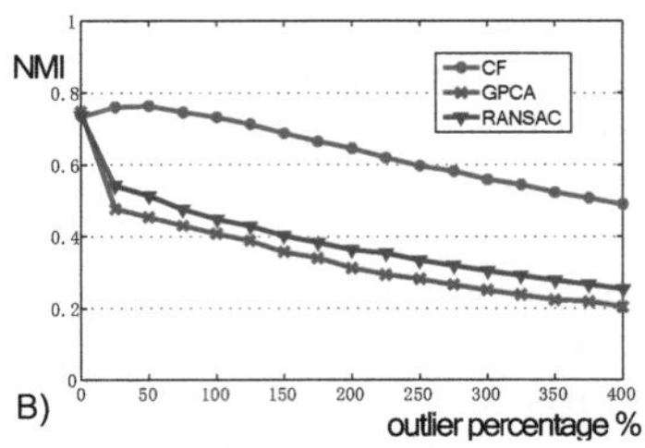

B)

Fig. 8. A) NMI of different methods on the Hopkins155 Database, along with the average computation time. Though Coherent Filtering is not specifically designed for 3D motion segmentation, it achieves comparative performance to other subspace segmentation methods with a better computational efficiency. B) NMI of different methods as the function of the outlier percentage(from 0% to 400%).

presence of outliers, we add outlier trajectories from 0% to 400% into the groundtruth trajectories of every 155 sequences, then test the performances of these methods. Outlier trajectories are generated by randomly choosing initial points in the first frame and then extending the trajectories with random walk. Figure 8B shows the NMI of these methods with different outlier percentages. Coherent Filtering works more robust with heavy noise.

4.3 Coherent Motion Detection in Crowd

Experiments are conducted on 8 video clips with coherent motion emerging in different scales and distributions. The first video clip is captured on the USC campus [4]. The scene is relatively sparse and the scales of pedestrians are high. The second one is from [26] with higher crowd density, and it contains both individual and groups of pedestrians. In the third one, many middle-sized people are coming in and out. The fourth is acquired from a far-view railway station. The resolutions of pedestrian are very small. And the last four clips are selected from Getty Image website, containing high-density crowd running and traversing. Some of them have been used in [7]. In initialization, KLT keypoint tracker [27] is used to automatically detect keypoints and extract their trajectories as the observation $\mathcal{I}$ for the input of algorithm. Tracking terminates when severe clutters or occlusions arise, and new tracks will be initialized later. For all videos, the parameters of Coherent Filtering are $\lambda = 0.6$, $d = 4$, and $K = 10$. We further discuss the influence of parameters on the clustering results in Section 4.4 .

Fig. 9. Representative frames and the coherent motion clusters detected by Coherent Filtering. Moving keypoints from videos exhibit a variety of coherent motion patterns at different scales in different scene context. A) The majority of detected coherent motion clusters result from the independent walking pedestrians, since the scale of pedestrians is rather big. B) Coherent motions from both individual pedestrians and groups of pedestrians walking together are detected. C) Different queues of walking-in-and-out people are detected. D) From the far view to the railway station, there are merely one or two keypoints tracked on each pedestrian in the scene. Thus the emergent coherent motions of keypoints represent the clusters of nearby pedestrians heading in the same directions, and they are related to different traffic modes. E) Two major lanes of vehicles on the road are detected, among them several small clusters representing jaywalkers are also detected because of their difference in motion directions to the major lanes. F) Two groups of pedestrians are detected to pass each other on the crosswalk. G) There is one circular coherent motion cluster detected as athletes running. H) The population density in the scene is extremely high, the detected coherent motion patterns characterize the dominant crowd flows. The crowd is separated into several bidirectional flows: the yellow flow is moving to the left, the orange flow is moving to the right, and the blue flow is moving against the orange flow dividing the orange flow of people.

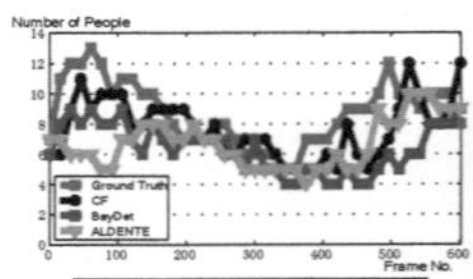

	CF	BayDet	ALDENTE
DR	0.62	0.57	0.41
FAR	0.22	0.20	0.34
CountError	1.95	2.88	3.15

A)

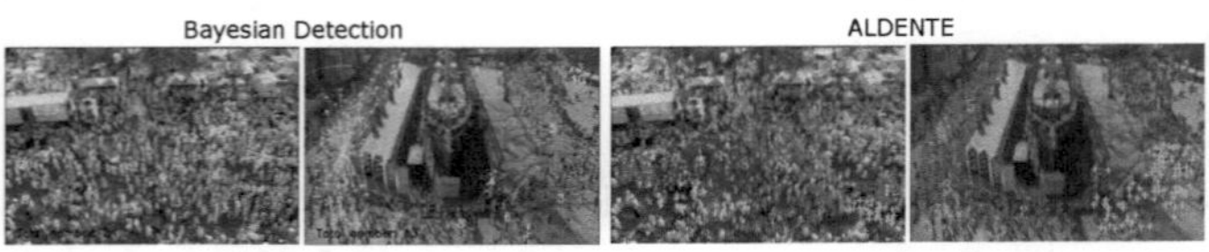

B)

Fig. 10. A) The number of pedestrians detected at each key frame with respect to Frame No., and Detection Rate(DR), False Alarm Rate(FAR), and counting error(CountError) for Coherent Filter(CF), BayDet[5], and ALDENTE[4]. B) BayDet and ALDENTE fail to detect the coherent motions when the crowdedness and the level of noise arise.

Figure 9 shows the representative frames and coherent motion clusters detected by Coherent Filtering in different scenes. Coherent Filtering detects well the underlying coherent motion patterns from the noisy time-series observations of detected keypoints. From these results, we can see that the detected coherent motion clusters correspond to a variety of semantic behaviors and activities, which are of great importance to further video analysis, surveillance and scene understanding. However, it is difficult to quantitatively evaluate these behaviors from detected coherent motions since it is hard to obtain the ground truth.

To quantitatively evaluate the detection performance, we conduct the people counting experiment on the scene shown in Figure 10, and compare with trajectory clustering-based people counting method ALDENTE [4] and Bayesian Detection counting method BayDet [5]. The experimental setting is the same as [5]. We count the number of pedestrian detected at each key frame (every key frame per 15 frames), and use the average people counting error as the evaluation criteria for the three methods. Meanwhile, since at each frame the detected clusters can be either True Positive or False Positive, and the False Positive also can be counted as the False Negative (the undetected one) in the number of pedestrians detected in each key frame. That makes people counting evaluation criteria not so accurate. Thus we further evaluate the Detection Rate (DR) and False Alarm Rate (FAR) as

$$DR = \frac{\sum_i TP_i}{\sum_i GT_i}, \quad FAR = \frac{\sum_i FP_i}{\sum_i TP_i + FP_i},$$

where TP_i, FP_i, and GT_i are the number of True Positive, False Positive, and groundtruth at frame i. Figure 10A shows the numbers of pedestrian detected by the three methods and the groundtruth at each key frames, and Figure 10B shows the average people counting error, DR, and FAR for the three methods respectively. Coherent Filtering achieves the best performance. On the other hand, ALDENTE and BayDet work poorly when the density of the crowd and the level of the noise increase. As shown in Figure 10C, they both fail to detect the coherent motions in crowded scenes.

4.4 Further Analysis of the Algorithm

Necessity of Two Filtering Steps in the Algorithm. The algorithm **CoheFilterDet** of Coherent Filtering can be divided into two steps: first removing variant neighbors and then filtering out the neighbors with low averaged velocity correlations. As discussed in Section 2.2, the coherent neighbor invariance of spatiotemporal relationships does not guarantee that *all* the dots in $\mathcal{A}$ are coherent dots, especially when d is small. Figure 11A shows the clustering results directly obtained from $\mathcal{A}$ without thresholding when d = 6, 10, and 20 respectively, and the plot of Normalized Mutual Information (NMI) under different d with thresholding and without thresholding respectively. No thresholding, when d is small there remains a significant amount of noise. As d increases, NMI increases, which means the clustering performance is improved. Then NMI with thresholding and NMI without thresholding gradually converge. In principle, all the incoherent dots can be removed by setting a large d, such as when d = 20. However in practice, it is difficult to obtain the correspondence of dots over a long period. Thus filtering with thresholding the averaged velocity correlations on $\mathcal{A}$ is necessary.

Influence of K. K decides the size of the neighborhood. Figure 11B shows the clustering results with $K = 5$ and $K = 25$ on the 2D synthetic data and the real data. When K is small, the detected coherent motion patterns are inclined to be divided into parts. However, when K is too large, some noise might be included. Thus the choice of K is related to the scale of coherent motion patterns to be detected in specific videos.

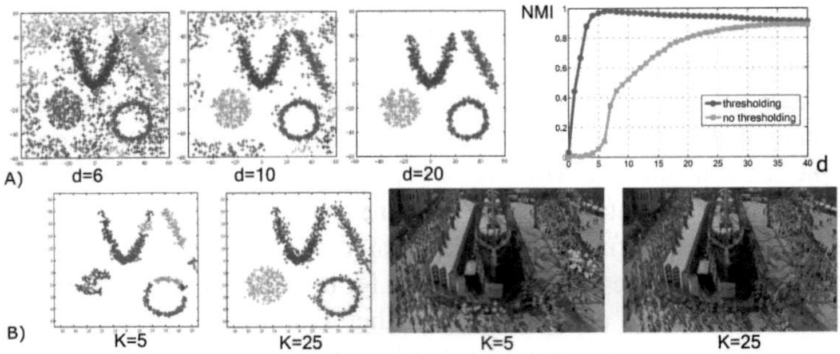

Fig. 11. A) The clustering results without thresholding when $d = 6, 10, 20$, and the plot of NMI under different d with thresholding and without thresholding. B) The clustering results on the 2D synthetic data and the real data with $K = 5$ and $K = 25$ respectively.

5 Conclusion

In this paper, we study the *Coherent Neighbor Invariance* as a prior of coherent motions and propose an effective clustering technique *Coherent Filtering*. Experimental evaluation and comparison on synthetic and real datasets show the existence of coherent neighbor invariance in various dynamic systems and the effectiveness of our technique under high-density noise. In the future work, we will study coherence neighbor invariance in a wider range of physical and biological systems and explore more potential applications.

Acknowledgement. This work is partially supported by the General Research Fund sponsored by the Research Grants Council of Hong Kong (Project No. CUHK417110 and CUHK417011) and National Natural Science Foundation of China (Project No. 61005057). It is also supported through Introduced Innovative R&D Team of Guangdong Province 201001D0104648280 and Shenzhen Key Lab of Computer Vision and Pattern Recognition.

References

1. Couzin, I.: Collective cognition in animal groups. Trends in Cognitive Sciences (2009)
2. Moussaid, M., Garnier, S., Theraulaz, G., Helbing, D.: Collective information processing and pattern formation in swarms, flocks, and crowds. Topics in Cognitive Science (2009)
3. Camazine, S.: Self-organization in biological systems. Princeton Univ. Pr. (2003)
4. Rabaud, V., Belongie, S.: Counting crowded moving objects. In: Proc. CVPR (2006)
5. Brostow, G., Cipolla, R.: Unsupervised bayesian detection of independent motion in crowds. In: Proc. CVPR (2006)
6. Ali, S., Shah, M.: Floor Fields for Tracking in High Density Crowd Scenes. In: Forsyth, D., Torr, P., Zisserman, A. (eds.) ECCV 2008, Part II. LNCS, vol. 5303, pp. 1–14. Springer, Heidelberg (2008)
7. Ali, S., Shah, M.: A lagrangian particle dynamics approach for crowd flow segmentation and stability analysis. In: Proc. CVPR (2007)

8. Wang, X., Ma, X., Grimson, W.: Unsupervised activity perception in crowded and complicated scenes using hierarchical bayesian models. IEEE Trans. on PAMI (2008)
9. Zhou, B., Wang, X., Tang, X.: Understanding collective crowd behaviors:learning a mixture model of dynamic pedestrian-agents. In: Proc. CVPR (2012)
10. Zhou, B., Wang, X., Tang, X.: Random field topic model for semantic region analysis in crowded scenes from tracklets. In: Proc. CVPR (2011)
11. Wang, X., Tieu, K., Grimson, E.: Learning Semantic Scene Models by Trajectory Analysis. In: Leonardis, A., Bischof, H., Pinz, A. (eds.) ECCV 2006. LNCS, vol. 3953, pp. 110–123. Springer, Heidelberg (2006)
12. Lin, D., Grimson, E., Fisher, J.: Learning visual flows: A lie algebraic approach. In: Proc. CVPR (2009)
13. Hu, M., Ali, S., Shah, M.: Learning motion patterns in crowded scenes using motion flow field. In: Proc. ICPR (2008)
14. Wang, X., Ma, K., Ng, G., Grimson, W.: Trajectory analysis and semantic region modeling using nonparametric hierarchical bayesian models. Int'l Journal of Computer Vision (2011)
15. Tron, R., Vidal, R.: A benchmark for the comparison of 3-d motion segmentation algorithms. In: Proc. CVPR (2007)
16. Vidal, R., Ma, Y., Sastry, S.: Generalized principal component analysis (gpca). IEEE Trans. on PAMI (2005)
17. Brox, T., Malik, J.: Object Segmentation by Long Term Analysis of Point Trajectories. In: Daniilidis, K., Maragos, P., Paragios, N. (eds.) ECCV 2010, Part V. LNCS, vol. 6315, pp. 282–295. Springer, Heidelberg (2010)
18. Fischler, M., Bolles, R.: Random sample consensus: a paradigm for model fitting with applications to image analysis and automated cartography. Communications of the ACM (1981)
19. Petit, O., Bon, R.: Decision-making processes: the case of collective movements. Behavioural Processes (2010)
20. Lamme, V.: The neurophysiology of figure-ground segregation in primary visual cortex. The Journal of Neuroscience (1995)
21. Shi, J., Malik, J.: Normalized cuts and image segmentation. IEEE Trans. on PAMI (2000)
22. Comaniciu, D., Meer, P.: Mean shift: A robust approach toward feature space analysis. IEEE Trans. on PAMI (2002)
23. Liao, W., et al.: Clustering of time series data–a survey. Pattern Recognition (2005)
24. Morris, B., Trivedi, M.: A survey of vision-based trajectory learning and analysis for surveillance. IEEE Transactions on Circuits and Systems for Video Technology (2008)
25. Strehl, A., Ghosh, J.: Cluster ensembles—a knowledge reuse framework for combining multiple partitions. The Journal of Machine Learning Research (2003)
26. Pellegrini, S., Ess, A., Van Gool, L.: Improving Data Association by Joint Modeling of Pedestrian Trajectories and Groupings. In: Daniilidis, K., Maragos, P., Paragios, N. (eds.) ECCV 2010, Part I. LNCS, vol. 6311, pp. 452–465. Springer, Heidelberg (2010)
27. Tomasi, C., Kanade, T.: Detection and Tracking of Point Features. Int'l Journal of Computer Vision (1991)

Robust 3D Action Recognition with Random Occupancy Patterns

Jiang Wang[1], Zicheng Liu[2], Jan Chorowski[3], Zhuoyuan Chen[1], and Ying Wu[1]

[1] Northwestern University
[2] Microsoft Research
[3] University of Louisville

Abstract. We study the problem of action recognition from depth sequences captured by depth cameras, where noise and occlusion are common problems because they are captured with a single commodity camera. In order to deal with these issues, we extract semi-local features called random occupancy pattern (ROP) features, which employ a novel sampling scheme that effectively explores an extremely large sampling space. We also utilize a sparse coding approach to robustly encode these features. The proposed approach does not require careful parameter tuning. Its training is very fast due to the use of the high-dimensional integral image, and it is robust to the occlusions. Our technique is evaluated on two datasets captured by commodity depth cameras: an action dataset and a hand gesture dataset. Our classification results are superior to those obtained by the state of the art approaches on both datasets.

1 Introduction

Recently, the advance of the imaging technology has enabled us to capture the depth information in real-time, and various promising applications have been proposed [1–4]. Compared with conventional cameras, the depth camera has several advantages. For example, segmentation in depth images is much easier, and depth images are insensitive to changes in lighting conditions. In this paper, we consider the problem of action recognition from depth sequences.

Although skeleton tracking algorithm proposed in [1] is very robust for depth sequences when little occlusion occurs, it can produce inaccurate results or even fails when serious occlusion occurs. Moreover, the skeleton tracking is unavailable for human hands thus cannot be utilized for hand gesture recognition.

Therefore, we aim at developing an action recognition approach that directly takes the depth sequences as input. Designing an efficient depth sequences representation for action recognition is a challenging task. First of all, depth sequences may be seriously contaminated by occlusions, which makes the global features unstable. On the other hand, the depth maps do not have as much texture as color images do, and they are too noisy to apply local differential operators such as gradients on. These challenges motivate us to seek for features that are semi-local, highly discriminative and robust to occlusion.

In this paper, we treat a three-dimensional action sequence as a 4D shape and propose random occupancy pattern (ROP) features, which are extracted from

A. Fitzgibbon et al. (Eds.): ECCV 2012, Part II, LNCS 7573, pp. 872–885, 2012.

randomly sampled 4D subvolumes with different sizes and at different locations. Since the ROP features are extracted at a larger scale, it is robust to noise. At the same time, they are less sensitive to occlusion because they only encode information from the regions that are most discriminative for the given action.

An Elastic-Net regularized classification model is developed to further select the most discriminative features, and sparse coding is utilized to robustly encode the features.The feature encoding step further improves the proposed method's robustness to occlusion by modeling the occlusion noise as the sparse coding reconstruction errors. The proposed approach performs well on the depth sequence dataset and is robust to occlusion. The general framework of the proposed method is shown in Fig. 1.

We evaluate our method on two datasets captured by commodity depth cameras. The experimental results validate the effectiveness of the proposed method.

Our main contributions are as follows: First, we propose a computationally efficient method to perform action recognition from depth sequences. Second, a novel weighted sampling scheme is proposed to effectively explore an extremely large dense sampling space. Third, we propose to employ sparse coding to deal with the occlusion in the depth sequences.

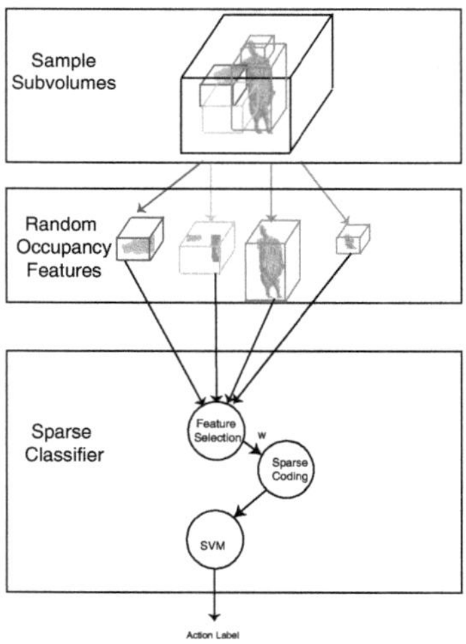

Fig. 1. The framework of the proposed method. The 3D subvolumes are shown for illustration purpose. In the implementation, 4D subvolumes are employed.

2 Related Work

The Haar wavelet-like features have been successfully applied in [5] for face detection. A boosted classifier is learned by applying AdaBoost algorithm [6] on a very large pool of weak classifiers. The weak classifier pool is constructed based on the features extracted from the rectangles at all possible locations and scales. While this approach is successful for 2D images, when the data becomes 3D or 4D, the number of possible rectangles becomes so large that enumerating them or performing AdaBoost algorithm on them becomes computationally prohibitive. [7] utilizes 3D occupancy features and models the dynamics by an exemplar-based hidden Markov model. The proposed ROP feature is much simpler and more computationally efficient than Haar-like features, while achieving similar performances in depth datasets.

Randomization has been applied in [8] and [9] to address this problem. [9] employs a random forest to learn discriminative features that are extracted either from a patch or from a pair of patches for fine-grained image categorization. [8] applies a random forest to mine discriminative features from binary spatial arrangement features for character recognition. Their work demonstrates the effectiveness of randomization in dealing with this problem. We exploit randomization to perform action recognition from depth sequences, in which the data is sparse and the number of the possible subvolumes is much larger.

[10] and [11] also employ randomization in the learning process. These approaches randomly map the data to features with a linear function whose weights and biases are uniformly sampled. Their empirical and theoretical results show that their training is much faster than AdaBoost's, while their classification accuracy is comparable to AdaBoost's. The proposed approach also randomly maps the data to features. Unlike [10] and [11], however, our approach exploits the neighborhood structure of depth sequences, and extracts features from the pixels that are spatially close to each other. Furthermore, we propose a weighted sampling technique that is more effective than uniform sampling.

Recently, a lot of efforts have been made to develop features for action recognition in depth data. [12] represents each depth frame as a bag of 3D points on the human silhouette, and utilizes HMM to model the temporal dynamics. [13] uses relative skeleton position and local occupancy patterns to model the human-object interaction, and developed Fourier Temporal Pyramid to characterize temporal dynamics. [14] also applies spatio-temporal occupancy patterns, but all the cells in the grid have the same size, and the number of cells is empirically set. [15] proposes a dimension-reduced skeleton feature, and [16] developed a histogram of gradient feature over depth motion maps. Instead of carefully developing good features, this paper tries to learn semi-local features automatically from the data, and we show that this learning-based approach achieves good results.

3 Random Occupancy Patterns

The proposed method treats a depth sequence as a 4D volume, and defines the value of a pixel in this volume $I(x, y, z, t)$ to be either 1 or 0, depending on whether there is a point in the 4D volume at this location. The action recognition is performed by using the value of a simple feature called *random occupancy patterns*, which is both efficient to compute and highly discriminative.

This paper employ four dimensional random occupancy patterns to construct the features, whose value is defined to be the soft-thresholded sum of the pixels in a subvolume:

$$o_{xyzt} = \delta(\sum_{q \in \text{bin}_{xyzt}} I_q) \tag{1}$$

where $I_q = 1$ if the point cloud has a point in the location q and $I_q = 0$ otherwise. $\delta(.)$ is a sigmoid normalization function: $\delta(x) = \frac{1}{1+e^{-\beta x}}$. This feature is able to capture the occupancy pattern of a 4D subvolume. Moreover, it can be computed in constant complexity with the high dimensional integral images [17].

As shown in Fig. 1, we extract ROP features from the subvolumes with different sizes and at different locations. However, the number of possible simple features is so large that we are not able to enumerate all of them. In this paper, we propose a weighted random sampling scheme to address this problem, which will be described in Section 4.

4 Weighted Sampling Approach

Since the number of possible positions and sizes of a 4D subvolume is extremely large and the information of these features is highly redundant, it is neither necessary nor computationally efficient to explore all of them. In this section, we propose a random sampling approach to efficiently explore these 4D subvolumes.

4.1 Dense Sampling Space

Recall that a ROP feature is extracted from a 4D subvolume. It is computationally prohibitive to extract the features from all possible subvolumes, thus we would like to sample a subset of discriminative subvolumes and extract the features from them. This subsection characterizes the *dense sampling space*, from which we randomly sample subvolumes.

Denote the size of a depth sequence volume to be $W_x \times W_y \times W_z \times W_t$. A subvolume can be characterized by two points $[x_0, y_0, z_0, t_0]$ and $[x_1, y_1, z_1, t_1]$, and is denoted as $[x_0, y_0, z_0, t_0] \sim [x_1, y_1, z_1, t_1]$. A normal subvolume has the property that $x_0 \leq x_1, y_0 \leq y_1, z_0 \leq z_1$, and $t_0 \leq t_1$, and the subvolume is the set of points

$$\begin{aligned}\{[x, y, z, t] : x_0 \leq x \leq x_1, y_0 \leq y \leq y_1,\\ z_0 \leq z \leq z_1, t_0 \leq t \leq t_1\}\end{aligned} \tag{2}$$

Our sampling space consists of all the subvolumes $[x_0, y_0, z_0, t_0] \sim [x_1, y_1, z_1, t_1]$ where $x_0, x_1 \in \{1, 2, \cdots, W_x\}$, $y_0, y_1 \in \{1, 2, \cdots, W_y\}$, $z_0, z_1 \in \{1, 2, \cdots, W_z\}$, $t_0, t_1 \in \{1, 2, \cdots, W_t\}$. If we take $(W_x, W_y, W_z, W_t) = (80, 80, 80, 80)$, the size of the dense sampling space is $80^8 = 1.67 \times 10^{15}$. This dense sampling space is so large that exhaustively exploring it is computationally prohibitive. However, since the subvolumes highly overlap with each other, they contain redundant information, and it is possible to employ randomization to deal with this problem.

4.2 Weighted Sampling

One way to sample from the dense sampling space is to perform uniform sampling. Nevertheless, since in the depth sequences many subvolumes do not contain useful information for classification, uniform sampling is highly inefficient. In this section, to efficiently sample from the dense sampling space, we propose a weighted sampling approach based on the rejection sampling, which samples the discriminative subvolumes with high probability.

To characterize how discriminative a subvolume is, we employ the scatter matrix class separability measure [18]. The scatter matrices include *Within-class scatter matrix* ($\boldsymbol{S}_W$), *Between-class scatter matrix* ($\boldsymbol{S}_B$), and *Total scatter matrix* ($\boldsymbol{S}_T$). They are defined as $\boldsymbol{S}_W = \sum_{i=1}^{c} \sum_{j=1}^{n_i} (\boldsymbol{h}_{i,j} - \boldsymbol{m}_i)(\boldsymbol{h}_{i,j} - \boldsymbol{m}_i)^T$, $\boldsymbol{S}_B = \sum_{i=1}^{c} n_i(\boldsymbol{m}_i - \boldsymbol{m})(\boldsymbol{m}_i - \boldsymbol{m})^T$, $\boldsymbol{S}_T = \boldsymbol{S}_W + \boldsymbol{S}_B$, where c is the number of the classes, n_i denotes the number of training data in the i-th class, and $\boldsymbol{h}_{i,j}$ denote the features extracted from the j-th training data in the i-th class. $\boldsymbol{m}_i$ denotes the mean vectors of the features $\boldsymbol{h}_{i,j}$ in the i-th class and $\boldsymbol{m}$ the mean vector of the features extracted from all the training data. A large separability measure means that these classes have small within-class scatter and large between-class scatter, and the class separability measure J can be defined as

$$J = \frac{\mathrm{tr}(\boldsymbol{S}_{\mathrm{W}})}{\mathrm{tr}\boldsymbol{S}_{\mathrm{B}}} \tag{3}$$

Denote V as the 4D volume of a depth sequence. For each pixel $p \in V$, we define a neighborhood subvolume centered at p, and extract the 8 Haar feature values from this neighborhood subvolume. These 8 feature values form an 8-dimensional vector which is used as the feature vector $\boldsymbol{h}$ to evaluate the class separability score J_p at pixel p.

A subvolume should be discriminative if all the pixels in this subvolume are discriminative, and vice versa. Therefore, we utilize the average of the separability scores of all the pixels in the region R as the separability score of R.

The probability that a subvolume R is sampled should be proportional to its separability score J_R, that is,

$$P_{R\ \mathrm{sampled}} \propto J_R = \frac{1}{N_R} \sum_{p \in R} J_p \tag{4}$$

where N_R is the number of pixels in the subvolume R.

We can uniformly draw a subvolume, and accept the subvolume with probability

$$P_{R\ \mathrm{accept}} = \frac{W_x W_y W_z W_t}{\sum_{p \in V} J_p} J_R \tag{5}$$

Note that $P_{R\ \mathrm{uniform}} P_{R\ \mathrm{accept}} = P_{R\ \mathrm{sampled}}$. Therefore, with the rejection sampling scheme, the probability that R is selected is equal to the desired probability as specified in equation (4). The derivation of the acceptance rate can be found in the supplemental material.

Because we are able to compute the average separability score in a subvolume very efficiently using the high dimensional integral image, this sampling scheme is computationally efficient. The outline of the algorithm is shown in Alg. 1.

Let N_S denote the number of subvolumes to sample, J_p the separability score at pixel p.
Compute $P = \frac{W_x W_y W_z W_t}{\sum_{p \in V} J_p}$
repeat
    Uniformly draw a subvolume R.
    Compute the average separability score in this subvolume J_R with integral image.
    Compute the acceptance rate $P_{\text{accept}} = P J_R$.
    Uniformly draw a number N from $[0, 1]$.
    if $N \leq P_{accept}$ **then**
        Retain the subvolume R.
    end
    else
        Discard the subvolume R.
    end
until *the number of subvolumes sampled* $\geq N_S$;

Algorithm 1. Weighted Sampling Algorithm

5 Learning Classification Functions

Given the training data pairs $(\boldsymbol{x}^i, t^i), i = 1, \cdots, n$, where $\boldsymbol{x}^i \in \mathcal{R}^L$ denotes a training data, and $t^i \in \mathcal{T}$ is the corresponding label, the aim of the classification problem is to learn a prediction function $g : \mathcal{R}^L \rightarrow \mathcal{T}$. Without loss of generality, we assume the classification problem is a binary classification problem, i.e., $\mathcal{T} = \{0, 1\}$. If the problem is a multiclass problem, it can be converted into a binary classification problem with the one-vs-others approach.

An Elastic-Net regularization is employed to select a sparse subset of features that are the most discriminative for the classification. Choosing a sparse subset of features has several advantages. First, the speed of the final classifier is faster if the number of the selected features is smaller. Second, learning a sparse classification function is less prone to over-fitting if only limited amount of training data is available [19].

For each training data sample $\boldsymbol{x}^i$, N_f ROP features are extracted: $h_j^i, j = 1, \cdots, N_f$, and the response is predicted by a linear function

$$y^i = \sum_{j=1}^{N_f} w_j h_j^i \tag{6}$$

Denote $\boldsymbol{w}$ as the vector containing all $w_j, j = 1, \cdots, N_f$. The objective of the learning is to find $\boldsymbol{w}$ that minimizes the following objective function:

$$E = \sum_{i=1}^{n}(t^i - y^i)^2 + \lambda_1\|\boldsymbol{w}\|_1 + \lambda_2\|\boldsymbol{w}\|_2^2 \tag{7}$$

where λ_1 is a regularization parameter to control the sparsity of $\boldsymbol{w}$, and λ_2 is used to ensure that the margin of the classifier is large. It has been shown that if the number of features N_f is much larger than that of the training data n, which is the case of this paper, Elastic-Net regularization works particularly well [19]. SPAMS toolbox [20] is employed to numerically solve this optimization problem.

The selected feature $\boldsymbol{f}$ is obtained by discarding the features x_j with corresponding w_j less than a given threshold and multiplying the rest of x_j by weight w_j.

All the training data is utilized as the dictionary $\boldsymbol{A} = [\boldsymbol{f}^1, \boldsymbol{f}^2, \cdots, \boldsymbol{f}^n]$. For a test data with feature $\boldsymbol{f}$, we can solve the following sparse coding problem:

$$\min \frac{1}{2}\|\boldsymbol{f} - \boldsymbol{A}\boldsymbol{\alpha}\|_2^2 + \lambda\|\boldsymbol{\alpha}\|_1 \tag{8}$$

where $\boldsymbol{\alpha}$ is called the reconstruction coefficients, and λ is a regularization parameter. This model assumes the feature vector $\boldsymbol{f}$ can be represented as the linear combination of the features of the training data plus a noise vector ϵ.

$$\boldsymbol{f} = \sum_{i=1}^{n} \boldsymbol{\alpha}_i \boldsymbol{f}^i + \epsilon \tag{9}$$

The reconstruction coefficients $\boldsymbol{\alpha}$ are employed to represent a depth sequence, and an SVM classifier is trained for action classification.

6 Experimental Results

In this section, we evaluate our algorithm on three datasets captured by commodity depth cameras: the MSR-Action3D datasets [12], Gesture3D dataset. The experimental results show that our algorithm outperforms the existing methods on these datasets, and is not sensitive to occlusion error. The β of the sigmoid function for ROP feature is set to be 10 in all the experiments.

6.1 MSR-Action3D

MSR-Action3D dataset [12] is an action dataset of depth sequences captured by a depth camera. This dataset contains twenty actions: *high arm wave*, *horizontal arm wave*, *hammer*, *hand catch*, *forward punch*, *high throw*, *draw x*, *draw tick*, *draw circle*, *hand clap*, *two hand wave*, *side-boxing*, *bend*, *forward kick*, *side kick*, *jogging*, *tennis swing*, *tennis serve*, *golf swing*, *pick up & throw*. Each action was performed by ten subjects for three times. The frame rate is 15 frames per second and resolution 640 × 480. Altogether, the dataset has 23797 frames of depth maps for 402 action samples. Some examples of the depth map sequences are shown in Fig. 2.

Those actions were chosen to cover various movement of arms, legs, torso and their combinations, and the subjects were advised to use their right arm or leg if an action is performed by a single arm or leg. Although the background of this dataset is clean, this dataset is challenging because many of the actions in the dataset are highly similar to each other. In this experiment, 50000 subvolumes are sampled unless otherwise stated.

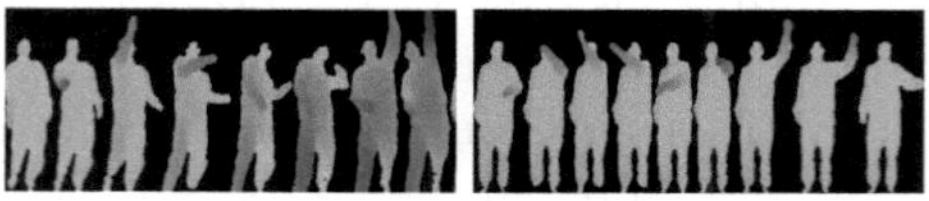

Fig. 2. Sample frames of the MSR-Action3D dataset

In order to ensure the consistency of the scale, Each depth sequence is resized to the same size $80 \times 80 \times 80 \times 10$. The separability scores of the MSR-Action3D are shown in Fig. 3. The regions with high separability scores are human's arms and legs, which is consistent with the characteristics of the dataset, and the beginning and the ending parts of an action is less discriminative than the middle part of an action. Moreover, in Fig. 3(d), it can be observed that the center of the human does not have high separability score, because the center of the human usually does not have many movements and does not contain useful information for classification.

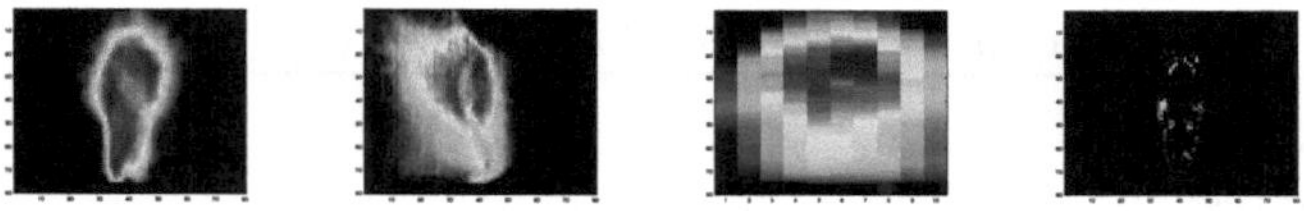

(a) (b) (c) (d)

Fig. 3. The projection of the separability scores for MSR-Action3D, where red color means high intensity. (a) the projection of the separability scores to x-y plane. (b) the projection of the separability scores to y-z plane. (c) the projection of the separability scores to y-t plane. (d) the cross section of the separability scores on x-y plane at $z = 40, t = 1$.

We compare our algorithm with the state-of-the-art method [12] on this dataset, which extracts the contour information from the depth maps, with half of the subjects as training data and the rest of the subjects as test data. Table 1 shows the recognition accuracy. The recognition accuracy is computed by running the experiments 10 times and taking the average of each experiment's accuracy. Our method outperforms this method by a large margin. Notice that our classification configuration uses half of the subjects as the training data and the rest of them as test data, which is difficult because of the larger variations across the same actions performed by different subjects. Our method is also compared with the STIP features. [21], which is a state-of-the-art local feature designed for action recognition from videos. The local spatio-temporal features do not work well for depth data because there is little texture in depth maps. Another method we compare with is the convolutional network. We have implemented a 4-dimensional convolutional network by extending the three-dimensional convolutional network of [22]. Finally we compare with a Support Vector Machine classifier on the raw features consisting of the pixels on all the locations. Although the Support Vector Machine performs surprisingly well on our dataset, the training time of the SVM is very long because the dimension of the features is very high. In contrast, the proposed method is simple to implement and is computationally efficient in both training and testing. Moreover, it outperforms all the other methods including SVM. In addition, we can see that the proposed ROP feature performs comparably with Haar features.

Table 1. Recognition Accuracy Comparison for MSR-Action3D dataset

Method	Accuracy
STIP features [21]	0.423
Action Graph on Bag of 3D Points [12]	0.747
High Dimensional Convolutional Network	0.725
STOP feature [14]	0.848
Eigenjoints [15]	0.823
Support Vector Machine on Raw Data	0.79
Proposed Method (Without sparse coding)	**0.8592**
Proposed Method (Haar Feature)	**0.8650**
Proposed Method (Sparse Coding)	**0.8620**

In order to test the sensitivity of the proposed method to occlusions, we divide each depth sequences into $2 \times 2 \times 1 \times 2$ subvolumes, i.e., we partition each depth sequences into two parts in y, x and t dimensions. Each volume only covers half of the frames of the depth sequences. Occlusion is simulated by ignoring the points that fall into the specified occluded subvolume, illustrated in Fig. 4. We run the simulation with one subvolume occluded, the performance is shown in Table. 2. It can seen that employing sparse coding can greatly improve the robustness.

The confusion matrix is shown in Fig. 5. The proposed method performs very well on most of the actions. Some actions, such as "catch" and "throw", are too similar to each other for the proposed method to capture the difference.

We also compare the classification accuracy of the proposed sampling scheme to that of the uniform sampling scheme in Fig. 6(a). It can be observed that the weighted sampling scheme is more effective than the uniform sampling scheme. Moreover, the proposed scheme does not suffer from overfitting even when the number of the sampled subvolumes is very large. [23] gives an intuitive proof of the generalization ability of classifier of the randomly generated features.

The depth sequences are downsampled into different resolutions, and we explore the relationship between the resolution of the data and the classification

Table 2. Robustness to occlusion comparison

Occlusion	Accuracy without using sparse coding	Accuracy using Sparse Coding
1	83.047	86.165
2	84.18	86.5
3	78.76	80.09
4	82.12	85.49
5	84.48	87.51
6	82.46	87.51
7	80.10	83.80
8	85.83	86.83

Fig. 4. An occluded depth sequence.

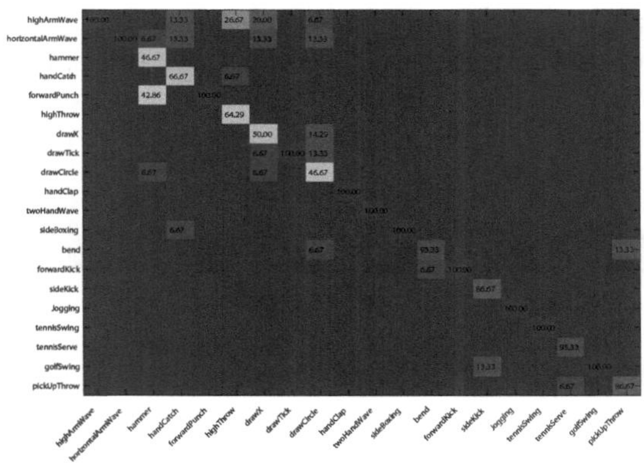

Fig. 5. The confusion matrix for the proposed method on MSR-Action3D dataset. It is recommended to view the figure on the screen

accuracy. The relationship found is shown in Fig. 6(b). Our observation is that the performance of the SVM classifier may drop when we increase the resolution of the data, but for our random sampling scheme, increasing the data resolution always increases the classification accuracy.

6.2 Gesture3D Dataset

The Gesture3D dataset [24] is a hand gesture dataset of depth sequences captured by a depth camera. This dataset contains a subset of gestures defined by American Sign Language (ASL). There are 12 gestures in the dataset: *bathroom*, *blue*, *finish*, *green*, *hungry*, *milk*, *past*, *pig*, *store*, *where*, *j*, *z*. Some example frames

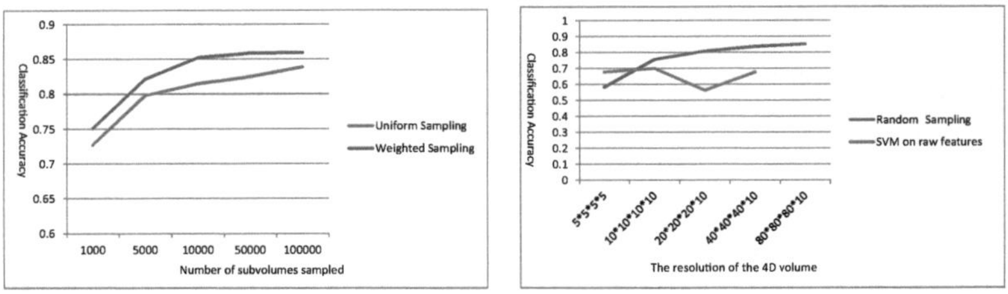

(a) (b)

Fig. 6. The comparison between different sampling methods, and the relationship between the resolution of data and the classification accuracy for SVM and the proposed sampling method.

of the gestures are shown in Fig. 7. Notice that although this dataset contains both the color and depth frames, only depth frames are used in the experiments. Further description of the gestures can be found in [25]. All of the gestures used in this experiment are dynamic gestures, where both the shape and the movement of the hands are important for the semantics of the gesture. There are ten subjects, each performing each gesture two or three times. In total, the dataset contains 336 depth sequences. The self occlsion is more common in the gesture dataset.

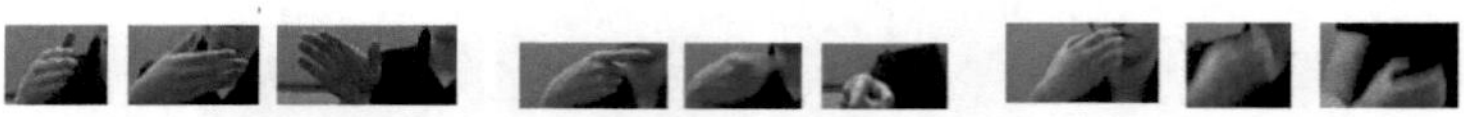

(a) blue gesture (b) green gesture (c) hungry gesture

Fig. 7. The sample frames of the Gesture3D dataset, (a) the blue gesture. (b) green gesture. (c) hungry gesture.

In this experiment, all gesture depth sequences are subsampled to size $120 \times 120 \times 3 \times 10$. The leave-one-subject-out cross-validation is employed to evaluate the proposed method. The recognition accuracy is shown in Table 3. The proposed method performs significantly better than the SVM on raw features and the high dimensional convolutional network. Our performance is also slight better than the action graph model which uses carefully designed shape features [24].

The separability score map for Gesture3D dataset is shown in Fig. 8. We observe that the score map of the gestures is very different from that of the actions shown in Fig. 3, because the movement pattern of the gestures and the actions is very different. In gesture depth sequences, the semantics of the gesture are mainly determined by the large movement of the hand, while the human actions are mainly characterized by the small movements of the limbs.

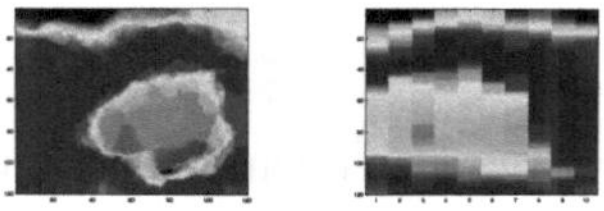

(a) (b)

Fig. 8. The projection of the scores for Gesture3D, (a) the projection of the scores to x-y plane. (b) the projection of the scores to y-t plane.

The confusion matrix is shown in Fig. 9. The proposed method performs quite well for most of the gestures. It can be observed from the confusion matrix that large confusion exists between the gesture "where" and "green". Both gestures involve the movement of one finger, and only the directions of the movement are slightly different.

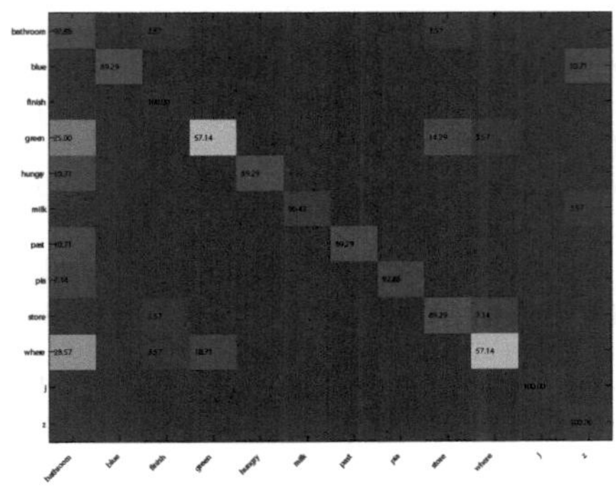

Fig. 9. The confusion matrix of the proposed method on Gesture3D dataset

Table 3. Recognition Accuracy Comparison for Gesture3D dataset

Method	Accuracy
SVM on Raw Features	0.6277
High Dimensional Convolutional Network [22]	0.69
Action Graph on Occupancy Features [24]	0.805
Action Graph on Silhouette Features [24]	0.877
Proposed Method (Without sparse coding)	**0.868**
Proposed Method (Sparse coding)	**0.885**

7 Conclusion

This paper presented a novel random occupancy pattern features for 3D action recognition, and proposed a weighted random sampling scheme to efficiently explore an extremely large dense sampling space. A sparse coding approach is employed to further improve the robustness of the proposed method. Experiments on different types of datasets, including an action recognition dataset and a gesture recognition dataset, demonstrated the effectiveness and robustness of the proposed approach as well as its broad applicability.

Acknowledgments. This work was supported in part by National Science Foundation grant IIS-0347877, IIS-0916607, US Army Research Laboratory and the US Army Research Office under grant ARO W911NF-08-1-0504, and DARPA Award FA 8650-11-1-7149. This work was conducted when the first author was at Microsoft Research Redmond.

References

1. Shotton, J., Fitzgibbon, A., Cook, M., Sharp, T., Finocchio, M., Moore, R., Kipman, A., Blake, A.: Real-time human pose recognition in parts from single depth images. In: CVPR (2011)
2. Hadfield, S., Bowden, R.: Kinecting the dots: Particle Based Scene Flow From Depth Sensors. In: ICCV (2011)
3. Baak, A., Meinard, M., Bharaj, G., Seidel, H.P., Theobalt, C., Informatik, M.P.I.: A Data-Driven Approach for Real-Time Full Body Pose Reconstruction from a Depth Camera. In: ICCV (2011)
4. Girshick, R., Shotton, J., Kohli, P., Criminisi, A., Fitzgibbon, A.: Efficient Regression of General-Activity Human Poses from Depth Images. In: ICCV (2011)
5. Viola, P., Jones, M.J.: Robust Real-Time Face Detection. International Journal of Computer Vision 57, 137–154 (2004)
6. Freund, Y., Schapire, R.: A Decision-Theoretic Generalization of On-Line Learning and an Application to Boosting. In: Computational Learning Theory, vol. 55, pp. 23–37. Springer (1995)
7. Weinland, D., Boyer, E., Ronfard, R.: Action Recognition from Arbitrary Views using 3D Exemplars. In: ICCV, pp. 1–7 (2007)
8. Amit, Y., Geman, D.: Shape quantization and recognition with randomized trees. Neural Computation 9, 1545–1588 (1997)
9. Yao, B., Khosla, A., Fei-Fei, L.: Combining randomization and discrimination for fine-grained image categorization. In: CVPR (2011)
10. Rahimi, A., Recht, B.: Weighted sums of random kitchen sinks: Replacing minimization with randomization in learning. In: NIPS, vol. 885. Citeseer (2008)
11. Huang, G.B., Wang, D.H., Lan, Y.: Extreme learning machines: a survey. International Journal of Machine Learning and Cybernetics 2, 107–122 (2011)
12. Li, W., Zhang, Z., Liu, Z.: Action recognition based on a bag of 3d points. In: Human Communicative Behavior Analysis Workshop (in conjunction with CVPR) (2010)
13. Wang, J., Liu, Z., Wu, Y., Yuan, J.: Mining Actionlet Ensemble for Action Recognition with Depth Cameras. In: CVPR (2012)

14. Vieira, A.W., Nascimento, E.R., Oliveira, G.L., Liu, Z., Campos, M.M.: STOP: Space-Time Occupancy Patterns for 3D Action Recognition from Depth Map Sequences. In: 17th Iberoamerican Congress on Pattern Recognition, Buenos Aires (2012)
15. Yang, X., Tian, Y.: EigenJoints-based Action Recognition Using Naïve-Bayes-Nearest-Neighbor. In: CVPR 2012 HAU3D Workshop (2012)
16. Yang, X., Zhang, C., Tian, Y.: Recognizing Actions Using Depth Motion Maps-based Histograms of Oriented Gradients. In: ACM Multimedia (2012)
17. Tapia, E.: A note on the computation of high-dimensional integral images. Pattern Recognition Letters 32, 197–201 (2011)
18. Wang, L., Chan, K.L.: Learning Kernel Parameters bu using Class Separability Measure. In: NIPS (2002)
19. Zou, H., Hastie, T.: Regularization and variable selection via the elastic net. Journal of the Royal Statistical Society 67, 301–320 (2005)
20. Julien Mairal (SPArse Modeling Software), `http://www.di.ens.fr/willow/SPAMS/`
21. Laptev, I.: On Space-Time Interest Points. IJCV 64, 107–123 (2005)
22. Ji, S., Xu, W., Yang, M., Yu, K.: 3D convolutional neural networks for human action recognition. In: ICML. Citeseer (2010)
23. Bartlett, P.: The sample complexity of pattern classification with neural networks: the size of the weights is more important than the size of the network. IEEE Transactions on Information Theory 44, 525–536 (1998)
24. Kurakin, A., Zhang, Z., Liu, Z.: A real-time system for dynamic hand gesture recognition with a depth sensor. In: EUSIPCO (2012)
25. (Basic America Sign Language), `http://www.lifeprint.com/asl101/pages-layout/concepts.htm`

Author Index

Abrams, Austin 357
Althoff, Tim 802
Alvino, Christopher 430
Appel, Ron 645
Avrithis, Yannis 788
Ayache, Nicholas 30

Baatz, Georges 517
Bahlmann, Claus 430
Bao, Hujun 601
Băzăvan, Eduard Gabriel 459
Belhumeur, Peter N. 502
Biswas, Arijit 502
Blaschko, Matthew B. 245
Boix, Xavier 744
Borji, Ali 414
Bristow, Hilton 59

Cao, Liangliang 688
Chai, Xiujuan 616
Chang, Shih-Fu 688
Chen, Zhuoyuan 872
Cheriet, Farida 30
Chia, Liang-Tien 230
Chorowski, Jan 872
Chum, Ondřej 774
Cour, Timothee 660
Cristani, Marco 273
Csurka, Gabriela 488

Dai, Qionghai 828
Dai, Zhenlong 385
Darrell, Trevor 702, 802
Dehghan, Afshin 343
De La Torre, Fernando 144
Del Bue, Alessio 273
Dollár, Piotr 645
Dorst, Leo 531
Dragon, Ralf 445
Dubbelman, Gijs 531
Dubuisson, Séverine 188
Dunn, Enrique 759

Efros, Alexei A. 73

Fei-Fei, Li 1
Felzenszwalb, Pedro 802
Fisher III, John 287
Frahm, Jan-Michael 759
Fritz, Mario 802
Fua, Pascal 400

Gao, Shenghua 230
Garvin, Gregory J. 557
Gehrke, Johannes 45
Geyer, Christopher 802
Girshick, Ross 802
Gong, Dian 315
Gonzales, Christophe 188
Gould, Stephen 202
Grady, Leo 30, 430
Grompone von Gioi, Rafael 572
Gu, Steve 816
Gunderson, Steinar H. 674
Guo, Yimo 631
Gupta, Abhinav 73
Gurdjos, Pierre 572

Haner, Sebastian 545
Harandi, Mehrtash T. 216
Hartley, Richard 216
Hasler, Nils 828
Hawley, Christopher 357
He, Kaiming 16
Heinly, Jared 759
Heyden, Anders 545
Hoffman, Judy 702
Hua, Gang 688
Huang, Dong 144
Hussain, Sibt ul 716

Inoshita, Chika 371
Itti, Laurent 414

Jacobs, David W. 502
Jégou, Hervé 774
Ji, Xiangyang 828
Jia, Jiaya 385
Jiang, Hanqing 601
Jiang, Yuning 730

Kankanhalli, Mohan 101
Katti, Harish 101
Kienzle, Wolf 645
Kobayashi, Takumi 474
Kohlberger, Timo 430
Köser, Kevin 517
Kress, W. John 502
Kulis, Brian 702
Kumar, Neeraj 502

Lang, Congyan 101
Law, Max W.K. 557
Leistner, Christian 744
Leung, Andrew 557
Li, Fuxin 459
Li, Shuo 557
Li, Yunpeng 400
Lian, Wei 259
Lin, Dahua 287
Lin, Yuanqing 1
Liu, Haomin 601
Liu, Yebin 828
Liu, Zicheng 872
Lombaert, Herve 30
Lopez, Ida C. 502
Lou, Yin 45
Lovell, Brian C. 216
Lucchi, Aurélien 400
Lucey, Simon 59

Mathe, Stefan 842
Matsushita, Yasuyuki 371
Medioni, Gérard 315
Mensink, Thomas 488
Metaxas, Dimitris N. 660
Mittal, Arpit 245
Moulin, Pierre 173
Mu, Yadong 688
Mukaigawa, Yasuhiro 371
Murino, Vittorio 273

Nakazawa, Atsushi 159
Natarajan, Pradeep 301
Natarajan, Premkumar 301
Natsev, Apostol 688
Nguyen, Tam V. 101
Ni, Bingbing 173
Nitschke, Christian 159

Ostermann, Jörn 445
Otsu, Nobuyuki 474

Park, Kyoungup 202
Park, Unsang 301
Pătrăucean, Viorica 572
Pennec, Xavier 30
Perronnin, Florent 488
Pietikäinen, Matti 631
Pijls, Henk 531
Pilet, Julien 674
Pless, Robert 357
Pollefeys, Marc 517
Prasad, Rohit 301

Ramnath, Krishnan 586
Rapantzikos, Konstantinos 788
Ravichandran, Avinash 329
Roig, Gemma 744
Rosenhahn, Bodo 445
Roshan Zamir, Amir 343
Russakovsky, Olga 1

Saenko, Kate 702
Sanderson, Conrad 216
Sangineto, Enver 273
Saurer, Olivier 517
Schauerte, Boris 116
Shah, Mubarak 343
Shan, Shiguang 616
Sihite, Dicky N. 414
Singh, Saurabh 73
Singh, Vivek 430
Sinha, Sudipta N. 586
Sminchisescu, Cristian 459, 842
Smith, John R. 688
Smith, Kevin 400
Snavely, Noah 45
Soares, João V.B. 502
Soatto, Stefano 329
Song, Hyun Oh 802
Stewénius, Henrik 674
Stiefelhagen, Rainer 116
Sun, Jian 16
Szeliski, Richard 586

Tan, Ping 601
Tang, Xiaoou 857
Tay, KengYeow 557
Theobalt, Christian 828
Todorovic, Sinisa 130
Tomasi, Carlo 816
Torr, Philip H.S. 245
Triggs, Bill 716

Van Gool, Luc 744
Varytimidis, Christos 788
Vedaldi, Andrea 87
Verbeek, Jakob 488
Vitaladevuni, Shiv 301

Wang, Jiang 872
Wang, Xiaogang 857
Wang, Zhengxiang 230
Wei, Donglai 287
Wu, Shuang 301
Wu, Ying 872

Xu, Li 385

Yadati, Karthik 101
Yagi, Yasushi 371
Yan, Shuicheng 101, 173
Yang, Ming 660
Ye, Genzhi 828
Yu, Gang 730
Yu, Kai 1, 660
Yuan, Junsong 730

Zhang, Guofeng 601
Zhang, Lei 259
Zhang, Shaoting 660
Zhao, Guoying 631
Zhao, Xiaowei 616
Zhao, Xuemei 315
Zheng, Ying 816
Zhou, Bolei 857
Zhuang, Xiaodan 301
Zickler, Stefan 802
Zisserman, Andrew 87, 245

MIX
Papier aus verantwortungsvollen Quellen
Paper from responsible sources
FSC® C105338
FSC
www.fsc.org

If you have any concerns about our products,
you can contact us on
ProductSafety@springernature.com

In case Publisher is established outside the EU,
the EU authorized representative is:
Springer Nature Customer Service Center GmbH
Europaplatz 3, 69115 Heidelberg, Germany

Printed by Libri Plureos GmbH
in Hamburg, Germany